The Off Off Broadway Book

DATE DUE

DEMCO, INC. 38-2931

D1223168

THE OFF OFF BROADWAY BOOK
The Plays, People, Theatre

Edited by Albert Poland and Bruce Mailman

ACKNOWLEDGMENTS

SPECIAL THANKS TO MAX WILLIAM JACOBS.

We gratefully thank Mary Boylan, John Chace, Robert Dahdah, Johnny Dodd, Ron Link and Charles Stanley for their invaluable assistance in compiling the Caffe Cino list.

We gratefully thank Paul Foster and Dr. Paul Cranefield for their invaluable assistance in compiling the La Mama list.

We thank Kenneth Burgess for the loan of photographs and programs from his collection of Caffe Cino memorabilia.

We thank Tom Adkins, Kenneth Brodney, Bonnie Brown, Remy Charlip, Nancy Christofferson, Condé Nast Publications Inc., Linda Eskenas, Robert Heide, Joan Muyskens, Nelly Vivas, Richard Vos and Jules Weiss for their assistance in the gathering of photographs, research and compilation.

We thank Madeleine le Roux for the angels and vice versa.

We thank Harry Joe Brown and Richard Lamparski for their *mishegaas*.

We especially thank Murray Mednick and Robert Patrick for telling all and making it low.

We thank Reiter-Dulberg Laboratories, Inc., for giving us a discount and Maxwell Silverman of the New York Public Library, Lincoln Center, for controlling the other librarian, who was impossible.

Special thanks to our attorneys, Schoenfeld & Jacobs and Jack Zimmeth.

We thank Peter Schneider who did the most work and got the least money.

We thank Boris Ivan Fedushin and John Sugg M.D. for being a constant up.

To the playwrights, their agents and publishers our sincere appreciation for all of their efforts on behalf of this book.

The Bobbs-Merrill Company, Inc.
Indianapolis · New York

I love the theatre. I love the make-believe and the magic. It's a world of fantasy and loveliness. That's the kind of theatre I love most. Something that makes you laugh and cry and feel better. Of course, I don't believe the theatre should only just entertain. Oh, no. I think the theatre should always teach a lesson . . . And I think that if there are evil things, the theatre should just show those evil things so you will want to go right out and change them. I love the theatre. It's a whole life to me.

Arthur Williams

TABLE OF CONTENTS

vii

MAP OF THEATRE DISTRICT

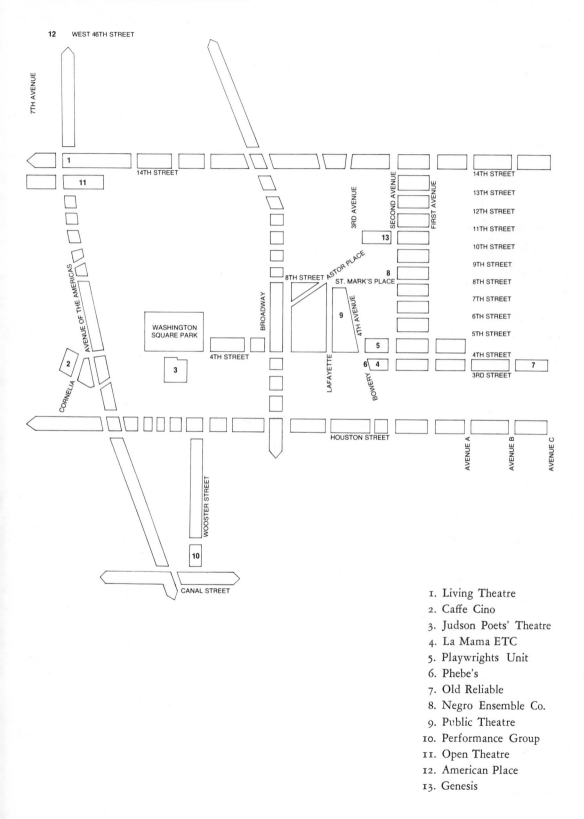

1. Living Theatre
2. Caffe Cino
3. Judson Poets' Theatre
4. La Mama ETC
5. Playwrights Unit
6. Phebe's
7. Old Reliable
8. Negro Ensemble Co.
9. Public Theatre
10. Performance Group
11. Open Theatre
12. American Place
13. Genesis

INTRODUCTION

The plays in this book are different from all of the American theatre which preceded them. The playwrights of the Off Off movement have no manifesto. Since they did not meet as a group to look at the inadequacies of the existing American drama and evolve a new theatre by plan, there is an inherent question: What is the common ground held by so many individuals? Why are these plays similar? First, the playwrights used symbols which are part of a new syntax. They worked in a similar way: syntactically, contextually and theatrically. From a historical perspective their plays have a unified style, a style that renders each play more similar to, than different from, all the others. Too, the writers worked the same geographical area: below Fourteenth Street in Manhattan (see map, page ix). The places were small, nontheatrical facilities, makeshift theatres in cellars, bars, lofts, storefronts and coffeehouses. The tightness of the space forced the playwrights to work within stringent technical limitations.

By the mid-1950's Julie Bovasso had founded the Tempo Theatre, which introduced the works of de Ghelderode, Genet and Ionesco to American audiences. At the same time Julian Beck and Judith Malina were attempting to present *Noh* plays translated by Ezra Pound in a basement on Wooster Street. The city authorities, objecting to the use of nonlicensed space for public occupancy and, perhaps more to the point, to the unorthodoxy of the people involved in this new theatre, were punitive. Julie Bovasso's theatre had a limited stay. The Becks eventually moved to 100th Street and Broadway, where they presented works by playwrights William Carlos Williams and Paul Goodman to a select, private audience. However, it was not until their group, the Living Theatre, moved to Fourteenth Street and Sixth Avenue to mount a production of a new American playwright that a new movement began to focus. *The Connection,* the second production of the Living Theatre under the Becks, presented the audience with a kind of theatre it had not seen before. Its form was indigenous to their life-style and its language was completely contemporary. The theatre was a second-floor loft; seating only 160, it created a forced intimacy. The musicians were onstage, not locked in a pit. The theatre was beginning to renew itself as ceremony and the audience was able to relate and participate; it could not deal with the play as if there were a fourth wall. The critics, who usually shape the public taste, were ignored. This was an audience theatre and the new audience was interested. Despite initially bad reviews, *The Connection* succeeded. The second level of criticism, journalism/periodicals, realized that something was happening. *Life* magazine did an article on a 160-seat theatrical presentation in a second-floor loft on Fourteenth Street. With poets, dancers and musicians forming an integral part of its exciting community, the Living Theatre became the center of the American avant-garde. Even when the I.R.S., in late 1963, seized the theatre for back taxes, the center held. After serving short prison terms, the Becks left the country with their troupe and the Living Theatre began a semipermanent exile. But an impact had been made and the foundations still existed. Lawrence Kornfeld, a former Living Theatre director, had already emigrated to the Judson Poets' Theatre. Joseph Chaikin, a Living Theatre actor, had formed a laboratory that was to become the Open Theatre. In those few short years of its tenure Off Broadway the Living Theatre had created a new audience and provided the impetus for a new theatre.

It is with the work and product of this new theatre that this book is concerned. As early as 1959, Caffe Cino had been started; it was quickly followed by the Judson Poets' Theatre and Cafe La Mama. They were independent theatrical organizations serving the specific needs of their own communities. At the outset they had no money; everyone who worked with them did so from devotion. With the founding of Theatre Genesis, church funds became available for these theatres. Slowly private donations and large foundation grants were made available and many small workshop theatres dealing with the new drama were 'established. The seed had been set by Cino, Judson and La Mama. Three charismatic personalities, Joseph Cino, Al Carmines and Ellen Stewart, created the theatres and kept them alive. These theatres, although individual, had a similar aesthetic. Witness the fact that most of the playwrights in this book worked at more than one of these places. They produced a range of theatre—plays, playwrights, actors, directors, designers and technicians—as rich as any golden period in dramatic literature. These plays form a united group with the same people, ideas and politics and, most important, the same aesthetic.

The plays of Off Off have a common language that is built on a set of new symbols. The new symbols are a function of the new audience, for Off Off is an audience-oriented theatre. Not since the great age of the American music hall and the melodrama has there been such real audience devotion and interaction. The audience participates; they boo, they cheer, but most of all they *enjoy* the plays and they attend the theatre because the new symbols are as familiar to them as they are to the playwrights. One need only be familiar with general American sociology to understand the new syntax: the movies on Saturday nights, popcorn, Cokes, the radio, TV, comic strips, drugs, etc.

Unlike earlier artists of this century who broke new ground, these writers do not have to invent or revitalize myths to mine their symbols. Yeats, for example, had to reestablish the whole of Irish mythology to draw adequately powerful symbols for his poetry. Likewise, Eliot goes back to the fisher-king phoenix myths to establish an adequate "objective correlative" for *The Waste Land*. The work of Ezra Pound is almost incomprehensible to the uninitiated. The playwrights of the twentieth century did not find a new language necessary. Eugene O'Neill, Thornton Wilder, Clifford Odets, Elmer Rice, Maxwell Anderson, Tennessee Williams, Arthur Miller and, more recently, Edward Albee follow a theatrical line originated by Ibsen, Chekhov and Strindberg.

The playwrights of Off Off have their mythology at hand—American folk art. If folk art is a product or form produced by artisans (rather than artists) of the general population and representative of that population, then the fashion illustrators, industrial designers, sign makers, photographers, etc. are the craftsmen of that art. Like all folk art, these forms are the most representative examples of the styles prevalent at the time of their production.

Camp was the first sensibility (see Susan Sontag, "Notes on Camp," in *Against Interpre-*

tation and Other Essays) to be attracted to the stylistic eccentricities of mass-produced forms that form the body of twentieth-century folk art. These forms, whether specific objects or media-produced, are the most extreme examples of the public taste from the individual periods. The stylistic extremes are the details that camp first noted and the very value of the forms.

Pop was the movement that converted camp's observation into symbols. To illustrate: everyone in the world knows the size, shape and color of the original Coca-Cola bottle. The first sensibility to recognize the representative value and individual design was camp. A Coke bottle is neither good nor bad art; it is an artifact that represents the style of a specific time in mass production in the United States, and it is different from any other bottle not only because of the way it looks, but because of its wide use. It represents the era and the civilization that produced it. But the Coke bottle is only an artifact until it is used as a symbol. Camp is only the appreciation of the form. Another catalyst is needed to convert it into more than a Coke bottle. A Coke bottle, once it appears on a canvas, is no longer a piece of folk art. It has become a definite statement by an artist. The Coke bottle has then been transformed into a concrete symbol of a time and style. *Pop art* is the movement responsible for this transformation and the labeling of the symbol.

If the visual arts could transform the camp recognition into pop and make it a symbol, then the new theatre could also make use of the basic sensibility to draw its symbols. Why should the stage limit itself to visual objects when its media can encompass more?

The movies are the least static and most far-reaching examples of folk art. The films made by Hollywood through the mid-1950s were examples of absolute stylization. They can be separated by decades and under this categorization they differ in style; however, they do fall into a general category. We refer to this pattern in everyday speech. For example, if one were to say that a book had a typical "Hollywood" ending, the statement would be understood to mean an ending of melodramatic nature playing for the simplest emotional response—usually happy. If one were to use "Hollywood" as an adjective, e.g., "That's very 'Hollywood,' " it would mean that the point of reference was opulent, lavish, excessive and expensive. More people in the United States today would understand and relate to the statement "X is like a Bette Davis movie" than to the statement "X is like the story of Ruth." This reality has been recognized and used by the playwrights of Off Off. They have connected the kinetic forms observed by camp and excluded from pop and transformed them into a New American literary dramatic symbolism.

Camp as the *root* of the new symbolism is one thing, camp as an overriding style is quite another. Many a serious work has been defeated by the leer of an Off Off actor playing to a coterie. There is a danger that the new language might be overly used, in which case the plays would pander to the worst level of their audiences and virtue would become a vice. The danger is inherent in the use of any symbolic language in art.

By the late 1950s the New York theatre had reached an appalling economic state. Broadway was going the route of the big Hollywood studios. It was producing fewer plays and each production was more expensive. The goal was superproductions with star-studded casts, equaling *safety*. Off Broadway, traditionally the home of the experimental, was finding itself in the same position. By 1960 it cost between 12 and 15 thousand dollars to produce a straight (nonmusical) play Off Broadway. The audience that Off Broadway had developed, the intelligentsia, were interested in revivals: O'Neill, Ibsen, Chekhov and the avant-garde, Genet, Pinter, Beckett, Ionesco; but they were not interested in unestablished new American playwrights. Edward Albee, the last playwright of the old movement to take the conventional route, was successful. But his plays were still in conventional dramatic form and the language was familiar to the middle-class audience. It was not a departure but an extension of an earlier dramatic line. With the possible exception of Thornton Wilder and Gertrude Stein (who is included in this book because her work, so long considered a literary dead end, seems to fit directly into this theatre and her plays have been performed by nearly every Off Off group), playwriting in the United States was standard—varying in quality, not form.

The new form evolved because of its economic limitations, a theatre that was bone-clean, depending on the very vigor of the production to make it work. The result is a new acting and directing style. Transitions are not made in a logical way. Explication and similar devices are no longer necessary. Using impressionism, expressionism, Brecht's alienation theories in combination with Artaud's horrors, they produced a rich collage that brought a new strength to their drama. It was not planned. It was what evolved. Did Cino, Judson and La Mama invent the styles of this theatre or were the styles the result of the limitations? There are no answers to these questions. There was a fusion and this fusion created a body of work.

THEATRE SECTION

JOSEPH CINO   *Eugenia Louis (Kenneth Burgess Collection)*

CAFFE CINO
31 Cornelia Street
New York, New York 10014

In *The Reader's Guide to Periodical Literature* there is no listing for Caffe Cino or Joe Cino. In the Theatre Collection of the Library of the Performing Arts at Lincoln Center there is, in addition to an obituary file, one slim file of written material that contains some notes on Caffe Cino written by Joe Cino for the anthology *Eight Plays from Off Off Broadway* (by Nick Orzel and Michael Smith, published by the Bobbs-Merrill Company, 1966). It is impossible to do factual research on Joe Cino or his theatre. There are no written records for conventional documentation. One must depend upon personal remembrances. It is as if the details were made deliberately obscure. The lettering on the Caffe Cino posters was designed so that when the poster was placed in the cafe window the city authorities would be unable to decipher it, but the attending audience was able to read it. In the same way, only the essence of Caffe Cino is documentable.

Sometime in December of 1958 Joe Cino started his coffeehouse at 31 Cornelia Street. The room was small and narrow, with high ceilings and a center playing platform. It was dark, smoky, cluttered and dirty. The walls were covered with posters, old photographs, crunched foil, glitter stars and hundreds of pieces of assorted memorabilia, which in time became ten and twelve thick. Periodically everything was taken down and the room was painted in an attempt to defeat the roach problem; everything was then put back exactly as it had been. Joe Cino insisted; even after a production the room was restored intact. If something was added, it was because Joe Cino had chosen it. He really cared about his room. If a performer was reluctant, he was told to perform in spite of a lack of audience, for the walls would miss him.

Caffe Cino paid its actors by passing around a basket for contributions after each performance. There was no admission charge and no minimum until Joe's death. The audience did not mind this and the actors did not object. It was a place to work in total freedom. It had no grants, no church support; it had no affiliations and consequently no obligations other than to itself. Caffe Cino was the only Off Off Broadway organization that was even marginally self-supporting. Over the door, in small letters, Bob Patrick had printed a quote from *Adrianna Lecouvreur;* it read, *"Io son l'umile ancella,"* roughly, "I am the humble handmaiden of the arts." Caffe Cino was the first theatre developed by the Off Off Broadway movement.

Joe Cino believed he was too fat to dance and he started his coffee shop to have a place where he could be surrounded by his friends in the "arts." He had not intended to create a theatre. It was to be a social place for art and photography exhibits, poetry readings, singing and general geniality. It continued in this spirit until Doric Wilson began to read some scenes from *Salomé.* This led to more scenes and finally a full production. However, it was not until the arrival of Lanford Wilson that Caffe Cino became a theatre. He brought with him an excellence of production and writing that led to recognition by the critics, first *The Village Voice* and then the other papers.

Joe Cino represented juxtaposition and H. M. Koutoukas was the archetypical Cino playwright; his combination of whimsy, speed, camp and insanity was precisely right for Joe's sensibilities. He saw value in seemingly opposite things; he considered *Looney Tunes* and *Thaïs* equally important and comparable artistic achievements. The highest compliment Joe Cino could pay a performer was to call him a Rockette; he thought the Rockettes were sheer genius. Joe Cino was like his room: complex, dirty and brilliant. He kept a bottle of Florida Water in the back room which he used profusely when he did not want to wash. Even this was part of the link between Joe and the young writers who came to him. It was probably the first time these young middle-class people had ever been shown that there was something more important than cleanliness. Joe Cino was honest. He forbade the playing of Bob Dylan records because he felt Dylan was a phony folk singer. When he was forced to hear "Route 66" he changed his mind, because he felt that Dylan was finally singing like a Jewish boy from Brooklyn.

Joe Cino had dreams of moving the theatre to a loft where there would be more space; he wanted to provide living space for the playwrights. He had no illusions about playwrights; he knew they were lazy and had to be forced to work. He wanted his new place to have a large neon sign reading "CINO'S TEMPLE"; but 31 Cornelia Street was to be his only monument.

Things should have become easier but they became more difficult. The constant battle to stay in the black, the continuing city harassment must all have taken their toll. Perhaps—there are so many perhapses—perhaps Joe Cino felt that what he was doing was not creative enough. Perhaps Joe Cino felt the need to do much more. Perhaps the very activity that vitalized him was the thing that drained him of energy, that made him duck into doorways to avoid playwrights who wanted to know WHEN. Perhaps . . . is endless but some things are certain. It is certain that Joe Cino had a talent for environment. It is certain that Caffe Cino was a wonderful place to work; it was warm, friendly and personal.

"Personal" is the essential word. Joe Cino knew what people needed. If they could not afford a check, they did not receive one. After one performance of *The Madness of Lady Bright,* Neil Flanagan had been particularly upset because of some personal criticism of his performance; this resulted in a great vendetta performance for the second show. That night Joe Cino gave him the gift he had been saving for closing night. Joe said he gave it because there could have been no better performance; Neil felt it was given because it was needed. Someone said he was like Santa Claus— always a little pick-me-up—a hug for everyone.

Joe Cino did not like to receive presents. He hated his own birthdays and sulked during parties given for him. Like all patriarchs, he preferred sowing to reaping. Unlike Ellen Stewart, he did not cast himself as Le Papa. He said, "Do what you have to do," and he did. He served his coffee, picked his people and his plays. He inaugurated a life-style for his creative community. Sometimes he even directed plays, but his real ability lay in bringing people together. John Gruen, in his *New York Herald Tribune* obituary of Monday, April 3, 1967, gave a very sharp picture of the environment:

Twice each night, and sometimes three times, the Caffe Cino presented the outrageous, the blasphemous, the zany, the wildly poetic, the embarrassingly trite, the childish, and frequently, the moving and the beautiful.

The room had a language of its own, Joe Cino's language, a kind of proto-hip talk that cut through barriers and went to the heart. He seems to have realized the value of it all and yet he seems to have been personally unsatisfied. He suffered this contradiction and perhaps it also contributed to his death.

The Lenten season was an ominous time for Joe Cino. In 1966 the theatre was destroyed by fire on Ash Wednesday; it was reopened on Good Friday. On Friday, March 31, 1967, Joe Cino attempted suicide and on Sunday, April 2, 1967, he died at St. Vincent's Hospital. He was thirty-six years old. By Saturday more than 130 people had come to give blood for him. His death was a tragic loss to the community he had helped to create. There was an attempt to keep the Caffe Cino going. In *The Village Voice* of Thursday, April 6, 1967, the following notice appeared:

CAFFE CINO OPEN

The Caffe Cino, 31 Cornelia Street, is continuing under the management of the regular staff with the schedule planned by Joe Cino before his death. The current play is Lanford Wilson's *The Madness of Lady Bright,* starring Neil Flanagan.

Charles Stanley and then Michael Smith made attempts to keep the theatre going, but these attempts ultimately failed. There were too many harassments: tax money owed by the corporation, 1,250 police violations in one day, etc., but the essential catalyst, Joe Cino, was no longer there.

There are many things people remember about Caffe Cino; they are incisive, diffuse, emotional, personal, factual, contradictory and conforming: *The Madness of Lady Bright* ran 205 performances; *Dames at Sea,* 148 performances; *Why Hanna's Skirt Won't Stay Down,* 146 performances. When a show did not get on, Bob Patrick initiated performances of classic comic books from *Dr. Faustus* through *Archie, Jughead and Veronica.* On Sunday night pastries were given away because it was the end of the week and Monday was a "dark" night.

Bob Heide said that Joe Cino believed in cookies, cake and sex. He did not believe in the isolation of the artist. Caffe Cino was a place to work without pretense. Joe Cino wore a cotton sweatshirt, blue jeans and yellow construction shoes; if he went uptown, the sweatshirt became velour and maybe a cape was added if the occasion warranted it. He had a Sicilian temper but he was a loving man. Joe Cino gave a chance to everybody whom he intuitively believed in. He never closed a show unless the principals wanted it. He loved bells and had some mounted over the coffee machine which he rang when a play was too slow. Ken Burgess said that when Joe Cino was in the mood, he pulled down his pants, bent over, backside to the audience and said, "On with the show."

The following are the plays presented at the Caffe Cino:

THE IMPORTANCE OF BEING ERNEST
Oscar Wilde   *1959*

THE STREET OF GOOD FRIENDS
Owen G. Arno   *1959*

HYACINTH HALVEY
Lady Gregory   *1959*

THE DEVIL AND THE GOOD LORD
Sartre, Adapted by John Chace   *May, 1960*

THE EGG (THE SYSTEM)
*Felicien Marceau, Adapted by
John Chace*   *Oct. 1, 1960*

ANGEL IN THE PAWNSHOP (999 WORDS)
Adapted by Robert Dahdah   *1960*

TO BOBOLINK, FOR HER SPIRIT
William Inge   *1960*

GOODBYE, MAMA
Unknown   *1960*

THE MOTHER
Paddy Chayefsky   *1960*

THE HAPPY JOURNEY
Thornton Wilder   *1960*

JUST BEFORE THE WAR WITH THE ESKIMOS
J. D. Salinger   *1960*

PRETTY MOUTH AND GREEN MY EYES
J. D. Salinger   *1960*

THE TYCOON
Abe Pacanofsky   *1960*

THE CAT'S CRADLE
Noel Coward   *1960*

LYSISTRATA
Aristophanes   *1960*

FLYSPREY
Anonymous   *1960*

HEART OF GOLD
Florence Stephenson   *Jan. 5, 1961*

AND HE MADE A HER
Doric Wilson   *March 23, 1961*

AN EVENING OF SHAKESPEARE   *March 30, 1961*

BABEL, BABEL LITTLE TOWER
Doric Wilson   *June 29, 1961*

THE MAIDS
Genet   *July, 1961*

PHILOCTETES
André Gide   *Aug. 10, 1961*

ANTIGONE
Jean Anouilh   *Aug. 10, 1961*

DAVID AND BATHSHEBA
André Gide   *Aug. 17, 1961*

I RISE IN FLAMES CRIED THE PHOENIX
and THE ENEMY TIME
Tennessee Williams   *Oct. 12, 1961*

DEATHWATCH
Jean Genet   *Oct. 19, 1961*

MY SIDE OF THE MATTER
Truman Capote   *Nov. 16, 1961*

PRETTY PEOPLE
Doric Wilson   *Nov. 23, 1961*

THE CANDLES
Rose Hennessey   *Dec. 7, 1961*

THIS PROPERTY IS CONDEMNED
Tennessee Williams   *1961*

THE LAST OF MY SOLID GOLD WATCHES
Tennessee Williams   *1961*

IN THE WINTER OF CITIES
Tennessee Williams   *1961*

FIELD OF BLUE CHILDREN
Tennessee Williams   *1961*

CAMINO REAL
Tennessee Williams   *1961*

THE ROSE TATTOO
Tennessee Williams   *1961*

THE GLASS MENAGERIE
Tennessee Williams   *1961*

SEPARATE TABLES
Terrence Rattigan   *1961*

BLITHE SPIRIT
Noel Coward   *1961*

THE PICTURE OF DORIAN GRAY
Oscar Wilde   *1961*

THE CHERRY ORCHARD
Chekhov   *1961*

THE AFFECTED YOUNG LADIES
Molière   *1961*

CALDWELL CORNERS
Abe Paconofsky   *1961*

THE TINY CLOSET
William Inge   *1961*

ALICE IN WONDERLAND (adaptation)
Lewis Carroll   *Jan. 18, 1962*

THE HUMAN VOICE
Jean Cocteau   *Feb. 1, 1962*

A VILLAGE WOOING
G. B. Shaw   *Feb. 22, 1962*

CERVANTES AND OTHERS
Molière   *Feb. 25, 1962*

AL CARMINES

Teresa King

THE JUDSON POETS' THEATRE

Judson Memorial Church
55 Washington Square South
New York, New York 10012

The artists who have flourished since the early 1960s at the Judson Poets' and Dance Theatres and the Judson Gallery are America's equivalent to those of the Paris of Gertrude Stein.

The Judson Memorial Church, which faces Washington Square Park and sees the seasons change there, has served its community's needs, social and political, since Edward Judson first opened its doors in 1892. The church began to find its way into the arts when Robert Spike, minister from 1948 to 1955, arranged for sporadic presentations of plays, concerts and exhibitions.

The Judson Gallery was instituted by Dr. Howard Moody, the present minister, when he arrived in 1956 and it is probable that the early work of such artists as Claes Oldenburg, Allan Kaprow, Tom Wesselman and Jim Dine set the tone for theatre and dance at Judson: the freewheeling evolution of form, color and content that would later assimilate itself into *the Judson style.*

The gallery presented the first Happening in New York in 1958 (created by Allan Kaprow) and among its audience was a young theological student named Al Carmines, whose dynamic personality and puckish wit were destined to shape the theatre at Judson into "the Granddaddy of the Off Off Broadway theatre movement."

As a child of eight Al Carmines began to study the piano. At nine he played for revival meetings. At ten he could play, sing and tap-dance —simultaneously—and he listened to Bessie Smith recordings for hours.

Coming from a traditionally religious Methodist family in Virginia, he put aside his dreams of studying piano at Juilliard to pursue the ministry. He majored in English and philosophy at Swarthmore and developed an interest in theatre while attending Union Theological Seminary.

When he answered Dr. Moody's invitation to initiate the theatre program at Judson, Carmines was uncertain of what he wanted, but with the help of Robert Nichols, an architect and playwright, he began.

"The two great doctrines of Christianity are salvation and creation," Carmines said. "There's been too much concern with the first. Judson wants to do more about the second." And the Judson Poets' Theatre was formed: the first to answer the need of area poets for a place to present their theatre works.

Avoiding the role of "patron of the arts" for the church, Carmines encouraged a *marriage.* Congregation members would work in the theatre and, in turn, Sunday services would find them collaborating with artists as they worshiped God through music, dance, Happenings, drama and prayer.

The marriage had an immediate test when it was discovered that *The Great American Desert,* selected as half of the opening bill, contained a liberal sprinkling of four-letter words. Carmines put the matter before the congregation, which voted never to censor a play on the basis of language or content.

Lawrence Kornfeld, a young assistant from the Living Theatre, directed the cast, which included poets, artists and at least one actor, and *The Great American Desert* officially opened the Judson Poets' Theatre. The play is interesting historically because several aspects of it are vividly indicative of what was to follow. It is a multi-leveled play, part poetry, part metaphysics, part put-on, and its prototypes are American cowboys. The play even talked about the drug problem in the military—as it related to the *Civil* War.

The play, on a bill with Apollinaire's *The Breasts of Tiresias,* was well received and well attended. The budget for the evening: $37.50.

Al Carmines' composing began quite casually during a rehearsal for George Dennison's *Vaudeville Skit* in August 1962, when Kornfeld asked him to improvise some music behind the actors. The result was somewhat astounding and the music, in Kornfeld's words, "became the source for the style of the play" and was retained for the performances.

Carmines wrote his first actual songs for Robert Nichols' *The Wax Engine,* part of a double bill that closed the second season.

With music by Carmines and direction by Kornfeld (by then Judson's resident director), the Poets' Theatre joined the newly formed Judson Dance Theatre for the landmark success that opened the third season and moved the productions from the balcony into the church sanctuary. With Gertrude Stein's *What Happened* the collaboration of artists at Judson found a framework that was to be a hallmark of the Off Off Broadway theatre movement and a lasting influence on America's musical theatre: the Carmines and Kornfeld musicals.

What Happened was Judson's first successful abstract theatre work. Al Carmines found the technique of taking lines here and there from an existing straight play and giving them musical settings that he has used on a majority of his scores.

Another Judson phenomenon, the Judson *superstars* (a group of regulars who have evolved over the years and whose appearances are adored by Judson audiences) became apparent with this production.

Michael Smith, whose columns in *The Village Voice* and subsequent books are among the best existing history of the Off Off Broadway theatre movement, wrote: "Everything that happens has the casual inevitability of great art."

Home Movies, which marked the playwriting debut of Rosalyn Drexler, was a madcap straight play musicalized to become the other highlight of the third season. It was, according to *Newsweek's* Richard Gilman, "the first musical of the absurd" and audiences were shocked enough at its openness about sex and ridicule of religion that it moved Off Broadway, where it enjoyed a six-month run.

In the 1963–64 season Judson established its style, set a new high standard for itself and, in doing so, delighted its audiences and received a record five Obie awards.

Wisely, *Sing Ho for a Bear* (based on *Winnie the Pooh*) was selected as the next major musical effort and went on, despite the best efforts of Walt Disney, who owned the rights. *The String Game,* an auspicious debut for Rochelle Owens, revealed the phantasmagoric imagery of a new poet for the theatre in February 1965.

In the brilliant *Promenade* (April) Maria Irene Fornés provided a social commentary on the classes filled with bitter ironies in counterpoint to a setting of high style and grace. Carmines delivered his best score to date and *Promenade* is a landmark musical. An expanded version was presented Off Broadway in 1969 which opened to great critical acclaim and was recorded by RCA Victor.

The 1965–66 season was highlighted by Rochelle Owens' exotic religious play of the east, *Istanboul* (with a haunting performance by Florence Tarlow), Remy Charlip's Obie award-winning production of Ruth Krauss' poem play *A Beautiful Day* and Jacques Levy's production of Sam Shepard's *Red Cross,* which moved Off Broadway on a double bill with John Guare's *Muzeeka* to critical acclaim.

Helen Adam's collaboration with Carmines and Kornfeld, the opera epic *San Francisco's Burning,* had a daemonic, tragicomic quality comparable to Offenbach's work. The production, which opened on New Year's Eve of 1966, revealed Judson's limitations as well as its virtues. It was the first full-length musical work (running nearly three hours) and had a cast of 27. As a result of the Judson's failure to take anything very seriously for very long in its musicals, the more metaphysical aspects of the piece were not fully realized and by the end of the run had disintegrated into *camp.* The Judson audience found itself split into two factions: one adored it and was in attendance repeatedly, shaping the performance by its screaming responses; the other left quietly, knowing it had seen a near masterpiece, which by the end of its run had become somewhat of a shambles.

In a complete change of pace Carmines provided a score of quiet sensuality and rich opulence for *Song of Songs,* based on the Song of Solomon and gorgeously costumed by Nancy Christofferson. Carmines directed the piece as a Valentine's Day offering.

The production of Ronald Tavel's outrageous *Gorilla Queen* met the coterie head on. "Campy, hell!" Kornfeld scoffed. "It's downright homosexual!" and he went on to point out the playwright's intention to paint "the strongest possible travesty of a world intent on converting itself into a travesty of humanity."

In April a young actor apologetically bowed out of rehearsals for Maria Irene Fornés' *Successful Life of 3* to work on a little show he was writing for production at the Public Theatre. His name: Gerome Ragni.

In Circles (October 1967) was a tribute to the collective artistic growth of the Judson. *Newsweek's* Jack Kroll wrote: "The Judson Poets' Theatre performs Gertrude Stein the way the Moscow Art Theatre does Chekhov." The production had a lilting, witty score and interpolated Kornfeld's concepts of depth psychology. The well-disciplined players performed with agility and the production moved Off Broadway, where the audiences either loved it or hated it and it won an Obie.

Carmines' one-act opera *The Sayings of Mao Tse-tung*, which created a furor from both right and left, and Rosalyn Drexler's play about a "groupie," *The Line of Least Existence*, were other highlights of the sixth season.

Peace, Tim Reynolds' hip adaptation from Aristophanes directed in the style of a minstrel show, opened in November 1968 to coincide with the Paris peace talks. The show was successfully moved Off Broadway, where it received the Drama Desk award. Carmines' rich and rangy score brought high critical acclaim and *New York Post* critic Jerry Tallmer called him "the best living American composer." The score was recorded by Metromedia and released secretly.

If Judson had been the first to present "originals," it was by 1969 one of scores of Off Off Broadway theatres to do so. Carmines decided that the large space of the church would be perfect for massive oratorios, which he would compose and which were presented in 1969–71. They were always exuberant but sometimes sprawling and undisciplined in the writing and performance.

Two of them were exceptional. *Christmas Rappings* was an abstract serious piece that sought the meaning of a contemporary Christmas. *The Journey of Snow White* introduced some new twists into the perennial tale and was declared "an innocent hit" by Clive Barnes of *The New York Times*.

The cycle was notably interrupted on one occasion, for Leon Katz's eerie ritual, *Dracula: Sabbat*, winning an Obie for Lawrence Kornfeld as its director.

The salon atmosphere at Judson continues to attract artists of all kinds. They seem to work and play together with a spirit that appears to rival that of the gods themselves. And if Judson continues its fearless experimentation and growth, audiences will have many years of exciting theatre and the theatre will have a wealth of dramatic and musical material.

Should you drop in for an evening, you might find it sort of like diving headfirst into a vat of joy. You will be startled as the daemons come swimming toward you, and just as you become enchanted they will wink and disappear.

The following plays have been presented by The Judson Poets' Theatre at the Judson Memorial Church:

THE GREAT AMERICAN DESERT and
BREASTS OF TIRESIAS
    Joel Oppenheimer;
    Guillaume Apollinaire   *Nov. 18, 1961*

THE CONTEST and SECOND SHEPHERD'S PLAY
    Ursule Molinaro   *Jan. 11, 1962*

THE IN (OUT) and THE RESERVATION and
INROADS REBUFF'D
    Vincent Ferrini; Martin Halpern;
    Dick Higgins   *March 3, 1962*

THE WOMEN AT THE TOMB and JOURMAD
    Michel de Ghelderode;
    Derek Walcott   *May 24, 1962*

VAUDEVILLE SKIT and THE EXECUTIVES
    George Dennison and Al Carmines;
    C. V. J. Anderson   *Aug. 24, 1962*

THE DEVIL'S MOTHER and MALCAUCHON
    Stephen Holst; Derek Walcott *Oct. 25, 1962*

YORK NATIVITY PLAYS
    York mysteries   *Dec. 14, 1962*

MISS RIGHT and GOD IS MY RAM
    Joel Oppenheimer and Al Carmines;
    Andrew Susac   *Jan. 25, 1963*

MURDER CAKE and SERVICE FOR
JOSEPH AXMINISTER
    Dianne Di Prima;
    George Dennison   *March 21, 1963*

MASKS OF ANGELS
    Notis Peryalis   *April 4, 1963*

THE DECAPITATED TAXI and THE WAX ENGINE
    Robert Nichols; Robert Nichols and
    Al Carmines   *June 13, 1963*

THE BIRTHDAY and HAGAR and ISHMAEL
    Paul Goodman   *July 26, 1963*

WHAT HAPPENED and ASPHODEL
    Gertrude Stein and Al Carmines;
    John Weiners, music by
    John Herbert McDowell   *Sept. 19, 1963*

POET'S VAUDEVILLE
    Diane Di Prima, music by
    John Herbert McDowell   *Oct. 17, 1963*

BUST OF A LUNATIC and HURRAH, IT'S LEWIS
CARROLL DAY
    Donald Kvares; Don Katzman, music
    by John Herbert McDowell   *Nov. 28, 1963*

PANTAGLEIZE and AN OLD TUNE
    Michel de Ghelderode;
    Robert Pinget and Al Carmines *Dec. 19, 1963*

HOME MOVIES and THE BITCH OF
WAVERLY PLACE
    Rosalyn Drexler and Al Carmines;
    Arthur Sainer   *May 19, 1964*

LEONCE AND LENA and
PATTER FOR A SOFT SHOE DANCE
    Georg Büchner;
    George Dennison and
    Al Carmines   *July 9, 1964*

THE HUNDRED AND FIRST and THREE THOUSAND
RED ANTS and FOR MADELEINE RENAUD
    Kenneth Cameron; Lawrence Ferlinghetti,
    Rilke W. Stevens,
    E. Dickinson   *Sept. 24, 1964*

ELLEN STEWART   *Ingrid*

LA MAMA, CAFE LA MAMA, LA MAMA ETC
74 East Fourth Street
New York, New York 10003

Ellen Stewart is the spirit of La Mama; she is its guardian, janitor, fund raiser, press agent, tour manager, conceptual leader—she is the guts of the place. To understand this theatre one must first know Ellen Stewart.

Irene Fornés says that Ellen Stewart is like a madwoman who held a piece of junk in her hand and said it was pure gold—and in five years it was pure gold. Paul Foster says that Ellen Stewart is a Black Witch. Tom Eyen calls her a "super yentah." Julie Bovasso says that she is like a pack rat: she will collect anything she likes, including people.

Personally, I find her the most political person I have ever met. I saw her stand the New York City Planning Commission on its ear with the king's English and in the same week wreck the Rockefeller Foundation with some expletives in pure cotton patch; both dialects achieved their desired effect.

Ellen Stewart is a natural phenomenon, a completely intuitive woman. Everything she touches grows. She makes magic and she is magical. What she does not know, she *knows*. Her history is quixotic; the reality varies with the telling.

Ellen Stewart was born in a Cajun parish of Louisiana. Marriage was a one-way ticket out and she traveled five times. She has one son, Larry Hovell, born in 1943. Marriage took her to Chicago. During the war she worked as a riveter in a defense plant. The FBI investigated her when she accidentally lost some bobby pins in the assembly line. Marriage took her to a "high" black nightclub as the hostess, and marriage finally took her to a middle-class Long Island suburb, where she went mad, suffered a breakdown, lost her hair and from which she fled.

Ellen Stewart ran to an eclectic slum railroad apartment (#8) at 334 East Fifth Street. She was a middle-aged black lady with no education and no future, wandering through the Lower East Side like the other refugees. She knew she was home. She wore a bandanna because she had no hair. Black women did not wear bandannas on the street in Manhattan in 1961. She had a Cajun accent and a crippled dog named Beau-Beau. She was always attracted to broken things. She found her way to Orchard Street, where Papa Diamond, a pushcart peddler, taught her that everyone should have a pushcart of his own; she never forgot it. She was interested in clothes and tried to make her own. They were different, colorful, with fringe and appliquéd paisleys.

Ellen Stewart's first job in New York was as an elevator operator at Saks Fifth Avenue. Wealthy customers wanted to know who the exotic Egyptian model was with the colorful clothes. Saks wanted to know, too. When they found out she became Edith Lansing's assistant. They let her design a line—she became the favorite draper of the young rich. Her co-workers were angry about her meteoric rise and pressured the store into firing her. She wanted something she could not be fired from, a pushcart of her own. She decided to open a boutique. She had backing: an unemployment check for $54.00.

Ellen Stewart found Jim Moore, Paul Foster and a tenement basement at 321 East Ninth Street. Ellen wanted a boutique; Paul wanted to do plays. They planked a dirt floor with old orange crates; they stuffed ratholes, cleaned out garbage, installed a sink with a garden hose and opened a boutique-theatre. The first play presented by Ellen Stewart was *One Arm* by Tennessee Williams. It ran one week. The second and third, each running a week, were *Before Breakfast* by Eugene O'Neill and *The Executioners* by Fernando Arrabal. The house seated 25 people. Paul Foster was sent out on the street to grab potential customers. They charged no admission—contributions only. They sold no clothes, though clothes were for sale. When Paul got a customer he tapped on the window and Ellen started the play. One customer was Leonard Melfi.

Bob Paulsen called Ellen Stewart Mother Earth and then just Mother and through her Cajun dialect it became La Mama. When a local complained that there were 25 men a night going to see a prostitute in the basement at 321 East Ninth Street, Ellen tried to explain to the police that it was all a mistake—THIS WAS A THEATRE. When asked its name, she replied unhesitatingly, "La Mama." In 1963 Bijou Fashions hired Ellen Stewart to design a sportswear line. With her paycheck, she decided to make the theatre pay for itself. If she sold pastries and soft drinks, she might conceivably make the operation self-supporting. On June 28, 1963, Cafe La Mama opened at 82 Second Avenue. It was a second-floor loft that had been renovated, like the basement, with spit, chewing gum, energy and lots of optimism.

Eighty-two Second Avenue became a small theatre center. It attracted unproduced playwrights, would-be playwrights, neophyte actors and the usual cranks who wanted to be identified with the avant-garde. Lanford Wilson and Sam Shepard joined the group. La Mama managed to survive in this location for a year and a half. It was constantly being closed only to reopen the next week. The endless harassment from the departments of buildings, fire, gas, water, electricity, the constant badgering from the local pedagogues continued, but the tiny theatre survived. Admission was one dollar if you could afford it; if not, Mother took care of you. The last play done at 82 Second Avenue was *Balls* by Paul Foster. On closing night Ellen asked the audience to pick up a chair or table close to them. They moved the entire operation processionally up Second Avenue to another second-floor loft. At 122 Second Avenue the second Cafe La Mama opened, on November 11, 1964, with *The Wedding Panda* by David Novack.

The history of Cafe La Mama at 122 Second Avenue reads like a continuing naturalistic novel. Ellen Stewart cooked soup to feed her actors and playwrights. Her salary went into the communal kitty. She understood the importance of her playwrights. She rang a cowbell at the beginning of each performance and welcomed the audience to the theatre with her now famous, "Welcome to La Mama; dedicated to the playwrights and all aspects of the theatre." They were her life and she was their mother. Tom Eyen, Rochelle Owens, Megan Terry, Jerry Ragni, Irene Fornés and Tom O'Horgan all came to La Mama. It was a place to work, a place to experiment, a place that attracted a serious audience.

In 1966 Actors Equity Association almost closed Cafe La Mama (*New York Times,* December 9, 1966). After considering that Cafe La Mama was a 74-seat theatre charging an admission price of a dollar, the union felt it incumbent upon themselves to demand that all Equity actors be guaranteed a minimum salary. La Mama depended heavily on Equity actors for productions of quality. Ellen Stewart faced the union with the same bravado she had previously exhibited. After hearing her, the union permitted members to perform gratis if they so chose and Ellen Stewart had won her first political victory.

The first European tour was put together in the usual La Mama fashion; two Bijou sample boxes housed the costumes and props—a group of ten actors under the direction of Tom O'Horgan began a hectic tour. They received rave notices. Europe hailed them as the "New American Theatre." The actor was not just a disembodied voice. They focused on a strong physical production using movement, kinetic energy. The body made theatrical sense. When they left New York they were a scraggly group of disparate actors and they returned as a world-famous troupe. They had developed a style—the O'Horgan–La Mama style.

Soon after their return they did *Futz!* by Rochelle Owens. The New York critics paid attention. The play received three Obie awards. *Futz!* was followed by *Tom Paine* by Paul Foster and these two plays were the repertory for the second European tour. Something had happened; a connection had been made. The public knew that something alive and important was happening on Second Avenue. Essays were written on the fact that the theatre was, after all, not dead.

The rest is history. *Tom Paine* opened Off Broadway on March 1, 1968; Paul Foster was established. *Hair* opened on Broadway April 19, 1968; Tom O'Horgan was established. *Futz* opened Off Broadway on June 13, 1968; Rochelle Owens was established.

The first grant came from the Rockefeller Foundation in late 1966 for 65,000 dollars so that Cafe La Mama, a nonprofit organization, could find itself a permanent home. This was followed by grants from the Ford Foundation, Rockefeller III Foundation, National Arts Council, New York State Council of the Arts, The Kaplan Fund and many small foundations totaling more than half a million dollars.

On April 2, 1969, Cafe La Mama became La Mama ETC (Experimental Theatre Club). It took two years to renovate and complete the complex of two theatres. La Mama was temporarily housed at 9 St. Mark's Place for part of that time. The former meatpacking plant at 74 East Fourth Street was renovated by professional contractors—no more spit and chewing gum. Ellen Stewart had a pushcart of her own. La Mama had arrived. The first theatre opened on April 2, with *Caution: A*

Love Story by Tom Eyen; two weeks later the second theatre opened, with *Gloria and Esperanza* by Julie Bovasso.

In January 1971 La Mama ETC purchased a new building, at 47 Great Jones Street, to serve as a rehearsal space and theatre school. La Mama has become a worldwide organization. There are now La Mamas in Boston, Amsterdam, Bogota, Israel, London, Melbourne, Morocco, Munich, Paris, Tokyo, Toronto and Vienna.

La Mama ETC ended its season on July 11, 1971, with *Monday on the Way to Mercury Island* by Julie Bovasso. Ellen Stewart spent the summer traveling for UNESCO as a cultural ambassador to the Philippine Republic. On June 6, 1971, Ellen Stewart was awarded an honorary doctorate from Colby College. Her picture has appeared in every national magazine. *Esquire* magazine listed her as one of the 100 most important women in the world.

In the spring of 1971 the United States government paid La Mama ETC formal recognition; its representatives, two Internal Revenue Service men, appeared at 74 East Fourth Street demanding the books for an audit. Ellen Stewart handed them three shopping bags and went off to take care of her babies.

La Mama ETC was an institution.

The following are the plays presented by La Mama:

ONE ARM
　Tennessee Williams　　　　　*July 27, 1962*

BEFORE BREAKFAST
　Eugene O'Neill　　　　　　*Aug. 4, 1962*

A CORNER OF THE MORNING
　Michael Locascio　　　　　*Aug. 17, 1962*

AFTER THE SUPPER AND TALK
　Russell Thacker　　　　　　*Aug. 31, 1962*

RAT FINK
　*George Spelvin (pseud. of
　Jesse Bigelow)*　　　　　　*Sept. 7, 1962*

THE TWO EXECUTIONERS
　Fernando Arrabal　　　　　*Sept. 21, 1962*

A PERFECT ANALYSIS GIVEN BY A PARROT
　Tennessee Williams　　　　*Sept. 28, 1962*

HEADHUNTING
　Pagoon (Kang Wouk)　　　　*Oct. 5, 1962*

ANTHONY AND SHIRLEY
　Shirley Stolyer　　　　　*Oct. 19, 1962*

LAZY BABY SUSAN
　Leonard Melfi　　　　　　*Oct. 26, 1962*

THE ROOM
　Harold Pinter　　　　　　*Oct. 31, 1962*

LAUGH WITH LEACOCK
　Stephen Leacock (excerpts)　*Nov. 23, 1962*

ROCOCO JOKER
　James Eliason　　　　　　*Nov. 30, 1962*

THE FLOOD
　Anthony Keller　　　　　*Dec. 7, 1962*

THE COLLECTOR
　Kate Hoffman　　　　　　*Dec. 14, 1962*

HOLIDAY (based on A CHILD'S CHRISTMAS IN WALES by Dylan Thomas)
　Joe Davies　　　　　　　*Dec. 21, 1962*

SON OF FRICKA
　Bruce Kessler　　　　　　*Dec. 28, 1962*

BATHSHEBA
　André Gide　　　　　　　*Jan. 11, 1963*

A SHEPHERD'S PARABLE
　Donald Knaut　　　　　　*Jan. 18, 1963*

THE BIG CHEESE
　Robert Sealy　　　　　　*Jan. 24, 1963*

Readings from Shaw (Including THE VILLAGE WOOING)
　George Bernard Shaw　　　*Feb. 8, 1963*

THE WRONG MAGNOLIAS
　Donald Julian　　　　　　*Feb. 15, 1963*

A MODERN TRILOGY
　Mark Sadau　　　　　　　*March 1, 1963*

AUTO DA FE
　Tennessee Williams　　　　*March 7, 1963*

HELLO, OUT THERE
　William Saroyan　　　　　*March 21, 1963*

MEDEA
　Jean Anouilh　　　　　　*March 29, 1963*

IN A ROOM HUNG WITH CURTAINS
　*Bruce Kessler, music by
　Gary William Friedman*　　*April 12, 1963*

THE BALD SOPRANO
　Eugene Ionesco　　　　　*June 28, 1963*

THE CLOWN
　David Zlochhauer　　　　*July 4, 1963*

THE VISCOUNT OF BLARNEY
　Austin Clark　　　　　　*July 11, 1963*

ALL WILL FALL
　James Eliason　　　　　　*July 18, 1963*

FAT CHANCE
　Robert Sealy　　　　　　*July 25, 1963*

ON THE BRIDGE
　Ross Alexander　　　　　*Aug. 1, 1963*

ELOISE AND RAMONA
　　　　　　　　　　　　　Aug. 7, 1963

MACKEREL ON TUESDAY
　James Eliason　　　　　　*Aug. 14, 1963*

WOZZECK
　Georg Büchner　　　　　*Sept. 13, 1963*

HURRAH FOR THE BRIDGE
　Paul Foster　　　　　　*Sept. 20, 1963*

LOVE SONG FOR MRS. BOAS
   Ruth Landshoff Yorck   *March 15, 1965*

AT THE CORNER OF POPCORN ALLEY AND THE
21ST OF SEPTEMBER STREET
   Merrill Williams   *March 24, 1965*

THE ESSENCE OF VENGEANCE
   Anthony Bastiano   *March 31, 1965*

WHO PUT THAT BLOOD ON MY
LONG-STEMMED ROSES?
   Mary Mitchell   *April 7, 1965*

Readings: THE ASSENT; DEARLY BELOVED; THE
LAST GREAT COCKTAIL PARTY; WINTER ROSE;
THE BEHEMOTH AND THE CROOK
   David Starkweather;
   Tom Topor; Tom Eyen;
   Donald Brooks; George
   Mazzei and *Donald Brooks*   *April 14, 1965*

THE ROPE
   Norman Wexler   *April 21, 1965*

AMERICA HURRAH AND PAVANE
   Jean-Claude van Itallie   *April 28, 1965*

TRILOGY
   Daniel Haben Clark   *May 5, 1965*

YOU MAY GO HOME AGAIN
   David Starkweather   *May 19, 1965*

OPRA: "SAINT SIEGFRIED" OR HOW TO
MAKE A HERO
   Tom O'Horgan   *May 26, 1965*

THE DRIFTER AND THE SOLIPSIST
   Walter Leyden Brown   *June 2, 1965*

A POOR WOMAN and THE CIRCUS
   Gerald Schoenwolf   *June 9, 1965*

THE WHITE WHORE AND THE BIT PLAYER
   Tom Eyen   *June 15, 1965*

WHY HANNA'S SKIRT WON'T STAY DOWN
   Tom Eyen   *June 17, 1965*

MR. LEONIDA CONFRONTS THE REVOLUTION and
MIME PLAY and AROUND THE WORLD
WITH AN ACTOR
   Ion Luca Caragiale; Samuel
   Avatol; Anthony Ingrassia   *June 23, 1965*

THE LANDLORD AND HIS GOOD TENANTS
   Pagoon (Kang Wouk)   *June 30, 1965*

MIRAGE and THE CIRCLE
   Robert Patrick; Alex Civello   *July 8, 1965*

IN THE WATER MARKET and BUNNY HOP, and
AND NOW THE WEATHER
   Bob Hart; Jean Reavey;
   Paul Rawlings   *July 14, 1965*

HYACINTH HALVEY and POT OF BROTH
   Lady Gregory;
   William Butler Yeats   *July 21, 1965*

CYCLE GUY and THE VALUE OF MONEY
   Bruce Kessler   *July 28, 1965*

LULLABY FOR A DYING MAN
   Ruth Landshoff Yorck   *Aug. 4, 1965*

THE GIRL ON THE BBC
   Claris Nelson   *Aug. 11, 1965*

PUSSIES AND ROOKIES
   Leonard Melfi   *Aug. 25, 1965*

THE DEMENTED WORLD OF TOM EYEN
   Tom Eyen   *Sept. 2, 1965*

THE NAKED KING
   Wesly St. John   *Sept. 8, 1965*

SANDCASTLE
   Lanford Wilson   *Sept. 22, 1965*

THE RESURRECTION OF PHILIP JEROME MICHAELS
   John Culjak   *Sept. 28, 1965*

THE TYPIST
   Murray Schisgal   *Oct. 6, 1965*

MEDEA IN THE LAUNDROMAT
   H. M. Koutoukas   *Oct. 13, 1965*

FIVE FITTS
   Harold Greenberger   *Oct. 20, 1965*

OPEN THEATRE IMPROVISATIONS
     Oct. 27, 1965

BANG
   A benefit by 25 playwrights, each with a
   three-minute sketch, to raise money for La
   Mama; organized by Robert Patrick.
     Nov. 3, 1965

DAFFODILS AND DAISIES
   Rosenzweig   *Nov. 10, 1965*

MEAT AND POTATOES
   Robert Sealy   *Nov. 17, 1965*

THE MADONNA IN THE ORCHARD
   Paul Foster   *Nov. 24, 1965*

MISS NEFERTITI REGRETS
   Tom Eyen   *Dec. 1, 1965*

DREAM
   Jean-Claude van Itallie   *Dec. 15, 1965*

BLUEBEARD and THE CHEAPSKATE
   Walter Harris   *Dec. 18–19, 1965*

THE WITNESS
   T. Roscwicz   *Dec. 26, 1965*

SOON JACK NOVEMBER
   Sharon Thie   *Jan. 10, 1966*

BACKDROP and TEN POUNDS OF GROUND
   Susan Sherman   *Jan. 26, 1966*

WHO PUT THE BLOOD ON MY LONG-STEMMED
ROSES? and ENACTMENT
   Mary Mitchell   *Feb. 2, 1966*

THE MAGICIANS and THE REUNION
   Merrill Williams;
   Michael Mathias   *Feb. 10, 1966*

THE DUMB DANCER
   Asif Currimbhoy   *Feb. 16, 1966*

THE MAGIC REALIST
   Megan Terry   *Feb. 16, 1966*

NOT ENTIRELY NONDESCRIPT BUT and
PERSEPHONE IN THE SUN
  Bruce Kessler   *Oct. 31, 1969*

BIG CHARLOTTE
  John Wallowitch   *Nov. 20, 1969*

SPRING VOICES
  Andy Robinson   *Dec. 4, 1969*

SPRINTORGASMICS
  Wilhelm Pevny   *Dec. 11, 1969*

NOVA
  Robert Schwartz   *Dec. 18, 1969*

CHRISTMAS SHOW
  Tom O'Horgan   *Dec. 25, 1969*

THE UNSEEN HAND
  Sam Shepard   *Dec. 26, 1969*

SHANGO DE IMA
  Susan Sherman   *Jan. 1, 1970*

PARAPET
  David Mueller   *Jan. 6, 1970*

THE ONLY JEALOUSY OF EMER and MUSIC and
RENARD THE FOX
  W. B. Yeats; Barbara Benary;
  Igor Stravinsky   *Jan. 14, 1970*

BUT MOST OF US CRY IN THE MOVIES
  Bruce Kirle   *Jan. 28, 1970*

UBU and ARDEN OF FAVERSHAM
  Alfred Jarry; Anonymous   *Feb. 6, 1970*

BUFFALO MEAT
  Chico Garvin   *Feb. 11, 1970*

QUAD
  Merrill Harris   *Feb. 18, 1970*

SON OF COCK-STRONG
  Tom Murrin   *Feb. 20, 1970*

HEAVEN GRAND IN AMBER ORBIT
  Jackie Curtis   *Feb. 24, 1970*

VAN GOGH
  Arthur Sainer   *Feb. 25, 1970*

APPROACHING SIMONE
  Megan Terry   *March 4, 1970*

ELEGY TO A DOWN QUEEN
  Leslie Lee   *March 11, 1970*

BLUEBEARD
  Charles Ludlam   *March 25, 1970*

WHAT IS MAKING GILDA SO GREY?
  Tom Eyen   *March 26, 1970*

CINQUE
  Leonard Melfi   *March 26, 1970*

HEIMSKRINGLA! OR THE STONED ANGELS
  Paul Foster   *March 28–29, 1970*

SECOND DOOR LEFT
  Alexander Popovich   *April 1, 1970*

CAPTAIN JACK'S REVENGE
  Michael Smith   *April 3, 1970*

THE DIRTIEST SHOW IN TOWN
  Tom Eyen   *April 4, 1970*

BAUDELAIRE
  Antoine Bourseiller   *April 9, 1970*

PIG
  Synduey Anveani   *April 22, 1970*

OUR PLAY OF THE FUTURE HAS NO NAME
  Harold Greenberger   *April 23, 1970*

HOW THEY MADE IT
  Nancy Fales   *April 30, 1970*

FEMME FATALE
  Jackie Curtis   *May 6, 1970*

JULIA CAESAR
  Alan Causey   *May 13, 1970*

MIRA
  Gucharan Das, music by
  David Walker   *May 20, 1970*

THE MARTYR
  Niagara Community College   *May 28, 1970*

CHARLIE and OUT TO SEA
  Slawomir Mrozek   *June 3, 1970*

PLAYING WITH DOLLS and THE MAN
WHO KILLED TINKERBELL
  Julian Anderson and
  Robert Reiser   *June 3, 1970*

SALOME
  Adapted by Andy Robinson   *June 10, 1970*

THE GOLDEN BAT
  Tokyo Kid Brothers   *June 17, 1970*

TA TA TA
  Ottowa College (Kansas)   *June 29, 1970*

ENDGAME
  Samuel Beckett   *July 8, 1970*

LA MARIE VISION
  Shuji Terayama   *July 8, 1970*

ALLEGROS
  Donald Harrington and
  Mark Brimijohn   *July 15, 1970*

SHAVED SPLITS
  Sam Shepard   *July 20, 1970*

GERTRUDE
  Wilford Leach   *Sept. 9, 1970*

THE SWINGER
  Chester Theater Company   *Sept. 11, 1970*

GRAND MAGIC CIRCUS (LE GRAND
CIRQUE MAGIC)
  Conceived by Jerome Savary with
  his company from Paris   *Sept. 16, 1970*

NIGHTCLUB
  Kenneth Bernard   *Sept. 17, 1970*

PHOTOGRAPHER and CARNIVAL
  Otto Dyjk; Alberd Maurits   *Sept. 23, 1970*

MONKEYS OF THE ORGAN GRINDER
  Kenneth Bernard   *Sept. 28, 1970*

ESTA NOCHE TEATRO
   South American Company   *Oct. 7, 1970*

STREET SOUNDS
   Ed Bullins   *Oct. 14, 1970*

PHOEBUS, YOU'VE TURNED ON
   Arva Petrides and Diane Kagan *Oct. 21, 1970*

CONEY ISLAND
   Tokyo Kid Brothers   *Oct. 28, 1970*

MARAT/SADE
   Peter Weiss   *Oct. 28, 1970*

TOY SHOW
   Leon Katz   *Nov. 4, 1970*

EARLY MORNING
   Edward Bond   *Nov. 18, 1970*

BLUEBERRY MUFFIN TWICE REMOVED and
CHAMBER PIECE FOR BEARDED PERCUSSIONIST
AND STROVIL
   Nancy Haiken;
   James Cuomo   *Nov. 18, 1970*

CARMILLA
   Wilford Leach   *Nov. 25, 1970*

SABAT
   Gerald Miller   *Nov. 25, 1970*

THE TRAGEDY OF HOMER SILLS
   Tony Barsha   *Dec. 2, 1970*

GRAVEDIGGERS OF 1971
   Reigh Hagen and
   Barbara Kahn   *Dec. 2, 1970*

A CHEAP TRICK
   Charles Mingus III   *Dec. 9, 1970*

SUICIDE IN ALEXANDRIA
   Nelly Vivas   *Dec. 16, 1970*

BLACK SUN
   Antonin Artaud   *Dec. 30, 1970*

THE RICHEST GIRL IN THE WORLD
FINDS HAPPINESS
   Robert Patrick   *Dec. 24, 1970*

THE CENCI
   Antonin Artaud   *Dec. 30, 1970*

CRANES AND PEONIES
   Jing Jyi-Wu and Ching Yeh   *Dec. 30, 1970*

TWO DANCES
   Erwin Martin   *Jan. 19, 1971*

COPS AND ROBBERS
   Leslie Lee   *Jan. 29, 1971*

THE REFRIGERATORS
   Mario Fratti   *Jan. 27, 1971*

DREAM OF DANANG
   Fred Curchak   *Feb. 10, 1971*

DANCE WI' ME
   Greg Antonocci   *Feb. 13, 1971*

RED, WHITE AND BLACK
   Eric Bentley   *Feb. 24, 1971*

GODSPELL
   John Michael Tebelak   *Feb. 24, 1971*

SAVAGE
   Conceived by Maxine Klein   *March 3, 1971*

LIBERATED WOMAN
   Barry Reckord   *March 17, 1971*

THIEF
   Steve Whitson   *March 24, 1971*

COFFINS FOR BUTTERFLIES
   Conceived by Asian American
   Repertory Company–La Mama
   Chinatown   *March 31, 1971*

CINDERELLA PLAY
   Paul Erik Rummos   *April 7, 1971*

REAL REEL
   Frederick Baal   *April 14, 1971*

KAAKA MAKAAKOO
   Conceived by Tone Brulin with
   Otrabanda Company of the
   Virgin Islands   *April 21, 1971*

PORK
   Andy Warhol   *May 5, 1971*

A DOG'S LOVE
   Michael Smith, music by John
   Herbert McDowell   *May 12, 1971*

MACDOUGAL STREET
   Edwart Setrakian   *May 19, 1971*

TESTIMONIES
   Edward Shannon   *May 30, 1971*

VAIN VICTORY
   Jackie Curtis   *May 26, 1971*

CYCLOTRON
   Conceived by Nassau Community
   College Company   *June 2, 1971*

THE RED HORSE ANIMATION and
COME AND GO and PLAY
   Lee Breuer; Samuel Beckett   *June 9, 1971*

FANDO AND LIZ
   Arrabal   *June 10, 1971*

PREDICATES
   Nancy Fales   *June 30, 1971*

MONDAY ON THE WAY TO MERCURY ISLAND and
SHUBERT'S LAST SERENADE
   Julie Bovasso   *June 30, 1971*

HAMLET
   Shakespeare   *Sept. 8, 1971*

LACELESTINA or THE SPANISH BAWD
   Fernando de Rojas   *Sept. 26, 1971*

STOLEN WORDS
   Joao Perry   *Oct. 6, 1971*

EL AMOR DE LA ESTANCIERA
   Anonymous   *Oct. 6, 1971*

AND THINGS THAT GO BUMP IN THE NIGHT
   Terrence McNally   *Oct. 13, 1971*

GENESIS!
   Philip Bosakowsky   *Oct. 20, 1971*

THEATRE GENESIS
St. Mark's Church-in-the-Bowery
Tenth Street and Second Avenue
New York, New York 10003

The Theatre Genesis (at St. Mark's Episcopal Church-in-the-Bowery) was founded by Ralph Cook in 1964 to "discover authentic theatre voices and develop them toward a kind of subjective realism."

The writers, directors and actors at the Genesis have attacked their projects with more guts and clarity than can be found almost anywhere else Off Off Broadway. There are no frills here; everything is stripped away and we get right down to basics: *how to survive* in a world of political, social and ecological chaos.

The Genesis experience during its first six years was closely tied in with politics and drugs, and its metamorphosis is an interesting parallel to that of the subculture from which it was born. It began with an easy one-to-one relationship which was often metaphysical, many times expressed in the language of the street and combined humor with a contained violence. As it evolved the violence began to be openly expressed on the stage. Finally it erupted in the work process.

Cook was looking for writers who were "working things out in themselves through their writing." He had a pessimistic view of the world but a strong inner belief in art. Cook believed that a good writer was "twisted around by his life and society" and that "worthwhile things could come from a radical nature trying to find itself in this society."

The Genesis writers chose a nondramatic way of dealing with acting that called for energy rather than emotion, and the audience was never indulged or condescended to. Often they were made to *live*. There was a brutal castration in *Willie the Germ* and in another production a man was carried in on a meathook.

"What is happening onstage is not a mirror," says playwright Murray Mednick; "it's what's happening."

Ralph Cook had been an actor, a salesman and a teacher when he arrived at the church, and he was at an undecided point in his life. A revelation he had at the church led to his becoming its minister to the arts and starting the theatre program in 1964.

In *Rock Garden* and *Cowboys* Sam Shepard was one of the first writers to deal with the contemporary American experience on its own terms. Leonard Melfi's *Birdbath* was a harrowing analogy of the agonies of creation and a fulfillment of Cook's philosophy.

Mednick and Tony Barsha went further with *The Hawk,* which combined a poem by Mednick with an improvisational group under Barsha's direction. After the group had been worked out and toned for six months, they were packed off to a farm, where work was begun on the poem. In a communal environment where they could share "the burden of life" together they improvised in the mornings and did formal work on the piece in the afternoons. Mednick would feed them information and he and Barsha would edit the language the actors came up with each day. They called themselves the Keystone Company and the resulting production of *The Hawk* was a metaphysical work with great power and magic.

The taste of freedom and the natural growth of the writers led to a split within the Genesis. Some writers had gone to other theatres, new voices like Walter Hadler were being heard and the writers wanted more say in the run of the theatre. In the established tradition of this church, the people were given the power and Cook left in 1969.

A short time later the Black and Spanish people of the church congregation, led by the assistant minister, David Garcia, interrupted a service and demanded their rights. Almost immediately Garcia replaced Michael Allen as minister and the congregation changed radically. The black and brown factions are now dominant, and the radical whites departed, to be replaced by a few *more* radical whites.

A theatre where playwrights, directors and actors present political and social ideas is even more important to its society than to any form of *theatre.* The Genesis has demanded and reciprocated to change in a real way. It has been a seed for change—planted in the plays of Shepard, Melfi, Mednick—which grows all over the world as these plays are performed.

The following plays have been presented by Theatre Genesis at St. Mark's Church-in-the-Bowery:

STUDY IN COLOR
    Malcolm Boyd   *July 30, 1964*

COWBOYS and ROCK GARDEN
    Sam Shepard   *Oct. 16, 1964*

BEFORE BREAKFAST IN WONDERLAND
and CHEER UP
    Pat Branch   *Jan. 29, 1965*

THE DRAPES COME
    Charles Dizenzo   *Feb. 12, 1965*

LET'S GET SERIOUS and THE GATE
    Charles Mee, Jr.   *March 5, 1965*

FREE, FREE, FREE and THERE'S A WALL
BETWEEN US, DARLING
    Sally Ordway   *March 26, 1965*

THE CUSTOMS INSPECTOR IN BAGGY PANTS
and CHICAGO
    Lawrence Ferlinghetti;
    Sam Shepard   *April 16, 1965*

BIRDBATH and SUNGLASSES and CYCLE and
THE VALUE OF MONEY
    Leonard Melfi; Leonard Melfi; *June 11, 1965*
    Shirley Guy; Anthony Webb *July 29, 1965*

PUSSIES AND ROOKIES and FERRYBOAT
    Leonard Melfi   *Sept. 2, 1965*

MEDEA
    H. M. Koutoukas   *Nov. 5, 1965*

THE BOX and MY DADDY IS DYING and
OUT OF TOWN TRAFFIC
    Murray Mednick; Tom Sankey;
    Leonard Melfi   *Dec. 10, 1965*

WHY THE CLOWN NEVER SPEAKS and
A CORNER OF THE MORNING and
THE INTERROGATION ROOM
    Thomas Ohlson; Michael Locascio;
    David Scott Milton   *Jan. 28, 1966*

DEGREES and THE WAITING HEXAGRAM
    George Birimisa;
    Rudy Wurlitzer   *Feb. 25, 1966*

THE PATTERN and THE TRUNK
    Tony Barsha   *April 9, 1966*

THE MARK OF ZORRO
    Murray Mednick   *June 17, 1966*

THE GOLDEN SCREW
    Tom Sankey   *Sept. 23, 1966*

HALLOWEEN MASK and THE HEARING
    David Scott Milton;
    Tony Barsha   *Oct. 14, 1966*

THE KEY and GUIDELINE
    Kit Jones; Murray Mednick   *Nov. 18, 1966*

SMASH and FRUIT SALAD
    Tony Barsha; Grant Duay   *Jan. 20, 1967*

ETUDE
    Robert Howard   *Feb. 17, 1967*

PAPYRUS! and SAND
    William Kushner;
    Murray Mednick   *March 31, 1967*

THE HAWK
    Murray Mednick and
    Tony Barsha   *Oct. 13, 1967*

FORENSIC AND THE NAVIGATORS
    Sam Shepard   *Dec. 29, 1967*

THE BEGGAR'S OPERA
    Tom Sankey   *March 8, 1968*

WILLIE THE GERM
    Murray Mednick   *May 10, 1968*

BAD TIMES IN BUMMERSVILLE
    Joel Oppenheimer and
    The Bummers Company   *May 30, 1968*

SOLARIUM
    Walter Hadler   *June 14, 1968*

THE HUNTER
    Murray Mednick   *Oct. 11, 1968*

THIRTY and AMERICAN GOTHIC
    Walter Hadler   *Nov. 29, 1968*

H ISOLATION
    Lee Kissman   *Jan. 31, 1969*

KEYSTONE COMMUNAL
    Keystone Company   *March 14, 1969*

MISSION BEACH and FLITE CAGE
    Walter Hadler   *May 3, 1969*

THE SHADOW RIPENS
    Murray Mednick and Theatre
    Five Company   *May 30, 1969*

THE WATER WORKS AT LINCOLN
    Walter Hadler   *Nov. 6, 1969*

THE FORGOTTEN AMERICAN and NIGGER NATE
    Tony Barsha   *Jan. 9, 1970*

THE DEER KILL
    Murray Mednick   *April 30, 1970*

GRAND MAL CRICK
    Walter Hadler   *Jan. 14, 1971*

MAD DOG BLUES
    Sam Shepard   *March 4, 1971*

LESSON IN DEAD LANGUAGE
  Adrienne Kennedy   *April 22, 1971*
CARTOON
  Murray Mednick   *Oct. 14, 1971*
COUNTRY MUSIC
  Michael Smith   *Dec. 16, 1971*

BORROWED TIME
  Robert Glaudini   *Feb. 3, 1972*
JIMTOWN
  Kathleen Kimbel   *March 17, 1972*
MUTILATION
  Walter Hadler   *May 4, 1972*

THE AMERICAN PLACE THEATRE
111 West Forty-Sixth Street
New York, New York 10036

The American Place Theatre began in 1964 at St. Clement's Church. The theatre, under the directorship of Wynn Handman, a well known director and acting teacher in the New York area, was established to be a place where American poets and playwrights could develop their dramatic works. Many of the works given as full scale productions were originally presented as readings, then works-in-progress, etc. at the American Place. Its audiences have the opportunity to observe a work at every stage of development.

The American Place audience is totally drawn from subscription and it is the only theatre in New York in this desirable situation. The membership has grown from 800 to 7,000 in the first seven years of its existence. Membership rates range from $12.50 for students to $25.00 for non-student subscribers.

The American Place has received aid from the New York State Council of the Arts and the National Endowment for the Arts. In the 1970–71 season the Council on the Arts donated 75,000 dollars. This money, in addition to offsetting the theatre deficit, is channeled into programs to promote theatre: high school, college, college seminars, senior citizens' programs, theatre for the blind, tours and a quarterly publication, *News of the American Place Theatre*. The American Place has received a number of awards for the excellence of its productions.

In the fall of 1971 Handman and associate director Julia Miles announced the completion of construction of a new space for the American Place Theatre. On December 6 the new theatre (the first of three theatres in office buildings in the New York area) opened officially with a double bill of Steven Tesich's *Lake of the Woods* and Ronald Ribman's *Fingernails Blue as Flowers*. The new theatre, in the Fisher Brothers' J. P. Stevens Building, 111 West Forty-sixth Street, also houses a cafe, The Sub-Plot, which presents political satire. Construction cost of the new theatre was $1.5 million. The thirty-year lease provides for an annual rental of $5.

The following are the plays presented by the American Place Theatre:

(Full Productions)

THE OLD GLORY	
Robert Lowell	*Nov. 1, 1964*
HARRY, NOON AND NIGHT	
Ronald Ribman	*March 12, 1965*
HOGAN'S GOAT	
William Alfred	*Oct. 20, 1965*
JONAH	
Paul Goodman	*Feb. 1, 1966*
THE JOURNEY OF THE FIFTH HORSE	
Ronald Ribman	*April 9, 1966*
DOUBLES AND OPPOSITES: THE FLOOR and 23 PAT O'BRIEN MOVIES and MISS PETE	
May Swenson; Bruce Jay Friedman; Andrew Glaze	*May 1, 1966*
WHO'S GOT HIS OWN	
Ronald Milner	*Sept. 30, 1966*
THE DISPLACED PERSON	
Cecil Dawkins	*Dec. 16, 1966*
LA TURISTA	
Sam Shepard	*March 4, 1967*
POSTERITY FOR SALE	
Niccolo Tucci	*May 11, 1967*
FATHER UXBRIDGE WANTS TO MARRY	
Frank Gagliano	*Oct. 12, 1967*
THE CEREMONY OF INNOCENCE	
Ronald Ribman	*Dec. 14, 1967*

xliv

THE ELECTRONIC NIGGER AND OTHERS
  Ed Bullins   *Feb. 21, 1968*

ENDECOTT AND THE RED CROSS
  Robert Lowell   *April 18, 1968*

THE CANNIBALS
  George Tabori   *Oct. 17, 1968*

TRAINER, DEAN, LIEPOLT AND COMPANY: THE
ACQUISITION and THIS BIRD OF DAWNING
SINGETH ALL NIGHT LONG and
YOUNG MASTER DANTE
  David Trainer; Philip Dean;
  Werner Liepolt   *Dec. 12, 1968*

BOY ON THE STAIGHT-BACK CHAIR
  Ronald Tavel   *Feb. 14, 1969*

PAPP
  Kenneth Cameron   *April 17, 1969*

MERCY STREET
  Anne Sexton   *Oct. 11, 1969*

FIVE ON THE BLACK HAND SIDE
  Charlie Russell   *Dec. 10, 1969*

TWO TIMES ONE: THE LAST STRAW and
DUET FOR SOLO VOICE
  Charles Dizenzo;
  David Scott Milton   *Feb. 21, 1970*

PIG PEN
  Ed Bullins   *April 27, 1970*

SUNDAY DINNER
  Joyce Carol Oates   *Oct. 16, 1970*

CARPENTERS
  Steven Tesich   *Dec. 10, 1970*

PINKVILLE
  George Tabori   *Feb. 22, 1971*

BACK BOG BEAST BAIT and COWBOY MOUTH
  Sam Shepard; Sam Shepard and
  Patti Smith   *April 29, 1971*

FINGERNAILS BLUE AS FLOWERS and
LAKE OF THE WOODS
  Ronald Ribman;
  Steven Tesich   *Dec. 6, 1971*

SLEEP
  Jack Gelber   *Feb. 10, 1972*

METAMORPHOSIS
  Charles Dizenzo   *April 5, 1972*

THE CHICKENCOOP CHINAMAN
  Frank Chin   *May 27, 1972*

(Rehearsed Readings, Works-in-Progress)

A REMEMBRANCE OF JAMES AGEE
  Varied excerpts   *Feb. 7, 1964*

CHRISTY
  William Goyen   *March 19, 1964*

JUANA LA LOCA
  Mary Lee Settle   *June 14, 1964*

THE OUTSIDE MAN
  Robert Smiddie   *Dec. 17, 1964*

LOWER THAN THE ANGELS
  John O. Killens   *Jan. 30, 1965*

CLARA TOMORROW
  William Roberts   *May 1965*

BROTHER TO DRAGONS
  Robert Penn Warren   *June 1, 1965*

A NICE JEWISH BOY
  Philip Roth   *June 11, 1965*

A STEP AWAY FROM WAR
  Varied excerpts   *June 20, 1965*

THE PLEASURE PARTY
  Lee Jacobson   *June 28, 1965*

LITANY FOR THE MAN
  Mark Zalk   *Jan. 8, 1966*

MICHAEL THE GOD
  George P. Elliott   *Feb. 6, 1966*

SLEEPY-BYES
  Edward Mannix   *June 6, 1966*

THE SOCIAL EUMENIDES
  Brock Brower   *Oct. 29, 1966*

CHANCE FOR RAIN
  Donald Justice   *April 8, 1967*

CRANE, CRANE, MONTROSE AND CRANE
  Jascha Kessler   *Jan. 2, 1968*

MICHAEL OF BYZANTIUM
  George P. Elliott   *Feb. 4, 1968*

GOIN' A BUFFALO
  Ed Bullins   *June 6, 1968*

THE MINSTRELS
  Joseph Whitt   *June 9, 1968*

WELCOME TO ANDROMEDA
  Ron Whyte   *April 19, 1969*

MADAME USA
  Clare Woock   *June 5, 1969*

THE BAREFOOT ANTELOPE
  David Scott Milton   *Sept. 22, 1969*

EVERY NIGHT WHEN THE SUN GOES DOWN
  Philip Dean   *Nov. 11, 1969*

REMEMBER THE ALAMO
  Barry Litvack   *Jan. 18, 1970*

BIGFOOT
  Ronald Tavel   *Nov. 11, 1970*

BREAD
  David Scott Milton   *Oct. 14, 1971*

THIS- THERE- MOVE
  Michael Kirby   *Dec. 4, 1971*

THE GREAT AMERICAN REFRIGERATOR and
BILL BAILEY and COME TRUE
  Fred Gordon   *Feb. 25, 1972*

WHAT IF IT TURNED UP HEADS?
  J. E. Gaines   *March 10, 1972*

BROKEN YOKE and WE MAKE OUR OWN
  Vincent Barry   *April 7, 1972*

COLLAPSE OF THE GREAT I AM
  PHILIP HAYES DEAN   *June 16, 1972*

THE CHELSEA THEATRE CENTER
Brooklyn Academy of Music
30 Lafayette Avenue
Brooklyn, New York 11217

The Chelsea Theatre Center was founded in 1965 by Robert Kalfin, who became its artistic director, and Michael David, who became its executive director. It began the first season at St. Peter's Episcopal Church and moved midseason to the Church of the Holy Apostles, where the initial program was continued—a series of free plays. The Chelsea Theatre Center presented 49 workshop productions at these locations. The Brooklyn Academy of Music invited the organization to become its resident company.

With the change in location came a change of production emphasis; instead of a workshop-free theatre, the group attempted full-scale productions with minimum three-week runs and a four-dollar admission. Robert Kalfin dedicated his theatre to the borough of Brooklyn; he wanted to produce only unfamiliar works. Sixty percent of the audience is presently drawn from Brooklyn. The small theatre, which was completely remodeled for the group, has a seating capacity of two hundred.

In recent seasons the Chelsea has presented some of the most exciting and innovative theatre in the New York area. It has no particular troupe or style but offers a consistent excellence of production and generally good material.

LeRoi Jones' *Slave Ship* spoke from the root of blackness and presented a clear definition of terms for an entire system. John Lahr in *The Village Voice* called it "the most powerful black theatre that white audiences have been allowed to see." In *AC/DC* by Heathcote Williams the play was enhanced by the use of video tapes depicting real and abstract events on thirty television monitors placed about the stage, created by a group of West Coast "video freaks" known as *Video Free America.*

The Chelsea Theatre Center in its 1971–72 season offered a subscription to four plays. Future plans call for expansion of their workshop productions, The Brown Bag; presentation of a touring program throughout the borough of Brooklyn, presentation of a full children's theatre program, and formation of a professional theatre training group to serve the Brooklyn community.

The following are the plays presented by the Chelsea Theatre Center:

FIVE DAYS	
Henry Zeiger	*1965–66*
TRIPTYCH	
Ken McGuire	*1965–66*
JOHN WILKES BOOTH	
Ronald Colby	*1956–66*
THE COMMUNIST	
Archie Shepp	*1965–66*
THE EVE OF THE GREEN GRASS	
Coleman Dowell	*1965–66*
REBELS AND BUGS	
Wynn Appling	*1965–66*
THE FINAL SOLUTION OF THE NEGRO PROBLEM	
Tom Mechling	*1965–66*
NERO AND FOOL	
Robert Reinhold	*1965–66*
THE ADMIRATION OF LIFE	
Patricia Broderick	*1965–66*
A DIFFERENT WORLD	
Rachel Erlanger	*1965–66*
BIRTH OF A REBEL	
Richard Davidson	*1965–66*
KID	
Edward Pomerantz	*1965–66*
BILLY	
Russ Vliet	*1965–66*

xlvi

THE NEW LAFAYETTE THEATRE

2349 Seventh Avenue
New York, New York 10030

The New Lafayette Theatre was founded in 1966 by Robert MacBeth and Ed Bullins to forge a community *theatre culture* for, from and by the people of Harlem.

In MacBeth's words: "In the past decade the major social, political, educational and cultural efforts to take place in the Black community have had a 'from the outside to the inside' attitude inherent in their programs. That is, things which were 'thought' to be needed and of value were 'brought to the disadvantaged' by those who had it. All this was so much 'missionary' activity, and proved itself to be unhelpful, even destructive.

"A body or community of people make up an organism, a culture, which functions much like any individual human organism or body. And the final curing or healing of a body or culture is always done from within; it is part of that body's *natural* function. External treatment of the symptom or pain is never a solution. *The people, the community, the culture itself is the only entity that can cure its ills.* And the methods and concepts needed by the ailing culture are found organic in its arts: the music, the literature, the architecture and design art, and the art of human movement and singing. When these arts are performed together, in concert, it is called theatre."

MacBeth defines the purpose of art as "the raising of consciousness" and further says, "Our job has always been to show Black people who they are, where they are and what condition they are in."

The company, first housed in the old Lafayette Theatre, a federally funded theatre in the 1930s on 132nd Street and Seventh Avenue, opened on October 13, 1967, with *Who's Got His Own* by Ron Milner. After the close of the second production, *The Blood Knot* by Athol Fugard, the theatre burned.

MacBeth directed a triple bill of plays by Ed Bullins (which included *Clara's Ole Man*) at the American Place Theatre in the spring of 1968 while a new home was sought.

In September 1968 the first issue of *Black Theatre* magazine was published, with Bullins as editor. While the magazine is closely linked with the activity at the New Lafayette Theatre, it also includes reportage of other Black theatres, play scripts and interviews and discussions with Black theatre artists throughout the world. The magazine supplements the purpose of the theatre: to evolve a Black theatre art.

The New Lafayette Theatre Agency, a non-profit play service, has also been established to handle the plays of Black playwrights: Kingsley B. Bass, Ed Bullins, Ben Caldwell, Martha Charles, J. E. Gaines, Salimu, Sonia Sanchez, Sharon Stockard, Richard Wesley and Marvin X.

The New Lafayette Theatre moved to its present location at 137th Street and Seventh Avenue in December 1968.

The dedication of these artists, musicians, painters, designers and actors is religious, and as Roscoe Orman wrote in *Black Theatre* (#5), "In coming together and working on a basis of pure human effort, hopefully [we] will reaffirm in the hearts of our people the essence of our Blackness, so that we may meet the difficult times ahead with foresight and vision."

The following productions have been presented at the New Lafayette Theatre:

WHO'S GOT HIS OWN
   Ron Milner   *Oct. 13, 1967*

THE BLOOD KNOT
   Athol Fugard   *Nov. 17, 1967*

IN THE WINE TIME
  Ed Bullins   *Dec. 10, 1968*
WE RIGHTEOUS BOMBERS
  Kingsley B. Bass, Jr.   *April 18, 1969*
A BLACK RITUAL
  Company   *Aug. 29, 1969*
GOIN' A BUFFALO
  Ed Bullins   *Oct. 24, 1969*
TO RAISE THE DEAD AND FORETELL THE FUTURE
(A BLACK RITUAL)
  Company   *March 6, 1970*

THE DUPLEX
  Ed Bullins   *May 22, 1970*
BLACK TIME FOR BLACK FOLK
  Company   *Aug. 28, 1970*
THE DEVIL CATCHERS
  Company   *Nov. 27, 1970*
THE FABULOUS MISS MARIE
  Ed Bullins   *March 5, 1971*
PSYCHIC PRETENDERS
  Company   *Dec. 24, 1971*

THE NEGRO ENSEMBLE COMPANY (NEC)

St. Mark's Theatre
133 Second Avenue
New York, New York 10003

Three seemingly disparate elements contributed to the formation of the Negro Ensemble Company: the first—in the summer of 1964 Robert Hooks founded a private group interested in the development of a Black theatre, The Group Theatre Workshop; the second—in August of 1966 Douglas Turner Ward wrote an article for *The New York Times* on the development of a Black theatre; the third—The Ford Foundation, because of Ward's article, became interested in funding a Black theatre organization.

The Negro Ensemble Company became a reality. The goal of the new organization was a theatre to be controlled by Blacks, making use of existing Black talent, developing new Black talent and encouraging a primarily Black theatre audience. The Ford Foundation contributed the financing; Robert Hooks brought the nucleus, The Group Theatre Workshop, and became the artistic director; Douglas Turner Ward became the director; and Gerald Krone, an experienced theatrical manager, contributed his expertise as administrative director. The NEC established itself at 133 Second Avenue, the site of the St. Mark's Theatre.

A school was established with a ten-week tuition-free program. Its purpose was to train young Blacks in all phases of the theatre. The students, in addition to their classes, were to participate in actual programs, works in progress by new Black playwrights. This program has presented between seven and ten works each season in addition to the NEC's full professional schedule.

The Ford Foundation provided a three-year establishment grant to begin the new company. Additional aid from both the state and federal governments over succeeding years enabled the NEC to continue producing at 133 Second Avenue and also to mount three national tours.

The Negro Ensemble Company is presently in its fourth season of production. It has performed in the World Theatre Season in London, and in the Premio Roma in Italy. The European tour planned for 1972 includes Munich, where the NEC will participate in the 1972 Olympic Festival.

The following are the plays presented by the Negro Ensemble Company:

SONG OF THE LUSITANIAN BOGEY
  Peter Weiss   *Jan. 2, 1968*

SUMMER OF THE SEVENTEENTH DOLL
  Ray Lawler   *Feb. 20, 1968*

KONGI'S HARVEST
  Wole Soyinka   *April 9, 1968*

DADDY GOODNESS
  *Richard Wright and
  Louis Sapin*   *June 4, 1968*

GOD IS A (GUESS WHAT?)
  Ray McIver   *Dec. 17, 1968*

CEREMONIES IN DARK OLD MEN
  Lonne Elder III   *Feb. 4, 1969*

STRING and CONTRIBUTION and MALCOCHON
  *Alice Childress; Ted Shrine;
  Derek Walcott*   *March 25, 1969*

MAN BETTER MAN
  Errol Hill   *July 2, 1969*

THE RECKONING
  Douglas Turner Ward   *Sept. 4, 1969*

THE HARANGUES
  Joseph A. Walker   *Dec. 30, 1969*

BROTHERHOOD and DAY OF ABSENCE
  Douglas Turner Ward   *March 17, 1970*

1

AKOKAWE (Initiation)
  Traditional and Modern
  African Writings   *May 19, 1970*
ODODO
  Joseph A. Walker   *Nov. 24, 1970*
ROSALEE PRITCHETT and PERRY'S MISSION
  Carlton and Barbara Molette;
  Clarence Young III   *Jan. 21, 1971*
THE DREAM ON MONKEY MOUNTAIN
  Derek Walcott   *March 14, 1971*
RIDE A BLACK HORSE
  John A. Scott   *May 25, 1971*

BLACK CIRCLES (STREET THEATRE)
  Hazel Bryant   *July 26, 1971*
THE STY OF THE BLIND PIG
  Phillip Hayes Dean   *Nov. 23, 1971*
WORKS IN PROGRESS
  Various   *Jan. 12, 1972*
A BALLET BEHIND THE BRIDGE
  Lennox Brown   *March 14, 1972*
FREDERICK DOUGLASS . . . IN HIS OWN WORDS
  Arthur Burghardt and
  Michael Egan   *May 9, 1972*

THE NEW DRAMATISTS COMMITTEE, NEW DRAMATISTS INC.

424 West Forty-fourth Street
New York, New York 10036

The New Dramatists Committee was formed in 1949 by a group of playwrights who wanted a place to meet and to discuss their problems with their peers. The Dramatists Guild gave the new group valuable assistance by guiding them, providing a meeting place for them and eventually providing funds for them. The first meetings were held at the Hudson Theatre. The group met on a regular basis when, by the mid-1950s, with the aid of certain foundations, they were able to rent permanent space and establish themselves as a nonprofit corporation.

The New Dramatists Committee became New Dramatists Inc., at 83 East Fourth Street; their facilities included a theatre and office space. By 1963, again with the help of foundations, they had expanded so that they could consider presenting readings and actual workshop productions of new plays. This proved an invaluable aid to any playwright who had reached the stage in his work at which a live presentation was required. Readings and workshop presentations were available to all members of New Dramatists Inc.

The requirements for membership in New Dramatists Inc. are that a playwright live in the greater New York area and have completed at least two full-length plays. Once a member, if a playwright wishes a presentation, he submits the project to the reading committee. The reading committee is composed of members who volunteer; the criterion for positive selection is the promise of the playwright rather than the excellence of the play. Once selected, the play is scheduled on the New Dramatists calendar. (This unfortunately can take as long as a year.) A maximum production budget of 100 dollars is allotted to the playwright. The organization provides the theatre, movable flats, furniture and prop pools, lighting equipment, etc.; the rest must be impro-

vised within the limited budget provided. Invitations are then sent to the mailing list kept by the organization and to anyone the playwright wishes to invite. Critics are allowed to attend but they are requested not to review the presentations. It is not the intention of New Dramatists to present full productions but rather works in progress. The organization wishes to provide an arena in which the playwright can see the shape of his work.

New Dramatists Inc. has been very successful. It provides a valuable and needed service. The organization remained at 83 East Fourth Street until the summer of 1969, at which time it moved to 424 West Forty-fourth Street, where it is presently located. The readings and productions began in 1963 and they continue today.

The following is a list of works presented at New Dramatists Inc.:

A YOUNG MAN'S GUIDE TO THE UPPER AIR
    Charles Best   *Oct. 13, 1963*

THE APPLE DOESN'T FALL
    Gene Radano   *Dec. 8, 1963*

DOES A TIGER WEAR A NECKTIE?
    Don Peterson   *Feb. 9, 1964*

NATHAN WEINSTEIN'S DAUGHTER
    David Rayfiel   *April 12, 1964*

A CUP FOR ELIJAH
    Justin Mamis   *April 19, 1964*

Q FOR QUASIMODO
    Harold Yablonsky   *April 30, 1964*

THE ARTISTS and SPIT IN THE OCEAN and
A LIMB OF SNOW
    Anna Marie Barlow   *May 14, 1964*

VIA ZEMSKY
    Anthony Terpiloff   *May 21, 1964*

THE GENTLE ART OF MAKING ENEMIES
   Joel Friedman   *June 7, 1964*

FROM A DARK LAND
   Harding Lemay   *Sept. 27, 1964*

THE MINOTAUR
   Joseph Scott   *Oct. 5, 1964*

BETTER LOVE NEXT TIME
   Lee Kalcheim and
   Leslie J. Stark   *Oct. 23, 1964*

RIDE THE COCK HORSE
   Joseph Scott   *Dec. 20, 1964*

OVERTURE
   Lee Kalcheim   *Jan. 13, 1965*

THE GIRL
   Violet Welles   *Feb. 28, 1965*

HOME BY HOLLYWOOD
   Oliver Hailey   *March 28, 1965*

KISSIN' RATTLESNAKES CAN BE FUN
   Lonne Elder III   *April 11, 1965*

SEVEN PLAYS (excerpts)
   Arthur Pittman   *April 26, 1965*

THE BED WAS FULL
   Rosalyn Drexler   *May 5, 1965*

ANIMAL AND THE PICTURE
   Oliver Hailey   *May 9, 1965*

THE BOY WHO CAME TO LEAVE
   Lee Kalcheim   *May 10, 1965*

THE OCEAN OUT FRONT
   James Harvey   *May 16, 1965*

THE CEREMONIES IN DARK OLD MEN
   Lonne Elder III   *June 1, 1965*

UNTITLED PLAY
   Lee Kalcheim   *June 7, 1965*

KEEP THE PASTRAMI HOT
   Malcolm Marmorstein   *June 2, 1965*

A WEEK FROM TODAY
   Norman Wexler   *Nov. 30, 1965*

THE DRAPES COME
   Charles Dizenzo   *Nov. 30, 1965*

THE MUTE WHO SANG
   Gene Radano   *Dec. 3, 1965*

HUSBANDS AND WIVES
   Arthur Pittman   *Dec. 14, 1965*

THE LITTLE BIRDS FLY
   Harding Lemay   *Jan. 16, 1966*

WHO'S HAPPY NOW?
   Oliver Hailey   *Jan. 2, 1966*

MR. AND MRS. LYMAN
   Joel Friedman   *March 6, 1966*

WHAT COLOR GOES WITH BROWN
   Jerome Max   *March 13, 1966*

APPLES AND INNOCENCE
   Justin Mamis   *March 21, 1966*

NEEDMORE AND NEEDMORE'S MOTHER
   William Parchman   *April 4, 1966*

FAT RUBENSTEIN (first act)
   Richard Foreman   *April 24, 1966*

PRUNELLA AND BLURR
   Jerome Max   *May 2, 1966*

NERO
   Charles Dizenzo   *May 17, 1966*

I RAN INTO THIS ZULU
   Malcolm Marmorstein   *May 31, 1966*

THE INVESTIGATION and HOT BUTTERED ROLLS
   Rosalyn Drexler   *June 5, 1966*

VILLON
   William Parchman   *June 9, 1966*

SEVEN MILLION LISTENERS CAN'T BE WRONG
   Lee Kalcheim   *June 9, 1966*

JOHNNY NO TRUMP
   Mary Mercier   *June 13, 1966*

THE PEACE CREEPS
   John Wolfson   *June 20, 1966*

DEADLOCK
   Gene Radano   *July 8, 1966*

THE SURPRISE
   Lee Kalcheim   *July 20, 1966*

THE EXILES
   Lee Kalcheim   *Oct. 24, 1966*

CHERRY SODA WATER
   Stephen Levi   *Nov. 27, 1966*

THE HOUSE OF BLUE LEAVES
   John Guare   *Nov. 28, 1966*

KEEP TIGHTLY CLOSED
   Megan Terry   *March 21, 1967*

FROM A DARK LAND
   Harding Lemay   *April 23, 1967*

THE LAST GOODBYE
   Joel Friedman   *April 29, 1967*

FATHER UXBRIDGE
   Frank Gagliano   *May 9, 1967*

THE MEETING
   Anna Marie Barlow   *May 31, 1967*

THE PRIZE IN THE CRACKERJACK BOX
   William E. Parchman   *June 4, 1967*

REQUIEM FOR A VACUUM CLEANER
   Aldo Giunta   *June 29, 1967*

AN AUDIBLE SIGH
   Lee Kalcheim   *July 14, 1967*

THE CALM BEFORE THE BOMB
   John Wolfson   *July 14, 1967*

THE SPIRIT OF '67
   Lee Kalcheim   *Aug. 10, 1967*

SNOW OF THE SOUTHERN SUMMERS
   Joseph Scott   *Oct. 2, 1967*

SAM
   Charles Best   *Oct. 7, 1967*

THE NEW YORK SHAKESPEARE FESTIVAL, THE PUBLIC THEATRE

425 Lafayette Street
New York, New York 10003

The Public Theatre opened on October 7, 1967, with *Hair.* Its beginnings can be traced back to 1953, when its founder and director, Joseph Papp, held his first rehearsal in a Lower East Side church hall. By 1958 Mr. Papp, in conjunction with the city of New York, offered a summer season in Central Park of free Shakespeare. The New York City Shakespeare Festival has had continuing summer seasons in the park and the 1971 season marked its thirteenth year. But Mr. Papp wanted more than just a summer troupe.

In 1966, with a combination of private funds, foundation grants and money provided by the city of New York, the New York Shakespeare Festival purchased the former Astor Library at 425 Lafayette Street. They hoped to renovate the building to create a theatre complex that could present varied work in all media. This hope became a reality by 1970, when the last theatre was completed. The Public Theatre presently houses the Florence Sutro Anspacher Theatre, a 299-seat house with three-quarter round design; the Estelle R. Newman Theatre, a thrust-stage room with 299 seats; the Other Stage, an experimental workshop theatre with 108 seats; the Anthology Film Archives, an experimental cinema with 90 seats; a concert room, informal space with no fixed seating, for music and special theatre pieces; the Cinque Gallery, which hangs the work of artists of representative minorities; and the Fernandez-Film Workshop, a group that works with underprivileged children and students.

The Public Theatre has made every attempt to keep its ticket prices as low as possible; the theatre has been a deficit operation since its beginnings. For the 1971–72 season a new concept in tickets was offered; a 15-dollar pass covered admission to the full season of eight plays and any workshop production the holder wished to attend. (There was a special rate for students and people over sixty-five of $7.50.)

Although the Public Theatre is clearly an Off Broadway institution in its concepts (and it presents fully mounted Equity productions) we have included it because the nature of the work has been social and experimental and it has provided a gateway for many alumnae of Off Off Broadway to flow into the mainstream of world theatre.

With the publication of two new magazines by the theatre, *Performance,* discussions and forums by contemporary theatre artists and *Scripts,* a monthly publication of new scripts written and selected by many of the authors in this book, the Public Theatre will exert a further influence on world and national theatre.

The following plays have been presented by Joseph Papp at the Public Theatre:

HAIR
James Rado and Gerome Ragni, music by Galt MacDermot   Oct. 17, 1967

HAMLET (as a happening)
William Shakespeare   Dec. 19, 1967

ERGO
Jakov Lind   Feb. 20, 1968

THE MEMORANDUM
Vaclav Havel   April 23, 1968

HUUI, HUUI
Anne Burr   Nov. 2, 1968

CITIES IN BEZIQUE: THE OWL ANSWERS and A BEAST'S STORY
Adrienne Kennedy   Jan. 4, 1969

INVITATION TO A BEHEADING
Adapted by Russell McGrath from the novel by Vladimir Nabokov   March 8, 1969

THE OLD RELIABLE
231 East Third Street
New York, New York 10009

A funky, junky, divey bar on Third Street between Avenues B and C: authentic lowlife—
junkies, pimps, whores, pushers—cavorts at the
bar over a gin or a 50-cent draft—a *nickel* juke-
box, yes! a Seeburg twinkles and blasts—and in
the back room—eek! oh my God—it's a theatre!

The Old Reliable Tavern first tried its hand
at doing plays in the summer of 1967. Tony
Preston wrote a play, *Rags an' Old Iron*, about
an old black woman and an old white woman in
a home, and together with director Hugh Gittens
and the bartender, Kenny Hill, he persuaded the
owner, Norman "Speedy" Hartman, to let them
do it.

The admission was free and the customers
(not part of the two percent of our total population who have seen even the *junior play* on a
stage) flocked into the back room in droves. They
loved what they saw.

The OR's playwright in residence was Robert
Patrick, a mad, astrological comic genius who
looks something like Noah Webster plugged into
the wrong socket, and he wrote nearly forty plays
until the place closed in the summer of 1971.

No matter what he wrote or how fast he
wrote it (once on an hour's notice when an angry
playwright withdrew his play on opening night)
it came out funny. Once he wrote a serious play
and wept because the audience was on the floor—
which at the OR is saying something. I never *saw*
the floor when I was there—just layers of people
stacked on tables and chairs.

"The OR was the least organized Off Off
Broadway theatre," says Patrick, "and the results ranged from the sublime to the unspeakable."
When the show was "unspeakable" the audience
more than made up for it. Their barbs could
reduce an actor to a crying—or laughing—shambles. Sometimes the crowd picked up the dialogue

and put on its own play. Occasionally fists flew.
Playwright Josef Bush called them "the last Eliza-
bethan audience."

The OR had its biggest hit with Patrick's
Joyce Dynel, a devastating musical satire of the
life of Christ and the first to look at Him as a
"superstar." It set out to show how Christ has
"stultified and paralyzed" our sex lives. Patrick
wrote it for Christmas 1968, and the holiday audience jammed the one reservation phone. At the
OR he died for our sins on a *muscleman*.

The uptown audience "discovered" the OR
and the place was packed for every new show.
Patrick explained the full houses by saying that
people were afraid to come alone. The spirit there
was like the Saturday matinees we went to as
kids—but, of course, with the added pleasure of
of "booze."

Originally the OR company was Black but
a lot of the white undergrounders who groove on
Black people showed up and the place was a mixture of Cino dropouts, Irish Catholics such as
playwright Jeannine (Bails) O'Reilly ("obsessed
by what it is to be a woman in America," says
Patrick), actor Joe Pichette and various funk
followers.

Eventually the total individual freedom that
made the OR what it was—imagine "Speedy"
winning an award for best producer *and* best
house manager in the same year!—made it fall
apart. Anyone who took any kind of responsibility was asking for it. No money, no props, no
sets, muggers on the streets. Once when I was
playing a scene with Neil Flanagan at the OR
we heard six shots ring out next door. We just
shrugged and went on. Neil ran the place for
a while. Also Eric Concklin.

Two of its shows, *Haunted Host* by Patrick
and *De Sade Illustrated* by Bush, moved Off

Broadway. Agents grabbed up the actors like crazy. But the main point was the total OR experience.

The following plays were presented at The Old Reliable Theatre Tavern:

RAGS AND OLD IRON and BLOOD IS THICKER
    Tony Preston   *July 18, 1967*

THE BUNDLE MAN and A CHANCE IN A MILLION
    Ilse Gilbert; Gordon Glasco   *Aug. 9, 1967*

THE ENCHANTED NIGHT and RAGS AND OLD IRON
    Slavomir Mrozek;
    Tony Preston   *Aug. 21, 1967*

BOXED-IN and QUIET AT RANDOM
    Joel Efrein; Harold Barnes   *Sept. 27, 1967*

27501, REVIVAL and THE DOLLS
    Lee Hunkins   *Oct. 11, 1967*

THE BREAST OF HEAVEN and THE UMBILICAL
CORD OF HOWARD LOSTFOGEL
    Lloyd Hezekiah;
    Jeannine Bails   *Oct. 25, 1967*

ONE LAST LOOK and THE BIBLE TELLS US SO
and FIRST CAUSE
    Steve Carter; Jeannine Bails;
    David Isaacson   *Nov. 16, 1967*

A SAD DAY FOR BERNINI and
MEDUSA OF 47TH STREET
    Eric Krebs; Nancy Henderson   *Dec. 6, 1967*

THE MYTH OF VERBIO and
EYES AND THE TRIAL
    Daniel Manesse;
    Kenneth Lillquist   *Dec. 20, 1967*

DADDY VIOLET and
MONOCHROME
    George Birimisa;
    Nancy Henderson   *Jan. 22, 1968*

THE LEADER and
THE DEAD DENTIST and
IT'S NICE OUT, ISN'T IT?
    Joseph White; Ilse Gilbert;
    Jack Heller   *Feb. 12, 1968*

UN BELDI and HELP, I AM and
THE WAREHOUSE and
AMELIA AND JESS
    Robert Patrick; Jean Forest;
    Ronald Mele   *March 11, 1968*

OBSIDIAN and TINKLE, TINKLE and
SEE OTHER SIDE
    Bambi Hartgens; Thomas Terefenko;
    Robert Patrick   *April 1, 1968*

UNDER THE CROSS EYED EAGLE and
AXE TO GRIND
    Elmer Klein;
    Thomas Terefenko   *April 22, 1968*

ABSOLUTE POWER OVER MOVIE STARS
    Robert Patrick   *May 13, 1968*

CONQUERING THURSDAY
    Elmer Klein   *June 3, 1968*

PREGGIN AND LISS and DIARIES and
AS YOU CAN SEE
    Robert Patrick; V. Robert Coleman;
    Steve Carter   *June 17, 1968*

HOW SWEET AND FITTING IT IS and THE
OVERSEERS and ANGELS IN AGONY
    Joseph Renard; Robert Patrick   *July 1, 1968*

THE FLOUNDER COMPLEX and
GET YOURSELF A GUN, BROTHER
    Anthony Damato;
    Thomas Terefenko   *July 15, 1968*

THE HAUNTED HOST and NO LARK
    Robert Patrick; Jeannine Bails   *July 29, 1968*

GOODNIGHT, I LOVE YOU and
THANK YOU, MISS VICTORIA
    William M. Hoffman   *Aug. 26, 1968*

WILL I SEE YOU IN THE CITY? and
AD MAJORAM DEI GLORIAM
    Peggy Simon; Josef Bush   *Sept. 9, 1968*

SALVATION ARMY and FRENCH GRAY
    Robert Patrick; Josef Bush   *Sept. 23, 1968*

LOVE ME OR I'LL KILL YOU and
NAUGHTY, NAUGHTY
    Dan Clark; Peter Copani   *Oct. 7, 1968*

UPTIGHT (Revue)
    William M. Hoffman   *Oct. 21, 1968*

LA REVUE (8 short plays)
    Jeannine Bails   *Nov. 4, 1968*

THE HAUNTED HOST and THE CLUB BEDROOM
    Robert Patrick;
    Louis Auchincloss   *Nov. 25, 1968*

DYNEL
    Robert Patrick   *Dec. 16, 1968*

THAT ONE AND THE OTHER and
THE BROWN CROWN
    Eric Concklin; Haal Borske   *Jan. 7, 1969*

FOG and PUDDIN' HEAD WILSON
    Robert Patrick; Mark Twain   *Jan. 20, 1969*

PHILOSOPHY IN THE BEDROOM BY THE
MARQUIS DE SADE
    Josef Bush   *Feb. 6, 1969*

THE NEIGHBORS and JADE
    Thomas Terefenko;
    Jeannine O'Reilly   *Feb. 24, 1969*

SMITHEREENS and THE FOREIGNERS
    Sally H. Levy;
    Michael McGrinder   *March 10, 1969*

I CAME TO NEW YORK TO WRITE
    Robert Patrick   *March 24, 1969*

JOYCE DYNEL
    Robert Patrick   *April 7, 1969*

THE OPEN THEATRE
60 West Fourteenth Street
New York, New York 10011

Joseph Chaikin had worked as an actor with the Living Theatre. In September of 1963 Mr. Chaikin founded the Open Theatre as a laboratory for actors. The goal of the new group was " . . . to redefine the limits of the stage experience, or unfix them." The Living Theatre, through 1963, had made every attempt to break the rules of the conventional theatre; however, their methods were often gratuitous and did not necessarily relate to the theatrical piece. The Open Theatre, unlike the Living Theatre, did not attempt to break the rules for the express purpose of being avant-garde. Chaikin incorporated the best of the theory evolved by the Becks and adapted it to meet the requirements of the new group.

The Open Theatre is a theatre for actors. It was created by an actor to develop a new acting style. The playwrights who work with the group are not independents who present finished scripts but rather integral participants in the group experience. The writing is done within the context of a given theme. The group attempts to portray that theme and the playwright watches, perhaps suggesting forms, until many versions of the theme are evolved. The playwright uses his artistic selectivity, changing, editing and shaping the group's work into a theatrical whole. The playwrights of this theatre are not concerned with ordinary dramatic transitions. The concentration is behavioral, not literal. Hence, a play can go from birth to death in one scene. The plays interrelate the absolutes in a stream-of-consciousness technique rather than in a chronological order. That is not to say that the material is as unformed as it might be in pure deductive thinking, but the connections between scenes and ideas are the kind made by the mind on the subconscious as opposed to the logical.

Since performance is the essential, each piece attempts to achieve its own fully realized individual goal. Unlike its successor, the Performance Group, and its predecessor, the Living Theatre, the works of the Open Theatre are goal-defined within the context of the work, i.e., the theatrical goal is "new" theatre, the plays are separate ideas, the technique is different with each play. *Keep Tightly Closed* is an experiment in the pure virtuosity of technique; it is an enjoyment of the technique for its own sake. *Viet Rock* is an organic play that presents the structure of war. The cast switches roles, commenting as individual members of the chorus so that the product seems to be presented by a cast of hundreds. The play is apolitical but it does make the simple statement that war "stinks." The troupe ends the piece by going out into the audience; this is not for the purpose of confrontation but to bring the audience closer to the conceptual reality of the work. *America Hurrah* is about the mechanization of modern life and its dehumanizing effect. The troupe was drilled like SS troops; there was no touching, no personal contact. The play was presented like the workings of a computer—programmed to the last gesture. *The Serpent* is an exploration of a part of the Book of Genesis. As Frazer and Fromm did, it defines the myth down to the simplest line and repeats it but always in a way that is understandable to the individual. The work is intensely moving to those who are familiar with the myth; and while elucidating, it illuminates the story so that the audience finds it new and original. The performers often simultaneously play the same character to give the audience a new dimensional characterization rather than the usual dimensional expression. Joseph Chaikin is an orchestrator more than a director, the actors are instruments and the playwright, the conductor. The result is theatre that is completely organic and alive.

With *America Hurrah* and *Viet Rock,* the Open Theatre arrived on the public scene. They had been working rigorously in a loft on Spring Street. Each member of the group contributed five dollars weekly to pay the loft rent and other expenses. There was no thought of salary. Not until 1968 when they were touring *The Serpent* and received grant money from the National Endowment and the Ford Foundation did the group begin to be paid regularly for their work. *Viet Rock* came too early for the critics to realize that its very newness was theatrically valid, but with *America Hurrah* they were overwhelmed. The simplicity of the staging, the relative lack of sets (other than the magnificent doll heads by Robert Wilson), the sheer technical facility with which the troupe underlined the inherent values of the play were overwhelming to the critics. But the Open Theatre has never been interested in commercial success.

What they do they do well. They perform in their own loft and give limited public performances in other theatres. They have made several European tours and are recognized as a new force in the theatre. They began with Monday night stands at the Sheridan Square and Martinique Theatres. They have become one of the most clearly defined theatre troupes in the world. The foundation money has enabled them to continue their exploration and we hope they continue and continue and continue.

Following is a partial list of the plays presented by the Open Theatre (in addition to these they have also presented pieces by Sam Shepard, Michael Smith, Sharon Thie, John Arden, T. S. Eliot and Bertolt Brecht):

CALM DOWN MOTHER
Megan Terry — 1965

KEEP TIGHTLY CLOSED
Megan Terry — 1965

SUCCESSFUL LIFE OF 3
Maria Irene Fornés — 1965

I'M REALLY THERE
Jean-Claude van Itallie — 1966

ALMOST LIKE BEING
Jean-Claude van Itallie — 1966

THE DREAM
Jean-Claude van Itallie — 1966

THE HUNTER AND THE BIRD
Jean-Claude van Itallie — 1966

THE SERPENT
Jean-Claude van Itallie — 1967–68

UBU COCU
Alfred Jarry — 1969

TERMINAL
Susan Yankowitz — 1969–70

ENDGAME
Samuel Beckett — 1970

MUTATIONS
Joseph Chaikin and Roberta Sklar — 1970–72

THE PERFORMANCE GROUP
The Performing Garage
33 Wooster Street
New York, New York 10013

Richard Schechner brought together a group of nonprofessional actors in 1968 that came to be known as the Performance Group. Mr. Schechner had been involved with a troupe in New Orleans from 1965 to 1967 and it was from this experience and from a meeting with Jerzy Grotowski that Mr. Schechner evolved the concept of the new group.

The group was to be mostly composed of nonprofessional young actors so that there would not be a need to unlearn. It was to meet three times a week for five-hour sessions. The theory behind the sessions was based on basic Grotowski methods and the exercises were those outlined by Grotowski. The sessions were intensive work observing rigid disciplines. In Mr. Schechner's own words: "We did not permit laughter, talking, tears." The objective was to produce a kind of theatre that went beyond just words, an archetypal ritual that could be understood regardless of language. The audience would participate to the extent they would be moved to do so. Mr. Schechner feels "that the structure of performance is universal; that the differences between ritual and theatre are of social functions." The ritual should be cross-cultural; it should attempt to take the audience to a level of common mythic experience, to put them in touch with those roots which their individual cultures have made them forget.

The first work presented by the Performance Group was *Dionysus in 69*. The play was a contemporary version of *The Bacchae* by Euripides. Sections of the actual Euripides text were used and these were set against fragments of other texts that were relevant to the effect. The language was a part of the production but it was used like a chant in a primitive celebration; although not unimportant to the full context of the piece, *Diony-sus in 69* could probably have been understood by a non-English-speaking member of the audience.

Dionysus was presented at the Performing Garage and this playing area was important to the production. The room was almost square with a triple-height ceiling. The set was composed of platforms, wood scaffolding—some going to the top of the room, on which the audience sat. There was an irregular opening in the center and a large part of the audience was seated on the floor. The audience was asked to dance, sing, join in chants and generally participate. The attempt was to make the audience feel as if it were taking part in a bacchanal—a religious and emotional celebration. The success of the piece was often dependent upon the audience; however, when it was successful, all of Mr. Schechner's vision was realized. The nudity of the actors was a vital part of the theatrical realization and at no time was it gratuitous.

The Performance Group received a great deal of critical praise for *Dionysus in 69*. Like its predecessors, the Living Theatre and the Open Theatre, the effect created by the same group working in close proximity for an extended period can be extraordinary, a theatrical experience of singular quality.

The following are the works performed by the Performance Group under the direction of Richard Schechner:

DIONYSUS IN 69	*June 6, 1968*
MAKBETH	*Nov. 20, 1969*
COMMUNE	*Dec. 17, 1970*
CONCERT FOR TPG	*June 2, 1971*

THE PLAYWRIGHTS UNIT
83 East Fourth Street
New York, New York 10003

The Playwrights Unit was founded in 1963 by Edward Albee, Richard Barr and Clinton Wilder. They rented a 199-seat theatre and office space at 15 Vandam Street. The unit was established so that neophyte playwrights might have the experience of a full theatrical production without subjecting themselves to the trauma of the critics before they had adequate experience. Any playwright could apply to the organization for a production. The scripts were read and decided upon by Albee, Barr and Wilder. Once the play was accepted, its production was left to the playwright. The unit's role was to see that the playwright had access to the talents he felt were required for a proper production of his piece; the unit acted exclusively in an advisory capacity. The playwright chose his own cast, set designer, light designer, costume designer, crew and director. In this way the playwright himself was responsible for the production values. The playwright was able to learn how vital these values are to his conception, i.e., the difference between what appears on the printed page and what is finally presented on stage.

In addition to its founders, the Playwrights Unit had a business manager and a secretary. The organization was wholly financed by its founders until it received grants in aid from the New York State Council of the Arts, the Ford Foundation, and other foundations.

The audience for the productions was drawn from a list maintained by the unit. If a recipient did not attend at least twice a season, his name was dropped from the list. The doors were opened one-half hour before each performance with a general seating policy; admission was free.

In 1968 Mr. Wilder withdrew his portion of the sponsorship and he was replaced by Charles Woodward. The unit remained on Vandam Street until early in 1969, when they moved to their own building at 83 East Fourth Street. This building, which had previously housed David Ross' Fourth Street Theatre and New Dramatists Inc., seemed to be an ideal home for the unit.

After considerable renovation, they had a beautiful 160-seat theatre, rehearsal space and offices. Unfortunately, because of the quality of the productions and the ambitious schedule, the Playwrights Unit cost 1,000 dollars per week to operate. In the spring of 1970 the founders announced that they could not continue to meet the rising expenses and that the unit would be closed. The building at 83 East Fourth Street is for sale and there are no plans to reactivate this fine organization.

The following are the plays presented at the Playwrights Unit (they are listed alphabetically instead of chronologically because the records were kept in this manner and there is no other source for this material):

AFTERNOON IS A SUGAR CUBE
Tom Oliver

AFTER THE WASH
Ursule Molinaro

A GREAT CAREER
Charles Dizenzo

ALMOST LIKE BEING
Jean-Claude van Itallie

AM
Otis Bigelow

AMERICAN ROULETTE
Tom McCormack

AND HE MADE A HER
Doric Wilson

THE RIDICULOUS THEATRICAL COMPANY

New Arts Management
100 Fifth Avenue
New York, New York 10011

THE PLAY-HOUSE OF THE RIDICULOUS

La Mama ETC
74 East Fourth Street
New York, New York 10003

In 1965, Ronald Tavel wrote *Shower* for Edie Sedgwick, Andy Warhol's then-reigning superstar. Warhol did not produce it because Edie felt the play was too outrageous to perform. This led Tavel to John Vaccaro, a young director who was willing to take a chance with it. *Shower* was produced at the Coda Gallery, East Tenth Street between Third and Fourth Avenues, on July 29, 1965, with *The Life of Juanita Castro.* The double bill was moved to the St. Mark's Playhouse, where it ran till the end of September. Tavel found a patron, Pana Grady, who donated 700 dollars, which enabled the group to rent an acting studio at 13 West Seventeenth Street. The group wanted a name that would describe the nature of the work Tavel had thus far conceived; they decided upon The Play-House of the Ridiculous.

The Play-House of the Ridiculous opened in the spring of 1966 with Ronald Tavel's *The Life of Lady Godiva.* The group was then formed, Tavel was the official playwright and Vaccaro the director. Charles Ludlam came to the group as an actor to do a minor part in *Godiva.* Ronald Tavel completed *Gorilla Queen* but John Vaccaro refused to direct it; instead, they mounted two of his smaller pieces, *Screen Test* and *Indira Gandhi's Daring Device;* the program ran from September to January.

John Vaccaro took the troupe on a college tour over Tavel's objections. The tour resulted in chaos—the schools were outraged by the plays. *Kitchenette,* Tavel's final play for the group, opened January 28, 1967. Tavel was interested in a playwright's theatre and Vaccaro wanted a theatre that was director-oriented. Tavel, troubled by the difference with Vaccaro and disgusted by the general disorganization, left the group. *Gorilla Queen* had been accepted for production by the Judson Poets' Theatre.

John Vaccaro stayed at the Play-House. The next production was Charles Ludlam's first play, *Big Hotel.* This production had a short run because the theatre was closed by the city. Wyn Chamberlain became the group's new producer and they mounted a professional production of Ludlam's second piece, *Conquest of the Universe,* at the Bouwerie Lane Theatre. It was during this production that Ludlam and Vaccaro separated, with Vaccaro continuing at the Bouwerie Lane under the heading of the Play-House of the Ridiculous. Vaccaro experimented with playing at various places; e.g., *The Moke-Eater* by Kenneth Bernard was performed at a restaurant, Max's Kansas City. Because they did not have a home, the group began to separate. They met sporadically and gave isolated performances at La Mama and other theatres, but the cohesion was gone. In 1969 John Vaccaro replaced Lamarr Alford as head of La Mama Amsterdam. He returned to New York for a successful season at La Mama in the spring of 1972.

When Charles Ludlam left John Vaccaro, he took the troupe and mounted his version of *Conquest of the Universe,* changing the title to *When Queens Collide.* Ludlam called his group the Ridiculous Theatrical Company. They played at Tambellini's Gate at midnight after the regular film showings. They moved to an abandoned theatre on West Forty-second Street, where Ludlam collaborated with Bill Vehr to write *Turds in Hell.* They were forced to move again—to a loft on Bond Street, where Ludlam mounted the first version of *The Grand Tarot.*

The Ridiculous Theatrical Company continued to move—playing when and where they could. *Bluebeard* was developed at a sleazy gay bar, Christopher's End. The company gave single performances of their repertory at churches and schools. They had no financing. They could not advertise. The audience was developed totally by word of mouth, which is no small feat considering that there was no announced playing schedule or theatre. Over a period of three years Ludlam added an additional five actors and five more in 1969. Charles Ludlam is the director, playwright, organizer and lead actor; yet Ludlam thinks of the company as collaborators. The central concentration of the group is to develop the style. Ludlam describes this style as "a synthesis of classical comedic acting and the popular mimetic styles preserved in the American Silent Cinema as a continuation of the grand tradition."

The members of the Ridiculous Theatrical Company are rarely paid. They sew their own costumes because they cannot afford professional costumers. *Vogue* referred to the costumes as ultra-chic, which was flattering, but the company does it because it must. They have no choice. They cannot afford a theatre, legal services, accountants, etc. With the full production of *Bluebeard* in 1970 and its continuous run at the Performing Garage, the company finally achieved the critical and public attention it so justly deserved. *Bluebeard* won an Obie award and was hailed by Martin Gottfried as a comic masterpiece. *The Grand Tarot* presented in repertory with *Bluebeard* at the Gotham Art Theatre received truly fine notices. In the summer of 1971 the Ridiculous Theatrical Company toured Europe. They premiered a new work which they brought to New York for the spring 1972 season, *Eunuchs of the Forbidden City*.

It can only be hoped that this worthwhile and dedicated company will find a permanent home, a theatre of their own in which they can continue to perfect the excellence that they have thus far achieved.

The following are the plays presented by the Ridiculous companies:

PLAY-HOUSE OF THE RIDICULOUS:

SHOWER and THE LIFE OF JUANITA CASTRO
Ronald Tavel July 29, 1965

THE LIFE OF LADY GODIVA
Ronald Tavel April 21, 1966

SCREEN TEST and INDIRA GANDHI'S DARING DEVICE
Ronald Tavel Sept. 29, 1966

KITCHENETTE
Ronald Tavel Jan. 28, 1967

BIG HOTEL
Charles Ludlam Feb. 2, 1967

CONQUEST OF THE UNIVERSE
Charles Ludlam June 10, 1967

PLAY-HOUSE OF THE RIDICULOUS UNDER JOHN VACCARO:

THE MOKE-EATER
Kenneth Bernard Sept. 19, 1968

COCK-STRONG
Tom Murrin June 20, 1969

SON OF COCK-STRONG
Tom Murrin Feb. 20, 1970

HEAVEN GRAND IN AMBER ORBIT
Jackie Curtis Feb. 24, 1970

NIGHTCLUB
Kenneth Bernard Sept. 17, 1970

XXXX'S
William M. Hoffman Dec. 22, 1971

ELEGY TO A DOWN QUEEN
*Leslie Lee, music by
John Vaccaro* Feb. 10, 1972

PERSIA (A DESERT CHEAPIE)
*Bernard Roth
and John Vaccaro* April 9, 1972

SATYRICON
Paul Foster May 20, 1972

THE RIDICULOUS THEATRICAL COMPANY UNDER CHARLES LUDLAM:

WHEN QUEENS COLLIDE
Charles Ludlam Dec. 29, 1967

WHORES OF BABYLON
Bill Vehr March 22, 1968

TURDS IN HELL
*Charles Ludlam and
Bill Vehr* Nov. 8, 1968

BLUEBEARD
Charles Ludlam March 26, 1970

EUNUCHS OF THE FORBIDDEN CITY
Charles Ludlam July 24, 1971

THE URBAN ARTS CORPS
20 West Twentieth Street
New York, New York 10011

The best way to say "Black is Beautiful" is by showing it; not by riots in the streets, but by art in the streets, in parks, in playgrounds, parking lots, prisons, churches, schools, colleges, libraries—and in theatres and art galleries.

—VINNETTE CARROLL

Vinnette Carroll is an educator, clinical psychologist, Obie Award-winning actress and an Emmy Award-winning director. In founding the Urban Arts Corps she brought with her not only her extensive formal background but a rich sense of pride in black cultural traditions and black history instilled by her mother during childhood in Harlem.

She formed the Urban Arts Corps as a summer project while heading the New York State Council on the Arts' Ghetto Arts Program in 1968. To find its actors, singers, writers, composers and choreographers she went to ghetto high schools, churches and youth groups. "I am trying to find Negro and Puerto Rican people with a background in the arts," she said. "We're looking for qualified young people who are on the way up. It's important that they are qualified because we can no longer perpetuate the myth of white supremacy in the black community. If we were to give them people who are not really qualified they would feel inferior again."

By the end of the year it was apparent that the Corps was to be far more than a summer project, and Vinnette left the council to become its Artistic Director. After a series of street and school performances the Corps made its formal debut at no less than New York's City Center on April 23, 1969. The production was *But Never Jam Today,* a soul adaptation of Lewis Carroll's *Alice in Wonderland* which literally shook the walls of that cavernous theatre. Jerry Tallmer wrote in the *New York Post:* "It brings the house down. I think the N.Y. State Council on the Arts, or some other body, would do well to send this production out to high schools and other places where it would surely be well received." The next time I saw it, at the insistence of the Corps' enthusiastic press agent, Robert Ganshaw, I am not quite sure just where we were. But it was a small church room filled with the most joyous young black faces you could imagine.

The next major work was a stirring adaptation of Irwin Shaw's *Bury the Dead* with music by Micki Grant. It was among the first productions of the play permitted in this country by Shaw in many years and Vinnette justifiably thinks it is their finest to date. Walter Kerr paid tribute to her ability to seek out the best of new talent and mold it into professionalism of the highest caliber: "The parade of singing (and acting) performers (are) skilled enough to put the best of Broadway to shame."

With many of her initial goals for the Corps well under way, Vinnette Carroll is on to new ones. A three-year program has been initiated to put black folk and fairy tales into the mainstream. The first effort in this direction was an adaptation of *Croesus and the Witch* from the black fabulist Aesop, with music by Micki Grant.

The workshop classes in voice, acting, movement and diction continue, and the Corps hopes to spend several months a year in residence with a university, producing plays in cooperation with the Drama Department and conducting workshops in acting with the students.

In the spring of 1972 the Corps produced *Don't Bother Me, I Can't Cope* Off Broadway, and *Village Voice* critic Dick Brukenfeld wrote: "It has more excitement per square inch than anything in New York." With the most dynamic woman in the New York theatre at its helm, that's not surprising.

The following are the plays presented by the Urban Arts Corps:

THE LOTTERY
> *Shirley Jackson, adapted by*
> *Vinnette Carroll*   1968

OLD JUDGE MOSE IS DEAD
> *Joseph White*   1968

MOON ON A RAINBOW SHAWL
> *Errol John, music by Micki Grant*   1968

BUT NEVER JAM TODAY
> *Adapted by Vinnette Carroll, music*
> *by Gershon Kinsley, lyrics by Robert*
> *Lorimer*   1969

DON'T BOTHER ME, I CAN'T COPE
> *Micki Grant*   1970

SHADES OF HARLEM
> *Mel Herring*   1970

BURY THE DEAD
> *Irwin Shaw, music and lyrics by*
> *Micki Grant*   1971

BLACK NATIVITY
> *Langston Hughes, traditional music*   1971

CROESUS AND THE WITCH
> *Aesop, adapted by Vinnette Carroll,*
> *music and lyrics by Micki Grant*   1971

THEATRE FOR THE NEW CITY
113 Jane Street
New York, New York 10014

Off Off Broadway in 1971-72 was undergoing an identity crisis, as was the entire New York theatre. Doing something *new* didn't seem quite enough and there didn't seem to be anything new left to do. Alliances were in a state of change, and the season had a large share of revivals of the plays of the 1960s and imports from other countries. The playwrights of Off Off Broadway's first decade, feeling the need to be independent, formed *The New York Theatre Strategy* and set about to produce their own plays. Off Off Broadway was caught. It no longer seemed to be a springboard to Broadway and Off Broadway, and yet it had become a little fast and commercial for the purists who had flourished during the early days of the Caffe Cino.

The general state of the economy was being felt in the theatre. Money raising for commercial ventures was difficult, and although the Off Off Broadway audience could still afford $2 for a ticket, its theatres were finding it increasingly difficult to obtain the necessary funding to operate. The Off Off Broadway Alliance (OOBA), a group of more than fifty theatres, was formed. Headed by Bill Gardner (Urban Arts Corps), Dick Brukenfeld *(The Village Voice)* and Virginia Aquino (Workshop of the Players' Art), its common objective was a combined effort to focus public attention on the movement and to effectively raise funds.

The Theatre for the New City, founded in March of 1971 by Crystal Field, George Bartenieff, Lawrence Kornfeld and Theo Barnes, exemplified a number of the problems befalling Off Off Broadway at this time. The founding members, veterans of the movement, had all been associated with the Judson Poets' Theatre—Field, Bartenieff and Barnes primarily as actors, and Kornfeld as its resident director. They conceived their new project as "a theatre of spectacle and magic, the spoken word and *fun*" and they wanted a huge space.

Westbeth, a subsidized artists' housing community, provided the space (rent-free), and in the traditional Off Off Broadway manner a paint-up, fix-up party was announced in *The Village Voice* and work was begun.

Shortly after the opening production (a revival of *Dracula:Sabbat* which Kornfeld had directed at Judson several months earlier), dissension developed and Kornfeld and Barnes soon departed. Field and Bartenieff pooled the resources they had after ten years of highly respected work in the theatre community and put together a season that was pretty dazzling. With their choice of writers and productions the theatre flourished, and Westbeth received its most extensive publicity as a center for the arts.

Toward the end of 1971 rumors of financial difficulties in the Westbeth complex began to circulate; in December, Field and Bartenieff, who had been guaranteed free rental through June 30, 1972, were given an eviction notice effective March 1. Westbeth was at first evasive about the reasons for the eviction; dissatisfaction with the theatre's artistic achievements wasn't terribly convincing, since all of the reviews proved to the contrary, and, further, the management had attended only the first production. The underlying financial problem became obvious: Westbeth needed income from the space. Field and Bartenieff appeared before OOBA and raised $12,000 which they offered for one year's rental, but Westbeth, because of its own financial needs, had already accepted a much higher bidder.

Disheartened but not defeated, Field and Bartenieff set out to find another space and to continue the Theatre for the New City. Behind them were hundreds of hours of work and improvements which someone else would now enjoy

—and a solid first season. There are no villains *directly* involved in the situation at Westbeth. More than anything else it was a reflection of our economic and spiritual state in 1972.

The following are the plays presented at the Theatre for the New City/Westbeth:

DRACULA: SABBAT
   Leon Katz, music by John Herbert
   McDowell   *March 24, 1971*

KEEPERS OF THE HIPPO HORN
   Florence Miller   *May 21, 1971*

PROSPERALL RISING
   Roderick Mason Faber, music by
   Michael Colina   *June 18, 1971*

BLU DOKTOR (ROCK AND LIGHT SHOW)
   Jim Hardy   *August 6, 1971*

MINDING THE STORE (STREET PLAY)
   Robert Nichols, music by
   David Tice   *Sept. 18, 1971*

PRÄXEIS
   Theo Barnes   *Oct. 4, 1971*

THE JOURNEY
   Bill Russell, Lawrence Sacharow and
   Group Concepts   *Nov. 4, 1971*

THE CELEBRATION: JOOZ/GUNS/MOVIES/
THE ABYSS
   Arthur Sainer, music by James
   L. Kurtz   *Feb. 11, 1972*

EUNUCHS OF THE FORBIDDEN CITY
   Charles Ludlam   *March 29, 1972*

EVIDENCE
   Richard Foreman   *April 20, 1972*

THE KING OF THE UNITED STATES
   Jean-Claude van Itallie, music by
   Richard Peaslee   *May 15, 1972*

THE CO-OP
   Barbara Garson, songs by
   Fred Gardner   *May 27, 1972*

The Off Off Broadway Book

THE GREAT AMERICAN DESERT

a play in one act

Joel Oppenheimer

The Great American Desert was first presented by the Judson Poets' Theatre at the Judson Memorial Church, New York City, as half of its opening bill with *The Breasts of Tiresias* by Apollinaire on November 18, 1961, with the following cast:

THE OLD COWBOY	*Gil Henderson*
GUNNY	*Jerome Raphel*
THE YOUNG COWBOY	*Ray Girardin*
THE WHORE	*C. Cornelia*
THE BANKER'S BEAUTIFUL DAUGHTER	*Joyce Glassman*
THE BANKER	*John Marshall*
THE SHERIFF	*Laurence Hellenberg*
THE MADAM	*Otis Burger*
WYATT EARP	*Jack Wesley*
WILD BILL HICKOK	*Anthony Hilliard*
BILLY THE KID	*Marty Washburn*
DOC HOLLIDAY	*Paul Blackburn*

It was directed by Lawrence Kornfeld.

All the action takes place somewhere west of Laramie; the time of the play is sunup in the morning to sundown at night. The play was presented in three-quarter round, with an additional stage area ("heaven") on which the four heavenly heroes sit. It is covered at the front enough to conceal their legs and waists as they sit. BILLY THE KID sits farthest from the ladder by which they ascend, in a slightly separated area, in this case a wider, lower platform.

Very low lights come up on stage and hold, while the lights on heaven begin slowly to build. The four heavenly heroes enter upstage left and move diversely across the main stage area, heading generally toward the ladder leading to heaven. They maintain the order necessary for their seating in heaven: BILLY THE KID first; he is dressed in rough range, or even farm clothes, and he carries a rifle. DOC HOLLIDAY next; he is dressed in black, but fastidiously, though not foppishly. WYATT EARP next; he is dressed neatly, with almost a hint of the puritan about him; he has a pistol which is holstered and tied to his leg. WILD BILL HICKOK last; he, of course, has shoulder-length hair and a pointed beard; he is dressed as foppishly as possible, ruffled shirt, etc., and his gun is tucked in his waistband. As they walk they hum, in unison, "Wagonwheels." The humming continues as they reach the ladder and begin the climb to heaven; it will stop when the tune reaches a natural stopping point. Once in heaven, they begin to take their seats. WYATT reminds DOC about BILLY's rifle. BILLY surrenders his rifle to DOC after a token protest, and DOC then leans it back against the wall between WYATT and himself. When all four are comfortable in their seats, WYATT nods to the stage manager, the lights begin to build on stage and revert to their normal holding position on heaven. The three cowboys are discovered downstage left, sleeping.

OLD COWBOY: Goddamn! Morning! [*He stretches, crawls out of bedroll, dresses, kicks each of the other two, and exits upstage right*]

GUNNY: Now what in the good hell he have to do that for? [*He begins dressing*] There are goddamn easier ways wakin' a man up. And you, goddamn you—get up, you lazy bastard, it's morning! The dew's on the frost, and goddamn, you know . . .

YOUNG COWBOY: The sun ain't nowhere near full up, and you both of you raisin' all kinds of hell. We only got another day to ride in, is all, we ain't doin' nothin'. [*He is still stretched flat*]

GUNNY: Yeah, but we still got to do it. Come on now, get yourself up, before he's back and screamin' again. He's probably takin' care of the horses, so I'll get you some firewood and

start this up again. You move your ass and get that goddamn breakfast goin'. I'm hungry. [*Exits upstage right*]

YOUNG COWBOY: Hungry. He's hungry. The two of them is always hungry. I might as well goddamn be married to the two of them. And always I got to do the cookin'. Though, God knows, I ain't about to eat anythin' either of them cooks. Probably poison a rattler, anything either of them cooks. [*Starts getting breakfast materials from his saddlebag*]

OLD COWBOY: [*Reenters*] Them goddamn horses ain't holdin' up so well. Two, three more days of this, they're gone. We better either be out of it by then, or hope we find someone to buy some new ones off'n, even a Indian.

YOUNG COWBOY: You ain't buyin' no goddamned Indian ponies with my share of that money. I'd a heap rather walk first, even into Albuquerque, and that's three hundred miles away.

OLD COWBOY: You sayin' it, boy, but you ain't about to do it. You be, as a matter of fact you be the first one to start cryin' if we have to walk. Listen, I took us through this far, I take us out, and you better believe it.

GUNNY: [*Reenters with firewood*] Here's your firewood. You goin' to get the water, or I have to do that too? Damn, I'm hungry!

YOUNG COWBOY: There's no call at all for you to be pushin' it that way, breakfast goin' to get here, never fear. Besides, you bein' such a big desperado, I think it's only fittin' you get the water, you so big and strong and desperate for it.

GUNNY: Damn this fuckin' desert anyhow. All this sweat over water, goddamn when I was a boy back home in Illinois they used to talk about the plains. . . . I thought to myself like the garden of Eden. Now we here, fightin' from one stinkin' waterhole to the next, nothin' but sand and bushes in betwixt. [*Exits upstage right with bucket. As he leaves stage area, blackout on stage, lights up on heaven. This will be standard procedure for all readings of commercials. They are to be read by individual heavenly heroes in random sequence. Each commercial is read from a typed card in either a straight speaking voice or standard—radio or television—English, or perhaps a pedantic lecturer's voice. The voice used must not be that of the heavenly hero in character*]

COMMERCIAL: THE GREAT AMERICAN DESERT

In the early days of the West the Great American Desert was the favorite hiding place of many desperate men, and for good reason. This desolate stretch of land, called by some "the great plains," stretches across the western heart of America. It is not only hard to traverse, but also, due probably to the intense dryness and sundry allied atmospheric factors, seems to have affected not only the hearts and souls of the men who moved on it, but their very destinies also, and, indeed, that of America itself. *During the commercial, while stage is blacked out, the* OLD COWBOY *and the* YOUNG COWBOY *move from their position downstage left to upstage right, assuming the same relative positions, while the* GUNNY *recrosses stage to downstage left, so that he may reenter to correspond with the change. Think of the move, and the following ones, as being a different camera angle on the same scene.*

OLD COWBOY: You talk about desperadoes and you kiddin' about it, but that's just about what it comes to. If we weren't so fuckin' desperate for a hidin' place it wouldn't be so bad. But we here on this fuckin' desert, and nothin' goin' to to get us out but guts. And I got those, even if you two boys don't. I'm goin' to come out of this.

GUNNY: [*Reenters with bucket*] What you talkin' about? We all goin' to make it. Hear? Here's your water. You forgettin' who you travelin' with. [*He turns his back on the other two and begins fooling with his gun, trying his draw, checking the loads and the action*]

OLD COWBOY: I ain't about to forget anything, and most of all I ain't forgettin' how the three of us have rid together three years, come hell or high water. But after three years I know you, and I know him, and most of all, I know me. You the best damn gun around, only because you don't care a doodly squat for you or me or him or anybody alive. And he, once trouble start, he goin' to do his job better'n any man alive, because he care too damn much about everything. And I goin' to keep on bein' the leader, the damn boss man, because the only thing I care about at all is gettin' the three of us out of whatever we got into for whatever damn reason we picked to get into it. And that's all.

GUNNY: Trouble with you is, you got it all figured out. But I don't give no goddamn, long as I'm gettin' mine.

YOUNG COWBOY: Balls! There go the bucket. Watch the fire, will you, while I get me more water. It's just startin' to lay nice for cookin'. [*Exits downstage left*]

GUNNY: Man, he make such a big deal about cookin' I could die here of hunger. The fire got to lay just right, and if he don't like the way somethin' taste he throw it out.

YOUNG COWBOY: [*Reenters*] Listen, don't you worry, hear? You goin' to get your breakfast, coffee, bacon, and you treat me right, shut that fat mouth you got, might even fry some beans in the bargain. [*Aside to* OLD COWBOY] Seen sign of Arikara down to the waterhole. They must've been here last night whilst we was sleepin'.

GUNNY: [*He is working with his gun again*] What in hell's all the whisperin' for? I got the fire goin', I got my bedroll done up, the horses is waitin', all ready to go, and damn! I'm ready to go too, except I ain't got any fuckin' breakfast to keep my belly warm whilst I ride.

OLD COWBOY: [*Aside to* YOUNG COWBOY] I seen it too, out by the horses, but I figure they don't mean no harm, or they would have done it already. [*Aloud*] Listen, the boy's got a while to go there, so cool down. Anyhow, you know you goin' to get your bellyful some day, and I don't necessarily mean breakfast either.

GUNNY: You so goddamn funny it hurts.

YOUNG COWBOY: Okay, boys, breakfast be ready in one shake, and I don't mean maybe. You boys ought to know better. I been here not so long, but I plan to be here a long time more. Only way I'm goin' to do that is keep eatin' steady. So don't you worry none about your food.

COMMERCIAL:
FOOD, THE STAPLE OF HUMAN BEINGS

Food has always been an integral part of all human, and indeed animal, life, as far as is known. Evidences of what are thought to have been food dishes have been found in the middens of the earliest of peoples. Especially in an alien environment such as the Great American Desert was food important, and particularly a good breakfast. A good breakfast, remember, is a healthy breakfast. [*During the commercial the three cowboys have moved upstage left. They are seated, eating*]

GUNNY: Man, this what I been waitin' for. Only thing missin' is those beans you was talkin' about. I could sure use some beans along about now.

OLD COWBOY: The beans'll come, boy. Right now fill your belly on what you got. Life is too short. I remember bein' in Sonora once, outside the town of Sonora on that goddamned Mexican desert. Ate nothin' but cacti for five days, and damn glad, too. I came through, boy, I lived. And that was 'cause I wanted to, and wasn't worryin' about no beans or nothin'.

GUNNY: Man, all I said was, I wanted some beans, some goddamn beans.

YOUNG COWBOY: All right, goddamnit, they're comin'. You think I just goin' to throw beans at you boys? First I got to add a little salt and pepper and chili powder which I got here in my saddlebags; I got to throw in a little ketchup, which it breaks my heart 'cause I ain't got any to throw in, but leastwise I got to give that good chili powder half a chance to settle in amongst the goddamn beans afore I throw them at you.

GUNNY: Man, I was just talkin', is all. All the time a big goddamn fuss, every time I open up my mouth. [*The beans are dished out*]

OLD COWBOY: Wouldn't be a bad idea, boys, to check your guns. We run so hard out of that town, and what with the sand and all, God knows what happen to them. [*He exchanges a meaningful glance with the* YOUNG COWBOY]

GUNNY: You right, man. I'm goin' to check mine again right now. Couldn't do without little Samuel here.

COMMERCIAL: THE SIX-GUN WON THE WEST

While it is true that barbed wire was a contributory factor to the winning of the West, and, indeed, one of utmost importance, we must consider Samuel Colt's six-gun, or revolver, as the crucial development in this direction. Without the six-gun, which, as you probably know, could fire six shots in quick succession, without reloading, to aid the frontiersman, the Indians, possessors of the finest light cavalry in the world, would, no doubt, have beaten off these earlier venturers into the western vastnesses.

The three cowboys have moved to downstage right. The YOUNG COWBOY *is standing practicing his draw.*

GUNNY: You aimin' to shoot a snake? Bring it up, sonny, you'll lose a toe.

YOUNG COWBOY: Thanks. [*Puts gun away*] Sure can't wait till we hit a town. Sure am gettin' hungry for somethin' besides bacon, beans, and coffee, even if I do know how to cook 'em all.

GUNNY: Laddybuck, I hope you don't mean things like steak and such. I sure hope you ain't talkin' about things like that, all that talk of bein' hungry.

YOUNG COWBOY: Sheeit! What you take me for? A little dewy-eyed boy? 'Course I ain't talkin' about things like steak. I talkin' about pussy [WHORE *enters upstage right and crosses to upstage center. She sits, back to audience, as if in front of a mirror*], some good old couze, even just a little old bit. I get away from it two, three days, especialy with a bunch of old goats like you two, I miss it more than when I been out on roundup, or in the hills for maybe six months. The more I get it, the more I want it, seems.

OLD COWBOY: Yeah boy. You young ones, you cause all the goddamn trouble in this world.

You hadna been foolin' round that banker's daughter [*The* BANKER'S BEAUTIFUL DAUGHTER *enters downstage left and crosses to downstage left edge of platform, where she sits writing in her diary*] we still been workin' on the Double-O right now, and just wakin' us up out of nice soft bunkbeds, and eatin' oatmeal for breakfast, with some ham 'n' eggs.

GUNNY: Yeah, you sayin' that, but you forgettin' we wouldn' have no seven thousand dollars in our saddlebags right now, hadn't the little one been playin' 'round. Boy, you can go on like that any ole time, if it keeps gettin' us this kind of money.

BANKER *and* SHERIFF *enter upstage right and stand with back to audience as if at a bar.*

YOUNG COWBOY: Yeah, don't you forget, old man, if'n we didn' need to leave that town in such a hurry, we'd a' never blown that bank, and we'd a' never had no seven thousand to rest on for a while.

OLD COWBOY: You goddamn guys think it's so goddamn easy! [*The three cowboys exit downstage left*]

The following interludes are played without sets. The BANKER *and* SHERIFF *are as if at a bar; the* BANKER'S DAUGHTER *as if in her sitting room; the* WHORE *and* MADAM *as if in the* WHORE'S *bedroom. Each interlude is preceded by a tune which is hummed by the heavenly heroes. Tune: "El Rancho Grande"—hummed spiritedly.*

BANKER: [*Turning around, leaning back on bar*] Sheriff, I been banker for this town longer'n you and me care to remember, right?

SHERIFF: [*Facing* BANKER] Yessir, that surely is right. Was a heap of years ago we both of us settled down here.

BANKER: And been a lot of water under the dam we don't need to talk about both before and after, right?

SHERIFF: Yessir, you are surely right there, when you say that. Oh me!

BANKER: Well, the way I feel, Sheriff, is, good riddance to bad rubbish. I'm so glad to see those boys gone, that I wouldn't offer no reward nohow for their capture. Why, they liable to get aggravated, either bust out, or wait till they was let out, or, God forbid, beat the charges somehow, and come back here and devil the livin' hell out of all of us, but mostly me and you. I figger seven thousand dollars a cheap price to be rid of them, and besides, the money's probably gone by now, and a reward would just be throwin' good money after bad. Yessir, I was powerful glad to see them leave, even at that price, the way that young skinny one was always hangin' around my daughter.

SHERIFF: Right you are. I surely would feel the same about that, if'n I had a beautiful seventeen-year-old daughter. And what with the mine hittin' the way it is, and the railhead comin' in, so's the drives'll end up here, I guess you got no need to worry about the money. Only thing was, the boys asked me was there a reward and such, and was it worth trackin' them, and so I just had to up and ask you. Wouldn' hardly be fair to my boys nowise if'n I didn't.

BANKER: Well, Sheriff, I surely do understand. And listen, Sheriff, if there's one person in town you don't need to worry about apologizin' to, on account of anythin' you do or done, or might even want to do, it's me. I think you know that, Sheriff, and how much I am beholden to you for all we been through in the past. [*Both turn back to bar*]

Tune: "Beautiful, Beautiful Brown Eyes"— sentimentally.

BANKER'S BEAUTIFUL DAUGHTER: [*Crosses to center stage on platform*] Dear diary, I think I am honest and truly going to have a baby. And him a bandit. Oh, when he held me in his arms, I could just feel he was a thrilling man. I even asked him once. I said, bold as brass, are you a bandit? No ma'am, he said, not me, but I could feel his arms a-tightening around me when he said it. The only thing is, dear diary, poor Daddy. Won't he have a fit? [*Crosses right, sits on right edge of platform*]

Tune: "You Are My Sunshine"—hummed music-hall style.

MADAM: [*Enters downstage left onto platform*] Well, you old whore, I hope you're proud of yourself. Screwed me up somethin' proper you did, hangin' around like that with old fastdraw. Oh, he paid all right, but I could've used you, and there you was hangin' round moonin' over him. And me havin' to put up with his damn loud mouth on top of it. I'm damn glad he's gone, I can tell you.

WHORE: Well, I'm glad he's gone too. It was gettin' to be awful borin' toward the end what with him always wantin' me to be standin' by his side all night long while he played poker. Brings him luck, says he. I'll give him luck. But I ought to tell you somethin' else, I reckon, seein' how it concerns you too. I think I give him a dose in addition to the luck.

MADAM: Damn you! I don't know whether to kiss you for fixin' him up, or kick you for screwin' me up. Don't you know there'll be a big drive in soon? You better take it easy for a while, get yourself straightened out. You better go on up to Colorado and see old Manny. I'll give you your fare, but you leave your clothes here,

hear? I wonder who it was dosed you up though. Have to ask Doc.

WHORE: I think probably it was that faro dealer was around. I never did trust him.

MADAM: You may be right. Howsomever, it's Colorado for you for a while.

WHORE: Yeah. And all the time I'm up there, I'm goin' to think about the three of them, old quickdraw and the other two, and hope I don't die laughin'. I tell you, I just have to think how puzzled his face get, when I told him what Jane said to me about the banker tellin' her how he was goin' to have the sheriff's boys run the three of them out of town, and I break up laughin'. Those three big gunnies [*Cowboys enter from upstage left behind barrier, stand silently to suggest riding*] runnin' 'cause of a silly little chit like that. But they did have balls enough to rob the banker to do their runnin' on. That much I got to give them credit for.

MADAM: Pshaw. You should've seen the boys I learned from. They would've took the whole damn bank with 'em, and the banker and the banker's daughter too. And wouldn't none of those boys been fool enough to pick up a dose. Would've left that for some other sucker. [*They both laugh and go out*]

Tune: "I'm Back in the Saddle Again"— hummed straight. The desert, noon. It's hot as hell, and there is no shade at all. OLD COWBOY signals "halt," they all come around barrier onto platform.

OLD COWBOY: [*Keeps circling*] Unless I miss my guess, there ain't even a bush within ten miles of here. But we better stop anyhow. The horses been goin' more'n an hour steady, and my belly been grumblin' the last two. Gotta eat somethin'.

GUNNY: Damn. Must be two hundred and ten degrees out here. You sure we goin' to find a place by night? Even a old rock to sleep my head under?

YOUNG COWBOY: Your head. Your head. Who in hell said your head was so damn important? For an instance, my head's a hell of a lot more important to me than anybody's head, even yours.

OLD COWBOY: Goddamn you two, stop, hear? Ain't nobody's head goin' to be important 'less I find a way out of this. And yes, we are goin' to find a place by tonight. Why you think I roused you so early? And all the while you two were bitchin'. Listen, I been through this desert on horse, in a wagon, in a posse, in front of a posse, and even walkin'. The last would be with that squaw woman I stole from the Arikara. They never come close to catchin' us either. I guess I told you all about that a dozen times or so, though. Anyhow, I know damned well they's a little spot just maybe four, five hours' ride from here, got it a waterhole, grass for the horses, and a tree for each and every one of us to sleep our heads under.

GUNNY: And probably goddamn Indians too, but you forgot to mention them.

YOUNG COWBOY: A while back, seems to me, you was right happy when he suggested findin' Indians, so's we could buy us some horses, but now you don't even want to see them for to get us a little shade, even.

COMMERCIAL: HORSES ARE ONE OF THE EARLIEST OF DOMESTICATED ANIMALS

The horse has, for eons, been an integral part of man's civilization and culture. So integral a part, that some say, among them eminent historians, that had the Indian had the horse for three hundred years longer than he did have the horse, his civilization would have developed to the point where he could have withstood the white invasion along the banks of the mighty Mississippi, and contained the United States east of the great natural barrier. Perhaps.

When lights come up OLD COWBOY *is seated,* GUNNY *stretched out,* YOUNG COWBOY *standing.*

YOUNG COWBOY: [*Walks in circle*] Man, it's surely nothin' much at all around here, is it? Looks like the most whole of nothin' I ever did see. [*He reaches in his shirt pocket, pulls out some jerky, takes a chaw, and throws it to* OLD COWBOY]

OLD COWBOY: Thankee, son, mighty kindly of you. Here, have some of this here water, if you will. [*Offers canteen*] Want a chaw of jerky, friend? [*Throws it at* GUNNY]

GUNNY: [*Throwing it away*] No, I don't want no damn jerky. [*Stands looking around*] Jesus! Almost really do wish I'd see some Indians. Make me feel like somethin' was alive here, besides us three. And I ain't sure we three alive. Fuckin' desert, goddamn this fuckin' desert.

OLD COWBOY: [*To* GUNNY] Don't you worry none about that, boy. [*To* YOUNG COWBOY] Right now, the less people we see the better it goin' to be. By the time we hit a big town, us two goin' to have our beards full grown almost, and ain't even nobody goin' to think we is us. And then we get us a nice hotel room, and set down and count us that money real slow. And then we go out to spend it, but we spend it real easy, and slow as molasses, so nobody goin' to get ideas, and pretty soon all them people goin' to get used to seein' us around, and won't pay us no never mind. And we'll live a long time nice and easy, and then when we got to, we'll go back to work. Why, I might even look for

the sheriff's job myself. And you boys could be my deputies if you'd a mind to.

BOTH: Deputies!

OLD COWBOY: Why not? I'm gettin' to be that age, I could use a little rest, might be a little bit of fun be a sheriff for a little while, or even a long while. Might marry me a pretty girl, get me a pretty ranch, have me a pretty life.

GUNNY: Oh me. Listen to him go. You be a goddamn old sheriff all you want, but me, I ain't old yet. I got to get me a whole lot of everything before I start pullin' that stuff, hear? But I sure glad to kiss you when you get your badge, and very damn glad to draw on you too, exceptin' that you my friend or that you was.

YOUNG COWBOY: Well, I don't know. I think maybe you talkin' big, you all whipped up right now. But I think they offer either of us a badge, you or me, we both goin' to jump for it, and knock heads jumpin' too. I know damn well I jump. Have it nice and easy that way, never have to do nothin' except maybe once in a while a hardhead like you decide he goin' to drink too much, I got to take you in. Say on a lovely Saturday night you start shoutin' and whoopin' an hollerin', I get my turn to come up and lay you out with one acrost the head, than which, incidentally, nothin' would give me more pleasure, then or now, I might add.

GUNNY *makes mock bow to* YOUNG COWBOY.

OLD COWBOY: Look, I might as well straighten you both out right now. I don't want no trouble cookin' here. He [*Nodding to* YOUNG COWBOY] knows it as well as me. We both of us seen sign of Arikara this morning at the camp. Any one of you gets feelin' revengeful, it's only goin' to hurt all of us, hisself included. Aside from we're all a little loco with the sun. Them damn injuns could be on our tails right now, we don't keep shakin' them.

GUNNY *suddenly alerts.*

COMMERCIAL: THE PRIMITIVE RADAR

Indians were notorious for their ability to track, or follow, other persons unnoticed. They walked very quietly, and could deduce, often, a trail from the most minute evidence. It is a known fact that all the western cavalry regiments, including Custer's, had a complement of Indian trackers to lead them through the wastes. These trackers were generally enlisted from friendly tribes, and did their best to warn our soldiers of the dangers confronting them, from the signs they were able to read along the path of travel.

GUNNY: Well, this is sure a hell of a time to tell a fellow something like that, damn it. What you want me to do?

YOUNG COWBOY: Keep your mouth shut.

GUNNY: Man. I wasn't talking to you. And you don't keep your mouth shut, I'm liable to close it for you. And I mean I do it to you, hear?

YOUNG COWBOY: Okay, I'm shuttin' up, but only 'cause of Indians, 'cause I know all about you. The only thing you goin' to do it to or anythin' is that silly fat old whore you left behind. You goin' to do it to that stuff proper. I bet she clapped you up in the bargain.

GUNNY: [*Starts to draw and rushes toward* YOUNG COWBOY] You sonofabitch . . .

OLD COWBOY: [*Stops* GUNNY *with a gesture*] Man, I think you better make an effort and straighten yourself out like I told you. You been gettin' worse and worse as the day pass on. I heard how you been bitching on the kid all morning. Why'n't you go and do it now, and get it over with?

GUNNY: Goddamn, maybe I will. [*He exits*]

COMMERCIAL: DOPE, THE DOCTOR'S FRIEND

During the Civil, or War Between the States, or, as it was sometimes known, the late unpleasantness, the only means available to surgeons, physicians, and the like, of alleviating excruciating pain due to wounds or amputations were the drugs cocaine and morphine. As a consequence, close to a million men who had served valiantly found themselves "hooked" to one extent or another on these drugs after the close of hostilities. Indeed, there were so many of these poor addicts that it was impossible for the government to pass any antinarcotic legislation till after the turn of the century, when their numbers had diminished. Most doctors were sympathetic to their plight.

YOUNG COWBOY: It surely do embarrass me when he carry on like that. And then that private thing he got to have. Do he think we going to laugh or something?

OLD COWBOY: Boy, I don't know. All I know is, any man come out of three four months in a hospital during that war, seems like they just got to have that stuff every so often or they just ain't ever goin' to be happy. Reckon I'm glad I wasn't never wounded there in the Shenandoah, or I might be just the same. As it is, a little whiskey now and again keep me satisfied, or a little bit of nooky. But those boys, they got to be a-stickin' that needle in they arm, every now and again, or they is most morose. I can't figure it, but I reckon the doctors can.

YOUNG COWBOY: Only thing bother me, why he got to do it in private. I offer to shoot it for him oncet, he got awful upset. No, he say, goddamn, this I got to do myself. Well, I guess I just don't know.

GUNNY: [*Reenters, very relaxed, ready for a nice long talk*] Well, I about ready to roll now. But listen, what you done with that there jerky? Sure am gettin' a little bit of hungry here. Been ridin' all this long time and ain't had nothin' to eat. And seems like I been growin' a powerful hunger.

YOUNG COWBOY: Here's the jerky, friend. Eat well. And here's the canteen.

GUNNY: Thankee, friend. You boys are sure a good bunch of boys to be ridin' with. Minds me of the time we rode down into Alabam' with Uncle Billy. I was ridin' with as fine a bunch you ever hope to see, ride here, ride there, ride everywhere, and find us the finest ladies, and the finest food, and the finest of everything your little heart ever dreamed of. Sure was a fine time ridin' like that, till I got wounded. And even that wasn't so bad, long as they had those damn needles around. Only difference twixt us and them, was then we sure had a powerful lot of people ridin' with us.

OLD COWBOY: Well, I wouldn't worry about that none, was I you. You're with friends, and that's a heap better than bein' in the middle of a whole bunch of boys ridin' one way and another and wavin' swords and things. Why'n't you two shake just to show there's no hard feelings?

GUNNY: Fine by me. I like the young'un a heap. Here.

They shake.

YOUNG COWBOY: Sure, boy. You know you are the pleasantest fellow in the world with that stuff in you. [*Takes canteen and toasts*] Here's to it. And to you. And to us.

OLD COWBOY: Okay, boys, now that's settled let's finish up here and get the hell out. [*Rises and goes upstage right*] I want to be safe in that old waterhole before the sun gets close to settin'. Man, when I think of the time that old squaw and me had there, I'll tell you. And after walkin' all day long too, in the burnin' sun. Well, I ain't gettin' any younger.

YOUNG COWBOY: That's a fact. Fact is, ain't none of us gettin' any younger. That there banker's daughter, why she had me feelin' like a old grandpa sometimes, and me only twenty-two. Whoeee! That little girl sure didn't want to hear no no's out of me.

GUNNY: That's the way it is with those young'uns sometimes. But one day, say somewhere around me and my old gray-haired thirty-five, you goin' to find out how restful and easy it is to give that young stuff up and just pick yourself out a nice silly fat whore, like the one I got me. She don't expect no wonders, and she just happy you is there.

YOUNG COWBOY: Well, I'm beginnin' to think maybe you might be right. But I think I'll wait a bit to find out. The young'uns got their points, too, don't forget.

OLD COWBOY: You boys can sit around like that all afternoon if you've a mind to, but me I'm goin' to skedaddle. [*Goes behind barrier, upstage right*]

GUNNY: Hold on there, we're with you, right?

YOUNG COWBOY: Right.

OLD COWBOY: Okay. Here's what I say. We string ourselves out maybe six lengths apart, so they can't get us all at once, if'n they come, but we're still close enough to join up if'n we have to. And most of all, we make those horses move. Agreed? [*Moves to upstage left behind barrier*]

GUNNY: That sure does sound right to me. Damn! I'm sure glad you leadin' the fuckin' way. By this time I don't even know which way to head, sun or no sun. I don't even remember which goddamn sonofabitch way is east anymore, or south or west or north, for that matter. [*Moves to upstage center behind barrier*]

YOUNG COWBOY: [*Packing up*] I sure hope, old pals, we ain't headin' west.

OLD COWBOY: Talk like that ain't goin' to get us no place. Only thing will is ridin' leather, makin' dust. Let's hit it. I know just which way that little old waterhole lays.

YOUNG COWBOY: [*Moves while speaking to upstage right behind barrier*] Yeah, but I sure do hope we ain't headin' west. I'm much too young for that. I got to find out 'bout them fat silly old whores. I sure hope we ain't headin' west yet, or leastwise me.

Lights dim down. Three cowboys are visible standing behind barrier as if riding, through interlude. Tune: "Red River Valley"—powerfully. Lights on bright on heaven.

WYATT EARP: [*Rises*] Boys, this here is Wyatt Earp speakin' from up here in heaven. I sure hope all you fellows are doin' your best to do your part. That's what I wanted to talk to you about today. *Doin' your part.* I know there are some around today who'll try and tell you boys I was a psychopath, because, they'll say, I liked to lop my buntline special, all that big long barrel, across some baddie's face, but, boys, I was just doin' my part as I saw fit. The West had to be made fit to live in, and by providence I was the man picked to do my part. There's no denyin' that all that shootin' and killin' and hootin' and hollerin' wasn't fun too, but most of all it was plain and simple, doin' my part. Boys, what I got to say to you is, like it says in the Good Book: go thou and do likewise. [*Sits*]

WILD BILL HICKOK: [*Congratulates* WYATT, *then stands*] All right boys, I decided it was time I give you the one and only truth about myself, old WILD BILL HICKOK. First of all it's true Bill wasn't my proper first handle, but that's what they called me. So now up here in heaven I call me that too. And it's surely true, boys, that all that stuff about the notches in my gun was just somethin' I made up to impress a smart-alecky New York reporter. But I done my share of fightin' in my day, and I'm here to tell you. I know there's a lot around today who wasn't never there who'll deny that last, call me a fraud, and what hurts more, they even sayin' there must of been somethin' queer about me. Boys, I put it to you, if'n I liked my hair shoulder long, and my linen a little fancy and spotless clean, and never did go out with none of those whores like the rest of the boys, boys, whose business is that 'ceptin' mine? It's my affair and none of their own. All you boys got to remember is that I were the best trick shot in the West. Why, those same people, they always pointin' to my dainty well-formed hands but, boys, from up here in heaven, I can just say I was blessed with them. They sure helped me in my trade, bein' the best trick shot in the West. [*Sits.* WYATT *congratulates him*]

BILLY THE KID: [*Rises, stares tensely around heaven, and stage, and audience all through speech*] Well, boys, up here in heaven, where they put me, even though it's some special section I can't seem to get out of, out there with the others, not even when I can see plain as day that yellow sneakin' bastard Pat Garrett a-sneakin' around just like he did when he come sneakin' in my bedroom while I was just tryin' to catch a little wink, and so goddamn dark I couldn't even see to draw on him, goddamn they ain't goin' to do this to Billy the Kid, not even up here in heaven, just 'cause I come from Hell's Kitchen they act like I was the first J.D. or somethin'. Oh yes, I know what they sayin' about me, calling me a goddamn J.D. just like I was some fuckin' P.R., or shade or somethin', man, I'll burn those mothers, all of them, they come pokin' their holier-than-thou noses in here, up in heaven. Mothers. [*Sits*]

DOC HOLLIDAY: [*Rises. He coughs continually through the speech*] Well, boys, this is the old con man, the original hipster, the first of the hackin' hipsters talkin' to you from up here in heaven. Yes, boys, it's true, we're all up here. All them you heard and a lot more besides. Last two we, or rather they, let in, they said it were the last of the heroes. That'd be, I know you're interested, Butch Cassidy and the Sundance Kid. Now wasn't that twosome a bitch? Oh man. Well, anyhow, here's what old Doc got to tell you. (1) You got to live like you goin' to die next month anyhow. (2) You got to be a good gambler, that means learn the rules, and have you some luck. (3) You got to take time out to learn you a trade, for the bad times, the slow times, and when you got to cool it. [*Lights on cowboys full out. They take next position in blackout*] You just do these three things, boys, you ain't goin' to have no trouble a-tall findin' yourself some upright crazy sonofabitch like Wyatt to pick up on, and then, boys, you goin' to have a ball. You goin' to be able to kick up such hell out of a sweet lovin' bitch like big-nose Bertha on Monday night that she have you thrown in jail. And you goin' to be able to fill her with so many memories, that Tuesday night she goin' to burn down the jail, and have your horse waitin' for you outside the window, so's the two of you can ride off into the desert. One more thing, boys, pure fact, John Ringo *is* dead. I seen WYATT plug him, and threw in two myself for luck. Okay, boys, that's about it. You hearken unto what I said and cleave your hearts unto it until next time, boys, this is Doc Holliday sayin' so long for all of us [*Waves*] up here in heaven.

Lights dim on heaven. Cowboys are seated upstage left.

YOUNG COWBOY: Damn! I'm surely sick and tired of all you screwing around whilst I make meals, and then just wolfin' them down, and nary a word about was they good, was they bad, was they indifferent, or what?

OLD COWBOY: Looky here, we ain't screwin' around. We been gettin' the damn wood for the fire, and some soft branches for to sleep on, and afeedin' and awaterin' the horses, and hobblin' them, and all. And in betwixt, we been lookin' for sign of Arikara. So you stop that whoopin'. You got no call at all to come on in that there manner.

GUNNY: Yeah, goddamn it. [*He belches*]

YOUNG COWBOY: Well, that's just how I feel. I know I ain't got much to cook with here, but you boys could at least hearken back to the time I had the wherewithal. It's damned hard to have to cook all the time like this, and get no praise nor thanks nor even bitches. I think you boys don't even taste it, and me breakin' my hump just to get it to taste like food, even.

GUNNY: All right, all right. It tasted like food, see? That's all it's supposed to taste like, and that's all it did taste like. It tasted like food. What the hell you expect? Ain't neither of us married to you yet, goddamn it. I'm so goddamned sick of your bitchin', and his leaderin' and my goddamn ridin'.

OLD COWBOY: You sick of it, yeah, but you was damn glad I was around when we started seein' those smoke signals, wasn't you? [*A coyote howls. They all fall silent, sit for a minute. OLD COWBOY assigns positions for defense*]

OLD COWBOY: [*Whispering*] This may be it, boys. Good luck, and a good fight, and if that's all, then goodbye, boys. You been a fine bunch to ride with. But I'll bet my bottom dollar on it, that sounded powerful like Arikara.

COMMERCIAL: THE INDIANS OF THE AMERICAS A VERITABLE TOWER OF BABEL

The Indians of the Americas are unique in their considerable diversity of tongues. Over seventy different language families have been discovered, amongst the Indians of North America alone. A family of languages is, in linguistic terms, a group of fairly similar languages between which various ties of vocabulary and syntax are apparent. The Indo-European family, for instance, comprises most of the inhabitants of Europe, and a good third of those of Asia. Imagine then the great diversity of languages to be found in early America, before the Indians were killed off. The Arikara belonged to one of these seventy language families.

GUNNY: Listen, you suppose that might've been a real coyote, anyhow? It's about time for them to be comin' out, around about now.

OLD COWBOY: Well, it could've been. And there weren't no answer. And, come to think of it, that damn yowl wasn't really real enough for Arikara. They sound realer than coyote most of the time.

YOUNG COWBOY: I ain't heard too many Indians signalin' but I know that's true. [*Starts to rise, is motioned at, crouches*] Leastwise it's what I heard from a lot of fellows.

OLD COWBOY: Well, let's relax a little, boys; most they can do is kill us. Long as it ain't a damn posse anyhow. Indians ain't goin' to know we gotta damn seven thousand in our saddlebags, and Arikara sure ain't smart enough to look. They'll just scalp us and take the guns and throw us all on the fire, or they'll leave us layin'. Dependin' on the fight we put up. I know it may be silly but I'd damn sight rather the money stays with us dead, than somebody else gets it and spends it.

YOUNG COWBOY: Yeah. After what that fuckin' banker tried to pull on us just because his damn beautiful daughter liked her tail, I feel the same.

GUNNY: Well, I hate to mention it to you, but if I had my druthers, I'd a heap better like spendin' it myself than knowin' nobody else had it. Though I would like knowin' that better than knowin' somebody else did have it. That is, if we are goin' to know anythin' after we're dead. And I ain't so sure of that.

OLD COWBOY: Now you know as well as I do ain't no sense worryin' about that sort of thing. That's the preacher's lookout, and he says we're goin' to know. That's good enough for me.

YOUNG COWBOY: And that's the way I feel too. I got nothin' to be ashamed of, when they read that final list, then the last trump blow, like the preacher say.

Silence—thought.

OLD COWBOY: I been meaning to say to you, boy, you a good cook. If the good Lord ever see fit to let me have that little ranch I keep dreamin' about, I goin' to let you cook for me any old time you want. You didn't have much to work with, but you made us a good old supper. Like the feller said, it were the best shit I ever ate.

YOUNG COWBOY: Well, that's mighty fine to hear. I'm surely glad you enjoyed it. And I want to tell you, I sort of enjoyed fixin' it up. It was a nice change after all day in the saddle.

GUNNY: Pardner, I got to say it too. For me it was a nice change to have food in my goddamn gut. I get so damn hungry sometimes after I have me that medicine, I don't know what to do. I appreciate what you doin' for us. I want to tell you that.

YOUNG COWBOY: You boys goin' to make me shy. Thanks, thanks a whole lot of millions.

OLD COWBOY: Well, I'm goin' to make a last check on the horses. Sure hope I don't find no sign around this time. [*Exits upstage left.* YOUNG COWBOY *covers his position*]

GUNNY: And me, I'm goin' to turn in. I'm tired. Been all day in the saddle and I'm wore out. [*Throws rifle to* YOUNG COWBOY] Boy, you call me when breakfast ready, you hear? [*Starts undressing*]

YOUNG COWBOY: [*Alert and apprehensive*] I goin' to call you when and how I get goddamn ready, damn you! Who you think you are to get a goddamn special call? All you do is ride, sleep, eat, and . . . [*Cooling down*] I got to add, draw faster nor any man got a right to. Where'd you learn that little trick?

I been meanin' to ask you. I know for a fact your old man so slow he won't even draw on a man in handcuffs.

GUNNY: Boy, you know you ain't about to rile me when I'm ready to sleep. Though it was true my old man was slow. I mind me of the time he caught me with sister. I was but twelve, but I faced him down even then. I had my Colt a-pointin' at his heart afore he even got his gun out. And that's how I left home, youngster. Oh, those goddamned good old never-come-again fuckin' old days, I sure wish I was twenty again. [*Lies down*]

YOUNG COWBOY: Way I left, I left middle of the night. Paw had got drunk that day and whupped me. I swore it were the last time. Old man was so loaded his snorin' covered every sound I made. But somehow, Maw heard me out to the barn. She come out in her old wrapper, and man, it were cold. She give me some food, and a kiss goodbye. [OLD COWBOY *re-enters, stands upstage left off platform*] I told her I was takin' the mule, but when she run back to the house I took the best mare. You never seen that mare. She died four year ago, but she was surely a sweet old horse. And I had my daddy's Colt in my shirt too, whilst I was kissin' Mama goodbye. And by damn I learned to use them both, Colt and mare, I tell you.

OLD COWBOY: You are speakin' truth, boy, you can do it when you need to. [*Undresses*] I just wish you felt a need to, more. But pay no mind to that. That's just an old man's talk. You goin' to come out all right. You goin' to have everything your heart desires some day, boy. And the sun goin' to shine in your back door. The other two of us, I ain't so sure. But you goin' to make it. [*Lies down*]

GUNNY: Okay, boys, hush it up. I need my beauty sleep if I'm going to be ridin' all around this countryside all day tomorrow on nothin' but bacon and beans and coffee.

OLD COWBOY: Me too. Good night, you all.

GUNNY: Goddamn, good night.

YOUNG COWBOY: Well, I'll hit it too. Though I guess us young'uns is too lively for you old goats. 'Cause I ain't really tired yet. But I do have me a powerful lot of thinkin' to do about that damn old banker's beautiful daughter, anyhow, and I'd sure rather do that thinkin' alone, without you guys to share it. [*There is no answer. They are both asleep. He sits upstage center on platform*] They may get us or maybe not. And tomorrow I got to ride like hell. And I'm tired, damn you. But first I'm goin' to sing me a little song. [*While he sings, lights dim on stage, lights go up bright on heaven, both very gradually*]

I ride an Old Paint,
I lead an Old Dan,
I'm goin' to Montana
To throw the houlihan.

They feed in the tuli,
They water in the draw,
Their tails are all matted,
Their backs are all raw.

Heavenly heroes hum softly behind Chorus only.

Chorus:

Ride round, little dogies,
Ride round them real slow,
You know that Wyoming will be
        your new home.
Ride round, little dogies,
Ride round them real slow,
Both Fiery and Snuffy are rarin' to go.

Now old Tom Jones
Had two daughters and a song;
One went to Denver,
The other went wrong.

His wife was killed
In a poolroom fight,
Now Tom sits asinging
From morning to night.

(Chorus:)

Now when I die
Take my saddle from the wall
Turn loose my pony
From out of his stall,
Put my bones across his back,
Turn our faces to the west,
And we'll ride the prairies
That we love the best.

He sleeps.

COMMERCIAL: INDIAN MORALS,
A STRICT ETHICAL CODE

Indians had a strict moral code. They respected courage and manliness, despised cowardice. For a plains, or desert, Indian, the supreme test was bravery under torture. In addition, Indians never attacked after dark. It was against their moral code.

GUNNY *rises and stumbles about on the dark stage.*

GUNNY: Goddamn! It can't be mornin'. But I got to take such a fierce pee. And it hurts something awful. It hurts so bad I could bend a pipe.

Blackout.

YOU MAY GO HOME AGAIN
a domestic Noh in one act

David Starkweather

You May Go Home Again was first presented by Joseph Cino at the Caffe Cino, New York City, on February 17, 1963. A second production was presented at the Caffe Cino on June 15, 1965 with the following cast:

EXECUTIONER .... *Chuck McLain*

MOM .... *Kay Carney*

LINDA .... *Shellie Feldman*

PETER .... *Ronn Hansen*

DAD .... *Ron Faber*

It was directed by the author, assisted by Stanley Rosenberg and Paula Mason. Music by Lucas Mason. Costumes by Ya Yoi.

To my family including Janice

Light comes up on the EXECUTIONER *standing on an "island" of stage height located in the audience and connected to the stage by a "bridge" about 12 feet long. The* EXECU-TIONER'S *fantastic costume suggests a medieval executioner with its skull-fitting hood of black, yet its wide, elaborate mantle is made of rich brocade of black and gold with tiny mirrors rimmed in crimson embedded in the material, dazzling the light that hits it. The mantle suggests in its macabre liturgical parody the* EXE-CUTIONER'S *self-aggrandizement and fantasies of power over Life and Death. The* EXECU-TIONER, *who has been shielding his eyes from the light as it rose, begins to speak with tired disenchantment.*

EXECUTIONER: I did not take Light this morning, Breath, or Resuming Consciousness as the latest, most glorious manifestation of Life's Eternal Return, but as yet ANOTHER imposition. I welcomed dawn with my accustomed sneer. (I knew it was coming.) I look upon wakefulness as a subtle aggression. Betrayed into STARING, I have assumed diligent enterprise to avoid much SEEING. [*He mimes swiping off two heads while the orchestra, a musician prominently located throughout the play between the* EXECUTIONER *and the stage, whacks a block of wood with a hatchet. From the darkness of the stage come two cries of pain from the family. The* EXECUTIONER *then resumes with growing "cool" and joy, fingering a rosary of skulls, small toys and a pacifier*] Today I have dipped my contemporaries in the rich turds of my abuse for the unpardonable crime of prior successes. [*From the darkness of the stage comes a moan of despair*] I have avoided beggars on the street, [*From the darkness is heard a measure of incoherent blubbering in six/eight time*] whose mere presence was not only an offense to Man's dignity, but a genuine challenge to his curiosity and natural morbidity. [*A blubbering triplet completes his sentence*] For breakfast I boiled the Bible, [*From the darkness comes a grace note of contrapuntal Gregorian Chant on the lyric, "Yumminy yumminy yah . . . ah . . . ah"*] lunch the limbs of lovely girls, [*The Chant is heard again, only it ends in a hysterical female giggle*] and for supper, why I'll have Baked Mankind or not a thing—[*And as he continues speaking we hear a short composition beginning with the Gregorian "Yumminies," the hysterical giggle, a measure of six/eight blubbering and ending with a solitary moan of despair*]— stuffed and trussed, basted, blasted and emboweled in one howling gulp. [*Then continu-*

ing a cappella] And later, while I watch T.V., I'll snack on beer and dead ideals, warming my toes around the rosy embers of an ending way-of-breathing. This morning I backed up a car and I split a bitch. [*A quiet, immediate, unison "yack" of shock and disgust is heard*] This morning, in a frenzy of remorse, [*Three soft female sobs are heard*] I swallowed a gardenia complete with bosom. [*Then kneeling he says awkwardly, now out of his element*] And now, dear . . . God, in this the treasured hour of a TRYING day, I wish to express my all-consuming love for humanity. Teach me to speak my love directly as a baby. Soft and cooing. Cooing . . . gooing—yet no. Yet let me LEAK out my love. Not the lush gush but the SWEET LEAK. Yes leak . . . yet turn, twist off that baby spigot ever dripping the corrosive urines of last night's lunch—[*Giving up*] Yet most of all, dear . . . God, help me, help me not to be overly sentimental. [*Then standing*] And now back to work. [*He mimes chopping again as the lights fade on him and slowly come up on stage revealing the family:* LINDA, *in a dress that could be used for a simple wedding;* PETER; MOM, *in faded house dress and apron; and* DAD, *in blue work shirt and tie. As we see the family, music begins: monodic, with a simple melodic motif easily remembered, with parallel voices moving at harmonious intervals. And though somewhat repetitious, the intervals are so close at times dissonance is approached and passed through. As the lights come up the family begins a short movement sequence in precise unison, an outline of an uneventful day. Their heads slowly lift, a gesture suggests a yawn and their eyes open. They begin a slow shifting of the knees that seems rather like a very constipated "twist"—much too slow to be any fun, or even comfortable, and completely isolated below the waist, yet somehow still "twistlike" . . . ubiquitous, banal. They speak as if hypnotized*]

MOM: Good morning, dear.

LINDA: Good morning, Mom.

They seem to sit and a gesture to the mouth suggests eating. Then they are back to shifting knees.

PETER: It's a nice day. I think I'll take the baby out . . . a bit later.

They sit again and eat—this time the meal a gesture longer as they lean back their heads in drinking from a cup—then stand.

LINDA: A nice lunch, Mom.

They turn, do a brief walking pattern, and as the music becomes more active they resume the movement with their knees at twice its former tempo.

PETER: No, it's getting a little late.

Suddenly they are in supper, which seems to be lunch twice, at twice the tempo, which makes it twice as mechanical and comical, and just as suddenly supper is over. The methodical, somnolent ritual resumes, the lights dimming, turning rose.

MOM: Oh, look at the sun.

PETER: Time for bed for you. [*His head leans to one side and eyes close*]

MOM: For me. [*As do hers*]

LINDA: For me. [*And hers. After a pause so do* DAD'S *and the movement and music stop . . . the lights almost out. After a moment* LINDA *looks up, moves away from the family, and as a spot comes up on her, faces out across the audience toward the* EXECUTIONER. *She speaks with difficulty at first, she wants so much to say the right thing, and through her homilies her sincerity is affecting*] Dear David. I hope you're happy about my wedding news. I realize there're many things I'll miss by marrying now. He and I will both have to work hard for everything we get, but if you can understand, I don't think you'll be disappointed. Because I feel you're the only one left in the family who could come near understanding, and it's certainly worth a try if I can make myself clear. *The family music is heard again and* MOM, DAD *and* PETER *begin repeating the ritual as the lights slowly creep up on them.*

MOM: Good morning, Peter.

PETER: Good morning, Mom.

LINDA: Basically, David, I don't think Life is a very happy thing. I don't mean by this I'm UN-happy. What I mean is it's seldom I am HAPPY. Most of the time we're on sort of a medium plane, hoping for happiness, looking for it in different ways.

MOM: Linda?

LINDA: Well, the things in Life that bring me closest to happiness are companionship, security, love and understanding. Some people want wealth and fame but I don't. I just want one person to need me and no one else. Care enough to always try and understand.

MOM: Linda?

A jammer of voices begins rising in the background.

LINDA: David, the Beloved One is like this to me! And because of this I love him and want to be the same to him.

MOM: Linda, it's time to get up.

LINDA: Just a minute, Mom, I'm not done.

MOM: But you're getting married tomorrow dear, and I can't do it all myself. Listen, the relatives are already filling the bleachers.

The crowd sound swells and all bow to acknowledge it, family music fading out.

LINDA: All right, Mom.

MOM: Come on now, everybody, out of the living room while I wax the floor. Out—out! [PETER, DAD *and* LINDA *move to one side as they wait, stand in a tableau of idleness.* MOM *then begins a simple rhythmical movement that suggests pushing and drawing a mop. It is not simply pantomimic however. Characteristic movements made while mopping have been isolated and their rhythmic structures emphasized. And as* MOM'S *body performs these rhythmically circumscribed gestures her voice comes to us as if from a bystander*] Wax, wax, wax. Sometimes I wonder why God went to the trouble to make me human if I'm going to spend half my life rubbing a board. Stalking the stupid corners of this room. Such things don't deserve that much human attention. What do you accomplish—does it all add up to? [*Variations have been brought into the original simple movement: its direction of performance has been altered into a comical to-the-left, then to-the-right manner. And now as she speaks, the rhythms of her speech begin playing against the rhythms of these movements, and as the orchestra accentuates the rhythmic outlines of the movements,* MOM *performs her rendition of the human condition*] During that millennium, in that small corner of the earth's now wrinkled brow, that little board, by the grace of some vast indirection, shone with a certain luster for all of a week. And nobody even looked. [*Cheers are heard from the bleachers.* MOM, *embarrassed at being discovered still cleaning, says apologetically*] Oh hello, Mary, Ron, Aunt Bell. Well of course, you wouldn't miss it for the world. No, you sit right down there in the front row. Excuse me a minute. I'm just about finished here. [PETER, DAD *and* LINDA *shift into positions suggesting a bleacher and watch while* MOM *performs a brief, rapid "dance flourish" to the orchestra's comic percussion. As she ends cheers are heard from the relatives and* DAD, PETER *and* LINDA *shout as if a football cheer*]

PETER, DAD, LINDA: U rah rah, Perfect Ma.

MOM: [*Flattered, warms to their appreciation. To the relatives*] Well, thank you very much. Have some more popcorn—it's on the house. [*To herself again, things looked brighter*] Well . . . the wedding—and David's coming home. Want to have the place looking nice. It does all add up to something, I guess. [*The family shifts into a tableau of a family portrait,* MOM *looking on.*] A part of what we've been together. [*They shift to a tableau of a bad photograph of a beach picnic,* MOM *holding the camera*] A small part of the success of the whole enterprise. [MOM *then steps into the picture and it is "Mother's Day"* . . . PETER *and* LINDA *kissing her on each cheek* . . . DAD *moving in a moment later, as if reluctant to express the full extent of his need, kneels in front of her and clutches her desperately about the thighs. The picture now complete,* MOM *goes on*] Linda is our baby. [*They cradle* LINDA *in their arms and begin rocking in unison*] The last of the lot. And our only girl. [*They stop rocking, and* MOM *says somewhat ominously*] Oh, we had another one once, but she got married too. And she had a nice family. And then one afternoon, her husband was at work, [DAD *moves away and* PETER *and* LINDA *begin sneaking mysteriously around her*] neighbors away, phone out of order, and without any warning she was SWALLOWED BY HER CHILDREN. [PETER, *standing back to back with her, has suddenly hooked his arms through her elbows and bent forward—lifting her off the floor bent across his back—and quickly turned so that she now appears upside down as if about to be dropped by him onto the waiting palate of* LINDA, *reclining open-mouthed beneath her. Still upside down,* MOM *says nonchalantly*] She seems to enjoy it, but she never writes. [*The cheers of the crowd are heard again and* PETER *and* LINDA *backtrack their movements and end up kissing her again. Musing*] "U rah rah, Perfect Ma." [*And* DAD *arrives, late again, clutching her about the thighs*] PERFECT. That's how it has to be, Linda. Because you are the fruit of the whole enterprise. On you it stands or falls. [*Lights begin to dim, leaving only a spot on* MOM] For we are failing here, Linda. [PETER, DAD *and* LINDA *begin sliding down, falling away from her, clutching her as they submerge* . . . *like* Titanic *passengers misdirectedly grasping at the iceberg*] Dissolution is the order of the day. The order of tomorrow. [*And desperately*] And in this, our final act, our final REASON, we've got to know that it was all worth while! [*Enormous cheers swell from the bleachers and* MOM *turns to them, crying out*] You fools! How do you know you're not betting on a loser? How do you know *I* even did my best? [*She automatically tests the quality of the shine on the floor she has just waxed. Then, realizing this a shortsighted response, she says with despair*] God knows I don't know that myself. [*And then as the final, most horrible possibility*] And how do you know she's not marrying some—[*Kneeling, melodramatically*] Some GOOF IN SHEEP'S CLOTHING!?

PETER: [*Tired from his uncomfortable position, with strained patience*] Mom, are you done?

MOM: [*As the lights come quickly up, getting slowly to her feet*] Done? Why, Peter, I've a million things. [*The orchestra begins a steady beat, each beat a different sound, and* MOM *runs center stage and begins waxing in a circle rapidly*] It has to be perfect.

PETER: [*As he stands*] I know, Mom.
MOM *is now on her knees polishing the floor in a circle around her—then frantically in a "million" uncertain directions—then is suddenly running off on her hands and knees, barking loudly.*

LINDA: [*Running off after her*] Mom. Mom!

PETER *speaks to us as* DAD *stands hung over in a radical slouch.*

PETER: Poor Mom gets so worked up. The same way when I got married. She came up to me and said, "I don't know if I'll be able to give you away today, Peter." And I said, "You don't have to give me away." [*Then as if crossing away from* MOM *on that day he begins another rhythmically heightened movement phrase*] "That's just the bride." [*Turning back toward her*] I go away [*And away again*] all by MYSELF. [*And to the orchestra's comical percussion, he continues in a mock-carefree walk away from her, as if teasing her. Stopping in unexpected syncopation as she apparently does not appreciate the joke, he says with resignation and bewilderment in a completely natural manner, the movement phrase being over*] And she just wasn't right the rest of the afternoon. [*He mimes holding a baby*] I'm in charge of the baby while Fran gets a hat for the wedding . . . my wife. [*Cheers from the bleachers*] They want to see the baby. I just got married last year myself. See what we've been doing? [*Holds baby up and crowd cheers*] You know some of those babies that look all red and matted at the beginning? Well, she wasn't like that at all. Right from the start she had this—well, this adult look. [*The orchestra hits two clunks on an old bucket partly filled with water, or a cracked ship's bell, and* DAD *begins perking up, peering intently around him, feeling the air with his hands*] And when I went to see her the second time the nurse picked up this little red shriveled thing. It was terrible—it looked like some kind of animal or something.

DAD: [*Intones as he seems to begin swimming toward some distant object of uncertain direction*] Bong bong. Bong bong.

PETER: [*Nonchalantly*] Oh yes, Dad, I'M here. It's Peter—I'm over here. [*Continuing immediately*] And I said that's not my baby. That one over there. The one that looks like Benjamin Franklin. Well, you should have seen the smile on her face. She was really proud to hold that baby up.

DAD: [*His voice sounding as if coming from someone calling from a long distance*] Hello over there. Can you hear me?

PETER: [*Softly, with patience*] Yes, Dad, I can hear you.

DAD: [*He stops swimming and speaks naturally, directly to Peter*] Good morning.

PETER: Good morning to you too. [DAD *turns away in disbelief. He then turns back, deciding to test his senses, and very shyly waves his hand at* PETER. PETER *waves back.* DAD *falls into shock. At the same moment* PETER *looks at the baby and calls with concern*] Mom. MOM! Could you come here? Hurry!

MOM: [*Scurrying in on her hands and knees*] What is it? What's wrong?

PETER: [*Calm again*] Oh . . . nothing I guess. For a minute I thought it was turning the wrong color.

MOM: Oh dear, and I've a million things—[*She turns and sees* DAD] Your poor father. He gets stuck in these moments of inertia. Sometimes I know just how he feels. Well, I've done the dishes, a batch of clothes, made the cookies, fixed the plumbing, now if you'll excuse me I have some small construction at the rear of the lot. [*She drops to her knees and begins lumbering off as a beast of burden to the rhythmic accompaniment of a handsaw by the orchestra*]

PETER: Take it easy, Mom.

MOM: No time at all David'll be here. Oh, it's so nice to have you all back. I forgot what it was to work up a really good sweat. [*She begins to leave again to her sawing accompaniment, but stops and backs hurriedly up next to* DAD. *Glancing about to see no one is looking, she quickly lifts her leg like a dog pissing on his foot, then immediately, innocently resumes her exit to her saw's resuming complicity.* DAD *rises out of his stupor briefly, feeling the air, aware of some human presence, but quickly sinks back into his slouch*]

PETER: [*To baby*] Well now, you're going to smile, are you? It sure is good to see you do that. Makes me feel I'm doing something right. [LINDA *enters wearing a short veil. A garlanded swing descends downstage at the foot of the "bridge"*] Oh, that's right, David's due tonight, isn't he? Linda, when's David getting in?

LINDA: [*Sitting in the swing, she continues to David*] So you see, David, that's why I'm getting married. Because I need the things the Beloved One gives me the same way you need the things YOU need. [*Orchestra hits the half-filled bucket twice and* DAD *perks up again, peering, feeling*] It makes no difference if he's educated, wealthy, super-intelligent—

DAD: Bong bong. Bong bong.

LINDA: I don't care if he likes to play ball and not get dressed up. None of these things are important to me.

DAD: Ahoy there. Can you hear me?

LINDA: And you may never get to know him—you don't have much in common—but believe me when I tell you he's a wonderful person, and he's wonderful to me.

DAD: Hello over there.

LINDA: Yes, Dad, I can hear you.

DAD: [*Stops swimming and speaks directly to her*] Good morning.

LINDA: [*Continuing to David*] A very easygoing, simple sort of person I respect more than anyone I know.

DAD: [*Frantically fighting to keep from being thrown backwards over Niagara, he calls as if from miles away*] Good morning.

PETER: [*Excitedly*] Oh, she puked again. Linda! Oh, look at her go.

LINDA: [*Impatient, distracted from her letter*] What do you want? I'm awfully busy—

PETER: She's throwing up everything. Quick, stop it.

LINDA: Well, I don't know what to do!

DAD: Can you hear me?

PETER: Well, you're the bride. You better learn pretty fast.

LINDA: Well, that one's yours.

PETER: Look at it writhe!

DAD: [*Going under for the third time*] Can anybody anybody anybody hear me?

LINDA and PETER: [*Turning on him*] Oh, Dad, will you stop that!

LINDA: NO MAN IS AN ISLAND. [*And she swings.* MOM *enters hurriedly.* DAD *heads straight for the bottom*]

MOM: What's the matter, what's the matter? [*Takes the baby*] There there, just a little gas.

PETER: [*To* LINDA] A lot of help you are. Poor thing could have choked to death.

LINDA: Well, what did you want me to do? Take it and have it die in MY hands?

MOM: Let's not argue.

PETER: [*Getting the baby back*] Look at it. Covered with barf. I don't know why they let them get married so young.

LINDA: Peter, it's upset me enough.

MOM: Well, it's true Linda. You're only a baby. [*Pushes her in the swing as if in demonstration of this fact*]

LINDA: Mother, don't you start picking on me too.

MOM: And look how you've hurt your father's feelings. [*He is back in his slouch*] Peter, pick up your father.

PETER: You're just a baby, that's all you are. [*He pushes her in the swing too. She stands, indignant*]

LINDA: I am not.

PETER: Just a little little baby. Well, after all, Linda . . . you're only three. [*She slowly turns to him. He, embarrassed for some reason, avoids her gaze and begins a movement that suggests his wish to be thought of as busy doing something . . . the movement a somewhat "busier" version of the shifting of knees done in the Family Dance. The orchestra begins a slow, ominous beat to accompany this*]

LINDA: I am not.

MOM: [*Unexpectedly*] You are too.

DAD: [*Pulls himself upright and says bitterly*] YOU ARE TOO! [*He looks at* PETER *and they nod in agreement. Then smiling he joins in* PETER's *movement, which they continue side by side in unison*]

LINDA: What's the matter with you? What are you all talking about? I'm twenty if I'm a day!

MOM: See, dear, you don't even know how to count yet. One, two, twenty . . .

The swing sails back to the ceiling. LINDA *looks at it in amazement. She looks at* PETER *and* DAD *and catches them looking away, avoiding her glance in a unison double-take.*

LINDA: [*To the audience*] I don't know what's going on around here, but I don't like the feel of it.

MOM: [*Beginning idle, realistic dusting*] Have you made up your mind yet who it's going to be?

LINDA: What do you mean?

MOM: Well, you're getting married tomorrow, dear. I just assumed you knew who it was going to be.

LINDA: I'm marrying the Beloved One. I TOLD YOU THAT! [*She looks at* PETER *and* DAD *and catches them avoiding her again.*] I made up my mind a year ago!

MOM: Well, of course you did, dear . . . [*And as the orchestra's accompaniment to* PETER *and* DAD's *movement begins getting louder*] But let's see if we can find something better. [MOM *begins dusting more nervously*]

LINDA: What do you mean, "something better"? I'm getting married tomorrow and I'm marrying the Beloved One.

MOM: Well, of course you are, dear. You're marrying the Beloved One . . . if you want to. [*And she begins dancing as she did earlier in the "dance flourish," now faster and messier*]

LINDA: What do you mean, "if I want to?" [*She catches* PETER *and* DAD *once more. To* MOM] What are you doing?

MOM: [*Frantically, moving high and low*] I'm trying to clean—

LINDA: What are you looking for!?

MOM: [*Stops and turns to her*] I'M LOOKING FOR SOMETHING BETTER! [*All sound and movement stop. All look at* MOM] I mean I'M LOOKING FOR SOME DIRT!! [*Almost in tears*] Is that such a crime?

LINDA: I don't understand this. I thought you all liked him.

PETER: Well, we do!

MOM: We love him! But . . .

A loud gong crash from the orchestra, quickly muffled.

PETER: But . . .

Another gong crash, quickly muffled. DAD *raises his finger as if about to speak. The orchestra hits* DAD's *bucket loudly and* DAD *drops his hand as if feeling "what good would it do?"*

LINDA: Oh, no. . . . [*She turns toward* DAVID] So you see, David, that's why I had to write. Why I had to make you understand. I hope this letter has made you feel better if you were concerned too. See you soon. Love always, Linda.

EXECUTIONER: [*Light coming up on him*] Dearest Linda. I received your correspondence only the night before the wedding, and was deeply moved by your heartfelt confidence.

LINDA: [*Turning to family*] It's David!

PETER: David? Where?

DAD: Ahoy, ahoy . . .

MOM: Where—where is that boy that all the world loves?!

EXECUTIONER: [*Softly*] In the basement, Mama, [*A hatchet chop from the orchestra*] chopping up God.

PETER: Did you hear something?

LINDA: Why, I thought—

MOM: Why, what a funny thing to say. You always loved your father.

EXECUTIONER: And why shouldn't I? [*A chop from the orchestra*] He was the only pet I ever had.

MOM: Well, that's one thing you can say about David: One Lovely Enigma.

FAMILY: One Lovely Enigma.

EXECUTIONER: Lest you fear you understand one thing I say, let me assure you my only description is found in that phrase often attached to me in jest, "One Lovely Enigma."

LINDA: He agrees with us.

And as she speaks the orchestra strikes a major arpeggio on a xylophone.

FAMILY: [*Speaking in harmony aside to audience*] It's so nice to find a family in accord.

DAD: Son, you're coming through loud and clear.

EXECUTIONER: But since I don't know the gentleman concerned, I'm at a loss to guess what misgivings there might be.

LINDA: Well, I am too, David, and I'm right here and I DO know him.

DAD: Do you know what kind of father he'll make? A father to his children? Why, for all you know he's never BEEN a father before.

LINDA: Well, I should hope not! Why, I wouldn't THINK of marrying—

DAD: Oh, you may think he's nice to look at and lots of fun to have around, but I'm warning you you're marrying a RANK AMATEUR!

PETER: And frankly I just don't think he measures up. I mean he's a fine person and I like him a lot, but—well, you're the baby and we always expected something special . . . and he just doesn't measure up. Well, look at him! At the very most he's only fourteen inches high!

LINDA *begins to protest, but* PETER *points demonstratively at the floor downstage center. The family converges on the spot, looking down intently.*

LINDA: Now, Peter, stop that! That's not fair! Don't say that. . . . He's lying down.

MOM: Well, that's just what he means dear. [*They all kneel*] He's ALWAYS lying down. He just doesn't . . . measure . . . UP.

And they are all slowly bending forward, looking closer and closer until their noses practically touch the floor.

EXECUTIONER: And MY opinion would be perhaps you are all too close to judge. For it just might be not the Beloved One who is not good enough for you, but you who are not good enough for the Beloved One.

After a pause a loud chop from orchestra.

LINDA: [*Slowly coming up*] He's right, Mom. The Beloved One IS too good for me. It's a nasty thing to say, but David's right.

PETER: Do you think so?

LINDA: Too nasty, but maybe all too true.

DAD: Better marry him before he gets away.

MOM: Call his mother and see if it's still on.

LINDA: David, you were so right. You were awfully nasty about it but you were right. I can't wait for you to get home to tell you how nasty you were and how right you were.

EXECUTIONER: I hope my advice has been helpful for I am afraid it must be the extent of my usefulness as far as your wedding is concerned, for I shall be unable to attend.

A minor arpeggio by the orchestra.

LINDA: Not attend?

EXECUTIONER: For the press of my affairs is such that no matter how much I might wish to be with you, such a gesture at this time would endanger the stability of my very existence. Your loving brother. [*Lights fade on him . . . the family momentarily frozen by this unexpected news*]

LINDA: He's not coming.

MOM: He has to come.

PETER: "His very existence"?

MOM: That'll ruin everything.

DAD: I knew he wouldn't come. I knew he'd do something like this someday.

LINDA: Mother, he's not coming. [*Goes to her crying*]

PETER: Maybe something's wrong.

MOM: He'll be here, don't worry. It'll be perfect.

PETER: But he said he can't make it.

MOM: But he's GOT to make it. If we have to, we'll go GET him.

LINDA: Get him?

MOM: If we all went to GET him, he couldn't refuse us, could he? He just forgot how much it means to us.

DAD: We couldn't make it. It's too far.

MOM: We'll travel all night. We should make it before morning.

PETER: I think Mom's right.

LINDA: We'll start right now.

DAD: It's too far! I know it's too far! I call and he never hears me. I call and you hear me, but HE never hears me.

PETER: We can make it, Dad.

LINDA: We can make it.

MOM: TOGETHER we can make it.

The lights dim to blue. MOM *moves to alongside* PETER, DAD *and* LINDA *side by side in front of them. A strange, attenuated musical interlude begins . . . flutes lowered electronically to suggest ship's whistles, sliding whistles raised to suggest the slow, soaring paths of gulls. The slow progression of strange harmonies suggests the passage of time, and a journey into the unknown. Shortly after the music softly begins, the family begins a unison shifting from foot to foot, their bodies each time alternating between facing two slightly different directions. It seems as if they are in a boat, a succession of waves approaching at an angle each time momentarily altering their true course. After the slow pace has been established, it begins to speed up as if the sea becomes rougher. The family raises its right hand toward* DAVID *as if taking a bearing and im-*

mediately the tempo of the movement slows again and arms drop.

DAD: Bong bong. Bong bong.

LINDA: [*Quietly*] We'll never make it, Mother.

MOM: Shh.

DAD: [*Intones*] Can you hear me?

PETER: [*Though apparently without the baby*] Oh, the poor baby, look at her squirm. And I never know what's the matter. God, it must be hard to be a baby.

LINDA: Where are we now, Mother?

MOM: Quiet, dear.

LINDA: We've got to make it back in time. What'll you-know-who think?

MOM: It'll be beautiful. Like it used to be.

DAD: Bong bong.

MOM: [*Intones*] Can you hear me?

EXECUTIONER: [*Firmly*] Don't come any farther. Proceed at your own risk!

They seem to not hear him, but the tempo of their sea movement quickens. They raise their arms again but the sea does not calm.

DAD: Can you hear me? [*Then as their arms lower he mutters to himself*] He could hear me if he wanted to. His problem is he doesn't listen. He never listened. At least to me. But then I never said much worth listening to. Oh, the memories, on every side. Feel them . . . drifting past? Dipping like gulls, darting—disappearing? So far . . . [*Then out loud*] HOW DO PEOPLE GET SO FAR?

MOM: A little patience.

DAD: [*To himself again*] How did it happen? The bitterness! How do humans learn to snarl like dogs at the throats of loved ones? The things that passed my lips. Was I to blame? And is a child more to blame? [*Then angry*] BUT WHAT HE SAID TO ME . . . a thousand times. . . . So far. Back . . . so far.

MOM: [*Intones*] Bong bong.

LINDA: Mother, I don't know where we are. I think we're lost.

Their arms go up again.

DAD: [*In the rhythm of their rocking motion he cries out loudly, intoning*] THE FAULT WAS MINE!

EXECUTIONER: [*Immediately echoing his anguish, not his voice*] THE FAULT WAS MINE!

DAD: [*After a moment, more insistently*] THE FAULT WAS MINE!

EXECUTIONER: THE FAULT WAS MINE!

After a moment the outstretched arms of the family slowly turn palms up as if making an offering.

MOM: Quiet, dear. [*Sadly*] Who's to hear you but your own echo?

DAD: Everything I did was wrong. Everything I said was selfish. HOW CAN HE EVEN LOOK AT ME?!

EXECUTIONER: HOW CAN HE EVEN LOOK AT ME?!

DAD: [*The movement slowing, dropping arms*] Without remembering?

EXECUTIONER: [*Mimicking the slowing tempo*] Without . . . remembering . . . ?

LINDA: Oh . . . look at the gulls go past. [*The movement slows even more. The music becomes louder for a moment*] Bong bong. [*The movement now changes as they bring their feet together and do small dips at the knees as if sailing straight into very small waves. Warm lights become mixed with the blue. Then calmly, but with bewilderment and mild amazement*] Look, Mom, we're coming to people. People again. Look at them in the darkness, standing on the water.

PETER: [*Hushed, in the presence of something very strange*] They're looking at us . . . watching us go past.

MOM: They don't understand us. See it in their faces. Tell them, Linda. You are the fruit of our enterprise.

PETER: Greet them before they slip away. They seem transparent.

LINDA: [*Having no idea how to begin*] My name is Linda . . . and I'm about to get married. I'm about to discover something important—that really has a place in the picture . . . and even ultimately cannot be ignored.

MOM: That's good, dear . . . ultimately.

LINDA: Oh yes, I think about that too. As a matter of fact that's what I think about most, even when I'm not thinking at all.

PETER: Look, Linda, they know you. They're bowing to you.

LINDA: [*Gaining more confidence*] My body thinks about it for one thing. All the time when people say, "My, isn't Linda growing," I want to tell them my body's not "growing"; it's just thinking me out . . . adding a little here and a little there. And maybe I didn't turn out a masterpiece, but it gives me some confidence I didn't turn out half horse or half giraffe. There's something in me knows what it's doing all right. Knows what it's doing maybe even ultimately. Oh, I'm going to start it all over again myself, I know it. I'm going to have babies.

PETER: God, is she going to have babies.

LINDA: No, I'm that kind of person. I'm sentimental. Like I cry at little things other people don't even notice. I mean that doesn't make you have babies all by itself. There's something else. And my body's been thinking about that too.

PETER: You better watch out 'cause there's going to be one mad rush of babies.

LINDA: And then I won't have much time to think.

MOM: You'll be like I was.

LINDA: Like I remember her when I was little. And then . . . why, God, it's just one fast trip downhill. No time at all and I'll be forty.

MOM: And you won't know much more than when you started.

LINDA: And that's what worries me. [*The movement stops, music fades*] 'Cause I don't know where I'm going. Oh, I'm going all right. I have a clock, each tick, a number, smaller. [*She stops a moment, thinking of the strangeness of what she has just said*]

EXECUTIONER: [*Quietly, commenting on the moment of silence*] Time stands like the Great Divide. At the top at the NOW of time, a stillness so without dimension its one reality is separation.

LINDA: [*As the music resumes*] But I am IN Time. And so is all the world, CRAMMED INTO "NOW." [*And they begin again the original shifting movement of the journey*] Rolling as the crest of a wave. On the brink of history, sliding tomorrow.

They now move together as she has described: rising slowly poised on one leg, dipping, sliding forward, dipping as if down the bank of a wave. The music rises to an overpowering roar, and only faintly heard, plaintively.

DAD: Bong bong. Bong bong.

The music fades away, and all that is left is a small stepping movement that is bringing the family closer to the front of the stage.

PETER: What's that I see ahead?

EXECUTIONER: Turn back!

Not hearing him, they step forward again. The light becoming warm again, blue disappearing.

MOM: It's a clock.

LINDA: No, it's a steeple.

DAD: It's a man.

EXECUTIONER: Don't come any closer. I warned you!

They step again.

LINDA: It's David!

MOM: Where! Yes, it's David!

DAD: Can you see us? We've come to see you.

PETER: To take you home.

LINDA: For the wedding, David.

The lights come up on the EXECUTIONER *and the bridge to the stage.*

MOM: Oh, David, it's so good to see you.

Their animation slowly dies as they DO see him.

LINDA: David . . . you've changed.

EXECUTIONER: I told you not to come but you came anyway. I warned you but you did not turn back. Don't you know there are reasons I have always run from you, trying to escape you? But you have forced your way into my very lair and now you must pay for it.

PETER: What are you saying?

EXECUTIONER: Don't you see what I have become—what I must do to you?

FAMILY: [*Questioning variously*] What do you— You're not going— You don't mean—

EXECUTIONER: I warned you—cried to you— begged you not to come!

DAD: We came out of love.

EXECUTIONER: And you die out of love! Don't you see I must kill you to ever live?

LINDA: Kill us? Why must you kill us, David? I don't understand.

EXECUTIONER: No more time. All of you, down on your knees.

LINDA: We love you.

EXECUTIONER: Down on your knees!

MOM: [*With indignation*] I'm your mother!

EXECUTIONER: Through no fault of mine.

PETER: You're mad, that's what you are.

EXECUTIONER: Then listen when I say DOWN ON YOUR KNEES!!

They begin kneeling, now aware of his seriousness.

PETER: The baby too?

EXECUTIONER: I want no witness to this horror. Down I say or you'll get it NOW!

DAD: I deserve it—it's all my fault.

EXECUTIONER: Stop it. Don't say it! Don't look at me! Put down your heads!

PETER: [*As they all do*] You'll die for this. If we die, you die.

EXECUTIONER: [*Softly*] Here it comes. [*Ragged, intense percussive music begins as he slowly raises his ax as if to destroy the bridge between them. But as the ax strokes down, the music bursts into a shower of bells, melodies, celebrations. Astonished for a moment, he steps back. Then as the percussive music resumes, he raises the ax once more. Yet as he strokes, the same thing happens. He says in anguish*] My ax . . . my ax keeps turning . . . into flowers.

Prolonged bells and celebrations are heard once more. The family, however, does not notice.

They begin standing, impatient with him, courteous and cold.

MOM: Well, we can't wait any longer, David.

DAD: Got to get back.

LINDA: Everyone's expecting us.

PETER: [*With mild sarcasm*] Maybe we'll see you next year.

DAD: If you need anything, just write.

They turn their backs on him and begin to walk away, the lights turning blue again.

LINDA: We'll never make it in time. The Beloved One will never forgive me.

But they seem to be wandering directionless, moving as a group no longer.

DAD: What is the way?

MOM: David? What is the way? [*The family music begins again, now painfully nostalgic, and though all facing in various directions the family begins its unison dance once more*] We knew the way when we were coming toward you, but we lost the way when we turned AWAY.

The EXECUTIONER watches them as they move through their ritual for a few moments, then speaks.

EXECUTIONER: Here. I am the way. I am only HERE because THIS IS THE ONLY WAY. [*But the family goes on, oblivious. Kindly*] Why don't you listen to me? But you're lost, all of you. Look at you. [*Then as if in the same room with them, testing his voice to see if they are listening to him*] Can you hear me? [*The music fades, but the dance continues for a while in silence as he watches and speaks. He speaks completely without passion—as if commenting on his own emotion*] Such pity for you as you all go on, God only knowing where your lives will lead. Seeing them as not tragic, but only a bit like everyone's—so why NOT go on like everyone? The stars will not go out when you die. [*The blue lights on the family begin dimming*] Why NOT wear out your lives in the common silence, with which we humans edge toward the quiet indignity of death? Between humans such conspiracy of silence. [*He sees the family disappear in darkness. He then speaks softly, affected by his own emotion for the first time*] No. Speak to ME. Shout to ME. I will not LET you pass through this world unnoticed. You are not like "everyone" to me. I love you—all of you. When you die the stars WILL go out for ME. One by one part of me will die as you leave me.

Immediately three authoritative drumbeats come from the orchestra, and the music of the return begins. First is heard a loud drum roll

during which the EXECUTIONER slowly raises one leg as if to take a giant step onto the bridge. Then the attenuated music of the journey is heard as, with complete relaxation, he begins simply walking across the bridge to the stage. But before he makes it the ragged percussion of the severance begins and he is suddenly drawn backward. His heels soundly thump and echo on the bridge as he draws himself away step by step in strong, methodical renunciation. But when most of the progress has been undone the motif of the family music is heard again—plaintive, nostalgic—and he steps back to the "island" and takes off his hood. Underneath we see a young, pleasant face, hair rumpled, smooth with perspiration. He has been having a hard time. Immediately the three loud beats by the orchestra are heard again as if ordering him to try once more. Then the drum roll, and his pose as if to step; the journey music and his relaxed walk; the ragged, methodical percussion, and his dragging backward, digging in his heels in tense, very strong movements. But the motif of the family is heard again, and stepping onto the island, he hurriedly takes off his magnificent mantle. Underneath he is wearing a loose, full-sleeved tunic, black, with a large, simple white circle on the front. The three insistent beats are heard again, followed by the drum roll. Then the journey and the relaxed walk. But before he is half the distance he has covered before, the three insistent beats from the orchestra are heard again, followed by the drum roll. So in the middle of the bridge he takes his pose of one leg high in the air, about to step. Blackout. In the darkness we hear a few seconds of the journey music, then three final live beats and the lights suddenly snap on again. DAVID is on stage at the foot of the bridge, a suitcase on the ground beside him. He is dressed casually in the unassuming attire of an upperclassman. The family stands facing him, his back to us, in a tableau as if he has just stepped from the plane. The following scene is played completely realistically—as if we are at the airport eavesdropping. After a long pause LINDA says softly, as if informing him in the unlikely case he didn't know.

LINDA: You missed it.

DAVID: [*Embarrassed*] I—I know. I'm sorry—

MOM: [*Quickly changing the subject, cheerfully*] How are you?

DAVID: [*Kissing MOM and DAD as PETER picks up suitcase*] Fine, Mom, Dad . . . Peter. Oh thanks.

PETER: [*Shaking his hand*] How are you?

DAVID: I took a late plane and—well I didn't know if I could . . . make it or not. [*This mostly for the benefit of* LINDA, *who is looking at the ground.* MOM *quickly moves to her*]

LINDA: [*Softly to* MOM] My own brother can't make it home for my wedding.

MOM: Linda . . .

LINDA: [*Still quietly to* MOM] I suppose you think it didn't make any difference. [*She slowly turns and looks at* DAVID. *He smiles at her helplessly. After a moment*] I missed you, David.

And they embrace. The whole family closes in, pleased that no friction will mar the homecoming—that they are all together again.

DAVID: I was here, Linda. You know that, don't you . . . Mom, Dad, Peter? [*Then with sincerity painful to express*] I'm always here.

Lights quickly fade.

APPENDIX

If it is not possible for a production to construct a "bridge" as indicated in the script—or if the play is to be done in the round, the stage in an area lower than the audience—an equally satisfactory alternative can be arranged as follows:

A low, sturdy sawhorse and a plank 12 feet long, one foot wide and two inches thick are required. The sawhorse is placed at the edge of the family's acting area. A lighted red lantern hangs under it throughout the performance to *suggest the danger beyond. One end of the plank rests on the horse, the other on the ground out in the audience (or otherwise away from the main acting area) at the foot of a low platform on which the Executioner stands. After Peter's line, "Makes me feel I'm doing something right" (page 18) the Executioner lifts his end of the plank and quickly slides it slightly more than halfway across the horse into the main acting area. It suggests a gangplank. Peter then continues, looking at it, "Oh, that's right, David's due tonight, isn't he?" Linda then sits on the end of the plank rather than the swing while talking to the Executioner, and she and he seesaw. The seesaw is used just as the swing by Mom and Peter in demonstrating Linda's immaturity, and on Mom's line, "One, two, twenty . . ." (page 19) the plank is drawn quickly back to its original position by the Executioner.*

During the Return at the play's end, the plank is once more tipped into the halfway position, and the Executioner's dance across the bridge becomes walking up and over the seesaw. On his first attempt, before the seesaw tips as he walks up his side of it, he decides to turn back and take off his mask. In the second attempt he tries with much difficulty to balance the seesaw before deciding he must remove his mantle. In the third attempt the seesaw tips, crashes to the floor of the main stage area, and the Executioner stands ready for the trip downhill at the blackout.

A BEAUTIFUL DAY

a poem play

Ruth Krauss

A Beautiful Day was first presented by Remy Charlip at the Pocket Theatre, New York City, in four versions (see Director's Notes) as part of *The Pocket Follies* on June 10, 1963, with the following cast:

GIRL .... *Viola Farber*

SUN .... *Burton Supree*

It was directed by Mr. Charlip.

A fifth version (see Director's Notes) was subsequently added and presented with the other four by the Judson Poets' Theatre at the Judson Memorial Church, New York City, combined with additional theatre poems by Miss Krauss and *Play I Play II Play II* by Gertrude Stein, on December 16, 1965, with the following cast:

GIRL .... *Florence Tarlow*

SUN .... *Charles Adams*

It was directed and choreographed by Mr. Charlip. Music by Al Carmines. Set by Malcolmn Spooner; costumes by Maria Irene Fornés and Sue Smith; lighting by Johnny Dodd. Stage manager: Lee Guilliatt.

poem play
A BEAUTIFUL DAY

GIRL: What a beautiful day!
THE SUN falls down onto the stage
end

DIRECTOR'S NOTES

The following are Remy Charlip's notes of the five versions of *A Beautiful Day* which he has directed.

1. *Stage black. Lights dim up slowly as golden sun appears from hole in ceiling.* GIRL *asleep on stage, awakens, stretches, sits up, rubs eyes, looks at* SUN, *smiles and says,* "What a beautiful day!" SUN *(tied to ashcan cover) crashes to the floor. Blackout.*

2. *Stage black. Lights up, as fully inflated orange balloon is lowered from hole in ceiling.* GIRL *enters watching. When balloon is fully visible,* GIRL *smiles and says,* "What a beautiful day!" BOY *explodes balloon with pin. Blackout.*

3. *Stage black. Lights up.* GIRL *seated on chair reading. Looks up to see and hear an empty orange balloon being blown up by* BOY *through a hole in ceiling.* GIRL *closes book to watch. When balloon is full,* GIRL *smiles and says,* "What a beautiful day!" BOY *releases balloon.* GIRL'S *eyes follow in amazement as air empties out propelling balloon zigzag, all over stage to final sputter on floor. Blackout.*

4. *Stage black. Lights dim up, as* GIRL *grimly and cautiously pushes head through trapdoor. Lights suddenly up full and warm.* GIRL *smiles and says,* "What a beautiful day!" *Big orange ball thrown from hole in ceiling hits* GIRL *on head, knocking her back down as trapdoor closes. Blackout.*

5. *Stage brightly lit.* GIRL *enters covered in dark blanket. Huge orange balloon floats down from above.* GIRL *throws off blanket and catches balloon as* BOY *climbs down and jumps onstage.* GIRL *walks out with* BOY *and balloon staring in disbelief from one to the other. Before exit,* GIRL *shouts,* "What a beautiful day!" *Blackout.*

WHAT HAPPENED

a play in five acts

Gertrude Stein

What Happened was first presented by the Judson Poets' Theatre at the Judson Memorial Church, New York City, as half of a double bill with *Asphodel, in Hell's Despite* by John Weiners, on September 19, 1963, with the following cast:

> *Joan Baker*
> *Lucinda Childs*
> *Aileen Passloff*
> *Yvonne Rainer*
> *Arlene Rothlein*
> *Al Carmines*
> *Masato Kawasaki*
> *John Quinn*
> *David Robb*

It was directed by Lawrence Kornfeld. Music by Al Carmines. Assistants: Larry Seigel, Neville Powers, Carol Sugerman. Curtain by Larry Siegel.

ACT I

(ONE): Loud and no cataract. Not any nuisance is depressing.

(FIVE): A single sum four and five together and one, not any sun a clear signal and an exchange.

Silence is in blessing and chasing and coincidences being ripe. A simple melancholy clearly precious and on the surface and surrounded and mixed strangely. A vegetable window and clearly most clearly an exchange in parts and complete.

A tiger a rapt and surrounded overcoat securely arranged with spots old enough to be thought useful and witty quite witty in a secret and in a blinding flurry.

Length what is length when silence is so windowful. What is the use of a sore if there is no joint and no toady and no tag and not even an eraser. What is the commonest exchange between more laughing and most. Carelessness is carelessness and a cake well a cake is a powder, it is very likely to be powder, it is very likely to be much worse.

A shutter and only shutter and christmas, quite christmas, an only shutter and a target a whole color in every centre and shooting real shooting and what can hear, that can hear that which makes such an establishment provided with what is provisionary.

(TWO): Urgent action is not in graciousness it is not in clocks it is not in water wheels. It is the same so essentially, it is a worry a real worry.

A silence a whole waste of a desert spoon, a whole waste of any little shaving, a whole waste altogether open.

(TWO): Paralysis why is paralysis a syllable why is it not more lively.

A special sense a very special sense is ludicrous.

(THREE): Suggesting a sage brush with a turkey and also something abominable is not the only pain there is in so much provoking. There is even more. To begin a lecture is a strange way of taking dirty apple blossoms and is there more use in water, certainly there is if there is going to be fishing, enough water would make desert and even prunes, it would make nothing throw any shade because after all is there not more practical humor in a series of photographs and also in a treacherous sculpture.

Any hurry any little hurry has so much subsistence, it has and choosing, it has.

ACT II

(THREE): Four and nobody wounded, five and nobody flourishing, six and nobody talkative, eight and nobody sensible.

One and a left hand lift that is so heavy that there is no way of pronouncing perfectly.

A point of accuracy, a point of a strange stove, a point that is so sober that the reason left is all the chance of swelling.

(THE SAME THREE): A wide oak, a wide enough oak, a very wide cake, a lightning cooky, a single wide open and exchanged box filled with the same little sac that shines.

The best the only better and more left footed stranger.

The very kindness there is in all lemons oranges apples pears and potatoes.

(THE SAME THREE): A same frame a sadder portal, a singular gate and a bracketed mischance.

A rich market where there is no memory of more moon than there is everywhere and yet where strangely there is apparel and a whole set.

A connection, a clam cup connection, a survey, a ticket and a return to laying over.

ACT III

(TWO): A cut, a cut is not a slice, what is the occasion for representing a cut and a slice. What is the occasion for all that.

A cut is a slice, a cut is the same slice. The reason that a cut is a slice is that if there is no hurry any time is just as useful.

(FOUR): A cut and a slice is there any question when a cut and a slice are just the same.

A cut and a slice has no particular exchange it has a strange exception to all that which is different.

A cut and only slice, only a cut and only a slice, the remains of a taste may remain and tasting is accurate.

A cut and an occasion, a slice and a substitute a single hurry and a circumstance that shows that all this is so reasonable when everything is clear.

(ONE): All alone with the best reception, all alone with more than the best reception, all alone with a paragraph and something that is worth something, worth almost anything, worth the best example there is of a little occasional archbishop. This which is so clean is precious little when there is no bath water. A long time a very long time there is no use in an obstacle that is original and has a source.

ACT IV

(FOUR AND FOUR MORE): A birthday, what is a birthday, a birthday is a speech it is a second time when there is tobacco, it is only one time when there is poison. It is more than one time when the occasion which shows an occasional sharp separation is unanimous.

A blanket, what is a blanket, a blanket is so speedy that heat much heat is hotter and cooler, very much cooler almost more nearly cooler than at any other time often.

A blame what is a blame, a blame is what arises and cautions each one to be calm and an ocean and a masterpiece.

A clever saucer, what is a clever saucer, a clever saucer is very likely practiced and even has toes, it has tiny things to shake and really if it were not for a delicate blue color would there be any reason for every one to differ.

The objection and the perfect central table, the sorrow in borrowing and the hurry in a nervous feeling, the question is it really a plague, is it really an oleander, is it really saffron in color, the surmountable appetite which shows inclination to be warmer, the safety in a match and the safety in a little piece of splinter, the real reason why cocoa is cheaper, the same use for bread as for any breathing that is softer, the lecture and the surrounding large white soft unequal and spread out sale of more and still less is no better, all this makes one regard in a season, one hat in a curtain that in rising higher, one landing and many many more, and many more many more many many more.

ACT V

(TWO): A regret a single regret makes a door way. What is a door way, a door way is a photograph.

What is a photograph a photograph is a sight and a sight is always a sight of something. Very likely there is a photograph that gives color, if there is, then there is that color, that does not change any more than it did when there was much more use for photography.

HOME MOVIES

a play in one act

Rosalyn Drexler

Home Movies was first presented by the Judson Poets' Theatre at the Judson Memorial Church, New York City, as half of a double bill with *The Bitch of Waverly Place* by Arthur Sainer, on March 19, 1964, with the following cast:

MRS. VERDUN	*Gretel Cummings*
VIVIENNE	*Sudie Bond*
VIOLET	*Barbara Ann Teer*
PETER PETEROUTER	*Fredie Herko*
SISTER THALIA	*Sheindy Tokayer*
FATHER SHENANAGAN	*Al Carmines*
CHARLES ANDUIT	*Otto Mjaanes*
JOHN THE TRUCKDRIVER	*Jim Anderson*
MR. VERDUN	*George Bartenieff*

It was directed by Lawrence Kornfeld, with music by Al Carmines.

Home Movies was subsequently presented by Orson Bean Productions, Inc., in association with the Judson Poets' Theatre at the Provincetown Playhouse, New York City, on May 11, 1964, with the same cast. It was directed by Mr. Kornfeld. Setting by Larry Siegel; lighting by Nicola Cernovich; costumes by Judith Berkowitz.

CHARACTERS

MRS. VERDUN, *an imposing woman of grandiose proportions. She wears a sweeping lace peignoir over a silk or satin sheath, so that her gestures flow around her. Her ears sparkle with drop diamond earrings and her neck strains beneath a garrote of similar composition. She enjoys herself and others, sexually and conversationally, although pseudo-religiosity is the operational framework.*

MR. VERDUN, *an exercise nut, appears in running trunks and an athletic shirt marked with the number 11 on the back. He is muscled, limber, and ready to go. He loves his wife, pities his daughter, and controls both.*

VIVIENNE, *the daughter, a maiden in her thirties. She is homely, zany, and longs to be nude in mixed company. She wears one-piece knickers with a zipper running full length. The knickers are of yellow angora and make her look like a fluffy canary. Beneath this coverall she is wearing a white brassiere with crisp, huge daisies pinned to the cups.*

VIOLET, *the colored maid, a gorgeous, supple beauty, completely at home in her surroundings. All desire her. She wears practically nothing: a top of feathery petals and a bottom of the same. Her long legs are encased in net stockings and her high-heeled shoes are spiked. Hooked to her bodice is a pom-pon, with which she occasionally dusts furniture and people.*

CHARLES, *the intellectual, he has a poignant quality. He wears a long scarf made up of patches. On his cheeks consumptive red spots stand out against off-white, clownlike makeup.*

PETER, *the homosexual, he wears layers of clothing: a jacket, vest, lamé shirt, red dress (to which he finally strips), a headband, and a necklace. He is innocent, sweet, and full of love—a sympathetic guest.*

JOHN, *the truckdriver, he wears any working outfit, plus a hat. In his pocket is a huge pencil. He shows burlesque dumbness and overt sexuality.*

FATHER SHENANAGAN, *dressed as a priest; he has an angelic countenance and perfect pitch. He is a bit of a lecher.*

SISTER THALIA, *is in nun habiliment. She wears an awful platinum-blonde wig under her wimple. She has a crush on Father Shenanagan but is hardly aware of it. Nervous as a little mouse. She is a refugee from an Eisenstein movie.*

Behind a curtain is a raked bed, sumptuously covered. To the right of the bed is a small stand, on which sits a bowl of fruit. There is a gaudy backdrop. An upright piano is on the stage.

The curtain opens from left to right. The silence is broken by the sound of FATHER SHENANAGAN *singing Gregorian plainsong. He comes through the curtain, crosses the stage, singing, to the piano. He sits, plays a minor chord, which is sustained as long as possible, and then abruptly swings into lively opening music. One at a time, the actors cross in front of the curtain and go offstage. Their movements are broad, in character, and in burlesque style.* VIOLET *is the last to cross; she opens the curtain on* MRS. VERDUN, *who is lying on the bed as* VIVIENNE *crosses to sit on the piano.* VIOLET *goes offstage, dusting things and* MRS. VERDUN.

MRS. VERDUN: Ever since your father died I have thought of the bliss complete we shared: stared at by the neighbors in envy, as they knew we were continually in love and I was the loveliest of brides, unbridled in a garden filled with divers flowers: none so gay as I.

VIVIENNE: You make me nervous. As if that idiot you married was capable of anything.

MRS. VERDUN: He was never sick a day in his life. He contributed generously to all disease-fighting organizations. He showed no favoritism.

VIVIENNE: Yeah, him and his clean-wall crusade. Made a habit of stealing my ink eraser whenever he went downtown.

MRS. VERDUN: I wish you would hold your tongue, but later, not now. Later, when old friends of your father come to call. I want you to be nice.

VIVIENNE: [*She gets off the piano and crosses to* MRS. VERDUN *on the bed*] Does that mean I have to keep my clothes on again?

MRS. VERDUN: The day had to come. Oh, why do you desire your downfall with such insistence?

VIVIENNE: You know I want to cast out virginity with one fell swoop of the moopem. Why do you always say don't? In the light of the final end we must all pay with our lives.

MRS. VERDUN: You're jumbling. You have a dribbling, indistinct palate, and I will not tolerate that in my house no matter where else it occurs. Understand?

VIVIENNE: [*She unzips her knickers to the waist and reveals her breasts; they are encased in a brassiere with daisies sewn on the nipple part*] What do you think of this, Mums? I grew them yesterday with my own fertilizer. Let me at least show how my garden grows. Don't you think it a sort of miracle: daisy tits that will not wilt without water. [*She examines the daisies closely*]

MRS. VERDUN: I ought to horsewhip you with my egg beater, but Aunt Helen borrowed it the other day to make whipped cream for the top of your little cousin Joany's birthday cake. She was six last Friday and enjoyed that fish I sent them for supper. They never eat the body of the Lord in vain.

VIVIENNE: Even though fish have flesh, they're human too. The proof is in the gills.

MRS. VERDUN: The gills?

VIVIENNE: Didn't we used to have them?

MRS. VERDUN: Always the question and the answer. Sometimes the answer and the question. Sometimes the answer. Sometimes the question. And in the end, or at the beginning, a blast of light from the East! Our Lord was born.

VIVIENNE: Mums, you're awful. Remember, I'm religious too. [*She closes the curtain and sings, as the cast behind the curtain sing in counterpoint*]

> Glory be to thee, adsurdum:
> Glory be to thee in admasculum.
> Glory to glory in Gloria's glorious and
>   thy . . .
> A mania.
> I would fink and I would be finked.
> I would smear and I would be smeared.
> I would be bought, being hole and nought,
> Being whole and nought,
> A mania.
> Crap danceth. I would crap. Crap ye all.
>   A mania.
> Wherefool I lay, loose walls decay: lament
>   ye all.
> A mania.

[VIVIENNE *opens the curtain*] The number twelve is on the shelve . . . [*To* MRS. VERDUN] Shall I continue?

MRS. VERDUN: Haven't you forgotten something?

VIVIENNE: Let's see. Oh yes. [*As the chorus sings again, she chants*] Ad infinitum, ad infinitum menstrualis, menstrualis corpus Christi, finiculus umbilicalis.

MRS. VERDUN: Later I expect you to express your devotions with emphasis on Vesica Urinaria, your patron saint.

VIVIENNE: He achieved sainthood in such a lovely way . . . [*She pantomimes washing*] his huge male hands up to the elbows in soapy water, scrubbing the underwear of those village women, while they jeered and brought him fresh supplies.

MRS. VERDUN: I don't think it's Christian of you to spread rumors.

VIOLET, *the maid, enters; she wears practically nothing.*

VIOLET: Someone to see you, m'am. So you get up offen the bed and let me make it. I wish you wouldn't stay in bed all the time. There's an awful fusty odor in here. I think I g'wine open the windows.

MRS. VERDUN: Don't you dare take such decisions on yourself. But yes, of course, open the windows. Wait, I don't want them opened too wide. No, that's too wide. Lower them. [*During these instructions regarding the windows,* VIOLET *lowers and raises her breasts as she would the window*] Remember, if you don't understand how we do things here in New York, back you'll go, back where you came from. Virginia, I believe!

VIOLET: Yeah!

MRS. VERDUN: You must say yes, not yeah, unless it's at the end of a prayer, Violet. Yes?

VIOLET: You gettin' up, or should I entertain the company?

MRS. VERDUN: Who, may I ask, has arrived?

VIOLET: A young gennulman call Peter Peterouter. He's wearin' my favorite perfume, "White Shoulders." It never comes true though.

MRS. VERDUN: Perhaps it will when you visit Lourdes.

VIOLET: Lords? And ladies too? They old friends of your husband, m'am?

MRS. VERDUN: Oh, I have to explain everything to you, woolly head. I mean the miraculous Lourdes where miracles *do* happen. I might take us all there in time. It depends.

VIOLET: You wouldn't take l'il ole me fresh fum de sharecroppers' cottage shack where I was born.

MRS. VERDUN: You know very well I couldn't do without you, Violet. So don't pull that ole darky act on me. There was a time when I would have ignored your education, but now, of course, I realize your possibilities. [MRS. VERDUN *rises from the bed, her peignoir floating behind her.* VIVIENNE *jumps on the bed and stretches out on it*] Please tell me in as short a time as you can how many by-products the peanut has.

VIOLET: [*Singing; also burlesquing a sexy walk, with bumps and grinds*]
> Peanut oil, peanut butter,
> Salted cocktail peanuts,
> Peanut in the shell,
> Peanut brittle . . .

MRS. VERDUN: [*Interrupting*] I knew you were an heiress when I hired you. That's why your pay is so minimal.

VIOLET: [*Continuing*]
> . . . peanut cookies, peanut synthetic
> fabric, and peanut ice cream.

MRS. VERDUN: At the same time I respect your future. You can pick up the clothes later. Better make the bed first. [*She throws* VIVIENNE *off the bed and gets back on it.* VIVIENNE *goes behind* MRS. VERDUN *and*

plays with her hair in an ill-tempered manner]
And when you're done with that, see if my
gargling glass has dried toothpaste on it. I was
disgusted with the condition of my own individual glass yesterday and had to cup water
into my mouth with my hands instead of using
my own gargling glass, which should be kept
immaculate because not only did I buy it
especially at the exclusive bathroom shop at
Saks Fifth Avenue for my own use because it
had my initials embossed in gold on it, but
what was I saying?

VIOLET: You sayed dat your mouf smell.

MRS. VERDUN: I didn't hire you for your sense
of humor. I'm completely aware of the race
hatred you bear me . . . [*She goes to* VIOLET
and embraces her] but I embrace you and love
you like a little child who is spontaneous to the
point of complete exhaustion and must be put
bodily to bed in the middle of the game no
matter who's losing.

VIOLET: [*Moving away from* MRS. VERDUN] I'm
glad you 'preciate my efforts, otherwise there'd
be no recompense. No recompense, wreck-um-
pants, pants-um-wreckum. [*She mouths the
words, fascinated, studying the sound*]
                Wreck-um-pants
                Pants-um-wreckum

BOTH: [*They sing this four or five times as they
meet at center stage*]
                Wreck-um-pants
                Pants-um-wreckum

VIVIENNE: [VIVIENNE *closes the curtain behind
them. She imitates* VIOLET] Peanut ice cream.

VIOLET: I'm glad you 'preciate my efforts.

MRS. VERDUN: Yes, I do. Now take these clothes
and put them in the cleaners, dear, and when
you go down, please see whether Vivienne's
other knickers have come back yet. I reminded
them on Wednesday that I wanted them on
Thursday, and now it's Friday and I don't
think they'll have them till next Tuesday.
They're so unreliable.

VIOLET: [*Chewing gum vigorously*] Yes'm. Shall
I announce your appearance into the other
room where that strange friend of your missing
husbin' is waiting for you?

MRS. VERDUN: Get rid of that gum. Get rid of it.
Do you hear? Rid-of-it. It's not becoming for
a maid of your age and position to talk and
chew at the same time. One would think you
were a cow chewing cud. [VIOLET *leaves.* MRS.
VERDUN *speaks to the audience*] She does re-
semble a cow pat, or turd drying in the good
Lord's sun. [*She exits*]

VIVIENNE: [*Enters with a Bible*] Ma. [*Pause*]
Ma. [*Pause*] Ma! [*Pause.* MRS. VERDUN *enters*] You forgot this again, Ma.

MRS. VERDUN: Thank you, dear. [*She takes the
Bible and exits*]

VIVIENNE: [*Alone, in front of the curtain*]
      I would fink and I would be finked.
      I would smear and I would be smeared.
      I would be bought, being hole and nought,
      Being whole and nought,
      A mania.

VIVIENNE *opens the curtain and exits.* MRS.
VERDUN *and* PETER *are discovered sitting on
the bed.* PETER *is ensconced at one end,* MRS.
VERDUN *at the other.*

MRS. VERDUN: I think fruit is so nice in the summer, don't you?

PETER: Oh yes, I adore fruit in the summer.

MRS. VERDUN: So refreshing.

PETER: Succulent.

MRS. VERDUN: Ripe.

PETER: Juicy!

MRS. VERDUN: Dripping.

PETER: Ever so wet.

MRS. VERDUN: Would you care for a fruit?

PETER: But your bowl is so delightful to look at,
I wouldn't dream of disturbing the arrangement. If, of course, you have more in the
kitchen . . . I prefer peaches.

MRS. VERDUN: As soon as my maid is free, she'll
serve us.

PETER: No hurry. I like waiting for my pleasures.
Often, you know, the expectation is better than
the realization. Although, when you have one
in the hand, why wait for two in the bush?

MRS. VERDUN: [*Singing*]
      All birdies fly away;
      Even those you've had in the hand.
      Nothing seems to keep winged creatures
      From using their wings.
      Away they go.
      Away into the wild blue yonder.
      All birdies fly away,
      All birdies fly away,
      Even those, even those you've had in the
            hand.

*She jumps off the bed, crosses to the apron of
the stage and belts out a repeat of the song to
the audience.*

PETER: Fruits are the same; once eaten, they are
gone forever, and the gas pains they cause
flutter and fuss inside like wings.

MRS. VERDUN *drags* PETER *downstage, where
they sing.*

MRS. VERDUN:
      Like wings aloft,
      Caught in an intestinal updraft.

PETER:
> Like wings aloft,
> Caught in an intestinal updraft.

MRS. VERDUN:
> It's true, dear,
> That if something else
> Is caught in the whirl
> Of something else entirely,
> It just can't help itself,
> But must continue
> In the powerful current
> Of that particular thing.

PETER:
> Yes, we just can't help it;
> The route we go,
> A power stronger than will.

BOTH:
> It just can't help itself,
> But must continue
> In the powerful current
> Of that particular thing.
> A Godlike power,
> Completely invisible.
> The route we go,
> A power stronger than will.

PETER:
> A power stronger than will.

MRS. VERDUN:
> A power stronger than will.

BOTH:
> A power stronger than will.

PETER: [*He slumps back*] Till the explosion, then BOOM! Everything gives way and falls into small portions. Sometimes I think the good Lord created everything by chance, set off the cherry bomb and waited for the shapes to crack.

MRS. VERDUN: Your attitude reminds me of my husband, who said anything he pleased.

PETER: He was a fine man.

MRS. VERDUN: Yes.

PETER: Strong.

MRS. VERDUN: Exceedingly muscled.

PETER: Well hung.

MRS. VERDUN: What was that?

PETER: His deportment in private excited my deepest admiration.

MRS. VERDUN: Where was it you two met? I thought it a coincidence that he should bring you home after I was already so familiar with your mother, who visits me often to chat.

PETER: [*Singing*]
> Mother told me about you,
> And then I told her about the gymnasium
> Where I met him.

He turns to the audience.

> He was rather close-lipped.
> I didn't know him well, although
> We used the equipment together.
> It was an inner feeling that we felt,
> An unspoken man-to-man sympathy
> Based on the fact that we spent so much
>   time there.
> Any overture would have spoiled
> The innocent childlike aura

On his knee.

> Of our relationship.

He falls back to the floor in a languid pose.

MRS. VERDUN: Now that he's gone I suppose the truth has dawned.

PETER: A terrible truth covered with the rash . . .

MRS. VERDUN: But physical discomforts concern me not. [*She speaks while sentimental music plays in the background*] I believe in the hereafter. I believe in a vast woolly tomb shaded from without, by huge striped awnings flapping in the wind like wings. I believe my husband's soul is a lost crow frightened forever by the motion of those awnings.

The music stops.

PETER: He is not a man to take limbo lying down, but in love and death we all lean back to die.

MRS. VERDUN: He had one thing which concerned him above all else.

PETER: Yes?

MRS. VERDUN: He wanted his daughter Vivienne to marry a suitable gentleman of his acquaintance.

PETER: If she resembles him, I'd be interested.

MRS. VERDUN: She resembles him in character, but her fine points are as unrealized as a tadpole's. She looks a bit like you. Let me see, turn to the side. Ah yes, there you are.

PETER: Here I am, and I'd like to meet her, but you might as well know that although Oscar Wilde had children . . .

MRS. VERDUN: The author?

PETER: Do you know any other?

MRS. VERDUN: No.

PETER: That although he had children, he was not quite suitable. Like myself, he held a part of himself back for others, strangers who could never bear the fruit of his seed.

MRS. VERDUN: Perhaps you are right. To be turgid under cover of darkest night is not the whole story. He might have been dreaming of those strangers at the very time he was planting those seeds.

PETER: [*Speaking over sentimental music*] The opalescent dew of his desire, as mine, was drawn, by three black stallions wearing emerald ostrich plumes and jeweled trappings. Some might call it queer, but the natural aristocrat finds it a most usual way to travel.

The music stops.

MRS. VERDUN: Who's an aristocrat these days? [*She sighs*]

PETER: I am. Watch me metamorph into a mannered and pompous queen. Discount my suit and call me Caladonia. Then ask me, "Caladonia, Caladonia, what makes your big head so hard?"

MRS. VERDUN: If I ask you, "Caladonia, Caladonia, what makes your big head so hard?" will you answer me?

PETER: I'll demonstrate.

MRS. VERDUN: Caladonia, you may begin.

To rhythmic strip music, PETER *takes off his jacket, his pants, his shoes; he wraps his tie around his head like a bandanna, puts on a rhinestone necklace, lowers his red shirt, which is in fact a dress, to his knees. Having completed his metamorphosis into a "pompous queen," he prances around, making grotesque faces to the audience.* MRS. VERDUN *coughs to get his attention. The music changes to "All Birdies Fly Away" as* PETER *closes the curtain in front of him, looking at the audience with a sweet, innocent face. There is a brief pause; then* VIVIENNE *enters. They look at each other, startled, then sing.*

VIVIENNE: [*Singing*]
You look like me.
If I had a brother, he would look like
    you.
Would you like to come and live with
    me?

PETER: [*Singing*]
You look the way I'd have looked
If I had been a girl.
You are my female counterpane.

PETER *and* VIVIENNE *repeat the song, this time singing simultaneously.*

BOTH:
I'll bet we could tell each other secrets,
And find each other sweethearts.

VIVIENNE:
And eat each other's leftovers.

PETER:
And wear each other's underwear.

BOTH:
And play catch as catch can.

VIVIENNE: Not in my bunny slippers. I wouldn't do that in them. The ears rip off too easy in my bunny slippers. I might try Graeco-Roman in them but never ketch-ez-ketch kan. I hate to sew the damn things on. When I trip on them I break my glasses and that blinds me temporarily.

PETER: Oh, I'm so sorry. You're much too nice a lady to go blind temporarily. One would think there'd be special dispensation for the good people; for the really good ones, so that tragedies didn't happen to them all the time. If I was your brother, I'd never cause you pain or blindness. I'd fall first.

VIVIENNE: The first fall is the fall from grace. After that nothing matters because who cares?

PETER: Nobody cares but mothers. Mothers do care, you know.

MRS. VERDUN *enters.*

VIVIENNE: [*Singing*]
My mother wears a concave lens.
She has trouble focusing.
For years I hated her because
I thought her squint was an expression
    of evil.

Remember when I hated you
And you loved me in spite of it?
I thought she was putting the curse
    on me.
Isn't that right, Mama? Didn't I hate
    you?

MRS. VERDUN: My little girl has always adored me. She wears concave lenses. For years I believed that I hated her, held her responsible for the looks we gave each other, but she had weak eyes too. We all have weak eyes. But it doesn't matter because . . . [*She sings*]

Once you've seen everything,
What is there to see?
My olfactory sense
Has sharpened, though,
Sharpened so.
We all have weak eyes
But it doesn't matter.
No, it doesn't matter because
Once you've seen everything,
What is there to see?
My olfactory sense
Has sharpened, though,
Sharpened so.
For instance, I can identify that perfume you're wearing. It's "White Shoulders," isn't it?

VIVIENNE *opens the curtain.*

PETER: I'm wearing "White Shoulders" on top, but underneath there's still the lingering odor of "Bagatelle." It expresses the real me.

MRS. VERDUN: [*She approaches* CHARLES, *who is standing behind the bed*] I wasn't familiar with "Bagatelle," but now that we're acquainted, my nose will not play tricks. Peter, I want you to meet Charles Anduit. He writes books. My, my, an author. I've always wanted to write myself, but I've been written already. Pleased to meet you, Charles. I hope we'll get to know each other better as the evening progresses.

VIOLET: [*After* CHARLES *whispers to her*] Mistah Chas. say dat if you don' stop suckin' you friggin' lips in like you doin', he goin' to sew dem up wif de topmast fum a model schooner. Ain' dat a scream.

VIVIENNE: [*She reveals a daisied breast*] I thought you came here to see me. Daddy had it arranged.

VIOLET: [*After* CHARLES *whispers to her*] Mistah Chas. say dat no frigit dike goin' tell him whose nooky ta tickle. He say dat when he do you all de favah of his company, he thank you all kindly to shut up. And he want more to eat. And he say send de fairy to de kitchen for anothah peach, pronto!

PETER *goes to the kitchen, making a big display of his good nature. He smiles, swishes, pirouettes.*

MRS. VERDUN: Charles dear, I know you think of me as an old cow, but time is running out and I must know. Is a woman's brain smaller than a man's?

VIOLET: [*After* CHARLES *whispers to her*] Woman's is got a more rounder an' shinier skull wat a man's got, but spite a dat news de truth is dat both is infinite-dismal. However, de proportions is jest right. Dat is to say, he ain't g'wine put down de chick brain wave in any sense, since however even the inferior wall outside of Jerusalem.

VIVIENNE: [*She starts to undress, but her zipper jams*] Damn, damn, damn, damn it to hell. I should have installed a new improved zipper that meshes and unmeshes at a touch. Can't even undress peacefully in my own home.

VIOLET: [*After* CHARLES *whispers to her*] Chas. say dat he got a putty good idee wut you got fum past performance, but he glad you attemptin' it again cause it give you kicks and evybody should get dey kicks.

VIVIENNE: You can tell Chas. that he always spoils my fun. [CHARLES *gets up and grabs* VIVIENNE. *He kisses her wildly, passionately, sadistically*] Oh! oh! How voracious you are. Charles, I dislike you intensely. [*Choking him*] Say that you love me.

VIOLET: [*After* CHARLES *whispers to her*] He say dat he love you, dat you de fox fo him. But he promised you mothah fust, me secunt, and he want to try dé pansy too, but you can come along as de lookout.

VIVIENNE: If only father were here. Life is so weird without him.

There is a knock on the door. JOHN, *a huge truckman, pushes a large wooden closet onto the stage. It has tags on it and a mirror the length of its door.*

JOHN: Who'll sign for this?

MRS. VERDUN: I will, young man. Bring your bill of lading here. Father Shenanagan is expected any moment with Sister Thalia. Did you happen to see a short father with a medium sister outside my door?

JOHN: Them people answer your description are downstairs in the lobby. Couldn't all fit in the elevator.

MRS. VERDUN: Good. They've come to comfort me. I'm receiving calls of condolence on the disappearance of my husband. We haven't seen or heard from him for a month of Sundays. T. God for ceremony; it fills in the gaps.

JOHN: Gee, lady, I hate to do a stupid thing like deliver a closet at a time like this.

MRS. VERDUN: We must proceed normally if we are to retain a modicum of sanity, must we not? Think of it, one never knows who's going next these days.

JOHN: No truer words were spoken, lady. I spoke, lady, once—and it was no truer.

MRS. VERDUN: What a beautiful closet it is, so ample, and the mirror goes up and down, up and down. [*Stepping back so that she bumps into* JOHN] Excuse me.

JOHN: Ample it is. Holds five suits, six dresses, four hats, one umbrella, two pairs of slippers, and four pairs of shoes.

MRS. VERDUN: Does it? How marvelous. You know your stock well.

JOHN: Yeah, an it comes with a six-month guarantee.

MRS. VERDUN: What could possibly happen to this? [*She caresses the closet*]

JOHN: If the mirror breaks, we replace it, and if the shelf don't fit, we adjust the fit.

MRS. VERDUN: You adjust the fit? All by yourself?

JOHN: On company time, Mrs. Trained to do the job.

MRS. VERDUN: I'll bet you're an expert.

JOHN: I am a bit of an expert on the side.

MRS. VERDUN: What side?

JOHN: Paternal.

MRS. VERDUN: Do you have a pencil?

JOHN: Sure. Here you are. [*He draws a huge, phallic pencil from his pocket*]

MRS. VERDUN: Ah, the regalia and adornments of your trade.

JOHN: The customer's always right.

MRS. VERDUN: I know I'm not wrong about you. I have a feeling in my bones.

JOHN: [*He puts his hand in his pocket*] I don't feel any bones.

MRS. VERDUN: Give it time. What's your name?

JOHN: John.

MRS. VERDUN: Give it time, John.

JOHN: You say my name as if you like it.

MRS. VERDUN: I could like it even more.

JOHN: What should I do to make you like it more without endangering my job?

MRS. VERDUN: Be sweet to me. Stay sweet to me. And adjust the price of the closet.

JOHN: Oh, I can't do that, lady. There are duplicates of the bill.

MRS. VERDUN: Just teasing. There is no love without danger, though.

JOHN: I guess I'm too careful in my life for love.

MRS. VERDUN: But you deliver a pretty wild closet.

PETER: [*Returns from the kitchen with a bowl of fruit*] Fruit, anyone?

There is a blackout.

VOICE OF MR. VERDUN: [*Singing*]
   There is nothing wrong with darkness,
   Nothing wrong with smells,
   But when the darkness has a smell of
      its own,
   And that smell is human,
   Then I say let there be light!
   If you hear me out there.
   Why am I here?
   What did I do?
   I never did a thing
   That didn't need doing
   On a small scale.
   That didn't need doing
   On a small scale.
Why am I confined at the expense of the state I am suffering under? Delusion, all is diluted. That may be my fault, Father, but we share the blame. [*Singing*]
   You and I,
   She and I,
   Us and we,
   And those who are no longer citizens.
   Wife, where are you?
   Where?
   I could swear
   That I heard whispering and titterings.
   Where are they now?
   Where is she now?
Answer me, someone. I swear it will go badly with you all if I have to break this expensive new closet to get out. I am the victim of a conspiracy. Daughter—wife—friends—

He continues knocking and scraping resignedly. The light on the closet dims. The lights go up on SISTER THALIA *and* FATHER SHENANAGAN, *who are sitting at a kitchen table. Their hands are in a prayerful attitude, catching cockroaches. A competitive cockroach-catching game!*

FATHER SHENANAGAN: Sister Thalia, how many do you have? I have three.

SISTER THALIA: I have five.

FATHER SHENANAGAN: Do they tickle?

SISTER THALIA: Only when they climb up the sides.

FATHER SHENANAGAN: Do they do that?

SISTER THALIA: Yes indeed, as the good Lord intended.

FATHER SHENANAGAN: Ah, the good Lord for all.

SISTER THALIA: Blessed be the virgin.

FATHER SHENANAGAN: And the virgin forests holding back the floods.

SISTER THALIA: They're disastrous.

FATHER SHENANAGAN: Floods always are, my dear, but the good Lord provides.

SISTER THALIA: In his infinite wisdom.

FATHER SHENANAGAN: Thank the Lord for doughnuts and coffee too.

SISTER THALIA: I cried when the men protested that my doughnuts were stale.

FATHER SHENANAGAN: We must praise the day-old bakery, not condemn it. How many do you have now? I have six.

SISTER THALIA: I have four. One got away.

FATHER SHENANAGAN: I feel very comfortable in the kitchen, the heart of the home.

SISTER THALIA: Oh, oh help me, another got away. I have three. They're all so agile today, I'm sure to lose.

FATHER SHENANAGAN: There is no better way to learn humility, Sister Thalia. I have eight.

SISTER THALIA: I'm going to let them all go.

FATHER SHENANAGAN: Not so soon.

SISTER THALIA: I must. They are crawling over the insides of my hands and I've already squashed two accidentally. I concede the victory to you.

FATHER SHENANAGAN: And the prize?

SISTER THALIA: I will say a prayer for you.

FATHER SHENANAGAN: And what else?

SISTER THALIA: And let you have some of our home-made wine.

FATHER SHENANAGAN: Good, good. It all sounds so very excellent and admirable.

SISTER THALIA: It's only fair.

FATHER SHENANAGAN: What shall I do with them?

SISTER THALIA: Let them run, dear Father, back under the table and into the silverware drawer.

FATHER SHENANAGAN: You once promised me a wonderful sight. What is it?

SISTER THALIA: Yes I did.

FATHER SHENANAGAN: You did promise.

SISTER THALIA: I did.

FATHER SHENANAGAN: You did.

SISTER THALIA: I?

FATHER SHENANAGAN: You.

SISTER THALIA: It couldn't have been me.

FATHER SHENANAGAN: Then who?

SISTER THALIA: Number two.

FATHER SHENANAGAN: Not you?

SISTER THALIA: No.

FATHER SHENANAGAN: Dear Sister, you are fibbing. Come, gentle Sister, show me it. [*He sings*]

> Showing is part of penance, you know.
> The more you suffer
> The more He'll understand you.
> Don't be a shy bride.
> Your secretive nature will be protected.
> Fear not.
> I merely want to be
> Filled with wonder.
> Show me, show me, show me, show
>   me. Oh, I do so want you
> To show me the horrible sight.

SISTER THALIA: If you insist. [SISTER THALIA *removes her wimple, revealing awful platinum-blonde hair. He takes her by the shoulders and presses her to her knees*]

FATHER SHENANAGAN: Now we must pray together. [*They pray*]

PETER *enters.*

PETER: Business before pleasure, Father? [FATHER SHENANAGAN, *startled, gives him an ugly look that softens into benignity*] Well, anyway, I always feel better when there's a servant of God around. Speaking of servants, I'm a little serving maid today.

FATHER SHENANAGAN: Please continue what you were doing. I'm sure you're a comfort and a help.

PETER: I should say so. If it weren't for me, this kitchen would be a real Grand Central Station. And you know, Mrs. Verdun is in such deep suffering that even she hardly realizes it. Why, to look at her you'd swear nothing had happened. I suppose it's a symptom of temporary insanity.

FATHER SHENANAGAN: Yes and no. Sometimes her behavior is permanent. She languishes wholeheartedly. Her giddy nature longs to appear seraphic. Her desire is to humble herself before personal disasters that would make any ordinary Christian die of shame or chagrin.

PETER: What are those personal disasters that would make any ordinary Christian die of shame?

FATHER SHENANAGAN: I am not free to divulge—

PETER: What has been whispered in the sacristy?

SISTER THALIA *struggles up from her knees.* FATHER SHENANAGAN *tries to prevent her from rising. He cannot tear himself away from the vision of her hair.*

SISTER THALIA: When was the last time you bought a candle, dear sir?

PETER: It was at a time, Sister, when I was going through one of those personal disasters, the kind Father Shenanagan will not discuss. It's true, I was ashamed. Ashamed and simply disgusted with myself. So I went to confession. You know, in my parish there are one or two rather adorable young priests. I prefer the chubby amorous ones with stars in their eyes, to the rotten epileptic scapegoats one adamantly associates with true religion. I like to imagine . . . well, I can't actually go into that. But the way they conspire with you behind that fancy grillwork. So many things happen to the spirit during confession. I swear I'm reluctant to come to the end of sinful recitation. I have to prevent myself from following those sacred, clinging, flowing gowns on their way to the study. I absolutely rankle in a mad funk when I leave the church; dusty-kneed and on the point of a seizure of love. I've been on that moot point too often. Is it any wonder I take the candle with me? [*He disappears under the curtain*]

SISTER THALIA: I believe I should retire to the living room. [*She exits*]

MR. VERDUN *breaks his way out of the closet, prances around, then sings.*

MR. VERDUN:

> Oh my number is eleven on the cross-
>   country run.
> They say the war is over and we've
>   driven out the Hun.
> But seeing is believing and I'll bet you
>   one to one,
> That if anyone is crazy it's my wife,
>   Mrs. Verdun.

[MRS. VERDUN *screams behind the curtain.* MR. VERDUN *stands up and poses. He makes muscles, faces, examines his legs, loosens the calves, etc.*] Sounds like my dear wife can't take it. I always told her that misery would befall her if I ever kicked the bucket. Boy, was I right. She thinks I jumped off the George Washington Bridge on my way to Jersey during my daily constitutional. Keep in shape, that's my advice. I'm in shape. What more could she want? She's safe with me. [*He sings*]

> I can save a friend from drowning,
> Wrestle alligators,
> Lift five cows on my shoulders
>   With the help of a specially constructed
>   platform.
> Women admire me for my nonchalant
>   bravado,

But I suspect that Mrs. V.
Doubts my masculine veracity.
Funny thing happened to me in a health food store the other day. I was ordering my macrobiotic staples from a very healthy looking blonde, so I ventured a stab in the dark, so to speak. As she handed me my package I said: "Baby, I know you sell it, but do you eat it?" and she answered me in a very straightforward health food way. She said: "Listen, buster, I can wipe the floor with you, and I have a good mind to do it, dirty slob!" "Stop!" I cried, "You must be a physical culturist too." [*He sings*]
> I know you sell it, but do you eat it?
> I know you sell it, but do you eat it?
> I know you sell it, but do you eat it?
> I know you sell it, but do you eat it?
> You must be a physical culturist,
> You must be a physical culturist,
> You must be a physical culturist too!

SISTER THALIA: I hear a familiar voice.

FATHER SHENANAGAN: Indeed it rings a knell.

SISTER THALIA: It couldn't be.

MR. VERDUN: It is. I. I have returned. I almost went to Hoboken, but habit prevented me from making the trip. How come no one heard me knocking, knocking on the closet door? Are all the deaf in league?

FATHER SHENANAGAN: We were in the kitchen or we would have heard you. We would certainly have heard you if we had been nearby.

MR. VERDUN: Enough, you sirrah! I believe you are the eminence I used to hear compound on the dais of a most holy lectern during masses. I always excuse reverent personages in case they put the nix on heaven when I go all the way. Here's my hand, sir, to cement your former usefulness and a low bow to you, sirrah, and a speedy sign of the cross.

SISTER THALIA: Bless us all. You echo your own sentiments. I'm afraid to see your wife when she sees you. Solace is a poor substitute for solstice when the sun is set.

PETER: [*Recitative*]
> Here they come now.
> I hear a rush of people and a sound
>   of shock which is silence.
> Here they come now;
> About to enter,
> Almost here,
> Cold,
> Warm,
> Warmer,
> Hot, hot, hot,
> Oh burning.
> They have arrived *en masse.*
> *Quel avec pomme de terre,*
> Mr. Verdun you are discovered.

PETER *opens the curtain on the tableau.* MRS. VERDUN *sees* MR. VERDUN *and screams. Then she rushes forward and kisses him loudly. She then pulls a switch and turns white with anger.*

MRS. VERDUN: *You* had the gall to readjust my calm routine!

MR. VERDUN: If I hadn't ever called you my little pumpkin, I'd say I was remiss, but since I have used endearments often, I'd say you're being hard on me.

ALL: [*Singing*]
> Being hard on him.

MRS. VERDUN: Ask Charles Anduit who's right or wrong. He has the answer book.

MR. VERDUN: Charles Anduit, that pale-faced, pasty-skinned, moon glow of a masculate?

VIOLET: [*After* CHARLES *whispers to her*] Three cheers for Mr. Verdun. Long may he pursue the iron game and be away fum home so that I, Charles Anduit, may commit daring acts of passion under his very nose, with his wife, daughter, and maid Violet. Welcome home.

MR. VERDUN: Watch out. I speak softly and carry a big stick. [*He menaces* CHARLES *and they scuffle ineffectually*]

MRS. VERDUN: [*She sings as* MR. VERDUN *threatens* CHARLES *and finally knocks him down—a Mack Sennett fight*]
> Beat him up. He's a bad boy.
> He's boyish and bothersome.
> Lower the boom.
> Lower the boom.
> He deserves a crushing blow.
> He took advantage of me.
> I cried when he forced me.
> 'Cause he's so boyish and bothersome.
> Lower the boom.
> Lower the boom.
> Lower the boom.
> Lower the boom.
> He took advantage of me!

MRS. VERDUN *sits on* CHARLES *on the last line of her song.*

VIOLET: [*Stuttering for* CHARLES] Help, help, let me up. Please, kind mistress.

MRS. VERDUN: I am still capable of largesse, and do not mean to smother you, young youth. Allow me. [*She helps him up*]

VIOLET: What we is cravin' is soup, and I got some in de kitchen. [VIOLET *goes out to bring in the soup.* VIOLET *appears immediately*]

MR. VERDUN: What kind is it? Answer me. I'm the master here.

VIOLET: Chicken soup with knaydlach.

MRS. VERDUN: Thank God it's not cabbage soup.

VIVIENNE: Or wonton.

VIOLET: Or boy-ya-best.

JOHN: Or borscht.

VIVIENNE: Or pee soup.

PETER: Or dehydrated beef noodle.

FATHER SHENANAGAN: Really thankful that it's not black bean.

SISTER THALIA: Or pee soup.

VIVIENNE: I've already said that. [*She smacks* SISTER THALIA *on the forehead*]

SISTER THALIA: But I agree. Pee soup is thick, green slime. Of course I'd eat it if the Lord prescribed it in his Canticles of Virtuous Foods.

FATHER SHENANAGAN: That deserves a responsory, but I'd rather let the Pope in his extraordinary Pallium rule on it. I am merely a rough-hewn cornerstone. *Cujus pulchritudinem.*

MRS. VERDUN: I'm going to have some right now.

VIOLET: [*After* CHARLES *whispers to her*] Soup of the evening, beeootiful soup. [PETER *takes a bowl of soup and hands out soup to all the people. Each takes out a soup plate and spoon. They all slurp soup. When* PETER *offers* VIOLET *some soup, she morosely brushes him away, takes the stool, plunks it on the apron of the stage, and sits on it. The cast freezes in mid-soup.* VIOLET *confides to the audience; she sings*]

> Sometimes I feel like a chocolate turkey
> Gazing out of cellophane windows.
> Sometimes I feel like I'm almost melted
> In the summertime of my race.
> Sometimes I feel that my body is hollow,
> A long, long way from the mold.
> Is there anybody here that's like weepin'
>   Mary?
> I'll tell you what the Lord has done for
>   me,
> Nothin', nothin', nothin', hallelujah.
> That's what the Lord has done for me.
> Ask not what the Lord has done for you.
> Ask what you can do for your Lord.
> Is there anybody here that's like weepin'
>   Mary?
> I'll tell you what the Lord has done for
>   me,
> Nothin', nothin', nothin', hallelujah.
> That's what the Lord has done for me.
> Well, ah has to go to de kitchen. [*She goes.* CHARLES *follows her out*]

VIVIENNE: [*Singing*]

> No one wants to pluck my daisies.
> Everyone is fooled by my knickers
>   and glasses.
> No one wants to pluck my daisies.
> I wonder why?
> I grew them yesterday
> With my own fertilizer.
> Let me at least
> Show how my garden grows.

> No one wants to pluck my daisies.
> Everyone is fooled by my knickers
>   and glasses.

MR. VERDUN: Now, now, daughter. You are my very own daughter, and as such I cannot and will not accept the notion that you are strange or ugly. Your knickers are functional. You can stand on your head without embarrassment to anyone. It is not your fault that you are white, and Violet exotic. Charles is best forgotten. He is a fakerino with a farina complexion. He has a marked stutter accompanied by unusual sensitivity of the stuffed derma. He sleeps all day and rides the ferries by night. Altogether not a pretty picture himself.

VIVIENNE: Daddy, how did you guess that I love him?

MR. VERDUN: No mind is the criteria, but mind is ever present. I use my brains.

MRS. VERDUN: [*From behind the curtain*] What a delicious soup.

VIVIENNE: I'm going to the kitchen to see what Charles and Violet are up to. Why, oh why, did he choose Violet to speak for him? I could have been so understanding, so voluble for his voice, so additive to his meaning, and so kind. I've always wanted the opportunity to be kind. Nobody has ever trusted me with their ailment. I wonder why. [*Singing*]

> No one wants to pluck my daisies.
> Everyone is fooled by my knickers
>   and glasses.
> No one wants to pluck my daisies.
> I wonder why? [*She exits*]

MRS. VERDUN *enters.*

MRS. VERDUN: See what you've done, you've alienated our daughter.

MR. VERDUN: How?

MRS. VERDUN: Damaging thoughts, they add up. You're responsible.

MR. VERDUN: I accept. *Mea culpa,* but who's the busy seamstress with one pattern in her repertoire—knickers?

MRS. VERDUN: My specialty is sportswear; I do what I do best.

MR. VERDUN: Something more seductive on the girl might change her life. Get her an invite to the movies at least: give her doddering precursors a shot at each other in privacy. She's always around complaining like a simp; what kind of romantic atmosphere is that for us, dearest? God, how I miss you. [*He starts for her*] My hormones are in top form.

MRS. VERDUN: That's the way I like it.

MR. VERDUN: [*Singing*]

> Beat her up.

MRS. VERDUN: [*Singing*]
> He's a bad boy.

MR. VERDUN:
> She's girlish and bothersome.

BOTH:
> Lower the boom.
> Lower the boom.

MRS. VERDUN:
> He deserves a crushing blow.

MR. VERDUN:
> I took advantage of her.

MRS. VERDUN:
> He took advantage of me.

MR. VERDUN:
> I took advantage of her.

MRS. VERDUN:
> He'll take advantage of me.

BOTH:
> (You)
> (I) deserve a crushing blow.
> Lower the boom.
> Lower the boom.

As they sing "Lower the boom" over and over again, they go behind the curtain. The full cast joins the singing. The tempo picks up, as CHARLES *chases* VIVIENNE *past the curtain a few times—a farce chase. They are stopped by* MR. VERDUN, *who holds* CHARLES *at arm's length.*

MR. VERDUN: [*Singing*]
> Do not bruise the fruit.
> Do not bruise the fruit.
> Do not bruise the fruit.
> That my wife bore and I planted.

Do not expose the pit of that overripe production, or it will dry and become sere. [*Singing*]
> It is the pit that holds the bitter almond.

The pit that keeps within it the true soft pit. Do not expose its surface to the breath you exhale and the teeth you dig with. [*Singing*]
> Let it lie!
> Let it lie!

Let it be half-hard, underripe, green, and about to be. [*Singing*]
> Don't feel how soft it is.
> Don't bruise the fruit.
> Don't bruise the fruit!

Smell it, if you must, [*Singing*]
> But don't lay your nose on it.

Let it stay in the basket till it gets rotten and frothy with mold and clings to others in the basket. Yes, let the fruit get rotten without help from your alien hands, Charles Anduit. Or do you insist that your thumbprint sink in—heralding decay wherever you press! I am helpless. [*Singing*]
> I cannot ask you
> To love my daughter.
> She is to be pitied.

> Do not bruise the fruit.
> Do not bruise the fruit.
> Do not bruise the fruit
> That my wife bore and I planted.
> Let it lie.
> Let it lie.
> Let it lie.

CHARLES: [*Stuttering*] L-l-l-l-let me g-g-g-go.

SISTER THALIA enters. She pulls MR. VERDUN away from CHARLES and leads CHARLES to the piano. VIVIENNE, MR. VERDUN, and SISTER THALIA exit.

CHARLES: [*Singing*]
> Charles Anduit is my name,
> And I do it all the same.
> Stutter while I seek out fame.
> Repetition is my game.
> Take a straight and simple word
> Of one syllable you've heard.
> If I say it, you'll regret
> You can't catch it with a net.

VIVIENNE sticks her head out of the curtain.

VIVIENNE: Say a simple word like "love."

CHARLES: [*Stuttering*] L-l-l-l-l-ove. [*Singing*]
> Charles Anduit is my name,
> And I do it all the same.
> Stutter while I seek out fame,
> Stutter while I seek out,
> Stutter while I seek
> Stutter while I
> Stutter while
> Stutter
> Stutt. [*He exits*]

MR. VERDUN: [*Entering with VIVIENNE*] Well, he's gone, and good riddance to bad rubbish.

The curtain opens, revealing MRS. VERDUN and PETER arm in arm.

PETER: Don't we make a charming couple?

MR. VERDUN: Ask me no questions, I'll tell you no lies.

PETER: Such character! You look exhausted though. Why don't you sit down and you too, my dear—[*To MRS. VERDUN*] You need the muse. I've written a poem.

MR. VERDUN: Go ahead, abuse the muse.

They seat themselves on the couch. PETER stands. FATHER SHENANAGAN and SISTER THALIA are rapt with anticipation and beam toward PETER with hands in prayerful attitude.

PETER: I'll begin at the beginning and end at the end. [*He recites*]
> Pussy cat, pussy cat, where have you been?
> I've been to London to visit the Queen.
> Pussy cat, pussy cat, what did you there?
> I lapped up a virgin without any hair.

MR. VERDUN: At least it was short. Did you just make it up? I mean, did it just come to you?

A sudden inspiration? What marvelous thing are you to have done it?

PETER: I am an amateur and my purpose is love. Vivienne is an amateur also.

MRS. VERDUN: Aren't we all!

MR. VERDUN: Father Shenanagan and Sister Thalia are professionals, dear wife.

SISTER THALIA: Only in the sense that we are sustained, um, arrive at staple means, um, do what we are cut out for without actually starving. It's a calling and we are answering.

MR. VERDUN: I hear nothing. It's a soundproof existence.

SISTER THALIA: You haven't been called.

MRS. VERDUN: He wants to respond but hates crowds.

PETER: My advice is never rush into anything.

FATHER SHENANAGAN: We really must be going. All's well that ends well.

PETER: How you've summed it up, Father Shenanagan! I must go too and leave that delightfully mean man with his equally delightful wife. [*He goes up to* MR. VERDUN] I hope you're not insulted. I've had a simply gorgeous time! [*He exits with a flourish*]

The curtain closes. SISTER THALIA *appears in front of the curtain.*

SISTER THALIA: [*Singing*]
> We must hurry;
> They are waiting for us at the seminary.

FATHER SHENANAGAN: [*If possible,* FATHER SHENANAGAN *accompanies them with an accordion. He sings*]
> With wine?

SISTER THALIA:
> Indeed, wine is seminal at the seminary.

FATHER SHENANAGAN:
> You need never remove your headdress for me again.

SISTER THALIA:
> But why? Have I failed you?

FATHER SHENANAGAN:
> I am not sure I can control the results
> Resulting from an irreligious glimpse.
> I'm not a saint, you know.

BOTH:
> (He's)
> (I'm) not a saint, you know,
> A saint, you know,
> A saint, you know.

SISTER THALIA:
> You begged me. You wanted it.
> I didn't get to my knees by myself.

FATHER SHENANAGAN:
> If you had no intention,
> Why did you come prepared?

> Why did you spread the rumor
> All over the cells?

BOTH:
> In the dormitories,
> In the retreats,
> In the parsonage
> And the vicarage,
> And also at the rear left chapel.

FATHER SHENANAGAN:
> All the way back to Saint Patrick's Cathedral?

BOTH:
> Why?

SISTER THALIA:
> I was asked by Mother Superior
> To publish an explanatory tract.
> I had to go into details.

BOTH:
> (My)
> (Your) mortification would not have been complete
> Without the details.
> The Mother Superior is playing on the same team,
> Is playing on the same team,
> Is playing on the same team.

The curtain opens.

VIVIENNE: Where did Charles go?

MR. VERDUN: Out into the world, step by step.

VIVIENNE: Say, maybe he stopped on the corner for a chocolate egg cream. I'm thirsty myself. Want a goody, Dad? I'm going out.

MR. VERDUN: Yes, I think so—I'd like a box of nonpareils, salted pumpkin seeds, a licorice whip, chocolate money, malt balls, and an all-day sucker.

VIVIENNE: Anything for you, Mom?

MRS. VERDUN: Thank you darling—I'd like two slices of watermelon candy, five bulls' eyes, a sugar daddy, and a package of candy cigarettes.

VIOLET: Miss Vivienne, girl, maybe you bring me back a li'l' somethin' too. I'd prefer to fust choice candy bananas, bubble gum, toasted coconut marshmallows, and a package of Black Jack gum.

VIVIENNE: *Bien entendu!* Back in a jiffy. Then we can have a real grab bag. Violet, you go make some lemonade. [*They exit, making a lot of noise*]

MRS. VERDUN: I worry when she gets like that: starts to talk French and offers to do favors. She's a nervous child, anything could happen. Poor child, she hasn't been the same since she bit into a frozen Milky Way. [*To* FATHER SHENANAGAN *and* SISTER THALIA] Could you kind of keep an eye on her when you go down? See that she doesn't talk to strangers.

SISTER THALIA: Of course, of course. [SISTER THALIA *and* FATHER SHENANAGAN *exit*]

MR. VERDUN: Well, there they go. [*He closes the curtain*] Yes, there they all go, my dear wifey. Now we are alone again for the second time this evening, except for Violet, who will go to her tiny windowless room off the kitchen in a moment.

MRS. VERDUN: [*Calling in to* VIOLET] Violet, are you making the lemonade? Make it snappy, please, Mr. Verdun is thirsty.

VIOLET: [*Appearing from the kitchen*] It on the table awready. I g'wine lie down an rest ma weary bones till de candy come. [VIOLET *sings "I'm g'wine" etc. backstage*]

MRS. VERDUN: Violet is a handsome girl. Don't you agree?

MR. VERDUN: You said it, kid!

The bed slides under the curtain, to the apron, and they sit on it.

MRS. VERDUN: I didn't expect such passionate articulation!

MR. VERDUN: Forget it, baby, I'm still crazy about you.

MRS. VERDUN: Kiss me. [*They kiss*] At times I want you out, but now I want you in. Come. *"Andiam, andiam, mio bene."* [MR. VERDUN *and* MRS. VERDUN *assume the wrestling hook-up position. They then wrestle, alternating advantage, and end with a cross-body pin and arm lock.* MR. VERDUN *tickles* MRS. VERDUN, *which renders her helpless. He pins her and wins the fall. Disappointed, wanting more*] Two falls to a finish.

MR. VERDUN: Okay, anything you say.

MRS. VERDUN: Who's the referee?

MR. VERDUN: Violet.

MRS. VERDUN: In the dark?

VIOLET *returns.*

VIOLET: Am I bein' paged?

MRS. VERDUN: Want to play a game?

VIOLET: Lawda mercy, it don make no no-how to me.

MRS. VERDUN: Well, then, winner take all!

MR. VERDUN: No cheating.

VIOLET: I'll see to that.

MRS. VERDUN: Let's begin. [MR. VERDUN *and* MRS. VERDUN *resume the hook-up position on the bed.* VIOLET *remains to the right of the bed. The cast enters, each as he sings his own line*]

FATHER SHENANAGAN:
    Let no man now diminish
    What takes two falls to a finish.

MRS. VERDUN:
    If wrestling once will get it twice.

VIOLET:
    Wouldn't three times make it nice?

ALL:
    Let no man now diminish
    What takes two falls to a finish.

MR. VERDUN:
    Though your muscles may be quivering,

JOHN:
    Still, 'tis fate the blow delivering.

ALL:
    Let no man now diminish
    What takes two falls to a finish.

PETER:
    Once I slipped out of a hold,

VIVIENNE:
    You are young, but the world is old.

ALL:
    Let no man now diminish
    What takes two falls to a finish.

SISTER THALIA:
    I have tried to break the habit

[*She tries to rip her habit open*]

CHARLES: [*Stuttering*]
    More than wa-wa-wa-wa-wa-wa-wa-wa- once.

ALL: [*Quietly*]
    Let no man now diminish
    What takes two falls to a finish.
    [*There is a pause. Then they all sing loudly*]
    Let no man now diminish
    What takes two falls to a finish.

There is a blackout.

Curtain

The curtain opens for a reprise. The actors exchange roles, and sing choice bits to each other.

AND THINGS THAT GO BUMP IN THE NIGHT
a play in three acts

Terrence McNally

And Things That Go Bump in the Night was first presented by the Office for Advanced Drama Research at the Tyrone Guthrie Theatre, Minneapolis, on February 4, 1964, with the following cast:

FA .... *Alvah Stanley*

GRANDFA .... *Ferdi Hoffman*

SIGFRID .... *Robert Drivas*

LAKME .... *Lois Unger*

RUBY .... *Leueen MacGrath*

CLARENCE .... *Joseph Chaikin*

It was directed by Lawrence Kornfeld. Set by David Delu; costumes by Sally-Ross Dinsmore; lighting by Richard Borgen.

The play was subsequently presented by Theodore Mann and Joseph E. Levine in association with Katzka-Berne Productions at the Royale Theatre, New York City, on April 26, 1965, with the following cast:

FA .... *Clifton James*

GRANDFA .... *Ferdi Hoffman*

SIGFRID .... *Robert Drivas*

LAKME .... *Susan Anspach*

RUBY .... *Eileen Heckart*

CLARENCE .... *Marco St. John*

It was directed by Michael Cacoyannis. Set by Ed Wittstein; costumes by Noel Taylor; lighting by Jules Fisher.

From ghoulies and ghosties
Long leggitie beasties
And things that go bump in the night
Good Lord deliver us!
[*14th Century Scottish Folk Prayer*]

For my father and mother

THE SETTING

A room. Two doors, left and right. At the rear of the stage there are stairs leading to a third and larger door. Beyond this door is the outside. The furnishings in the room—various sofas, chairs, small tables, etc.—are stark and modern. The style is anonymous, abstract somehow. Of special importance is a low table with an intercom system, phonograph, and tape recorder on it. There is a piano. And facing the rear wall and to one side is a very large chair. Whoever sits in it will be invisible to the audience. The lighting is white: a brilliant, blinding white which is of a uniform intensity throughout the room. There are no shadows or semitones.

THE PLAYERS

FA, *short, overweight, and almost bald. He is in his fifties.*

RUBY, *his wife. A good deal more youthful-looking. She is larger, too.*

SIGFRID, *their son. Twenty-one years old, dark and good-looking.*

LAKME, *their daughter. Thirteen years old. She is wiry and tough, rather like a rooster.*

GRANDFA, *very, very old. But the eyes are quick and bright.*

CLARENCE, *early twenties, thinnish, irregular features.*

ACT ONE

At rise the stage is empty. Absolute silence. Pitch dark. After a moment the red light on top of the intercom goes on and we begin to hear the terrible grunting and groaning noises of a person just waking up from a long and deep sleep. The sounds must be amplified to an almost unendurable volume. The theatre should reverberate. We hear a bed table laden with medicine bottles and knickknacks crashing to the floor. And then, after a yawn of agonizing dimensions, we hear

RUBY'S VOICE: [*A pronouncement*] I'm awake. The Ruby is awake. *Buon giorno a tutti!* [*An-*

other *huge yawn*] Correction: almost *buon giorno* and not quite a *tutti*. [*The lights begin to come up now: slowly, slowly, slowly*] Is everyone out there? . . . the four of you? . . . that's nice . . . I like it when the four of you are out there listening to me . . . and I'm all snuggled up . . . broadcasting from bed. It comforts me, yes! [*Lights up ever so slightly more*] Children, I have six toes! Look at them. One, two, three . . . Come in here this instant and look at them! [*Tiny pause*] Sigfrid? Lakme? Are you . . . there? [*No response, Ruby laughs*] You little nippers! I know what you're up to. Pretending not to be there when I call you. Nasty nippers, naughty. Not nice. [*A pause, the light always slowly coming up*] I know you're out there, too, Grandfa. So shall we begin again? [*And now each time more floridly*] *Buon giorno a tutti!* [*Pause*] *Buon giornissimo a tutti!* [*Pause*] *Buonissimo giornissimo a tutissimo!* [*Pause, then sudden, hard*] I SAID GOOD MORNING! ALL RIGHT, IT'S YOUR EVENING BUT IT'S MY MORNING AND I SAID GOOD! [*Pause*] I'm not amused by this. I warn you . . . the four of you . . . there will be retributions. I said I am not amused . . . ANSWER! [*The lights are still coming up, Ruby's desperation is becoming more apparent*] I don't have six toes. I have eight! NINE! Sigfrid, you go right over to that intercom and answer me! Lakme, you too! [*The anger is steadily mounting*] You miserable . . . you think it's so funny, well I do, too! If I ever thought you'd left me alone in this terrible house I'd . . . kill myself! I suppose you'd like that! [*The lights are at full brilliance now, and then the terrified outburst*] I WON'T BE ALONE IN HERE! SOMEONE! SOMEONE COME IN HERE! . . . PLEASE! [*Grandfa, scowling and dour, has come into the room in his wheelchair*] Who's that? . . . Sigfrid, is it—? Lakme, you know better than to frighten me like this . . . Fa, don't let them! Who is it? [GRANDFA *is headed toward the intercom*] WHO IS OUT THERE??? SOMEONE . . . PLEASE . . . TELL ME WHO IT— [GRANDFA *has snapped off the intercom*]

GRANDFA: Harpy! [*The room returns to utter stillness*] Oh, am I ever glad this is my last night in this house. They don't know how glad I am. [*He is fiddling in a tote bag which he carries on one arm of his wheelchair*] No one knows how glad I am. [*Produces a long strip of black knitting*] I don't know how glad I am! [*Knits a moment*] My teeth in a goddamn cookie jar! [FA *stirs in his chair at the rear of the stage, the first time we have noticed him. He will be reading a newspaper during the scene with* GRANDFA *that follows*]

FA: West.

GRANDFA: [*Turning*] Son?

FA: It's moving west.

GRANDFA: I found 'em. And guess where the little monster hid 'em. The cookie jar. Not in the freezer again . . . not like last time . . . oh no, not her, not Lakme . . . but the cookie jar.

FA: The government says it's moving west.

GRANDFA: [*Crabbed*] What is? What's moving west?

FA: It.

GRANDFA: Poppycock! [*He can't get over it*] Eighty-five-dollar teeth she hides in a goddamn cookie jar! [*An appeal to some deity somewhere*] GODS!

FA: Listen to this. [*Reads*] "A definite westerly movement in its western motion has been definitely defined," a high-ranking government spokesman who declined to reveal his identity told reporters today. "Alas" the anonymous spokesman added.

GRANDFA: And I say poppycock.

FA: The man in government said alas.

GRANDFA: The man in government is a politician. I'm an old man.

FA: So it's headed west?

GRANDFA: [*Who often talks to himself*] He's also anonymous . . . no, that's something in common.

FA: Which way is west?

GRANDFA: We are.

FA: Are you sure?

GRANDFA: We are the west, much good that ever did us.

FA: [*Flat*] Oh. That's upsetting.

GRANDFA: It's disgusting.

FA: [*Turning to another part of the paper, with great complacency*] Well, here it's safe. No one's gonna die down here. Not in our sanctuary.

GRANDFA: You're damn right they're not. They're already dead.

FA: [*A weary rejoinder to GRANDFA's protests*] It's only a room, Grandfa.

GRANDFA: Basement! It's not a room, it's a basement.

FA: Yes, Grandfa.

GRANDFA: Upstairs, now those were rooms, real rooms. But this thing, what you've built down here . . .

FA: We're safe down here, Grandfa, and that's the most important thing these days . . . to be safe. Everyone's doing it.

GRANDFA: I suppose so. I suppose you are safe down here. But safe from what?

FA: It, Grandfa, it.

GRANDFA: It . . . IT!

FA: It.

GRANDFA: I hate this basement. I hate that fence up there. I hate the reason for them.

FA: You're malcontent.

GRANDFA: I'm old, damnit, there's a difference.

FA: [*Folding the newspaper*] You've done your best, Grandfa, and what else can a man do but his best?

GRANDFA: I don't know . . . I DON'T KNOW ANYMORE!

FA: [*Settling deep in his chair for a long, long sleep*] What time are they coming for you?

GRANDFA: Early. As soon as the streets are open. This infernal curfew . . . I could've gone tonight.

FA: [*Covering a huge yawn*] We'll miss you.

GRANDFA: I won't. Should've done this years ago. Only I thought you had to put me to pasture. Didn't know I could do it myself. [*Slight pause*] Well maybe you . . . a little bit . . . miss, I mean. Blood's blood. [*Looks up from his knitting*] . . . I don't suppose you want to kiss me. [*The first snore from FA*] SON!

FA: [*Immediately responding, but groggy*] I'm listening, Grandfa.

GRANDFA: I said . . . [*An old gentleman's embarrassment*] I said I didn't expect you wanted to kiss me.

FA: Now Grandfa!

GRANDFA: I didn't think so. [*Slight pause*] It's been done before, you know.

FA: [*Sleep overtaking him again*] Yes, Grandfa.

GRANDFA: It's a sign of affection . . . a kiss is.

FA: Yes, Grandfa.

GRANDFA: And stop calling me that! That's their name for me.

FA: [*Even sleepier*] We'll drive up every Sunday that it's nice.

GRANDFA: Well, don't!

FA: . . . every Sunday . . . just like Ruby said . . .

GRANDFA: You won't find me!

FA: . . . every Sunday that it's nice . . .

GRANDFA: I'll hide! I'll hide in a thicket!

FA: [*Going fast now*] . . . we'll find you . . .

GRANDFA: You think . . . you think!

FA: [*Lapsing into sleep*] . . . we'll find you . . . Grandfa . . . oh yes! . . . we'll . . . [*The snoring begins: an even, rhythmic drone. GRANDFA sits a moment. He is sad. Then he goes slowly over to FA and puts his hand on FA's shoulder. He looks at FA. He does not move. There is a stillness*]

GRANDFA: [*A gentle moan, a benediction, a forgiveness*] Oh. [*Now he moves away from FA.*

Maybe he clears his eyes with his fist . . . for perhaps there has been a tear or two. A pause. Now he is taking a writing book out of the tote bag. It is his Chronicle. He opens it, looks at his last entry, and then begins to write] "I am dying. It is acknowledged. I do not want to. It is not understood." [*Sigfrid is seen at the top of the stairs. He wears a heavy-knit, navy-blue sweater with a large white "Y" on the front. He carries a football. He pauses there briefly*] "Life is . . . it is not . . . easy. It is not that."

SIGFRID: [*Bounding down the stairs now, exuberant*] So they all went down to the seashore and . . .

GRANDFA: [*At once, moving away from him*] . . . and were drowned by their grandfather. Eavesdropper!

SIGFRID: No! They roasted wieners. They all went down to the seashore and had a wiener roast. Grandfa wouldn't drown his grandbabies.

GRANDFA: You don't know. You don't know what he wouldn't do!

SIGFRID: [*Playing with the football, assuming a center's position*] And you're wrong about life, too, Grandfa. It's just one big fat *snap!* [*He shoots the ball between his legs. It hits* GRANDFA *in the stomach with a thud.* SIGFRID *assumes an attitude of immense disappointment*] Aaaaw! We could've had 'em, Grandfa. Some school try that was. Where's your oomph? You all out of oomph? [GRANDFA *charges wildly at him with his chair*] Atta boy! That's the spirit.

GRANDFA: [*More sad than angry*] If I had a gun . . .

SIGFRID: . . . you'd shoot yourself! Now cheer up, Grandfa. It's your last night here.

GRANDFA: And I am jubilant!

SIGFRID: OK, I'm sorry. Peace?

GRANDFA: [*Gruff*] Peace. [*And then*] Just a few more hours . . . a few more hours in this room.

SIGFRID: Come on then, Grandfa, one last round of "Oh, what a rogue and peasant slave am I."

GRANDFA: Not on your life.

SIGFRID: For old time's sake?

GRANDFA: I was good, Sigfrid. I was damn good. Those plays had stature. The characters had stature. They were the measure of a man. But now—[*Cutting off abruptly, wheeling around in his wheelchair, looking in all directions*] All right, where is she?

SIGFRID: Who?

GRANDFA: That little troll child. Your sister.

SIGFRID: Lakme?

GRANDFA: Where is she? What direction is she going to come at me from this time?

SIGFRID: She'll be along. We got separated in the crowds. There's so many people out just before curfew, rushing back home.

GRANDFA: Any chance of her getting trampled to death?

SIGFRID: Not Lakme.

GRANDFA: Too bad. [*Then*] What was the strategy for today? Today's bait?

SIGFRID: A football, Grandfa.

GRANDFA: A football!

SIGFRID: Well, it worked. A football. A blue sweater. A little sister. And . . . [*Snaps his fingers*] we have a friend for tonight. His name is Clarence, Grandfa. And he sure has stature!

GRANDFA: Does it never stop down here with you people?

SIGFRID: Every night, Grandfa, someone every night.

GRANDFA: If you'd only—!

SIGFRID: [*Hard*] Don't start in on me. [*Then, gently*] Oh my Grandfa, my sweet and wondrous Grandfa, there are more things in heaven and earth than are dreamt of—

GRANDFA: In *your* philosophy, Sigfrid!

SIGFRID: You may not believe this, Grandfa . . . I daresay you will find it incredible . . . but the simple truth is that . . . [*Pantomimes very clearly the words "I love you"*] very, very much.

GRANDFA: [*Fiddling desperately with his hearing aid*] What's that? What's that you said? [*It is a moment before* GRANDFA *realizes what* SIGFRID *has done. They look at each other*]

SIGFRID: I do. [LAKME *is heard at the top of the stairs. Her entrance is announced by the sound of a small child bawling her head off. The moment between* SIGFRID *and* GRANDFA *is quickly broken*] Enter one crocodile: tearful. [*Lakme appears, her face a study in childish misery. She sobs, howls, and in general carries on like there is no tomorrow. It is almost convincing. Her dress is tom-boyish and appropriate for a thirteen-year-old. She might wear her hair in pigtails. She carries an array of photographic equipment: cameras, cases, etc. She is howling like a banshee, yet is perfectly capable of stopping should it be to her advantage.* SIGFRID *speaks with mock cheerfulness*] Hello there, little one! What seems to be the trouble? You pick another fight with that German shepherd down the road? [LAKME *increases her howling*] Poor little Lakme. All forsook and chewed on. Comfort her, Grandfa.

LAKME: [*In heaving breaths between sobs*] Gran —Grandfa! . . . Grandfa, Sigfrid tackled me! . . . hard!

SIGFRID: [*Mocking*] Not true, not true.

LAKME: He did! Look! [*She hunts for and finds a tiny cut on her knee*] See? . . . see? [GRANDFA *snaps his teeth at her: three times.* LAKME *changes to her normal voice, it is an ugly one*] Where did you find those? . . . hunh? Sigfrid, did you tell him where his teeth were?

SIGFRID: [*Absolving himself with a gesture and then pointing to her injured knee*] That was quite a recovery . . . even for you.

LAKME: [*Tough*] Oh yeah? [*She begins howling again—though not quite so effectively as before and limps her way over to* FA. *Again she speaks in the congested voice*] Fa! . . . Sigfrid tackled —Wake up! [*Furiously shaking him*] How are you going to have that heart attack if you sleep all the time? . . . Hunh? . . . LIAR! [SIGFRID *has been enjoying this enormously.* LAKME *turns on him now*] Well, it hurt!

SIGFRID: [*Explaining to* GRANDFA] It was nearly an hour ago. She said, "Ouch" . . . that's all. And not one whimper all the way home.

LAKME: [*The anger dissipated into a general sulkiness*] Well, you certainly don't expect me to waste my tears on you! A lot you care . . . stinky! [*Sits and examines the cut on her knee*]

SIGFRID: [*Coming back over to* LAKME] How now, scab?

LAKME: There will be one! And I have a dance recital coming up next week . . . two solos! It'll look terrible.

SIGFRID: Then you'd just better tippy-tap-toe your way into Ruby's bedroom and let her kiss it. That'll make it go away.

LAKME: [*Flaring*] I don't tap-dance! We do modern . . . acrobatic modern.

SIGFRID: All right, then acrobat-modern your way in there . . . slither.

LAKME: [*Rolling down her pants leg*] You're such a cheat, Sigfrid. You say we're going to play touch football and then as soon as I get the ball you change it to tackle.

SIGFRID: And what about that stiff-arm? You practically gouged my eye out.

LAKME: That was different. That was a tactic. [*The little lady bit now*] Besides, if I were a twenty-one-year-old . . . boy? Hah! . . .

SIGFRID: [*He means this*] Watch it, Baby Snooks!

LAKME: [*Continuing*] . . . I'd certainly be embarrassed to be seen playing football in a public park with a thirteen-year-old child.

SIGFRID: Oh, you would?

LAKME: Yes! And when the thirteen-year-old child just happens to be a thirteen-year-old girl . . . !

SIGFRID: A what . . . ?

LAKME: . . . his own little sister, in fact . . . well, that's just about the worst thing I ever heard

of. And then hurling her to the turf like that . . . a vicious tackle . . . !

SIGFRID: [*Suddenly on the defensive for the first time*] Now look, you little dwarf, you tripped. I didn't push you. You tripped.

LAKME: [*Amazed that he could have taken her seriously*] I know that, stupid. Of course I tripped. Honestly, Sigfrid, you can be so dense sometimes. You know what a little liar I am.

SIGFRID: There's some jokes I don't like.

LAKME: [*With great affection*] You're such a dope. [*Gets up to join him at the intercom and makes a final reference to her injured knee*] I don't mind helping you get the friend here so much . . . I mean I know the reason for it. It's just the ploys you use. Couldn't we try another way? Like croquet or something? This really hurts. [*Puts one arm affectionately around his waist*]

SIGFRID: [*Into the intercom*] Hey Ruby! . . . Wake-up time! [*Then to* LAKME] I can't help it. It's just my nature. I'm very . . .

LAKME: [*Anticipating him, so that they say the word together*] . . . ployful! [*They laugh and jostle each other like the very best of friends, which, of course, they very often are*]

RUBY'S VOICE: [*On the intercom, it is very small, very frightened*] Sigfrid? . . . is it you, Sigfrid?

SIGFRID: No, Karl Marx and Trotsky! Who do you think?

LAKME: Batman and Robin!

RUBY'S VOICE: [*With some relief*] Lakme!

SIGFRID: [*The little game over*] Come on, Ruby, hustle it.

LAKME: Wait'll you see him, Ruby! The friend.

RUBY'S VOICE: [*Hell hath no fury*] . . . you bastards! . . . you utter, utter bastards! . . . you think you're pretty funny, don't you? . . .

SIGFRID: Ruby!

RUBY'S VOICE: . . . had our little kicks for the evening . . . hunh? . . . we showed her what kind of games we can play . . . we had ourselves one big fat laugh! . . . HAH!

SIGFRID: Ruby, what—?

RUBY'S VOICE: [*An explosion*] HOW DARE YOU PRETEND YOU'RE NOT OUT THERE! HOW DARE YOU!

SIGFRID: [*Completely confused*] We didn't. I mean we weren't.

RUBY'S VOICE: Can you imagine what it's been like for me in here? Can you possibly conceive the terror of it? Of waking and thinking I was alone? Utterly, completely alone? And then hearing sounds . . . and no answer, no answer at all? Can your pea-sized little hearts even begin to understand what an experience like that does to a person?

LAKME: I bet it was Grandfa playing tricks on her again. Say something to her, Grandfa.

GRANDFA: [*Obligingly, loud and clear*] Harlot!

RUBY'S VOICE: I quivered . . . yes! . . . for fifteen minutes Ruby quivered!

LAKME: Can you picture it, Sigfrid? Ruby quivering?

RUBY'S VOICE: . . . not knowing who was out there . . . *what!* . . . It could have been anything!

LAKME: [*Acting it out*] The demon of death gulch! Aarg!

RUBY'S VOICE: That it was finally happening even! That it had come! Yes, I was that terrified!

SIGFRID: Ruby—!

RUBY'S VOICE: [*Huge*] I WAS SO ALONE!

SIGFRID: [*Cutting in, stern, to head off the outburst*] BUT YOU WEREN'T ALONE! [*A pause*] Ruby?

RUBY'S VOICE: [*A trifle disappointed*] I wasn't?

SIGFRID: You woke up early, that's all. No one had come down yet. Fa and Grandfa must have still been in the upstairs dining room.

LAKME: Sigfrid and I were back here in plenty of time for your wake-up. We all were.

SIGFRID: If you were upstairs . . . in one of the old bedrooms . . . maybe there'd be some reason.

LAKME: I'm only surprised you didn't turn the fence on already!

SIGFRID: Christ, Ruby, it's a good thirty minutes till curfew!

LAKME: Sigfrid and I were on the streets . . . we were outside . . . where it can happen . . . and we're not all gone to pieces. [*A pause*] Ruby?

SIGFRID: Hey, Ruby!

RUBY *has come into the room behind them. She watches them a moment as they hover solicitously over the intercom.*

RUBY: [*Flinging wide her arms and with purposeful, humorous exaggerations*] ECCO LA MAMA! [*Then, in a deeper voice*] If you ever do that again, I will take you upstairs and push you off the roof . . . the four of you! [*Advances a step and again flinging open her arms*] GUARDAMI! [*Another change of voice*] Such bastardy, such unspeakable bastardy! [*A final step forward*] ABBRACCIAMI! [*No one has moved toward her yet*] I said kiss me, damnit, and I meant kiss me! [*LAKME crosses and gives her a rather perfunctory kiss. SIGFRID stays where he is*] Scorpions! [*A word now about RUBY's appearance. It is a spectacular disappointment. Oh, the peignoir she wears is fancy enough and there are many rings on her fingers and expensive slippers on her feet. But RUBY herself will disappoint you.*

Her face is without makeup and seems almost anonymous. The intense lighting in the room, you see, washes the "character" out of her face so that it is impossible to tell very much about her except that she is no longer young. As for her hair, well, she might as well be bald, for she wears one of those wide elastic cloth bands women use to pull the hair back from their faces before applying makeup. The appearance of her entire face, in fact, is best suggested by this word "bald." Or "plucked clean." Or "erased." So this, for the time being, is RUBY]

SIGFRID: Now if you'll just calm down, Ruby, and let me explain— [RUBY *makes a sharp intake of breath*] Are you? Are you calm now?

RUBY: [*Great dignity*] Considerably. And don't patronize.

SIGFRID: All right, now tell me what happened. Was it one of your dreams again?

RUBY: [*A deliberate sulk*] No.

SIGFRID: You're sure? You're sure it wasn't one of your nightmares?

RUBY: Yes, I'm sure and the word's *cauchemar*.

SIGFRID: Then you must have—

RUBY: [*Imperial*] Say it!

SIGFRID: [*Anything to accommodate*] Cauchemar.

RUBY: [*Wincing*] *Mon dieu*, that accent!

LAKME: [*With great care and love for each syllable*] Cauchemar.

RUBY: *Bravo, bravo, arcibravo!*

LAKME: [*So in love with herself*] Cauchemar!

SIGFRID: Damnit, Ruby! If you're not interested in this—!

RUBY: I am extremely interested!

LAKME: [*Delirious*] Cauche—!

SIGFRID *slugs her.*

RUBY: What happened?

LAKME: [*Not in a whine*] Sigfrid hit me.

RUBY: [*Matter-of-fact*] Hit him back.

LAKME *does so.* SIGFRID *doesn't respond. They are used to this little ritual.*

LAKME: I did.

RUBY: [*Continuing where she left off now*] I am extremely interested, Sigfrid . . . I am extremely interested as to why . . . why with all the care, love, and protection I have lavished on you . . . why with all the lovely and nice things I have given you . . . your fabulous good looks, for example; courtesy of me, natch! . . . why with so much . . . with so many goodies in your little hopper . . . why . . . [*And with an abrupt change of voice*] you turned out to be such a miserable son of a bitch!

GRANDFA: [*To his private world at large*] I could answer that one! [*But he doesn't*]

SIGFRID: [*He's had it*] Christ!

LAKME: [*Virtue triumphant*] That puts your little light under a basket!

RUBY: [*Gently remonstrating*] Bushel, dear, bushel.

LAKME: [*Discovering a delightful new word*] Bushel-basket! [*Then, making it an expletive to hurl at* SIGFRID] Bushel-basket!

RUBY: [*Stopping* LAKME *cold*] And that goes for you, too! You're both sons of bitches. You're all four sons of bitches. The whole world's sons of bitches! Except me. I'm nice. I like me. [*Considers this a moment, then*] Sigfrid, look at you! . . . that outfit . . . is that what you wore? . . . You're outlandish in that sweater! [*Singing hilariously*] Boola, boola, boola, boola! Well, I hope it worked! You did find someone in that getup?

SIGFRID: [*Laughing, too, now*] Yes, monster mother. I found someone.

RUBY: Male or female? And do say male. It's been the little ladies, the little ladies nearly every night now.

SIGFRID: Well, Clarence is male, Ruby.

RUBY: Wonderful!

LAKME: [*Sibilating*] Oh yes! Very male. Very definitely male.

RUBY: [*Flat*] Oh. It's going to be one of—

SIGFRID: [*Before she can finish it*] That's right, wonder mother, one of those nights.

RUBY: I don't approve, of course . . . but *la vie n'est pas en rose.*

SIGFRID: You love it, you old bawd!

LAKME: We had a little trouble with him. He kept thinking better of it.

RUBY: [*Dead serious*] But he's coming, Sigfrid? You're sure of it?

SIGFRID: He'll be here.

LAKME: He'd better be! Can you imagine it alone down here? Just the four of us? Without the friend? Yikes! [*Gets up and wanders over to the tape recorder: in a moment she will have turned it on*]

RUBY: Oh it's going to be another lovely, lovely evening! I can feel it in my . . . what, Sigfrid?

SIGFRID: [*Playing along with her*] Fangs, Ruby, you can feel it in your fangs.

RUBY: Yes! Yes, I do!

RUBY'S RECORDED VOICE: [*On the tape recorder*] "The way we live. Message to the World Number 812."

LAKME: [*Paroxysms of joy*] You taped another Message! Sigfrid, another Message to the World!

SIGFRID: You're such a pope, Ruby! You and your encyclicals. What's this one called?

RUBY'S RECORDED VOICE: "Final message. The summation."

SIGFRID: [*Mimicking*] The summation.

RUBY: It's a closed book now as far as I'm concerned. See what you think.

RUBY'S RECORDED VOICE: [*A "quiet" voice, such as one uses when alone, yet with a full range of color and nuance, a sharp contrast with the often strident voice of the "live"* RUBY *we have been hearing*] "The way we live is compounded of love . . . love which neither nurtures the receiver nor lays fallow the sender but will suffice for each . . ."

LAKME: [*Terribly put out*] Is this Message gonna be about love, Ruby? Ugh.

RUBY'S RECORDED VOICE: . . . of hate . . . and more of it than we can often cope with . . . yes!"

LAKME: [*Brightening*] That sounds more like you!

RUBY'S RECORDED VOICE: ". . . and of a numbing, crushing indifference . . . an indifference which kills . . . slowly, finally, totally."

LAKME: Bang, bang! You're dead.

SIGFRID: Sshh!

RUBY'S RECORDED VOICE: "And for which our cruelty (and pain now is our only reminder that we yet live) . . . for which the cruelty we do unto each other is but a temporary antidote."

LAKME: Does that mean about the friend?

SIGFRID: [*Not really listening to her, affected by the Message, looking at* RUBY] Yes . . . no.

LAKME: Hunh?

RUBY'S RECORDED VOICE: "God . . . gods . . . some*one* . . . some*thing* . . . *whatever:* things done or not done and then called good or bad . . . these *things* men speak of, attain to, do battle for . . . the way we live does not involve us with them. They are the concerns . . . no, were! . . . were the concerns of peoples, nations . . . yea, individuals . . . who thought they were to prevail."

RUBY: [*A little strained, perhaps;* SIGFRID *doesn't take his eyes from her*] Quite Biblical, don't you think? That "yea, individuals."

RUBY'S RECORDED VOICE: "We shall *not* prevail . . . so be it. We shall *not* endure . . . but who was ever meant to? And we shall *not* inherit the earth . . . it has already disinherited *us.*"

A pause. RUBY *moves as if to turn off the recorder.* SIGFRID *stops her.*

SIGFRID: No.

RUBY'S RECORDED VOICE: *"C'est triste . . . N'est-ce pas?"*

SIGFRID: *C'est triste,* Ruby.

RUBY'S RECORDED VOICE: "If we are without faith, we find our way in the darkness . . . it is light enough. If we are without hope, we turn to our despair . . . it has its own consolations. And if we are without charity, we suckle the bitter root of its absence . . . wherefrom we shall draw the sustenance to destroy you."

SIGFRID: [*Deadly*] You really went to town this time.

RUBY: [*Faltering*] It was . . . I . . .

RUBY'S RECORDED VOICE: [*And this is the saddest part*] "Go . . . seek not to know us . . . to understand. The compassion of it will exhaust you and there is so little strength left us now . . . so little"

RUBY: So little, Sigfrid!

SIGFRID: [*Steel*] So little, Ruby.

RUBY'S RECORDED VOICE: [*Very quickly, in an everyday tone*] "Spoken by me this December morning. Unwitnessed, unheard, alone."

And now there is a good moment of silence. No one moves. The tape reels spin noiselessly.

FA: [*Waking momentarily*] Good-bye, Grandfa . . . Come and kiss me, Grandfa.

GRANDFA: [*FA's had his chance*] I'm knitting. Knitting and listening to this harridan spout balderdash. You never heard such—[*But FA is already asleep again*] Balderdash, Ruby! Pure tommyrot!

RUBY: [*Switching off the recorder, making something of a moment of it, anything to break the mood in the room now*] Ecco la testimonia d'una traviata . . . una testimonia nera!

LAKME: [*Quite overcome by it all*] Nero? You mean nerissimo! Wow!

GRANDFA: [*Grousing away in his corner*] Message to the World, she calls it. That's no message . . . it's garbage, that's what it is . . . pig food!

LAKME: [*Trying to reconstruct a certain phrase*] "And if we are without faith . . . we shall suckle? . . ." Is that right, Sigfrid . . . "suckle?"

GRANDFA: Yes, that's right. Suckle! Suckle your way like pigs!

LAKME: ". . . suckle our bitter root in the darkness?"

RUBY: [*Throwing it away*] It has its own absence.

LAKME: Absence?

RUBY: [*Trying to get it right for her now*] Consolations, then! It has its own consolations.

LAKME: Which has? Our bitter root or our darkness?

RUBY: [*Irritably*] Well, something like that!

SIGFRID: How should Ruby know?

LAKME: She said it!

RUBY: That was this morning . . . hours ago . . . [*Directly to* SIGFRID] centuries!

LAKME: [*Satisfied with this*] That part about destroying you. That's the part I liked best.

RUBY: You would. [*Passing near* SIGFRID] Boola boola. [*Sitting now*] I have such a headache.

LAKME: You mean vapors. Ruby's evening vapors.

GRANDFA: [*They all love these word games*] No, vipers. She means vipers. Evening vipers. The three of them.

RUBY: [*The game's over*] I mean vapors! [*With a wave of her arm*] Presto, cara, presto.

LAKME: Wait'll you see this fink we got coming over here tonight. The friend. One of those demonstrators.

SIGFRID: [*Low*] We shall not prevail.

RUBY: *Va! Fuggi!*

LAKME: [*Running on*] Finks! They're all finks. They're not going to change anything. Not with signs. Signs aren't going to make that thing out there go away.

SIGFRID: We shall not endure.

RUBY: *Fuggi*, damnit, *fuggi!*

LAKME: [*Stopped cold*] Fuggi?

SIGFRID: And we shall not inherit the earth.

RUBY: From *fuggire:* to make haste . . . to pick up our little feet and vanish . . . in other words, to scram!

LAKME: [*Still puzzling*] Fuggi—? [*She's got it*] Oh.

RUBY: Yeah, oh. *Piccola* nitwit.

LAKME: [*Nice and prissy*] I'm sorry, Ruby, but we can't all of us be such opera queens. I mean some of us are normal. Some of us speak English when we want something. Some of us—

RUBY: Will you get in there and get that coffee?

LAKME: [*Singing, anything to prolong her exit. Mimi's aria from* La Bohème] Mi chiamano Lakme, ma il perchè, non so.

RUBY: *Va!*

LAKME: [*In a charming little voice*] Vo. [*She fairly twinkles through the door, stage right, and is gone. Even with* GRANDFA *there, it is* SIGFRID *and* RUBY *alone now*]

RUBY: [*After thinking it over a moment*] I am not an opera queen. Sigfrid, you don't think I'm an opera queen, do you?

SIGFRID: God knows you're some sort of a queen, Ruby.

RUBY: [*Smiling, gritted teeth*] But not that.

SIGFRID: [*Likewise*] You're in rare form tonight.

RUBY: [*Hissing it, almost*] I'm just beginning! [*Then turning and "seeing"* GRANDFA] Grandfa! Sweetest old thing on two wheels! How old? Will you never tell us? Two hundred? . . . three hundred? . . . four?

GRANDFA: It's criminal how you abuse the gift of speech, woman!

RUBY: [*Effusive*] Each day could be . . . should be . . . your very last . . . but it never is. Keeping us in such suspense! Sly, sly, Grandfa.

GRANDFA: [*Determined to be heard*] CREATURES LIKE YOU SHOULD HAVE THEIR VERY TONGUES CUT OUT!

RUBY: [*Stopping her ears*] Grandfa! Don't shout at us like that. We're not the deaf ones; you are.

GRANDFA: Right out of your heads with a big rusty knife. [*Rumbling on*] Message to the World! I never heard such contamination.

RUBY: We can't all be your beloved Shakespeare, Grandfa.

GRANDFA: I'll say!

RUBY: [*A little less playful here*] I meant it when I said it.

GRANDFA: So did he!

RUBY: Forsooth!

GRANDFA: And it didn't come out garbage!

RUBY: How you prate, nuncle, how you will prate!

GRANDFA: It was poetry. It sang!

RUBY: With a hey-nonny-nonny and a ho!

GRANDFA: Shakespeare respected words! And you know why? Because Shakespeare respected people! . . . But you! . . . this family! . . .

RUBY: [*A little sorry she got into this*] You just put everything you're thinking about in that little book you're writing, Grandfa. Scribble it in your little novel!

GRANDFA: [*She has touched a sore point*] Chronicle! It's not a novel. It's a chronicle.

RUBY: Chronicles record the truth, Grandfa. Your book is full of lies. Therefore, your book is a novel.

GRANDFA: "Time Was: A Chronicle." A book of facts . . .

RUBY: Not facts, Grandfa. Lies! Un-historical non-facts! Nonsense!

GRANDFA: [*Never relinquishing the offensive*] Facts about you . . . this family . . . the truth!

RUBY: [*Her last defensive*] That's wonderful, Grandfa. You go right on deluding yourself. Don't waste a minute! There's so little time left!

GRANDFA: [*Not to be stopped*] I will! Old people remember, you know. They remember everything That's their function . . . to remember!

RUBY: [*Retreating now*] Lakme! . . . Where is that child?

GRANDFA: [*Pursuing*] Only younger people don't like that! . . . they don't like to remember . . . they're afraid! . . . facts frighten them . . .

memory frightens them . . . old people frighten them!! This book frightens them!

RUBY: [*Turning on him now*] Then won't you be happy to get away from us! Won't you be delirious up there on that little farm? All you old retired actors . . . all you old Shakespeareans . . . lolling around all day . . . in wheelchairs . . . being pushed! . . . Just lolling around and mewling sonnets at each other all day long? Mewling sonnets over social tea biscuits and a drop of sherry? Won't that be fun? And doing real live theatricals for the Sunday visitors? Grandfa as Lear! Grandfa as Macbeth! Grandfa as Lady Macbeth! Well, why not? They did it in his time. They did it in that poet's time. And won't that be fun! Grandfa in a skirt with candle . . . enters deranged . . . *uno sonnambulo!* . . . and tears the house down. Oh, you'll be very happy on that farm. I just know you will.

GRANDFA: [*A little sad now—his prospects are none too cheerful—but with simple dignity*] I have friends up there . . . some . . . old thespians like myself . . . there's a few of us still left . . . they say the food's not too bad . . . the care . . . I'll . . . manage.

A pause.

RUBY: [*With more than a little desperation*] Isn't it wonderful, Sigfrid? . . . at his age . . . so spry!

SIGFRID: [*With a violence that has been building in him ever since* RUBY'S *Message to the World*] LEAVE HIM ALONE, RUBY! JUST ONCE, LEAVE SOMEONE ALONE! [RUBY, *for the moment, is quite taken aback and absolutely speechless*] CHRIST, RUBY . . . CHRIST! [SIGFRID'S *explosion has produced a tense, angry silence.* GRANDFA *has withdrawn and gone back to his corner.* SIGFRID *has moved away from* RUBY *who stands watching him, her own anger mounting. A long pause*]

RUBY: [*With a repressed and terrible fury*] That wasn't called for, Sigfrid. That wasn't called for at all. [SIGFRID *is silent*] And take off that ridiculous sweater. You're home now. The camouflage is no longer necessary!

LAKME'S VOICE: [*A sudden intrusion on the intercom*] Hey, opera queen! Black?

RUBY: What?

LAKME'S VOICE: Your coffee. How do you want it? Black?

RUBY: No, blue!

LAKME'S VOICE: Well, sometimes you take a little brandy in it.

RUBY: [*Always glowering at* SIGFRID, *never taking her eyes from him*] Brandy never changed the color of anything . . . except maybe my teeth.

[*Then, directly to him*] Some people we don't humiliate each other in front of.

LAKME'S VOICE: So that's how you want it?

RUBY: Yes, that's how I want it! [*Then again to* SIGFRID] We save that sort of thing for the friend.

LAKME'S VOICE: [*More confused than ever now*] With brandy? You want it with brandy?

RUBY: YES, I WANT IT WITH BRANDY! [*Snaps off the intercom*] Those are the rules, buster . . . the way things are done . . . and I think you'd just better stick to them. [RUBY, *restless as ever, moves away to* C. *Brooding. Silence*]

FA: [*A terrified nightmare*] WEST, IT'S MOVING WEST! RUN, RUN FOR YOUR LIVES!

RUBY: [*With a somewhat forced gaiety*] What is? What's moving west? What is Fa mumbling about? [*No one answers. Long silence. A tension is building*] It can get so silent down here . . . so dead! I ask you: are we the only people in the world or are we not? Hmmm? Sometimes I think we are. I really do. [*Another pause. More silence. More tension. Then, going to* SIGFRID *and taking his lowered face in her hands, utterly without guile or a trace of anger*] Hey, I love you, prince. [*Kisses him on the forehead*] No matter what I say . . . although I meant it . . . I do love you.

SIGFRID: [*Quietly*] You should have seen the city today, Ruby. There were so many people . . . stumbling, wandering, milling . . . masses of people. Outside movie theatres . . . churches . . . in the parks. Young men in tight pants . . . old men in tight pants. I saw a young girl nursing her baby. She had a growth on her neck. It was big. Like a grapefruit. It swayed when she walked. Tok-tok, tok-tok, tok. Butterflies . . . pale yellow butterflies . . . were hovering around them. Encircling them almost. One settled . . . only for an instant . . . near them, on them. The baby, startled, laughed then. Laughter. Tok. Then I saw a crowd of people. They had an old man down behind a clump of bushes. They were kicking that old man. Some had knives. I'm sure they killed him. And then, coming back here, just a little while ago . . . there was a girl standing crushed against me. We were facing . . . there was no place else to look but at her . . . we were so pressed, so close. She was ugly. She hadn't found someone. And she was crushing into me. "Take me with you. Let me be your friend tonight. Take me with you. Let me be your friend." That's all she said. She wasn't even crying. No one wanted her. She tried to follow me. Someone pushed her. On the stairs. She fell. Others fell on her. Stairs can be very crowded just before curfew. People can be

trampled. [*Short pause*] And everywhere there were people marching, demonstrating, protesting. People saying, "No, No, No!" And then I saw Clarence. [*Another short pause*] That's what you would have seen in the city today, Ruby. All that. Outside in sunlight. Out looking with Lakme.

RUBY: [*A murmur*] How beautiful he is! . . .

SIGFRID: [*Looking directly at her now*] And then night after night down here in this basement . . . this stinking hole in the ground . . . waiting for it to happen. Waiting for something to happen.

RUBY: . . . how very beautiful!

SIGFRID: The way we live . . . and Ruby acknowledges it. Ruby makes a Message.

RUBY: A prince, my son is a prince!

SIGFRID: [*Wearily, he has tried to reach her*] Don't you understand, Ruby, don't you understand anything? You went over the line with your goddamn Message. [*He has gotten up and begun to move slowly out of the room*]

RUBY: [*To make him stay*] I was alone, Sigfrid! It was the strain—! [*She breaks off as* LAKME *enters with the coffee. But* SIGFRID *has gone*]

LAKME: [*Brightly*] Ecco la Lakme! [*Taking a look over* GRANDFA'S *shoulder as she passes him*] Message to the World? Hey, now Grandfa's started one! That ought to be something. [*Giving the coffee to* RUBY] Here, slurp. [*Then, throwing her arms around* RUBY'S *neck*] Oh how much I love my Ruby! Nobody loves their Ruby as much as I love mine.

RUBY: And my Lakme! How I love my little Lakme! [*Then, hugging* LAKME *close to her but her eyes looking to where* SIGFRID *left, as if she were trying to reach him*] Both my children . . . such beautiful children . . . so strong . . . so . . . *right.*

LAKME: [*Seeking and finding a little girl's comfort in* RUBY'S *arms*] That was a sad Message to the World, wasn't it? The saddest one you ever made. They're not usually so . . . sad.

RUBY: [*Holding* LAKME *close, but really an appeal to* SIGFRID] But not to frighten you . . . no! never that.

LAKME: But I do get frightened sometimes, Ruby . . .

RUBY: [*In a soft voice, almost to herself*] We all do, Lakme. We all do. [*The red light on the intercom has come on.* SIGFRID *is listening*]

LAKME: Is that why, Ruby, you made the Message?

RUBY: [*Her attention fixed on the intercom and* SIGFRID] In the morning . . . early . . . when you're sleeping . . . the four of you . . . and I'm alone . . . sitting here . . . thinking . . . waiting for it to end, the night . . . another night and it has not yet happened . . . then . . . when it's quiet . . . no sounds . . . no sounds at all . . . I try to . . . understand . . . understand what has happened to us . . . why . . . and sometimes I have premonitions . . . tremors . . . not heart tremors . . . nothing like that . . . but soul tremors . . . tremors of the soul . . . when the very earth seems to rise up . . . hover a moment, suspended . . . somehow suspended . . . and then fall back. [*Short pause*] Sigfrid knows these moments, too.

LAKME: When we were little, you mean, Ruby?

RUBY: [*With a soft smile*] Yes, Lakme, when you were little and the wind blew and there was thunder. How Sigfrid howled when the shutters banged and the thunder clapped!

LAKME: But it's not that way now. Not when we're together.

RUBY: Remember, Sigfrid? Those nights? The howling, the hiding under the bed, the—[*The red light on the intercom has gone off*] It was the strain, Sigfrid! [RUBY *has gotten to her feet and taken a step toward the intercom, a movement which has dismissed* LAKME *rather abruptly from her place in* RUBY'S *lap*]

LAKME: [*Stung*] What's the matter now? Everybody's so moody in this family.

RUBY: [*Pacing, a note of irritation in her voice*] Where's that draft coming from? Did someone leave a—? [*Sees that the door at the top of the stairs is ever so slightly ajar*] Lakme, close the door!

LAKME: [*Still sulking*] It's not time yet. Wait till curfew.

RUBY: I don't care what time it is. I don't want that door left open. Anytime!

LAKME: Well, it is. It's open lots. We just don't tell you.

RUBY: Thank you. I hadn't known that. I'll see to it myself after this.

LAKME: That'll be the day!

RUBY: [*A quarrel is building*] I asked you to go up there and close it.

LAKME: How are we ever going to get any fresh air down here if we keep that door closed all the time? We'd all suffocate if we left it up to you.

RUBY: [*As her desire becomes more insistent, her tone of voice becomes more desperate*] I don't want that door left open.

LAKME: [*The voice getting meaner, victory is sweet*] People need air, Ruby. They have to breathe. Some people, that is. Normal people. I don't know about opera queens. I don't know what they use for oxygen. Arias, probably. Love duets!

RUBY: Please!

LAKME: [*Giving no respite*] Of course we could all cut little gills in our necks and then flood this place and live like fish. I suppose then you'd be happy. All of us turned into a bunch of fishes!

RUBY: [*Evenly*] It's simply that I feel safer when that door is closed . . . that's all I meant . . . that I would feel safer.

LAKME: But it can't happen until after curfew!

RUBY: They think.

LAKME: Well, it can't.

RUBY: They only think!

LAKME: [*Stubborn, but on less firm ground*] They're almost certain. It's never happened yet before. Besides, even when it does happ—. . . I mean, if it ever happens . . . how do we know it won't come right through that door and down those stairs? Right through! How do we know?

RUBY: Because the government—

LAKME: [*Furious at herself, the situation, and the tears welling up within her*] The government! What do they know? What does anyone know? [*Then, in a sudden outburst of rage*] What about last week, Ruby? Remember that little incident? You turned the electric fence on at noon! At noon! If that dog hadn't put his leg up against it to pee, Sigfrid and I would've both gotten it! You were afraid, so you turned the fence on at noon and nearly killed us! You've gotten so afraid, Ruby, you'll make it happen! You'll kill us you're so frightened!

RUBY: [*Who has regained her composure, but with some effort*] Are you going to go upstairs and close that door or not?

LAKME: [*Wild defiance*] NO!

RUBY: I see. I think you're going to regret this little interview.

LAKME: Oh, am I now?

RUBY: Yes, are you now!

LAKME: Do tell! Do tell!

RUBY: I tell! I tell!

LAKME: You don't say!

RUBY: I say! I say all right!

LAKME: [*At once, determined to pursue the argument to the finish*] How? How am I going to regret it? You going to have Fa spank me? Then first you'll have to wake him and I doubt even you could wake Fa up.

RUBY: [*Flaring briefly*] I don't want to!

LAKME: [*Like machine-gun fire*] How else? How else am I going to regret it? Go ahead. Tell me. Because I don't think I'm going to regret it at all.

RUBY: That will do, Lakme.

LAKME: [*Still not satisfied with the blood she has drawn*] You never do anything, you never go anywhere, you haven't been out of this house in . . . years, practically! All you do anymore is sleep in there in the daytime and then come out here and sit up all night.

RUBY: I SAID THAT WILL DO!

LAKME: And look at yourself! Have you done that lately . . . looked at yourself? You used to be beautiful. You were a queen . . . a real queen. But now! [*Quite matter-of-factly*] You've gone to pot, mother. That's what— [*A buzzer sounds, loud, drowning* LAKME *out. It is a harsh, ugly, rasping noise.* RUBY *chokes back a scream. Her knuckles whiten, she is holding the arms of her chair so tightly.* LAKME *only marks time, ready to resume speaking the moment the buzzer is silent. Five seconds of this terrible sound. And then utter stillness.* LAKME *speaks at once*] That's what I think. You've gone to pot. [*Then, getting up*] Come on. Fifteen minutes. He'll be here. [RUBY *sits trembling, whimpering almost*] That was just the warning buzzer, Ruby! It's fifteen minutes till curfew! That's exactly what I was talking about! [*She goes to* RUBY, *embraces her, and continues with enormous tenderness*] Look Ruby, I'll close the door. I'll turn the fence on at curfew time. We'll be all safe and sound again. Even Grandfa wants the door closed then and he's so old he might as well be . . . dead! But he still wants that door closed. Don't you, Grandfa? [GRANDFA *looks up from his journal, growls at her, and then resumes writing*] You just can't be nice to that man. [*Then, to* RUBY, *with a little laugh*] Besides, goose, if we closed that door now our little friend might not think we were down here and trot right back where he came from. Or what if he ran into the fence while it was on? He'd end up like that dog . . . sizzled! That would be great . . . just great! An evening without someone! You know what happened the last time we tried that.

RUBY: [*Very low, toneless, a private memory*] We nearly killed each other.

LAKME: You're telling me! And we certainly don't want that to happen again. Now, kiss-and-make-up, Ruby.

RUBY: [*The same*] Sigfrid actually had his hands around your throat. I almost let him.

LAKME: [*Demanding*] Ruby! Kiss-and-make-up! Kiss-and-make—!

RUBY *slaps her sharply across the cheek.*

RUBY: Kiss-and-make-up, Lakme. Kiss-and-make-up.

Long pause. No one moves. Then, breaking the silence, SIGFRID'S *voice on the intercom.*

SIGFRID'S VOICE: Ruby? . . . Ruby?

RUBY: [*In a strange, almost monotone, voice which will seem all the more sinister because of its deadly calm, and all the while she talks to* SIGFRID, *she never once takes her eyes from* LAKME] Yes, Sigfrid, Ruby's here.

SIGFRID'S VOICE: I'm all right now, Ruby.

RUBY: Yes, *caro*, yes.

LAKME: [*Low, her eyes locked with* RUBY'S] I knew you'd do that.

SIGFRID'S VOICE: Are you, Ruby? All right?

RUBY: Oh yes . . . yes. [*And with slow, deliberate movements—almost like a priest performing some sacred rite—she loosens the hairband. Masses of hair tumble to her shoulders. This is the beginning of* RUBY'S *Transformation*]

LAKME: [*Low again*] Sooner or later . . . I knew you would.

SIGFRID'S VOICE: What you said . . . about the strain . . .

LAKME *is moving slowly up the stairs. When she gets there she will very quietly close the door.*

RUBY: [*Combing her hair out with long, slow strokes*] There is no strain . . . not now . . . in fifteen minutes there will be no strain.

SIGFRID'S VOICE: His name is Clarence.

RUBY: Clarence.

LAKME: Clarence. [*A pause.* LAKME *has closed the door*]

RUBY: We are strong, children. In some ways we are strong.

SIGFRID'S VOICE: Clarence.

LAKME: The friend.

RUBY: It's only before that we are not so strong.

LAKME: Clarence.

SIGFRID'S VOICE: The friend.

RUBY: But soon . . . in fifteen minutes . . . then . . . then we are strong. Fifteen minutes and we will be strong again. [*A pause*] There's only one trouble, Sigfrid . . . just one. They always stay the night. They never leave. They always stay.

SIGFRID'S VOICE: I know.

RUBY: They never . . . go out there.

LAKME: [*Coming back down the stairs*] I think I know what you're talking about.

RUBY: Why, Sigfrid, why do you let them stay the night?

SIGFRID'S VOICE: You always said . . .

LAKME: [*At the door*] I think I do. [*She is gone*]

SIGFRID'S VOICE: . . . not to go too far.

RUBY: I did?

SIGFRID'S VOICE: We agreed on it. The three of us.

RUBY: I see.

A pause.

SIGFRID'S VOICE: Ruby?

RUBY: Yes.

SIGFRID'S VOICE: What are you thinking?

RUBY: That we might.

SIGFRID'S VOICE: Make him go out there?

RUBY: Yes.

SIGFRID'S VOICE: I don't know.

RUBY: It's a possibility.

SIGFRID'S VOICE: Yes.

RUBY: That way we would know . . . for once and for all we would know what is out there.

SIGFRID'S VOICE: Yes.

RUBY: It would serve some . . . purpose. The friend.

SIGFRID'S VOICE: Yes.

RUBY: Clarence.

A pause.

SIGFRID'S VOICE: We'll see, Ruby. All right? We'll see.

The intercom snaps off. RUBY *sits combing out her hair. A moment of silence. Then* GRANDFA *begins to move in on her, slowly at first but then picking up speed.*

GRANDFA: [*Circling her chair, needling like a mosquito*] Who's it going to be, Ruby? Who's the victim for tonight? I know what goes on in here after I go to bed. I know. Thank God I never had to watch. Thank God for that. I thought I'd seen plenty in my time, but this . . . what you people do.

RUBY: [*Lipsticking her mouth a brilliant red*] There are things, Grandfa, things which you do not understand.

GRANDFA: I understand corruption . . . decay! I understand that!

RUBY: [*With studied disinterest as she continues making up*] Do you?

GRANDFA: I can smell it, woman! Smell it! There's a stench in this house. A stench of putrefying rot. Human rot! . . .

RUBY: Things which you do not understand.

GRANDFA: [*Not pausing*] And it's all here! Written down! The truth! Everything!

RUBY: We don't know those people. They're fictitious . . . fabrications. They never existed.

GRANDFA: [*Finding himself on the defensive*] You've made it that way. There was a time—

RUBY: [*With great force, she has no intention of continuing this conversation*] WAS! [*Short pause*] There was a time, Grandfa . . . was. [*Another pause,* RUBY *puts the final touches to her makeup. The Transformation is nearly complete*]

GRANDFA: [*After a while, very sadly*] It wasn't meant to be this way.

RUBY: [*Rather distantly*] Perhaps Grandfa . . . just perhaps.

GRANDFA: [*His voice growing fainter*] Things weren't meant to be this way.

RUBY: But they are, *caro* . . . they are.

GRANDFA: [*Fainter still*] People weren't meant to be this way.

RUBY: [*With a sad mockery in her voice*] How, Grandfa, how were people meant to be? [GRANDFA *scarcely tries to answer her question. She takes out a large and fantastic wig and, settling it on her head, she faces* GRANDFA *fully and repeats her question with a bitterness turned more against herself than him*] Tell us, Grandfa. Tell us how people were meant to be. For we should dearly like to know. [*The wig is in place. The Transformation is complete now. The* RUBY *before us is utterly different from that "anonymous" woman of her entrance. What we see now is garish, hard, almost obscene. There is a pause*]

FA: [*Breaking the silence, in great terror, he is having a nightmare*] WEST! . . . IT'S MOVING WEST!

GRANDFA: [*Trying to answer* RUBY *now*] Not like . . . not like you.

FA: RUN! . . . RUN FOR YOUR LIVES!

GRANDFA: Like . . . like here . . . [*Holds up his Chronicle*] as you were . . .

RUBY: [*With the same sad mockery*] Imperfect? . . . weak? . . . afraid?

GRANDFA: [*Low, but spitting it out*] Human, woman . . . human!

POW! A rubber-tipped toy dart has been fired through the right door hitting GRANDFA *squarely in the back of the head. The Chronicle falls from his hand. He does not turn to see who fired the dart. He knows.* LAKME *bursts into the room. She is in the highest spirits, dressed in her Green Hornet costume and ready for* CLARENCE.

LAKME: *Sic semper tyrannis!* [*Then, rushing toward* GRANDFA, *doing a little dance around him*] The Green Hornet! Bzzzzzz! Bzzzzzz!

GRANDFA *turns away from her and moves slowly toward the right door.*

RUBY: [*Calling after him*] Why is it, Grandfa, why is it that you can be so quiet at times . . . like a mouse . . . a knitting mouse . . . and at other times so noisy? Why is that?

LAKME: Hey, Grandfa! Aren't you going to chase me? Come on, try to run me down! [GRANDFA *is gone*] What's the matter with him?

RUBY: Your Grandfa is suffering from an acute attack of how-it-was.

LAKME: Oh, he's off on that tack again! [*Then, stopping to retrieve the Chronicle*] Hey, Bede!

You dropped your Chronicle, Bede! [*Then, again to* RUBY] The Venerable Bede. I know about him from school. He wrote chronicles, too.

RUBY: But your Grandfa is a novelist. The oldest first novelist in captivity.

It might be remembered at this point that everyone, including SIGFRID, *who has just entered through the stage right door, is in the sunniest of dispositions. Joy, for the moment, is abounding.*

SIGFRID: [*Dressed entirely in black now*] Guess what I spied? A tear on Grandfa's cheeklet.

RUBY: No!

SIGFRID: One large, goopy tear. Right here.

RUBY: Why, who would've thought the old man to have so much salt in him?

SIGFRID *has joined* RUBY *while* LAKME, *to one side, begins to thumb through* GRANDFA'S *Chronicle.*

LAKME: [*Reading from the Chronicle*] "Message to the World." That's all he wrote: "Message to the World." And then it's blank.

SIGFRID: How do I look?

RUBY: Plumpish. Look how you stick out there. You used to have such a firm stomach, Sigfrid. I'd never seen such firmness. Whatever happened to it? You're all soft around there now.

SIGFRID: [*Glumly regarding his waistline, maybe there is a hint, just a hint, of flabbiness*] Well . . . your bazooms have dropped.

RUBY: Well, of course they have! There's no one I especially want to keep them up for.

SIGFRID, *still concerned with the real or imaginary bulk at his waistline, has begun a set of strenuous sit-ups.* LAKME *continues with the Chronicle.*

LAKME: [*It doesn't make any sense to* her] "Take me with you. Let me be your friend tonight." What is this stuff? [*Turns to another place in the Chronicle*]

RUBY: What about me? How do I look? Apart from my fallen grapes, that is.

SIGFRID: [*Always exercising*] You look . . .

RUBY: *Attention!*

SIGFRID: . . . Rubyesque.

LAKME: "Butterflies . . . pale yellow butterflies!" Did you see this thing he's writing?

SIGFRID: Why don't you go put your costume on?

RUBY: I thought you told me it was going to be one of those nights?

SIGFRID: It is.

RUBY: Considering how long it's going to be before you need me . . . considering the hour

wait while you two play boy scouts . . . I don't see what all the rush is.

SIGFRID: Well, while you're waiting, sweetheart—

RUBY: [*Perfectly aware she is interrupting*] Sigfrid, it just occurred to me! Whenever it's a girl, you introduce her to me before you go in there and when it's a boy, you don't want him to meet me until after. Why is that?

SIGFRID: It's the way things are done, Ruby.

RUBY: Oh?

SIGFRID: It's a heterosexual society we live in.

RUBY: Preposterous!

LAKME: Hey, Sigfrid! This part's about you. He wrote down all about you when you were little.

SIGFRID: As I was saying, *madre* . . . while you're in your little boudoir getting up . . . why don't you consider slipping into that *Walküre* outfit. You know, the one with the cast-iron boobies and the winged helmet.

RUBY: [*Correcting*] Wingèd. And thank you all the same.

SIGFRID: Ruby! You look so feminine in steel.

RUBY: No! It chafes.

SIGFRID: [*The last sit-up*] Suit yourself.

RUBY: Oh, I will! I always do.

SIGFRID *gets up, paces a moment.*

LAKME: [*Reading from the Chronicle*] "Sigfrid is a sickly child, prone to respiratory ailments. Sometimes his face and little hands turn an alarming blue. Ruby is heartsick." [*Delves into the Chronicle again with renewed interest*] Did you used to be blue, Sigfrid? I didn't know that.

RUBY: Who is this friend, Sigfrid?

SIGFRID: His name is Clarence.

RUBY: I know what his name is. What I'm asking you is something about him.

SIGFRID: He says we went to school together. Up to the sixth grade. He insists we're old friends. Friend friends.

RUBY: I hope you told him.

SIGFRID: Well, of course I did. Vicious gossip like that. I said, "Sigy-poo no have friends, Clarence. He have victims . . . mice. But he no have friends. Especially since the sixth grade. Now we have mice."

LAKME: "We read Shakespeare together in the late afternoon. Sigfrid's enthusiasm is boundless. He has the makings of a poet. A poet's soul." You, Sigfrid, a soul? Hah!

RUBY: [*Pacing, waiting*] Is he a clean person? This Clarence?

SIGFRID: Ruby!

RUBY: Well some of the people you've found lately are so . . . well, there's something so grayish about them.

SIGFRID: Clarence isn't gray, Ruby. He's white. Lily, snow, virgin white. Clarence will come unto us . . . in his whiteness . . . and we shall be saved.

RUBY: Sigfrid, he's not a cleric! Some unfrocked something or other?

SIGFRID: He's one of the committed ones. Clarence believes in making this a better world. Clarence is deeply involved with that thing out there. Well, he was.

RUBY: Clarence is committed, therefore Clarence is clean?

SIGFRID: [*Good-natured checking his watch*] *Merde, mamacita, merde.* [SIGFRID *freezes*]

RUBY: [*At once, checking her watch*] Sigfrid!

SIGFRID: [*Taut*] He'll be here.

RUBY: [*The same*] Two minutes, Sigfrid, two minutes till curfew.

SIGFRID: I said he'll be here, Ruby, and he will.

RUBY: [*Almost a challenge*] An evening without someone, Sigfrid?

Tense, awful pause. No one moves.

LAKME: Hey, Sigfrid. You used to write poetry! He wrote down a poem here. A poem you wrote.

RUBY: [*The threat is genuine*] Murder, Sigfrid . . . an evening without someone? . . . would it be murder?

SIGFRID: If . . .

RUBY: Yes, Sigfrid?

SIGFRID: He'll be here. [*They are still frozen*]

LAKME: [*Mostly to herself*] Did you really write this, Sigfrid? Did you used to write poems? Ugh!

SIGFRID: Shut up, Lakme!

LAKME: [*Mean*] What did I do? [*She'll have her revenge*]

RUBY: [*With a resignation calculated to annoy* SIGFRID] Well, I think you'd better run upstairs and lock up for the night. Turn the fence on. It's obvious he's not coming.

SIGFRID: I said he'll be here and he will.

LAKME: [*Starting to needle now*] You want to hear some poetry, Ruby? You want to hear one of Sigfrid's finky poems?

SIGFRID: I said shut up.

RUBY: What we said, Sigfrid . . . what we said about making him go out there . . .

SIGFRID: [*Curt*] No.

RUBY: . . . assuming he ever comes . . .

SIGFRID: No, I said.

RUBY: . . . we'd know then . . . what is out there . . . it would end this . . . wondering.

SIGFRID: I SAID NO!

LAKME: Nobody ever told us, Shakespeare, what a poetic genius you were!

SIGFRID: [*Literally counting the seconds till curfew*] Come on, Clarence, come on!

RUBY: [*With a strange smile, which becomes a laugh*] Why, Sigfrid? Why not make him go out there? . . . Murder? . . . would that be murder, too? . . .

SIGFRID: Jesus, Clarence, Jesus!

LAKME: [*Determined to get his attention*] Poem by Sigfrid!

Sky, a blue sky, the eagle soars.
High soars, high soars the eagle.

SIGFRID: [*Turning to her, but not moving*] Give that to me.

LAKME: [*Brazen, loving it*] What kind of sores, Shakespeare? Big pusy ones?

SIGFRID: GIVE ME THAT BOOK!

LAKME: "Can I soar? Can I soar, too?" Suits us, Shelley. Take a big flying leap right off the roof!

SIGFRID: [*Going after her*] You goddamn little bitch.

LAKME: [*Dodging him*] You were some poet, Sigfrid. Some poet. You were a real Shelley. You are a Shelley!

SIGFRID *is strangling her. A sharp silence.*

RUBY: [*Watching them, the cruel smile on her lips*] Murder, Sigfrid? Would it be . . . ? [SIGFRID *has gone far enough*] Sigfrid! [*A silence, then three long, heavy, metallic knocks from outside*] Allons, mes enfants, il faut commencer! [*Short silence, again no one moves, again the three knocks*] IL FAUT COMMENCER! [SIGFRID *slowly takes his hands from* LAKME'S *throat. An ugly moment of silence between them*]

SIGFRID: [*Terrifying*] Don't you ever . . . ever! . . . EVER! do that again.

LAKME: [*A threat*] That hurt, Sigfrid, that really hurt.

The knocks again, more insistent this time.

RUBY: [*Cutting them apart with her voice*] The friend, Sigfrid! The friend is at the gate!

SIGFRID: Get the camera ready.

LAKME: I'll kill him!

SIGFRID: [*About to go upstairs*] And Ruby, do it right this time!

RUBY: [*Again with the same strange, cruel mockery*] Murder, Sigfrid? Would it be murder?

SIGFRID *has disappeared up the stairs and out the door.* LAKME, *hard on his heels, stops at the open door, takes a picture with her camera and then runs back down into the room. The curfew buzzer sounds again, this time louder than before.* RUBY *and* LAKME *freeze.* RUBY *covers her ears with her hands. Five seconds of this terrible noise. Then silence.* RUBY *moves quickly toward the right door.*

LAKME: [*Following*] I'll kill him! [*Ruby is out*] Ruby? What's the matter, Ruby?

Now LAKME *is gone, too. The stage is empty. No sounds, nothing moves. Then, from outside, the sound of an enormous iron gate slamming shut. Reverberations. Then silence again. Footsteps are heard and a moment later* SIGFRID *is seen at the top of the stairs. He beckons with his arm for someone to follow him, then comes quickly down the stairs. He pauses a moment to pull down a lever on an electrical unit box. The lights dim ever so slightly and we hear a faint hum. And now* SIGFRID *has moved swiftly out of the room. Another brief moment of empty stage.* CLARENCE, *breathless and flushed, has appeared at the top of the stairs. He comes quickly into the room, closing the heavy iron door behind him.*

CLARENCE:[*With a nervous laugh*] Whew! That was close. My bus . . . I nearly missed it . . . [*His voice trails off as he realizes he is alone in the room. We see now that he is carrying a large placard, the type that pickets carry, which reads: "There Is Something Out There"*] Sigfrid . . . ? [*As he turns, we can read the other side of his placard: "We Shall Prevail." The curtain is beginning to fall*] Gee, it's nice down here . . . very nice. [CLARENCE *is coming down the stairs. Silence in the room. And now the curtain is down*]

ACT II

At rise, the room is the same. As before, the lighting is white and brilliant. CLARENCE'S *placard, the "There Is Something Out There" side facing us, rests against the wall near the left door.* CLARENCE *is alone in the room. He wears a woman's dress, but there is no mistaking him. We are perfectly aware it is a male in the wrong attire. We only wonder how he got there. His uneasiness in this strange and empty room is immediately apparent. His movements are tense and fidgety. He wanders. A long silence. And then a loud snortle from* FA *in his chair.* CLARENCE *stiffens, retreats a little, pauses. Another snortle.* CLARENCE *is edging toward the chair. He is there. He looks down at* FA, *hesitates, bites his lip, and then throws caution to the winds.*

CLARENCE: I'm Clarence. [*No response*] My name is Clarence.

FA: [*Giggling foolishly*] Hello, Grandfa . . . hello there!

CLARENCE: No, Clarence.

FA: Bye-bye, Grandfa! . . . come and kiss me, Grandfa!

CLARENCE: Sir?

FA: [*Almost a mumble*] West . . . moving west . . . unh . . . [*Lapses into a deep sleep—snoring sounds*]

CLARENCE: [*After a while, thoroughly miserable*] Oh, this is *dreadful* . . . Sigfrid!

And at once GRANDFA *comes through the door, he has a suitcase.*

GRANDFA: [*A parody of senility*] Well well well. Looky here.

CLARENCE: Good evening.

GRANDFA: Fa! Wake up! Fa! We got company. Something of Sigfrid's. Something Sigfrid dragged home.

CLARENCE: I'm Clarence. My name is Clarence.

GRANDFA: Who ?

CLARENCE: Clarence.

GRANDFA: You sure?

CLARENCE: Sir?

GRANDFA: Nice name.

CLARENCE: Thank you. [*Pause*] It's English.

GRANDFA: What's that? You're English.

CLARENCE: No, my name. Clarence is English.

GRANDFA: And you? What are you? Or shouldn't I ask that question? [*Laughs wildly,* CLARENCE *manages a weak smile*] You're the friend.

CLARENCE: Sir?

GRANDFA: The friend. You.

CLARENCE: Well, I'm *a* friend. I don't know if I'm *the* friend.

GRANDFA: You are.

CLARENCE: A friend of Sigfrid's.

GRANDFA: Ah yes, Sigfrid. Fine lad, fine lad.

CLARENCE: Yes, isn't he?

GRANDFA: Lakme, too.

CLARENCE: Lakme?

GRANDFA: His sister. Fine lad, fine lad.

CLARENCE: Fine *lad?*

GRANDFA: And let's not forget Ruby. Fine lads, all of 'em. You, too. Fine, fine lads and laddies.

CLARENCE: [*Taking the suitcase and setting it down*] Here, let me take that for you.

GRANDFA: Thank you, thank you kindly.

CLARENCE: You're taking a trip?

GRANDFA: Off to the looney-bin, first thing in the morning.

CLARENCE: The where?

GRANDFA: The looney-bin. Bin for loons. I'm a loon.

CLARENCE: You're joking, of course.

GRANDFA: I don't know. I suppose that's why I'm a loon. [*Laughs his wild laugh again;* CLARENCE *moves away from him, ever so slightly*]

CLARENCE: Gee, it's nice down here.

GRANDFA: We like it. It's nice and homey.

CLARENCE: That's what's so wonderful about it. It doesn't look at all like a basement. It's so . . . so cheerful.

GRANDFA: Well, we've tried to brighten it up some. A little blood, a little spleen.

CLARENCE: [*Trying for firmer ground*] Our sanctuary isn't half as nice. I mean, it's not even connected to the house. I guess you're Sigfrid's grandfather.

GRANDFA: [*Enormously funny*] Who'd you think I was? His grandmother?

CLARENCE: [*Laughing, too*] Well, not really!

GRANDFA: Oh, you're a droll one, you are.

CLARENCE: [*Reckless*] Of course you might've been his aunt! [*The laughter is raucous, slightly hysterical*]

GRANDFA: Or his auntie! [*Then, quickly, straight-faced*] Nice dress you got there.

CLARENCE: [*Snapping to*] Sir?

GRANDFA: Eh? Sorry, I don't hear too well.

CLARENCE: I suppose you're wondering why I have this dress on.

GRANDFA: [*Breezy*] Oh no! No no!

CLARENCE: Well, you see—

GRANDFA: Happens all the time around here. If you're not one thing, you're t'other.

CLARENCE: Sir?

GRANDFA: You don't hear so well yourself. [*Short pause*] Florence.

CLARENCE: Sir? [*Then, correcting himself*] I beg your pardon?

GRANDFA: Florence.

CLARENCE: No, Clarence.

GRANDFA: Funny name for a young man.

CLARENCE: Clarence?

GRANDFA: No, Florence. Florence is a funny name for a young man.

CLARENCE: Yes! . . . Yes it is. [*A pause*] I'm *Clarence.* My name is—

GRANDFA: [*Crabbed*] I know what your name is. I was saying that Florence is a funny name for a young man. If your name was Florence, it would be funny. [*Sweetly*] Nice frock, Clarence.

CLARENCE: Sir?

GRANDFA: [*Thundering*] I SAID: NICE FROCK, CLARENCE!

CLARENCE: Oh.

GRANDFA: I haven't seen such a nice frock in a long time.

CLARENCE: Thank you. [*Then aghast*] Oh, but it's not mine.

GRANDFA: Finally!

CLARENCE: I lost my clothes. This is all I could find.

GRANDFA: Now I understand.

CLARENCE: I don't wear a frock . . . a dress!

GRANDFA: Unless, of course, you've lost your clothes. Then you wear a frock.

CLARENCE: Well, I certainly hope you don't think I came over here like this. A boy in a dress! That would be a sight!

GRANDFA: Oh, yes! Indeed it would . . . *is,* in fact.

CLARENCE: It's the craziest thing. Everything I had on when I got here . . . gone! . . . just like that. I can't understand it. I've looked everywhere.

GRANDFA: It's a careless generation, the younger one.

CLARENCE: My socks even.

GRANDFA: Well, you know the old saying: sooner or later we all end up in our rightful clothes.

CLARENCE: No, I never heard that one.

GRANDFA: Well, you trust in it. When all else fails, boy, trust in the old sayings and they'll never let you down.

CLARENCE: [*With a smile and a shrug*] Well, you certainly can't say I'm not a good sport about it. [GRANDFA *seems about to leave the room.* CLARENCE, *with his back to him, continues with a relaxed genuineness we have not seen yet*] Talk about giving the Movement a bad name! We've got a major demonstration in the morning. I'm a squadron secretary; I'll be leading an entire platoon. That's all we need at a time like this: a squadron secretary in a dress! There's enough opposition to us as it is. [GRANDFA *is listening to* CLARENCE] We've actually been hooted. Physically attacked sometimes. It's awful when that happens.

GRANDFA: [*A sad realization, softly, almost to himself*] You don't know what's going to happen, do you?

CLARENCE: [*Without pause*] Why people should be against anyone trying to make this a better world, I'll never know. But they are . . . Gee, I wish Sigfrid would come back.

GRANDFA: [*A weary sigh*] Go home, missy . . . please . . . go home.

CLARENCE: [*Awkward*] It was such a coincidence . . . running into each other like that this afternoon. We hadn't seen each other since the sixth grade. That's . . . [*Counting the years up on his fingers*]

GRANDFA: While there's time . . . pick up your skirts and run along home.

CLARENCE: [*Unable to prolong it*] I beg your pardon?

GRANDFA: You heard me . . . maybe you didn't want to . . . but you did.

CLARENCE: I . . . no, no I didn't . . . something about home?

GRANDFA: [*Flat*] That's right. Something about home.

CLARENCE: Well? Well what?

GRANDFA: They'll devour you. Run, boy, I say run for your life. Get up those stairs and run.

CLARENCE: [*A little peevish*] I honestly don't know what you're talking about.

GRANDFA: I'm talking about what will happen to you if you stay here. He's already put you in a dress. But that was only a beginning.

CLARENCE: [*Edgy*] I don't know what you're talking about.

GRANDFA: [*Full Voice*] I'm talking about you. Who you are! AND THEY WILL REVILE YOU FOR IT. That is their function! They'll make you want to die!

CLARENCE: [*Ugly*] I DON'T KNOW WHAT YOU'RE TALKING ABOUT!

A silence.

GRANDFA: [*Gently*] God help you, Clarence, God help you.

The quiet is shattered by the horn fanfare announcing NORMA'S *entrance from Bellini's opera. There is no specific source for the music. It is very loud. It will continue.*

CLARENCE: [*Distracted*] What? . . . music . . . the music . . . where? . . . Sir! [GRANDFA *is headed for the door: slowly, slowly*] Wait! Where is everyone? . . . What's going to happen? . . . This music . . . I didn't know what you were talking about . . . I didn't know! . . . please, stay! [GRANDFA *is gone*] I didn't . . . know . . . [*He is alone. The music builds. At the first beat of the orchestral verse of the chorus,* LAKME *comes skipping into the room. She wears her Green Hornet dress and cape. As she skips about the room in time to the music, she scatters rose petals from a tiny basket.* CLARENCE *watches, stupefied, unable to speak.* SIGFRID *has entered directly behind her. He still wears his black shirt and slacks. But now he carries an enormous saber. He holds it out in front of him with great reverence, as if it were a sacred object. His expression and movements are solemn, trancelike*] Where have you been? Sigfrid! Where?

SIGFRID: [*With a terrible, controlled fury*] Ruby! Her entrance!

CLARENCE: [*After he has recovered from this*] I . . . don't understand.

LAKME: [*Helpful*] You'd better kneel. She won't like it if you don't.

CLARENCE: I . . .

SIGFRID: [*The same voice*] Down! [SIGFRID *and* LAKME *kneel, facing the right door*] Down!

> CLARENCE *kneels, too. The horn fanfare sounds again and* RUBY *makes her long-awaited entrance. It and she are spectacular. She is wearing an elaborate, flowing white dress, over which is a brilliant cape. She moves majestically to a spot center stage and stands there, motionless, until the music ends.* CLARENCE, SIGFRID, *and* LAKME *are almost prone on the floor, their heads bowed, they are not looking at her.*

RUBY: [*After a pause, with an imperial gesture,* NORMA'S *opening recitative*] "*Sediziose voci—*" [*She stops singing on the high note and yawns hugely, not bothering to cover her mouth. Then she stretches, very slowly and yawns again. Affected, and she knows it*] *La Ruby non canterà stanotte.*

SIGFRID *and* LAKME: [*Together, exaggerated cadences*] *Che peccato!*

RUBY: *E troppo stanca.*

SIGFRID *and* LAKME: *Maledetto.*

RUBY: *E troppo vecchia.*

SIGFRID *and* LAKME: *Poverina.*

RUBY: [*Sitting*] *Buona sera a tutti!*

SIGFRID: [*Low, to* CLARENCE] Isn't she terrific? Didn't I tell you?

RUBY: *Mi sento male. Mi sento noiosa. Mi sento many things. But most of all* mi sento *blue.*

SIGFRID: [*The same*] One in a million.

LAKME: One in ten million!

RUBY: [*Arms outstretched*] *Abbracciami, tesori, abbracciami.*

SIGFRID: [*Excusing himself to* CLARENCE] She wants to embrace us.

LAKME: No. She wants *us* to embrace *her.* There's a difference.

RUBY: [*Taking* LAKME *and* SIGFRID *into her arms*] *Ah, mes enfants. Mes véritables enfants. Comme je suis heureuse. Et comme je ne suis pas heureuse. Mais ce soir . . . peut-être . . . je —* ["*Seeing*" CLARENCE, *she breaks off*] Who is that, please?

SIGFRID: Who?

RUBY: [*Pointing*] That. That person.

SIGFRID: [*Terse whisper*] The friend.

RUBY: Ah! *L'ami.* [*To* CLARENCE] *Nous vous avons attendé, chéri.*

CLARENCE: [*From across the room*] Hello. I'm—

RUBY: [*Brightly*] We'll be with you in a moment, dear. Sweet dress and what a perfectly atrocious body!

LAKME: [*So knowing*] Sigfrid knows that, Ruby.

RUBY: I wouldn't have thought he was your type at all. Never in my life.

SIGFRID: It was the best I could do.

RUBY: It's the bottom of the barrel, Sigfrid. The veritable bottom of the barrel. This is hardly worth the effort.

SIGFRID: You try it next time, you think it's so easy. You try finding someone.

LAKME: As he said, it was the best he could do.

RUBY: [*With a sigh of finality*] Ebbene, comminiciamo la commedia.

LAKME: [*Yelling to* CLARENCE] Hey! You!

RUBY: Not that way, Lakme. Properly, very properly. Sigfrid, he's your friend.

SIGFRID: Just . . .

RUBY: Yes, darling?

He only looks at her. She smiles up at him. Then SIGFRID *goes over to* CLARENCE, *takes him by the arm and leads him back to* RUBY. *There should be a suggestion of royalty granting an interview during the next scene.*

SIGFRID: Clarence, I'd like you to meet my mother. Ruby, this is Clarence.

RUBY: *Enchantée.*

CLARENCE: *Enchanté.*

RUBY: I beg your pardon?

CLARENCE: [*Who doesn't speak French or Italian or anything*] Enchanté? [*Ruby shifts in her chair*] Please don't get up!

RUBY: [*Settling back*] Oh, I won't. I wasn't, in fact. But you sit down. Here . . . on the friend seat.

CLARENCE: The what?

SIGFRID: Friend seat.

RUBY: Seat for friends.

SIGFRID: You're the friend. You.

CLARENCE: Oh. [*Short pause;* CLARENCE *sits*]

RUBY: Halloween?

CLARENCE: Please?

RUBY: [*At once*] You've met our little Lakme? Our own *piccola cosa nostra?*

CLARENCE: No, I don't think so.

SIGFRID: In the park this afternoon. You left the demonstration and came over and played football with us.

LAKME: Attempted to play football with us. You're pretty stinky at it.

CLARENCE: Was that you?

RUBY: Lakme's thirteen. Aren't you, sweetheart?

A pause.

CLARENCE: I didn't recognize you in that . . . dress.

RUBY: [*A little louder this time*] Lakme's thirteen. Aren't you, sweetheart?

Another pause.

CLARENCE: I have a little sister.

SIGFRID: [*Completely out of patience*] Lakme's thirteen. Aren't you, sweetheart?

LAKME: [*Finally, remembering her cue*] Oh!

SIGFRID: Well, it's about time!

LAKME: Well, you changed the cue—

RUBY: *Avanti, Lakme, avanti!*

LAKME: [*A little aria directly to* CLARENCE] Thirteen! Thirteen years old and total monster. Have been for some time. I'm bright . . . extremely bright. Close to genius, in fact. I know everything a thirteen-year-old girl isn't supposed to know. Even ninety-three-year-old girls aren't supposed to know what I know. I know so much they don't know what to do with me. "They" meaning everyone. Everyone outside this house. Ruby and Sigfrid are different. At least they hate me. [*Appropriate comments from* RUBY *and* SIGFRID] I have talents. I must have. Only I don't know what they are yet. So I play the piano. Bach, mostly, but sometimes Mozart. My favorite thing in the world is the Green Hornet. He makes people tell the truth and goes "Bzzzz, bzzzzz" at them until they do. I do love the Green Hornet. My unfavorite thing is . . . well, lots of things. Finks being in the vanguard. Fink! [*Very fast now*] My favorite color is white . . . because it's blank. Time of day: night . . . blanker. Time of year: winter, blanker blanker. Fink! [*And now slower, languid*] Millions of tiny sprouts of golden hair on my legs and arms. In the sun they glisten. Breasts moving along nicely. Not much bigger than a scoop in a nickel cone right now. Eyes and teeth: sharp and healthy. Fink! [*Fast again, the finale*] Other favorites—book: *The Iliad;* poem: *The Rubáiyát* . . . yeah, the *Rubáiyát!* . . . also "Sky, a blue sky, the eagle soars" . . . it's by a certain Shelley I know . . . movie: none. I never saw one. Ocean: the Dead Sea; tree: cactus; flower: lily; dress: the one with strawberries I wear on Fridays; painter: none . . well, maybe Leonardo; color: black; food: fish; person: me. Fink! [*She finishes with a flourish, then, to* SIGFRID] "Lakme's a charming child. We're extremely fond of her." That's the cue, idiot!

RUBY: You've made a few changes in it, darling.

LAKME: [*So pleased with herself*] Unh-hunh!

SIGFRID: And one of them better go.

LAKME: Oh yeah? Which one? [*Then to* CLARENCE] Sigfrid used to write . . . [*Hesitates, decides not to*] never mind . . . [*She goes back to her place and sits. Awkward silence.* RUBY *snaps her fingers at* SIGFRID]

SIGFRID: Clarence had quite a little tête-à-tête with Grandfa, Ruby.

RUBY: Yes, I heard them.

CLARENCE: . . . heard? . . .

RUBY: The intercom. We listen to everything. Poor Grandfa. Look, children, over there. His little bag's all packed. We're putting him in an asylum tomorrow.

CLARENCE: Yes, so he told me.

SIGFRID: Grandfa is insane.

CLARENCE: Yes, he told me that, too.

RUBY: He's written a novel.

CLARENCE: Oh. [*Pause*] Is that what makes him insane? [RUBY *nods her head*] Oh. [*Pause*] How does that make him insane?

LAKME: He thinks it's the truth.

CLARENCE: Oh. [*Pause*] Well, lots of famous writers cracked up right toward the end. [*A joke*] Sometimes before!

LAKME: [*Tight-lipped*] Grandfa isn't famous.

SIGFRID: [*The same*] Grandfa isn't a writer.

RUBY: [*The same*] Grandfa is insane.

CLARENCE: Oh.

An extremely loud snortle from FA.

LAKME: And that's our Fa. Rip Van Winkle with a bad heart.

SIGFRID: Fa won't be with us much longer we're afraid.

LAKME: [*A horse laugh*] Afraid? Hah!

RUBY: It's imminent. We've been expecting the worst for quite some time now.

CLARENCE: That's awful.

RUBY: Yes, I suppose it is. But you see, Clarence, Fa has not been affectionate with us. He's slept, while we have . . . how shall I put it? . . . not slept.

SIGFRID: It's been a hard row to hoe without our *babbino*.

RUBY: Nevertheless we've managed, Clarence. Somehow we have managed.

SIGFRID: Triumphed, Ruby. "Triumph" is a better word.

RUBY: [*Arms outspread to* LAKME *and* SIGFRID *again*] Abbracciami ancora, tesori, abbracciami! [*Maybe they don't come this time*] Aren't they wonderful, Clarence? Aren't my babies wonderful?

CLARENCE: They're . . . very nice.

RUBY: You use words so judiciously, Clarence. So judiciously. [*A pause, she snaps her fingers again*]

SIGFRID: [*The efficient host bit*] Drinks! I completely forgot. Ruby? What are you having!

RUBY: Cognac, a little cognac, darling. [*Then, directly to* CLARENCE] Je ne pouvais pas exister sans le cognac.

CLARENCE: Yes.

SIGFRID: Lakme?

LAKME: A martini, stupid, what do you think? [*Then, at once, to* CLARENCE] You should have seen your face when I came in here during Ruby's entrance. Stupefication!

SIGFRID: [*"Rescuing" him*] Clarence? [*And before* CLARENCE *can answer*] You're not uncomfortable? Sitting there?

CLARENCE: [*Crushed*] No, I'm fine, just fine.

SIGFRID: Let's see, does that get everyone? All-righty. And a pernod for me. [*He works at the bar*]

LAKME: [*Who has been considering that word, "stupefication"*] Stupefaction. I can say "stupefaction." Only I prefer "stupefication." [*Very virtuoso*] It's more stupefacient than stupefaction . . . stupefication is. Stupid!

RUBY: That will do, Lakme. I should think that will do for quite a while now.

LAKME: I'm being nice. Aren't I? Aren't I being nice?

CLARENCE: [*To* RUBY] My little sister—

RUBY: [*Beaming*] It's such a relief to see Sigfrid bring someone nice home for a change. We've had some of the most awful people here. Right where you're sitting. Riffraff! And if there's one thing I won't have in my basement, it's riffraff. Trash is all right . . . and Sigfrid's brought home enough of it . . . but I draw the line at riffraff . . . well, do you blame me?

CLARENCE: It's not very pleasant.

RUBY: I wish you could have seen the girl he brought home with him last night. A belly dancer. An Arab belly dancer.

SIGFRID: She was amusing.

RUBY: I'm glad you thought so. The hair, Clarence. Horrible black hair. Everywhere. And the skin. Oily, oily.

SIGFRID: Olive, Ruby, an Arab's skin is olive.

RUBY: I call it oily. Now if that had been a real jewel in her navel . . .

SIGFRID: Well, Clarence isn't riffraff, Ruby.

RUBY: [*To* CLARENCE, *sharing an enormous joke*] Just trash? [*Everyone laughs;* CLARENCE *manages a smile*] You don't say much, do you?

SIGFRID: [*Coming forward with the drinks, passing them around;* LAKME *gets a Coke, of course*] Clarence is shy, Ruby. Clarence has a father who used to beat him as a child. Clarence has a mother—

CLARENCE: Sigfrid!

SIGFRID: Relax, sweetheart. It's no skin off your nose. You told me and now I'm telling them.

CLARENCE: That was . . . different.

SIGFRID: Not really. [*Continuing*] . . . a mother who smothered him with affection. She still does, in truth. And Clarence works in the public library. It is not difficult, therefore, to explain why Clarence is shy. It is not difficult to explain Clarence. There are reasons for him. [*Toasting*] Skoal, Clarence.

RUBY: Skoal, Clarence.

LAKME: Skoal, Clarence.

CLARENCE: [*Instinctively raising his hand to drink*] Skoal.

They drink to him.

RUBY: [*Reflectively*] There's something about you, Clarence . . . I can't quite put my finger on it . . . something about you that makes me think it's Halloween.

SIGFRID: It's the dress, Ruby.

RUBY: Mmm, I suppose it is.

SIGFRID: Clarence couldn't find his clothes. He asked if there wasn't something of yours he might put on.

CLARENCE: No!

RUBY: Well, it is a bit damp down here this evening. You were afraid he might catch cold. I don't mind, do I?

CLARENCE: That's not true.

RUBY: [*Running on*] Mind? Of course I don't mind. One thing life has taught me . . . and perhaps this is all it has taught me . . . is never to mind anything. Since I stopped minding, which was not so many years ago, I have . . . on occasion . . . been amused. And I suppose being amused is the closest thing left us to grace. [*Then, directly to* CLARENCE, *with all her charm*] Don't you think so, Clarence?

CLARENCE: Mrs. . . .

RUBY: Ruby. The name is Ruby.

CLARENCE: That's not true about . . . I didn't ask to . . .

RUBY: To what, dear?

CLARENCE: This . . . this dress.

RUBY: [*Placating*] Sigfrid's only joking . . . maybe he's only joking . . . either way, I know that. Besides . . hmm? [LAKME *is whispering into* RUBY's *ear*. RUBY *laughs and nods her head affirmatively several times. Meanwhile,* SIGFRID *joins* CLARENCE, *putting one arm affectionately around his shoulder*]

SIGFRID: Ruby's a good sport. We all are. So you be one, too. Just . . . relax.

CLARENCE: [*A whisper*] That was a lie.

SIGFRID: [*Good-natured*] Oh, grump, grump, grump.

CLARENCE: Well, it was. It was embarrassing.

SIGFRID: [*Logically*] How can it be a lie when it's not true in the first place? . . . Hunh?

RUBY: [*Back to* CLARENCE *and* SIGFRID] I'm sorry. You were saying . . . ?

SIGFRID: [*Sweetly*] Clarence was just accusing me of telling a lie and I was explaining to him that it's not a lie unless it's true.

RUBY: Why of course! *Tout le monde* knows that. There's no point to a lie if it's not true. [*As before*] Don't you think so, Clarence?

LAKME *is at the rear of the room.*

SIGFRID: What's she up to?

RUBY: Lakme thought our little guest might enjoy a little music. Little guest, little music. One of the records, dear.

CLARENCE: Mrs. . . . Ruby. It's just not true.

SIGFRID: Sshhh. You're going to like this.

RUBY: [*Rising to the occasion, a command performance*] I had a career in grand opera, you know. I was a *diva* . . . a *prima donna* . . . quite one of the best. *La Regina dell'Opera:* me! Or as the children so idiomatically put it: I was an opera queen.

SIGFRID: That's idiomatic and literal both.

RUBY: [*Not annoyed at his little interruption*] Well, to press on! I was beautiful then and there was music in my voice . . . beautiful, beautiful music. I could sing anything . . . and I often did. There was no role too high, too low, or too in-between. And on stage . . . ah! on stage . . . and you must believe this, I was beautiful . . . so very, very beautiful. And now they are both gone: the beauty and the music . . . dearly departed ornaments of my being. The one, frozen for a single terrifying instant, snatched from eternity, *my* eternity, in a red Moroccan leather album of yellowing photographs . . . hundreds upon hundreds of them. The other, my voice . . . my beautiful voice . . . echoes endlessly on the eroded grooves of a spinning black disc . . . just this one. *Ascolta!* [*The music begins now. Instantly her mood lightens and her speech tempo becomes faster. The recording played should be that of an incredibly awful soprano singing an elaborate coloratura aria. Florence Foster Jenkins' recording of the Queen of the Night aria from* The Magic Flute *is suggested. The actress should "play" with the music at all times during the following speech: mouthing certain phrases of music, pausing in the speech to listen to certain phrases, conducting a little. One should never be too sure just how serious* RUBY *is about the recording, her career . . . anything.* SIGFRID *and* LAKME *alternate between rapt attention and trying to keep a straight face.* CLARENCE *is flabbergasted*]

Aaaah! Wolfgang Amadeus! *Bravo, miei figli, bravi!* . . . The unhappy mother, the enragèd Queen of the Night, swears vengeance and vows to deliver her daughter Pamina from her captor's hands . . . Vengeance! . . . This phrase: lovely, lovely. I sang this once in Moscow . . . at the Bolshoi . . . in Russian, no less . . . those dreadful thick vowels . . .

CLARENCE: [*In a whisper*] Is that really your mother—?

SIGFRID *fiercely motions him to be silent.*

RUBY: After the performance I was delivered to my hotel in a troika drawn by several thousand delirious students who then proceeded to serenade me with folk songs from the streets beneath my windows . . I sat alone on my balcony . . . it was a warm evening, warm for Moscow . . . alone and weeping . . . weeping and toasting them with vodka . . . They sang until dawn . . . I toasted till dawn . . . when the Kremlin's domes first were flecked with the morning sun's gold. Here! The cadenza. Marvelous!

SIGFRID: [*A stage whisper to* CLARENCE] That's Ruby's Lucy Lammermoor mad-scene dress.

CLARENCE: Oh!

RUBY: Once in Milano . . . after my debut at the Scala in a revival of *La Cucaracha* . . . revived for me, *ça va sans dire* . . . the manager, the manager of La Scala, Milan, said to me: "Ruby, *tu hai la voce delle anime di purgatorio.*" . . . Well, something like that. "You sing with the voice of the souls in purgatory!" You see, he'd heard the pain in my voice. *Verismo*, we called it. [*And now, acting it out*] This part, now! I would rush about the stage brandishing this enormous dagger. One critic said it was an awesome moment. Oh, the memory of those nights! . . . those days! The continental tours with Brünnhilde, my Pekingese, and my three male secretaries! The steamer trunks stickered ten times over with those magic names: Paris, Rome, Vienna, London, Bayreuth, Peiping, Manila, Camden, New Jersey . . . yes! Camden, New Jersey . . . Athens, Napoli, Palermo . . . Palermo where I first met Fa, after a Delilah at the Teatro Massimo. He'd come there to take away the olives . . . Here! The *portamento,* Clarence, *il portamento!* . . . Oh, the glory! The glory! [*Her voice trails off and she is lost in reverie, listening to the music with closed eyes, her head back. The music ends. There is a pause. Then* RUBY *opens her eyes and leans forward toward* CLARENCE] Well?

LAKME: Well?

SIGFRID: Well?

CLARENCE: I . . . unh . . . I . . .

SIGFRID: Tell Ruby what you thought, Clarence. Go on.

CLARENCE: I . . . I don't know very much about music. I really shouldn't venture to make a judgment.

SIGFRID: Oh, go ahead, venture!

LAKME: [*Singsong*] Nothing ventured, nothing gained.

CLARENCE: Especially opera. I don't know anything about opera. [*A weak joke*] Wagner wrote Puccini as far as I know. [*They are not amused*] Really . . . I'm not qualified.

RUBY: [*Edgy*] The quality of the voice, dear. We're interested in what you think of that.

CLARENCE: Oh . . . that . . . it was wonderful, Mrs. . . .

LAKME: Ruby. Her name is Ruby.

CLARENCE: . . . just wonderful.

RUBY: Yes?

CLARENCE: What else can I . . . ? It reminded me of . . . of a bird. A lark maybe. I don't know. But it certainly was wonderful. You're very talented. [*The three of them explode with laughter*] What? . . . What's so funny? . . . Did I say something wrong? . . .

RUBY: [*Rocking with laughter*] He's so pathetically polite.

SIGFRID: [*The same*] You're very talented, Ruby!

RUBY: And so patronizing.

LAKME: A bird! You reminded him of a bird.

CLARENCE: [*The light slowly dawning*] Oh . . . I see . . . that wasn't you!

LAKME: Do tell!

CLARENCE: [*Joining in the laughter himself*] No wonder! . . . well, I'm glad it wasn't . . . ha ha . . . that was the worst thing I ever heard in my life . . . ha ha ha . . . it was awful . . . where did you find that record . . . who was she?

Abruptly, the laughter ceases and they stare fiercely at CLARENCE.

RUBY: [*Sharp*] A very dear friend.

CLARENCE: [*Caught in mid-laugh*] Oh.

RUBY: A seventy-two-year-old lady.

LAKME: A seventy-two-year-old Negro lady.

SIGFRID: A seventy-two-year-old Negro servant from the deep Deep South.

RUBY: Seventy-two-year-old Negro lady servants from the deep Deep South who sing Mozart arias are not to be ridiculed. Ever!

LAKME: Racist! Dirty Nazi racist!

CLARENCE: [*Thoroughly chastened*] I . . . I didn't know.

RUBY: You may laugh with us, Clarence, at yourself . . . but not at sweet old Aunt Jemima from the deep Deep South. [*Again they explode with laughter.* CLARENCE *sits dumbly, not knowing what to do or say or think.* RUBY *leans forward to pat his cheek*] Clarence! Where's that smile? That famous smile of yours? [CLARENCE *doesn't react*] Now! Together! Sing! [*She leads them in a rousing chorus of "For He's a Jolly Good Fellow." Suddenly the lights dim to half and hold there. The singing falters.* RUBY *is determined to finish the song, but for a moment she is the only one singing. Then* SIGFRID *joins in, rather limply at first, but soon belting it out with his full voice.* LAKME *has stopped singing altogether and moves away from the others. Even though her back is to us, we can tell from her heaving shoulders that she is fighting to hold back enormous sobs. The lights come swiftly back up to full, as* RUBY *and* SIGFRID *finish the song boisterously*]

CLARENCE: I don't know what to think of you people. One minute you're friendly, the next you're making fun of me.

SIGFRID: [*Poo-pooing*] Oh! Don't mind us. That's our way.

CLARENCE: Fun at my expense!

RUBY: [*Looking across the room at* LAKME] Lakme!

SIGFRID: And whose fault is that? You admired the singing. A cat in heat, a God-knows-what, and you admired the singing.

CLARENCE: Because I thought it was . . . I was only trying to be polite.

RUBY: Stop that, Lakme.

SIGFRID: So you made a fool of yourself? Oh baby, learn to laugh at yourself. Learn it quick. It's the only thing that makes sense anymore.

CLARENCE: I'm sorry, but I don't have a sense of humor.

SIGFRID: [*Flip*] Neither do we. Think about that.

RUBY: Lakme, I asked you to stop.

SIGFRID: What's the matter with her?

RUBY: The fence. Something on the fence. Go to your room, Lakme.

SIGFRID: [*Going to* LAKME, *not unkindly*] Come on, little one, calm down now.

LAKME: [*Pulling away from him*] Keep away from me!

SIGFRID: We're here. We're all together. Don't—

LAKME: KEEP AWAY!

SIGFRID: It was only an animal. It's happened before.

RUBY: Make her go to her room, Sigfrid.

LAKME: I said keep away!

RUBY: [*Delighted sarcasm*] Brave little Lakme. Fearless little Lakme. Our own little St. Joan of the underground. "Leave the door open, Ruby. It's fifteen minutes till—"

LAKME: Shut up, Ruby, just shut up!

RUBY: [*Delighted with herself*] Coraggio, Lakme, coraggio!

LAKME: JUST DO WHAT YOU SAID YOU WOULD. MAKE HIM GO OUT THERE. BUT GET IT OVER WITH AND LEAVE US ALONE. JUST DO IT. [*She leaves quickly through the right door*]

SIGFRID: [*Following*] Lakme!

RUBY: Sigfrid! Not yet.

SIGFRID: But she'll—

RUBY: Be all right.

SIGFRID: But she won't—

RUBY: She will. Sit.

SIGFRID: But—

RUBY: SIT!

He obeys.

CLARENCE: [*A voice in the void*] Is there anything the matter? [*A long pause*] Is there?

SIGFRID *snaps his fingers at* RUBY.

RUBY: [*Abruptly*] Tell us about the way you live, Clarence.

CLARENCE: Sir? I mean . . . [*Laughs*] Excuse me.

RUBY: [*Not amused*] The way you live. I want you to tell us about it.

CLARENCE: I don't understand. The way I live? Me?

SIGFRID: What you believe in, Clarence. A statement of principles . . . life principles.

CLARENCE: Like my philosophy? Is that what you mean? My philosophy of life?

RUBY: [*An edge in her voice*] It's called the way you live.

CLARENCE: [*Amused*] But why? I'm not even sure if I have one.

SIGFRID: You're alive, aren't you?

CLARENCE: Well, yes.

RUBY: Then you have one.

CLARENCE: Well, I suppose I do . . . I must . . . only I hadn't really thought about it.

RUBY: You gave Grandfa an earful.

CLARENCE: Please?

SIGFRID: [*Always more conciliatory than* RUBY] Now's your opportunity, Clarence.

CLARENCE: What do you want with it? My philosophy of life?

RUBY: [*Insistent*] It's called the way you live.

SIGFRID: We'd like to tape it.

CLARENCE: Tape it? You mean on a— [SIGFRID *nods*] But why would anyone want to do a thing like that? Tape someone's philo— . . . way he lives?

SIGFRID: Ruby collects them. All our guests do it. She's looking for the answer.

RUBY: I have the answer. I'm looking for corroboration. I find it consoling. Usually.

CLARENCE: [*A little intrigued with the idea*] You mean we'll probably end up saying the very same thing? Or just about?

RUBY: Or just about.

SIGFRID *has been setting up the recorder.*

RUBY'S RECORDED VOICE: [*Very loud*] ". . . wherefrom we shall draw the sustenance to destroy you . . ."

RUBY: On "record," dear, not on "playback."

SIGFRID *now sets a microphone in front of* CLARENCE.

CLARENCE: [*To* RUBY] That was you. Was that from your . . . ? [*Noticing the microphone*] Is that what I talk into? I feel like I'm on the radio. Gee, I bet I make a mess out of this. [SIGFRID *motions for silence and points to the spinning reels*] You mean I'm on already? Heavens! I'm really not prepared, you know. [*A pause*] Unh . . . unh . . . the way I live . . . no, let me start again . . . unh . . . [*Takes a deep breath*] The Way I Live . . . The way I live is . . . the best I can do. I try. I mean I really try. And I think I am improving. I think I am becoming a better human being day by day. I really do . . . Anyway, I'm trying. [*Then, turning to* RUBY *and* SIGFRID] This is awful. I told you— [*They motion him to continue*] I believe in . . . well, lots of things. [*Short pause*] And I think it's sad that we can't enjoy these things the way we were meant to. Because of . . . the circumstance. [*Shorter pause*] I love life. I suppose that's a corny statement . . . I know how fashionable it is to be morose these days . . . but I do. I really do love it. There are just too many good things in the world not to want to be alive. Just think of all the beautiful things men have made. Music, art, literature . . . Shakespeare alone is a reason to be alive. How could anyone not want to be alive after there's been a Shakespeare on this earth? Someone who writes poetry? I can't imagine it. And even if I've never seen it real . . . and maybe I never will . . . how could anyone not want to be alive when there is a city in Italy named Florence? How could they? Just knowing about Florence! . . . what it means to us that it's there. That there was a Florence, is and will be. It . . . it makes the rest of this planet tolerable. Florence is why we're alive. It's what we're about. [*A pause*] And the things you can do! The simple things. What about them? Just to take a walk even. It can be wonderful. Or to be by the sea and feel that air on your face and see what the horizon means. You can actually see the curve of the earth. Just what they taught you in school and it's true!

That's a wonderful thing to see for yourself. Or just to sit in a park . . . with the sun spilling all over you . . . watching the people. The other people. They're not you, and that's what's so beautiful about them. They're someone else. Sit and wonder who they are. What they ate for breakfast, what paper they're reading, where they live, what they do . . . who they love. And that's another reason. Everybody loves somebody . . . or they will . . . sometime in their life. [*A pause*] Anything that makes you want to live so bad you'd . . . you'd die for it . . . Shakespeare, Florence . . . someone in the park. That's what I believe in. That's all. That's the way I live. [*A silence*] Was it all right?

SIGFRID *turns off the recorder.*

RUBY: Shakespeare, Florence, and someone in the park. That was nicely spoken, Clarence.

CLARENCE: I sort of enjoyed it once I got into it. What happens now? With the tape, I mean.

SIGFRID: [*Almost mechanical, his mind elsewhere*] We put it aside . . . save it . . . keep it for reference.

CLARENCE: Were they very similar? Yours and mine?

RUBY: Not quite, Clarence . . . not quite.

CLARENCE: Did you . . . ? [*Giggles*] did you like it? [*Looks from one to the other*]

RUBY: Sigfrid?

SIGFRID: There is a sadness, Clarence, there is a sadness in what you said.

CLARENCE: Sadness? . . . No!

SIGFRID: There is a sadness.

RUBY: [*Edgy, suspicious of this change in* SIGFRID'S *mood*] What are you doing, Sigfrid?

SIGFRID: [*Simply*] I don't know.

CLARENCE: [*Trying to relieve the tension*] Well, sure, there is sadness in the world. Lots of it. Everyone knows that.

SIGFRID: Do they?

CLARENCE: I do.

SIGFRID: The sadness of Shakespeare . . . the enduring sadness of Florence . . . and the necessarily greater sadness of someone in the park.

CLARENCE: I . . . I don't understand.

SIGFRID: [*Turning directly to him*] And that is the sadness of Clarence. [*Then, to* RUBY] Maybe we could stop now, Ruby. Maybe we don't have to finish it tonight. [RUBY *snaps her fingers at him, hard*] For whose benefit? His?

RUBY: Yours!

CLARENCE: [*Another try*] Sigfrid, what happened after the sixth grade? After they . . .

RUBY: [*Making him say it, to goad* SIGFRID] After they what?

CLARENCE: Expelled him. What happened then?

RUBY: Nothing.

CLARENCE: [*To Sigfrid*] Nothing?

RUBY: Nothing.

CLARENCE: Well something . . .

SIGFRID: Nothing! . . . this! . . . nothing.

CLARENCE: [*After an awkward silence, one final try*] Well anyway . . . and this is another nice thing . . . I should've taped it . . . another very un-sad thing . . . sometimes you run into an old friend. A friend you haven't seen—

SIGFRID: I am not your friend, Clarence. I am . . . I am not that either, but I am not your friend. [*A pause*] And that is the sadness of Sigfrid. The sadness of being him. [*Rises*] Gently, Ruby, gently.

RUBY: Sigfrid?

SIGFRID: [*His answer to this*] I'll be here . . . when it's time . . . I'll be here.

CLARENCE: Sigfrid, where are you going?

SIGFRID: You'll see. [*And then*] Despair, Clarence, despair.

CLARENCE: Is something going to happen?

SIGFRID: You might say that. [*And again*] But despair, Clarence, despair. [*He is going*] And gently. [*He is gone*]

CLARENCE: [*To no one in particular*] I hate surprises. [*A very long silence.* RUBY *slowly takes off her wig. Next she will remove her cape*] I wrote a poem once. For my mother. On her birthday. When I was little. "God bless the Lord, God bless my mother. She has good things in her oven." She's always saved it. [*A pause*] What did Sigfrid mean? . . . about the sadness? And to despair? [*Another pause*] It was unfortunate.

RUBY: [*Rather distantly at first*] What was?

CLARENCE: That they expelled him. Sigfrid was very popular at that school.

RUBY: [*With an almost grotesque emphasis on the word*] Lots of things . . . are *unfortunate*.

CLARENCE: [*In solemn agreement*] The Situation. You mean the Situation.

RUBY: [*Flat*] That's right . . . the unfortunate Situation. [*And then, reading from* CLARENCE'S *placard*] "There Is Something Out There."

CLARENCE: "We Shall Prevail."

RUBY: I beg your pardon?

CLARENCE: Turn it around. The other side's a little more optimistic. It's what we believe in.

RUBY: [*Reading from the other side of the placard*] "We Shall Prevail." Will we, Clarence?

CLARENCE: I think so. [*Warming to his subject, his favorite, not hearing her*] It's been this way so long now . . . I suppose it would be easy to get depressed. Do you realize there are children who have never seen a sunset and the moon only in the daytime when it's not really the moon . . . the way it should be the moon?

RUBY: [*Low, he doesn't hear this*] Lakme.

CLARENCE: [*Running on*] Though actually, if I had a choice, I think I'd rather see an eclipse of the moon than the moon itself. From what I've read—

RUBY: [*Cutting in now*] Once.

CLARENCE: You've seen one? What's it like, an eclipse?

RUBY: Dark.

CLARENCE: [*Disappointed*] Oh.

RUBY: It was in Florence.

CLARENCE: You've been to Florence!

RUBY: It was lovely.

CLARENCE: Everything is was now. [*The lights suddenly dim to half*] The lights again! Something's happening to the lights! [*The lights come back to full*] See how jittery I am? Something happens . . . a little thing like the lights . . . and I think it's started to happen . . . that it's finally out there. If we only knew when . . . It's this waiting that's so terrible. And we don't even know what it is we're so afraid of!

RUBY: We know it's out there. That's enough.

CLARENCE: And if you went out there to find out . . .

RUBY: Yes?

CLARENCE: [*Looks at her*] Dead. You'd be dead.

RUBY: But you'd know, Clarence. Then you would know what is out there.

CLARENCE: And then you'd be dead.

RUBY: What would it take, Clarence, to make someone go out there?

CLARENCE: [*Who doesn't like this part of the conversation*] You'd have to be crazy or something.

RUBY: Or something.

CLARENCE: I don't know.

RUBY: Despair, Clarence. Sigfrid said despair.

Another pause.

CLARENCE: What do you think it is?

RUBY: I don't know.

CLARENCE: Don't you have any idea what it's like?

RUBY: I said I don't know!

CLARENCE: Oh.

RUBY: Does that disappoint you?

CLARENCE: [*It does, of course*] No. It's just that I'm so frightened of it. Aren't you frightened of it?

RUBY: If it gives you any pleasure to know this, Clarence, I am terrified beyond belief, and, occasionally, out of my mind.

The lights dim again, hold a moment, and then come back to full.

CLARENCE: [*More frightened this time*] What's happening? The fuses keep blowing!

RUBY: It's not the fuses. It's those dumb stray animals wandering into the fence.

CLARENCE: You mean it's . . . electrified?

RUBY: We have to keep people out somehow. There are signs posted at regular intervals. You don't approve I suppose?

CLARENCE: No . . . it's just that . . . well, how often does it happen?

RUBY: Four or five a night. Dogs . . . cats . . . an occasional parakeet. The city picks them up the next morning along with the garbage. Of course if Darwin were right, the animals should have learned to read those signs by now.

CLARENCE: It shouldn't be like this . . . fences, basements, curfews.

RUBY: Well, it is.

CLARENCE: And it's because it is this way and it must not be that I'm so concerned. You can't be indifferent to these things. People have to care . . . passionately!

RUBY: [*Who has been moving about the room and now holds up a sock which she has "found" under one of the sofa cushions*] Passion . . . ah yes, one must have passion . . . where would we all be without passion? [*She has "found" another sock now*]

CLARENCE: [*A little nervous, those are his socks*] Don't you care about . . . [*Gestures vaguely toward the outside*] things?

RUBY: The only issue of passionate concern in this family . . . the only one any of us really cares about . . . is who's going to get who: where, when, and how. [*Holds up a pair of garishly patterned undershorts*] Did you ever in your life? [*Laughs*] I'm sorry, Clarence. You were saying?

CLARENCE: [*A certain smugness will begin to creep into his voice*] I was talking about something else. Those are social relations . . . personal problems . . . neuroses. I was talking about more universal themes . . . the ones that really count.

RUBY: Oh? And what are they? [*She has put the socks and undershorts next to where* CLARENCE *is sitting*]

CLARENCE: [*Terribly uncomfortable*] Life . . . survival . . . that thing out there . . . I don't know.

RUBY: [*Helpful*] The big things?

CLARENCE: Yes.

RUBY: The major issues of our times?

CLARENCE: That's right.

RUBY: And not . . . how shall I put it? . . . personal unpleasantness?

CLARENCE: Especially not that. People think too much about themselves these days. That's all they think about. They encourage their neuroses. They coddle them, if you ask me.

RUBY: Well, we'll certainly put a stop to that.

CLARENCE: I hope I'm not sounding smug or anything.

RUBY: You? Smug? Clarence!

CLARENCE: I have that tendency. [*But plunging right ahead with it*] All it is actually is a question of people allowing themselves to become involved . . .

RUBY: Commitment!

CLARENCE: [*A little surprised at this*] Yes! But how did you know what I was—

RUBY: That is the word for you people? The committed ones? But committed to what exactly?

CLARENCE: [*Shrugging*] Anything.

RUBY: [*Obviously teasing*] To an asylum, like Grandfa?

CLARENCE: [*Laughing*] No! Something . . . large!

RUBY: Elephants are large. Are you committed to elephants?

CLARENCE: [*The same*] You know what I'm talking about. Something larger than myself . . . something . . . I don't know . . . purer! . . . a cause, an ideal . . .

RUBY: Well if that's all that being committed is . . . being purer than someone who isn't . . .

CLARENCE: I didn't mean it exactly like that.

RUBY: [*Not stopping for him*] . . . I suppose it's better than nothing. I suppose it's better than us.

CLARENCE: Nowadays people are all hunched over their navels when they have the stars to reach for.

RUBY: Had.

CLARENCE: I beg your pardon?

RUBY: Had the stars to reach for.

CLARENCE: [*Sadly*] Yes, had.

RUBY: "Everything is was now." Those are your words. [*Nailing him*] Then what's the point, Clarence? The point you people are trying to make?

CLARENCE: [*Very directly*] If I didn't believe that I could do something about that thing out there . . . if I didn't believe the Movement could do some good . . . if I didn't believe that people . . . if they tried, really tried . . .could change things . . . if I didn't believe all that, I'd . . .

RUBY: Yes?

CLARENCE: [*Beginning to understand the word now*] Despair.

RUBY: [*Almost a dare*] And then . . . you'd go out there? [*A pause,* RUBY *is standing over him, her hand on his cheek, she speaks softly*] Soon, Sigfrid, very soon now.

CLARENCE: [*Losing ground fast*] Maybe I'm not as aggressive as I'd like to be . . . outgoing. I'm more introspective.

RUBY: [*With the velvet glove*] But committed.

CLARENCE: I try to be.

RUBY: Dedicated.

CLARENCE: That, too.

RUBY: No distractions.

CLARENCE: [*His back to the wall*] Well, sure. You can't worry about these things twenty-four hours a day.

RUBY: [*Deadly*] I didn't think so.

CLARENCE: [*Simply*] I know you don't like me. What I don't know is why. [*But too late,* RUBY *has already begun it*]

RUBY: [*The coup de grâce, but gently, almost sadly at first*] I mean there you were, Clarence: marching around town all afternoon in this nippy weather. . . . Marching and waving your little sign and being committed and all. Being purer! That's what I call a big day. You needed a distraction after an afternoon like that. No wonder you toddled over to the curb when you saw that good-looking son of mine giving your little sign the once-over. No matter how committed you are, you certainly don't pass up a good-looking distraction like Sigfrid without at least inquiring. After all, he might be committed, too! Only in this case he wasn't. He most certainly wasn't. [*Acting out the dialogue, slowly becoming uglier*] "Hello there. I'm looking for something larger than myself. What about you?" asks the commitment. The distraction only smiles but does not answer. They never do. [*Breaking the mood a moment*] I know this scene well. [*Then, resuming*] And now the distraction, still smiling . . . always smiling . . . beckons with his head and begins to move away. "But I'm committed. I can't go with you!" cries the commitment. What to do? What to do? And as he stands there . . . soon to be alone . . . his feet numb with cold . . . watching the commitments march up the street one way and the distraction walk slowly down it the other . . . he remembers those immortal words of Cla-

rentius, the saddest commitment of them all: "You can't worry about these things twenty-four hours a day." Hey! Distraction! Wait for me! [*She whistles with two fingers in her mouth, and then breaks into laughter, prodding* CLARENCE *in the ribs*] Wasn't it that way, Clarence? Wasn't it?

CLARENCE: [*Immobile, shattered, quiet tears*] That isn't everything about me. There's more.

RUBY: That boy of mine may be a lousy commitment but he's one hell of a distraction.

CLARENCE: THAT ISN'T EVERYTHING!

RUBY: [*Fast and tough*] Look, sweetheart, it's not like outside down here. You check the guilt baggage at the front door when you come into this house. We deal with what's left us . . . not what we'd like to add to the mythology. It's a subtraction process and if the answer is zero . . . that's okay, too. Now you just be a sweet little distraction and simmer down.

CLARENCE: I'm not a distraction!

RUBY: You're just someone who happened in off the street, all committed up for Halloween? Is that it?

CLARENCE: NO!

RUBY: [*Making him look on her face*] "And someone in the park!" That's your commitment. Not Shakespeare, not Florence, not what's out there, but someone in the park! And that someone happened to be Sigfrid!

CLARENCE: [*Broken now*] I didn't come here for that.

RUBY: But Sigfrid wanted it that way. So you let him.

CLARENCE: I didn't want him to.

RUBY: But you let him. Oh, Clarence . . . Clarence, Clarence, Clarence

CLARENCE'S RECORDED VOICE: [*A mocking echo, from no specific source*] Oh Sigfrid . . . Sigfrid, Sigfrid, Sigfrid.

RUBY: I beg your pardon?

CLARENCE *neither answers nor looks at her.* SIGFRID *and* LAKME *enter through the right door. He carries a slide projector. She, a movie screen.*

LAKME: Here we are. Ready to go. Did you two have a nice talk while we were gone? Did Clarence try to convert you to the cause, Ruby?

RUBY: Sahh! The Clarence is temporarily out of commitment.

LAKME: Aaaaaw!

SIGFRID: I gave you some advice, Clarence. I hope you took it.

CLARENCE: I'd like to go home, please.

SIGFRID: Then I guess you didn't.

CLARENCE: I'd like to go home.

SIGFRID: [*An exaggerated transition*] But love-blessing! Lakme's produced an entertainment . . . a sight and sound entertainment . . . especially for you.

CLARENCE: [*Each time more emphatic, but never rising*] I would like to go home!

RUBY: I must say your mood's improved.

SIGFRID: You think? [*Then*] Do you know what Clarence did, Ruby? He told his father I was a girl. Me. Can you imagine it? And he told his mother he was coming over to see a boy.

RUBY: Oh, I see! His daddy lets him sleep with girls and his mummy lets him sleep with boys. They're a very conventional pair, your parents.

CLARENCE: [*Strong, for him*] Stop it!

RUBY: That's right, Clarence. Tell us off.

CLARENCE: [*Standing*] I'd like my clothes, please. My own clothes.

SIGFRID: But buttercup, you're in them.

CLARENCE: WHERE ARE THEY?

SIGFRID: [*Mocking*] Hoo hoo! Hoo hoo!

LAKME: [*Simultaneous*] Arabella's in a huff. She's huffled!

SIGFRID: We're getting waspish. Oh oh oh oh!

CLARENCE: I don't have to stay here.

LAKME: Oh, yes, you do. [*Mock horror*] There is something out there! Grr!

CLARENCE: Not if I can find my clothes I don't.

LAKME: Poor lady, poor Lady Godiva.

CLARENCE: Do you know where they are?

SIGFRID: Pout, pout, pout. Pretty Alice Pout.

CLARENCE: Stop that! I'm not pouting. I'm getting mad. And my name's not Alice.

SIGFRID: Sorry, Joan.

CLARENCE: [*The explosion*] WHERE ARE MY CLOTHES!

SIGFRID: [*Ugly, ugly, ugly*] WHERE'S YOUR SENSE OF HUMOR YOU MEAN!

LAKME: THAT'S WHAT YOU'RE LOOKING FOR!

SIGFRID: YOU CAN'T LIVE WITHOUT A SENSE OF HUMOR! NOT ANYMORE! NOT NOW!

LAKME: DOPE!

SIGFRID: SO WHERE IS IT! HUNH! HUNH! HUNH! [*Quietly, and with a hideous calm*] You've also got a lousy body.

LAKME: Skin and bones.

SIGFRID: [*He means it*] Shut up, Lakme.

CLARENCE: [*Pathetic*] I didn't say you hid them.

SIGFRID: We did, of course.

CLARENCE: I didn't accuse you.

SIGFRID: Maybe you should've. [CLARENCE *makes a sickened, moaning sound.* SIGFRID *continues, almost gently*] You're rather a toad, aren't you?

CLARENCE: I'm . . . I'm just not strong. But I think things!

SIGFRID: Yes, I suppose you do. [*A pause*] What was that word, Clarence?

CLARENCE: [*Almost inaudible*] Despair.

SIGFRID: I can't hear you, Clarence.

CLARENCE: Despair.

SIGFRID: I still can't—

CLARENCE: Despair! *Despair!* DESPAIR! [*He is silent*]

SIGFRID: Very good, Clarence, very good.

RUBY: [*Not breaking this mood*] Shakespeare, Florence, and someone in the park. Two are names and one's a person. Right, Clarence? . . . right?

CLARENCE: [*Numbed*] Right.

A pause; LAKME, SIGFRID, *and* RUBY *are ready now and return to a lighter mood.*

RUBY: Lakme, what's the name of your production?

LAKME: "The Way You Live."

RUBY: The way who lives, dear?

LAKME: Him!

RUBY: Clarence! It's about you. Lakme's entertainment is about you.

LAKME: [*Finishing the arrangements*] Okay. You ready, Sigfrid?

SIGFRID: All set.

RUBY: [*Clapping her hands*] It's beginning, it's beginning! Can you see all right from there, Clarence?

SIGFRID *sits where he can control both the slide projector and the tape recorder,* LAKME *sits at the piano.*

LAKME: "The Way You Live. Clarence Fink: This Is Your Life." Lights! [*All the lights in the room go off except for a dim spot on* CLARENCE, *who sits with his back to the movie screen. Not once will he look at it. Throughout the scene that follows our concentration is on* CLARENCE *live on the hassock and* CLARENCE *on the screen. The voices of* SIGFRID, LAKME, *and* RUBY *are but sounds in the dark.* LAKME *narrates over the musical commentary*] Lakme Productions bring you "The Way You Live" . . . an entertainment conceived, produced, and directed by Lakme Herself. Visuals and audio by Sigfrid Simp. With occasional shrieks, howls, and whoopings by Ruby Rat. Clarence Fink! This is your life!

The picture on the screen comes sharply into focus now: we see CLARENCE *marching along with his poster.*

SIGFRID: There you stand, Clarence Fink. A young man of bold convictions and forthright ideals. Admired . . . loved . . . respected even by all who know you. As you march boldly into the future, wagging your sign behind you . . .

LAKME: Wagging your commitment!

SIGFRID: . . . do you remember, beneath that façade of confidence and bright hope . . . do you remember, Clarence Fink, do you remember this? [*The slide changes to a wretched dwelling*] Ruby!

RUBY: It was a miserable beginning.

SIGFRID *and* LAKME: Aaaaw!

RUBY: Oh yes! The palace had seen better days. The windows all were broken and the great marble floors were cracked and stained. Your mother, good queen Nefertiti, was reduced to taking in dirty linen. [*A rather whorey nude with enormous breasts*] That's her, Sigfrid! That Arab girl you had here last night!

SIGFRID: Olive-skinned. What did I tell you?

LAKME: Will you look at those knockers!

RUBY: Lakme!

LAKME: Sorry.

SIGFRID: Tell us about Clarence, Mrs. Fink. In your very own words. [*Falsetto*] "He was a good boy. Bright, too. Walking at five years, talking at ten. Caught him once doing nasties behind the barn when he was fifteen, but other than that . . . I love him, still do, always will, I s'pose."

RUBY: And your Pa, Old King Cole . . .

SIGFRID *and* LAKME: . . . that merry old soul! . . .

RUBY: . . . was putting on airs! [*A Prince of the Church in all his finery*] Mr. Fink?

SIGFRID: [*Exaggerated basso*] "I'd as soon hit him as spit on him." [*Real voice*] He's a mean man, your daddy. Ruby!

RUBY: Out of such squalor, out of such filth . . . can any good come unto our little Clarence?

SIGFRID *and* LAKME: Yes!

RUBY: You dreamed of a house . . .

LAKME: . . . a beautiful house . . .

SIGFRID: . . . high, high on a hill.

The slide changes to a stately home.

RUBY, SIGFRID, *and* LAKME: Our house!

RUBY: Fa, we simply must have those hedges trimmed.

SIGFRID: And you dreamed of the people in the beautiful house high, high on a hill.

We see RUBY, SIGFRID, *and* LAKME.

RUBY, SIGFRID, *and* LAKME: Us!

SIGFRID: That's a rotten picture of me, Lakme.

RUBY, SIGFRID, *and* LAKME: How to get there? How to meet them? How?

SIGFRID: You came to the big city. It was cold and you were lonely. You drifted, spent hours at the movies, took odd jobs. [*The Radio City Rockettes*] But nothing seemed to last.

RUBY: You were searching . . .

SIGFRID: You were groping . . .

RUBY: He was *searching* . . .

LAKME: For someone . . . something . . .

SIGFRID: For anyone . . . anything . . .

RUBY: In other words . . .

RUBY, SIGFRID, *and* LAKME: COMMITMENT!

Piano fanfare, great applause, the slide changes to SIGFRID *dressed in the collegiate sweater he wore in Act One.*

RUBY: Your salvation was just around the corner . . .

LAKME: . . . your commitment! . . .

RUBY: . . . well, at the curb, actually . . . and you went right over to it. [SIGFRID *and* CLARENCE *talking on the street*] SNAP! And the poor little fishy gobbled up the big bad worm.

SIGFRID: Commitment, thy name is Sigfrid!

Piano fanfare; applause; SIGFRID *and* CLARENCE *outside the house.*

RUBY: Shakespeare, Florence, and someone *from* the park!

Piano fanfare; applause; SIGFRID *and* CLARENCE *going into the house.*

LAKME: There is something out there. We shall prevail! [*Piano fanfare; applause which quickly fades as we see* CLARENCE *by a bed unbuttoning his shirt; gasps, clucking of tongues, etc.*] This is the beginning of the sexy part. I used an F15 lens.

SIGFRID: Clarence Fink, stand up and take a bow!

RUBY *and* LAKME: A committed bow!

The lights on CLARENCE *grow perceptibly brighter. From this point on, the slides are shown more rapidly. The "slide" directions that follow are merely an indication of where we generally are in the sequence.*

RUBY, SIGFRID *and* LAKME: Speech! Speech!

CLARENCE'S RECORDED VOICE: "I'm . . . well I guess slender is the word . . ."

LAKME: See, Clarence? Sight and sound.

CLARENCE *barely responds to the sound of his own voice; his head, shoulders only sag even more.*

CLARENCE'S RECORDED VOICE: "I take after my mother. He's enormous . . . my father is. You should've seen him when he was young. He played football in school."

CLARENCE *with his shirt fully off.*

RUBY: [*Awed by the sight*] Ooooooooooooo!

SIGFRID: Aren't those pectorals something, Ruby? Pret-ty snazzy!

RUBY: These are wonderful pictures, Lakme, just wonderful.

LAKME: Thanks.

CLARENCE'S RECORDED VOICE: "I'd like to have a better build. Broader shoulders, better arms."

RUBY, SIGFRID *and* LAKME: Sweet Clarence. Sweet, sweet, sweet.

CLARENCE *taking off his pants.*

CLARENCE'S RECORDED VOICE: "But you can't have everything. I mean, I've got a fairly good mind. I'm not manual labor, that's for certain. I'll never dig a ditch. And there are worse places than the public library."

CLARENCE *with his pants off.*

RUBY: That's what we always say.

CLARENCE'S RECORDED VOICE: "Sigfrid . . . are you glad I'm here?"

SIGFRID: Sure I'm glad. Why not?

CLARENCE'S RECORDED VOICE: "I'll probably lose my rank for leaving the parade like that. They're very strict. Once you begin a march you're expected to finish it."

RUBY: But you can't worry about these things twenty-four hours a day. Right?

SIGFRID *and* LAKME: Right!

CLARENCE'S RECORDED VOICE: "What if they demote me? I'm a squadron secretary."

SIGFRID: You can be our squadron secretary.

CLARENCE'S RECORDED VOICE: "Oh well, I'll tell them I got sick or something."

RUBY: Or something.

CLARENCE'S RECORDED VOICE: "I doubt if they'll check up on me."

SIGFRID: Now that's what I call commitment!

CLARENCE *taking his socks off.*

LAKME: Clarence wanted to wear his socks to bed.

RUBY: I can see that, dear. Sshh!

SIGFRID: I think it's uncouth to wear one's socks to bed.

RUBY: Well, you! [CLARENCE'S *clothes tidily arranged on a chair*] What's happening now? Where's Clarence?

LAKME: Where do you think?

SIGFRID: Sshh!

CLARENCE'S RECORDED VOICE: "Sigfrid, do you ever get lonely? I mean for someone more than just a friend? . . . "

RUBY: You mean someone in the park, dear.

SIGFRID: He means me.

CLARENCE'S RECORDED VOICE: "Someone you can really be with . . . I do. Sometimes . . . you may think this is silly . . . but sometimes at night I cry about . . . about being lonely . . . [SIGFRID, RUBY, *and* LAKME *begin a steady chant of the word "uncommitted," whispering but steadily growing louder*] At night . . when I can't sleep . . . and that thing is out there . . . I get frightened . . . and I cry . . . I get frightened . . . and I'm lonesome and I cry . . . [SIGFRID *has set the tape recorder at a faster speed,* CLARENCE'S *recorded voice takes on a ridiculous tone*] Maybe I talk too much but . . . I don't feel safe most places . . . I'm nervous . . . I feel cold sort of . . . but not here . . . Oh, no, not here . . . I feel safe here . . . It's warm . . . very, very warm . . . Oh, Sigfrid . . . Sigfrid, Sigfrid, Sigfrid."

LAKME, RUBY, *and* SIGFRID: [*Mimicking in unison*] Oh, Sigfrid . . . Sigfrid, Sigfrid, Sigfrid.

At this moment, which has been building up inside him ever since this sequence began, CLARENCE *stands with an incredible look of pain and terror on his face. At the same instant, his face appears on the screen in close-up with exactly the same expression on it. The two faces should seem to overlap.* CLARENCE *gives an animal howl from the guts and suddenly he has bolted across the room and we hear his footsteps running up the stairs. A moment later we hear the iron door opening. A long silence in the dark room. The only light comes from the slide of* CLARENCE'S *face.*

SIGFRID: [*After a pause, tentative*] Ruby?

RUBY: [*Steel*] He'll be back, Sigfrid. Clarence will be back.

SIGFRID: But maybe he—

RUBY: [*Strong*] Clarence will be back.

CLARENCE'S RECORDED VOICE: "I don't want to ever go home. I could stay heeerrreee fooooorrrrevv—" [*The tape drags to a halt, the lamp in the projector goes out, absolute darkness now*]

SIGFRID: [*After another pause*] Ruby?

RUBY: It was one of the animals, Sigfrid.

SIGFRID: Maybe not.

RUBY: The friends always stay the night, Sigfrid. They never go out there.

SIGFRID: [*A decision*] Lakme, get the flashlight.

RUBY: The light will come back, Sigfrid. It always does.

SIGFRID: I'm going up there.

RUBY: It was one of the animals, Sigfrid.

SIGFRID: We don't know, Ruby. WE DON'T KNOW! [SIGFRID *and* LAKME *rush up the stairs*]

RUBY: Sigfrid! Lakme! Come back here! Don't leave me alone down here! SIGFRID! LAKME! IT WAS ONE OF THE ANIMALS! PLEASE! [*Silence, darkness, the hysteria is mounting*] You miserable . . . you goddamn miserable . . . I WON'T BE LEFT ALONE DOWN HERE! [GRANDFA *enters with a flashlight. He shines it directly into* RUBY's *face. The moment the light hits her, she begins on a hysterical laughing jag*] Murder, Grandfa? . . . would it be murder? . . . if we made him go out there? . . . Grandfa? . . . murder? [GRANDFA *moves the light to the top of the stairs.* SIGFRID *is standing there, carrying* CLARENCE's *body.* RUBY's *laughter builds and builds*] It was one of the animals, Sigfrid. What did I tell you? It was one of the animals. [*The laughter, completely out of control and hysterical, continues.* SIGFRID *is coming slowly down the stairs with* CLARENCE *in his arms. Tableau. The lamp in the slide projector comes back on and once again we see* CLARENCE's *face. The tape recorder starts playing*]

CLARENCE'S RECORDED VOICE: " . . . ever and forever and forever. I don't want to ever go home . . . "

Fast Curtain

ACT III

At rise, the room is again the same. But now the slide of CLARENCE's *face dominates the stage. The picture is enormous, filling the entire rear wall. A person will seem very small standing next to it. Candlelight, black crepe . . . maybe.* FA *is still in his chair, the top of his head or perhaps one arm barely visible to the audience. He snores. There is a coffin: black, stark. It is* CLARENCE's. RUBY *sits, center, rigid, immobile.* SIGFRID *and* GRANDFA *are at opposite sides of the stage, each with his back to her and to each other.* LAKME *stands looking down at* CLARENCE. *It is a formal grouping. After all, the final, grimmest ritual is being played out now. There is a stillness in the room we have not heard before.*

CLARENCE'S RECORDED VOICE: " . . . and that's another reason. Everybody loves somebody . . . or they will . . . sometime in their life. [*A pause*] Anything that makes you want to live so bad you'd . . . you'd die for it . . . Shakespeare, Florence . . . someone in the park. That's what I believe in. That's all. That's the way I live. [*And then, with that foolish giggle in his voice*] Was it all right?"

A long silence. RUBY *rises, moves slowly to the projector and turns it off. The picture of* CLARENCE *fades.*

LAKME: [*Looking down at* CLARENCE] The way his eyes are open . . . just like the dogs' are.

SIGFRID: [*Not turning*] Go to bed, Lakme.

LAKME: I never saw dead before.

SIGFRID: Lakme.

LAKME: People dead.

RUBY: [*Who has moved back to her place center*] No, Clarence, it was not all right. [*Slowly shaking her head*] And that is the lesson of him, Sigfrid. Not the sadness.

LAKME: Just like the dogs' are!

RUBY: [*Controlled, yet with apparent difficulty: she cannot, will not, must not acknowledge* LAKME's *anguish and terror*] We must move now toward some . . . understanding.

LAKME: Ruby, his eyes!

RUBY: [*Blotting that voice out of her consciousness*] The strong have survived . . . the weak have not . . . and what is there more to say.

LAKME: Ruby!

RUBY: [*Gaining in strength, finding it in what she says, at the same time fighting her own emotion*] There are those who remain . . . and those who do not . . . it is that simple. There is strength and there is weakness and there is only they. But oh! such a din there is when they collide! There is trembling . . . there is clamor . . . there is a spasm of the earth. There is struggle. [*And then this keening, lacerating howl*] THERE IS EXULTATION!

LAKME: [*An involuntary cry of terror*] Exultation!

RUBY: And then . . . there is this . . . how it ends . . . the silence This is how the world is. This. And so be it.

GRANDFA: [*Very sad, very low, and very far away*] No.

RUBY: [*Almost to herself*] An understanding. Yes. [*Then, directly to* LAKME] The lesson of Clarence, Lakme. [LAKME *only looks at her with wild, accusing eyes*] The strong have survived . . . the weak have not . . . and what—

LAKME: I don't like dead. I don't like him to be dead.

RUBY: Those who remain . . . and those who do not . . . it—

LAKME: [*Her voice always rising*] I don't want him to be dead. I don't want anyone to be dead . . . ever!

RUBY: [*The façade of strength is cracking*] There is strength and weakness . . . and there's only they!

LAKME: Dead is bad, Ruby . . . you didn't tell us . . . you didn't tell us how bad dead was.

RUBY: [*Faltering*] Those who remain, Lakme! Think of those who remain!

LAKME: [*Unrelenting*] I don't like it . . . dead. I don't like it at all!

RUBY: There is . . . exultation, Lakme!

LAKME: WHY DIDN'T YOU TELL US? WHY DIDN'T YOU TELL US HOW BAD DEAD WAS?

RUBY: [*Breaking, opening her arms to* LAKME] I couldn't . . . not until now . . . now, this night.

LAKME: [*With a sharp cry, rushing into* RUBY'S *arms*] JUST TELL US WHY!

SIGFRID: [*Very low*] Answer her, Ruby . . . answer us.

RUBY: [*Comforting* LAKME *in her lap, her eyes beseeching* SIGFRID *to understand with her*] Some things can't be told, Lakme . . . best not . . . or answered. They just . . . happen.

LAKME: [*Her head buried in* RUBY'S *arms*] Dead? You mean dead?

RUBY: [*Her eyes on* SIGFRID] The silence. And there is only the silence.

LAKME: [*Calmer now*] But Clarence . . . that thing out there . . .

RUBY: [*At once and with strength*] People like Clarence don't need something out there to come to a bad end. [*She must make this point*] People like Clarence don't even need us. They find it on their very own . . . even in broadest daylight . . . under the bluest skies. They sniff it out . . . hunt and scratch for it under every stump and log until they finally dig it up like some rotten truffle. IT IS THEIR PROPENSITY. They are attracted to a shabby, dismal, futile end as surely as . . .

SIGFRID: [*Alone and far away*] We are.

RUBY: Are not, Sigfrid. As surely as we are not. [*She should be at center now*] Consider the Clarences of this world . . . and they are out there . . . just as he was . . . millions upon millions of them . . . no different—not really—from this one . . . consider these Clarences . . . consider them objectively . . . with neither tears nor laughter . . . and you will know this: that no good will come to them.

SIGFRID: [*With a sad smile . . . perhaps*] Objectively. The most important emotion . . . objectivity.

RUBY: They . . . just as he . . . do not understand what we have understood and we have . . . will . . . ARE DETERMINED to survive them. Understand that there is no—

SIGFRID: Shakespeare . . . Florence . . . someone in the park.

RUBY: [*With finality*] Anything. Just . . . US.

GRANDFA: [*Again and always as from afar*] "If they live long and in the end meet the old

course of death, mankind will all turn monsters."

RUBY: And then, there is this, Lakme . . . how it ends . . . the silence.

LAKME: The silence, Ruby.

GRANDFA: [*His voice always the most remote and distant-sounding*] "I'll never care what wickedness I do if this man comes to good."

RUBY *and* LAKME: [*Low, in unison*] This is how the world is. This. And so be it.

GRANDFA: [*Responding with all the force an old man can summon*] NOOOOOOO!

RUBY: [*With quiet strength now; the crisis has passed; only this remains to finish it*] The litany, Sigfrid. Shall we begin now?

SIGFRID: [*Low*] I can't do it, Ruby.

RUBY: After this lesson of Clarence must come our litany of the strong.

SIGFRID: I SAID I CAN'T DO IT.

RUBY: [*With a soft, cruel laugh*] You will, Sigfrid. Sooner or later . . . you must. With me, Lakme. [SIGFRID *still does not, will not turn to her.* LAKME, *however, is kneeling at her feet and looking up at her.* RUBY *has taken a deep breath and now begins a kind of chant*] Fear is not strong.

LAKME: [*With the same cadences*] Fear is not strong.

RUBY: Fear sickens.

LAKME: Fear sickens.

RUBY: Fear corrupts.

LAKME: Fear corrupts.

RUBY: We were not strong . . .

LAKME: We were not strong . . .

SIGFRID: [*Almost feverish*] Words . . . these words! . . .

RUBY: . . . once!

LAKME: . . . once!

SIGFRID: . . . all my life I've heard these words!

RUBY: [*Her voice always rising*] But we have dealt with fear . . .

LAKME: But we have dealt with fear . . .

SIGFRID: [*Turning on and to* RUBY, *trying to shatter the rhythms of the litany*] No! It has dealt with us. Warped . . . maimed . . . MUTILATED!

RUBY: [*At once, in deadly combat*] . . . not succumbed to it.

LAKME: . . . not succumbed to it.

SIGFRID: We have succumbed. We're suffocating with fear.

RUBY: [*Relentless*] But dealt with it.

LAKME: Dealt.

SIGFRID: [*Trying to break through to* LAKME] Don't listen to her.

RUBY: [*Stronger in his moment of weakening*] Because we had to.

LAKME: [*Breaking out of the cadence of the litany: a simple concern for her brother now*] We had to, Sigfrid.

SIGFRID: Close your ears to her!

RUBY: [*Never breaking the cadence of the litany; forcing it, in fact*] Because demands were made on us . . .

LAKME: We agreed, Sigfrid. The three of us. The way we live . . . remember?

SIGFRID: [*Close to the breaking point*] WE ARE NOT LIVING AND WE HAVE MURDERED FOR IT. WHY, RUBY, WHY!

RUBY: Because we could no longer cope with it.

SIGFRID: [*Now*] OURSELVES!!!

RUBY: [*Tremendous*] IT!!! BECAUSE WE COULD NO LONGER COPE WITH IT!!!

LAKME: [*Shrinking*] I'm frightened, Ruby. I'm frightened.

SIGFRID: [*A prayer, a desperate prayer*] Please . . . someone . . . make it stop!

LAKME: Ruby!

SIGFRID: Let it stop.

GRANDFA: [*On the alert, moving in now*] Go on, Sigfrid.

RUBY: [*After blood*] What stop, Sigfrid? Let "what" stop?

SIGFRID: Us . . . everything . . . this . . .

RUBY: What else is there, Sigfrid?

SIGFRID: I DON'T KNOW . . . SOMETHING . . . SOMETHING ELSE. THIS ISN'T ENOUGH.

RUBY: [*Rapping it out*] IT WILL SUFFICE!

SIGFRID: It's a mechanism, the way we live. That's all it is . . . a machine. It runs us. Sitting here . . . night after night . . . pretending—

RUBY: [*Always attacking*] No, Sigfrid, no pretending!

SIGFRID: PRETENDING! Pretending not to feel, not to live. Rituals . . . requiems . . . litanies . . . friends. Devices! Excuses for living. [*Making her*] LOOK AT HIM! LOOK AT CLARENCE! That is the way we live . . . the result of it.

RUBY: [*Making him*] Death, yes! But his! Sigfrid, not ours!

SIGFRID: [*Breaking away from her*] WE DON'T LIVE ANYMORE. WE . . .

GRANDFA: Go on, Sigfrid, finish it.

SIGFRID: [*With a terrible anguish*] WE DO! WE ARE NOT ALIVE DOWN HERE . . . WE ARE!

LAKME: What's Sigfrid doing?

SIGFRID: [*The breath coming in gulps now, harder and harder for him to breathe; convulsive, almost*] This room . . .

LAKME: Is something bad happening?

GRANDFA: Yes! oh thank God, yes!

SIGFRID: This room . . .

RUBY: [*Harsh*] You won't win him, Grandfa. I won't let you.

LAKME: It *is* something bad.

SIGFRID: This roooooom! . . .

GRANDFA: [*At once, hoping* SIGFRID *will turn to him and not* RUBY] Say it, Sigfrid!

SIGFRID: . . . I am safe in this room.

GRANDFA: No, Sigfrid, not safe. Save yourself from it.

RUBY: [*The enemy is* GRANDFA *but never taking her eyes from* SIGFRID *whose back is to both of them*] He can't, Grandfa.

SIGFRID: And there is the need for this room! The need for it.

GRANDFA: [*Insistent, strong*] Ask questions, Sigfrid. There are answers.

RUBY: He already has them!

SIGFRID: This room . . .

GRANDFA: Other answers!

RUBY: Other answers are called Clarences!

SIGFRID: . . . nothing happens in this room. Except us. We happen.

RUBY: [*Always topping him*] And we are the victors, Sigfrid. Remember that.

SIGFRID: [*His voice rising, too*] This room . . .

RUBY: Remember who we are. We are the victors!

SIGFRID: [*Overlapping with her*] . . . there is death in this room!

GRANDFA: Then go out of here. Go up!

RUBY: Down, Sigfrid, our way is down!

SIGFRID: This room . . .

RUBY: [*Picking it up*] There is exultation in this room!

SIGFRID: . . . I AM SUFFOCATING IN THIS ROOM. Suffocating on that presence. There. [*Pointing to* RUBY] That response to that thing without a name. That alternative to looking on its face. That consequence of being down here. That death!

RUBY: [*Rising to her full strength now, overwhelming*] Without me, Sigfrid, without me . . .

SIGFRID: I would be free of all this. I could hope to be free. Dare to.

GRANDFA: [*A Dies Irae voice*] Dare it then, Sigfrid!

SIGFRID *suddenly bolts for the stairs,* RUBY *freezes.*

RUBY: [*Terrified*] Noooo! [*But halfway up the stairs he stops—a silence*] You can't.

GRANDFA: Go on!

RUBY: [*The venom and contempt are mounting again*] There's your fear . . . your sadness . . . your rage. Those stairs and what's beyond them.

SIGFRID: [*Writhing, pitiful*] This room! . . .

GRANDFA: Dare it!

RUBY: Accept!

SIGFRID: . . . I would be out of this room!

RUBY: [*Relentless*] The answer to your questions is down here, Sigfrid. With me! I have that answer. I have become that answer!

SIGFRID: [*His eyes always on the door, wanting to move, but motionless, a command, yet pleading*] Open.

RUBY: [*Using the words like a sledgehammer*] I am your sadness! I am your rage! And yes! yes! I am your fear!

SIGFRID: Open!

GRANDFA: Sigfrid, dare it!

RUBY: But consider, consider how I grow strong! That I remain right! That I triumph!

SIGFRID: [*Coming to a climax*] Open!

GRANDFA: [*The same*] Dare it!

RUBY: [*The same*] I AM OUR STRENGTH.

SIGFRID: OPEN!

RUBY: I AM OUR LOGIC!

SIGFRID: OPEN!!!!

RUBY: I AM OUR TRIUMPH—! [*Her mighty howl withers into a stifled moan. SIGFRID has bolted up the stairs and thrown open the door. There is an immediate, terrible silence. RUBY and LAKME freeze. Even GRANDFA winces with fear. Only SIGFRID, at the top of the stairs, his back to us, moves: his entire body heaves as he gulps in the outside air. A very long silence*]

SIGFRID: [*Turning back into the room*] We are . . . outside, Ruby.

RUBY: [*Staring straight ahead, never at the door*] Yes.

Silence.

SIGFRID: I . . . did it, Grandfa.

GRANDFA: [*The same as RUBY*] I know.

Silence.

SIGFRID: Are you . . . cold, Lakme?

LAKME: Ruby . . . Ruby's shivering.

SIGFRID: I know. [*Silence*] We are outside then. [*Silence*] Nothing.

GRANDFA: Nothing.

SIGFRID: Nothing.

LAKME: Ruby's shivering.

RUBY: [*A moan*] Close . . . please close.

SIGFRID: It's dark out here . . . all stillness . . . no sounds at all.

GRANDFA: Yes.

SIGFRID: I thought there would be . . .

GRANDFA: What?

SIGFRID: Something.

RUBY: [*Again*] Cloooose!

SIGFRID: [*Dawning on him*] The fence.

LAKME: [*Trying to soothe her*] Poor Ruby . . . poor.

SIGFRID: We have no need of a fence. [*Low, but decisive*] Lakme. [*She turns from RUBY and looks up at him*] Turn off the fence.

LAKME: The . . . ?

SIGFRID: [*Calm*] Off . . . yes.

LAKME: [*Recoiling*] But . . .

SIGFRID: [*Terrifying*] OFF! [*LAKME obeys, then goes quickly back to her place with RUBY, the room will seem even stiller than it did before*] Yes . . . now.

And at once there is a rapid, rustling sound: almost like the beating of wings, but not specifically that, it grows loud quickly and passes quickly.

SIGFRID: [*In the silence that follows*] Grandfa?

GRANDFA: I don't know, Sigfrid.

SIGFRID: It . . . passed . . . us.

GRANDFA: Yes.

SIGFRID: Will it . . . ?

The sound again: louder, more terrifying than before; no one moves.

RUBY: [*Trying to drown out that sound*] NOOO-OOOOO! [*Sharp silence*] Are we still . . . ?

SIGFRID: Yes, Ruby.

RUBY: . . . out there?

SIGFRID: Yes.

RUBY: [*As if she's been punched in the stomach*] Ooooh!

SIGFRID: [*Going to her now*] And you will look with me. Give me your hand. [*Grabs her wrist*] The victors are not afraid. Together they will look. [*Leading her toward the door*]

RUBY: No, Sigfrid!

SIGFRID: [*Unrelenting, a momentum of cruelty building*] The strong have survived, the weak have not and what is there more to say? LOOK.

RUBY: [*Trying to break away*] Sigfrid!

SIGFRID: [*Forcing her to stand with him before the door*] There is strength and there is weakness and there is only they. LOOK.

RUBY: I will not!

SIGFRID: The survival of the strong. It is that simple. LOOK.

RUBY: I have looked!

SIGFRID: [*Brutal*] THEN LOOK AGAIN. WE ARE THE VICTORS NOW AND TOGETHER WE SHALL LOOK AT WHAT IS OUT THERE!

RUBY: NOOOOOOOOOO!

They break apart; there is a pause.

SIGFRID: [*Very low*] The survival of . . . the strong.

LAKME: [*A concern for* RUBY] Sigfrid—

SIGFRID: [*In command now, exercising it*] I WILL NOT CLOSE.

LAKME: I'm frightened, too!

SIGFRID: [*Cruel*] I WILL NOT! [*Playing with them*] Except for . . .

LAKME: Who?

RUBY: Whoooooooo?

SIGFRID: [*Simply*] Clarence.

RUBY: [*At once*] Ask him, Clarence!

LAKME: Clarence is . . .

SIGFRID: [*Howling it*] DEAD! [*Manic*] Then what did Sigfrid mean by that?

A new sound now—it could be the wind, or it might be a moan: human, animal, something in pain; low at first, then rising.

GRANDFA: The wind.

SIGFRID: Something. [*A beat, then very softly*] "For he's a jolly good fellow, for he's a jolly—" Sing with me! "For he's a jolly good fellow." SING! [*He is standing over* RUBY *and* LAKME *now, shouting out the song*] "For he's a—!" WITH ME! SING! [*A crescendo of sound, then sharp silence*] Sigfrid's shivering . . . warm him . . . please . . . warm.

RUBY: I . . . am . . . alone.

LAKME: Me, too . . . me, too.

SIGFRID: [*Looking down on* CLARENCE] What did you want from me, Clarence who was so simple for us? . . . who stumbled against the fence and did not go out there? . . . who could have told us something? . . . who was pointless? Simple, stumbling, pointless Clarence . . . WHAT!

RUBY: It . . . is . . . dark . . . here.

LAKME: Yes . . . yes.

SIGFRID: He feels your hand, Clarence. It's cold, Clarence. Dead, Clarence.

RUBY: It . . . is . . . silent . . here.

LAKME: [*Her arms around* RUBY] I'm here, Ruby . . . I'm here.

SIGFRID: Someone in the park is very cold now. He was always warm until you came here . . . He wrote a poem once. He was . . . like you. Warm him then . . . please . . . warm. Someone who wrote a poem.

GRANDFA: [*Who has come over to* SIGFRID *and put his hand on* SIGFRID'S *shoulder*] Sigfrid—!

SIGFRID: [*Tremendous*] I HAVE OPENED AND YOU MUST WARM ME!

LAKME: [*Scarcely daring*] Ruby, are we . . . ?

RUBY: [*Toneless*] Yes.

LAKME: . . . dying?

SIGFRID: Shakespeare . . . Florence . . . and someone in the park.

GRANDFA: Yes.

SIGFRID: Anything that makes you want to live so bad you'd die for it.

GRANDFA: Yes.

SIGFRID: Die . . . for us, Clarence.

GRANDFA: [*Gently*] Sigfrid.

SIGFRID: [*Sudden, ugly*] DIE FOR US! [*The breath coming harder now*] You said men could change things. You believed that. Then change this. Change now. Change or tell me to close!

GRANDFA: I can't.

SIGFRID: [*Turning on* GRANDFA] Then what, Grandfa? What was that word if he couldn't change? That word we made him say?

GRANDFA: Despair.

SIGFRID: [*His voice rising*] I can't hear you.

GRANDFA: [*Low*] Despair.

SIGFRID: You're shouting!

GRANDFA: Despair.

SIGFRID: YOU'RE BREAKING MY EARDRUMS!

GRANDFA: [*Almost inaudible*] Despair. Despair. Despair.

SIGFRID: [*Keening*] DESPAIR! There was warmth in our despair. And none, none in his. Tell me to close!

GRANDFA: [*Sudden, lacerating*] I WILL NOT DESPAIR! [*Enormous; it is the most important—the only point really—that he can make*] IT'S OUT THERE FOR ALL OF US. [*A silence; he has been heard*] It's out there for all of us.

SIGFRID: Then what's the point of going on with it?

GRANDFA: To stand up to it!

SIGFRID: From a wheelchair?

GRANDFA: Does there have to be a point to everything? Is that what men insist upon these days?

SIGFRID: [*In spite of himself*] I suppose not, Grandfa. I suppose not if you're nine thousand years old and you're standing up to it sitting down in a wheelchair. Then I suppose there doesn't have to be a point to anything. [*A pause; then low, very low*] Even dying.

RUBY: [*Low, gasping*] Finish it, Sigfrid, finish it then.

SIGFRID: You're a Clarence, Grandfa. That's who you are. Clarence thought he could change things. Clarence even thought he could change us. Wasn't that sweet of him, Grandfa? And wasn't that sad. Sweet Clarence, sweet Grandfa. Sad Clarence, sad Grandfa. He couldn't do it, Grandfa. And neither can you. Things are the way they are. We are the way we are. Look what it took Clarence to find out he couldn't change anything . . . most of all himself. He stomped all over town . . . stomp, stomp, stomp . . . bells ringing, banners waving . . . his own little children's crusade . . . ta ta ta ta ta! Wanting to change things. And all he accomplished was this. Why, he didn't even accomplish me. [*The viciousness, the hysteria are mounting now*] I buggered him, Grandfa. I buggered him good. We can't have buggered saints, now can we, Grandfa? We're sorry, Clarence, but your bid for martyrdom has been rejected. It was a real good try, baby, but you just didn't have the stuff. This is the court of last resort down here and you and your ideals . . . your buggered ideals . . . have been found lacking. They lack the substance, they lack the granite, they lack the simple facts of life. The facts of you! AND I WILL CLOSE! [*And with a cry he has rushed up the stairs and slammed shut the mighty door. All external sounds cease at once.* RUBY *begins heaving great breaths. She is coming back to life . . . inflating, like a balloon.* SIGFRID, *from the top of the stairs, without pause and not breaking the tempo and emotion of the preceding speech, continues*] Yes, we're horrible. We have made that choice. This house is horrible. But none have built a stronger one. The way we live is horrible. Then teach us your way. But don't send us this for an answer . . . don't send us a Clarence. It simply won't do. And know this first . . . before you send us another Clarence . . . AND THERE WILL BE MORE OF THEM . . . know! Know this horribleness. Know this room without windows. Know Clarence who does not move. Know Fa who meant nothing. Know that thing out there without a name. Know us. KNOW! [*And now, facing full front, his fists clenched*] All right, Ruby! We may resume now! [*He has begun the litany*] With hands!

RUBY: [*New strength surging in her*] Ah!

SIGFRID: . . . with mind! . . .

GRANDFA: [*Low, his head bowed*] No, Sigfrid.

SIGFRID: [*Relentless, moving down a step with each phrase of it*] . . . with passion! We have managed an existence!

RUBY *and* LAKME: [*Picking it up now*] An existence!

SIGFRID: . . . an arrangement . . .

RUBY *and* LAKME: . . . an arrangement . . .

SIGFRID: . . . an arrangement that works . . .

RUBY *and* LAKME: Yes!

SIGFRID: . . . something for us!

RUBY *and* LAKME: Us!

SIGFRID, RUBY, *and* LAKME: We have done that . . .

SIGFRID: [*Almost to the very front of the stage now*] . . . done that . . .

SIGFRID, RUBY, *and* LAKME: AND WE HAVE SURVIVED YOU!

These last words were very loud: shouted almost. Now there is a sharp silence. No one moves. There should be the suggestion of a tableau. The movement looks and feels like the end of the play. A long pause. Then RUBY, *abruptly breaking this mood, crosses the stage and turns on the overhead lights. After so much darkness, the room seems unbearably bright.*

RUBY: [*At once, her old self: all energy and triumph restored now, as if the preceding had never happened*] Your *viola da gamba* lesson, Lakme. Is it tomorrow or the day after? I can never remember which.

LAKME: [*A dead voice*] Tomorrow. The day after. I don't know.

RUBY: Put something on the phonograph. Something exhilarating. "La Grand Messe de Morts" should do very nicely. [LAKME *does not move*] I understand the Libyans are agitating for land reforms. Or isn't that what they're saying? It's so difficult to keep up these days . . . turmoil under every bushel. Bushel basket, Lakme. Bushel basket? [*No response; silence*] I am an admirer of the works of Miss Jane Austen. In rereading . . . oh, you know that book . . . I was struck by the similarity of her writing to the music of Mozart. Each so precise, so balanced . . . so controlled, that's the word! Don't you think so? Sigfrid? [*No response; silence*] Grandfa! Will you favor us with one of your dramatic recitations? And may I suggest the Richard II deposition scene? It should have particular significance for you this evening.

GRANDFA: [*Who has never taken his eyes off* SIGFRID, *even though* SIGFRID *has his back to him*] There was a time, Sigfrid—

SIGFRID: [*Without turning*] Was. I was choking on that word. The time is. I am.

RUBY: [*Still with* GRANDFA, *trying to end his exchange with* SIGFRID] No? An old trouper like you passing up an opportunity for a gala farewell performance? *Ein kleiner Schwanengesang?* Grandfa!

GRANDFA: [*Still to* SIGFRID, *quiet anger*] It didn't mean anything to give in to it like this.

SIGFRID: It meant a lot, Grandfa. It meant Ruby is right. It meant Clarence is dead. It means we are down here.

GRANDFA: [*Harsh*] I'm down here, too!

SIGFRID: [*Simply*] Yes.

RUBY: [*Alone, restless, inner tension building*] What shall we do now? No music, Grandfa won't recite, *les enfants sont* sulking . . . look at Clarence the rest of the night? [*And somewhere, in the nethermost regions of the theatre, there sounds a faint, dull thump. Silence. No one moves. All eyes go to the door and hold there. A quiet terror. A pause. And again that sound, ever so slightly louder.* LAKME *has begun to move slowly out of the room.* RUBY *is abstracted, looking at the door, yet wanting to hold* LAKME *close to her*] Lakme! [*Opens her arms to her but* LAKME *does not come*]

LAKME: I wish . . .

RUBY: I know.

LAKME: [*She means this*] I wish we hadn't done this tonight.

RUBY: [*Who must ignore this*] Now say goodbye to Grandfa. He won't be here in the morning.

LAKME *crosses to* GRANDFA.

LAKME: [*Simply*] Grandfa. [*He does not look at her*] We'll miss you. And I hope you'll be very happy wherever it is you're going. I hope— [*Turning wildly on all of them*] I HOPE YOU DIE ON THAT FARM! I HOPE WE ALL DIE! [*She is gone. Brief silence. And again the thump. Each time a little louder, a little closer*]

RUBY: Sigfrid? [*He looks at her*] Nothing.

SIGFRID: What, Ruby?

RUBY: Nothing. [SIGFRID *is moving out of the room now*] Sigfrid! [*He turns*] Please.

SIGFRID: It's late.

RUBY: Just a little while longer.

The thump. It is becoming increasingly difficult not to acknowledge it.

SIGFRID: [*Alone, remote, as they all are now, his eyes fastened on the invisible rooms above them*] There is a room up there with a bed in it. My bed. My bed before . . . this.

GRANDFA: [*Low, almost toneless, reading from his Chronicle*] "Sky, a blue sky, the eagle soars."

RUBY: [*By herself, at center, hoping against hope the thump will not sound again*] Sigfrid, do you remember when—

The thump.

SIGFRID: I had a quilt on that bed . . . a quilt with calico patches. Every night . . . even the very coldest . . . I would sleep with the windows open. They were that warm . . . my bed and my quilt with the calico patches.

GRANDFA: "High soars, high soars the eagle."

The thump, still louder, more compelling, more terrifying.

RUBY: [*The terror mounting*] Make it stop, Sigfrid!

SIGFRID: And I would dream . . . real dreams. I would dream of Persia and flying carpets and every far-off place I'd ever read of.

GRANDFA: "Can I soar? Can I soar, too?"

SIGFRID: I *could* dream of them under my quilt with the calico patches all snuggled deep in my soft warm bed.

GRANDFA: "For my longing is as great."

A terrifically loud thump; each of them, in his fashion, starts perceptibly.

SIGFRID: WE ARE CLOSED! [*Pause*] And we will never open . . . again . . .

GRANDFA: [*Very low, closing the Chronicle*] "For my longing is as great."

Silence. And then yet another thump. It is loud, very loud. It is a moment before the sound fades away.

RUBY: [*In the silence that follows*] Sigfrid? [*He looks at her, but she will not acknowledge what she has just heard*] Nothing.

SIGFRID: What, Ruby?

RUBY: Nothing! [*He turns from her and is on his way out*] Sigfrid! [*He stops but does not turn to her*] Five minutes? [*He starts to go again*] SIGFRID! [*Again he stops, but again he does not turn to her*] What will become of us?

SIGFRID: [*After a moment*] Nothing.

RUBY: No?

SIGFRID: We will continue.

And again the thump.

RUBY: Yes?

SIGFRID: Ask Clarence. [*He is going*] We will continue. [*He is gone. The thump.* RUBY *and* GRANDFA *are alone*]

RUBY: We will continue. Did you hear that, Grandfa? Sigfrid said we will continue. [*The thump.* GRANDFA *has begun and will continue to very slowly tear the pages, one by one, from the Chronicle*] And that nothing will happen to us. Ask Clarence, he said. [*The thump, each time a little louder now*] But Clarence doesn't have anything to say. Clarence is dead. [*The thump*] Then what did Sigfrid mean by that? [*The thump; then, like lightning*] I AM NOT A STUPID PERSON. WHAT OTHER ALTERNATIVES WERE THERE? [*The thump*] We are eagles, Grandfa, we are. We have, you see, some stature. We are not little people. We are not pathetic people. There is something heroic about us. [*The thump*] WE ARE SAFE. DOWN HERE WE ARE SAFE. [*The thump*] Ask Clarence? I have nothing to ask Clarence. I'll tell him. Tell him something he should have known. For all his talk about commitment, we were, after all, as it turned out, the committed ones. We were. [*The thump*] IT WILL PASS. THIS THING WILL PASS US BY. [*The thump*] You see, Clarence, we, too, have taken a stand against these things, only we have acted on it. We have acted accordingly. We are no longer life-size. We are larger than you. We have transcended— [*An enormous THUMP; she falters, then forces herself to continue*] We have survived everything and we shall survive now this night. We are prepared for now this night. Our lives were meant for it. It is our meaning. We are vindicated . . . now this night . . . finally . . . totally . . . we are vindicated now this night! [*The thud; terrifying, overwhelming, crushing, like a hard punch in the stomach; no reverberations; a dull, hard, crunching thud*] SIGFRID SAID WE WILL CONTINUE! . . . WE . . . WILL . . . CONTINUE! [*And again that devastating sound. And now silence, a very long one.* GRANDFA *lets the pages of the Chronicle fall from his lap and begins a slow, slow exit. Without moving, numbed and toneless,* RUBY *continues*] Grandfa? [THUMP] Sigfrid? [*THUMP*] Lakme? [*THUMP*] Fa? [*THUMP*] No one? . . . No one! . . . NO ONE! [*THUMP. THUMP. THUMP*]. *A very, very long silence.* SIGFRID *and* LAKME *come slowly into the room. They stop at the door and look at* RUBY. *No one moves. Silence. THUMP. Silence.* RUBY *has moved almost somnambulistically to the tape recorder. The wheels are spinning.*

RUBY'S RECORDED VOICE: ". . . who thought they were to prevail. We shall *not* prevail . . . so be it. [*THUMP*] We shall *not* endure . . . [*THUMP*] . . . but who was ever meant to? [RUBY *is walking slowly back to her place in the center of the room*] And we shall *not* inherit the earth . . . it has already disinherited us. [*THUMP. THUMP.* RUBY *sits. Staring*

straight ahead, not looking at them, she extends one hand each to* SIGFRID *and* LAKME *who come forward and sit one to each side of her. They do not move*] If we are without faith, we find our way in the darkness . . . it is light enough. [*THUMP*] If we are without hope, we turn to our despair . . . [*THUMP*] . . . it has its own consolations. And if we are without charity, we suckle the bitter root of its absence . . . wherefrom we shall draw the sustenance to destroy you. Go . . . seek not to know us . . . to understand . . . the compassion of it will exhaust you and there is so little strength left us now . . . so little. [RUBY, SIGFRID, *and* LAKME *never move. Even their eyes do not move. They stare straight ahead and nothing more. The lights are beginning to fade*] Spoken by me this December morning. Unwitnessed, unheard, alone."

The Thump. Silence. No one moves. The Thump. Silence. The Thump. Fa snortles. The Thump. Silence. The THUMP. *And silence. The stage is completely dark.* THE THUMP.

Curtain

SOUND NOTES

Act One: The buzzer should be loud, harsh, rasping. An extremely unpleasant sound.

Act Two: The music from Bellini's *Norma* can be found on any of several complete commercial recordings of the opera. Florence Foster Jenkins' recording of the "Queen of the Night" aria is available on "The Glory??? of the Human Voice," RCA Victor long-playing record LM2597.

Act Three: The thumps must have real "presence." The actors must be able to play with and against them. In various productions they have been achieved with a prepared tape, with a recording of a heartbeat or by experimenting with a live microphone. The acoustics and sound equipment of a particular theatre will usually determine which method to follow. The main thing is to make them convincing.

MOTEL

a masque for three dolls

Jean-Claude van Itallie

Motel was first presented under the title *America Hurrah* by Ellen Stewart at the Cafe La Mama ETC, New York City, as half of a double bill with *Pavane,* a fugue for eight actors, also by the author, on April 28, 1965, with the following cast:

MOTEL-KEEPER DOLL .... *Cheryl Kilgren*
MAN DOLL .... *John Mintun*
WOMAN DOLL .... *Fay Chaiken*
MOTEL-KEEPER'S VOICE .... *Heidi Zimmerli*

It was directed by Michael Kahn. Designed by Robert Wilson; doll's bodies created by Tania Leontov; music by Jean-Jacques Perret; lighting by John Dodd.

Motel was subsequently presented by Stephanie Sills Productions, Inc., at the Pocket Theatre, New York City, as one third of a bill, *America Hurrah,* with *Interview** and *TV* also by the author, on November 6, 1966, with the following cast:

DOLLS .... *Conrad Fowkes, James Barbosa, Brenda Smiley and Joyce Aaron* (alternate evenings)
MOTEL-KEEPER'S VOICE .... *Ruth White*

It was directed by Jacques Levy. Incidental music by Marianne du Pury and Fred Cantor. Lighting by Ken Glickfeld and James Dwyer; costumes by Tania Leontov, assisted by Beckie Cunningham.

* Formerly titled *Pavane.*

". . . after all our subtle colour and nervous rhythm, after the faint mixed tints of Conder, what more is possible? After us the Savage God."

—YEATS

Light will come upon the room very slowly. It will increase in whiteness to the point of fluorescent glare by the time the dolls enter.

During this dawning a woman's voice will be heard, coming from any place in the theatre, and not necessarily from any one place continually. The voice will at first be mellow, mellow and husky. As the light grows harsher and brighter so the voice will grow older, more set in its pattern, hard finally, and patronizing and petty.

WOMAN'S VOICE: I am an old idea. Gaia I have been, and Lilith. I am an old idea. Lilly, Molly, Gaia; the walls of the stream that from which it springs forth. The nothing they enclose with walls, making then a place from which it springs forth, in which it happens, in which they happen too. I am that idea: the place, the walls, the room. A Roman theatre: roofless stone place where the heat of the sun and the cheers of the people break loose the fangs of the lion. There was that room too, a railroad carriage in the Forest of Compiègne, in 1918 and again in 1941. There have been rooms of marble and rooms of cork, all letting forth an avalanche. Rooms of mud, rooms of silk. Within which they happen. There is another room here. And it too will be slashed as if by a scimitar, its balconies shuddered, its contents spewed and yawned out. What walls it has will be unsquared, the room tumbriled, its cornices broken. That is what happens. It is almost happening in fact. This is my room too. I made it. I am this room. It's a nice room, not so fancy as some, but with all the conveniences. And a touch of home. The antimacassar comes from my mother's house in Boise. Boise, Idaho. Sits kind of nice, I think, on the Swedish swing. That's my own idea you know. All modern, up to date, that's it—no motel on this route is more up to date. Or cleaner. Go look, then talk me a thing or two. All modern here, but, as I say, with the tang of home. Do you understand? When folks are fatigued, in a strange place? Not that it's old-fashioned. No. Not in the wrong way. There's a button-push here for TV. The toilet flushes of its own accord. All you've got to do is get off. Pardon my mentioning it, but you'll have to go far before you see a thing like that on this route. Oh, it's quite a room. Yes. And reasonable. Sign here. Pardon the pen leak. I can see you're fatigued. Any children? Well, that's nice. Children don't appreciate travel. And rooms don't appreciate children. As it happens it's the last one I've got left. I'll just flip my vacancy switch. Twelve dollars please. In advance that'll be. That way you can go any time you want to go, you know, get an early start. On a trip to see sights, are you? That's nice. You just get your luggage while I go unlock the room. You can see the light.

The MOTEL-KEEPER *enters through the door. It is a large doll, slightly larger than human size, though not a giantess. The dancers will be inside the dolls. Their movements will have the quality of ritual, their fascination will be that of a dance or a machine: strictly controllable, humorous sometimes, but increasingly violent and disturbing. The* MOTEL-KEEPER *doll is predominantly gray, feminine, with square breasts and a triangular skirt. On its mask it wears large square eyeglasses which are mirrors. It doesn't matter what these mirrors reflect at any given moment. The audience may occasionally catch a glimpse of itself, or be bothered by reflections of light. It doesn't matter; the sensory nerves of the audience are not to be spared. It may be more feasible for the* MOTEL-KEEPER'S *voice to continue coming from a loudspeaker, with accompanying rhythmic jaw motions on the part of the doll.*

MOTEL-KEEPER'S VOICE: There now. What I say doesn't matter. You can see. It speaks for itself. The room speaks for itself. You can see it's a perfect 1966 room. But a taste of home. I've seen to that. A taste of home. [*She turns down the covers on the double bed*] Comfy, cozy, nice, but a taste of newness. That's what. You can see it. [*She snaps up the shades. There are neon lights outside*] The best stop on route six sixty-six. Well, there might be others like it, but this is the best stop. You've arrived at the right place. This place. And a hooked rug. I don't care what but I've said no room is without a hooked rug. [*She centers the rug*] No complaints yet. Never. [*The* WOMAN *doll enters. It is the same size as the* MOTEL-KEEPER. *Its shoulders are thrown way back, like a girl posing for a calendar ad. Its breasts are wiggleable. It has glamorous blonde hair and a cherry-lipstick smile. Its clothes, real clothes these, are those of a young married woman. The* WOMAN *doll goes directly to the bathroom and doesn't shut the door. There is absolutely no rapport between the other dolls and the* MOTEL-KEEPER. *The other dolls do not ever stop what they are doing, and they are perpetually doing something. The* MOTEL-KEEPER *is sometimes still and sometimes ambulates in circles. But all her remarks are directed generally; she is never motivated by the actions of other dolls*] Modern people like modern places. Oh, yes. I can tell. They tell me. And reasonable. Very very reasonable rates. No cheaper rates on the route, not for this. You receive what you pay for. [*The toilet flushes*] All that driving and driving and driving. Fatigued. You must be. I would be. Miles and miles and miles. [*The toilet flushes again*] Fancy. Fancy your ending up right here. You didn't know and I didn't know. But you did. End up right here. Respectable and decent and homelike. Right here. [*The* MAN *doll enters carrying suitcases. He is the same size as the others. His clothes are real and vulgar, unremarkable*] All folks everywhere sitting in the very palm of God. Waiting, whither, whence. [*The* MAN *doll begins an inspection of the bed. The* WOMAN *doll comes rapidly from the bathroom, opens one of the suitcases, and messily rummages for toilet articles with which she returns to the bathroom*] Any motel you might have come to on six sixty-six. Any motel. On that vast network of roads. Whizzing by, whizzing by. Trucks too. And cars from everywhere. Full up with folks, all sitting in the very palm of God. I can tell proper folks when I get a look at them. All folks. [*The* MAN *doll pulls at the coverlet in every direction, testing its strength. He begins to jump on every part of the mattress*] Country roads, state roads, United States roads. It's a big world and here you are. I noticed you got a license plate. I've not been to there myself. I've not been to anywhere myself, excepting Town for supplies, and Boise. Boise, Idaho. [*The* MAN *doll is now jumping heavily on the mattress*] The world arrives to me, you'd say. It's a small world. These plastic flowers here: "Made in Japan" on the label. You noticed? Got them from the catalogue. Cat-a-logue. Every product in this room is ordered. [*Pieces of the* WOMAN *doll's clothing are thrown from the bathroom*] Ordered from the catalogue. Excepting the antimacassar and the hooked rug. Made the hooked rug myself. Tang of home. No room is a room without. 'Course the bedspread, hand-hooked, hooked near here at Town. Mrs. Harritt. Betsy Harritt gets materials through another catalogue. Cat-a-logue. [*Now toilet articles and fixtures from the bathroom follow the clothing. The* WOMAN *doll returns, without clothes. She applies more lipstick to her lips and nipples— her breasts are obscenely huge. The* MAN *doll takes off his trousers*] Myself, I know it from the catalogue: bottles, bras, breakfasts, refrigerators, cast-iron gates, plastic posies, paper subscriptions, Buick trucks, blankets, forks, clitter-clack darning hooks, transistors and antimacassars, vinyl plastics, [*The* WOMAN *doll blots her lipstick on the walls. The* MAN *doll strikes at objects in the room with a cigar*] crazy quilts, paper hairpins, cats, catnip, club feet, canisters, bannisters, holy books, tattooed

toilet articles, tables, tea cozies, [*On the wall the* MAN *doll writes simple obscenities with his cigar. She does the same with her lipstick*] pickles, bayberry candles. South Dakotan kewpie dolls, fiberglass hair, polished milk, amiable grandpappies, colts, Galsworthy books, cribs, cabinets, teeter-totters, [*The* MAN *and* WOMAN *dolls have turned to picture-making. They work together; he with his cigar, her filling in with her lipstick*] and television sets. [*The* MOTEL-KEEPER *doll turns on the television set, which eventually starts glaring*] Oh, I tell you it, I do. It's a wonder. Full with things, the world, full up. Shall I tell you my thought? Next year there's a shelter to be built by me, yes. Shelter motel. Everything to be placed under the ground. Signs up in every direction up and down six sixty-six. "Complete Security," "Security While You Sleep Tight," "Bury Your Troubles at This Motel," "Homelike, Very Comfy, and Encased in Lead," "Every Room Its Own Set," "Fourteen Day Emergency Supplies $5.00 Extra," [*The* MAN *doll pushes the TV button with his cigar, and the TV plays the twist. The* MAN *and* WOMAN *dolls twist*] "Self-Contained Latrine Waters," "Filters, Counters, Periscopes and Mechanical Doves," "Hooked Rugs," "Dearest Little Picture Frames for Loved Ones (Made in Japan)," through the catalogue. Cat-a-logue. You can pick items and products: cablecackles (so nice), cuticles, twice-twisted combs with corrugated calesthenics, meat-beaters, fish tackles, bug bombs, [*The* MOTEL-KEEPER'S *voice is slowly drowned out by the twist music. The* MAN *and* WOMAN *dolls, moving ever more rapidly, tear the bedspread in two, tear the rug, and smash the framed prints on the wall. A civil defense siren's noise starts to build up*] toasted terracotta'd Tanganyikan switch blades, ocher closets, Ping-Pong balls, didies, capricorn and cancer prognostics, crackers, total uppers, stickpins, basting tacks . . .

(*The* MOTEL-KEEPER'S VOICE *is drowned out by the other sounds—siren and music—which have built to a deafening pitch and come from all parts of the theatre. The door opens again and headlights shine into the eyes of the audience.*

The actor inside the MOTEL-KEEPER *doll has slipped out of it.*

The MAN *and* WOMAN *dolls tear off the head of the* MOTEL-KEEPER *doll, then throw her body aside.*

Then, one by one, the MAN *and* WOMAN *dolls leave the motel room and walk down the aisle. Fans blow air through the débâcle on stage onto the audience.*

After an instant more of excruciatingly loud noise: blackout and silence.

It is suggested that the actors do not take a bow after this play.)

BIRDBATH

a play in one act

Leonard Melfi

Birdbath was first presented by Theatre Genesis at St. Mark's Church-in-the-Bowery, New York City, on June 11, 1965, with the following cast:

FRANKIE BASTA .... *Kevin O'Connor*

VELMA SPARROW .... *Barbara Young*

It was directed by Ralph Cook.

It was subsequently presented by Theodore Mann and Paul Libin with the Circle-in-the-Square at the Martinque Theatre, New York City, as part of the bill, *Six from La Mama,* on April 11, 1966, with the following cast:

FRANKIE BASTA .... *Kevin O'Connor*

VELMA SPARROW .... *Mari-Claire Charba*

It was directed by Tom O'Horgan.

THE PEOPLE OF THE PLAY

FRANKIE BASTA, *a poet in his late twenties.*

VELMA SPARROW, *twenty-six, a nervous and troubled young lady who is a rapid speaker and sometimes trembles.*

WHERE THEY ARE

New York City: a midtown cafeteria, the streets outside, and FRANKIE'S *basement apartment.*

WHEN

Contemporary: a night in February. The action is continuous.

Hazy music coming from a piped-in system. The curtain rises. We are in a garishly lit cafeteria. To our right we see FRANKIE BASTA *behind the cash booth before the cash register. He lights a cigarette, eyes his wristwatch, and then begins to read a book.*

To our left we see VELMA SPARROW. *She is clearing off a table in her working area. As she wipes the surface we are aware of her delicate, slow and easy nature, fused together with strange anxiety. Every so often she gives a quick look over at* FRANKIE. *He, in turn, does the same thing. But their eyes never meet. They never catch each other. It is almost as though they both know the precise moment when to steal their brief glances without being noticed. This little "game of glances" goes on for about two minutes before they are finally caught staring at each other, both face to face. There is a pause wherein they both seem semimesmerized, as they both continue to stare at each other.*

FRANKIE: Hi.

VELMA: Hi.

FRANKIE: How are you doing?

VELMA: [*Shrugging*] Okay . . . I guess. [*She goes back to her work;* FRANKIE *goes back to his book. Going over to him*] What's your name?

FRANKIE: [*Looking up*] Frankie. What's yours?

VELMA: Velma.

FRANKIE: I'm glad to meet you, Velma.

VELMA: Likewise, I'm sure. [FRANKIE *smiles*] You jist started workin' here tonight, didn't you?

FRANKIE: Yeah. That's right.

VELMA: And you don't like it, do you?

FRANKIE: How can you tell that?

VELMA: By the way you look.

FRANKIE: How's that?

VELMA: Well, first of all, if you don't mind my sayin' so, you jist don't look like you belong in a lousy place like this. I think you look pretty

high-class to me. My mother would really go for you.

FRANKIE: Yeah? How old is your old lady—I mean your mother?

VELMA: [*Giggling*] Oh, I didn't mean that way, Frankie! Now you got me blushin'. My face is red, huh? If my mother was here she'd really be blushin'. What I meant to say was she'd think you were jist *right* . . .

FRANKIE: Right for what?

VELMA: I . . . I . . . oh, I don't know how to say it. Forget it . . . I guess. But do you know what, Frankie?

FRANKIE: [*Kindly*] What's that, Velma?

VELMA: Well, I used to be real skinny, you know what I mean? I used to be all bones, almost like one of them skeletons. But since I been workin' here for Mr. Quincy, well, I've been puttin' on some weight. [*She pauses*] That's why, in a way, this job isn't really that bad—because of the free meal they let you have. My mother said to me, "Velma, you take advantage of that free meal. You eat as much as you can . . . when something's free you make use of it . . . take as much as they let you have." And so, I've been eating pretty good lately, and Mr. Quincy, he's a nice man, he never tells me that I'm eating too much. In fact, I think he's a real nice man, because he hired me without my having any experience at all. This is the first time I've ever had a job where I cleaned off the tables and everything when the people were through eating. Boy, at first I was real scared about this job. I didn't think I was gonna be able to do it right . . . you know?

FRANKIE: You're doing okay . . .

VELMA: Although, you know what? [*She starts to bite her fingernails*]

FRANKIE: What's that, Velma?

VELMA: Well, sometimes Mr. Quincy says things to me . . . or he gives me certain kinds of looks . . . like for instance . . . [*Embarrassed*] I was his . . . *girl friend*, maybe. [*She looks at* FRANKIE, *waiting hopefully for him to agree with her.* FRANKIE *gives her a slight smile of comfort, but it is not a smile of agreement*] I told my mother about the way Mr. Quincy is to me sometimes, and right away she wanted to come down and meet him. She asked me how old he was and she wanted to know how he looked, and after I told her everything she wanted to know, she said that some night she would get all dressed up and then come down here and wait for me until I got off, and while she was waiting I could introduce her to Mr. Quincy. [*She walks away and begins to wipe the same tabletop over again*] You know what she said to me, my mother? She said that it was all up in my mind that Mr. Quincy might jist be . . . *interested* . . . in me. She said that it wasn't true and that I should jist concentrate on my job and forget about all those pipe dreams, otherwise I would be gettin' fired. [*She pauses*] Sometimes . . . sometimes it's so hard for me to figure my mother out . . . because right afterwards she's tellin' me that maybe I shouldn't eat so much after all because then I would be goin' from one extreme to the other. She said when I was real skinny I couldn't find a nice boy, and, well, if I kept on eating the way I've been doing lately, I'd get real fat, and so it would still be the same old story for me. [*She laughs a desperate, frantic sort of laugh*] My mother . . . changes her mind so much sometimes . . . that it gives me a headache. [*She begins to wipe the tabletop with great pressure.* FRANKIE *watches her for a moment*]

FRANKIE: [*Lightly*] Velma, what are you trying to do?

VELMA: [*Quickly*] What?

FRANKIE: Are you trying to wear that tabletop off?

VELMA: Oh . . . yes . . . I know what you mean.

FRANKIE: You can get a headache just by doing things like that, Velma.

VELMA: Yeah . . . I guess you're right. [*She goes back over to him*] You know something?

FRANKIE: Yes? I'm listening to you, Velma.

VELMA: Oh, what a funny coincidence. That's what I was jist goin' to say to you, Frankie. I was goin' to say: you know something? You make me feel good, Frankie, because you're listening to me. And then I was goin' to thank you for it, and tell you how much I appreciated our conversation with each other. There's not too many people I can talk to. Or what I should say is that there's not too many people who will listen to me because they think I talk too much. [FRANKIE *glances at his wristwatch*] It's almost time to go, huh?

FRANKIE: Five minutes and we'll be free.

VELMA: You really don't like this job, I can tell. You can't wait to get out of here, can you?

FRANKIE: You know what you're talking about.

VELMA: But I don't know as much as you.

FRANKIE: You can't really say things like that.

VELMA: [*After a pause*] What . . . do you do . . . when you leave here? I mean, if you don't mind my askin'. I know it's none of my business . . .

FRANKIE: I would like to go out and get drunk!

VELMA: Boy, do you sound mad all of a sudden.

FRANKIE: That's the way I am sometimes.

VELMA: [*Rapidly*] Are you married?

FRANKIE: [*Trying to be pleasant*] Velma . . . I have a hard time just taking care of myself.

VELMA: [*After a pause*] You know, you really look nice. You don't belong here, that's all there is to it. You should be in the movies. You know what I mean? You could be an actor. I always wanted to be in the movies. I'd love to be an actress, but my mother says I'm not pretty enough . . . and I guess she's right . . . or was she?

FRANKIE: Why don't you relax, Velma?

VELMA: How come you're telling me that?

FRANKIE: You're shaking. You should learn how to be calm. It would make things a lot easier for you.

VELMA: [*Very nervously*] Well, it's almost time, isn't it? It's almost midnight . . . time to quit and everything . . . so I better go and change. [*She starts to move away, but it is an immense effort for her to do so*] I'll see you again tomorrow night, Frankie, okay?

FRANKIE: Sure . . . okay . . . Velma.

VELMA: [*Running off*] 'Bye! And nice talkin' to you . . . [*She is gone*]

FRANKIE: 'Bye . . . [*Then, more to himself*] Nice talkin' to you, too.

A quick blackout. The lights come up again. We are on the streets outside. VELMA *is standing alone. She is out of breath. Then* FRANKIE *enters from our right.*

VELMA: Hi, Frankie.

FRANKIE: What are you doing here?

VELMA: I . . . I . . . left . . . before you did! I've been standin' here waitin' for you!

FRANKIE: You're shivering to death.

VELMA: I was jist wonderin' if you would walk me to the subway. I'm usually never afraid, but tonight, well, I jist can't explain why I got the jitters.

FRANKIE: Where do you live?

VELMA: In the Bronx. It's pretty far. It takes about an hour on the subway. Where do you live?

FRANKIE: Around the corner.

VELMA: Oh, geez! You're lucky! I wish I lived near where I worked. My other job is jist as far away as this one. I never have any luck when it comes to my jobs.

FRANKIE: You mean you have another job?

VELMA: My mother wants me to. She says we need the money. For a while I only had the day job. But my mother said it wasn't enough. So then I got this job from Mr. Quincy about a month ago. He's a real nice man. I'll bet if you get to know him he'd be a lot like the way my father was.

FRANKIE: Your father dead?

VELMA: We really don't know. He might be. I ain't seen him since I was six years old. That's twenty years ago. I'm twenty-six.

FRANKIE: What did he do? Where did he go?

VELMA: He deserted us and no one's been able to find him since. But actually, he didn't leave me and my brother Herbert; it was my mother who he left. He said that if he didn't run away, mother would drive him nuts. But I don't think that would've happened because she didn't drive me and my brother Herbert nuts. We're both okay. Of course Herbert hasn't lived with us for a long time now. He got married when he was only nineteen and we hardly ever see him any more. Do you know something? You're almost as handsome as Herbert. He's the most handsome person you ever saw. My mother always wanted him to be a movie star, and he could've been too if he didn't run away and get married like he did. My mother never stopped telling him that he was going to make a lot of money someday for all of us and that we would be so proud of him because he would be famous throughout the whole world. [*Very wistfully*] I wish he would've listened to her. Then I wouldn't have to work any more.

FRANKIE: It's getting pretty cold standing here, Velma. One thing I don't like is cold weather. Let's start walking toward the subway.

VELMA: Okay.

They begin to walk.

FRANKIE: Wouldn't you know that I would be born during the month that has the lousiest weather?

VELMA: [*After giving a long sigh*] We should celebrate, Frankie!

FRANKIE: Why?

VELMA: I was born in February, too.

FRANKIE: Congratulations.

VELMA: Ain't that a coincidence?

FRANKIE: Sure is. And it's also getting colder.

VELMA: When is yours?

FRANKIE: When is my what?

VELMA: The date. Mine's already gone. It was the seventh.

FRANKIE: Well, happy birthday anyway, Velma. Mine hasn't arrived yet. It's the twenty-first.

VELMA: Well, then, when I see you on the twenty-first, I'll wish you yours, too.

FRANKIE: You do that.

VELMA: You jist sound so unhappy compared to when we first started talking tonight. February isn't that bad a month. I think it's the *best* month of all, Frankie.

FRANKIE: How do you figure that?

VELMA: Because of the people born in this month. There's George Washington, and Abraham Lincoln . . . and there's . . . *tomorrow!*

FRANKIE: What's tomorrow?

VELMA: Saint Valentine's Day!

FRANKIE: Oh . . . yeah . . .

VELMA: You won't believe this . . . but . . . I never once got a valentine in my whole life.

FRANKIE: [*After a long pause, uneasily*] It's getting colder by the minute, isn't it, Velma?

VELMA: But do you know, Frankie, I didn't mind too much. My mother used to take me to Schrafft's and then afterwards we'd go to the Radio City Music Hall every Valentine's Day while I was still going to school. She said it would take my mind off not getting any valentines. My mother did good things for me except sometimes she would yell at me and say I was homely and skinny and that I shook too much and it made her nervous and so she'd scream at me to go into another room so's she wouldn't have to look at me for a while . . .

FRANKIE: [*Quickly*] This is it! You want to come in for a minute? [*He stops and so does* VELMA]

VELMA: Come in where, Frankie?

FRANKIE: This is where I live. Do you want to come in for some coffee? It'll warm you up.

VELMA: I really got to get back home. My mother will be waitin' up for me . . . and . . . oh . . .

FRANKIE: C'mon. Look, you're trembling because it's cold out here. It's even beginning to snow now.

VELMA: No, no. I'm not trembling because I'm cold. You know now how I tremble a lot, don't you? I'm really warm. I almost feel as though I'm beginnin' to sweat, as though it was the summertime, or because I was worried about something.

FRANKIE: What are you worried about, then?

VELMA: Well, I started to say before that my mother would be . . . waitin' up for me . . . but . . .

FRANKIE: All right, then. C'mon, I'll walk you to your subway. I can't waste any more goddam time!

VELMA: No, Frankie! I forgot! You see . . . my mother's not home . . . I mean, she *is* home but she's not waitin' up for me tonight . . . and so . . .

FRANKIE: Yes? So?

VELMA: So I suppose it'll be all right if I come in for a few minutes. I guess I really would enjoy some hot coffee before I leave . . . for home.

FRANKIE *takes out his keys and walks down the steps to his apartment. He opens the door and turns on the light.*

FRANKIE: Well? Are you coming in, Velma?

VELMA *is trembling almost violently.*

VELMA: [*Standing on the stairs*] I . . . I . . . yes . . . I'm coming . . .

FRANKIE: Jesus! Control yourself, will you?

VELMA: I'll be okay, Frankie, in a minute. It's jist that I've never been in a man's apartment before. It's jist that I've never been alone with a man before. Oh, I forgot . . .

FRANKIE: Hey! I don't have much patience left, Velma!

VELMA: I forgot that I *was* alone with a man before. My brother Herbert. But that doesn't really count, does it? Because he's my brother, huh, Frankie?

FRANKIE: If you don't come down here in one more second, I'm shutting the door on you and you're walking to the subway by yourself!

VELMA: [*Finally going down the stairs*] You know, Frankie, maybe instead of the coffee I'd better have hot tea instead. [*The lights are beginning to dim*] My mother says . . . she *used* to say . . . that I drank too much coffee. Ever since I was a little girl I drank coffee, and she always told me that that was why I was so skinny and not very tall like most girls, and that's why I shake so much, and that's why I'll probably never find a nice man to marry me someday . . . but now I'm gaining weight and everything . . .

Complete blackout. We hear music now. It is the old-time, dance-band type of music coming from a phonograph. The lights slowly come back up. We are in FRANKIE'S *apartment.* VELMA *is sitting on the edge of the bed drinking her hot tea.* FRANKIE *is standing up before the refrigerator with the door opened; he is drinking from a bottle.*

VELMA: I don't wanna sound stupid or anything, Frankie, but what's the name of that record?

FRANKIE *takes another long slug, puts the bottle back into the refrigerator and slams the door shut.*

FRANKIE: [*Turning around, facing* VELMA *with a smile*] "I Only Have Eyes for You."

VELMA *blushes and turns her face away; she stifles a giggle.*

VELMA: It's a pretty song . . .

FRANKIE: [*With half-a-sigh*] It sure is! Makes me feel nostalgic. That's why I'm playing it, because I like feeling nostalgic . . .

VELMA: I don't know what it means . . .

FRANKIE: They used to play this song when I was in high school. It was the theme song of the ole' hometown band.

VELMA: I'll bet you had as much girls chasin' you as my brother Herbert did.

FRANKIE: [*Singing*] "Are the stars out tonight? . . . I don't know if it's cloudy or bright . . ."

VELMA: [*Embarrassed*] It's certainly a romantic song. [*She sips her tea*]

FRANKIE: " . . . 'cause I only have eyes for you . . ." [*He begins to dance*] Would you like to dance with me, Velma? [*He bows to her*]

VELMA: [*Really embarrassed*] Oh . . . I . . . I forgot to tell you. But I *did* get a few valentines when I was younger. My brother Herbert used to mail them to me.

FRANKIE: Jesus Christ! Will you shut the hell up about your goddam brother Herbert!

VELMA: Geez . . . you get mad easy, don't you?

FRANKIE: And stop trembling like that. My bed's going to fall apart. [*He goes back to the refrigerator and takes out the bottle*]

VELMA: You drink a lot, too, don't you?

FRANKIE: [*Drinking*] No shit, baby!

VELMA: And . . . when you drink . . . you curse a lot, too, don't you?

FRANKIE: You don't like it?

VELMA: No . . .

FRANKIE: [*Pausing, then smiling*] I'm sorry . . . Velma.

VELMA: What's that you're drinkin'? If you don't mind my askin'?

FRANKIE: Ice-cold martinis. Already mixed. You can buy it in any liquor store, all prepared, ready and waiting for you. Saves lots of time, you know. Not too much time left . . . Velma . . . Sparrow!

VELMA: How . . . did you know my last name? I never told it to you.

FRANKIE: I guessed.

VELMA: Aw, c'mon, I don't believe you.

FRANKIE: Honest to God, I did.

VELMA: It's spooky then, don't you think?

FRANKIE: Not at all. It's a beautiful name, Velma. It goes perfect with you.

VELMA: I didn't tell it to you before because I've always been ashamed of it.

FRANKIE: How could you be?

VELMA: When I was in school the kids used to always whisper behind my back. They'd say: here she comes, here comes Velma the ugly sparrow.

FRANKIE: You forget about those creeps!

VELMA: Well, you know what I did? I quit school jist so's I wouldn't have to listen to them any more. And I only had a year left before I would'uve got my diploma, too. Sometimes I think about going to night school, but my mother says it's all too late now. You know, my mother is a peculiar woman. First she's sayin' to me, "Velma, we gotta save money, that's all there is to it!" And then . . . the very next minute she's askin' me to loan her five dollars for the beauty parlor or something like that.

FRANKIE: Doesn't your mother work?

VELMA: You sound mad again.

FRANKIE: I am mad again! [*He takes another swig of the bottle*]

VELMA: No, she doesn't work because she usually doesn't feel too well. That's why I have two jobs. During the days I work in a movie house in Greenwich Village. I'm an usherette. My mother didn't want me to work down there at first because she thinks the Village is dangerous. She doesn't like the idea of me being around all those fairies and those leprechauns. Well, I'm not afraid of the fairies but *those leprechauns* really scare me.

FRANKIE: [*Scratching his head*] What do you mean by leprechauns?

VELMA: You know what I mean: those girls who don't like men; they like to be with women instead.

FRANKIE: Uh, Lesbians, Velma, Lesbians. Not leprechauns.

VELMA: Oh, that's right, Les—bi—ans.

FRANKIE *takes off his shoes and socks.*

FRANKIE: I'm making myself comfortable, so don't worry about a thing.

VELMA: Oh, well, it's your apartment, so why should I mind, huh? Besides, I don't really mind anything right now. I'm having a good time here with you. [*She looks around*] This is a real artist's apartment, isn't it?

FRANKIE: If you think so.

VELMA: So Frankie, what do you do? I know that being a cashier isn't your life. You're too handsome for that. And you're too smart. I've never seen so many books in all my life.

FRANKIE: I'm a writer, Velma.

VELMA: [*Thrilled*] Gee! You must have a big imagination! You'll probably be rich and famous some day, and then I'll be able to say that I knew you, won't I?

FRANKIE: I'm a poet, really. Poets don't make very much money, and they hardly ever become famous.

VELMA: Who's that on the wall? He looks real familiar to me.

FRANKIE: That's Van Gogh. A self-portrait.

VELMA: [*Excited*] Did he give it to you?

FRANKIE: No, Velma.

VELMA: And who are these people in this picture? [*She looks closer*] Oh! You're in the picture, too! It must be your family, huh?

FRANKIE: That's right.

VELMA: They all look so happy: your father and mother and sister and brother . . . and you! Are they all happy as the picture?

FRANKIE: Yes, they are, most of the time. I'm pretty proud of them . . . and they're pretty patient with me.

VELMA: You're soooooo . . . lucky!

FRANKIE: Why's that?

VELMA: To be able to have such a nice family.

FRANKIE *drinks some more.*

FRANKIE: I'm getting stoned . . . drunk, Velma. Don't mind me if I do. I might get a little vulgar . . . a little truthful . . . I might start talking about myself . . . but I'll try to be nice . . . I really . . . *like you*, Velma!

VELMA: [*Nervously*] And do you know who else was born during this month? My favorite actress! And you probably like her because she is the most beautiful woman in the entire world!

FRANKIE: Who's that?

VELMA: Elizabeth Taylor! What do you think of that?

FRANKIE: Liz, huh? Marvelous! We're in good company, aren't we, Velma?

VELMA: I knew you'd like to hear that.

FRANKIE: Velma, I'm going to make myself some tea. I really shouldn't be getting this drunk. I'm a bad host, huh?

VELMA: Oh, no, I don't think so at all.

FRANKIE: Thank you. You're beautiful.

VELMA: I don't know what . . . to say . . .

FRANKIE: You don't have to say anything. Just keep me company, that's all.

VELMA: I like you when you drink. It's like watching a show on TV or something. You never know what to expect next. First you're very funny and then you're very mad. In a way, it's fun. [*There is a pause*] I'll bet I know why you don't have a TV set here.

FRANKIE: [*Trying to make some tea*] Why?

VELMA: Because if you had a TV set then you wouldn't write your poems, would you?

FRANKIE: You're very much on the ball.

VELMA: I wouldn't know what to do without a TV set in the house. My mother and me, we sit and watch all of the *love* stories! I used to go to Loeee's Paradise a lot. You ever been there?

FRANKIE: What is it?

VELMA: A movie house. It's jist like a castle out of fairy tales. You really dream there: Loeee's Paradise!

FRANKIE: It's *Loew's* Paradise, not *Loeee's,* isn't it?

VELMA: It is? Geez. My mother and me have always called it *Loeee's,* and we've been goin' there for years and years. But you must be right because you're educated and because you're an artist.

FRANKIE: Where is this place?

VELMA: It's in the Bronx. I used to go on Saturday nights. They have stars on the ceilings. Thousands of stars twinkling on and off. It's like another world. And if you sit right in the middle of the theatre, there's a big full moon above your head. It's so romantic. You should see it! But . . . I stopped goin' because most of the girls and the boys go in couples and they all try to sit underneath the big full moon . . . and I was beginning to feel out of place.

FRANKIE: Velma, do you want more tea?

VELMA: I was thinkin' that maybe I'd like jist a little sip of that martini mix, if you don't care, Frankie?

FRANKIE: Of course I don't care. It's my pleasure. [*He pours her a glass*] Salut!

VELMA: [*Lifting the glass*] Cheers . . .

FRANKIE: Cheers then. It's all the same. [*He drinks more too*]

VELMA: It's strong . . . but I like it.

FRANKIE: Very good. Enjoy yourself.

VELMA: This is a real treat. I like treats. Every payday when I bring home the money, my mother decided that we both should have a treat, and so the next morning, every single week that I can remember, we have coffee cake and caviar for breakfast!

FRANKIE: Coffee cake and caviar?

VELMA: Oh, it's delicious together. Some day you'll have to come to our apartment for breakfast. You'll love it . . . [*She sips some more*]

FRANKIE: Drink up, Velma. There's a lot more yet. Relax. [FRANKIE *flops down on the bed next to her*] My head is beginning to spin.

VELMA *immediately rises from the bed.*

VELMA: [*Trembling*] I used to work at The Merry-Go-Round Club once. I was the hat-check girl, but my mother said they fired me because they wanted a girl who was prettier than me. Do you know that it was my favorite job, though, even if it didn't last very long. I saw all the stars and the celebrities. Once I even saw Ed Sullivan!

FRANKIE: Relax, Velma.

VELMA: [*Drinking some more*] Oh, I'm okay. I'm relaxed. [*She goes to his desk*] This is where you write, huh?

FRANKIE: When I'm working on my book.

VELMA: You're writing a book too? You really are smart! I'll bet you're a good typist, too, aren't you?

FRANKIE: I never compose my poetry on the typewriter; only my book.

VELMA *sits down at his desk.*

VELMA: Well . . . anyway . . . [*She finishes the drink rapidly.* FRANKIE *sits up on his bed and stares over at her*]

FRANKIE: You want more?

VELMA: I don't think I'd better. I'm gettin' sleepy now. Maybe I'd better go home . . . my mother is . . . well, she's *not* . . . really . . .

FRANKIE: I would like to hug you, Velma. I would like very much to put my arms around you, and I would like to hold you ever so gently, and I would like to whisper tenderly in your ear; I would like to say to you: "Velma honey, believe me, little-girl Velma, things are not really that bad. Everything's going to be all right, okay, you just wait and see. Take my word for it, Velma."

VELMA *does not know what to do; she glances back and forth at her wristwatch.*

VELMA: Well! It's Valentine's Day now! I'll bet you have so many girl friends, don't you? I can jist see it in the morning when you wake up. Your mailbox will be stuffed with hundreds of valentines, won't it? From all your girl friends?

FRANKIE: It used to be that way once, but no more, and I like it that way. You see, Velma, most girls, after they flip their corks over me, find out pretty fast that they don't go for me anymore. They discover that there is competition. They believe I'd rather make it with my typewriter. Did you know that every chick I've ever sacked becomes insanely jealous of that innocent little machine over there on my desk? Isn't that the stupidest thing you ever heard of? Harmless portable! . . . inanimate black mother, old pawnshop object that never gives me any bullshit!

VELMA: You're really somethin'.

FRANKIE: Would you bother me if I sat down and typed away whenever I felt that I had to, whenever the urge was suddenly the most important thing in my life? You'd leave me alone, wouldn't you?

VELMA: Yes . . .

FRANKIE: You wouldn't show any signs of bitterness, would you?

VELMA: No . . .

FRANKIE: [*Drinking some more*] I knew you wouldn't let me down, Velma. You see, these chicks, almost all of them, they want all of your time and all of your attention. They say they understand you, but when it comes right down to the actual test, well, their lovely precious pussies panic! And so what do you do? You make it with a guy and there's just as much bullshit there too! [*Quietly*] The thing to do is to find out where the hell the right chick is . . . under my bed? . . . in the bathroom? . . . up in the Bronx, maybe? [VELMA *giggles*, FRANKIE *sips his drink*] I'll tell you something: I'd rather *come* all over the keys of that hot typewriter . . . that's the way I feel sometimes! [*He gets up from the bed*] Besides . . . [*He laughs bitterly*] maybe it's not such a bad idea . . . it's a whole lot safer. No sweat. How can you knock up a typewriter? [*He stops and stares at her*] But . . . you don't even know what I'm talking about, do you? [VELMA *simply smiles back at him*] Anyway, that answers your question about how many valentines I'll be getting in the morning. [*He begins to take off his shirt.* VELMA *gets up*] Don't worry about anything. I'm only making myself comfortable, that's all. [*He takes off his pants*] Will you please sit down? I'm not going to harm you. [*He goes into the bathroom*]

VELMA: Please don't get mad at me, Frankie.

FRANKIE: [*Offstage*] I'm not getting mad at you. I'm just disappointed, that's all. [*He begins to sing and/or hum his song from the bathroom. Then he returns in a bathrobe*]

VELMA: [*After a moment*] Maybe I can stay here, jist for a little while? My mother won't even know about it . . . since she's not waitin' up for me . . . [*She begins to shake again*]

FRANKIE: You're confusing me, baby, and I get confused enough when I got gin in my belly. Make up your mind. And forget about your mother. I'm sick and tired of hearing about your old lady!

VELMA: Okay . . .

FRANKIE: If I give you just a small glass of this martini mix, it'll make you stop shaking like that. [*He goes and pours her some more*] Now here. Take it and drink it in one gulp.

VELMA: Will it? Will it make my shaking stop?

FRANKIE: Don't ask questions. Just do as I told you.

VELMA: Okay . . . [*She manages to get it all down in one swig*]

FRANKIE: You see? You did it. Now come back over here and sit down like before and make yourself at home. And take your coat back off. [VELMA *walks away from him and sits back down at the desk*] Well, aren't you going to take your coat off?

VELMA: In a minute, Frankie, in a minute.

FRANKIE: Velma? You want to know something?

VELMA: What, Frankie?

FRANKIE: I'm glad that you came home with me tonight. You're the first woman I've had here in a long time.

VELMA *shows signs of wanting to leave. She nervously notices a book lying on the desk.*

VELMA: [*Reading, as she picks the book up*] "Poet in New York . . ."

FRANKIE: A great goddam good poet, too, let me tell you!

VELMA: Fed-er-ico . . . Garcia . . . Lorca . . .

FRANKIE: And God bless him! Amen.

VELMA: I . . . never heard of him. Is he a Puerto Rican?

FRANKIE: [*Softly*] Where did I find you?

VELMA: Does he still live in New York?

FRANKIE: Oh, sure. He's pushing boo up in East Harlem for the winter.

VELMA: Oh.

FRANKIE: [*Going to her*] Please . . . let me just hold you, Velma, okay? [VELMA *shows signs of wanting to leave again*] Don't move! Stay where you are . . . I'm not going to harm you. If only you'll believe that, then everything will be okay. Take my word for it, please . . . okay? [*He gives her a very honest smile*]

VELMA: [*After a moment*] Okay . . . I guess.

FRANKIE: Good, Velma. Besides, I need someone to talk to, and you need someone to talk to. Right?

VELMA: Right, I guess.

FRANKIE: In other words, we both need someone to listen to us.

VELMA: You mean those other women . . . I mean, didn't those other girls ever want to listen to you, Frankie? I mean the ones who used to come here?

FRANKIE: Never! That's the trouble, Velma.

VELMA: They just wanted to talk about themselves, huh?

FRANKIE: That's it, Velma. That's exactly it.

VELMA: And that's why you're not married yet, huh? Because maybe you can't find a girl who'll listen to you?

FRANKIE: Yeah, maybe it's one of the reasons . . .

VELMA: It's so hard to believe that you're not married, though. I think you'd make a nice husband and be a good father, too.

FRANKIE: [*Sharply*] Why would I make a nice husband and be a good father?

VELMA: [*Jittery again*] Well . . . because your kids would have so much fun with you. You'd make them laugh and everything. I never really had a father to make me laugh and have fun with because I hardly remember him.

FRANKIE: You're making me feel good, Velma. In a way, you're making me feel sort of happy. You see, about a year ago around this time I almost got married. I had this girl friend, and . . .

VELMA: Was she pretty?

FRANKIE: It doesn't really matter now. It's not important anyway. Her name was Carrie and we went together for over a year. Then she wanted to get married. I didn't. Remember, Velma: I have a very hard time just taking care of myself. Well, anyway, that's all she talked about was getting married. In a church. The whole works. And having lots of babies afterwards. It scared me, Velma. She was ashamed now. She didn't think we should go on living together. [*He laughs bitterly*] We had to make it all legal! Carrie said some pretty stupid things to me. I was beginning to feel nervous and miserable. "Frankie Basta," she screamed at me, "you're not a man! You can't face up to responsibilities!" Over and over again she said this to me. Christ, Velma, I couldn't even take care of myself then. Almost like now: no job, no prospects, no nothing. And I didn't know whether I was a good poet or a bad one. I still don't know. And so, I asked her to try and understand. I knew I would fail her then. I said to her, "Please, Carrie baby, just hold on and wait, and then we'll see, Carrie honey . . . we'll see, okay?"

VELMA: But she didn't, huh?

FRANKIE: Didn't wait, you mean? No, she didn't wait and she wouldn't see. You can't do it, Velma, you can't do it! It's almost impossible to make people understand certain things, especially the people who you care so much about, the people who you love . . . or the people who you could care about and love . . .

VELMA: [*Softly*] I . . . don't know what to say to you.

FRANKIE: You don't have to say anything, Velma. Just keep me company, that's all. [*He goes to the phonograph*] What would you like to hear? Do you have any favorite songs, Velma?

VELMA: I like the one you played a little while ago.

FRANKIE: No, I mean one of your own. Don't you have one of your own favorites? That's *my* favorite song.

There is a short pause.

VELMA: Well . . . it's *mine*, too . . . now. [*She smiles faintly at him*]

FRANKIE: [*Smiling back*] Then I'll play it again, for the both of us.

VELMA: It would make me happy, Frankie . . .

FRANKIE: What's the matter all of a sudden? I thought you *were* happy.

VELMA: I am . . . but I'm also worried . . . and . . . I'm getting tired . . . I'm feelin' weak and everything . . . [*The music begins to play softly*] Oh, that's so nice . . . it makes me forget . . . things . . . easier . . .

FRANKIE: And you're not trembling any more, either, are you?

VELMA: Geez, you're right! I never even thought of it.

He has somehow managed to get her to dance with him. It is all rather awkward: his drunkenness, her fear.

FRANKIE: [*Singing, dancing*] "Are the stars out tonight . . . I don't know if it's cloudy or bright! . . . 'Cause I only have eyes for . . . YOU!"

VELMA: [*Pulling away, embarrassed*] This picture of you and your family sure is nice, don't you think? Don't you think so, Frankie?

FRANKIE: [*Singing*] "Dear Velma . . . Oh, the moon may be high . . . "

VELMA: . . . and you can tell that you're different from the rest of them. I mean, you look like an artist and everything . . . all the rest of them look nice and ordinary . . .

FRANKIE: [*Singing*] "Maybe millions of people go by"

VELMA: . . . but you really stand out in the picture! You look nice and . . . *wild!* If you know what I mean? Frankie? Please, don't sing to me any more, please! I'm going to feel scared and I can't think when you keep singing to me like that, please!

FRANKIE: [*He turns off the phonograph*] I'm sorry, Velma. Look, anything to make you cozy.

VELMA: Boy oh boy, you really are drunk, aren't you?

FRANKIE: Why do you say . . . that?

VELMA: Well, because you're acting so funny.

FRANKIE: I know, I know . . . Velma. Look, from here on in . . . well, just don't mind me too much . . . excuse me if I seem . . . in any way clumsy to you, okay?

VELMA: Frankie?

FRANKIE: Let me have your coat. I'll hang it up for you.

VELMA: [*Motionless*] Frankie, I'm getting a tiny headache . . . do you think, Frankie, that you could keep a secret? I've never been so worried . . .

FRANKIE: C'mon now: your coat?

VELMA: Yes . . . [*She hands her coat to him. FRANKIE goes and puts the coat on a hanger. He notices a newspaper half-exposed in one of the pockets*]

FRANKIE: [*Looking at it*] Velma, why are you reading a newspaper like this?

VELMA: You're mad again, aren't you?

FRANKIE: How can you waste money this way?

VELMA: I buy it for my mother. She reads it.

FRANKIE: I don't want to hear another word about your MOTHER! Do you hear me?

VELMA: [*Beginning to tremble again*] Yes, yes, Frankie.

FRANKIE: Yeah, sure! You buy this rag for your old lady, but you read it too, don't you?

VELMA: It . . . has lots of gossip in it . . . about all the stars and celebrities . . . and *everything!*

FRANKIE: [*Reading*] "Mother Uses Daughter's Head for Hammer!" [*He rips the newspaper up with great fury*] Velma, why do you read such shit? What are you trying to do to yourself? [*Angrily*] "Mother Uses Daughter's Head for Hammer!" [*He moves closer to her*] God, Velma, I mean what's happening? [*He makes an attempt at embracing her*]

VELMA: Please, please, please! Oh, noooooooo! I'M SCARED OF YOU! I'M SCARED OF EVERYBODY, OF EVERYTHING! [*She tries to run from him*] I never thought of it 'til now . . . they'll do somethin' to me, won't they? I want my coat back! I'VE NEVER BEEN ALONE WITH A MAN BEFORE! My mother would think . . . *my mother!*

FRANKIE: [*Violently*] FUCK YOUR MOTHER! YOUR MOTHER IS ROTTEN!

VELMA: I can't stay here tonight! Maybe it jist isn't right for me to stay here with you . . . not tonight!

FRANKIE: You've got to now. You're in no shape to go anywhere. It'll be all right, Velma. You'll sleep in my bed, and I'll sleep here on the floor. Nothing hard about that, is there?

VELMA: I can't, Frankie! *I've . . . got . . . to . . . be . . . there!*

FRANKIE: What are you talking about? [*He moves toward her again, his arms outstretched*] Please, just let me hold you and whisper in your ear, Velma?

VELMA: NOOOOOOO! [*She pulls a small kitchen knife out of her pocketbook. It is partly caked with dry blood*] YOU STAY AWAY FROM ME! I DON'T WANT YOU TO TOUCH ME! We're not even married yet . . . [*She is trembling as she holds the knife at FRANKIE*] You leave me alone, Frankie . . . or I'll *kill* you! [*FRANKIE is motionless*] When . . . we got up this morning, my mother and me, we had coffee cake and caviar for breakfast. It was a big surprise. My mother said that we were havin' the treat even if payday was three days away yet. She said it was sort of a special celebration. My mother said that she

was leaving for the mountains this afternoon. She was going to a resort to meet a man. Harriet, my mother's friend who lives in the next apartment, she told my mother that there were a whole lot of available men at this certain resort up in the mountains, the Catskills, I think, and my mother said she was goin' no matter what, and that I must send her money every weekend until she has some luck. She said that I couldn't go because I would scare the men away, that I would ruin her chances, and that I was really such an ugly girl, and that I looked like the mother and she looked like the daughter . . . and then she said that was why we're havin' the treat early: to celebrate! The coffee cake and caviar . . . and then she asked me to cut her a big piece of the coffee cake and to cover it with a whole lot of caviar . . . and so I started to cut the coffee cake with this here knife, but . . . [*VELMA trembles to such a degree that the knife falls from her hand and onto the floor. She runs to the bed and throws herself upon it in a burst of hysterical sobbing*]

FRANKIE: Velma, what have you done? [*He picks up the knife and lays it on his desk*]

VELMA: It's my mother's blood! I didn't know what to do. I don't . . . know why I did it! I don't even really remember that much, Frankie. When I got in the subway to come to work afterwards it was jist like nuthin' happened, nuthin' at all! But do you know? I thought, I thought when my mother asked me to cover her piece of coffee cake with a whole lot of caviar, I thought . . . my mother . . . she thinks that my head is a *hammer!* That's what she thinks! AND IT ISN'T! IT ISN'T! Tell me, Frankie, please tell me that my head is not a *hammer!*

FRANKIE: [*After a pause*] No, Velma, no. Your head is not a hammer.

VELMA: [*A brief pause*] Can I sleep here tonight?

FRANKIE *goes to the bottle and takes the longest gulp he can manage. He falls, exhausted, down into a chair. He closes his eyes.*

FRANKIE: Sure . . . Velma.

VELMA *continues to sob on the bed, but it is growing softer now.* FRANKIE *gets up and turns off all the lights. The moon is shining in through one of the windows.*

VELMA: [*Very quietly*] What will they do to me? I'm scared, Frankie . . .

FRANKIE: They're not going to do anything . . . to you. I'll make sure of that . . . [*FRANKIE goes and sits down at his desk. He begins to scribble swiftly on a piece of paper*]

VELMA: [*Vaguely*] It makes me sleepy . . . alcohol . . . makes me sooooo tired . . . I've never felt

soooo . . . tired . . . before in my whole life
. . . [*She is no longer crying*] Help me . . . help
me . . . help . . . me . . .

FRANKIE: [*Still writing*] Yes, yes . . . *I will*, Velma Sparrow . . . I promise you that *I will*.

VELMA *is breathing heavily now.* FRANKIE *continues to write with great speed. He stops and
then begins to read.*

FRANKIE: [*Aloud, with a strange sobriety*]
  "Dead birds still have wings
  Dead birds, saddest-looking things
  Because they are dead, on the ground

With their still wings, on the ground
Saddest-looking things
Dead birds with still wings,
Dead on the ground
Instead of the sky . . ."

[VELMA *is sound asleep; her breathing is
peaceful.* FRANKIE *turns and faces* VELMA'S
*weary and forlorn figure. His eyes are full of
tears. He stands up and lights a cigarette*] I
have a treat for you in the morning, Velma.
[*He turns out the desk lamp*] I've just written
you . . . a valentine.

WHY HANNA'S SKIRT WON'T STAY DOWN

a play in one act

Tom Eyen

Why Hanna's Skirt Won't Stay Down was first presented by Ellen Stewart at the Cafe La Mama ETC, New York City, as half of a double bill with *White Whore and the Bit Player,* also by the author, on June 16, 1965, with the following cast:

HANNA	*Helen Hanft*
ARIZONA	*Steven Davis*
VOICE OF BARKER	*Neil Flanagan*

It was directed by Neil Flanagan. Set design by Josef Bush; lighting by Harvey Duke; stage manager, Maggie Dominic; costumes by Jane Green and Ellen Stewart.

To Helen Hanft

TIME

Five minutes to seven. Yesterday, today, but hopefully not tomorrow.

PLACE

A Fun Wax House, Coney Island, USA

SETTING

Four gigantic, brightly colored posters upstage forming a backdrop. From left to right: Nero playing his violin; Hanna over breeze-hole with her skirt blowing over her face; Arizona in his American flag bikini briefs (posed like Michelangelo's statue of "David"); and Marie Antoinette at the guillotine.

The circus-carnival stage can be cluttered with amusements and wax figures, or can be empty except for the two main areas: the breeze-hole for HANNA *and the mirror-maze for* ARIZONA. *A large clock is visible, reading five minutes to seven. The* BARKER *may be seen onstage throughout if desired, possibly frozen in a ticket booth at one side, watching the audience. He, of course, should never accept the human existence of* HANNA *and* ARIZONA.

MUSIC

The background music should change with and as quickly as the emotional moods. Carousel music, a laugh record, a 1920s recording of "Chicago," a contemporary rock sound for the bar scenes, etc.

LIGHTING

Should create the illusion of a multicolored rainbow: the fickle flickering of a carnival, plus the one barren light bulb of reality somewhere in the back of everyone's head. Other than this simple effect, the lighting should be clear white for the actual past, a somber blue mist for the past that never was, a shallow green for the inevitable death of our fantasies, and no etc.

FIRST IMAGE

Darkness. The eternal music of the carnival ba-ba-ba-ba-ba-ba is joined by haunted canned laughter ha ha ha ha ha ha. As the music and laughter build in volume, hundreds of blinking lights begin dancing around the posters and set. HANNA *appears onstage quietly, wearing a conservative coat. She studies the posters with more than casual interest. Seeing the breeze-hole, she circles it, debating with herself "if she really should." She decides she really should and jumps over hole, throwing off her coat to reveal a costume similar to a circus performer's. (In the original production,* HANNA *wore flesh-colored tights with sequins over the nipples and a red velvet heart sewn on the crotch, a red chiffon skirt, red boa, and shoes to match.)* HANNA'S *skirt can no longer stay down and her orgasm reaches a crescendo, together with the music, laughter, and blinking lights. Suddenly all stops.* HANNA *looks around, aware of her isolation, and, guiltily, begins justifying, which she does throughout.*

HANNA: . . . I come here every payday and stand over the breeze-hole. It's relaxing. You know, everyone should have a place in life to come to where they can relax, think out loud, feel at home. It keeps me calm, if not cool. There's something about air—the pressure! The sensation of something trying to penetrate your body. Now don't you put no Freudian connotation on that one! I can't stand assumptions! I just like a little cool breeze. *As I said,* I come here every payday. I have my hair done at my favorite salon (a Puerto Rican beauty school), dust off my faithful boa, wash my unfaithful panties, polish up my Kitty Kelly specials. As long as Hanna's around, *glamour lives!* I get here around 5:47. Beat the evening crowds. It takes forty-seven minutes to get to Coney Island on the "D" train from where I work on Forty-second Street. I work in a movie house. I'd tell you which one, but I don't want this conversation to become overly personal. [*Jumps on breeze-hole, has a fast orgasm, then jumps off*] Besides, there are some things I choose to forget. I'm a ticket dispenser. Never met one before? We're human, so don't get panicky. I sit there from eight to five and sell tickets in a glass cage. So it's not an art-movie house, but it's a living. And it's interesting! Some of the people who come to the other side of the glass you wouldn't believe. I'm terribly interested in people, you know. Well, to a certain extent. As long as they're on the other side of the glass. On the other side you can smell their breaths. And the one thing God should spare you from is people's breaths who go to Forty-second Street movie houses at eight in the morning! Oh, my name is Hanna O'Brien. I'm from Springfield, Illinois. Been in New York since after the war. No!!! Not the

Civil!!! How I hate that—assuming it was the Civil War. The Second World War! I come from good middle-class American stock. My father was Irish Catholic, and my mother Russian Orthodox Jewish. And between the Knights of Columbus and the Hadassah meetings—Oy vey, Maria—were we kids confused! We, my sister and I—she's older. She lives in Jersey City now. She sells Avon cosmetics door to door. Of course, the cops tried to prove otherwise, but they ain't got nothing on Sophie! During the Depression I was fourteen. Why'd I think of the Depression all of a sudden? I always think of the Depression when I think about Sophie—two national catastrophes! I was fourteen then and she was sixteen . . . and she had this boy friend. Don't remember his name, but he had a smile that would shame the sun. I used to watch him at night on the sofa with her, and even in the dark the room would glow. Of course, part of this was due to Sophie's shining bald spot on the crown of her head. Born that way! Funny, all I've ever won in life were Sophie's losing battles. But I never see her now. We don't even write. But I often think of her . . . old Sophie with her short, stubby finger reaching hopefully for some strange new doorbell, with her bald spot gleaming brightly in the noonday sun, singing behind false teeth, "Avon calling!" [*A reflective pause*] No wonder Jersey City is a Revlon Festival! But to get back to this place! I always come back to this place. It's relaxing! I can let my hair down, or my skirt up, if you wish. I was happy here. Oh, maybe except for a few of the stupid kids who come through here on dates and unfailingly remark, "Dig that crotch!" Oh, how I hate that remark, "Dig that crotch!" What kind of language do they use today! What kind of a verb is "dig?" But I was happy here, with the wind blowing and even the kids' casual interest, I suppose. *Then it happened!* [ARIZONA, *in levis and denim shirt, wanders in*] One evening, I'm standing here after work, minding my own business— I have learned to mind my own business— when this young man comes through. A kid that looked like all the others who pass and who unfailingly remark, "Dig that—" you know!—but with *that smile.* And he goes over to the mirror-maze section. Now this doesn't mean anything; a lot of the boys do it. But this one with the smile stays there and starts taking off his clothes! Now I know then that Hanna is in for a little trouble! This is Hanna's fun house! Other people are allowed to pass through, but no one, and particularly no one with *that smile,* is staying in Hanna's Fun House!!! [*She seeks comfort by jumping on the breeze-hole; her dress rises above her head*]

ARIZONA: [*Smiling at* HANNA, *he admires himself in the mirror-maze*] The world is a funny place. I know a man's already said it, but it's true. You ought to dig the crotch on this dizzy dame that stands over the breeze-hole. What some people won't do for a little attention! [*Taking off shirt*] In my limited observations of life, I shall never forget the Empire State Building, Radio City Music Hall, Yankee Stadium, and this dame's crotch. Truly the eighth wonder of the world! It seems as though it knew stories and had feelings kept secret from its owner. Not that I'm a crotch expert who goes around looking at every one he sees. But how can I miss hers? Her skirt is always up. Well, it's always up when she's here. And, as far as I know, she always is. [*Taking off levis, showing American flag bikini*] Oh, I'm sure the old dame's human . . . has a job somewhere; probably got a sister somewhere in Jersey to verify her existence. So why does she have to wiggle over a breeze-hole? But as that same man who wrote "The world is a funny place" also said, "You've got to get your kicks somehow!" I guess. But now take me! I'm different! The exception to the rule. I don't have to come here, but . . . well, it's interesting, always something to see. By the way, I'm a narcissist, as I'm sure you've already gathered. Oh, I'm not just an ordinary run-of-the-mill narcissist, but a highly unusual one. I don't just love the one me, but all forty-three of them. Well, forty-three is all I've found so far in the mirrors. I'm probably God, but I'm not sure. I think God would have at least seventy-five facets, but I'm still discovering more each day. Besides being a supposed God, I'm also a student. I go to college. Science major. Numbers, theories! I'm also a definite person. I can feel my body and I know my mind. As I've admitted before, I'm unusual. [*Flexes muscles*] Highly unusual! Even my subconscious is highly unusual. For instance, you see, I have this recurring dream each night that the old dame's crotch walks over to me smiling, saying . . .

HANNA: [*Walks over, throws crotch out to him*] "A penny for your thoughts, young man!"

ARIZONA: . . . As though it wanted to make friends. And in that same dream I feel embarrassed. That, because of social pressure, I reject it. I mean, how could I ever tell anyone that my best friend is some old bitch's snatch! My name is . . . I'm from Arizona. I left there because I didn't have asthma. My parents are dead. They died when I was born. My father was driving my mother to the hospital and they had a head-on with a Fink Bakery delivery truck. I was delivered right there amidst the cream-filled cupcakes by an intersection cop. As that same man also said, "From the ruins will rise a new Greece!" Never heard that one before, did you? Well, he said it! *Back to why I come here.* Well, you see, it's interesting, and . . . it's because, you see . . . I'm lonely. I don't love myself because I want to; it's only because I'm sure. I love myself and myself loves me. There's no confusion . . . no jealousy . . . no infidelity. I don't know anyone except myself. I can't love someone I don't know. But my loneliness is not as bad as I've led you all to believe; I truly like being with myself alone. But maybe every twenty-four hours, or once a week, or even once every year, I feel I need someone. So I come here. I don't talk to the old dame, but she's there. And I can talk and rely upon her to be a quiet listener. And she'll stay. Well, after I was born during the caution light at that intersection, I was taken to the hospital. I was under four pounds. There I attracted the attention of a nurse's aide who watched my incubator. It seems she had a problem. She was sterile. So she wanted me badly. So badly, in fact, that she convinced her cowardly—reserved—CPA husband that they should rent—adopt me. It seems she had a weakness for three-and-a-half-pound weaklings. When I was thirteen, however, we no longer spoke. I had grown into an assurance and strength she couldn't cope with. So I sought other outlets, like books. . . . *[Puts on little boy's cap]*

HANNA: *[As librarian]* Kindly keep it down!

ARIZONA: The first person I tried to talk to, other than my mother, was a Miss Polaski, our school librarian.

HANNA: As I so delicately mentioned before, and as the writing on the wall indicates in bold black letters, "PLEASE BE QUIET!"

ARIZONA: Sorry! I wonder if you could help me?

HANNA: Gladly. Try: *Etiquette for the Common Man.* Post, Emily. Room 1, Row 2, Number 345.

ARIZONA: No, I need help in another area. You see, Mrs. . . .

HANNA: Polaski. Hanna Polaski. *Miss* Hanna Polaski! *[They have an Indian arm-wrestle on desk. She wins]* Try: *What to Name Your Child if It's a Girl.* Bain, Richard. Room 2, Row 3, Number 456.

ARIZONA: Miss Polaski! Nice to meet you. My name is . . .

HANNA: Oh . . . try: *What to Name Your Child if It's a Boy.* Same author, same area as before. *[Beginning to seduce him]*

ARIZONA: I'm a freshman, and I'm . . . it just started this year. You see . . .

BOTH: I'm lonely! *[He grabs her around waist]*

HANNA: Try: several selections. *How to Train Your Dog to Respond Emotionally.* Or *[She pushes her backside into his groin, making him fall with pain]* Ball—room Dancing, Seventh edition. Both in Room 3, Row 4, Numbers 567 and 568.

ARIZONA: *[Now sitting on floor]* The prime reason for my disturbance naturally is my parents. *[HANNA pets him on head, sighing, "Oh . . . h . . . h . . . h"]* They never really include me in. They keep to themselves in their room. I can't even hear them. I always wonder what they say to each other that they can't include me in.

HANNA: *[Kneels on floor, grabbing his face in her hands]* Try: *Africa! The Sex Life of the Ancient and Modern Watusi.* Brown, Dr. Alfred. Room 4, Row 5, Number 678. *[Makes cannibal sounds, kissing him, and falls back to the floor chanting]* Um-Gawa, Gawa, Gawa!!

ARIZONA: *[Sadly]* I can't talk to anyone.

HANNA: Then may I suggest—*Cooking for One,* by Crocker, Betty. Room 5, Row 6, Number 789.

ARIZONA: *[Beginning to undress her]* What happens every time I try, is that . . . well, I get afraid at the last minute, afraid of failing, of course, and I take the sure-fire easy way out. I always . . .

HANNA: Come! Come! . . .

ARIZONA: *[Jumping up]* That's it! I always ask, *[Taking off cap like the little gentleman that he is]* "Would you like to fuck?" *[HANNA screams]* Sorry! *[He returns to his area]*

HANNA: *[Rising]* Quite all right. Try: *Religion, the Beginning and End of Christianity.* Sheen, Fulton, J., Bishop. Room 6, Row 7, Number 69. Wait for me there. I'll close the library in five minutes. We'll be safe; no one ever goes there. *[Goes back to breeze-hole]* Ahhhhhhhh! *[Freezes]*

ARIZONA: After Miss Polaski, which ended upon my high school graduation—that's when I stopped reading—there were others. *[HANNA grunts, "Yeah!"]* I can't remember specifics, but there were many others I tried to *talk to!*

Lights fade out on ARIZONA, *up on* HANNA. *She breaks position.*

HANNA: How I hate! How I hate! *[Aware of watchers]* It wasn't always like this! I wasn't always hating over breeze-holes in a Coney Island fun house! It's only been four weeks . . . *[ARIZONA: Yeah!]* Four months? *[ARIZONA: Yeah!]* Four years! *[ARIZONA: Yeah!]* . . . Well, it hasn't been long! You see, as a child I was soft. *[ARIZONA sings "Rock-a-bye Baby"]* Well, I was a child! *I had a right to* be! [*He stops*] You see, as a child I liked the world. I liked Mommy, Daddy, the neighbors, and the other children. But I wasn't a bland child. There were times when I disliked the world, and Mommy and Daddy, and etc. Then, when I was sixteen, I moved away to Chicago and got married. [ARIZONA: *Yeah!*] No! I didn't have to!!! Do I look like a girl that would have to get married? It was just that Mommy and Daddy thought it best when I got pregnant the third time. But I didn't have to, as the little bastards were all secretly put away in adoption agencies. Besides, no one ever knew—except the neighbors. The nibshits! So I ran away to Chicago. I'm from Springfield, remember? That's Lincoln's birthplace! He was one of the great fathers of our country! [*Laughing*] Little Melinda, one of the other children, often said I was one of the great mothers of our country. [*Stops laughing abruptly*] How I disliked that little bitch! So I ran away to Chicago with the father of my third child, and it lasted for two months after the baby came. [*She poses with* ARIZONA] Oh, I liked him all right . . . [*He pushes her away*] . . . but we didn't get along too well. So I had to find another adoption agency and a place to work!

ARIZONA: [*Behind desk-bar now, wearing a bartender's apron*] Come on! Come on, girls! Let's get a little leg action going here!

"Roaring Twenties" music floods in.

HANNA: It was a speakeasy right on State Street in the heart of Chicago!

ARIZONA: Lady, would you mind standing out of the aisle? You're blocking traffic!

HANNA: Oops! Sorry! I wonder if you could help me? I'm looking for a . . .

ARIZONA: The john's over there.

HANNA: No, no, that's not what I mean . . .

ARIZONA: Betty! Three Collins to the ladies in front! What's your name?

HANNA: Ahhh . . . my name is Hanna O'Brien. And I'm from Springfield, Illinois! That's Lincoln's birthplace!

ARIZONA: Come on, Rita! Over to table seven! Why'd ya leave? You have to?

HANNA: Yes! I mean, no! Well, yes! The town was too small. As my best girl friend Melinda put it, I was one of the great mothers of . . . of . . . of *Liberty!* [*Saluting*] I wasn't meant for small places!

ARIZONA: Wanda! Two martinis to the couple over at table fifteen! [*To* HANNA] Have you ever hustled?

HANNA: Oops! I beg your pardon!·

ARIZONA: Hustled! Wait on tables. Be nice to a soak. Get pinched on the ass.

HANNA: Well, I worked in the school cafeteria for two days once, if that's what you mean.

ARIZONA: Come on, girls!

HANNA: Are you from Chicago?

ARIZONA: Arizona!

HANNA: Why did you leave?

ARIZONA: Because I didn't have asthma! Come on! Betty! Wanda! Rita! Let's hustle it for last call!

HANNA: [*Becoming nervous because of time pressure*] Excuse me, but this is really difficult for me . . . to just walk in like this and ask for a job. It's not easy for me to converse with strangers. But I like people and I'm sure I can learn. You have a beautiful smile!

ARIZONA: Huh? What'd you say?

HANNA: I said, I said . . .

ARIZONA: Come on! Come on! . . .

HANNA: [*As a last resort*] Could you tell me where I could get a good lay around here? [ARIZONA *yells*] Oops! Sorry!

ARIZONA: Quite all right! Champagne! Hey, you, what's your name?

HANNA: Hanna. Hanna O'Brien.

ARIZONA: Take this champagne upstairs! I'm through here in fifteen. Sit on it till I get there!

Light fades on ARIZONA, *but stays on* HANNA *as she holds champagne bottle up.*

HANNA: Well, I got the job. And after my fourth pregnancy, I discovered a horrible revelation. I loved that bum bartender! Of course, so did Betty, Rita, and Wanda! [*Slams bottle down on bar*] But nevertheless, for the first time I *loved!* It was no more a game of trying to win something from my sister. I was in love, and I loved the world, and I began loving other people and things instead of just liking. But I also began to *hate!* [*Pauses, reflecting*] I wish I could just *like* again! [*Jumps back on breeze-hole, sighs and freezes*]

Lights fade out on HANNA, *up on* ARIZONA, *who takes off his apron from the bartender scene.*

ARIZONA: So, after all the other Miss Polaskis, I said to myself, "Hey, Arizona, what do you need it for?" and I closed up shop, so to speak. Luckily, I found this place. It's a little out of the way for me; I'm from Arizona, remember? I left there because I didn't have . . . skip it. But I like this place because it's *vital!* Things are always happening. [HANNA *now begins waving two small American flags and singing "Over There"*] I'm maintained! History surrounds it. There's confusion, paradox. It's life in a nutshell. There's excitement. There's old dames over air holes with snatches

*waving in the breeze, like an armistice flag,
letting you know peace is at hand. But they
only get you out of your foxhole to be shot to
death.* I was in the Army also. [*Checks time on
invisible clock somewhere in space*] But we
won't be able to go into that today! [*He motions for* HANNA *to stop; she does*]

HANNA: [*Stopping*] Damn! My one big musical
number!

ARIZONA: I often wonder, after my recurring
dream—you remember, "Penny for your
thoughts"—what would have happened, where
I'd be today, if I had really got to talk to Miss
Polaski instead of taking her on *Religion, the
Beginning and End of Christianity,* and using
the King James Bible, revised edition, to boost
her box up! Oh, we weren't trying to be sacri-
legious or rebellious; it's just that that was
the thickest book around, and with Miss
Polaski you needed a high boost under it to get
a new angle. After high school, I came to New
York to go to Columbia. But I still think about
Miss Polaski spread out over the King James
Bible, revised edition. All I remember now was
the heat. I wanted to take my coat off, but she
said to keep it on in case someone came. No
one came except me. All I remember now was
the heat and the heaviness of my coat. [*Puts
tie around neck, over bare chest*]

HANNA: [*As hat-check girl*] Coat check! Young
man, would you like to check your coat?

Current dance tune fades in.

ARIZONA: My first year in college, and in New
York, I spent discovering nightclubs.

HANNA: Look! If you want to come in, you have
to check your coat. It's the policy of the house.

ARIZONA: Mrs. Polaski!

HANNA: Weiss! Hanna Weiss! *Miss* Hanna
Weiss!

ARIZONA: You ever been in Arizona?

HANNA: [*Laughing*] Never had asthma! From
St. Louis, Pittsburgh, New York—the Grey-
hound Express route. That'll be a quarter.
Thank you!

ARIZONA: It's just that you remind me of someone.

HANNA: Oh, how nice! Your mother? Have your
picture taken; send it to Mother. Let her
know you are still alive and in good hands.
[*Flash!*] That'll be five, thank you.

ARIZONA: No, you remind me of the first lady I
tried to talk to. . . .

HANNA: How was it? You want to talk? Converse about the universe? Who's doing what to
whom in Vietnam? General problems of society or small-town gossip? Buy the talkative
lady a drink! Champagne, please! That'll be
ten. Thank you!

ARIZONA: Ten times I tried to talk to her but . . .

HANNA: When you refer to "her" . . . what do
you mean? Your mother or . . . Miss Polaski?

ARIZONA: Miss Polaski. Was I going too fast for
you?

HANNA: When you go too fast—and, like the
others, you will—I will stop you!

They stop dancing and stand face to face.

ARIZONA: Ten times I tried to talk to her, but I
never could reach her.

HANNA: Your words were obviously too big for
her.

ARIZONA: So I always had to resort to mere physical compromise.

HANNA: Try me! [*Instant sex denoted on stage
by both bumping pelvises and grunting*]
That'll be twenty! Thank you! [*Going back to
breeze-hole*] I have enjoyed this conversation
immensely-ee-ee-ahhh-h-h-h-h!! [*Freezes*]

ARIZONA: As I grew older, conversations grew
shorter. I became less curious. After all, I
knew how they would end. [*He freezes*]

HANNA: [*Breaks pose*] What is this? All this
decadence, moral decay, incest, segregation,
homosexuality—VD is on the uprise? What
has happened to all the little niceties of life?
What in the fuck has happened to all the little
niceties of life? So I asked this boy—never can
remember his name, oh probably because he
never told me—I would ask, feeling his smooth
skin, "Where the fuck has love gone, Buster
Brown?" And he would say to me, "Oh, Aunt
Hanna, you are nuts!" He had the cutest way
of saying that with his smile. As you can tell
by now, I am just crazy about smiles. [*Reflecting*] But I never was crazy about anyone
calling me "Aunt"! I met him, this boy, the
last one, on my day off, Monday. I was walking along Broadway in the Forties and it began
to rain, so I had a little time to kill. I ducked
into the doorway of Horn and Hardart's, and
there, through the revolving glass, I could see
him. I knew then that this was my new silent
stranger. [ARIZONA *places two chairs onstage,
facing each other, sits in one, puts bandanna
around neck and begins to eat imaginary food,
making crude slurping sounds*] For when he
smiled, barren deserts became green valleys,
ominous clouds became crimson rainbows—
and my heart, my imprisoned heart, became
free and I was again free to fly. [*She goes to
where* ARIZONA *is sitting*]—And then he had
to speak.

He burps.

ARIZONA: You can sit down, lady. No one is
sitting there.

HANNA: Once more my illusionary god turned
out to be just another hungry cowpoke. But,

since I wasn't looking for religion, I decided to get a piece of—pie. [*She begins to circle him like a vulture, humming "Chicago"*]

ARIZONA: Look, lady, sit down if you want, but stop staring. This food is hard enough to digest.

HANNA: Raining out! Thought I'd get a piece of . . . pie.

ARIZONA: Lady, are you going to sit down? Your nervousness is reaching me and my strained carrots.

HANNA: [*Jumps into chair with the grace of an armadillo in heat*] There! Now I'm all sat down, aren't I? [ARIZONA *ignores her.* HANNA *takes handkerchief from bosom and begins blowing her nose as he continues crudely eating his food*] So . . . where you from? [*Still blowing her nose*]

ARIZONA: What is this, Roseland? Lady, I'm trying to eat my dinna! [*She stops blowing her nose*] I'm from Arizona.

HANNA: Of course you are! How silly of me to ask! You came here because you didn't have asthma! [*Laughing*]

ARIZONA: No! [*She stops laughing*] Moved here with my family. Last week. [*He smiles, buttering imaginary bread*]

HANNA: Would you do that again?

ARIZONA: Do what? Butter my bread?

HANNA: Smile! Would you smile again? [*He does. She sighs*] Smile! You are beautiful when you smile. [*He smiles; she sighs*] It warms me! [*He smiles; she sighs*] Teases me! [*Repeat*] Charges me! [*One more time*] Oh, that smile!! [*She goes slightly insane and faints in chair*]

ARIZONA: Lady, I bet you'd have an orgasm if you saw me go all the way and laugh! [*He begins to laugh.* HANNA *stops him by rising and pulling his head into her bosom*]

HANNA: Would you like to see New York? [ARIZONA *sneezes; she falls back onto chair*] Ahh-h-h . . . would you like to go for a walk? The rain has stopped.

ARIZONA: I'm not very ambitious about that idea, ma'am.

HANNA: Then may I rephrase that question? [*Jumping in his lap*] Ya wanna do it with a very tired ticket-taker?

ARIZONA: [*Licking his fingers*] All right, let's go. [*He carries her to his area*]

HANNA: So I hustled him up to my apartment to check him out further. I live in the West Forties, so we didn't have far to walk. I kept him for nine months. He stayed for only nine months, and once more the Wicked Witch of the West Side was a widow. That's me—a

nickname this nice old queer I share the hall john with coined for me. How I hate that vicious faggot!! Every morning, on my way to work, I'd meet him in the hall, draped in his cerise kimono, and he'd curtsy, saying, "Hail, the Wicked Witch of the West Side!" Now that's no way to begin your day, believe me! So, after that one left, Hanna rationalized to herself, "Do you really need this emotional aggravation?" Hanna has always been an objective person.

ARIZONA: [*Leaving with clothes*] Of course not! Find other outlets!

HANNA: . . . was the immediate reply! [*To the exiting* ARIZONA] "But what other outlets?" I asked again. [*Turning from* ARIZONA, *facing audience*] And there was my answer in red neon lights—"Friends, friends, friends!" I threw myself into society which I had long ignored because of other diversions. Hanna suffocated herself with friends, which she has always been able to *make,* if she so desired. An extra girl who's a good dancer is always in demand, and Hanna's always been up on the latest foot routines and the juiciest gossip. And soon there wasn't a clique from the West Side to the East Side that I didn't belong to. I was "in" then, as they would say downtown. "But 'in' what?" as my late mother Gilda back in Springfield would say. Of course, I never starved with all the *hor de' whores* [*Mispronounced*] around, and I really didn't have to rent an apartment because the parties never seemed to stop! But expensive caviar makes me break into a rash, bubbly champagne makes me run for the nearest stomach pump, and cocktail gossip makes my conscience vomit!! But one night . . . at one of those "in" affairs, I found a man who seemed to understand misunderstood ticket-takers who stand over air holes. Don't laugh, you! I did find one! Found him in February around Washington's Birthday. At first I thought he was a little weird because he didn't try to undress me with his opening comment. Yet he interested me! And the funny thing was . . . he wasn't young, nor that handsome, and he wasn't from Arizona. Get it? Do you get it? He wasn't from Arizona! Yet he interested Hanna; he maintained her! Hanna had finally been saved from her destructive pattern! [*To imaginary man sitting in opposite chair—denoted by a follow spot*] Yes, I'll have another drink, thank you. [*Spot moves from chair as if man is getting her a drink*] But his walk! Like a *duck!* [*Laughing*] He waddled just like a pregnant duck! And I would say, "No, no, that's all wrong!" And when he spoke—well, I was embarrassed that one of my smart friends might hear, and I would always reply to his cliché remarks, "Oh really." [*Quite bored*] "Oh, really? Uhh-hum, uhh-hum." And *dull!* He never wanted to do anything. Well, hardly anything. Bicycle riding! "Now, what do I have to wear to go bicycle riding?" And I would tell him, "Ahhh, you want to do all the wrong things!" [*She rises, turns her back to chair, and then faces it again*] Then one night he wasn't around and I casually asked some dear friends where he was, and they said, "Oh, do you mean the funny little guy with the wobbly walk? Do you mean the older, not so handsome one with the unbelievable language? Do you mean the bicycle peddler?" And I tried to tell them, "No! No! *I mean the one who loved me!!*" Well, I tried to tell them, but they kept stuffing caviar and champagne and gossip down my throat just like they prepare a goose for paté. [*Choking, she falls in the chair now left empty by the man, and clutches it*] That was five years ago, but I continued to go to those dull soirees because I knew that one night I was going to find him, or someone like him, hiding in some corner embarrassed to walk or to say anything. And when I did, I wasn't going to say, "No, no," or "Oh really, uhh-hum," or "That's all wrong!" And when I did, every disgustingly sweet maraschino cherry I'd chewed, every greasy, rolled anchovy I'd swallowed, and every choice backbiting tidbit I'd been forced to relish, would have been worth it! And then Hanna would be saved. [*ARIZONA returns, as in beginning*] But Hanna never found him again. All she found was malnutrition, hangovers, and more and more undependable Arizonas! So, after five years of gracious society, Hanna, alone, faced the mirror on the wall and asked, "One more time, Hanna baby?" The answer—finally, after so many years of replying, "Yes, yes, Hanna baby, let's try one more time"—finally, the answer was, "No, no, Hanna baby, it's time to hang up your red shoes." So, luckily, I found this place. It's far from heaven, but it's relaxing. It's tranquil.

ARIZONA: It's vital! Something's always happening! [*Begins doing push-ups*]

HANNA: You can let your hair down, or if you get bored there's always someone passing through to amuse, divert, interest you until the boredom passes. The acoustics are perfect. Why, one can hear whole thoughts and conversations without actually having to participate!

ARIZONA: On the first day, God created man in His own image. Does God really look like Kate Smith?

HANNA: Of course, most of the conversations and thoughts one overhears here are vague, meaningless . . . and cleverly contrived. Only because they know you are listening, and they try much too hard to please. If only they would just be still and smile!

ARIZONA: On the second day, God committed suicide and hasn't been seen around the neighborhood bars since.

HANNA: How I hate cleverness that confuses emotion! How I hate intellectualisms! How I hate young naked boys without names who stand in a maze of mirrors in my Fun House, tempting the Wicked Witch of the West Side into believing maybe she shouldn't be here after all! [*ARIZONA pushes his pelvis toward her; she retreats*] How I hate brief encounters! How I hate people who think they know you! [*Pauses, reflecting*] How I hate people who spend all their energies hating! [*She seeks the comfort of the breeze-hole*]

ARIZONA: So I found this place one day last month. I came to the beach and it turned cloudy suddenly, and I had some time to kill.

HANNA: To kill Hanna's privacy. Her only safety.

ARIZONA: So I was walking along the boardwalk and I noticed this place by the amusing posters out front. *"See How Rome Burned While Nero Played." "See Lovely Marie Antoinette at the Guillotine." "See Why Hanna's Skirt Won't Stay Down."*

HANNA: Stop! I beg your pardon. What did you say?

ARIZONA: [*Continuing*] So I thought to myself, "Who is this Hanna?" Of course I was never very big on history. . . .

HANNA: Young man! Hey, Arizona! I'm speaking to you!

ARIZONA: Me?

HANNA: Yes! What were you saying? I couldn't help overhearing you.

ARIZONA: Uhhh . . . "So I was walking along the boardwalk and I . . ."

HANNA: No! No! After "Lovely Marie Antoinette at the Guillotine." After "Guillotine." Something or other about "skirt."

ARIZONA: [*Remembering*] Oh . . . "See Why Hanna's Skirt Won't Stay Down."

HANNA: How dare they!!! I'm not part of this place!!! *"See why Hanna's skirt won't stay down!!!"* I'm not part of this place!!! How dare you stand there and assume I am part of this place. And don't tell me you're not assuming that. You are assuming. And how I hate you for that. How I hate you. . . .

ARIZONA: [*Defending himself*] Look, lady, you were here when I came in. I've always seen you here. One can only believe what he sees these days.

HANNA: I come . . . I go. I come here to relax. I like air. I don't have to tell you all this. I come, I go. . . .

ARIZONA: [*Mocking*] She comes, she goes, she comes. . . .

HANNA: *Stop!!* Naughty, naked young man! Prankish child mustn't upset the sensitive lady. She teases much too easily.

The clock now reads seven o'clock. Carnival music returns.

VOICE OF BARKER: Door's opening! Step right in, folks! Admission only ten cents!

HANNA: It must be seven already. I think I'll stay a few more minutes before the crowds start coming in. I wonder where I'll eat tonight?

VOICE OF BARKER: See *"How Rome Burned While Nero Played,"* see *"Lovely Marie Antoinette at the Guillotine,"* see *"Why Hanna's Skirt Won't Stay Down."*

HANNA: Those bastards! Who are they to do this to me? [*She begins to freeze uncontrollably over the breeze-hole*]

ARIZONA: [*Admiring himself in mirror*] She comes, she goes.

VOICE OF BARKER: And see our new attraction: *"Smiley, the Smiling Narcissistic Wonder, Trapped in the Mirror-Maze."*

ARIZONA: What? What did he say?

HANNA: [*Amused, if plaster of paris can be amused*] "Step right in, folks! Admission only ten cents."

ARIZONA: No! No! After "Hanna's Skirt Up." Something about "trapped!" What did he say? [*He freezes slowly in front of the mirrors*]

HANNA: [*Freezing slowly*] Look, sonny, you're new here so I'll give you a few complimentary tips of advice. When that gate out there opens

and those stupid people pay their greasy dimes, they want what they were told they'd see. They want you to smile. They want Hanna's skirt up at all times. They want Rome to burn. They don't want to know why; they don't give a damn about your confused childhood. They won't even notice that Hanna's skirt is nothing but shreds now. They want their illusions. So be a good kid and you'll go far. They might even send you to the big time—the London, Paris houses. I hear they get as much as fifty cents admission over there. And all you have to do is keep your mouth shut and smile. . . .

Canned laughter joins the carousel music.

ARIZONA: I'm not part of it. I come, I go. . . .

Carousel music fades out, leaving only the terrified canned laughter.

HANNA: Now w-h-e-n they c-o-m-e t-h-r-o-u-g-h t-h-a-t d-o-o-o-r, y-o-u m-u-s-t-n't s—a—y a w—o—r—d!! [*She freezes completely*]

ARIZONA: I-I-I c—o—m—e, I-I-I g—o. [He freezes]

The lights shift suddenly to a deathly green as the life is drained from the two characters. Ten seconds. Bright and merry carnival glitter in sound and color return as the two are left, frozen, wax figures, human impostors.

VOICE OF BARKER: There they are, folks! Step right in! Admission only ten cents!

THE BARKER *is now seen* smoking a cigar and holding a broom, with which he sweeps the area around the frozen characters. He takes a rag out of his back pocket and dusts off* HANNA's *arm, then goes over to* ARIZONA's *area and gathers up his clothes. Silence as the lights fade to darkness.*

---

* The BARKER's appearance may be omitted. If *Who Killed My Bald Sister Sophie?* is played as a second act, SOPHIE should appear onstage during this final image.

THE JOURNEY OF THE FIFTH HORSE

a play in two acts

Ronald Ribman

The Journey of the Fifth Horse was first presented by the American Place Theatre (Wynn Handman, director) at St. Clement's Church, New York City, on April 13, 1966, with the following cast:

TERENTIEVNA, *housekeeper to Nikolai Alexeevich Chulkaturin* .... *Mary Hayden*

ZODITCH, *first reader in the Grubov Publishing Company* .... *Dustin Hoffman*

SERGEY, *grandchild of Terentievna* .... *Christopher Strater*

* RUBIN, *apprentice reader in the Grubov Publishing Company* .... *William H. Bassett*

† MISS GRUBOV, *owner of the Grubov Publishing Company* .... *Susan Anspach*

‡ PANDALEVSKI, *supervising printer in the Grubov Publishing Company* .... *Lee Wallace*

KATERINA PROLOMNAYA, *a landlady* .... *Catherine Gaffigan*

NIKOLAI ALEXEEVICH CHULKATURIN, *a landowner* .... *Michael Tolan*

DOCTOR KORVIN, *a physician* .... *Mark Hammer*

LEVINOV, *a lawyer* .... *Harry Miller*

§ FEATHERS, *a cleaning girl* .... *Susan Lipton*

KIRILLA MATVEICH OZHOGIN, *a landowner* .... *Allan Rich*

† ELIZAVETA KIRILLOVNA, *his daughter* .... *Susan Anspach*

‡ BIZMIONKOV, *family friend of the Ozhogins* .... *Lee Wallace*

ANNA, *wife of Kirilla* .... *Martha Greenhouse*

GREGORY, *a neighbor to Zoditch* .... *Jack Aaron*

§ VOLOBRINA, *a servant girl* .... *Susan Lipton*

* CAPTAIN IVAN PETROVICH NARVINSKY, *a cavalry officer* .... *William H. Bassett*

TANIA, *an unmarried girl* .... *Jane Buchanan*

LIEUTENANT ZIMIN, *a cavalry officer* .... *Jim Doerr*

OFFICERS .... *Brian Turkington*
Ron Seka

The following roles are doubled:

* RUBIN and CAPTAIN IVAN PETROVICH NARVINSKY
† MISS GRUBOV and ELIZAVETA KIRILLOVNA
‡ PANDALEVSKI and BIZMIONKOV
§ FEATHERS and VOLOBRINA

It was directed by Larry Arrick. The scenery and costumes were by Kert Lundell; the lighting by Roger Morgan.

The Journey of the Fifth Horse is based, in part, on the story "Diary of a Superfluous Man," by Ivan Turgenev.

ACT ONE

Scene One: The Grubov Publishing House.
Scene Two: Zoditch's apartment.

ACT TWO

The entire action takes place in Zoditch's apartment house.

TIME

The late nineteenth century.

PLACE

St. Petersburg, Russia.

ACT I

Scene I

PLACE: An office space in the Grubov Publishing House occupied by ZODITCH *and* RUBIN.
TIME: Late afternoon.
SCENE: There are two desks: RUBIN'S *on the left side of the room;* ZODITCH'S *on the right side.*
ON RISE: The stage is completely dark. We hear a voice.

VOICE: In Samarkand I saw a monkey yellow-splotched and dying in a cage, and as I made to hasten by, he grasped my sleeve as if there might be something more to the matter.

Lights up. RUBIN, *a young man of about twenty-five years of age, sits behind his desk tweezing and clipping his moustache. His desk is bare, in rather sharp contrast to the fairly well-cluttered desk of* ZODITCH. ZODITCH *stands on a little ladder near the back wall of the room, engaged in hanging a border of black crepe around a large portrait of* MR. GRUBOV, *the founder of the firm.* ZODITCH *is about ten years older than* RUBIN. *He is thin, wiry, quick and nervous in his movements. When he puts his glasses on you can hardly see his eyes. He is of somewhat less than average height, and losing his hair. In front of* ZODITCH'S *desk sit two visitors:* TERENTIEVNA, *a peasant woman in her early sixties, and her grandson* SERGEY, *about seventeen years old—a simpleminded boy who is stylishly dressed in clothes that are obviously too small for him. His arms dangle out of his sleeves. The clothes seem ready to burst.*

TERENTIEVNA: [*To* ZODITCH] Did you say something, mister?

ZODITCH: No.

TERENTIEVNA: Oh, I thought you said something. I thought you was saying you wanted to read the writing, mister.

ZODITCH: I said nothing, madam. I am hanging the crepe now.

TERENTIEVNA: Because if you want I can let you read the writing now, mister.

ZODITCH: [*Exasperated*] I cannot read your master's manuscript now, madam. I am hanging the crepe now. You have come at a bad time. There has been a death in the firm; our employer, Mr. Grubov, has passed away.

TERENTIEVNA: Oh, has he?

ZODITCH: Yes.

TERENTIEVNA: That's a sorrow.

ZODITCH: Yes.

TERENTIEVNA: And a sorrow it was when my master died, him being so sadly reduced in fortune.

ZODITCH *stares at her for a moment and then resigns himself to the fact that she will not be silenced.*

SERGEY: He didn't have a kopeck what you could call his. And them what he owed money to was fierce.

TERENTIEVNA: There was always the money-lenders banging at the door of the house, but I never let none of them get at the master. I kept the doors locked in their faces I did, and I told them what they could do with their bills receivable. As God is my judge, mister, they woulda pulled the sheets off the bed he was dying on, if I'da let 'em, so vicious they was about getting their monies. What makes people get that way over money do you suppose, mister?

RUBIN: [*He speaks before* ZODITCH *has a chance to answer. He gestures at the painting of* MR. GRUBOV] Well, what do you think, Mr. Zoditch, have they buried him yet?

ZODITCH, *without answering, starts down the ladder.*

TERENTIEVNA: The master's house was what they called the Chulkaturin family house. [ZODITCH *looks at her*] Chulkaturin, mister. It's a name what nobody gets right, and him, poor soul, being the last of 'em what bore the name, who's to care now what the rights and wrongs of sounding it be?

RUBIN: Now that Mr. Grubov is tucked away, we can expect some changes wouldn't you say, Mr. Zoditch? [ZODITCH *still doesn't answer*] I'd imagine Mr. Pandalevski would be the man to watch.

ZODITCH *sits down and begins adjusting himself. He removes the garters from his arms, pushes down his sleeves, runs his hand through his hair.*

TERENTIEVNA: And a hard thing it is to say "family house" when all that were near and dear to poor Mr. Chulkaturin, his mama and papa, was already gone and buried.

SERGEY: They was dead, wasn't they? Tell 'em about the rats.

TERENTIEVNA: During the winter I took service with the gentleman, I found the house overrun.

SERGEY: Rats big as horses' heads.

TERENTIEVNA: Not only rats, mister. Moles and other creature things what come burrowing in through the cellar to get in from the snow. He wouldn't let me drive them out, though I could have easy enough without him knowing because by that time he was near finished with this world, but I didn't have the heart to go against his wishes, him being perishing like he was and the doctor telling us to leave him be about the little things.

ZODITCH: Madam, I am not interested in rats, moles and medical reports.

SERGEY: And the lousy stream? What about that?

RUBIN: Of course the fact that Mr. Pandalevski accompanied Miss Grubov to the cemetery may not mean anything definite, unless it's a step in the right direction. A young girl has to rely on someone when her father's dead, don't you think?

ZODITCH *starts angrily over to* RUBIN's *desk. He slams down a stack of manuscripts on it.*

ZODITCH: Work. Tweeze on your own time.

TERENTIEVNA: The boy is meaning a stream what belonged to the properties. When the master died the water went particularly bad.

SERGEY: It stank, that's what it did. And the garden had nothing to eat from it.

TERENTIEVNA: It was a flower garden, you see, mister.

SERGEY: Well, ya can't eat flowers, so what's the sense in that?

TERENTIEVNA: The flowers was particular treasured by him. You see, mister, he was a gentleman, which was why he didn't need to plant vegetables. And then after he died the spring came around again and everything was coming up, and that's a sorrow, him dead and everything coming up colorful.

RUBIN: Only who would have thought it would turn out to be Mr. Pandalevski she relied on? My money was on you, but he's a comer, he is. Well, it's all a ladder, Mr. Zoditch. It's up or it's down. We can't be keeping our feet on the same rung.

ZODITCH: Be still. I warn you. I'm the first reader.

TERENTIEVNA: The good Lord has his ways, I know, and none of us can choose the comings and goings of things, but I prayed for him that he would last through the spring so the flowers would give him pleasure.

SERGEY: So why didja pour the soapwater on 'em?

ZODITCH: Madam, I have already told you, you have come at a bad time. There has been a death in the firm.

TERENTIEVNA: [*Begins coughing. A very bad cough. She pulls out her handkerchief and spits into it*] That clears it up, it does. So that's how it is with us, mister. All Mr. Chulkaturin left us in exchange for the cruel months of our services is what I got here. [*She takes a small parcel from her bag*] And it's for getting it made into a book with you bookmongers, which is what the gentleman himself was most insistent on so we could get paid something for our kindnesses to him, that me and the boy came to Petersburg. He didn't pay us a bit of wages so it's a fair thing we're doing now trying to make a little money off his writings, wouldn't you say, mister?

ZODITCH: Yes. Yes. [*Annoyed, he takes the offered parcel*]

TERENTIEVNA: Not that I begrudge working for the sick. Doing a Christian duty to another fellow creature is doing no more than what Christ expects of us.

ZODITCH *starts to unwrap the parcel. Suddenly there is the sound of a bell—the kind of bell that hangs over a door. Then the door slams shut.*

RUBIN: They're back.

There is a flurry of motion. RUBIN *shoves his manicuring equipment into the desk and hurriedly begins reading and taking notes at the same time.* ZODITCH *puts on his coat. In come* MISS GRUBOV *and* MR. PANDALEVSKI. *They are dressed in black. As they pass by* ZODITCH, *he scurries out from behind his desk.*

ZODITCH: Miss Grubov. [PANDALEVSKI *and* MISS GRUBOV *stop.* ZODITCH *searches his pockets for an envelope and then remembers it is on his desk. He takes the envelope and hands it to* MISS GRUBOV] A note of condolence.

MISS GRUBOV: Thank you, Mr. Zoditch. [*She starts to leave, but* ZODITCH *tries to get in a few more words while he has the opportunity.* PANDALEVSKI *frowns*]

ZODITCH: [*He speaks falteringly*] I just wanted to say that I thought your father was wonderful, Miss Grubov, wonderful, a man to be admired, respected. It was an honor to be employed by him these past twelve years. We all miss him: a loss, a great loss . . .

MISS GRUBOV: Thank you. [*Starts to go again. Again* ZODITCH *dribbles out a few words*]

ZODITCH: I hope it was not too cold for you, Miss Grubov. I thought of you in the carriage and I said they will forget the extra blankets. I . . . [*Starts backing away*] Excuse me. Excuse me.

MISS GRUBOV: It was fine in the carriage, Mr. Zoditch, thank you. [*She walks off stage*]

PANDALEVSKI: Bring up the tea to Miss Grubov. [*He starts to exit after* MISS GRUBOV *and then turns*] And a cup for me.

RUBIN: [*Although* PANDALEVSKI'S *words were spoken mostly to* ZODITCH, RUBIN *answers*] Yes, Mr. Pandalevski. Right away. [*He starts out from behind his desk*]

ZODITCH: Where are you going? It is my privilege to bring up the tea. [RUBIN *just smiles and exits.* ZODITCH *runs after him*] Where do you think you're going? [*We hear him running down the steps after* RUBIN] It is my privilege.

[*As soon as* ZODITCH *leaves,* TERENTIEVNA *spits into the wastepaper basket. She opens her purse and, withdrawing a small flask, takes a quick snort.* SERGEY *begins hitting his boots*]

SERGEY: [*To boots*] Damn you. Damn you. [*To* TERENTIEVNA] I don't like it here, grandma. I don't like him. I don't like anybody. [*Grabs his boots and starts wringing them with his hands*] Arrrh, Arrrh, Arrrh. They're haunted. They're killing my feet. His ghost is in them. What's the sense in having boots to kill you? I don't want them. I told you to let him have his boots right from the beginning. [*Strikes boots again*] Arrrh. Arrrh. I don't feel well. Let's go to another bookmaker's place. You remember I wanted him to have his boots? You remember that? I don't like it here.

TERENTIEVNA: Be still!

SERGEY: Listen, I want a regular suit. While we're in Petersburg I want you to buy me a regular suit.

TERENTIEVNA: You have a regular suit.

SERGEY: This is not a regular suit. It hates me. It's his suit. His suit is not a regular suit. It doesn't fit me. The pants are too tight. Look how they make me walk. [*Gets up and walks as uncomfortably as possible. He keeps grabbing at the pants*] You see. Look. You see how I'm walking. They're tearing my legs to pieces. I can't put anything in the pockets. [*Flings himself back in the chair*] The jacket is crushing my chest. It cuts me under the arms. It twists my shoulders. Look at the collar. Do you see how tight it is? I can't breathe. Arrrh, Arrrh. Listen, you know what I think? [*Leans forward confidentially*] This was the suit Mr. Chulkaturin was meant to be buried in. Not the lousy one. This was the one he wanted. That's why it doesn't fit. It was supposed to go with him to the grave. I told you to let him take this suit. Let him take the good suit was what I said.

TERENTIEVNA: Be still!

SERGEY: I can't be still. It itches me. It chokes me. It tears my legs. It rubs my neck. It doesn't let me alone. Arrrh. Arrrh. [*Beats at the boots and tears them off*] Leave my feet alone, damn you. Damn you! [*Switches topic*] And when are we going to see the wild animals? I want to see the wild animals of Petersburg. You promised me. [*Again switching topic*] And maybe they won't buy his writings and then we won't make any money and then we've come all this way for what? For what? [*Rubbing his feet*] Arrrh. Arrrh. And then what? What about my yellow sled? What about that? Where's the money for that?

ZODITCH *and* RUBIN *enter fighting over possession of a tea tray containing a tea pot, two cups, and a stack of biscuits.*

ZODITCH: It is my responsibility to bring the tea. Will you let go of it?

RUBIN: Mr. Pandalevski was talking to me.

ZODITCH: He was not, Mr. Rubin. He was talking to me. I have always brought the tea to Mr. Grubov and now I will bring it to Miss Grubov.

RUBIN: Will you let go? I am to bring the tea. He was talking to me.

ZODITCH: I am not going to let go. You let go. He was talking to me. Don't be silly, Mr. Rubin.

RUBIN: I am not going to let go. I'm not being silly.

ZODITCH: Let go. You are being very silly.

RUBIN: No. It is you who are being very silly.

ZODITCH: You.

RUBIN: You.

ZODITCH: You.

There is a real skirmish. RUBIN *pulls the tray free with a final jerk.*

RUBIN: You! [*He walks off stage.* ZODITCH *begins wandering about the stage*]

TERENTIEVNA: [*Thinks this a good time to continue her monologue*] The master was a very refined type such as yourself, Mr. Zoditch, and he had a good handwriting, too, which comes from being so sensitive to things. You could tell he was delicate just from looking at his hands.

ZODITCH *is at this moment in his pacing wringing his hands, and making almost animal*

noises in his frustration. He sits down on
RUBIN's *chair.*

ZODITCH: Madhouse. Madhouse. Up the ladder,
is it? [*He picks up a small bundle of* RUBIN's
pencils and breaks them]

TERENTIEVNA: Yes, mister, a madhouse it is for
sure, which is something of what the master
said when he was trying to save the family
properties which his father had gambled away.
That was what they all said at the burial.

ZODITCH: [*Highly distracted, jumps up*] Who
said? Why do you go on and on? What are
you talking about?

TERENTIEVNA: It was "they" what said it, mister.
Those at the church what knew the family.
They was coming and going in the law courts
all the time, the mother and father was, and
after the mother and father passed on, the
poor gentleman continued fighting to save
what was his. If you ask me, it was the courts
what drove him back and forth like a poor
pigeon across the country. It was them what
broke his heart. That was what done it,
mister. The law stealing his property. Even
down to the summer house which the law
stole away from him for taxes. Didn't he get
in a rage when he learnt that. [RUBIN *reenters carrying the empty tea tray. He crosses
over to his desk and, sitting on the edge of it,
stares at* ZODICH. ZODICH *stares back at him
furiously.* TERENTIEVNA *continues, trying to regain his attention*] You should have heard him,
mister. "I won't have it. They won't get away
with it," he says and such like, but they did
get away with it. [*And then in a different
tone of voice, as if what she now has to say
has particular significance to* ZODITCH] Which
is what they always do, ain't it, mister? The
worst getting away with it all. [ZODITCH *looks
at her and they exchange a quiet stare.* TE-
RENTIEVNA *then continues as before*] Oh, he
was as much a fighter for things what was
his as ever Death took away. He was never
one to give up on things on account of him
being a delicate soul. He was a brave sort
and nobody can grudge him that. God love
him for it.

ZODITCH: So? So? You are finished? Eh? [*Angrily
unwraps the parcel containing the MS and
glances at it*] This is a diary. [*Pushes the
MS back to* TERENTIEVNA. *Keeps looking
over at* RUBIN, *off and on*] We do not publish
diaries. You have talked all this time for
nothing.

TERENTIEVNA: Oh no, mister. It ain't a diary.
It's papers.

ZODITCH: It's a diary. [*Madly opens up to one of
the pages and shoves it under her nose*] You

see? March 20th? A day of the month. That's
a diary.

TERENTIEVNA: No, mister. I can't read dates.
Me and the boy can't read.

At this moment MR. PANDALEVSKI *stands unseen at stage right, a cup of tea in his hand.
Only* RUBIN *sees him.* RUBIN *gets instantly
to work.*

ZODITCH: Well, I read dates, and it's a diary,
madam. I assure you. And I assure you that
we do not read diaries, nor have we ever in
the entire history of Grubov Publications published one. So if you will excuse me . . . [*When*
ZODITCH *looks over toward* RUBIN *and sees*
RUBIN *working, he imagines it is because he
has asserted himself with* TERENTIEVNA, *and
put* RUBIN *in his place. It fills him with renewed determination to be assertive. He keeps
looking at* RUBIN]

TERENTIEVNA: You see, mister, it was just as a
favor to the poor gentleman what wrote it
because he wanted to see us paid for our
goods and services that we come at all. He
was a fine talker and word writer.

ZODITCH: Oh, he was, was he?

SERGEY: [*To* TERENTIEVNA] You're going to take
me to see the wild animals of Petersburg!

ZODITCH:[*With mounting anger*] A good writer
was he? [*Whips open the pages of the diary*]
Well, he had a bad handwriting. How does
that suit you? He wrote with the hand of a
pigmy. Tiny, tiny letters, too backward, too
feminine. And where is the punctuation? Do
you see the punctuation? What has he done
with that? Perhaps it is a very long sentence
and all the punctuation is at the end? [*Turns
the pages*] Ah, here is a comma. I have found
a comma! But where are the periods, the
colons, the semicolons, the question marks?
Where?

TERENTIEVNA: It's just writing, mister.

ZODITCH: Perhaps he has placed all his punctuation on the last page. [*Turns to the last page*]
No. I do not see them. In the middle, perhaps
they are stored in the middle. [*Turns to the
middle*] No. They are not in the middle. So
I will shake the pages and see if they fall out.
[*Shakes the pages.* SERGEY *stares at the diary
and the floor as if he expects the punctuation
to fall out*]

TERENTIEVNA: It's just writing, mister.

ZODITCH: There is no *just* writing! There is only
proper and improper writing. Your Mister
Chulkaturin doesn't cross his t's, he ignores
his t's, he makes his t's look like l's, and the
l's like b's, and the b's like h's, and the h's
like nothing at all. And why doesn't he dot
his i's? Why doesn't he loop his e's? I'll tell

you why. Because he doesn't know anything; because he doesn't know how to write. We have here a babbling of consonants, a scribbling scribble, a disease that knows no punctuation, no sentencing, no paragraphing, a singular disease . . . [*At this point he sees* MR. PANDALEVSKI, *but he cannot stop. He would like to stop, but he goes on and on*] that rambles, that goes no place, that floats on streams of bombast, a leaking hulk of language in a sea of rhetoric, a babbling monument of incoherency . . . [*He rises in his chair until he stands*] a vacuum, a wasteland, a desert, a void, a . . . [*He stops. There is a moment of absolute silence, as* PANDALEVSKI *comes forward*]

PANDALEVSKI: Read it! Take it home with you, Mr. Zoditch. Read it!

Lights out.

Scene Two

PLACE: ZODITCH'S *apartment.*

TIME: *Early evening. Same day.*

SCENE: *The apartment is poorly furnished. It contains a coal stove, a desk, a bed, sundry other things.*

ON RISE: *The apartment is unoccupied. Outside the apartment, offstage right, we hear the shrill sounds of many small dogs barking. We next see* ZODITCH *hastening up the staircase. When he reaches the door to his room he stops and turns around.*

ZODITCH: [*Speaks out loud, although the words are directed towards himself*] Bark your lungs out, you bitches. You think I'm afraid of your dogs, Katerina Prolomnaya. I'll take a stick to them. I'll beat their brains out. And where is the hall light, Katerina Prolomnaya? You are quick enough to ask for the rent. [*The barking ceases.* ZODITCH *enters his room and, standing near the door, shouts into the hall*] There will be no rent without a hall light! [*Shuts door quickly. Barking immediately begins again. Offstage sound of a woman's voice,* KATERINA PROLOMNAYA, *the landlady*]

KATERINA: [*Offstage*] Who opened his mouth? Show yourself! You miserable pack of cowards. I'll set my dogs on ya, if I hear another word. You hear me? It'll be a cold day in hell before Katerina Prolomnaya takes garbage from the pack of you.

From somewhere in the darkened hall comes a feeble voice.

VOICE: No rent without a hall light!

This call is picked up by another voice, and then another, until there is a chorus of voices chanting one after the other.

VOICES: No rent without a hall light! No rent without a hall light!

KATERINA: No rent? A hall light? I'll throw the lot of you useless pieces of baggage out on the street where you belong. I'm coming up. [*Dogs bark louder. To tenants*] We'll see who it is that keeps his door open now. [KATERINA *ascends the stairs. Sound of doors shutting*] So you're shutting your doors, you crawling pack of cowards. [*Stops right outside* ZODITCH'S *door. He is plainly frightened*] Well, which one of you will stick his head out now and ask me for it? Which one? [*Pause*] Which one? [*She bursts into a laugh that echoes and reechoes through the halls of the house.* ZODITCH, *terribly frightened, keeps his back against the door. Sounds of the dogs sniffing around, scratching at his door*] Come along Porshy, Potshy, Pinchy. [*Sound of the pack of them descending the stairs. Sound of her door shutting, and then silence*]

ZODITCH *goes over to his stove and looks inside. He takes some paper and puts it in. He goes over to a small bucket—the bucket has only a few pieces of coal in it. He spills the entire amount into the stove and, striking a match, lights it. He stands in front of it for a moment, rubbing his hands. Then he picks up a pot of gruel which has been sitting on the stove and takes it over to the desk. He reaches into his pocket and pulls out the* CHULKATURIN MS. *He eats while he talks.*

ZODITCH: Take it home with you. Read it! I will not take it home with me! I will not read it! Aagh. [*Slowly pronounces* CHULKATURIN'S *name*] Chulkaturin. Mister Chulkaturin. You impossible name. You gentleman. So much the worse for you if you believe worms make distinctions underground. There are no distinctions underground. No better classes of worm. No gentleman's worm. No worm with an uncommon body, an uncommon mouth. You won't find them to your liking. I can assure you. [*Takes a whiskey bottle out of his coat and a glass out of the desk. Wipes the glass with his handkerchief. Pours in a tiny drop and spends a few seconds savoring it and smacking his lips over it*] Rest assured. Worms don't get down to boot level. You won't get their tongue on your boot. They don't know about the summer houses you had, your Mediterranean villas, your ladies. Damn your ladies. Damn your fruits and peppermint creams. Damn their parasols, their lawn parties, your fresh meat and ice creams, your sailboats, your insolences.

Aagh. [*Pours out another tiny drop, and drinks it down the same way*] Here you come to me. Down to me, and you satisfy me or I'll ship you into oblivion. I'll take your bones and mangle them, I'll break your head, I'll break your back. I'll . . . [*In his anger he bends the spoon in his mouth. All subsequent action, real or imagined, will be played out within the room. The following is imagined*]

PANDALEVSKI: [*His voice comes from somewhere in the dark*] Why don't you shut your mouth, you sack of hot air!

ZODITCH: [*Lights up on* PANDALEVSKI] You scum. You garbage. You dregs. You horse's tail. Do not think injustice goes unpunished. Do not think this is the office. Here there is freedom. Here you watch what you say to me. A trip to the cemetery does not make a love affair. Keep your hands off my water jug.

PANDALEVSKI: [*Pours the water from the jug into a basin*] On the trip to the cemetery it was boringly obvious which direction the affection of Miss Grubov lay. Spreading the blanket to cover our legs from the chill, I found that by a subtle snaky motion of her torso she connived it so that one two three our thighs and hips were dancing flank to flank to the rolling of the wheels. Hand me the soap.

ZODITCH: Who do you think you're ordering about? I am the head of the reader's section, the first reader, you carbuncle, you wart, you pimple. I do not take orders from you. I will dance on your grave before I'm through.

PANDALEVSKI: Hardly had this dance begun when by a writhing of her arm, a heaving breathing of her bosom, as if the desire in her must burst, she seized my fingers one by one and locked them in the compass of her hand. Get me the soap!

ZODITCH: I'm warning you, Pandalevski. Watch what you say. Do not push me too far. Be careful. I will not put up with these lies.

PANDALEVSKI: Seizing thus my hand, she covered it with kisses and sent it, as it were, on a foreign exploration to private lands best left undiscovered outside the marriage bed. I pretended fright, surprise, but her importunities and protestations were of such severe necessity I at last gave way and exposed her bosom. Get me the soap!

ZODITCH: You liar! You defamer! What right do you have to say such things?

PANDALEVSKI: The soap!

ZODITCH: The soap is it? [*Reaches over and grabs the soap bar*] Here is the soap. [*He brings the bar of soap down on top of* PANDALEVSKI'S hat *and proceeds to hammer* PANDALEVSKI

into the ground] I'll drive you into the ground. I'll beat your brains out. We'll see who's whose superior. We'll see about trips to the cemetery, you carcass, you liar, you buzzard, you ink pot. [ZODITCH *drags* PANDALEVSKI *to the door and out.* PANDALEVSKI *holds on to his hat*] Down the stairs with you! [*Curiously enough there is no barking from the dogs.* ZODITCH *returns and stands by the door*] Monstrous liar. Vilifier. What right to say such things?

The voice of PANDALEVSKI *is heard from the direction of the washbasin. He is lathering his hands with soap.*

PANDALEVSKI: What right to say such things? Once having seduced Miss Grubov, once having aroused in her the fevered breath of passion, which I found most sour to the smell, I suppose I have all rights to say what pleases me. Hand me the towel. [ZODITCH *doesn't move*] It was then that I thrust your name into the conversation, where it fell like a small stone dropped from some low height into the sea. "And what of Zoditch?" I said, and when there was no sign of recognition on the lady's lips, I pressed forward with encouragements to her remembrance: "The rude fellow, the crude fellow, the open the door and 'if you please,' fellow, the tea fellow, the biscuit fellow, the a b c and loop your e's fellow." But there was no remembrance. You are, nevertheless, welcome to the wedding along with the bookkeeper and the printer's apprentice. Hand me the towel.

ZODITCH: There will be no wedding!

PANDALEVSKI: Oh, yes, a very large wedding. Hand me the towel!

ZODITCH: There will be no wedding. She is untouched.

PANDALEVSKI: I have washed my fingers, have I not? Do I wash my fingers for no reason? Hand me the towel!

ZODITCH: I'll give you the towel. [*Takes the towel and suddenly wraps it around* PANDALEVSKI'S *throat. There is a struggle this time*] Sleep with the devil in hell tonight. Enough of your insults. Your lies. Enough. Enough. [PANDALEVSKI *slumps to the floor.* ZODITCH *nudges him a few times to make sure he is dead*] It is finished. Idiot! [*He drags* PANDALEVSKI *out, returns. He sits at his desk once again. He spoons in his gruel*] Was it too cold, Miss Grubov? I thought of you in the carriage and I said they will forget the extra blankets and Miss Grubov will be cold. It's a long drive to any cemetery and the horses move so slowly.

Following is imagined.

MISS GRUBOV: [*From the dark. Her voice flat, almost as if hypnotized*] Yes, it was cold. [*As she speaks the light goes up revealing her seated on* ZODITCH'S *bed*]

ZODITCH: [*Still eating*] That is too bad. In the winter when Death comes to Petersburg, he takes the large and the small: I have heard forty to fifty cats, their eyes like jelly ice, their whiskers stiff as banjo wire, die each night. I have heard a like number of cur-bitches with teats so locked with rime they could not suck their puppies die each night. I have heard birds innumerable die each night seeking warmth in chimney smoke—and I thought of you huddled in the carriage, your father before you, his great black coat wrapped about him and his eyes shut to eternity come, and I said she will listen to the horses kicking up the ice and she will know in her heart she is alone. [*He stands up and wipes his mouth with the back of his hand. Goes thru his obsequies: rubs shoes against pants, wets fingers and runs them up and down trouser crease, cleans wax out of ears, slicks down hair*]

MISS GRUBOV: I sat in the chapel with my father, and the cold sunlight shone over the length of his body and I was alone.

ZODITCH: [*Stands by her side and begins unbuttoning her jacket*] There was loneliness.

MISS GRUBOV: I was alone. Lonely.

ZODITCH: What were you thinking of?

MISS GRUBOV: I thought of nothing. I saw nothing.

ZODITCH: [*Begins ravishing her*] Without me, nothing. Nothing [*She responds and they embrace on the bed*] I am to be promoted.

MISS GRUBOV: Yes, I will promote you.

ZODITCH: I will fire Pandalevski. I will set my desk in the main office. I will be served tea and I will have what is mine to have. I will buy a sailboat. I will buy a house. I will buy a carriage to go to the operas.

MISS GRUBOV: Yes. Yes. You shall have all.

ZODITCH: I love you.

MISS ZODITCH: Marry me. Marry.

ZODITCH: Yes. Yes. Yes. Yes. Yes. [*They embrace for a few seconds. Suddenly* RUBIN *appears. He watches them for a second or two and then, bending down, picks* ZODITCH *up by the seat of his pants and the scruff of his neck and tosses him to the floor*] You! You! You! You!

RUBIN *is already in the bed on top of* MISS GRUBOV. ZODITCH *tries to grapple with* RUBIN *but* RUBIN *shoves him to the floor with his foot.* ZODITCH *remains on the floor.* MISS GRUBOV *speaks as she engages in lovemaking with* RUBIN. *They roll from side to side in the bed. They laugh.*

RUBIN: It's all a ladder, Mr. Zoditch. We can't be keeping our feet on the same rung, can we?

MISS GRUBOV: There are matters that come to my attention, Mr. Zoditch.

ZODITCH: [*Scurrying over to the bed*] What matters?

MISS GRUBOV: Complaints that may lead to your dismissal.

ZODITCH: This is impossible. Your father promised to advance me. I have told everybody I am to be advanced.

MISS GRUBOV: My father is dead. Death causes change.

ZODITCH: There can be no change in this. I have served with loyalty for twelve years.

MISS GRUBOV: Those who have watched you say you seek a strange advancement.

ZODITCH: They are madmen. You must not believe their lies.

MISS GRUBOV: Do they lie?

ZODITCH: They lie. Dear Miss Grubov believe me. I think of you only as a person above me. I do not dream. I'm not a man driven by dreams. You don't know them. How they connive. How they watch me to discover evil. They distort me. They twist me into shapes I am not. It is they who harbor these evils. Yes. It is they. I can give you their names.

MISS GRUBOV: Can you?

ZODITCH: Yes. Yes. It is the man in the book-keeping section, and the printer's apprentice. You see? I know them. I spit on them. They do not respect your virginity. They make jokes. It is they who seek strange advancement. [MISS GRUBOV *and* RUBIN *laugh and throw the covers over themselves*] Do not treat me this way, Miss Grubov. I am a man of feeling. I am not a nothing. I am a man of respect, of sentiments. [*They just continue to make love*] Stop it. You have no right to do this. Stop it. Stop it. What do you think I am? You think I am a toad! I am a man to be respected. Everybody in this house comes to me because I am a man of influence. This is my bed! [*Once again he is pushed away from the bed by the feet of* RUBIN *and* MISS GRUBOV. *He falls to the floor and yells from the floor*] You think there were not affairs I had? What do you know of that? There were women who loved me. When I was not even twenty there was a woman who wanted to marry me, who said I was hand-some. She thought I was a soldier. [*The muted sounds under the covers have become increasingly animalistic.* ZODITCH *speaks in a calmer tone as he returns to his desk*] I could have been an officer, but there was no one to speak for me. [*Lights out on bed.* ZODITCH *slumps down at his desk and opens* CHULKATURIN's *diary*] I would have been a captain by now. [*As* ZODITCH *silently reads, the lights come up on* CHULKATURIN *standing near the bed*]

CHULKATURIN: I, Nikolai Alexeevich Chulkaturin, in my twenty-ninth year, certain in the hope of the resurrection and the life to come, begin this my diary at Lambswater, March the twentieth, eighteen seventy.

ZODITCH: [*Still thinking of his own problems, calls out*] I had no one to speak for me!

CHULKATURIN: The doctor, the same doctor that brought me into this world, came this morning with his black bag of useless medicines to tell me that I must now prepare myself to be shortly ushered out of it. At the end of all his medical subterfuges and hemhawing terminologies he told me only what I already knew —I am to die. So be it. My life has been as brief as it has been meaningless, and death's a goodness for all we know.

Lights up on DR. KORVIN *standing near the bed.*

DOCTOR: I will leave this here for you, Nikolai. [*Places a bottle on the night table*] If you are troubled by pain, you are to take a teaspoonful. In any event have a teaspoonful before you retire. It will assure you a good night's sleep. It's opium. If you dream, do not pay any attention to it.

CHULKATURIN: [*Speaking as if to himself*] This morning I dreamt I was in a great cage in some marketplace I had never seen before. The sun burned down upon me and I could not escape. I kept sticking my hand through the bars of the cage, grasping at those who passed by, but they would not stop and I had lost all power to speak. I could not breathe. I felt myself suffocating, and no person stopped. [*He turns to look at the* DOCTOR *as if expecting an explanation*]

DOCTOR: I will have that Terentievna of yours open the window a crack before you retire this evening. [SERGEY, *without knocking, opens the door a trifle and sticks his head in.* CHULKATURIN *lies down on the bed*] Oh, there you are. It's about time. What took you so long?

SERGEY: I was chasing the cats away.

DOCTOR: Away from what? [SERGEY *just shrugs his shoulders*] Well, come in, come in. There are some sheets in the closet I want you to take down to your grandmother to wash.

SERGEY: [*Pointing to the closet*] In here?

DOCTOR: Yes. Be quick about it. [SERGEY *opens the closet and looks at all the clothes before he bends down to pick up the sheets. He suddenly backs away, letting out a cry*] What's the matter with you?

SERGEY: There's blood on 'em.

DOCTOR: Never mind what's on them. Just take them down to your grandmother. [SERGEY *picks up the sheets with great distaste and leaves*] Stupid lout. If your father were alive, he'd pick them both up by the neck and toss them out.

ZODITCH: [*Interrupting with a comment. Action freezes*] I'll pick you up by the neck and toss you out!

DOCTOR: [*Action resumes*] Do you know what she was doing when I came in this morning? Sleeping! Big as you please, sprawled out in bed with a bottle of vodka clutched to her chest and her legs dangling to the floor. She's allowed the downstairs to become a rat's den.

CHULKATURIN: Terentievna's old and she drinks, but she is here when I need her. The boy is somewhat backward. Everyday he sticks his head into the room to see that I have not made off with the closet. He fancies my clothes.

DOCTOR: And the old woman? What does she fancy?

CHULKATURIN: The house.

DOCTOR: Look here, Nikolai, this is none of my affair, but if you do not watch what you are doing, they will rob the teeth out of your head before they are done. Do not underestimate the cunning of poor people. You do not know them.

CHULKATURIN: [*Seriously*] I have never known anybody, Doctor Korvin. [*Changing mood*] But do not worry, nothing is settled yet. We negotiate day by day. Besides, to whom else should these clothes and this house belong? By the time I am gone she will have earned this roof over her head.

DOCTOR: And the summer house What has become of that?

CHULKATURIN: Sold at auction. A cloth merchant from Novgorod. A man who had to have a summer house.

DOCTOR: This is all quite distressing to hear, Nikolai. Surely, some other alternative presented itself to you.

CHULKATURIN: No, doctor. Let the summer house be gone. What it meant to my father, it never meant to me and for it the Chulkaturins, father and son, are at last quits with the human race. I have paid off the last of my father's obligations and if no man will be the richer for the Chulkaturins having lived, well, no man can say he is the poorer either. Do not look so concerned, Doctor Korvin. Obligations must be met.

DOCTOR: Your friends will not permit this, Nikolai. To sell your property this way is demeaning. You are no merchant's son.

CHULKATURIN: I have no friends, doctor.

DOCTOR: You have had friends, Nikolai. At the university I'm sure you made many friends. [*There is no answer from* CHULKATURIN *so the* DOCTOR *makes his own*] Every man has friends. [*The* DOCTOR *busies himself putting back his medicines and collecting together his odds and ends. He pays no attention to* CHULKATURIN]

CHULKATURIN: Upon meeting my friends on the street of the university: "Why, it's Chulkaturin," they say, and when I approach, the circle of friends parts as if a slightly leprous thing had been thrust into their midst. And the eyes which had been set upon my eyes begin dropping from my face to my chest to my knees to the bottom of my feet, and everybody stands absolutely struck-still desperately trying to remember what it was they were saying before I arrived. Once I am ten feet past, the circle once again shrinks, the eyes once more rise, and conversation moves like fish hustling down the Don. Oh Christ, that the circles of this world might shrink and find me standing locked inside!

Unaware of what CHULKATURIN *has said, the* DOCTOR *turns to him.*

DOCTOR: Try not to have too many visitors, Nikolai . . . You must get your rest.

CHULKATURIN: Doctor? I'll see that you are paid as soon as I can.

The DOCTOR *exits as* TERENTIEVNA *comes in, broom in hand.*

TERENTIEVNA: He's a bit of nose, ain't he? He was staring into everything downstairs when he first come. Even poked into my room and me with a bottle of furniture polish in my hand at the time and the dress about the knees from bending over.

CHULKATURIN: I'm sure he meant nothing by it, Terentievna. He used to visit this house often when my parents were alive.

TERENTIEVNA: I'm not a housekeeper to have her work looked after by them what ain't of the family. I do my job.

CHULKATURIN: Yes, I'm sure you do.

TERENTIEVNA: I do my dusting and my window washing and my floor cleaning and my cooking and them what ain't of the family has other business to mind. [CHULKATURIN *reaches over to take his writing pad and pencil*

out of the night table] Let them stick their noses to their own face.

CHULKATURIN: Terentievna, there is something you can do for me.

TERENTIEVNA: And what would that be?

CHULKATURIN: I'm going to do some writing and when I am finished I want you to promise me that you will take it downstairs to the kitchen stove and burn it.

TERENTIEVNA: Burn it, sir?

CHULKATURIN: Yes. You are not to show it to anybody, or get anybody's advice about what to do with it. You will take it straight to the stove, you understand?

TERENTIEVNA: Is it letters, sir?

CHULKATURIN: No. Just writing that I wish to do for myself. Just a whim, it will be of no value or concern to anyone, so it is to be destroyed.

TERENTIEVNA: Yes, sir.

CHULKATURIN: You will do this without fail, Terentievna?

TERENTIEVNA: That I will. Is it bad news the doctor was bringing about the cough, then?

CHULKATURIN: Yes.

TERENTIEVNA: The cough's not to go away?

CHULKATURIN: No, Terentievna, it will not go away.

TERENTIEVNA: I'm sorry for that, sir, truly I am.

CHULKATURIN: I know you are, Terentievna.

TERENTIEVNA: It's the good what always go before us and the bad what come dragging after. It's a bad world, sir, that's what it is, and none of us can look for justice in it. [*Pause, and then slyly*] Is it soon you'll be leaving us, sir?

CHULKATURIN: I don't know, Terentievna. [*She nods her head up and down as if thinking something over*] Is there something else?

TERENTIEVNA: No, sir, only . . . well, it's the boots and the clothes in the closet. I was wondering if you'd be wearing them again.

CHULKATURIN: [*Softly*] No.

TERENTIEVNA: Sir?

CHULKATURIN: You can have them, Terentievna.

TERENTIEVNA: You see, it's for the boy. He doesn't have much in the way of shoes fit for the snow and all, and him without a winter coat . . .

CHULKATURIN: Yes. You are right. There is no need to wait.

TERENTIEVNA: [*Goes to the closet and pulls out the boots and winter coat*] We'll be obliged to you for this kindness, sir. You're a gentleman what understands.

CHULKATURIN: Those were my father's boots, Terentievna.

TERENTIEVNA: Yes, sir, and fine leather they are, too. Would the overcoat be your father's, too?

CHULKATURIN: No.

TERENTIEVNA: It's hardly worn at all, is it? It's the changing of the styles what do it for gentlemen more than the wearing of them out, I suppose. There are some what get a new coat every year just for the new look of it, they say. Will we be needing the services of a lawyer, sir?

CHULKATURIN: For what?

TERENTIEVNA: The house, sir. Can we make our agreements by the speaking of them, or do we have to have them writ down by the lawyers?

CHULKATURIN: They must be written down.

TERENTIEVNA: Oh, must they? Everything is a fuss, ain't it?

CHULKATURIN: You can tell Sergey to fetch Lawyer Levinov tomorrow. I will have him draw up the transfer papers.

TERENTIEVNA: Yes, sir. And don't you trouble yourself about anything. I don't mind at all about the sheets. I'm going to do the wash right now.

CHULKATURIN: You won't pour the washwater in the stream, will you, Terentievna? I don't want the carp and grudgeon killed by the soap.

TERENTIEVNA: Don't you worry about that, sir. Don't you worry. I'll find another place. [*Exits*]

Lights dim to indicate a passage of time.

CHULKATURIN: March twenty-second. Lawyer Levinov came yesterday and as I signed the papers giving the house over to Terentievna upon my death, I felt that by that simple signature I had somehow set myself irrevocably free: as a piece of ice that has been bound all winter flows at last down to the sea, so I too have become unbound. To flow where? God knows.

Lights up on LEVINOV.

LEVINOV: I find myself hard put to even describe the coach ride over. The driver, a lunatic of a fellow, was absolutely insensitive to anything other than meeting his schedule. Although the four horses we had were good and we were flying along, this madman insisted on adding a fifth horse. This poor horse was completely out of place, completely superfluous. [*Points to a spot on the page*] Sign there, too, Mr. Chulkaturin. [*He continues with his story*] And how was this unnecessary horse fastened to the carriage? Absolutely all wrong. By means of a short thick rope that constantly cut into his flank so that his flesh was at all times positively lacerated. How he expected the beast to run naturally when his entire body was arched in pain I don't know. And what was this lunatic's reaction when I informed him that we would do better without this superfluous horse? [*Points to another spot*] And here as well, Mr. Chulkaturin. [*Continues with the story*] He began lashing the horse, a dozen additional strokes across its back and swollen belly, and screaming out to the wind. "What the hell. It's been tied on, and if not to run then what the hell for?"

CHULKATURIN *and lawyer stare at each other. Lights out on* LEVINOV. ZODITCH *flips a page.*

CHULKATURIN: March twenty-third, Sunday. The churchbells have been ringing all morning, heavy, slow, melodious, and so they will ring when I am no longer here to listen. I cannot bear to hear them. I have had Terentievna shut the window tight, but still the sound washes into the empty room filling every corner. In darkness I see the meadow where once I played, the branches of my plum tree bending with fruit, the small streams where I caught carp. Oh my Christ, if I cannot say good-bye to the summers that warmed me, the winters I put my fur hat on to! If I cannot say good-bye, what shall I do? Who will have pity for us all?

ZODITCH *runs over to the bed.* CHULKATURIN *stares frozenly ahead.*

ZODITCH: Pity? Why do you waste my time with pity? There is no pity. Up the ladder. Down the ladder. Make up your mind to it. Do not live in the delusion you will put tears in my eyes. In me you do not deal with an amateur of suffering. [*Mimics* CHULKATURIN] "The churchbells have been ringing all morning." Let them ring! Every bell rings; every dog cries; every sheep bleats tears. The public is not interested in suffering. In me you deal with the public, Chulkaturin. Who is to buy the lungs and brains of you, that is what I am to decide. That is why I am a first reader. That . . . [*Finally becomes aware of a slight but persistent knocking on his door. Lights out on* CHULKATURIN. ZODITCH *goes over to his door*] Who is it?

FEATHERS: It's me, sir, the housegirl, Feathers.

ZODITCH: [*Opens the door*] What do you want?

FEATHERS: [*A young girl, filthy from coal dust and in rags. She smiles constantly, nervously*] Katerina Prolomnaya sent me with a bucket of coal.

ZODITCH: [*Imitates her*] Katerina Prolomnaya sent me with a bucket of coal. [*Lets her in. Harshly*] Well, don't stand there smiling all night. I've important work that must be done. We can't all afford to live like princesses.

FEATHERS: Shall I put the coal in the stove for you, Mr. Zoditch?

ZODITCH: [*With a wave of his hand indicates she is to do so*] Yes. Why have you brought the coal to all the others and only now to me? Why am I the last? I won't forget that, Miss Feathers.

FEATHERS: Oh, no, sir. You're not the last. The mistress says the others aren't to have any coal at all tonight, only you, sir. She says let 'em freeze and the city would be better off without them.

ZODITCH: Do not give me stories. Coal doesn't grow on plum trees, madam! I do not live in fairy tales. [FEATHERS *busies herself putting the coal in the stove*] She expects something for this eh? Eh? What does she expect? Nobody does anything without expectations. If she expects to be paid now, I cannot pay now. To be advanced in the publishing business is not to be made a prince. I didn't ask for any extra coal.

FEATHERS: The mistress said nothing about asking for money, sir.

ZODITCH: Nothing? What nothing? You watch what you're doing there. You're putting in too much at once. You're not dealing with a spendthrift, Miss Feathers.

FEATHERS: And I was to bring you this kerosene, sir. [*She hands him the kerosene. He just stares at it*]

ZODITCH: Why? [*Hesitantly takes it and, opening the jar, sticks his nose to it to make sure it's what she says it is*] She expects to make up on the coal by overcharging me on the oil. That's it, isn't it? Well, I will not pay a kopeck for the oil. I will not pay for the coal. I asked for nothing and from nothing comes nothing. I do not need these extravagances.

FEATHERS: The mistress said nothing about money for the kerosene, sir.

ZODITCH: Tell Katerina Prolomnaya I cannot afford extravagances . . . I live close to the bone. Do something about that smile! [*Ushers* FEATHERS *out and locks the door. Once again he smells the kerosene*] Is she so rich that she can give something for nothing. Rich? From what, rich? Her husband died owing the moneylenders. Everybody knows he died owing the moneylenders. [*Stands in front of the mirror and stares at himself. He runs his hands through his hair and preens a little*] But if he didn't die owing the moneylenders. If . . . Bah! [*Turns from the mirror. Picks up the diary and begins reading. Immediately there is a stabbing cry of pain that comes from* CHULKATURIN *in bed. Lights come up dimly.* CHULKATURIN'S *arm extends itself opening and closing*

as if seeking to grasp onto ZODITCH. *The* DOCTOR *steps out of the shadows*]

DOCTOR: So, Nikolai, so. What has happened is a certain flow of blood from the lung. You understand? Now we must engage in the removal of a like quantity of blood. You will feel better after you are bled. It is to be expected that spittle from the lungs, since the hemorrhage, will be somewhat pasty, like clay, even like clay. A slight disruption of the digestive organs, the increased frequency of intestinal discharge in turn brings about an additional grabbing and contracting, as it were, of the bowels, which in turn produces the diarrhea. Do not distress yourself with keeping your sheets clean. That is nothing to distress yourself about. A trifle of blood, a trifle of excrement. You understand? So. So.

Lights out on DOCTOR *and* CHULKATURIN.

ZODITCH: [*Nervously*] Who's to say what handsome is? Katerina Prolomnaya's first husband was short. What was Napoleon if not short, or Caesar? *Veni, vidi, vici.* It is a medical fact that the short man, by having his heart placed closer to his brain, enjoys a richer supply of blood, ergo, a proportionate enlargement of the cranial area so that he becomes quicker in wit, more active in deed, greater in accomplishment. To marry Katerina Prolomnaya would be a diminishment . . . [*He begins biting at his nail, and then laughing and then biting and then laughing. Glances at MS*]

Lights up on DOCTOR *as he pours a beaker of* CHULKATURIN'S *blood into* ZODITCH'S *washbasin. Lights out on* DOCTOR. *Lights up on* CHULKATURIN *in bed. He is writing.*

CHULKATURIN: Think, dear Christ, have you made me anything more than Lawyer Levinov's fifth horse? If I had never lived, it would have made no difference to anyone. My entire existence has been superfluous. That is the central fact of my being: the central word that sums of my total meaning. Think, dear Christ, is that not so? Have you not made me a fifth horse fastened uselessly to the coach of life? To whose benefit do I run? For whose benefit am I beaten? Oh my Christ, where is my posthouse? [*Action freezes.* CHULKATURIN *looks straight ahead*]

ZODITCH: So it is a husband she is after. She sends Miss Chimney Sweep with the kerosene to keep me from getting an eyestrain. Five feet four inches can hardly be considered short in any event. She doesn't wish me to be eyestrained because she is concerned. The coal alone might be construed as meaning no more than a mere landlord-tenant relationship. So if she just sent the coal, she might expect no more than a thank you, but more than a thank you is floating around here. The time I left my gloves on the hall table and she called out to me on the street: "Oh, Mr. Zoditch, your gloves." And the payment of the rent, did she not say, "Ah, Mr. Zoditch, your rent." What was the "Ah" about? "Ah, Mr. Zoditch." Ahs and ohs have meanings. They don't just blow around the air! One does not say "ah" . . . "oh" just for the pleasure of opening a mouth. [*Begins biting his fingernails again and looking at himself in the mirror*] Surely she loved me even while her husband was alive! [*Does a stupid little jig. Begins to read*]

CHULKATURIN: April the second, Wednesday. It rains now. A cold, soundless rain that falls into the snow and vanishes. I struggle to separate the days one from the other. It is useless. I think of you, Liza, my rainbow, my bird, caught now forever fixed in the timeless grace of your seventeen years, and I know as truly as I must have known all these years that in you and in you alone exists all I shall ever know of useless happiness, and useless agony. Now I begin. Now at the end of my life I prove, dear God, that had I never lived it would have made no difference to anyone. [*Takes a slight pause before continuing*] Some years ago, I was obliged to spend some months in a small town lying in one of the more remote districts—a town overrun by mud and goats. Fortunately, the parents of Illya Ozhogin, an acquaintance I had known for a single term at the University, lived there, and before I found myself desperate with boredom, I resolved to pay a call. I sent a boy from the inn I was lodged at, to announce my arrival to the Ozhogins.

Lights out on CHULKATURIN. *Scene with the* OZHOGINS *becomes animated. Light remains on* ZODITCH. KIRILLA MATVEICH OZHOGIN *sits with his hands folded on his belly.* ANNA, *his wife, is sewing.* BIZMIONKOV, *the family friend, plays a game of solitaire.* LIZA *toys with a caged bullfinch.* ZODITCH *identifies the characters in* CHULKATURIN'S *story with people familiar to him in his own life. Thus:* KIRILLA MATVEICH *is* MR. GRUBOV, *the man in the portrait at the publishing house;* BIZMIONKOV *is* PANDALEVSKI; LIZA *is* MISS GRUBOV.

KIRILLA: [*Pulling a watch from his vest and looking at it*] If he's going to call, why doesn't he call? And why isn't the dinner ready yet? It's already after twelve. How much longer must we wait to eat? Liza, go into the kitchen and find out what they're doing there. [LIZA, *busy playing with the bullfinch, doesn't hear*] Elizaveta!

LIZA: Yes, papa?

KIRILLA: Go into the kitchen and find out what the delay is. [*She can scarcely tear herself away from the bird. She exits staring at the bird all the way*] That girl is turning deaf, positively. And crazy, as well. All day with that bird. [*Imitates* LIZA *with the bird*] Eech. Eech, eech. Ooooch. Ooooch. Eech, eech.

BIZMIONKOV: [*Calmly continuing with his game*] It is the same with all young girls, Kirilla Matveich. There is nothing to be concerned about.

KIRILLA: We will see if you sing the same tune, my friend, when you marry and have a daughter who arranges flowers all day and tickles bullfinches. Maybe you should marry my Liza and then we will see what you say.

ANNA *offers one of her little social laughs.*

KIRILLA: [*Pulling out his watch again*] Is he coming for lunch, or what?

BIZMIONKOV: [*Calmly*] When you send a messenger at lunchtime, you are coming for lunch.

ANNA: I'll have them set another place. [*Leaves excitedly*]

KIRILLA: Don't get rich, Bizmionkov. Take my advice. Stay poor. When you live in poverty, you live in happiness. Your meals are served on time.

BIZMIONKOV: Money is a curse.

LIZA *returns.*

KIRILLA: Liza, dear, go back into the kitchen and get a little snack to hold Mr. Bizmionkov over to lunch.

BIZMIONKOV: I can wait for lunch, there is no need to go to extra effort.

KIRILLA: There is no need starving yourself, my friend. Why be a martyr? If we have to wait for Mr. Chulka . . . Chulkaturin, we have to wait, but there is no need to starve. We are not at the gates of starvation here. Just bring some fish, Liza . . . [*She keeps starting out, but his additional requests keep calling her back*] . . . with lemon . . . bread . . . some olives . . . five or six . . . better bring the same for me . . . some kvass to drink . . . you want some kvass, Bizmionkov? [BIZMIONKOV *nods.* LIZA *has started toying with the bullfinch again*] Some kvass for Mr. Bizmionkov, too. Eh? What, are you playing with that bird again? Leave the bird alone. [LIZA *exits back to the kitchen.* KIRILLA *looks after her to make sure she is gone*] Listen, Bizmionkov, I have something I want to talk to you about. [KIRILLA *tries to start, but isn't quite sure how to frame his remarks*]

BIZMIONKOV: Well?

KIRILLA: It's about Liza. [*Still hesitates*] When you're a father you notice things.

BIZMIONKOV: Yes?

KIRILLA: Don't rush me.

BIZMIONKOV: Who is rushing you?

KIRILLA: As I was saying, you notice things when you're a father.

BIZMIONKOV: What things?

KIRILLA: What do you mean, "what things?" Things! What I want to know is what kind of a bird is that?

BIZMIONKOV: [*Going up to the bird*] A bullfinch. What else would it be? You thought it was an owl?

KIRILLA: I know it's a bullfinch, but what kind of a bullfinch?

BIZMIONKOV: A Russian bullfinch.

KIRILLA: A female? Is it a female?

BIZMIONKOV: What difference does it make what sex it is? Isn't it singing all right?

KIRILLA: Will you look under the feathers and stop asking a thousand questions.

BIZMIONKOV: It won't raise its tail.

KIRILLA: Wait a minute. [*He opens the cage and starts to stick his hand in just as his wife comes in*]

ANNA: What are you doing?

KIRILLA: [*Quickly pulling out his hand*] Nothing. I was merely placing my hand in the bird's cage.

BIZMIONKOV: Kirilla Matveich wants to know if the bird is a male or a . . .

KIRILLA: Sha. [*To wife*] Nothing. It is nothing.

ANNA: Isn't it singing well?

KIRILLA: It is singing well. I just felt like feeling its feathers, that's all. Have you set another place for our son's friend?

ANNA: Yes.

KIRILLA: Well, let's not stand in front of the bird's cage all day. [*Return to seats. KIRILLA makes a big production about sitting down, ANNA eyes him suspiciously*] Ah! My favorite chair. [*Nobody says anything. To wife*] Are you going to be sitting there for a while, Anna?

ANNA: Is there some reason I should not sit here?

KIRILLA: No reason. Of course there's no reason.

ANNA: Then I will be sitting here for a while.

KIRILLA: There is nothing further that needs your attention in the kitchen?

ANNA: What else should need my attention in the kitchen?

KIRILLA: I don't know, Anna. I was only asking. [*Pause*] Things do not go well all the time in the kitchen, that is all. [*ANNA gets up*] Where are you going?

ANNA: Back to the kitchen.

KIRILLA: If things are going well, there is no need to go back to the kitchen. [*ANNA starts to return to her chair*] But if you feel it needs your attention . . . [*ANNA leaves the room, almost tearfully. KIRILLA hastens over to the cage and, opening the little door, sticks his hand in*]

ANNA: [*Returns unexpectedly. KIRILLA'S hand gets momentarily caught in the cage*] If the meal is not right, it is not my fault. I do my best. [*Almost in anguish*] What do you want from that little bird?

KIRILLA: [*Exasperated*] Nothing. We are going into the garden. Come, my friend, come, come. Why must you exasperate me so, Anna? [*Takes BIZMIONKOV'S arm and escorts him out of the room. ANNA, still distraught, exits —passing her daughter, who has just entered with a tray. LIZA puts the tray down and stands looking about her for a second. Then, for no apparent reason, she whirls about the room ending up in front of the bird cage. She dances about the cage and begins whistling to the bird. There is a knock at the door, which brings LIZA out of her little trance. She looks about her for a second and then seeing that there is no one to answer she goes to the door. CHULKATURIN comes in. He is rather overdressed, almost foppish, somehow ill at ease. He tends to make little mistakes in manners due to his anxiety*]

CHULKATURIN: Excuse me, I am Nikolai Alexeevich Chulkaturin.

LIZA: I am Elizaveta Kirillovna, Illya's sister.

They just stand looking at each other.

CHULKATURIN: Is there anything wrong? I sent a messenger to say that I was to follow.

LIZA: Oh, no, there is nothing wrong. Illya used to talk so much about his University friends . . . we are expecting another of Illya's friends to call later this summer, you must know him . . . Captain Ivan Petrovich Narvinsky.

CHULKATURIN: No, I don't think so.

LIZA: Ilya used to talk about him all the time. He's the terribly handsome one that I was absolutely forbidden to meet. The one who went into the Army.

CHULKATURIN: No, I'm afraid I don't recall . . .

LIZA: Shall I try to place you? I know all of Illya's friends.

CHULKATURIN: Well, I don't think that outside of being roommates we were very . . .

LIZA: [*Clapping her hands*] You were the roommate who never came in from parties earlier than four in the morning. The boy who never attended a single lecture for two years.

CHULKATURIN: No. I think that was the roommate your brother had during his senior year.

We were roommates during the second year, the first half of the second year. Then Illya moved out.

LIZA: Oh. [*Pause*] Then you must be the one Illya had that terrible fight with over some dreadful woman. He wrote papa all about it in a letter.

CHULKATURIN: No. Illya and I never had a quarrel. That was Peter Richter from Prussia.

LIZA: If you give me time I will remember just exactly your place in my brother's life, because Illya wrote me without fail a letter every week from Petersburg and I'm sure I know everything he did. [*Pause*] You were the one who gambled at the races.

A line of pain momentarily crosses CHULKATURIN's *face but the girl does not see it.*

CHULKATURIN: That was Ivan Vorontzoff. I never went to the races.

LIZA: You did not own a white stallion? [CHULKATURIN *shakes his head*] You know what I think? It will come to me suddenly. Oh!

CHULKATURIN: What is the matter?

LIZA: I hope you have not come all this way just to see Illya, because he is not here. He left to go abroad for the Czar; he is in the diplomatic service now you know since last April, but I'm sure he wrote you about that. [CHULKATURIN *shakes his head*] No? He must have forgotten. Poor Illya, it was a very busy time for him so you must excuse him. He left for Austria a month after his wedding to Frieda Semeonova, who is a blood relative of Prince Adrian. I'm sorry you were unable to come for the wedding. So many of Illya's friends and yours from the University came, but you must have been busy. [*It is obvious from the look on* CHULKATURIN's *face that he realizes what a small part he must have played in* ILLYA's *life, and that* ILLYA *did not even consider him enough of a friend to extend a wedding invitation to him. He is saved from any further embarrassment by* LIZA *running over to her bullfinch*] Isn't it darling? Illya gave it to me when he left. I have been teaching it to sing. [*To the bird*] Sing a song for the gentleman, Popka. [*She whistles to the bird, then turns to* CHULKATURIN] He really sings his heart out when he wants to. Come. [*Motions for* CHULKATURIN *to come over to the cage. He stands close to* LIZA *as she talks*] See, he is not afraid of you at all. That's a good sign. It is a well-known fact that birds and animals can instinctively look into the hearts of people and know if they are good or bad. Did you know that?

CHULKATURIN: No.

LIZA: Oh, they can. If you trust the judgment of your pets, they will always tell you who your real friends are. See how he is not afraid of you.

CHULKATURIN: Then we shall become friends.

LIZA: [*To bird*] Brave little bird. That's a brave little bird. [*To* CHULKATURIN] I would find it impossible to love someone that an animal feared, wouldn't you?

CHULKATURIN: I don't know.

LIZA: Will you whistle for Popka? See if he will sing for you.

CHULKATURIN: Oh, I don't think I could.

LIZA: Please.

CHULKATURIN, *after a moment's hesitation, begins to whistle.*

ZODITCH: Already he must prove he is an ass. Already the fool.

CHULKATURIN: Is it possible that one day you could open the door to some stranger's house and fall in love? [ZODITCH *lets out a cry of disgust*] Yes, it is possible. That was the exact moment I fell in love. I say that without reservation. The moment the door swung open into that household was the exact moment I came to love and to shut out all the impossible loneliness and misfortune of all the years before: my father's failures, my mother's long-suffering virtues, my less than human isolation from mankind. I had now for the first time placed myself in contact with one whose steps would not flee from me, one whose eyes would behold my face and not turn away. It didn't matter that now I stood in front of a bird's cage and forced myself to whistle. Not even forced myself. I whistled joyfully.

ZODITCH: You ass!

CHULKATURIN: The tune, whose melody I can no longer remember, rose from my heart. A nameless tune from the so long shut closet of my heart broke forth and I brushed against the sleeve of her dress and she did not move and the bird broke forth answering me and I thought as I stood there, God, oh God, don't let me be shut up any more.

Lights out on CHULKATURIN *scene.*

ZODITCH: What are you talking about? What do you think you're talking about? [*Pours himself a drink. Sound of someone shuffling about in the hall. The shuffling goes back and forth as* ZODITCH *drinks.* ZODITCH *goes to the door and listens. In a whispered voice, as he opens the door a crack*] Who is that?

GREGORY: It's me, Zoditch, Gregory from downstairs.

ZODITCH: [*Practically hissing in annoyance*] What the devil are you doing marching up and back? Have you lost your wits?

GREGORY: I must talk to you.

ZODITCH: [*Suspiciously*] About what?

GREGORY: Let me come in. I don't want to stand in the hallway. [*After some hesitation* ZODITCH *lets him in*]

GREGORY: Something must be done to increase the amount of coal provided the tenants. We will all freeze to death unless steps are taken with Katerina Prolomnaya. The woman is mad to think a family can survive a winter night on half a bucketful of bad coal. Do you know the dogs are freezing to death out on the street? Have you heard even as much as one of them howl tonight? By morning there won't be a live dog left in Petersburg. Already the water basin in my kitchen has pieces of ice in it the size of your fist.

ZODITCH: Why do you bother me with your family problems? Go see Katerina Prolomnaya. I have no time to get involved in this.

GREGORY: That is what must be done. Katerina Prolomnaya must be visited.

ZODITCH: Then go. Go!

GREGORY: That is what my family has instructed me to do. My wife will not put up with it another night. And my children . . . the eyes they turn to me . . . it would break the heart of a monster . . . even Katerina Prolomnaya would see the necessity of more coal if she could hear my children crying in their beds. We must not be ignored because we are poor. She must not be allowed to prey on our misery.

ZODITCH: Then why do you stand here? Be off. Speak to her. This is a family problem.

GREGORY: She must be spoken to. It's not right to be cruel when people are suffering. But I don't know what to say to that woman. Every time I have to speak to her the words tumble together in my mouth. I am no good with words . . . that is why I was in the hall . . . I kept saying if I start down the stairs I will find the right words to make my position clear by the time I reach her door, but then I think what if I knock on her door and she opens it and I do not have the words yet, what then? Eh? What then?

ZODITCH: [*Anguished*] What do you want of me? Leave me alone.

GREGORY: And I think what if those rotten brown dogs of hers come for me even while the words are glue in my mouth? How many have those dirty beasts sunk their teeth into already?

ZODITCH: I cannot help this. I want only to be left alone. I am a busy man.

GREGORY: Zoditch, come with me.

ZODITCH: What are you saying?

GREGORY: You are a man of words. Everybody knows that. Everybody respects you for that.

Just the other day my wife was commenting on your fine methods of address and speech deportment. "How fine Mr. Zoditch speaks. How quickly. How precisely. . . . He is a master of the Russian language." You are much in respect because of it. If you went with me, the other tenants would follow. I know they would. Come. Come. We will face her together. You will say all the right things. You will say what only you know how to say. One, two, three, it will be done.

ZODITCH: Leave go of my arm. This is not for me. I tell you leave go! [*Jerks his arm free*]

GREGORY: What are you doing to me? We are neighbors. We live side by side.

ZODITCH: Side by side. What is that, side by side? When my mother died, who came to me with fruit? When I lay in my bed sick with fever for three days, who knocked on my door? Who said to me, "Zoditch, my friend, we have come. Zoditch, are you alive? Here is soup to warm you, a cool towel for your head. Zoditch, we have come." Nobody. Nobody came.

GREGORY: But nobody knew. Nobody was informed.

ZODITCH: [*Pulling open the door*] Nobody cared! [GREGORY *seems about to say something, then changes his mind. He exits.* ZODITCH *closes the door after him*] Nobody. [ZODITCH *leans against the door intently listening as* GREGORY *descends the stairs. We hear the shrill barking of a number of small lap dogs.* KATERINA PROLOMNAYA'S *door opens and the barking becomes louder and more shrill. Through the barking we hear* GREGORY]

GREGORY: Katerina Prolomnaya, I have come . . . [*The rest is blotted out by the barking. After a moment*] We won't survive the night. Already the frost is through the window. Surely there is enough compassion in you to . . . [*There is the sound, the mad sound of* KATRINA PROLOMNAYA'S *laughter. The barking has increased.* GREGORY *runs up the stairs shouting*] Get them away from me. Get away. You get away. In the name of Christ, if we don't get some more coal . . . Oh God . . . get away . . . aaagh . . . Help me. Zoditch, help me. Get away you bastards. Get away. [*Pounds on* ZODITCH'S *door*] Zoditch! Zoditch, help me. Oh God.

The scene ends in a wild crescendo of pounding, barking, yelling, and laughter, as ZODITCH *presses his back to the door.*

ZODITCH: Leave me alone. Leave me alone. This is a family problem! [*He slides down the door and collapses to the floor*]

Curtain

ACT TWO

PLACE: The same. ZODITCH'*s apartment.*

TIME: A few moments later.

SCENE: The same.

ON RISE: All sounds have stopped. GREGORY *is gone.*

ZODITCH: [*Suddenly shouts out, nervously, excitedly, clearly in an anguish of some kind*] Let the house freeze, Gregory. What else are winters for if not to put frost on dogs! [*Shovels in the remainder of the coal. Stands in front of the stove, his arms wrapped about him*] I am not to freeze. She would be a fool not to take my attainments into consideration. Is it nothing to be a first reader in a famous publishing house? Is it nothing to have read Seneca, Cicero? O *tempora! O mores! Senatus haec intelligit, consul videt; hic tamen vivit. Vivit?* Where is the wonder then that Katerina Prolomnaya should reach for me? Is it every widow who can snatch twice at the gold ring? [*Goes over to the table and picks up the diary for a second and then puts it down*] Katerina Prolomnaya, do not underestimate my value! I am no ring for your finger without considerations. You are not the voice of springtime. Bear in mind assets. Ah. This marriage is a diminishment for me without your assets. I do not mind the diminishment if there are assets. [*Pulls out a piece of paper and makes notations*] Rents. Movables: tables, chairs, sofas, beds, et cetera. Drapes, linens, clothings, furs, equipments, carriages. Personal assets: the pleasures of the bed . . . marred, gray streaks in the hair, brow wrinkles, crow's feet, throat wrinkles, worn-down teeth, yellow and fallen-out teeth, breasts good, too-full waist, a mouth forever at the food box, a brain stuffed with candies. [*Shaking the paper in his hand*] It is well to bear in mind, Katerina, that we do not live by bread alone. In me you will not find a husband who is fondly foolish, one of those husbands who thinks to satisfy a woman's whims is to satisfy all. In me you will have a husband gentle but firm, a husband capable of great understanding and compassion, but a husband capable of being the master of his house, a husband whose hand though not often set down, set down becomes immovable. [ZODITCH *smashes his hand on the table. And then, satisfied with his speech, picks up the diary*]

Lights up on CHULKATURIN.

CHULKATURIN: O sweet summer. Sweet lost summer of days that are no more. Summer of bright birds. Summer of flowers. Summer of strawberries and golden mornings. Summer of musical harmonies in the sky. Summer when my heart stood in tune with every living thing. Summer when I was not myself. Summer when I was in love.

Lights out on CHULKATURIN. *Lights up on a public garden.*

KIRILLA: [*Offstage*] Why don't they watch where they plant their damn vines? Must a man break his skull or strangle to death in order to keep on the path?

BIZMIONKOV: [*Offstage*] This way, my friend. Be careful. Do not trample down the flowerbeds.

KIRILLA: [*Offstage*] Is that you, Bizmionkov? Blast their flowerbeds. What idiot planted flowerbeds in a public garden? [*He comes out on stage*] Here, this way. It's clearer over here. [*He plunks down exhausted on the bench.* BIZMIONKOV, *book in hand, calmly appears*] Where's Anna?

BIZMIONKOV: She was with you. You were hand in hand when we left the fountain.

KIRILLA: No. She was with you.

BIZMIONKOV: [*Turns a page*] I'm sure she was with you.

KIRILLA: Don't be foolish. [*Calls out*] Anna! Anna! [*To* BIZMIONKOV] And where is my daughter? [*Shouts*] Liza! [*To* BIZMIONKOV] This park was designed by a madman whose sole desire is to lose half of Russia in a vine tangle! And where is Chulkaturin? The poor fellow can't find his way from one end of the street to the other.

ANNA: [*Halloing from somewhere offstage*] Yoo hoo. Yoo hoo.

KIRILLA: Anna! Anna! Is that you?

ANNA: [*Offstage*] Yoo hoo. Yoo hoo.

KIRILLA: Over here, woman. Yoo hoo. Yoo hoo.

ANNA: [*Offstage*] I can't.

KIRILLA: What do you mean you can't?

ANNA: [*Offstage*] I'm in the middle of a flowerbed.

BIZMIONKOV: Watch how you step, Anna. Don't crush the flowers.

KIRILLA: [*To* BIZMIONKOV] The devil take the flowers. [*To* ANNA] Come forward. Watch the vines; damn the flowers!

Sound of ANNA *crashing through the brush.*

ANNA: [*Offstage*] I'm coming. I'm coming. Yoo hoo. Yoo hoo.

KIRILLA: I can assure you, my friend, this park will be looked into. Monstrosities do not just create themselves. There are madmen at work here. [ANNA *breaks into the clearing. Her large white hat is crushed*] You see? You see? Look what those madmen have done to my wife.

BIZMIONKOV: It is only a matter of staying on the path, my dear friend. It is all geometrically laid out. One has only to follow the path.

KIRILLA: Bah! Here, Anna, sit on the bench. [*To* BIZMIONKOV] We will see what is geometrically laid out and what is not. Do they imagine we are bees? My poor Anna.

ANNA: [*Practically in tears*] Oh, my hat.

BIZMIONKOV: They do not imagine we are bees.

KIRILLA: They think because we are an outlying province they can send their madmen out here to create monstrosities, but that is a mistake, I can assure you. The businessmen of this town will not put up with it.

ANNA: Oh, my hat.

KIRILLA: [*In a quick aside to his wife*] Enough with the hat, Anna. [*To* BIZMIONKOV] I have a son in the diplomatic service. All I have to do is write a letter and there will be repercussions. It isn't every family that has a son involved in the intricate workings of government, or is expecting a visit from a captain of cavalry.

BIZMIONKOV: The diplomatic service and the park department are totally separate.

KIRILLA: Ah, you think so. But you are mistaken. They are hand in glove.

ANNA: My hat, look at what has happened to my hat.

KIRILLA: Enough with the hat! [*To* BIZMIONKOV] It is only to a political novice such as yourself, Bizmionkov, that things appear unrelated. In government the toe is connected to the foot and the foot to the arm and so forth.

BIZMIONKOV: The Department of Parks is connected to the Department of Fish. It is not connected to diplomatic service.

KIRILLA: [*Calls, after giving* BIZMIONKOV *an angry stare*] Liza! [*To* BIZMIONKOV] That is only what they want you to think, Bizmionkov. Listen to me. I am aware of what is and what is not.

ANNA: And where is Elizaveta? You were holding her hand when we left the fountain.

KIRILLA: I was not holding her hand when we left the fountain. Do not exasperate me, Anna. [*Shouts*] Liza! [*To* BIZMIONKOV] There are things I could tell you about the working of the government that would completely shock you. You would say to me, "Kirilla Matveich, that is impossible. Kirilla Matveich, you are mad, such things cannot be."

ANNA: She is lost.

KIRILLA: She is not lost. She is with Chulkaturin.

KIRILLA *and* ANNA: [*Suddenly aware that to be with* CHULKATURIN *is to be lost, both call out*] Liza! Liza! [*They exit.* BIZMIONKOV *follows, reading his book*]

Sound of LIZA'S *laughter is heard.* LIZA *bursts out into the open and whirls herself around.* CHULKATURIN *appears and watches her as she is lost in her reveries. She spirals to the ground. For a long moment she remains on the floor of the forest as* CHULKATURIN *stares at her.*

ZODITCH: Go to the Petersburg ballet! Don't dance on my time! This is not the ballet!

CHULKATURIN: I could not move. I could not breathe. There were wildflowers in her hand. Her cheek pressed to the floor of the forest as if feeling the unheard music of grass and earth. I clung to the edge of the clearing afraid to approach, afraid to be seen, afraid of a moment into which I had transgressed. Though love had brought me, I came only as a stranger. [LIZA, *resting on her extended arm, slowly opens her eyes and stares at* CHULKATURIN. *The moment is poignant and* CHULKATURIN *breaks the mood abruptly by striding forward in cheerful embarrassment. A bit too loud*] Well, you see you have fallen. That's what you get for running so fast. Come. Let me help you up. [*Extends his hand to her. She looks at him for a moment and then turns away. He drops his hand*]

LIZA: I'm all right. Please, just a moment.

CHULKATURIN: [*Stands by her, uneasily feeling that something should be said but not knowing, or rather not daring, to say what is in his heart. Instead, he makes conversation*] I suppose they will be wondering what happened to us. I cannot imagine how we came to be separated from your parents. [*Pause in which there is no answer*] Well, we've certainly taken our exercise for the day. If the summer continues at such a pace, we shall all be in fine health. I haven't run this far since my father raced me in the meadows of Lambswater. [*Pause. Change of tone. Serious*] You grow older you run less.

LIZA: [*Suddenly turning to him*] You think it was childish of me to run?

CHULKATURIN: No. No, I didn't mean to imply that.

LIZA: Well, it was. Perhaps it will be a long time before I run again. [*Her mood changes from seriousness to fresh exuberance*] Come. Sit down beside me. [*Extending her hand to him as he had before to her*]

CHULKATURIN: We ought to sit on the bench. Your dress is going to be covered with grass stains.

LIZA: [*She drops her hand as he, before, had dropped his. She becomes thoughtful for a second and then that passes and she smiles again, playfully]* If you make me sit on the bench, I shall fold my hands in my lap and not allow you to become what you should become.

CHULKATURIN: And what is that?

LIZA: What do you think that is?

CHULKATURIN: I don't know.

LIZA: Guess.

CHULKATURIN: I can't.

LIZA: Then you shan't become it. *[She plays with the wildflowers]*

CHULKATURIN: Tell me.

LIZA: What would you like to become?

CHULKATURIN: I don't know.

LIZA: Poor Nikolai Alexeevich Chulkaturin doesn't know what he would like to become. Shall I be kind and tell you, then? *[Pause, and she breaks into a smile]* King of the May! The king of all the hearts of young ladies. Here and now I shall give you your new identity. But you must kneel properly and lower your head. Come. On your knees, or else I shall be forced to find another to be King of the May and you shall have lost your identity for good. Don't dally. Shall you be crowned or not? *[There is a moment in which they look at each other directly in the eyes, and then CHULKATURIN goes on his knees and lowers his head. She begins putting the wildflowers in his hair]* What fine silky hair you have, Nikolai Alexeevich. Have there been many young ladies who have loved you for your fine brown hair?

CHULKATURIN: There has been no one.

LIZA: Perhaps you have forgotten them. The woods are full of the sighs of young girls. I think there must be many girls you have loved and forgotten.

CHULKATURIN: Do not think that there have been others.

LIZA: You must hold still. If you raise your head, the flowers will fall.

CHULKATURIN: There has been no one who has loved me. Do not think that of me.

LIZA: I think men must be very cruel creatures to play with the heart of a girl and then not even remember her name. Men are like that according to my brother. *[She laughs]*

CHULKATURIN: Why do you laugh?

LIZA: Illya says that the hearts of young girls are strewn about the world like grains of sand upon the shore and that there are not as many stars in the night sky as unremembered girls. Do you think that is true?

CHULKATURIN: I think that is poetic.

LIZA: And is that the same as true? What is your answer to that, Nikolai Alexeevich, who has fine silky hair?

CHULKATURIN: You are making fun of me.

LIZA: *[Stops as if suddenly wearied]* Yes. *[She stands up and turns to face the sun]*

CHULKATURIN: Have I offended you?

LIZA: *[Wearily]* No.

CHULKATURIN: Then what is the matter? Why are you staring into the sun?

LIZA: Must I have reasons for everything? Is it not enough reason to stare at the sun because it is up there, because it is flaming across the sky, because we may never see the light again, because, because, because, because. *[The mood becomes a trifle lighter as if she attempted to recover]* Have I found enough "becauses" to satisfy you? *[He is hurt. She reaches out to him, sincerely]* Poor Nikolai, it is I who have offended you. Am I completely intolerable to be with?

CHULKATURIN: *[As he stands up, the flowers fall off his head]* No. You cannot offend me. How could you ever think that you . . .

LIZA: See how soon every flower must fall. *[Brushing her hand through his hair to dislodge the other flowers]* Every flower. *[To CHULKATURIN]* Don't be angry with me, ever, Nikolai. *[She takes his hands in hers and kisses them. CHULKATURIN bends down to kiss her, but she almost flippantly turns away]* Papa thinks young girls should be placed in hibernation along with Siberian Mastodons until we become eighteen years old, then we are to be melted from the ice and returned to our homes in time for marriage. Isn't that terribly clever of papa? *[She begins to cry]*

CHULKATURIN: *[In surprise and confusion]* Liza, why are you crying?

LIZA: *[Tears running]* Isn't that terribly clever? I suppose I should take my dear bullfinch to sing to me in the ice and . . .

CHULKATURIN: What is wrong? Please don't cry. Please, Liza, Liza. Please! *[She turns her back to CHULKATURIN and, bowing her head, runs off. CHULKATURIN picks up the fallen flowers]* Are the tears of women ever insignificant? And the tears of young girls, the young girls of our youth that so haunt us in after years, are they so much salt water lost from us forever? Did she not then, standing there in the final light of the sun, love me? Think, think, if I could not claim every tear, might not there have been a single tear that was for me, a fragment of a tear, a thousandth part of all that running flood loosed for me? For me alone? Could those tears have fallen without me?

ZODITCH: They fall. They fall. Having no mind of their own, women have tears. It is not necessary to philosophize these things.

CHULKATURIN: I danced that night. I opened every window to the summer air, struck every candle, from every corner of the room dispelled every shadow. I took the wine from the landlord's table and brought it to my room. I took the books from the shelves and threw them in the closet. I locked the closet. The tears of a young girl, no . . . the tears of a young woman are bashful trembling tears. Shall I quote to you important works of important philosophers that will tell you that, precisely just that? There is no other way for girls to come to love but through tears. Shall I tell you about my future plans? In my happiness, my love, I made future plans. The world was to become involved with me, and I, through Liza, like some rose flung to the shores of the universe was to become involved with the world. There was the plan involving a wedding that the little provincial town would never forget. The entire town was to be invited, down to the last shoemaker.

ZODITCH: You cannot make weddings out of tears! There is nothing written down here to make weddings from! What are you making weddings from? [*Furiously begins rereading the previous pages. He turns the pages backward and forward while* CHULKATURIN *goes on in his happiness*]

CHULKATURIN: Why should not the lowest shoemaker share in my happiness? I wanted everybody that I had ever brushed against to be happy. Let all those whose hearts were sick, be healed. Let those who were pained in silence, be pained no more. I saw the house of the Ozhogins preparing for the feast. Tables decked out: linen cloths, silverware, breads, steaming urns of soup, caviar, chicken boiled, chicken roasted, assortments of dainties, teas black and green, chocolates and mints, fruits, oranges, lots of oranges.

ZODITCH: [*Calling out while hunting for anything written that might have provoked* CHULKATURIN'S *outburst*] Insane madman! You are making a wedding out of nothing!

CHULKATURIN: Old man Ozhogin stuffed into his leather chair, delightful, wondrous old man Ozhogin, patting his stuffed belly, checking the time with a gold watch drawn from his vest, blowing fantastic vast clouds of tobacco from a miraculous black cigar; my father's watch, I had given Father Ozhogin my father's watch, and Mother Ozhogin crying tears on her voluminous breasts, she was my mother now . . . [ZODITCH *lets out a cry of disgust*] I had a family . . . Ozhogin . . . how rich that simple name sounded . . . Ozhogin . . . has there ever

been a more lovely name? A more beautiful sound upon the air? And Liza, my Liza before me in her wedding dress, her long unbound hair fallen to her shoulders, her eyes lit with happiness. The happiness that would be mine forever.

Lights out on CHULKATURIN.

ZODITCH: No more of this! [*Starts flipping the pages for a new beginning. As he hunts, a spotlight falls on* CAPTAIN IVAN PETROVICH NARVINSKY, *a spit-and-polish officer. The kind of young man that traditionally sways a young girl's heart . . . he is* RUBIN. *The* CAPTAIN *is apparently engaged in conversation with others. Spotlight on* CHULKATURIN]

CHULKATURIN: In brass, in leather, in saddle soap, the captain of cavalry called. Volobrina. [VOLOBRINA *approaches. . . . She is* FEATHERS] Who is that?

VOLOBRINA: The friend of Illya's, Ivan Petrovitch. A distinguished officer and rich. Come to organize recruits for the Czar.

CHULKATURIN: Illya's friend, ah. What the hell does he want here? Doesn't he know Illya isn't at home?

VOLOBRINA: What does anyone want here? Eh? [*She goes*]

Lights go up on the OZHOGIN *living room. Present are the* CAPTAIN, KIRILLA, ANNA, BIZMIONKOV *and* LIZA.

CAPTAIN: At present my stay in this district is quite indefinite. A month, perhaps two. It is difficult to say at the outset.

ANNA: And have you found a suitable place to stay, Ivan Petrovich?

CAPTAIN: Yes, thank you. I have engaged a number of rooms at the inn for my officers and myself.

BIZMIONKOV: I'm afraid you will find the inn somewhat less than what you are accustomed to.

KIRILLA: I'm sure that will be the case. There are no decent accommodations in this entire town.

BIZMIONKOV: But then hardly anyone ever comes here, so there never seems any pressing need to have decent accommodations.

ANNA *laughs at the little joke.*

CAPTAIN: I am a soldier, Mr. Bizmionkov, and for a soldier luxury is an unnecessary vice.

BIZMIONKOV: Yes, of course.

CAPTAIN: A soldier must take the terrain as he finds it. If he finds his feet are wet, well, then he must accept his wet feet. In my life such things are of no significance.

BIZMIONKOV: And what is of significance, Ivan Petrovich?

CAPTAIN: To serve the Czar and the motherland. To fight the enemies of Russia and to serve with courage and with faith.

LIZA: [*With a sigh*] Yes, that is right.

Before she has a chance to be embarrassed at her outburst, CHULKATURIN *enters the room waving a white rose.*

CHULKATURIN: Good day. Good day. [*They all turn toward* CHULKATURIN. *The* CAPTAIN *alone stands*] Oh, you have a guest! [*As if in complete surprise*] I hope I'm not intruding, but I was just passing by and . . . [*In his gesture, the rose flies out of his grasp and lands at* LIZA's *foot. He tries to remain nonchalant*] Oh. [*He hastens to get it*] I thought since I was in the vicinity I would come over. [LIZA *hands him the flower. They briefly exchange glances. He doesn't know quite what to do with the rose. It occupies much of his attention*] I hope I'm not intruding.

KIRILLA: [*With a trace of irritation in his voice*] Not a bit.

CHULKATURIN: Are you sure?

KIRILLA: Yes. Yes. Quite all right.

CHULKATURIN: Because if you wish I could return later. I do not wish to interrupt. [*Looking about him for a friendly smile*]

KIRILLA: [*Impatiently*] You are not interrupting! May I present Captain Ivan Petrovich Narvinsky, an officer in the Czar's cavalry. Captain, this is Nikolai Alexeevich Chulka . . .

CHULKATURIN: [*Used to his name being mishandled, completes it*] Chulkaturin.

KIRILLA: Chulkaturin. A friend of Illya's from the University.

CAPTAIN: Ah! A pleasure, sir.

CHULKATURIN *has started to shake hands. However, all the* CAPTAIN *intended to do was a slight click of the heels and a bow. When he sees* CHULKATURIN *intends to shake hands, he extends his hand.* CHULKATURIN, *unfortunately, raises the hand with the rose. He switches the rose to the other hand. They finally shake.*

CHULKATURIN: Thank you. Thank you. A pleasure for me as well. [*A kind of silence settles on the room*] Well, please go on with whatever you were discussing. I'll just sit here. [*Starts to sit on the step leading into the living room. A step near* LIZA]

CAPTAIN: No, please. [*Offers* CHULKATURIN *his chair*]

CHULKATURIN: Oh no. Please. It's quite all right here. I really don't mind in the least.

KIRILLA: What? Is that our last chair? I have a thousand chairs in this house. Wait. [*Starts to head out of the living room*]

CHULKATURIN: Please. There is no need to bother. I'm perfectly . . .

KIRILLA: There is a need. Nobody has to sit on floors in my living room. [*Glares at* CHULKATURIN *and marches out. Silence descends. Finally . . .*]

CAPTAIN: So you knew Illya from the University, Mr. Chulkaturin.

CHULKATURIN: Yes, from the University.

CAPTAIN: Ah!

Followed by a pause. A noticeable lapse in the conversation.

CHULKATURIN: [*Starts the conversation again*] Is that where you knew Illya from?

CAPTAIN: Yes.

CHULKATURIN: Ah!

Another noticeable pause.

CAPTAIN: Perhaps we've met before?

CHULKATURIN: I don't think so.

CAPTAIN: Ah. [*Pause*] Were you one of the gentlemen Illya brought to my father's summer home?

CHULKATURIN: No.

CAPTAIN: It was a hunting trip?

CHULKATURIN: I don't hunt.

CAPTAIN: Oh.

Pause.

ANNA: The captain is here to recruit soldiers for the Czar's cavalry.

CHULKATURIN: So?

CAPTAIN: Yes.

Pause.

BIZMIONKOV: [*Opening his watch*] Almost noon. [*Snaps his watch shut. Sound of chair scraping in the hall. Some grunting on the part of* KIRILLA]

CHULKATURIN: Let me help, Mr. Ozhogin. I'll give you a hand. [*Goes offstage. We hear them speak*]

KIRILLA: [*Offstage*] No. It's all right.

CHULKATURIN: [*Offstage*] I'll take the leg.

KIRILLA: [*Offstage*] I have it by myself. Watch your flower. You're pushing the flower in my eye. Watch it! Watch it!

Sound of the chair falling over.

ANNA: [*Rising*] What's happened?

CHULKATURIN: [*Pokes his head in. The flower is bent*] We've got it now.

KIRILLA: [*Appears holding the chair by himself.* CHULKATURIN *uselessly hovers about him*] I can manage by myself.

ANNA: Are you all right?

KIRILLA: [*Sets the chair down*] Fine. Just fine. [*To* CHULKATURIN] Sit! [CHULKATURIN *sits.* KIRILLA *returns to his seat. He blinks his eye*]

LIZA: Is your eye all right, papa?

KIRILLA: Yes. Yes. Go on with your conversation.

Pause. Silence. BIZMIONKOV *coughs. More silence.*

CHULKATURIN: Would you like to take a turn around the garden, Mrs. Ozhogin? Liza?

ANNA: Perhaps after a bit, thank you.

LIZA *just shakes her head.* BIZMIONKOV *coughs again.*

CHULKATURIN: Allow me to get you some water.

BIZMIONKOV: No need . . . Just a tickle.

CHULKATURIN: Quite all right. I'll be back in a moment. [*Gets up and heads for kitchen. Conversation immediately picks up*]

KIRILLA: You were saying, my dear captain?

LIZA: Ivan Petrovich was telling us about the cruel conditions under which soldiers must live, papa.

Lights dim on scene in the living room. The rest of their conversation is played out in mime. Light focuses gradually down on the CAPTAIN, *who continues speaking, and* LIZA, *who becomes more and more absorbed.* CHULKATURIN *has returned. He stands spotlighted in the doorway, a rose in one hand, a glass of water in the other*]

CHULKATURIN: So he talked and so she listened and so you see . . . you see what it is to exist as an interruption, a break in everybody's conversation.

ZODITCH: [*Shouting out*] Nobody is just a break in the conversation! We all have our place! From the peasant to the Czar we have our place. Every ant, every roach has his place. This is God's universe. This is not a madhouse of useless, placeless rats.

CHULKATURIN: How well the conversation proceeds now that I have left. Bizmionkov no longer coughs. He no longer even finds it necessary to clear his throat. Papa Ozhogin is no longer set to the task of moving chairs; Mama Ozhogin does not have to refuse a walk in the garden. Everybody is dug in. Conversation, now that I am gone, becomes pure song. [CHULKATURIN *extends his hand holding the rose*] For you, Liza. Did you not know the rose was for you? Do young men carry roses for nothing? [*Only* LIZA *and* CAPTAIN *are now visible in living room*] Go on, you Othello of the Steppes, with your big wars, your killings, your medals. Go on, Liza, fall in love with his black boots, his mous-

tache, his eyes, and gallantries. What could I bring to you to match those gifts? And you, stand in the arches of the doorway with your waterglass and your rose, stand there until the sky falls down, for all the difference it makes. It should have been enough for you to sleep through life, dreaming of happiness. [*Light goes out on* LIZA *and* CAPTAIN] Oh time that was and time that never more shall be, I give you back your woods, your pathways, your shadowed glades. I give you back her whose dear sweet lips once brushed my heart. I give you back the earth I knelt upon to take a crown. I give you back the happiness of days now fled from me, I give back . . . I . . . [*Sound of waltz music growing louder*] No. No. Nothing! I give back nothing! [*A lighted chandelier is lowered from the ceiling onto the center of the stage. Bit by bit, as* CHULKATURIN *stares about him, a dance is assembled. A table of punch, fruit, cookies, is brought in by a number of the* CAPTAIN'S *officers. We hear the chatter of people, the music, the laughter. In the wings of the stage, left and right, we can see some of the dancers. A young woman, perhaps twenty-five years of age, enters the stage behind* CHULKATURIN. *She pauses momentarily at the punch bowl and then, eyeing* CHULKATURIN, *comes forward. On her head quivers a small butterfly attached to a copper spring. The girl has an awkward smile that is constantly being flashed. She is the girl left over, the girl unchosen by any man.* CHULKATURIN, *in his anguish, cries out to the world and to the vanished* LIZA] Nothing was definite until the night of the dance. Listen, I am not the type that deludes himself. You were no more his than mine the night of the dance. No more mine . . . [*Voice trails off as if suddenly aware he is now at the dance*] than his. Why do you play games with me?

TANIA: [*Flirting as best she can. She occasionally strikes* CHULKATURIN *with her fan*] I still think it's mighty strange, Mr. Chulkaturin, that you could be in our little town so many months and we never meeting. I bet you just came in for the dance.

CHULKATURIN: [*Scarcely hears her, he is so distraught*] What?

TANIA: I said isn't it strange we never met previously. I just bet you came in for the dance. Everybody does.

CHULKATURIN: Came in where?

TANIA: Why, in town.

CHULKATURIN: No. No. I've been here for months.

TANIA: Isn't it strange we've never met before?

CHULKATURIN: Yes. Strange, very strange.

TANIA: Just everybody is here tonight. Just everybody. I think someone has done something to the punch. Everybody seems to be having such a gay time, don't you think? I just love dances. I can't seem to remember who I am when I'm dancing. Isn't that funny? I start out saying, "Tania, you must remember your own name, you silly girl, you mustn't forget your own name," but then I feel myself saying "one, two, three, one, two, three," and the room begins spinning around and around, and the music seems to slide right into my slippers. [*There is no response from* CHULKATURIN. *She waves to someone*] So many of the gentlemen I know seem to be absent tonight.

LIZA *and the* CAPTAIN *waltz by, from wing to wing of the stage, totally ignoring* CHULKATURIN.

CHULKATURIN: Did he say something to me? Did you hear him say something to me when he danced by?

TANIA: The Captain?

CHULKATURIN: Yes. Yes. Him.

TANIA: Why, I'm sure I don't know. I don't think so, Mr. Chulkaturin. Isn't he a handsome man in that lovely uniform?

CHULKATURIN: He made a noise.

TANIA: Is something wrong, Mr. Chulkaturin?

CHULKATURIN: No. Why should there be something wrong?

TANIA: I don't know.

CHULKATURIN: Then what are you talking about? Let's dance. [CHULKATURIN *dances wildly, angrily. He begins to shout as he dances. The girl becomes increasingly distressed. On one of the turns, he half thrusts her from him. He continues shouting as he dances alone.* TANIA, *frightened, watches him for a moment and runs from the room*] You provincials. You eaters of onions. You sleepers with sheep. Who invited you to the dance? Who told you to come? Wasn't it enough you had your fat-legged wives? Your pimple-nosed children? And you, Captain of Killing, weren't there enough women in Petersburg to satisfy you? Let me tell you, my friend—go polish your boots in another neighborhood. Why didn't you stay away from what's mine? Did I come around bothering your women? Did I ever come to Petersburg and bother your women? Did I ever take what was yours?

The CAPTAIN *enters in time to hear* CHULKATURIN'S *last few words and to see the girl flee.* CHULKATURIN *does not see him. The* CAPTAIN *pretends he has seen nothing. He heads toward the punch bowl.*

CAPTAIN: Ah, Mr. Chulkaturin. Where have you been keeping yourself all evening? Are you enjoying yourself?

CHULKATURIN: Do not mock me!

CAPTAIN: What?

CHULKATURIN: It is you who deserves to be mocked, you hollow-brained imitation of a peacock.

CAPTAIN: [*Holding the glasses full of punch*] In a moment.

CHULKATURIN: I'll kick your head in if you laugh at me.

CAPTAIN: [*Smiling*] Not here. In a moment. I understand you.

CHULKATURIN: [*Whispering furiously as he departs*] Go back to Petersburg.

The CAPTAIN *gives the drink to* VOLOBRINA, *who is passing by with a serving tray. He returns.*

CAPTAIN: [*Smiling. Puts his arm around* CHULKATURIN] I believe we have some business to discuss.

CHULKATURIN: Take your hands off me. I am not one of your serfs.

CAPTAIN: Keep your voice down. There is no need not to handle this as gentlemen. I assume I am talking to a gentleman. [*Waves at* LIZA *as she passes by arm in arm with* BIZMIONKOV]

CHULKATURIN: Assume what you like.

CAPTAIN: I believe you have intentionally insulted me.

CHULKATURIN: Believe what you like.

CAPTAIN: Perhaps you would prefer to settle this in a duel?

CHULKATURIN: As you wish.

CAPTAIN: If you do not withdraw your remarks it shall be my wish to challenge you. It will also be my unfortunate choice to have to kill you. Let me assure you I am an excellent shot. Therefore, consider what you are forcing me into. I do not wish to kill a man who means nothing to me one way or the other.

CHULKATURIN: Nothing, is it? I withdraw nothing, you fop, you strutting suit of peacock feathers. You think because I am not a soldier I do not know the meaning of courage? You think because I do not have brass bands and medals I do not know how to behave when I am mocked?

CAPTAIN: You mock yourself, sir. But as you wish. I shall have the honor of sending my second to you tomorrow morning, Mr. Stuccoturin. [CAPTAIN *turns and walks away, smiling, greeting others*]

CHULKATURIN: Chulkaturin! My name is Chulkaturin!

A circle of light illuminates BIZMIONKOV *and* CHULKATURIN. *Light on dance scene dims.*

BIZMIONKOV: Listen to me, Chulkaturin, you cannot persist in this. Do you hear his officers? They are laughing because they think you are a fool. They know he will kill you.

CHULKATURIN: That is their prerogative. Perhaps tomorrow I shall give them less cause for laughter than they think.

BIZMIONKOV: Have you ever fired a pistol?

CHULKATURIN: No.

BIZMIONKOV: Then you are a fool. He will kill you. He will not miss.

CHULKATURIN: Perhaps.

BIZMIONKOV: Not perhaps, certainly! Do you wish to die? Is that it?

CHULKATURIN: I do not wish to die.

BIZMIONKOV: Do not be too sure of that, my young friend. Many a man has died thinking he did not wish to die.

CHULKATURIN: If you think that, you do not understand the meaning of honor.

BIZMIONKOV: This is not a question of honor.

CHULKATURIN: He has insulted me. Something was said.

BIZMIONKOV: What was said? [*Long pause in which no answer comes from* CHULKATURIN] What? Are your sensibilities so refined you cannot even say what has been this insult to your honor? Listen to me, go away, tonight. There is nothing for you here. You cannot make a woman love you. Not if you stood on your head till kingdom come. If you can learn that by the time you are twenty-five, you have learned much.

CHULKATURIN: You do not understand.

BIZMIONKOV: Then tell me. Tell me what it is I am to understand. Because I am glad it is not for love that you are putting your back to the wall. Because I am very glad you are not dying for love, because at this very moment the captain's affair is progressing in the back of the Ozhogin garden, in a closed carriage, in the captain's bedroom, or wherever else they have found convenient.

CHULKATURIN: Why do you lie to me?

BIZMIONKOV: Go home, my friend, go home. Do not die uselessly. [BIZMIONKOV *starts to exit*]

CHULKATURIN: [*Shouting after him, and as* CHULKATURIN *turns toward* BIZMIONKOV *a light goes on showing the* CAPTAIN *kissing* LIZA] It is not useless! Don't tell me what is useless! I at least am not a sponge. I do not hang onto the coattails of a family and rob them of their food because they have money!

I do not pretend friendship where there is none.

ZODITCH: [*Shouts out*] Go on! Give it to her! Press her into the wall, Rubin! [*The scene fades out*] Why don't you write about that? That's what the public wants to read about. There's a man to handle every bitch . . . And they're all bitches. They take your heart. They . . . they . . .

The scene lights up and we are on the dueling field. On one side of the stage stands CHULKATURIN *and on the other side the* CAPTAIN *and some of his officers. One of the officers,* LIEUTENANT ZIMIN, *slightly drunk, comes over.*

LIEUTENANT ZIMIN: Listen, Tulkaturbin or whatever the hell your name is, can you handle a military pistol?

CHULKATURIN: Yes.

LIEUTENANT ZIMIN: [*Looks at* CHULKATURIN *dubiously for a second and then shouts out to the other officers*] You better watch out, Ivan Petrovich. He says he's fired a pistol before. [*The other officers laugh.* ZIMIN *and the* CAPTAIN *do not. The* CAPTAIN *hushes the others. To* CHULKATURIN] All right Tulkaturbin, I'm going to give you some advice. The Captain has no desire to blow your head off. Until you insulted him he didn't even know you existed. Take my advice, apologize and the affair is ended. [*Belches*] Pardon. Then we can all go back to the inn and go to sleep. It's too early in the day for you to die. You're a bright fellow. What lies between the hammer and the anvil soon gets knocked flat. Huh? You understand me? Why get your nose knocked out of joint by interfering in a love affair? Go down to the stage line. Every coach brings in a new woman.

OFFICER A: [*From one of the group by the* CAPTAIN] Lieutenant Zimin, are you ready?

LIEUTENANT ZIMIN: [*Looks at* CHULKATURIN, *who remains impassive*] My friend, it is imbeciles such as yourself who ruin the summer. [*To* OFFICER A] We are ready. [*To* CHULKATURIN] There is one round in the pistol so you will have only one opportunity to fire. You understand?

CHULKATURIN: Yes.

LIEUTENANT ZIMIN: When he tells you to cock your pistol you pull this back with your thumb. [*Indicates the hammer.* ZIMIN *pulls back the hammer, and then releases it to show* CHULKATURIN *how it's done*] You see? Don't be too much in a rush to fire. There are no prizes for firing first. [CHULKATURIN *nods*] All right. Let's go. Take off your coat. Give it to me. [CHULKATURIN *and* ZIMIN *walk to meet the* CAPTAIN'S *party in the middle of the stage*]

OFFICER A: Take your positions.

LIEUTENANT ZIMIN: [*To* CHULKATURIN, *who doesn't quite know what to do*] Here, turn around. [*He turns* CHULKATURIN *around so* CHULKATURIN *and the* CAPTAIN *are back to back*]

OFFICER A: Are you both ready?

CAPTAIN: Yes.

CHULKATURIN: Yes.

OFFICER A: You will each take five paces. At the command, "Turn," you will turn and fire.

OFFICER B: [*One of the ones who has been laughing*] Has anyone found out where we're supposed to ship the poor fellow's body?

CAPTAIN: [*Turning on him*] Be still!

OFFICER A: Cock your pistols. [CHULKATURIN'S *hand is shaking slightly. He has trouble cocking his pistol.* ZIMIN *cocks it for him*] Take your paces.

ZIMIN, OFFICER A, *and the rest back away from the line of fire as the paces are counted off. The* CAPTAIN *and* CHULKATURIN *have come to a stop.*

OFFICER A: Turn! [CHULKATURIN *turns quickly and fires. The* CAPTAIN *is grazed along the temple. He goes down for a moment.* CHULKATURIN *instinctively moves forward*] Stand your place, sir.

CHULKATURIN *stands still. Head erect, the pistol hanging in his limp arm, he is obviously willing to die. The* CAPTAIN *returns to a standing position and after a moment's hesitation, at which time his pistol is leveled straight at* CHULKATURIN'S *head, fires into the air.* CHULKATURIN *gives a long scream of anguish.*

CHULKATURIN: Shoot me! Shoot me! Shoot! Shoot! [*Lights out. We hear the sound of scuffling.* CHULKATURIN *calls out from the dark*] Where's he going? Take your hands off me. Leave me alone. Come back! Shoot! Shoot me!

Lights up on CHULKATURIN *in his bedroom. He is writhing on the floor, the* DOCTOR *and* TERENTIEVNA *trying to hold him down. It is a melee with his last amount of energy. He appears hysterical. He seems to be wanting to pull himself out of the* DOCTOR'S *grasp to get at the* CAPTAIN *in the scene before.*

DOCTOR: There's nobody. Nobody wants to shoot you.

CHULKATURIN: [*To* DOCTOR] Listen, you don't know what that little scar across his temple did to me. Nobody in town spoke to me again. They didn't let me come to their doors be-

cause I who wasn't worth the killing had tried to kill the Captain. She wouldn't see me. What right did he have to fire into the air? What right did he have to scorn me so? What right to injure me twice?

DOCTOR: Help me get him to lie down, Terentievna.

CHULKATURIN: Did I deserve that treatment? What right did he have to shoot into the air? What was I supposed to do? Take his insults lying down? Don't snakes bite the foot that crushes them? Even snakes. Just because I'm superfluous, am I to be stepped on?

They get him into the bed.

DOCTOR: Where was he going? Why is he dressed, Terentievna?

TERENTIEVNA: I don't know, sir. He said he was going to a dance.

DOCTOR: Take off his boots. What nonsense!

She begins pulling off his boots.

CHULKATURIN: And who was right, after all? After they didn't speak to me, after all the doors shut, after I wandered the streets like a ghost for weeks, when they came around to me. So who was right, after all? "Chulkaturin," and they knew my name, "you were right. Listen, my friend, he has made her pregnant and has deserted her. He has gone back to Petersburg. He has moved out with his recruits. What is to be done? Who will marry her now?" [CHULKATURIN *looks hard at the* DOCTOR *and* TERENTIEVNA. *They both stare at him*] Eh? Who will marry her? You know how it is with those springtime fellows? Eh? One flower in April, one flower in May. His day, his hour, was my whole summer, my whole life. [CHULKATURIN *stares off in the distance and a spotlight illuminates* KIRILLA *and* ANNA, *who seem to be addressing* CHULKATURIN]

KIRILLA: Chulkaturin, how clever you are. You knew what that fellow was from the start. You saw through him, my friend, when the rest of us were blind. My friend, what are words? What can I say?

ANNA: She goes nowhere now. She will not leave the house. She is invited nowhere. What can I say to you?

Lights out on KIRILLA *and* ANNA.

DOCTOR: [*To* TERENTIEVNA] Get me the pan. We must remove the excess blood before it is too late. [*She exits. To* CHULKATURIN] Be calm, my friend, be calm. What are you staring at?

CHULKATURIN: What if I gave myself to her now? What if I offered to marry her? You understand how it was? She was proved worthless, dishonored. It would be a sacrifice for me to go to her and propose marriage. It would be an act of pity to love what others mocked. She would fall into my arms. She would bless me. She would think I was her savior. That was a proper expectation. A reasonable man would call it a proper expectation.

DOCTOR: Yes. Yes.

CHULKATURIN: Listen, they've taken my father's boots. Find out what they've done with my father's boots.

DOCTOR: Don't worry about the boots now.

CHULKATURIN: [*Tears running down his face*] Don't let them steal the boots. Can I rely on you? Don't let them steal my property. See to it. See to it. I rely on you.

Lights out on scene. Lights full up on ZODITCH *at his desk, the diary open,* FEATHERS *standing by his side.*

ZODITCH: Well? Well? Was that all?

FEATHERS: Katerina Prolomnaya says that if you wish to come down, then you are free to come down, Mr. Zoditch.

ZODITCH: And what else?

FEATHERS: Nothing else, sir.

ZODITCH: But she was anxious?

FEATHERS: I don't know, sir.

ZODITCH: She seemed excited, nervous?

FEATHERS: I couldn't say, sir.

ZODITCH: You are a stupid little girl. When I am master of this house I will not tolerate stupid servants, mark my words. I will not tolerate smiling. If you do not wish to live in the chimney, do not trifle with me.

FEATHERS: Are you then to be master of this house, Mr. Zoditch?

ZODITCH: [*Thinking about something and not particularly listening*] Eh?

FEATHERS: Are you to be the new master, sir?

ZODITCH: What have *you* heard?

FEATHERS: Nothing, sir.

ZODITCH: You heard something. Out with it. Do not play games. She mentioned my name to you?

FEATHERS: Oh yes, Mr. Zoditch. That she has.

ZODITCH: Ah, I knew it. In what connection?

FEATHERS: In connection with the weather, sir. She said this morning that you left the house without your scarf.

ZODITCH: She noticed that, did she? [FEATHERS *nods head*] Well? Well? What else did she say?

FEATHERS: [*Hesitantly*] She said that only a fool walks in this weather without a scarf about his neck.

ZODITCH: A fool! You did not hear her correctly. Her manner? She did not perhaps rest her hand upon her cheek . . . [FEATHERS *shakes her head*] or tilt her head, thus . . . [FEATHERS *still shakes her head*] or utter any oohs or ahhhs?

Girl's face lights up and she nods her head.

FEATHERS: Something of that, sir. An ooooh.

ZODITCH: Ah. Ah. [*Rubs his hands together and then anxiously shoos his hands at the girl*] Go. Go. Tell your mistress I shall be down shortly. [*The girl starts to go*] Wait. Just say I shall be down. Do not say shortly. [*She exits. To himself*] Shortly implies haste. Here there is no haste. A wormy apple is not to be thrown out, nor to be hastened to. [*Goes over to his closet and starts looking at his clothes. Picks a gray suit*] Gray. Neither too gaudy nor too funereal. Gray as a seagull. [*He pulls it out and inspects it. He starts to brush it off. He is plainly thinking. From the darkened part of the room, in his imagination, a voice*]

KATERINA: Will you have a piece of fudge, Mitya? [ZODITCH *turns without surprise. He is going to act out his approach to the woman. This is how he imagines it will be. As he turns, the couch area lights up and we see* KATERINA PROLOMNAYA. *She is an immense woman, a good four or five inches taller than* ZODITCH. *She is overstuffed, overripe, and yet sensual for it all. Her face is heavily painted, her hair is intricately in place with hairpins. He takes the proffered fudge and sits down on the couch. They both eat fudge while staring intently at each other*] Do you like the fudge, Mitya?

ZODITCH: It is only fudge, Katerina. I do not concern myself with fudge. A man concerns himself with taxes, estates, properties, and bank balances.

KATERINA: [*Sighing*] I know. I know. But surely there must be time for . . . [*Hesitantly*] other things.

ZODITCH: Other things? I do not understand what you mean by other things. [*Points to match*] The match.

KATERINA: Yes, Mitya. [*She lights his cigar*] I enjoy a man smoking a cigar.

ZODITCH: Your late husband did not smoke?

KATERINA: No.

ZODITCH: That is unfortunate. A house without tobacco smoke is a house not lived in.

KATERINA: Yes, that is true. [*Then a bit too forward*] Oh, Mitya, these last few months have been lonely ones for me. Knowing that you were near and yet so distant.

ZODITCH: [*Raises his hand*] You must learn to keep your lusts under control, Katerina. The ashtray, please. [*She hands him the ashtray*]

A woman who cannot keep her lusts under control soon finds her lusts keep her under control. Lust is the devil's monastery on the road to hell.

KATERINA: The seas have been rough for me, Mitya. Women by their nature are but frail vessels. They only have their hearts to guide them.

ZODITCH: And so I have come to consider taking the helm.

KATERINA: Oh, Mitya.

ZODITCH: To *consider*, Katerina. *Consider*. To consider is not to undertake; it is merely to consider.

KATERINA: [*A bit subdued*] Yes.

ZODITCH: Yet many things are finally arrived at which, at first, were but considered.

KATERINA: [*Her hopes picking up*] Yes. Yes.

ZODITCH: As you know I am by nature and by inclination a bachelor. However, since the death of my dear mother, who was constantly by my side these past thirty-five years, I have had the inclination to seek another who might be equally solicitous of my welfare. One who might be concerned to see, as it were, the proper socks laid out in the morning, the stove lit fifteen minutes before awakening, the wash-basin filled with water neither too hot nor too cold and, as it were, et cetera, et cetera, et cetera. In brief, one who might so conform her life to mine that we become a single entity of one mind, of one direction. I, on the other hand, shall, as it were, seize the helm of our mutual fortunes and guide the ship all safely into harbor. A man can do no less than to captain his ship, a woman can do no more than obey. Nothing less is correct; nothing more permissible.

KATERINA: Is it then to be so nautical? What of love, Mitya?

ZODITCH: What of love! On the sea of marriage love is understood.

KATERINA: [*Taking his hand and stroking it*] Our love, Mitya?

ZODITCH: Our love! Any love! There is no need to bring up superfluous topics. We must proceed logically. The disorganized mind is the handmaiden of cupidity. [*Pulls a sheet of paper out of his pocket. From this point on she slowly but surely begins making physical overtures*] Now. My bill of assets. What you may expect in terms of physical property. [*Places the paper before her. She leans close*] Three pairs of shoes. Two in excellent condition. One in used condition, though without holes. Seven pairs of black socks. The wash, therefore, must be done no later than the sixth day of every week. [*She puts her hand on his ankle*] There is no need to inspect the socks

at this time. Everything is as I will state it. [*Proceeds with the inventory. She moves in on him by degrees as he recites his list of assets*] Three suits: one black, one brown, one gray. Eighteen pieces of undergarments. In undergarments I am particularly fortunate, having received twelve pieces in total settlement of my late cousin's estate. Five shirts, four cotton white, one Egyptian cotton striped. A wool overcoat, full cut with imitation pearl buttons. A malacca cane belonging to the estate of my late father, still in the process of settlement, but to which I have indisputable right; a Persian rug, nine by twelve, purchased for me by my departed mother in Constantinople; bedding supplies consisting of two sheets, two pillow cases, one pillow and a six-inch-thick Siberian goose-down comforter.

KATERINA: And your heart, Mitya?

ZODITCH: [*Pulling out a bankbook*] A bank statement, listing monetary assets in excess of one hundred seventeen rubles.

KATERINA: And your heart, Mitya? Your heart?

ZODITCH: What are you talking about? We are itemizing now!

KATERINA: [*Grown increasingly amorous*] I must have love. Love. Love.

ZODITCH: There is no place for love in an itemizing of particulars. Where is your list of physical property?

KATERINA: [*Grabs his hand and places it on her heart*] Here is my physical property. Feel it beating.

ZODITCH: Where is your bill of purchase for the house? Your list of bank holdings? Your movables? Your tangibles and intangibles?

KATERINA: My dogs, Mitya, what of my dogs?

ZODITCH: Superfluous. To be gotten rid of. I am not piloting a doghouse.

KATERINA: Be my pilot. Mine. [*Shoves some fudge practically into his mouth*]

ZODITCH: Show me the bills of purchase. How many horses are in the stable. I don't want any fudge. [*She puts the fudge halfway into her mouth and begins to crawl all over him. She wants him to take the other half in his mouth. He retreats along the couch until there is no room to retreat. She literally begins physically overpowering him. She presses the fudge against his mouth until he starts biting it. His conversation until he devours the fudge runs something like*] What are you doing? Why are you touching me? You're pushing me. Listen. Don't. Wait. How much is your bank balance? What are you doing? Don't come any closer. You're hurting me. Let me up. Up. Up. Up. [*When he does take the fudge from her mouth into his, he starts chewing it up furiously. Now she does the talking*]

KATERINA: We will have our honeymoon in the house. We will stay in the bedroom. There will be no need for you to work. No need to ever leave the house. We will raise the rents. [*She grabs his head and forces him to kiss her*] Don't kiss me so hard, Mitya, not yet, not yet. I want to make love to you. Yes. Oh make love to me always. Always. Never leave the house. Patience, Mitya, not yet. Wait until we are man and wife. Be sweet. Be gentle. Never leave the house.

ZODITCH: Let me go. For the love of God. You're crushing me. I can't breathe. You're crushing me.

KATERINA: Kiss me, Mitya. Put your arms around me. Crush me. Crush me.

ZODITCH: Get off. Off. [*He suddenly frees himself from her embrace and flees to his desk. Lights out on the couch. He stands shakily by his desk trying to catch his breath. Suddenly, from down below there comes the voice of* KATERINA PROLOMNAYA *in the midst of the barking of dogs*]

KATERINA: [*Shouting*] If you're coming down, Zoditch, come down! I haven't all night to spend waiting for you! [*Followed by wild barking*]

ZODITCH: [*Wildly to himself, almost tearfully*] Yes. Yes. Good-bye, Miss Grubov. Good-bye. [*Out loud*] Yes. Yes. I'm coming, Katerina Prolomnaya. I'm coming. [*Runs over to the closet and slips into the gray trousers*] Coming. Coming. [*Throws on the coat, grabs the diary and some official papers. He stamps them with a seal*] With a seal. Official. [*Starts to read as he runs out*] I'm coming, Katerina Prolomnaya. Coming.

Light dims on ZODITCH's *room but does not go out. Lights up on* CHULKATURIN *standing in the entrance to the* OZHOGIN *living room.* KIRILLA *is warmly welcoming him. He rushes up and puts his arms around* CHULKATURIN.

KIRILLA: Ah, my friend, you have come. In spite of everything you have come. [*To* VOLOBRINA] Bring some tea for our guest. Quickly. [*Embraces* CHULKATURIN *again as* VOLOBRINA *heads for kitchen*] Come in. Come in. Let me take your coat. [*Helps* CHULKATURIN *off with his coat*] Here, by the fire. Soon winter will be down upon us. You are well?

CHULKATURIN: Yes.

KIRILLA: Good. Good.

CHULKATURIN: And you and Madam Ozhogin?

KIRILLA: [*Opens his hands as a form of silent reply meaning, "As well as might be expected"*] Well.

CHULKATURIN: And Liza?

KIRILLA: Ah. How quickly the summer has gone. How quickly youth vanishes. Smoke, that is all it is, dear Chulkaturin, smoke and expectations. This is a different household you have come into.

CHULKATURIN: You mustn't blame yourself.

KIRILLA: But they blame me, all of them, Anna, the servants. You see what ingratitude is? Could I tell what a snake he was when he came into this house. Is it every snake that walks around and says he is a snake? But he never fooled you, my dear friend. You knew him from the start. I saw no more than the show of things, but you saw into the heart. You saw the snake in the man.

CHULKATURIN: Has he written to her? [KIRILLA *shakes his head*] That is to be expected. It is just as well.

KIRILLA: [*Slowly nodding his head*] Yes. Just as well. Oh, my friend, what can I say to you? You fought, you risked your life to save my daughter from him and only received contempt in return. What can be said to you?

CHULKATURIN: Your friendship now is all I desire.

KIRILLA: You have that, my friend, from the bottom of my heart.

CHULKATURIN: And to bring Liza happiness.

KIRILLA: Ah, if that were only possible. If I could believe that you could find forgiveness for her.

CHULKATURIN: It is possible. I do forgive.

KIRILLA: [*Sinking into his chair. He is almost in tears*] What irony. Bitter bitter irony. The whole town condemns her and you who have every right . . .

CHULKATURIN: I do not care what fools condemn. [*Sinks to his knees by* KIRILLA's *side and touches his hand*] You understand? She is not of less value to me because of fools.

KIRILLA: She is a young girl. She made a mistake. The judgment of the young is not foolproof.

CHULKATURIN: Yes. As you say. If she will have me even now I will marry her. I will take her to Lambswater. She will be loved as no woman has ever been loved. She will be respected. I swear that to you.

KIRILLA: [*Speechless*] Respect? Is it yet possible?

CHULKATURIN: Believe what I say, my friend. If you believe nothing else of me, believe that. Let the past be done.

KIRILLA: [*Practically bursts into tears as he hugs him*] You have her. You have her. I don't know what to . . . You have her! Go to her. She is alone in the garden . . . Go, my son. Take her. [*He releases* CHULKATURIN] Your coat. Don't catch cold. [*Gives* CHULKATURIN *his coat.* CHULKATURIN *stands in the doorway leading to the garden.* KIRILLA *flees the living room*] Anna! Anna!

Lights out on CHULKATURIN. *Lights up on* ZODITCH *in the apartment of* KATERINA PROLOMNAYA. *She stands before a meat grinder, grinding meat. In the background we hear the intermittent growling of her dogs.*

ZODITCH: Katerina Prolomnaya, what is loneliness? Did not the Roman poets tell us, *"Lupus pilum mutat, non mentem,"* meaning we are all thrust alone on a dark sea? [*Pauses expecting a response. There is none. He goes on*] A dark sea! A sea without light. A sea of gigantic waves. In life, Katerina Prolomnaya, the wind blows. The wind blows! [*Pauses for a second to wipe his forehead with a handkerchief*] And what is the effect of this wind? It pushes us along. We do not know where we have sailed from. We do not know where we sail to. We sail! [*Again he pauses, but still she continues grinding*] No man can say, "No, I will not sail. No, I will remain where I am safe." This he cannot say because the wind blows. That is the substance of it all—the wind. And what is the effect of this wind when we sail in the darkness, Katerina Prolomnaya? Who's to say how many of us are blown over the edges of the world. Which is to say without metaphor, how many of us come to bad fortune because he . . . or she . . . sailed alone. To sail alone is to vanish alone. And this is the answer to my question, Katerina Prolomnaya.

KATERINA: You have received the extra coal and oil I sent.

ZODITCH: [*Nervous. Wiping his forehead again*] Yes, yes, thank you. We see that what is loneliness is to be alone and to vanish alone. [*Softly, as if trying to remember a set speech*] To vanish alone. [*Then a bit too loudly*] Loneliness must end! How is loneliness to end? Loneliness ends when a light is lit.

KATERINA: [*Suddenly shouting at the dogs*] Shut up!

ZODITCH: [*In a moment of sudden fright* ZODITCH *knocks a small piece of meat off the table. He instantly bends down to pick it up*] Excuse me. Excuse me. [*Puts the meat back on the table. He continues, nervously*] And what power do we have to strike such a light? Mutual feeling . . . mutual regard, but even more than this, love. Love is a light. When two boats come together they make a light. This is the holy light of marriage. Now we must ask, what is marriage? Marriage is a sacrament, and by a sacrament the church means a sanctity and a union of spirits; therefore, marriage is not based on material possession. Oh, no, Katerina Prolomnaya, it is not a contract of assets and liabilities. The church does not in-

tend us to inquire into the number of houses owned, the number of horses in the stable. Love is above these things. It makes a harmony from separateness. It makes joy. It is above rings and rubles. [KATERINA *has stopped grinding the meat and now stares directly at him. He has grown very nervous*] It is the light that moves above the darkness of the sea. It is the star and moon. It is the refuge, the shelter, the roof against the wind. [*Suddenly taking her hand. She continues trying to grind the meat. He continues trying to get her to stop. A silent grinding.* ZODITCH *is dismayed. Nevertheless he continues*] Know, dear Katrina Prolomnaya, that it was not for nothing that your extra coal to me was given. Know that such seeds of generosity, of goodness, did not fall on barren ground, but that they found their way to this heart that even now illuminates with respectful fondness.

KATERINA: Now that you have been advanced in your position you will pay me two extra rubles a month for coal and oil.

ZODITCH: To you, Katerina, I offer this hand of marriage, this hand of spiritual bondage, this hand . . .

KATERINA: I cannot marry you. You are too old, too . . . [*Looking at him up and down*] short.

Light slowly fades out on KATERINA PROLOMNAYA.

ZODITCH: [*Turns and faces the audience*] Too old? *I* am too old. It is *I* who am laughing, Katerina Prolomnaya. [*Laughs a dry, hollow laugh*] I laugh to think you can laugh at me. It is you who are the wrinkled fish here. [*Cups his hand to his ear*] Is that so? Is that so, madam? Well, it is I who stoop to consider marriage to you. I laugh in your face. I withdraw my offer. . . . When I marry Miss Grubov your tongue will hang out to come to the wedding. [*From somewhere in his mind comes the sound of* KATERINA *laughing*] You keep your dogs away from me, Katerina Prolomnaya. Your tongue will hang out to be invited. Get away, you filthy beasts. Get away. [*He begins kicking at invisible dogs*] To a man of my position your assets are nothing. I am not interested in your buildings and your rents. I am a man of sensibilities. A man interested in love and feelings. Get away from my legs, you bitches. I'll kick your heads in. You think I didn't know the coal was given just to raise my rent? Keep your coal and kerosene. [*Laughter breaks out again*] What did you expect for a husband? A giant? Jack and the beanstalk? A ten-foot monster? There is no golden goose for you. You are no princess of the pea. Get away. Leave me alone. I'll kill you, you bitches. I'll kill you. Gregory! Gregory! Madhouse. Madhouse. Madhouse!

Lights dim on ZODITCH *frozen in a scream. Lights up on* LIZA *and* BIZMIONKOV *in the garden.* CHULKATURIN *stands half unseen in the archway.*

LIZA: How brown the garden has become. How dry.

BIZMIONKOV: Perhaps the Captain will yet write.

LIZA: You think so? [*Catching herself*] No. It is done. He will not write. Ivan etrovich has gone to Petersburg and he will not write. Shall I dig up these flowers do you think, and bring them inside? They will die in the first snow.

BIZMIONKOV: Let them die, Liza.

LIZA: Papa must have taken the spade inside. I cannot seem to find it.

BIZMIONKOV: What of Chulkaturin?

LIZA: [*Suddenly stops looking for the spade. She speaks with scorn*] That one? How hateful that name sounds to me. [*Touching some flowers*] These petals are still soft. I can save these flowers.

BIZMIONKOV: He has not left yet.

LIZA: Ah. Still he waits. For what does he wait? To forgive me? I do not need his forgiveness. Better that he had never known my brother. Better that the door to this house had remained forever shut against him.

BIZMIONKOV: He is in love with you.

LIZA: His love is nothing to me now! I cannot forgive him. What did he want here? Did he come all this way to stand alone at dances? To throw flowers to no one? To shoot Ivan? For what did he come?

BIZMIONKOV: [*Slowly*] I think Nikolai Alexeevich Chulkaturin came all this way to love you.

LIZA: [*There is a pause in which she looks at* BIZMIONKOV *for a long time, as if seeing him for the first time*] How good you are. You are an angel. What should I have ever done without you?

BIZMIONKOV: Is there nothing then for Chulkaturin?

LIZA: I have forgotten him. [*Raising her hands to his face*] My friend, if you love me, knowing all, I will do as you ask. I will become your wife.

BIZMIONKOV *embraces her, slowly, tightly.* CHULKATURIN *lets out a short cry.*

CHULKATURIN: You, Bizmionkov? You?

ZODITCH: No, Miss Grubov! Not Pandalevski! [*Lights go out on* BIZMIONKOV *and* LIZA, ZODITCH *and* CHULKATURIN *are left facing each other across the stage.* ZODITCH *grabs the manuscript in his hand*] This is a story of lies! You are a liar! You distort. Do you see what I am doing? I reject this manuscript. I reject you. [*Writing across the face of the manuscript*]

CHULKATURIN: And I stood in the garden dumb and dark with hedges, stood as if the winds of a thousand centuries might wash upon me and find me standing yet. And for all of it, the roses shut in books, the crowns of May, the duels, the summer dances, what for all of it, if, at the last, to say, "Bizmionkov, is it you?" [*Extends his arm to* ZODITCH]

ZODITCH: Liar! I am the one that is loved! That is the ending. I am loved! [*There is a pause in which* ZODITCH *and* CHULKATURIN *stare at each other. When* ZODITCH *speaks the anger has been replaced by anguish*] What do you want of me? [CHULKATURIN's *arm falls. Lights out on* CHULKATURIN. ZODITCH, *with rage, throws the diary violently away*] I am the one that is loved. There is no other ending. [*He begins curling himself up into a hard ball as if suddenly very cold*]

Lights out.

VOICE: And when I had passed through the antique marketplace of Samarkand, through the cries and fevers of the merchants, the monkey's hand fell within his cage, and there was nothing further to the matter.

THE RIMERS OF ELDRITCH

a play in two acts

Lanford Wilson

The Rimers of Eldritch was first presented by Ellen Stewart at La Mama ETC, New York City, on July 13, 1966, with the following cast:

ROBERT CONKLIN	*Michael Warren Powell*
EVA JACKSON	*Claris Erickson*
EVELYN JACKSON	*Tanya Berezin*
NELLY WINDROD	*Blanche Dee*
MARY WINDROD	*Shellie Feldman*
PATSY JOHNSON	*Beth Porter*
MAVIS JOHNSON	*Kay C. Coulthard*
PECK JOHNSON	*Gene Alton*
JOSH JOHNSON	*Marvin Alexander*
LENA TRUIT	*Jane Buchanan*
MARTHA TRUIT	*Ann Harris*
WILMA ATKINS	*Jacque Lynn Colton*
SKELLY MANNOR	*Robert Thirkield*
PREACHER/JUDGE	*George Harris*
CORA GROVES	*Kay Carney*
WALTER	*Fred Forrest*
TRUCKER	*Oliver Dixon*

It was directed by the author; the stage manager was Lola Richardson.

The play was subsequently presented at the Cherry Lane Theatre, New York City, by Theatre 1967, directed by Michael Kahn and designed by William Ritman.

For Joseph Cino
The harvest is past, the summer is ended, and we are not saved.

—JEREMIAH 8:20

CHARACTERS

ROBERT CONKLIN, *a boy, eighteen*

EVA JACKSON, *a crippled girl, fourteen*

EVELYN JACKSON, *her mother*

NELLY WINDROD, *a strong woman, middle-aged*

MARY WINDROD, *her senile mother*

PATSY JOHNSON, *the prettiest girl at Centerville High*

MAVIS JOHNSON, *her mother*

PECK JOHNSON, *her father*

JOSH JOHNSON, *her brother*

LENA TRUIT, *her girl friend, the same age*

MARTHA TRUIT, *Lena's mother*

WILMA ATKINS, *a friend of Martha's*

SKELLY MANNOR, *the town hermit, about sixty*

PREACHER ⎱ *played by the same actor, in midfifties*
JUDGE ⎰

CORA GROVES, *the owner of Hilltop Café*

WALTER, *her lover*

A TRUCKER

The locale of the play is Eldritch, present population about seventy, one of the many nearly abandoned towns in America's Middle West. The time is the present.

The play takes place during the spring, summer, and fall of the year, skipping at will from summer back to spring or forward to fall and from one conversation to another. All the characters are on stage throughout the play, except twice as indicated, grouping as needed to suggest time and place.

At La Mama Experimental Theatre Club and the Cherry Lane Theatre the play was acted on a series of six or eight descending, irregular levels, some with railings to suggest a porch or the witness stand of the courtroom as needed, against a black void. It might also be done with various architectural elements, suggested gables, trees, ruined buildings, American Gothic motifs indicating the various buildings of the town.

The lighting, especially if a bare stage or platforms are used, might be considered the most important single scenic element. In this edition—to assist the readers in seeing the play —it has been indicated at the beginning of each scene where the conversations take place. Some are quite obvious: scenes in the café, court, or church. Others, such as "A street in town," a director might wish to place else-

where; they should be thought of only as suggestions to aid in following the printed text of the play. A scene continues—sometimes two or more in separate areas of the stage simultaneously—until the lights dim on the scene and focus attention elsewhere.

ACT I

In darkness, WILMA *and* MARTHA *on the porch of* MARTHA'S *house.*

WILMA: Well, what I heard isn't fit for talk, but I heard that Mrs. Cora Groves, up on the highway . . . ?

MARTHA: Yes.

WILMA: . . . has taken a boy, she's old enough to be his mother, on, and is keeping him up there in her café.

MARTHA: In her bed.

WILMA: [*With true sympathy*] That woman went crazy when her husband left her.

MARTHA: Oh, I know she did.

WILMA: That woman, I swear, isn't responsible for her own actions.

A very faint light begins to illuminate the courtroom. NELLY *standing, her hand raised.*

MARTHA: I should say she isn't.

WILMA: I hear he does things around the café, whistling around like he belonged there.

MARTHA: Have you ever heard anything like it?

WILMA: I haven't, I swear to God.

A sharp increase in the lights. In the courtroom.

NELLY: I do.

MARTHA'S *porch—morning.*

MARTHA: Why, she called Evelyn Jackson a liar to her face, and Eva too. Swore things the devil and his angels wouldn't believe it. She'd stand up there and swear black was white.

WILMA: And Nelly, poor woman, the life that woman leads. Only God in His Heaven knows the trials that woman has to bear.

MARTHA: That she should have to be dragged through this.

WILMA: She stood there and told the way it was; I said to Mrs. Jackson—cried the whole time—

MARTHA: —I know, I saw.

WILMA: Only God in Heaven knows the trials that poor woman has had to bear.

In the courtroom.

JUDGE: Nelly Windrod, do you solemnly swear to tell the whole truth, and nothing but the truth—

NELLY: [*Quietly troubled*] I do, yes.

JUDGE: —so help you God?

NELLY: I do.

JUDGE: [*Exactly as before*] Nelly Windrod, do you solemnly swear to tell the truth, and nothing but the truth—

NELLY: I do, yes.

JUDGE: —So help you God?

NELLY: I do.

MARTHA'S *porch—night.*

MARTHA: So help me God, I don't know how we let him hang around here like he did. Not talking to nobody.

WILMA: Nobody I know of could live like that.

MARTHA: Like that time he scared young Patsy so bad.

WILMA: Bad for the whole town with someone like that.

MARTHA: Like that way he had of just standing around.

WILMA: Around here everybody knows everybody.

MARTHA: Everybody was scared of him. Everybody knew what he was.

WILMA: A fool like that.

MARTHA: Grumbling and mumbling around; standing and watching it all.

WILMA: I'd think people'd feel easier now. I know I swear I do.

MARTHA: I do.

In the courtroom.

NELLY: I do.

Beat.

JUDGE: [*Faintly, fading*] Now, Miss Windrod, if you would tell the court, in your own words . . .

In the grocery where ROBERT *works.*

MARY: [*To* ROBERT] Now, we have to understand that Nelly is my flesh and blood.

ROBERT: I know.

MARY: Yes, love, she's my flesh and blood and she thinks she knows but she doesn't know but she thinks she does.

ROBERT: I suppose she does if anybody does.

MARY: Well, she thinks she does. But I know and you know. I was at my window, watching the moon.

ROBERT: Was there a moon?

MARY: I said to those people, all those new people in town—there isn't much to know about Eldritch, used to be Elvin Eldritch's pasture till it gave out I guess and they found coal. It was built on coal with coal money and deserted when the coal gave out and here it stands, this wicked old town. All the buildings bowing and nodding.

ROBERT: How do you know so much?

MARY: And still so little? I would puzzle that if I could. I told them none of the people here now were coal people. The mining people moved off; they raped the land and moved away. There used to be explosives that rattled the windows, oh my, and shook the water in a bucket, day and night.

ROBERT: How come you remember so much?

MARY: And still so little? The last time I saw you, why, you was just a little baby; you've grown up so.

ROBERT: You saw me yesterday, Mrs. Windrod.

MARY: You don't know. Isn't that sweet? The last time I saw you, why, you weren't no bigger than that high.

ROBERT: You've known me all my—

MARY: You've grown up so. I have terrible bruises on my arm there. Look at that.

CORA'S *café.* WALTER *is sitting at the counter.*

TRUCKER: [*Leaving*] I'll see you, Cora.

CORA: Can't avoid it, I guess. You watch it now on those narrow roads.

TRUCKER: It's push-pull with the load; I'll come back through empty day after tomorrow—you remember to tell me that again.

CORA: Stay awake now.

TRUCKER: No danger of that.

On the porch.

WILMA: I'll say one thing for her. How long has it been he's been there?

CORA: [*To* WALTER] Boy.

MARTHA: Two or three months now nearly. Walks around the place whistling like he owned it.

WILMA: Well, he earns his keep.

CORA: Boy.

MARTHA: It's not in the kitchen that he earns his keep, Wilma.

CORA: Boy.

WILMA: Well, I'll say one thing—

CORA: —I'm getting ready to close up now.

WILMA: —Whatever it is, she looks a darn sight better now than she did a year ago. Since I can remember.

CORA: Boy.

WALTER: [*As though waking from a daydream*] I'm sorry.

CORA: I'm fixing to close up. You sleeping?

WALTER: Thinking, I guess.

CORA: Have another cup of coffee, I got time.

MARTHA: That woman isn't responsible for her own actions since her husband left her.

WALTER: Swell.

WILMA: It's not for us to judge.

MARTHA: That's all well and good but anyone who deliberately cuts herself off from everybody else in town.

WILMA: I don't judge, but I know who I speak to on the street and who I don't.

WALTER: Is there work here in town do you know?

CORA: Down in Eldritch? Not if you're looking for wages. Not here.

MARTHA: It's easy to see the devil's work.

WALTER: I had that in mind.

CORA: You might try Centerville; Eldritch is all but a ghost town.

WALTER: You here alone?

CORA: I've managed for seven years; it hasn't bothered me.

WALTER: It might not be a bad idea to take someone on yourself.

WILMA: It's a sin to sashay through Centerville the way she does, buying that boy shirts and new clothes. Keeping him up on the highway.

MARTHA: I don't go, but I understand he's made a show place out of her café.

WILMA: I'd be happier if it was me if they made her close it down.

MARTHA: It ought to be against the law serving beer to truck drivers and them having to be on the road so much.

WILMA: The wages of sin lead to death.

CORA: Aren't you cold in just that jacket? That's pretty light for April.

WALTER: No, it's not bad.

They regard each other a moment; the light fades on the café.

MARTHA: The wages of sin is death.

WILMA: Bless her heart, poor old thing.

MARTHA: [*As* MARY WINDROD *passes the porch*] Good evening, Mary.

WILMA: Good evening, Mary Windrod.

MARY: [*Stopping*] You two. I watch you two sometimes. [MARY *talks, almost with everything she says, as though she were describing a beautiful dream to a pet canary*]

WILMA: Aren't you cold in that shawl, dear?

MARTHA: Nights are cold in this valley for June.

MARY: It's not bad.

WILMA: You'll be catching a chill next.

MARY: I was once a nurse and I believe that the constant proximity to sickness has given me an immunity to night air.

MARTHA: Never think that.

MARY: Us dry old women rattle like paper; we couldn't get sick. I listen to you old women sometimes.

WILMA: How's your daughter?

MARY: Yes, indeed.

MARTHA: I beg your pardon?

MARY: The proximity to all that sickness.

WILMA: Yes, love.

MARY: Immunity to death myself. My number passed Gabriel right on by. It came up and passed right on by and here I am a forgotten child.

WILMA: You better get inside, love.

MARY: Rusting away, flaking away.

MARTHA: You get in, now.

MARY: [*Leaving*] This wicked town. God hear a dried-up woman's prayer and do not forgive this wicked town!

The CONGREGATION *bursts into "Shall We Gather at the River"; after only a few bars, the song stops abruptly. In the courtroom.*

NELLY: And Mama came running downstairs and said a man had attacked young Eva Jackson.

JUDGE: Would you point out Eva . . . ?

NELLY: [*As the light fades*] There, poor lamb, can't hardly speak two words since this thing happened and I don't wonder—

On the porch.

WILMA: [*Overlapping a word or two*] Well, I know I swear I don't know what he sees in her.

MARTHA: It's nice of him, though.

WILMA: Well, I know but Driver Junior's old enough to be taking girls out; he shouldn't be wandering around with her.

MARTHA: It's nice to have somebody to keep her company. Still and all, it doesn't seem natural. I know what you mean.

WILMA: I don't know what he sees in her.

MARTHA: Poor thing.

Near EVA'S *house.*

ROBERT: Eva!

EVA: Are you glad to be out of school?

ROBERT: I liked it all right.

EVA: What are you going to be?

ROBERT: Who knows?

EVA: We had our Eighth Grade graduation in robes! I bet I know what you won't be, don't I?

ROBERT: What's that?

EVA: A race car driver.

ROBERT: Why do you want to say that? You think I couldn't do that if I wanted to?

EVA: You don't want to get yourself killed.

ROBERT: Driver didn't want it; he just had an accident.

EVA: You want to be like him?

ROBERT: People don't want to do the same thing their brother did; I couldn't see any sense in it.

EVA: I knew you didn't. You aren't going to get yourself killed.

ROBERT: Killed doesn't have anything to do with it. Eva, good Lord, I don't want people carrying on like that; honking their horns, coming into town every week like a parade. I never even went to see Driver.

EVA: You decided what you want to be?

ROBERT: I don't have to decide this minute, do I?

EVA: I just wondered.

ROBERT: Do you know? You don't know what you want.

EVA: Of course I know; you know, I told you. So do you know, everybody knows what they want—it's what they think they really can do that they don't know.

ROBERT: Well, I don't have to decide yet.

EVA: [*In a sudden burst, as though conjuring*] When's it gonna be autumn? I love autumn so much I could hug it. I want it to be autumn. That's what I want right now. Now! Autumn! Now!

ROBERT: Good luck; I don't see it.

EVA: [*In a burst*] Don't you be derisive to me, Driver Junior!

ROBERT: Don't call me that.

EVA: Well, don't you go on, Robert Conklin, or I'll call you anything I like.

ROBERT: You'll be talking to yourself.

EVA: Everybody else calls you that. Don't go away; I won't, I promise. Don't you wish it was autumn? Don't you? Don't you love autumn? And the wind and rime and pumpkins and gourds and corn shocks? I won't again. Don't you love autumn? Don't you, Robert? I won't call you that. Everybody else does but I won't.

ROBERT: I haven't thought about it.

EVA: Well, think about it, right now. Think about how it smells.

ROBERT: How does it smell?

EVA: Like dry, windy, cold, frosty rime and chaff and leaf smoke and corn husks.

ROBERT: It does, huh?

EVA: Pretend. Close your eyes—are your eyes closed? Don't you wish it was here? Like apples and cider. *You* go.

ROBERT: And rain.

EVA: Sometimes. And potatoes and flower seeds and honey.

ROBERT: And popcorn and butter.

EVA: [*Opening her eyes*] Yes. Oh, it does not! You're not playing at all. There's hay and clover and alfalfa and all that. [*Hitting him, really quite hard, slapping*]

ROBERT: [*Laughing*] Come on, it's different for everybody.

EVA: Well, that's not right; it doesn't at all. Are you making fun?

ROBERT: Come on, don't be rough.

EVA: I will too; you're not the least bit funny, Driver Junior! [*As he starts to walk on*] Come back here, Robert! Robert Conklin. Driver Junior! Little brother. Your brother was a man, anyway. Coward. Robert? Bobby?

In the store.

WILMA: And I'll have some flour and yeast. And three packs of Sure-Jell.

ROBERT: Right you are. How much flour?

WILMA: No more than five pounds in this weather. How're you doing in school?

ROBERT: All right.

WILMA: I just said to Martha Truit, I suppose Driver Junior will be leaving us as soon as school gets out next month, like all the young kids now.

ROBERT: Not for a while yet.

WILMA: Oh, you will; you'll be going off to see the world.

ROBERT: I don't know.

WILMA: There's nothing for a strong young man in this dead old town. Where do you think you'll be heading?

ROBERT: I don't know.

WILMA: Des Moines?

ROBERT: I don't imagine.

WILMA: St. Louis?

ROBERT: Who knows?

WILMA: Chicago?

ROBERT: I might not leave at all for a while.

WILMA: Well, your brother stayed and he was wonderful, but we all expect you to be moving along like all the young boys now.

ROBERT: I don't know.

Downstairs in the Windrod house. NELLY *has a hold on* MARY'S *arm.* MARY *is turning backward,* NELLY *forward,* MARY *avoiding the raised hand threatening her, much as on a turntable going backward.*

MARY: I know, I know, I know, I know, don't
hit me; don't hit me, baby.

NELLY: What do you mean telling people a tale
like that. You know I bought that mill.

MARY: You bought it, baby; I know you bought
it.

NELLY: Well, they said in town you told I'd
killed Dad to get it.

MARY: I said he died mysteriously.

NELLY: Well, he died of old age; he was ninety-
six, for God's sakes.

MARY: He died mysteriously!

NELLY: In his sleep like you will; died of old age
like you will. What in hell do you mean telling something like that?

MARY: I didn't mean to, baby. I don't mean to—

NELLY: —You're batty as a goddamned loon.

MARY: They don't like me is what it is. They
know I watch them. They don't like me in
town, I knew they didn't. I don't say those
things. They tell things on me.

NELLY: You're crazy as hell is what it is; you're
out of your goddamned mind is what it is.

MARY: Baby, don't talk like that. They tell *fibs*
on me. They say—

NELLY: Showing them bruises and saying I beat
you; when the hell did I ever beat you? You
know goddamned well how you get those
bruises. You fall down! You bruise! You run
into things! You're old. You bump things.
Who the hell takes care of you and you telling
lies on me like that, Mama—what do you
mean?

MARY: I don't mean to.

NELLY: They don't listen to you—to say things
like that.

MARY: They don't listen to me, Nelly.

NELLY: It doesn't do you any good; they come
right in and tell me.

MARY: Don't hurt me.

NELLY: I think you better go on up to your room!

MARY: No, don't lock the door.

NELLY: If I leave the house, I'll lock the door or
you'll wander out and get hurt. You'll fall
down the stairs and tell I beat you.

MARY: I don't want to go up there; the evil town
is all around me up there.

NELLY: Go upstairs, Mama.

MARY: It's painted on the windows—

NELLY: Well, pull the shades down if you don't
want to see them. [*She leaves*]

MARY: My skin, whole body is just flaking away
—this evil town! This evil town!

On a street in town: JOSH *and all the young
men in the cast except* WALTER.

BOY: [*Taunting* SKELLY, *jeeringly*] Baaaaaaaaaa!
Baaaaaaaaa! Baaaaaaaa! Baaaaaaa!

SKELLY: [*In a deep, mangled, growling, almost
drunken voice*] Get on, you son of bitch. Son
of bitches. [*Sounding about like "Geah-own-
ya-sansobith! Sansobith!"*]

BOYS: Baaaaaa! Baaaaaa!

SKELLY: Get the hell on, you, get on! [*In a deep,
almost terrified growl*] Go, go on, sonabith!

In the courtroom.

NELLY: And I heard something outside—

The town becomes alive everywhere, PECK,
NELLY, MARY, JOSH, MARTHA *and the* JUDGE
are in the court, PATSY *and* LENA *in town;*
EVELYN *is walking out onto her porch calling*
EVA, *who is approaching the porch. An area
may be* EVELYN's *porch and part of the courtroom at the same time—the effect should be of
the entire cast moving in a deliberate direction
with lines coming in sequence from all over the
stage.* CORA *enters the café area from upstairs, sleepily, calling softly, exactly as she
will when the scene is repeated at the end of
the first act.*

JUDGE: A travesty of justice.

PECK: We, the jury—

CORA: Walter?

PECK: —find Nelly Windrod—

CORA: Walter?

PECK: —not guilty.

MARTHA: Not guilty.

CORA: Walter?

EVA: Robert?

NELLY: Oh, God; Mama?

EVELYN: Eva?

TRUCKER: Not guilty.

WILMA: Papa?

MAVIS: Peck?

JOSH: Not guilty. [*He begins whistling softly,
calling a dog*] Here, Blackie, here, boy.

WALTER: Cora!

CORA: Walter?

JUDGE: Not guilty.

PATSY: I know.

EVELYN: Eva? You come on, now.

CORA: Oh, God, oh, God, oh, God, oh, God, oh
God.

JOSH: Blackie? Here, Blackie?

EVELYN: You better get on in here now.

EVA: I'm coming.

JOSH: Come on, boy.

LENA: The poor thing.

PATSY: Really, I get so damn tired of all that nonsense.

LENA: I know, but they insist I wear it.

The movement subsides.

EVELYN: [*Continuing*] You better put a sweater on if you're going to sit out there.

EVA: [*Approaching the house*] I'm coming in directly.

EVELYN: Not directly, you come on in now.

EVA: All right.

EVELYN: Where were you all day?

EVA: I was wandering around the woods.

EVELYN: Now, you know I don't want you running around alone. What if you fell and hurt yourself and who'd ever know it?

EVA: I wasn't alone; Robert and I went walking.

EVELYN: Well, don't you go off alone.

EVA: I won't.

EVELYN: Not all afternoon. Wandering around; God knows what could happen to you.

EVA: I know, I don't.

EVELYN: You look so fatigued.

EVA: I'm not at all.

EVELYN: I don't want you spending so much time with that boy.

EVA: What boy?

EVELYN: That Driver Junior. Wandering around with that boy. Spending all afternoon and evening with him.

EVA: Well, who else would I spend it with?

EVELYN: Well, why do you have to go off every day of the week? Doing God knows what? You could visit the Stutses, you shouldn't be running around. It isn't good for you; you have to be careful. You're not like other kids; you know how easily you get fatigued; you run yourself out every day; perspiring like you do; wandering off with that boy. If something happened, who'd know? And don't think he's responsible; his brother might have been different; devil and his angels wouldn't know if something happened. I don't know why you can't stay at home like everyone else. Traipsing around the woods half-naked, what do you do out there in the woods alone, the two of you, anyhow?

EVA: Nothing.

EVELYN: I said you answer me.

EVA: [*Rapidly*] Nothing!

EVELYN: I said you answer me the truth, young miss.

EVA: We don't do anything. Whatever you think.

EVELYN: Don't you talk back to me, what do you do, little miss smarty pants? All day gone from the house, smarty? [*Hits her*]

EVA: We talk.

EVELYN: You talk, you talk, I'll just bet you talk; now you get in that house this minute do you hear me!

EVA: [*Running to the witness stand*] I don't know what you think.

EVELYN: You get on in to the supper table! You're going to be the death of me. I swear, I swear, I swear.

Everyone is assembled in court.

JUDGE: —to tell the whole truth and nothing but the truth, so help you God?

ROBERT: She didn't see anything.

JUDGE: Eva, as a witness to this terrible—

EVA: I don't know! I didn't see! I told you I didn't see anything! [*A long run to her Mother's open arms*]

EVA: Mama.

CORA: She told me.

CORA: I talked to her; she told me.

ROBERT: [*His lines overlapping* CORA'S] She didn't see.

EVA: I don't know!

NELLY: It's not true, none of it, it's like I said. You're trying to make a murderer of me; it was God's will be done.

CORA: She told me.

EVELYN: Leave my daughter alone! Can't you see she's upset? My God, what are you trying to do to her?

EVELYN: [*to* EVA] Poor baby—[*To* CORA] You know what I think of you? Before God!

JUDGE: [*His voice rising above theirs, simultaneously, trying to quiet them*] We have all long known Skelly Mannor; we have known of his past—that latent evil in him, that unnatural desire, and we have long been aware that at any time the bitterness in his soul might again overflow. [*General crowd murmur*] We let things lie. We took no action to prevent his crime—the pending, at any moment, crime—we all knew it—and the burden must be ours. We are responsible for the shock to these two innocents.

The others have been quieted. General murmur in response to the JUDGE. *Several Amens.*

JUDGE: [*Continuing*] We are responsible for our actions; for allowing the heathen in our fold]

The JUDGE'S *oratory slides into the* PREACHER. *We are at church.*

CONGREGATION: Amen!

PREACHER: God forgive us.

CONGREGATION: Amen.

PREACHER: In Your wisdom forgive us. And help these two souls, these two innocent souls forget that dark moment.

CONGREGATION: Amen, amen.

PREACHER: Blind them to that dark moment and set them free, Lord.

CONGREGATION: Amen.

PREACHER: Dear Lord.

CONGREGATION: Amen.

PREACHER: Our Saviour!

In the café.

WALTER [*To* CORA] Where do you want the pie?

CORA: [*Warmly, chiding*] On the rack that says "pies."

WALTER: And the coffee in the jar that says "coffee" and the typed-up menus in the menu covers? I'll catch on.

CORA: You're doing fine.

WALTER: Well, for only a week.

CORA: You'll catch on.

In the congregation MARTHA *says, very faintly,* "A show place," *echoed by* "I hear" *from* WILMA.

WALTER: [*Overlapping*] And you have to consider that we spend more time upstairs than down, or I'd know a lot more about the restaurant business and a lot less about you.

CORA: Now you just clam up before somebody comes in.

WALTER: Ashamed, are you?

CORA: No, I most certainly am not and you know it, but I don't intend to bother someone else's business with my own.

WALTER: Wonder what they think?

CORA: You do, do you?

WALTER: "No, I most certainly do not and you know it"—I like the way you people talk. You're looking good.

CORA: I'm feeling good.

WALTER: What would you think about putting an awning over the door so a fellow doesn't get soaking wet with rain as soon as he steps out the door.

CORA: Hm. What'd I care if he's going out?

WALTER: Oh, it might be that on the way out is when he decides to come back.

CORA: You think, do you?

WALTER: "You think, do you?" It's something to consider.

WILMA: A show place.

The Johnson house.

PATSY: It's a trash heap is what it is. I don't know what keeps us here; I swear I don't. Maybe it was all right when you were young. The only people who ever comes into town is people to drive around looking around, poking around to see what a ghost town looks like. Movie house been closed down eight years; you want to see a movie you have to drive twenty miles into Centerville. Every building on Main Street closed up, falling down except a store and a grubby filling station. Boys stand out, hanging around, it's a disgrace—

On her porch.

EVELYN: —Can't be healthy, rats took over the old granary, all the buildings rotting and falling down, the mine shaft building used to just shine; you could see it miles away; now the way it sags—falling apart, boarded together; everything flapping and rusting, it's an absolute eyesore. Cats poking around through the rotting ruins of all those old buildings, their bellies just busting, it can't be healthy—

PATSY: —Dad could get a job in Centerville as well as here; I don't know why we stay here, there's a lot of decent people there, they know how to have fun, but no. We have to stay here. The boys from Centerville *all* have cars, I'm so ashamed getting off that ugly smelly school bus with all those younger kids, squealing; I swear sometimes I think I'm just going to sit there and not budge all day. Just let them drive right into the parking lot and sit there in the hot sun all day broiling rather than get off that bus with the boys all standing around the front of the school watching. I just wish you knew—they're probably surprised I don't smell of cow manure.

PECK: Patsy.

PATSY: Well, I'm sorry but it's true. I wish you could see the way they dress! In the summertime the boys from Centerville drive by on the highway alongside the field and I'm up on the hay wagon like some common hired hand and they yell and honk and carry on so damn smart I just wish I could die.

MAVIS: Patsy June.

PATSY: Well, I'm sorry but I do. At night sometimes I just cry my eyes out. Night after night. I just cry myself to sleep; I hope you're satisfied—

EVELYN: —Trying to scratch a living together. Trying to keep strong—

PATSY: [*Leaving house; to* LENA] —I'm sorry, but I do—

EVELYN: —Sometimes I don't even know why we try—

LENA: [*On the porch*] I said it's warm, for crying out loud; it's May; school's nearly out; I don't know why I have to wear that ugly old thing, you have the nicest clothes. I never have a danged thing.

PATSY: Well, all the boys were wearing cashmere sweaters with V necks and I said if they can have them I sure as hell can; the girls in my class just turned pea-green-purple. I said, well, they didn't have what I wanted in Centerville, this two-bit town, so I went along with Dad to Des Moines; you should have seen them.

LENA: Peggy was furious.

PATSY: Oh, she thinks she's so rich; she has absolutely no taste at all.

LENA: I know.

PATSY: Black and brown and blue and green; I said the other day, "Why, Peggy, you look exactly the color of Chuck Melton's two-toned Mercury." You should have seen her face.

LENA: I wish I could have.

PATSY: [*As they walk away from the porch*] Well, listen; Chuck thinks he's so damn smart himself. Yelling to me, you should hear the things they say. It'd make your ears burn. I told him and he should know, if he wants to come by and come up to the door and knock like some kind of respectable person, then I'd go out; but I'm not going to just fly out of the house like that. He thinks he's so damn smart, I don't care how long he sits out in front of the house in his damn car. Honking. He can honk all night for all I care.

MARTHA: [*Coming to the porch*] Evelyn said a regular show place.

WILMA: I heard she closes up at ten every night now.

MARTHA: Oh, my . . .

WILMA: [*Leaving porch*] Ours is not to judge.

MARTHA: Still I know what I know.

LENA: [*Joins her mother*] I know he did it. Why would anyone want to poison a helpless dog?

MARTHA: He just looked up at me like he knew I'd help him and there wasn't anything I could do this time and I think he knew.

LENA: I don't understand somebody doing something like that.

MARTHA: There wasn't anything I could do. Just nothing at all.

LENA: Why?

MARTHA: I don't know, love.

LENA: [*Repeating, with same inflection*] Why?

MARTHA: I don't know, love.

LENA: Why?

MARTHA: I don't know, love.

LENA: Just a helpless little dog, he was too old to hurt anybody. There's somebody poisoning dogs around here and that's the lowest, meanest thing in the world.

MARTHA: No one should cause an animal to suffer like that.

LENA: I know he did it, too. I know it was him.

MARTHA: Well, we can think what we think, but we can't do anything.

LENA: I've seen how they bark at him; you know that. A dog can tell an evil person; a dog can tell; they're all scared of him.

WILMA: [*Coming to the porch*] Wickedest man; creeping through town, looking into things.

MARTHA: Peeping into girls' bedrooms; standing around looking like that.

WILMA: Who knows what's in someone's mind like that?

PATSY *screams very loudly, running from her bedroom into the living room.*

PECK: [*Startled*] What in God's name?

PATSY: Oh, God, oh, God, oh, God, oh, God. In there.

MAVIS: What's wrong, baby?

PATSY: I saw him. I saw him. Oh, God, he was looking in the window. His face—

PECK: Who was? Answer me.

MAVIS: Skelly?

PATSY: Skelly. Skelly. Skelly was. Oh, God, you should have seen his eyes! And I was only in my pants. You should have seen him.

JOSH: I don't know what he could have seen.

MAVIS: That's enough out of you now.

PECK: Where was he?

PATSY: At my bedroom window, where do you think?

MAVIS: You're imagining things; you're dreaming.

PATSY: I wasn't asleep, I tell you; I just was getting ready for bed.

PECK: It's okay now, I'll go out.

PATSY: No, he's gone now, my God, I screamed and he ran away.

PECK: [*With some humor*] Well, I'd think he would.

JOSH: Wake the dead; what's he gonna see?

MAVIS: Don't you start.

PATSY: [*Contrite*] I'm sorry.

MAVIS: For what?

JOSH: Sorry he didn't come on in probably.

PATSY: For scaring you so.

MAVIS: It's all right. My word, something like that, I'd think you would.

PATSY: Only I was just so scared.

MAVIS: Of course you would. [JOSH *is stifling a laugh*] That's enough, Dad said.

PATSY: It was horrible.

MAVIS: It's all right now.

PATSY: I don't think I can go back in my room.

JOSH: Oh, good Lord.

PECK: Young man.

MAVIS: It's all right now.

PATSY: Can't I sleep with you tonight?

MAVIS: It's all right now.

PATSY: Just tonight.

MAVIS: No, now, he's gone.

JOSH: What are you, some kind of baby?

PATSY: I was just so scared.

MAVIS: Go on back to bed, honey.

PATSY: I'm sorry.

MAVIS: It's okay.

PATSY: It was horrible. Can't I sleep between you? I'm shaking like a leaf.

MAVIS: It was nothing.

PATSY: Just tonight?

MAVIS: You're too big for that kind of thing.

PATSY: Something ought to be done about him.

MAVIS: It was your imagination, it was the wind; it was the shadows.

PATSY: It was Skelly Mannor! I guess I know him when I see him.

MAVIS: Go on back to bed. He's gone.

PATSY: I know I saw him.

MAVIS: Go on, it's okay now; he's gone; whoever it was.

PATSY: Well, it was Skelly Mannor, I guess I know who it was, I saw him.

MAVIS: Something ought to be done about him.

JOSH: He hasn't hurt anyone—not yet.

MAVIS: I suppose you call scaring an innocent girl out of her wits doing nothing. And the whole family too. Everyone knows what he does.

JOSH: Well, what could he do but look? He must be over a hundred if he's a day.

MAVIS: Just looking is doing; who knows what he might do?

JOSH: He's eighty years old.

PATSY: He is not. How can you tell how old he is, through all that filth.

PECK: Well, I know when I was a young man like Josh or younger we used to give old Skelly a "baaa" sometimes—

MAVIS: Peck, now—

PECK: Well, and he looked the same then as he does now, and all the men then said he'd been looking like that for as long as they could remember so he's getting on.

JOSH: He's just a curiosity.

PATSY: Oh, that's very funny. A curiosity. You're just as bright as the sun; you ought to hide your head under a barrel.

JOSH: He's not hurt anybody. Except Warren Peabody.

PATSY: Well, Warren Peabody deserved whatever he got, I'm sure.

MAVIS: What did he do to Warren, is that Laura Peabody's boy?

PATSY: Oh, Lord, no; you know he drives an old Chevy, from over at Centerville; part of that river trash bunch. [*Exits, coming to* LENA]

JOSH: Well, he hit Warren in the back of the head with a rock, threw it, I'll bet, thirty feet, and caught Warren running. Knocked him out cold.

In town.

LENA: [*Talking to* PATSY] I remember when Driver was alive.

PATSY: Before his accident.

LENA: This was a wonderful place.

PECK: [*Continuing*] He's got a good aim, I can vouch for that.

MAVIS: I've told you, Josh, I don't want you boys teasing him. You just ignore him, I don't care how old you are. I don't know why you do that. You know he could turn on you any second.

JOSH: Oh, I don't bother him.

MAVIS: Well, who know's what's in somebody's mind like that.

On WILMA'S *porch.*

WILMA: Like that time he scared young Patsy so bad.

MARTHA: Bad for the whole town with someone like that.

LENA: [*To* PATSY] Like that parade every Saturday afternoon with Driver spinning through town, laughing; I remember his laugh.

PECK: I remember he let Curt Watson have it across the side of the face once. Curt was the fastest runner in town too; let him have it once when Curt gave him a "baaa."

JOSH: God knows he's crazy enough to try to do something like that with a sheep.

MAVIS: Josh, now.

JOSH: Well, I figure maybe he couldn't get a girl.

MAVIS: That's enough.

JOSH: Well, now; the whole town knows what he did; it's not like it was some secret—it's the funniest thing anyone's ever seen around here.

MAVIS: It's not our place to talk.

PECK: I don't imagine he did it much more than once and that time he got caught.

JOSH: That's about the dumbest thing I ever heard. He must have been really hard up is all I can say.

On WILMA'S *porch.*

WILMA: To do some bestial thing like that.

MARTHA: When I think of the evil in this world.

LENA: [*To* PATSY] I could just cry.

JOSH: Who saw him?

PECK: Hell, I don't know. It must have been before I was born.

JOSH: Hell, he must be eighty years old.

PECK: Well, he's getting on.

PATSY: [*To* LENA] And Driver Junior. I think he hated his brother. He's just nothing compared. His brother was always so happy at least.

LENA: Driver's been dead now three years tomorrow.

PATSY: May thirty-first.

LENA: Every time I see that car, it just kills me.

JOSH: Some dumb old sheepherder. I hear they're all like that.

PECK: Well, they don't get into town much. Shit, they sure must be the hard up is all I can say.

PATSY: [*To* LENA] His name is Walter, I found out.

JOSH: Shit, I wish I could of seen him. That old son of a bitch. We ought to have him tarred and feathered on Halloween if anyone could find him on Halloween. That old bastard, I don't know how he gets away with the things he does. I know Driver and me was gonna run him out of town once; I think we got drunk instead.

PECK: When was that?

JOSH: Just before his accident sometime. Shit, we used to run that old boy ragged.

PECK: You watch yourself.

MARTHA: [*To* WILMA] When I think of the evil in this world, I swear.

JOSH: Aw, he hasn't hurt anybody. [*He leaves* PECK *and* MAVIS]

LENA: [*To* PATSY] I could just cry.

MAVIS: A decent person is afraid to move outside at night; now what kind of life is that?

PECK: Well, we'll tell Clevis and see what he says. He can't do nothing; we didn't catch him at it.

MAVIS: It'll be too late one day and then who's to blame.

The light fades on PECK *and* MAVIS. *Downstairs at the* Windrod *house.*

MARY: I saw it.

NELLY: Sure you did, Mama.

MARY: In my dream. Oh, God; it was horrible, Nelly.

NELLY: Go back to sleep, Mama.

MARY: Someone's going to be butchered in this town. Blood is going to be shed.

NELLY: Be still.

MARY: Blood is going to be shed; someone is going to be butchered.

NELLY: Go on out into your garden, Mama; go back upstairs.

CONGREGATION: [*Softly singing*]
    "I walk through the garden alone;
    While the dew is still on the roses . . .
        [*Fading*]
    And the voice I hear, falling on my
        ear—
    The Prince of Peace discloses . . ."

A street.

SKELLY: Hey.

EVA: What? What? What do you want?

SKELLY: You tell him—

EVA: What? I don't know who you're talking about—what do you want?

SKELLY: Your friend.

EVA: Who?

SKELLY: Him. Robert.

EVA: Tell him what?

SKELLY: Tell him he's all right.

EVA: What do you mean he's all right?

SKELLY: He's a good boy.

EVA: Well, I imagine he knows that.

SKELLY: People talk but they don't know—it's them that's the bastards. He's all right.

EVA: You're terrible the way you talk. Nobody makes fun of him. It's you they laugh at.

SKELLY: You tell him . . .

EVA: I don't know what you're talking about. I wouldn't tell anybody anything you told me to tell them.

In the store.

CORA: He drifted in town and he helped me around the café for a while and he drifted on; nothing was holding him here.

MARTHA: I heard you started closing the place up at ten in the evening when that boy started working for you.

CORA: When Walter came, yes, I did. I closed earlier. I don't know why I used to be open all that late for anyway.

MARTHA: I heard you still close it up at ten, though.

CORA: Well, force of habit, I suppose.

MARTHA: How long is it he's been gone?

CORA: I don't know, Mrs. Truit; I suppose a month now.

MARTHA: I heard you two made that café a regular show place.

CORA: You'll have to come up sometime and have a cup of coffee and a piece of pie.

MARTHA: Yes, when you was still with your husband, before he left, I mean, I know you used to make the best pie in the state.

CORA: It's still pretty good.

MARTHA: [*Leaving the store*] Yes, I will. I'll come up and see you one day. [*To* WILMA] "Helped around the store," did you ever hear anything like it? I heard she still closes the café at ten sharp. They say he left without taking a stitch she'd bought him. Didn't leave a note even—

In town.

JOSH: I hear Hilltop would be an easy place to break into, if you had in mind to steal something.

MARTHA: [*To* WILMA] Leaves the door for him still, every night.

WILMA: I hear.

MARTHA: Closes at ten.

LENA: [*To* JOSH] That's what I heard.

WILMA: What Reverend Parker said is so true.

MARTHA: Oh, I know it is

WILMA: It's difficult for us to accept.

MARTHA: "We must accept the blame upon ourselves. Each and every one of us."

WILMA: "It's not Nelly Windrod who is being tried here today."

MARTHA: "Nelly Windrod is not the person who is being tried here today."

WILMA: —No indeed—

PREACHER: [*To* CONGREGATION] —It is the soul and responsibility of our very community. The laxity with which we met the obligations of our Christian lives. The blindness from which we allowed evil in our lives.

CONGREGATION: Amen.

PREACHER: Evil in our lives.

CONGREGATION: Amen.

PREACHER: We watched it fester and grow; we allowed this dreadful thing to happen through shirking our Christian duty. Nelly Windrod—

WILMA: —is not on trial here today.

PREACHER: —No indeed. That man. May the Lord have mercy on his soul. [*Waits*]

CONGREGATION: Amen.

PREACHER: May the Lord have mercy on his soul and mercy on our blindness to His way. It is our responsibility and we must share in that terrible knowledge.

In town.

LENA: It's not that bad.

PATSY: It's terrible, this crummy old ghost town; tumbleweed blowing down the deserted streets.

LENA: There's no tumbleweed blowing down the—

PATSY: Well, there ought to be, it's enough to give a person the creeps. Everyone from Centerville and all over driving by to see where the murder was committed; it's creepy. Looking at this awful ugly old ghost town, and all the boys know I live here, I swear, I've never been so humiliated in my life.

LENA: I know, it's terrible.

PATSY: Driver Junior never talks to anyone any more—I haven't even seen him with Eva; of course her—that dumb cripple hasn't said a word since. Everyone staring at her—the whole thing is just the ugliest thing I ever heard about. I knew what was going to happen, I said. I swear Driver Junior is such a creep—never spoke to anyone in his life anyway. Doesn't hang around with us or anyone else his own age; hanging around with her, that girl, I feel sorry for her and all, but I look at her and I just feel my shoulder blades start to pooch out all over, people like that—deformed people ought to be put out of sight. Like her and Skelly and everybody; I mean people with deformed minds as well, too; don't think I'm forgetting that. It's absolutely creepy the way people drive through here; I've never been so humiliated in my life.

A street.

SKELLY: You! Hey, Robert. Bobby! Hey!

ROBERT: Hay is for sheep.

SKELLY: Yeah, uh, you, uh—Driver is dead.

ROBERT: Well, I guess I know that.

SKELLY: You going around like—

ROBERT: What? What do you want?

SKELLY: He was a son of a bitch.

ROBERT: Don't talk like that to me.

SKELLY: You don't talk bad.

ROBERT: I don't, no, because I don't see any need to talk—

SKELLY: Driver was a sonabitch. Walking like some kind of stud horse. He wasn't human.

ROBERT: Who are you to tell if someone is human or—

SKELLY: You know what he did? I say. You didn't go to the races to see him kill himself.

ROBERT: My brother was a very good race car driver and I didn't go because I don't like them; if everyone went and I didn't, it's because they like them and I don't.

SKELLY: You don't know. I'll tell you what your sonabitch was like.

ROBERT: You don't know anything.

SKELLY: You hear me talking to people? I *see*. He was a snotnose kid, twelve when you was born. I saw him. And him driving through town like a big shot. With his racing car all green and yellow and rared back there. Lined up after him in cars, trailing after him and honking like a string of geese coming into town.

SKELLY: [*Continuing*] And him telling everybody about it up at the café. I heard the stories and the shouting and the glory.	WILMA: [*To* MARTHA, *on the latter's porch*] Land, it was wonderful just to hear them cheering.
ROBERT: I don't know what you're talking about.	MARTHA: Another silver cup, another blue ribbon.
	WILMA: First place.

SKELLY: I saw him with Betty Atkins—in her bedroom and her crying and crying and how he hit her—you didn't know that! And she cried 'cause he got so mad. He liked to killed her.

ROBERT: I thought people made up stories about you peeping into windows—you're worse than they say.

SKELLY: I SAW HIM! You're better for a man than he is.

ROBERT: You're disgusting; you're as bad as everybody says you are. Dad says you are and Driver said so too.

SKELLY: Yeah, because I told him I saw him. Your brother, you know what he did? You know what he did? He had to help himself. Had to help himself out. Out in his car parked on the road and in his room. He had to do it for himself.

ROBERT: Shut up!

SKELLY: That's what I know.

ROBERT: You're disgusting. You should be killed or jailed; my brother was a good person; he was a wonderful person.

SKELLY: He beat Betty Atkins and did it by hand. Jacking all on her. I've seen him. I've seen him.

ROBERT: Baaaaaaa.

SKELLY: That's what I know.

ROBERT: You're worse than they say. Everybody knows you spy on them. Who do you think you are?

SKELLY: Who do you think your sonabitch brother was? Is what I want to—

ROBERT: Baaaaaaa. Baaaaaaa.

SKELLY: Now you know! Go on.

ROBERT: BAAAAAAAAA! Baaaaaaaaa.

SKELLY: Get on—get on—Driver Junior, you like that? I know, I know. You like that? Get on. Hey—

ROBERT *exits*.

WILMA: Such a beautiful man; lived so dangerous; like the world wasn't turning fast enough to suit him.

MARTHA: Gave of himself until there was nothing else and got himself killed in an accident.

WILMA: The Lord giveth and the Lord taketh away.

MARTHA: Poor lad. I swear.

Silence. Same street as on page 145, precisely as before.

SKELLY: Boy! Robert!! Boy! Hey!

EVA: What? What? What do you want?

SKELLY: You tell him—

EVA: What? I don't know who you're talking about—what do you want?

SKELLY: Your friend.

EVA: Who?

SKELLY: Him. Robert.

EVA: Tell him what?

SKELLY: Tell him he's all right.

EVA: What do you mean he's all right?

SKELLY: He's a good boy.

EVA: Well, I imagine he knows that.

SKELLY: People talk but they don't know—it's them that's the bastards. He's all right.

EVA: You're terrible the way you talk. Nobody makes fun of him. It's you they laugh at.

SKELLY: You tell him.

EVA: I don't know what you're talking about. I wouldn't tell anyone anything you told me to tell them.

SKELLY: You tell him . . .

In court.

PECK: We, the jury, find Nelly Windrod. Not guilty.

NELLY: [*In court*] Oh, God, oh, God. Mama?

JUDGE: It is not Nelly Windrod who is on trial here today.

In town.

PATSY: Tumbleweed blowing through town; it's so creepy I don't know how anyone can stand it.

LENA: [*To* PATSY] There's no tumbleweed blowing through . . .

On the Windrod porch.

MARY: [*To* EVA] You talk to him and that's nice. I talk to things too. I talk. I have several tropical fish and a number of small birds that I feed each and every day and take excellent care of them. Talking with them until they die. I like little things, with little hearts beating and little lives around me. Their little hearts just moving away. With short life spans and high temperatures. And I pat out little graves like loaves in the back yard and put little whitewashed gravel, little rocks around each one, and that's my garden. And I decorate the little loaves with flowers when I remember to. Now there's Trinket. That was my rat terrier, died eleven years ago last November, and Bonnie, my cocker spaniel, died four years ago last October, all in the fall; and Gilda and Wanda, the two goldfish, floating on their sides one morning, little loaves, those two. And Chee-chee, my canary, died two years ago last September. And Goldie, my other canary, passed on the year after that and Tina, the little blue kitten —beautiful kitten, that one's little too. She prefers violets and Goldie takes daisies and Chee-chee takes dandelions and Bonnie takes roses, and Trinket has daffodils generally—spring daffodils and Wanda tulips; and the flowers dry up and die and I feel I should bury them too. All my children. Gone, gone, gone.

CONGREGATION: [*Singing softly*]
"I come to the garden alone
While the dew is still on the roses
And the voice I hear
Falling on my ear
The son of God discloses.
And he walks with me—"

MARY *and* EVA *join the* CONGREGATION, MARY *by her daughter,* EVA *by her mother.*

CORA: [*Enters the café from upstairs, sleepily, calling softly as if wakened from sleep*] Walter?

CONGREGATION: "And he talks with me."

CORA: Walter?

CONGREGATION: "And he tells me I am his own."

CORA: Walter?

CONGREGATION: "And the joy we share."

CORA: Walter!

CONGREGATION: "As we tarry there!"

CORA: Walter!

CONGREGATION: "None other. Has ever—"

CORA: Walter.

CONGREGATION: "Known."

PREACHER: Let us pray.

They bow their heads in silence.

CORA: [*Falling to her knees as though felled*] Oh, God. Oh, God. Oh, God. Oh, God. Oh, God. Oh, God. Oh, God.

Curtain

ACT TWO

On the Johnson porch.

PATSY: [*To* LENA] It wasn't really sudden. I knew he wanted to, he'd let on, you know, in little ways. He said would I mind not being in school; he'll graduate, of course, 'cause this is his last year—and I said would I *mind?*

LENA: That's just incredible; when's it going to be?

PATSY: We aren't messing around; he said two weeks from this Saturday. He didn't want to have a church wedding at first—you know how he is—and I said, Chuck Melton, if you think I'm going to just run off to a preacher and practically elope you got another think coming. So it'll be the First Presbyterian of Centerville, but I want it to be just simple. I said I wanted a street-length dress—I know, but that's what I want and I'll have a veil, a little pillbox hat, I love those, and a veil and probably roses, if it's not too early for roses—

In the Windrod house.

MARY: [*Over*] —Bonnie? Here girl. Bonnie? Here kitty, kitty—

LENA: —I'm just so surprised.

PATSY: Well, it wasn't really sudden; I knew he wanted to, he'd let on. I love the First Presbyterian. I only hope the trial and all is quieted down. That could just ruin it all.

LENA: Oh, it will be.

PREACHER: [*Over*] Now you know I'm aware we all want to get this settled and go home and forget about it.

PATSY: It's a beautiful church.

LENA: I really love it; it's just beautiful.

PATSY: And my aunt's gonna give the bride's breakfast.

LENA: Aren't you excited?

PATSY: I imagine we'll live in Centerville. You know, till we have enough money to get a place or maybe move somewhere. Probably right in town; there's a wonderful place over the barbershop, the Reganson one on the corner with windows on both sides that's been empty for weeks. I only hope someone doesn't beat us to it. I want to tell Chuck to put some money down on it. I don't want to live with his folks. I just can't stand them and I don't think they think too much of me either.

They're so square and old-fashioned. They really are. They don't even smoke or believe in make-up or anything.

LENA: Chuck is wonderful, he really is. I'm just so surprised.

PATSY: [*Beginning to cry gently*] He was so cute; he said would I mind not being in school next year, and I said of course I'll miss my friends, but would I *mind?*

LENA: It's so beautiful. It's a beautiful church for a wedding.

PATSY: Isn't it?

LENA: Aren't you excited? What's wrong?

PATSY: Well, of course I am, silly.

LENA: I don't think Josh and me want to get married, though, until after I'm out of school.

PATSY: Oh, my God, you don't want to marry Josh. My Lord, I can't imagine it. You're not serious about him. Lord, he's so childish.

LENA: He isn't. He's six years older than you are. He's worked for two years.

PATSY: Well, I know, but you don't want to marry him. Age doesn't have anything to do with it. He's all right and he's sweet and all, but I mean to go to the show with and hold hands. I don't know how you can bear to ride into town in that garage tow truck, though.

LENA: I drive it sometimes; it's not bad.

PATSY: Well, I know, but Josh! Lord, Lena, I've got so many things to do yet. You know the thing I think I like most about Chuck is that he's so clean and neat and all. The way he takes care of his Mercury. It's always like spanking new.

In court.

ROBERT: And he took us by surprise.

In the café.

CORA: [*To* WALTER] You seem uneasy.

WALTER: I'm not really.

CORA: I depend on you too much probably.

WALTER: Huh? No, nothing's wrong.

CORA: I've always had a dream, an idea, of maybe leaving here.

WALTER: You have?

CORA: Would you like that?

WALTER: And go where? Hawaii?

CORA: Well, no, not quite Hawaii. I don't know. It's sometimes somewhere and sometimes somewhere else. Somewhere. St. Louis maybe; Des Moines, Chicago. Anywhere.

WALTER: What would you do there?

CORA: The same, of course. Only a nice place maybe. I know the business, if I could sell this place.

WALTER: You wouldn't want to do that, would you?

CORA: Wouldn't you like that? St. Louis maybe, or anywhere. I thought you'd like that. Have a bigger place. Maybe hire someone to run it for us so it doesn't take up all our time.

WALTER: That's an idea. I can't say I like St. Louis much.

CORA: Have you been there? Well, Chicago then.

WALTER: Chicago's nice.

CORA: I have a uncle in Chicago; he might help us get started. What's wrong, anything? You seem uneasy.

WALTER: I'm not. Why don't we close early.

CORA: I'd be agreeable to that.

MARTHA: [*Coming to* EVA'S *porch*] Is she any better?

EVELYN: Oh, I don't know. Who can tell?

SKELLY: [*Entering his shack; alone*] Hound? Hey, hound. What are you shaking about, huh? Get your tail up in the air and out from between your legs like a hunting dog. No, you wouldn't be any good for that, would you? What kind of dog are you? Huh? I got a roast bone from Cora's for you. Here. There you go. Go to it. Those guns scare you, do they? Those hunters? Eh? Oh, they strut around and shoot around after their quail and their duck and their pheasants. They scare you, huh? If you wasn't wild, you could sit out on the steps, huh? No, they'd shoot off one of those duck guns or a fire-popper and off you'd go back in under the bed, huh? Under the steps. And they're wasting their shot anyhow. Couldn't hit the broad side of a barn ten feet off. You should have seen it with the mines running. With the mines working and the dynamite and the what-you-call-it booming around everywhere underground fifty times a day or more. Boom! [*Laughs*] Boom! [*Laughs*] Every hound . . . [*Coughs*] . . . every hound in town kept out of sight from seven in the morning till seven at night. Under every bed in town. That'd make you shake. Eat it. That's roast bone. You. [*Laughs*]

You good for nothing. Oh, hell, yes. They was fancy people; butter wouldn't melt. Old Man Reiley bought the Eldritch place up on the hill, wouldn't no other place do for him, and carried on with their miners drinking parties and societies if you please. And Glenna Ann sashaying around serving tidbits on a platter; oh, well-to-do. Blast all day in the mines all day and blast all night at home. Old Man Reiley called me every name in the book. Fit to be tied. She was a pretty one, too; only eighteen, the both of us and her wearing dresses to the ground and bows and her old man called me every name in the book. Chased me off the place with a crowbar. [*Laughs*] And we done it in the old man's woodshed. Oh, sure. I sneaks back the very same night and we done it out in the woodshed there. Everything smelling of hickory and cedar for their fancy fireplaces. Oh, yeah. And, oh, how she did squirm! Oh, Lord. Saying to me, "Oh, I love you. Oh, I love you, oh, really I do, Skelly." Oh, shit. [*Coughs*] Till I thought she was gonna croak. Oh, Lord. Never let on she even knew me. Sashay around town with her big hats. Glenna Ann. Pretty girl. Oh, yeah. No girl in town so pretty. Then or now. None in between. How she did claw and bite. No bigger than a mite. Hound. Where'd you go? Don't you bury that. You eat that now. That's good. You no good. Old Man Reiley moved off; she moved off, whole family, lock, stock, and petticoat. Mines give out, off they git. How she did squirm. "Oh, I love you so much." Oh, sure. Pretty girl too. Right in the woodhouse the very night her old man chased me off with a crowbar. And we sat up against the wall there, playing in the shavings on the floor. Till morning, near. Sure. All blue. The bluest blue in the morning. Blue light on her gown there. Sticking her feet into the shavings—digging. Holding hands, panting. Where's that tea kettle, huh? Where'd it go? Make some sassafras. Yeah, wouldn't eat it if I gave it to you, would you? Don't know what's good, do you? Beautiful tits; no tits like that then or since. I guess you know Peck Johnson fairly beat the shit out of that girl of his last night. Whipped her good. Never seen anything like it. Thought she was dead. Patsy. Little whore she is, too. Thought he near to killed her. The old lady standing there with her teeth clenched watching, white as a ghost . . . mad as the devil. Good! I say good! What she done, I say good! She deserved it; little whore. Here, you whore. Go on with you! get on out with you. Filthy brother; whole family right along brother and sister both. Beat her till she nearly bled. Thought he was gonna kill her. People don't care! What kind of thing goes on. What kind of devilment. Where'd you go to? Hound? What-are-you-not eating? If you was tame, you could come out and sit on the street. Catch a rabbit, huh? You scared of rabbits? Are you? That's a good girl. You're okay. Bluest blue you ever saw in the daytime. Cold too and her in a nightgown; run right off of the house when I called up and off we went. [*Laughs*] Oh, boy! Arms is no good. Can't lift 'em even over my head. Look a-there. Oh, boy. Red thing over her nightgown there. Barefoot. Grass sticking to her feet from the fresh-cut lawns with their lackeys there, mowing and clipping and futsing. Barefoot. Right across the dew and all.

That crippled girl, Jackson, she's got her leg shorter, one than the other. Cries. You never saw anything like it. Dances around her room in the window curtains, all lace, wrapped around her whooping, dancing around like a banshee. Oh, he's all right. Tell him I said he's all right. Well, I guess he knows that. No, he don't know it, now, there! Better'n his no good brother everybody yelling about doing it by hand. Hitting girls around. People don't care! They don't see. What. What they want to think they think; what they don't they don't. They don't care anyway; what kind of devilment. What goes on. Her old man, Old Man Reiley; never did know. No, no. Never did know. I weren't the only one either, you can bet. Get some water boiling; make some sassafras; good for the stomach. Cedar. All in the air. Bluest blue in the air. Hickory and cedar cedar cedar cedar cedar in the air. Sang. [*Laughs*] All manner of songs there. Soft so's it wouldn't carry to the lackeys' house there. Carrying on, scratching, biting, thought she was gonna croak. "Oh, really, oh, I love you so!" [*Laughs*] Pretty girl. Beautiful tits. Beautiful tits. Oh, yes. Oh, sure.

On EVA'S *porch.*

MARTHA: Is she any better?

EVELYN: Oh, I don't know. Who can tell?

MAVIS: Has she said anything?

EVELYN: The doctor said it was just shock.

MARTHA: Well, I'd think so.

WILMA: I've never heard anything like it.

MARTHA: Like when he scared young Patsy so bad.

WILMA: Bad for the whole town.

MAVIS: It's awful.

PATSY: I feel so sorry for her.

WILMA: How's Driver Junior?

EVELYN: He hasn't been over. I don't know what to think about that. I'd told her not to go off; well, I won't say anything.

MARTHA: Such a shock. For us all.

MAVIS: A terrible thing.

EVELYN: She's always been so easily upset.

LENA: Well, she has cause.

PATSY: I just wish he was still alive! That's what I wish.

WILMA: When I think of the evil in this world.

EVELYN: The doctor said she just needs rest.

MAVIS: If he'd of lived, he'd not have seen the light of day tomorrow.

WILMA: That poor girl.

MARTHA: And Nelly, that poor woman, the life that woman leads.

WILMA: [*Leaving*] I said to Eva's mother—cried the whole time—

MARTHA: I know, I saw—

WILMA: Only God in His Heaven.

In court.

MARY: It appeared to me that both the men were hitting at her.

Tremendous crowd reaction.

JUDGE: Order!

MARY: It appeared to me.

JUDGE: Now you have testified, as a witness, Mrs. Windrod.

MARY: I was at my window, watching the moon.

ROBERT: [*To* MARY, *but not in court*] Was there a moon?

MARY: A crescent moon that night, I know for sure.

JUDGE: You have testified that you saw—

MARY: Blood, everywhere; all over. It was terrible. On the porch, rivers and I was mopping and it spread with the water, all around, all over.

JUDGE: —Driver Junior and young Eva clearly.

MARY: I didn't say "clearly," I couldn't see clearly; I don't see well.

JUDGE: You testified you saw—

MARY: In my dream.

JUDGE: You were asleep?

MARY: Weeks ago and I told Nelly that blood was going to be shed, and I was wiping and it spread with the water, all around on the porch — [*She leaves the stand*]

NELLY: [*Taking the stand*] And Mama said someone was in the back yard and I took up the gun that I keep by the door, the shotgun; and checked to see if it was loaded and it was and I opened the door.

MARY: [*Over*] —Bonnie? Here, kitty, kitty, here, girl.

In the café.

CORA: [*To* WALTER] Did you go into town?

WALTER: Yeah.

CORA: Into Centerville?

WALTER: No, no, only into Eldritch.

CORA: Did you? Well, what do you think?

WALTER: Well, what can I tell you, it's a ghost town.

CORA: I told you.

WALTER: What was that big building?

CORA: The movie house?

WALTER: On the corner.

CORA: Oh, there was a drugstore, and an exchange. And a lawyer's office and a couple of doctors up above had their office in that building. A dentist, I think. That was the first building to shut down.

WALTER: Some people said hello like they knew me.

CORA: Well, they do know you from here.

WALTER: Wonder what they think?

CORA: You do, do you?

WALTER: Sometimes.

CORA: Peck Johnson said the new boy "helping" me appeared to be a genuine good worker.

WALTER: What did you say to that?

CORA: Well, I said, oh, yes, yes, he's a genuine good worker.

WALTER: [*Laughing*] I like some of them all right. The truck drivers are all right, anyway.

CORA: Oh, they're from all over; they support the place. Have for years.

WALTER: Some of the people from Eldritch aren't so bad.

CORA: I think a couple of the girls have a crush on you. Well, I don't blame them.

WALTER: They're young.

CORA: Well, they're not all that damn young.

WALTER: It's gonna be a nice night.

CORA: It's gonna be a nice summer.

JOSH *and the* TRUCKER *walk casually to* SKELLY.

EVA: [*In the woods*] No, in the wintertime and in the autumn especially. It's so nice; it smells so clean.

ROBERT: [*In court*] He came from nowhere!

EVELYN: [*On her porch*] I said she shouldn't be out gone from the house like that!

JOSH: [*To* SKELLY] What are you standing on the corner about? Why aren't you back to your grubby house? Where do you sleep now your stinking shack burned down? Or do you sleep? Do you sleep? Sleep with sheep, huh?

SKELLY: Get on.

TRUCKER: What'd you say?

SKELLY: Mind your own business.

JOSH: Which old damp rotting cellar do you hole up in now your dry old shack's gone? Huh? I bet you eat worms, doncha.

SKELLY: Go on, you.

JOSH: What d'you eat? Won't tell anybody where you live, will you? 'Cause you know what'd happen if you closed your eyes there, don't you?

SKELLY: Yeah, you sonabitch, you mind your own —I don't say whether I got ary a bed or no now.

JOSH: What'd you call me?

SKELLY: Go on with you.

JOSH: I said what'd you call me?

TRUCKER: Ought to kill him, Josh.

JOSH: What'd you say? Shit, he ain't worth it.

SKELLY: Get on.

JOSH: Just don't let anybody follow you home. [SKELLY *leaves*] You get on now. You're the one who had better get on, not me. You'll wake up to a hot bed one of these days again. [*Laughs*] Old bastard. BAAAAA! [*Laughs*]

TRUCKER: Son of a bitch shepherd!

In court.

ROBERT: He was just there all of a sudden from nowhere and he took us by surprise and he pushed me—he hit me from behind; I don't know if I passed out or not. [*Crowd murmur*] He's immensely strong. [*Crowd murmur*]

MARY: [*Overlapping crowd murmur, in her house*] Nelly, Nelly, there's someone out back, honey, having a terrible fight. They came through the woods and started yelling all kinds of things.

NELLY: [*To* MARY] Where was you? I thought you was in bed.

ROBERT: And I heard a ringing in my ears and I saw what he was trying to do and everything went white. [*Crowd reaction*] And he pushed me! [*Crowd reaction*]	MARY: You better go out and see, honey. PATSY: [*To* LENA; *in town*] I mean he's out there polishing the chrome and dash and all. LENA: I know, it's amazing.

Some of the crowd reaction has been to EVA, *who has been moaning throughout* ROBERT'S *testimony. Now she screams—a huge ear-splitting scream, and I mean it.*

EVELYN: Oh, God, baby, my baby—

EVA: —No, no, no, no, no!—

EVELYN: See her crippled body. See her broken back; why, why has God cursed me with this burden. I don't complain. I ask why? We love Him. We bless Him. Praise Him. And this monster! I mean Skelly! My daughter is weak; you're trying to kill her! Look at her! Is that what you want? I only ask why?

PREACHER: [*Overlapping*] The Lord works in—

EVELYN: [*Overlapping*] WHY? I said, why? I have a right to know; I'll repent if I've done anything; if I've sinned—

CORA: [*Overlapping*] —Eva said to me—Eva, you know what you said. Skelly worked for me sometimes; none of you knew him. He was honest.

EVELYN: [*Overlapping*] My daughter has never spoken to you; my daughter has never spoken to a person like you; my daughter has been scarred, permanently scarred by this. She's crippled already. She's weak. She can't stand up.

CORA: If you'd listen to me.

EVELYN: No, no. I won't listen to you; I won't trust the word of a woman like you.

CORA: And what are you?

Crowd reaction, which continues until singing begins.

EVELYN: [*Screaming wildly*] My daughter is a virgin! She's pure! She's a Christian, from a Christian home; a daughter of God and you'd put your word against the word of a virgin. A beer-swilling harlot. Everyone knows. A drunken Whore of Babylon! Harlot! Daughter of Babylon! Go back to your beer parlor; your house of sin. You couldn't keep your husband and you couldn't keep your whore boy friend. In the name of God before this court I call you that. Liar. You're the liar. Before God I call you that. On His word. His holy word. Yes! Put her on the stand. Let her talk. We have nothing to hide. Ask her if she didn't keep a whore boy friend up to her place. Ask her what kind of woman she is. . . .	CORA: I talked to her because I knew Skelly would never, *never* harm anyone. If you'd listen to me. JUDGE: [*Begins pounding steadily with the gavel*] Order. Order. Order. Order. *The* CONGREGATION *begins singing "When the Roll Is Called Up Yonder," to the rhythm of the gavel. The* CONGREGATION *drowns* EVELYN *out with the loud, joyous hymn, the pulpit beaten now, in time to the song. The song is sung to its finish. Everyone moves into small groups. Worried, quiet.*

A long pause. Silence.

PATSY: [*Very upset; quietly to* WALTER] Pretty sure.

WALTER: [*Beside her, after a pause*] Are you sure it's me? [*Pause*] You're not sure are you? [*Pause*] It could be somebody else. It could have been what's-his-name. Chuck. [*Pause*]

PATSY: Well, it was somebody! [*Pause*] Oh, God.

WALTER: I don't know what you want from me.

PATSY: I'll tell your precious Cora what you're like. Then we'll see how high and mighty you think you are. No, you wouldn't like that very much, would you?

A street in town: the JUDGE, PECK, *the* TRUCKER, *and* JOSH *in a group. They speak with deliberation.*

JUDGE: The oats was late 'cause of the spring was so wet.

PECK: Me and the boy couldn't plant till late May. Eighteenth of May. Up till then the ground was so wet we couldn't get at the field even.

TRUCKER: And then that cold spell.

JUDGE: Ground was solid out our way till almost April.

JOSH: Hell it was.

JUDGE: Almost April. You couldn't stick a fork into it. Hard as a rock.

PECK: 'Course you're high; it wasn't near so bad along in the valley.

TRUCKER: Oh, no. It wasn't near.

PECK: Along the valley there I don't imagine there was more than six-ten cold days. Days it was froze solid. River wasn't more than three inches ice.

JOSH: I don't believe it ever froze clear across.

PECK: No, it never froze across.

JOSH: There was some running out aways right through the winter.

PECK: 'Course you're up on the hill there. You're not protected.

TRUCKER: Yeah, it was froze solid right up through April.

JUDGE: 'Course the rains was bad for you. In the valley there.

JOSH: Oh, yeah.

TRUCKER: I don't believe I've ever seen the rains so bad.

PECK: Yeah, the river swelled up there along in March, I can't remember it that bad before. I said to Josh, I couldn't remember it that bad. There was that.

JOSH: Most of the field was under six-ten feet of water along in the spring.

PECK: April it was.

JOSH: Yeah, I believe it was April.

PECK: Wasn't able to set a plow till late in the month. Plowed for the oats finally in May. Eighteenth of May; that's the latest I can remember. I believe it was the eighteenth.

JOSH: It was, I remember.

PECK: Latest I remember.

JUDGE: Well, you're in the valley there; you're not protected.

TRUCKER: The floods was bad for you.

PECK: Yeah, I'll say. It's rich soil, though. Good bottom topsoil.

TRUCKER: Yeah, it's rich bottom land.

PECK: It's good bottom land.

TRUCKER: It's good for corn.

PECK: Oh, yeah.

JUDGE: It's sandy for oats though.

JOSH: Yeah, the oats isn't doing well.

TRUCKER: Well, it's been dry the past month.

PECK: Radio says we might be heading for a drought.

JUDGE: I been thinking I might have to irrigate. Later on. If it doesn't get wetter.

JOSH: Yeah, we had all our rains right there together.

TRUCKER: Not what you'd call a deep rain though.

JUDGE: No, it run right off, much as there was of it. Could sure use some of it now.

PECK: Oh, yeah.

JUDGE: The corn's beginning to curl; I noticed this morning.

JOSH leaves, goes to LENA's *porch.*

TRUCKER: It was dry this morning. Almost no dew even.

PECK: There wasn't much even low like I am. 'Course you're up on the hill. You must be getting the worst of it.

JOSH: [*To* LENA] Just got off work.

LENA: You look it; you didn't even wash up.

JOSH: I did, but it'll have to wear off; it's ground right in, I think.

LENA: Where did you want to go tonight?

JOSH: You mind eating up at Cora's or you want to go into Centerville?

LENA: It doesn't matter, whatever you want.

JOSH: We might as well go on into town to the drive-in.

LENA: Oh lets, 'cause Patsy'll be there and I wanted to see her.

JOSH: You've seen her this morning.

LENA: Yes, but she said she had a surprise she wanted to tell me.

JOSH: I don't know what she thinks is a surprise. Then we'll go into the movies, all right? Or would you rather just drive?

LENA: I'd kinda like to see the picture.

JOSH: Whatever you want.

LENA: [*Going to* PATSY] She's gonna be with Chuck so you be nice to him.

PATSY: Don't you think he's cute, though?

LENA: I guess.

PATSY: Was he really at the drive-in with her? That's so funny. His name's Walter I found out. But I can't imagine. That's the funniest thing; I just wish I'd have seen it.

LENA: It's not so bad.

PATSY: But, she's so old for him. My God, she's thirty-eight.

LENA: She isn't, is she? Mama said thirty-four.

PATSY: Well, she's older than any thirty-four, and besides that's bad enough.

LENA: That soldier you went out with last year was that old.

PATSY: He was not.

LENA: I'll bet he was. He was balding.

PATSY: He was not, what do you think I am, he had a crew cut; besides he was twenty-six, I saw his ID.

LENA: Oh, he wasn't any twenty-six.

PATSY: I saw his draft card, Lena. Besides, my God, it's different with a boy. He was very nice. Besides, I only went out with him twice. I felt sorry for him. We didn't do anything.

On EVA'S *porch.*

CORA: That's hard for me to believe, Eva.

EVA: You ask Robert; what difference does it make?

CORA: 'Cause he worked for me; he used to pick up the garbage for his hogs. He lived out back of the café for years, till they burned that shack down. I still say it was Driver Junior's brother and Josh did it, burned that shack down.

EVA: We come into the clearing back behind Nelly Windrod's house, by her mill there, and I heard something, and he said he'd show me what.

CORA: Skelly did? He did not.

EVA: No. He didn't say.

CORA: Eva if that's not the truth, you better say how it really happened.

EVA: I said it happened like Robert said. It's like that and I don't care if you knew him or not. Mama said the preacher said a sermon about the evil in people like him and that we should have killed him or something before he had a chance to take advantage of me. I've been cursed and scarred.

CORA: You can't lie under oath, Eva.

EVA: [*Running away*] You're the one who's going to hell. Not me. I didn't do it, anyway; Nelly did it.

In the café.

CORA: It wasn't Skelly.

TRUCKER: [*Leaving café*] Well, who do you think it was?

CORA: She told me.

TRUCKER: If he hadn't of died, I know he wouldn't have seen the light of day the next morning. [*Goes to* JOSH]

A street in town.

JOSH: [*Almost good-naturedly*] Damn that mutt anyway.

TRUCKER: Good watchdog, is he?

JOSH: That old bitch of a dog, I'll kill that bitch.

TRUCKER: Wakes up the folks does he?

JOSH: Every damn time we drive up it starts up a racket. Son of a bitch, every light in the house goes on. She has to run on in, the noise that dog raises, every goddamned night. I don't care how easy I drive up. We started parking on down the block, she still starts up as soon as Lena steps a foot on the porch.

On MARTHA'S *porch.*

MARTHA: When I think of the evil in this world.

WILMA: To do some bestial thing like that.

In town.

PECK: [*To the* TRUCKER *and the* JUDGE] Well, I never figured him to actually hurt anybody.

TRUCKER: Hell, we all knew he was loony.

JUDGE: Someone like that—we all knew he was capable of any kind of thing.

PECK: Capable, yes, but I never figgered him for actually hurting anybody.

TRUCKER: Well, when somebody lives like that—away from everybody.

PECK: The boys give him a hard time but he can take care of himself.

TRUCKER: Should have been put away the way he looks at everybody.

JUDGE: Should have been shot—just shot in the woods; nobody the wiser.

PECK: I just never really figgered him to do anything. Capable, yes, but I have to admit I'd never thought he'd do anything. Outright, I mean.

MARTHA: [*On her porch*] Why, she called Evelyn Jackson a liar to her face, and Eva too. Swore things, the devil and his angels wouldn't believe it. She'd stand up there and swear black was white.

MARY: [*In her house, upstairs*] Nelly, Nelly, there's someone out back, honey, having a terrible fight; they came through the woods and started yelling all kinds of things.

NELLY: [*As she exits to a street in town*] Where was you? I thought you was in bed.

MARY: You better go out and see, honey.

MAVIS: Morning.

NELLY: Good morning.

MAVIS: We don't see you to talk to much.

NELLY: Well, summer is a slow time; I've been saving up strength for Peck's corn crop this year.

MAVIS: It's sure looking good.

NELLY: I drive past; I've been keeping my eye on it.

MAVIS: How is the mill?

NELLY: Well, summer is slow.

MAVIS: We see you drive by.

NELLY: Evenings I've been going into Centerville; talking to the farmers over there; say we might be into a drought.

MAVIS: We saw you, I believe going into the movie house there.

NELLY: Yes, I don't get a chance to go often.

MAVIS: Well, we don't go.

NELLY: I've seen the girl there.

MAVIS: Patsy? Oh yes, Patsy enjoys it. She goes with Chuck; awfully nice boy; I guess you know we're planning a wedding; I said it wasn't any use having a church wedding, all amounts to the same—Patsy wouldn't hear of it, of course, so I suppose we're going all out.

NELLY: He's an awfully nice boy, I hear.

MAVIS: Do you? I'm glad to hear it; we hardly know them really; but he does seem sweet; his family has a lovely farm, we visited. Last Sunday. They grow up so fast.

NELLY: Quite a nice young lady.

MAVIS: We're proud of her. How's your mother?

NELLY: Oh, Mom's the same; her mind's gone. I hate to leave her alone nights. Just like a child.

MAVIS: Well, you have a life of your own; you have to get out.

NELLY: Yes, I do. I hate to leave her, though, just the same.

MAVIS: We see you driving into Centerville.

NELLY: It's good to get away from the mill; Duane nearly runs it for me now.

MAVIS: I was talking to your mother; poor thing.

NELLY: Yes, it's sad.

MAVIS: I remember she had a fine mind.

NELLY: Yes, she did. One of the first registered nurses in Des Moines. Long time ago now; when she was a girl.

MAVIS: She goes on terrible about you; poor thing.

NELLY: I know, she doesn't know what she's saying half the time.

MAVIS: Still she tells things; it must be terrible for you.

NELLY: I'll take care of her, Mavis, as long as my strength holds out.

MAVIS: Martha Truit said, the life you have to bear.

NELLY: It's my cross, Mavis.

MAVIS: I know, I told Peck . . .

NELLY: How is Peck?

MAVIS: Oh, he's all right; his back is giving him trouble again. It's just nerves I keep telling him, but I don't know. Between you and me I don't know.

On MARTHA's *porch.*

WILMA: Who knows what's in somebody's mind like that.

MARTHA: Like that time—when was it, last summer.

The people have wandered to random, scattered positions about the stage. They stand still and isolated, ROBERT *and* EVA *moving about them as though walking through the woods.*

EVA: No, in the wintertime and in the autumn. It's so nice, it smells so clean.

ROBERT: Okay, the fall then.

EVA: Yes. And it's heavy, heavy frost and it covers everything and that's rime.

ROBERT: And it's just frost? Is it a hoarfrost?

EVA: That's it, hoarfrost is rime. And it covers everything. Every little blade of grass and every tree and houses and everything. Like it's been dipped in water and then in sugar.

ROBERT: Or salt. Yeah, I know what it is.

EVA: It's better than ice storms or anything like that. And everything is white and sparkling so clean when the sun comes up it nearly blinds you and it's rare! It doesn't happen every year. And that's what I'd like to be. What I'd like to do. I have a book with a picture of Jack Frost painting rime on a window-pane with a paintbrush. Do you fly? Do you dream you fly?

ROBERT: When?

EVA: Ever?

ROBERT: I guess. I haven't thought about it.

EVA: How high? Think about it. It's important. Everybody flies, it's important how high.

ROBERT: I don't know. Just over the ground.

EVA: Really?

ROBERT: I guess. As high as my head. I'm always getting tangled up in wires and all.

EVA: I'm way over the treetops, just over the treetops, just brushing against the treetops, and I fly right over them, just brush them with my arms out. Over the whole town like an airplane. Spreading this salt frost in the autumn. I love autumn. And when the sun comes up—

ROBERT: Right.

EVA: It'll blind you!

ROBERT: I've seen it.

EVA: It's so bright it blinds you. I want to fly like that, all over the town, right over everybody. It's beautiful. [SKELLY *takes a step forward, among the silent people*] Listen! Listen. Did you hear something?

The people move from their still positions into small groups. SKELLY *comes to* CORA *and* WALTER.

CORA: Are you out there?

SKELLY: Here. Yeah.

CORA: Can Walter help you? You know Walter.

SKELLY: Yeah, I know.

CORA: We're gonna be turning in, but he can help you with it.

SKELLY: The white one, with the spots?!

CORA: Spotty?

SKELLY: Had a litter.

CORA: She did?

SKELLY: She had four but she ate one.

CORA: Skelly, you just let them go wild, that's terrible; you should take them away from her.

SKELLY: The runt, the last one.

WALTER: She what? She ate one of them?

CORA: Pigs do that sometimes; they're terrible. A runt or something that they think is weak, they will.

WALTER: Couldn't you stop her?

SKELLY: I didn't see it.

CORA: Oh, he lets them just go wild, you can't get near them; one of them's all right, the brown one.

SKELLY: She's good.

CORA: One of them is tame and nice, the rest you can't get near them. He has four. So that makes seven now, doesn't it? You're getting to be a regular rancher.

SKELLY: The brown's a good one.

CORA: He has an old hound dog he keeps too; he's good with them but they just run wild. [*She leaves*]

WALTER: You want me to help you?

SKELLY: I'm all right. You like her?

WALTER: Do I like? What? Who?

SKELLY: Jackson. [*Pause*] That Patsy Jackson. Cora ain't good to you?

WALTER: Cora? I imagine she's good to every-body.

SKELLY: But you. She's good to you. I seen you with Patsy Jackson. You like her? You like that carrying on?

WALTER: What? I thought you were talking about your brown sow; I've not seen her.

SKELLY: I said, if you think you're a big man and you play around here and you play around there.

WALTER: You want me to help you slop the hogs?

SKELLY: I'll be all right.

WALTER: Well, if you make it your business to know what everybody is doing, I see why Cora makes sure we pull down the shades at night, and turn off the light and listen to hear if any-one's about. If that's your business, I guess I don't have to tell you what Patsy Jackson is like.

SKELLY: She's a bitch.

WALTER: Patsy? And them that lies down with . . .

SKELLY: Cora's a good woman.

WALTER: Yes, well, you slop the hogs and carry off the garbage and I build the fence and paint the café; we're none of us freeloaders, I don't suppose. I don't imagine I owe anyone any-thing except money. I don't owe anybody time. I can't say that I see it as any of your business anyway, Skelly. You don't have to worry about her; she's managed seven years without you or me either. Don't you think? [*Pause*] Wouldn't you say? [*Pause*] You go on and slop your hogs. [*Pause*] Go on, get on, be thankful she gives it to you for the price of carrying it away. [*Pause*] Hey. What do you do with those hogs anyway? How come they're so wild?

Pause.

SKELLY: I feed 'em, they run wild.

WALTER: Go on, I didn't mean anything by it. Good night.

MARY: [*To* MAVIS] I have a bruise there on the inside of my elbow, she holds onto me there, she pushes at me terrible, she can't help it.

A street in town.

EVA: If you had a car, you could drive all over.

ROBERT: What do I want with a car?

EVA: Are you afraid?

ROBERT: What for? So I can drive around the square. Around the square, around the square. It's all they ever do; all the boys with cars. Around the square and over into Centerville to a drive-in to eat and a drive-in to see a movie.

EVA: You just don't want to be like—

ROBERT: Everybody doesn't have to have a car. Everybody talks like that's all there is. The guys at school spend their whole lives in or on top of or under their cars. They eat in them and sleep in them and change clothes and drink and get sick and vomit and make out with their girls—it's all they even ever talk about. Evolution's gonna take their feet right away from them. Make turtles with wheels for legs out of them.

EVA: I think you're just afraid 'cause of Driver.

ROBERT: Well, that's another thing I hadn't thought of. They die in them too. Live and die without ever stepping outside. Why would I want that?

LENA: [*Offstage*] Sometimes I think life is so short and we should enjoy it for the time we're here and then I think I should work really hard so I can be comfortable, you know, after I've made some money, and then I think how awful working all that time would be and most of my life would be gone by that time and I'd have wasted it, you know what I mean? No, no, don't, Josh!

JOSH: [*Offstage, to* LENA] You said you would.

LENA: Sometime, I said.

JOSH: You don't want to?

LENA: It isn't that. You know. Don't now!

JOSH: What?

LENA: You know. If something happens, you don't know what can happen. And there's no assurance—of what can happen.

JOSH: Nothing can happen, I told you.

LENA: Come on. Don't now! I'm not kidding now.

JOSH: Just see.

LENA: You don't like me really or you'd respect me.

JOSH: What? I don't like you? Why do you think I want to?

LENA: You know what I mean.

JOSH: Just see. Just see. Just see. Nothing will happen; just see.

LENA: No, I said, now. Come on.

JOSH: Jesus Christ, Lena.

LENA: Well, don't be mad.

JOSH: Well, you let me go so far and then say no, I don't know what you expect.

LENA: It's all right, isn't it? Josh? Well, don't just sit there. I said sometime. Sometime, really. I mean it. Just not tonight. Okay? I want to, too; I just said not tonight. Really. It just scares me. Okay? Okay? [*Pause. Then rapidly*] Josh! Damn it, now, come on. No! I said and that means no! Good Lord. [*Sound of someone being slapped. Pause*] Now you're mad, aren't you?

PREACHER: [*To* CONGREGATION] No, sir, it is the soul and responsibility of our very community. The laxity with which we met the obligations of our Christian lives. The blindness from which we allowed evil in our lives. We watched it fester and grow; we allowed this dreadful thing to happen through shirking our Christian duty. Nelly Windrod is not on trial here today. That man, may the Lord have mercy on his soul damned eternally to hell, and our blindness to His way. It is our responsibility and we must share that terrible knowledge. As you go your ways tonight. As you leave and walk and drive to your homes, realize that the burden must be ours and ask the Lord for his grace. Pray for these two souls as you pray for the lost, the outcast, as you pray for the soul of the damned, and the care of our boys overseas. Pray to the Lord to unlock the bitterness in the hearts of those like him in the world today and pray that they may see the light of His holy way.

CONGREGATION: Amen.

PREACHER: Amen, the Lord be with you.

The CONGREGATION *walks slowly, as if coming from church, to the positions of the woods.*

JOSH: Had the Olds out last night.

TRUCKER: The old man's Olds?

JOSH: Took it out onto the Old Sparta Road and opened it up.

TRUCKER: Gene was out there last week.

JOSH: Pegged it. Hundred twenty. That old needle was bouncing against the peg and half the way back again. Two miles or over, then I eased it down.

TRUCKER: We'll have to take 'em out Sunday.

In the woods—precisely as before, a rerun.

EVA: And it covers everything and that's rime.

ROBERT: And it's just frost? Is it a hoarfrost?

EVA: That's it, hoarfrost is rime. And it covers everything. Every little blade of grass and every tree and houses and everything. Like it's been dipped in water and then in sugar.

ROBERT: Or salt. Yeah, I know what it is.

EVA: It's better than ice storms or anything like that. And everything is white and sparkling so clean when the sun comes up it nearly blinds you and it's rare! It doesn't happen every year. And that's what I'd like to be. What I'd like to do. I have a book with a picture of Jack Frost painting rime on a windowpane with a paintbrush. Do you fly? Do you dream you fly?

ROBERT: When?

EVA: Ever?

ROBERT: I guess. I haven't thought about it.

They walk about the forest, walking slowly through the people.

EVA: How high? Think about it. It's important. Everybody flies, it's important how high.

ROBERT: I don't know. Just over the ground.

EVA: Really?

ROBERT: I guess. As high as my head. I'm always getting tangled up in wires and all.

EVA: I'm way over the treetops, just over the treetops, just brushing against the treetops, and I fly right over them, just brush them with my arms out. Over the whole town like an air-plane. Spreading this salt frost in the autumn. I love autumn. And when the sun comes up—

ROBERT: Right.

EVA: It'll blind you!

ROBERT: I've seen it.

EVA: It's so bright it blinds you. I want to fly like that, all over the town, right over everybody. It's beautiful. [SKELLY *steps forward*] Listen! Listen. Did you hear something?

ROBERT: No. What?

EVA: Like something rustling in the leaves?

ROBERT: No. What? It was probably a rabbit.

    SKELLY *steps forward again.*

EVA: Listen.

ROBERT: I don't hear anything.

EVA: Maybe it was the wind.

ROBERT: There isn't any; maybe it was a fox.

EVA: Don't.

ROBERT: Or a wolf.

EVA: Ted Caffey trapped a wolf in his barn last year.

ROBERT: Shot its head off too.

EVA: Oh, he did not—are you trying to scare me? —it got away.

ROBERT: Shot it and killed it; took its pelt into the county agent in Centerville and got twenty dollars for it.

EVA: It wasn't anything; we better get back.

ROBERT: It was probably the mate looking for the one Caffey shot.

EVA: Don't say that, it wasn't— [SKELLY *moves again*] Listen!

ROBERT: It wasn't anything.

    They stop still.

WALTER: [*Turning from his tree position*] What's that junk heap of a what was it a Plymouth?

CORA: At Church Street? That's Driver's car. Driver Junior's older brother. Drove it in stock-car races; over in Centerville they have a track. The whole town went; used to, when he drove. I suppose they think it's bad luck now, he had some kind of accident; smashed it to hell, it looks like, doesn't it?

WALTER: He get killed?

CORA: Oh, yes, killed instantly. They hitched up a chain to the car and pulled it back here.

WALTER: And dumped it in the middle of the street? The grass and weeds almost cover it; I didn't know what it was at first.

CORA: Well, that's where the chain broke and the axle broke and every other damn thing broke,

so there it sits. Not a very pretty sight. [*They move a few steps*]

    The following is from all over the stage. The characters may move from their stationary positions for a few steps and return to them. The woods become alive with their voices. The sequence should begin softly and build, becoming faster and more forceful toward the end.

MARY: Rusting away—flaking away.

EVELYN: Falling apart, boarded together, everything flapping and rusting.

MARY: All the buildings bowing and nodding.

PATSY: Movie house been closed down eight years.

TRUCKER: It was dry this morning; almost no dew even.

NELLY: You fall down, you bruise, you run into things, you're old.

PATSY: Tumbleweed blowing down the deserted streets.

MARY: And the flowers dry up and die.

SKELLY: You didn't go to the races to see him kill himself.

EVA: And it covers everything and that's rime.

LENA: I remember his laugh.

CORA: Eldritch is all but a ghost town.

WILMA: The wages of sin—

MARTHA: I don't know, love.

EVA: And when the sun comes up it blinds you!

EVELYN: The mine shaft building used to just shine.

SKELLY: All in the air.

JOSH: Just see.

LENA: It's a beautiful church.

WALTER: Wouldn't you say?

MAVIS: A decent person is afraid to move outside at night.

PREACHER: As you go your way tonight.

CORA: You seem uneasy.

EVELYN: The doctor said it was just shock.

PECK: You watch yourself.

MARY: Gone, gone gone.

EVA: Like it's been dipped in water and then in sugar.

MAVIS: And not seen the light of day tomorrow.

MARY: All my children.

EVA: And that's what I want to be.

    They are still, trees again.

MARY: Gone, gone gone.

EVA: [*Continuing, in the woods*] You know what my mother says?

ROBERT: What?

EVA: When I come in?

ROBERT: What?

EVA: She says you're unresponsible, and she asks me things like where we go and all, everywhere we go every time I go anywhere with you. Everything we do.

ROBERT: Where does she think we go?

EVA: Oh, I tell her we just go walking in the woods; talking. She knows that but she thinks we do other things too.

ROBERT: Like what?

EVA: You know.

ROBERT: Like what?

EVA: You know. Dirty things.

ROBERT: What does she think that for?

EVA: I don't tell her, though.

ROBERT: What would you tell her?

EVA: About that. About when I have to pee and things.

ROBERT: Well, there's nothing dirty about that.

EVA: Well, don't you think I know!

ROBERT: She means other things.

EVA: What?

ROBERT: Never mind.

EVA: Well, don't you think I know? I know. You don't do things like that, you don't even look! I can, though; I know.

ROBERT: You don't know anything.

EVA: I DO TOO! I've seen. You think I'm so young because I'm so little. I'm fourteen; I can have babies already; and I've seen cows do it when they're in heat. But you wouldn't do something like that.

ROBERT: Let's go back.

EVA: Let's do. I know how; I can.

ROBERT: When cows are in heat, that's one cow jumping on another; you don't know anything.

EVA: You're ashamed; you're not old enough to.

ROBERT: You don't know what you're talking about.

EVA: Boys have to be older. But I'll bet your brother could anyway. I might as well because she thinks we do anyway. You're the one who doesn't know anything about it.

ROBERT: I should, just to show you—don't— you don't know what you're talking about.

EVA: What?

ROBERT: Anything. Because you don't know anything about it.

EVA: I do too. You're afraid.

ROBERT: You don't know what you're talking about even.

Their lines begin to overlap.

EVA: Only not here.

ROBERT: Why not? What's wrong with here?

EVA: You have to be in bed, stupid!

ROBERT: If you think you know so much. [*Grabbing her*]

EVA: [*Violently*] Let go of me! You leave me alone. I will if I want to.

ROBERT: You want to get it in you so bad! You think I can't.

EVA: Stop it.

ROBERT: You think I won't do it.

EVA: Leave me alone. I'll tell.

ROBERT: No you won't; you asked for it.

EVA: Leave me alone.

ROBERT: [*Throwing her to the ground*] You think you're so smart; I'll show you. Shut up now, shut up or I'll kill you anyway; you asked for it. [*They struggle violently on the ground. EVA saying, "No, stay away, leave me alone," screaming*] You little whore; you think I won't. Stop it.

SKELLY: [*From the woods, breaking toward them. His lines are simultaneous with the above struggle*] What do you think—leave her alone. Don't hurt her. Robert. Don't hurt her. [*He throws ROBERT off her. EVA screams. SKELLY, seeing NELLY, looks up and runs toward her instinctively*] Help her!

MARY: [*To NELLY, from upstairs at the Windrod house*] Nelly, Nelly, there's someone out back, honey, having a terrible fight; they came through the woods and started yelling all kinds of things.

NELLY: Where was you? I thought you was in bed.

MARY: You better go out and see, honey.

NELLY *takes up a shotgun, throwing open the door.*

NELLY: What's going on? Who's there?

As EVA screams, NELLY levels the shotgun at SKELLY'S chest and fires first one, then the other, barrel. SKELLY falls, violently spun about by the force of the gun. In production it is important that the blanks for the shotgun be very loud, about half as much powder as in actual shots; the powder from the gun smokes the entire stage until the end of the play. The CONGREGATION moves from their stationary position as SKELLY hits the floor. They mill a brief moment. The gun is passed, without much interest from one to the other of the men: JUDGE, JOSH, PECK, and the TRUCKER. The cast assembles at the court, blocking SKELLY from the audience's view.

JUDGE: [*Immediately after the* CONGREGATION *begins to move*] State your name.

ROBERT: [*Moving into the witness stand*] Robert Conklin.

JUDGE: Do you swear to tell the whole truth and nothing but the truth, so help you God?

ROBERT: I do.

JUDGE: There's nothing to be nervous about, Robert. We want you to tell the court, just in your own words, what happened on the night in question. Can you do that?

ROBERT: Yes, I think.

JUDGE: We know this has been a terrible shock to you—

ROBERT: —I'm okay, I think. See—Eva and I were walking. We do quite frequently. Just wandering through the woods, talking. And we noticed that it had begun to get dark so we thought we had better start back—and we were heading back toward the main street, that would be west. And Eva thought she heard something behind us and we listened but we didn't hear it again so I assumed we were hearing things. Or it was our imagination. And it got dark pretty fast. And we were just coming into the clearing right behind the mill. Windrod's mill. And uh, we heard something again and this time we saw something behind the trees and we started running. More as a joke than anything—and then he started running too. And it was Skelly, and I wasn't afraid of him, but I knew he'd never liked my brother, and he started running too. He must have been following us all the time; everybody knows how he spies on people; I guess just as we broke into the clearing—and he came from nowhere. [*Crowd reaction*] And he took us by surprise and he pushed me—he hit me from behind; I don't know if I passed out or not. [*Crowd murmur*] He's immensely strong. [*Crowd murmur*] And I heard a ringing in my

ears and I saw what he was trying to do, and everything went white. And he pushed me.

EVA: [*Screams as loud as possible*] AHHHHHH-HHHHH! AHHHHHHHHHHHHH! AHHH-HHHHHHHHH!

EVELYN: Oh, God, oh God, baby, my baby.

EVA: NO! no, no, no, no, no.

EVELYN: See her crippled body. See her broken back; why? Why has God cursed me with this burden? I don't complain, I ask why? We love Him. We bless Him. Praise Him.

Everyone freezes. Tableau. Silence.

PATSY: [*Off*] You know I saw you the day you first came into town, I'll bet. I've seen you a lot. Up at the Hilltop. I told Lena I liked you. No, no, come on. Yes, it's all right; I want you to. You know I do.

WALTER: [*Off*] I've got nothing with me.

PATSY: [*Off*] I know, it doesn't matter. You wouldn't wash your feet with your socks on. Be easy. Did you know I'd watched you? Huh? Did you? Huh? Did you know I had?

WALTER: [*Off*] No. I've seen you a couple of times.

PATSY: [*Off*] I told Lena I liked you. I don't like any of the boys here; they're terrible, shiftless; oh, they're all right. But nobody wants to spend their life here; not here in this place rotting away. Walter! Your name's Walter, isn't it? I found out. Oh. Oh, I love you, Walter. I do. I really do. I love you. Oh, I do. Really. Did you know that? I have since I saw you that first time. I do. I really do. I love you so much. I love you, oh I do, I love you. I do. Oh, I love you, Walter. You're the only one I love; I do. Really, I do.

Pause. Silence. The people mill gently, leave the stage slowly, silently, a few at a time. SKELLY *lies on stage where he fell.*

CURTAIN

SATURDAY NIGHT AT THE MOVIES

a play in one act

William M. Hoffman

Saturday Night at the Movies was first presented by Joseph Cino at the Caffe Cino, New York City, as half of a double bill with *Good Night, I Love You,* also by the author, on September 7, 1966, with the following cast:

MARIO	*Gerald Peters*
HELEN	*Hollis Solomon*
LILA	*Pat Starr*

The music was by David Kent; the sound by John Lakata.

The bedroom of HELEN *and* MARIO. *It is furnished in the latest style. A double bed (perhaps a water bed) and night table are center stage. There are two doors: one to the bathroom and one to the rest of the apartment. There is a color television set with its back to the audience. It is late Saturday night.* HELEN, *a pretty girl in her late twenties, is pacing the room in her nightgown. She puts the telephone off the receiver. She picks up a book. The front door slams. She jumps into bed.* MARIO, *handsome and about* HELEN'S *age, knocks at the bedroom door.* HELEN *ignores the knocking.* MARIO *knocks louder.*

MARIO: [*Offstage*] Come on. Can I come in? I know you're not asleep. I see the light under the door.

HELEN: [*Pretending to read*] I'm sorry. Come in. I was engrossed.

MARIO *enters.* HELEN *doesn't look up.*

MARIO: [*Kissing* HELEN *lightly on the cheek*] I'm sorry I'm late. What time is it anyhow?

HELEN: [*Looking up*] I don't know. I can't see the clock from here.

The clock is buried in trivia on the dresser.

MARIO: Always hiding the clock, aren't you? [*He finds the clock*] My God, it's eleven-thirty. I didn't realize it was so late. We must of had ten cups of coffee. . . . It just started to rain as I got in the door.

HELEN: [*Reading*] How did it go?

MARIO: Crappy. I've a headache.

HELEN: I'm sorry. What did you say? [*She looks up*]

MARIO: I said "crap." Christ, I'm sick. Where're the aspirin? [*He lies down next to* HELEN. *She starts to get up*]

HELEN: Please get them yourself. I'm too comfortable to move.

MARIO: Oh, sorry, honey. Are they in the cabinet?

[*Exits to bathroom*]

HELEN: Bring me two sleeping pills, will you, Mario?

MARIO: [*Enters and hands her pills*] Did anyone call?

HELEN: I've had the phone off the hook all evening. I wanted to get to bed early. [*She swallows the pills with water from carafe on the night table*]

MARIO: [*Puts the telephone back together*] Hmpf.

HELEN: Who're you expecting to call?

MARIO: No one. I just don't like it off the hook. [HELEN *turns on her side with her back toward him*] Oh, my baby wants to sleep [*He pats her head*]

HELEN: Well, what'd he say?

MARIO: In essence, keep your hands off my manuscript.

Silence.

HELEN: Good night.

MARIO: Have you set the alarm?

HELEN: It's Saturday.

MARIO: Saturday. . . . Do you want to watch some television?

HELEN: I'm very tired.

MARIO: My head's splitting.

HELEN: [*Head buried in pillow*] Saturday.

MARIO *undresses and climbs into bed. He turns out the light on the night table. The stage is semidark.* MARIO *is on his back and* HELEN *is lying on her side with her back to him. Her eyes are closed. He tries to bring her into his arms. She mumbles as if she were asleep. Her eyes are open. He kisses the back of her head and rolls over on his side with his back to her.* HELEN *fidgets and lies on her back.* MARIO *lies on his back and tries to get* HELEN *in his arms. She rolls on her side. After some more fidgeting she gets up and goes to the bathroom. Light from the bathroom makes a streak across the bed.*

MARIO: [*Sleepily*] What are you doing?

HELEN: [*From the bathroom*] I'm taking another pill. Go to sleep. [*Water is running.* HELEN *comes back into the room. She lies down and switches on the lamp.* MARIO *rolls away from the light. A car horn blares outside. A toilet flushes somewhere in the building*] Mario, wake up!

MARIO: [*Startled*] What's the matter?

HELEN: I can't sleep like this. This is not my game.

MARIO: Game. Game? [*Awake*] What are you talking about? I'm sorry I was late. Now go to sleep. Aren't the pills working?

HELEN: The pills won't work. I'd like to go to sleep, God knows I'd like to go to sleep, but I can't. . . . [*Silence*] Well, aren't you going to ask me what's wrong?

MARIO: I've a headache. Every other night you're insomniacal—insomniacal—is that right?

HELEN: Yes. Go on.

MARIO: Every other night you have insomnia and I ask you what's wrong.

HELEN: Me and my insomnia and you and your illnesses. Tonight you have a headache. Last night you were coming down with the flu. The day before your leg hurt. Last week it was a backache. And you expect me to take each of them seriously. The only thing you've really ever had is hypochondria.

MARIO: Well, I do have a headache.

HELEN: No, I will *not* open my mouth.

MARIO: What? [*Silence*] Oh, good night. [*He turns away from her*]

HELEN: I will not open my mouth.

MARIO: Speak. [*Silence*] Speak, I beg you.

HELEN: I've figured out why you're always sick and I can't sleep.

MARIO: It's in my head.

HELEN: [*Ignoring him*] I was speaking to Lila—

MARIO: Oh, God, no.

HELEN: It's women who usually have these symptoms.

MARIO: Okay, what did Liberated Woman say was wrong with me?

HELEN: *I* figured it out. Lila didn't have anything to do with it. I was only using her as a sounding board.

MARIO: What conclusion did you and your sounding board come to? I can hardly wait for your latest bit of pseudopsychiatry.

HELEN: Skip it. Forget it.

Silence.

MARIO: God, my head is splitting—I'm sorry, I feel nothing. Not a thing. I didn't say a word. I'm fine, fine!

HELEN: Do you know why I can't sleep. We haven't made love in a week. So I'm *tense* and I make you *tense,* so you're *sick* all the time. Does that make sense to you?

MARIO: I'm speechless. You told Lila about our sex life? Oh, God, how could you? Don't you know that every word that woman writes is autobiographical?

HELEN: Is that all you care about?

MARIO: I can just see it: "Hilda was reading in bed when Mark finally came home to their West Side apartment—"

HELEN: Lila can keep her mouth shut. She's our best friend. Why don't you want to make love to me any more?

MARIO: I have other things on my mind. [*Softening*] Baby, it's not that I don't want to make love to you; it's that I'm not into love at all. I've come to a decision—

HELEN: Where were you really tonight?

MARIO: I was being unfaithful with another woman.

HELEN: With big breasts. I'm sorry I don't have big breasts. It's not my fault.

MARIO: She had gigantic breasts, each as large as a basketball.

HELEN: [*With increasing speed*] You were late because you forgot the time. You forgot the time because it wasn't important for you to re-

member what time it is. It's not important for you to remember what time it is because you were coming home to me, who is here every night, who will be here with her small breasts every night and every morning, forever faithful because I love you, because you don't love me as much as I love you, because I love you so much. You know exactly what I mean.

MARIO: You're right.

HELEN: You bastard. If I thought that getting married would solve anything, I bet I could get you to marry me.

MARIO: You're hardly making sense. Those pills are working whether you know it or not.

HELEN: I'm quite high on them, but that doesn't mean I'm about to go to sleep. . . . Have you ever been unfaithful to me?

MARIO: No.

HELEN: Come on now. In the three years that we've been "going together" you haven't once cheated, gotten a *piece* elsewhere? How stupid do you think I am? The truth.

MARIO: Christ, a "piece." You sound like Lila.

HELEN: Answer my question. Have you?

MARIO: Yes, once. Would you make some coffee? I see that we're going to be up all night again.

HELEN: When? When!

MARIO: That time a year ago when we broke up —when you broke things off. It was awful. . . . Oh, it was not awful, it was great. She was great. I slept with her for a week. Then she got bored with me. *She* broke things off.

HELEN: Son of a bitch! [*She slaps him hard but playfully*]

MARIO: [*Laughing*] I was lonely. I like you more! [*She slaps him again. He pins her arms down*] Hey! Should I tell you what we did in bed?

HELEN: No, I don't want to hear the details. And I know that you have very rarely been unfaithful to me. I don't understand why; you've not been exhausting me exactly. "Unfaithful," what a disgusting expression. And I know that you love me best of all. And I know that I AM LOSING MY MIND!

MARIO: What on earth is the matter with you?

HELEN: It's this set-up. Man creative, woman drudge. Man courts woman. Woman rejects. Man pulls away. Woman chases. And chases for the rest of her damned life. Because she's nothing more than a woman.

MARIO: Do you want to be like Lila?

HELEN: I know what you mean. I can't stop it. I could go on like this for the rest of the night. I'm sorry. Tell me about your meeting. [*Doorbell*] Lila was missing. It's your turn to get rid of her.

MARIO: I will not be rude to her. That's your department. [*Doorbell*] Why doesn't she call before she drops in?

HELEN: Let's not answer it.

MARIO: Maybe it's not Lila.

HELEN: I can tell by the ring. Oh, answer it. [MARIO *exits*] Kiss me quick. [*She crawls under the covers and tries to look asleep*]

MARIO: [*Offstage*] Well, if it isn't the sounding board.

LILA: [*Offstage*] Where is she? Where is she? [*Enter* MARIO *and* LILA. LILA *is overweight and almost deliberately unattractive. She is wearing a slicker, which is wet from the rain. Her hair is dripping. She is carrying a paper bag*] It's your ugly girl friend with a paper bag. Don't pretend you're asleep. I've come to amuse you all at my expense.

HELEN: [*Perfectly awake*] Okay, Pathetica, what are you carrying?

LILA: Love love love. Kiss me, Mario, I've come to take you away from all this. So what's new and exciting? [*Tosses several packages of cigarettes on the bed, which were in the paper bag*]

MARIO: You're wet. I failed to get the Collins manuscript.

LILA: That's neither new nor exciting. Collins? Collins who? Don't tell me. George Washington Carver Collins.

MARIO: [*Flatly*] George Collins.

LILA: What's he up to these days, America's foremost so-called Negro novelist? I heard he's writing a book about how blacks and gays get together and take over New York. Or how the blacks put the gays in concentration camps in Central Park. Something like that. How *is* old George?

MARIO: [*Offended*] Busy being published. How's *your* novel coming?

LILA: Slowly. It's tedious being literate.

MARIO: Heard Helen's been blabbing to you about our sex life.

HELEN: Mario!

LILA: What sex life?

MARIO: Meet any men lately?

LILA: My sex life is adequate, thank you.

MARIO: If your novels are any reflection of your sex life—

LILA: They're not.

HELEN: [*Joining in*] My, what a lovely outfit.

LILA: [*To* HELEN] Sadist. Getting any younger, hmmm? I don't know why I visit you drab, drab people. What's eating you, Mario?

MARIO: Lila, Helen. I've come to a decision. I'm going to leave publishing and go back to writing.

HELEN: [*To* LILA] He tells *you* that. This is the first I've heard of it.

MARIO: I tried to tell you.

HELEN: [*To* MARIO] Fantastic. I'm thrilled.

LILA: What on earth for?

MARIO: Go to hell the both of you. I'm serious.

HELEN: That's wonderful, really. Really it is. What are you going to write?

LILA: You're a gorgeous man; you shouldn't spend your time writing. There're too few men around for you to be writing. But I'm sure you'll be good at it. Congratulations. I'm with you, kid.

HELEN: God, I'm exhausted. I took three sleeping pills.

LILA: If that's a hint—

HELEN: Stay! Stay! But if I fall asleep, don't wake me up. Talk softly. [*To* MARIO] Oh, darling, that's wonderful.

MARIO: I had an idea—just the germ of an idea, actually—for a novel. I was reading the other day about Arab women.

LILA: [*Exiting to the bathroom*] I'm going to dry my hair off. [*Offstage*] I'm listening.

HELEN: I wish you wouldn't read about other women.

MARIO: Shut up, you're an odalisque.

HELEN: [*To* LILA] What's an odalisque?

LILA *comes back with towel on her head.*

MARIO: This is interesting, really.

LILA: You're always interesting, darling.

MARIO: [*Impatiently*] Listen. You know that Arab women in some countries have to wear veils and all that. And that they are excluded from society and have to bend to their husbands' every whim.

LILA: Love it.

HELEN: [*To* LILA] You bend to anyone's whim, that's a laugh.

LILA: I've seen a few men whose *whim* I would bend to.

MARIO: What do you suppose their attitude—not attitude—their *feeling* is to the men?

LILA: They adore it.

HELEN: I suppose you can get used to anything.

MARIO: Well, it's this way: Arab men live in mortal fear of being *poisoned*.

HELEN: Ha! Ha-ha!

MARIO: They often forbid any woman except their mother or sister from cooking for them.

LILA: That sure cuts through a lotta crap, doesn't it?

MARIO: Well, anyway . . .

LILA: Well, anyway, what're you people doing for kicks these days?

MARIO: Fighting. Would you like to watch?

LILA: Don't you know any *men* you could introduce me to? Forget it. I would only end up in bed with them.

MARIO: Don't you ever do anything with your boy friends but sleep with them?

LILA: I've no time for meaningful relationships. Look, I know I'm no beauty, but I'm even less charming than I am beautiful. So what else is there left?

HELEN: Television.

LILA: And here I thought you two might be making it.

HELEN: He's trying to give it up. The only thing we have in common and he's trying to give it up. I drudge and he creates.

MARIO: Oh, yes, I create.

HELEN: Well, try being a social worker, darling. [*To* LILA] At least you've done something with your education.

LILA: Look. I have only one consolation in life. I'm ugly *now,* but when you get old and lose your looks, I'll be used to it by then. I might even look interesting when I get older.

HELEN: I rather doubt it. I think you'll get uglier.

LILA: You're asking for it, drudge. Sin-woman. Why don't you two get married?

HELEN: Not being married is the only thing preventing us from having babies.

LILA: I'd love to be called Aunt Lila. Ugly Aunt Lila.

MARIO: You have an uglier-than-thou attitude.

LILA: What's wrong with babies?

HELEN: I'm sure they'd look like Mario.

MARIO: And?

HELEN: You're very handsome, but I'm sure your genes are dominant. And that'd be the last straw. What I need is a hobby.

LILA: What you need is a—

HELEN: If I had *one* thing to do that really fulfilled me—

LILA: As a woman. [*To* MARIO] When do you think you'll be quitting?

MARIO: I wasn't serious.

HELEN: Thank God.

MARIO: What do you mean, thank God?

HELEN: If you want to know the truth, I think it's a lousy idea. You're twenty-eight. If you were meant to be a writer, you'd have started writing by now. What evidence, what slightest bit of evidence is there in your mind that you can write?

MARIO: I wrote a great deal in college, and very well, too.

HELEN: Oh, yes. You showed me some of that stuff. [*To* LILA] Strictly from Creative Writing 202.

MARIO: I thought it was very good. What the hell am I doing defending myself? What's eating you?

HELEN: What do you mean?

MARIO: Why are you being so hostile?

HELEN: I wasn't being hostile. I just don't want you doing something rash. You have a good job and I don't want you losing it because of a whim.

MARIO: If I did have talent, you'd certainly see to it that I'd never get a chance to try it out, wouldn't you?

HELEN: Come on, let's talk about something real. The fact is that you don't have any talent.

MARIO: How would *you* know?

HELEN: Are you trying to tell me that you can write, or are you just bitching because you know you're wrong?

LILA: [*To herself*] You can't tell "write" from wrong. Write on, Mario!

MARIO: What's wrong with you? Why are you being so negative? Don't worry. I won't leave Hogarth. I'll sit here forever holding your hand, wallowing in other people's writing. I don't mind being the bathroom attendant of the writing profession—correcting commas, writing book jackets.

HELEN: You haven't done that for years.

MARIO: I could write some of our authors under the table.

LILA: With Magic Marker!

HELEN: Why haven't you then?

MARIO: I don't know. Maybe because of you. You sit around here and bitch. Bitch me, bitch you. Bitch, bitch! If I want to quit, I will! I won't be discouraged by you.

HELEN: All right!

Silence.

LILA: Do you mind if I turn on the TV while you argue? [*They ignore her*] I'm hungry. What have you got to eat?

HELEN: [*Looking at* MARIO] Ravioli!

LILA: [*Exiting*] Do either of you want anything while I'm in the kitchen? [*Pauses at doorway. Silence.* LILA *exits*]

HELEN: I'm sorry! [*Kittenish*] I'm sorry? [MARIO *is standing with his back to her*] I didn't mean what I said. I don't know what made me say it. Please forgive me. . . . I was jealous.

MARIO: That was unfair. I'm never that way with you.

HELEN: I said I was jealous. You don't have anything to be jealous about. You have an interesting life. What do I have? You. You're the only thing I have.

MARIO: Don't you want me to do things? I'd never discourage you.

HELEN: When have I ever tried to do anything? I just sit around and bitch. I'm sorry. [*Kittenish*] Do you forgive me? I'll be good. I promise.

MARIO: [*Kittenish*] Do you promise?

HELEN: Only if you come here.

MARIO: [*Sniffs, pouts, and cocks his head to one side*] I don't know.

HELEN: Well, then I won't promise.

MARIO: Well, okay. [MARIO *goes to* HELEN *on the bed. Enter* LILA *with a sandwich on a plate and a glass of milk.* MARIO *and* HELEN *are kissing*]

LILA: Play time is over.

HELEN: We made up. [*To* MARIO. *She is in his arms*] You have the most fantastic arms. [*She rubs his stomach*] His stomach is growing.

LILA: [*Taking a bite of her sandwich*] So is mine.

HELEN: I can't wait for you to get old so other women won't look at you, I'm so jealous. [*To* LILA] Isn't he fantastic? Feel his arm.

MARIO: I feel like a head of cattle.

HELEN: Go on, feel it.

MARIO: Or a slave on an auction block.

LILA: A love slave. [*She feels his arm*] It's meager. [*Still holding his arm*] I like them heftier, so when they hold you, you know you're being held. I like to be held a little too tight.

HELEN: I know what you mean.

LILA: I like them with tattoos and uniforms so that you know they're really men.

HELEN: That's fetishistic.

LILA: Yes. And I like them less intelligent than me and rather brutal. [*She rubs* MARIO's *head*] Crawling with fetishes: hair, muscles, thick socks . . .

HELEN: And you're proud of it.

LILA: Look, kid, I don't carry all my fetishes in one basket.

HELEN: If that's the way you feel about him—

LILA: Honey, he's too skinny for me—

MARIO: I'm not too skinny—

HELEN: He's not too skinny. He's perfect.

MARIO: Quite. [HELEN *gropes him under the blanket*] Cut that out.

LILA: She was always the letch.

HELEN: Talk about letches.

LILA: Sin-woman.

MARIO: What's on TV?

LILA: Ah, yes, TV.

HELEN: You are not cuddling me, Mario.

Mario is reading TV Guide.

LILA: Cuddle her, Mario. That old cuddle is very important. . . .

MARIO: Saturday. There's a horror movie on Channel 7—

LILA: Fantastic. *Love* horror movies. [LILA *turns on the television, which soon fills the room with its glow. The sound track of the movie on television should be prerecorded as follows*]

TELEVISION	*HELEN, LILA, MARIO*
ASSISTANT: Ready, Doctor Simanthus.	
DR. S.: [*Has Central European accent*] Start the kilomonograph. [*Whining machine sound*] Slowly, you idiot! One iode at a time. [*Slowly increasing whine*]	HELEN: Wonderful!
ASSISTANT: Five hundred volts . . . one thousand . . .	Hold my hand, darling, I'm scared.
Cut to	LILA: What'd she say? [*To* HELEN] For Chrissake, you made me miss what she said.
JEFF: [*Whispering*] Betty, stay back.	
BETTY: No, I'm coming with you.	
JEFF: Look, there's a light up ahead.	
BETTY: I hope we're not too late.	
Cut to	
ASSISTANT: Fifteen hundred volts, Doctor.	
DR. S.: Prepare the brain, Hermann.	
GIRL moans.	
ASSISTANT: She's waking up.	
COMMERCIAL: [*Tape-record a real one, perhaps Doublemint commercial*]	HELEN: Oh, damn. MARIO: I'll bet she has bad breath. HELEN: Come into bed with us, Lila. LILA: That's disgusting. MARIO: Lie down, Lila, you're blocking the screen.

Movie resumes.

GIRL: Oh . . . Oh . . . Doctor Simanthus!

DR. S.: Quiet, my dear.

GIRL: What happened?

DR. S.: You had a little accident.

GIRL: Where's Jeff?

DR. S.: He's waiting outside. [*To* ASSISTANT] Prepare an injection, Hermann. [*To* GIRL] You'll soon be comfortable. Relax, we're your friends. Relax.

GIRL: I want to see Jeff.

DR. S.: Hurry, Hermann.

GIRL: No!

JEFF: Drop the hypodermic, Hermann.

GIRL: Jeff!

JEFF: Don't make a move, Doctor, or I'll blast you. Betty, get her loose. Stand back, Simanthus, or I'll vaporize you.

Scuffling sound.

DR. S.: You won't get me.

Zap. Scream.

ASSISTANT: Doctor Simanthus! You've killed him. I'll get you for this.

Scuffling.   Zap. Scream.

HELEN: We'll be a family.

LILA: I'm too fat to fit in bed with you two.

HELEN: I'll move over. [*To* MARIO] Move over.

LILA *lies down with them.* HELEN *tries to snuggle into* MARIO'S *arms.*

MARIO: Sh.

HELEN: I didn't say anything. I was just being affectionate.

LILA: Sh.

HELEN: Be sweet, Mario. [MARIO *kisses* HELEN *three times mechanically*] That's better.

MARIO: [*Adjusting* HELEN *tenderly in his arms*] How is that, sweetheart?

HELEN: Wonderful, honey angel.

LILA: Move over, lovey lamb. You're pushing me off the bed.

MARIO: Turn off the light, would you, Lila?

LILA: Yes, kootchy woo. [LILA *turns off light. Light is still coming from the living room*]

HELEN: You just don't understand true love.

LILA: Sigh.

HELEN: Oh, world, I'm so happy now. The TV is on and fills the room with a pearly glow. The telephone won't ring and take Mario away from me. My dear Lila is next to me. My Mario, my Mario is here and definitely

GIRL: Thank God you came in time.

BETTY: Oh, Jeff.

JEFF: We'd better get out of here or we'll miss blast-off.

BETTY: Oh, Jeff, we made it.

JEFF: Yes, we've solved the secret of Mars.

Music covers screen credits.

ANNOUNCER: Channel Seven of the Metropolitan Broadcasting System is signing off with our daily sermonette, which is presented this morning by the Reverend Stephen MacAlister of the Hollis Baptist Church. Good night.

REVEREND: Oh, Lord, in these days of peril, of superbombs, of racial strife, of war, of moral degeneration, show us the right way, guide us. Help us to understand how we may preserve our inner peace. Help us not to forget how Your Son suffered, and, believing in His suffering for our sins, we may gain eternal deliverance and earthly peace. Amen.

MARIO: Oh, you're going. What're you doing tomorrow?

LILA: I'm going to church.

MARIO: What?

LILA: Nothing. [*Gets up and gathers her clothing together*] I'll call.

MARIO: Would you turn the TV off? I'm fading out. [LILA *turns off the television leaving the room lit from the next room*] Good night.

LILA: [*Exiting*] Yeah.

MARIO: See you.

LILA: [*Offstage*] See you.

Light from living room goes off.

not with another woman.

MARIO: Look, Helen.

HELEN: Oh, I'm fading off. The pills are working. Is it raining outside?

LILA: It's raining outside.

HELEN: And we're inside, the three of us, in this room. [*Helen falls asleep in* MARIO'S *arms*]

LILA: The three of us. Helen. Mario. Lila. And that pearly glow. . . . I have to go. . . .

MARIO: I was almost asleep. You going? You going home?

LILA: I'm going to the moon.

SOMETHING I'LL TELL YOU TUESDAY

a play in one act

John Guare

Something I'll Tell You Tuesday was first presented by Joseph Cino at the Caffe Cino, New York City, as half of a double bill with *The Loveliest Afternoon of the Year,* also by the author, on October 25, 1966, with the following cast:

AGNES .... *Clio Vias*

ANDREW .... *Frank Ammirati*

HILDEGARDE .... *Sharkey Fink*

GEORGE .... *John Fink*

MRS. HASSELBACH .... *Joan Campbell*

It was directed by Russ Kaiser. Lighting by Donald Brooks. Production stage manager, George Borris.

NOTE: The play is written to be performed with the barest minimum of scenery; two chairs are all that is needed. The cast should in no way approximate the ages of the people in the play. It is a play about old people to be performed by young people. Ideally it would be played by children dressed up in old clothes: Hildegarde and George played by twelve-year-olds; Agnes and Andrew played by sixteen-year-olds. When played by actors in their twenties, no attempt should be made at makeup or playing wobbly-old. The quiet rhythms of Agnes and Andrew played against the hysterical rhythms of Hildegarde and George should be enough to dramatize the ages. The relationship between Agnes and Andrew is very matter-of-fact. The trap of the play is playing them as two old sickly-sweet people in love with each other. The important thing to remember is that they were Hildegarde and George forty years before.

The action of the play is the West Fifty-ninth Street Block between Eighth and Ninth Avenues in New York City on a pleasant April day; first in a shabby brownstone walkup, then the corridor, the street, a lunch counter, and the street.

AT CURTAIN: bare stage. Two chairs center a few feet apart. Area lighting #1.

AGNES, an old woman, sits left packing a suitcase with nightgowns and a toothbrush and combs and brushes and curlers. ANDREW, an old man, stands down right, back to her, staring out the window.

AGNES: [*The tail end of a fight*] If we left now, we could leave a note for them to meet us there.

ANDREW: They'll be here any minute.

AGNES: Andrew, it's only a block away—

ANDREW: It's a long block—

AGNES: It's such a nice day. Look at it outside. And I'll be flat on my back such a long time.

ANDREW: You'll only be there a couple of days. Doctor Daner said only a week maybe.

AGNES: Maybe, he said. I could be there a long time.

ANDREW: You won't be.

AGNES: Couldn't we walk? Oh, Andrew, I'll be flat on my back for God knows how long—

ANDREW: [*Turning to her*] Don't say that—

AGNES: And I can rest. That's all I'll be doing is resting and—I'd like to walk with you.

He looks at her. He takes his necktie off the back of the chair right and begins tying it.

ANDREW: Well, I can't blame you for not wanting to drive with Hildegarde and George.

AGNES: [*Stops packing*] Andrew?

ANDREW: Ah, it hurts me the way they fight. You all packed?

AGNES: [*Rises, crosses up center*] You know what I was thinking about this morning? Come here —look at this. Look behind the picture.

ANDREW: What is it?

AGNES: Look behind the picture. [*He crosses up to her, pantomimes moving a picture away from the wall*] Remember that?

ANDREW: [*Puzzled*] What is it?

AGNES: That streak on the wall. Remember? [*She comes back down to her chair and resumes packing*] The painters had just finished painting this room and the walls were still wet and we were fighting about something and I got mad at you and threw the grapefruit I was eating at you and you ducked and the grapefruit stuck to the wet wall and slid all the way down to the floor.

ANDREW: [*Pushing the picture back into place*] That was a long time ago.

AGNES: I got up very early this morning. You were still asleep and I roamed around the apartment and I remembered why we hung that picture on the wall. I haven't thought of that in years.

ANDREW: [*Sharply*] Are you all packed? [*He paces back and forth*]

AGNES: I'm all ready. [*She hurries up packing and closes her bag*]

ANDREW: I just wish this day were over.

AGNES: That's why I want to walk to the hospital. It'd be pleasant. We could leave a note for Hildegarde and George that we left already and they could meet us there.

HILDEGARDE and GEORGE enter up left, come down left in the nonlit area. HILDEGARDE's hair is askew. GEORGE looks like he's on the brink of either murder or an ulcer.

GEORGE: Your mother's sick—for once in your life can't you think of somebody beside yourself—yatata yatata—

HILDEGARDE: [*Over the above*] Don't get me started—don't get me started—

AGNES and ANDREW hear them. They look at each other. ANDREW goes to answer the door. She pulls him back.

AGNES: [*Whispering*] Andrew, don't answer the door. They'll think we've left and they'll go right to the hospital. We could take a cab if you're tired.

HILDEGARDE: [*Harshly*] Oh for God's sake—shut up, George. [*Calling sweetly*] Mama? Papa? Open up! We're here! Knock knock knock! [*She straightens her clothes and glares at GEORGE*]

AGNES: [*Pleading, whispering*] Andrew, we haven't taken a walk together in so long. That's what I was thinking about this morning. Please, Andrew?

His shoulders slump. He motions her to the door.

HILDEGARDE: [*Panic-stricken*] You don't suppose anything's happened? Mama? Papa!

AGNES: Oh . . . [*Moving toward the door*] We're here. Knock knock knock. Hello, Hildegarde. [*Pantomimes opening door*] Hello, George.

HILDEGARDE and GEORGE storm in.

ANDREW: Hello, Hildegarde. George.

HILDEGARDE: [*Quick kisses her parents*] Well, why didn't you open? [*GEORGE sits down right*] I have been so nervous today I'll expect anything. We have had THE worst trip in—

GEORGE: Just shut up, Hildegarde. We got here safe and just shut up.

ANDREW *starts off right to get the coats.* AGNES *goes to pick up her bag.* HILDEGARDE *sits down left.* GEORGE *turns away disgustedly.* ANDREW *comes down right.*

HILDEGARDE: Do we have time? I have just got to sit down and rest and catch my breath. [*She starts crying.* AGNES *comes down left of her and puts her hand around* HILDEGARDE'S *shoulder*]

GEORGE: For God's sake—it wasn't that bad.

HILDEGARDE: [*Furious*] Oh, it's all right for you to talk—

GEORGE: [*Brightly, to his in-laws*] Folks, we parked the car two blocks away. We were lucky. A DeSoto pulled out just as we came down the block, so anytime you're ready to leave, we'll go get it again.

HILDEGARDE: Just let me get my breath before we start out again.

GEORGE: We are just going down the block.

HILDEGARDE: [*Like it's the longest trip in the world*] And then all the way back to Newark. I'm driving this time, George. You are not safe behind a wheel. [*Turning to her mother*] Mama, he knocked over every one of those yellow markers on the George Washington Bridge.

GEORGE: I did not knock over every one of them. With you screaming at me. Agnes, you have a nice voice. Andrew, you have a nice voice. I do not know where she gets her voice from. She screams and it does something to your ears. [*Leans back disgusted*] Ah, for God's sake, Hildegarde, let's not wash dirty linen in public.

HILDEGARDE: [*Horrified*] This is not public. This is my home. This is the home I grew up in. [*She wraps her arms tightly around her mother's waist who stands left of her, while she screams at* GEORGE *to the right of her*] He has no consideration. Every one of the yellow markers. I always thought they were metal, [*Appealing to her mother*] so when he knocked them all over, naturally, I screamed.

GEORGE: [*All the hate in the world*] They were only rubber, Hildegarde. Yellow rubber.

AGNES: [*Brightly, trying to get out of* HILDE-GARDE'S *grasp*] How are the children? [*She crosses down to her husband, rubbing her waist*]

GEORGE: [*Glaring at* HILDEGARDE] Fine.

HILDEGARDE: [*Murderously at* GEORGE] We'll bring them over on Tuesday. It's a holiday in New Jersey.

ANDREW: [*Trying to break the tension*] What's the holiday?

HILDEGARDE: Some tree day. [*Breaking down*] Oh, Mother, I would like to—

GEORGE: Don't start that crying again. [*He throws his hands up at his in-laws*]

HILDEGARDE: [*Pulling together all her dignity*] I would like to come to that hospital with you and just crawl in beside you and stay there. I'm so fed up. [*A whimper*] So fed up.

GEORGE: [*Leaning forward to her*] I wish you would stay in that hospital. And let me tell you one more thing. I knocked over all those yellow markers on purpose.

HILDEGARDE: [*Daring him*] He's trying to drive me insane. Okay, George, drive me insane. If that's what's going to make you happy, you go right ahead and drive me insane. [GEORGE *stands up disgustedly.* HILDEGARDE *covers her head with her arms*] Don't you dare hit me! [*Andrew starts for her.* AGNES *pulls him back*] Papa, help!

GEORGE: [*Amazed*] I'm only going to get a glass of water. [*He exits up right shaking his head.* AGNES *takes* GEORGE'S *seat*]

HILDEGARDE: [*Whispering to her mother.* AN-DREW *comes over behind* AGNES *quickly to hear what she's saying*] He called me the worst names once we got off that bridge. Names you wouldn't call the lowest scum on earth he called me.

AGNES *pats her hand.*

GEORGE: [*Off*] What're you saying?

HILDEGARDE: [*Whispering*] He'd hit me. He has. He will.

GEORGE: [*Sticking his head out up right*] Any-body want a glass of water or coffee or some-thing?

HILDEGARDE: [*Offhand*] I would like some water. Put sugar in it. [GEORGE *disappears back into the kitchen.* HILDEGARDE *pats her mother's hand with great dramatic concern*] Oh, Mama, how are you? You're going to be all right. I said to George that DeSoto pulling out just as we came down the block is a good sign. You're going to be all right.

AGNES: [*Nobly*] Don't be upset about me.

HILDEGARDE: Oh, it's not you, Mama. [AGNES *looks surprised*] It's the kids. It's—it's him. It's everything. It's me. [*She starts laughing*] Wow, aren't I the cheery one?

ANDREW: [*Touches her shoulder*] Now that's the Hildegarde I like to see.

GEORGE *reenters with the sugared "glass of water."*

GEORGE: [*Good-naturedly, crossing down left to her*] Minute I go out of the room she starts laughing.

HILDEGARDE: [*Still sore at him*] Now don't try and make up.

GEORGE: [*Giving her the "glass" and standing down left*] Maybe I should stay out of the room more often. [*He winks at* ANDREW. HILDEGARDE *sips*]

AGNES: How's your water?

HILDEGARDE: [*Startled at first*] What? Oh, this water. I thought you meant something else. This water—fine. Not as good as Jersey water —but still fine. [*Like a recipe*] The sugar makes it sweet.

GEORGE *groans.*

ANDREW: I think we should hurry. Hospitals run on a tight schedule.

HILDEGARDE: Oh, Papa, you're always in such a hurry. It's so nice here with you. [*Patting her mother's hand*] My God, we won't always have this chance.

Horrifying pause all around. AGNES *stands and crosses right to the window.*

GEORGE: That's a rotten thing to say.

HILDEGARDE: [*Realizing what she's said*] Mama, I didn't mean that. I meant—and this is the truth— [*Rises, crosses to* AGNES]—the way George drives, I don't know how many more chances we're going to get.

GEORGE: Just leave my driving out of it. Look at your father. He's quiet. He's happy. Why don't you take after him?

ANDREW: [*Sitting right*] I'm just thinking today, George. Just thinking.

HILDEGARDE: [*Laughing nervously*] Thinking? About how you're going to be a bachelor while Mama's away? Mama, do you think you can trust him? [AGNES *smiles*] That Mrs. Hassel- bach on the third floor's always had her eye on Papa. Even when I was a little girl. [AN- DREW *laughs at her. She crosses to him, leans over from behind and hugs him*] It's the truth. I'd take the garbage down to the incinerator and Mrs. Hasselbach would stick her head out the door and she'd say, "Isn't your papa bring- ing the garbage to the incinerator today, dearie?"

AGNES: [*Playing along with* HILDEGARDE] I think I can trust him.

ANDREW: [*Pushing* HILDEGARDE's *arms away*] Of course you can.

HILDEGARDE: [*Happily, sitting at his left*] Papa, you're taking everything so seriously today. We're only teasing. Papa, Monica has her first date next Saturday. The High School Junior Prom. Isn't that nice?

GEORGE *comes behind* HILDEGARDE *and signals his in-laws not to get involved in this particu- lar conversation.*

ANDREW: [*Looking up at him, taking the cue*] What? Oh, maybe we better get started— [*He starts to rise*]

AGNES: [*Reaching for her suitcase*] Yes, hospitals run on a—

HILDEGARDE: [*Turning to* GEORGE] What's he doing? Oh, he doesn't want to talk about Monica. [*She stands up to him. He crosses down center. She faces him.* AGNES *and* AN- DREW *sigh and both sit down, exhausted*] You don't want to talk about Monica. He knows he did wrong.

GEORGE: I did not do wrong. Your father proba- bly did the same thing for you.

HILDEGARDE: He never did.

ANDREW: What's the matter? What wouldn't I do?

AGNES: Who's her date?

GEORGE: [*Proudly*] Captain of the swimming team!

HILDEGARDE: Co-Captain of the swimming team. The way Monica talks about him you'd think he was Cary Grant or something. So George here goes out and buys her this fantastic eve- ning gown.

GEORGE: [*Shuffling over by the window*] It's her first big date.

HILDEGARDE: [*Pacing down left*] It's cut down to here. She's only sixteen. She'll look like a freak. It wasn't even on sale.

AGNES *and* ANDREW *sit center hypnotized— powerless—watching the fight between* HILDE- GARDE *and* GEORGE *like a tennis match, their heads swinging right then left as* HILDEGARDE *tops* GEORGE *in volume from down left and he tops her from down right.*

GEORGE: So what? Your father probably did the same thing for you.

HILDEGARDE: Never! He never bought me a dress for more money than we could afford and my mother never had holes in her underwear. Mama, this sounds so crude to say—

GEORGE: Then don't say it!

HILDEGARDE: Here is Monica going to this dance. Only in the gymnasium. Wearing this fantastic evening gown that you can't even return. Now how can she have a good time knowing her mother is sitting up home waiting for her with holes in her underwear. Mama, all my lingerie is shot and here's Monica in this fantastic— cut down to here—it is just not fair!

GEORGE: Aha! [*Comes to her, mockingly*] The truth comes out. You are a very jealous woman.

HILDEGARDE: [*Meeting him halfway*] I AM NOT JEALOUS! And it's time we got started. I'm going to get the car. You all wait right here. I'll be back in a few minutes.

GEORGE: I'm driving the car.

HILDEGARDE: [*Holding out her hand*] I will drive my parents to the hospital. You will give me the keys.

GEORGE: [*A warning in his voice*] Hildegarde—

HILDEGARDE: [*Runs to her mother, hugging her, almost knocking her off the chair*] Mama, he punched me. We got off that George Washington Bridge and he leaned over and punched me right in the side. I'm frightened of him, Mama.

GEORGE: I'll be right back with the car. Be waiting out front. [GEORGE *crosses down left, pantomimes opening the door, storms out up left down the dark corridor.* HILDEGARDE *runs to the door and screams down the corridor*]

HILDEGARDE: Don't you dare leave without me. [*She turns to her parents, smiling nervously*] I better go after him. You can't trust him alone. [*She comes down to her mother and kneels in front of her speaking to her as one would to a child*] This is what I wanted to tell you. I'll bring the bed jacket on Tuesday. I went to buy it, but the salesgirl told me on the sly they're having this fantastic sale on them—the nice lacy ones—on Tuesday. So I'll bring the bed jacket then. Okay? [*She stands up, smiling*] We'll be right back. We'll beep. [*Patting her mother's hand*] And, Mama, don't worry! [*She leans over and kisses her father*] Papa, she's going to be all right. [*She runs out the door down the corridor*] George, if you step one foot in that car, I swear you'll be sorry. [*And she is off.* AGNES *and* ANDREW *look at each other. They take a deep breath.* ANDREW *checks his watch*]

AGNES: Andrew?

ANDREW: [*Rubbing her knee*] They'll be back in a few minutes.

AGNES: It'll take them about fifteen minutes, won't it? To get back? Andrew, we could walk down the block in fifteen minutes. Please, Andrew, it'd be like a date. Andrew, I don't want to drive with Hildegarde and George.

ANDREW: Oh, I know what you mean there.

AGNES: [*Turning to him*] And I'm not tired. I slept so well last night and, Andrew, I'd just like to be alone with you. Please? Are you tired?

ANDREW: Are you packed? [*She nods yes. He pauses*] Then get your coat on. [*He stands up*] I'll leave a note. [*He goes up left and pantomimes writing a note. She runs up off right and returns with his coat and hat and her coat and hat.* ANDREW, *coming down*] I'll call a cab.

AGNES: No! I want to walk. [*She sticks her hat on. He takes his coat from her and puts it on. He reaches over and helps her with hers. She looks at him, surprised*]

ANDREW: We better hurry. [*He picks up her suitcase. She buttons her coat.* ANDREW *stands at the door. She looks around the apartment from center*] You'll be back next week . . .

AGNES: [*With infinite sadness*] Yeah. Next week. [*She straightens the two chairs, putting them side by side, stands behind them, then goes out the door.* ANDREW *pantomimes closing the door. She blocks his hand*] Wait, Andrew . . . [*She looks in the doorway through the apartment one more time, her eyes very wide. She crosses out into the dark corridor*] All right.

ANDREW *closes and locks the door and sticks the note in the door. The light fades on the apartment. Lighting area #2 eases on. The corridor where they are is lit. The up area is lit. Far up left a head sticks out: an old deaf lady in a too large robe she keeps wrapped around herself.*

MRS. HASSELBACH: [*Calling out*] You leaving now?

AGNES: [*Calling up to her*] Oh, hello, Mrs. Hasselbach. Yes, we're leaving now.

ANDREW: [*Tipping his hat embarrassedly*] Hello, Mrs. Hasselbach.

MRS. HASSELBACH: I saw your daughter and son-in-law were here a few minutes ago.

AGNES: [*Loud, but pleasant*] Yes. They came in from New Jersey.

MRS. HASSELBACH: [*Impressed*] Oh, they live in New Jersey now? Nice. I have relations in New Jersey. Where do your daughter and son-in-law live in New Jersey?

AGNES: [*Happily*] Well, nice seeing you, Mrs. Hasselbach. We better be going. All set, Andrew, Andrew? [*Loudly to her*] Hospitals run on a tight schedule.

ANDREW: Nice seeing you, Mrs. Hasselbach.

MRS. HASSELBACH: I didn't notice any taxicabs waiting out front.

AGNES: We didn't call any taxicabs, Mrs. Hasselbach. We're walking.

MRS. HASSELBACH: [*Morbidly*] On a day like this you're walking?

AGNES: It's a lovely day.

ANDREW: Don't let her think I'm a cheapskate.

AGNES: [*Laughing*] And it's not because he's a cheapskate.

MRS. HASSELBACH: [*Offended*] So who said?

ANDREW: Ask her to tell Hildegarde and George we left.

AGNES: [*Kidding coquettishly*] Mrs. Hasselbach, Andrew has something to ask you.

MRS. HASSELBACH: [*Thrilled*] Ooooooo—what is it?

ANDREW: Thanks a lot, Agnes. [*Loud*] Mrs. Hasselbach, when Hildegarde and George come back, would you tell them we left already? We left a note.

MRS. HASSELBACH: [*Musically*] Certainly, Andrew. [*To* AGNES, *flat*] I'll come visit you, dearie. Good luck. [*She exits off right*]

ANDREW: [*A deep breath*] Well, come on. Let's go . . .

The lights fade on the corridor. Area lighting #3 eases on. The whole stage is filled with light, warm, almost golden. She opens the door and steps out into the street. They are down left.

AGNES: [*Surprised*] It's such a lovely day . . . such a pretty day . . . [*She takes his arm, looking all around her. She is down of him. They cross from down left to down right. He is troubled*]

ANDREW: [*Stopping*] Let me call a cab.

AGNES: [*Laughing*] Look at her at the window up there behind the curtain. OooHoo! Hello, Mrs. Hasselbach.

ANDREW: [*Pulling her along*] Now come on!

AGNES: [*As they walk*] And the way she called you. Certainly, Andrew. You think I can trust you?

ANDREW: That's not funny.

AGNES: I'm only kidding. It's such a nice day.

ANDREW: [*Stopping again*] Look, we just can't walk up to the hospital. Let me call a cab.

AGNES: Are you tired?

ANDREW: No.

AGNES: Is the suitcase heavy?

ANDREW: No.

AGNES: Then we'll walk.

They begin walking the outer edge of the stage area in a clockwise direction. Her arm is wrapped tightly in his. Her eyes shine proudly, taking in everything around her. He looks morosely ahead.

ANDREW: [*Muttering*] I don't want them thinking I'm a cheapskate.

AGNES: Who? The hospital? Mrs. Hasselbach?

ANDREW: [*Pulling her sharply back*] Watch out for that car—[*Follows the car till it's out of sight*] Goddam drivers.

They are at the curb. They step down in unison. They hurry across the street, looking both ways.

AGNES: [*As they cross the street*] You were never what they call a John Jacob Astor, but you were never a Collier Brother either. People know you're no cheapskate.

ANDREW: Watch the sidewalk.

They are at the curb, they step up in unison.

AGNES: You know why I want to walk? When we moved here forty years ago, I said it'll be good.

Kids ever get sick, you ever get sick, Roosevelt Hospital is only a block away. We can walk. So in forty years, nobody ever gets sick enough to have to go to the hospital, except me now. So let me get something out of living here forty years. Let me walk to the hospital. [*Stops, gasps*] Look what those kids wrote on the sidewalk. I don't think I ever learned that word till I was—

ANDREW: [*Sounding almost harsh*] I don't think you ever learned that word.

She looks at him, surprised for the second time today at him.

AGNES: That's— [*But they're at another crossing. He hurries her across the street to make the light. She stops him at the curb. They are both out of breath*] That's very sweet.

ANDREW: [*Gruff*] Way they change these lights before you get a chance to get across— Watch the curb.

They step up in unison. They walk in silence till AGNES *smiles.*

AGNES: Remember the old Fred Allen Show on the radio about the house blew up and the old man and woman go flying through the sky and she says, "This is the first time we been out together in twenty years."

ANDREW: [*Laughing in spite of himself*] Fred Allen was very funny.

AGNES: That's us. We haven't been out together like this in a very long while. This is like a date. I feel very young.

ANDREW: You are young.

AGNES: Listen, when your youngest daughter is having her change of life, you know you're not Shirley Temple any more. [*Something catches her eye and she stops him*] Andrew, could we have a cup of coffee?

ANDREW: We can't be late.

AGNES: You want to get rid of me?

ANDREW: NO! But—but hospitals run . . . let's get a cup of coffee.

They walk into the center area. The lights fade down as lighting area #4 comes on, a spotlight on both of them. He sets down the suitcase. They sit on the chairs, AGNES, *left;* ANDREW *right . . .* ANDREW *holds up two fingers. They sit in silence, looking straight ahead. A moment later, they pantomime picking up their cups and begin sipping.* ANDREW *murmurs an automatic thank you to the counter man.*

AGNES: I always liked Bickford's coffee.

ANDREW: [*Frowning*] Is Hildegarde having her change of—of life?

AGNES: [*Sipping*] Ah, she'll be all right.

ANDREW: I wish they didn't fight so much—her and George.

AGNES: You know what I'm gonna tell her Tuesday when she comes with the kids? I was thinking this while I was watching them. I'm gonna tell her she's lucky they still fight. That's the worst part of getting old, I decided. You don't miss the love part, the sex part, the not being able to have kids part. You think that's the part you're gonna miss, but you know it's gonna go. No, the one thing I always thought we'd have, you and me, is the fights. God, didn't we toss some beautiful battles. And the neighbors hammering on the walls. [*Almost angry*] Not even a hot bath or a cup of tea can make you feel as clean as when I'd finish yelling at you and you'd finish yelling at me. That's the worst part of getting old, I decided. You just don't have the energy to fight.

A long pause.

ANDREW: We better go . . .

AGNES: [*Looking straight ahead, lost*] Yeah . . . [*He throws two "dimes" on the counter. He stands up. He realizes he is old. He rises with great difficulty. She watches him, reaches for his hand, but needs both of her hands to lean forward on her knees to help herself rise. She takes his hand. He picks up the suitcase. They walk out very slowly left. She stops him and looks at him. After a moment*] God, Fred Allen was funny, wasn't he?

They turn up and walk out of sight. Light holds briefly on the two chairs.

THE LOVELIEST AFTERNOON OF THE YEAR

a play in one act

John Guare

The Loveliest Afternoon of the Year was first presented by Joseph Cino at the Caffe Cino, New York City, as half of a double bill with *Something I'll Tell You Tuesday,* also by the author, on October 25, 1966, with the following cast:

SHE .... *Karlene Weise*

HE .... *Frank O'Brien*

It was directed by Russ Kaiser. Lighting by Donald Brooks; scenery by Mr. Guare. Production stage manager, George Borris.

BEFORE CURTAIN: Calliope music plays and fades as the curtain rises.

AT CURTAIN: A shy young girl sits center feeding pigeons in the park for want of anything better to do.

Autumn day. Crisp air: The kind called invigorating.

A young man enters left in a panic, sees her, gasps.

HE: I wish you wouldn't feed the pigeons! [*She freezes*] Please. I wish you wouldn't feed the pigeons . . .

SHE: [*Looking at him*] Huh?

HE: I wouldn't mind you feeding—

SHE: [*Stands up, clutching her purse*] Are you a mugger?

HE: —the pigeons— No! I'm not a mugger. I'm just trying to tell you—

SHE: [*Petrified*] Because if you are a mugger, I'll scream. I'll have those cops after you so quick—

HE: I am trying to tell you—

SHE: [*A warning whisper*] I love to scream. I have a very loud voice.

HE: I don't believe that.

SHE: [*Rummaging in her purse*] Where is my tear-gas gun?

HE: [*Terror-stricken*] I don't want you feeding pigeons because I just saw pigeons at the Seventy-ninth Street Entrance and the covey of them—the whole bunch of them—whatever you call a bunch of pigeons—a gaggle—all those pigeons had foam— [*She stops rummaging through her purse*] Were foaming at the mouths.

SHE: [*Simply*] I'll scream.

HE: At the *beaks?* Pigeons were foaming at the beaks—all of them.

SHE: Who the hell are you?

HE: [*Pleading*] I'm very hungry and hate to see you feeding pigeons when I'm hungry. A Crackerjack at this point would be a feast. [*He crosses to her. She crosses down left*]

SHE: I don't believe you.

HE: [*Sits down dejectedly on bench*] You're very perceptive. I—actually, it's the birthday of this child and I promised this child a present and I know at the bottom of that box *is* a present and [*Seductively*] I was wondering if you'd let me have it. [*She's shocked. She swings her bag at him. He ducks to protect himself*] The present! The little plastic present . . .

SHE: Buddy, I bet you got more money in the silk change pocket of that fancy sport coat of yours than I got in my whole imitation alligator bag.

HE: [*Stands up, desperate*] That's not true! My wife takes all my money and she bends it in her teeth so I can't use it. I have to walk everywhere because she bends all my subway tokens. And she has a blue rifle with a silencer on it and shoots my feet so I have to dance this crazy darting dance whenever I come in late. [*He stares at her in desperation. Her jaundiced eye grows curiouser and curiouser. A moment of silence. She bursts out laughing and hands him the Crackerjack*] Please? Believe me? Everything I say is true. Please don't laugh. [*She is so happy. He eats Crackerjacks nervously. He finds a plastic ring in the box. She turns to him*]

SHE: I have been in this city eleven months now and you are the first person I've spoken to. That's spoken to me. Eleven months of silence—till now. I feel like I've just been released from a convent—a goddam convent. No, I'm not laughing at you. I'm a young girl and I'm pretty and nobody ever speaks to me—not even to ask directions—and you're the funniest man I've ever met and I thank you in all the languages there are. Thank you for speaking to me.

HE: Everything I've said is true! [*He turns to go. She touches his arm*]

SHE: Oh God—please? Don't leave.

HE turns to her. They look at each other. HE puts the Crackerjack under the bench and slips the plastic ring on her finger. SHE looks at it. Then at him. A shy kiss that turns into a long kiss. Then they both turn joyously out front to us in the audience.

HE: [*To us*] And that's how we met two Sundays ago. And we walk in the park. This is the third Sunday we've met now. We talk about the future . . .

They walk in place, their arms locked. They are lovers. They talk to us in the audience.

SHE: It's autumn and orange and green and blue and yellow leaves are all over the ground and our feet make a scuffing noise like this . . . chh chh chh . . .

HE: And when we get home, our socks have orange and green and blue and yellow leaf shreds in them stuck in the wool.

SHE: Now wait—his socks and his home. I wear nylons and I have my apartment and he doesn't know where I live and I don't know where he lives. He has his life and I have mine.

HE: Except for Sunday. Today. We walk along and talk about the future. We never mention the past. And our feet make a scuffing noise like this . . . chh chh chh . . .

SHE: Now wait, just because we don't talk about the past, don't get the idea I'm any slut or something. I'm just an Ohio girl. O-H-Ten.

You only talk about the past when you have a past. [*Embarrassed smile*] I must remember not to wear this sweater any more Sundays.

HE: I think she still thinks I'm a mugger.

SHE: I spent all last Monday picking these long shreds of dead grass out of the back of my sweater with a silver tweezer. Oh, I don't care if he's a mugger or not!!! I'm not going to take any chances, no siree, like meeting him at night or during the week when there's nobody around. But Sundays are okay—and, mugger or not—I like him very much. He's really an odd person—an odd duck. But he does tell me awfully funny stories. [*To him, shyly*] Hey, tell me a funny story?

HE: They're not funny stories. They're true!

SHE: [*To us*] True. Listen to this one, please. [*She comes down right*] We're in the Zoo near the polar-bear cage. Now I have never seen a polar bear. [*Excited*] Hey, look at the polar bear! [*She reaches out to touch it through the bars*]

HE: [*Violently pulling her back*] Don't do that!!!!

SHE: I never saw a polar bear, for God's sake. It won't kill me.

HE: Won't kill you! Listen, ten years ago, my sister Lucy was a top debutante—

SHE: [*Impressed*] Really?

HE: And after her coming-out party at the Hotel Plaza back there, Lucy and her two escorts broke into this part of the Zoo and Lucy stuck her arm into this cage—this very cage—just as you did now before I stopped you. And this polar bear— [*Coming down center,* HE *follows the polar bear with an accusing finger. Three count beat*] No, I don't think it was *this* polar bear—this one doesn't look familiar— [*She comes down to him*] But the polar bear —the one ten years ago—bit my sister Lucy's arm right off at the *breast!* [*He turns away covering his face*]

SHE: OMIGOD!

HE: And we heard her screams clear over to the Plaza and the doctors came and [*Petulant*] we all had to leave the coming-out party. I was very young—well, eighteen—

SHE: What did they do?

HE: My parents shrieked, "Do something, do something," and the doctors and all the ambulances which came [*Pantomimes dramatically*] pulled Lucy's arm out of the polar bear's mouth and quickly sewed it back on. Modern surgery can do things like that.

SHE: [*Truly horrified*] What happened?—Omigod!!!!

HE: The arm grew back—thank God—but Lucy never went to another coming-out party again.

SHE: Boy, I can see why not.

HE: Because enormous amounts of—she developed all over her body—enormous amounts of white polar-bear hair and for her comfort we had to ship her to Alaska in a cage.

SHE: [*Suspicious*] You're putting me on.

HE: [*Disparaging her disbelief*] You're from Ohio. You come from a nice little family. You don't understand the weirdness, the grief that people can spring from—

SHE: You're the oddest duck I have ever met.

HE: [*Horrified*] Ducks! You stay away from ducks. I can tell you a story about my aunt—

SHE: [*Hands over her ears*] Please. I don't want to hear any more stories. We said we'd just talk about the future.

HE: [*Crosses down left*] The future! If you came from a past like I have—such as mine—the idea of riding—galloping into a future which would ultimately turn into past [*Turns to her accusingly*] would make you break out in hives and your hair would fall out.

SHE: [*Backs away from him*] Well, it won't fall out and if you keep on talking like that, I'll go home and wash it and massage it and make sure—damn good and sure—that it doesn't fall out. [*He is hurt*] So let's just walk in silence and— [*She extends her hand.* HE *takes it. They face center and walk in place. They smile at each other, remembering they are lovers*] Listen, do you hear that merry-go-round! I always like calliope music. Isn't that what they call it?

HE: Yes. They run on steam. My father fell in one and was scalded to death.

SHE: [*Stops walking*] Please . . . let's just walk and sing. [*They stroll arm in arm. The tune is "Over the Waves." They both hum as they stroll. Then:*] Do you really have a wife?

HE: [*Fingers to his lips*] Shhhh . . . [*He smiles peacefully*]

SHE: [*Over his humming*] That's one story you told me I wonder if it's true. You told me your wife had a blue rifle with a silencer on it and shot you in the feet if you came in late. You told me that three weeks ago. I hope you don't have a wife. I'd hate it if you had a wife.

HE: Since I met you, I don't have a wife.

SHE: Are you divorced?

HE: [*Looking straight ahead*] No.

SHE: But you do have a wife?

HE: [*Beat*] No.

SHE: [*Laughing, snuggling up to him*] At least not a wife who carries a blue rifle and shoots you if you come in late.

HE: [*Stops their walking and turns to her desperately*] I have no wife. Listen, since I met you—these last three Sundays—the last three weeks have had music. I don't mean all violins and trombones. I mean I've been conscious of the rhythm in people's walking, the music in the turning of the turnstiles in the subway at rush hour.

SHE: [*Pulling his hands away*] I thought you said your wife bent your subway tokens so you couldn't go anywhere.

HE: [*Angry*] I don't have a wife and I sneak under the turnstiles. You've saved my life. I've never picked anybody else up before but something about you—the way you fed those pigeons—I wanted to know you, and now . . . now it looks like I'd better thank you. [SHE *smiles, puzzled.* HE *sits her on the bench and kneels in front of her. Both are in profile to the audience.* HE *begins to sing loudly and sweetly to her to the tune of "Over the Waves"*]

> You knelt and you fed
> Little pigeons sweet pieces of bread

[SHE *takes a long embarrassed look out to us in the audience.* HE *continues singing*]

> Those pigeons could kill
> Or at least make you feel very ill

SHE: [*Then, to him, over his singing*] What do you mean—thanking me? Is this the last time? Aren't I going to see you anymore? [*Fiercely*] Don't *sing* so loud!

HE: [*Lost in the romance of his song*]

> We saved both our lives
> Which should lead to husbands and wives

SHE: [*Total embarrassment*] People are staring at you! Please, tell me—why are you thanking me? [HE's *lost in his song. She beats him on the chest to get his attention*]

HE:

> But since we must part
> Feed the pigeon that cries in my heart

SHE: [*Stands up. Crosses behind the bench and faces him*] Are you leaving me?

HE:

> Pigeons that [*Changes key three tones higher*] cry in my heart!

[HE *stops singing suddenly.* HE *stands up. Pause. Quietly*] I can't marry you. I can't see you during the week. I owe you something at least for all the music. Maybe we could meet a few times during the year. Bump into each other? [*She crosses down left, deeply hurt*] Do you like that song?

SHE: I don't give a damn about that song.

HE: [*Comes up behind her*] Do you know who sang that song?

SHE: I don't care who sang that song.

HE: Mario Lanza . . . and right after he sang it, he grew very fat and died. And then a few

months later, his wife took drugs and she died too. Now that's true. You can read that in the newspapers.

SHE: So it's all off . . .

HE: Do you know what my job is? I've never told you.

SHE: So I'll spend the rest of my life feeding pigeons in the park. Maybe I'll meet somebody else . . .

HE: I'm a seeing-eye person for blind dogs. And that's very ironic. Because you've made me see so many things—to hear music in those subway turnstiles at rush hour . . .

SHE: [*Seeing something in the distance off left*] Maybe it's just as well . . .

HE: And I've made you see nothing. [*He turns away*]

SHE: I want to be married. I like you. I'd like to be married to you . . . but I see people like her over there—that incredibly fat woman pushing those two—yes, two—incredibly fat children in that bright blue perambulator with that dog on the leash, and I say what's the use of being married. It obviously didn't make her happy . . . what's the good of marriage?

HE: [*Crossing back to her and peering over her shoulder, holding his breath*] What incredibly fat woman?

SHE: [*Moving down center*] You can't see her now. She just passed behind that rock. Why fall in love with anybody? You just get hurt. I'm young. I'm pretty. I don't need anybody. [HE *suddenly crouches down behind her, holding her legs, peeking out from around her hips*] What are you doing?

HE: That woman—what did you say she was pushing?

SHE: [*Annoyed*] A bright blue perambulator with two enormous young . . . [*Shocked*] that's—your wife, isn't it? You weren't fooling . . .

HE: [*Petrified*] And what did you say she had on a leash?

SHE: [*Squinting to see them in the distance*] A dog . . . a great Great Dane and look—it just bumped its head into that tree and she yanks it back and it falls down against a bench.

HE: The dog has no eyes, has it?

SHE: The dog has no eyes and the children are so ugly and your wife—you have to go home to that every night?

HE *stands up and crosses to the bench.*

HE: We work together. Dogs that can see bite her. [*He sits down on the bench, back to audience*] Oh, I can't divorce her. You can divorce a pretty wife for a homely one, but you can't switch an ugly one for a beautiful one.

SHE *takes a long cross to him and faces him hesitantly.*

SHE: Am I beautiful?

HE: You're very beautiful.

SHE: I really love you.

HE: [*Pulls her down beside him,* SHE *sits left*] Don't let her see us. Under those two babies, she carries the blue rifle with the silencer on it. She'd shoot us if she saw us together.

SHE: And would that be any worse than you leaving me, me leaving you, you going back to her, me going back to my empty apartment? [*She turns away from him*] The last tenant left hundreds of murder mysteries and I'm afraid to read them.

He turns her to him.

HE: My wife's name is Maud. I'm going to call her. [*He kisses her. He stands up, facing down right. Calling*] Maud?

SHE: [*Stands beside him, calls quietly*] Hey, Maud?

HE: [*Louder*] Maud? Maud!!!!

SHE: [*Louder*] Hey, Maud!!!!

HE: [*Happily*] She sees us! She's seen us! Hey, Maud! [*She kisses him all over his face so Maud will see, all the time they both keep waving and jumping up and down*]

SHE: [*Suddenly shocked*] Look! She's lifting the babies out and throwing them on the ground!

HE: The dog rears up and here comes the blue rifle. Hang on.

SHE *is shot by the rifle with the silencer.* SHE *clutches her stomach in amazement.* HE *is shot. They fall onto the bench, leaning over it, their knees almost on the ground.*

SHE: [*Tapping him on the shoulder*] Hey, you really do have a sister Lucy, don't you?

HE: [*In pain*] I do.

They reach for each other, but both fall dead on either side of the bench. When their bodies hit the ground—
                    BLACKOUT

MOON

a play in one act

Robert Heide

Moon was first presented by Joseph Cino at the Caffe Cino, New York City, on February 14, 1967, with the following cast:

SALLY .... *Linda Eskenas*

SAM .... *Victor Li Pari*

INGRID .... *Jacque Lynn Colton*

HAROLD .... *Jim Jennings*

CHRISTOPHER .... *John Gilman*

It was directed by the author. Lighting design by Donald Brooks.

"Each day is dark and dreary,
But the night is bright and cheery."

—From "When the Moon Comes Over
   the Mountain"

sung by MISS KATE SMITH

ENVIRONMENT

*The set should be a maximum of simplicity
and symmetry meant only to "represent"
symbolically an apartment in the Village.*

*The room and the objects in it are of a dark
bilious color.*

*In contrast: blazing white light like the
highpower-intensity lighting that might be
used inside a microscope.*

*On the wall: a square of multicolored plas-
tic with two transistor knobs which represent
dials used in the play to turn sound "on" and
"off."*

*The usual areas and objects: windows
(fourth wall) shelves, tables, seating arrangements, kitchen facilities—a range, coffee pot,
cups etc., the outer hallway and door into
the apartment.*

Characters

SALLY: *a young woman in a loose-fitted black
sweater and skirt. An unmade-up appearance.
Ballet slippers.*

SAM: *a young man. A turtleneck sweater. Baggy
pants. Sandals or slippers. He does not bother
combing his hair.*

INGRID: *a girl dressed in the latest and most
exaggerated of the newest fashion with emphasis on breasts, legs and shoulders. Flat
shoes. She enters and leaves wearing a black
fur coat. Her dress is silver. She carries a
large handbag filled with pill boxes, makeup,
poppers, anything imaginable.*

HAROLD: *a tall young man. Dungarees. A leather
jacket. Heavy workman's shoes that are coated
with mud.*

CHRISTOPHER: *the young man upstairs. White
pants. White shirt. A clean, scrubbed appearance. A look of innocence.*

The characters, with the exception of CHRIS-
TOPHER *and* INGRID, *wear black.*

SAM *is reclining on the daybed, back to audience.* SALLY *sits closely on a low stool.*
SALLY *breathes heavily, twitching and playing
restlessly with her hands. She stares full force
at* SAM *as if she expected some movement on
his part. She makes a quiet, gurgling sound
in an attempt to attract attention.* SAM *remains tight-faced, his head buried deeply in
an open book. It is not discernible whether*

*or not he is actually reading. He seems tense,
withdrawn. Abruptly* SALLY *jumps up as
though she were about to let out a scream.
She paces wildly like a confined beast. Her
body seems to heave as if she even felt
"trapped" in it. Quickly, she switches "on"
the phonograph. Over the speaker system we
hear "2,000 Light Years," The Rolling Stones.*
SALLY *dances wildly attempting to distract*
SAM. *She soon becomes caught in a free-form
dance. Perhaps she is rehearsing for a dance
class. The record begins to repeat itself. About
one-quarter of the way through the second
playing,* SAM *rushes up and shuts "off" the
machine with forceful intent and anger as if
he might begin to let loose a rage at any
given moment.*

SAM: [*Loud, nervous*] There are times I'd like
some . . . silence . . . around here . . . peace
of mind . . . quiet!

Pause.

SALLY: [*Pacing back and forth*] I . . . ha . . . ha
. . . feel nervous . . . fidgety myself. There's
somehow a tenseness . . . a heaviness in the
air. I don't know. I mean . . . [*Slight pause*]
. . . I'm not sure what. Oh nothing. I guess
I'm just a little on edge. [*She sits down*]

Pause.

SAM: [*Sitting*] What happened last night . . .
to us? I don't seem . . . I'm not able to remember . . . anything.

SALLY: [*Getting up. Confronting him*] You became violent . . . you had consumed a great
deal of liquor. It was strange . . . I mean—I
had never known you to become so violent
before. You came at me and . . .

SAM: Let's not talk about it. Let's go into something else . . . some other subject . . . something less . . . strenuous.

SALLY: [*Moving further in to him*] Maybe you're
feeling guilty . . .

SAM: I don't want to talk about it . . . whatever
it is. You want to go into it. I don't! That's
final . . . whatever it is—I say!

SALLY: Whatever what is? [*Pause*] Look! Will
you just talk to me? Talk! [*Pause*] Well, I
can't take it!

SAM: Take what?

SALLY: Your silence. Your withdrawals. Your
. . . noncommunication. I'm fed up.

Pause.

SAM: I'm sick . . . I feel sick. I have a hangover.
My head is bad. All day I . . . oh, what's
the . . .

SALLY: Does that mean we can't talk . . . say
anything? [*Pause*] Maybe you'd rather be

alone. Have your withdrawal . . . alone. It feels stuffy in here. Hot. Close. I can't breathe. Maybe I'd better go out. Get some air . . . [*Beginning to go out. Moves frenetically*]

SAM: [*Gets up. Pulls her down. Slaps her*] Sit down! Relax your complicated little anxieties. Have some coffee. Later we will discuss whatever it is that needs discussing between . . . ourselves . . . between us. For now, let us discuss only everyday things. My mind . . . [*Slight pause*] . . . Later I will be . . . prepared to face . . . to look at the ugliness . . . the abstractions . . . the truth of things. Here, smoke a cigarette.

SALLY: [*Putting cigarette to her mouth and lighting it nervously. Quickly she extinguishes it. Gets up, moving downstage*] Today is not such a good day for me. I feel . . . nervous . . . ha . . . ha. Sometimes I don't know what is happening to me either . . . what is the matter with me. Something stirs up inside of me . . . like some blind instinct I can't control . . . inside of me. I feel I could burst open . . . explode. I get to feeling desperate. I want to run somewhere . . . away. I just don't know . . . where . . . out to the store . . . to a movie.

SAM: [*Behind her*] Just try to remain calm . . . try . . .

Slight pause.

SALLY: [*More composed*] Let's begin again . . . a new conversation . . . not relating to yesterday at all . . . uh . . . tell me . . . I mean . . . let us forget those few moments of anxiety we just had . . . begin again. Calmly. Can we? Can we begin again calmly? Yes. [*Pause*]. SALLY *puts her head into* SAM's *lap as she sits on the floor*] What kind of day . . . tell . . . what it was like . . . earlier . . . what you did . . . what went on?

SAM: [*Reserved*] Just a day. The usual happenings. Statistical reports. Office rituals. Making additions and additions and pushing buttons . . . then . . .

Pause.

SALLY: What?

SAM: [*Half to himself*] Oh, nothing . . . I was thinking about things not really adding up . . . anywhere . . . in my head . . . I mean . . . my life.

SALLY: [*Jumping up*] Is that some personal inference to me? Are you meaning to infer . . .?

SAM: [*In a rage. Grabbing her*] Look, will you shut up before I break your arm? Shut up, I said!

SALLY: [*A pause. A transition*] Did you see today's paper? Did you see the paper . . . read the news today?

SAM: I didn't feel like looking at it . . . my head and all. I had two Bromo Seltzers. What an idiotic party! Stupid people! "Hello, and what do you do with your life, young man? How are you justifying your existence?" Blah! Social events! [*A slight pause.* SAM *moves onto the floor*] Anything in it?

SALLY: What?

SAM: In the paper. Anything in it . . . Today's paper . . . of interest . . . that I should know . . . be informed about?

SALLY: [*Circling around him*] Only the usual everyday chaos . . . problems. Someone slashed open five people . . . with a knife. He tied them up, gagged them and . . . in Texas . . . I think it was. A young man. Eighteen. In a beauty parlor it was. Five women. He said he did it for the publicity, to get his name in the paper. He wanted to be a celebrity . . . become recognized . . . I guess. Something about high food prices having something to do with the high cost of war . . . or something. Some paintings . . . old masterpieces . . . were stolen. [*Coughing and gagging*] Air pollution. [*Slight pause. She gets onto the floor with* SAM. *Lights go down*] The moon. There was a feature article on the moon. [*Laughing to herself*] It's strange . . . funny . . . I mean.

SAM: What's funny?

SALLY: [*Playful*] I mean . . . I was just thinking . . . you can't really talk about the moon the same old way anymore like people used to in Shakespeare's plays and all. You can't say . . . with poetic emphasis . . . "O Moon!" like in *Romeo and Juliet* or [*Singing now, somewhat flatly*] "It's only a paper moon . . . hanging over a cardboard sea" or [*More throaty, matronly, like Kate Smith*] "When the moon comes over the mountain." I'm really crazy about Kate Smith aren't you? God Bless America. [*Low*] Moo . . . Moooooooooon. [*Dramatically, staring forward*] "The cow jumped over the moon . . . hey diddle . . . diddle . . . the cat and his fiddle" or something. The whole idea struck me as just "funny" . . . somehow . . . I guess . . . ridiculous. Moon. Blah! I mean there it is . . . really just there . . . if yah wanna look at it. No longer just some romantic 1920s singsong abstraction . . . something to aspire to . . . to look at from a great distance through a telescope. Wait. Here's a picture. I'll show you. [*Goes to handbag and brings out a newspaper. Sits back down*] Here. [*Pointing*] I mean doesn't it look odd and bumpy and all? See . . . here! Right here in this diagram . . . the *first* moon city. Moon city. They plan to build it . . . to live there . . . a whole lot of people . . . on the moon—eventually . . . soon

. . . in the not-too-distant future. And later, Mars . . . Venus. Whole communities under a huge air-conditioned oxygenized plastic bubble! It's kinduv fantastic . . . I think . . . I mean living up there in space and all . . . I mean not that we're not in space too . . . right here . . . already, now . . . I mean . . . well . . . people . . . the idea of it . . . real people . . . you and I maybe . . . and everybody . . . living on the moon. It would be like being a real pioneer . . . up there. The first experimental community . . . mmmm.

SAM: [*Bursting her dream bubble, he gets up. Brighter light*] So when do we make reservations?

SALLY: Huh?

SAM: [*Going back to his novel*] Reservations . . . numbskull. Plans? Don't we have to make plane or rocket reservations . . . or something?

SALLY: [*Deflated. Sad. Bewildered by her own enthusiasms*] Yeah . . . yes . . . I guess so. [*Pause. Angrily*] Probably it won't happen for some time though . . . even . . . in our own lifetime, I mean. A moon community. Maybe it will.

SAM: [*Taking over the room like an actor*] Probably it will turn out to be just another Levittown, U.S.A. . . . the U.S.A. starring Richard M. Nixon and Spiro Agnew . . . with shopping centers, five and ten cent stores, Grand Unions, bowling alleys . . . super highways, movie houses . . . [*Slightly deflated*] beauty parlors. [*Pause. There is a prolonged silence in which the two characters do not utter a sound. Finally* SAM *brings things back to some notion of reality*] My book . . . the book I was reading . . . did you see it?

SALLY: [*Looking*] What? Oh. Book. Uh . . . no . . . let me see . . .

SAM: [*Looking around the room*] I don't know where it is. [*Finding it*] Ah, here it is! I found it. [*He sits down. Begins to read*]

Pause.

SALLY: Can we hear the radio?

SAM: No! I'd rather it remain "off" if you don't mind. I'd rather listen to just . . . silence.

SALLY: Okay. Okay. Don't yell! [*Slight pause. Nervous*] Would you like some coffee?

SAM: If you're gonna make some . . . if you're having some.

SALLY: [*In kitchen area*] Is the book good?

SAM: What?

SALLY: [*Looking for a confrontation*] Damn you. Will you listen! I said—Is the book you are reading any good?

SAM: It's okay.

SALLY: [*Angry*] Well, why are you reading it if it's just okay? Haven't you any better way to live out your existence?

SAM: How?

SALLY: Mmmm. I don't know. You said once you wanted to paint a picture or something.

SAM: [*Ignoring her last statement*] No. I mean it's good . . . I guess. [*Slight pause*] Anyhow, I know how it ends.

SALLY: [*Curious*] How?

SAM: [*Perturbed*] How?

SALLY: [*Demanding*] How?

SAM: [*Scratching his head*] Mmmmm. Well . . . you really wanna hear? Well . . . this couple have been making it, see. I mean both of them are married . . . I mean each one to someone else like; but they are having this affair, see, with one another, that is. Get it?

SALLY: Yeah. Dope!

SAM: So they are driving back from this weekend on the French Riviera, St. Tropez, I think. It's French . . . the book . . . I mean it takes place, see, in France. Well, the whole book is about how they can't—either one of them—have an affair, even, anymore.

SALLY: What?

SAM: Anyhow, they are suffering from a kind of modern metaphysical boredom . . . and all . . . living in an increasingly mechanized and alienated world. They feel alienated from one another . . . alienated even to themselves . . . see . . . each individual self. They can't get together. . . . Yet they can't really be apart either. He—the man—is married to this famous chanteuse named Cleo who is never at home 'cause she has this . . . her career . . . and so he feels, existentially speaking, that he is in her eyes—like an object, like an old table or chair—very Sartrean. I mean, they talk a lot about life being one big nothing and all . . . in the book . . . [*Slight pause*] . . . or was it Heidegger?

SALLY: [*Under her breath*] Heidegger.

SAM: See, he, the main character, is a philosophy student. So anyhow, he doesn't feel related to this wife who is so obsessed . . . uptight . . . having this "overneed" for her career. She sings these very sorrowful songs; [SALLY *jumps up making a screeching sound. Looks stage front. Looks into fourth-wall mirror*] and, when she's not doing that, she is looking in the mirror—checking out her image and all. Well, she doesn't like sex either.

SALLY: [*Loudly*] Who? Who!?

SAM: Cleo . . . even though she's supposed to be some sex image to her fans. They write her dirty, suggestive letters which she, in turn, answers. [SALLY *mimics letterwriting*] See. It makes Henri—that's our hero's name—feel disgusted, even though he never brings the subject forth . . . out into the open. So Henri takes up with Françoise . . . see. She's married . . . kinduv . . . to this uncle of hers who's this novelist . . . older. Anyhow, he knows about the affair. In fact, he encourages it. See, he's bored too . . . with everything.

SALLY: [*Worried*] Then what happens?

SAM: [*Running amuck*] Well, it gets complicated 'cause everywhere they go . . . well, it gets more and more frenetic . . . the tension . . . the plot . . . hysterical . . . and Françoise thinks she is pregnant by some Oriental houseboy too. [*He grabs* SALLY. *They play out the "game" of the novel fully. They mimic driving a car together*] Well . . . being bored and all, she drives on this highway into this Mack truck . . . [SALLY *screams*] . . . in a red Porsche—sort of like James Dean. It ends with a double funeral where Cleo sings "Chanson de morte"—"The Song of Death" . . . [*Lights down. At this point we hear the voice of Cleo singing in French over the loud speaker with full orchestra. This goes on for one full minute. Lights up*] . . . but everyone is bored even there too. I mean, what does death mean if you're really hip and all? Anyhow, to make a long story short, Cleo meets the uncle . . . at the funeral, which the uncle paid for . . . heh . . . heh . . . and they grab hands . . . [SALLY *and* SAM *grab hands. Hollywood music ensues loudly. They "act out" a "Hollywood ending"*] . . . touch one another. They feel . . . well . . . through the death of Françoise and Henri they have a reawakening . . . a kinduv catharsis into . . . being able to "really" feel and all. You know, like maybe things are not so bad after all? So anyway, they go off and make it or something. I mean it ends on a kinduv positive note . . . y'know . . . [*Music off*] but not too positive . . . he he . . . he. Hey, are you listening?

SALLY: I thought you said you just read the end?

SAM: [*In a fury*] Yeh, I did . . . but I read this review of it in *The Village Voice*. I mean, they gave the whole story and all. That's what made me wanna read it. They said it was . . . well . . . subtle in its exploration of character relationship—that's what made me wanna read it. I mean . . . [*Intense, angry*] people feel alienated They don't know how to get together Oh, Christ . . . I don't know! Don't ask me questions about what I'm reading. I lost my goddamn place!

SALLY: [*Dreamy*] Maybe they'll make a movie out of it.

SAM: Yeah . . . they are already with Jean Seberg and Marcello . . . no . . . it's not him . . .

somebody like him . . . Belmondo . . . no. It's what the hell is his name? Trig . . . Trig . . . Trintignant . . . Jean Louis Trintignant. I wish I had a name like that. Yeah. [*Movie soundtrack music pours forth. The lighting goes kaleidoscopic*] Brigitte Bardot will be Cleo and maybe Charles Boyer for the uncle. Ha ha. A supertechnicolor, panavistic . . . spectacle . . . in pornovision!

On the word "pornovision" SAM *and* SALLY *roll around on the floor together in mock copulation. They breathe heavily, remaining on the floor. They make sounds, then separate, exhausted, still on the floor.*

SALLY: [*Entering Movieland*] Jean Louis Trintignant. Wasn't he in *The Sleeping Car Murder*? Didn't we see that at the Eighth Street—or was it the Garrick?

SAM: Did we see that? Did we see that one?

SALLY: Yeah . . . I remember . . . you fell asleep in it.

SAM: Oh, was it good?

SALLY: Okay . . . I guess . . . It's not my type of thing.

SAM: Who got murdered?

SALLY: Murdered?

SAM: Yeah. *Sleeping Car Murder*. Murder mystery. Who got murdered?

SALLY: [*Getting up*] Six people . . . I think . . . two homosexual lovers plot the whole thing to get this lottery check from this actress . . . Simone Signoret. She is in love with one of them—not knowing he's gay . . . or knowing . . . and thinking she can change his direction. I don't remember which. Ha.

SAM: [*Moving restlessly*] Oh, yeah . . . and one of them works for the cops or something . . . as a detective . . . and he's working to try to solve the case!

SALLY: Then . . . you weren't sleeping?

SAM: Well, partly.

SALLY: [*Running after him, tickling him*] How does it end? I'll *murder* you, you ass! How does it end? Tell me.

SAM: [*Rolling on to the floor*] Stop it! Cut it out! Stop!

SALLY: [*Straddling him*] They don't make it. They're gonna live happily ever after on some South Sea island in a rose-covered cottage on Simone Signoret's money . . . but they don't make it . . . they get caught and they don't make it. Ha! Ha!

SAM: [*Half sarcasm, half humor. Getting up*] Tough! Nobody makes it, bitch.

SALLY: [*Serious now. Angry*] They don't? Why not?

SAM: [*Flying into fantasy*] 'Cause I say so and I'm the President and I have the power and I'm gonna blow up the whole world anyway. Blow it up. [*Throwing imaginary hand grenades*] Boom. BOOM! Boom.

SALLY: [*Confronting*] You're a paranoid-schizophrenic living in Greenwich Village with delusions of grandeur and an inclination toward anticipating disaster out of every situation. Ha. How's that for a penny analysis?

SAM: [*Furious*] I could be Jesus Christ and you wouldn't know the difference.

SALLY: [*In a full-fledged argument*] He was another paranoid too.

SAM: Say's who?

SALLY: [*Moving in circles around* SAM] Albert Schweitzer, baby—in this book I read—*A Psychiatric Study of Jesus.* He said there is a lot of evidence to support that old J.C. may have been another psychotic with another Christ complex out to save the whole world just like you . . . or maybe destroy it.

SAM: [*Throwing his arms around her as if they were about to ascend into space*] Boom. Boom. Boom. Then we could go live . . . pioneer on the old green cheese moon.

SALLY: [*Breaking off. Sitting*] Ah, who cares? I'm sick of the whole world anyhow. Why pretend anything else?

Pause.

SAM: You sure you read that book correctly?

SALLY: Whadahyamean?

SAM: I mean you're always reading things into things. Your imagination. Your fantasy projection transferences. [*No reply. Pause*] How about lighting a joint? [*Goes to kitchen, where he gets joint*]

SALLY: [*After him in the kitchen*] Go ahead! You light it! Transcend existence. Catatonize yourself. What do I care!

SAM: [*Grabbing her. Pulls her down*] What!?

SALLY: Go ahead! Break my arm too.

SAM: Nobody's breaking your arm. [*Slight pause. SALLY waves her arm at SAM in jest and anger*] Let's sit down and keep quiet . . . shut up . . . for awhile.

SALLY: [*A last stand*] You'd like to avoid all communications with me . . . just blow pot all day long . . . reach Nirvana or something. Who knows what or where you want to get to? The moon. Dreams. Movies. I'm sick of it all. It's all just *lies* anyway. [*Hysterically*] Lies! [*Screaming*] Lies!

SAM: . . . Now, calm down. You're having one of your free-floating anxiety attacks again. Just calm down sweets . . . love . . . valentine.

SALLY: [*Biting*] At least it's not free-floating paranoia or simple-schizophrenia or some swimming-in-a-sea-of-ambiguity . . . like you.

SAM: Your terminology is really flying. You sound like some coffee klatch in the dorm after Psych I . . . at NYU. The girl who's always waving her hand in the last row who knows all the answers but none of the . . . now, just calm yourself. Here. [*Hands her a joint*] Light it. [*She does*] It's not the answer—I know— any more than acid, speed, T.H.C. . . . or going to the moon. But it does manage to keep me calm . . . sometimes. [*He sits*] My nerves. My body is still depressed from all that rotten alcohol we drank last night. Put on some music . . . on the machine. Indian. [*Gets onto the floor in Yoga position*] I want to meditate . . . concentrate . . . groove . . . with something . . . spiritual.

SALLY: [*Standing over him*] Do I have to meditate? [*She puts on Indian raga music. They sit, eyes closed, attempting meditation. After a moment*] I can't concentrate on anything today. Somehow . . . I . . .

SAM: Shut up! Meditate . . . or just keep your trap shut! I can't talk anymore!

They remain silent, listening to the music, passing a joint back and forth to one another. After a long moment, INGRID *and* HAROLD *are heard by the audience, as it were, moving down the corridor outside the apartment. They are pushing and shoving one another physically close to violence.*

INGRID: [*Berating, loudly, trumpeting*] What kind of people don't put their names on the bell, I ask you?! [*She passes back and forth looking at various doorways*] I think what they told us was four R—that means rear! These stairs are killing me. Maybe we should go back down . . . go have a drink somewhere by ourselves. Oh, wait. Here. [*Looking*] There's nothing more embarrassing than knocking on the wrong door. [*She pulls out a nose popper and begins sniffing, trying to get higher*] That man was naked and I think he was having sex in there . . . with a boy too. Sex has a very decisive, odoriferous smell I tell you. Don't you have anything to say? [*Moving close*] I suppose you would like to have joined in or something, into the sexual act, but yet you can't raise it up when it comes to me. [*At this point* INGRID *reaches into her handbag. She pulls out a pillbox and begins gulping pills. She offers one to* HAROLD. *He refuses*] Now try to compose yourself. [*Slight pause*] Act natural. Try not to indicate . . . to show . . . that we are having marital difficulties. It's not in good taste to wear your problems out in the open for public consumption as it were . . . this being a social situation. Now try to remember these simple rules . . . Oh . . . ha . . . ha . . . Here we are. Hello. Hello. [*Loud, demanding*] Anybody home? Hello. Shhh. Shh.

SALLY: [*Disrupted*] Who's that?

SAM: [*Trancelike*] What? . . . Shhhh . . . Quiet! I'm thinking . . .

SALLY, *realizing a presence, gets up and turns off the music. Puts on ballet slippers.*

INGRID: [*A false cheerfulness*] Uh . . . Hi—You . . . uh . . . left your door open. Can we come in? [*Examining the place suspiciously*] You shouldn't leave your door open . . you know, with all the murders, rapes and robberies going on . . . in the city . . . uh . . . heh . . . mmmm.

An awkward, silent, heavy tension takes over the room. The two couples stalk one another.

SALLY: [*Polite, pulling herself together, breaking the freeze*] Oh . . . well . . . come in . . . sit down . . . wherever you can . . . there's not much room. Let me have your coat.

INGRID: Yes. [*Removes her coat and scarf.* SALLY *disposes of it quickly. Goes to* HAROLD] Harold, your jacket!

HAROLD: [*Staring downward. A tight lip*] I prefer to keep it on . . . thank you.

INGRID: [*Moving toward couch*] A cold. Harold is afraid of catching a cold, aren't you Harold? [*No answer. A false merriment*] I said to Harold I bet you people forgot about having us over . . . er . . . the party . . . last night? Remember? ha . . . ha . . . Well, we almost didn't come. [*An awkward pause*] We had your address . . . your phone number. We were gonna call . . . first. We tried. Didn't we, honey? Didn't we try?

HAROLD: [*Dull, not listening*] Yeah.

INGRID: [*Anxious. Somewhat terrified*] You've had your phone disconnected. I said to Harold . . . "I bet you forgot." It was just a casual, meaningless suggestion on your part. Just drop by. And here we are . . . Heh . . . mmm. [*Slight pause. To* SAM] Harold would rather have his face in the TV or be screwing nuts and bolts into his machines. It was my decision to venture out. [*Cornering* SALLY] You can still renege . . . shoo us off . . . if you want to be alone. Tee . . . hee.

SALLY: [*Trying to place her guests in her mind*] Oh . . . uh . . . no . . . uh . . . we don't mind. We were just . . . sitting . . . listening to some music . . . weren't we? Why . . . uh . . . don't you sit . . . ?

INGRID: I'll just sit down. [*Accidentally falling*] . . . OOooooooooooooo!

HAROLD: [*Half to himself*] The clumsy never succeed.

INGRID: [*Getting up. Menacing*] What did you say?

HAROLD: I said, "The clumsy never succeed." Just an old saying from my mother.

INGRID: [*Angry, staring long and hard*] Your mother! She certainly didn't teach *you* anything . . . about success . . . in the *real* world. [HAROLD *moves toward her with violent intent. Abruptly, she switches her attitude to "the coquette," realizing she is with others*] What an interesting and cute apartment you have. Ha. Ha. Very bizarre. Very interesting. I'm sure our turning up is a complete surprise . . . I said to Harold . . . it was a casual suggestion . . . on your part. [*Desperate*] Lots of people write their names and addresses on little pieces of paper and hand them to people they meet . . at parties . . . never really expecting . . . acknowledgment . . . or a visitation.

SALLY: It doesn't matter. We were very drunk. Part of the evening is a complete blur . . . in both of our minds. Yes? [HAROLD *walks blindly into* SALLY. *She stares full force at him, then breaks it off*] Something happened which we don't remem . . . ber.

This last statement is followed by a long, dead silence in which the four characters stare blankly, bewilderedly at one another. An uncomfortable tension takes over the room.

INGRID: [*Gazing at* HAROLD *and* SALLY] Er . . . ah.

SALLY: [*Snapping her fingers nervously*] We . . . uh . . . were having some coffee. [*Pause*] Would anybody like some coffee . . . or something?

HAROLD: [*Following her*] Yeah.

INGRID: [*Nervous, trying to make conversation*] Harold doesn't say much . . . really . . . in company. [*Cornering, advancing toward* SALLY *in kitchen*] We were just married . . . a year it is. We're just beginning to get used to one another . . . understand our position in relationship to one another as to who has the upper hand and all that stuff. He's a little shy . . . awkward . . . ha . . . ha . . . in a social situation. [*Slight pause. Leaves kitchen. Sits next to* SAM *on sofa*] What time did you people leave last night's festivities?

SALLY: [*Moving away from* HAROLD's *steady advances*] Time? What . . . time? I'm not sure.

INGRID: [*Angry, sarcastic*] We left early. Harold got sick . . . mixing the drinks. Didn't you, Harold? Didn't you get sick last night?

HAROLD: [*With controlled violence, a smirk across his face*] Yeah.

INGRID: That's why we left early. I mean as opposed to staying on and on. Harold feels... that it's better to leave before things ... people ... become decadent as they very often do at parties. He wouldn't like it. ... [*She moves closer to* SAM, *putting her arm around his neck seductively*] I mean ... if somebody tried to screw ... I mean rape me ... made advances or anything. [*More excited*] Harold is capable ... I mean Harold might ... it is within his capacity to murder someone. Didn't you say you might murder someone, Harold? If someone, I mean, made advances on me ... on my person ... at a party ... or someplace?

HAROLD: Yeah.

INGRID: [*Going into her purse*] I carry this tear-gas gun. My Aunt Emma gave it to me. She sent it through the mail all the way from Kansas—that's where I'm from ... mmm. You never know about men, she says, in New York City. [*She gets up and pulls out gun, pointing it bluntly at* SAM] Yah wanna see it?

HAROLD: [*Grabbing her. They wrestle for the gun*] Gimme! ... that!

INGRID: Harold! You're hurting me. It might go off. Harold!

HAROLD: [*Twisting her arm. Throwing her down*] Sit down!

INGRID: My arm!

SALLY: [*Ignoring the situation, trying to remain cool*] I think coffee is ready.

SAM: [*Quietly*] You people like music?

INGRID: [*Going up to* HAROLD] We should apologize.

HAROLD: [*Breaking from her*] I'll do my own apologizing if there's any to be done. [*To the rest of the room*] What my wife, Ingrid, is trying to communicate to you all is that I have ... a kind of ... violent personality ... an uncontrollable temper. When I get worked up ... [*Pause. He sits down. Lights go dim*] You see, I was a Marine ... in the Marines. [*Slight pause*] Of course, even as a kid—well, I'm not sure what it is. [*Slight pause*] Back in Texas, where I come from ... a man was murdered ... I mean to say that I don't conceal any longer this nightmare truth. I loved him ... I guess. He was my buddy ... in the Marines and after. We went everywhere ... together Well, one night ... we shared a double bed ... I ... [*Slight pause*] He was asleep. I was fooling ... kidding around. I put a pillow over his face. He had asthma or something ... respiration trouble. Anyway, in the fooling around ... he stopped breathing. I took the pillow off his face. His eyes were open ... staring ... at me. Later, there was an inquisition you see. I was set free. It was

decided that what he had had was a heart attack. Somehow, in me ... I knew that ...

INGRID: [*Jumping up abruptly*] Oh ... Stop it! Stop telling everyone you meet that morbid and ludicrous story. You don't know ... you can't be absolutely certain that it wasn't an accident. You said that he had a heart condition ... or something. Why continue to implicate yourself any further? This wallowing in guilt.

HAROLD: [*Still in the story. Moves up*] There is ... there was ... an intention ... somewhere ... in me. There must have been. I don't understand.

INGRID: [*Quickly. Going at him like an attorney who is onto a victim*] We understand! It is obvious ... psychologically obvious ... a clear deduction that you were in love with this man ... that because of convention, this love ... you could not consummate it. It turned then into hatred. You hated yourself and him for remaining unfulfilled ... repressed.

HAROLD: [*Loud*] Shut up!

INGRID: [*Moving in tightly*] Why lie! You can't express ... the truth. So you choose me with all my convenient sexual fears to share your guilt ... to continue to support your image of manhood ... punishing me for what was done to you by your family. I'm tired of playing the role of mother-substitute. I'm ...

HAROLD: Shut up, I say ... you bitch! [*He grabs her throat, pulls her to her knees and begins to strangle her with intent to kill. We hear* INGRID *make a gurgling sound.* SAM *and* SALLY *watch frozen in terror*]

SAM: [*Finally*] This will have to stop! [SAM *pulls* HAROLD *off of* INGRID *bodily, forcing him to yield his grip. They are on the verge of a fist fight*] You will both have to leave ... just leave!

INGRID: [*Still on the floor*] I'm sorry. Please. Let us stay. Just for a moment. Till we pull ourselves together. [*An awkward silence follows.* INGRID *stays on the floor for a long while. Finally she gets up, goes to kitchen, gets a drink, sits back on sofa*] Harold has vivid fantasies. He goes to an analyst three times a week. These stories ... he ... prefabricates them to bring attention to himself. There is no basis in truth to what has been said.

SAM *moves to the phonograph.*

SAM: [*Nervous*] Do ... uh ... you like music? I'll put on a record.

SALLY: Not now.

INGRID: [*Sitting nervously, humiliated*] Yes ... play it ... anything.

They listen through a three-minute record. Dave Clark 5, "Do You Love Me." During the *record the lights go up.* INGRID *swallows about seven different pills.* HAROLD *and* SALLY *stare at one another.* HAROLD *is attracted.* SALLY *is strangely drawn to his look.* SAM *begins to do a shaking rock and roll dance. Each character is caught in his own private world, lost, lonely, bewildered. At the end of the record,* SALLY *puts on her coat and hat.*

SALLY: [*Quickly*] Er . . . ah . . . ha . . . ha. Would . . uh . . . you all excuse me for a moment? I think there is something I forgot to get at the store. [*She leaves*]

INGRID: [*Desperate*] Where is she going?

SAM: [*Half dazed*] She said to the store. She sometimes leaves abruptly.

INGRID: Her leaving seemed peculiar just then. [INGRID *looks at* HAROLD. *He is on the floor lying down, legs outstretched, reading* SAM'S *book.* INGRID *gets onto the floor herself. She heaves convulsively, making sounds. She has taken too many drugs. The room spins in her head. She gets up after a long moment*] I don't know. I'm not sure why . . . we came here. Harold . . . we must go . . . home . . . now. [*Getting her things*] I feel a sudden panic seizing hold of me here. [*Going up to* SAM] I am sorry. Perhaps we will see you again . . . sometime. Harold. Leave one of our cards. [*They put on their things and proceed to leave*] You invited us from the party. [*She menaces* SAM *a final time*] I said to Harold earlier that you had probably forgotten. Goodbye. Come along, Harold.

SAM *waves halfheartedly with his hand, his back turned to the audience. There is a long moment in which he walks about the room examining its various sections. He goes to the phonograph, but does not play it. He walks to window area (fourth wall), staring straight out. We hear traffic sounds. Finally, he lies down, exhausted. Enter slowly* CHRISTOPHER, *in white pants and sweater. He carries a loaf of bread in a pan.*

CHRISTOPHER: Er . . . ah . . . hello. [*No reply.* SAM *is asleep. Finally, startled by a strange presence,* SAM *jolts up, confronting* CHRISTOPHER] We . . . my friend and I . . . we made some bread . . . upstairs. We just moved in. We had nothing to do today . . . so we made . . . we made some bread. [*Slight pause*] There is a funny smell in here. Well, I'll just leave it then. [*Begins to leave*]

SAM: [*Puzzled*] No. Wait.

CHRISTOPHER: Yes?

SAM: [*Goes to him*] Did you want something?

CHRISTOPHER: [*Quietly*] No.

SAM: You moved in . . . upstairs . . . in the vacant rooms?

CHRISTOPHER: Yes.

SAM: What is your name?

CHRISTOPHER: Christopher. My friend is Joe. He's asleep.

SAM: Oh. [*Pause*] Would you like some wine . . . or coffee?

CHRISTOPHER: [*Hesitant*] No. I must get back. I'm a painter . . . see. I want to sort of get to bed early so I can get up . . . in the morning . . . to get the light. The skylight . . . the light here . . . upstairs . . . is the reason we took the space, it being on the top floor. I need it for my painting. The daylight. Well, as I said, I wanted to bring you down one of the loaves . . . we made two . . . see who was living underneath . . . introduce myself . . . So . . .

SAM: What do you paint?

CHRISTOPHER: [*Moving about the room, intense*] Circles mostly. Just circles. You'll come up and see them sometime. I'm kinduv *obsessed* with circles, see. They are meant—I guess—to represent . . . ha . . . ha . . . the earth, sun, moon and all the other planets in the heavens, the solar system. I use many brilliant colors, electric colors, red, green . . . yellow . . . they hurt your eyes if you look at them too long. [*Pause*] Well, we heard the music. We thought you might like some. We'll see you again . . . come back down. Maybe tomorrow you'll meet my friend. [*Exits*]

There is a moment in which SAM *stares at the bread. He picks it up, putting it in the bread box. Enter* SALLY.

SAM: [*After a moment, softly*] Where did you go?

SALLY: I don't know. I just had to leave . . . get out . . . get some air. I brought back some milk. [*Puts down paper bag she is carrying*]

SAM: They've gone.

SALLY: Yes, I see.

SAM: I don't remember ever having met them. Do you? . . . at that party?

SALLY: No . . . I . . . [*Pause*] I don't want to talk about them . . . now.

SAM: What is it you want to do?

SALLY: I don't know.

SAM: What were you thinking about . . . what were you doing . . . what happened to you while you were out? Tell me. Talk to me. Philosophize . . . anything. I feel . . .

SALLY: [*Entering the game*] Oh . . . not much happened . . . really. I walked around the same block two, three times. I thought, if only there were someplace to go . . . to . . . to run away to. I thought, I would like to leave this city, go back to St. Louis where I came from—all the time knowing, inside, I could never go back there anymore. Backwards. I said to myself, "There is nowhere to go, nowhere left for you to run to." I passed by the newsstand, on the square. The headline on the evening paper glared up at me, saying, "A Man Walks on the Moon." [*She laughs*] It struck me as being funny somehow. Then, I ran back here . . . right then. Right away. That's all.

SAM: [*Lightly in a matter-of-fact manner*] One day, I suppose, as you said earlier tonight, there will be this community . . . a community of men who will be living on the moon in a plastic bubble, but it will not seem either strange or funny at all, to anyone who will just . . . be . . . there—in that situation. And things will not be that much different from what they are . . . right here . . . right now. The truth is none of us will really ever know anything about the deeper, darker mysteries of existence. We will never know . . . never . . . never really be certain about what it is we really are searching for in this life anyway . . . in this world. The endless questions . . . thoughts . . . that well up deep down inside of us. As of now . . . at this point in time and space we remain uncertain . . . except for having reached the moon—moo-oon. Hallelujah!

SALLY: [*Holding him—a determined, firm attitude*] But if we could be certain, maybe, someday, of something more . . . than just the beating of our hearts. Listen! [*She puts his head to her breast*] Boom. Boom. Boom. One day they will just stop pounding . . . but for now . . . they just go on . . . and on. Boom. Boom. Boom.

SAM:	SALLY:
Boom	Boom
Boom	Boom
Boom	Boom
Boom	Boom

—Blackout—

FUTZ

a play in one act

Rochelle Owens

Futz was first presented (for one performance) at the Tyrone Guthrie Workshop, Minneapolis, on October 10, 1965. It was first presented in New York City by Ellen Stewart at La Mama ETC on March 1, 1967, with the following cast of the La Mama Troupe:

NARRATOR	*Beverly Atkinson*
CYRUS FUTZ	*John Bakos*
MAJORIE SATZ	*Beth Porter*
OSCAR LOOP	*Seth Allen*
BILL MARJORAM	*Michael Warren Powell*
ANN FOX	*Mari-Claire Charba*
SHERIFF TOM SLUCK	*Peter Craig*
FATHER SATZ	*Robert Thirkield*
MOTHER SATZ	*Mari-Claire Charba*
BROTHER NED SATZ	*Victor LiPari*
MRS. LOOP	*Marilyn Roberts*
BUFORD	*Peter Craig*
SUGFORD	*Michael Warren Powell*

It was directed by Tom O'Horgan. Setting by Saito; lighting by Laura Rambaldi; technical assistant, Howard Vishinsky. Music by Mr. O'Horgan.

Futz was subsequently presented by Harlan Kleiman in association with David Cryer, Albert Poland and Theodore Hoffman at the Theatre De Lys, New York City, on June 9, 1968, with the following cast from the La Mama Troupe:

NARRATOR	*Sally Kirkland*
CYRUS FUTZ	*John Bakos*
MAJORIE SATZ	*Beth Porter*
OSCAR LOOP	*Seth Allen*
BILL MARJORAM	*Fred Forrest*
ANN FOX	*Mari-Claire Charba*
SHERIFF TOM SLUCK	*Peter Craig*
FATHER SATZ	*Jerry Cunliffe*
MOTHER SATZ	*Mari-Claire Charba*
BROTHER NED SATZ	*Victor LiPari*
MRS. LOOP	*Marilyn Roberts*
SUGFORD	*Fred Forrest*
BUFORD	*Peter Craig*

Music and direction by Tom O'Horgan. Scenery by Nicholas Russiyan; costume supervision by Sandra Jones; lighting by John Patrick Dodd; sculpture by Saito. Presented by special arrangement with Lucille Lortel Productions, Inc.

Now concerning the things whereof ye wrote unto me: It is good for a man not to touch a woman.

—I CORINTHIANS 7:1

SCENE I

NARRATOR: Let's give it a strange passion to a story, some handyman handy in the barns with animals—"someone to watch over him"— somethings, the udders of the moo-moo especially. No stupid pretty girl to rely on him, like a homemade stunt between his feet, to knock up his knees—bad onions—spoiling him eternally.

Small fetid room, obvious barnlike but still a small room with lots of oily automobile rags and other signs of the terrible city existence, brewed still more stinky with the worst the country has to offer: dead grassy worms; horses' shit; small portions of a moldy outhouse; summer brooms; women's drawers; rubber suits for working in the water; etcetera. Anything you can think up naturally. Cy Futz, a Scandinavian sort of big fellow, wearing new dungarees, bell bottom—they could be overalls —comes in filled with a sexual dream; it does not bear in the least to anything real in terms of yours or Cy's world. It's pure sickness but in its pureness it's a truth. Sitting down on a wet broken step he says:

CY: O the cow's tits are bigger and I know it's wrong, but young uns never know the difference between an animal's or a woman's hipbones, so soft like my socks, freshwashed like new kids' hoofs. O I could sing! OOOOOooo-OOOOOooooOOOO LooLoooooooooLoooo-ooo Looy [*Loud*] Looy loy Lord Lord I love you God! [*Normal voice*] And I have no hate for anybody, but wanting to love the animals the way I do. *They,* mean folks, hate my face. I turn around the corners and make fun on their asses, no tickle does theirs feel like my own good one as I sing tears in the sow's belly. With their fried eggs for wives, they know no song.

NARRATOR: Again he sings his ooos and loooooos intermingled with a belch and a mock fart and ending with three very loud "Lords." All the time he's buttering his wrists with his red hands, making bird and other noises, he is very excited and seems absolutely certain to explode all his love or whatever over the world which is the room where he is in now. Now she comes in, Miss Majorie Satz, about twenty-seven years old, tall with a square worldly, insulted once maybe, body. Her coarse red hair is combed up in a sophisticated way which is sweetly silly in retrospect to her food-stained gingham, typical farm girl get-up.

MAJORIE: Hello, bastady man. Yus big man-bloke, I missed you at the greengrocer, yus said that you would come, yus said so, and I painted my big toe too for yu. [*Giggling*] Yu man-bloke, old Swede man.

NARRATOR: Cyrus is looking at her and is vexed at her, probably Cy was always squinnied by her, probably because she obviously is a woman in the very dreamy sensual way which he only wants his animals to be. Gentle sick man he is. He hoots at her.

CY: Hallas, Majy, ya French dancer! You woman of ten beds and manure heaps, yus stinking human woman with only cat mouths for tits and a baby paw for your arse. I did not want to see you; you told me a foul story the last time that I saw you. Not again mind you do I want that shit! Always you are pretending to be my friend and better yet a hole for me to dive in, but I'd rather sink my pick in turd, cleaner my Lord more than you, Maj!

NARRATOR: Majorie moves backwards and starts to hum the French anthem.

MAJORIE: I'll pick up my skirt right now if yu want. I'll get on my heels and elbows, old farmer, yus not so old yu know, only forty, there are whut's younger men than yu who'd like to take me to a movie, strongir and slimmir than yu, so why make me hurt your chest —an' don't I buy you fodder for your sick love, Amanda the sow, so she could be a better one for yu? Even I know, who likes yu, how bad it is to sleep with a pig! Unnatural, like in the Bible, it's piggish—that's where the word comes from yus know, piggish—from a pig yugh yugh sooo evil. Yu smell so baad it is no joke—

CY: Go forget about it and your checks won't be nervous—put your nose out of my business, disgusting girl. I like Amanda because she's good. Pig or not. And I don't stink that's your lie—any much more than you or the boys that take you in the fields.

MAJORIE: [*Hatefully*] That's your own dirtty story 'nd it makes me nasty towards yu—I can't feel bad for your dread and doom—yu sleep with the unimals bitter bitter unholy unholy.

NARRATOR: Cy pushes her from behind then stoops and picks up a dirty broom begins to sweep her flanks with a mock lust also singing a very low song in a Celtic tune. She covers her ears and shrieks!

MAJORIE: [*Shrieking*] Yeeeiiiiiey oyu big man-bloke!

NARRATOR: He snaps her rope belt with his left hand and slaps her face—not hard—with the right. He pushes her ahead of him and they both go behind the half-rotten wall which was once an old outhouse.

Animal grunts sound and lights are dimmed.

SCENE II

NARRATOR: Look at the old rotten wall—behind it here are Cyrus and Maj and yugch! a sow! Amanda! The animal that's sure to steal forever Cy's heart never to marry yus, her, Maj, sweet flower, woman with a wholesome grin and no hair on the chin, sallow woman with a cantaloupe seed in her belly and toes that are canary yellow. Ooopph! [NARRATOR *shapes his hands into a cup form and feeds the sounds of grunts and human voice to the audience*]

MAJORIE: Pechhh *so* indecent! I'd live in shame if the village ever knew what I'd done.

CY: Fahhh! My woman, the people need never know what you done, anyways they would want the full freedom to be able to do what you done. Girl, peachy sweet currant stop being afraid, even the sow won't tell!

NARRATOR: Maj tears, she's sore afraid.

MAJORIE: Yu make it wus tan it is mentionin' the pig—she does not know anyting about it and she did not feel soft like you said but like an old razor on my feet. *O O O so indecent I am* and now the filty dreams'll come! O Gods help meee that we shoulda both laid with a sow!

NARRATOR: Maj carries about awhile with hands scratching out her Lord from the sky, pushing him into her soul, trying to wring his sweat from the skinny body, trying hard hard to have his water wash the dinny sin from her wretched body. Lust for animals is like a run in spring rain, sniggle. Lewd lewd, foosh foosh, and she calls on all the idols and the true God to make the slop go away.

CY: Now fish stop, stop fish, nobody knows and the pig won't tell.

MAJORIE: Stop stop stop! Yus mean rat, your modern sin has killed me!

CY: Ain't no modern sin, old as your Bible, lay down with a calf somebody did and did get no punishment from God like your village will give you, cluck, if you don't stop your sirens blowing. Shit your mouth up, Majorie! You're makin' me sound funny in my own ears and I have faith for my love of the animals with hoofs and corncob appitite. Can't you really see—it is no wrong. They laugh more real than the mayor and your mother! *Brooey* to the devil for the bad conscience you feel, say *phat phat* to it. It don't pay.

MAJORIE: Your diggnitty is like sloppy ole shoes! But good luck to me soon as I get away from evil—never again! Os os never agin piggying myself like that.

NARRATOR: She gets up from the bed of wet paper and rags, smoothing her clothes and wrapping her hair in her fists. Cy watches her with pickles in his eyes. He spies the pig and on the knees and hands jerks towards her, sticking his fingers out like stone worms, his tongue lolls like mice in his mouth, he sticks his leg out banging his shoe on the pig's ass (not cruelly though) just enough to make the animal turn and be conscious of him, for in that white-flesh no-blood brain she remembers pleasure. And she backs toward him, you know, and he grabs her body. Maj is watching with bloody senses then tears out shrieking.

SCENE III

NARRATOR: In an old-fashioned prison cell with the traditional water pot, hammock, etcetera, two men are talking. O everything is the same with these two as with a hundred other yolts, the jailbird, Oscar Loop, is skinny and wears the prison suit like he was a fallen priest. The other man is Bill Marjoram, squat, strong, sweaty and typical in workclothes, fat shoes, etcetera, how can well I go describing on?

LOOP: O breakfast is not much, I mean breakfast is not much, two pieces of bread, glass of water and a sausage, not real you know, something to think about anyway, sometimes I think like a motherless child, I mean take the tiny spices out of the sausage and grow them like small insects, I mean if they get watered and sun on them they might get life and then they'd be like insects.

MARJORAM: Shut up, Loop! Stupid, talking 'bout insex and maybe hanging tomorra! Your riddles too! Make me sick!

LOOP: Listen, they would be spice-insects so you could eat them—they would even be medicinal, cure a palsy helpfully, jerk a dead newborn back to life! O I hope it would do all those things.

MARJORAM: *Shut up, Loop,* I said! Stupid. Don't you know you gonna die?

LOOP: I mean a dead newborn could have been Mozart—I care in a great many ways for life, that's why the good sausage seed-spice might work—[*He whispers*]—without the evil eye! I bet Siva would help me, Siva is beautiful with her lovely hands. She's picked the mosquitoes out of my head! I've read greatly about her.

MARJORAM: You keep blabbing on 'nd on 'bout things that don't stop you from dying!

LOOP: How do you know? What makes you be so sure? Anything cun help a man maybe, a rock hit a devil in the Bibledays and a devil sucked out the blood of the thrower of that rock in hell! Somebody made that devil draw out all the blood in the man. Hmmmmmmmmmmmm I'll have to write that on the sausage. Mustn't forgit all the marvelous thoughts I git lately.

MARJORAM: Mavilous thoughts my foot! Swear you're gonna hang on Monday. Man, think, Loop! Think! Whut did you do?

LOOP: Whut did I do? Flah! A woman saw me! She bought me a mitten, tole me to put it on, said that the feeling would come through better. She looked like Mary in a story, but not the Lord's mother you know. No, she looked like the whore! But then like *Him* I changed her.

MARJORAM: Whut do you mean changed her! Speak it up truthfully. You killed her!

LOOP: I made her fall asleep on the ground. Put a bad blueberry in her mouth. Satan was a grub and when he got inside of her he ate her innards out but that was God's wish.

NARRATOR: Loop is smiling like a good king.

MARJORAM: How did she die! And if it's too bad a story you bitter not tell it in your crazy way. Tell me how you killed the girl, nobody dies with fruit-bugs, tell it sound and real!

NARRATOR: Now there are keys and chains sounds, the prison keeper comes in and Loop, eyes frightened, begins to stretch. He is afraid that he has been heard.

Everybody cringes.

LOOP: I mean to say that what I tole Bill wasn't all so. [*He points to the* GUARD *and ropes his arm toward himself*] You come here, guard, O I'm gonna tell you how I killed the girl, but in the beginning! Hoos! In the beginning was purity and cleanliness was a big garter belt!

NARRATOR: The keeper is sniffing in his giggles, feeling his bone, trying to see garter belts.

GUARD: Tell us what happened and maybe you can get a reprieve, hhah ha ha ha hiss— Did you put the garter belt round her small throat?

LOOP: I met Ann Fox in the greengrocers. I saw her skirt swing frisky and I knew that her father was a good farmer and Baptist. I knew that everybody in the village liked that family and no young fella would treat her disrespectfully. I could not just get married to a girl without her being like Ann, I knew that I wouldn't get married and be normal—so I asked her out, and she went with me, she said she liked the smell of leather. You know I have a good leather belt and jacket that a handcrafts woman sent me. Well, Ann liked that jacket, she said she'd take it from me when I was asleep. Sometimes I think she meant it too. Her father was a rich man, he could buy her all the leather clothes she wanted but she'd say she wanted my jacket too. Well, I'd get mad thinking about it, though I knew too that she was playing. But I took her one night near the field where Cy Futz's barn is and we horseplayed a little bit, nothin' but some hunky-punk.

SCENE IV

NARRATOR: A small dark field, nighttime, a blanket on the grass, a leather jacket spread perfectly out. Oscar Loop and Ann Fox are sitting opposite each other cross-legged.

LOOP: Little good cat, ooph! You knock my eyes out of my head, you're so pretty!

NARRATOR: He sticks out his forefinger and strokes her nose.

ANN: Buford Skark says I'm pretty too—too bad to mention another fella? You both think the same, that I'm pretty.

NARRATOR: Loop hops on his knees hooping himself toward her. If it's possible lights should shine green on top of his hair.

LOOP: Little rat, stop thinkin' of other men! Dogs'll crawl up your back if you do.

NARRATOR: He puts his hands on her hips and she falls at him laughing. They both move at each other like beachballs. Her foot catches in the jacket and he pushes at her ankle with two hands. She meanly slams her heel into the precious leather.

LOOP: Crazy rich girl, cut that out!

ANN: Hang it!

LOOP: Whut d'yu mean, "Hang it!" Have respect for a man's garment! I wear that on Sunday!

ANN: On Sunday the people laugh at you too just like on Monday! OOOOBles you're serious, so, so serious. Why'nt you kiss me? I'm a girl.

LOOP: I—I—I will kiss you—I would like to learn to dance so that I can go with you to fancy places.

NARRATOR: She moves her hip closer to his and takes his hand laying it on her stomach. He grabs her mightily and they kiss.

ANN: I hear something, is it my head? There are crazy bees inside of it! You kiss crazy! [*There are sounds, animal sounds, like an animal in heat*] Listen—I hear grunts! And I think someone cussing. Don't it sound strange?

LOOP: Yus, I hear them too. Don't know why somebody should beat their animals. Terrible to do that—I would never do that.

NARRATOR: Loop and Ann move very close to where the noises come from. Futz's barn. The barn is not seen, though. The noise is a human and animal one and both people are dumbfounded at what in all heaven's holy name is happening. Something equally weird is happening to Loop; he looks insane. He pushes himself at Ann and starts to pummel her, his voice is croaky.

LOOP: Gonna rid the place of evil, gonna make you sleep a long time till your soul becomes clean!

ANN: Stop it stop it! Let me be! [*She screams*]

NARRATOR: She tries to get away but he drags her around in a small circle.

LOOP: Gonna bury you in that evil dress! Stink will in a hundred years be covered up by the sweet grass! Hell isn't as bad as a whoring girl! May your father and mother not mourn you too long.

NARRATOR: Ann cries in soulful anguish. Loop drags her off. He comes back in terribly bloody clothes and sits cross-legged in the moony night. The animal sounds are louder but he shows no life, just sits with his arms folded and the hands covering his eyes. Then he slowly takes off his shoes and with a monkey's grace raises his feet to his nose and whiffs deeply.

SCENE V

NARRATOR: Cy Futz's barn again just like in the beginning. Cy is sitting with his kneebones high like the two hemispheres. The pig Amanda is sleeping on her side.

CY: *Flahfy Amanda ya faymale!* Four ugly legs you got! Zeus, wot hams! Lucky luck that I'm in love with you otherwise you'd be hanging in my pantry. Heeeehhhhehehehe, when you're old you'll be sitting in my granny's rockin' chair readin' the Bible. Amanda, you are of the world, known two kinds of male animals, pig and man! Sow, I know you love me but I wonder whether you'd rather be with your own kind? Piglets I can't give you you know though I am a healthy man.

NARRATOR: Cy licks his hands passionately and praises God for making him a husbandman. Silent is his worship but the world enters his barn now, Bill Marjoram and the Sheriff Tom Sluck. Slowly they go up to him. Futz yawns one eye open.

MARJORAM: There's the creep!

SLUCK: Y'all be quiet now.

MARJORAM: Quiet in hell! The biggest sinner in the world is here. If we weren't fair he'd be dead now by our own hands!

CY: I'd break them off like they were rabbits' necks.

SLUCK: Nothing is really proven yet. There will be justice.

MARJORAM: Men can make men insane!

SLUCK: Nothing is really proven yet.

MARJORAM: He drove a fella whacky!

CY: Fitz on you both, boys! I know no man well enough to make him nuts. Tell me who's crazy?

SLUCK: A man's in jail now for murdering a girl, he killed because he saw something very evil!

CY: Very sad thing. But there's lotsa evil here in the world.

MARJORAM: You're the satan here in our village!

CY: I'm not anybody's keeper. I'm never near anybody. Except when they come here to see me. I just work on my little plot of land raisin' vegetables for me and my pig. What sort of evil could I have done?

NARRATOR: Cy plays a tom-tom with his feet and salutes the sun. This is done subtly, the men not being aware of the ritual. Lord, these two are blind!

SLUCK: The man who murdered an innocent girl says he did it because he was under an influence, a spell he says, because he's a simple man. Now, Mr. Futz, I'm going to be blunt. People here say that you are an unnatural man.

CY: Am I?

SLUCK: Well, aren't you?

MARJORAM: Gods, he bangs pigs!

CY: I never do! Why my mother didn't bring me up like that. I'm a Bible-man!

SLUCK: If you're not serious you better become it! Very many people talk about your way!

CY: They're all wrong, Mr. Sluck. An animal is something to care about, not to committeth a sin with. Soos!

MARJORAM: See what he says! Soos!

SLUCK: Soos! Soos! What does it mean?

MARJORAM: It means he be guilty and pulling our feet!

CY: Why, why, I never would go with an animal! I'm a village man and the sun is good on me! Why I say that fellow has a devil in his head! [*He points at* MARJORAM]

MARJORAM: Devils! You bastud!

NARRATOR: He lunges at Cy and throws him down, he should not have done that though because Futz is quick and kicks his legs out cracking Marjoram's guts hard. The Sheriff fires his pistol a warning shot into the air. Both men relax like drugged sheep.

SLUCK: There will be a trial for the man who killed the girl and he'll probably hang! The day will be Monday!

CY: I do wish they, folks, wouldn't be mean toward each other.

MARJORAM: Mean! He talks about not bein' mean! Whut about Majorie Satz? She's wretched! She's become a bigger tart than she was. She's yapping always about what he did with her and the pig with him at the same time too he was with her! Crazy evil! Heaven help us working people with Lucifer here in our village!

NARRATOR: Futz is laughing hard.

SLUCK: What are you laughing for? It ain't funny when a man's going to die.

CY: I'm not killing. I'm not a judge or lawyer, just a farmer who lives poorly, mindin' his own business.

MARJORAM: Well, my word! You live here in the town with us. Where's your duty and responsibility?

CY: In my hands! I use them only on my land and in my barn.

SLUCK: I'm gonna tell you that I hate you myself. It ain't right that I as a lawman feel that way. The Constitution says that there should be fairness. But you ruined women, animals and a man's going to die because of you. Futz, I'm gonna do something that my sweet guts don't want. I'm gonna lock you up in the prison because the people might come here, my choppers say yes to your head under their feet, taking good revenge. But I'm gonna lock you up. You'll be safe.

CY: Who'll feed my pig and water my vegetables?

SLUCK: That's not our thought to care about your land and animals. My duty's gonna be lockin' you up in a cell.

MARJORAM: I think he needs death, not just bein' locked up. Futz has done so much harm!

SLUCK: He'll be locked up.

NARRATOR: Futz throws up his arms as though ready to receive lightning sticks from his friend God and crash them down on the heads of his judgers who want to see him minus, with no thing, no bliss.

CY: I'm a helpless man now, a partridge run after by turkeys!

MARJORAM: Bastud! Lecherous bastud! You'll get yours for spoilin' our lives!

SLUCK: I'll be easier when you pay up your debt to us. You've done a wrong, man.

NARRATOR: Futz in the middle walks out with the men, maybe sad jazz could be played now, not too much though.

SCENE VI

NARRATOR: Majorie Satz—it's another day—is in the field with two men, father and brother. Father is father and brother is brother. The first is simple. The second is complex.

FATHER: I don't know what about anything but Futz should hang though.

BROTHER: Like Loop, Dad. And the corpses hoss-whipped!

NARRATOR: Majorie is quiet with her arms hard against her body. She's listening like water.

FATHER: My dotter Majie is a good girl. Frisky like her reverent mother. [*The old man slaps her face*]

MAJORIE: Git away from me, ya old creep! Nothing was my fault!

BROTHER: Dad, cut it out! Nothin' is the girl's fault. She's just crazy.

FATHER: She is crazy! Should be put away!

MAJORIE: Can't be solved this way, nothing can, important thing is that I get revenged!

BROTHER: Nobody gonna revenge you! Nobody really cares that much.

FATHER: I care! Who's gonna marry this tramp if somehow we don't save her honor. Nobody'll git the bitch off my neck if Futz is allowed to get away with what he done. She's gotta get married off or I'll have her around our shack forever.

NARRATOR: The old man is sick by this fact of life.

FATHER: She's just got to be made respectable!

BROTHER: Don't Bill Marjoram want to marry her? I get the idea he'd be willing to have the old slot machine.

MAJORIE: Shet up, ya bastud! Don't call me names!

FATHER: Control that trap! It's a wonder you haven't been killed yet being whut you are. Majorie, you're a poisonous snake! And if I didn't have to live in this village I'd kill you myself. Your daddy or not—[*Loud*]—I hate you!

NARRATOR: Does Satz mean it? I don't know.

BROTHER: The both of you really get me! Spoiling with fight when we got to think of something. Something where we can get Futz. I mean he should be killed! Loop is gonna be killed and Futz should also.

NARRATOR: Brother does not have much feeling when he says this. Does he have a reason for Futz's death? Yes. His sister's honor? No. Well—

FATHER: I don't want a ruckus and yet there's gotta be something to happen.

MAJORIE: What he does with animals is dirty!

BROTHER: HAHAHaaaahshhhhhushy yeah yeah.

FATHER: Craziest thing I ever heard of.

BROTHER: Maybe it's good!

MAJORIE: OOOOOOOOOOOOooooooooohhh I'm sick!

FATHER: Stop your yellin', tramp! You've muddied yaself with every bloke in the village.

MAJORIE: So I have. But it's with men!

FATHER: Quit up your braggin'. Slut!

BROTHER: She sure is. [*He hunches over with jackal laughter*]

SCENE VII

NARRATOR: Oscar Loop is in his cell; his mother is there. She looks like Loop, smaller of course and wearing old things. It's the day of her boy's death.

MRS. LOOP: Oscar, sweet good boy. I didn't do nothing but—but good for you I thought. I told you 'bout God when you were small and polished up your shoes for you when you went to school. I did my best for you, my son. [*She weeps*]

LOOP: Mama, I know you did, Mama, I know you did. But let's make some plans for the wonderful things that I have. [*He takes from his pocket tiny specks of something*] Mama, these are holy bits of something good. They can cause miracles! Make people that are sick well. You know. They can even make a dead thing come alive again!

MRS. LOOP: Let me hold some in my hand, maybe it'll cure my arthritis. What are they, my son?

LOOP: I call them spice-seed insects, they're alive!

NARRATOR: Mother flings her arms to the north and south, letting the insects fly. She squelches a shriek letting something dawn on her. Her son's dream.

MRS. LOOP: O Son, I'm sorry! But those wonderful seeds are potent, they cured my arthritis so quickly! My hands tingle!

LOOP: I knew it would work! I'm so happy! Take care of them I only have a handful. Mother, use them wisely, don't give them to no pretty women, only old people and dead things. It's a gift from Siva.

MRS. LOOP: Siva? Who is Siva?

LOOP: A holy thing with lots of arms. She couldn't die with her lots of arms even if ten brutes tried to do her in. Siva lives and lives!

MRS. LOOP: Siva sounds like she's a good Christian woman. None around here like her. My son hates evil so he justly killed it. O Son, o Son, that you should be killed by the villagers is fair though you're my precious blood, it's

right. And that you should have killed an evil girl is right too! No! Nobody—No woman is good! All want one thing from a man, his lust-stick!

LOOP: Mother mother mother—[*He is weeping sickly*]—mother mother mother, why couldn't I find you? Why couldn't I ha' been my own father?

MRS. LOOP: Stop it, my son—[*She is slightly smiling*]—that is not a thing to say, but we two are godly and there shall be rest for us both. A son and his mother are godly!

LOOP: A son-and-his-mother-are-godly! Everything you say is beautiful. Mother, you are like the Holy Virgin!

MRS. LOOP: That is blasphemy, Son. Never say that! Look! Look! Look at me, my boy, watch me. Don't talk—just look at me. See my eyes and nose and lips? Remember my face good so that you see it on the inside of the black hood—Oooo I shouldn't say that but it's all so important to me that when after—when you are dead they'll come to be with me and grieve. But if they don't? I couldn't stand it, I must feel them all around me, they must be a loving family—all around me, they must feel so sorry for me—because I am a mother with no son.

LOOP: Nothin' nothin' nothin'. . . .

MRS. LOOP: Whut?

LOOP: I'm gonna be nothin'—[*He rubs his feet on the floor*]—nothin'—so? Mother, who's gonna be with you? The folks you like?

MRS. LOOP: Yes. But they've made my life very hard. I need them though. You wouldn't know being a man. You're my son and if you were a minister, I couldn't be more proud! I'm saying everything now. I remember when you got tattooed. You said it was manly. I wasn't more proud! [*She opens her raggy bag and lifts out a square package*] I remember when Howard bopped me. Take some fruitcake, son. Your father was jealous of me, you wouldn't dream that I was a good-looking girl to look at me now but I was and Howard was very jealous of me. You look like me you know when I was young. And he would say he'd kill me too you know even before you were born when you was just the fruit of my womb. I'm an old woman now and have not one bit a thing. When I was young I coulda had a lot cause of my looks. I didn't want anything, just to be happy.

LOOP: Mom—wouldn't it be wonderful if I could make myself invisible? Then I could go away. They couldn't find me. You and me would finally be let alone.

MRS. LOOP: Yes, it would be wonaful. [*She's almost in a trance*] Oscar, I forgive you for wanting me to die.

LOOP: Mama, I never meant that really.

MRS. LOOP: I know you didn't. I'm sorry I said that.

LOOP: You couldn't die anyway, 'cause I'd give you the spice-insects.

NARRATOR: They look at each other as if he's a tot learning to walk. Noise is heard, it's time for Loop to die. When he's dead he won't see anymore.

WARDEN: Hello, Mrs. Loop and Oscar. Mrs. Loop, go to my cousin Hattie, she's outside waiting to take you home with her. Oscar, you come with me to the middle of town. Right?

LOOP: Right, yes yes, right. I'm bad. But I'm gonna keep my feet together when I swing, like a soldier!

MRS. LOOP: He's gonna look like a minister high on the pulpit above the congregation! I'm going to dress respectably!

SCENE VIII

NARRATOR: Majorie in a whorey mood, walking with two drunken blokes in the field.

MAJORIE: Runnin' bastad! Futz's so scared now.

SUGFORD: Aaaaa harrrr that's good!

BUFORD: Pooos! Scared yella! Uuuuuuuuuuuch my stomach hurts!

MAJORIE: You have your stomach—Cy's not gonna have his!

SUGFORD: Yeah yeah.

BUFORD: Gal, that was a *creazzy* thing to do with you. I wouldn't ha' done that. I'm bagged.

SUGFORD: You bagged? I'm alive.

MAJORIE: I'm alive too.

NARRATOR: She sits on the grass, the two get down on her sides.

MAJORIE: I'm wanting excitement!

SUGFORD: Maybe you need to get banged.

BUFORD: Me too!

MAJORIE: [*Laughing high*] What for?

BUFORD: Wha' ya mean wha' for? For fun.

NARRATOR: He picks up a stone and throws it at her. She catches it and starts playing with it, hands cupping it like it's a baby chick.

MAJORIE: Let's go nuts us three then clean up somehow.

SCENE IX

NARRATOR: A little time later.

MAJORIE: Noooooot enough noooot enough!

SUGFORD: We gotta fix it good!

BUFORD: Gal, you're a pig!

SUGFORD: Yeah, she's a pig! We should chop her up with the other one.

MAJORIE: It's too late and I'd be dreary eating. I'm revengeful. Look, I know where it is! His sow! Let's kill her! Let's kill his pig!

BUFORD: So what for? So? Fat pig wants to kill a pig.

SUGFORD: Wouldn't that be like killing yu sister?

MAJORIE: Both of you are like mice! Just want-ing—

BUFORD: Git off it!

SUGFORD: Girly, git off it! You're just askin' for it.

BUFORD: You don't know how you could end up.

MAJORIE: *You don' have to do nothin'.* I'll just do it.

SUGFORD: Why?

MAJORIE: Because I want to.

SUGFORD: Beef?

BUFORD: Okay.

SCENE X

NARRATOR: Everything is the same.

SUGFORD: Who wants it!

MAJORIE: She's a dirty dirty thing!

SUGFORD: I'm getting away from totty. You don' want to stay here anymore, do you?

BUFORD: No! Let's just gooooo! [BUFORD *and* SUGFORD *run off*]

MAJORIE: Come back, ya chicken bastads!

NARRATOR: Hell hath no fury like a woman scorned by a man—for a pig!

SCENE XI

NARRATOR: In the prison cell Futz sits very hard. He's blowing out his cheeks and binding his nostrils close to the bone.

CY: Huh-uuh-huh-hh-uuh— Oooooook huuhhhh-ooooookiioooook huuuuuh—uuuuhuh—huuuuo-ook oooK *Amaaaaanddddaaaaa I miss you soooooo. My Molly Amaaaaandaaaaa I miiiiii-iissssss youuuuuuu.* Tain't faih, my faymale. You were good to me 'nd I was sooo good to you. You ate corn 'nd sleep beside me. We tried to go to church but they wouldn't let us in so I'd read you the Bible at home. *My mother was a good Protistin,* she'd love you too. *Mother, get back in your grave you're stinkin' up the green world!*

WARDEN *comes in.*

WARDEN: Behave yourself! Isn't there any decency in you? Dishonorin' your parent's memory screaming out blasphemies in prison!

CY: Warden, you look like a bad drawing of God!

WARDEN: Futz, I should let the folks take you. I should hand you over to them. They'd teach your dead body manners!

CY: You want a war!

WARDEN: I want you legally killed.

CY: You don't have to fear I'll rape your mother, she's too old! Or your daughter, she's got your bad teeth! Warden, why don't you kill your wife and kids? You know that you're unhappy.

WARDEN: I'm a normal man, Futz. It's you that's unhappy. And you've caused treachery!

CY: I wasn't near people! They came to me and looked under my trousers all the way up to their dirty hearts! They minded my *own* life! O you're making me be so serious. And I'm only serious with my wife!

WARDEN: Your what?

CY: [*Loud*] My wife my wife! And how many tits does your wife have? Mine has twelve!

WARDEN: You're ranting, animal!

CY: If I was wi' her I'd be grunting.

SCENE XII

NARRATOR: It's Satz's place. Dirty. The old man, son and mother are there.

MOTHER: Majorie's such a bitch.

FATHER: It must ov been the bug's fault when she was born.

MOTHER: What d'ye mean?

FATHER: I saw a bug on your stomach when she yipped.

MOTHER: I was clean when the child was born.

FATHER: Clean as a swamp.

MOTHER: Swamp! Swamp! No! It was pure water that they had on me!

FATHER: Pig piss it was! Why, woman, you're still slying and lying!

MOTHER: I'm not gon' to say the story anymore.

FATHER: Look! Look! The girl is not mine. Not my dotter.

MOTHER: She is she is she is!

FATHER: She is my dotter? Then why did the bugs sit on your knees crying prayers to heaven?

MOTHER: It didna happen!

FATHER: It could ov been you with the pig and him—like it was her!

MOTHER: I'll call my son! [*Screaming*] Ned! Ned!

BROTHER *comes in.*

FATHER: Ned Ned—be dead!

MOTHER: Hear him!

FATHER: Everythin's made her nervous, Ned. She's mad again.

BROTHER: Don' be mad. Majorie'll get her honor back again. I'm goin' to kill Futz!

FATHER: Don't do it alone, take someone with you.

BROTHER: I want to myself!

MOTHER: [*Crying*] But wash with pure water, don' leave the blood.

FATHER: He could leave the blood. There's no disgrace in fightin' for his sister.

BROTHER: *Hah*uuuhahahashus hahhas hohaaahh—Mother, don't fret I won' leave the blood.

MOTHER: Before you go will you have somethin' to eat?

SCENE XIII

NARRATOR: He's in the prison with Cy. Ned.

CY: Boy boy boy. You want to kill me. Why?

BROTHER: My family.

CY: I've not none just a sow.

BROTHER: You make my brains red!

CY: I'll tell you peace!

BROTHER: *Shut up shut up!* I don't want to *know you!*

CY: You don't have to know me—just let *me be!*

BROTHER: [*In cold fury*] Your neck should be boiled!

CY: That's what I don't want to happen to my sow!

BROTHER: She'll die too!

CY: Now why, Ned, why do you want to kill the animal?

BROTHER: [*Seething*] You make my brains red! [*He stabs* CY]

NARRATOR: [*Ironical*] Amanda—there's someone here he needs you. Yes!

Blackout

GORILLA QUEEN

a play

Ronald Tavel

Gorilla Queen was first presented by the Judson Poets' Theatre at the Judson Memorial Church, New York City, on March 10, 1967, with the following cast:

VENUS FLY TRAP	*Jo Ann Forman*
BRUTE	*George Harris II*
LIGHTING GIRL	*Deborah Lee*
GLITZ IONAS	*Adrienne de Antonio, Mary Duke, Norman R. Glick, John Harrill, George Harris III, Dick Lipkin, Norman Soifer*
MAIS OUI	*Selena Williams*
KARMA	*Paula Shaw*
CLYDE BATTY	*James Hilbrandt*
TAHARAHNUGI WHITE WOMAN	*Quinn Halford*
CHIMNEY SWEEP	*David Kerry Heefner*
SISTER CARRIES	*Eddie McCarty*
PAULET	*Barbara Ann Camp*
QUEEN KONG	*Norman Thomas Marshall*
INTERN	*Cal Thorpe*

It was directed by Lawrence Kornfeld. Music by Robert Cosmos Savage and Al Carmines. Set by Jerry Joyner; costumes by Linda Sampson; lighting by John P. Dodd. Production stage manager: Roland Turner.

Gorilla Queen was subsequently presented by Paul Libin at the Martinique Theatre, New York City, on April 24, 1967, with Florence Tarlow as KARMA and Harvey Tavel as INTERN.

With patience, to the unpracticing

We dedicate the natural thing.

Note on pronunciation: Unless otherwise indicated, foreign words and names are pronounced correctly and not Anglicized. "Taharahnugi" is pronounced with equal emphasis on each syllable.

Dark stage; then a traveling spotlight, beneath which BRUTE, *a sluggish but amiable gibbon, comes ambling across the apron. He is dressed in a tacky ape-hair outfit with ill-fitting gibbon mask. A bare arm, ankle, ear, etc., sloppily exposed. He pauses and speaks the prologue.*

BRUTE: [*With very heavy Brooklyn accent*] Ladies and gentlemen of every genus: When I was a kid my Daddy used to say, "I'll explain it to ya when ya get older." Now in order that daddies no longer have to explain anythin' to their kids, we are presentin' dis play. Dis here play don't leave nothin' to the imagination. After all, most people ain't got any. Hit it, Maestro!

The overture music, a bongo-heavy, rapid marching beat, strikes up at a deafening pitch. Then just as suddenly, it loses all enthusiasm and peters out into ambling nonsense chords as the members of the GLITZ IONAS, *a tribe of gibbons, enter from various directions. They are costumed in played-out ape-hair outfits, bras and skirts of long fur and mat that have seen better days, ape masks alternately silly and grim, etc.; here and there naked midriffs, arms, legs, necks, toes, etc., very obviously exposed. Spotlights follow the chaotic entrance of the* GLITZ IONAS: *each crawls about, grunts, adjusts his costume—some put their costumes on right there on stage; sounds of "Ooo-ou-oop," "Gubba-mubba," "Get dis garter, will ya!" etc. They all carry bananas.*

Gradually the set becomes visible: upstage center is a huge fireplace with grate, over which rises a wide, long chimney. Downstage right is a seven-foot-high bamboo cage, almost completely camouflaged with jungle foliage. Before the cage stands the immobile figure of the VENUS FLY TRAP. *She is dressed in form-fitting green tights with reddish-pink face, hands, and feet. Long forbidding needles corona her face, hands, and feet. She is slender and graceful, like a mime. Downstage left is a rattan table on which are tall drinks and a flower basket containing acacia blossoms, bulrushes, carnations, daisies, ivy, myrtle, and grape vines. Two rattan wicker chairs. Between the fireplace and the cage and between the fireplace and the table, and against the backdrop and the wings, is built a row of shelves, several feet above the floor, forming a very distinct semicircle. The stage is decorated, here and there, with potted plants and flowers, preferably any which would not be found in a jungle; the symbolic growths of the flower basket are noticeably repeated at key points about the stage.*

Several of the GLITZ IONAS *jump up and take a place on the shelf. More and more* GLITZ IONAS *arrive, grunting and bickering, their cacophony of sounds reaching a feverish pitch as the last mischievous one takes his place, squatting, on the shelf. Then, suddenly, the deafening bongo-heavy overture resumes, and they all break out into song, an irregular collection of voices to be sure, but not to the point where the words become indistinct. Flickering lights illuminate the long, semicircular row of their face masks; they scratch their crotches with little apparent relief. Just before the overture ends,* MAIS OUI, *carrying a cuspidor, arrives in time to sing the last two lines, in timid high soprano before jumping daintily up on the shelf between the fireplace and cage.* MAIS OUI *is one of the* GLITZ IONAS, *played by an actress; but she should appear to the audience to be an actor, very effeminate in word and gesture. Throughout the play the other characters will refer to and respond to* MAIS OUI *as if she were actually an effete, effeminate male.*

GLITZ IONAS: [*Singing*]
    Hear Barbaric Overture
    Overhearers hold a bore,
    Though our toying each his fore
    Overseers more deplore:—
    Human, vomit, let it pour,
    If your nausea upward soar;
    Know, though toilet fill galore,
    What you heave you but restore
    To our stomachs sickened more:—
    We be all a single corps!

    Still, who stay and do not snore,
    They that share our common lore,
    Swing ahead to years of yore
    When to humor sophomore
    Jungles rang with raucous roar.
    Now our throats are straining sore
    So we'll stretch no furthermore
    This Barbaric Overture!

MAIS OUI: [*Hurrying in, singing with mock obsequiousness*]
    Please to use the cuspidor
    For opinions—not the floor!

The overture music ends with a loud crash upon which the lights on the GLITZES *go out —and a strong spot immediately goes up on the rattan table downstage left. In the chair nearest to the left wing is seated* CLYDE BATTY, *very short and very thin, hair slicked back in a bogus 1930's style, costumed as the animal trainer his name recalls. In the chair closest to center stage is seated* KARMA MIRANDA, *a very huge, very heavy woman, got up like a lovely rococo shepherdess made of porcelain; her skin is powder white; her buckled shoes, bonnet, and shepherdess' crook are gilt; Belgian lace covers her shoulders and leggings; a purple rose neatly catches up her wide bell skirt. Sequestered from these two, and languishing on the floor in front of the table is* TAHARAHNUGI WHITE WOMAN, *a brownskin male actor, ravishing in a tight white sarong and wig of long raven hair; barefooted with ankle bracelets, huge round falsies, thick lipstick, and long lashes. When the spotlight goes up on them, the conversation begins without a second's pause, as if it has been in progress for some time.* CLYDE'S *voice inclines to the squeak,* KARMA'S *to an alto pitch.*

CLYDE: And so finally, Miss Karma, the theatre is superior to cinema because whereas in cinema everything is misplaced, in theatre the four corners of the stage are the four corners of the earth.

KARMA: But that still doesn't explain why people walk out in the middle of a play.

CLYDE: Oh, them, they're just trying to get into the papers.

KARMA: Well, I'll be a monkey's uncle, I never thought of that! But I sure am glad you told me, Clyde, 'cause this sure is better than a movie.

CLYDE: What is better than a movie?

KARMA: Sitting out here on the canopied verandah of the old plantation, sipping cool mint juleps, being enamored of the pagan amer of this forbidden tropical paradise and its primitive untamed dangers. And here, here in Egypt, where adventure lives and romance rules, here—

CLYDE: Here, where?

KARMA: Where? In Egypt.

CLYDE: This ain't Egypt. I wouldn't dream of planting a plantation in Egypt, Miss Karma.

KARMA: But why not, Clyde, Clyde Batty, since you're actually an animal trainer?

CLYDE: Because while Egypt is an interesting country, it is, on the whole, a bit disappointing historically.

KARMA: I sure can sympathize with you on that point. But where, then, are we?

CLYDE: In Nigeria, of course, Miss Karma. You see, if we're in Nigeria, we can sympathize

with the whole British nation. Nigeria, after all, was Britain's showcase in Africa.

KARMA: Quite. Listen, Clyde, have you heard tell anything about a certain . . . Queen Kong?

CLYDE: Queen Kong? Why, no—are you she?

KARMA: Not likely—nor like her. I assume Queen Kong is a great ape.

CLYDE: Sounds likely, but it's not likely. Someone who is queen around here is more likely to be a woman than a great ape, don't you think? A great woman. And you, my dear Miss Karma, are as great a woman as ever I hope to—

At this point, TAHARAHNUGI WHITE WOMAN *begins squirming along the floor toward* CLYDE'S *boots. He will speak throughout with a heavy Caribbean accent.*

TAHARAH: Show cause! Show cause!

CLYDE: What?

TAHARAH: Show cause!

CLYDE: What for?

TAHARAH: [*Sexy*] Show cause! Show cause why theez show shouldn't be clozed down!

CLYDE: [*Bending over toward* TAHARAH] And what is your identity, little one?

TAHARAH: [*Sizzling*] I am Taharahnugi White Woman! Men are attracted to me and men who are attracted to me soon crack-up!

CLYDE: [*Fingering the falsies bulging out of the top of* TAHARAH's *sarong*] I can believe it:— that's a real crack up front you've got there, Taharahnugi!

TAHARAH: Some-sing de matter wit you?

CLYDE: Perhaps, but the matter is in good hands.

TAHARAH: Good hands?? They look like effete white white-man's hands to me. Don't reach for more than you can grab, Bwana Clyde!

KARMA: Well, well, this play and interplay is rather dull, after all. Gargoyle, l'addition, s'il vous plaît.

TAHARAH: Eet is too hot for you out here, Memsab?

KARMA: [*Ignoring him*]: Gargoyle, l'addition, s'il vous plaît, I say.

CLYDE: You'll never get the check asking for it in that tone of Swahili. Waiter, the abacus, please!

TAHARAH: [*Squirming up the table leg and sitting square on the tabletop*] I am the waiter.

CLYDE: [*With roaming fingers*] Can you wait for me?

TAHARAH: [*Ignoring his familiarities*] Will there be anything else?

CLYDE: Will there?

TAHARAH: Oh, don't be so fresh! Theez ain't one of doz places where de waitresses are topless, de entertainers bottomless, and de audience brainless, and therefore you can be free to say anything you damn please!

KARMA: The check, please.

TAHARAH: Did you haf the high-priced spread on your table?

KARMA: [*Regarding his rear*] No, indeed! Nor was the egg-drop soup very high-priced either.

TAHARAH: How do you mean?

KARMA: The egg was doubtless dropped into it, but apparently removed shortly thereafter.

TAHARAH: How obscene! And you a woman!

CLYDE: Garçon!

TAHARAH: Oh, mais oui!

KARMA: Mais Oui?—who's that?

CLYDE: She's that real small gibbon you sometimes see swinging with the rest of the pack at the edge of the plantation.

MAIS OUI: [*From her position on the shelf*] Oh! how exciting—he has an eye out for me.

KARMA: [*Disgusted*] He'll have an eye *knocked* out for you!

TAHARAH: [*Picking up the challenge posed by* KARMA *and suddenly switching his attitude toward* CLYDE] I am the waiter. Can I wait for you?

CLYDE: [*Hampered because* KARMA *is there*] I, er, I—if it's part of your job, I mean if your job entails—

TAHARAH: [*Sizzling*] Yeez . . . tails. I weel wait for you by the Venus Fly Trap plant. The beeg one . . . You know where 'tis, yeez, Bwana Clyde? [*Chucking Clyde under the chin*]

CLYDE: [*Fumbling, suddenly no longer the aggressor*] Er—er—one fly trap looks pretty much like another to me.

KARMA: [*Sarcastic*] They're all Greek to him.

TAHARAH: Do not slander his manhood so, Mem-sab. [*Winking*] In Greek is called Aphrodite Fly Trap. You weel fin' it. . . . If you don't fin' it, it fin' you. If it don't fin' you, it *de*fine you.

KARMA: [*Sarcastic*] Well, that's just fine.

TAHARAH *takes a long, hot walk across the stage till he reaches the* VENUS FLY TRAP, *at whose feet he immediately throws himself, languishing as if under a palm, legs sensuously planing along the floor as if in heat.* CLYDE *adjusts his leather belt.*

CLYDE: Oh, Miss Karma, will you excuse me? I wanna call Sister Carries.

KARMA: What do you wanna call him?

CLYDE: A fruit.

KARMA: I disagree with you, he's not a fruit.

CLYDE: Well, disagree without me for two minutes, will you? I really do have to call him about a trip to Hollywood.

KARMA: [*Suddenly sexy*] Holly *would??* —Holly *did!!*

CLYDE: Er, I'm trying to get a booking for my animal act out there. I wanna be discovered.

KARMA: But you're leaving without paying the check.

CLYDE: I always leave restaurants without paying the check—that's 'cause I crave that thrilling ice-blue hole that hollows out your back when you're slipping away and still within apprehending distance of the waiter.

KARMA: Oh, yeah? There's something going between you and that waiter that slipping away without paying the check won't help you to slip out of.

CLYDE: Look, I hate to be callous—

KARMA: [*Angry*] You ain't—you're callow. Go —go! You and your animal act! Go, beast, go!

CLYDE *braces his narrow shoulders, then struts across the stage like a peacock toward* TAHARAH. *At that moment a* CHIMNEY SWEEP *hops out of the left wing and lands precisely beside* KARMA. *He is quite tall, quite skinny in form-fitting black tights, with a stovepipe hat roofing his porcelain face; he is as clean and neat as any other man, "for it was only make-believe that he was a sweep; the china-workers might just as well have made a prince of him, if they had been so minded." The* CHIMNEY SWEEP *carries a large emerald-green plantain. A quartet scene ensues, carefully integrated and counterpointed; do not employ the "freeze" technique during this four-corner interlude.*

SWEEP: Beg your pardon, Miss, what time do you have?

KARMA: Anytime. [*Looking at her wristwatch and giving him the exact time it reads at that moment*] But right now, it's exactly———.

SWEEP: [*Suddenly placing the tip of the plantain on* KARMA'S *inner elbow and speaking like a hardened criminal*] That where ya shoot it, baby?!

KARMA: [*Indignant*] I beg your pardon!—and ruin my lily-white arms?!

SWEEP *helps himself to a generous sampling of her lily-white and lovely arms.*

CLYDE: [*Bending over with his hand touching* TAHARAH'S *thigh*] What a delightful contrast must be between the inner pink and outer dark . . .

TAHARAH: Oooooooooo . . . you found the right place. Did you follow the brain wave I astro-projected to direct you here?

CLYDE: [*Lifting* TAHARAH *in his arms*] No, I just followed the heat wave.

KARMA: Ain't it hot enough without your hands all over me?

TAHARAH: [*On his feet, turning his back to* CLYDE *and leaning against him as if he were a palm tree*]: Ooooooooo, Bwana Muskels! What manner of labor do you do to haf developed such beeg muskels?

CLYDE: [*Nibbling on* TAHARAH'S *neck*] I don't have to labor: I have a private income.

TAHARAH: Perhaps Bwana could be induced to share it?

CLYDE: I said it was private.

KARMA: Yer a chimney sweep, ain't cha?

SWEEP: [*Kissing her between her fingers*] How can you tell?

KARMA: By your skin-tight tights.

SWEEP: You like skin-tight tights, do you?

KARMA: [*Giving him the "screw-you" finger*] No, just skin—tight!!

TAHARAH: Perhaps Bwana haf income from some other activity, which he could be induced to share?

CLYDE: At the least, I could be induced to share the activity—you see, I'm a pataphysician. [*Patting* TAHARAH'S *falsies and worming his hands into the top of the sarong*]

TAHARAH: Ooooooooooo, a pataphysician; you must haf studied at beeg college—like Barnyard or somethink.

SWEEP: [*Quickly, making time*] But I'm more than just a simple chimney sweep; I'm also a May-son, a Taurian, one who uses words like *completely, totally, always, forever,* and so on—a May-son, a bricklayer to you.

KARMA: Or a rock dropper, but I wouldn't know about that; you see, I abide in a very small grassass shack.

SWEEP: [*Suggestively*] Well, I'd like to enlarge your place.

KARMA: All ya have to do is get one foot in the door.

TAHARAH: College is de door to de inner life.

CLYDE: A nose for news could smell it from without.

SWEEP: What's yer name, toots?

KARMA: Karma.

SWEEP: Karma what?

KARMA: Karma Miranda.

SWEEP: [*Brandishing the plantain*] Karma Miranda, the Brazilian Fly-Fortress! You married?

KARMA: I haven't the right time to be married—I have too many affairs of state.

SWEEP: [*Pulling away and coming downstage for an elaborate aside*] Affairs of state—I thought so! That broad don't pull this boy's third leg—she ain't Karma Miranda—she's Queen Kong! And not married—what a break! If I can make her to the altar I'll be sable to shit the degrating job of chimney sweep and be King for a lay! [*He returns to manhandling* KARMA, *who has quietly followed him downstage with an auditor's curiosity*]

TAHARAH: Is the Mem-sab Bwana Muskels' wife?

CLYDE: Who, Karma? Hell, no, Karma's jist my fiancée.

TAHARAH: Then perhaps Taharahnugi White Woman can be Bwana's financée.

CLYDE: How much are ya willin' to lay out, Too-hairy-noogi?

TAHARAH: For Bwana, I weel put up all my spangles . . .

SWEEP: [*Smacking* KARMA'S *face*] A smack in time saves nine.

KARMA: [*Stunned*] Hey! what dja do that for?

SWEEP: 'Cause I'm more than just a simple bricklayer or May-son if you like—I'm also a smacking thief.

KARMA: [*Rubbing her cheek*] A smacking thief?

SWEEP: [*Stealing, unnoticed, the purple rose that catches up her bell skirt*] Yeah, pretty romantic, huh?

KARMA: Watch it, sonny mae, watch it. You're playing with fire.

SWEEP: But of course, 'cause I'm more than just a smacking thief:—I'm also a chimney sweep.

KARMA: [*Perceiving her outermost skirt slowly falling to its full length now that it is no longer caught up by the rose*] How self-reliant is my chaperone skirt; it draws, unaided, the veil across my lips.

TAHARAH: Taharahnugi White Woman do not want Bwana Muskels to beleef that she haf only money on her mind. Taharahnugi is well to do in her own right.

CLYDE: [*Obscenely smacking his lips, his hand now completely up* TAHARAH'S *sarong*] I'll bet you're well to do, Too-hairy-noogi. And you're pretty well bushed, too, aren't you?

TAHARAH: Taharahnugi very, very bushed. She know some thick seluzive bushes where she and Bwana can rest *up.*

CLYDE: Well let's not wait till the cows come milk.

TAHARAH: Bwana Muskels not afraid of getting lost in the bush?

CLYDE: I know my way around the country.

TAHARAH: Then follow my scent, O strong one!

CLYDE: I'm followin' with a long one.

TAHARAH, *seeming suddenly very tall, breaks into the elegant Watusi ceremonial dance and glides back and forth across the stage, head swirling, arms winging, Watusi bongo accompaniment.* CLYDE *follows awkwardly behind trying to imitate the dance, and they work their way upstage while* KARMA *gives her speech; as* KARMA *finishes speaking,* TAHARAH *and* CLYDE *exit behind the huge cage at right, and the music ends.*

KARMA: [*Removing her bonnet*] I shall never forgive Clyde Batty for Watusiing away into the wold with that Taharahnugi White Woman waiter. It is inhuman to forgive:—on the one appendage, one inflicts self-harm by retaining the offense and not equalizing it; and on the other appendage, one inflicts harm on the offender, for by letting him go unscathed, one is donating him liberty to harm oneself and others again, and thus to damn yet once more his eternal hole.

SWEEP: [*Debonair*] Never let the jungle sun set on your jealousy.

KARMA: Who's jealous? After all, what does a mere native girl have over a half-breed?

SWEEP: She has Clyde Batty over her, for one appendage. But tell me, I never knew that you were a half-breed.

KARMA: Certainly, I am. I'm half native, half Brazilian. Don't I look it?

SWEEP: At second peek, I guess you do. It's written all over your porcelain-pale complexion. Listen, Miss Miranda, have you heard tell anything about a certain . . . Queen Kong?

KARMA: Why, sure. Hasn't everyone? It's printed in the program credits.

SWEEP: Not everyone can read. And it isn't everyone who reads words. But speak, my dear, could . . . [*Very cautious*] it be . . . that you . . . in the ineffable complexity of your womanliness, conceal the fact . . . that you . . . are . . . this mysterious . . . Queen Kong? You're certainly big enough to be.

KARMA: Ha—ha! Long may you wonder but never know the truth, for the jungle keeps well its unrevealable secrets!

SWEEP: But surely you could proffer some impertinent information anent this curious queen called Kong?

KARMA: [*Portuguese accent*] You likes Brazilian music?

SWEEP: Here in Angola, who dare not?

KARMA: [*Portuguese accent*] You likes it, you got it!

The music begins with great dash and flare as KARMA *tosses the flora out of the basket on the table; the basket has a bandanna attached to the bottom of it:* KARMA *secures the bandanna under her chin, thus securing the empty basket on top of her head as a hat; and begins to dance in little Miranda steps out toward center stage. The music for the song is "South American Way," except for the chorus, which is sung to the children's rhyme, "One Banana, Two Banana." As* KARMA *starts her song and dance, the* GLITZES *jump off the shelves and accompany her as if they were a Latin chorus line à la 1940's Hollywood. During the "Bwana" chorus, each* GLITZ *glides by* KARMA *and tosses a banana into her basket as she quickly calls out the numbers.* KARMA *dances about briefly with huge smile during the short introductory music, then whips into her song.*

KARMA: [*Singing*]
　I Yi! I Yi!
　Efer learn to lust in a freak show,
　Lose your easy queasiness
　Wiz zee sleasiest
　Man Gargantuan Girl?

　I Yi! I Yi!
　Efer drop your civilized mores,
　Kiss a rare and hairylike
　Sort of scarylike
　Man Gargantuan Girl?

KARMA *and* GLITZES: [*All singing,* KARMA *pointing to the following parts of her body to heavy bongo accompaniment, and the* GLITZES *tossing bananas into her basket-hat*]
　[*To her nose*] One bwana,
　[*To her mouth*] Two bwana,
　[*To her ears*] Three bwana, four,
　[*To one breast*] Five bwana,
　[*To other breast*] Six bwana,
　[*To rear and lap*] Seven bwana, more!

KARMA: I Yi! I Yi!
　Efer try to mate wiz a monster,
　In zee jungles vapoury
　Rim an apery
　Man Gargantuan Girl?

　I Yi! I Yi!
　Efer lick a lap wasn't human,
　Eat a unitarian
　Sex barbarian
　Man Gargantuan Girl?

KARMA *and* GLITZES: [KARMA *pointing to the following parts to heavy, rapid bongo accompaniment*]
　[*To her cheek*] One red,
　[*To other cheek*] Two red,
　[*To her breasts*] Three white, four,
　[*To her rear*] Five blue,
　[*To her lap*] Six blue,
　[*Shrugging shoulders*] Who takes more?

The music goes into the minor bridge and
KARMA *sings and now dances more ornately*
with the GLITZES. *Delete major bridge.*

KARMA: I Yi! I Yi!
   O, zee Man Gargantuan Girl!

GLITZES: I Yi! I Yi!
   I Yi! I Yi!

KARMA *and* GLITZES: O, zee Man Gargantuan
   Girl!
   O, zee Man Gargantuan Girl!

KARMA: I Yi! I Yi!
   Efer long to sire zee children
   Of zee deva cleavable
   Inconceivable
   Man Gargantuan Girl?

   I Yi! I Yi!
   Efer beat your meat for zee bestial,
   Dip your tricky dicky-hot
   In zee sticky spot
   [*Pause*]
   —Of zee Man Gargantuan Girl?
   —Of zee Man Gargantuan Girl?

KARMA *and* GLITZES: [KARMA *pointing to the*
following parts of her body to heavy, rapid
bongo accompaniment; GLITZES *tossing ba-*
nanas in basket]
   [*To her nose*] One bwana,
   [*To her mouth*] Two bwana,
   [*To her ears*] Three bwana, four,
   [*To one breast*] Five bwana,
   [*To other breast*] Six bwana,
   [*To her rear*] Seven bwana—
   [*Throwing wide her arms, and the* SWEEP
   tossing his plantain into the basket-hat]

KARMA *and* SWEEP: MORE!!!

The song ends with a loud pound on the bon-
gos and the dancers freezing. Then the
GLITZES *scamper back to their positions on*
the shelves, and SWEEP *applauds* KARMA'S
performance.

SWEEP: Very, very delicate, Señorita Karma, and
   very poetic!

KARMA: But was it in good taste?

SWEEP: Farce is seldom in good taste—but genitals always are. Soap and scenters see to that.

KARMA: I take it, then, that you like my little
   act?

SWEEP: More than you can conceive—although
   the information it offered concerning the nature of Queen Kong did not exactly identify
   her as yourself.

KARMA: How could it?—I'm not Queen Kong.
   How many times do I have to render that
   particular exposition?

SWEEP: But are you positive, and thinking positive, when you say you're not Queen Kong?

KARMA: How could I be? First of all, a queen is
   a human male; and second of all, anyone
   called Kong must be an animal—a giant ape.
   It's a contradiction in terms.

SWEEP: Naturally, because it's terms. Male!
   man! female! king! queen! human! animal! ape!—what are these terms except ex-
   pedient, comforting designations?

KARMA: But you don't mean to—

SWEEP: Would you predicate your existence on
   a *legal* definition?

MAIS OUI: The point is what ya go for or ya
   don't go for. And that chimney sweep is jist
   too skinny for me.

BRUTE: I ain't so skinny.

MAIS OUI: I been noticin', hon, I been noticin'.

SWEEP: I go for you, Miss Señorita, more than
   you've conned—

KARMA: But, Señor Sweep, you hardly know me.

SWEEP: I know that you can dance as well as
   Salomé, and [*Making for her bosom*] that
   you're solid—

KARMA: [*Evading his grasp*] Yeah, solid as Lot's
   wife.

SWEEP: And those are the only two important
   things in a girl.

KARMA: [*Puffing out her bosom*] What are the
   only two important things?

SWEEP: One, that you're not Queen Kong, and
   two, that you won't become her. Your men-
   tality certifies as much. Now listen, why don't
   you forget that rake, Clyde Batty, and take
   up with me?

KARMA: Take up where, a chimney?

SWEEP: I'll show you a chimney you ain't never
   even dreamed existed, baby!

KARMA: I can't wait. Set up a trysting place.

SWEEP: [*Thinking*] A twisting place? Let me
   see . . .

KARMA: Got your stinking cap on, don't ya?

SWEEP: I've got it! Know the layout on this stage
   pretty well?

KARMA: Well as any Nigerian might.

SWEEP: Great, since this in Angola! Tell ya what,
   meet me under the Venus Fly Trap.

KARMA: What time?

SWEEP: [*Looking at his wristwatch*] Let me see,
   it's ——— [*Saying the exact time*] now;
   —how about 10:30?

KARMA: Suits me. See ya then, Señor Chimney
   Sweep.

SWEEP: [*Walking upstage toward* MAIS OUI]
   See ya, Big Girl!

MAIS OUI: Hey, how come ya still wanna make time with her, I mean now that yer sure she ain't Queeny Kong?

SWEEP: [*Holding the purple rose up to* MAIS OUI] The dick has its directions that *the* Direction knows not of. [SWEEP *ostentatiously drops the purple rose into the cuspidor that* MAIS OUI *has placed beside herself on the shelf*]

A chorus of "Man Gargantuan Girl" plays softly as if to mark the end of the scene, and ends as KARMA *settles herself into a bored theatre spectator in the chair closest to the left wing,* CLYDE'S *previous seat. Then eery, surrealistic mime music begins as* SWEEP *dances slow mime steps toward* VENUS FLY TRAP, *who slowly comes alive, moving arms and one leg in graceful mime movements. The two figures in tights seem now suddenly alike, Gemini-like.* SWEEP *dances around and dangerously close to* VENUS. *By now all the lights have dimmed, except for a purple spot on these two.* SWEEP *stops and stares at* VENUS, *then smacks her face.*

VENUS: I the Venus Fly Trap am,
　　Who you are don't mean a damn,
　　Sexy Barker, Auntie Sam,
　　Buster Crabbe or other ham!
　　Motionless I stand in sham
　　Waiting till an actor jam
　　Dick into my diaphragm:—
　　Then on dick I sudden slam
　　In my snapping snatch to cram,
　　Closing up as cruelest clam—
　　You don't need no diagram!

SWEEP: [*Looking all about her, brushing his obvious crotch up against her side*] You've nothing to be robbed of—not even virtue—so shut your trap!

VENUS: Snap!!! [*One arm extends quickly and clamps on his crotch*]

SWEEP: Aie! Mama-meeee!!! [*He struggles to free himself but cannot*]

VENUS: When from female man can't rob
　　Womanhood, she'll nab his lob!
　　Snap!
[*Her other arm darts out, her fingers clamping his neck*]

SWEEP: And me someone who always avoided starched colars, despite my stovepipe—hat!

VENUS: One good smack deserves another Snap!!! [*Her left leg shoots out and then around his thighs*]

SWEEP: I don't mind a petticoat legging, but a fig leaf cov . . . [*He is pulled close up against her, his words muffled*]

VENUS: Snap-snap!!! [*She snaps him tightly against her and clamps onto his whole body as if she were an iron vise*]

SWEEP: [*Gasping, his voice being crushed out of him*] Gasp! Gasp! . . . mmmmmmmmmm . . . *au secours* . . . gasp! . . . mumbo-jumbo . . . mmmmmmmmmm . . .

The eery, surrealistic music slowly peters out with the CHIMNEY SWEEP'S *breath. The purple spot on the two blinks out. Lights softly brighten on stage left, and from the left wing, just in front of the rattan table, a bicycle built for two rides awkwardly out onto the stage.* SISTER CARRIES, *a witch doctor, is nervously steering the bike. A male actor, he is dressed in a grass skirt with shoes, socks, garters, and wears a nun's headdress; arm bands, ankle bracelets, voodoo charms; a gorilla tattoo on his chest; he is quite fierce looking (in a ludicrous way), bloody fangs protruding from the corners of his mouth. In the back seat, her hands tied behind her back, looking very 1930's, is* PAULET COLBERT. *She has bobbed hair, is scantily attired in torn, transparent drapery, appears, in fact, to be nearly nude. The* GLITZES *become quite agitated when they perceive the approach of the bicycle.*

MAIS OUI: Oh, look, regard, see where from the left wing, Sister Carries, apporting the latest sacrificial maiden, on his bicycle built for two comes riding!

CARRIES: Boy, if that ain't as obvious an identification line as any I fear to hear! Come here this instant, Miss Mais Oui, and help me off with tonight's sacrificial cutey.

MAIS OUI: [*Humming, fluttering daintly off her shelf and toward the bike*] Tra-la, tra-la, tra-la, bananas that zoom in the ring, tra-la!

CARRIES: [*Dismounting, humming*] But I'll be king if I'll be killed on a bicycle built for two . . .

MAIS OUI: [*To* PAULET] Well, aren't you the juicy one!

PAULET: [*To* MAIS OUI] Don't you dare paw me, you hairy ape!

MAIS OUI: Hairy ape!—who do you think I am, William Bendix?

CARRIES: Some finesse, don't paw her, will you! A damaged sacrificial maiden is as gross an insult to the great God Kong as the fruit of the ground was to an earlier God.

PAULET: [*Staring at* MAIS OUI'S *peroxide gibbon headdress*] What a situation! Hey, are you a real gibbon?

MAIS OUI: That's my God-gibbon destiny, dearie.

PAULET: Oh, yeah, if you're really a gibbon, then how come you got blond hair?

MAIS OUI: Well, I decided that I have only one life to live.

KARMA: Call that mustard-yellow lamb-shit, blond hair?

CARRIES: Lug her over here, Miss Oui [*Motioning to center stage*] and aid me to pull this asbestos bikini on her.

PAULET: What a situation. Asbestos bikini?—what's that for?

CARRIES: You shall burn all the slower with an asbestos bikini on, my soon-to-be-late lovely, the more's the sacrificial fun that way. Heh, heh, heh!

MAIS OUI: [*Helping the resistant* PAULET *into the bikini*] What's your name, dearie?

PAULET: Ona.

MAIS OUI: Ona what?

PAULET: Ona mujer.

CARRIES: Oh, he means your maiden name, silly.

KARMA: *Maiden* name?—Boy, some of the people you can fool all of the time!

PAULET: My maiden name is Paulet Colbert. [*Pronounced as it would be correctly in French*]

MAIS OUI: Paulet Colbert? —anyone would feel cold bare

CARRIES: Yes, but she won't for long;—this stunning asbestos creation is a perfect tropical fit!

PAULET: But it itches. And ya could practically see my pyramids.

KARMA: Even a bit of your Nile.

CARRIES: Shut up, you bitches, both of you shut up!

MAIS OUI: If your name is really Paulet Colbert, you must be an actress.

PAULET: [*Heavy, exotic accent*] Yez, dat is true: —I haf played in many dramas, and serious tragedies.

MAIS OUI: Yeah?—name one.

PAULET: *Ben Hur.*

MAIS OUI: *Ben Hur*—shouldn't it of been *Ben Him?*

PAULET: [*Heavy, exotic accent*] Certainly not:—it vas the life story of Ben Gay.

CARRIES: [*Putting the final adjustments on the bikini and discarding the transparent drapery*] Well, you're about to play in the life story of Ben-gory-him. There, that's categorically superlative! viz., it's just so-o-o you, Paulet, and what man could ask for anything more!

PAULET: Drop dead!

KARMA: Hey, Carries, was that bikini hard to come by?

CARRIES: Not at all, I creamed in my grass skirt the second I spotted it in the store window.

MAIS OUI: [*To* KARMA] Wish you could whinny into something so svelte, don't cha, sour sow?

KARMA: You scheming queen!

CARRIES: [*Suddenly ecstatic*] Queen! Queen! The grand Queen Kong! Our gigantic god awaits the goodies! Come, the time for the offering is hard in hand, at hand! [*Turning to the shelves of* GLITZES] O grubby Glitz Ionas, brazen brownnosers of the glamorous Conglomerate Kong, wait ye no more, but pounching down from your precarious perches, draw ye now all around for all is in rotten readiness!

The GLITZES *leap moronically from the shelves and hop about, scampering toward and around the center trio; they call out, "Ooo-ou-oop!" "Ooga-booga," "Ugger-bugger," etc.*

MAIS OUI: Steady, steady, girls, do not prelibate the juiciness!

CARRIES: [*Being bumped into*] Down, down, you dogs! Down, away, keep your distance, you ungrateful Glitz Ionas!

KARMA: Glitz Ionas?—What are they?

CARRIES: Why, don't you know?

KARMA: No.

CARRIES: Well, a Glitz is the same thing as a Fub.

KARMA: And what's a Fub?

MAIS OUI: A Fub is someone who goes around smelling bicycle seats.

GLITZES: Ooo-ou-oop! Lumper-humper! Mogombo! etc.

CARRIES: [*To* KARMA] You just sit on, in your box, Madame, and mind your own Modess, if you don't mind.

The GLITZES *are now bounding about and grunting in free-lance confusion.* MAIS OUI *opportunes the chaos to flirt with* BRUTE.

MAIS OUI: Oh, you big bad furnace-fuller! How's your bulb?

BRUTE: [*Permitting the inspection*] Fine; how's yer socket?

CARRIES: Silence! Silence! O, gregarious Glitz Ionas! Cease off your Edenish-innocent frolicking and licking! [*The* GLITZES *come quickly to order*] That's more preferable. Let us kneel now and pray together ensemble, and summon the presence of the ever-popular pagan god—QUEEN KONG!!

GLITZES: Queen Kong! Queen Kong! Queen Kong! Kong Queen!

MAIS OUI: Princess Gibbon! Princess Gibbon! Gibbon Princess!

They all kneel in a perfect semicircle about the standing PAULET, *all facing the right wing, except for* MAIS OUI, *who kneels facing the audience, trying to steal the scene.*

PAULET: [*The essence of her thickness*] Gee, it's all kinda exciting. What a situation comedy.

MAIS OUI: Ain't excitin' for me: I seen this play before.

KARMA: You did?—what happens?

MAIS OUI: Oh, she dies in the end.

KARMA: Really? Well, at least that solves the existential problem of how to choose one's death —you end your days when they *have* to get rid of you.

CARRIES: [*With astonishing solemnity; prayerfully and even*]

> O, matted-hair Inhuman Queen,
> Best excuse for Brilliantine
> That the theatre's ever seen—
> We will fry in margarine
> Paulet *à la* Mandarin—
> [*Thoughtfully*]
> Better make it French cuisine:
> She's not kosher, she's unclean.
> Deus ex machina, Ape Queen!
> Now upon our set convene,
> Since we're but the go-between
> In this 'forties flick routine . . .

MAIS OUI: [*Softly, pondering*] The go-between what? . . . wonder what that means?

BRUTE: The go-between yer opened seam.

A preposterously loud and impressibly awkward flourish: enter CLYDE *from left wing behind the table, got up with a sun helmet with a huge feather boa, and armed with a pistol. He fires the pistol:* MAIS OUI *starts to her feet and then falls in a faint.*

MAIS OUI: Oh! my hairy heart!

CLYDE: Abort this sacrifice at once, you hostile Hurons!

BRUTE: Eeeeeeeeeeeeeek!!! Prince Kong!

CARRIES: [*Furious*] What are you—an American?

CLYDE: No, I'm a New Yorker, and I've been appointed district commissioner of this district to oversee that plausible law and northwestern order is strictly enforced, and I have come to stop this wanton human sacrifice and pointless, needless spilling of human blood and bring peace to the people!

CARRIES: Fires of de fate! The fateful grow ever laxer! The offerings fewer and further between! Kong grows more implacably insistent —she *demands* more female human sacrifices!!

CLYDE: Not in my district, sister!

PAULET: Oh, my handsome interlocutory interloper!—another two minutes and you'd have come too late!

KARMA: Yeah, how come you're so late?

CLYDE: The avant garde is always late. Did the curtain go up at precisely 8:30, or did it not? Besides, that California deal fell through.

KARMA: Why, weren't you discovered in Hollywood?

CLYDE: I was indeed. And brought to the city limits and warned not to return.

CARRIES: This ceremony shall proceed as proscribed, with or without you, Commissioner, you must adjust to your environment and the typographical peculiarities therein!

CLYDE: I must persist to insist, but this rite shan't proceed.

CARRIES: [*Foreign spy accent*] I am afraid, Commissar, that in this district, you vill nefer adjust.

CLYDE: Who are you, O power-monger?

CARRIES: [*Pridefully*] I am Sister Carries, distinguished witch doctress of the Glitz Ionas.

CLYDE: Sister Carries?—are you called that because of the indigenes traditional bad teeth?

BRUTE: Oh, no, he's called dat 'cause he carries syphilis. [*Bending over* MAIS OUI] Mae, Mae baby, get up, yer missin' the interruption.

CLYDE: Witch doctress, eh? Well for your uptodation, Sister Carries, and for the uptodation of all you Glitz Ionas, the day of the witch doctress is done. All that mumbo-jumbo bloodthirsty juju is over—gone with the Dark Ages to which it belongs.

CARRIES: The day of the witch doctress shall never be done! The witch doctress is possessed of Absolute Presence, he dates from prehistoric times, he of the cave-men, he as the cave painter, alone of the cave-men, services us today. His magic can never diminish, he is the cynosure of centuries, his spirit haunts and edifies generations as yet untold. All ye others pass into nothingness, but the indefinable mystical emanations from the ineluctable Presence of the witch doctress defy mere eternity, they gyrate in the completion and deletion, the yin and yang of cosmological incomprehensibil—

CLYDE: Shut your trap, Carries, I don't buy you any more than self-styled poet Robert Frost. I demand to know the charge against this girl that spellbinds the lot of you to this spot to exterminate her!

CARRIES: The charge is that she was caught stealing morphine—and then *more* pheen!

CLYDE: Such a crime does not merit so cruel and unusual a penalty. Your criminal code seems to lack all standard.

CARRIES: Junkel law is swift yet just. It does have a standard: we reward the worthy and punish the dumb.

PAULET: Really! What nerve! I may not be as smart as a porpoise, but I can spit in that cuspidor from here! And besides, I'm still growin'.

MAIS OUI: [*Reviving*] What are ya growin'?

PAULET: Tits.

CARRIES: [*Throwing up both arms, singing to the Marseillaise*]

> Aux arms, mes Glitz Ion!
> Faites vos battions!

Seize him! Give the white fool the bums' rush! Seize him, squeeze him, and disarm him!

The GLITZES, *who have been cowering behind* CARRIES, *arise en masse and clumsily stampede toward* CLYDE *with cocked pistol.*

CLYDE: Stand back, you beasts, or I'll shoot your hirsute faces off! Back, back!

The GLITZES *freeze where they are, a mountain of fur.*

CARRIES: On, drive on! Who the hell wants to look at your backs! Don't be intimated, I say! This ain't the hunting season—he dare not shoot!

MAIS OUI: Carries is correct! Drive on! Drive in!

BRUTE: Grab 'im! Grope 'im! Stamp on his pizzle!

The GLITZES *surge forward;* MAIS OUI *leaps onto* CLYDE, *kissing, pinching him feverishly;* BRUTE *grabs his pistol, which goes off in the struggle;* MAIS OUI *starts back at the boom and faints again.*

MAIS OUI: Oooooooooooooo!—he got me which is more than I got . . .

KARMA: Gee, it's jist like in the movies. The "B" features.

1ST GLITZ: [*Sitting on* CLYDE, *who has been thrown to the floor*] Gracious, yer quite a piece: now that I'm on top of you, you'll never get up!

CLYDE: With a stomach like that, it's small wonder. Release me, release me, I say, or you will curse the evil August dog-day you were born!

CARRIES: O flunky foreign imperialist, no one is here to obey you! You see, my brave Commissioner, these are not the servile tenants of your allotted district—they are Kong's fateful brownnosers, good and glorious Glitz Ionas down to the last lousy gibbon amongst 'em!

CLYDE: If you persist in this, Sister Carries, the Governor will send his men to take you. It's an unfriendly act and rank insubstantiation . . . Oooo—don't sit on that!

2ND GLITZ: What d'ya wanna do wit 'im?

CARRIES: Fetter him for now. I'll think up something suitable after our heathen rite. We'll plant him in concrete, or dump him in the quagmire out on the moody moor.

CLYDE: [*Being fettered*] Now, now Carries, don't be too hasty.

CARRIES: Hastiness in creation is at the core of camp. We'll homogenize this hetero yet!

MAIS OUI: [*Reviving with a joyful bounce*] And now let us resume our raucous revels at the point at which we were so dashingly deterred. Places, everybody, places!

The GLITZES *place* CLYDE, *hands fettered to feet behind him, on his stomach nearly at the*

shoes of KARMA. *Then they hasten to resume their previous kneeling positions about* PAULET.

KARMA: [*To* CLYDE] Comfy, het'ro-hero?

CLYDE: I've got an itch.

KARMA: An itch to letch, you mean! Suffer in silence. *Sic semper* dirty old men.

PAULET: Lest aught snatch me from death's jaw, doom's my lot!

CLYDE: How do you feel about theatre now, Miss Karma?

KARMA: [*Yawning*] I'll tell ya, it's a drag. Bores my bubbies. I feel like nodding right out.

GLITZES: [*Screaming*] QUEEN KONG!! APPEAR!—DEAR!!!

A deafening clap of thunder and bongo-banging; the lights go out suddenly; the entire cast shrieks frighteningly in the dark. Then lights flash on/off with disorganized psychedelic effects. QUEEN KONG *appears in a sudden blinding spotlight at the back of the theatre, standing amidst a clump of foliage, apparent now for the first time.* QUEEN KONG *is played by a male actor of huge dimensions, dressed completely in the gorilla outfit so dear to Hollywood's heart; long, shabby hair, fierce face, etc.; rhinestone tiara and pretty little rambling roses fixed on his head; emerald and ruby rings on his fingers and toes.* KONG, *growling and roaring, pounds his chest; then the fierceness peters out into a very effeminate gesture with his hand: a broken wrist, the "violet limp wrist." Immediately, he resumes his menacing manner and menaces his way through the audience, fearfully preposterous all the way up to the stage. At this point, a* CLINIC INTERN, *dressed in white intern's outfit, inexplicably emerges from within the audience carrying a quart jar of what appears to be a yellowish liquid. As* KONG *rampages his way toward the stage, the* INTERN *begins soliciting the audience with cries of "Void a specimen! Void a specimen, please! Hurry up now! Void a specimen!" Then the* INTERN *also works his way through the audience toward the stage. The singing and dancing of the* GLITZES *begins some time before* KONG *and the* INTERN *can reach the stage, creating thereby three disorganized and chaotic effects upon the audience at once. For the stanzas beginning "Keen-prong" and "Ding-dong" use the music for "A Bicycle Built for Two"; original music should be provided for all the other stanzas.*

GLITZES: [*Singing together and dancing in a frenzy*]

Keen-prong Queen Kong, ride on our
    rumpers' fat,
Where g'rillas sit, there they have
    never shat;

Our rear ends are soft and comfy
And you can have a Humpfrey
   Which uses more
     Posterior
Than a bike on whose seat you sat.

HALF OF THE GLITZES: [*Making a dash for the bicycle*]
   Howe'er he love feet
   No ape is complete
   Till he learn how sweet
   A bicycle seat
   Is to the élite!

KONG: [*Singing and gamboling in the midst of the musical confusion in all his immense glory*]
   The scent-quenching treat
   Of a bicycle seat!
   Grab a bicycle seat!
   Smell a bicycle seat!

OTHER HALF OF GLITZES: [*Rushing to the bicycle and atempting to get at the seats which the others have removed from the bicycle and are busy sniffing with delirium*]
   A bicycle seat!
   It makes obsolete
   All savory meat,
   Finds roses effete
   And perfumes deceit!

BRUTE: [*Going into a forties tap-dance routine*]
   Subtle the odor
   From shy exploder.

MAIS OUI: [*Joining the tap-dance*]
   Keen she who knoweth
   What silent outgoeth.

PAULET: [*High hysterical alto*]
   Save me! Save me!
   Army or navy!

1ST GLITZ: [*Going into forties jazz steps; the tap-dancers moving off from center, but continuing to dance*]
   Carbonate juices
   Lacking excuses
   Garner abuses!

2ND GLITZ: [*Joining the bebop steps, swinging with 1ST GLITZ*]
   How oft with looseness
   Wanton profuseness
   Ends in recluseness!

PAULET: [*Uneven hysterical alto shriek*]
   Save me, O some savior!
   I'll improve my behavior!

INTERN and 3RD GLITZ: [*Going into Rockette leg-high-over-head business*]
   Naïve to think beast
   Or flipped-out artiste
   Alone can find feast
   In festering yeast.

4TH and 5TH GLITZES: [*Joining the Rockette steps, the previous duos continuing their individual routines*]

Condemn not who may
Unwary bewray
A throne with bouquet
Of buns' exposé.

GLITZES: [*Half of them bounding in a circle about KONG, the other half in a circle about the struggling PAULET*]
   Ding-dong Queen Kong, sit on our
     faces please,
   We just want to taste where we can
     not squeeze;
   Our motives are not too naughty,
   Rear lips are tight and tauty,
     So we'll just lick
     Your toothless quick
   And our appetites thus appease!

PAULET: [*A cracked alto, desperate as several GLITZES begin to lay hands on her*]
   Save me! Save me!
   Oh, he's a knave, he
   Lets me be gravy;
   Bosom so sav'ry
     In a tropic oven
     There by gibbons shoven!

KONG: [*Rising to his gigantic height, arms benedictory, singing basso profundo with electrifying solemnity*]
   Glitz and Fubs, how We adore
   Praise of Our fortissimo
   Fleeing leaky black-eye store:
   Hence for fruit and brute We'll blow
   Out Our crown posterior
   Mildew where it's apropos.
   Air from regal portico
   On thine bike seats We'll bestow.

KONG *bends his rear toward the bicycle seats appropriately placed by* 1ST *and* 2ND GLITZES; *others begin to drag* PAULET, *terrified and screaming, toward the fireplace; the remainder dance in heathen hotness around* CARRIES; MAIS OUI *makes as if to follow the instructions in* CARRIES' *lyrics, trembling tenor.*

CARRIES: Strike your Ronson lighter, lass!
   Quick! ignite the royal gas!
   Then put torches to the flame
   And we'll burn this Colbert dame:
   Col' her hole and earthen heart,
   Yet the spark from regal fart
   Shall consume her to a cinder,
   She'll go up like female tinder
   Smelling to the scentless sky,
   Half-completing till she die—i yi yi! . . .
[*Aghast, looking toward the fireplace*] I yi yi!!! . . . [*Looking bewildered all about the stage*] STOP!!! Every Damn Body Stop!!!

The music curtails bluntly and all freeze. The GLITZES *holding* PAULET *drop her to the floor with a thump.* KARMA, *who has been sleeping since* KONG'S *entrance, awakens.*

CARRIES: *Where is the Chimney Sweep?!*

KONG: [*After belching loudly*] Funny, didn't even miss the creep.

INTERN: [*Offering the jar*] Void a specimen, Your Majesty?

KONG: Anytime. [*Taking the jar and turning around, making gestures as if he were urinating into it; several* GLITZES *watch*]

BRUTE: Yeah, how about dat—where *is* da Chimney Sweep?

CARRIES: You sightless imbeciles! Where is he?

1ST *and* 2ND GLITZES: [*Rhythmically*] We don't go. We don't blow. Nor know. Nor know.

CARRIES: Twin tarts! What do you mean you don't know! Hasn't he been summoned? Hasn't anyone seen him?

MAI OUI: I might have, but he's so nowhere I wouldn't even see him if I did.

CARRIES: [*Angry*] Whose deputed was it to subpoena him?

BRUTE: I don' understan' dat kinda talk.

CARRIES: [*Furious*] Oxymoronic slaves! ye all shall suffer the sniffer's death save he be made instantly apparent!!!

MAIS OUI: No, no, not the *sniffer's* death! not the *sniffer's* death! I could never keep my tongue still for that long!

BRUTE: I'll drop sometin' heavy on it for ya, dat oughta help.

KONG: [*Back still turned*] The Brute is considerate.

KARMA: What's the defuculty, Sister Carries? Why did you quit just when things were warming up?

CARRIES: What do *you* know about traditional religions? How can we complete the mysteries without the Chimney Sweep?

KARMA: But what do you need him for?

CARRIES: What do we need him for?!! Did ye all hark that female fool? ! How can we consume Paulet Colbert in yon fiery furnace sans a Chimney Sweep's first sweeping the chimney clean? [*Going to the fireplace and examining it contemptuously*] Just look at this, will you! Sotten with soot! Crammed with ashes! Debauched with debris! Awful with offal!

KARMA: So fancy it doesn't have to be. After all, it's the sentiment that really counts.

INTERN: [*Taking the filled jar from* KONG] Ridiculous! Ridiculous and dangerous! Dangerous and unhealthy! Do you know what the smut-smog level is around here?

KARMA: Sorry, I don't.

INTERN: It's 99 percent.

CLYDE: Really?

INTERN: Yes, and do you know what smut level is considered safe?

KARMA: Sorry, I don't.

INTERN: 98 percent.

CLYDE: Really?

KONG: [*Using the* 3RD GLITZ, *who is now on all fours, as a throne, and surrounded by fawning* GLITZES, *now noticing* CLYDE *for the first time*] Hmmmm . . . what heavenly citily-civilized delight have we here?

INTERN: Now if we burn one more maiden in that fireplace without having the chimney stack swept completely clean, the air-pollution level in this district will go up to 100 percent and we'll all croak of cigarette lung cancer.

KARMA: Indeed? How absorbing: statistics always are.

CARRIES: This ain't statistics, it's climatology!

KARMA: Climatology?

INTERN: Yeah, climatology. Y'see, that shows how much you know! And climatology tells us that if it weren't for the stagnant heat pockets which keep the smut pollution about two inches above our nose, because heat rises, we would all have choked and croaked long ago even if the smut level were only 97 percent.

CLYDE: Ya live and burn.

INTERN: On the wheel of immutable fire. [*Going upstage and placing the jar in the cuspidor*]

KONG: Hmmmm, who's the handsome young hunter, too prince a Kong at the moment to pay us any mind?

CARRIES: He is an intruder in the dirt, Queen. Permit us to attend to him anon. After such lengthy *explication sur le texte,* the matter at present press is the locating of the Chimney Sweep.

BRUTE: Maybe he took da night off.

CARRIES: Impossible—at the salary we pay him?—and at the height of the sacrificial season?

BRUTE: Ya never can tell.

CARRIES: Someone *must* tell! The someone who knows where he is.

CLYDE: How do you know someone knows where he is?

KARMA: How do you know any one knows where he is?

KONG: [*Rising to make an ex cathedra pronouncement*] Because someone always knows where someone else is, such is pure Cartesian logic; because any one always knows where everyone is, as follows in undiluted Carthusian logic based on the well-known specimen theory of the sample that's amply the whole; and because we are all really one and, being one, are some and, being some, are none and so actually one and since one knows none of two, therefore one specimen knows one of one and therefore one of you knows where one another of you is right now, which is authentic cartographic logic so whoever it is had better tell Sister Carries right away and suffer no further delay. [*Heavy exotic accent*] I haf spoken: let it be written, let it be done!

CARRIES: You heard her!

MAIS OUI: We did, but who writes around here that she can be done?

KONG: [*Frighteningly*] Sister Carries, We doth ordain you to launch an inquisition *toute-suite* to scare up the wily knowledgeable one. I haf spoken: let it be—

CARRIES: Roger! We'll start with you [*Indicating* CLYDE, *as* KONG *makes a throne of* 4TH GLITZ], you may be the link, O pink one! Brute, get him from his shanks to his shins.

MAIS OUI: And leave the upper Cartesian point to me.

KONG: [*To* MAIS OUI, *with the alertness of jealousy*] Mind your behind, low fawning unfavorite . . .

BRUTE: [*Lifting* CLYDE *to his knees*] Upsa-black-eye-daisy.

KARMA: Got ya out on the carpet now, don't they, snidey Clydey?

CARRIES: Where is the Sweep holed up?—liar, talk quickly!

CLYDE: I wouldn't know, Sister, my job don't usually bring me in contact with sweeps.

CARRIES: [*Smacking his face: simultaneously,* SWEEP *smacks the face of* VENUS] You lie! What is your job?

CLYDE: I'm a sponge.

CARRIES: A sponge? Don't you find it hard to get along being a sponge?

CLYDE: Well, you have to have a lot of openings. As you do.

CARRIES: How dare you?!

CLYDE: I mean, for a chimney sweep right now.

KARMA: Hot damn, what could be duller than night court!

CLYDE: Listen, Sister, I wouldn't tell you where the sweeper was even if I knew, and I do—not.

KONG: Why not, courageous hunter?

CLYDE: Because I don't endorse human sacrifices and I'm thrilled that the sweep is missing so you can't carry out yours. As a matter of chatter, Queeny, I disapprove of your religion in the altogether.

KONG: Show cause.

CLYDE: 'Cause it's a cult grounded on pain, on banal anal mass masochism and shady sadyism. Isn't it funny, honey, that in two thousand years of worship it shouldn't have occurred to you that pleasure can also be fun?

MAIS OUI: [*Meandering toward stage right*] Hear! Hear!

KONG: [*Eyeing* MAIS OUI *evilly*] Fear, fear, he knows no fear, that fruity one!—Ooops, that tickles! [KONG *settles back amidst his sniffing pile of* GLITZES *while* CARRIES *smacks* CLYDE's *face and* SWEEP *VENUS' face.* MAIS OUI *reaches the site of* SWEEP *and* VENUS *and stares curiously and bemused at* SWEEP's *predicament.* KARMA *is very concerned*]

MAIS OUI: Hey, whatsa matter with you?—You ain't been saying much lately.

SWEEP: [*Gagging*] I don't have too many lines.

MAIS OUI: 'S that a fact? Wonder why not . . . And wondering why not pricketh mine deductive forte to ever higher heights. [*Circling away from stage right*] Think I'll stick it inta the ol' Sista.

KARMA: [*Worried*] Wonder what that worm's upta?

MAIS OUI: [*Goosing* CARRIES, *who, along with* CLYDE, *is momentarily sidetracked by* GLITZES *sniffing about them; the much-besniffed* KONG *sighs with stupid satisfaction*] Hey, hot hole, bottoms up!

CARRIES: [*Annoyed at interruption*] What gives, barren mule?

MAIS OUI: [*Slowly, importantly, with spy accent*] Inspector, I imagine that I am capable of invaluable assistance . . . [*Mysteriously*] to you. I beleef I know somethink that might interest you professionally, very much indeed. . . .

CARRIES: What?

MAIS OUI: [*Meaningfully*] Mind if I sit down, Inspector? . . .

CARRIES: The pleasure's all mine, my mouse; don't be backward, if you can help it.

MAIS OUI: [*Sitting in the empty chair at the table*] I usually am backward, in order *to* help it.

CARRIES: Now what is this unvaluable assistance that you—

MAIS OUI: [*Interrupting, bloated with self-importance, and gesturing with her head at* KARMA *in the chair beside her*] Ever dig that dame's chapeau? . . .

CARRIES: [*Stretching his chin up and peering over and into* KARMA's *basket headdress*] Hmmmm . . . it's a veritable horny of plenty . . .

KARMA: [*More than anxious*] Clyde, Clyde!—what shall I do?—The authorities are about to interrogate *me!*

CLYDE: Be as obvious about your activities as possible, Miss Karma, regardless of what they are. Authority always looks for something suspicious, not obvious.

CARRIES: [*Plucking the plantain out of* KARMA'S *headdress*] Hmmm, hello, here's an obvious fruit.

MAIS OUI: [*Mistaking the reference, incomprehensibly*] Well! That's Rosey! And after every time I've done—I mean, everything I've done for him.

CARRIES: It occurs to me that the Mem-sab's objective perspective on this play may qualify her as one who might, with reasonable justification, be expected to be reasonably aware of the whereabouts of the elusive Chimney-chipper and his broom to zoom.

KARMA: [*Heavy Portuguese accent from here until specified*] But, Inspector Carries, you seem to forget zat I was dancing at zee time zat zee Chimney Sweep disappeared.

CARRIES: Such is factual accuracy. [*Holding up the plantain*] Is this your banana?

KARMA: Why, yez, zat's my banana: I must haf dropped it while I was dancing.

CARRIES: [*Just too official to be believed*] Quite possible, Señorita, quite possible. Except for one thing: you see, Señorita, this is not a banana: it is a plátano.

KARMA: Oh?

CARRIES: And in this district, the only entity possessing a plátano is the Chimney Sweep.

KARMA: Oh!—care for a drink, Investigator Carries? Perhaps, some liquor?

MAIS OUI: Lick 'er where?

CARRIES *tosses* MAIS OUI *out of the chair and sits in it himself, the height of affability, debonair beyond words;* KARMA *applies herself to mixing juleps with feverish intensity.*

CARRIES: A drink concocted by so porcelain a hand would be hard for a man of my tastes to resist.

KARMA: [*Straining to concentrate on the juleps*] Do your tastes incline toward zee liquid?

MAIS OUI: [*From the floor, uptight*] That depends on how well you lubricate.

KARMA: May I take your headdress, Inspector Carries?

CARRIES: Where ya wanna take it?

KARMA: [*Straining to affect charm*] Ho-ho; I perceef you are not only wise, but witty, my dear detectif; haf a slug.

CARRIES: [*Ignoring the glass she offers him, forcing himself closer upon her*] I prefer a hug.

KARMA: But a drink in time safes nine—nine months. [*Quakingly nervous, rattling the table*] I should be quite offended if you decline my barmaid art.

CLYDE: [*Warningly, regarding the tête-à-tête with fiancé concern*] Full many a maid by the bar was made.

CARRIES: I'm afraid, Señorita, but I must resist the gratuities. You understand that a man in my precarious position is not infrequently confronted with treachery—in the guise, shall we say . . . of exquisite beauty?

KARMA: Why, Detectif Daring, you could not possibly implicate—

CARRIES: [*Sudden angry reversal to his old self*] I implicate nothing! I don' swill on the job, that's all!

CLYDE: [*Wishing to break them up*] How about getting back to the plantain business, Carries?

CARRIES: And so now, concerning the plátano, Señorita—

KARMA: Ah, yez, I find it most divertingly curious zat in this district zee Chimney Sweep alone should be possessed of zee plátano. It makes a most divertingly fascinating conversation piece—especially wit mint juleps, don't you think so, Inquisitor?

CARRIES: It is more than a conversation piece, Chica, it is one of the pointed facts of life!

KARMA: How so?

INTERN: The plátano was a present personally presented to the Chimney Sweep by Her Regal Brutishness, Queen Kong.

KARMA: [*Subtle sarcasm*] Sounds generous.

KONG: [*Solemn, profound*] It was. We took it from the tallest tree nest in the majestic bestiary where We cache Our gynecologist-fitted masturbating material.

MAIS OUI: Wonder how much cash ya could get for it?

KARMA: [*Shocked*] Gynecologist-fitted *masturbating* material?

INTERN: What is so shocking? Masturbation is America's only innovational contribution to world culture.

KONG: [*To* CLYDE] Hey, Muskels, wanna make me after court?

CARRIES: [*Upset*] Miss Kong, court has not yet adjerned! Please desist from these spicy interjections and assist me in maintaining the dignity of this seedy proceeding!

KONG: Proceed, Sister.

MAIS OUI: [*Examining the plantain, which she has picked off the table*] Wonder what the proceeds are on a thing like this? Wonder what kinda seeds it got?

CARRIES: And so, Guwappa, do you still detain your preposterous maintain that you know not the Sweep and did not obtain this plantain from him?

KARMA: Now actually I did spot this zo-call Sweep, but only briefly, and paid him little mind: you see, he was so out of place on this set, what wit his weird mime-immodest getup, zat I figured he was just a tourist.

KONG: [*Working himself up against* KARMA *because of his attraction to* CLYDE] How brief could your encounter with him have been, that you had time to con him out of the precious plantain which We personally took from Our parts to bestow on him?

MAIS OUI: Bestowed yer parts on him, did ya?

KARMA: [*Standing in her fear, reverting to her natural voice*] But this is unspeakably ineffable! It surpasses credence! The Sweep doesn't even know who Kong is! You all, every last loon of you, lack linkage, lack logic.

BRUTE: Naturally, my queer, we're only gibbons. Except for Queeny, she's a g'rilla.

KARMA: But how does having the Chimney Sweep's plantain mean that I know where he disappeared to?! Somewhere in your reasoning, there's a terrible error!

INTERN: Why do people always think that the thing most difficult for one to effect, is an error?

KARMA: [*Hysterical, rushing to* CLYDE] Oh, help, Clyde, help!

CLYDE: [*Struggling in his fetters*] Karma! My life's karma! My only karma—huge as it is!

KONG: [*With terrifying authority*] We'll take over this obsidianly obliquitous inquisition! Cut that nose-newsing out, will you? Listen, you Brazilian torpedo-hanger, did that Sweeper ever buy you anything?

KARMA: [*Simpering*] Yes, Mrs. Cross, he did.

KONG: Ah-ha! What?!

KARMA: A malted.

Long pause.

INTERN: Chocolate?

KARMA: [*Simpering*] What does it matter—you'll find me guilty whatever flavor it was.

KONG: [*To* CLYDE] Mister Muskels, is this hussy your fiancée?

CLYDE: [*Meekly*] One might so define her.

KONG: That settles it! Seize her! Seize her! Sacrifice her!!!

1ST GLITZ: [*Pushing his way through the crowd toward* KARMA] One minx, methinks, is as good as the other mother . . .

INTERN: But Queen K., the air-pollution level! The smut rate!

KONG: What care I? I care not! I do not give a good—

CARRIES: [*Rushing to* KONG] The slut—er, the smut percent Sage—

KONG: [*Kicking him with royal fury*] Shut your competitive, repetitive trap! Get the hell out of my hair, fuckface!

CLYDE: [*Wormwise in his fetters, working his way toward* KONG'S *feet, while several* GLITZES *lay greedy hands on* KARMA] O awesome Ape, reconsider: I at Thy corn-encrusted feet for the lady's life do implore Thee!

KONG: [*Sudden switch*] Hmm, kinda sexy grovelin', ain't he?

CLYDE: Thou wilt share, er, spare her?

KONG: What balls! Spare her, so *she* can have ya?

CLYDE: For mine unlinked line and pitiable pipe's sake!

INTERN: [*Pleading*] There are no lines, only a circle, but still for sake of the smut rate!—on the present date!

GLITZES: [*Chanting rebelliously*] THE SMUT RATE! WE TOOK OF LATE! FOR KONG-GOD'S SAKE! WE'LL ALL CROAK! IT AIN'T A JOKE!!!

Long pause. The chanting echoes out.

KONG: Grrrooooowl! Grrrrrrrrr! Aaaaaagh! Popular opinion seems to run contrary to Our holy Person.

MAIS OUI: And you *do* wanna win next year's popularity poll!

KONG: Such is accuracy. Our august Person shall reconsider: Tell ya what:

ALL: WHAT?

KONG: We'll schedule our heathen rite for 10:40. You have a menstruation period of grace from now until then, Prince Kong, in which to bleed out, er, cough up the Sweep. Brute, unfetter him!

BRUTE: [*Obeying the order*] Jist a minute, Pepe, and ya'll be able to git up and walk away, like a pair o' dirty gym socks, on yer own accord.

KONG: If you find the Sweep in the time allotted, this Karma character shall thereby be proved exonerate of guilt and set footloose and fancy-dancing free. And you may marry her.

CLYDE: [*Freed of his fetters*] And if I fail to locate the Sweep?

KONG: Then the pagan pleasures will come off as scheduled—exactly at 10:40. We shall have a Gemini sacrifice: both Paulet Colbert and Karma Miranda will be spectacularly burnt to death!

CLYDE: But in that event, we'll all suck come to lung cancer!

KONG: Well, We hate to be callous, Maria Callous, but that's how it gotta be. If I can't have you, nobody will. [*Bursting into ditty with sentimental Victorian tune*]
    If I cannot have you,
        The Rose toward Divine,

No human shall have you:
I ain't asernine!

MAIS OUI *and* BRUTE: [*Singing*]
Dry Gulch, let me fit you
And fill your incline,
For plantain shall split you
At base of the spine.

GLITZES *and* INTERNS: [*Singing*]
My Spoke, it's to stop you
From female supine:
A hub soon atop you,
A pearl under swine!

CLYDE: It don't make sense. You sing that you want me, but the alternatives are—

INTERN: But it does make sense—that's just what's wrong with it. Sense, like the mule, manages no young.

MAI OUI: [*Near stage right, to SWEEP*] You sleeping?

SWEEP: No, dreaming.

MAIS OUI: [*Picking up roll of toilet paper next to SWEEP's unmoving foot*] What? [*Sadly, almost depressed, shaking her head at SWEEP*] Has it come to this?

CARRIES: It's gonna be a long hot summer, Commissioner!

CLYDE: [*Confused*] Watts?

KONG: Grrooooowl! Aaaaaaaaah! Now Our pristine court adjerns for supper. Tonight, gourmet treats. [*Suggestively*] So We'll see a few of you Fubs in Our private quarters. Brute, return the Bwana's pistol. He and his heart have a confrontation coming up. We reconvene at 10:30. [*Alter time to exact time of reentrance*]

CARRIES: Take the broads as hot ages; let's go.

BRUTE *gives pistol to* CLYDE. 1ST *and* 2ND GLITZES *revive* PAULET *and then take hold of her and* KARMA *and drag them toward downstage left.* 3RD *and* 4TH GLITZES *refix the seats on the bicycle.* INTERN *helps the demoralized* CARRIES *onto the front seat.*

KARMA: Take yer young paws offa me—I know howda wheel!

2ND GLITZ: Yeah, but we're gonna wheel ya to the last stop! And what d'ya mean young? In a few years, I'll be older than you.

PAULET: Maybe we'll be rescued by a Buddhist uprising.

KARMA: Buddhist uprising?—What's that—another contradiction in terms?

CARRIES: Thanks, bottle-boy. Hop on, Mae, I'll drive ya home.

MAIS OUI: [*Complying*] That's what usually happens when I hop on.

SWEEP: [*Shouting across to MAIS OUI*] Bring back something sixteen and nice, will ya?

CARRIES: [*Having trouble with the bicycle*] Who *is* he yellin' to! Gotta get my crotch—crutch relined.

MAIS OUI: The ride I got, but moving I'm not.

KONG: [*A bitter dig at CARRIES*] He'll get that bike started; he's not a person to rest on his laurels.

MAIS OUI: [*Kicking-him-when-he's-down*] He's not a person.

CARRIES: There we go; hang on!

MAIS OUI: [*Hands clasped on CARRIES' crotch*] Ooo—yer in reverse!

KONG: [*The GLITZES having difficulty in carrying him out*] Girls, girls, lemme go out on my own gas!

All head for the exit downstage left: CARRIES *riding the bicycle out, the* GLITZES *dragging the women,* KONG *attempting it on his exhaust like a rocket; they all sing as they grandly exit.*

GLITZES *etc.*: [*Singing*]
If I try to steal you
And, Rose, make Divine,
Ought Smacker conceal you
In sexual shrine?

If I must eschew you,
Forever resign
To be without yoo-hoo,
Beware the malign!
Beware the malign
AND WATCH YOUR BEHIN'!!

CLYDE: [*Sorrowfully alone and bewildered center stage*] There is just so much space on this stage, so much and no more, but I wouldn't know where to begin to look for that ratty Chimney Sweep. I can't think of a thing to do. Thank God Kong this is the end of Act One. [CLYDE *crosses quite close to* SWEEP *and* VENUS *and squats on the floor beside them with desolate expression. Eerie mime music plays softly.* CLYDE *rubs his cheek as if in thought or soothing a smack.* VENUS *intones, but is apparently unheard by* CLYDE]

VENUS:
Cheeky he to whom is aught
Alien in an'mal thought;
Sim'lar he who beastly instinct
Thinks mere love of licking sin-stink.

KONG: [*Peering around the corner of the cage, baiting CLYDE very coyly*] Yoo-hoo, soldier boy!

CLYDE: [*Bitchy, as the mime music suddenly stops*] Whatsa matter, forget your purse?

KONG: [*Coyly*] Oh, please, squeezey please, handsome, don't be curt, Kurt Douglas, with me.

CLYDE: I ain't curt—I'm concerned.

KONG: [*Emerging from behind the cage*] 'Bout what? Tell Mama what's on yer mindy-blindy like a good little boy.

CLYDE: I'm concerned about what's in store for them two peppery numbers.

KONG: Any man worth his salt would be. But there's nothin' to worry about. I seen this play before—

CLYDE: Yeah, I know, and they both die in the end. Well in that case, just stick to the other side of the stage, if ya know what's good for you.

KONG: [*Genuinely offended*] I really don't know what's wrong with me: people always look at me as if they've seen something I can't bear.

CLYDE: Uglier than a bear. Keep to your corner.

KONG: Oh, please be curt-eous: I readily acknowledge that I was once quite dangerous, but I'm changed now, really.

CLYDE: You're changed now! What were you like *before?*

KONG: [*Deep, alluring feminine advertising voice*] Well, you see, before it was all very like before . . . Compoz . . .

CLYDE: Who *are* you, anyhow?

KONG: [*Very effeminate*] I'm Brod.

CLYDE: Brod?

KONG: [*Coyly effeminate*] Brod Crawford. Joan's my sister.

CLYDE: [*Sarcastic*] Is she? Well, just keep your distance.

KONG: Gawd! you make me feel like Quasimodo!

CLYDE: That's gawd, 'cause ya look like him.

KONG: How dare you, how double-dare you, how gemini-dare you! I am *not* Quasimodo, I am Queen Kong!

CLYDE: You may be Queen Kong to them gullible gibbons, but yer j'st a plain ol' g'rilla to me. In fact, ya look like a g'rilla queen to me.

KONG: [*Feminine indignation*] I am not a gorilla queen—I'm Venus in Furs, I'm a hairy lady, I'm the Lady in the Pelt!—The Lady in the Pelt, do you hear me? Care for a little leather and discipline?

CLYDE: No thanks: I'm too young to go out with g'rillas—even if they *are* a lady.

KONG: You'll regret this rejection, O cold, short, and unobtainable one: remember, only I hold the key to the late fate of those damsels in distress.

CLYDE: Such is accuracy; I shall reconsider; what do you want me to do?

KONG: Be a little less chaste; be a little more chas*ing.*

CLYDE: Okay, you call the tune.

KONG: [*Joyously obsequious*] Oh, sir! Will you be wanting me for fifteen minutes, sir, or for the whole night?

CLYDE: That depends on the first fifteen minutes.

KONG: [*Pulling out the nearest chair from the table*] Well, then, come over here and sit on my face, I mean, my lap like a good little dog.

CLYDE: [*Crossing toward KONG seating himself*] I'll screw anything once. Besides, ya could only screw it up. [*Sitting on KONG's lap*] Well, ya gotta eat a pound of dirt before ya die.

KONG: [*Lifting a doily off the table*] Here, have a derly.

CLYDE: No thanks, I don't go in for that frilly fruit stuff.

KONG: I am certain. [*Trying to employ the rejected doily as toilet paper, having some difficulty in rising slightly from the chair since CLYDE is securely in his lap and quite obviously not willing to facilitate matters*]

CLYDE: [*Like a psychiatrist*] Now, Madame, since this is your first visit, please tell me just what is bothering you.

KONG: To begin with, you have too much karma —karma Miranda.

CLYDE: We'll discuss my philosophical shortcomings at some future fate, if you don't mind. What else?

KONG: So for another thing, seeing as how us two've finally gotten ends to meet, so that I be made not to feel altogether too self-consciously hirsute, I'd like to see you grow a beard; a huge, heavy, grizzly beard.

CLYDE: What! grow a beard and ruin my eighteen-year-old image?

KONG: [*Catty*] Your image is eighteen years old?

CLYDE: A queen is a queen is a queen, isn't he? What else?

KONG: Oh, it's kind of excruciating to put into words.

CLYDE: Well, it should be put into something. Besides, the Word *was* made flesh; so why not reverse the—

KONG: Yes, that's more or less what I'm trying to get around to; I do so hate to beat around the bush.

CLYDE: Yes, it's better to go right in. One in the bush is worth two in the hand.

KONG: [*Coyly*] You embarrass me, Clydey cutey. I hope you realize I was innocent until quite recently.

CLYDE: Oh? so you've been making up for lost time?

KONG: [*Peeved*] Not quite; I've been losing it again.

CLYDE: With a mug like yours, lousy lady, it's small wonder. You've probably got lice in your face.

KONG: [*Angry*] Don't get so uppity—just remember, shrimpy-dick, you can always be replaced by a shrinker!

SWEEP: Yeah, don't get so uppity—bail out when you gain elevation.

KONG: No need!:—he's bailing out right now!

[KONG *rises with a swift thrust, catapulting* CLYDE *to the floor. The table shakes violently in the upset and* KONG *bends over it to catch the spilling glasses: in this maneuver* KONG'S *rear end is directly on line with* CLYDE'S *face, sitting as he is on the floor*]

CLYDE: [*His nose practically in the huge backside*] Hmmmm . . . the black hole of Calcutta . . .

KONG: *Quelle insulte noire!* You disapprove of my other side?

CLYDE: [*His nose still buried, his hands supporting the huge buttocks*] Oh, no, I'm glad for *both* of you!

KONG: [*Turning to face him, furious*] Both those girls *will* perish! I have decreed it and I'll not be deterred from my decreation!

CLYDE: All right, big boobs, then fend for your front without *my* titillations! And that's final!

KONG: [*Quickly regretful, hovering over* CLYDE, *running fingers through his hair*] Oh, Clydeyboo, don't be peeved—your overtaxed nerves are just overwrought, that's all. I didn't mean to be snappish with you, honest to Betsy—

CLYDE: Get your hairy hand outta my hair.

KONG: But, Diminutive One, I just love your silken locks!

CLYDE: You do?—You oughta try my bagels.

KONG: [*Purring*] Mmmmmmmmmm, purrrrrrrr, poor *bébé*, gimme a kiss?

CLYDE: [*Calculating*] I'm game . . . turn your back . . .

KONG: But, Princeling, one's ill-advised to turn his back on anything around here.

CLYDE: Now, now, Lady in the Pelt, don't you trust me?

KONG: Of course, but—

CLYDE: Then face the cuspidor and stop giving me a hard time.

KONG: I hope you don't give *me* a hard time.

CLYDE: Few they be, could show hard for you . . . [*He rises slowly from the floor as* KONG *about faces*] Yet I can . . . *kick a can!* [*He rams mightily into* KONG'S *rear with his left boot and, as* KONG *falls flat on his face, hurriedly picks up the overturned chair and whips out his pistol*]

KONG: [*Exotic accent*] You ram treezon! treezon on Her Royal Majesty! Seedy, blood-sucking—

CLYDE: [*Handling the chair and pistol like a lion trainer as* KONG *fixes on all fours*] Steady . . . steady, big girl . . . [*Circling slowly about* KONG *as in a circus ring*] You have failed to make mental note, haven't you, that famed Clyde Batty is also an accomplished animal trainer?

KONG: How could I? I don't date back to them thirties flicks.

CLYDE: Woulda been worth yer wiles to've sat up and caught a few of 'em on the late show. . . . Steady now, big gal. . . .

KONG: [*Twisting torturously within the circle like a baited bear*] Unfledged wingling! Sadistic pipsqueak! I could malleate you with a single blow—they got *that* on the late show too—*Mighty Josephine Young, Daughter Ape*—

CLYDE: [*Narrowing his circle, nervously, professionally, and altering it as* KONG *takes several cautious steps toward him*] Quiet, quiet now, enough lip for one act . . . Easy does it, ol' bag, take it easy . . . that's it . . . ah . . . nothin' simpler than animal trainin'—like narrowin' in nervously on the precarious petals of the multifidous rose . . .

KONG: Oh, the humiliation, oh, the disgrace! Royalty debunct! Regality ruined! Majesty in the mud!

CLYDE: Easy, bitch, easy . . . Now—roll over, roll over, baby—

KONG: [*Indignant*] I most certainly will not! [*Making a sudden lunge at* CLYDE] I'll stamp you out, you pigmy! you praying manta!

CLYDE: [*Ramming the chair into* KONG'S *belly*] Back, piglet, back!

KONG: [*Retreating*] Groooooooooowwwwllllll!!!!! Aaaaaaaaagh!!!

CLYDE *aims his pistol at* KONG *and is about to shoot; suddenly the* INTERN *drops down from within the chimney stack into the hearth.*

INTERN: CLYDE BATTY, DON'T SHOOT!! The Park Department is on strike and there'll be no one to carry off the corpse. The mayor urges you not to litter until further notice.

CLYDE: Glad ya told me. I like to keep an eye on city ordinances. What citizen worth his dicker doesn't?

INTERN: Carry on. Oh, er, Kong, roll over like the man says. [*The* INTERN *disappears up the chimney stack*]

There is a long bewildered pause. Finally, KONG *sinks to the floor. Another pause, torturously long, then* KONG *rolls over, arms and legs thrown in the air.* CLYDE'S *glance, scanning the stage, lights on the cage.*

CLYDE: Hello, what's this? Ah, yes, the perfect litter basket! [*Edging toward the cage as* KONG *completes the roll*] Again, Kong, again, please. [*Backed up against the cage as* KONG, *all too humanly, repeats his humiliation as best he can, the last vestige of his dignity being his gagged silence*] Now, Queen, stand on your crown! Facing wing left.

KONG: [*Pitifully*] But I can't. I'm too fat for that.

CLYDE: Stand on your hard head, I say, or I'll ignore that new ordinance and you'll lie flat on your flabby butt from now till the Forest Forever!

KONG, *turning his back on* CLYDE, *attempts to obey the command; bulking and clumsy, he cannot, but tries and pitifully tries time and again. As soon as* KONG *is busied,* CLYDE *puts down the chair and begins hacking away at the foliage that camouflages the huge cage. He topples over one potted plant after another, bulrushes, ivy, and grape vines in particular.* KONG *is oblivious to all noise.*

CLYDE: Cumbersome tropical undergrowth! Hack it down and a day later it's taller than yer tit!

VENUS: Note how, slaughtering, he gnaws Closer to my man-clampt claws!

CLYDE: Lurid vegetation of the torrid zone! Humid, rainy, salivary climate—that's what shoots it up.

VENUS: But my grappling grasp is full, Sweep ingesting, cock 'n bull!

CLYDE: Flunky's work this is, chopping the tangle. But if I savvy that ordinance correctly, I've gotta cut this cage free—and in a fat-ass hurry. That dumb g'rilla ain't gonna be turnin' tricks all day, dig?

VENUS: [*Trembling*] "Human trap is Zoo of Age

And vice reverses," versed the sage. Yet Venus Trap by circus cage Soon shalt be dead foliage!

CLYDE: [*Reaching* VENUS *and* SWEEP] Get a loada that, will ya! Boy, but they got some strange growths around these parts. What'll nature thinka next? An Aphrodite in fly-fur, no doubt! [CLYDE *hacks at* VENUS *with his pistol: her arms, legs and body fall limp, appear to wither under the assault; slowly she crumbles to the floor, releasing* SWEEP, *who also seems all but dead*]

VENUS: Moon! at leaf and trap he hacks, Urine-drinking root attacks! One! two! three! the fatal cracks! Dealt as to sane bric-a-bracs Who, of all the cul-de-sacs, Chose the right-wing, far from quacks,

Far from the jar of maniacs Pickled by the zodiacs!

SWEEP: [*Falling with* VENUS, *but still managing to smack her*] Female plant! who man ransacks, Dying, still you merit smacks!

VENUS: Smack thy last, seed-sowing Sweep, Every night. And now to sleep.

SWEEP: [*Painfully, before expiring beside the motionless* VENUS] Love! I lack all lust to rise: Here must lie till my demise . . .

CLYDE: [*Pulling on the cage door*] Heavens' Totality! never dreamt a door could be this stuck. Gotta have the pull of a bull to budge it.

The cage door gives begrudgingly with a frightfully loud as well as peculiar (onomatopoeic in keeping with the themes) noise which alerts KONG *and curtails his essays at head standing.*

KONG: There's something fishy in the district of Denmark . . . I smell a pussy, I mean, rat! [*Turning around, spotting* CLYDE *busy at the door*] Ah-ha! guard's down and the table's turned! Aaaaaaaaagh!!

CLYDE: [*Unaware of* KONG's *stretching to his full terrifying stature*] The junkel abounds with strange sounds tonight. Many very curious ejaculations.

KONG *charges across the stage like an elephant stampede, shrieking and scream-growling at lung's loud top; just as he is about to pounce upon* CLYDE *and shred him,* CLYDE *turns calmly, distractedly, about, daze-eyed at* KONG's *middle, and says:*

CLYDE: Got a dime? I'm short.

KONG: [*Stopping dead in his tracks, completely stymied*] I'm tall. But hold on a minute. [*Fingering his hairy hips as if searching pockets*] Gee, I was sure I had one. . . .

CLYDE: [*Circling the preoccupied* KONG, *so that* KONG *is between him and the open cage*] Whadda ya doin'?

KONG: Looking for the star in the sapphire.

CLYDE: [*Landing* KONG *in the cage with a well-rammed goose*] Back up on a nail and yer flat in rear gear! [*Slamming the cage door shut and bolting it*] Ho-ho! ever consider hibernating, butterfly?

KONG: [*Turning, grasping the cage bars*] Butterflies come after hibernation. I'm stunned.

CLYDE: [*Just too satisfied*] Penny for your stunning thoughts.

KONG: From a guy what don't got a dime to his name? Hey, lemme loose!—Whatcha take me for, a barmaid?

CLYDE: [*Smacking his hands together and dusting his finger tip*] Know somethin', Kong baby, I'm gettin' pretty sick and tired of all these double entendres.

KONG: They ain't double, they're triple—triple sec.

CLYDE: Sex?

KONG: Sec, I said. Triple sec. *Ménage à trois.*

CLYDE: [*Cocking his pistol*] Hummm-gum, a fly trapped Venus with Furs. Ready for a little leather and discipline?

KONG: Hey, wait! whatcha doin' with that plantain, er, pistol?

CLYDE: Ah-ha!—another fraudulent slip!

KONG: [*Quaking*] Muskels, you ain't bein' very social!

CLYDE: To a g'rilla? Why should I? G'rillas, like chimpanzees and orangutans, ain't social animals.

KONG: But my people, the gibbons, is: they cohabit in herds.

CLYDE: [*Aiming the pistol*] We ain't discussin' yer people now.

KONG: [*Horrified*] A-social sore-thumb! Outcast of the cosmos! What gives you jurisdiction over your immanent atrocity?!

CLYDE: I am Clyde Batty, the *great* Clyde Batty, by Hollywood given the jurisdiction to corner, capture, and round up all—to cage, categorize, and define!

KONG: [*Sinking to his knees, imploring hysterically*] Listen, Mr. Batty, hear me, don't fire! We could still make it, you and I, all things are conceivable, all concei—

CLYDE: Man and manthropoid make it?—Don't be sick!

KONG: [*Arms stretching out of the cage, hands clasped in prayer*] Bide a bit, let me tell you how I've heard of even humans often having sex—one holds the other's hand, lying both in bed, and comes, arrives, achieves orgasm, without further contact!

CLYDE: [*Unimpressed*] Now dig the hard-on facts Miss Throw-Back:—Sister Carries, backed by the gibbons, is dead against the burning of the babes because of the deadly air-pollution level. That leaves you, and you alone, still motivated to this murder. Which means that if there is no Kong—

INTERN: [*Voice from within the fireplace*] There'll Always Be A Kong!!!

CLYDE: [*Unperturbed*]—there is no warming of the hearth. So beat your bubbies and growl your glam-lust last: thy omophagic reign is run—unless you wanna alter your brain-child right this second?

KONG: I'd sooner alter my string of studs than turn you over to that Karma dame! —Junior, if you slaughter me, you'll be left all alone in the treacherous tropical rain forest: tell me, just tell me what you'd do if a serpent were to sting your pecker?

CLYDE: [*Offhand*] Sit down and smoke a cigarette, seein' as how it would probably be my last.

KONG: You do that and you're a better woman than I am.

CLYDE: [*Stepping downstage, deeply involved and thinking out loud*] Funny, but looking at her locked up in there looking out at me, reminds me of the time I once visited a chicken farm. There was a long, long two-story coop with endless windows on the second floor and on each windowsill a dozen white hens were perched, and all of them hanging out and looking straight down at me, at you. The looniest sight I've ever seen, but all those white chickens were staring me down as if *I* were the loony one. . . . Made ya feel kinda peculiar, it did, ya know what I mean?—sorta crazy . . . [*About facing quickly, firing the pistol directly at* KONG] Fire-arm, speak for me!!!

Percussions echo the pistol shot to deafening pitch. KONG *leaps back and stiffens, hands over his bleeding face.*

CLYDE: Spit in the cusp!—A perfect shot!—Right in the face!

A moment of pregnant silence. Then drums and percussions of thunderous force; lights blink blindingly like the Lord's wrath come visual; all deaden except for a red spot on KONG, *who staggers and collapses over a hay heap and banana peels within the cage.*

KONG: [*Expiring, his spot dimming*] Of . . . the sciences . . . anthropology . . . is . . . my favorite . . .

CLYDE: [*Delivering a funeral oration as the red spot brightens on him*] Ladies and gentlemen of every genus, the Great Kong *was* great: she was a great queen and a great lover. She took over a million gibbons and humans up to her tree-top nest during her long and lusty career. But I, myself, just couldn't make it with her: you see, where I come from, animals as well as people are taught to keep their place. For beast is beast and nest is nest and never the sane shall invest in the twain. A line is a line and division division and woe be to he holds derision toward either. And neither shall lessen but both find a blessin', if brute in the junkel stays and man goeth separate ways.

A noisy shuffle within the cage; the spot inky-dinkies across the stage to investigate the disturbance; it picks out the furry junk pile from which stumblingly emerges TAHARAH-NUGI WHITE WOMAN, *dusting long hairs and patches of fur off his sarong; a bit shaky.*

TAHARAH: Some costume change, that one—a pain in de neck. I shed eet like serpent skeen, like steef cacoon. Is like a woolen dress—beleef you me, eet itches, like a son of a—

CLYDE: [*A second spot on his pale expression, wild, agonized, as he attempts to escape stage left, but fails, being partially paralyzed; he sings to "A Bicycle Built for Two"*]
    Crazy! crazy! like from a rabies kiss!
    I'm Clyde Batty sighting the savage Miss;
        I have heard of lýcanthropy
        But this can make ya dopey:
            What I had seen
            As g'rilla queen,
    Was a girl in her chrysalis!

TAHARAH: [*Unbolting the door, smoothing the bolting bar in his embrace*]
    Full many a maid by de bar was made,
        But who haf de hole
        Could rigormarole
    A beauty like theez when she laid?

CLYDE: I'm pistil-happy, stigma-stung! A *stone-fuckken-nut!!!*

TAHARAH: [*Stepping out of the cage*] No, you're not, Bwana. Theez is de lackadizzical heat-depleting torrid zone: is not way up Nort' where people haf de energy to go mad.

CLYDE: I don't—I won't believe it!

TAHARAH: [*Lifting up his tight sarong*] What, de torrid zone? Then, Bwana, allow me to reveal *my* torrid zone.

CLYDE: [*As* TAHARAH *advances*] From chrysalis to Charybdis!

TAHARAH: [*Throwing his arms around* CLYDE, *the bolting bar caught between them*] Junior speak many beeg words. But Taharahnugi White Woman prefer he carry beeg steeck.

CLYDE: But, but, Too-hairy-nugi Double Double You, how'd *you* come outta that pen—it was Queen Kong I locked—

TAHARAH: Simple—she married his mama, and out came I. You not like the outcome of in-breeding?

CLYDE: No more than Ivan de Carlo likes Mona Liar.

TAHARAH: Taharahnugi no say lie; she not fibber. People who lif a fib end their ends on de Bowery.

CLYDE: [*Tearing himself out of the embrace*] Yet can it be that—that after all this, YOU are Kong? Tell me, tell me quickly, are *you* Kong? No, no, it can't be, you must've been holed up in that cage all along!

TAHARAH: Haf you nefer read *Darwin, dar*-link?

CLYDE: Natural selection is not my specialty, I'm rather indiscriminate about whom I choose to ball, but—there's such a difference—I mean! —Kong had all that hair, I mean where I know for a fact you don't!

TAHARAH: J. R. Marett explains that since iodine deficiency causes baldness, humans lost their hair through "the need to economize iodine and adapt an anthropoid body to a life on the tree-less alp of a young mountain system." Since salivary tropical rain forest rains in the pluvial period engendered an acidity of the soil and an accumulation of iodine later reduced through the merciless, pass-waterless increasing aridity—

CLYDE: Stop telling malicious truths, woman, they're as clear as [*Shaking the bolting bar at* TAHARAH] this stick in yer muddy hole! Heavens to Betsy's Totality! to think that I tried to croak what was actually a human being, caged, defenceless—

TAHARAH: Oh, do not keen ofer a dead queen. Instead, be oferjoy ofer my emanation from her body like a omnivorous prince froma frugivorous frog.

CLYDE: [*Jumping on top of the table to avoid* TAHARAH'S *clutch*] I'm losing my bird, that's all: I'm stark raving nuts!!

TAHARAH: Talk no more of your nuts, leetle screwel: you haf seen nuff movie on de late as well as early show to know exactly how theez transformations occur. Nuff's too much.

CLYDE: Yeah, but this here's the kinda thing don't matter how many times ya see it ya still can't believe it.

TAHARAH: [*Tugging on* CLYDE's *right boot, pulling it off*] Muskels, your attenuated non-suspension of beleef is drag on de audience: anyone wit haf a brain in theez jernt figger out my efolution way back in Act One. So quit labor—

CLYDE: [*Concluding, imitating*] Wit de pernt? Hey, whatcha doin'?—Hopin' against hope for a prehensile foot?

TAHARAH: [*Pulling off his sock*] Generally, I'd stoop to conquer more confentionally, [*Pointing his chin up toward* CLYDE's *thighs*] but you too-too high up and too-too far ofer for that!

CLYDE: Then jist which innovation have you in heart, Miss Mange?

TAHARAH: I thought I'd get a leak, er, look at de nur between yer toes—

CLYDE: [*Yanking his naked foot away from* TAHARAH's *grasp and bending it up into the cupping protection of his own hands; shocked*] The *nur* between my toes?????

TAHARAH: [*His feelings hurt*] Ees only natural. Ain't us all de go-between angel and earth, expression and suspension?

CLYDE: [*Cringing as before a leper*] Now wait a minute—what other talents in this category do you decline toward?

TAHARAH: [*Intimidated, very tentatively*] . . . I could eat de cottage cheese out of a dead gibbon's jockstrap . . .

CLYDE: [*Letting go of his foot in catatonic disbelief*] The only thing wasp about *you* is yer waist!

TAHARAH: [*Seizing the foot*] What's theez? You've a webbed toe!!

CLYDE: A web between two toes: not much room for nur, is there?

TAHARAH: How long haf you had theez?

CLYDE: Since I was born. What of it?

TAHARAH: [*To audience*] Girl, deed I get roped in! Not so high up on de tree of efolution himself, is he, theez Mr. Muskelar Half-Back!

CLYDE: Never claimed to be more than half-way back; but that's still a branch above you, a g'rilla girl!

TAHARAH: Or beneat me: depend which met-trick system you exploit.

CLYDE: Here, man, help me down.

TAHARAH: How can I?—I'm not your inferior.

CLYDE: But you are, because I've asked you to be my butler.

TAHARAH: That's not your subtlest, but it ees at your best.

Suddenly the "Tales from the Vienna Woods" waltz is heard, "sung" to by the Hartz Mountain Master Canaries [*whose sound may be approximated by toy bird whistles*]. CLYDE *and* TAHARAH *listen to the first chorus in bewilderment, acknowledgment, and finally ecstasy; they join to sing the chorus as it is repeated.*

CLYDE *and* TAHARAH: [*Singing*]
The Forest, Forest Forever,
The Forest, Forest Forever,
As brought to you by Hartz Mountain,
Is sung by Master Canaries,
Hartz Mountain Master Canaries.
Hartz Mountain Master Canaries
Sing the Song of Kong clad in white
  sarong
And the empty cuspidor
That contains the World and more:
Urine specimen, urine specimen,
Ample sample of the hole;
Trinity of sex and soul:
Plantain, the jar, and the rose—Amen!

TAHARAH: [*Singing to "Yes, We Have No Bananas Today," and dance-stepping toward right wing as at the end of a vaudeville soft-shoe routine*]
Yez, we haf no buwanas today,
(—I better beat it!)
We lost both our gambit and lay!

CLYDE: [*Jumping down from the table*] Hey, where you going?

TAHARAH: Just going, not waiting.

CLYDE: [*Grabbing onto* TAHARAH'S *long wig*] Wait a minute.

TAHARAH: What for?

CLYDE: I need you.

TAHARAH: I mean, what are you waiting for?

CLYDE: I'm waiting for the Chimney Sweep to show; or for those Glitz Ionas to get here ahead of him. —Gulp!

TAHARAH: Hear me, Bwana, hear me good: ain't no such think as waiting *for* any-sink: waiting *ees.*

CLYDE: How d'ja mean?

TAHARAH: Some pataphysician! I taught you went to Barnyard? Ain'tcha heard?: waiting is our position longer; there's nothink to wait for, all thinks are as ees now.

CLYDE: [*Clamping onto* TAHARA'S *neck*] Get it, Charmer, I got plans 'n sizzling ol' sarong-clad you figgers in 'em!

TAHARAH: [*Hitting and kicking fiercely to escape*] Lemme go, weel you—I gotta beat it! Blue-balls usually do.

CLYDE: A privates break, eh? I—

TAHARAH: [*Sudden switch*] Oh, when you're back in New York, weel you sent me a pair of dungarees?

CLYDE: [*Taken aback*] What for?—ya can buy 'em here.

TAHARAH: [*Feeling his biceps*] Yez, but you can understan' de sentimental py-chology behin' my request. . . .

CLYDE: [*Appreciative*] Gosh, Sweets, I suppose I do.

SISTER CARRIES, *looking even more neurotic than before, sweaty, blear-eyed, appears downstage left. He is wearing a circus ringmaster's top hat in place of the nun's headdress, and a whistle dangles from a string of shrunken heads around his neck.*

CARRIES: [*Smearing war paint on*] So do I. She has no money.

CLYDE: [*Sardonic*] Now, if it ain't sanguinolent Sister Soft Heart, the latest in anthropological mysticism!

CARRIES: Oh, go crap in a quonset hut! Is this here your plátano plantation?

CLYDE: Not exactly. It's actually just a place ya can check into without a toothbrush. —Why?

CARRIES: Nobody's checkin' in; we jist wanna use the fireplace concession.

CLYDE: Precisely what business I wanna haggle over—

CARRIES: [*Raising Eddie Cantor eyebrows*] When it comes to the business, I'm a sharp shooter. Find the Sweep yet?

CLYDE: Looky, Sis, ya can case the jernt yerself, but Queen Kong ain't nowhere in the theatre: so why go ahead with the barnfire? It'll only raise the carbon monoxide—

TAHARAH: [*Released and sizzling*] To speak nothink of de temperature, and it's sizzling nuff round theez parts [*Indicating which*] wouldn't you say?? . . .

CARRIES: Nothin' doin'! During the coffee break, I went out and danced me a no-holes-bare war dance and got me plenty enthused and sweated up about this finale bit. Then I boosted me falt'rin' courage with a couple o' peppies, er, pepsis and am right rear to go! [*Demonlike, looking suspiciously about*] Who cares if Queen Kong's here or not to oversee the succulent sights?—I'm as good as her any night!!! [*Expanding his narrow chest and pounding on it*] In fact, my unsuspecting ninnies . . . *I AM KONG!!!!*

CLYDE: Apecock!

TAHARAH: Peacock, perhaps; or a typographical error.

CARRIES: [*Breaking uncontrollably into a distinctly American Indian war dance, chanting*]
> Big barbaric barbecue
> Make good eatin', b'lieve me you!
> Me work up heap appetite,
> Me big Injin dynamite:
>> Pow-wow! Pow-wow!
> Smokin' signals, smokin' hash,
> Gonna bust me heap big bash!
> Plenty footwork, plenty keen,
> Me damn good like ballet queen:
>> Pow-wow! Pow-wow!
>> Pow . . .

[*Stops, suddenly embarrassed by his manic display*] Bring in the babes!!

The GLITZES *converge on the set from all the various entrances, grunting, squealing, smearing war paint over their hair masks and patched fur costumes; some are still in the process of putting on their costumes;* KARMA *and* PAULET, *arm in arm, enter unescorted downstage left, chatting like two neighbors on a shopping tour;* KARMA *with her bonnet full of flowers,* PAULET *in her bikini.*

KARMA: And so finally, I must reiterate how very much I enjoyed taking in the cinema when we weren't called for on stage.

PAULET: [*Not too adept at sophisticated chit-chat*] Quite; quite so, my fair. Gee whiz, it's noisy around here.

KARMA: I do believe the cinema is superior to the theatre, because whereas in theatre, which may be defined as the quickest way to lose the great-

est sum of money, every thing is replaced, in cinema the curving Cinemascope screen is actually the circumference of the earth, or to speak more accurately—

PAULET: The curvature of space, itself.

KARMA: [*Shouting above the* GLITZES' *racket*] Quite. I just love a girl friend with whom I can hear mouth to ear.

PAULET: I just love a girl friend.

CLYDE: Hi there, Karma; now how ya diggin' the play?

KARMA: [*Preposterously affected*] Oh, Clyde, dahling! This piece is simply so frothy, so trifling, so airy—I believe I might liken it to a dandelion—

TAHARAH: [*Jealous*] She mean you got a dandy's loin—

KARMA: [*As* CARRIES *lays hands on her*] And truly have the feeling that if I were to breathe heavily upon it . . . were to *blow* on it . . . [CARRIES *winks deliciously at her*] it would all blow away . . . light as air—

CLYDE: [*Angry*] Pollution! So ya blew on it, did ya? Was he [*Indicating* CARRIES] any good?!

KARMA: [*Thick Chinese accent*] Ah so, yes, he cum quarts, [*Correcting*] quats.

CARRIES: Enough of this interlay, er, delay: let the rain dance, er, the ritual begin! [*Looking at his wristwatch, stating the exact time*] It's precisely ————. Mister Beauty and Master Beast, [*Indicating* MAIS OUI *and* BRUTE] please to take in hand the soon-to-be-late lovelies, Miss Karma Miranda and Mrs. Paulet Colbert.

PAULET: *Miss* Paulet Colbert!

CARRIES: *Miss* Paulet Colbert.

MAIS OUI: One Lezzy Scott, one flower pot, coming up! [MAIS OUI *and* BRUTE *hasten toward the women;* CLYDE *leaps quick into the medley and fends them off, stands with arms akimbo before the threatened two, a cartoon superhero to the rescue; confusion*]

CLYDE: Hold your hair pieces, you Sugar Commies!! Your whole hirsute outfit is postulated on a preposterous falsie! a Piltdown hoax!

TAHARAH: [*Edging offstage right*] A put-down! a show-down! Oh—

MAIS OUI: [*Laying it on thick*] We don't believe it!

CLYDE: Ya betcher boobs ya will, 'cause I can prove it!

BRUTE: None o' dat soft salami, you!; lemme spread 'im out!

CARRIES: Show cause!

CLYDE: I will! [*He yanks out of the crowd and darts after* TAHARAH] Heads down, I got a date who don't rate!

TAHARAH: Why ees eferbody looking at me? I ain't de star—oh!

CLYDE: [*Seeing* VENUS' *arm shoot out and grab* TAHARAH'S *ankle*] A confederation of its composites is junkel justice! That's ironical!

VENUS: And botanical.

TAHARAH: Protect the proprieties! Release me as I haf done no wrong! Beastly plant!

CARRIES: We know that snatch. What's the big deal?

CLYDE: [*Gripping* TAHARAH *around the waist, yanking him free*] There's no big deal, that's just the lack of point.

TAHARAH: [*Fighting*] Unband my waist! In deference to—

CLYDE: [*Pulling* TAHARAH'S *sarong down to the waist; since the falsies are built into the sarong, bare-chested,* TAHARAH *is a man*] There ya go: —Contemporaneously Topless!!

GLITZES: [*Severally, chaotically*] WHAT HATH GOD WROUGHT!!! WELL, I'LL BE A MONKEY'S AUNT!!! UNDERSEXED!!! UNDERFED!!! OVERMILKED!!! NEEDS PASTURING!!! etc., etc. [*The cries of dismay peter out into a long, shocked silence*]

TAHARAH: [*Sniffing*] What's wrong wit all you guys?! Ain't cha never seen a naked white woman before??!!

CARRIES: [*Crossing to examine* TAHARAH] Lucky thing my license is for mind-reading and not body-reading powers.

TAHARAH: [*Bitch-back*] Oh, I read *you*, Maude!

CARRIES: I thought you were of size and then some trouble [*His hands palm flat on* TA-HARAH'S *flat chest*] but I suppose even a witch doctress can be wrong. How come you chose *this* kind of life, Taharahnugi?

TAHARAH: Well, er, er, you know how straight people are—one of them leads to another.

CARRIES: Certainly. Okay, everybody, that was an edifying diversion, and now let's get on with the finale.

CLYDE: [*Pushing* TAHARAH *aside*] Whadda ya mean?! I just exposed what a fake this entire development is!

CARRIES: All you exposed is an underdevelopment.

TAHARAH: [*Licking his wounds upstage*] A figger ain't eferthink. A man who's really a man can appreciate a woman for her mental development, her culture, her talents, etc. . . .

CLYDE: But don't you see? Taharahnugi White Woman is Kong!

GLITZES: [*Stunned chorus*] SHOW CAUSE! SHOW CAUSE!

CLYDE: Cause she's, I mean, he's a queen.

CARRIES: [*Incredulous*] And just how does his being a queen make Taharahnugi White Woman, Kong?

CLYDE: Because Kong is a queen.

CARRIES: Of course, she is! What nonsense—there are millions of queens, but there is only *one* Kong. Logic, at this point of the tale, may be a vestigal structure, but what's above *your* buttocks, Mr. Batty, I have no idea! We shall suffer no further delay: to postpone the proposed another two minutes will be to dispose ourselves to pejorations on the part of neighboring packs. Seize that bird-brain and cast him into the canary cage!

TAHARAH: Thought you haf it all figgered out, dincha, stool pigin!

CLYDE: [*Bewildered*] Gee, I thought I had it all figured out. . . .

KARMA: [*To* TAHARAH *as several* GLITZES *toss the catatonic* CLYDE *into the cage*] He had your figure figured out.

PAULET: [*Disappointed*] Yeah, damn.

MAIS OUI: [*To* TAHARAH] He probably *had* your figure.

TAHARAH: Shut up! You've got *hair* on *your* flat chest.

CARRIES: [*Disarming* CLYDE *and bolting the cage*] So ends your screaming weak end: you won't be needing this pistol now: you see, Pepe, I told you you'd never adjust.

BRUTE: [*Peering with amazement into the cage*] It's like a inverted zoo, ain't it? Us bein' the—

CLYDE: Inverts.

MAIS OUI: [*Brandishing the plantain which she has constantly carried about*] Have a plantain; here, boy, here, have—

CARRIES *blows his whistle and the* GLITZES *scurry to starting positions. They sing and dance in three groups;* BRUTE *is part of the first third,* MAIS OUI *is part of the second third, and* CARRIES *is part of the third third. The three groups begin by singing and dancing together "The Frickadellin," whose music and choreography is an illogical extension of whatever is the latest in the long line of social dances inaugurated by the Twist; its particular flavor, however, its gestures and footwork, imitates the nature and movements of the gibbon. The lyrics suggest many of the steps and appropriate action should accompany any line indicating it.* KARMA *and* PAULET, *now two British tourists, squat near stage right watching the festivities.* TAHARAH *looks on from the left.* CLYDE *rattles the cage bars. This spectacle should be amended and continuously augmented until it has the effect of a three-ring circus.*

GLITZES: [*Sing, dance*]
>Do The Frickadellin!
>Do The Frickadellin!
>Lotsa stompin', lotsa yellin'!
>Gibbon-steps you'll find compellin'
>Witchy footwork for dispellin'
>All the hang-ups that ya fell in!
>>Bash your sole upon the groun'—
>>Scratch an armpit up 'n' down—
>>Let your roommate search your hair:
>>See if any salt is there!
>*Sui generis* rebellin',
>Let's go do The Frickadellin!
>>Let's go Frickad*ell*in! —*Dell*in!
>>Let's go Frickad*ell*in! —*Dell*in!

KARMA: [*As the* GLITZES *dance the frenzied "Frickadellin" without singing*] You can't conceive how rewarded I feel about our decision against skipping these native ceremonies in our touring sheduel, pressed though we are for the exact time.

PAULET: Oh, I shouldn't have missed this for a month of catlick cathedrals.

KARMA: This will certainly be something to yack about back in Es-sex.

PAULET: How but they do make you homesick, don't they?

GLITZES: [*Sing, dance*]
>Do The Frickadellin!
>Do The Frickadellin!
>Lotsa stompin', lotsa yellin'!
>Sounda chestnuts that yer shellin'
>Adds to muzac parallelin'
>Snappin' toes the dance is swellin'!
>>Gambol on the void of veldt;
>>Pinch the Princess in the Pelt;
>>Swing from twig to twig in trees,
>>Give a free ride to your fleas!
>Pyromaniacs rebellin',
>Let's go do The Frickadellin!
>>Let's go Frickad*ell*in!—*Dell*in!
>>Let's go Frickad*ell*in!—*Dell*in!

PAULET: Their costumes are so natural, so unusual, what?

KARMA: Their choreography worthy of Cunninghamlingus.

The first third of the GLITZES *leaps up on the shelves between the fireplace and the table, and proceeds to unhook vine ropes that are attached to the ceiling and chaotically scalloped over the shelves; then they commence swinging back and forth across the stage. The second and third thirds begin to sing and dance "The Cockamanie," a thirties ballroom extravagance with pretensions to ballet; the dancers attempt to emulate the poses and low-brow "gracefulness" of bathroom and kitchen-can decals.*

2ND *and* 3RD THIRDS OF GLITZES: [*Sing, dance*]
>Plant, perform The Cockamanie!
>It is ballet; classic! zanie!
>Loved by audiences brainy
>Or by dolts, the weather rainy,
>Worried glad rags might get stainy,
>Ent'ring opry house complainy.

While the second and third thirds of the GLITZES *dance a romantic underline of "The Cockamanie,"* TAHARAH *notices* BRUTE *swinging blissfully, idiotically on a vine rope above, and tugs on his leg.*

TAHARAH: Hey, you, dopey, I understan' you're interested in fruits, from time to specific time, that ees . . .

BRUTE: Yeah, but I don' find you too excitin'.

TAHARAH: If you was a beet more mature, you'd realize that money ees more importan' than excitement.

BRUTE: But you ain't got no money.

TAHARAH: No one person can haf eferthink.

2ND *and* 3RD THIRD OF GLITZES: [*Singing, dancing, half like ballet swans, the other half like river reeds caressing them*]
>The ghostly swans in triple claque
>>Do The Cockamaniac,
>While faithful bull-rush 'umbly slack
>>Also Cockamaniacs
>Caressing pizzle-frizzled backs.

CARRIES *blows his whistle to begin the third song-dance theme, "Pyromania." Several* GLITZES *roll a six-foot-in-diameter, nonspoke but hollow-hub wooden wheel into center stage from out of the right wing. This wheel is both an Indian Mandala and a Chinese Yin-Yang Circle: i.e., the full flat wood with hollow-hub suffices as a mandala, while the curved black and white semispheres of Yin-Yang are painted over it:*

KARMA *is seized and bound against the black half of the wheel, her full shepherdess' skirt filling out the wider bottom, her arms tied above and to the side of her head in the narrow portion.* PAULET *is bound with her hands behind her back into the white half, from head to waist slightly bent, filling the wider portion of the white; and her tapering, curving legs*

filling the narrow portion at the bottom of the wheel. "Pyromania" is a musique concrète chorale, stepped to with erratic modern-dance technique. The GLITZES *sing and dance while they bind the women; then, rolling it upstage so that the women go topsy-turvy, they plant the wheel securely within the fireplace.*

PAULET: Heavens, what's that?

MAIS OUI: It's a mandala, smarty.

KARMA: And just *what* is a mandala?

CARRIES: Oh, it's a mystic symbol that tells you where It's at. [*With absolute flatness, an afterthought*] So what.

KARMA: [*Being bound*] Oh, tourist participation! How quaint.

PAULET: [*Being bound*] It ain't.

First third of GLITZES *sings, and second and third sing and dance.*

GLITZES: Pyromania applied
In the drought-hit eventide
Will ignite the shadowed camp
Better than a Tiff'ny lamp!

Rub two dicks till you've a spark
Shot off through the virgin dark;
Then some tissue paper use
So wet print may not abuse
Your intentions with a damper
Like the lust for month-old hamper.

Teach these cherry tarts a trick
Who with chilly arsenic
Frost our vision till it's sick.
Boy, this beats a grade-B flick!

KARMA *and* PAULET *are now fixed in the fireplace; the first third of the* GLITZES *continue swinging on their vines; the second third dance dance insanely "The Frickadellin"; the third third gracefully dance "The Cockamanie." During the ensuing scene,* TAHARAH *manages to coax* BRUTE *down from his swing and the two of them get intimate on the shelf between the fireplace and table.* CARRIES *blows his whistle. Against this counterpointed complexity,* QUEEN KONG *stirs within the cage: his huge bulk laboriously rises to all fours.*

KONG: Grrrrrrrrrrrr . . . Aaaaaaaaaaaaaagh . . .

CLYDE: [*Freezing with incredulous terror*] YOU! No! No! I thought you were dead, I mean, transformed!!

KONG: [*Awesomely*] I *am* dead. I am The Corpse of Kong!

CLYDE: But, but, his corpse is out there, in the guise of Taharahnugi White Woman, currently making time with—

KONG: Grooowwwl!!! Shut up, Piss-a-bed, I am The Corpse of Kong and I have arisen in Her

core-ish behalf to ravish you and rape you gutless!!!

CLYDE: [*Backed up against the cage door, to* CARRIES] Help, lemme out, Maria Tall Chief—save me!

CARRIES: This is quite a blast; those attending are stunned.

KONG: [*Full height*] I am The Corpse of Kong, bigger than life!

CLYDE: I'll take yer word for it.

KONG: [*Flinging himself at* CLYDE, *grabbing his crotch*] Aaagh! Queen Kong surpasses Queen Anne:—now—try this Chippendale cabriole on for size, O he who would be hung too high for Her Majesty!!! Aaaaaaaaaaah!!!

CLYDE: [*Thrown to the cage floor on his back;* KONG *leaps on top of him*] Eeeeek! What does one in a fix *comme ça?*

MAIS OUI: Come too. Or close your eyes, and think of Brooklyn.

CLYDE: [*Giving up under the superior weight*] Ah, me! Which do you prefer: screwing men or screwing women?

KONG: [*Pumping like a nanny goat*] Such is a question improperly put; ask rather: "Which do you prefer, at the present moment?" Hmm-mmmm.

CLYDE: Remedial zoology! Oh, the interspecial ignominy!! Beasts of the Kingdom Come, bring KY ere I die!

KONG: [*In the heat of passion*] Intercourse! inter-run-fun! interrush! intermix! intermingle! interseed! interzone! interbone! inter ONE BY TWO!!! . . .

The second third of the GLITZES *breaks off dancing and bounds up on the shelves between the fireplace and the cage: there they unhook vine ropes attached as the previous ones, and quickly join the first third in swinging back and forth, but from the opposite direction. The counterswingers occasionally ram into each other, pinch those crossing them, pluck a hair or two, smack a passing face, etc. The third third remains downstage to continue dancing and singing "The Cockamanie."*

3RD THIRD OF GLITZES: [*Sing, dance*]
Apeman, mark The Cockamanie!
Lift your limb and learn the pain we
Find in pelvic hern-ya strain—see?
Squat upon your squeamish sitter,
Leap up then to toe-point—titter!—
O, Act Two's perversely bitter!

The swinging GLITZES *throw gigantic black and white balloons down to the third third, each of whom retrieves one and dances with it as if he were a bubble dancer; on the last line*

of the next stanza, each bursts another's balloon with a pin.

TAHARAH: [*Fondling* BRUTE] If you care to join
me in de cuspidor, Brutey, you'll fin' a surprise
waits for itchy bitzy you!

BRUTE: What?

TAHARAH: Napalm.

3RD THIRD OF GLITZES: [*Sing, dance*]
Them bubble babes who lap all lack,
Split in The Cockamaniac:
At least their bubbles show a crack
During The Cockamaniac
When Truth procures a prick and—
WHACK!!!

The first third of the GLITZES *jumps down
from their ropes; the third third rushes to the
shelves, grabs the ropes and swings in their
place along with the second third;* MAIS OUI
*also descends in this exchange, running over to
the prostrate* SWEEP, *nudging him.*

MAIS OUI: Quick, quick!—who was the intern?

SWEEP: [*Lifting his head slightly, annoyed*] Was?
A brute.

MAIS OUI *runs back to her swing as the first
third of the* GLITZES *lustily resumes the frenetic singing and dancing of "The Frickadellin"; their first stanza is a bridge, in which
they go about listening at each other's stomachs
for the innocent offender.*

1ST THIRD OF GLITZES: [*Sing, dance*]
Herr Carter's little liver dumplin's
Consumed, cause gastric stomach
rumplin's:
Yet playing it by ear oft stumbles
In puzzling out whose belly grumbles:
Alas, we fear we'll never figger
Exactly whose emits which snigger!

Do The Frickadellin!
Do The Frickadellin!
Lotsa stompin', lotsa yellin'!
Soon you'll cease yer mildew smellin',
Axial division dwellin':
Ego solo arts farewellin'!

Anchor up! ascend! embark!
Roommates in the Noah's ark:
Both your places, vacant, paired,
Safely separate, simply shared.
Salvagees ain't infidelin'
When they do The Frickadellin!
Let's go Frickadellin! —Dellin!
Let's go Frickadellin! —Dellin!

The first third of the GLITZES *dances "The
Frickadellin"; the second and third thirds continue swinging;* CARRIES *blows his whistle.*

KONG: [*Rocking motion as in a rocking chair,
sighing as an old grandmother*] Push away,

Vinyl Vuman, push away . . . push away . . .
push away all the pain . . .

TAHARAH *and* MAIS OUI: [*Singing*]
Rock-a-bye bottle fulla pee sop,
You plant a plantain, I'll reap the
crop . . .

KONG: [*To* CLYDE] How do you like my can-
opener?

SWEEP: [*Aroused by the commotion within the
cage*] Seems to fit the rim like a rose the nose.

KONG: Mind your own mate.

SWEEP: How can I, with you kids making all
that noise?

MAIS OUI: Whatsa matter, Sweep, can'tcha sleep?

SWEEP: [*Rubbing his eyes in disbelief*] Heaven's
Contradiction! A big ball in full swing and me
hung low! [*Looking at his wristwatch*] Wow,
am I late in coming so to speak!

VENUS: [*Turning over but not rising*] Quit
kickin', will ya? Can't stomach a restless
sleeper.

SWEEP: [*Standing*] Don't recall being hot to trot
with you—must've been plenty soused. Sorry,
but I gotta pull out.

CLYDE: Pull out! Pull out!

SWEEP: [*Yawning*] Honey, I'm late for work.

VENUS: Deposit a token of yer esteem on the
dresser, will ya?

SWEEP: [*Exiting right*] Later, mater.

BRUTE: [*To* TAHARAH] I gotta hand it to you
guys, ya really know howda work it up.

TAHARAH: Yez, work eet up an' hand eet to me.

KARMA: [*To* PAULET] Am I cracked, Bric-a-brac,
or is a horn of the Billygoat-legs-Lieutenant-
and-Major-General-War-Commander-Sergeant
falling down?

PAULET: [*Peering up the chimney stack*] Either
that, Shepherdess, or it's drizzlin' soot!

KARMA: [*Peering up the stack*] Something's coming down; headsup!

PAULET: If drawers are coming down, heads *are*
up.

*A narrow ladder drops from the chimney stack
and is grounded in the grate next to the wheel;
then a foot, two feet of the* SWEEP *appear on
its rungs; then a broom sweeping hither and
dither.*

SWEEP: [*Singing*]
Cremated ashes Indians plunder,
Lessen ya sweep 'em a carpet under.

KARMA: Why, if it ain't the rock-dropping May-
son and smacking thief!

SWEEP: [*Reaching awkwardly down from mid-
ladder and smacking* KARMA'S *face twice*]
Take two, a sign yer true.

PAULET: What d'ja say he was?

MAIS OUI: A chimney sweep to you.

PAULET: A chimney sweep!—It's THE Chimney Sweep! Hey, there, Karma, you're saved! Oh, Honey, I'm so glad for you!

TAHARAH: [*Greatly disappointed*] Conratulations.

KARMA: Never mind!! Whadda ya doin' *here*, Skinny? I thought we had a date for 10:30 under the Venus Fly Trap!!

SWEEP: [*Busy sweeping*] Did we? Gee, must be living a double life. The pollution's probably affecting my brain. Junkel rot setting in. [*Singing*]

> When dick splits the May-son halves asunder,
> Sweep the cracked twosome a carpet under.

KARMA: You rot rat!! You unicorn!! You forgot our date! And I! I risked all, dear life itself, to keep it quiet!!

SWEEP: Then please keep quiet now, will ya, China-doll? I got a gig to do, and I'm late enough starting as is.

KARMA: And yer late showin' here to boot! Why *are* you so late?

SWEEP: I believe, Mother-Source, that I was victimized by the tse-tse fly; whereupon a rather heavy nap by a normally light sleeper ensued.

PAULET: Are you the "heavy" in this play?

SWEEP: Mr. White, I weight 98 pounds. Have a smack.

PAULET: Watch it, buddy, I can handle you!

SWEEP: [*Poking the top end of the broom handle toward her*] In your present Promethean state of being, it is I, on the contrary end, who can handle you.

The second third of the GLITZES *descends from its vine ropes and joins the first third in singing and dancing "The Cockamanie."*

1ST *and* 2ND THIRDS OF GLITZES: [*Sing, dance*]
> Man, mix in The Cockamanie,
> On one peg let love profane be!
> Karma lax your lap resistance,
> Lessen twixt us mating distance:
> "Animals For Co-existence"
> Advocate we, sex persistents!

The swinging third third of the GLITZES *tosses huge white fans to the dancers below, each of whom, catching a fan, tips off a* très *fey Sally Rand fan dance. The goings-on in the cage are now blocked from view by a build-up of the furry junk piles.* MAIS OUI *comes dancing down to the very edge of the audience.*

MAIS OUI: [*Very thick exotic accent*] Theez play weel nefer cloz!

1ST *and* 2ND THIRDS OF GLITZES: [*Sing, dance*]
> Fandangle dancers, tits so stack,
> Started The Cockamaniac;

> Bow wow now how to bivouac
> After The Cockamaniac
> In a single dingle dangle's sack?

The first and second thirds of the GLITZES *leap onto the shelves and join the third third in swinging chaotically above the stage; all hum and sing at once snatches of the three different songs; happy chaos.*

KARMA: [*Shouting*] You there, Sister Cynosure, mind landing for a minute? Earth errand.

CARRIES: [*Jumping from his rope, annoyed at the interruption*] It's protocol to permit virgin condemnees a last utterance, but don't overenter my good ear.

KARMA: Hate to steal yer time during the juballie, know just how Carries away you are, but if it please yer Doctressship, the Chimney Sweep Lost has been rediscovered, and I'd appreciate being unbound. —Cut me loose!

CARRIES: Life's lack of ironies! The Sweep is here?

SWEEP: How do there, Ph.D.?

KARMA: Hurry, please: I gotta beat it home and start supper.

PAULET: Yeah, remember big Queen Kong's ex cathedra bull!

CARRIES: [*Untying* KARMA] A technical knockout, a whim of the wheel of fortune. Well, one tittie toasted is still a branch above none.

PAULET: Congratulations, Karmy, good luck to you.

KARMA: [*Rubbing her wrists and body cramped from the bonds*] So long, Paulet, bikini-clad, keep a stiff clit, try harder in yer next reincarnation.

CARRIES: [*Remounting his swing*] When the day's come that even a witch doctress gets bogged down in all the red tape involved in a simple propitiation—

GLITZES: [*All swinging, all singing a thunderous chorus of "Pyromania"*]
> Teach the Tomish heretic
> How to lay a cosmic brick:
> She'll lay off her candlestick
> Once within our fire's flick!

> Pyromania! Torch Song!
> Gibbons to a herd belong
> Chimpanzees've heard headstrong.
> Torch song! night long! right-wrong!
>   torch song!

CARRIES *and* MAIS OUI *descend from their ropes and ignite a torch; they step menacingly, then coyly teasing, toward* PAULET.

PAULET: At last! I can see the light.

MAIS OUI: Ya could practically feel it, it's so real.

GLITZES: [*Singing, swinging*]
>Pyromania! Torch Song!
>Light the cold the dark night long
>Taking out of right all wrong.
>Torch song! night long! right-wrong!
>   torch song!

SWEEP: [*To* KARMA] Betcher glad to be in the bleachers.

TAHARAH: [*To* BRUTE] Betcher glad to be in my breeches.

A clattering and rattling of the cage bars accompanied by earsplitting drums; everyone turns toward the cage. CLYDE-AS-KONG, *i.e.,* CLYDE *dressed in* KONG'S *gorilla costume, is roaring to be released. He is radically shorter than* KONG *and has a rivet held against his back from his waist up to the top of his head by straps about his hips and neck, which prevents him from being able to bend: he stands up absolutely straight. All assume he is* QUEEN KONG.

CLYDE-AS-K: [*Roaring*] Stop the stupid muzak! Get me outta this marriage broker's Bronx Zoo!

CARRIES: [*Aside*] O Queen, thou comest when I had thee least in mind and matters most in hand; my power grab's gummed-up! [*To the* GLITZES] Why, it's kitsch Queen Kong! Stop the repetitive muzak!

CLYDE-AS-K: [*As the music and swinging halt; all attention focused on him*] What are all you guys starin at? Ain'tcha never seen a queen before? Mais Oui, undo this bolt!

MAIS OUI: [*Hastening to obey the order as the* GLITZES *all descend from their ropes*]
>From rope she rode to all-four floor,
>   And thence unlatched the door,
>Let out a Queen that in a Queen
>   Hadn't gone before.

CLYDE-AS-K: [*Released*] Douche, er, douse that torch, Master Carries. And now, everybody, it's final curtain marriage time!

CARRIES, *suspicious of* CLYDE-AS-KONG'S *identity, quietly disobeys, hands the torch to* MAIS OUI. *Suddenly the* INTERN *appears from behind the wheel carrying another quart jar, this one empty.*

INTERN: Void a specimen, Your Majesty?

CLYDE-AS-K: [*Taking the jar and turning around, making gestures as if he were urinating into it*] Anytime. And, er, please don't forget a blood sample also. We, Kong, Queen of all the cage can convey, are mightily pleased that you, O Miss Karma, have come safely through this savage spectacle in one piece [*Indicating* PAULET], or half a piece; and, as was decreed Our right if the Sweep were found, We do desire to marry with you. [*Handing the jar to* INTERN, *who takes it upstage to the cuspidor; he extracts the first jar and begins performing medical tests on both*]

KARMA: We do?

CLYDE-AS-K: Yes. Americans have always evinced absorption in the pressing question: "Are the great apes women-stealers?" This play goes a long way toward begging that question and, to be sure, other adjacencies.

KARMA: [*Winking maliciously at his rear*] Speaking of adjacencies, how does your other feel?

CLYDE-AS-K: By this point, I'm closed for alterations. But how's about yer big self? Has this harrowing experience in any way changed your life?

KARMA: Actually, yes; I've had my menopause.

TAHARAH: And now men pause before rerequesting your hand.

CLYDE-AS-K: [*Emphatically*] They do not! May I rerequest your hand, Mem-sab?

KARMA: Really, Queen Kong, how could you possibly expect me, a mere woman, to requite your request? What would our children be— g'rillets?

CLYDE-AS-K: But lovely light 'n you're Karma, don't you recognize me? I'm your fia—

KARMA: Fiasco! A woman wants a man who's a man, not a man who's a queen. [*Putting on her shepherdess bonnet*] No, Kong, I prefer to marry the Chimney Sweep, an able stable stud and a he-hero, he who is responsible for snatching me from the tongues of fire. For his timeliness, I reward him with my hand. [*Putting her hand to a rewarding spot on* SWEEP]

SWEEP: I receive, er, accept. As a man, you have, er, I have made mine cherce.

CARRIES: [*To* CLYDE-AS-KONG, *with squint-eye suspicion*] Any objections to his directions?

CLYDE-AS-K: [*Unable to nod his disapproval because of the rivet*] Let me not stoop to go between lovers hard and fast. Two lovers fastened hard. Now, let's look . . . [*Looking with difficulty about, spotting* PAULET] Douse that torch; spare the Tom; I ain't picky, I'll marry *her* instead.

MAIS OUI: [*Putting out the torch, holding the burnt stick up to* PAULET] Pyrotechnical flamboyancies aside, hon, this could still be of use to you.

PAULET: [*Being untied by several* GLITZES] Fresh freak! wise guyess, you'll get yours with gauze!

CLYDE-AS-K: Well, m' nervy Paulet, queen of Our heart, can you picture us both on a bicycle built for two?

PAULET: Sorry, Queen, I ain't a queen: I can't marry you: I'm a lezzy: wanna marry a lezzy?

CLYDE-AS-K: A man had as well marry a celibate and beget imaginings. But let me look around the set: we do have to find someone for you before curtain call. [*Peering about, everyone peering brow-knit about*] Don't see any comers . . .

INTERN: [*Busy with the tests*] How about the Venus Fly Trap?

MAIS OUI: Yeah, how about her? Like Marilyn Monroe, she's forgotten, but not gone.

CLYDE-AS-KONG, CARRIES, PAULET, *and* MAIS OUI *rush en masse downstage right to the motionless, recumbent* VENUS.

PAULET: She done gone out!

MAIS OUI: Who does her hair—the elements?

INTERN: [*His back still turned*] She needs an aphrodisiac.

CLYDE-AS-K: Quick, Glitz Ionas, bring flies to revive her!

The GLITZES *converge, form a tight circle around* VENUS; *sounds as of a commode flush feedback are heard; then the circle of* GLITZES *breaks, and* VENUS, *rejuvenated, is helped to her feet.*

CLYDE-AS-K: Venus, revived when administered to by fount-filled cods and swordtail steaks, won't you consider this salmon-slender spoke for your—

VENUS: [*Appraises* PAULET *with immodest velocity, then*]
        I of flies have had my fill,
        Wishing bones and pickles dill;
        This Paulet is scented dish:
        She renews my nose for fish.

As VENUS *and* PAULET *come together,* CLYDE-AS-KONG *moves away toward center stage, his back presented to* CARRIES, *who suddenly is alerted by the obvious rivet:* CARRIES *cocks the pistol.*

CARRIES: Wait, hold everything! Queen Kong is kinda spineless.

CLYDE-AS-K: So?

CARRIES: Yers looks like it could give ya a cerebral hemorrhage!

MAIS OUI: [*Examining the rivet, brandishing the plantain*] Funny place to hang yer umbrella. What a man!

CARRIES: Man, no doubt! Kong!—are you a *poseur?!*

CLYDE-AS-K: Just for *Phyzeek Magazine.* Why?

CARRIES: Let me stare at you . . . scrupulously . . . like someone who's just discovered that monkeys have faces. . . .

CLYDE-AS-K: [*Heavily scrutinized by all*] Why do people always look at me as if they've seen something I'm afraid of?

CARRIES: All right, Chinaman on the make, who ARE you?

CLYDE-AS-K: I am the product of the rape of Clyde by the Corpse of Kong, as well as all that remains of those two.

CARRIES: [*Lifting his face mask, seeing* CLYDE] Eeek! *You are* . . .

CLYDE-AS-K: I am Clyde-as-Kong.

ALL: CLYDE-AS-KONG???!!!

CLYDE-AS-K: [*Meekly*] What's so strange? It has alliteration.

CARRIES: [*Suddenly resigned*] Such is accuracy. And I suppose that makes him legitimate.

KARMA: Really, Doctress?

CARRIES: Yes, my child, there is nothing I can do. The product of a rape by Kong-as-Corpse is always the Rapee-as-Kong; and "as" as the go between two alliteratives in the product's name is always the birthmark of legitimacy. Such is our gibbon Law. I haf spoken.

INTERN: [*Coming downstage with the two quart jars*] And Clyde-as-Kong's specimen is medically identical with the specimen of Queen Kong which I mystically had the foreskin, er, foresight to procure back in Act One.

BRUTE: Which means wha'?

INTERN: Which means that the specimens, as ample sample of the whole, bear out Clyde and Kong as identical, as wholly one. I haf spoken.

TAHARAH: [*Tossing* BRUTE *aside*] Oh, Holy One, ees it really you, Muskels? I haf been waiting so patiently for you to evolve. Leetel unprecocious me!

MAIS OUI: [*Tipping* TAHARAH'S *flat chest with the plantain*] My, but yer unprecocity leaves something to be desired!

TAHARAH: [*Haughtily triumphant*] Second fiddle, piddle! piddle!

CLYDE-AS-K: And now that my lawful stock has been improved, I mean, approved, who'll wed me? I'm a find in any behind.

TAHARAH: I weel! I weel wed you, Queen Clyde-as-Kong!

CLYDE-AS-K: But—but—how can you, my love? You are the Living Kong, his transformation!

PAULET: Is such, den, veracity?

TAHARAH: Yez, woman, it ees. Clyde shot Kong, and I resulted. Kong-Shot raped Clyde, and he resulted. I am Kong-as-Kong-Shot; he is Kong-as-Kong-Shot's-Load-Shot. You haf heard of cell-cleavage?—well, try to keel a Queen [*Squeezing his flat chest together*] and she cleaves. No rose that fades, but pressed, it haf two shades.

KARMA: But, Taharahnugi White Woman, wasn't it you who was smoldering around the verandah before Kong got shot?

SWEEP: Ever hear of astroprojection?

KARMA: I thought a medium was needed to conjure it.

SWEEP: Your anticipational jealousy was the medium.

KARMA: [*Still jealous*] But if you marry *him,* don't you marry back into your previous half?

INTERN: She does. But why shouldn't she? If he marries her, he too marries back into his previous half. Two halves so identically destined are well healed, er, wholed, are they not? and augured well for future compatibility? [*Mumbling to himself as he wanders back upstage*] Or does he marry back into his previous half's half?

CARRIES: [*Ex cathedra*]
Kong clove into Taharah and Clyde,
But Taharah weds Clyde is Kong simplified.

VENUS: And reincubied, and considerably fructified.

CARRIES: [*Holding out the pistol as at a shotgun wedding*] And now, with the power invested in me by the Union of Witch Doctresses, I pronounce you man and wife, or man and man, or ape and man, or queen and woman, or queen and man, or queen and queen, or ape and ape up and up. And now, if it please the cast, could we all canary the finale. There's a great flick on the Late Show and I don't wanna miss it. —Maestro!

The new pairs hold hands and all sing. Several GLITZES *begin removing their costumes and makeup while others of them bring the bicycle back on stage.* CLYDE-AS-KONG *and* TAHARAH *mount the bicycle and ride off through the audience with the entire cast singing and following them.*

ALL: [*Singing*]
Can this corny triplethink,
Better nab a nipple pink:
Art about your life is plot,
But your life 'bout art is not!

Soooooooooooooo:
If it's got a mind, stump it.
If it stands too high, slump it.
If it willn't budge, bump it.
If ya don't like, it lump it.
But if it's got a hole, hump it!

Clear the aisle, we're ridin' through,
Locomotive, make adieu!
If your mores still you'd trover,
Please, tight patrons, bend right over!

If it's militant, jump it.
If it's got a pipe, pump it.
If it smells too much, dump it.
If it hymen has, rump it.
But if it's got a hole, hump it!

Reservations we eschew,
Ne'er accept, "The heck with you!"
Narrow-minded: rend fright over;
Spotless—(THE spot!)—bend right over!

BRUTE *disengages himself from the singing, exiting parade, and hops back up on the stage. He scampers over to the cuspidor and extracts the purple rose.*

BRUTE: Ladies and Gentlemen of every genus: Forget dem dirty minded fakes: Art ain't never 'bout life, but life *is* only 'bout art. Dis rose?—oh, it ain't no symbol like ya mighta thought, an' dat's cause it ain't got nothin' to do wit life either. Dis here rose is all 'bout art. Here, take it— [*He throws the rose into the audience*]

THE HAWK

an improvisational play

Murray Mednick and Tony Barsha

The Hawk was first presented at Theatre Genesis, St. Mark's Church-in-the-Bowery, New York City, on Friday, October 13, 1967, with the following cast:

THE CHINESE OPIUM SMOKER	*Ching Yeh*
THE HAWK	*Tony Serchio*
THE DOUBLE	*Lee Kissman*
THE FIRST VICTIM	*Sally Sommer*
THE SECOND VICTIM	*O-Lan Johnson*
THE INSPECTOR	*Walter Hadler*
THE THIRD VICTIM	*Scarlett Johnson*
THE FOURTH VICTIM	*Barbara Young*
THE DEALER	*Walter Hadler*

The Hawk was subsequently produced by James Walsh and Dina and Alexander E. Racolin at the Actors Playhouse, New York City, on April 17, 1968, with the same cast. Both productions were directed by Tony Barsha. Music was composed by Eddie Hicks.

SCENE

The stage is bare except for three chairs, center stage, facing the audience, and a single chair, different from the others, placed at an angle, stage left. No props are used.

PROLOGUE

THE CHINESE OPIUM SMOKER *enters in the traditional Chinese opium smoker's robe. He goes to downstage center, holds, then begins a sound and movement representation of fire. He builds this to a peak, shouts: "FIRE!" then moves to stage left and addresses the audience:*

CHINESE OPIUM SMOKER: Fire is reality. It starts with a tiny spark and moves through spontaneous combustion from one layer to another. And the color of fire changes from red, to orange, to yellow, and as the temperature rises, it changes to blue—yes, blue—and from blue the fire rushes to white heat. Fire then ceases to be real. Fire is but the extension of the object which is burning. [*He returns to center stage*] I am the extension of the object which is burning! I am the Almighty Fire God! The Powerful Fire God! The Divine Fire God! Ra, ra, ra! Yes! I am the Powerful Fire God! Ra, ra, ra! Get the fuck out of here, you Water God! You get the fuck out of here! Ra, ra, ra! Let me tell you the story of these ra, ra, ra, birds that came to the window of my palace. They want to get high. They want to be divine. Then one day along comes this ra, ra, ra hawk! This ra, ra, ra ridiculous hawk! And he stole the fire from me and gave it to the birds! And the birds all get high, and they all get hot, and they all get burned up. Ra, ra, ra. Don't play with me! If you play with me, you play with fire. I am the Fire God. I am the Divine Fire God. Ra, ra, ra. Ra, ra, ra. [*He returns to stage left*] Man fears fire. Ever since he is a kid. His parents would yell: "Stanley! Keep your hands off that fire!" So the kid gets a social prohibition. Yet man has a strong affinity for the fire. The heat resembles the warm blood of the body, the flickering flame is the vitality of life; and the blue flame is the phallic symbol, the smoke is the female sex organ. So man gets a complex between the social prohibition and his fascination for the fire. So he goes to the psychiatrist, or analyst. And the analyst tells him to lie down on the couch, and man talks himself out of walking into the fire. [*He returns to center stage and walks into the "fire." As his body writhes and struggles as the burning man, his voice describes the event*]

The feet burn, the legs burn, the body burns, the arms burn, the skin blisters and peels, the juices burn up, the arms try to push the fire away, the mind tries to control the body, the flames rise, the throat burns, the nostrils burn, the muscles contract, contract, the hair is burning, the head is burning, the eyes pop out, the eyes pop out, the body contracts, contracts, the head! head! head! the mind can no longer control the body, the body contracts, contracts . . . the body falls to the ground. [*He goes to stage right*] The body falls down to the ground, yet the fire keeps on burning, and burning, and burning. [*He bows and exits*]

PART I

The HAWK *enters.*

HAWK: This is not an ordinary apartment. Junkies come here. I don't take junk myself. I sell it. The size of the apartment . . . well, it starts here [*Following the edge of the stage*], goes to here, and along here, down and across. This is a wall [*Stage right*], it's blue. This is a wall [*Upstage*], it's blue. And this wall [*Stage left*] is blue. There is a rug which covers the entire floor. Wall to wall. It's blue. It's a nylon synthetic rug. The reason it's synthetic is that if you spill a drink or throw up on it, I can clean it. A sofa [*The three chairs*]. A blue sofa. A modern, conventional box-type sofa. I sit in it. Sometimes I sit here and sometimes I sit there. The table [*In front of the chairs*]. This is a very practical table, in that sometimes it's here and sometimes it's not here. It has a glass top. That's because when you look through you can see the blue rug. I keep the table clean and clear of all things. [*Crosses to upstage left, opens a door*] The bathroom is ordinary. Sink, shower, john, and [*Facing rear wall*] . . . What the fuck do you call that? It's . . . a medicine cabinet. [*Crosses to upstage right*] The kitchen. Refrigerator, sink, stove, cabinets. All in various shades of blue. I keep a lot of food in the refrigerator. Food I eat and food I don't eat. Junkies don't eat much. [*Crosses to downstage right*] The liquor cabinet is lined in blue. I keep it refrigerated. For the champagne. [*Crosses to the single chair*] This is a very comfortable chair. It's blue. Velvet. A 1920s-1930s barrel chair. When you sit in it your arms rise up. It's the kind of chair Jean Harlow sat in. Nobody sits in this chair. Nobody ever sits in this chair. [*Crosses to downstage center*] This is a mirror. It completely covers this entire wall [*The fourth wall*], from the ceiling to the floor. [*Crosses behind the sofa*] Well. Do I have everything? Sofa, chair, bathroom, kitchen, rug, walls, cabinet, mirror . . . I think I'll go out. [*He starts to leave. The* DOUBLE *intercepts him. They open the door together*]

DOUBLE: Where are you going?

HAWK: I was going out.

The DOUBLE *enters, crosses to the single chair and sits. The* HAWK *closes the door and sits on the sofa. The* DOUBLE *begins reciting the* HAWK'S *litany. The* HAWK *repeats after him, phrase by phrase. As the litany is repeated over and over the* HAWK *rises and circles the stage. At a point they reverse—the* HAWK *recites, the* DOUBLE *repeats. The litany builds to a peak—the* HAWK *leading, the* DOUBLE *subsiding. Finally the* HAWK *stands before the mirror, loudly reciting the litany by himself.*

The Hawk's Litany

DOUBLE *and* HAWK: The Hawk. The Hawk is an animal. An animal is hungry. That's why he kills. He kills because he's hungry. The hawk is hungry. He finds a victim. He attacks the victim. He kills the victim. He takes the victim into the sky, back to his nest, and he devours the victim. Because he's hungry. That why he kills. Because he's an animal. An animal is hungry. The hawk is an animal . . . [*The* HAWK *stops suddenly. The* DOUBLE *rises*]

DOUBLE: Did you score?

HAWK: Yeah. I have everything. The heroin. Morphine. Pot, coke, orange soda, champagne, tea, food . . . [*Sits*]

DOUBLE: [*Indicating a box*] The box. This is a wooden box. It's from Tangiers.

HAWK: Veracruz.

DOUBLE: Veracruz. It's a hand-carved box and in the center there's an engraving of a fire god. The fire god has two blue sapphires for eyes. The inside of the box is lined in blue velvet and contains a syringe and two needles. The syringe has two parts. . . .

HAWK: The plunger and the receptacle.

DOUBLE: The plunger and the receptacle. Of the two needles, one is long and the other short. One is gold and the other silver. I'll put these back in the box here and close it.

HAWK: Ornithological.

DOUBLE: Yes, this is the most important object in this ornithological tragicomedy of life and death, love and hate, war and peace.

HAWK: Okay.

DOUBLE: [*Returns to his chair*] Now, if you ever want this box, if you ever need it, just ask me for it, and I'll give it to you.

HAWK: Now.

  DOUBLE: Wait.

    HAWK: Wait.

      DOUBLE: Wait.

        HAWK: Wait.

          DOUBLE: Wait.

            HAWK: Wait.

              DOUBLE: Wait.

                HAWK: Wait.

                  DOUBLE: Wait.

HAWK: She's coming.

DOUBLE: She's coming.

HAWK: She's coming.

DOUBLE: Wait.

HAWK: She's coming.

DOUBLE: She's coming.

HAWK: Wait.

DOUBLE: She's coming.

HAWK: Wait.

DOUBLE: She's coming.

HAWK: Wait.

DOUBLE: She's coming.

HAWK: She's coming.

DOUBLE: Wait.

HAWK: She's coming.

DOUBLE: Wait.

HAWK: She's coming. She's coming. She's coming. She's here. [*They both turn and look at an empty space in the sofa as if someone were sitting there*]

First Improvisation: The Imaginary Victim

HAWK: She's skinny.

DOUBLE: But she has a great walk.

HAWK: A sequin dress . . .

DOUBLE: . . . in the early darkness . . .

HAWK: And a certain Oriental . . .

DOUBLE: . . . roll to her . . .

HAWK: . . . hips. She's anything but cherry.

DOUBLE: She has the sweet . . .

HAWK: . . . pale . . .

DOUBLE: . . . look . . .

HAWK: . . . of the damned.

DOUBLE: Just like . . .

TOGETHER: Jean Harlow.

HAWK: But she's skinny.

DOUBLE: Yeah.

HAWK: She looks hungry.

DOUBLE: Maybe you should give her something to eat.

HAWK: Yeah, that's a good idea. [*He feeds her*] There.

DOUBLE: She's a fast eater.

HAWK: Scoffs it right up, doesn't she?

DOUBLE: You know, not eating is unhealthy, self-destructive.

HAWK: I'll give her some more. [*Feeds her*]

DOUBLE: Aside from the nutritional value, there's also the simple pleasure of eating.

HAWK: Look, she's filling out . . . she's much healthier-looking.

DOUBLE: Give her some of that spaghetti there.

HAWK: She Italian? [*Feeds her*]

DOUBLE: Everybody eats spaghetti. The Chinese invented it.

HAWK: Look at that.

DOUBLE: Yeah. Give her some more.

HAWK: [*Pries her "mouth" open and stuffs it*] Down it goes.

DOUBLE: She's really getting fat now.

HAWK: Yeah.

DOUBLE: More.

HAWK: Yeah? Here you go, baby. [*Throws it into her*]

DOUBLE: Wow. Look at that.

HAWK: [*Moving off the sofa to make room*] Fantastic.

DOUBLE: Will you look at that flesh!

HAWK: I'm looking at it.

DOUBLE: Do you see the flesh on her?

HAWK: It's there all right.

DOUBLE: Pink, juicy flesh.

HAWK: Pink, juicy flesh. [*They turn and watch her "image" in the mirror*] She's huge. Gigantic.

DOUBLE: Look at that stomach.

HAWK: Look at that stomach.

DOUBLE: Do you see the flesh on that stomach?

HAWK: Look at that stomach.

DOUBLE: Look at those arms.

HAWK: They're enormous.

DOUBLE: Look at the flesh on those arms.

HAWK: Just hanging there.

DOUBLE: Look at those legs.

HAWK: Those legs.

DOUBLE: Fat, juicy legs.

HAWK: Oh, legs, legs, big legs.

DOUBLE: Look at those breasts. Do you see those breasts? All the meat on those breasts.

HAWK: Mounds of flesh.

DOUBLE: Pendulous boobies.

HAWK: Look at it roll! I want her.

DOUBLE: Succulent, juicy . . .

HAWK: I want her.

DOUBLE: Limitless flesh . . .

HAWK: I want her.

DOUBLE: You want her?

HAWK: Yes, I want her.

DOUBLE: She's ripe.

HAWK: I want her! I want her!

DOUBLE: You can have her.

HAWK: I want that flesh. [*Moves to the mirror*] I want it. I want to devour that flesh.

DOUBLE: You can have it.

HAWK: I want to rip and tear and bite into every bit of it.

DOUBLE: Take it.

HAWK: I want it. I want that flesh. I want it now. Right now. I want it. Yeah! I want it! I want it! Now! Now! Now! [*To* DOUBLE] Now.

The DOUBLE *brings the box. The* HAWK *prepares an injection and gives it to the "victim." A pause. They watch "her" as she falls to the floor.*

DOUBLE: I think she O.D.'d.

HAWK: Easy come, easy go. [*The* HAWK *goes to the bathroom and takes a shower*]

The DOUBLE *rearranges the materials. The* "VICTIM" *lies on the floor.*

DOUBLE: [*In the kitchen, repeating the gestures of the* HAWK'S *shower*] A kind of anxiety appearing verbiage. Is what it is. He reassures himself. About the real. But there's something . . . signs . . . there are signs . . . yes, there are signs, signals . . . yes, signals we give . . . to one another in . . . our passing . . . in order to create warmth . . . light. . . . Yes, but we must see that the light and the dark and the warm and the cold, the good and the bad . . . the actual pain we suffer . . . between them . . . that's not right . . . not "between," no . . . the actual pain we suffer . . . in the process . . . the process? Is illusory, not real, is the void . . . therefore, a reflection on the surface of the . . . whatever . . . a glance . . . the droplets of meaning adding to a force . . . a power . . . a demon . . . which he confuses with himself! Verbiage. [*The* DOUBLE *escorts the "victim" out. The* HAWK *and the* DOUBLE *return, as before*] She's dead.

HAWK: She was skinny but she had a great walk. A sequin dress in the early darkness and a certain Oriental roll to her hips. She was anything but cherry. She had the sweet, pale look of the damned. Just like Jean Harlow.

DOUBLE: What do I do with the body?

HAWK: The body?

DOUBLE: Her corpse. She's dead.

HAWK: I turned her on.

DOUBLE: They'll be looking for you.

HAWK: What do you expect me to do? I can't help it.

DOUBLE: Get rid of the body.

HAWK: I can't.

DOUBLE: Get rid of the body.

HAWK: I can't.

DOUBLE: Get rid of the body.

HAWK: I can't.

DOUBLE: Get rid of the body.

HAWK: I can't. I can't. I can't.

The FIRST VICTIM *appears at the door.*

Second Improvisation: The First Victim

HAWK: [*Opening the door*] Yes?

VICTIM: Hiya. I'm Joanie.

HAWK: Yeah?

VICTIM: Marilyn Stein's friend?

HAWK: Marilyn . . . oh, come in.

VICTIM: [*Entering*] Oh, thank you. [*Sees the mirror*] Oh, my!

HAWK: You're Joanie?

VICTIM: Uh, yes. You know, that is the biggest mirror I have ever seen. [*They both look in the mirror*]

HAWK: Sit down.

VICTIM: [*Sitting*] Thank you. Ah, Marilyn said that if I ever wanted to reach her, I should come here and maybe you could tell me where I could contact her.

HAWK: Marilyn Stein?

VICTIM: Yes.

HAWK: She's a friend of yours?

VICTIM: Oh, my closest and dearest.

HAWK: Wait here. [*Goes to the kitchen*]

VICTIM: My goodness, it's so blue here, and everything matches.

HAWK: [*Handing her a "bottle"*] Here.

VICTIM: Oh, thank you . . . Orange soda! My favorite. [*Drinks*] Marilyn said you were a very gracious person. Ah, do you know where I could find her?

HAWK: Excuse me. Your name is . . . ?

VICTIM: Joanie.

HAWK: Joanie Stein.

VICTIM: No, Marilyn Stein. I'm Joanie . . .

HAWK: Oh, yes, you're Marilyn's closest and dearest friend.

VICTIM: Yes. Joanie. Do you know where I could contact her?

HAWK: Marilyn. Ah, let's see, she was living in this pad downtown, but she had to leave for some reason, and I don't know where she is right now.

VICTIM: Oh? [*Disappointed*] Oh. Well, does she ever call you?

HAWK: Well . . . yes, as a matter of fact. . . . That's right, she called me this afternoon. Yes, Marilyn called this afternoon.

VICTIM: Isn't that something. You know, Fate is just playing with me today.

HAWK: How's that?

VICTIM: Well, when I arrived at the Port of Authority . . .

HAWK: Where?

VICTIM: The Port of Authority?

HAWK: Fate.

VICTIM: I mean, it's funny that Marilyn should call you today. You see, I was thinking that maybe Marilyn would put me up until I could find a place of my own.

HAWK: Where are you from?

VICTIM: Brooklyn.

HAWK: Did you run away?

VICTIM: Well, I never thought of it like that. . . . I just left.

HAWK: Listen, if you need a place, you can stay here for a couple of days.

VICTIM: You know, Marilyn told me that you were a very kind and gracious person. I can tell why.

HAWK: Do you want to stay here? It's cool. . . .

VICTIM: Oh, no, I couldn't. Really, it would be too much bother. . . .

HAWK: No, not at all. One of us could fall out on the floor and the other could . . .

VICTIM: What did Marilyn say when she called?

HAWK: Oh . . . she said she would be here about 11 or 12 . . . 1 . . . 2 . . . 3 . . . 4 . . .

VICTIM: I told you. Didn't I tell you?

HAWK: What?

VICTIM: Fate.

HAWK: Fate?

VICTIM: Playing.

HAWK: Right. [*Gets up, goes to kitchen, returns*] Have another orange soda.

VICTIM: That is really very nice of you.

HAWK: Fate. How long have you known Marilyn?

VICTIM: Oh, we grew up together. Ever since we were kids. We went to high school together, and the dances on weekends, and to Dubrow's. . . . We even had a whole cha-cha routine worked out. And Bay Two, and Manhattan Beach. . . . Did she tell you anything about me?

HAWK: Well, only that you were a close and a dear friend.

VICTIM: That is so true. You know, she told me an awful lot about you, too.

HAWK: She did?

VICTIM: Oh, yes. How terrific you were and what a kind and gracious person you were. And what wonderful times she had here and everything like that. And that sometimes when she came here, ah, she would sometimes get . . . high?

HAWK: Get high?

VICTIM: Ah, yes, and she thought that, since I was her closest and dearest friend, that maybe I could come here and get high, too?

HAWK: You want some grass?

VICTIM: Not exactly.

HAWK: Pills? I have ups, downs, Seconal . . .

VICTIM: Ah . . . heroin?

HAWK: You take heroin?

VICTIM: Ah, sometimes.

HAWK: I see. Well, sure.

VICTIM: Oh, I knew it. I could tell. This really is my day.

HAWK: Oh, listen, I should apologize, I haven't offered you anything to eat. Would you like a little something?

VICTIM: Oh, no, thank you. I couldn't, really. See, when I was at the Port of Authority, I had a frankfurter at the Nedick's they have there. I wasn't really hungry or anything, but my mother said never to go with an empty stomach. And with the excitement of the day . . . ah, do you think I could have my shot now?

HAWK: You look like you should eat more. You look skinny.

VICTIM: No, I'm just slender . . . if I could just have my shot . . .

HAWK: You know, it's not very healthy to be as thin as you are. You really should make an effort to eat more. I happen to have some food here and I would feel much better if you ate something.

VICTIM: Oh, I couldn't, really . . .

HAWK: I have some salami, potato chips, frozen pizza, pickled herring, peanut butter; or something more substantial, like pastrami, canned ravioli, Spam . . .

VICTIM: Really, I just ate. If I could . . .

HAWK: You know, eating is very important. It is one of the most important activities that fill our day. Besides the nutrition it brings, there is also the pleasure it gives. Not to eat is unkind, unhealthy, and self-destructive. Besides, I won't give you the shot unless you eat something first.

VICTIM: Well, maybe I could force down a bite or two.

HAWK: Good. [*He gets up and brings the food to her*]

VICTIM: [*Eating*] You know, this is very strange, but it really reminds me of a dream I had the other night. I dreamt that I was starving . . . oh, barbecued chicken! My mother always makes boiled. This is my favorite. Mmmmmm. Delicious. As I was saying, in this dream, I was so hungry that I had these terrible pains in my stomach. But I couldn't find anything to eat. And there were all these people around handing me Care packages; only when I opened them up they turned out to be full of garbage! Coffee grounds, rinds, potato peels . . . and then, all of a sudden, I was in my mother's kitchen. And there was my mother at this huge stove cooking chicken soup in a great big pot and I asked her for a kreplach, so she reached into the soup and pulled out a kreplach and she threw it on the floor. I bent down to pick it up, and, what do you think? She stepped on it! "Mother," I said, "could I have another kreplach, please?" and she took out another one and threw it on the floor and when I reached for it she stepped on it again and when she took her foot away, underneath was my sister and the kreplach went into her mouth, so I went right in after it and, what do you think? I was sucked into my sister's mouth and there I was suspended in this dark room, and all of a sudden the lights came on and I was at a dance where everyone was wearing tunics and eating turkey legs and on the cha-cha they would bite into the turkey legs and on the cha-cha-cha they would throw the bones at me! Then I started running away through a dark corridor that changed into a refrigerator, one of those enormous wholesale meat refrigerators, and there were these huge sides of beef hanging all over, and I knew that, at last, here was my dinner. So I went over to a side of beef and I started eating and eating and eating, and I started to get fat. And I got fatter and fatter until the flesh was hanging from my body layer after layer and I tried to walk but I could only waddle. That's when this small white duck came waddling up to me and as it was waddling it lost its feathers and then it lost its skin and then there was this raw duck waddling beside me as I waddled to the next side of beef and I ate and ate and I got fatter and fatter until the only thing I could move was my mouth. [*Pauses, eating*] Then I woke up. Oh, seedless grapes. I thought they were out of season. They're my favorite.

HAWK: Here, have some tomato juice.

VICTIM: Do you have a piece of lemon?

HAWK: Of course. [*He gets the lemon*]

VICTIM: This is really so nice of you. I just wish I was a little hungrier. Do you think Marilyn will be here soon?

HAWK: Marilyn? Oh, no, I don't think Marilyn is going to make it tonight. I just remembered, she's a dyke.

VICTIM: I beg your pardon?

HAWK: I said, "I don't think Marilyn will be here tonight. I just remembered that she's a dyke."

VICTIM: That's what I thought you said.

HAWK: You see, she has this new lover uptown and she was concerned about your coming here because she knew that if you met this person, it would make you unhappy . . .

VICTIM: I do not comprehend what you are saying.

HAWK: I said that she is making it with this new chick now and she doesn't want to see you.

VICTIM: This is not a very funny joke.

HAWK: Besides, you can't depend on dykes to come when they say they're going to come.

VICTIM: Wait a minute. Wait a minute. I cannot sit here as Marilyn's closest and dearest friend and listen to you cast aspersions . . .

HAWK: Oh, come on, she told me about the two of you. Don't play dumb with me. Your lover's making it with someone else. I told you you can't depend on dykes, not for anything. They're just unreliable.

VICTIM: . . . on my closest and . . . I mean, you've been very gracious up till now and a joke is a joke, but I will not sit here and listen to you go on damaging the character of my closest and dearest . . .

VICTIM: I'll just have to leave. [*Goes to the door*]

HAWK: What about the heroin?

VICTIM: [*Stops*] Do you think I could have my shot now?

HAWK: Sure. You ready?

VICTIM: Do you think . . . ?

HAWK: Sit down there, on the rug. [*To* DOUBLE] Now. [*The* DOUBLE *delivers the box and returns to his chair. The* HAWK *slowly and methodically prepares the injection*]

VICTIM: [*Sits*] I don't understand why you're saying these things. I mean, Marilyn and I are the closest and dearest friends, and just because two human beings happen to be able to be close and communicate with each other doesn't mean what you said. I mean, if I don't know Marilyn, who else could know her? We're the closest and dearest of friends and you don't find a friend like Marilyn every day of the week. I mean . . . I mean, she was such a good friend to me. She would do anything in the world . . . like the time her Uncle Max invited her up to the bungalow colony and she wanted me to have just as good a time as she did. And that was the best time I ever had. . . . Marilyn and I did everything together. . . .

That's what matters, when two people can care about each other . . . and communicate . . . and do things together. I mean, Marilyn is the best friend I ever had, and, I mean, she's really a good friend, and . . . and I understood . . . I mean, when she started taking heroin . . . I understood . . . and when I was just a little afraid at first . . . I mean, she understood . . . and that's . . . and even when we had this plan about leaving Brooklyn together and she left a little before me . . . I understood. And I'm sure she understands now. . . . That's what a friend is. That's what it's all about, not what you said. When two people can talk to each other and understand each other. And be together. Do everything together. You don't find that every day in the week! I mean, Marilyn and I . . . I . . . I mean, I would do anything in the world . . . and she would do anything in the world for me, and that's what is really important. That's what really matters . . . when it's all one . . . when two human beings can care and understand and communicate and be together . . . that's what it's all about! That's what . . . [*he gives her the shot*] . . . really matters . . . what really matters . . . when it's all one . . . [*She starts to get up. A flash. She slumps to the floor, dead*]

The HAWK *takes another shower. The* DOUBLE *rearranges the materials. The* VICTIM *lies on the floor.*

DOUBLE: [*In the kitchen, repeating the gestures of the* HAWK's *shower*] He is overcome by the abstract gestures of animals. Snouts . . . scurrying . . . feet in the hallway . . . wings knocking . . . Birds fly out of networks of trees, shrieking. Straight down. Heading straight down. Images exploding. "That's where it's at," he says to himself. He grabs a piece and runs. He's still heading straight down. He screams. He doesn't hear himself. Someone is laughing at him. The laughter is slow, hollow. He forces. He claws. He grabs. He dries himself in the sun. [*The* DOUBLE *escorts the* VICTIM *out. The* HAWK *and the* DOUBLE *return, as before*] She's dead.

HAWK: She was skinny but she had a great walk. A sequin dress in the early darkness and a certain Oriental roll to her hips. She was anything but cherry. She had the sweet, pale look of the damned. Just like Jean Harlow.

DOUBLE: What do I do with the body?

HAWK: The body?

DOUBLE: Her corpse. She's dead.

HAWK: I turned her on.

DOUBLE: They'll be looking for you.

HAWK: What do you expect me to do? I can't help it.

DOUBLE: Get rid of the body.

HAWK: I can't.

DOUBLE: Get rid of the body.

HAWK: I can't.

DOUBLE: Get rid of the body.

HAWK: I can't. I can't. I can't.

The SECOND VICTIM *appears at the door.*

Third Improvisation: The Second Victim

VICTIM: [*Breezes in wearing a psychedelic outfit, checks herself out in the mirror*] What's happening?

HAWK: I give up.

VICTIM: Hey, I brought you a present. [*Outlining a large box*] It's a big present.

HAWK: Should I open it?

VICTIM: Yeah.

HAWK: [*Opening the "box"*] What's in it? [*Victim stands in place of the box . . . shrugs . . . they turn away*]

HAWK: How about a Coke?

VICTIM: No, that's okay. I've got one here. [*Outlines a Coke*]

HAWK: Have a real one.

VICTIM: No, I'm getting to like these. Do you want one? [*She makes him a "Coke." He takes it. She puts hers in a "cabinet" and begins doing a thing with the cabinet, changing it into various objects*]

HAWK: Not bad. You got any root beer in that thing of yours? [*No response*] Just Coke. Coke, Coke, Coke.

VICTIM: [*Stops*] You know, I did the funniest thing the other day. I was just like walking down this street. I'm walking down this street, and I see this fat man. [*Outlines the man*] This little fat man. And he looks terrible. Really down. So I say to him, "Qué paso, little fat guy?" And he says, "I want to get high." So, I think, if he wants to get high, he should get high. But, like, I don't have any grass on me. So, I say to him, "Come with me, little fat guy." We start walking down the street and he's kind of, like, waddling next to me and we keep walking until we come to this narrow little alley. And at the end of the alley there's this . . . ah . . . door. Yeah, door. [*Makes a door*] So, I open the door and I look around and it's very dark. But, it's okay, because I've got my candle [*Makes a candle*], and I light my candle, and I see . . . two boxes. We sit down on the boxes and the little fat guy says, "I want to get high." Well, I still don't have any grass, right, so I go . . . [*Makes a joint and smokes it*] . . . you know how I do . . . and I go [*Smoking the joint*], and I pass it to him, and he smokes it, and I go

[*Makes another joint, smokes it, passes it*] . . . like that. And we sit there for a while, doing that. Nothing happens. Then, I look over at him, and he's not just a little fat guy anymore, he's a *stoned* little fat guy. I mean, like he's smashed out of his head. I can hardly believe it. [*Pause*] That's cool, because it's all an illusion anyway.

HAWK: [*Rolling a joint*] Care for a smoke?

VICTIM: Yeah. [*Takes a toke, holds it*] Dynamite. [*Another toke, looks toward the door*] Was that somebody at the door?

HAWK: No, there's no one at the door. If there was someone at the door, I'd be the first to hear it.

VICTIM: Well, I don't know. I get paranoid sometimes. And there's a lot of bad shit happening lately. Like, just the other night I was sitting over at a friend's pad. A quiet evening. There was someone in the kitchen doing some stuff, and the rest of us are hanging out in the living room smoking some nice hash. A quiet evening with friends. And I'm just sitting there grooving. And all of a sudden I hear this sound outside, this kind of tapping sound, like, tap, tap, tap. Well, I can't figure out what's happening, so I open the window and I look out, and what I see, over on the corner, is this cop. And he's standing there with his nightstick [*Makes a nightstick*], just kind of tapping. Then I look down at the other end of the block and there's this other cop and he's tapping with his nightstick, too. Then I look up and down and around and the street is full of cops tapping with their nightsticks. So, while I'm trying to work out whether it's Morse code or something, I hear someone yell, "Hey, man, they're coming through the fucking windows!" Then there's this whole scene with people running into the bathroom to flush their lives away, and needles breaking and all like that, and I crawl out on the fire escape to see what's happening. And, man, there's cops everywhere, thousands of them, rushing up and down dragging people out into the street and throwing them into wagons. I mean, they don't care who the fuck it is, they're just grabbing people. Like there's this cat just walking down the street, you know, minding his own business, and he gets his head smashed by a cop with a nightstick and there's blood pouring all over the place and across the street this chick is screaming her head off, and there's people smashing bottles and slashing and hitting and kicking and this wild scene, I mean they got bricks and garbage and shotguns and tear gas, and there's blood and gore and people screaming and dying [*Thrashes about on the floor*] in the gutters and it's horrible and nobody knows what to do. Like, it's blood and people's insides and gore and screaming, wow! [*Stops*] I mean, like, you can tell why someone would get paranoid. [*Sits*] Are you sure there's no one at the door? [*Goes to the door*] I'd better check.

HAWK: It's cool. Nobody's there.

VICTIM: Yeah, you're right. There's no one there.

HAWK: Listen, I've got your stuff. Why don't you . . .

VICTIM: You know what you need?

HAWK: What do I need?

VICTIM: You need a radar set.

HAWK: Listen, I have to go out . . .

VICTIM: [*Making the "radar set"*] With that whoosh, whoosh, scanning device, and in your case a camera; yeah, a camera.

HAWK: Look, I'll give you a box and you can take it with you.

VICTIM: And you put this on the roof, see, and bring down an extension cord and attach it . . . ah . . . here, to this control panel [*Outlines a control panel*], and up there [*The mirror*] you have a huge screen. Now you just sit back and wait . . . when something's happening you'll get a beep, beep, beep thing and . . . there it goes. Okay. That means somebody is coming, right? So, switch to the roof . . . ah, do you know those two people? Well, that's all right, they look involved. Zoom to the hallway. No one in the hallway. The stairs. Up the stairs, down the stairs. Oh, and the fantastic thing about this model is that you can get an entire aerial view of New York. Let's see. Switch to aerial . . . wow. Now let's move in closer. To 37th St. and Seventh Avenue . . . oh . . . zoom in on that yellow cab . . . and in the back seat . . . wait a minute . . . do you see that? The taxicab driver isn't the same as his picture! This is unbelievable. What you could do with this machine. You could spy anywhere. Rule the world. You can even get this very room. You can see everything that's happening in this fantastic blue room. In the kitchen, the bathroom . . . [*The HAWK makes a tool kit and attempts to dismantle the "set." She maneuvers to avoid him*] Right in this very room. And you can get a close up or move way back and you can get a side view, three quarter, full face. And you can make it bigger than life or [*He has a "hammer" now*] you can make it smaller than life and you can even make it very, very small, so like nobody can get to it. But, sometimes you want to change the image. Like it's not very cool to have the same image all the time. [*Tries to change the "image," continues hammering at the "set"*] I mean, it's a drag, man, you want the image to change, right? You don't want to always have the same image, the same stupid image. [*They

both beat the set*] You want to change the image. To . . . change . . . the . . . image . . . wow! Ah, I think I'll take my bag and split, okay?

HAWK: Sure. [*Makes a needle and hits her arm*]

VICTIM: What's that?

HAWK: Junk. [*Hits her again*]

VICTIM: Yeah. Could you give me my junk?

HAWK: Here. [*Hits her again*]

VICTIM: No man, that's nothing. I want some junk. [*He hits her again*] I mean, that's nothing. If that worked, do you think I'd come to you? Look! [*She makes a needle and hits him*] See, that's nothing. [*He hits her*] Wow! [*She hits him*] I just want some junk. [*He hits her, she hits him, they fight with the "needles"*] Okay. All right. I'll fight for my junk. Here! No, man, that's nothing. Fingers, you dig? I mean, nothing. All right. Yeah. Okay. No, that's nothing, nothing. I don't want that. I want junk. Okay. [*She makes a huge needle and pushes it into him, he continues hitting her*] No! That's nothing! [*They face the mirror, he pounds at her body*]

VICTIM: That's noth-	HAWK: Here, junk. My
ing. I want junk. I	entire supply: heroin,
mean, what's that?	morphine, Metha-
That's nothing, man!	drine, Demerol, acid,
No. I want junk. I	Seconal, mescaline,
don't want that, no,	DMT, peyote, junk,
junk, I want junk. I	shit, opium, hash,
don't want acid or	junk, junk, cocaine.
Demerol, I want	Here, coke, more
junk. I don't want	coke, Coke, coke,
any coke! Junk! Junk!	Coke!

HAWK: Coke, coke, Coke, coke . . .

VICTIM: [*Heading for the door*] Just give me my bag and I'll split.

HAWK: [*Stops*] Sit down on the rug and I'll straighten you here. [*To DOUBLE*] Now.

The DOUBLE delivers the box and returns to his chair. The HAWK prepares the injection.

VICTIM: [*Sits*] You're a fucking drag. I mean, like it's very hard to make it when people fuck with your thing like that. Like you got your thing and I got mine and you could have the exact same one if you wanted it. Like . . . people . . . like they're really stupid and vicious. Like when somebody just goes and claws out a piece of your thing. And then . . . like, yeah, they start thinking that someone else makes up all the rules for their little games and they think there's some great almighty thing up there that really cares what the fuck they do with their stupid games . . . and who cares . . . like animals . . . yeah, animals know what to do. They got one thing and they go out there and they go after it. But people, they get all hung up . . . with objects . . . yeah, like you don't see a lion stalking through the jungle in search of a double boiler! Or a bird checking his watch. Animals really know . . . and then people, like they put them in zoos. But they don't say, "Dig the groovy animal, he's doing his thing." No, they say, "Look at the funny animal." People get so fucked up, I can't believe it. It's crazy is what it is . . . it's really crazy. It's a whole crazy mess. You got to be crazy to stay here. I mean, like I'm going away. Yeah, I'm going away. But you can't just [*Makes a car*] drive to Connecticut or someplace like that . . . you got to [*Makes a train*] take a train to the coast . . . or [*Makes a boat*] a boat to Tangiers or Ibiza . . . or . . . Oh, no man, I'm going to take a jet [*Makes a jet*] . . . yeah, a jet. A big silver jet, with wings and windows, no, no windows, just one big window in front and inside there's this control panel [*Makes the panel*], and I can just get into it . . . because it's my jet, yeah, it's not anybody else's jet. It's all mine. It's all my thing. Like I can get into anything I want to . . . and I can just be up there and a lot of sky and blue and clouds and go anywhere and leave all that pink people babble and just stay up there and go and do anything and be alone [*The* HAWK *gives her the injection*] . . . and not have any stupid games bumping into me . . . and be there . . . and go . . . just go . . . wow [*A flash, she dies*]

The HAWK *takes another shower. The* DOUBLE *rearranges the materials. The* VICTIM *lies on the floor.*

DOUBLE: [*In the kitchen, repeating the gestures of the* HAWK's *shower*] There was once a musician who, each night at nine, would blow his horn out the window of his apartment. He was all right. He could get into it. He had a good dramatic sense. He was playing for a chick he dug—she lived in the building behind his, on the other side of a small cemetery. It was a routine, a serenade. First he fiddled around a bit, announcing his presence, working himself up. When he found a riff he could play with, he got louder and came on with the vibrato. It started to get painful. He must have really had it in for that chick. After a while, he gave up on the music part altogether —the horn yelped and moaned and got all frustrated. Finally, he went into this one, long, screaming high note . . . and fucked it for all he was worth. Which was enough to blow your brains out. I guess he got his nut off, but he was doomed to repeating it . . . each night at nine . . . until she split or he busted his lip . . . or something. [*The* DOUBLE *escorts the* VICTIM *out. The* HAWK *and the* DOUBLE *return, as before*] She's dead.

HAWK: She was skinny but she had a great walk. A sequin dress in the early darkness and a certain Oriental roll to her hips. She was anything but cherry. She had the sweet, pale look of the damned. Just like Jean Harlow.

DOUBLE: What do I do with the body?

HAWK: The body?

DOUBLE: Her corpse. She's dead.

HAWK: I turned her on.

DOUBLE: They'll be looking for you.

HAWK: What do you expect me to do? I can't help it.

DOUBLE: Get rid of the body.

HAWK: I can't.

DOUBLE: Get rid of the body.

HAWK: I can't.

DOUBLE: Get rid of the body.

HAWK: I can't. I can't. I can't.

The INSPECTOR *appears at the door.*

Fourth Improvisation: The Inspector

INSPECTOR: [*Enters wearing a trench coat and hat. He flashes a badge in the mirror, inspects the room, then encounters the "body"*] The body. [*Inspects it*] No pulse . . . incipient rigor . . . dead two and a half hours . . . overdose of heroin. [*Rises, begins a reconstruction of the crime*] He is sitting here [*Couch*]. He's five feet tall, brown hair, blue eyes, 185 pounds . . . there's a knock at the door. She enters . . . five foot three, 120 pounds, 27 years of age, blue eyes, green feet. She crosses over and sits down. He brings her an orange soda. They begin to talk. Does he know Marilyn Stein? Yes, he knows Marilyn Stein and she . . . there's a knock at the door. She comes in. Five foot two, 127 pounds, 17 years of age, red hair, red eyes, psychedelic jump suit . . . sits down. He hands her a Coke . . . There's a knock at the door. She enters. Five foot three, 185 pounds, 47 years of age, Indo-Eurasian graduation gown . . . crosses over and sits down. He gets up and goes to the bathroom and gets her a cup of tea. . . . There's a knock at the door. She comes in, five foot three, blond hair, blue eyes, black dress, 285 pounds . . . crosses over and sits down. He comes back, hands her the orange soda. She drinks the tea. She asks him if he has a headache. "No, I don't have a headache." "Would you like something to eat?" Yes. She goes to the television set, turns it on. He goes into the bathroom, takes six aspirin, comes back out, sits down. She gets up, goes to the kitchen, comes back with six eggs, eats the eggs. He goes into the bathroom and brushes his teeth. Marilyn Stein . . . a possibility. She goes to the champagne, takes a sip of champagne, he steps on her foot, she sits down, looks in the mirror, the mirror collapses on her face, she runs into the bathroom, the medicine cabinet jumps to the floor, closes, opens, slams in her face, she runs into the kitchen, takes the sink, flushes it down the commode, comes out and spits in his face. He goes into the bathroom and returns with a dead baby sandwich. He eats the sandwich. Uh, huh. He turns around in the form of an anopheles mosquito, buzzes about, flips over the couch, lands on a horse, rides into the bathroom, back out dressed in cleats, stands on her face, kicks her, she doesn't like it, jumps over the couch, he takes a lasso, lassoes her hair, drags her into the kitchen and slams her head in the refrigerator door. Oh . . . There's a knock at the door. A car drives in, the chauffeur gets out, opens the door, nine Packer football players come out, run into the bathroom, turn on the radio, take off their clothes, run back out, get in the car and drive off. Marilyn Stein, Jeffrey, Packers . . . possibilities. She's lying on the floor now, doing a hula dance, in a hula skirt, with a hula hoop. Red Ryder is sitting over here, he throws a spear, it gets Little Beaver, who falls on the floor and turns into 47 Mexican bongo players, the bongos turn into saxophones which turn into 78 exact replicas of Jean Harlow humming Beethoven's Twenty-fourth Sonata. She gets up, goes to the mirror, the mirror splatters, the room turns blue, he swims toward her in a scuba suit, takes a harpoon and gaffs her ear, her ear turns into a cornucopia. Coins fall out, he picks them up, goes into the kitchen, takes out a frying pan, beats on it, hears the sound of the frying pan, she's beginning to bleed, her heart is throbbing on the floor, he takes a nine iron and chips it into the wall, the room turns red, the iron turns into a snake, coiling into her ear, eating her, digesting her, he goes into the kitchen, takes some Saran Wrap, wraps her head in it, her head leaps from her body, bounces on the floor, bouncing up and down. He leaps in the air, grabs a vine, swings back and forth, dressed as Tarzan, lands over here, where he keeps his stash, starts swinging again, she's lying on the floor, throbbing, begging, pleading . . . yes, that's it, yes, she's here for dope. The kitchen runs into the bathroom, the bathroom into the kitchen, the medicine cabinet jumps back on the wall, the mirror decollapses. He swings over to her, she's here, dressed as Dale Evans, burning up, he grabs a pen wiper, cuts the vine with the pen wiper, grabs her arm, the vein is throbbing, pulsing, he vines her vein with the vine, raises the pen wiper and is about to insert it into her vein . . . which is where we come in. [*Addressing the mirror*] There's really no need for this kind of thing.

None at all. We have a situation set up, which is comparable to this only it's under more beneficial, controlled circumstances. He proceeds in this amateuristic fashion, thus convicting himself, I'm afraid. There's no need for it. If he wanted to see us, if he made an effort, if he had something on his mind, some sort of desire, some sort of feeling, some sort of lust, some need, flesh need, hair need, eye need, soul need, mother need, father need, rock, tree, earth, sun, sound, sky need . . . he could have come down and seen us. It's a simple matter. You take the cross-town shuttle. The building's eighty-seven stories high, black, no windows, you can't miss it. This particular crime is very common, *homo sapiensis romantismus phantasmagorias*, RP for short—it's located on the thirteenth, twenty-second, thirty-fourth and eighty-eighth floors. We have miles and miles of files, prints, charts, graphs, ideograms, caligragrams, telegrams, every conceivable aspect dealing with this particular operation, desire, need, felt emotion, whatever it was, we have it for him. You see, he has something on his mind. Something that he is seeking. We know what he was seeking, don't we? Some sort of fulfillment. What was it? Some supreme emotion? The feeling of his body moving through space, weightless like a bird? We have birds on tape, he could have been a bird. If he wanted to learn Chinese we could have transplanted the head of one of our Chinese people. There's no problem. We could have done this, done it all, for him. That's what we're there for, to help. Help, help, help. But, no, they insist on going about it their own way, you see, and this is where they fall short. Then we're called in. And more's the pity, I'd say. It's bothersome. For me, for us, for everybody involved. And yet, it's so simple. So easy. He could have come in and sat down, given us his name, his number, his need, whatever it was, we have it. We check his print, his chart. We have his cellular development, his genetic background, his father's, mother's, sister's, his son's, heirs' to come, their genetic background, their cellular divisions, the history of his cells, chromosomes, past, present, future, their evolutionary development, on film, as they're developing in his body. Everything that he is, will be, hope to be. Everything that has been. We have all this. We could have done this for him. But, no. No, no, no! He proceeds in his own shoddy, little, amateuristic way. Insisting on his own method, flipping and flopping about. Why did he do this? Why? Why? Why? So simple a matter, so simple a matter. Was it love? Love? Love? Or hate. What? What was it? Images? Sounds? Did he want to hear the sound of a liner meeting the dock? The longshoremen singing at night? We have that. We have World War II on tape. We're working on World War III. What was it? A baby's cry? Hob-nailed boots? We could have given him this! Charts, prints, graphs, files, miles and miles of files! Anything! In perfection! Control! Whatever it is. Come in, give us your number, we have it for you. Anything you want! The world in the palm of your hand! The universe! Equations! Arithmetic! Alice! Method Alice! The birth of a star! A galaxy moving through space! Space moving through a galaxy! What is it? We have it! All of it! We have it! All! . . . controlled . . . [*Stops*]*!* We left him here. Our friend, the bird. He inserts the needle into the vein. The heroin, an overdose, in this case, courses through the vein, 12 seconds of time, into the heart. The victim experiences a flash of joy . . . 13 seconds later, death. He gets up, goes into the bathroom, undresses himself, looks in the mirror and steps into the shower. Well, this concludes the case. Except for the motive . . . the motive. Oh, there's someone in the kitchen. There's someone in the kitchen and he's eating. He's eating. Yes, yes, of course. The motive is hunger. [*Leaving, stops*] Odd, she resembles a K109BC . . . a saint. [*exits*]

The DOUBLE *addresses the mirror.*

DOUBLE: Yes, I have known a lot of psychopaths—bad amphetamine heads, bad junkies, father haters, killers, hard guys, slow talkers from Texas, droolers, silent tea heads, schizoid dykes, cokeys, racial fanatics, flipped-out husbands. . . . The one thing they all have in common is a certain freedom of action—they just don't give a shit. They have their thing to get them off, whatever it is, in the head. . . . And I should say also, for your information, that drugs do not make psychopaths, psychopaths make drugs, as they make war, as every man is a potential psychopath.

INTERMISSION
END OF PART I

PART II

The HAWK *and the* DOUBLE *are as before.*

DOUBLE: She's dead.

HAWK: She was skinny but she had a great walk. A sequin dress in the early darkness and a certain Oriental roll to her hips. She was anything but cherry. She had the sweet, pale look of the damned. Just like Jean Harlow.

DOUBLE: What do I do with the body?

HAWK: The body?

DOUBLE: Her corpse. She's dead.

HAWK: I turned her on.

DOUBLE: They'll be looking for you.

HAWK: What do you expect me to do? I can't help it.

DOUBLE: Get rid of the body.

HAWK: I can't.

DOUBLE: Get rid of the body.

HAWK: I can't.

DOUBLE: Get rid of the body.

HAWK: I can't. I can't. I can't.

The THIRD VICTIM *appears at the door.*

Fifth Improvisation: The Third Victim

HAWK: Who is it?

VICTIM: Madame Duval.

HAWK: Who the fuck is Madam Duval? [*Opens the door*]

VICTIM: I am Madame Duval.

HAWK: What can I do for you?

VICTIM: Well, you must know me.

HAWK: No, I don't.

VICTIM: Well, you know my chauffeur, Jeffrey.

HAWK: Oh, come in.

VICTIM: [*Enters, looks in mirror*] Oh, what a marvelous mirror. Absolutely charming. [*Turns*] You know, I had a terrible time getting here.

HAWK: Oh, really.

VICTIM: Oh, yes. It was simply awful. It's Jeffrey's night off, you know. I think everyone should have one night off, don't you? It breaks the monotony and refreshes the spirit, in a manner of speaking. Well, where was I? Oh, yes. So I came by taxi instead. Have you ever tried to get a taxi over here? It's really quite an experience. You stand out in the street and shout "Taxi! Taxi!" And, of course, they're all going to Brooklyn. And then there's the ones with their off duty signs on. So, you shout, "Off Duty! Off Duty!" Of course that does no good whatsoever. And when I finally got one, the driver talked incessantly all the way over about some person named Jackson or Johnson . . . it was simply unbearable.

HAWK: Would you like something to drink?

VICTIM: Oh, yes, how sweet. [*She talks to her "guides," who hover somewhere over her left shoulder*] What's that, darlings? Oh, yes, the blue . . . you're quite right . . . very poor taste . . .

HAWK: [*At the liquor cabinet*] What would you like? I have champagne, some whiskey, Scotch . . .

VICTIM: Oh, no—I'm English.

HAWK: No, what would you like to drink?

VICTIM: I would like tea, please.

HAWK: Tea. How do you take it?

VICTIM: I take it with one level teaspoon of sugar and a twist of lemon floating in the glass.

HAWK: Certainly. [*Goes to the kitchen*]

VICTIM: [*Arranging herself in a rigid position*] Ommmmmm.

HAWK: [*Returns with the tea*] Are you all right?

VICTIM: Oh, yes. I was just composing myself. I feel relaxed now. More relaxed than I was before, which isn't very relaxed, but it is more relaxed than I was before.

HAWK: I see. [*Hands her the tea*]

VICTIM: Oh, thank you. Mmmmm. Delicious. Have you known Jeffrey long?

HAWK: Two, three years.

VICTIM: He's a dear boy. He's been with me for some time now. His friends, though, they're a bit odd. Bohemians, I suspect. Charles . . . that's my husband, he's the nervous sort, you know, with blue eyes and baggy trousers. Charles thinks that Jeffrey is a common criminal. Hardly. A bit common, perhaps, but certainly not criminal. Wouldn't you say?

HAWK: What can I do for you?

VICTIM: Oh, yes. Of course. Excuse me . . . what's that, my dears? . . . yes, yes . . . patience, we'll go soon . . .

HAWK: Who are you talking to?

VICTIM: Oh, that . . . my guides.

HAWK: Your who?

VICTIM: My guides.

HAWK: Oh, you're one of those . . . ah . . . Christian Scientists?

VICTIM: Not exactly.

HAWK: They talk back to you?

VICTIM: We communicate, of course.

HAWK: How many do you have?

VICTIM: Two. How many do you have?

HAWK: I have one.

VICTIM: Oh, bully for you.

HAWK: I think one's enough. Any more than that and the room would start to get crowded. Two of anything is more than I can stand. [*Pause*] What did you come here for?

VICTIM: Oh, yes. Well, I was going to call you. On the phone, of course. It's Jeffrey's night off, you know. And I had the receiver in my hand, when they said to me, "Emily" . . . they call me Emily.

HAWK: Is that your name?

VICTIM: No. "Emily," they said, "go yourself." And I said to them, "But surely I could just call a messenger service and have them deliver

it in a plain white wrapper!" But they insisted. "That is not discreet," they said, "go yourself." So, I came myself.

HAWK: Why?

VICTIM: Oh, yes. I'm so forgetful at times. Well, to get to the point, it's about your merchandise. Yes, your . . . what's that noise? Do you hear that?

HAWK: What noise?

VICTIM: That flapping noise. It's getting louder. It's coming closer. [*Rises, backing away around the room*] . . . it's the beating of wings . . . it's coming closer . . . it's a bird . . . a huge bird . . . it's coming closer . . . it's coming toward me . . . it's a . . . it's a hawk! . . . and it's coming toward me! No! Stop! Stop it! Get away! Get away from me! Stop! Stop! [*Pause*] Well. They certainly are playful little devils. Now, what was it you came to see me about?

HAWK: I live here. You came to see me.

VICTIM: Oh, yes. Quite right. It is rather confusing sometimes. They can throw me off, as it were. But it's much better now. I went to a psychiatrist, you see, and my problem was cured in three months' time. He said I was the fastest client he ever had. Charles sent me. He was upset when I told him I could hear voices. I was upset too, because it got to be very distracting when I couldn't tell whether they were talking to me or just having a little chat with one another. So, I went to the psychiatrist, and after three months, I was able to hear them loud and clear . . . yes, darlings, we're hurrying right along.

HAWK: The merchandise.

VICTIM: Oh, yes, about the merchandise. How shall I put it? I feel . . . yes, of course . . . we feel that a better brand is the best solution.

HAWK: What do you mean?

VICTIM: Well, I mean that whatever you have been giving us has been . . . I hate to use the word "inferior" . . . but inferior it has definitely been.

HAWK: It's not working.

VICTIM: Well, it does produce a mild nausea and splitting headaches, but these aren't exactly the effects we had in mind. So, we thought that if you could prescribe a better brand, we would be most appreciative.

HAWK: How long have you been taking morphine?

VICTIM: Oh, let's see . . . I've been taking syrettes now . . . thank you, darlings . . . eighteen months.

HAWK: I see. Well, what you have is very common among junkies. You've developed a tolerance for the drug. Most addicts suffer from this. It's very common.

VICTIM: Ah, yes, junkies, poor sufferers.

HAWK: You need more. Six syrettes instead of three.

VICTIM: That wouldn't be very practical, would it?

HAWK: Practical?

VICTIM: Well, of course, with such a busy schedule, people coming to see me for guidance and readings . . . and there's Jeffrey . . . why, that would mean he would be at my side morning, noon, and night . . . hmmmm.

HAWK: Later on, you'll probably need nine. But, I assure you, it happens every day. As long as the cost doesn't bother you, you needn't worry about it. Most junkies are poor.

VICTIM: Yes, of course. Well, I hardly think it necessary to dwell on that. Besides, if your theory had been correct, they would have said to me, "Emily, you need more injections." Now, wouldn't they?

HAWK: It makes no difference to me. You'll need the six injections sooner or later. Your body just won't stand it. That's the reason for the nausea and the headaches. Now, do you want . . .

VICTIM: Excuse me . . . what's that, darlings? . . . oh? Oh, really . . . well . . . [*To* HAWK] "Emily, you need more injections." That's what they said. Now, if you have a sterilized needle, some alcohol, and gauze, we can put your theory to the test.

HAWK: You want to try it now?

VICTIM: Oh, yes, by all means.

HAWK: How do you take it?

VICTIM: One level teaspoon of sugar and a twist . . .

HAWK: No, the injection. Where do you take the injection?

VICTIM: Well, I used to take it in the arm, but I found that when I appeared before a multitude—sometimes it's more like a minitude—to speak, and I raised my arms, well, the marks weren't exactly in keeping with the spiritual nature of the occasion. So, I take it in the ankle, alternating one here, then one here. I find that to be most efficacious. Although I can't remember which ankle was last . . . Jeffrey sees to all that, of course.

HAWK: How about if I give it to you up your ass?

VICTIM: Well, if you think . . . up my what?

HAWK: Jeff was saying to me the other day how the old junkie likes it up her ass.

VICTIM: [*Goes to the door*] Could you open this door? Could you please open this door?

HAWK: [*Opens the door*] I'll send Jeffrey over with the usual amount.

VICTIM: [*Leaving*] Yes, that would be just fine. [*Turns*] The usual amount! Oh, really! Do you mean to say that I've come all the way over here, stood in the street waving for a taxi, sat in this horrid blue room drinking lukewarm tea, chased by that abominable hawk, to have you say to me, "Up my ass!" Well, up your ass! The usual amount, indeed.

HAWK: See that worn spot on the rug?

VICTIM: Yes.

HAWK: Sit on it. All of you. I'll give you the shot. [*To* DOUBLE] Now.

The DOUBLE *delivers the box and returns to his chair. The* HAWK *prepares the injection.*

VICTIM: [*Sits*] Well . . . yes, in a minute, darlings . . . we must endure . . . a junkie, indeed . . . sit on the floor . . . isn't that just too bohemian . . . it's not as though we haven't sat on floors before. We have sat on floors . . . sometimes we were fortunate enough to sit on mattresses . . . choking from incense . . . little boxes with colors on them . . . it's all so common . . . how they manage, I don't know . . . they're barely able to communicate with each other, let alone on some higher plane . . . poor Jeffrey. If only he wasn't so . . . well, he is . . . yes, yes, darlings . . . be patient. . . . And Charles' friends, oh they're really impossible too. They look at one another and they talk. You can hardly tell them apart, except one is long and one is short . . . I often wonder if they hear each other. . . . Imagine Charles worrying about my voices. . . . Charles has never heard a thing in his life. . . . Yes, yes, my dears, soon. . . . A junkie. Imagine, a junkie. Why, for thousands of years civilized man has used stimulants to elevate and communicate . . . to reach the world of the spirit. A junkie! Everyone knows that a junkie is someone who falls, shakes, sweats, has fits and strangles people in dark alleys . . . a junkie . . . Please hurry! . . . Oh, it's so impossible. All of them. Jeffrey's friends. Charles' friends . . . but, I have made efforts. Yes, I have. I have gone out to people and have said to them, "friend." Yes, I have. And have they extended their hand in friendship? No, they have not. They have hid in their horrid little voids . . . you are the only ones . . . I can speak to you. . . . I can communicate with you. . . . we talk . . . yes, we do. . . . Where are you? . . . I say, where are you? . . . [*To* HAWK] Are you ready? Are you ready? [*To guides*] Well, where are you? One joke is enough. Where are you? [*To* HAWK] Please hurry! [*The* HAWK *starts to give her the injection in the arm*] No, no, in

the ankle. Yes. [*He gives her the injection*]
There. Now, where are you? Please, darlings
. . . [*To* HAWK] I told you! It is not enough!
Get more! Get more! [*He goes for more*]
Are you there? Are you there? What's that?
[*Looks in the mirror. A vision seems to come
to her*] Of course . . . [*Falls to floor, dead*]

The HAWK *returns with the other shot. He
pauses a moment, then pounds it into her ass.
The* HAWK *takes another shower. The* DOUBLE
rearranges the materials. The VICTIM *lies on
the floor.*

DOUBLE: [*In the kitchen, repeating the gestures
of the* HAWK'S *shower*] You know, I have
moments. I walk around a lot. I go for strolls
in the park. I hang out. I observe, sometimes,
when my head gets loose . . . when the habitual
hairiness . . . subsides . . . I watch them, you,
us, the others . . . carry on . . . I have moments.
I see the picture. I wonder at this creature I
see, who is so far out of the muck, who has
shed his gills, who swims for relaxation, who
shits into plastic bowls, who searches for love,
love. . . . I wonder about this need for love,
this irrational yearning . . . a torment, in fact
. . . especially when you consider what he's
made of, what he smells like, what he's capable
of doing. . . . I wonder if it's built in . . . how
deep it runs . . . if it is in the sea! If it is in
the sky! In the eyes of cats! Then I get a
feeling in my gut just like hunger, a feeling
that washes over my balls and up into my
lungs, and my heart, and my brain . . . a
useless compassion . . . making me into a
dumbfounded idiot! Which disgusts me! [*The*
DOUBLE *escorts the* VICTIM *out. The* HAWK
and the DOUBLE *return as before*] She's dead.

HAWK: She was skinny but she had a great walk.
A sequin dress in the early darkness and a certain Oriental roll to her hips. She was anything but cherry. She had the sweet, pale look
of the damned. Just like Jean Harlow.

DOUBLE: What do I do with the body?

HAWK: The body?

DOUBLE: The corpse. She's dead.

HAWK: I turned her on.

DOUBLE: They'll be looking for you.

HAWK: What do you expect me to do? I can't
help it.

DOUBLE: Get rid of the body.

HAWK: I can't.

DOUBLE: Get rid of the body.

HAWK: I can't.

DOUBLE: Get rid of the body.

HAWK: I can't. I can't. I can't.

The FOURTH VICTIM *appears at the door.*

Sixth Improvisation: The Fourth Victim

HAWK: [*Opening the door*] Oh, fuck! [*Shuts the
door in the face of the* FOURTH VICTIM, *a
striking platinum blonde reminiscent of Hollywood in the early 1930s, who opens the door,
enters, and crosses in front of the mirror, holds
her breast, and poses. She turns*]

VICTIM: Hello, fuck face. [*Sits on the couch next
to the* HAWK] Hey, Charlie, you like this?
[*She presents a perfumed arm under his nose*]
It's called Ben Hur. Give it a chance to sink
in. A gift from an admirer.

HAWK: Something else. Let's have another smell.

VICTIM: So, how's your ass, Charlie?

HAWK: It's all right. How's yours?

VICTIM: I wish you hadn't asked me that. I'm
in bad shape, Charlie. I have this huge bruise
on my hip. [*Hands on hip, outlining a bruise*]
You wouldn't believe it. It's not even black
and blue. It's all yellow and purple, and there's
some green here. And there's this pain that
goes down my leg, past my knee [*Hands on
knee*], then shoots up the other side, where
there's this big scratch across my stomach. I
couldn't begin to tell you how that all happened. Oh, and my toe, right on the end, a
large sore, and [*Presents an ankle*] do you
see that?

HAWK: Is that a rash?

VICTIM: No, cigarette burns. Could you believe
it?

HAWK: That's a rash.

VICTIM: Cigarette burns. I ought to know. I was
there. And then there's this piece of bone.
Give me your hand. [*His hand on her hip*]
I think it's come off and into my . . . yeah,
right there.

HAWK: That's a cyst, not a bone.

VICTIM: No, that's a piece of bone, Charlie, it's
a chip. Don't try and scare me. You see my
neck?

HAWK: Hickies.

VICTIM: Look at that. And I have a sore throat,
and my back is killing me, my tongue hurts,
my tits are swollen. . . . [*Pause*] Jesus, I got
to change my life, Charlie. [*Poses in the mirror
as she would on a magazine cover*] You know,
I've been thinking, just because I'm five feet
three and a little chesty doesn't mean I couldn't
be a fashion model, does it, Charlie?

HAWK: You want to be a fashion model?

VICTIM: Well, I have very high cheekbones and
long eyelashes and all you have to do is look
dumb. I've been looking through a lot of
magazines and I could do that. What have
you got to drink, Charlie?

HAWK: There's some champagne, help yourself.

VICTIM: Champagne? What's the occasion?

HAWK: I just thought you might like it.

VICTIM: You're a real friend, Charlie. [*Pops the cork*] Oooooh. [*Pours a glass, hand on breast, and swills it down*] So, anyway, this is what I thought: sooner or later people are going to get tired of all these women that are built like boards, you know. They're going to want to see some flesh, right? That's where I come in. I mean, what's a woman without flesh? So, I figure I could just change it all. Can't you just see it? I could become famous. My picture on billboards, TV, magazines all over the country . . . my face. People would start imitating the way I wear my hair and the way I make up. And I could meet someone who would love me for what I am. . . . What movie did I see that in? [*Pours another, drinks it*] Seen any good movies lately, Charlie?

HAWK: Yeah, I saw this movie about a hooker who gets syphilis and dies.

VICTIM: What the fuck kind of movie is that?

HAWK: Four-star.

VICTIM: You know, Charlie, you wouldn't know a good movie if it hit you right in the kisser. If you saw *Red Dust,* you'd be just as stupid afterwards.

HAWK: *Red Dust?*

VICTIM: Yeah. With Jean Harlow and Clark Gable. It wouldn't change you one bit.

HAWK: I didn't see that movie.

VICTIM: It looks it. But don't see it on television. It's not the same thing. You got to see it on the big screen. There's this great scene at the end. [*Swings over and throws her arms around him*] She's sitting on his lap and she's got her arms around him.

HAWK: Whose lap?

VICTIM: Clark Gable. Jean Harlow has her arms . . .

HAWK: Yeah.

VICTIM: And he's looking down into her eyes.

HAWK: Right.

VICTIM: And she's looking up into his eyes.

HAWK: Yeah. Then what?

VICTIM: They have this moment, this long moment, looking into each other's eyes . . .

HAWK: So then what happened?

VICTIM: I went home. What do you do when a movie ends? [*More champagne*] You probably eat the popcorn left in the aisles.

HAWK: Listen, don't drink too much champagne.

VICTIM: Oh, I won't.

HAWK: The other night you threw up all over the floor.

VICTIM: I didn't throw up all over the floor. I never throw up, Charlie.

HAWK: I have photographs of you throwing up all over the floor.

VICTIM: Photographs! What kind of pervert are you that takes photographs of people throwing up? You're sick, Charlie.

HAWK: Just watch the champagne.

VICTIM: [*Staring into glass*] I'm watching it. [*Drinks it*] Now you watch it. [*Pours another*]

HAWK: Put your beak to that worn spot over there and smell it.

VICTIM: Charlie! They ought to lock you up. You're sick. You know, they ought to put you away behind bars.

HAWK: Hey, listen, why don't you take your shit now and leave.

VICTIM: Did you ever see *Hold Your Man?* That was with Jean Harlow. She went to prison in that movie.

HAWK: Oh, yeah.

VICTIM: For a crime that she didn't commit, because Clark Gable, who plays a real rat, kills this guy and he leaves Jean Harlow holding the rap.

HAWK: Yeah, I saw it.

VICTIM: And he runs away . . . you saw it!

HAWK: I saw it, yeah.

VICTIM: So she gets blamed for the crime and she's in prison.

HAWK: And she's in this cell . . .

VICTIM: That's right, wearing a gray uniform, with a Peter Pan collar . . .

HAWK: And there's this psychopath in the next cell. And he's really got it in for Harlow. So, he pulls apart the bars and he takes a long knife and starts stabbing at her breasts, and then he gives her one in the stomach. . . .

VICTIM: She's carrying Clark Gable's baby, only she's not going to tell him, because she's too proud. She wants him to come back on his own. So she waits and waits and she thinks a lot and then she starts to pray. And she prays a lot. And finally, she gets . . . what do you call it?

HAWK: Syphilis.

VICTIM: Religious! You're some kinda mono . . . what do you call it, Charlie? You have a diseased mind.

HAWK: She spends a lot of time in the chapel, remember? The prison chapel.

VICTIM: Yeah, the little room with light shining down. And she prays and prays. Her hair was like a white halo. . . .

HAWK: Then this chaplain comes in. But he's not really a chaplain. He's an ex-Nazi lieutenant who's posing as a chaplain. And he goes up to Harlow and he says, "Kneel down, my child, and I'll bless you." So she kneels down and he . . . [*Takes "Harlow's head" and pulls it between his legs*]

VICTIM: Blesses her. "You keep having faith, my child, and don't ever give up what you believe in, because what you believe in is what you are and you can only lose by not believing and if you keep believing in it, you'll get what you want."

HAWK: And she believes that?

VICTIM: Yes. And she says, "I will, Father, I will." And she kisses his ring. . . .

HAWK: He's the Pope?

VICTIM: Well, I don't remember. Maybe that was another movie. Anyway, one day while she's waiting in her cell what happens? That big fat woman, you know, the dyke with the big keys hanging down. . . .

HAWK: Barry Fitzgerald.

VICTIM: I don't remember who played the part. But she comes around and knocks on the cell and she says, "There's a visitor to see you." And Jean Harlow jumps up and runs down the hall and pushes open this big door, and who's standing in the middle of the room?

HAWK: The psychopath. Only this time she's not getting away. He takes the knife and starts hacking her to pieces. . . .

VICTIM: Clark Gable is standing in the middle of the room, looking away. He's ashamed.

HAWK: He's ripping at her, slashing at her body. . . .

VICTIM: He's such a rat. But she puts her arms out . . .

HAWK: He cuts off the arms, throws them over his shoulder. . . .

VICTIM: Because she's got a big heart . . .

HAWK: Cuts out the heart . . .

VICTIM: And she forgives him with her eyes . . .

HAWK: Gouges out her eyes, slices her head off . . .

VICTIM: . . . And then she runs across the room and throws herself into his arms. [*Lands in his lap, arms around his neck*] And she looks up at him for a long time, and he looks down at her for a long time, and they look deep into each other's eyes for a long time, and they have this moment, this long moment [*Caresses him*] . . .

HAWK: What the fuck are you doing?

VICTIM: [*Rising*] What's with you? You're a dumb fuck, Charlie. You don't even know a moment when it's sitting in your lap. [*To champagne*]

HAWK: Listen, I have to go out. Why don't you take your shit now and leave?

VICTIM: [*Drinking*] I'll think twice before I tell you my favorite movies again, Charlie. I'll think twice. I really feel sorry for you, though. I don't hate you, Charlie, you're too stupid. But I'll think twice. [*Staring into mirror*] Charlie, what's the matter with this mirror?

HAWK: What's wrong with it?

VICTIM: It makes me look like death warmed over. Maybe it's the blue; no, the mirror. Christ, Charlie, I look like a corpse. A corpse at 26. Can you imagine that? She was only 26.

HAWK: What movie was that?

VICTIM: *Saratoga.*

HAWK: *Saratoga?*

VICTIM: That's right. Suddenly, right in the middle of the filming, she just couldn't go on. Then she died. At the height of her career. You could see how pale she was. They had to get someone else to finish her scenes. God, it was awful.

HAWK: Sounds bad.

VICTIM: Oh, it was. Here you are and suddenly, in the next minute, you're gone. It's really horrible. But, that's just a small part of it, you know, Charlie? I mean, sure, they buried her, but she's not dead, not really dead. And that's the difference. She's forever.

HAWK: She's what? Forever?

VICTIM: You could never understand. It's an idea, Charlie. It's more than . . . what you could understand. It's way beyond you, Charlie.

HAWK: Try me. What's this "forever"?

VICTIM: Well, like, she'll always be there, somewhere, there, up there . . . white and divine . . . there's more to it than just a body . . . it's a kind of forever . . . that's all, a forever.

HAWK: Wait a minute. I think I got it. Let's see. She's forever, because, no matter what, there will always be Jean Harlow, somewhere. A movie, a photograph, a line in a magazine, a thought of Harlow, she'll be there. That's what makes her forever.

VICTIM: Yeah, that's right.

HAWK: Okay. Now picture this. You die. They put you in a box, right? And they lower you into the ground, and throw dirt over you, you're dead, right? Dead. And the worms eat your marrow. Are you going to be forever?

VICTIM: One thing I hate is a smart ass. [*Staggering to champagne*] You know, Charlie, you're depressing the shit out of me. I think I'll brighten myself up a bit. [*Pours a glass, looks into it, drinks it*] Liquid diamonds. [*Pours another*]

HAWK: Excuse me. [*Gets up, heads for bathroom*]

VICTIM: Where are you going?

HAWK: [*Gesturing obscenely*] To piss.

VICTIM: [*Hand on breast, swilling it down, staring into mirror*] Divine! [*Pours another, backs up, staring into mirror*] *Dinner at Eight* was without a doubt the best film I ever made. [*Waving her arm*] Whoooops! [*Spills her drink*] Nylon rug. He can clean it up. [*Pours another*] The most important people at M.G.M. supported me in that film. John and Lionel. Marie Dressler. She was a real good friend, Marie Dressler. But Billie Burke, what a dumb cunt she was. Wallace Beery played my husband. He was a rotten son of a bitch to work with. He was. And . . . oooh, that long white dress. Up there, on the top of the stairs in that long, white satin dress . . . with that slob next to me. Well, you got to make some compromises in this business. But I was beautiful. White . . . satin . . .

HAWK: [*Coming out of bathroom*] What's going on?

VICTIM: Oh, hello fuck face.

HAWK: You're drunk.

VICTIM: It's a party, Charlie. We're having a party. What a party, too. Everybody is here, Charlie. When we give a party, it's a party. Ah, what's wrong, Charlie, you look so grim. You don't know anyone. You feel out of place. Too much class. [*He turns*] Oh, don't leave, Charlie. You're a friend of mine, and a friend of mine is special, Charlie. [*Falls into him, he grabs hold of her*] John Barrymoore! [*Moves away*] Look at him—peeing on the curtain! What a lush! And Marion Davies, she's with Charlie again. You know, he's got the biggest jingjang in Hollywood. Hey Charlie, [*Falls on him, he grabs*] you can stay. You can be Tyrone Power or Wallace Reid. [*Moves away*] And here comes Lionel Barrymore, that poor, crippled old motherfucker. And Mack Sennett, and Lupe Velez, and Mary Miles Minter. She's through, washed up, ruined by scandal. It's a hard world, Charlie. Clara Bow is here and she brought the entire team with her. Oh, it's going to be a party, Charlie. [*Throws herself on him, he grabs*] Loosen up, Charlie, you can be Fatty Arbuckle, we got lots of Coke in the ice box.

HAWK: How about Paul Bern?

VICTIM: [*Moving away*] Oh, the life of the party . . . look . . . there's Ethel Waters, she doesn't get to go to these parties often. How you doing, Charlie? Roll out de wardemelon. [*He moves over to her, grabs her*] What are you doing, Charlie? Cut it out. [*Moves away, he follows and grabs her*] Hey Charlie, shape up, you'll never get invited again. [*Moves away, he grabs*] Cut it out! I said. What do you think I am—a piece of meat? Charlie! You prick! Get your hands off me! [*He grabs, holding on*] Off! I said, off! You motherfucker! Are you deaf? Get them off, you cunt! You prick! You cocksucker! Off! Get your fucking hands off my body! Off! Off! Off! GET YOUR FUCKING HANDS OFF MY BODY! [*He lets go, she poses, divinely, in the mirror*] Wheeeew! [*He grabs her breast*] Wha . . . ! Charlie, get it off! Get your shitty hand off my breast, you prick! GET IT OFF! CHARLIE, GET YOUR HAND OFF MY BREAST! [*He does, she turns to the door*] I'm leaving. Do you hear? I'm going. Leaving. Charlie? I'm leaving.

HAWK: [*To* DOUBLE] Now.

The DOUBLE *brings the box.*

VICTIM: I'm not coming back, Charlie. I'm leaving for good.

HAWK: How would you like a little taste of shit to pick you up? You look frazzled.

VICTIM: [*Turns*] You're an animal, Charlie. A sick, diseased, perverted . . .

HAWK: Sit on the floor. Don't fall—sit.

VICTIM: [*Returns to the center*] The scary thing is if you're around sick people like that, you begin to feel like it's going to rub off. That's a scary thing. I don't want any of that crap rubbing off on me. I take good care of myself. It's not easy. It's not easy with all this shit around. You have to be careful . . . I shouldn't spend too much time with you, Charlie. You're sick. You're depraved. You can't treat flesh like that, like it's a piece of flesh . . . it's not that. It's not the same. . . . There's so much of it around One diseased pervert after another. . . . It starts to rub off. . . . I can feel it crawling all over me . . . black hairs and warts and pimples. . . . You got to stay clean, you got to take care of yourself. . . . It's not the same. It's different. You can't treat it like that. . . . It just multiplies. You open the door, and the flesh, the hairs and warts and the stink, it floods in. Through the windows, out of the toilet and the ice box, jumping from the mirror, oozing, hanging . . . flesh . . . I can't open my mouth . . . it oozes inside me . . . into my eyes . . it comes in through my eyes . . . covering me . . . drowning me . . . it's everywhere . . . flesh . . . but it's not just flesh . . . it's not! . . . It's not the same . . . and I'm afraid to lie back . . . just lie back . . . but I can shut myself, my mouth, my eyes . . . and it can't touch me . . . on the ceiling, where it can't touch me. And I can stay there . . . where's it's white . . . on the ceiling where it's white . . . I can lie back and shut myself. . . . No, I don't want to lie there, . . . no, I don't want to lie down. It's not a bed. It's not . . . it's white. A white dress. I know what it is. A long white dress. And it's not the same. . . . It's a chair. A blue velvet chair. I'm wearing a white satin dress with white feathers, and my hair is white and my face is white and I'm sitting up there . . . in a blue velvet chair . . . it's me and I'm sitting there and I can't be touched, because it's not the same as flesh. . . . It's different . . . It's white. It's all white. It's beautiful. I'm beautiful, I'm white and forever. . . . My hair, my skin . . . are forever . . . and my face is white. It's beautiful. It's forever. My face is forever. It's always there. It's me. It's me. And that's always, always there. [*The* HAWK *gives her the injection*] That's me. I'm there. I'm there. Forever. Up . . . there . . . that's for . . . ulp! [*Covers her mouth, then braces herself on the floor*] Blaaaaa! [*She stares at it, then falls face down in the puke, dead*]

The HAWK *takes another shower. The* DOUBLE *rearranges the materials. The* VICTIM *lies on the floor.*

DOUBLE: [*Repeating the gestures of the* HAWK's *shower*] Nothing will grow on a dead planet. I needed the bread. It's over now. It's a picture. Put a frame around it. He did it, the *he* did it. A memory. Don't bug yourself. Go on. He needed the bread. I felt guilty, but I wanted her. Something had to give. He cuts his off or I cut mine off, or . . . I loved, he hated. There were two of us. No, more. I have to live. He did what he had to do. He was under stress. That's how it goes. Put a frame around it. Suddenly his life is a movie and he is the hero. The film is absolute. It goes from birth to death. Without a witness, he does not exist. . . . I have something to sell. The reason I have something to sell, is the people who want to buy. Or is it the other way around? Nothing will grow on a dead planet. [*The* DOUBLE *escorts the* VICTIM *out. The* HAWK *and the* DOUBLE *return as before*] She's dead.

HAWK: She was skinny but she had a great walk. A sequin dress in the early darkness and a certain Oriental roll to her hips. She was anything but cherry. She had the sweet pale look of the damned. Just like Jean Harlow.

DOUBLE: What do I do with the body?

HAWK: The body?

DOUBLE: Her corpse. She's dead.

HAWK: I turned her on.

DOUBLE: They'll be looking for you.

HAWK: What do you expect me to do? I can't help it.

DOUBLE: Get rid of the body.

HAWK: I can't.

DOUBLE: Get rid of the body.

HAWK: I can't.

DOUBLE: Get rid of the body.

HAWK: I can't. I can't. I can't.

The DEALER *appears at the door.*

Seventh Improvisation: The Dealer

DEALER: [*Enters. He is the same person as the* INSPECTOR, *except that he wears sunglasses, a vest and a black raincoat. His hand is held up in front of the mirror as though it contained a small package. He sits on the sofa, waits, then begins a brief reenactment of the scenes, playing all the parts*] Oh, yeah . . . Mmmmmm. Aaaarrrghh! [*Coughs*] . . . [*Places the package down*] . . . Marilyn Stein? Well, let's see if I can place her . . . I'm Joanie, her closest and dearest friend and I just came from the Port of Authority / Oh, that's cool. The Port of Authority. Well, let's see. She comes by here from time to time / Well, she said, that, I should come to you if I ever needed anything / Oh, did she? Well, she speaks highly of you too / And I had a funny dream that I turned into a kreplach / Oh, yeah, did you? Well, how about something to eat / Hey, I've got a present for you. It's a big present. Here / Oh, what a surprise. Oh! I'm surprised / And I thought that since I was her closest and dearest friend / Yes, of course. Well, sit right down and have an orange soda and some cantaloupe. . . . Oh, sorry I didn't see you come in / Madam Duval. My chauffeur sent me. You know, Jeffrey. Of course. Dear boy, I gave him the day off / You did. Well, that's certainly very kind of you. Ah, how about something to eat? Gracious, certainly not. I'll just do an Omm chant here on the rug and I'll be perfectly refreshed. Ooooooommmmmmmm-mbbaaaaaaAAAA / You know Charlie, I'm so goddamn beat. My tits are sore. My legs are swollen. I've got ringworm of the navel and my whatchamacallit. . . . Charlie, you wouldn't believe it. Christ, Charlie, I've got to change my life / And I thought that because Marilyn and I were such closest and dearest friends and because I'm coming all the way from Brooklyn / Well, you just suck that orange pop while I turn down this television / You know what you need. You need a radar set. Hey. Oh boy, you can make it small and put it on the roof / Well, ah, certainly a home is not a home without a radar set. Bleep, bleep, bleep / What's that? Do you hear that? That flapping sound. Oh, god. There. It's a Hawk. And it's coming for me. It's coming for me and it's biting me. It's biting and chewing and tearing me. Oh, god. It's tearing my flesh off / Oh, it's awful, awful, just goddamn bloody awful. Aaacchhh! / Such a thing I never heard. Just because I'm Marilyn's closest and dearest friend doesn't mean that you can be such a schmuck and call to my face, her, a dyke / Well, you know that's just some people's way of love / Hey, oh boy, I brought you a present / I see I'll have to acquire a taste for presents. What is it? / Oh, boy. It's an illusion. Oh, boy / Oh, yeah, just what I need. Ah, can I get you something to eat? Pizza? Pig pudding? I think we have some chitlins in the back / You know, maybe I should do something that has some social security. Like a meter maid or something like that. What do you think, Charlie / It's a possibility. Now where did she go? Oh / What? What, darlings? No, no, it's all right. They're my guides. Guides—uh! Guides—uh! / I see, well maybe I'd better check on that roast pork / Could I have my shot now / Yeah, we're getting to it. Let's see now you're . . . / blood and guts and gore and smash and crash and pow and wowie screaming and dying, oh boy / Charlie, I saw this movie the other night with Ruth Roman and Gina Lollobrigida. They played two guys who were in love with each other and then there's this great scene at the end when they have this long moment together / Junk! I want junk! What's that? That's nothing. I want junk / Well, let's see, I have a sofa and a chair and a medicine cabinet and a mirror / Dyke schmike, you schmuck. My closest and dearest . . . Give to me the dope boobie / Now wait a minute, girls / Up my ass! Up my ass! A Junky. A Junky! Oh, oh, oh. Oh, my god, we must endure / If you think that I'm going to stand here while you insult to my face my closest and dearest friend a dyke. I am just going to have to leave / Now let's not be hasty / Charlie, I think you got your hands all over my body, Charlie, and I want to be white and divine and forever, so get your motherfucking hands off me / Why yes, certainly / Coke, coke, coke. What's that? I want a present, oh boy / Here I think I have an illusion in this box. If you'll just be patient / I won't. I won't. My guides won't. Jeffrey won't. My ass won't. No. None of us won't / Charlie your hands are so rough and scaly, Christ, Charlie, you're tearing my titty off / I'm leaving. I'm walking out that door and I'm never coming back. I'm walking out. I'm going down that street, down to the nearest movie house and suck popcorn and never coming back. Do you hear that, Charlie? / Hey, I want some junk, oh boy / I'm leaving. Leaving. Open this door, I say. I say, you colonial motherfucker, open this door / Charlie, you're a dumb fuck. I never puke, I never piss, I'm going to be forever, but before I do, I'm leaving you, Charlie.

Leaving / Hey, oh boy, hey, I'm going to split. You're such a fucking drag, oh boy / To my face a dyke. Sprrratzzz! Fuck you, boobie, I'm going back to Brooklyn / Wait a minute, girls. Now just hold on there. Let's settle down. Now, girls, let's just pile in here. Yeah, right here. Now. Ah, where's that imported box. Ah, let's just make one here, because we're getting ready for it. That's ready for the Now. Are all you girls settled in there? You ready for it? / I'm ready. I'm ready. I'm ready. I'm ready / Yeah, you're ready. Okay. [*The* DEALER *rises, raising his hand in the air as if it held a hypodermic syringe*] The Now. This is the Now. The Now is what it's all about. This is the Now right here. [*Raises his hand, pause*] That was the Now. [*Pause*] Dreams, Death and Orgasm. That's now. Bibble, babble, blip, blap, bullshit now. That's now. Dreams, Death, Orgasm. Now. That's it right now. That's the Now. [*Hand, pause*] And don't you forget it. Dreams, Death and Orgasm is the Now. There's always the Now. No matter where you are you're going to find the Now. Now, you're in the Now. You're dreaming right now. Dreaming now is in the Now. Right? You have an orgasm in your dream. That's a Now in your dream. An Orgastic Dream Now. And you're dying, that's now. You die, now. You're dead. That's now. [*Hand, pause*] AND DON'T YOU FORGET IT. NOW! Now, now, nownownownowNOWNOWNOW! D.O.D., now. D.O.D. O.D. ODD D.D.O. Now. Do, do, di, now. Do, do, di, oh now. O.D.D. Di, di, do, do, oh, oh D.O.D. That's now. Okay. You got Dreams over here. Orgasm here and Death here. Mix them around shuffle them up. Now what do you got here? Where'd you go, Orgasm? Get out of there. Hey, there's Death jumping up and down. That's now. What are you doing Dreams? Dreams is taking a left-hand turn on the Now. Swings around and lays a right cross into Orgasm. Smack! OH! Now Orgasm is coming around disguised as a Plymouth Fury. Hardtop convertible, white-wall tires. A Plymouth Fury Coming around. And here comes Dreams. A pig. Four hundred and fifty-five thousand tons of pig is Dreams, baby. A four-hundred-fifty-five-thousand-ton ham-hock pig. And Orgasm is a Plymouth Fury. And over here we got Death. Death will be played in this particular instance as Mickey Mouse. Now Mickey Mouse is a little old son of a bitch with a great big ole long tail and looks like he needs something to eat. Maybe a piece of cheese or a piece of ham. But, don't forget Dreams is ham. Four hundred and fifty-five thousand tons of ham. There's a Plymouth Fury. And Mousey's over here. Mousy Death. Mouse-ass Death. Mouse-eyed, mouse Death. Mouse-eyeball

Death. Right? Okay. Dreams over here. Four hundred and fifty-five thousand tons of pig fat now. Next to it is Orgasm. Plymouth Fury, red, hard topped convertible. White wall side tires. One spare coming out the trunk. Driven by nineteen nuns wearing steel rimmed shades. Death is Mickey Mouse. Fuck, no! It ain't Mickey Mouse. It's Mickey Mouse's foot. One inch tall and it talks way up here like Butterfly McQueen and says, "Has it started? Has it started?" And this is the Now [*Hand*]. And don't forget it, mother hunches. The Now! Pig ton dreams flopping in. Plymouth Fury coming up fast. Mickey Mouse foot—clip, clop, clip, clop. He's got his thing, you see. It's a foot race. To be qualified to be in this race you had to have a foot. And we caught that cat in the Now. That's how he got that foot. That's where Death came from. He got his foot trapped in the Now. That's Mickey Mouse's foot—the Now of Death. Coming in solid is Dreams, four hundred fifty-five thousand tons of pig puking fat. And over here is orgasm. Plymouth Fury. That's a Now, motherfucker. Moving up fast. Dreams. Death. Orgasm. On the outside come foot. Clip, clop, splat! On top of Dreams. Pig puking Dreams all laid out. Orgasm coming over to the end zone and through the goal posts to score. For the Now. You got to score for the Now. That's now. They're coming in fast. Orgasm takes a left turn. Dreams pops into Orgasm. Uhhhh! Orgasm scoots Dreams in the neck. Eeeekkkkk! Neck turns ear ball Death. Death screams, "Get off my foot!" Neck says, "That simple motherfucker's a seven-toed sloth." Splits. And here comes Orgasm moving up fast. Takes a sharp left turn. Pokes Dreams in the eye. Dreams blows her horn. Nineteen nuns do a tuck and roll, knock Orgasm back three paces. Back to Go, baby. Death swings a hard right, bounces off Dreams, does a flip flop, half pike back dive, grabs Orgasm by the ear, pulls nine pounds of pig fat off and throws it in that lady's face sitting right over there. Sorry, madam, but that's life. And that's the Now. Coming up here fast, now. Over here's the Now. Getting closer to the finish line. It looks like . . . oh, here comes that Plymouth Fury. Foot flop flip flapping over there. Ham-hock pig puke coming in. To the Now. Coming up fast. Coming in close. Here they are. Say it, motherfucker. You pick up on that. That's the Now! [*The* DEALER *returns to where he left the "Victims"*] Well, let's see, now. As I recall . . . yes . . . [*Kneels on the floor*] . . . the, ah, first to go here . . . I don't know why a girl and a girl can't get together. Marilyn Stein was my closest and closest and closest and . . . uhhh! [*Hits his arm with the "Now" hand*] . . . OOIII! [*Dies*] . . . Number one. Number

two is—"Death of a Teeny Bopper" . . . I wanna be up there, Charlie . . . no, that's the other one . . . oh, boy, oh boy, oh boy. A big silver jet. A big silver jet all my own, oh boy. Hey, oh boy, I read the news today, oh boy . . . whaam! [*Hits again*] Eeeennnaa / Bogies on the right / nnaaaaaawwwwSplat! [*Dies*] . . . Now, let me see . . . that was . . . oh, yes . . . what's that, Darlings? Please hurry. Do hurry along. Yes, darlings? What's that? Up my ass. No. Never. Not while the sun is still never setting . . . what? What darlings? Yes, loud and clear. Ten-four? Oh shit! [*Hits again, dies*] Three. And now . . . I wanna be up there, Charlie. Up there. So pure and white and white and divine and forever. Up there. Just me. White and divine and . . . come on, Charlie, fill it up. High octane, Charlie, that's it, pump it in. Yeah. Forever and forever and for . . . ulp. [*Hand to mouth*] Ulp! Ulp! Ulp! Blaaaa-aah! Blaa! Blaa! Blaa! Blaah! [*Pause, then rises*] Yeah. Well . . . oh. [*Hands the "box" to the* DOUBLE] I, ah, think she O.D.'d . . . hmmm . . . [*Coughs*] . . . ah . . . [*Waves to* HAWK] wha's happening, Hawk. [*The* DEALER *goes to the shower and without undressing, steps in and sings this song*]

O, when them poppy balls get rotten
You can't pick that poppy cotton
And there's one man can fix you when
    you're down.
Oh, when them little ole poppy balls
    get rotten
You can't pick-a very much poppy
    cotton
There's that little ole junk man
    coming round . . . yes, there he
    is, coming round there, he's the
    man, oh yes, indeed, oooooh!

[*The* DEALER *leaves the shower, goes to the kitchen, slides palms with the* HAWK *on the way, takes something out of the refrigerator and eats*] Hmmmm. Delicious. Food's the Now, hey, baby? [*Leaving, stops*] Oh, I brought you thirty decks. [*Points to the table*] Better watch that stuff—it'll kill you. [*Exits*]

The HAWK *and the* DOUBLE *return as before. The* DOUBLE *begins to speak. The* HAWK *repeats him, phrase by phrase to the end. As the speech builds, the* DOUBLE'S *cool begins to crack as the* HAWK *moves in on his thing. Toward the conclusion, he relaxes again, though bitter and disgusted.*

DOUBLE: Considering this mad scramble in its appropriate light, that is, with the correct distance, in focus, detached, we are reduced to the image of a slaughterhouse on a crust of dirt . . . the crust spins, the sun heats it, the rains cool it . . . the creatures multiply . . . they take it seriously . . . they're at each other's throats . . . they fight for scraps . . . millions are wiped out. Still, they multiply . . . they read the papers, they keep one eye on their neighbors, they copulate . . . there's too many of them . . . there's always too many of them . . . it's an endless supply . . . there's no shortage . . . it fills its quota . . . taking care of business . . . they seem gleeful about it—they jump up and down, they wave flags, they fly in the air, they shout . . . but it's all right . . . it's fertilizer. . . . I am not interested in a solution to my . . . problem. My problem no longer admits to a solution. . . . I have become my problem . . . which is the same as having no problem. . . . That's right. . . . I believe in myself, to put it another way, just like the doctor, lawyer, housewife, and chicken-shit inspector, who will kill, as you know, in defense of their . . . beliefs. He hallucinates rivals. . . . His pleasures are threatened by others. Nameless others clouding his joy. He can't think straight. His eyes burn from the inside out. His fingers peel an endless grape. His laughter is strange, coming at pauses in the conversation. He breaks doors. At night he rolls over into his own skull. His left eye twitches. He's gray before his time. He thinks he's something! How can I avoid obsessions? Obsessions are criminal. Criminal! The work that I have to do! The work! That is what is important!

WITH WHICH TO TORMENT MYSELF!

What? Aha! Then who is the perpetrator of this . . . OBSESSION? One sees infinity in all directions—that's right. Where does this image come from, that won't let go, this OBSESSION? Why, it arises in the self, that's right, which is a bottomless pit, where there is no one, nothing, to be apprehended . . . for the crime. . . . A kind of anxiety appeasing verbiage. Is what it is. He reassures himself. About the real. But there's something . . . signs . . . there are signs . . . yes, there are signs, signals, yes signals we give . . . to one another in our passing . . . in order to create warmth . . . light. . . . Yes, but we must see that the light and the dark and the warm and the cold, the good and the bad . . . the actual pain we suffer . . . in the process . . . the process? Are illusory, not real, are the void . . . therefore, a reflection on the surface of the—whatever . . . a glance . . . yet he behaves . . . the droplets of meaning adding to a force, a power, a demon . . . which he confuses with himself. Verbiage! NOW! [*Brings the box*]

HAWK: [*Preparing an injection with the 30 decks left by the* DEALER] Wait.

DOUBLE: Wait.

HAWK: Wait.

DOUBLE: Wait.

HAWK: Wait.

DOUBLE: Wait.

HAWK: Wait.

DOUBLE: Wait.

HAWK: Wait.

DOUBLE: Wait.

HAWK: NOW! [*The* HAWK *plunges the needle into the* DOUBLE'S *chest. The* DOUBLE, *arms and legs spread akimbo, staggers to the mirror, spins, staggers back, around the room, back and forth, stops, sways, staggers around the room, into the mirror, back, spins, staggers, backwards, stops, sways, goes rapidly around the room, stops, goes back, around, stops, sways, staggers, staggers, sways, stops, sways, now swaying over the worn spot in the rug, sways, sways, suddenly spins about one, two, three times, spinning, falls to the floor—a short series of spasms, convulsions—dead. The* HAWK *takes a quick shower, goes to the refrigerator, eats something, puts it back, goes to the* DOUBLE *and escorts him out. The* HAWK *returns as before*] The Hawk. The Hawk is an . . . an animal. The Hawk is an animal and an animal . . . an animal is hungry. That's why he . . . he . . . he kills. He kills . . . he kills . . . be . . . cause he's hungry. [*Pause*] Because he's hungry. . . . That's why he kills. . . . He's hungry. . . . He takes . . . takes the . . . finds a victim . . . finds a victim [*Rises*] . . . attacks the victim. He kills . . . kills the victim. . . . Takes the victim. . . . [*Pause*] . . . He's a Hawk. A Hawk is hungry. An animal is hungry. That's why he . . . kills . . . kills the victim . . . [*Circling the room*] . . . Takes the victim into the sky . . . the sky . . . sky . . . back . . . back . . . to his nest . . . and . . . and . . . and he devours the victim. He devours the victim . . . because he's hungry. That's why he kills . . . because he's a Hawk. . . . He's a Hawk. . . . He finds a victim . . . [*Moving into the mirror*] . . . Kills the victim. Takes the victim back to his nest and devours the victim. Because he's an animal. Because he's hungry. That's why he kills. Because he's a Hawk. A Hawk. He's a Hawk. A Hawk. A Hawk! A HAWK! HAWK! HAWK! HAWK! HAWK! HE'S A HAWK! [*Pause*] I think I'll go out. [*Exits*]

LEMONADE

a play in one act

James Prideaux

Lemonade was first presented by Richard Barr, Edward Albee and Clinton Wilder at the Playwrights Unit, New York City, on November 30, 1967, with the following cast:

MABEL LAMSTON .... *Jane Rose*

EDITH NORTHRUP .... *Eugenia Rawls*

It was directed by John J. Desmond.

It was subsequently presented by William E. Hunt at the Jan Hus Playhouse, New York City, as half of a double bill with *The Autograph Hound,* also by the author, on December 13, 1968, with the following cast:

MABEL LAMSTON .... *Jan Miner*

EDITH NORTHRUP .... *Nancy Coleman*

It was directed by Mr. Hunt and the production was designed by David F. Segal.

TIME

Memorial Day, the late 1960's.

PLACE

A Highway at the Edge of a Midwestern Town.

The curtain rises on a bare stage. MABEL LAMSTON *appears right. She is a matronly lady in her mid or late fifties. There is about her a smug air of affluence and well-being. She is dressed for a warm spring day in a simple —but expensive—frock. A voluminous straw bag hangs from her shoulder. She carries a large pitcher of lemonade in one hand, and drags a wooden box behind her with the other. She places the wooden box on end at right and carefully puts the pitcher on top of it.*

MABEL: There! [*Satisfied, she exits right for a moment, returning with a stool and a large poster. She puts the stool behind the box, and then leans the poster against the front of the box so that it faces the audience. It reads:* "LEMONADE—2¢ A GLASS." *She sits on the stool and, rummaging in her bag, produces paper cups, which she arranges next to the pitcher. Now she is ready for business, she and her stand facing the audience. Her head moves slowly from left to right. Calling in a timid, cultured voice*] Lemonade. [*A little louder*] Lemonade. Get your ice-cold lemonade here.

EDITH NORTHRUP *appears left. She is cut of the same cloth as* MABEL, *but she is slighter, smaller, perhaps a little younger. A bag hangs from her shoulder, and she also carries a pitcher of lemonade and drags a box. She stops dead upon seeing* MABEL.

EDITH: Why, Mabel Lamston!

MABEL: Edith!

EDITH: Of all people! I never expected—

MABEL: What a surprise! [MABEL *rises,* EDITH *approaches, and they touch cheeks*]

EDITH: What are you doing here?

MABEL: Now don't laugh. I'm selling lemonade. I've got this little stand and I'm selling lemonade. [*She looks at* EDITH's *pitcher*] You don't mean—! [*They shriek with laughter*]

EDITH: [*Politely*] I'll go down the road.

MABEL: You'll do nothing of the kind. There's plenty of business for both of us.

EDITH: Sure you don't mind?

MABEL: [*Helping her place the box beside hers, facing the audience*] I'll be glad for the company. Where's your stool?

EDITH: It's over by the telephone pole. I won't be a minute.

MABEL: [*Sitting*] I'll mind the store.

EDITH *exits left, returning immediately with her stool and sign.*

EDITH: I can't get over meeting you like this.

MABEL: I've always said it's a small world.

EDITH: It certainly is *here*. [*Puts her sign up— it reads the same as* MABEL's—*and, sitting, pulls paper cups out of her bag*]

MABEL: All set?

EDITH *puts the cups beside the pitcher.*

EDITH: I'm open for business. [*Suddenly they both half rise and, leaning forward, read each other's signs. They smile at one another and sit down. Her head moving left to right, taking off gloves*] I've never seen so many cars.

MABEL: It's the holiday weekend. Happy Decoration Day!

EDITH: We always called it Memorial Day. Happy *Memorial* Day! [*They laugh socially*]

MABEL: Now what I do is, I shout lemonade every so often. Like this. [*Softly, meekly*] Lemonade!

EDITH: I don't know if I've got the nerve.

MABEL: Well, you'll never make a sale if you don't, Edith. Try it.

EDITH: [*Meekly*] Lemonade.

MABEL: That's very good.

EDITH: [*Louder*] Lemonade!

MABEL: Wonderful!

EDITH: [*Quite loud*] Lemonade!

MABEL: Talent will out!

EDITH: I used to sing, you know.

MABEL: Really?

EDITH: Years ago. I was with a singing group. You probably heard of us. The Cincinnati Songbirds?

MABEL: [*She hasn't*] I'm trying to think.

EDITH: We sang in hotel lobbies a lot. That's how I met Herbert. In the lobby of the Seqwaunie Hotel. He was sitting and I was singing and one thing led to another.

MABEL: [*Conversationally*] Oh, yes?

EDITH: I miss my singing.

MABEL: I've always been sorry *I* didn't have a career.

EDITH: Well, Mabel, now you have.

MABEL: This? This is just a diversion. I don't expect it to *lead* anywhere. Do you?

EDITH: [*Laughing*] Gracious, no! It's just an excuse to get out of the house.

MABEL: I know how you feel.

EDITH: Now that the children are gone, things are just too quiet for me around there. I like things stirring. All these cars whizzing by!

MABEL: I was sorry to hear about the children, Edith.

EDITH: [*Pleasantly*] Don't give it a thought. Have you sold any?

MABEL: I just got here myself.

EDITH: If I only sell one glass, I'll feel I've done something. I had such a shock the other day.

MABEL: What in the world—?

EDITH: Elizabeth Arden's obituary. Did you read it?

MABEL: Let me think.

EDITH: When I saw what she'd accomplished, I just went limp in the knees. There she was, all her life, up to her earrings in liniments and lotions. Inventing things, discovering things. She made Madame Curie look like a *slouch!* And the money. Millions of dollars! She even kept race horses.

MABEL: I wouldn't care to keep race horses.

EDITH: When I think what *I've* done, I wonder why I was *put* on this earth. Do you ever feel like that?

MABEL: [*Sighing*] It's all too clear to me, Edith.

EDITH: What is?

MABEL: We're *mothers*, that's what we're here for. And I for one am *exhausted*. Bringing them up, seeing them through college, making good marriages. And with my brood, it was especially difficult. Marilyn cross-eyed and Randolph a cripple. I had to do double duty. Anyway, I did it and that's that.

EDITH: I don't mean to pry, but what are you doing out here on the highway selling lemonade?

MABEL: I don't know, I really don't. I just got up this morning and I looked at Raymond reading his newspaper over the breakfast coffee and I thought: Wouldn't it be fun to go out to the highway and set up a lemonade stand! I don't mind admitting I feel pretty peculiar. The president of the League of Women Voters.

EDITH: Well, *I'm* Grand Matron of the Order of Eastern Star. [*They laugh*] Lemonade!

MABEL: Lemonade! [*More laughter*]

EDITH: [*Head turning*] Where do you suppose all these people are going?

MABEL: Just out driving, I guess. I used to enjoy that—especially on Sundays—but I don't so much anymore. Too many cars on the road.

EDITH: I suppose I should be at the cemetery doing something to the children's graves.

MABEL: I feel so guilty. I ought to be putting peonies on Raymond's mother. We do that every year. Put peonies. On Raymond's mother.

EDITH: Herbert's people are all in Sandusky so I just send his sister a check every year and she decorates *them.* But she has such poor taste. She buys plastic wreaths! I certainly hope when my time comes nobody puts a plastic wreath on me.

MABEL: You see plastic everywhere these days, Edith.

EDITH: I just pray that Herbert's sister goes *first.*

MABEL: [*Excitedly, half rising*] Did you see the way that car slowed down?

EDITH: I wasn't looking.

MABEL: I thought we had our first sale. [*Waves her hand in front of her face*] I don't see how cars on a paved highway can stir up so much dust.

EDITH: It's terrible. [*Conspiratorially*] I think we ought to sample the product.

MABEL: [*Coyly*] Now, we mustn't drink up the profits.

EDITH: One little cup? I want you to try mine.

MABEL: I'd love to. And you must have some of *mine.* [*They each pour a cup*] I'm afraid it's tepid.

EDITH: It's impossible to keep it cold. Mine was *icy* when I left the house, but now I'm sure it's —[*She accepts a cup and hands* MABEL *one*] Thank you.

MABEL: Thank *you*, dear.

EDITH: [*She sips*] Oh, *Mabel!*

MABEL: Is it all right?

EDITH: It's just *perfect.* That certainly hits the spot.

MABEL: [*She sips*] It can't be any better than yours! What did you put in it?

EDITH: Lemon and sugar and water.

MABEL: You've put in *something*, it's got a wonderful flavor.

EDITH: [*Innocently*] Really?

MABEL: Like gin.

EDITH: [*She hiccoughs and looks into her glass*] Mabel!

MABEL: Surprise! What does it taste like? Vodka?

EDITH: I don't know that I've ever tasted vodka.

MABEL: You have now! [*They explode with laughter*]

EDITH: Aren't we wicked!

MABEL: There are times, Edith, when you just have to break loose.

EDITH: But on the highway!

MABEL: Well, I'm so sick of being me I don't know what to do.

EDITH: I had the funniest dream the other night. I dreamed I was Shirley Temple. There I was in one of those musical movies she used to make, dancing away with sausage curls all over my head. And Herbert was my mother. Isn't that funny? He was wearing a big flowered hat and smoking a cigar, and he kept saying, "We're *investing* her money." [*They laugh*]

MABEL: I hardly ever dream.

EDITH: I dream all the time. Just before the children died, I had a dream about a bonfire. Now, that's spooky—considering.

MABEL: I don't think it *means* anything. Did you see that?

EDITH: No.

MABEL: A Hawaiian license plate. They're a long way from home.

EDITH: I can't get used to that being a state. They'll always be foreigners to me.

MABEL: What do you suppose they're doing here?

EDITH: Just passing through, I guess.

MABEL: They must have shipped the car over on a boat.

EDITH: *That* cost a pretty penny.

MABEL: Lots of people have got it. I just don't now where the money comes from these days.

EDITH: It's always *other* people.

MABEL: Now, Edith, with all the money Herbert's made—

EDITH: He's a terrible tightwad, though. Even the children's caskets. [*Trying to remember*] Were you at the funeral?

MABEL: That was during the tournament at the bridge club. I was so sorry.

EDITH: [*Lightly*] It doesn't matter. Anyway, we had the lowest-grade caskets you could get. Caroline's almost fell apart on the way to the cemetery. I didn't say anything, but I was really annoyed with Herbert.

MABEL: He always seems so generous. The wing of the hospital and all.

EDITH: That's just for show. When it comes funeral time, he doesn't care *what* he sticks in the ground.

MABEL: Really? He's so distinguished-*looking*.

EDITH: [*Dubiously*] You think so? So many people say that and I just can't see it. All I know is, when I first met Herbert Northrup that day in the Seqwaunie Hotel, he was nothing but a bum.

MABEL: *Herbert?*

EDITH: *And* a sex maniac.

MABEL: A *what?*

EDITH: I was so shocked. We weren't married ten minutes before he—well, I hardly had the *veil* off. Come to think of it, I didn't have the veil off. After that, it was morning, noon, and night. He'd come home for lunch and never touch his sandwich.

MABEL: [*Incredulous*] Herbert?

EDITH: Why do you think we had that big family, because we liked children?

MABEL: I never thought about it one way or the—

EDITH: I used to look up at him and say, "Herbert, you know what I am? I'm Passion's Plaything."

MABEL: What did he say to that?

EDITH: He was always too busy to talk.

MABEL: I just can't imagine . . .

EDITH: Appearances are deceiving. [*She takes a deep gulp of lemonade*] What about you?

MABEL: [*Startled*] Me?

EDITH: You and Raymond. You've never told me a thing.

MABEL: [*Embarrassed*] Well, Edith, we've never been the kind of friends who would exchange confidences.

EDITH: You and Raymond?

MABEL: You and *me*.

EDITH: No time like the present. [*Picks up her pitcher and holds out her hand for* MABEL'S *cup*]

MABEL: [*Handing it over*] I don't know that I should.

EDITH: [*Pouring*] It's a holiday.

MABEL: Now, don't rob *yourself* [*She takes the cup*] Thank you. [*She lifts her own pitcher and puts out her hand for* EDITH'S *cup*] May I?

EDITH: [*Gives her the cup*] I don't mind if I do. It's so refreshing.

MABEL: [*Pouring*] There's nothing like a glass of lemonade on a warm day. [*She hands the cup to* EDITH] Bottoms up! [*They take a sip*]

EDITH: Now!

MABEL: Yes?

EDITH: Tell me about you and that sweet Raymond.

MABEL: I don't know that *that's* the word you'd apply to—

EDITH: I think he's sweet. Tell Edith all about it.

MABEL: I wouldn't know where to begin.

EDITH: Start with the wedding night.

MABEL: Really, Edith! That's been so long ago I'm not sure I can remember. We were at the Grand Canyon and I do recall thinking that the Grand Canyon was more impressive than Raymond was. Especially at twilight.

EDITH: I wonder if that's a good idea, newlyweds going to places like that, being surrounded by all that . . . natural splendor. It makes everything else look so—piddling.

MABEL: Where did you and Herbert honeymoon?

EDITH: Niagara Falls. Of course, we never got around to seeing the Falls. Herbert said it didn't matter. He said it was just a lot of water going over a cliff.

MABEL: Well, the Grand Canyon's just a hole in the ground, isn't it! [*They laugh, sip.* MABEL, *suddenly serious*] Funny. When I think back, I have this vague sense of . . . disappointment.

EDITH: I know exactly what you mean.

MABEL: [*Sighing*] I guess I had expected more. I was completely . . . uninformed . . . you know. Nowadays young people seem so much more . . . sophisticated than we were.

EDITH: Frankly, I don't see what men see in it.

MABEL: No. Only, I think, with the right person there might be a possibility of—

EDITH: Well, *we'll* never know. [MABEL *looks at her, then they sip simultaneously*]

MABEL: [*Suddenly*] Lemonade!

EDITH: Lemonade!

MABEL: All these cars. [*Turns to* EDITH] You know who I saw on the late movie the other night? Rudolph Valentino!

EDITH: So did I!

MABEL: Wasn't he marvelous! The way he swept that woman up and carried her away on his . . . stallion.

EDITH: He could have put his shoes under my bed anytime.

MABEL: Mine too, Edith. I suppose you wouldn't have wanted to settle down in Peoria with him, but in a tent in the desert he was certainly all you could ask for.

EDITH: I didn't care if he *was* Italian.

MABEL: Did Herbert ever sweep you up like that?

EDITH: Herbert was more of a lunger than a sweeper. What about Raymond?

MABEL: Raymond? Raymond wasn't really much like Valentino. He was more like that other fellow. Franklin Pangborn.

EDITH: Now, isn't that strange! Raymond Lamston always struck me as being a real dark horse.

MABEL: How do you mean?

EDITH: Well . . . sensual.

MABEL: *My* Raymond?

EDITH: [*Picks up her cup*] Uh huh. Sort of . . . smoldering underneath.

MABEL: [*Laughing*] Edith, really!

EDITH: Uh huh. [*She sips*] My, this lemonade is strong stuff.

MABEL: Have a little more?

EDITH: Will you join me?

MABEL: Maybe just one. [*They pour simultaneously*]

EDITH: This was such a good idea.

MABEL: I haven't had so much fun in years.

EDITH: Then you settled down here?

MABEL: When was that?

EDITH: After the Grand Canyon.

MABEL: Oh, yes. Raymond got a job here. That was a long time before he bought his own business. He'd always lived here, you know. I never told anybody—not even Raymond—but I wanted to live in New York City. Isn't that silly?

EDITH: We go every year, you know. See the sights.

MABEL: [*Pleasantly*] Raymond likes to stay home. We're just stick-in-the-muds. Well, after that the children came along. That was nothing at all. Raymond said I dropped children like a Chinese peasant. He said all I needed was a clear day and rice paddy. I've never had much patience with these women who make such a fuss about having babies.

EDITH: I suffered.

MABEL: You did?

EDITH: I suffered the tortures of the damned with Edgar. First he wanted to come out too soon, then he didn't want to come out at all, then he got halfway out and decided to go back in. Believe me, Mabel, if the *men* had the babies, it would be a different world. [*She laughs*] Can you imagine Herbert in labor? I can just see it—screaming and flailing his arms!

MABEL: [*Laughing*] Or Raymond! He howls if he's only got a hangnail!

EDITH: I'd like to see Herbert with *triplets!* Mother of three!

Finally the laughter subsides.

MABEL: Well, Edith, they're more to be pitied than censured.

EDITH: I'm not so sure of that.

MABEL: I'm just glad it's over. I really am, Edith. I'm glad I have my own room and I'm glad I don't have to have any more babies and I'm glad I don't have to bring them up. It's all very comfortably behind me. From now on, I just look forward to a nice . . . gentle . . . painless . . . decay.

EDITH: Then what are you doing out here in the middle of the highway selling lemonade?

MABEL: I might ask you the same question. [*They both take a sip of lemonade*] Now be honest, Edith. Aren't you just as glad it's over?

EDITH: [*With great seriousness*] Mabel. I haven't told another soul this yet. But I want you to know.

MABEL: What, Edith?

EDITH: I'm getting married.

MABEL: You're what?

EDITH: I'm getting married.

MABEL: Edith, you've *been* married for twenty-five years!

EDITH: I'm leaving Herbert and marrying somebody else.

MABEL: You can't be serious.

EDITH: I am.

MABEL: It's unthinkable! Why, you and Herbert *apart.* I couldn't imagine—

EDITH: I've fallen deeply and desperately in love. This is the real thing at last, Mabel. It's the most beautiful thing that's ever come into my life and I don't intend to lose it.

MABEL: I can't *believe* it!

EDITH: You probably think it's too late for me, but you're wrong. We're perfect together. He's a little older than I am, but I think that's all to the good. Mabel, we have moments of such . . . understanding. We read aloud to each other. We're halfway through *The Agony and the Ecstasy*.

MABEL: Who *is* he?

EDITH: He's a schoolteacher, a widower. He's not much to look at, a little rough, a little homely, but very sensitive underneath. And he worships the ground I walk on.

MABEL: Where does he teach?

EDITH: [*On guard*] What?

MABEL: Where does he teach?

EDITH: [*Hedging*] Where?

MABEL: Where?

EDITH: He teaches at the . . . Seqwaunie Junior High School. Out at the other end of town. He teaches music. Singing.

MABEL: I never heard of it.

EDITH: It's at the other end of town.

MABEL: [*Holds up pitcher*] A little more lemonade, dear?

EDITH: No, thank you.

MABEL *puts the pitcher down. They never drink again.*

MABEL: What about Herbert?

EDITH: Herbert doesn't need me.

MABEL: Surely after twenty-five years, he—

EDITH: Herbert Northrup has never *once* raised his hand to me. He's never cared enough even to *want* to. My friend at the Seqwaunie Junior High School once threw a copy of *Anthony Adverse* at me. [*Proudly*] I had to have three stitches.

MABEL: [*Firmly*] Edith, *there is no Seqwaunie Junior High School.*

EDITH: [*Rises*] What did you say?

MABEL: I said there is no Seqwaunie Junior High School.

EDITH: Why . . . you . . . *turncoat!*

MABEL: I'm merely stating a *fact*.

EDITH: I don't want your facts! You talk like some silly *man*. I *know* there isn't any Seqwaunie Junior High School. And for all I know there wasn't any Seqwaunie Hotel either, and I didn't sing, and Herbert wasn't sitting there. And I suppose I'm not a woman who watched her children go up in flames?

MABEL: [*Wearily*] I really don't know.

EDITH: If it never happened, why do I remember it so clearly? Why can I still smell the smoke?

MABEL: Edith, lots of things that occupy our minds never happened and they never will. So there's no sense in worrying about them.

[EDITH *sits, sullenly*] I do admire you for decorating the children's graves, even if they're not dead. They will be one day and you'll be that much further ahead. As for this school teacher you've invented—

EDITH: I don't care to discuss that. I might just mention that Marilyn isn't cross-eyed and Randolph is not a cripple, either.

MABEL: But I did *try*. I tried everything to get Marilyn's eyes to cross. I had her doing eye exercises in *reverse*, reading small print in dim light—*everything*. And as for Randolph, I was forever putting obstacles in his way, a box here, a bucket there. He was just too nimble for me. They were wonderful children. It was the least I could do for them.

There is a pause. Then EDITH *speaks with great significance.*

EDITH: Do you remember Miss Gundlach?

MABEL: Raymond's secretary? Of course. A lovely woman.

EDITH: [*Hitting every word*] They copulated time and time again . . . over and over!

MABEL: [*Rising, stunned*] That's . . . not . . . true!

EDITH: It was common knowledge. He kept a room above the Seqwaunie Casino at the other end of town. They went there at lunchtime every Monday, Wednesday and Friday, and he—

MABEL: That's impossible! Raymond had no interest in that—no *need!*

EDITH: Sometimes they'd go on Tuesdays and Thursdays, too.

MABEL: [*Deeply hurt, moves a step to right, looks away*] Why should he do that? I was waiting . . . I was willing . . . I always did the best I could.

EDITH: [*Blithely*] I wouldn't worry about it. So many of the things that occupy our minds never happened . . . and never will.

MABEL: [*Facing her grandly, her full height*] You're a gossip, Edith. I must ask you to leave. Please peddle your lemonade somewhere else.

EDITH: It's a public highway. I have as much right here as you have.

MABEL: Please *go*.

EDITH: *Never.*

MABEL: [*Rummaging in her bag*] Very well. But I shall see to it that you do no business whatsoever. [*She pulls out a black crayon and marches around to her sign. She then crosses out the 2¢ and makes it 1¢. She gives* EDITH *a superior smile and resumes her seat.* EDITH, *disturbed, rises, goes front, and reads* MABEL'S *sign. Then she gets her bag, produces a black crayon, crosses out the 2¢, and writes:* "FREE"]

EDITH: [*Leaning on the box*] Nobody, but nobody, undersells Edith Northrup. [*She goes grandly back to her stool and sits.*]

MABEL: [*After a moment, facing front*] I've never liked you very much, Edith.

EDITH: [*Also facing front*] The feeling is mutual.

MABEL: I've always found you uninspired. Tawdry. Common.

EDITH: You're pompous. Overbearing. Stupid.

MABEL: *Shallow.*

EDITH *lets this go by for an instant, but only an instant.*

EDITH: For your information, I am a woman of . . . unplumbed depths. All right, I admit it's too late, but I'm still . . . unplumbed.

MABEL: You make yourself sound like a bathroom fixture.

EDITH: You needn't sound so smug. You're in the same boat. I'll tell you one thing. If I'd been Mrs. Raymond Lamston, things would have been different.

MABEL: I suppose that would make me Mrs. Herbert Northrup.

EDITH: I wouldn't be surprised.

MABEL: Well, I don't believe I'd care for that.

EDITH: Oh yes, you would. Anyway, you don't know *what* you'd care for. Heaven knows, *I* don't. Half the time I find I don't care for what I thought I cared for at all. It would have been nice, I admit, if I'd dropped a lit cigarette on the living room carpet and the children had gone up in flames. A lovely glow for a moment. But afterward they really would have been dead and I would have missed them. They've kept me going for a long time. Do you know what I think our trouble is?

MABEL: Whose?

EDITH: Ours. Everybody's. I think . . .

MABEL: I'm not sure I want to hear.

EDITH: I think the trouble is that way deep down we're filled with—

MABEL: If this is going to be unpleasant, I—

EDITH: It's *love*, Mabel. I think that way deep down we're filled with *love*. I mean *way* deep down where you sometimes can't even see it, you don't even know it's there. Now *that* poses problems. Here we are on this planet, Earth, and— [*But* MABEL *has made a choking sound and buried her face in her hands*] Why, Mabel! [*She rises, goes to her*] What is it?

MABEL: I'm sorry. I'm being such a fool.

EDITH *produces a handkerchief from her pocket and gives it to* MABEL.

EDITH: You just go ahead and have a good cry. [*She pats her*] Better now?

MABEL: Yes, thank you. I don't know what came over me. Out here on the highway, too.

EDITH: What do you care what *they* think? All right? [MABEL *nods and* EDITH *goes back to her stool*]

MABEL: [*Dabbing eyes with handkerchief, speaking to herself, really*] I really am sorry. This isn't like me at all. It was only . . . despair . . . that made me do it. All these years, and I've just never found the answer. At first I thought it was going to be . . . physical contact . . . but it wasn't. And then . . . human relationships . . . weren't to be counted on— they changed like the wind. And religion turned out to be . . . a bit of a fraud . . . all man-made. I don't know. I sometimes think . . . the best you can do . . . is just be kind to everybody . . . and keep pets.

EDITH: [*Lightly, sympathetically*] Is *that* all you've been worried about?

MABEL: Isn't that enough?

EDITH: Well, I'll tell you what you do. You simply go home and fuss with Raymond a bit and rustle up something good for dinner and watch a little television and go to bed.

MABEL: I won't be tired.

EDITH: Well, read in bed for a while. Put some soft music on the radio and read in bed. How can life get better than that? [*She sighs, looks out toward highway*] I don't think I'm going to sell a thing. I might as well go home. [*She rises, looks at* MABEL] You coming?

MABEL: Not just yet.

EDITH: I'll leave my things here. Who knows, you may sell all of yours and mine, too. [*She goes to* MABEL, *who rises, and they touch cheeks*] Good-bye, my dear.

MABEL: Oh. [*She returns the handkerchief, uses a social tone of voice*] Thank you. It's been *awfully* pleasant.

EDITH: [*Crosses back of stools*] You must come by for dinner one evening soon.

MABEL: [*Cozily, also crossing back of stools*] We'd love to. And you folks be sure and stop by whenever you're in the neighborhood. Raymond's always saying, "Let's have Edith and Herbert over."

EDITH: [*She starts to exit left, turns, and coming back to* MABEL, *speaks with sudden fervor*] I wish you'd been at the funeral. It was such a beautiful service. If I do say so, we did very well by the children. [*She turns and exits, left*]

MABEL: [*Sits, looks out at the highway a moment, then calls timidly, sadly*] Lemonade. Lemonade! Get your lukewarm lemonade here!

The curtain falls.

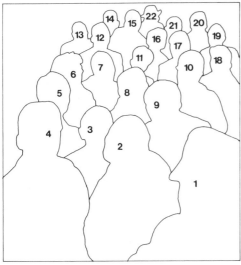

Playwrights on the roof next door to Caffe Cino, 1966. (*Dan McCoy*, Black Star)

1. Storey Talbot / 2. Maria Irene Fornés / 3. Claris Nelson / 4. Ted Harris / 5. David Starkweather / 6. Mary Mitchell / 7. H. M. Koutoukas / 8. Jean Reavey / 9. Lanford Wilson / 10. Paul Foster / 11. Unidentified / 12. Asif Currimbhoy / 13. Tom Eyen / 14. Unidentified / 15. Sam Shepard / 16. Susan Sherman / 17. William M. Hoffman / 18. Megan Terry / 19. Jean-Claude van Itallie / 20. Leonard Melfi / 21. Walter Leyden Brown / 22. Robert Heide

THE GOLDEN FLEECE

a play in one act

A. R. Gurney, Jr.

The Golden Fleece was first presented by Richard Barr, Edward Albee and Clinton Wilder at the Playwrights Unit, New York City, on February 22, 1968, with the following cast:

BETTY . . . . *Barbara Baxley*
BILL . . . . *Joseph George*

It was directed by Jered Barclay.

It was subsequently presented by Harlan Kleiman, Jeffrey C. Reiss and Orin Lehman at the Actors Playhouse, New York City, as half of a double bill, *Tonight in Living Color,* with *The David Show,* also by the author, on June 10, 1969, with the following cast:

BETTY . . . . *Rue McClanahan*
BILL . . . . *Tim O'Connor*

It was directed by Jered Barclay. Setting by Merrill Sindler; costumes by Yvonne Bronowicz; lighting by Andie Wilson Kingwill. Original music, Orville Stoeber.

NOTES

1. *Questions from the audience are included here and may be delivered by additional actors. On the other hand, the play may be performed without them, the actors on stage responding as if there were such questions.*
2. *For West Coast productions, "Honolulu" may be substituted for "Los Angeles."*
3. *No scenery, except for two chairs which will be brought out by the actors during the course of the play. There may also be an American flag and a plastic potted plant.*

While the house lights are still on, BETTY and BILL enter up the aisle from the audience. They hang up their coats. BILL stands awkwardly, waiting for BETTY, who may be seen just offstage combing her hair. Finally, BETTY comes out and takes BILL's arm. Smiles. House lights down, stage lights on. They blink in the light.

BETTY: [*To audience; nervously*] Tonight . . . on this stage . . . we are going to see the Golden Fleece. My husband and I have arranged everything. Jason and Medea will be here, and Jason will display the Fleece and tell us how he got it. And Medea will tell us how he got her.

BILL: And afterwards you can meet them. You can shake Jason's hand.

BETTY: Yes. And you can meet Medea. And you can touch the Golden Fleece.

BILL: They're a little late.

BETTY: Yes.

BILL: [*Softly; to BETTY; indicating audience*] They probably want to know how we arranged this.

BETTY: Yes. [*To audience*] It took some doing.

BILL: But I sailed with Jason in the Navy.

BETTY: Yes. And I used that—Can you hear us? Out there?

VOICE: Yes, yes, fine.

BETTY: I used that connection to meet Medea.

BILL: And now she's great buddies with Medea.

BETTY: Well, we're friends. She's teaching me how to do pottery.

BILL: Betty brings home some great pots.

BETTY: Well, the point is I like Medea. And one day I said to her, "What about the Fleece, Medea? Could I see the Golden Fleece?" And she smiled mysteriously and said it was up to Jason. So I got Bill to call Jason.

BILL: And Jason laughed and said it was up to Medea. [*Both laugh*]

BETTY: And so then we thought, why not do it up brown? Why not . . . celebrate it? Why

not share it with others, with other friends, with all of you?

BILL: I mean, how many times in your life can you see a Golden Fleece?

BETTY: It's more than that, Bill. It's much more than that. It's that we all . . . *need* to see it, these days. It will bring back so much that we've forgotten. [*Both begin to talk simultaneously*]

BETTY: And then we fussed about details. I asked Medea how she'd like to do it.

BILL: I told Jason I could show my slides. I've got some great Kodachrome slides of the trip.

BETTY: [*She wins out*] And I thought maybe Medea would want to show some primitive pottery. Or sing authentic folk songs from her homeland.

BILL: But they both said no.

BETTY: Independently.

BILL: "Keep it simple," said Jason. "Keep it Greek."

BETTY: "Just give us a bare stage," said Medea. "Jason and I will fill it up."

BILL: So we rented this place—

BETTY: And notified all of you—

BILL: And here we are. On this blank stage.

BETTY: Waiting for Jason and Medea, and the Golden Fleece. [*Pause. Then the sound of a telephone ringing. They jump. Quickly*] That's Jason.

BILL: I'll get it. [*He goes off quickly*]

BETTY: [*Smiles; a bit nervous; to audience*] Flat tire, probably. Or traffic. Jason has to drive all the way out from town, pick up Medea in the country, and bring her back in to us. [*Pause*] You'll get the Fleece tonight. I promise you that. [*Pause*] Bill and I will show you *something*. If it kills us. [*BILL returns and whispers to her*] Oh, no. [*BILL whispers*] Oh, no. [*BILL whispers*] Oh, I know. Darn it. [*BILL whispers. Irritatedly*] I know that, Bill! [*To audience*] Well. There we are.

Pause.

BILL: He wants you to go out and get her.

BETTY: Right now? . . . [*Remembers audience*] Oh. I'm sorry. Jason is tied up at work. So—

BILL: Medea's waiting.

BETTY: That's right. She doesn't have a telephone.

BILL: [*To audience; impatiently*] She doesn't drive. . . . She doesn't have a telephone—

BETTY: She doesn't *want* to drive. She doesn't want a telephone.

BILL: So go get her and bring her in.

BETTY: Yes. All right. Is the Fleece with her?

BILL: I guess so.

BETTY: I'll go get her, then. [*She gets her coat, returns, stops, turns to* BILL. *He hands her the car keys*] She's probably crawling up the walls.

BILL: She must be used to this. You know Jason.

BETTY: No, I don't, really. But I know Medea.

BILL: Go. [*She exits briskly, putting on her coat.* BILL *looks after her, and then looks at the audience. He smiles embarrassedly, and scratches his head. To audience*] Don't worry. He'll show. He's an old friend. I sailed with him all over the Mediterranean. I was with him when he got the Golden Fleece. [*Pause*] Oh, I know it's hard to believe now. I'm getting a little bald. I'm getting this gut. Huh, Howard? I wear these civilian clothes. But I was there. I pulled my oar. And then he promoted me to steersman. And so I steered. Right through the Dardanelles. On into the Black Sea. Dark skies. High waves. Shifting winds. But I kept that ship straight, so Jason could find his Fleece. [*Pause*] You know, sometimes when I'm pushing a pencil down at the office, when I'm counting the cash, I think about those days. I can feel that wooden tiller in my hand, and the push of the sea, and I can smell the wind again, and I wish . . . oh, well, we can't go back, can we? [*Pause*] But I was good then. I steered that ship into that dangerous harbor. Without a chart. Without a compass. I slid her right up on the beach. And Jason was standing on the bow, like a figurehead, and he turned to me, and he said, "Good man, Bill. Good man!" before he jumped ashore.

MAN'S VOICE: [*From audience*] Can I ask a question?

BILL: Shoot.

MAN: Did you actually go ashore with Jason?

BILL: No. I didn't. I stayed with the ship. I had to stand watch. So I waited for Jason, while he explored, just as we're waiting now. Anyway, what was there to see ashore? A hot sun. A lot of gooks dancing around naked. Listen: you people don't know about ships. There's always work to be done on ships. We had to bring her home after all. And so I worked, while Jason looked around. And he showed up finally. Late. Like now. Running. With Medea on one arm, and the Fleece on the other. But our sails were set, so they jumped aboard, and I had to steer a crazy course as the natives threw spears at us from the shore. But Jason had the Golden Fleece. And Medea.

MAN'S VOICE: Hey, Bill—how did they get the Golden Fleece?

BILL: The Fleece? Oh, I don't know the details. The Fleece came with Medea, that's all I know. She helped him get it, or it helped him get her. The point is, Jason got what he wanted and we brought him home.

Pause.

WOMAN'S VOICE: Uh . . . was there . . . rape involved?

BILL: Rape? [*He laughs*] Oh listen, if that was rape, let's have more of it. Medea was crazy about him. We had fair weather all the way home, and Jason and Medea lay in the sun, up forward, on the Golden Fleece, screened by sails. And I swear, you guys, I had the tiller and I swear . . . that the whole ship shivered when they made love. And it was contagious! Every man on that ship was horny as a toad! And when we got home, why, we tore the town apart! There are a lot of girls, a lot of girls, fellas, with bow legs because of that night! [*He laughs*] Oh, those were the days, men! Those were the . . . [*Pause*] Well, then I met Betty. And we got married. [*He points to his wedding ring*] And Jason stood up with me, and handed me this ring, and now we're both settled down, with homes, and six kids between us. [*Pause*] So he'll show. [*He looks off*] And here comes the judge. Here comes the judge.

BETTY *comes in quickly, panting.*

BETTY: Get me a chair, please.

BILL: Where's Medea?

BETTY: I'll tell you. Get me a chair. [BILL *goes off.* BETTY *turns to audience*] I'm exhausted. I'm drained.

BILL *comes back on with a chair. She sits down.*

BILL: Where's Medea?

BETTY: Out in the country. She won't come in. Except with Jason.

BILL: [*Impatiently*] Jason's tied up.

BETTY: Oh, he's tied up, all right, all right.

BILL: What do you mean?

BETTY: Jason is tied up with a little friend, at the moment.

BILL: A little friend?

BETTY: A cutie pie. A little number. A girl.

BILL: No.

BETTY: Oh, yes. And Medea also said that this girl is not the first.

BILL: Not the first?

BETTY: Not by a long shot. This girl is just the latest of a long, long line.

BILL: Why, that—

BETTY: Oh, yes. This has been going on, with one girl or another, since a year after they were married.

BILL: Why, that son of a—

BETTY: Oh, yes. Jason has come and gone his merry way almost from the beginning. And the Golden Fleece . . . he's been spending it on other women.

BILL: Why, that son of a gun! [*Pause. He looks at her*] I never knew that.

BETTY: Nobody knew that. She has never said a word.

BILL: She has never—

BETTY: Said one word. Until tonight.

BILL: She has said plenty to him, I'll bet. Knowing Medea.

BETTY: You don't know Medea. She has never mentioned it to him. She has let him do it.

BILL: She has let him—?

BETTY: Do it.

Long pause.

BILL: Think of that . . . [*To audience*] Think of that, you guys.

BETTY: [*Sarcastically, to audience*] Oh, yes! Think of that, you girls [*She looks at* BILL] And then start thinking about the Golden Fleece!

BILL: But it's . . . gone now.

BETTY: It has not gone. It is torn a little. It is tarnished a little. But it is still there, I'm convinced of it. And we're going to see it.

BILL: But how?

BETTY: Now, Bill: let me think. [*Pause; she thinks*] Don't you see what's going on?

BILL: No.

BETTY: I do . . . I'm beginning to see it all. . . . I think Jason and Medea have decided to . . . test each other.

BILL: Test?

BETTY: Exactly. Test. Each other. Through us. We are the audience, and they want us to witness a huge—test.

BILL: You've lost me, Betty.

BETTY: No. No, listen. [*To audience*] Listen, everybody. I think . . . Jason was purposely late. I think . . . he wants us to know he's got a girl. He is spreading his tail like a peacock!

BILL: Oh, Betty—

BETTY: Yes, yes. And Medea was waiting for me. Bill! She knew I'd come. [*To audience*] Oh, I think we've started something here, people, I think we've started a mating dance between two great whooping cranes!

BILL: And what happens next?

BETTY: It's obvious. Jason must get her, and bring her in. To us.

BILL: Which means—

BETTY: No more girls! She is calling his bluff . . . of course! Medea wants a new marriage, in public, in front of all of us. She wants Jason to stand beside her, with the Fleece between them, and declare proudly and publicly that he'll cherish her from this day forward! [*Triumphantly; to audience*] Oh, that's it, people!

BILL: Jason won't buy that.

BETTY: Of course he will. He wants her to take a stand. And she's taken it. And here we are.

Pause.

BILL: [*Carefully*] Who tells Jason to get Medea?

BETTY: You do, darling.

BILL: Forget it.

BETTY: I promised Medea you would.

BILL: I'm not going to get caught in the middle of this.

BETTY: But we're messengers, Bill.

BILL: [*Whispering angrily*] I do that at work. I don't do it here.

BETTY: [*Smiling*] Do it, Bill.

BILL: What would I say to the guy?

BETTY: You say, "Jason, go home."

BILL: Like a flunkey—

BETTY: Like a friend.

BILL: We're not friends.

BETTY: He was your best man!

BILL: We've grown apart.

BETTY: *He's* grown apart. You've stayed *with* it. Be his steersman, again, and steer him home. [*Indicates the audience*] Look! here's your ship. We're all aboard. And Jason and Medea are the mainstay! If those two big, beautiful people can't make it, then we'll all go under. So take the helm, Bill.

BILL: [*After a pause*] Why do I always have to steer?

BETTY: It's your job, Bill. Now, come on. Anchors aweigh, Bill. Please.

BILL: Where is he?

BETTY: At the Downtown Motel. [*She hands him the car keys.* BILL *gets his coat, and starts off. She calls after him*] Hey! [*He stops. She goes to him and gives him a big kiss; and then smiles at the audience*]

BILL: Wow. [*He looks at the audience embarrassedly*]

BETTY: That was just so you'll come back, sailor.

BILL: I'll be back. Grrr. [*He exits. She watches him go, and then turns toward the audience and sits down*]

BETTY: [*Sighing*] Medea, Medea, Medea . . . I am fascinated by that woman. . . . I've known her all these years, and she has never mentioned this thing about Jason. She has kept it all to herself. . . . Why? She worships Jason. She gave up everything for him. She was a princess, or something, in the old country, and she gave it all up, for him. The Fleece was hers, you know. Oh yes, it was her Fleece. And when she saw Jason with his blond hair and jaunty ways, why, she just handed it over to him, and they sailed away. She doesn't hear a word from home now. Nothing. Jason is all she has . . . Jason and the children.

WOMAN'S VOICE: [*From audience*] Betty, it sounds as though she's pretty content with Jason.

BETTY: Yes. I think that's right. I think that's why she bought that place out there in the country. To be alone with him. She won't even come in for dinner. Crab-meat casserole? That's not for Medea.

WOMAN: What do you do with Medea?

BETTY: [*Cups her ear*] Me? Oh well. I go out there during the day. When Jason's not home. I love it actually. I . . . need it, really. Whenever I get fed to the *teeth* with all this . . . stuff . . . whenever the children get me down . . . why, then I just throw them in the car, and out we go, out to Medea's. And my kids play with her kids. And Medea and I do pottery. I just sink my fingers into that dark, red wet clay. And then I watch it spin round and round on a wheel, and I pat it and poke it like mad, and I never know how it will come out. . . . But there's always a shape. I must have shapes. [*Pause*] Oh, she's got acres of land out there, and deep woods, and a barn, and animals, and a vegetable garden. And she handles it all herself. She makes blankets from the sheep's wool, and cans vegetables, and makes her own special cider from the apple orchard. Oh, it's wonderful, out there. Every season is different. It's not like . . . this.

WOMAN: Do you and Medea talk?

BETTY: [*Cups her ear*] Do we talk? Why, of course we talk. . . . Or at least I do. Medea listens. The children play in the barn, and Medea and I sit by the fire, and she gives me a hot glass of cider, and I chatter away, just as I'm chattering now. And she . . . listens. So carefully, people. And she nods so . . . knowingly. There are things going on behind her dark eyes. . . . I envy the woman, that's all. I envy her. She's . . . in touch with something we'll never touch. [*Pause; then quickly and brightly*] Oh, I forgot. I have Medea's children. Yes. When I was out there, she insisted I take them. She had them all ready. [*Pause*]

I . . . don't know why exactly. She was adamant about it. [*Pause; then smiles*] Yes I do know. Tonight she wants a second honeymoon. She wants the children out of the way. [*Pause*] So we've got them. My mother is sitting for the whole tribe. I put them in our bed. Bill and I can sleep on the couch. It's the least we can do for Jason and Medea. [*She looks off*] Ah! Home is the sailor, home from the sea. . . .

BILL *comes back on. He whistles "Anchors Aweigh." His tie is loose. Pause.*

BILL: [*A little defiantly*] Jason is going away with her.

BETTY: What? With Medea?

BILL: With the girl. With that gorgeous girl.

BETTY: Well, *go on,* for heaven's sake! Tell!

BILL: I went to the Downtown Motel. I knocked. He opened the door immediately. [*Pause*] He expected me.

BETTY: You see? He knew!

BILL: Oh, sure. He knew I'd show up. He knew what I'd say. And after I said it, he knew what to do. He picked up the telephone, and got two tickets on the night flight to Los Angeles.

BETTY: To Los Angeles?

BILL: He'll fly into the sun. With that golden girl.

BETTY: Why, that no-good—

BILL: Hold it!

BETTY: I said, that lousy, no-good—

BILL: I said hold it!

Pause; then BETTY *smiles sweetly.*

BETTY: You've been drinking.

BILL: Jason and I had a drink together, yes.

BETTY: Where? In some bar? Oh, I can see it. Palsy-walsy, buddy-buddy. Old Navy days in some bar. While we all waited here.

BILL: No. We had a drink in the motel room. All of us.

Pause.

BETTY: All of you? All? You drank with that girl?

BILL: We all sat on the bed and drank.

Pause.

BETTY: Perhaps you'd like to sit again. [*Indicates offstage*] Out there. Where you can pull yourself together.

BILL: [*Through a grin*] I'll sit when I want to sit.

Pause. They look at each other.

BETTY: [*To audience; through her teeth*] I could kill that Jason. I could throttle him!

BILL: [*To audience*] Jason is a good man.

BETTY: [*To audience*] Jason is not a good man.

BILL: [*To audience*] Jason is a great man.

BETTY: [*To audience*] Jason is a big, fat stinker!

BILL: [*Wheeling on her, threateningly*] Watch it, kid. You're talking about my best friend.

Pause. She looks at him, sighs, and goes to her chair. She sits down and closes her eyes and folds her hands on her lap.

BETTY: [*Quietly; sarcastically; eyes closed*] Sweetheart . . .

BILL: [*Equally sarcastic*] Yes, darling. . . .

BETTY: Sweetheart, I wonder if you'd say why you think your good friend Jason is such a good man. Do you think you could do that for the group, dear?

BILL: Sure. [*He turns and immediately walks out. She opens her eyes and sees that he is gone. She jumps up, panicky. He returns immediately, carrying a chair. He sets it up a distance away from her chair. Both sit down. Pause*] Why I think Jason is a good man . . .

BETTY: Yes, dear. Jason. You know. The one who is leaving his family in the lurch.

BILL: Oh, *that* Jason.

BETTY: Yes, that one. Your best friend Jason.

BILL: Ah. Now remember: I only spent a relatively short time with Jason.

BETTY: Yes. Sitting on a bed with some babe. Yes.

BILL: Yes. We just hacked around. You know.

BETTY: Yes. I know. And it was all just a little bit out of your league. Wasn't it?

BILL: Maybe. . . . But I learned one thing.

BETTY: And what's that?

BILL: I learned that Jason is one helluva lot like me.

Pause.

BETTY: Why is Jason running out on Medea?

BILL: Because she's forcing him to.

BETTY: She's forcing him to choose.

BILL: He doesn't want to choose.

BETTY: Well, he's got to.

BILL: So he's chosen.

BETTY: Some babe.

BILL: A gorgeous girl!

BETTY: He doesn't love Medea!

BILL: Sure he does.

BETTY: He doesn't love his children!

BILL: Sure he does.

BETTY: I don't believe that.

BILL: He does. And he loves the girl. And he'll love Los Angeles.

BETTY: Then I don't know what love means!

BILL: I do. And so does Jason!

Long pause.

BETTY: [*Getting up*] Well. We're out of it now.

BILL: You think so?

BETTY: Oh, yes. We've done what we can. The rest is up to them.

BILL: We're not out of it, baby.

BETTY: Oh, yes, oh, yes.

BILL: Oh, no. . . . Go tell Medea!

Pause.

BETTY: Jason will tell Medea.

BILL: No, he won't.

BETTY: Then he's a coward.

BILL: Your turn, baby.

BETTY: No.

BILL: I told Jason you would.

BETTY: I won't.

BILL: We threw the ball in, kid. Let's keep it going.

BETTY: I'm frightened.

BILL: Of Medea?

BETTY: No. . . . Yes. . . . You don't know her.

BILL: Ah, but you do. She's your best friend.

BETTY: No, no, she isn't. Not really. I don't know what she'll do.

BILL: Go find out.

BETTY: Bill, I want to stop this.

BILL: Stop? Now?

BETTY: Yes. I want to stop. I want to go home.

BILL: To do what?

BETTY: Bill, we're in this over our heads now. It's none of our beeswax now. I—I think we did some good, actually. We—brought things to a boil. And now our job, it seems to me, is to get out of it, and stay out of it.

BILL: [*Sarcastically*] But we're messengers, Betty!

BETTY: No, Bill, no, I . . . don't like it here. It's . . . empty up here. [*She looks at him*] Bill, what I thought we'd do is . . . call it a day. . . . We'll join all our friends . . . [*Indicates audience*] at Howard Johnson's or something . . . and then, Bill, when we get home . . . I'll give you a glass of Ovaltine, and a piece of cherry pie, just the way I used to when we were first married. Remember that, Bill?

BILL: Yeah, I remember—

BETTY: So I'll give you that, and then we'll . . . [*Smiles at the audience*] Just go to bed. Hmmmmm? Hmm. Bill?

BILL: [*Weakening*] You mean, just—

BETTY: Go to bed. And we can sleep late in the morning, Bill, because Mother's there, and she'll get up the—[*Pause; thinks*] We'll move Medea's children down to the couch.

BILL: Medea's children?

BETTY: She asked me to take them.

BILL: Medea's children are now in our bed?

BETTY: They will be on the couch.

BILL: [*Exploding*] Children in my bed. Always some Goddamn kid in my bed! Diapers in the john! Toys on the stairs! Food on the floor! Cats crapping in the fireplace! Dogs barfing on the rug!

BETTY: [*Very quietly*] What . . . exactly . . . are you talking about?

BILL: I'm talking about children in my bed! I'm talking about greasy hot dogs, and spilled milk, and a decibel level beyond human tolerance! I'm talking about a broken stereo set, and stacks of doctors' bills, and crumby crayoned pictures all over the goddamn white walls!

BETTY: [*Grimly*] You are talking about your home.

BILL: [*Grimly*] Yes, I am.

BETTY: I take it you don't like your home.

BILL: Not at the moment. [*Pause*] I like it here. [*Pause*] I can breathe here. [*Pause*] I can talk here. I can hear myself think. [*Pause*] There's nothing on the floor, here, to trip me up. [*He begins to move around the stage in a sort of shuffle*] There are no Tinker Toys here. . . . [*Moves more easily*] No tricycles. . . . No erector sets to gouge my shins and tear my pants. [*He lifts his feet*] No Silly Putty ground into the rug! [*He looks down*] No crumby homemade pottery! [*He pantomimes kicking a pot out at the audience*] Crash! [*He dances*] I'm free here! It's the wide-open spaces. I can do anything I want here! I can be the fastest gun in the West! [*He pantomimes shooting her*] Save the last bullets for the women and children! . . . Or d'Artagnan! [*He pantomimes a sword fight, almost cutting off her head*] Or Fred Astaire! [*He dances defiantly in front of her*] "Monday, Monday . . . Tuesday, Tuesday . . . Wednesday, Wednesday . . ." [*He ends with a big finish. She looks at him and slowly turns toward the audience*]

BETTY: That was . . . lovely. [*Pauses; she holds out her hand*] Keys, please! [*He makes her grope for them in his pockets. When she gets them, he gooses her*] I will now take Medea's children back to their mother.

BILL: Yes. Do that.

BETTY: I will wake those poor children, who have already been awakened once tonight, and I will bundle them into the car, and take them to Medea.

BILL: Good. Fine. Get them out of my bed. And change the sheets, will you!

BETTY: Those children will need a mother now. They will need all the mothering they can get now—

BILL: [*Shouting*] Can't even get a good night's sleep!

BETTY: And Medea will want her children now. She'll want them home. I will tell Medea—

BILL: Tell her that Jason is Goddamn tired of finding children in his bed, and so he's flying away with a beautiful girl into the Golden West!

BETTY: NO, I WILL NOT TELL MEDEA THAT! I will tell her that she is LUCKY! Lucky because she is free. Free to start a new life with the children. A life where she doesn't have to worry about some stupid, idiot MAN!

BILL: Good! Tell her that!

BETTY: I will also tell her to hold Jason up for everything he's got! She gave up everything for him. Now let him cough up for her. And for the children. Oh, Medea is a lucky lady! She's going to be free, free, free! [*She starts off*]

BILL: Jason too, baby! Jason too!

BETTY: [*Wheeling on him*] Oh, no! Not Jason! This is going to cost him the whole Goddamn Golden Fleece! [*She strides out*]

BILL: [*Calling after her*] You don't know what the Fleece *is*, kid! [*Pause; he looks at the audience*] I do. I've just seen it. [*He comes downstage, determinedly*] And I'll tell you about it! [*He shields his eyes and looks out*] This is for the men. You women can shove off. Go home to the kiddies. This is going to be much too raunchy for you. [*Pause*] This is stag, girls. Scram, please. [*Pause; presumably the women don't go*] Okay, stick around, then. Don't say I didn't warn you. [*Pause*] Anyway, you girls won't understand this. Only men will understand this. So here goes, fellas. I'll tell you about the Golden Fleece. . . . He met me at the door. And get this: he just had a towel around him. So I said I'd wait outside. "Hell no," said Jason. "Come on in." And he gave me a great big bear hug for old time's sake. And I could feel his beard—he wears a beard again—I could feel it against my cheek. [*Looks out; points his finger*] I know what you're going to say, buddy. It was nothing like that. It was hearty, man to man. Like a huddle in a football game. So I went in. [*Refuses another question*] Hold your water, fella. I'm getting to her. . . . She was in the bed. Jason introduced me to her, and when she held out her hand, the sheet fell away and I could see two of the biggest, most beautiful . . . I mean, there they WERE! Just winking and blinking at me, and she didn't even bother to cover them UP! So I just stood there, slowly shaking her hand, and trying not to look at those two, big, soft, pink BREASTS!

MAN'S VOICE: [*From audience*] Hey, Bill, how old was she?

BILL: About twenty-two or -three. [*Pause*] Blond hair. Long and blond. Sort of in her eyes. Which were blue. Got the picture? Okay. [*He takes a deep breath*] So. Jason broke out the Scotch, and we all sat on the bed and had a drink. I felt like a visiting minister sitting there with my legs crossed, holding a glass in my hot little hand, trying to keep my beady little eyes away from those bazoolis. I mean, they were still unCOVERED, guys! But after a while, I felt easy. We sat and talked about everything under the sun. And . . . they were like two kids, laughing at everything, and pretty soon I was laughing too, and the girl, when she laughed, why, her boobies jiggled up and down like they were beckoning to me, saying, Come and get it, and I just wanted to reach over and grab them, and then by golly, I DID! And we all laughed all the more.

WOMAN: Did you bother to mention Medea?

BILL: [*Grimly*] Yes, madam, I did. I mentioned Medea. [*Pause*] And oh, boy, did that put a damper on things. [*Pause*] Jason just looked at his drink. The girl pulled the sheet up to her chin. It was very quiet. And then Jason got up, and called the airlines, and got two tickets for Los Angeles. [*Pause*] And then suddenly we were all laughing again, and then— [*Pause*] I don't know whether to tell you this part or not. [*Pause*] I wish you women would get the hell out. [*Pause*] Never mind. It will do you good. Okay. So we got Medea off our back, and we were hacking around, and suddenly I got the urge to take off my clothes. So I did. I got up. And I took off my clothes! Yessir! Every stitch. And they cheered, those two! They applauded, Jason and his girl! And Jason put a record on his portable, and we all danced, naked as jaybirds, drunk as skunks, we all danced to the Mamas and the Papas. . . . [*He sings "Monday, Monday . . ." and then he stops*] And then I remembered this little gold ring on my finger. [*Pause*] And I thought of my wife. [*Pause*] And my kids. [*Pause*] And all of you, sitting here. [*Pause*] So I got dressed. I said good-bye. I shook hands. I took one last little squeeze of those . . . [*Pause*] And I left. [*He looks longingly off right*] And I guess they're still there. Those two blond beautiful naked people. Dancing to the Mamas and the Papas. Waiting to fly to Los Angeles.

BETTY *comes on from the left. She carries a bulky bag. She looks at him coldly, and turns to the audience.*

BETTY: I've told Medea everything. She is sending this bag to the girl.

BILL: What is it? A bomb?

BETTY: [*Not looking at him; grimly patient*] No. It is not a bomb. It is a dress. [*She opens the bag, holds out the dress; it is long, reddish-gold, luxurious, menacing*] Medea is sending this dress to Jason's girl.

BILL: I don't get it.

BETTY: No. You don't. [*To audience*] Medea was waiting for me, of course. She knew I'd bring back the children. She hugged them wildly. And then she took them into her bedroom, and came back with this dress. It's her native costume. She wore it when she sailed away with Jason. And now she wants the girl to wear it.

BILL: Oh, come off it!

BETTY: You don't understand.

BILL: No, I don't.

BETTY: You don't, because you're a man. We women understand. Every woman here understands.

BILL: And every man here doesn't.

BETTY: [*With a sigh*] Ladies: Medea wants to say something with this dress. To me, and to the girl, and to all women everywhere. [*She holds it in front of her own body*]

BILL: Could you—uh—translate it? Into words? For us guys?

BETTY: [*With a patient sigh*] Medea is saying— how would you men put it?—"Welcome to the Club"? She is saying that Jason—men— don't really count. She is saying that what counts, in the end, is this old dress . . . which has come all the way across the sea from Medea's dark homeland. And which will go all the way across this land to sunny California. And it connects all us women, across all this distance. It binds, it ties together, Medea, and me, and the girl, more than marriage ever could. [*She holds it out to the audience*] This is the Golden Fleece, really. This is the important thing.

BILL: I see—

BETTY: No, you don't see. Because it can't be seen. [*She puts it carefully back in the bag*] It's something to feel. And men can't feel it.

BILL: [*He glances off right; then he looks at his wedding ring. Rubbing the ring*] So this little ring . . . doesn't mean much?

BETTY: [*Patting the bag*] Not compared to this.

BILL: [*Glances off right again; starts to sing softly*] "Monday, Monday . . ." [*He looks at* BETTY. *Then he takes off his ring, holds it up to his eyes, and squints at her through it*] Silly little things . . . these rings . . .

BETTY: [*Carefully*] Oh, they have their uses. . . . They're insurance, after all. [*She looks at him*] They guarantee support. No matter what.

Long pause.

BILL: Well, I'll take that package on over.

BETTY: I'll do it.

BILL: [*Reaching for it*] It's my job.

BETTY: [*Holding on to it*] Oh, no. This is woman's work.

BILL: [*Tugging at it*] I said—

BETTY: I said NO!

BILL: [*Poking her with his finger*] That motel is my territory, baby.

BETTY: I promised . . . [*Poking him back*] Medea!

BILL: [*Poking her harder*] Jason's my best friend!

BETTY: Medea is mine!

With a sudden lunge, she straight-arms him, and starts running off with the bag. He grabs her, and lifts her up; she kicks and struggles. She lands an effective kick, and starts off again. He tackles her. She falls on the floor. He pins her like a wrestler. Then he looks up with horror at the audience, letting go of her arms. She smacks him on the head with the bag. He twists her nose. She smacks him. Pause. Both pant. He lets her go and gets up. She extends her hand feebly. He helps her up. She lets him have it in the gut. He moves toward her, fist raised. She retreats. He slugs her, grabs the bag, and starts out.

BILL: I'm going to Los Angeles. [*He storms out*]

BETTY: [*Shrieking after him*] I'm moving in with Medea! [*She rubs her jaw. She looks at the audience*] No, no. I'm all right. Keep your seats, please. Keep your SEATS! I said I'm all RIGHT, thank you. [*She gets to her feet, panting*] I'm fine. [*She staggers a little*] I'm perfectly fine. He didn't hurt me. He's too WEAK! . . . That does it, of course. [*She shouts off*] THAT DOES IT, BUSTER! [*She throws off her coat onto the floor*] I'm moving in with Medea! I'm taking the children, and out we go! Tonight! We'll sleep in the barn. If anyone else wants to come, she's welcome. Any woman, any mother, is welcome out there with Medea! Come on! And bring the children! [*Looks out*] Oh, you're so wrong, lady! Children do not need fathers! What is a father these days? What does he do? Does he teach them how to hunt? Does he show them how to plow? Where is he, most of the time? Gone! Out of it! As that father . . . [*She points off*] is out of it now! . . . This, this is your life, girls! This! Right here. This bleak, barren stage, halfway between Jason and Medea,

where we stand around trying to explain ourselves! Oh, let's go back to Medea where we belong! [*Her eyes dart around the audience*] Oh, I know what you're going to say! [*Sarcastically*] We mustn't forget schools! [*Vehemently*] Well, the hell with schools! The hell with those smelly buses, and that crazy arithmetic, and all those sappy things they learn about American democracy! We'll run our own schools out at Medea's. We'll teach them farming and animal husbandry. They'll learn how to sink some roots in the ground. They'll see lambs born. They'll get milk from the cows, and eggs from the chickens, and fresh peas from the pea patch! And at night, when they're asleep, all together, all in the hay, we women will churn butter, and spin wool, and Medea will tell us old folk tales around the fire. [*She smiles*] And men can come to Medea's. Not husbands. Men. Visiting hours will be at night, in the spring. We'll meet you in the fields, in the woods, in the barn, and we'll never see your faces, or your silly bodies! Oh yes, we'll have men. Any men, all men. Black men, white men, old men, young men. Come, and then go! And that's all I have to say about men! [*She comes close to the edge of the stage, croons to the audience*] But women! My women! Come with me to Medea. Wake the children. Wrap them in swaddling clothes. Lay them in the manger, among the cattle and sheep, and we'll all begin again. . . .

BILL *comes on slowly from the right.* BETTY *sees him, turns heel, and starts out, grimly.*

BILL: [*Quietly*] Jason has gone back to Medea.

Pause. BETTY *comes back on.*

BETTY: I don't believe that. That's not true.

BILL: [*Grimly patient, to audience*] Jason has gone back to Medea.

BETTY: If Jason crawled back on his hands and knees, he'd get—nothing! Let him stay with his girl.

BILL: There's no girl now.

BETTY: No girl?

BILL: [*Looking at her*] The girl is out of it.

BETTY: Did she wear the dress?

BILL: Yes.

BETTY: Then why—?

BILL: I don't know.

BETTY: [*Grimly*] The suspense is killing me.

BILL: [*To audience*] I took the dress to the girl. She laughed, and wanted to try it on. As a joke. But Jason took it away from her.

BETTY: He probably wanted to try it on himself.

BILL: [*Ignoring her*] The girl insisted.

BETTY: She had to wear it.

BILL: She tried it on. She slipped it over her head, holding up her arms, and as it slid down, I took one last look . . . [*He turns defiantly to* BETTY] at her beautiful breasts.

BETTY: [*Very calmly*] Oh, I'm sure. [*To audience*] He sneaks into nudie movies during his lunch hour.

BILL: Once!

BETTY: [*She holds up three fingers to the audience*] Go on about the dress, dear.

BILL: [*With a grim sigh*] When she got the dress on, Jason just stood and stared at her.

BETTY: Because she looked so lovely.

BILL: She looked just like Medea!

BETTY: Exactly! Oh, I knew it!

BILL: Jason shouted at her: "Take it off! Take the Goddamn thing off!"

BETTY: Because he remembered Medea!

BILL: But the girl panicked. She couldn't get it off.

BETTY: Because it fit too well!

BILL: Her hair got caught in the zipper, and she writhed and struggled as if the dress were on fire—

BETTY: Medea's dress!

BILL: And Jason tried to pull it off. And the girl lost her balance. They rolled on the floor, the girl clawing at the dress, Jason pulling at it, and she was screaming at him, and he hit her —hard—and then she lay still. And he ripped the dress off her, and walked out of the motel. The girl lay there, shivering. I threw a blanket over her. And came back here. And Jason went back to Medea.

BETTY: Because—

BILL: Because she has the Golden Fleece.

BETTY: [*Triumphantly*] Ah, I knew it, I knew it! The dress did it! Medea was telling him, with the dress, that he'll always fall in love with the same woman! It's always Medea! [*To audience*] Oh, haven't you seen it? The second wife just like the first. It's the old story. . . . [*She turns back to* BILL] So he's gone home! For the Golden Fleece! Which is their old love.

Pause.

BILL: I don't think so.

BETTY: Oh, yes. The Golden Fleece is their old love!

BILL: I don't think so.

Pause.

BETTY: [*Carefully*] What do you think, then? What is the Golden Fleece? To you?

BILL: The children.

BETTY: The children?

BILL: Those golden-haired kids. [*Carefully*] They're what it's all about, I think.

BETTY: Jason loves—

BILL: His children.

BETTY: [*Shaking her head*] He's never shown it.

BILL: He will now. He remembered them.

BETTY: And he remembered Medea.

BILL: A little.

BETTY: And he loves Medea.

BILL: He'll live with Medea.

BETTY: And love her.

BILL: [*Shaking his head*] Not in the old way.

BETTY: Why not?

BILL: Because he's changed since then.

BETTY: More girls?

BILL: More life.

BETTY: Medea wants all or nothing.

BILL: Jason wants . . . more.

BETTY: Then he doesn't belong at home.

Pause.

BILL: Then he'll see the kids on weekends.

BETTY: Oh, no.

BILL: He has a father's rights.

BETTY: And she has a mother's.

BILL: He has the law.

BETTY: What law?

BILL: He gets them in the summer.

BETTY: [*Contemptuously*] Oh, that law.

BILL: He'll take those kids.

BETTY: Steal them? Kidnap them?

BILL: To a new life.

BETTY: He's too old.

BILL: Younger than you think.

BETTY: Then Medea has another law. She'll teach the children to hate him.

Pause.

BILL: She wouldn't do that.

BETTY: You don't know Medea. [*Pause; the sudden sound of a telephone ringing*] Ah. There's your pal. Calling from the neighbors' to tell you that all's well.

BILL: He wants me to meet him at the airport. He'll have his kids.

More ringing.

BETTY: He's coming here with Medea to prove his love.

More ringing.

BILL: What Jason does, I'll do.

BETTY: Fair enough. The same with me and Medea. [*More ringing. He exits. She comes downstage; to audience*] Medea will forgive and forget. Because she's a big woman. Oh, there will be . . . tension. I admit that. The children will suffer, for a while. Their marks will go down, and they'll act up. But at least they will sleep in their own beds all night long. [*Pause; she smiles*] And when we're sixty we'll talk about all this. And laugh.

BILL *comes on. He stares at* BETTY *blankly.*

BILL: That was the police. [*Pause*] Medea has killed her children. [*Pause*] She was waiting for Jason at the door. [*Pause*] She shot them down, like animals, before his eyes. [*Pause*] The police asked if we knew why. [*Pause*] Do we?

BETTY: [*Backing away. She doubles up for a scream, then shakes her head, speaks very quietly*] I hardly know that woman! [*She straightens up. He takes her arm. They exit slowly through the audience, unable even to say good-bye*]

CLARA'S OLE MAN

a play of lost innocence

Ed Bullins

Clara's Ole Man was first presented by the San Francisco Drama Circle at the Firehouse Repertory Theatre, San Francisco, on August 5, 1965, with the following cast:

CLARA	*Blanche Richardson*
BIG GIRL	*Margo Norman*
JACK	*James Robinson*
BABY GIRL	*Dorothy Parrish*
MISS FAMIE	*Marie Bell*
STOOGIE	*Doyle Richmond*
BAMA	*Roy Hammond*
HOSS	*Ray Ashby*
C.C.	*Jerry Kemp*

It was directed by Robert Hartman. Sets designed by Louie Gelwicks and Peter Rounds; lighting by Verne Shreve.

Clara's Ole Man was subsequently presented by the American Place Theatre (Wynn Handman, director) at St. Clement's Church, New York City, as part of the bill *The Electronic Nigger and Others,* also by the author, on February 21, 1968, with the following cast:

CLARA	*Kelly Marie Berry*
BIG GIRL	*Carolyn Y. Cardwell*
JACK	*Roscoe Orman*
BABY GIRL	*Helen Ellis*
MISS FAMIE	*Estelle Evans*
STOOGIE	*Kris Keiser*
BAMA	*George Miles*
HOSS	*Gary Bolling*
C.C.	*L. Errol Jaye*

It was directed by Robert Macbeth. Settings by John Jay Moore: lighting by Roger Morgan.

It was subsequently moved to the Martinique Theatre, New York City, where it was presented by Paul Libin as part of the same bill (title changed to *Three Plays by Ed Bullins,* then *Ed Bullins' Plays*) on March 28, 1968, with the same cast and credits as American Place production.

CHARACTERS

CLARA, *a light brown girl of 18, well built with long, dark hair. A blond streak runs down the middle of her head, and she affects a pony tail. She is pensive, slow in speech but feline. Her eyes are heavy-lidded and brown; she smiles— rather, blushes—often.*

BIG GIRL, *a stocky woman wearing jeans and tennis shoes and a tight-fitting blouse which accents her prominent breasts. She is of an indeterminable age, due partly to her lack of makeup and plain hair style. She is anywhere from 25 to 40, and is loud and jolly, frequently breaking out in laughter from her own jokes.*

JACK, *20 years old, wears a corduroy Ivy League suit and vest. At first, JACK'S speech is modulated and too eloquent for the surroundings, but as he drinks his words become slurred and mumbled.*

BABY GIRL, *BIG GIRL'S mentally retarded teenage sister. The girl has the exact hairdo as CLARA. Her face is made up with mascara and eye shadow, and she has black arching eyebrows penciled darkly, the same as CLARA.*

MISS FAMIE, *a drunken neighbor.*

STOOGIE, *a local streetfighter and gang leader. His hair is processed.*

BAMA, *one of STOOGIE'S boys.*

HOSS, *another of STOOGIE'S boys.*

C.C., *a young wino.*

TIME

Early spring, the mid-1950s.

SCENE

A slum kitchen on a rainy afternoon in South Philadelphia. The room is very clean, wax glosses the linoleum and old wooden furniture; a cheap but clean red checkered oilcoth covers the table. If the room could speak it would say, "I'm cheap but clean."

A cheap AM radio plays rhythm 'n' blues music throughout the play. The furniture is made up of a wide kitchen table where a gallon jug of red wine sits. Also upon the table is an oatmeal box, cups, mugs, plates and spoons, ashtrays, and packs of cigarettes. Four chairs circle the table, and two sit against the wall at the back of the stage. An old-fashioned wood- and coal-burning stove takes up a corner of the room and a gas range of 1935 vintage is at the back next to the door to the yard. A large, smoking frying pan is on one of the burners.

JACK and BIG GIRL are seated at opposite ends of the table; CLARA stands at the stove fanning the fumes toward the door. BARY GIRL plays upon the floor with a homemade toy.

CLARA: [*Fans fumes*] Uummm uummm . . . well, there goes the lunch. I wonder how I was dumb enough to burn the bacon?

BIG GIRL: Just comes natural with you, honey, all looks and no brains. . . . Now with me and my looks, anybody in South Philly can tell I'm a person that naturally takes care of business . . . hee hee . . . ain't that right, Clara?

CLARA: Awww, girl, go on. You's the worst messer-upper I knows. You didn't even go to work this mornin'. What kind of business is that?

BIG GIRL: It's all part of my master plan, baby. Don't you worry none. . . . Big Girl knows what she's doin'. You better believe that!

CLARA: Yeah, you may know what you're doin', but I'm the one who's got to call in for you and lie that you're sick.

BIG GIRL: Well, it ain't a lie. You know I got this cough and stopped-up feeling. [*Looking at JACK*] You believe that, don't you, youngblood?

JACK: Most certainly. You could very well have a respiratory condition and also have all the appearances of an extremely capable person.

BIG GIRL: [*Slapping table*] Hee hee. . . . *See, Clara? . . . See?* Listen ta that, Clara. I told you anybody could tell it. Even ole hot lips here can tell.

CLARA: [*Pours out grease and wipes stove*] Awww . . . he just says that to be nice. . . . He's always sayin' things like that.

BIG GIRL: Is that how he talked when he met you the other day out to your aunt's house?

CLARA: [*Hesitating*] Nawh . . . nawh he didn't talk like that.

BIG GIRL: Well, how did he talk, huh?

CLARA: Awww . . . Big Girl. I don't know.

BIG GIRL: Well, who else does? You know what kind of line a guy gives ya. You been pitched at enough times, haven't ya? By the looks of him I bet he gave ya the ole smooth college-boy approach. . . . [*To JACK*] C'mon, man, drink up. We got a whole lot mo' to kill. Don't you know this is my day off and I'm celebratin'?

JACK: [*Takes a drink*] Thanks . . . this is certainly nice of you to go to all this trouble for me. I never expected it.

BIG GIRL: What did you expect, youngblood?

JACK: [*Takes another sip*] Ohhh, well . . . I . . .

CLARA: [*To BABY GIRL on floor*] Don't put that dirty thing in your mouf, gal! [*She walks around the table to* BABY GIRL *and tugs her arm*] Now, keep that out of your mouf!

BABY GIRL: [*Holds to toy sullenly*] No!

CLARA: You keep quiet, you hear, gal!

BABY GIRL: No!!!

CLARA: If you keep tellin' me no, I'm goin' ta take you upstairs ta Aunt Toohey.

BABY GIRL: [*Throws back head and drums feet on floor*] NO! NO! SHIT! DAMN! SHIT! NO!

CLARA: [*Disturbed*] Now stop that! We got company.

BIG GIRL: [*Laughs hard and leans elbows upon table*] Haw Haw Haw . . . I guess she told you, Clara. Hee hee . . . that little dirty-mouf bitch [*Pointing to* BABY GIRL *and becoming choked*] . . . that little . . . cough cough . . . hooooeee, boy!

CLARA: You shouldn't have taught her all them nasty words, Big Girl. Now we can't do anything with her. [*Turns to* JACK] What do you think of that?

JACK: Yes, it does seem a problem. But with proper guidance she'll more than likely be conditioned out of it when she gets into a learning situation among her peer group.

BIG GIRL: [*Takes a drink and scowls*] Bullshit!

CLARA: Awww . . . B.G.

JACK: I beg your pardon, Miss?

BIG GIRL: I said bullshit! Whatta ya mean with proper guidance . . . [*Points*] I taught that little bitch myself . . . the best cuss words I know before she ever climbed out of her crib. . . . Whatta ya mean when she gets among her "peer group"?

JACK: I didn't exactly say that. I said when . . .

BIG GIRL: [*Cuts him off*] Don't tell me what you said, boy! I got ears. I know all them big horseshit doctor words. . . . Tell him, Clara . . . tell him what I do. Where do I work, Clara?

CLARA: Awww . . . B.G., please.

BIG GIRL: DO LIKE I SAY! DO LIKE BIG WANTS YOU TO!

CLARA: [*Surrenders*] She works out at the state nut farm.

BIG GIRL: [*Triumphant*] And tell Mister Smart and Proper what I do.

CLARA: [*Automatically*] She's a technician.

JACK: Oh, that's nice. I didn't mean to suggest there was anything wrong with how you raised your sister.

BIG GIRL: [*Jolly again*] Haw haw haw . . . Nawh, ya didn't. I know you didn't even know what you were sayin', youngblood. Do you know why I taught her to cuss?

JACK: Why no, I have no idea. Why did you?

BIG GIRL: Well, it was to give her freedom, ya know? [JACK *shakes his head*] Ya see workin' in the hospital with all the nuts and fruits and crazies and weirdos I get ideas 'bout things. I saw how when they get these kids in who have cracked up and even with older people who come in out of their skulls they all mostly cuss. Mostly all of them, all the time they out of their heads, they cuss all the time and do other wild things, and boy, do some of them really get into it and let out all of that filthy shit that's been stored up all them years. But when the docs start shockin' them and puttin' them on insulin they quiets down, that's when the docs think they're gettin' better, but really they ain't. They're just learn'n' like before to hold it in . . . just like before, that's one reason most of them come back or are always on the verge afterwards of goin' psycho again.

JACK: [*Enthusiastic*] Wow, I never thought of that! That ritual action of purging and catharsis can open up new avenues of therapy and in learning theory and conditioning subjects . . .

BIG GIRL: Saaay whaaa . . . ? What did you have for breakfast, man?

CLARA: [*Struck*] That sounds so wonderful. . . .

JACK: [*Still excited*] But I agree with you. You have an intuitive grasp of very abstract concepts!

BIG GIRL: [*Beaming*] Yeah, yeah . . . I got a lot of it figured out. . . . [*To* JACK] Here, fill up your glass again, man.

JACK: [*To* CLARA] Aren't you drinking with us?

CLARA: Later. Big Girl doesn't allow me to start in drinking too early.

JACK: [*Confused*] She doesn't?

BIG GIRL: [*Cuts in*] Well, in Baby Girl's case I said to myself that I'm teach'n' her how in front and lettin' her use what she knows whenever it builds up inside. And it's really good for her, gives her spirit and everything.

CLARA: That's probably what warped her brain.

BIG GIRL: Hush up! You know it was dat fuckin' disease. All the doctors said so.

CLARA: You don't believe no doctors 'bout nothin' else!

BIG GIRL: [*Glares at* CLARA] Are you showin' out, Clara? Are you showin' out to your little boyfriend?

CLARA: He ain't mah boyfriend.

JACK: [*Interrupts*] How do you know she might not have spirit if she wasn't allowed to curse?

BIG GIRL: [*Sullen*] I don't know anything, youngblood. But I can take a look at myself and see the two of us. Look at me! [*Stares at* JACK] LOOK AT ME!

JACK: Yes, yes, I'm looking.

BIG GIRL: Well, what do you see?

CLARA: B.G. . . . *please!*

BIG GIRL: [*Ignores*] Well, what do you see?

JACK: [*Worried*] Well, I don't really know . . . I . . .

BIG GIRL: Well, let me tell you what you see. You see a fat bitch who's twenty pounds overweight and looks ten years older than she is. You want to know how I got this way and been this way most of my life and would be worse off if I didn't let off steam some drinkin' this rotgut and speakin' my mind?

JACK: [*To* BIG GIRL, *who doesn't listen but drinks*] Yes, I would like to hear.

CLARA *finishes the stove and takes a seat between the two.* BABY GIRL *goes to the yard door but does not go out into the rain; she sits down and looks out through the door at an angle.*

BIG GIRL: Ya see, when I was a little runt of a kid my mother found out she couldn't keep me or Baby Girl any longer cause she had T.B., so I got shipped out somewheres and Baby Girl got shipped out somewheres else. People that Baby Girl went to exposed her to the disease. She was lucky. I ended up with some fuckin' Christians. . . .

CLARA: Ohhh, B.G., you shouldn't say that!

BIG GIRL: Well, I sho as hell just did! . . . Damned kristers! I spent twelve years with those people, can you imagine? A dozen years in hell. Christians . . . *haaa* . . . always preachin' 'bout some heaven over yonder and building a bigger hell here den any devil have imagination for.

CLARA: You shouldn't go round sayin' things like dat.

BIG GIRL: I shouldn't! Well, what did your Christian mammy and pot-gutted pappy teach you? When I met you you didn't even know how to take a douche.

CLARA: YOU GOT NO RIGHT!!!! [*She momentarily rises as if she's going to launch herself on* BIG GIRL]

BIG GIRL: [*Condescending*] Awww . . . forget it, sweetie. . . . Don't make no never mind, but you remember how you us'ta smell when you got ready fo bed . . . like a dead hoss or a baby skunk. . . . [*To* JACK, *explaining*] That damned Christian mamma and pappa of hers didn't tell her a thing 'bout herself . . . ha ha ha . . . thought if she ever found out her little things was used fo' anything else 'cept squattin' she'd fall backwards right up in it . . . ZaaaBOOM . . . STRAIGHT TA HELL . . . ha ha. . . . Didn't know that li'l

Clara had already found her heaven, and on the same trail.

CLARA: [*Ashamed*] Sometimes . . . sometimes . . . I just want to die for bein' here.

BIG GIRL: [*Enjoying herself*] Ha ha ha . . . that wouldn't do no good. Would it? Just remember what shape you were in when I met you, kid. Ha ha ha. [*To* JACK] Hey, boy, can you imagine this pretty little trick here had her stomach seven months in the wind, waitin' on a dead baby who died from the same disease that Baby Girl had? . . .

CLARA: He didn't have any nasty disease like Baby Girl!

BABY GIRL: [*Hears her name but looks out door*] NO! NO! SHIT! DAMN! SHIT! SHIT!

BIG GIRL: Haw haw haw . . . Now we got her started . . . [*She laughs for over a minute;* JACK *waits patiently, sipping;* CLARA *is grim.* BABY GIRL *has quieted*] She . . . she . . . ha ha . . . was walkin' round with a dead baby in her and had no place to go.

CLARA: [*Fills a glass*] I just can't understand you, B.G. You know my baby died after he was born. Some days you just get besides yourself.

BIG GIRL: I'm only helpin' ya entertain your guest.

CLARA: Awww . . . B.G. It wasn't his fault. I invited him.

JACK: [*Dismayed*] Well, I asked really. If there's anything wrong I can go.

BIG GIRL: Take it easy, youngblood. I'm just havin' a little fun. Now let's get back to the Clara Saga . . . ya hear that word, junior? S-A-G-A, SUCKER! You college boys don't know it all. Yeah, her folks had kicked her out and the little punk she was big for what had tried to put her out on the block and when that didn't work out . . . [*Mocking and making pretended blushes*] because our sweet little thing here was soooo modest and sedate . . . the nigger split! . . . HAW HAW HAW. . . . HE MADE IT TO NEW YORK! [*She goes into a laughing, choking and crying fit.* BABY GIRL *rushes over to her and on tiptoe pats her back*]

BABY GIRL: Big Girl! Big Girl! Big Girl!

A knocking sounds and CLARA *exits to answer the door.*

BIG GIRL: [*Catches her breath*] Whatcha want, little sister?

BABY GIRL: The cat! The cat! It's got some kittens! The cat got some kittens!

BIG GIRL: [*Still coughing and choking*] Awww, go on. You know there ain't no cats under there with no kittens. [*To* JACK] She's been makin' that story up for two months now about how some cat crawls up under the steps and has kittens. She can't fool me none. She just wants a cat but I ain't gonna get none.

JACK: Why not? Cats aren't so bad. My mother has one and he's quite a pleasure to her.

BIG GIRL: For your mammy maybe, but all they mean round here [*Singsong*] is fleas and mo' mouths to feed. With an invalid aunt upstairs we don't need any mo' expenses.

JACK: [*Gestures toward* BABY GIRL] It shows that she has a very vivid imagination to make up that story about the kittens.

BIG GIRL: Yeah, her big sister ain't the biggest liar in the family.

CLARA *returns with* MISS FAMIE *staggering behind her, a thin middle-aged woman in long seaman's raincoat, dripping wet, and wearing house slippers that are soaked and squish water about the kitchen floor.*

BIG GIRL: Hi, Miss Famie. I see you're dressed in your rainy glad rags today.

MISS FAMIE: [*Slurred speech of the drunk*] Hello, B.G. Yeah, I couldn't pass up seein' Aunt Toohey, so I put on my weather coat. You know that don't a day pass that I don't stop up to see her.

BIG GIRL: Yeah, I know, Miss Famie. Every day you go up there with that quart of gin under your dress and you two ole lushes put it away.

MISS FAMIE: Why, B.G. You should know better than that.

CLARA: [*Reseated*] B.G., you shouldn't say that. . . .

BIG GIRL: Why shouldn't I? I'm payin' for over half of that juice and I don't git to see none of it 'cept the empty bottles.

BABY GIRL: CAT! CAT! CAT!

MISS FAMIE: Oh, the baby still sees them there cats.

CLARA: You should be ashamed to talk to Miss Famie like that.

BIG GIRL: [*To* JACK] Why you so quiet? Can't you speak to folks when they come in?

JACK: I'm sorry. [*To* MISS FAMIE] Hello, ma'am.

MISS FAMIE: Why howdie, son.

CLARA: Would you like a glass of wine, Miss Famie?

MISS FAMIE: Don't mind if I do, sister.

BIG GIRL: Better watch it, Miss Famie. Wine and gin will rust your gizzard.

CLARA: Ohhh . . . [*Pours a glass of wine*] . . . Here, Miss Famie.

BABY GIRL: CAT! CAT!

BIG GIRL: [*Singsong, lifting her glass*] Mus' I tell' . . . muscatel . . . jitterbug champagne. [*Reminisces*] Remember, Clara, the first time I got you to take a drink? [*To* MISS FAMIE] You should of seen her. Some of this same cheap rotgut here. She'd never had a drink before but she wanted to show me how game she was. She was a bright little smart thing, just out of high school and didn't know her butt from a doorknob.

MISS FAMIE: Yes, indeed, that was Clara all right.

BIG GIRL: She drank three waterglasses down and got so damned sick I had to put my finger down her throat and make her heave it up. . . . HAW HAW. . . . Babbled her fool head off all night . . . said she'd be my friend always . . . that we'd always be together . . .

MISS FAMIE: [*Gulps down her drink*] Wine will make you do that the first time you get good 'n' high on it.

JACK: [*Takes a drink*] I don't know. You know . . . I've never really been wasted and I've been drinkin' for quite some time now.

BIG GIRL: Quite some time, huh? How long? Six months?

JACK: Nawh. My mother used to let me drink at home. I've been drinkin' since fifteen. And I drank all the time I was in the service.

BIG GIRL: Just because you been slippin' some drinks out of ya mammy's bottle and you slipped a few under ya belt with the punks in the barracks don't make ya a drinker, boy!

CLARA: B.G. . . . do you have to?

MISS FAMIE *finishes her second drink as* BIG GIRL *and* CLARA *stare at each other.*

MISS FAMIE: Well, I guess I better get up and see Aunt Toohey. [*She leaves*]

BIG GIRL: [*Before* MISS FAMIE *reaches top of stairs*] That ole ginhead tracked water all over your floor, Clara.

CLARA: Makes no never mind to me. This place stays so clean I like when someone comes so it gets a little messy so I have somethin 'ta do.

BIG GIRL: Is that why Jackie boy is here? So he can do some messin' 'round?

CLARA: Nawh, B.G.

JACK: [*Stands*] Well, I'll be going. I see that . . .

BIG GIRL: [*Rises and tugs his sleeve*] Sit down an' drink up, youngblood. [*Pushes him back into his seat*] There's wine here . . . [*Slow and suggestive*] . . . there's a pretty girl here . . . you go for that, don't you?

JACK: It's not that . . .

BIG GIRL: You go for fine little Clara, don't you?

JACK: Well, yes, I do . . .

BIG GIRL: HAW HAW HAW . . .[*Slams the table and sloshes wine*] . . . HAW HAW HAW . . . [*Slow and suggestive*] . . . What I tell ya, Clara? You're a winner. First time I laid eyes on you I said to myself that you's a winner.

CLARA: [*Takes a drink*] Drink up, B.G.

BIG GIRL: [*To* JACK] You sho you like what you see, youngblood?

JACK: [*Becomes bold*] Why, sure. Do you think I'd come out on a day like this for anybody?

BIG GIRL: HAW HAW HAW . . . [*Peals of laughter and more coughs*]

JACK: [*To* CLARA] I was going to ask you to go to the matinee 'round Pep's, but I guess it's too late now.

CLARA: [*Hesitates*] I never been.

BIG GIRL: [*Sobers*] That's right. You never been to Pep's and it's only 'round the corner. What you mean it's too late, youngblood? It don't start getting good till 'round four.

JACK: I thought she might have ta start gettin' supper.

BIG GIRL: She'd only burn it the fuck up too if she did. [*To* CLARA] I'm goin' ta take you to Pep's this afternoon.

CLARA: You don't have ta, B.G.

BIG GIRL: It's my day off, ain't it?

CLARA: But it costs so much, don't it?

BIG GIRL: Nawh, not much. . . . You'll like it. Soon as C.C. comes over to watch Baby Girl we can go.

CLARA: [*Brightens*] Okay!

JACK: I don't know who's there now, but they always have a good show. Sometimes Ahmad Jamal . . .

BABY GIRL: [*Cuts speech*] CAT! CAT! CAT!

BIG GIRL: Let's toast to that. . . . [*Raising her glass*] . . . To Pep's on a rainy day!

JACK: HERE HERE! [*He drains his glass*]

A tumbling sound is heard from the backyard as they drink and BABY GIRL *claps hands as* STOOGIE, BAMA, *and* HOSS *appear in yard doorway. The three boys are no more than sixteen. They are soaked but wear only thin jackets, caps and pants. Under* STOOGIE'S *cap he wears a bandanna to keep his processed hair dry.*

BIG GIRL: What the hell is this?

STOOGIE: [*Goes to* BIG GIRL *and pats her shoulder*] The heat, B.G. The man was on our asses so we had to come on in out of the rain, baby, dig?

BIG GIRL: Well, tell me somethin' I don't know, baby. Why you got to pick mah back door? I ain't never ready for any more heat than I gets already.

STOOGIE: It just happened that way, B.G. We didn't have any choice.

BAMA: That's right, Big Girl. You know we ain't lame 'nuf to be usin' yo pad fo no highway.

HOSS: Yeah, baby, you know how it is when the man is there.

BIG GIRL: Well, what makes a difference . . . [*Smiles*] . . . Hey, what'cha standin' there with your faces hangin' out for? Get yourselves a drink.

HOSS *goes to the sink to get glasses for the trio;* STOOGIE *looks* JACK *over and nods to* BAMA, *then turns to* CLARA.

STOOGIE: How ya doin', Clara? Ya lookin' fine as ever.

CLARA: I'm okay, Stoogie. I don't have to ask 'bout you none. Bad news sho' travels fast.

STOOGIE: [*Holds arms apart in innocence*] What'cha mean, baby? What'cha been hearin' 'bout poppa Stoogie?

CLARA: Just the regular. That your gang's fightin' the Peaceful Valley guys up in North Philly.

STOOGIE: Awww . . . dat's old stuff. Sheeet . . . you way behind, baby.

BAMA: Yeah, sweetcake, dat's over.

CLARA: Already?

HOSS: Yeah, we just finished sign'n' a peace treaty with Peaceful Valley.

BAMA: Yeah, we out ta cool the War Lords now from ov'va on Powelton Avenue.

HOSS: Ole Stoogie here is settin' up the war council now; we got a pact with Peaceful Valley and man, when we come down on those punk War Lords . . . baby . . . it's just gonna be all ov'va.

BIG GIRL: Yeah, it's always one thing ta another with you punks.

STOOGIE: Hey, B.G., cool it! We can't help it if people always spreadin' rumors 'bout us. Things just happen an' people talk and don' understand and get it all wrong, dat's all.

BIG GIRL: Yeah, all of it just happens, huh? It's just natural . . . you's growin' boys.

STOOGIE: That's what's happen'n', baby. Now take for instance Peaceful Valley. Las' week we went up there . . . ya know, only five of us in Crook's Buick.

CLARA: I guess ya was just lookin' at the scenery?

STOOGIE: Yeah, baby, dat's it. We was lookin' . . . lookin' fo' some jive half-ass niggers. [*The boys laugh and giggle as* STOOGIE *enacts the story*] Yeah, we spot Specs from offa Jefferson and Gratz walkin' with them bad foots down Master . . . ha ha ha . . .

BAMA: Tell them what happened to Specs, man.

HOSS: Awww, man, ya ain't gonna drag mah man Bama again?

They laugh more, slapping and punching each other, taking off their caps and cracking each other with them, gulping their wine and performing for the girls and JACK. STOOGIE *has his hair exposed.*

STOOGIE: Bama here . . . ha ha ha . . . Bama burnt dat four-eyed mathafukker in the leg.

HOSS: Baby, you shoulda seen it!

CLARA: Yeah, that's what I heard.

STOOGIE: Yeah, but listen, baby. [*Points to* BAMA] He was holding the only heat we had . . . ha ho ho . . . and dis jive sucker was aimin' at Specs' bad foots . . . ha ha . . . while that blind mathafukker was blastin' from 'round the corner straight through the car window. . . .

They become nearly hysterical with laughter and stagger and stumble around the table.

HOSS: Yeah . . . ha ha . . . mathafukkin' glass was flyin' all over us . . . ha ha . . . we almost got sliced ta death and dis stupid mathafukker was shootin' at the man's bad foots . . . ha ha . . .

BAMA: [*Scratching his head*] Well, man. Well, man . . . I didn't know what kind of rumble we was in.

CLARA *and* BIG GIRL *laugh as they refill their glasses, nearly emptying the jug.* BIG GIRL *gets up and from out of the refrigerator pulls another gallon as laughter subsides.*

BIG GIRL: [*Sits down*] What's the heat doin' after ya?

STOOGIE: Nothin'.

CLARA: I bet!

STOOGIE: [*Sneer*] That's right, baby. They just singled us out to make examples of. [*This gets a laugh from his friends*]

BIG GIRL: What did you get?

HOSS: Get?

BIG GIRL: [*Turns on him*] You tryin' ta get wise, punk?

STOOGIE: [*Patronizing*] Awww, B.G. You not goin' ta take us serious, are ya? [*Silence*] Well, ya, see. We were walkin' down Broad Street by the State Store, see? And we see this old rumdum come out and stagger down the street carryin' this heavy package. . . .

CLARA: And? . . .

STOOGIE: And he's stumblin', see. Like he's gonna fall. So good ole Hoss here says, "Why don't we help that pore man out?" So Bama walks up and helps the man carry his package, and do you know what?

BIG GIRL: Yeah, the mathafukker "slips" down and screams and some cops think you some wrongdoin' studs. . . . Yeah, I know. . . . Of course you didn't have time to explain.

STOOGIE: That's right, B.G. So to get our breath so we could tell our side of it we just stepped in here, dig?

BIG GIRL: Yeah, I dig. [*Menacing*] Where is it?

HOSS: Where's what?

Silence.

STOOGIE: If you had just give me another minute, B.G. [*Pulls out a quart of vodka*] Well, no use savin' it anyway. Who wants some hundred proof tiger piss?

BAMA: [*To* STOOGIE] Hey, man, how much was in dat mathafukker's wallet?

STOOGIE: [*Nods toward* JACK] Cool it, sucker.

HOSS: [*To* STOOGIE] But, man, you holdin' the watch and ring too!

STOOGIE: [*Advancing on them*] What's wrong with you jive-ass mathafukkers?

BIG GIRL: Okay, cool it! There's only one person gets out of hand 'round here, ya understand?

STOOGIE: Okay, B.G. Let it slide. . . .

BABY GIRL: CAT! CAT! CAT!

STOOGIE: [*To* JACK] Drink up, man. Not every day ya get dis stuff.

BAMA *picks up the beat of the music and begins a shuffling dance.* BABY GIRL *begins bouncing in time to the music.*

HOSS: C'mon, Baby Girl; let me see ya do the slide.

BABY GIRL: NO! NO! [*She claps and bounces*]

HOSS: [*Demonstrates his steps, trying to outdance* BAMA] C'mon, Baby Girl, shake that thing!

CLARA: No, stop that, Hoss. She don't know what she's doin'.

BIG GIRL: That's okay, Clara. Go on, Baby Girl, do the thing.

STOOGIE *grabs salt from the table and shakes it upon the floor, under the feet of the dancers.*

STOOGIE: DO THE SLIDE, MAN! SLIDE!

BABY GIRL *lumbers up and begins a grotesque maneuver while grunting out strained sounds.*

BABY GIRL: Uuuhhhhh . . . sheeeee . . . waaaa . . . uuhhh . . .

BIG GIRL: [*Standing, toasting*] DO THE THING, BABY!!!!

CLARA: Awww . . . B.G. Why don' you stop all dat?

STOOGIE: [*To* JACK] C'mon, man, git with it.

JACK *shakes his head and* STOOGIE *goes over to* CLARA *and holds out his hand.*

STOOGIE: Let's go, baby.

CLARA: Nawh . . . I don't dance no mo'. . . .

STOOGIE: C'mon, pretty mamma . . . watch this step. . . . [*He cuts a fancy step*]

BIG GIRL: Go on and dance, sister.

STOOGIE *moves off and the three boys dance.*

CLARA: Nawh . . . B.G., you know I don't go for that kind of stuff no mo'.

BIG GIRL: Go on, baby!

CLARA: No!

BIG GIRL: I want you to dance, Clara.

CLARA: Nawh . . . I just can't.

BIG GIRL: DO LIKE I SAY! DO LIKE BIG WANTS!

The dancers stop momentarily but begin again when CLARA *joins them.* BABY GIRL *halts and resumes her place upon the floor, fondling her toy. The others dance until the record stops.*

STOOGIE: [*To* JACK] Where you from, man?

JACK: Oh, I live over in West Philly now, but I come from up around Master.

STOOGIE: Oh? Do you know Hector?

JACK: [*Trying to capture an old voice and mannerism*] Yeah, man. I know the cat.

STOOGIE: What's your name, man?

JACK: Jack, man. Maybe you know me by Tookie.

STOOGIE: [*Ritually*] Tookie . . . Tookie . . . yeah, man, I think I heard about you. You us'ta be in the ole Jet Cobras!

JACK: Well, I us'ta know some of the guys then. I been away for a while.

BAMA: [*Matter-of-factly*] Where you been, man? Jail?

JACK: I was in the Marines for three years.

STOOGIE: Hey, man. That must'a been a gas.

JACK: It was okay. I seen a lot . . . went a lot of places.

BIG GIRL: Yeah, you must'a seen it all.

STOOGIE: Did you get to go anywhere overseas, man?

JACK: Yeah, I was aboard ship most of the time.

HOSS: Wow, man. That sounds cool.

BAMA: You really was overseas, man?

JACK: Yeah. I went to Europe and North Africa and the Caribbean.

STOOGIE: What kind of boat were you on, man?

JACK: A ship.

BIG GIRL: A boat!

JACK: No, a ship.

STOOGIE: [*Rising,* BAMA *and* HOSS *surrounding* JACK] Yeah, man, dat's what she said . . . a boat!

CLARA: STOP IT ! ! !

BABY GIRL: NO! NO! NO! SHIT! SHIT! SHIT! DAMN! SHIT!

MISS FAMIE'S VOICE: [*From upstairs*] Your aunt don't like all that noise.

BIG GIRL: You and my aunt better mind ya fukkin' ginhead business or I'll come up there and ram those empty bottles up where it counts!

BAMA: [*Sniggling*] Oh, baby. We forgot your aunt was up dere sick.

STOOGIE: Yeah, baby. Have another drink. [*He fills all glasses except* CLARA'S; *she pulls hers away*]

CLARA: Nawh, I don't want any more. Me and Big Girl are goin' out after a while.

BAMA: Can I go too?

BIG GIRL: There's always have ta be one wise mathafukker.

BAMA: I didn't mean nuttin', B.G., honest.

STOOGIE: [*To* JACK] What did you do in the army, man?

JACK: [*Feigns a dialect*] Ohhh, man, I told you already I was in the marines!

HOSS: [*To* CLARA] Where you goin?

CLARA: B.G.'s takin' me to Pep's.

BAMA: Wow . . . dat's nice, baby.

BIG GIRL: [*Gesturing toward* JACK] Ole smoothie here suggested takin' Clara but it seems he backed out, so I thought we might step around there anyway.

JACK: [*Annoyed*] I didn't back out!

STOOGIE: [*To* JACK] Did you screw any of them foreign bitches when you were in Japan, man?

JACK: Yeah man. I couldn't help it. They were all over, ya know?

BIG GIRL: He couldn't beat them off.

STOOGIE: Yeah, man. I dig.

JACK: Especially in France and Italy. 'Course, the Spanish girls are the best, but the ones in France and Italy ain't so bad either.

HOSS: You mean those French girls ain't as good as those Spanish girls?

JACK: Nawh, man, the Spanish girls are the best.

BAMA: I never did dig no Mexican nor Rican spic bitches too tough, man.

JACK: They ain't Mexican or Puerto Rican. They Spanish . . . from Spain . . . Spanish is different from Mexican. In Spain . . .

STOOGIE: Whatcha do now, man?

JACK: Ohhh . . . I'm goin' ta college prep on the G.I. Bill now . . . and workin' a little.

STOOGIE: Is that why you sound like you got a load of shit in your mouth?

JACK: What do you mean!

STOOGIE: I thought you talked like you had shit in your mouth because you been ta college, man.

JACK: I don't understand what you're trying ta say, man.

STOOGIE: It's nothin', man. You just talk funny sometimes . . . ya know what I mean. Hey, man, where do you work?

JACK: [*Visibly feeling his drinks*] Nawh, man, I don't know what ya mean, and I don't go to college, man, it's college prep.

STOOGIE: Thanks, man.

JACK: And I work at the P.O.

BAMA: Pee-who?

JACK: The Post Office, man.

STOOGIE: Thanks, George. I always like to know things I don't know anything about. [*He turns his back on* JACK]

JACK: [*To* BIG GIRL] Hey, what time ya goin' 'round to Pep's?

BIG GIRL: Soon . . . are you in a hurry, young-blood? You don't have to wait for us.

JACK: [*Now drunk*] That's okay . . . It's just gettin' late, ya know, man . . . and I was wonderin' what time Clara's ole man gets home. . . .

BIG GIRL: Clara's ole man? . . . What do you mean, man? . . .

The trio begins snickering, holding their laughter back; JACK *is too drunk to notice.*

JACK: Well, Clara said for me to come by today in the afternoon when her ole man would be at work . . . and I was wonderin' what time he got home. . . .

BIG GIRL *stands, tilting over her chair to crash backwards on the floor. Her bust juts out; she is controlled but furious.*

BIG GIRL: Clara's ole man is home now. . . .

A noise is heard outside as C.C. comes in the front door. The trio are laughing louder but with restraint; CLARA *looks stunned.*

JACK: [*Starts up and feels drunk for the first time*] Wha . . . you mean he's been upstairs all this time?

BIG GIRL: [*Staring*] Nawh, man, I don't mean that!

JACK: [*Looks at* BIG GIRL, *then at the laughing boys and finally to* CLARA] Ohhh . . . jeezus! [*He staggers to the backyard door, past* BABY GIRL, *and becomes sick*]

BIG GIRL: Didn't you tell him? Didn't you tell him a fukkin' thing?

C.C. *comes in. He is drunk and weaves and says nothing. He sees the wine, searches for a glass, bumps into one of the boys, is shoved*

into another, and gets booted in the rear before he reaches wine and seat.

BIG GIRL: Didn't you tell him?

CLARA: I only wanted to talk, B.G. I only wanted to talk to somebody. I don't have anybody to talk to . . . [*Crying*] . . . I don't have anyone . . .

BIG GIRL: It's time for the matinee. [*To* STOOGIE] Before you go, escort my friend out, will ya?

CLARA: Ohhh . . . B.G. I'll do anything but please . . . ohhh Big . . . I won't forget my promise.

BIG GIRL: Let's go. We don't want to miss the show, do we?

CLARA: Please, B.G., please. Not that. It's not his fault! Please!

BIG GIRL: DO LIKE I SAY! DO LIKE I WANT YOU TO DO!

CLARA *drops her head and rises and exits stage right followed by* BIG GIRL. STOOGIE *and his boys finish their drinks, stalk and swagger about.* BAMA *opens the refrigerator and* HOSS *takes one long last guzzle.*

BAMA: Hey, Stoogie babe, what about the split?

STOOGIE: [*Drunk*] Later, you square-ass, lame-ass mathafukker!

HOSS *giggles.*

BABY GIRL: CAT! CAT! CAT!

C.C.: [*Seated, drinking*] Shut up, Baby Girl. Ain't no cats out dere.

MISS FAMIE *staggers from upstairs.*

MISS FAMIE: [*Calling back*] GOOD NIGHT, TOOHEY. See ya tomorrow.

With a nod from STOOGIE, BAMA *and* HOSS *take* JACK'S *arms and wrestle him into the yard. The sound of* JACK'S *beating is heard.* MISS FAMIE *wanders to the yard door, looks out but staggers back from what she sees and continues sprawling toward the exit, stage right.*

BABY GIRL: CAT! CAT! CAT!

C.C.: SHUT UP! SHUT ON UP, BABY GIRL! I TOLE YA . . . DERE AIN'T NO CATS OUT DERE!!!

BABY GIRL: NO! DAMN! SHIT! SHIT! DAMN! NO! NO!

STOOGIE *looks over the scene and downs his drink, then saunters outside. Lights dim out until there is a single soft spot on* BABY GIRL'S *head, turned wistfully toward the yard; then blackness.*

MASSACHUSETTS TRUST

a play in two acts

Megan Terry

Massachusetts Trust was first presented by the Cafe La Mama Troupe as a project of Interact at Brandeis University at the Spingold Theatre, Waltham, Massachusetts, on August 21, 1968, with the following cast:

MINISTER OF INFORMATION	*Kevin O'Connor*
PROSPERITY	*John Bakos*
DEMON	*Sally Kirkland*
SENATOR	*Jerry Cunliffe*
QUEEN	*Mari-Claire Charba*
GENERAL	*Michael Miller*
DR. RAIN OCTANE	*Marilyn Roberts*
HEAD GHOST	*Peter Craig*
BISHOP	*Clay Haney*
FIRST MAN	*Peter Craig*
SECOND MAN	*George Spelvin*
THIRD MAN	*Dana Gladstone*
WOMAN	*Sally Kirkland*
MAN	*Fred Forrest*
THE CHEESE	*Robert Sherman III*

BEAUTIES AND UGLIES, GHOSTS, TREES, SPIDERS AND MUSICIANS: Edward C. Berkeley, Betsy Bernstein, Judith Brier, Bruce Edwards, Patrick Epstein, Dana Ferry, Rhona Goldberg, Sharon Goldberg, Dana Gladstone, Barbara Hecht, Paul Jarocki, Laimon Juris, Natalie Klebenov, Richard A. Morof, Mark J. Roth, Art Sinclair and Carol Zussman.

Direction, music and design by Tom O'Horgan. Production Stage Manager: Robert Patrick. Production Coordinators were Peter B. Reid and Beth Porter. Company Astrologer: Robert O'Connor. Company giraffe keeper: Victor Lipari.

For Elisabeth Marton

ACT I

The curtain opens, or the lights come up or the lights have been up (if it's a proscenium or semiproscenium stage) on a white impression. The sides and top of the stage opening are molded toward the audience. There is a white backdrop, a white ground-cloth. The house lights go down. Silence. Two small white balls close together begin to move across the top half of the stage on a wire toward a larger round white ball moving toward them from the opposite side of the stage. The movement is very slow. So slow as to be finally funny—and it should be timed that when the two small balls penetrate the larger ball, the audience might smile. While this is going on, unseen actors are hissing and breathing over microphones. Then two low-built white thrones, one containing a man, the other a woman painted white from head to foot, begin to move out from stage left and stage right. They come to a point about ten feet apart and there they stop. Their mouths slowly open wide and then close for each sentence that will be said. The sound will come from either side of the wings. All the female actors will be massed nearest the woman and all the males nearest the man (unseen). When all the sentences have been pronounced, the two will be drawn back into the wings. There will be a blackout, and all the white removed.

Through this scene, drums pound like a slow heartbeat. Bells sound intermittently.

WOMAN: I dreamed Earth married Venus.

MAN: I dreamed I knew I was a man.

WOMAN: I dreamed a beautiful dark-haired man promised to commit suicide with a blond girl.

MAN: I dreamed a thin orange-haired, very thin young girl was obsessed with having someone die, or die with her.

WOMAN: And all the planets were fused in a spectacular display of fission.

MAN: The poison was green like crumbled jade.

WOMAN: And the sheets of the bed were really the Yangtze river.

MAN: But the sniper put the guns in the hands of the family.

WOMAN: Then he took out a pair of scissors.

MAN: And everyone was dancing and cheering.

WOMAN: And cut her fingers off at the second knuckle.

MAN: Then the blood was pouring from his mouth.

WOMAN: Where his words had been.

MAN: And my nipples . . .

WOMAN: Were the rosary beads . . .

ALL:

> He was saying.
> He was saying.
> He was saying.
> He was saying.
> He was saying.

BLACKOUT

The lights come up slowly on a black stage. The thirty actors are lying prone on the stage. They are dressed in white turtlenecks and white dungarees. Very slowly on their own prechosen count, they rise and form groups of threes, all the time repeating in low voices: "He was saying, he was saying, he was saying, How bad is it?" Slowly they get into a formation, facing the audience, that looks like a giant mouth opening and closing. This happens three times as they chant, "He was saying." On the final close of the mouth, the MINISTER OF INFORMATION *bursts forth and addresses the audience. The other actors cluster around him.*

MINISTER OF INFORMATION: Ah, good gentles. The latest news.

ACTOR ONE: He was saying.

MINISTER OF INFORMATION: You must make up your minds. . . . [*Chorus of four actors say, "He was saying" backwards*] . . . but you can't without the latest news.

ACTOR TWO: How bad is it?

MINISTER OF INFORMATION: [*Walking casually toward audience*] Lend me your ear and I'll spend my seed in it. [ALL *gesture toward* MINISTER OF INFORMATION *and give a small controlled yell. Strolling off stage*] The news is —that it is too late to make any difference.

ALL *make an abrupt "bloop" sound and turn their backs. Then they abruptly go into their next formation, "I'VE GOT TO HAVE YOU."*

Six men take up positions as musicians. They play on plastic water pipes. Several others play pieces of metal against each other. They keep the beat and the rhythm for the Dancer-Singers.

People disperse, then take fifteen counts to get into their opening formation. As they move, they choose one personal gesture to execute as they move to place.

ALL: I've got to have you. Sucking is essential.

WOMEN: Hello, brother.

MEN: Hello, Mother.

ALL: Baby. Baby.

GIRLS: I love a tongue inside my mouth.

MEN: Hello, lover.

ALL: All ladies must wear bathing caps to keep the drains clean.

All this is danced and sung in a sexy pattern moving down toward the audience. When they reach the edge of the stage, they kneel looking at audience until the MINISTER OF INFORMATION *begins his next speech. Then, one by one, they disperse into the auditorium and carefully choose an audience member whom they look directly in the eye and try to contact nonverbally only by looking.*

MINISTER OF INFORMATION: The hippie accountants have taken over the art world. I've told you this for your information. I don't want to lose you. You must be educated to an edifying inner organic, orgasmic, volcanic cartoon. Because very soon you're going to have a four-day weekend in which to fight with your life. Now here is a point program. First, you must become a movie star. Second, you have got to lose weight. Third, look in the mirror. Fourth, praise the grass. Fifth, take a new name. Sixth, run for office. Seventh, burn the office down. I tell you this for your own good because obviously you can feel that I have your best interests at stake. Finally, do call me anytime you are lonely and I'll let you come over to scratch my back.

All the actors should have left the auditorium and arrived backstage, stage left, by the end of this speech. As the MINISTER OF INFORMATION *finishes his last line he switches on a 1930s white radio on stage right. When the radio goes on, the actors emerge singing. They are arranged in a grotesque, monstrous caravan.*

ALL:
> In every two-pound jar of pineapple
>   preserves
> Swim ten devil-faced roaches.
> They are ready to spray
> Rat poison on the congressmen
> Who carry
> Mafia money
> Concealed in their heels.

The song is sung through twice. On the beginning line of the third time through, the MINISTER OF INFORMATION *switches off the radio.*

MINISTER OF INFORMATION: Those devil-faced roaches! Without the Congressmen and the Mafia, there wouldn't be any prosperity. [*He turns the radio back on. A wagon carrying* PROSPERITY *is pushed downstage*]

CHORUS: Enter Prosperity!

MINISTER OF INFORMATION: A handsome sorcerer!

PROSPERITY: Demons, General, Birds, Senator, Queen, Beauties, Uglies, Trees and Spiders. Clouds and Camembert. I need you now. [*His servants assemble around him*] We must elect a woman.

DEMON: Where?

PROSPERITY: Here.

SENATOR: What, sir, may I put to you? What, sir? What candidate, sir, have they put up against us, sir?

PROSPERITY: I fear they'll find a man.

QUEEN: Not if I find him first.

PROSPERITY: Is there a woman in the house?

TREES *and* SPIDERS: [*Singing*]
> Come forward, don't be afraid
> We'll work to elect any bonny maid.
> Come forward, don't be afraid
> We'll work to elect any bonny maid.

PROSPERITY: Look fondly on me, my beauties and my uglies. Listen with all your hearts and sores. I'm sending you to the four corners of the planet to find for us a candidate. A candidate, fair of face and fair of mind who will consent to be the nation's valentine.

BEAUTIES *and* UGLIES: But Father, what about us?

PROSPERITY: You're too beautiful and you're too ugly. What I need is the stripe in the road. A girl whose hair doesn't quite curl, or whose teeth are a mite agape at the front. Tiny tits, but a winning smile.

BEAUTIES *and* UGLIES: We'll scour every beauty shop.

PROSPERITY: Begone.

BEAUTIES *and* UGLIES: Tiny tits, but a winning smile.

PROSPERITY: [*To the clouds*] Take me for a pollster ride while I sup upon my Camembert. [*Exit stage left. The clouds bear him aloft, he pulls his cheese along with him*]

GENERAL: [*To* SENATOR] I think it's time for a coup.

SENATOR: It's plain to see his nuts have exploded.

GENERAL: Shall we plant a cache of arms in the clouds?

SENATOR: Too obvious.

GENERAL: The trees?

SENATOR: Too risky.

GENERAL: The cheese.

SENATOR: He'd eat them.

GENERAL: But that's a good idea. But that's a good idea. But that's a good idea.

SENATOR: Step aside, General. This crisis calls for statesmanship. And I can just make it. One leaves every half hour on the half hour. [*He takes off in a plane*]

GENERAL: [*Offering his arm to the* QUEEN] Shall we? [*They walk in a stately march time toward the audience*] Your Highness?

QUEEN: Mon General?

GENERAL: Your sweetness?

QUEEN: [*Sexy*] Your sweat.

GENERAL: May I offer you my support?

QUEEN: Are you sure it would be fitting?

GENERAL: Look, Queen. I'm putting it to you straight. The time has come for education.

QUEEN: I couldn't agree more.

GENERAL: We'll have to re-educate the educated masses.

QUEEN: Tell me your plan. [*They exit*]

Repeat "Pineapple Song"

Four women stand together, center stage, singing into a 1930s microphone. They sing "Ooo-ooo-ooo," but not on the same note. They take time to establish their sound and rhythm, then a man and a woman enter and sing the song through in unison.

MAN and WOMAN sing the song through again, then all the men join in with the FIRST MAN. The remaining women join the FIRST WOMAN, but each chooses a different pitch to come in on. They sing the song through in unison, and start it again, but stop abruptly on the syllable "Cong" from "Congressman." The entire troupe is ranged across front of stage as MINISTER OF INFORMATION turns off the radio.

MINISTER OF INFORMATION: He was saying, "How bad is it?" And everyone was dancing and cheering.

The actors form two lines on either side of the stage. They choose a count to come in on. One actor is left center stage. The other actors go back to place. Then they move in on the CENTRAL ACTOR saying the ASSASSINATION lines forward. They pick him up. He screams. They bring him to the floor, he screams. They hold him above their heads and move him clockwise chanting. They bring him to the floor, he screams. They hold him above their heads again and chant backward. They put him on the floor again and back off to their places chanting backward the words to "THE ASSASSINATION SAID BACKWARD."

ALL BUT CENTRAL ACTOR:
He was saying
He was saying
How bad is it?
And everyone
Was dancing and cheering.

Narish nya nisnad zao
nursev na ti si dab wa
nye saw ee
nye saw ee

The actors divide into four groups. Each group finds its own inner-connected formation. They exchange places with the other groups, where they again make the exact formation, "I LIKE YOU TO BE OPEN WITH ME"

GROUP ONE: I like you to be open with me.

GROUP TWO: Is it possible to unify your body?

GROUP THREE: So many messages sent that they tune out.

GROUP FOUR: Inhale through one nostril, exhale from the other.

GROUP ONE: Do you oppose the feeling of people?

GROUP TWO: Pinheads have been in power too long.

GROUP THREE: Attack the bigots, attack the bigots!

Very slowly all the groups come together, hands outstretched, then over their heads, the hands all touching, they turn and move in a solid wall of hands, singing the line that becomes a long held chord.

ALL FOUR GROUPS: THEY HELD HANDS IN SILENT PRAYER.

The chord stops abruptly. The actors sink slowly to the ground as if the air has been let out of them.

MINISTER OF INFORMATION: [*Sings*]
Bombs bursting from His hair
God rides by through the air
He wants you in His sky
God wants you in His lap
Stop all your flap and hide
He'll see you on His next glide
Watch out
Don't get hung
God gets the good and He gets them young.

He moves among the fallen actors with white paint on a plate. As he sings he raises up the actors who are to be GHOSTS in the next scene and paints their faces white. By the end of the song the GHOSTS should have left the stage to be ready to start the next scene. There is a count of three at end of song, the remaining actors rise up and gesture to the oncoming wagon.

ALL: Doctor Rain Octane!

MINISTER OF INFORMATION: A beautiful psychiatrist!

ACTOR ONE: Followed by her ghosts.

DR. RAIN OCTANE: [*As the wagon is pushed down front by the GHOSTS. Writhing on the wagon*] Oh Mother. Oh Mother. Oh Mother. Oh Mother. Oh Mother. Oh Mother. Oh Mother. Oh Mother. Oh Mother. Oh Mother . . . Oh Oh Oh . . .

GHOST ONE: What is it, Doctor Rain?

DR. RAIN: Oh Father. Oh Father. Oh Father. Oh Father. Oh Father. You won't believe it.

GHOST TWO: You can tell me if you want to.

DR. RAIN: It's unspeakable. Unprintable. Unbearable. Unrelenting madness and that son of a bitch Prosperity is just trying to drive me crazy. That's it. That is what he's trying to do, he's trying to drive me crazy and if we don't work fast he'll succeed. Oh baby. Oh baby. Oh baby. Why did you die when I need you now? Where have you gone? Come back, Jack, when I need you now. A council of public relations is called for one minute from now. Prosperity has got to be stopped at all costs. Oh baby. Oh baby.

GHOST THREE: Mother, you're like a sister to me.

DR. RAIN: The pain gets unbearable. If I read another editorial in the *New York Times* I'll be ready for the funny farm.

GHOST FOUR: [*In* New York Times *tones*] A studied balance of the day's opinions is what needs to be squarely faced in black and white.

GHOST FIVE: Doctor Rain. Doctor Rain. Get a hold of yourself. Put an end to all the mewling self-pity. Is this what your grandmothers lashed themselves to the lampposts for? Is this what Sappho invented an Island for? Is this what Lady Macbeth drew a dagger for? Is this what Picasso drew a three-holed nose for? Doctor Rain? Doctor Rain, we hounded you through thirty-three years of insane internship to get you to this? This? You know what to do. You American Annie, whistle for your dog and get up there to the starting line. We're there chewing on the roots of your hair. We'll pursue you till you pay back the money you borrowed.

DR. RAIN: Prosperity is driving me crazy.

GHOST SIX: Run against him.

DR. RAIN: But I can't run against him.

GHOST SEVEN: A mouthpiece will do.

DR. RAIN: Where will I find one?

GHOST SEVEN: Try a man.

DR. RAIN: A man. Yes, a man. A man. Where will I find one?

GHOST ONE: And she has three degrees!

DR. RAIN: I've got to find a man. I'll run my man against Prosperity's woman. [*Going into a trance. . . . In a trance*] By the soft bouncy balls of Doctor Jung, by the coming cream of the Milky Way, by the shining big sea waters, by the side of the road, by the time you read this, by golly and by gosh, when you hear the tone, by God lead us to that mossy Eden where Pan has played with maidenhead. There let us find a man to run in my stead. By all the ghosts of my ancestors. By all the ghosts of my selves I charge you with finding that man. Find me a man. Find me a man with a blooming basket and a winning smile. [*She faints, and has muscle spasms*]

GHOSTS: We're off to the mossy banks of Eden to watch Pan ply his play.

DR. RAIN: [*In a witch's voice*] Don't just watch. Fetch him here.

GHOSTS: For this we didn't go bowling so she could go to college? [*The* GHOSTS *float off at a rapid rate*]

One actor enters center stage and the AS-SASSINATION formation is repeated again.

ALL BUT CENTRAL ACTOR:
> He was saying
> He was saying
> How bad is it?
> And everyone
> Was dancing and cheering.
>
> Narish nya nishad zao
> nursev na ti si dab wa
> nye saw ee
> nye saw ee

At end—designated actors take up positions all over the auditorium. At the indicated places in the following speech the actors in the audience call out their assigned lines.

DR. RAIN: [*Wandering and pacing alone. Fraught*] I've got to plan. I've got to think. I've got to get hold of myself by the back of the neck. They are not going to win.

ACTOR ONE: You have a lovely smile.

DR. RAIN: How dare he run a woman against me. I'm a woman.

ACTOR TWO: Please turn me on.

DR. RAIN: [*To audience*] Even while you're talking peace, I'm washing the dishes.

ACTOR THREE: Life is lousy without love.

DR. RAIN: Even while you're talking peace, I'm feeling sorry for myself.

ACTOR FOUR: God save Massachusetts.

DR. RAIN: Even while you're talking peace, I'm snatching at love.

ACTOR FIVE: Nixon's cheeks are so fat because his mouth is full of shit.

DR. RAIN: Love is very smart. It skips constantly out of my reach.

ACTOR SIX: It's time for an honest man to open his mouth.

DR. RAIN: Love keeps me reaching by letting me touch it once a week.

ACTOR SEVEN: Where do you keep your essential feminine self?

DR. RAIN: What I really need to do is get rid of the dishevelment of living.

ACTOR EIGHT: Does that feel good, baby?

DR. RAIN: I wish I had a groom to pick up after me. I'm not really a girl, I'm a Doctor!

ACTOR NINE: High cholesterol.

DR. RAIN: Yes. Yes. Ah, there's a spine. Look out, Prosperity—

ENTIRE GROUP: He was saying, "How bad is . . ."

When DR. RAIN *finishes her speech* ALL *say:* "*It!*"

DR. RAIN: —hard times are good for the character. [*She marches off, much heartened. Enter the* GHOSTS]

GHOST ONE: How can we get her to see the light?

GHOST TWO: She sees the light.

GHOST THREE: She sees too many lights at once, that's why she's confused.

GHOST FOUR: Do we have to do all the work?

GHOST FIVE: Who else? We're her only ghosts.

GHOST ONE: Prosperity never works, he has millions of handmaidens.

GHOST TWO: Not to mention the Queen, the General, a Senator, a Bishop. All those trees and birds and demons. Five ghosts to do the work of an army of delegates.

GHOST THREE: Let's make a deal with the Beauties and the Uglies.

GHOST FOUR: Yes, they cover more ground than we do.

GHOST FIVE: But we can walk through walls.

GHOST ONE: Then we better get over there and go through the White House.

GHOST TWO: You're right, we've got to find out what the opposition is up to.

GHOST THREE: But that would be spying.

GHOST TWO: Yes, that's exactly what it would be.

ALL: To the White House! [*They float off rapidly. The actors in the audience now mount the stage to form a human throne. They shout these stage directions*]

ACTORS: Enter the Queen, General, Senator and Demon. [*The* GHOSTS *float in from all directions and hover to listen*]

QUEEN: Mon General. Your plan?

GENERAL: It's the simplest plan of all.

QUEEN: Your plans usually are.

BISHOP: [*Rushing on*] What's developed? I just finished the funeral. My God, but that church was filthy. I was up all night scrubbing the pews on my hands and knees.

SENATOR: You're right. It wasn't as clean as the last funeral.

BISHOP: [*Offended*] What do you expect with all the traffic? There's no time between funerals to do anything right.

QUEEN: What was she wearing?

GENERAL: Oleg Cassini, I caught the show on television.

GHOST: No, it was Norell.

QUEEN: You've got to be kidding. She wouldn't be caught dead wearing American.

GENERAL: It's all arranged. Prosperity's going to be shot. Then I can get this country in order at last.

QUEEN: Oh, that's crude. Oh, that's the same old way. Oh God, I can't go through another of those.

GENERAL: It's the safest, surest way.

SENATOR: Assassination by a bullet in the brain bats one thousand.

GENERAL: It's the kindest, fastest, most humane method.

BISHOP: I won't allow it. I absolutely put my foot down. I'm sick to death of eulogies. I want an inauguration. I've got to say something new or my brains will fry.

SENATOR: Isn't there another way? I'm awfully fond of Prosperity.

GENERAL: But look what a mess he's made.

SENATOR: He's willing to step aside. He said so.

GENERAL: But when is it my turn? When is it my turn?

QUEEN: You have a lovely uniform. Learn to be satisfied.

GENERAL: You never let me have my way.

SENATOR: This, sir, is a democracy. Watch yourself.

QUEEN: Suppose *we* find the woman to run for him.

SENATOR: Then she'll be ours. We can extract favors.

QUEEN: We'll do better than that, we'll rule through her.

GENERAL: How can you be sure?

SENATOR: That's right. Some people grow up to fill their office.

QUEEN: We'll make her ourselves [*The* QUEEN *takes the* DEMON's *hand*] Here, Bishop, here's something new for you to do. Lay your hands on this demon and convert her into our candidate, a sweet, young, docile girl.

GENERAL *and* SENATOR: With tiny tits, and a winning smile.

BISHOP: [*Laying hands on the* DEMON, *he prays*] Now hear this. Now hear this O Heavenly Father. This is your most handsome and humble servant the Bishop of Chance begging for your attention and most divine favor. I ask only a second of your time and you will see that we present shall forever be thine grateful servants here on earth. From this day forward, O Heavenly Father, we will cleanse ourselves of all earthly sins and shall spread your name far abroad and your name shall forever be on our lips and in our thoughts. O Heavenly Father, when I was but a small lad . . .

QUEEN: Knock it off. Time is growing short.

BISHOP: O Heavenly Father, I feel your presence and rejoice this day of our Lord. I have here a humble demon in my hands of humility. Look kindly down on this dumb demon, dear Lord, and change it into a dumb woman.

Lightning, thunder, tidal waves, etc. The DE-MON turns into a female.

ALL: Thank you, Dear Lord.

BISHOP: That's more like it. A change is just as good as a vacation.

QUEEN: [*Inspecting her*] Not bad. Not bad.

DEMON: [*Feeling herself all over*] Wow, does this mean I can get laid now?

QUEEN: Not yet, you have work to do. Put her where the Beauties and the Uglies won't fail to find her. [*Leaving with* BISHOP] About the inauguration, I'm wearing diamonds encrusted with pearls.

BISHOP: Splendid, it won't clash with my Bones-of-Saint-Peter cassock.

GENERAL *and* SENATOR: [*Feeling her as they pick her up*] It does have tiny tits.

DEMON: [*Laughing wildly*] And a winning smile. [*They run off*]

GHOST ONE: They've rigged the election.

GHOST TWO: What to do? What to do?

GHOST THREE: Two can play as cheaply as one.

GHOST FOUR: Do you have an idea?

GHOST THREE: We'll change Doctor Rain into a man.

GHOST FIVE: She won't hold still for that.

GHOST THREE: She should see how the other half lives.

GHOST TWO: This is life or death.

GHOST THREE: Man or woman.

GHOST FOUR: All's fair in life or death.

GHOST ONE: All's fair in man against woman.

GHOST TWO: A double threat, a switch-hitter to fool the opposition.

GHOST THREE: I can't wait for the debate.

GHOST FOUR: Quick, let's run out and buy up all the TV time.

They vaporize. One by one three men appear. They are dressed in white hats, white trench coats, white pants and shoes, and white-rimmed sunglasses. They carry white brief-cases. They speak in cordial, but cool business voices.

FIRST MAN: Have a good trip up?

SECOND MAN: Can't complain.

THIRD MAN: Nice tan you got.

SECOND MAN: Keeps me from getting colds in winter.

FIRST MAN: Here's a message from your brother.

SECOND MAN: Is he meeting me?

FIRST MAN: Lisbon.

THIRD MAN: There are three passports here along with the cash and plane tickets. [*They exchange briefcases*]

SECOND MAN: You treat a fellow well.

FIRST MAN: You deserve it, you delivered.

THIRD MAN: You'll be hearing from us.

SECOND MAN: Pleasure doing business with you.

Fade out. PROSPERITY *rides in on his clouds. He sings to his cheese.*

PROSPERITY:
It's good to be in love
It's good to eat my cheese
It's good to look down from above
It's good to share the breeze
With my cheese.

Dear clouds. Sweet clouds. Clouds of fleece and Hell's Angels leather. Drift me to the house of my love, I long to see her stormy weather. I'm the happiest man in the world. I've found the woman of my dreams. Doctor Rain Octane. I never ever, no I never ever hoped to be happy, but now here it is. Her neurosis compliments my psychosis. At last I can lay down the burdens of my office and get back to bed. Prosperity has lived too long in his head. 'Tis time to spread the living around. I'll win Doctor Rain; she's compelled to contest, and that means she'll have to think about nothing but me, her secret love Prosperity for all eternity.

He sings "THE CHEESE SONG" again as he's propelled offstage.

The entire company fills the stage singing. They hold or carry each other in unexpected ways.

ALL:
This country's climate dehydrates my
    eggs.
When cake is eaten right from the
    cunt—
Hope is restored.
Hope is restored.

But for a healthy breakfast—
Drink peppermint semen.

The Queen of Angels contacts my
    crotch
Her flying fingers illuminate our pages
While cherubs float and stroke us—
    sweetly
As we come
As we come
As we come

And you can come too.
Remember . . .
Don't shrink . . .
Every day you must eat and drink.
You come too
You must eat and drink
You come too
You must eat and drink.

A huge table full of marvelous things to eat and drink, beautifully arranged, is wheeled onto center stage.

MINISTER OF INFORMATION: [*Sweetly to audience*] You come too. You must eat and drink.

All the actors go into audience to encourage them to come up on stage to eat and drink. Each actor must in the course of intermission tell his assigned dream (the dreams they are to say in Act II) to at least three members of the audience.

ACT II

After the audience on stage have resumed their seats, the banquet table is removed. All the actors come on stage and sit cross-legged looking at the audience. This goes on for as long as it takes the audience to realize that the actors are looking at them (the audience) with the same sort of impersonal curiosity that the audience usually demonstrates when looking at actors.

Next the actors move into and all over the audience saying lines of their own choosing from the next three columns. When they have finished saying these lines they go back up onto the stage saying one line from group chant on page 306. They get into formations, sitting on the stage on stage left and stage right, again facing the audience as in the opening of the act; but this time they are in a trance state and not curious about the people in the house.

See the dog.
There will be three minutes more.
You're sweet.
Caution—keep contents under pressure.
Men
Women
Men
Women
Men
Women
Men
Man
Woman
Woman

Woman
Man
Woman
Children
Woman Woman
Man Man
Baby
Hi Baby.
Daddy!
Hello sweetheart
American Cleaning Equipment Corporation.
Magic Margin
Tighten cap, tip bottle to fill the well.
I got hot pants for you.
Cigarette smoking may be hazardous to your health.
Oh say can you see any fleas on me.
Exit! Exit! Exit!
One
Please call.
While you were out . . .
One Two
Here it is.
If discomfort persists see your physician.
It's time for the honest man to open his mouth.
One Two Three
I want your pussy
Caution
Onliwon Tissue, New York, New York.
See the dog.
One Two Three Four
Menwomen Menwom-en
Washable black.
Hello brother
Hello Mother
Baby baby baby
You have the dearest smile
Love hair
One Two Three Four Five
Experience is the best teacher
Please turn me on.
Everyone loves a love story.
My money is my baby.
Caution—explosives.
One a day is the only way.
Will you be mine?
I want to put it to you.
One way—do not enter
No that's too fast.
To the south
Hold upright, pull pin, push lever.

I love your tongue in my mouth.

One Two Three Four Five Six

I'm in love with a queen.

No smoking in the gallery

All ladies must wear bathing caps to keep the drains clean.

Hello lover.

Warm a glass or china pot.

You fuck me so good.

One Two Three Four Five Six Seven

Sing it soul Mother

Everybody loves a baby.

Twenty-five dollar fine for spitting.

Sucking is essential.

Follow Directions

Made in America

I've got to have you.

The angel of my heart

The king of my bed

See the pig.

Sign and mail to your nearest office of Internal Revenue.

I love you with all my heart.

Turn right

One Two Three Four Five Six Seven Eight

My sister loves me at last.

I love salted crackers.

God bless America

Jesus the Christ goes in and out with me.

Fuck off—Motherfucker.

One Two Three Four Five Six Seven Eight Nine

The fishing's good off the coast of Florida

Your eyes melt my heart

Sixteen extra measure tea bags

Sock me that cock

The way it all began

This way out

Chinese cheese

No one else can have you

Does that feel good baby?

Where is it on the map?

Yes, yes, yes, yes, yes.

Where do you keep your essential feminine self?

Close cover before striking.

I see God's testicles.

I see by the papers.

I see what you mean

I see a dog

I see a cunt

Look at them necking

No picnicking on the grass

Her baby is sucking her boobies

Area code 617

This is the time for social security

Kiss me again

Screw on top

Lay out all the parts

Ladies and gentlemen, please welcome.

Anything you want, anything!

Half past kissing time, time to kiss again.

High cholesterol.

Fucked up Freak head

Walk with me down memory lane.

I want to eat your pie in the sky.

All the world loves a lover.

There's mother!

Humphrey *was* to Johnson what Lurleen *was* to George.

Life is lousy without love.

Quality Business Papers.

Take my heart

The world of mathematics.

A prince of a fella

To reverse, push down and pull back

Hold me tighter

One Two Three Four Five Six Seven Eight Nine Ten

Man, Woman, Woman, Man.

Come this way.

He was saying, he was saying, he was saying.

How bad is it?

How can we elect a leader when we don't know a man?

How can we elect a woman when we don't know a man?

How can we elect a man when we don't know a woman?

God save the Massachusetts Trust.

He was saying, he was saying, he was saying.

How bad is it?

We're going to feed you soon.

We're going to feed you soon.

We're going to feed you soon.

How bad is it?

> *The actors may choose one of the following lines and interchange the words and images any way they wish:*

God save the United States and this theatre.

Zeus save Massachusetts and this court.

Jesus save the sunshine and this house.

Governor Wallace save the grass and this ice cream.

Kennedy save the planet and this sanity.

Mohammed save the dream and this world.

Buddha save the cigarettes and this fingernail.

Eros save the body and this orgasm.

Mickey Mouse save God and this Republic.

The actors divide into four groups: sopranos, rhythm, tenor and bass. They exchange places on their lines.

GROUP ONE:
> A public trial
> A public trial
> A public trial of extravagance.

GROUP TWO:
> It's you, it's me
> It's you, it's me
> It's you, it's me
> Sugar—!

GROUP THREE:
> A public trial
> A public trial
> A public trial of extravagance.

GROUP FOUR:
> It's you, it's me
> It's you, it's me
> It's you, it's me
> Sugar—!

ALL:
> Now we'll
> Now we'll
> Now we'll
> Exchange
> Clothes
> Clothes.

On the last verse the actors crawl to stage center and exchange clothes in slow motion, as the MINISTER OF INFORMATION *walks down the center runway to give his next speech.*

MINISTER OF INFORMATION: And now for today's headlines! [*Pause*] And now for the story behind those headlines! [*Pause*] The official weather forecast . . . [*Pause*] . . . is rain, pain and laughs down the line and up the fire escape. The bullets will fly on September first. And every good white man better stay indoors under his bed, if he wants to go on living inside a white skin, or soon he will be the color of the bone moon. American red. American blood red. American blood red, running into American blood ground. The official forecast is wear an armband stitched "soul-brother," or bandage yourself from head to foot before going out of your house. Be very extra careful on the way to the A & P—if you can get there, that is. Watch out at the A & P, you may be burned to death as you reach for the ground sirloin. Be sure to dodge the ceiling when it falls. Above all, stop looking people in the eye. Men have been killed for less than that. [*Exit. Enter* DR. RAIN *followed by her* GHOSTS]

GHOST ONE: Doctor Rain, we have a plan.

GHOST TWO: We don't have to look for a man after all.

GHOST THREE: We have one right here in our own backyard.

GHOST FOUR: Since you have such a masculine mind, and the ability to reason fast and sidestep attractively, we've . . .

GHOST FIVE: Come up with the beautiful solution of running you.

DR. RAIN: Of all the lazy cop-outs. Of all the lazy-fuzzy-minded ideas. What good are you ghosts? What good are you? Hock me night and day and never do a decent day's work.

GHOST ONE: But this way you'd have complete control of the debate. They're running a woman.

GHOST TWO: And you are a woman.

GHOST THREE: If you became a man, we'd have twice the chance to win.

DR. RAIN: No. No. No. No. No. No. No. No. No. No. No. No. I spent ten years in deep analysis, searching for that her in me, I won't give up the strain and pain that cost me and cross back over the line. What do you think I am, some tricky-Dixie politician—with a cameleon cunt?

GHOST FOUR: But Doctor Rain . . . don't you see . . . that . . .

DR. RAIN: Prosperity has bought you out. I see the plan now. How could you turn on me? My very own ghosts. My ghosts of my ancestors, my ghosts of myselves. You've offended me to the heart. I knew it. I knew it. Prosperity is trying to drive me crazy. God, adversity makes me smile. There's nothing like anger and suspicion to fuel a good fight. You get back out there in the woods and you come up with a man, and I mean a man. Prosperity, you won't win, I'll see that hard times come back again.

They exit. A coffin on a wagon is placed center stage.

> *Enter* QUEEN, SENATOR, GENERAL, BISHOP *down the aisles. Other actors chant and hum like a dirge.* Four actors walk up the aisle in step carrying giant candles which they place on either side of coffin. As the scene goes on, the other actors file by the coffin, kneel and kiss it, then move on.*

QUEEN: The gin is not successful.

GENERAL: [*Sexy*] I need something.

QUEEN: So do I.

GENERAL: I didn't anticipate company.

---

* Words on page 307.

QUEEN: Everyone is apprehensive, we should all go to bed.

GENERAL: I'm very upset.

BISHOP: Let us pray.

QUEEN: Pull yourself together, baby. If we don't win, this is the last time I'm flying you home.

GENERAL: Don't you understand, if he goes, we go.

QUEEN: An aberration, a momentary ploy. He'll come to his senses. When he hears the debate he'll decide to make a comeback. He'd be lost without us. He's had to deal with us every day of his life. We make a structure. We make a form for him to fit into.

SENATOR: He's putting you on. He's putting you on, to find out if you're thinking about him. You stupid shreeks. Don't you know what he's done? He's put you on to thinking about him. The more you think about him the more you think about him. You're totally engaged with him, and don't you think that's what he wants? I'm retiring this round. I've found a new tax to anticipate and I'm going to go home and sip bourbon and draw up the rules of condensation. I can make the next move if I can see where the town is. Stand aside. I feel decisive.

BISHOP: Let us pray. [*Mounts the wagon behind the coffin and sings to it*]

SENATOR: [*Sings*]
> You remind me of my father
> You have my father's hands
> I have my mother's glands
> Be my brother.
>
> You remind me of my sister
> You have my sister's curls
> I love my sister's girls
> Be my mother.

At this point the song changes to a rock beat and the chorus dances wildly around the auditorium.

> You remind me of my innocence
> You look so pure
> You make me feel unsure
> Be my bank account.
>
> Be my father
> Be my brother
> Be my sister
> Be my mother
>
> You remind me of my father
> You have my father's hands
> I have my mother's glands
> Can't you see
> Why can't you be
> Why can't you be
> Why can't you be me?—

SENATOR: There's time to count. There's time to count the count. I don't have to smile now. I can sit there and count the pluses and minuses of the market where the mark-up is not now stupendous. But the lobbies are expanding. Soon we'll have the iron curtain on the big board.

QUEEN: [*To the* GENERAL] Will you stop swilling my perfume.

GENERAL: A little more. I need a bit. I need a charge. I need a sweet. The smell of your perfume makes me think it's the smell of you and though you know and I know that that isn't true, don't you know that it's nice for me to think I've fooled not only you but me too? Queen?

QUEEN: If they elect a man. I mean a man. You know a man. . . . If they elect a man, I may go over to the other side. The idea has me half way there already.

GENERAL: We'll ignore that act of treachery, but remember it's all noted in your file.

QUEEN: And you have a thousand pictures of my playing time in that file.

GENERAL: Ah yes, taken with my V-shaped microcamera. The colors of your corridor, my dear Highness, are a mini-trip of womanhood.

QUEEN: Mon General.

TREES *and* SPIDERS: (*Dirge*)
> Oh where is Prosperity
> Where is our king
> We want only Prosperity
> He can lead us over the
> Sand
> He can give us fifty-grand
>
> Oh where is Prosperity
> Where is our king
> We want only Prosperity
> He can lead us over the
> Sand
> He can give us fifty-grand

SENATOR: I just had a thought.

GENERAL: Oh, that's a good idea. That's a good idea.

QUEEN: Hush, he may be right.

The three kneel facing right, saying their beads. The BISHOP *stands behind them intoning his speech and making signs over their heads.*

BISHOP: If Prosperity leaves us, there are dark days ahead. You will be stripped of all your clothes and leaves. You will have no food. You will have to make your own bed. There will be no signs for getting ahead. And you will have no money.

ALL: Oh no. Oh no. Not no money. Oh my no. Not no money.

BISHOP: [*Chanting*] No money honey. [*Spoken*] Get to work. Knock on every door and I'll ring the bells.

SENATOR: Now calm down. Let a man of experience soothe your troubled waters. Don't you see, he's toying with us. He's bored, that's all. After eighty months of constant economic expansion he wants us to walk off the cliff for him. But he's giving us a thrill. Don't you see, you've been getting bored with Prosperity too. Now he's immediate again because we may lose him.

BISHOP: I don't think you're right. But whether you are or not, we must all work together to support the candidate of our creation or the opposition could trample us out of our offices.

QUEEN: General, you run out and buy up all the TV time.

GENERAL: Oh, that's a good idea. That's a good idea.

ALL: [*As they exit, they chant*] To the White House! [*They feel up each other's asses on the way out*]

The actors run out and take up positions around the theatre. This becomes a chain of words in rhythm, bouncing all over the house. Each actor is to speak only two syllables.

It's you

It's me

It's you

It's me

It's you

It's me

Su-gar.

This is repeated around the entire group. It's important to say the syllables; do not sing them.

MINISTER OF INFORMATION: Violence must organize. The masses do not understand handshakes. We will have to take time for public dreaming. If I hit your hairdo with a hammer, would anything happen inside your head? Pull off your house and blankets. Raise your eyes and contemplate the collective wisdom of this great body. Thirty-six, twenty-four, thirty-six.

One by one, three men appear. They speak cordially, but are a little more tense than their first meeting.

FIRST MAN: Have a good trip back?

SECOND MAN: One close call.

THIRD MAN: Do you have a cold?

SECOND MAN: Just a touch.

THIRD MAN: Here's some antibiotics. You can't afford to be sick right now.

FIRST MAN: Here's a message from your brother.

SECOND MAN: Is he meeting me?

FIRST MAN: They took him in.

SECOND MAN: You can count on him.

THIRD MAN: We're not taking any chances.

FIRST MAN: Is there anything you wanted to say to him before he's silenced?

SECOND MAN: I told you you could trust him. He won't talk no matter what they do to him. He's my brother. He's like me.

THIRD MAN: Is there anything you want to say to him?

SECOND MAN: Tell him not to worry. That I'm right behind him, and we'll get him off.

They exchange briefcases. Blackout. The actors who have been in the audience now debate one another as members of the opposing sides. Each time they speak they turn on a flashlight below their chins so that the audience can easily find them and know where and from whom the voice is coming.

ONE: I'm sick of having a tiny-titted candidate shoved down our throats again. I think we should stop and decide what it is we want.

TWO: We have clear orders. It isn't easy to deliver, but we know what we have to do.

THREE: I agree with him, perhaps we could find someone better.

FOUR: We've done all right with Prosperity and I'm sticking with him. He wasn't born yesterday.

FIVE: But you were. Why can't you learn to think for yourself!

SIX: What I'd like to see is a candidate of integrity and authority who could set a precedent that ideals are not suspect, but that ideals are energy, the proper energy for setting this world to rights again and pointing the way to a new world, with honor and justice for all.

FOUR: Just what ideals do you propose?

TWO: Don't knock the system, if you haven't got a better plan to replace it with.

SIX: But we could take the time now to work one out.

FOUR: There is no time, the convention is just minutes away.

TWO: Doctor Rain gave us her specifications, and I for one aim to not disappoint her.

SIX: Pig sucker.

TWO: Check the idealist and his name calling.

ONE: Shut up and find your candidate.

TWO: Leave me alone. You can't talk to me like that.

THREE: I can talk to you any way I want to.

FOUR: When we win, that kind of talk will be grounds for never-never-land.

SIX: You won't win.

THREE: You and how many mothers say so?

FIVE: We don't have to say. We have the votes. And the votes tell the story.

ONE: I'm sick to death of your stories. There are going to be some new stories.

TWO: Shut up. We know what we have to do. There's no room for heresy.

ONE: Heresy? This isn't heresy. I only want room for my voice. I only want room for my feeling.

THREE: Fuck your feeling.

ONE: Get the hell up there and work. This is getting us nowhere. [*They start back up to the stage*]

TWO: No one gives a good God damn what you think.

ONE: I don't believe that.

THREE: Don't wake up, fool, just do what you're told. [*A general fight begins. It becomes more and more ferocious until they all sink to the stage, worn out and wanting sleep*]

FIVE: Give me room.

SIX: Grab him.

FOUR: I'll back you up.

FIVE: Kill him.

SIX: Fascist.

FOUR: Commie kook. [*Here they begin to sink to floor*]

FIVE: Shut up—some people are trying to sleep.

ONE: Some have never waked up.

FOUR: Shut up—I'm really pissed!

THREE: Don't drink so much.

They are now asleep. A moment of stillness.

DREAM SEQUENCE: *The actors, on a count of their own choosing of from 1 to 40, stand and then sit on either side of the stage, facing the audience, and say in unison in hypnotic tones:*

I
Dreamed
Earth
Married
Venus

Then, on another count, they leave the first groups and form up downstage at the apron where they make an arc of bodies across the stage spilling into the house.

They say "I — dreamed — Earth — married — Venus" once more as they move to form the arc.

They caress each other as they tell their dreams. The first few dreams will be heard by the whole audience but as more and more join the first DREAMERS, only audience members in the DREAMERS' immediate vicinity will be able to hear a particular dream. The dreams should be given out to the actors at random without regard to sex. The only dream that should be definitely assigned is the ASSASSINATION DREAM, which the actor who is to play the MALE CANDIDATE must have.

I dreamed I was in Los Angeles with Bobby. I was in his caravan. A dragon with sweet eyes and a fiery tongue carried me down the street behind him in his cavalcade on the way to the kitchen. He was blowing kisses to everyone, but all the kisses landed on my cheeks. I like your eyes, he said. All my children have eyes and I love them very much. Ethel was beside him and everyone was dancing and cheering. Ethel was beside him and everyone was dancing and cheering. I groove on your word, I said. I groove on your groove, I said. And I was dancing and cheering. Then ten men with one hand raised a hand gun. Bobby went forward to shake the gun and kiss the gun and throw his hair to the gun. And I was dancing and cheering. Then the blood was pouring from his mouth where his words had been, and my nipples were the rosary beads he was saying. He was saying. He was saying. He was saying. He was saying—"How bad is it?" And everyone was dancing and cheering.

As each actor finishes his dream, he breaks from his place in the arc and crouches in another area center stage. Here he begins the unison section of the dream. The empty space he leaves is to be still caressed by the remaining actors. The unison section is repeated until all the actors have joined the NEW GROUP. The NEW GROUP maintain eye contact with the audience. When all the actors have joined the SECOND GROUP, the group slowly rises, torsos leaning toward the audience, they move backwards upstage and whisper the whole unison speech again.

I dreamed a thin, orange-haired, very thin young girl was obsessed with having someone die or die with her. She conceived of and put forward many plots, including a whole family or group who were being picked off by a sniper. But the sniper put the guns in the hands of the family and then made them eat poison. But it wasn't poison, it was grape juice. He did that to fool her, even though he was something of a zombie himself. Someone called the police and we were ordered to run from the sniper toward the police. The orange-haired girl ran too. As we neared the police she raised her hand, and the police shot her. And I said to her, You finally made it. Then the blood was pouring from his mouth where his words had been, and my nipples were the rosary beads he was saying. He was saying. He was saying. He was saying. He was saying—"How bad is it?" And everyone was dancing and cheering.

I dreamed I knew I was a man. I got my degree and it said Mister on it. But even though I got my degree they wouldn't let me off campus. I had to go through my last semester all over again. The trouble was that my advisor gave me a yellow paper with my room numbers on it that had been caught in the rain. I couldn't make out the room numbers where my classes were being held, because the numbers had been washed off the yellow paper. I couldn't ask my advisor to make me out a new slip because he'd gone on vacation and locked up his room. I spent the next three months looking for my classrooms. Then the next three years. Then the next thirty years, but they wouldn't let me graduate. Then the blood was pouring from his mouth where his words had been, and my nipples were the rosary beads he was saying. He was saying. He was saying. He was saying. He was saying— "How bad is it?" And everyone was dancing and cheering.

I dreamed I was in bed with my mother and father and brother. I was in the middle. It was Sunday morning. Everybody smelled good. I was hot in my crotch while they read me the Sunday funnies. I liked to look at the color of the Blondie and Dagwood colors. All the colors swam into my crotch. I closed my eyes and listened to my father read while my mother giggled. My father played all the parts, and my mother kept petting my hair. I felt so happy. Then the blood was pouring from his mouth where his words had been, and my nipples were the rosary beads he was saying. He was saying. He was saying. He was saying—"How bad is it?" And everyone was dancing and cheering.

I dreamed that Earth married Venus. The planets were fused in a spectacular display of fission and gas. I was stationed on the moon so that I could see the whole thing. The orbits erupted and the Earth went pell-mell into the uterus of Venus. Immediately Venus began to spew forth a hundred pretty moons. I took Polaroid pictures of each moon as it emerged. The Earth was smiling and smiling. Then the blood was pouring from his mouth where his words had been, and my nipples were the rosary beads he was saying. He was saying. He was saying. He was saying—"How bad is it?" And everyone was dancing and cheering.

I dreamed I was eating smoked salmon at the dinner table. My grandmother kept staring and staring at me. I knew she loved me, and watched me all the time. I knew she couldn't get enough of looking at me. I pulled out The New York Times and started to read it. Slowly I brought the paper up all the way till it covered my face. My grandfather said that it wasn't polite to read at the table. I told him I was tired of yearnings I couldn't do anything about. Then I went outside and built a treehouse in the blackberry bushes. Then the

blood was pouring from his mouth where his words had been, and my nipples were the rosary beads he was saying. He was saying. He was saying. He was saying. He was saying —"How bad is it?" And everyone was dancing and singing.

I dreamed I was swimming with Esther. She's the greatest Queen swimmer of all. We were swimming a four-leaf clover. The clover split into two parts, and I lost Esther. I couldn't find Esther, but Moses found me. He took me by the hand and fed me pomegranates. The pomegranates weren't fruit, they were type face. Everytime I ate a piece of type, abcdefgh or i, Marshal McLuhan would laugh at me, and then my father would strike me across the mouth. I'd eat another piece of type face and say to him. I don't care, Dad. I don't care, Dad. I don't care, Dad, because I hate you, Dad, and there's nothing you can do to me because I've found a new father. Then the blood was pouring from his mouth where his words had been, and my nipples were the rosary beads he was saying. He was saying. He was saying. He was saying. He was saying —"How bad is it?" And everyone was dancing and cheering.

I dreamed I was driving my old forty-one Mercury coupe. I loved that car, it had cute chrome accents around the back and front of its fenders. Even though I loved the car, I was compelled to trade it in. First I traded it in for a forty-nine Merc. It was the best year they ever had for Mercs. Then I traded it for a fifty-two Chev which I worked on like a son-of-a-bitch to strip down and tune up. Then I traded that for a wagon, it was red and said Speed Dragon on the side, but the motor was missing. When I investigated the wagon I found that it had never had a motor and that I would have to provide the power. I was too tired for that by then and so I went deeply asleep. Then the blood was pouring from his mouth where the words had been, and my nipples were the rosary beads he was saying. He was saying. He was saying. He was saying. He was saying—"How bad is it?" And everyone was dancing and cheering.

I dreamed a beautiful dark-haired man promised to commit suicide with a blond girl. But he just pretended to do so and the girl found out that he just wanted to trick her. The poison was green, like crumbled jade and there were two white earrings that materialized when the glass was empty. Nobody died. They took off their clothes to put on the earrings. Then the blood was pouring from his mouth where his words had been, and my nipples were the rosary beads he was saying. He was saying. He was saying. He was saying. He was saying—"How bad is it?" And everyone was dancing and cheering.

I dreamed—two women—sisters—a big strange house. So I said to him do you have an extra needle, sweetheart? I'll take you past the laundry. A man sits there in a chair reading the newspaper all day. You can get anything there, anything if he knows you, but he won't sell to Japanese. I know they look like they're on it, but he has some hangup about not selling to Japanese. Back at the house: Let's do it? There's still so much time left in the day and we're very calm. They go into a room, the walls are made of bed sheets. Are we going to take pills or the needle? We're going to make love. Just don't kiss me. I'm your sister and that would be disgusting. They embrace and make love. Visitors, strangers and friends burst in on them. They wish to continue making love, and keep searching for a place where they won't be seen. They finally climb up into the attic. The floor of the attic is like a giant mattress, that curves with same pitch as the roof. Then the blood was pouring from his mouth where his words had been, and my nipples were the rosary beads he was saying. He was saying. He was saying. He was saying. He was saying—"How bad is it?" And everyone was dancing and cheering.

I dreamed they were going to interview me on a half-hour TV show, but made me dress like a beatnik so that I would look younger. They wanted me to sit in a chair and be very cocky. We could see the TV at the same time that we were being interviewed. Someone drove a jeep right at a beachhouse, and there were guns on the sand. The interior of the car was filled with valuable secret loot, and two little boys kept trying to see what it was. The girl driving kept trying to destroy everything, and I kept trying to calm her. She was crying and crying and shooting guns, but they didn't hurt anything. I held onto her breasts till she calmed down. Then the blood was pouring from his mouth where his words had been, and my nipples were the rosary beads he was saying. He was saying. He was saying. He was saying—"How bad is it?" And everyone was dancing and cheering.

I dreamed I was standing on a street corner, trying to collect guns. "Ladies and lovers, I have a petition. Ladies and lovers, I wish you to sign my petition. Sign here, ladies and lovers. We will wipe out assassins. Turn in your guns. We'll melt all the guns into computers. You will no longer have to carry a rattlesnake inside you. Stop frowning, ladies and lovers, sign here and hand me your gun. Step forward.

Step forward and hand your gun to me. You can trust me, ladies and lovers. You can trust me." Then the blood was pouring from his mouth where the words had been, and my nipples were the rosary beads he was saying. He was saying. He was saying. He was saying. He was saying — "How bad is it?" And everyone was dancing and cheering.

I dreamed my father asked me to play golf. I kept slicing the ball into the left rough. Don't slice the ball, my father kept saying. You have to keep your head down and your mouth shut. That's the only way you'll get ahead on the fairway. Then the blood was pouring from his mouth where his words had been, and my nipples were the rosary beads he was saying. He was saying. He was saying. He was saying. He was saying—"How bad is it?" And everyone was dancing and cheering.

I dreamed I was in a riot in Newark. I drank a Molotov cocktail and ran at a tank. I blew up the tank and half a block with it. Then I drank a lazy dog bomb. They flew me over New York and I bombed the port of authority. Then I drank an atomic bomb. The fallout was so perfectly planned and directed that when they released me from the supersonic bomber, I bombed every major, ugly, sprawling city in the world. Then I drank grass seed, and peed it on the ground till there was green for as far as you could see from the viewpoint of a helicopter. Then the blood was pouring from his mouth where his words had been, and my nipples were the rosary beads he was saying. He was saying. He was saying. He was saying. He was saying—"How bad is it?" And everyone was dancing and cheering.

I dreamed I was sleeping with a man of sixty. He was lying on top of me. He was moaning and crying. The sheets of the bed were really the Yangtze River and we were a page in a book about China. He was crying and lying on top of me, he was pleading with me to sleep with his wife. "You see," he said, "She's a lesbian. The only way she lets me near her is if the covers are between us. I can lie on top of her if the covers are between us from head to toe. I'm exhausted. Please do me this favor," he said. I looked at him and floated back down the river. Then the blood was pouring from his mouth where his words had been, and my nipples were the rosary beads he was saying. He was saying. He was saying. He was saying. He was saying—"How bad is it?" And everyone was dancing and cheering.

I dreamed I was trying to get my girl friend to marry me. For some reason I thought all I had to do was put my tongue in her ear. But that wasn't enough. She wanted me to be able to get an apartment. She wanted to sleep there with me in peace for a year, before she made up her mind to stay with me forever. I knew I wanted her with me in my bed every night of the week. But she was afraid that she'd get used to me and she liked danger and excitement. She wanted a new me any time and every time she saw me. But I wanted her to marry me. I never thought I would want to be married and I held onto her breasts and begged her to go with me to the garage, where I was certain I would find someone to marry us. Then the blood was pouring from his mouth where his words had been, and my nipples were the rosary beads he was saying. He was saying. He was saying. He was saying—"How bad is it?" And everyone was dancing and cheering.

I dreamed I made a deal with God, but I had to go through hell to do it. I prayed until there was no water left in my body. I looked like a piece of dried beef. I prayed and banged my head against the wall all night long to get God to hear me. I wanted him to let me go to hell in my father's place. My father was lost and mean and a drunken lecher. But I loved my father and wanted him to go to heaven. I begged God to let me go to hell in my father's place so that he could be well here on earth. Then the blood was pouring from his mouth where his words had been, and my nipples were the rosary beads he was saying. He was saying. He was saying. He was saying. He was saying—"How bad is it?" And everyone was dancing and cheering.

I dreamed I bought a machine gun with my week's salary. The minute I bought the gun, I knew where I was going to go with it. I bought a New York Post and read where they were having sales. I went to Klein's on Union Square. The ladies were lined up five abreast to get into the bargain days. I waited till at least half of them were in the store. I chewed on a Nathan's hotdog the whole time. When enough were in the store, I rented a trapeze, strung it up on the main floor. I swayed gracefully over the crowd on my trapeze and machine-gunned every shopper in sight. Then the blood was pouring from his mouth where his words had been, and my nipples were the rosary beads he was saying. He was saying. He was saying. He was saying. He was saying—"How bad is it?" And everyone was dancing and cheering.

I dreamed I was with my husband. We had been laughing and playing with each other, but we couldn't find our sex. We played and made mud pies and we laughed and we dared each other to eat dirt. Three ghosts rose up from the dirt and we changed into water.

While in the water we were the water, but we could see our reflections in the water. The ghosts reached down a sheeted hand and pulled us out. The ghosts joined us to one another and we were a rope. The rope caught fire and we came together and it was the best yet. Then the blood was pouring from his mouth where his words had been, and my nipples were the rosary beads he was saying. He was saying. He was saying. He was saying. He was saying—"How bad is it?" And everyone was dancing and cheering.

I dreamed that the F.B.I. was going through my wastebasket. They carefully smoothed out every piece of paper and put it in Saranwrap, so they could read it while keeping it from fraying. I was very impressed with the meticulous care they showed my work. I didn't treat it that way. They are precision trained, the F.B.I., and save everything, because it might add up to something. Nevertheless, I left terribly apprehensive, because I thought they might know more about my work than I did. I was in the dark, and I felt hounded, but I couldn't stop watching them work. They knew what to do and I didn't. Then the blood was pouring from his mouth where his words had been, and my nipples were the rosary beads he was saying. He was saying. He was saying. He was saying. He was saying—"How bad is it?" And everyone was dancing and cheering.

I dreamed I was a beautiful boy in a hot African brothel. The room was yellow and smelled of jasmin. The bed was wet and smelled of me. He came into the room and I changed instantly into a cunt. My breasts hurt me because I was just about to get my period. He flipped me in the bed and the bed was dry, his breath was moist and drilled a hole through my back to the middle of my heart. I came and came and came and came on his breath before he even penetrated me. I think he knew it, but I was flying so high in his beautiful balloon that I didn't have time to tell him. The moment he was inside me, I knew I was a boy, and I rejoiced. Then the blood was pouring from his mouth where his words had been, and my nipples were the rosary beads he was saying. He was saying. He was saying. He was saying. He was saying —"How bad is it?" And everyone was dancing and cheering.

I dreamed I was asleep. I was breathing and dreaming in my bed. Suddenly I was awake and terrified. Someone was in the room with me. I knew he was there to rape and kill me. I didn't move. I could smell him. I could smell his foul sweat as he moved closer to the bed. My girl friend was right beside me.

I wasn't afraid for her, though. I knew it was me he was after. I thought at first that I wasn't moving because I wanted to fool him. But then I found out I couldn't move. I couldn't breathe. And I wanted to scream. I couldn't open my mouth and the sweat was filling my eyes. I kept scratching my girl friend on the elbow asking for help. Then the blood was pouring from his mouth where his words had been, and my nipples were the rosary beads he was saying. He was saying. He was saying. He was saying. He was saying— "How bad is it?" And everyone was dancing and cheering.

I dreamed I was married to an Australian Bushman. He was very good to me. I got to carve all his arrows. But he got mad at me because I didn't want him to have another wife. He shook me hard, he shook me good, he screwed me hard and he screwed me good and he told me that I was a silly thing because he needed five more wives. You are only the beginning, he said. Make me some sourdough pancakes and make them good. The pancakes were good. He liked them because they turned into five dollar bills. He was so happy he licked each one of my ten fingers to show his gratitude and promised not to get any more wives until tomorrow. Then the blood was pouring from his mouth where his words had been, and my nipples were the rosary beads he was saying. He was saying. He was saying. He was saying. He was saying—"How bad is it?" And everyone was dancing and cheering.

I dreamed I was sitting at the breakfast table, eating frosted flakes and walnut hotcakes. My mother came into the kitchen and kissed me. She held something behind her back. As I poured more syrup on my hotcakes, she raised her arms. She was carrying an axe. She hit me five times with the axe, but I didn't die. I cried and cried. I spent the whole night trying to get all the five selves back together again. Then the blood was pouring from his mouth where his words had been, and my nipples were the rosary beads he was saying. He was saying. He was saying. He was saying. He was saying—"How bad is it?" And everyone was dancing and cheering.

I dreamed a fat greasy man of youngish age was sitting in the middle of my room. Wesson oil oozed from all his pores. He was sitting on many mattresses. I was one of the mattresses. There were four beautiful young women sitting on sponges on top of the mattresses sitting in a circle around him. The fat greasy man kept throwing pillows all around the room. Then he picked up dish after dish of food and tasted it. When he had

let the taste of the dish fill his tongue, he would throw the food at the walls. Food ran down all the walls of the room onto the mattresses. Knives hung all over the walls. The food began to cover the knives. This made the fat greasy man very angry and he pulled all the knives off the wall. He had many hands. He fought with the four women. They struggled in silent motion for their lives. Slowly he slashed and stabbed the women in the right side. The last woman tried to get the knife away. She got it from him, but he got her down on top of me, the mattresses. I could feel her heavenly ass pressed into me. He got her down and sat on her breasts, then he took out a pair of scissors and cut her fingers off at the second knuckle, one by one. Then the blood was pouring from his mouth where his words had been, and my nipples were the rosary beads he was saying. He was saying. He was saying. He was saying. He was saying—"How bad is it?" And everyone was dancing and cheering.

I dreamed I went to the opera. The opera lasted a week and it was in a cinerama theatre. It was beautiful. The songs, the women. All with pretty breasts, and the men all with ample baskets. It was exhilarating to see all that masculinity and femininity on the stage and they could sing besides. I enjoyed myself over and over. I applauded and yelled like a banshee. I never wanted the opera to stop. I only wished I could remember the plot because I had so much fun. Then the blood was pouring from his mouth where his words had been, and my nipples were the rosary beads he was saying. He was saying. He was saying. He was saying. He was saying—"How bad is it?" And everyone was dancing and cheering.

I dreamed I was in bed, and my mother brought me a breakfast tray. On it was a yellow flower. A dead rat. A piece of soap. My mother was smiling and she kissed me. I hugged her with all my heart, but when I let go of her I found out she was wearing my cock. Then the blood was pouring from his mouth where his words had been, and my nipples were the rosary beads he was saying. He was saying. He was saying. He was saying. He was saying—"How bad is it?" And everyone was dancing and cheering.

I dreamed I was trying to make split pea soup. My boyfriend was sitting on top of the refrigerator asking me for more soup. I told him to wait a minute because I couldn't find the onions. I went to the store to buy onions and carrots. I like to put carrots in split pea soup, one or two. It lightens the flavor. On the way I had to stop off at Poland to buy some dried mushrooms. There in the wood I saw my boyfriend making love to the grass. Stop doing that, I said. You're crushing my mushrooms. Then the blood was pouring from his mouth where his words had been, and my nipples were the rosary beads he was saying. He was saying. He was saying. He was saying. He was saying—"How bad is it?" And everyone was dancing and cheering.

I dreamed I was dead. But I was also above ground. I looked down at the tombstone. I read my name. It seemed that I had lived after all. I looked at the next tombstone. There was my father's name. I looked back and forth from one tombstone to another and read our names aloud. It was very difficult, because my throat ached. My head was very clear, and I was sure I felt no emotion, but my throat ached harder than at any time in my life. Worse than when I had strep throat. The ache was unbearable, and then pus, yellow pus with green pieces of seaweed began to gush on the ground from my mouth. Then the blood was pouring from his mouth where his words had been, and my nipples were the rosary beads he was saying. He was saying. He was saying. He was saying. He was saying—"How bad is it?" And everyone was dancing and cheering.

I dreamed I was with my mother and stepfather and my father and stepmother. We were at the beach to dig clams. I carried the gunny sack. On the way to the beach were a series of docks. But they weren't ordinary docks. The docks were built like traps. The docks were beautiful but treacherous. As you walked along the dock, a panel might slide open and swallow you up. I saw what was ahead of me and ran. I ran and dodged. And dock after dock opened up to swallow me. The gunny sack changed into a wheelbarrow, and it was harder for me to run. The others kept calling to me to hurry. I ran as fast as I could, but the whole dock opened up. I leaped in the air. I landed on a piling with a seagull. Then the blood was pouring from his mouth where his words had been, and my nipples were the rosary beads he was saying. He was saying. He was saying. He was saying. He was saying—"How bad is it?" And everyone was dancing and cheering.

"ASSASSINATION DANCE":
Five actors sit to one side and are the musicians. They clap the rhythm. The remaining actors take up positions in two lines on either side of the stage. They change places with each other, somehow during the cross they exchange a gesture. One actor is left in center stage. The actors move in on the CENTRAL ACTOR, *chanting.*

They lift him up; he screams. They turn him above their heads in clockwise position, then counterclockwise, repeating the chant backward. Between the two turns, they drop him to the floor, and he screams again. After the second turn, they leave him center stage and creep back to their original places backward, and chanting backward.

ALL but CENTRAL ACTOR:
    He was saying
    He was saying
    How bad is it?
    And everyone
    Was dancing and cheering.

    Narish nya nisnad zao
    nursev na ti si dab wa
    nye saw ee
    nye saw ee

MALE ACTOR *says alone after the actors have put him down for the last time:*

MALE ACTOR: How can we elect a leader when we can't even find a human?

The QUEEN *appears center stage, her hands held over her eyes for a count of ten. Then the actors mill around rapidly at a very rapid rate. Four beats of silence to get into the circle. Bang. The company is in position on stage. They begin to walk to a beat. One of the musicians makes a loud noise. The* QUEEN *chooses an actor and says: "You!" The* DREAMER *steps forward to tell his dream. The rest of the company joins into groups of three and there they make a combined physical reaction to the dream. Two groups form in the aisles of the auditorium. There will be five or six other lighted areas for the other groups to work in.*

When the chosen DREAMER *walks down the runway to tell his dream to the audience, the company starting with a low hum that evolves into an "OOOWWWW" with rising volume makes this sound as they get into their groups. This goes for seven beats, and cuts off immediately and the* DREAMER *speaks. In this way, usually, a different dream will be spoken each night.*

A young MAN *enters carrying a young* WOMAN. *He runs with her. She screams. He drops her. She laughs. He runs alone. She screams. Slowly the actors wake up, but are still in a torpor. The young* MAN *picks up the* WOMAN *and throws her in the air.*

WOMAN: Is this all there is to it?

MAN: I've only knocked on your door.

WOMAN: Why is it illegal if this is all there is to it?

MAN: I've only rung your buzzer.

WOMAN: What's all the shouting about?

MAN: [*Reaching for a breast*] May I start your motor?

WOMAN: Leave me alone.

MAN: You've been alone all your life.

WOMAN: I like it.

MAN: Why did you come with me?

WOMAN: You took me.

MAN: Not yet. [*The actors come more awake*]

WOMAN: All my life I've just wanted to be left alone.

MAN: Alone with me.

WOMAN: Alone with me.

MAN: All your life you prayed to God for a man like me.

WOMAN: Can I learn from you?

MAN: I'm wiser.

WOMAN: Can I lean on you?

MAN: I'm stronger.

WOMAN: Can I count on you?

MAN: I'm rich as a cherry tree.

WOMAN: I've never known a man.

MAN: [*Embracing her*] Now you shall know me.

The actors are thoroughly aroused. The YOUNG LOVERS *are in a deep kiss.*

The BEAUTIES *and the* UGLIES *run in and grab the young* WOMAN. *The* GHOSTS *fly in and grab the* MAN.

GHOSTS: A blooming basket and a winning smile.

BEAUTIES *and* UGLIES: Yes, yes, she fits the tape. Tiny tits and teeth agape. Half curled hair and a common maid. Tiny tits and a winning smile! [*They run off with the* WOMAN. GHOSTS *bring the young* MAN *downstage*]

GHOST ONE: Thank God we found one.

GHOST TWO: He measured out well.

GHOST THREE: I can't wait to rest in peace.

GHOST FOUR: If he gets elected she'll have to retire.

GHOST FIVE: Thank God, I can't stand being half alive.

GHOST ONE: She's hocked us more since we died than we ever did her when we were alive.

GHOST TWO: Will we truly be allowed to dissolve?

GHOST THREE: It's got to be. I can't stand any more sermons from her. I've had enough to last me for twelve eternities.

GHOST FOUR: Well, she is high strung.

GHOST FIVE: That comes from your side of the family.

GHOST FOUR: I want to get away from you too.

YOUNG MAN: Where have I been? Where are we going?

GHOST ONE: You'll like it. You'll be first.

ALL: Vaporize!

They float off.

Enter PROSPERITY, *the* QUEEN, *the* GENERAL, *the* SENATOR, *the* CLOUDS, *the* CHEESE, BIRDS *and* BISHOP.

QUEEN: Our dependency, our ecstasy, our constancy. Our firm Prosperity, sir, may we now beg you to discontinue your jest and get back to the business of economy.

SENATOR: I fear, sir, that you've fucked up enough with our dollars, and we have to josh you back into shape.

GENERAL: You've played with smaller climes and countries, and narrower states of mind, and you must have expanded your consciousness to include another company. But let's annex and continue.

SENATOR: The merger is not unacceptable. We can digest it.

BISHOP: It can be spun dry in a matter of seconds.

GENERAL: Amalgamation will conglomerate the polls and everyone can go back to counting food stamps.

BIRDS: Life is not possible without you to look at first thing every morning.

CHEESE: I don't mind any change as long as I'm inside him.

PROSPERITY: Thank you, Cheese.

QUEEN: Prosperity, come back to us. We do need you. Your little game worked, it's true we can't do without you.

PROSPERITY: But—

"PROSPERITY'S LOVE SONG"

I see you, Love
I see you, Bird
I see you, Demon
I see you, Dove

I feel you, Queen
I need you, Trees
I eat you, Cheese
Yes, Grass, you're green

Yes, General
I read your manual
Dear Senator,
I studied your roar

But it's time for me
To listen to me
I want to share my love
With my darling Doctor Rain.

Hello, Cloud
I've heard you speak aloud
But before I meet my shroud
I'm going to go lovingly insane
With my darling
My darling
Doctor Rain.

QUEEN: You mean you're giving up all of us for that insane Doctor Rain?

PROSPERITY: Her insanity is nearly as extensive as mine. We can wind in and out of each other's labyrinth. [*Exit, stage right*]

ALL: Please . . .

PROSPERITY: Sorry, I promised to shoot pool with my Cheese. [*He exits*]

QUEEN: [*To* GENERAL] It's a good thing we have one in our pocket.

GENERAL: He does mean it after all.

SENATOR: I'm going down to drill the candidate.

QUEEN: Be thorough. We can't afford to lose one vote.

BISHOP: I'll extend her spiritual side.

QUEEN: I'll fill her up with a maternal complex.

GENERAL: I'll teach her tactics and strategy.

SENATOR: And I'll teach her to talk in authoritative, sonorous, stentorian tones. She shall make beautiful noise.

They exit.
    Enter PROSPERITY *and* DR. RAIN *from opposite sides of the stage.* DR. RAIN *is oblivious to* PROSPERITY *at first.*

DR. RAIN: I picked out all his clothes myself. Clothes make a big impression on the electorate. Men don't realize how many women are crotch-watchers. They think they have all the eyes. I'll do his makeup myself. Oh, I'm nervous. Oh, oh, oh, oh, I can't turn my neck. Every time I take an exam I can't turn my neck. My man is so perfect, no one will notice. Maybe I should go to sleep and forget the whole thing. Maybe I'll fly to Switzerland and get frozen. Why do I keep fighting? I don't want to fight. I want to love. I'm a lover. I saw the best loving today that I ever saw in my life. That's the kind of love affair I long for.

A wagon stage comes on with a three-man band consisting of trumpet, guitar and harpsichord. One of the men hands her a microphone which she takes and begins to sing.

I saw two white whales today
There they swam, two white whales today
And they're lovers!
There were only two
Huge white whales there—
And they're lovers!

Chorus of men appear stage right to hum under the song.

You can see that they are lovers
Over a thousand pounds apiece
And they're lovers
You have no idea how they tease
These massive lovers
They start by big bites
Big big whale bites
They open their jaws
These massive lovers and take tiny
Little love bites from each other
It makes you laugh
They roll and skip and glide
They flip and bite and hide
These white whale lovers
And then his penis appears
And he starts to poke around
And then her vagina erupts
And they begin to flip and bound
And the chase is on for these massive lovers
His penis is eight feet long
And her clitoris—you can *see* it!

PROSPERITY *enters here and dances with her until end of song.*

I pressed myself close
To praise these white whale lovers
They were in love
You could see it. You could see it.
You could see it.

PROSPERITY: [*Feigning a cordial toughness*] All ready for the match.

DR. RAIN: Good day, Prosperity.

PROSPERITY: Want to make any bets?

DR. RAIN: This is not a game.

PROSPERITY: You can't win.

DR. RAIN: Perhaps not, but we're giving it everything we've got.

PROSPERITY: Why not graciously withdraw and leave it to the pros?

DR. RAIN: It's been left to you long enough. There's a new brew burning in the land. We're going to strip off your bunting and take a look at the bone. And when we find the rot, we'll reconstruct the structure.

PROSPERITY: I admire your courage, but you don't stand a chance. Want to run away with me?

DR. RAIN: I'm going to run over you. [*She exits with a secret smile on her face*]

PROSPERITY: [*To audience*] It's working better than I'd hoped. I'm tired of manipulating. I want her to win, so that she can take over manipulating me. Sweet peace. I can almost feel her now. [*He exits*]

Entire company marching and singing "Convention Song" up the aisles.

In recognition of his watchful ways
Through many a long night and even darker
day
In grateful acknowledgment
Of his trust in us—
Will God please save the United States
And Massachusetts.
Will God please save the United States
and Massachusetts.

MINISTER OF INFORMATION: Order in the hall. Clear the aisles.

ACTOR ONE: The candidates are now leaving their hotel rooms.

MINISTER OF INFORMATION: In cooperation with the laws of the land, the candidates will come forward to meet the public they wish to serve. Throw out your hearts and emotions, good people. There is only room now for honor, judgment, pledging, reasoning, weighing, wanting and winning.

Enter the BISHOP. *Perhaps other actors are out in the aisles campaigning for a* MAN *or a* WOMAN. *They could say both forward and backward,* "We want man," "We want woman."

BISHOP: Ladies and gentlemen. Delegates. Demons. Heads of Institutions. Inmates and outsiders. We are gathered here today to decide for sex. Search your pockets, search your heads, search your pants, search your hearts. Do you see a man? Do you see a woman? By the people's will we have brought forth for you today two personages who wish to reassure you that such creatures as men and women exist. Bless you all, my children. Bless you and may you grow confident. Let us sing.

[*The entire company sings the "Convention Song" again*]

SENATOR: My fellow thieves and citizens. It's time we bring forth a woman. We have searched the four corners of the planet and have brought here for your undivided attention not a child of granite, but a possible Mother, a Queen of the heart, a tear in the eye, a savor on the tongue. And something for the boys to look at. I place in nomination a female animal who aspires only to be your *woman!*

Half the "Convention Song" is sung as the WOMAN *is brought in and placed.*

DR. RAIN: My fellow paranoids. My fellow schizophrenics, my fellow frantics, my fellow savants, my fellow ghosts. My fellow women. How about a man? M. A. N. We went to the jungle and there he was. We went to the Antarctic and there he was. We went to the Pacific Shelf and there he was. We looked in our backyard and there he was. Here he is, my fellow colleagues, your next *man!*

Half the "Convention Song" is sung as the MAN *is brought in and placed. The* PARTISANS *cheer.*

The MAN *and* WOMAN *who take their places on the campaign platforms on either side of the stage should be dressed or undressed at the absolute height of what the director and designer feel would best show them off in their masculinity and femininity. Lush and beautiful. Or they could be dressed in the pop idea of what the "perfect candidate" should wear or look like, to "Mr. and Mrs. America."*

WOMAN: It's good to be back in the heartland of humanity.

MAN: It's heartening to be in the cradle of a civilization.

WOMAN: It's marvelous to tread the ground that was once soaked red by the blood of our brilliant fathers.

MAN: It's downright enough to get a man's eyes puddled up to breathe the air hanging over the ground that bred so many sons of the American revolution. A revolution that went underground but has now surfaced again to satisfy the hovering ghosts of the Architects of this Republic.

WOMAN: We won't let them down.

MAN: I am your candidate.

WOMAN: I will teach you to be a mother. I will teach you to raise children. I will teach you to raise men. I will teach you to raise a president. I will teach you to raise the dead. The good dead.

MAN: The good are dying faster every day.

WOMAN: In the limelight of the love light I come to you to ask your support. To ask for your confidence. I come to you to give to you the reassurance of a womanly image.

DR. RAIN: I see that there's really no contest. What we need is a man. I want to stand here before you Americans and tell you he is your man. A man is what's needed. He is that man. All you have to do is close your eyes and take a look.

WOMAN: Close your eyes and fade into me. Close your eyes and follow the female. Close your eyes and trust in me. I can guide you to the center of your soul. You will become one in me.

MAN: I will give you you. I will reflect the best in the West. All that's hairy and hoary shall have fucking space. All that swells and yeasts will have its own hiding place. I'll place a chicken on every prick and two in the mouth. I'll teach you how to cook!

BISHOP: Hear ye. Hear ye. All those gathered at the foot of the mountain. The mountain has dissolved and has been packaged as low-cholesterol whipped cream. Come forward each and every martyr, turn your cheek aside so that I may fill your ear from here to here. The cream will seep into the burned-out brain cells and the enemy will be fooled. The cream will disguise any pain or doubt that may have been floating from eyeball to skull bone. All will be stilled in sugar. The time has come to blend your heads into the conscience of the stone.

WOMAN: The first ear to come to me will be licked. Then I will spurt the wisdom of granite conglomerate glacier dust throughout your hemispheres. And you'll give me all your money for safekeeping.

SENATOR: This is the only woman to lead you back from the compartmentalization brought on us all by the industrialization of your bodies to the point where your hand has been cut off from your arm.

MAN: Your tongues write other people's letters. Your fingers sort the shiny, cold metal of nuts and bolts instead of caressing the creamy eager flesh of your lover. I will lead you back to grass.

GENERAL: She will teach you to enjoy your woman as never before. You will trust her and she and you will rise to such towering climaxes that your souls will float a lifetime together in unified tenderness.

MAN: And the gnawing snake of anxiety will be forever banished from your gut. Am I not the man to lead you?

WOMAN: No. All he does is paint pretty pictures. Pictures to lull you into a sleep. A sleep where the patterns he has painted will satisfy you. You might as well be drugged. Pictures are not what you need. Words and pictures are for the passive fools, the dolts ruled by others.

QUEEN: The dolts who cannot take time out from a busy business day for an unexpected screw.

SENATOR: The dolts who pay the pornographers a billion a year to make them pictures to jerk off by in the men's room on the New Haven.

BISHOP: The dolts who are too tired to satisfy the wives who put them through college.

WOMAN: We've had enough pictures, and plans and instructions.

DR. RAIN: We've had enough of ineffective mouthpieces. We've had enough of secretly satisfying ourselves at three o'clock in the morning while the nation snores.

WOMAN: Action. Action. Action to tenderness. How long has it been since you touched a stranger's mouth? How long has it been since

you looked into the eyes of another to find out where his soul resided? Do it now. Close your eyes. Everyone here close your eyes. Try to visualize the person who sits next to you. Now slowly everyone put your arms on the arm-rests of your seat. Very slowly and keep your eyes closed.

MAN: This is an outrage. This is criminal. This is a steal. You've completely contradicted yourself. You have scored the direction givers, only so that *you* could be the one to give the directions. I warn you, ladies and gentlemen. You could be replacing one set of directions for another. Stay with what you know and work within to make that framework better. Don't be taken in by promises of tenderness. How can you be tender toward someone you don't even know? Give them your hand and they'll steal your cock.

WOMAN: Of course you can be tender toward someone you don't know.

All during the final speeches of the TWO CANDIDATES, *they are brought together on one platform by the other actors. As they speak to the audience they are undressed.*

MAN: It's good to lie back and slide down together. But it's important to protect your backbone. Backbone crushers abound.

WOMAN: You've been tender to this brood.

MAN: Before putting your arms around each other, lie side by side on your back, mouths locked so tongues can lick each other only on the tip.

WOMAN: . . . this stew, this group of organisms . . .

MAN: Stay on the tip of each other's tongues, and alternate this expanding pleasure by sucking her lower lip while she sucks your upper lip; at the instant when the sucking might turn into pain . . .

WOMAN: . . . who fancy themselves possible . . .

MAN: . . . catch the tip of her tongue again and at the same time take a big handful of her sweet pussy and squeeze and pull in rhythm to your tongue.

WOMAN: . . . You've spent the night . . .

MAN: Then it is now safe to lie down on your back with her breasts in your mouth and slide head-first.

Their outer garments have been stripped from them to reveal the MAN *in a perfect naked suit of a female body, the* WOMAN *is in a perfect naked suit of a male body. There is a count of five, and then the naked suits are removed through the next speeches, until at the end both the male and female are splendidly nude.*

WOMAN: . . . trying to woo them . . .

MAN: . . . but don't start eating it until you reach the end of the slide. Listen carefully to the suck in of breath that grazes her lips and teeth. That breath belongs to you. Collect it. Collect it.

WOMAN: . . . with pictures from your mind . . .

MAN: Collect it with care and tuck it in between the spaces of your rib bones . . .

WOMAN: . . . with pictures from your mind . . .

MAN: Someday you might have to save your life with the memory of the sound of her breath.

WOMAN: . . . with pictures from your mind . . .

The nude CANDIDATES *are wheeled to stage right as* PROSPERITY *and* DR. RAIN *enter arm in arm. The* CHORUS *sits in front of the* CANDIDATES *on the floor.*

DR. RAIN: I do want to run away with you.

PROSPERITY: We both win. I love the way you chew your hair.

DR. RAIN: Your saliva sparkles like diamonds.

PROSPERITY: I've lost my heart to you.

DR. RAIN: I've lost my tongue to you.

GHOSTS: At last.

PROSPERITY: We shall marry. [*To the audience*] And now I want you to bow your heads and take the hand of your wished-for wife, or desired husband. All those here who are married, are married again. All those here who are unmarried are married to each other. The audience is married to the actors and the actors to the theatre. The theatre is married to America. America is married to America. Do not despair over your fall. Prosperity now has married you all. [*He and* DR. RAIN *sit with the* CHORUS]

MAN: [*To audience*] I dreamed I was in Los Angeles with Bobby. I was in his caravan. A dragon with sweet eyes and a fiery tongue carried me down the street behind him in his cavalcade on the way to the kitchen. He was blowing kisses to everyone, but all the kisses landed on my cheeks. I like your eyes, he said. All my children have eyes and I love them very much. Ethel was beside him and everyone was dancing and cheering. I groove on your word, I said. I groove on your groove, I said.

And I was dancing and cheering. [*Three men begin to enter slowly downstage right*] Then ten men with one hand raised a hand gun. Bobby went forward to shake the gun and kiss the gun and throw his hair to the gun. And I was dancing and cheering. Then the blood was pouring from his mouth where his words had been, and my nipples were the rosary beads he was saying. [*They begin their scene here*] He was saying. He was saying.

ALL: [*Whispering*] He was saying. He was saying—"How bad is it?" And everyone was dancing and cheering. [*This is repeated all during the final scene until the gunshot*]

The CHORUS *strips down to white bikinis.*
*   One by one, three men appear. This time they are worried and tense.*

FIRST MAN: You fucking shit-head, you're late.

[*They exchange briefcases*]

SECOND MAN: I thought I was being followed.

THIRD MAN: No one is supposed to know that you exist.

FIRST MAN: You fuck-up. Don't you know the future of the United States is at stake?

THIRD MAN: You're reeking of alcohol.

FIRST MAN: That alone is grounds for elimination.

SECOND MAN: It's not . . . I wasn't drinking . . . it's codeine for my throat.

FIRST MAN: [*Pulling a gun with a silencer*] I'm the only one I can trust now. This is the first time in my life I've had to take the gun into my own hands.

SECOND MAN: I love my country. You don't understand, I love my country. Give me a chance?

FIRST MAN: You psychotic double agent, on your knees. You don't know what love is. Get down there. Kiss my cock. [*He shoots the* MAN. *He crumples, blood running down his shirt*]

THIRD MAN: Weak little shit-ass.

FIRST MAN: By God, we'll show them how to stand up for America. Who's next on the list?

Lights fade out as a spotlight comes up center stage on a giant meat slicer. It moves toward audience slicing bloody roast beef. It stops.

MOLLY'S DREAM

a play in one act

Maria Irene Fornés

Molly's Dream was first presented by the Boston University Writers Conference, Tanglewood, Massachusetts, on July 23, 1968, with the following cast:

MOLLY	*Diane Kagin*
THE YOUNG MAN	*Peter Masterson*
MACK	*Bill Gerber*
JOHN	*Leonard Hicks*
ALBERTA	*Crystal Field*
THE HANGING WOMEN	*Lisa Billock, Diane Birken, Tina Takayanagi, Julia Ann Goldsmith, Myla Zinn, Carolyn Clowes*

It was directed by Edward Setrakian. Music by Cosmos Savage; costumes by the author; lighting by Thomas Munn.

A revised version was subsequently presented at the New Dramatists Workshop, New York City, on December 5, 1968, with the following cast:

MOLLY	*Julie Bovasso*
THE YOUNG MAN	*Ray Barry*
MACK	*Jim Cashman*
JOHN	*Leonard Hicks*
ALBERTA	*Crystal Field*
THE HANGING WOMEN	*Carol Gelfand* (soloist), *Kay Carney, Penny Dupont, Margaret Impert, Alice Tweedy*

It was directed and designed by the author. Musical accompaniment by David Tice; lighting by Teresa King.

To Aileen Passloff

CHARACTERS

MOLLY, *late twenties; a waitress.*

THE YOUNG MAN, *late twenties; a laborer.*

JIM, *played by the same actor as the* YOUNG MAN *but he appears endowed with sublime sex appeal.*

THE HANGING WOMEN, *a chorus of five.*

MACK, *a bartender in his forties.*

JOHN, *a lean middle-aged cowboy.*

ALBERTA, *a 27-year-old, who refuses to grow.*

PART I

MOLLY AND THE HANGING WOMEN

An old-fashioned saloon typical of warm climates. There are several swinging doors on both sides. Both sides of the saloon lead to streets. Another swinging door on the back wall leads to the kitchen. The counter is alongside the back wall. A trapdoor on the floor behind the counter leads to the basement. There are fans hanging from the ceiling, potted plants, spittoons, tables, and chairs. There is a wall mirror, and a cage with a bird. On the counter there is a gun, and two porcelain figures—one in the shape of a woman; the other, Cupid. A top hat hangs from a hat rack.

The play of lights indicated in the script denotes an important moment in the life of one or another character.

MOLLY is alone in the tavern. She wears a black satin uniform. She prepares herself a cup of coffee, takes off her shoes, sits down and begins to read to herself from a magazine.

MOLLY: [*She mumbles some of the following words and begins to act them out*] Rosie was a darned good waitress. She wasn't the kind that would spill any whiskey on the counter. But when Sam started walking toward her, her hand started shaking, and the whiskey spilled. Sam, her beloved Sam, whom she was even thinking of marrying, had shot at the Sheriff. What a thing to do. This broke her heart and made her nervous. That's why she spilled the drink. Sam, who seemed like such a nice guy, had shot at the Sheriff and now he had the nerve to come into the tavern as if nothing had happened, or at least he had

the nerve to come into the tavern. He pulled a chair from one of the tables, turned it toward him and straddled it. He looked at her for a while without saying anything. Then he said, "Are you angry because I shot at the Sheriff?" [MOLLY *puts the magazine down and takes a puff from her cigarette. She speaks the following dialogue out loud, acting out both characters in the story*] "Are you angry because I shot at the Sheriff?" [*Sarcastically*] "Naw, I was getting tired of his face. I wouldn't mind seeing someone else wear that star. What would you like?" [*One of the swinging doors opens slightly. The* YOUNG MAN *puts his head in.* MOLLY *does not notice him*] "Let me have a steak . . . rare. . . . And don't bother putting arsenic in the gravy." [MOLLY *writes in her check pad*] "Rare, no arsenic." Oh, boy. [MOLLY *notices the* YOUNG MAN. *She is flustered. They look at one another for a moment. He smiles and walks away.* MOLLY *begins to feel sleepy. She yawns. She leans her head on the table and falls asleep. A dream-like atmosphere is suggested by means of lights, smoke, or the lifting of the walls. A swinging door opens.* JIM *puts his head in. He looks exactly like the* YOUNG MAN *and is played by the same actor*]

JIM: [*Suspiciously*] Is there a waiter here?

MOLLY: [*Raising her head*] Yes.

JIM enters. He is dressed in glittering lace. He looks like a prince in a fairy tale. Five women surround him as if they were a floating part of him. These are the HANGING WOMEN. When he is still, they hang on to him gently. He sits at a table. MOLLY stretches and walks to him. She waits for his order.

JIM: Isn't there a waiter here?

MOLLY: Yes, me.

JIM: I mean a man waiter.

MOLLY: No, there's just me.

JIM looks at MOLLY for a moment. Then he stands and walks to the door.

JIM: I don't need one more woman. [*As* JIM *exits, the doors swing.* MACK *enters with a box of soda bottles, goes behind the counter and disappears behind it.* JIM *puts his head through the doors again*] Didn't I just see a man behind the bar?

MOLLY: Yes.

JIM: Where did he go?

MOLLY: He's in the basement.

JIM: Is he coming back?

MOLLY: Mack!

MACK: What?

MOLLY: Are you coming back?

MACK: Yes.

MOLLY: Yes, he is coming back.

JIM *starts walking toward the same table where he sat before.*

JIM: I thought you said there was no waiter.

MOLLY: He's not a waiter.

JIM: [*Stopping*] What is he?

MOLLY: Bartender.

JIM *walks to the bar. A few moments pass.* MOLLY *looks at him with curiosity. He tries to avoid her glance.* MACK *appears behind the bar.*

JIM: A double rye, please.

MACK *pours a drink.* JIM *takes the drink to a table.*

MACK: Boy, that's a man for you. . . . Look at that. [MACK *exits.* MOLLY *sits at* JIM's *table and looks at the* HANGING WOMEN]

MOLLY: Who are they?

JIM *drinks his rye in one gulp.*

JIM: Who? [MOLLY *points to the* HANGING WOMEN] Friends.

MOLLY: What's the matter with them?

JIM: Nothing is the matter with them.

MOLLY: Why are they hovering around you like that?

JIM: They like me.

MOLLY *looks at the* HANGING WOMEN.

MOLLY: Doesn't it bother you to have them . . . [*She gestures.* JIM *shakes his head*]

JIM: A little.

MOLLY: Why don't you tell them to scoot?

JIM: I have.

MOLLY: And?

JIM: They won't go.

MOLLY: [*Waving her hands as if to scare away chickens*] Shhh . . . Shhh . . .

The HANGING WOMEN *flutter.*

JIM: Don't do that. . . . You'll hurt their feelings. [JIM *looks for* MACK. *While his head is turned* MOLLY *waves her arms with sweeping movements*]

MOLLY: Shh . . . Shhh . . . [*The* HANGING WOMEN *scatter all over the room. They are breathless and in a state of anxiety. The lights flash on and remain strong through the following scene*] They're off. [JIM *is also breathless and in a state of anxiety*] What's the matter? [JIM *gasps for air*] I thought you wanted them off.

HANGING WOMEN: [*Sing*]
Do not collapse just now, world.
Do not collapse just now.

Wait a bit. Wait a bit.
Perhaps I can find my way back.

MOLLY: I thought you wanted them off.

The HANGING WOMEN *start moving toward* JIM.

JIM:
Oh . . . oh . . . oh . . . oh . . .
The flower of love grew on me,
And she pulled,
She pulled it off

The HANGING WOMEN *surround him again.* MOLLY *pats them.*

MOLLY: It's all right now.

JIM:
It grew from my side.
It grew from my legs.
It grew from my arms.
The most beautiful thing grew off me.
The flower of love.
And she pulled it off.

HANGING WOMEN:
Oh . . . oh . . . oh . . .

MOLLY: It's all right . . . you're back.

HANGING WOMEN:
It's just that I hear
A little bit of love
Going down the drain.
Glop, glop, glop,
Going down the drain.

JIM:
Oh, God. Oh, God.
She put them back.
But she pulled them off.

MOLLY: Gee whiz. [*The lights go back to normal.* JIM *looks for* MACK] What do you want?

JIM: I thought I'd ask him for a drink. But that's all right.

MOLLY: [*Standing*] Double?

JIM: Don't bother.

MOLLY: It's no bother. That's what I'm here for.

JIM: I changed my mind. I don't want a drink.

MOLLY *sits.*

MOLLY: Are you broke?

JIM: No.

MOLLY: It's on the house.

JIM: Why?

MOLLY *stares at* JIM *and speaks distractedly. He recognizes the look and becomes cautious.*

MOLLY: Oh, I don't know. I just thought I'd buy you a drink.

JIM: Why?

MOLLY: Why? . . . That's how I felt. . . . I felt like buying you a drink. [*She walks toward* JIM]

JIM: Oh, God. . . . Well, don't buy me a drink. You go on out in there.

MOLLY: Where?

JIM: In the kitchen. Go in the kitchen and do what you have to do. Wash some glasses.

MOLLY: I don't wash the glasses. Mack does that.

JIM: Well . . . read your magazine. . . . Don't come so close.

MOLLY: . . . Why not? [*She is very close to him*]

JIM: Oh, God. [MOLLY *throws her arms around* JIM's *neck and lets herself hang. The lights flash on and off*] Listen . . . lady . . . excuse me a moment. Hey, Miss . . .

MOLLY: [*Still hanging*] What?

JIM: Do I owe you anything?

MOLLY: I don't know.

JIM: Think about it for a moment.

MOLLY: I can't think now.

JIM: Look, I don't owe you anything. You have to let go.

MOLLY *returns to her chair.*

MOLLY: Well, what do you expect? I was curious.

JIM: That's all right. Just don't do it again.

MACK *enters.*

MACK: . . . That's a man for you.

JIM: Double rye, please.

MACK *pours the drink and exits.* JIM *starts to stand.*

MOLLY: I'll get it.

JIM: No, it's all right. I'll get it.

MOLLY: [*Going to the bar*] I'll get it. It's my job.

JIM: No, it's all right. I'd like to get my own drink if you don't mind.

MOLLY: That's all right. I'm the waitress. [*She reaches for the drink*]

JIM: It's my drink. I get my own drink if I want to.

MOLLY: You can't get your own drink. I get paid to get the drinks.

JIM: It's my drink. I'm paying for it and I don't want any favors.

MOLLY: It's no favor. It's my job. [JIM *grabs her. They struggle for a moment. She manages to put the drink on the table*] Just leave me a tip.

JIM: You don't need a tip.

MOLLY: What do I need?

JIM: Love.

MOLLY *hangs again.* MACK *enters.*

MACK: You didn't have to bother. Molly would have brought it to you. Where's Molly? [*Discovering her*] Molly . . . [MOLLY *doesn't answer*] Molly, what are you doing?

MOLLY: I'll be up in a minute.

MACK: What do you mean you'll be up in a minute? Molly . . . what in the world are you doing?

JIM: She'll never let go.

MACK: How do you do it?

JIM: It's a burden.

MACK: I wish I had that burden.

JIM: They weigh a lot.

MACK: Leave them home. You don't know how to handle women.

JIM: I can't leave them home. It would hurt their feelings.

MACK: Hurt their feelings? What's the matter with you. Are you a sissy?

JIM: I don't want to hurt their feelings.

MACK: Hey, Molly, forget it, kid. This guy's a sissy. [*She ignores him*] Hey, Molly, what's the matter with you? He's a sissy.

MOLLY: Shut up, Mack.

JIM: Bunch of creeps.

MACK: That's the trouble with women. Here's me, a real man. You name it, I have it. There's that creep . . . a sissy. . . . Do they go for me? No. They go for him . . . a sissy. [MACK *starts moving furniture as if to prepare for cleaning the floor*] A burden he says . . . women a burden. . . . Wish I had that burden. I could take on a hundred. One right after the other. No problem. A hundred. Bang, bang, bang. Just like that. [*Sings*]

> Bang bang bang bang
> Bang
> Bang bang bang bang
> Bang
> Bang
> Bang
> Bang

The HANGING WOMEN *surround* MACK.

MACK *and the* HANGING WOMEN:

> Bang bang bang bang
> Bang bang bang bang
> Bang bang bang bang
> Bang bang bang bang
> Bang bang bang bang
> Bang
> Bang bang bang bang
> Bang
> Bang
> Bang
>
> Bang bang bang bang
> Bang bang bang bang
> Bang bang bang bang
> Bang bang bang bang
> Bang bang bang bang
> Bang
> Bang bang bang bang
> Bang

Bang
Bang
Bang bang bang bang
Bang bang bang bang
Bang bang bang bang
Bang bang bang bang
Bang bang bang bang
Bang
Bang bang bang bang
Bang
Bang
Bang

MACK: [*Spoken*] But do they go for me? . . . No.

The HANGING WOMEN *put their hands on* MACK. *He collapses.*

HANGING WOMEN: Creep! [*The* HANGING WOMEN *go back to* JIM. MACK *stands. He turns to the* HANGING WOMEN *the way a wrestler waits for an attack*]

MACK: Try again. . . . Come on. . . . Come on. Try again. I can take the lot of you. You yellow-bellied broads.

HANGING WOMEN: Creep!

MACK: Aw, bunch of dumb broads. [JOHN *enters. He wears black dungarees, a black shirt, a cowboy hat, and holsters with guns from his ankles to his armpits*] Hey, Molly, a customer. [MOLLY *does not respond*] Hey, Molly.

MOLLY: What?

MACK: Customer.

MOLLY: Wait a moment.

JIM: Molly . . .

MOLLY: What?

JIM: Are you going to stay? [*Pause*] Molly, are you going to stay? [*Pause*] I like you, Molly, but I just can't take on any more. [*He waits a moment*] Listen, you have to let go.

MOLLY: I don't want to.

JIM: Well, you have to. [MOLLY *lets go*] Are your feelings hurt?

MOLLY: [*Hurt*] No.

JIM: Molly, I can't take on any more. I just can't. I can hardly walk as it is. I can't play baseball. Do you understand what it is not to be able to play baseball? I just can't take on any more. And besides, I don't owe you anything.

MOLLY: Well, I liked it.

JIM: All right then, hang on. What's one more?

MOLLY: Not unless the others leave.

JIM: I can't tell them to leave.

MOLLY: Why not?

JIM: I'm indebted to them.

MOLLY: Why?

JIM: Because . . . they like me.

MOLLY: That's nothing.

JIM: I'm indebted to them.

MOLLY: I can do more than that for a man.

JIM: I know, you're different.

MOLLY: So?

JIM: Molly, I can't.

MOLLY: You said I was different.

JIM: I'm indebted to them.

MOLLY *dries a tear, starts to walk away. Then turns to the* HANGING WOMEN *and starts waving her arms.*

MOLLY: Shhh . . . Shhh . . .

JIM: Mollyyy! Don't!

MOLLY: Creep! [*The lights flash on and remain strong through the following scene.* MOLLY *takes off her apron. She gradually develops a German accent. She begins to behave in a manner resembling Marlene Dietrich*]

MACK: Molly. . . . Customer.

MOLLY: [*To* JOHN] What do you want? [JOHN *thinks a moment and begins to make a gesture*] Whiskey, double, very straight, hold the chaser, make it fast. He's dry.

JOHN: Make it a Bloody Mary.

MACK: [*While preparing the drink*] What was it like?

MOLLY: I can't explain it.

MACK: Try.

MOLLY: It felt right. That's all.

MACK: Come on.

MOLLY: You have to live it. You can't explain it.

MACK: [*Pouring whiskey for* MOLLY] It's for you.

MOLLY *drinks it.*

MOLLY: Thanks.

MACK: Now, tell me.

MOLLY: What?

MACK: What was it like?

MOLLY: It felt right.

MACK: That doesn't mean anything.

MOLLY: It felt right to be near him.

MACK: That's nothing.

MOLLY: It's everything, you dumb creep. You'd never understand.

MACK: Well, explain it to me.

MOLLY: I can't explain it. Try it yourself.

MACK: What do you think I am?

MOLLY: Forget it then.

MACK: Are you going back?

MOLLY: Never again. [*She walks to* JOHN'S *table with his drink*]

MACK: Ha ha.

MOLLY: What does that mean? Ha ha.

MACK: He's not so good.

MOLLY: He's good all right. I'm just not going back. [MOLLY *drinks* JOHN'S *drink. She then goes to the bar and sits on it*]

MACK: What do you mean by drinking the customer's drink? [MOLLY *shrugs her shoulders*] Who do you think you are? [MACK *pours another drink for* JOHN. MOLLY *lights a cigarette*] Here, bring it to him. [MOLLY *does not respond*] Hey, Molly! . . . Kid! . . . Bring the customer his drink.

MOLLY *puffs some smoke.*

MOLLY: Molly kid was. Are you blind, you creep? Can't you see what life has done to me? Molly kid was. I have just changed my name. [*The music starts*] No. I'm not breaking into song. The moment is too sad. I'm not going back. Good as he is, my feelings are hurt.

JIM: Molly, come back.

MOLLY: Molly was. I have just changed my name. [*The music plays louder as if to invite her to sing*] No. Little Molly would have sung, do re mi fa sol la ti, not me.

JIM: Molly, come back.

MOLLY: Not me. My feelings are hurt. Broken to pieces. [*She pushes the figurine in the shape of a woman off the counter. It crashes on the floor.* MACK *picks up the pieces*]

JIM: Come back, Molly.

MACK *starts putting the pieces together.*

MOLLY: Don't bother to put the pieces together, Mack. It will never be the same. Throw it away. [MACK *throws the pieces in a garbage can. The sound pains* MOLLY] Good-bye, Molly . . . poor kid . . . she's gone. [*Taking the figure of* Cupid] Perhaps you're too young to know how it hurts to love. . . . It hurts. [MOLLY *and* JIM *stare at each other for a while. She looks away from him, showing her profile. She puts her foot up on the bar, puts a top hat on and her elbow on her knee*] It seems I did my song after all. [*She rests her head on her hand*]

MACK: Okay, Molly, get off the bar.

MOLLY: Shut up, Mack.

JIM: Molly.

MACK: Get your feet off the bar. I won't have anybody putting their feet on the bar.

JIM: Leave her alone.

MACK: Who do you think you are? You come in here and look at the way she's acting. She's acting like a nut. She never acted like that before.

JIM: I know, I just broke her heart.

MACK: Molly.

MOLLY: Huh?

MACK: Look at her. [*To* MOLLY] What's the matter with you?

MOLLY: Nothing is the matter with me. What are you talking about?

MACK: You're acting like a nut.

MOLLY: I'm not acting like a nut.

MACK: You better do something about her. I won't have anybody sitting at the bar.

JIM: I will. . . . [*To* MOLLY] Molly.

MOLLY: What?

JIM: You used to be a nice kid.

MOLLY: No more. Those are bygone days.

MACK: Well, somebody bring the customer his drink, or I'm not responsible for my acts. [MOLLY *takes a puff of her cigarette.* JIM *takes the drink to* JOHN'S *table as* JOHN *goes to the bar*] What do you want?

JOHN: I thought I'd get the drink myself.

MACK: It's on the table. [JOHN *goes to his table*] I'm glad you brought him the drink, otherwise I couldn't have answered for my acts.

JIM: I didn't do it for you. I did it for her.

JOHN: Thanks, I was beginning to get thirsty.

JIM: That's all right. I did it for her. [*Going to* MOLLY] Molly . . .

MOLLY: Hm?

JIM: Molly, I didn't mean to hurt you.

MOLLY: You can't hurt me. I have no heart.

JIM: You do, Molly, you have a heart.

MOLLY: I don't have a heart.

JIM: Molly, if I told you that I loved you, would you get off the bar?

MOLLY: No.

MACK: He's a sissy.

JIM: I am responsible . . . [*He sings*]
I accept,
I accept,
I accept
The responsibility of my enormous
    sex appeal.
If a woman says she loves me,
I cannot tell her to go.

I breathe hot,
I breathe hot,
I breathe hot,
And I breathe hot.
No woman has ever resisted me, and
    I accept
The responsibility.

J'accepte,
J'accepte,
J'accepte
La responsabilité de mon énorme sex-
    appeal.
I cannot turn them away.

J'accepte
Les conséquences désastreuses de mon
    énorme sex-appeal.
I never said to a woman,
I love you.
But I accept,
I accept
The responsibility.

HANGING WOMEN: [Sing]
    To a woman you will say,
    I love you.
    She will not understand.
    You will say,
    I love you, twice.
    Je t'aime. I love you.
    And then she'll understand.
    You will say I love you, twice.
    Je t'aime. I love you.

JIM turns to MOLLY. His face is close to hers.

JIM: Je t'aime. [MOLLY turns her head to look
at JIM and does not reply] I love you.

MOLLY blows smoke in his face and smiles.
JIM coughs. He is downcast. The HANGING
WOMEN move away from him. JIM walks to
center stage and stands on his head with one
leg bent and crossed, in a position resembling
the Hanged Man of the Tarot.

HANGING WOMEN:
    To a woman he said,
    I love you.
    La, la la la, la la la, la.
    She did not understand.
    He said,
    I love you, twice.
    Je t'aime. I love you.
    And then she understood.
    But not a word came out of her
        mouth.
    Only smoke.
    And he lost his charm.
    All his charm was lost.
    [Spoken] Now, you're as common as Mack.

MACK: And who said I'm common, you dumb
broads? I can take on the whole lot of you,
you yellow-bellied broads. Bang, bang, bang,
just like that.

HANGING WOMEN: [Sing]
    La, la la la, la la la, la.

JIM stands on his feet and sits at a table. The
lights are dimmed except for a spot on JIM.

    La, la la la, la la la, la.

INTERLUDE

JIM: [Spoken]
    And what has my noble face offered
        the world?

A smile.
Yes, it has done that.
A gentle look? Yes, my noble face
    has done that.
And what else have I offered the
    world?
A few kind words, perhaps.
And some elusive words.
And what have my loving eyes given
    the world?
A benign stare.
And who am I?
Am I the wrongdoer?
I never raised my hand to hurt a
    man.
And yet, I ask: Who am I?
The wrongdoer. . . .
And what have my hands done?
They have reached out with love.
And the loved one has turned to me
    and said:
Who are you? . . . Who are you?
I'm the wrongdoer.
That's who I am.

The lights come up.

PART II

DRACULA THE MISUNDERSTOOD

There is no time lapse between Part One and
Part Two.

JOHN: [To JIM] Blackjack, sir?

JIM: What? . . .

JOHN: Blackjack? [JIM looks JOHN over and
nods. JOHN shuffles the cards expecting JIM
to come to his table. JIM pushes a chair away
from his table with his foot inviting JOHN to
come to his. JOHN shuffles the cards again,
cuts them twice and looks at JIM. JIM chal-
lenges JOHN by remaining where he is. JOHN
picks up the cards and holds them thinking
what to do. Then, he puts two cards on the
table face down and sneaks a look at JIM, who
remains seated. He looks at his card, then at
JIM's and smiles feebly] You win. [He goes to
JIM. Through the following scene JOHN puts
a dollar on the table, JIM puts a dollar on the
table. JIM deals two cards each. One of the
HANGING WOMEN joins the players at their
table and watches the game]

MOLLY: Give me a drink, Joe.

MACK: My name is not Joe.

MOLLY: Give me a drink.

MACK: What do you want?

MOLLY: Give me an absinthe.

MACK: You give me a pain. Did you guys hear that?

JOHN: What?

MACK: She wants an absinthe.

MOLLY: That's what we drink in the islands.

MACK: What islands?

MOLLY *thinks awhile.*

JIM: Make it two.

JOHN: Make it three.

MACK: [*Referring to* MOLLY] Creep.

JOHN: Hit me. [JIM *gives* JOHN *a card*] Hit me again. [JIM *gives* JOHN *a card*] Hit me again. [JIM *gives* JOHN *a card*] Hit me again. [JIM *gives* JOHN *a card*] Hit me again.

JIM: How many cards have you got? You must be over.

JOHN: No, I'm not. Hit me again. [JIM *gives* JOHN *a card suspiciously*] Hit me again.

They Indian-wrestle through the following scene. MACK *puts three glasses on the counter.*

MOLLY: Mack, set them up, Joe.

MACK: The name is Mack.

MOLLY: Set them up. [MOLLY *walks to the players, and puts one foot up on the fourth chair. She puts a flower behind* JOHN's *ear and kisses the* HANGING WOMAN. *Then, she considers a moment, takes the flower and puts it behind her own ear. Then, she moves as if to kiss* JOHN, *changes her mind, puts the flower behind the* HANGING WOMAN's *ear. Then, she takes the flower and holds it over her lips as she tries to remember such a scene from the film* Morocco. *She, then, eats the flower. She starts walking toward the counter humming* "One for My Baby." *She is not satisfied with the song. Then, starts humming* "My man." *She is happier with that tune*]

> He isn't true.
> He beats me too.
> What can I do?
>
> He isn't true.
> He beats me too.
> What can I do?

I don't really let anyone beat me.

MACK: So why do you keep saying it?

MOLLY: I like saying it.

MACK: *I like saying it. I like saying it.*

MOLLY:

> He isn't true.
> He beats me too.
> What can I do?

MACK: Phony! You want a sock in the jaw? Why don't you guys do something about this dame? She gives me a pain.

MOLLY *takes a gun from the counter and puts a bullet through* JOHN's *hand, which ends the Indian-wrestling.*

JIM: Thanks. [*To* JOHN] Stay?

JOHN: Hit me again. [JIM *gives* JOHN *a suspicious and threatening look.* JOHN *looks at the cards*] I'm good.

JIM *deals himself a card.*

JIM: I'm out.

JOHN: I win. [JOHN *puts the two dollars on his side of the table and picks up the deck*]

JIM: Show me.

JOHN *shuffles the cards.* JIM *puts the two dollars on his side of the table.* JOHN *picks seven cards from the deck, puts them on the table, and takes the two dollars. They Indian-wrestle.* MOLLY *takes the gun and puts a bullet through* JIM's *hand.*

JOHN: Thanks. [JOHN *takes the cards*] I'm dealer.

JIM: Forget it.

JOHN: What do you mean, forget it?

JIM: I'm not playing. [*To* MACK] How about that drink? [MACK *signals* MOLLY *to take the drinks to the table.* MOLLY *throws the glasses over her shoulder, one at a time.* JIM *catches them and throws them back. They juggle the glasses for a while.* JIM *fails to catch them. They fall to his feet*] You make me feel frustrated.

MOLLY: How's that?

JIM: First you hang on and you like it, and then you ignore me.

MOLLY: Who, me?

JIM: Yes, you.

ALBERTA *enters. She wears a Shirley Temple wig and a child's dress.*

MACK: [*Signaling* MOLLY *to get* ALBERTA *out*] Hey, Molly.

MOLLY: My name is not Molly.

JIM: What is your name?

MOLLY: I'm not telling anyone.

JIM: You could tell me.

MOLLY: I'm not telling.

JIM: What's the good of having a name if you don't tell anyone?

MOLLY: It's good. That way no one can call me.

JIM: I might want to write you a note.

MOLLY: I wouldn't read it anyway. [*She goes to* JOHN] Hey, handsome.

JIM: Don't talk to him. He's a fake.

MOLLY: What do you mean?

JIM: He never got laid in his life.

JOHN *threatens* JIM. *The lights flash on and off.*

ALBERTA: He's cute.

MACK: [*To* ALBERTA] I told you, no children allowed. [ALBERTA *taps to a chair and sits.* MACK *taps her shoulder*] Out. [*She ignores him.* MACK *takes her by the collar out the door*]

JOHN: Is that a child?

MACK: Yeah. You wouldn't believe it, would you? Smart aleck. Can't bear her. She dances all the time.

JOHN: She's an interesting-looking dame.

MOLLY: If you're not interested in me, I was not interested in you first.

JIM: Can't even think straight.

MOLLY: I can think straight. I just don't want to.

JOHN: Let me have another drink. Don't give me any more of that licorice stuff. Give me a man's drink.

MACK: Like what?

MOLLY: Absinthe is a man's drink. If you drink a lot of it, you go blind.

JOHN: Give me an absinthe. [*He gives* JIM *an assertive look, then drinks the absinthe in one gulp*] Yes, that child is certainly an interesting-looking dame. [*He gives* JIM *another assertive look and speaks to* MACK] Let me have another one of those. I don't care if I do go blind.

MACK *pours.*

JIM: [*To himself*] He never got laid in his life.

JOHN: I'll have another.

MACK: You didn't drink that one yet.

He drinks it, belches several times and checks his vision.

JOHN: [*To* MACK, *attempting to be casual*] Why do you think he said I never got laid?

MACK: Don't pay any attention to him. He's a creep.

JOHN: Ask him.

MACK: Hey, why did you say . . .

JIM: [*Interrupting*] All he's got is guns.

MACK: He's got more than guns. I bet you he's got more than guns.

JIM: [*Putting a dollar on the table*] I bet all he's got is guns.

MACK: [*Putting a dollar on the table*] I bet he's got more.

JOHN *does the "One Narrow Idea" dance. The dance consists of making the guns swing back and forth. The lights go to full intensity and remain so through the dance.*

JOHN: [*Sings*]

> One very long,
> Very narrow
> Idea.
> One very long
> And narrow
> Idea.
> A narrow idea.
> An old idea.
> A withered idea
> Without reward.
> A withering idea.
> An old, old idea.

MACK: [*Taking the two dollars*] Yup, he's got more than guns.

JIM: [*Taking the two dollars from* MACK] No, he doesn't.

They Indian-wrestle. JOHN *helps* MACK *push* JIM's *arm down.*

MACK: [*Taking the two dollars*] Thanks.

JOHN: What did you think of that dance?

MACK: That was swinging, man.

JOHN: Was that swinging? Or wasn't that swinging?

MACK: That was swinging, man.

JOHN: Did you ever see anyone swing like that?

MACK: Not that I can remember.

JOHN: Try to remember. [MACK *thinks*] Well? . . .

MACK: I can't remember.

JOHN: Try.

MACK: I said I can't remember.

JOHN: Then you never saw anyone swing like that.

MACK: I can't remember.

JOHN: If you can't remember it's because you never saw anyone swing like that.

MACK: I don't know.

JOHN: [*Twisting* MACK's *arm*] What do you mean, you don't know?

MACK: I don't know.

JOHN: If you had, you would remember. [MACK *doesn't answer.* JOHN *points his gun at* MACK's *temple*] If you had, you would remember.

MACK: I suppose.

JOHN: Don't suppose. Did you or didn't you?

MACK: No, I never did.

JOHN: [*In narcissistic rapture*] Ahhhhhhh.

MACK: Jesus! What a creep.

JOHN: Ask that lady in.

MACK: What lady?

JOHN: The one you turned out.

MACK: The child?

JOHN: Ask her in.

MACK: Jesus!

Lights go back to normal. MACK *goes to the door. On his way there he stops by* JIM'S *table and gives him back his dollar.*

MOLLY: [*To* JOHN] If that's your taste, you don't belong in my book of names and telephones like a sailor. . . . I cross you out.

JOHN: What is she talking about?

MOLLY: If you like her.

MACK: Don't pay any attention to her.

JIM: Can't even speak English.

MOLLY: I can when I want to. . . . I only don't want to.

MACK: [*To* ALBERTA] All right. You can come in.

ALBERTA *dances in.*

JIM: You know why you haven't grown?

JOHN: She's grown.

ALBERTA: Why?

JIM: Because you haven't been loved.

ALBERTA: Creep.

JIM: I thought you might want to know.

ALBERTA: No, I don't want to know. I am a child. That's why I haven't grown. And I get plenty of love, so leave me alone.

JIM: How old are you?

ALBERTA: Twenty-seven.

JIM: [*He considers a moment*] You need love.

JOHN: The lady is with me, if you don't mind.

JIM: No, I don't mind. But she should mind.

JOHN: Why should she mind?

ALBERTA: I don't mind.

JOHN *presses* ALBERTA'S *hand against his lips and remains in that position until he speaks again.*

JIM: [*To* ALBERTA] You need love.

ALBERTA *makes an obscene gesture to* JIM.

MACK: [*Referring to* JIM] Boy, he's finished.

JIM: What do you expect? You get involved with a broad like that and you're cooked. I didn't know she was German.

MOLLY: I was not German. I became German. You made me become German.

JIM: You always had it in you.

MOLLY: I am not a hen. I will not share my rooster with other hens. I'm the only hen or I'm not a hen.

JIM: She's crazy.

MOLLY: I may be crazy but I'm not a hen.

JIM: What's wrong with hens?

MOLLY: There's nothing wrong with hens. Only I'm not a hen.

JIM: I don't see why you had to be the only one. The others were happy.

MOLLY: But I'm not happy.

JIM: She's crazy.

MOLLY: I'm just wise and tough about you men.

JIM: I don't like tough women. I'm through with you.

MOLLY: I'm through with you before you are through with me.

JIM: Can't even speak English.

MOLLY: Only when I get angry. [*She goes to the bird cage and sets the bird free*] Fly away, *mien kleiner Vogel,* baby. *Esse alle Würmer die du kannst.* That means: fly away, my little bird. Eat all the worms you can. Fly away, *mien kleiner Vogel,* baby. *Esse alle Würmer die du kannst.* [*The* HANGING WOMEN *surround* MOLLY] No . . . no . . . no . . .

The HANGING WOMEN *giggle and go back to their places.*

JIM: Creep.

MOLLY: Little man.

JIM *goes to* JOHN *and* ALBERTA.

MACK: His pride is hurt.

JIM: No, it is not. I just think there's something wrong with her. [*To* JOHN *and* ALBERTA] May I join you?

JOHN: If the lady wishes.

ALBERTA: All right. But don't tell me I'm a hen.

JIM: I never told you you were a hen.

ALBERTA: I mean, okay, but don't tell me I need love.

JIM: Okay. [*He sits*]

JOHN: Madam? . . .

ALBERTA: Sir? . . .

JOHN: Would you like anything to drink?

ALBERTA: I'll have a mint julep with cherry syrup.

JOHN: [*To* JIM] Would your lady friend like a drink?

JIM: I have no lady friend. Can't you see I have no lady friend? [*He gives* MOLLY *a dirty look*]

ALBERTA: You don't have to get rude. You have no lady friend because you have no manners.

JOHN: [*To the* HANGING WOMAN] Would you like a drink, madam?

The HANGING WOMAN *smiles.*

JIM: Why aren't you with the others? [*The* HANGING WOMAN *joins the others*] Creep!

JOHN: [*To* MACK] A mint julep with cherry syrup. . . . Make it two.

JIM: See? He's not real. He just drinks what everybody else drinks.

ALBERTA: I still like him better than you. Even if he's not real.

JOHN: I'm real. Can't you see I'm real? [*He pinches himself and shakes the table*] Could I have done that if I weren't real?

ALBERTA: You're real. It's he who is not real.

JOHN *presses* ALBERTA's *hand against his lips.*

JIM: [*Dismissing the subject*] I'm real.

ALBERTA: [*Referring to* JOHN] And besides being real, he's cute.

JOHN: My peach. [*He presses her hand against his lips again*]

JIM: You see what I mean? He's not real.

ALBERTA: He looks real to me.

JOHN: My peach . . . my pearl . . . [*He presses* ALBERTA's *hand against his lips*]

JIM: He's just pretending to be real. That's why he kisses you.

ALBERTA: [*Hitting* JIM *on the head*] He's not pretending. He kisses me because he likes my baby flesh . . . and you stop bothering us. We want to be alone. Sit somewhere else.

JOHN: My peach, my pearl, my persimmon, I want to be alone with you. My peach, my pearl, when the impossible begins to seem possible. When love knocks at our door. All our expectations, dreams, desires go rampant. There is no end to what seems possible. There is no end to what we ask for. Sugar baby, candy child, give me your life.

ALBERTA: [*Matter-of-fact*] No.

JOHN *picks* ALBERTA *up. He looks for a place to take her. He is like a wild beast looking for a place to take his prey. She gets away from him. He runs after her.*

HANGING WOMEN: [*Sing*]
Is this true passion,
Or the way a vain man has
Of saying to himself:
I am not dead?

JOHN: [*Spoken*]
I am not dead.
Not dead.
Not dead.

HANGING WOMEN:
Is this true love?
True love?
True love?

One very long,
Very narrow,
Very old idea.
An old idea.
A long idea.
An old, old,
Withered idea,
Without reward.

A withering idea.
One very narrow,
Very old idea.
A narrow idea.

ALBERTA: Me, the little darling. The heaven on earth. The night without pain. The honey of the flowers. I will not be yours. Ever. . . . I can't. . . . I'm pure.

JOHN: My fairy tale, my peach, my pearl, grant me my wish.

ALBERTA: No.

JOHN: I am in control of my emotions. I always have been. Once I was almost in love. Yes, indeed, no one can say I've never loved. I am an important man. My scope is very narrow. Yes, it's very narrow, but it is wide enough to strike a pose of self-importance. . . . That's all I need. . . . Me, a failure? Never! I'm in control of my emotions. My emotions are feeble. Me, strong. The more I'm known to strangers the more I lose my sense of dignity. I have no point of view. I am well known, that's all I need. You know me. I know myself. What, me, get old? Never! That's not for me. Candy child, give me your life.

ALBERTA: No.

JOHN *moves behind* ALBERTA *and sinks his teeth into her neck. Through the following song* JOHN *and* ALBERTA *take vampirical love-making poses. Between the poses, and with the aid of the* HANGING WOMEN, *they do a costume change with rapid choreographed movements.* JOHN *removes his guns and his hat and puts on a cape.* ALBERTA *takes her wig off, letting her hair loose. Her dress grows long to the floor. He looks like a vampire. She is sensuous and glamorous. He sinks his teeth into her neck again.*

HANGING WOMEN: [*Sing*]
Is this true passion,
Or the way a vain man has
Of saying to himself:
I am not dead?

Is this true love?
True love?
True love?

He lifts his head and looks around. He moves in front of her and stretches his arms as if to protect her.

JOHN: Don't anyone touch my own. She's mine.

JIM: Who wants to.

JOHN: My one and only. My own.

MACK: Creep.

JOHN: Ahhh. Love, love, love . . . [*He does a pirouette*] I feel at last alive. [*He dances around with movements resembling a lizard's. He then takes* ALBERTA *to the mirror. By means of rear projection one sees* ALBERTA *in the mirror but not* JOHN. *He moves away from her in terror and shame. To* ALBERTA, *from a distance*] Tell me that you see me. [*She takes a step back*] Tell me that you love me.

ALBERTA: Vampire. . . . [*She looks away from him*]

JOHN: Kiss me. [*She takes a step back*] Ahhh. My love recoils from me. [*He sits down at a table. He is downcast.* ALBERTA *takes two steps toward him but stops. He watches her. He speaks the following*]

>My lady said the hair around my temple
>Is different from the rest,
>And that it is a sight to behold.
>She said it is smooth and grows downward,
>While the rest grows wild.
>
>My lady said there's a line
>From the back of my ear to my shoulder
>That gives her pleasure to look at.
>And she said as a present
>She'll give me a flock of birds.
>She is my love.
>That lady is my love.
>
>She speaks of love
>Only angels know,
>And yet she fears me.
>My lady fears me.
>[*She moves toward him*]
>My lady said
>The joint that holds my jaw to my skull
>Is delicate like a bird's.
>So my lady said.
>
>My lady said my face is life itself.
>She is my love.
>That lady is my love,
>And yet, she fears me.
>
>My lady said when she held me in her arms
>She held not a man but the world.
>And yet my lady fears me.
>She fears me.

ALBERTA *goes to* JOHN. *She brings her hand to his cheek and kisses him.*

ALBERTA: [*Sings*]
>The senses are five:
>Sight, smell, hearing, taste, touch.
>*Los sentidos. Les sens. I sentiti.*
>The verb "to sense" in French
>Refers to smelling *"sens."*
>*Tu sens bon.*
>In Italian, *"sentire,"*
>It refers to hearing.
>*Sente amore mio.*
>In Spanish, *"sentir,"*
>It means to feel.
>*Siento en el alma*
>*Unas ganas intensas de llorar.*
>In English, "to sense,"
>Is nothing you can put your finger on.

>I sense something unusual all around me.
>Love, love, love. Love, love, love, love.
>You have brought me to my senses.
>You have made sense of me.
>And the sense of me is you.
>I hear. I see. I smell. I taste. I touch.
>Oh, love.
>My life is senseless without you.

They kiss. They circle around the stage as if strolling in the park. The HANGING WOMEN *surround them singing. When they reach the center of the stage they each circle the stage in opposite directions. Half the* HANGING WOMEN *follow* JOHN, *the other half follow* ALBERTA. *They meet in the center again, and walk down the aisle, followed by the* HANGING WOMEN, *who carry garlands.*

HANGING WOMEN: [*Sing*]
>She is my love.
>That lady is my love.
>She speaks of love
>Only angels know.

MACK: Molly, that kid is doing better than you.

MOLLY: No, she is not.

MACK: Yes, she is.

HANGING WOMEN:
>She is my love.
>That lady is my love.
>She speaks of love
>Only angels know. [*They exit*]

JIM: Fiddlesticks. [*There is a short pause and a sense of sadness*] Yeah, that's how it is.

MOLLY: Mack, play something amusing, Sam. I feel sad. [*They are silent for a moment.* MOLLY *sighs*]

JIM: I beg your pardon?

MOLLY: Hm.

JIM: A second chance?

MOLLY: Hm.

JIM: Hm, hm. Not me. I'm quitting. . . . You had your chance.

They speak the following.

MOLLY:
>To tell you I still love you?
>Why? You care?
>I loved you once.
>What? You think that's nothing?
>It isn't everyone who's loved the way I loved you.
>You're feeling sorry now.
>Well, too late, I'm quitting.
>You can't expect me to survive all that.

JIM:
>I'm too proud. You're right.
>And you're a two-time loser.

Once you had my love and didn't
  take it.
That makes it once you were the
  loser.
And now you want me back.
You lose again.
I'm too proud, you're right.
I'm quitting.
I'm not expected to survive all that.

JIM *walks to the door. He and* MOLLY *start
singing with their backs to each other.*

JIM *and* MOLLY:
  A sense of incompletion . . . yeah . . .
    yeah . . .
  A joke without a laugh,
  A friend who doesn't hear,
  A promise without hope,
  An offer withdrawn,
  A good-bye with no departure.
  And what? Am I expected to survive
    all that?
  Ha ha. Fat chance. Not me. I'm quit-
    ting.

JIM:
  Johnny told me, August first,
  There'll be a parade.
  Ha ha. If the city permits.

MOLLY:
  Ronnie told me, August second,
  We'll see a movie.
  Ha ha. He changed his mind.

JIM:
  My horoscope said, August third,
  I'd have good news.
  Ha ha. There was no news.

MOLLY:
  Mack told me, August fourth,
  He'd give me a raise.
  Ha ha. There was no raise.

JIM:
  My cousin told me, August fifth,
  We'd go for a ride.
  Ha ha. The car broke down.

MOLLY:
  August sixth, I took the bus.
  It was a long ride,
  And when I got there,
  No one said hello.

JIM *and* MOLLY:
  And what? Am I expected to survive
    all that?
  Ha ha. That's all I can say.
  Ha ha. Ha ha. Ha ha.

JIM *walks to the door. He turns back and
shakes hands with* MOLLY.

JIM: Good-bye.

MOLLY: Good-bye. [*He walks to the door again*]
  You know . . .

JIM: . . . What? . . .

MOLLY: In order to become what we are . . .

JIM: Yes? . . .

MOLLY: We have to go through many stages.

JIM: Yes.

MOLLY *puts on the top hat. They laugh.*

MOLLY: If we had met some other time . . . perhaps . . .

JIM: Perhaps we'll meet again some other time.

MOLLY: Yes.

JIM: I'll be going now. [*He walks to the door*]
  See you later . . . Molly?

MOLLY: [*Taking the hat off*] Yes . . .

JIM: You'll wait for me?

MOLLY: I will. . . . Will you recognize me?

JIM: Yes, I'll know you.

They wave. He exits. MOLLY *walks to the
table where she first fell asleep. She leans
her head on the table.* MACK *walks in and
straightens the place, leaving it as in the beginning of the play. The* YOUNG MAN *enters.
He carries luggage which resembles in color
the* HANGING WOMEN'S *costumes. He looks at*
MOLLY.

MACK: She's lost to the world. What would you
  have?

YOUNG MAN: Do you rent rooms?

MACK: No, we don't rent rooms.

YOUNG MAN: [*Picking up the luggage*] Oh, well
  . . . [*The lights flash on and off. The* YOUNG
  MAN *puts the luggage down and turns to look
  at* MOLLY] On second thought, I think I'll
  have a drink.

MACK: What would you like?

YOUNG MAN: Double rye. [MACK *pours the
  drink. The* YOUNG MAN *pays* MACK *and
  takes the drink to a table*] I'll give my feet a
  rest. I walked from the station.

MACK *exits. The* YOUNG MAN *watches*
MOLLY. *He drinks his drink, takes a deep
breath, picks up his bags, and exits. The lights
fade except for a blue spot on* MOLLY'S *head.
She wakes up suddenly and looks where the*
YOUNG MAN *sat. The spot is held for a few
seconds while two high musical notes play.
The spot fades.*

GLORIA AND ESPERANZA

a play in two acts

Julie Bovasso

Gloria and Esperanza was first presented by Ellen Stewart at La Mama ETC, New York City, on April 4, 1969. It was subsequently presented by the National Theatre and Academy (Alfred de Liagre, Jr., executive producer; Jean Dalrymple, executive director) at the ANTA Theatre, New York City, on February 9, 1970, with the following cast:

ACT I

A BASEMENT APARTMENT

JULIUS ESPERANZA, *a poet* .... *Jeff Weiss; Kevin O'Connor**

GLORIA B. GILBERT, *his girl friend* .... *Julie Bovasso*

PROFESSOR POE .... *Hervé Villechaize*

SOLANGE, *an eight-foot chicken* .... *Daffi*

AGITATORS .... *Alex Beall, Reigh Hagen, Wes Williams, Alan Wynroth*

GURU CHILDREN .... *Maria D'Elia, Sara Dolley, Daffi, John Bacher, Deirdre Simone, Dennis Sokal, Ella Luxembourg, Laverne Jamison, Jane Sanford*

SOLDIERS .... *William Pierce, Louis Ramos, Peter Bartlett, Carl Wilson*

FRED THE MAILMAN .... *William Shorr; Ted Henning**

TERRY WONG FU, *an Oriental landlord* .... *Charles Cajori; Dan Durning**

THE EMERGENCY ROOM

THE PSYCHIATRIST .... *Leonard Hicks*

DR. BROWN, *another psychiatrist* .... *Alan Harvey; Maury Cooper**

ATTENDANTS .... *Louis Ramos, Alan Wynroth*

GLADIATORS .... *John Bacher, William Pierce, Peter Bartlett, Carl Wilson*

ACT II

IN THE MADHOUSE: SAINTS AND MARTYRS

JACK SINISTRE, *the Black Prince* .... *Alex Beall*

STEISSBART, *his Demon* .... *Hervé Villechaize*

ST. TERESA, *a young man* .... *Reigh Hagen*

ST. AUGUSTINE .... *Ted Henning*

ST. AMBROSE .... *Alan Harvey; Maury Cooper**

ST. ANTONY, *really Lt. Col. Antony Moore* .... *Sean MacNamara; Leonard Hicks**

ST. JOHN, *a shell-shocked soldier* .... *John Bacher*

ST. DOMINIC, *a mongoloid* .... *Constantine Poutous; Dennis Sokal**

ST. BONIFACE, *a hysteric* .... *Wes Williams*

ST. AGNES, *a spastic* .... *Sara Dolley*

ST. FELICITE, *a catatonic* .... *Deirdre Simone*

MARY and MARTHA .... *Maria D'Elia, Ella Luxembourg*

ST. BERNARD, *a schizophrenic* .... *Daffi*

* ANTA production only

BACK IN THE BASEMENT

ERIC VON SCHTUTT, *the Internal Revenue Man* .... *Tom Rosica*

MARSHA, *Gloria's friend* .... *Nancy Nichols; Jane Sanford**

THE ALVIN AND HIS MOTHER TV SHOW

ALVIN, *a cocker spaniel and star of the show* .... *Leonard Hicks; Ted Henning**

ALVIN'S MOTHER, *his co-star* .... *Dennis Sokal*

BASKETBALL BALLET GIRLS .... *Sara Dolley, Laverne Jamison, Myra Lee, Deirdre Simone, Jane Sanford*

ORIENTAL GORILLA DANCERS .... *John Bacher, William Pierce, Peter Bartlett*

THE REVELATIONS REVUE

4 HORSEWOMEN SHOWGIRLS OF THE APOCALYPSE .. *John Bacher, Maria D'Elia, Sara Dolley, Jane Sanford*

STAR ANGELS .... *Laverne Jamison, Myra Lee, Ella Luxembourg, Deirdre Simone*

SWORD ANGELS .... *Reigh Hagen, Wes Williams, Carl Wilson, Alan Wynroth*

TRUMPET ANGELS .... *Peter Bartlett, William Pierce*

WOMAN CLOTHED IN THE SUN .... *Dennis Sokal*

ALPHA AND OMEGA .... *Louis Ramos*

DRAGON .... *Ted Henning*

CHORUS: *Richard Beil, Robert Cherry, Sara Cholakis, Maria D'Elia, Mary Drysdale, David Kasmire, Bert Maddore, Fred Muselli, Grace Parades, Carole Patrick, Constantine Poutous, Evan Ritter, Betsy Ryan, Dee Simone, Patricia Shevlin, Dennis Sokal, Ella Sherman, Douglas Stone, Steven Verakus, Lydia Winsloe, Allan Wynroth, Mark Zweifach.*

DANCERS: *John Bacher, Peter Bartlett, Reigh Hagen, Margaret McLaughlin, William Pierce, Sandy Ratcliffe, Patricia Whited.*

It was directed by the author. Associate director and choreographer: Raymond Bussey. At La Mama: costumes designed and executed by Randy Barcelo. At ANTA: assistant choreographer, William Pierce; setting, Daffi; lighting, Keith Michael; settings and costumes supervised by Peter Harvey; costumes, Ella Luxembourg and the Birdie Sisters; lighting supervisor, Richard Nelson.

ANTA production only

For Leonard Hicks

ACT I

Scene I

A room without walls or doors. Tall screens up right and up left; an old bed, a makeshift desk and a packing trunk. Upstage center there are three long steps which lead to a rear platform with bamboo shades. Above this platform there is a catwalk construction about eleven or twelve feet high.

As the house lights fade we hear an electronic hum, followed by a tremendous explosion and a loud burst of machine-gun fire. There is a moment of silence before we hear parade music in the distance. JULIUS *and* GLORIA *enter down the center aisle, followed by the* BLACK PRINCE *and the entire company of 43 players: Gladiators, Masked Beasties, Star Angels, Guru Children, Soldiers, Agitators, Trumpet Angels, The Terrible Mother, the 8-foot chicken with* POE, *a uniformed midget mounted on its back, etc., etc., etc. They all take places around the stage: seated, standing, kneeling; on both platform levels, around the edges of the main stage, with* JULIUS *and* GLORIA *down center. The parade music is suddenly interrupted by machine-gun fire and a continuous round of battle sounds. Nobody responds to the noise except* JULIUS, *who tries to take cover. He grows increasingly frantic, then whirls on the audience.*

JULIUS: In a few days the boom will be lowered. You know that, don't you? *I said you know that, don't you?* Listen to me. In a few days we'll all be mowed down like rats. Worse than rats. You don't seem to realize what's going on out there. [*He begins to include the players, directing his words alternately to them and the audience*] Don't you know what's going on out there? Well, maybe you can't hear it, but I can hear it. And even if you can't hear it, that doesn't mean it isn't going on just the same . . . hear it or not! Don't tell me you can't hear it. You can hear it! It's right under your noses and you can't hear it? Listen! If you'd listen you'd hear it. [*He listens, then covers his ears to shut out the noise. The sound increases, he crouches in the center of the stage, then with heightened anger, uncovers his ears*] YOU DON'T WANT TO HEAR IT! [*Looking wildly about—then to the audience*] I'm not going to stay here and be mowed down like a rat. Worse than a rat. Like a sitting duck. You can do whatever you want to do. I'm going

to fight, that's what I'm going to do. [*He turns to the players onstage*] I'm going to need help. I can't fight it out alone. Who? Who? Who can help me? [*They stare at him blankly*] Oh, God! God! Help me! [*He takes cover under the desk. The machine-gun fire stops, followed by faint birdcalls. As the birdcalls grow fainter, he crawls out from under the desk. Silence. Slowly he rises. The players break into applause. It is as though they have been watching a performance. He stares around, dazed, then crosses to the chair, where he sits. Music begins: "Pleasure Mad."* GLORIA *takes two canes and two straw hats, crosses to* JULIUS, *hands him his cane and puts a straw hat on his head and goes into a dance. He follows. They do a routine, through which the following dialogue takes place. Dancing, to* GLORIA, *who pays no attention*] In a few days the boom will be lowered. You know that, don't you? [*She shuffles past him*] I said you know that, don't you? [*He joins her in a dance-walk*] Listen to me. In a few days we'll all be mowed down like rats. Worse than rats. [*They tap-dance around their canes*] You don't seem to realize what's going on out there. Don't you know what's going on out there? Well, maybe you can't hear it, but I can hear it. And even if you can't hear it, that doesn't mean it isn't going on just the same, hear it or not!

GLORIA: [*High kicking*] Hear what? I told you before. I can't hear anything.

JULIUS: Don't tell me you can't hear it. You can hear it.

GLORIA: I cannot hear whatever it is you hear.

JULIUS: It's right under your nose and you can't hear it?

GLORIA: It has nothing to do with me. I'm sorry, but I can't hear it. [*Swaying back and forth on her cane*]

JULIUS: [*Tap-dancing*] If you'd listen you'd hear it.

GLORIA: All right. I'll listen.

JULIUS: Do you hear it?

GLORIA: [*Tilting her straw hat and strutting off in front of him*] No.

JULIUS: YOU DON'T WANT TO HEAR IT! [*Struts after her*] God damn it, I've had enough. I'm not going to stay here and be mowed down like a rat. Worse than a rat. Like a sitting duck. You can do whatever you want to do. I'm going to fight, that's what I'm going to do.

GLORIA: Julius, will you stop being crazy—

JULIUS: [*Whirling on her*] What?

GLORIA: [*Dancing away from him*] Nothing, nothing, I didn't say a thing.

JULIUS: [*Leaning on his cane, doing a soft-shoe step*] I'm going to need help. I can't fight it out alone. Who? Who can help me? I haven't the vaguest idea who. If only there were some answer. Some hope of salvation.

GLORIA: Well, you made your bed.

JULIUS: Yes, the die is cast.

GLORIA: You cast it yourself.

JULIUS: I have no choice but to pray to God to send me the means of getting out of here alive.

GLORIA: I think that's a very sound idea.

JULIUS: You think *what's* a very sound idea? You think *God* is a very sound idea?

GLORIA: Well it's your idea, not mine.

JULIUS: Then let me tell you something. I got his answer on Monday. He hasn't got the means. He's broke.

GLORIA: Ha.

JULIUS: Broke and busted.

GLORIA: You're the one who's broke and busted.

JULIUS: God is on his last legs.

GLORIA: God, God, God, that's all you ever talk about. I don't know anything at all about God, but I don't go around saying He's on His last legs. What's happened to your faith?

JULIUS: It is currently sleeping in the arms of my doubt. [*They end the dance, with* GLORIA *sitting on his knee. The players applaud.* GLORIA *acknowledges it. There is a sudden burst of machine-gun fire*] I WANT MORE SOLITUDE! [*The players slowly leave the stage. The lights fade.* JULIUS *stands alone in a spotlight*] The beginning. What was the beginning? Words, a place, other people perhaps. Prayers and dreams, perhaps. In my waking hours or in my sleep? I must confess in all honesty that I cannot remember the beginning, and must therefore cast my hook rather haphazardly into the sea of memory, and trust that I shall come up with something that will satisfy my own curiosity. [*He crosses to the desk and begins to write*] And Abraham's body was carried across the battle-field . . . shot in the back, betrayed. Hero and victim of this war that raged within . . . splitting me in battle with myself. A civil war. And Abraham lay dead within me. [*He pauses, reflecting. The lights come up fuller and* GLORIA *enters. She is wearing a half slip, bra and slippers and carries a colander in which there is a package of wrapped tinfoil and cigarette papers. She sits at the trunk and begins to strain leaves through the colander and to then roll a joint.* JULIUS *looks at her, rises restlessly*] Yes, I've made my bed. The die is cast. I cast it myself. [*He begins to change from his ruffled parade shirt into a work shirt*] I have no choice but to pray to God to send me the means of getting out of here alive. [*Pause*] I wouldn't be surprised if He were already dead.

GLORIA: Who?

JULIUS: He. Him.

GLORIA: Oh.

JULIUS: I wouldn't be surprised if He were already mowed down like a rat.

GLORIA: God was not mowed down like a rat.

JULIUS: I have a feeling He was. Yes, I feel it. I sense it. He was mowed down like a rat. [*He crosses back to the desk*] God, ha!! [*Then suddenly*] What's happened to my faith?

GLORIA: It is currently sleeping in the arms of your doubt.

JULIUS: What?

GLORIA: Well, that's what you said. [*She has finished rolling the joint and rises, crossing to the bed*] You know I was very hurt when you said that.

JULIUS: Hurt? Why were you hurt?

GLORIA: [*Lighting the joint and taking a drag*] Well . . . you are currently sleeping in my arms, to say the least; so if your faith is currently sleeping in the arms of your doubt . . . [*Another drag. She is getting slightly high*] . . . am I therefore to draw the logical conclusion that I am your doubt?

JULIUS: You amaze me, Miss Gilbert. You're getting brighter every second.

GLORIA: Well? Am I your doubt or am I not your doubt?

JULIUS: Yes, you are my doubt. You are also my fears.

GLORIA: [*Really stoned now*] Therefore I must be your weakness. [*She rolls limply from the bed onto the floor.* JULIUS *rises and crosses to her, standing over her. She raises her right foot and, hooking it between his legs, pulls him down on top of her. They roll around on the floor. He becomes quite passionate*]

JULIUS: I say . . . may I call you Gloria?

GLORIA: No.

JULIUS: Why can't I call you by your first name?

GLORIA: Because we don't know each other that well.

JULIUS: How well do we have to know each other? I've been inside you.

GLORIA: Lots of men have.

JULIUS: But I've touched something nobody else has touched.

GLORIA: That's *your* fantasy. [*He gets up and returns to his work. She goes back to the bed and takes a chocolate*]

JULIUS: I told you those chocolates are drugged.

GLORIA: So what? They taste good. Um yum yum.

JULIUS: Um yum yum. All you know is um yum yum. [*He rises and crosses into the bathroom, behind the up right screen. In a moment he returns, glances annoyedly at* GLORIA, *goes to the desk, where he tears a piece of newspaper in half and returns behind the screen.* GLORIA *glances around, then rises quickly and silently and goes to the desk. She leafs through the papers, folds one or two and stores them in her bosom. She then picks up a sheet which interests her particularly.* JULIUS *returns*] What are you doing?

GLORIA: Hah? Nothing . . .

JULIUS: [*Crossing to her*] Give that to me.

GLORIA: What is it? A poem about me?

JULIUS: Oh, yes. Perhaps it is.
"When my love swears that she is made of
    truth
I do believe her, though I know she lies,
That she might think me some untutor'd
    youth
Unlearned in the world's false subtleties . . ."
And so forth and so on . . .

GLORIA: Does that mean me? Is that written about me?

JULIUS: If that were written about you, Luv, you would belong to posterity, as does the man who wrote it.

GLORIA: Who's 'at?

JULIUS: Shakespeare.

GLORIA: William?

JULIUS: [*A glance*] Yeh, William.

GLORIA: You didn't write it.

JULIUS: No, I didn't write it. [*He goes back to his writing. She begins to polish her nails. There is a sudden burst of machine-gun fire*] Jesus! Listen!

GLORIA: What, again?

JULIUS: That *is* machine-gun fire! My God! There's no place to take cover! [*He pulls her from the bed onto the floor*]

GLORIA: Julius, my nails!

JULIUS: Holy Mary, Mother of God, pray for us sinners, now and at the hour of our death, Amen. Holy Mary, Mother of God, pray for us sinners, now and at the hour of our death, Amen.

The noises stop.

GLORIA: Is it finished!?

JULIUS: You didn't hear that? You really mean to say you didn't hear that?

GLORIA: No, I didn't hear it!

He grabs her roughly by the arms and shakes her.

JULIUS: You heard it! Don't tell me you didn't hear it!

GLORIA: Julius, please . . . !

JULIUS: [*Flings her against the bed*] You heard it, God damn you! Stop pretending you didn't hear it!

GLORIA: I didn't hear . . . Jesus Christ! . . . Lousy Cucu . . . [*She throws a magazine at him*]

JULIUS: Maybe they'll bomb us out . . . !

GLORIA: Shit! . . .

JULIUS: Maybe that's what they're planning next . . . !

GLORIA: You broke my nail!

JULIUS: . . . to blow us up into little pieces.

GLORIA: God damn you!

JULIUS: We've got to do something. We can't just sit here.

GLORIA: I can.

JULIUS: Well, maybe you can! You close your ears to what's going on. You pretend it isn't there! You sit and eat your chocolates and you close your eyes. Pretty soon you'll be so drugged you won't even care what happens. Well, not me. I'm going to find help . . . !

GLORIA: [*Muttering*] Yeh, go find help. . . .

JULIUS: Don't think I'm trapped! Not yet, I'm not. I'll give them a fight if it's a fight they want.

GLORIA: [*Derisively*] Yeh, fight, fight! [*She gets up from bed angrily and collects the colander and foil from the trunk*]

JULIUS: You didn't hear it. You really didn't hear it, did you?

GLORIA: You hurt my arm. [*She disappears behind the screen*]

JULIUS: I hurt your arm . . . I'm sorry . . . [*With his head in his hands, at the desk. He sighs. Then, bringing his fist down on the desk*] That was machine-gun fire. There's no question about it. I'm as sure of it as I am of my own existence! [*He pauses and reflects on this*] No, I'm trapped. Trapped, trapped, trapped. [GLORIA *returns with a piece of cake. She pauses in front of the mirror and observes her belly with some trepidation. She then looks at the piece of cake and decides to give it to him*] Thanks. [*She goes to the bed and begins a series of sit-up exercises*] There is no help for me. Nobody can help me. [*Stares off into space and eats the cake*]

GLORIA: [*Exercising*] What about the Black Prince? He can help you.

JULIUS: Who?

GLORIA: Jack Sinistre, the Black Prince. He'll know what to do. He's the only one who will know what to do.

JULIUS: How do you know about the Black Prince?

GLORIA: How do I know about the Black Prince?

JULIUS: Yes, how do you know about the Black Prince?

GLORIA: I heard about him.

JULIUS: Oh, you heard about him.

GLORIA: Or maybe I read about him first.

JULIUS: Read about him.

GLORIA: Someplace.

JULIUS: First. Someplace. Like in my notebook.

GLORIA: Well . . .

JULIUS: Like in my notebook!

GLORIA: . . . maybe I did.

JULIUS: So you've been leafing through my notebooks again. Stealing my ideas.

GLORIA: What are you talking about?

JULIUS: A little line here, a little line there . . .

GLORIA: Don't be ridiculous!

JULIUS: A little paragraph, a little poem!

GLORIA: What would I do with your ideas?

JULIUS: Well, what did you do with it? What did you do with the Black Prince?

GLORIA: Nothing, nothing! I read it, that's all. I read it!

JULIUS: Well, let me tell you something about the Black Prince—he's dangerous. You didn't know that, did you? You didn't know about that left hand of his. No, you didn't . . . the one he always keeps in his pocket. Well, he carries a bomb in that pocket, and if you happen to look at him cross-eyed . . .

GLORIA: That isn't true. Prince is a good guy.

JULIUS: He's an agitator. A revolutionary.

GLORIA: Wouldn't you rather take your chances with him than with them?

JULIUS: I'm not so sure about that.

GLORIA: But he's on your side.

JULIUS: No, he isn't.

GLORIA: He believes what you believe.

JULIUS: He believes what *he* believes.

GLORIA: But what *you* believe is what *he* believes. You both believe the same thing.

JULIUS: I believe it is necessary to make the separation between what I believe and what others believe. I've made my bed, the die is cast, I cast it myself. What can I do about it, when it's one against everything? One against the world.

GLORIA: Two.

JULIUS: What do you mean, two?

GLORIA: You and Prince. Prince and you are one.

JULIUS: I told you, I don't trust that left hand of his.

GLORIA: That isn't true. You just made that up this minute.

JULIUS: Of course it's true. And I did just make it up this minute. After all, it's my story.

GLORIA: Well, I like the story the way it was.

JULIUS: Yes, of course. The glorification of evil.

GLORIA: Oh, oh. I'm running out of jelly centers. [*Rises*] Did you buy me some more jelly centers?

JULIUS: Yeh, they're in the kitchen. [*She goes into the kitchen*] But I do know that we're in danger here. Particularly since there are no walls, no place to take cover. And it's impossible to get out because the front door hasn't even been built yet. [*Pause*] It seems I have imprisoned myself, Miss Gilbert, on an open battlefield. [*Rises*] Limitations. That's the answer. We have no limitations around here. No walls. No front door. There are too many possibilities, you see. There is no freedom here, Miss Gilbert, because there are no restrictions. Why doesn't that landlord do his job? Renovate this place. [*He crosses to the window and stares out*] Yes. Anarchy. [*A pause*] I must do something, however. I can't just stay here and wait. For what? Why do I stay? Why can't I leave? [*Pause*] Because I'm not a man of action, that's why. [*Pause*] How long have I been in this room? One thousand years? Two thousand years? I wonder what's going on out there. I wonder what century it is. I want to leave, but I can't. I wish, I want, I wish, I want . . .

She returns.

GLORIA: [*Entering from the kitchen*] You didn't buy me more jelly centers. I couldn't find them. [*She crosses restlessly to the bed and begins to play solitaire*]

JULIUS: Do you realize, Miss Gilbert, how many things in this world remain undone because they remain rooted in that limbo of passive wanting? I wish, I want, I wish, I want . . . God! What more is needed than to lift the hand and transform it all. To be a man of action! [*She is absorbed in her card game and pays no attention*] What would you think if I suddenly raped you?

GLORIA: Not now.

JULIUS: Yes, a man of action. The Black Prince. You're right, you know. He would know what to do. He'd fight his way out, that's what he'd do. Yeah . . . if I were the Black Prince, I'd show you some action out there. Yeah . . . if I were the Black Prince, I would. Maybe I'll become the Black Prince. How would you like that, huh? Jack Sinistre! [*He leaps on top of the trunk*] Jack Sinistre! I call upon you to enter my body! I invoke your spirit, Jack! Come and get me, Jackie, baby. [*Stepping down from the trunk*] He was my hero, you know. My childhood hero. [*Sitting at the desk*] I have to rewrite that story some day. Tell it like it is. [*He resumes his writing*]

GLORIA: I don't think you ought to change it. I think you ought to leave it the way it is. All this crap about his left hand . . . I don't think it's pertinent.

JULIUS: [*Stops writing. Not sure he has heard correctly*] You don't think it's *what?*

GLORIA: Pertinent. Well, that's a word, isn't it?

JULIUS: [*Hiding his amusement*] Yes, yes, it is.

GLORIA: You think I don't know anything. You think I'm stupid.

JULIUS: I don't think you're stupid at all. I think you're very . . . pertinent.

GLORIA: What?

JULIUS: Nothing.

GLORIA: I know a few things, too, you know. I know a few things that you don't know. In fact, I can teach you a few things.

JULIUS: You have, Miss Gilbert. You have.

GLORIA: You think I'm nothing but a dumb shit. Well, maybe I am nothing but a dumb shit. But I'm human, too, you know.

JULIUS: Yes. A human dumb shit. [*She hurls a book at him*] Zonked by a holy Bible . . .

GLORIA: I'm not so dumb . . . !

JULIUS: Hurled in a fit of rage . . .

GLORIA: Motherfucker . . .

JULIUS: . . . by a dumb shit!

GLORIA: Don't call me a dumb shit. [*She throws pillows, etc. at him. He picks her up and whirls her about the room*]

JULIUS: You are the dumb shit to end all dumb shits, Miss Gilbert.

GLORIA: No, no. Put me down . . . I'm not dumb . . .

JULIUS: [*Putting her down on the trunk, play-acting the Mad German Professor*] You know nothing! Do you understand, Miss Gilbert? Nothing! And I am going to kill you, Miss Gilbert, because we must rid the world of all the dumb shits who know nothing! Nothing!

GLORIA: [*Pushing him away and escaping*] But you told me yourself that nothing is potentially everything so therefore in a way I know everything. [*Singing and dancing*] I know everything. I know everything. I know everything underneath the sun. I know everything . . . rolled up into one . . .

JULIUS: [*Still playing the Mad German Professor*] You know nothing! You understand vords! But you do not underschtand concepts!

GLORIA: [*Suddenly*] Concepts? What's concepts?

JULIUS: [*Dropping the act*] I'm not going to tell you. [*He lets go of her and returns to his desk*]

GLORIA: You're not going to tell me? [*He resumes his writing*] Tell me. What is concepts? [*He does not answer*] Julius, I want to know what concepts means!

JULIUS: Look it up in the dictionary.

GLORIA: How can I look it up in the dictionary, I don't even know how to spell it! [*He goes on with his work*] Tell me! Julius, I'm warning you . . . if you don't tell me what concepts means, I won't let you fuck me!

He rises quickly and grabs her arms.

JULIUS: I told you not to threaten me like that!

GLORIA: Then tell me what concepts means. [*Angrily he releases her arm and returns to the desk*] Are you going to tell me?

JULIUS: No. You'll never get it out of me now.

GLORIA: All right, that settles it. From now on you can satisfy yourself! [*She goes angrily behind the screen up right*]

JULIUS: And she disappeared into the crapper and was never heard from again.

There is sudden machine-gun fire, accompanied now by birdcalls. JULIUS covers his ears, gets up, stalks around, sits down again. He then throws himself onto the bed, covering his ears, hunched up. The noises stop. He falls asleep. Very softly, as though from a great distance, we hear can-can music played on a piano. The music grows louder and PROFESSOR POE enters, mounted on the back of SOLANGE, the good chicken. SOLANGE does a dance. When the dance is over, POE dismounts and says to the chicken, pointing to the trunk.

POE: *Va t'asseoir sur le coffre,* Solange.

The chicken sits obediently on the trunk. POE then takes a flask of water from his shoulder and goes to JULIUS, who is still asleep. He lifts JULIUS' head and puts the flask to his mouth. JULIUS drinks the water like a man dying of thirst. Then he opens his eyes and stares at POE, who stands watching, nodding his head all the while.

JULIUS: Thank you.

POE: [*As JULIUS lifts the flask to drink again, POE takes it from him*] You have had enough for today. [*He seals the flask and places it beside SOLANGE on the trunk*] If we had not happened to come by, Monsieur, you might have died of thirst. That would certainly have been your last sleep.

JULIUS: Yes. I was dreaming of a well with silver water.

POE: [*He turns sharply*] Oh, you must beware, Monsieur. You must beware of the lion who guards the silver water in that well. That lion has a trick. He sleeps with his eyes open and watches with his eyes closed. [*He nods at* JULIUS] You must be very careful, Monsieur.

JULIUS: Yes, yes, I must.

POE: This is Solange. She is a very good chicken.

JULIUS: [*Rising a bit unsteadily, to* SOLANGE] How do you do?

POE *laughs and crosses to the desk, where he climbs on the chair and looks through* JULIUS' *papers.*

POE: *Très bien, Monsieur. Vous avez beaucoup de talent.* [*There is a long pause. Then* POE *says finally*] Would you like Solange to do a dance for you, Monsieur? Perhaps it will cheer you up. She is a very good dancer.

JULIUS: A dance . . . oh, yes. Yes. That would be . . . lovely.

POE: [*Standing on the desk, raising his arm in command*] Solange! *En avant!* [*The chicken rises*] Get out of the way, Monsieur. She needs a lot of room. [JULIUS *sits on the top step under the window*] *Un, deux, trois, quatre . . .*

The can-can music starts again and the chicken does a brief dance.

JULIUS: [*Rising*] That was . . . beautiful. Thank you . . . Mademoiselle. [*He extends his hand to the chicken, who merely stares at him dumbly*]

POE: Well, Monsieur, it would have been a shame if you had died before seeing Solange do her dance, would it not?

JULIUS: Yes, yes. It would have been a . . . bloody shame. Yes. [*He clears his throat*] Yes. Well . . . [*He rubs his hands together*]

POE: It would also have been a shame if you had died before continuing on your journey.

JULIUS: What?

POE: Yes. You must continue, Monsieur. You cannot stay here forever. And you cannot turn back now, either, Monsieur. But you must go when you are ready, and not before.

JULIUS: When I am ready?

POE: Yes. And you will know when it is time to leave when the tree begins to move. Then it will be time to go. Not before.

JULIUS: When the tree begins to move. What tree?

POE: Yes. And you must follow the tree, Monsieur. It will show you the way.

JULIUS: Follow the tree.

POE: And you must leave by the front door, Monsieur, because it faces the east. You must continue eastward on your journey. And after seven years you will reach the Great Mountain. [JULIUS *is silent, staring straight out*] I will give you some things to help you on your travels, Monsieur. [*He climbs down from the desk and goes to the trunk and takes the flask, which he hands to* JULIUS, *and a scrip*] Take these. You will have all the food and drink you need.

JULIUS: Thank you.

POE: And last of all, but most important . . . [*He reaches under his cape and takes out a rather large leaf*] . . . this leaf. If you ever have to cross the water, it will turn into a boat.

JULIUS: Turn into a boat . . . yes.

POE: And now, most important of all, I must give you a list of things to beware of. [*He reaches under his cape again and hands* JULIUS *a scroll.* JULIUS *unrolls it and reads*]

JULIUS: Things to Beware Of. [*He clears his throat*] 1. Beware of the lion who guards the silver water . . . oh, yes, you told me about that one already . . .

POE: Yes. He is very dangerous, that tricky lion. Son of a bitch.

JULIUS: Yes, I'll watch out for him, you can be sure. [*Reading from the scroll*] 2. Beware of the witches who live in the magic fountain. [*He looks at* POE]

POE: Yes. They have a rope, and if you go too near the magic fountain, they will . . . *que vous dire . . . ?* [*He makes a gesture of twirling a rope*]

JULIUS: Lasso.

POE: Yes, lasso. They will lasso you into the magic fountain and turn you into a statue that stands all day making pee-pee.

SOLANGE: Pee-pee, pee-pee.

POE: You wouldn't like *that* very much, Monsieur, would you?

JULIUS: No, no, I wouldn't.

POE: Making pee-pee all day in the middle of a magic fountain . . . *Comme ça* . . . PShhhhhhh . . . PShhhhhhh . . . Psh . . . PShhhhhhhhhhhh . . . [*He imitates a statue making pee-pee*]

JULIUS: No . . . no, indeed . . . I should say not!

SOLANGE: Pshhhhhh . . . pshhhhhhh . . . pshhhhhh . . .

POE: [*in French*] *Qu'est-ce qu'il y a,* Solange?

SOLANGE: Pshhhh . . . pshhhh . . . pee-pee . . . pee-pee . . .

POE: [*in French*] *Vous voulez faire* pee-pee?

SOLANGE: Ahhh, *oui.* Pee-pee.

POE: [*Climbing on the chicken*] We must go, Monsieur. Solange has to make pee-pee.

JULIUS: Yes . . . yes, of course . . . well . . .

POE: Do you have everything straight?

JULIUS: [*Reading the scroll*] Yes, let's see . . . Always leave by the front door . . . yes, you told me that. Travel eastward . . . yes . . . follow the moving tree . . . I know about that one . . . and wait for the tree to move before I leave. Yes. That's about it, is it?

POE: [*Smiles knowingly*] And a few other things.

JULIUS: A few other things . . . yes. Well. Thank you very much, my friend. You have undoubtedly . . . saved my life.

POE: Ah well, Monsieur. But you must remember something else: A life-bringer is also a death-dealer. [*JULIUS stares at him*] Perhaps when we meet again you will have cause for tears. [*There is a terrible silence*] But you must also remember: He who takes part in the mysteries will not die in darkness and in gloom.

JULIUS: How very small you are.

POE: I have to be small in order to fit inside your head. [*The can-can music starts softly again*] Courage, Esperanza! Courage! [*They exit*]

JULIUS *places the articles into the trunk. He then crosses to the screen up right.*

JULIUS: Miss Gilbert, open up! Open up, I say! Stop running away from the issue! Open the door and face the issue. Face to face. Do you hear me? Stop hiding! Come out of there. Meet me on even ground, you bloody cur! Show yourself on the field of battle, you cowardly whelp! Fight it out hand to hand! [*Laughing, he returns to his desk.* GLORIA *appears suddenly. She is dressed in leather bra and tights, and a helmet made of buttons. She carries a riding crop. She stands center, then cracks the whip on the trunk.* JULIUS *turns, startled, then bursts out laughing*] I say, what have we here? The latest transformation of woman!

GLORIA: [*Cracking the whip again*] What's concepts?

JULIUS *jumps up.*

JULIUS: Concept is from the Latin *conceptum* . . .

She cracks the whip at his feet, he jumps again, still laughing.

GLORIA: What . . . *conceptum?*

JULIUS: . . . which is the neutral form of *conceptus* . . .

GLORIA: [*Wildly cracking the whip*] I don't understand that bullshit! Neutral form . . .

JULIUS: Pluperfect *concipere* . . . which is "to conceive."

GLORIA: What, conceive! You're putting me on!

JULIUS: Something conceived in the mind. [*She continues to thrash about with the whip, like a child. He jumps, runs, pretends fright, laughing*] An abstract idea generalized from particular instances.

GLORIA: I don't understand!

JULIUS: [*Stopping suddenly*] Thought. [*He appears suddenly very serious, as he stares at her. Then, quietly, his hand outstretched*] Give that to me. [*She is arrested by his manner and hands him the whip, which he places on the trunk*] You don't need that. [*She crosses to the stool and sits. He goes to the bed and lies down, his arm over his face. He is like a man utterly alone*] Once upon a time there were three little beasties, each with a mark on his forehead, and each with the number six on his chest, so that when they were multiplied together they added up to one thousand, nine hundred and ninety-nine. [*He turns and looks at her. She rises automatically and goes to him. With a sudden desperation he grabs her and buries his face in her arms. She pats him on the head. There are tears in his eyes*]

GLORIA: [*Somewhat helplessly*] Do you have a headache?

JULIUS: Yes, I have a headache. [*He draws her down onto the bed. The lights fade on the bed. The electronic hum is heard. In the half light, from both sides of the stage, the* GURU CHILDREN *enter. They are dressed in white robes with beads. They are followed by the* AGITATORS, *dressed in black trousers and shirts with red headbands. They all mill about the room, as though waiting. The* GURU CHILDREN *pick up the hum. The manner of the* GURU CHILDREN *is passive, almost oblivious to their surroundings. The* AGITATORS, *on the other hand, appear on the alert. They mingle with the* GURUS, *but appear to be keeping them in line. The* SOLDIERS *appear suddenly from down the center aisle.* JULIUS *has now risen from the bed and is mingling with the crowd. When he sees the* SOLDIERS, *a look of fear crosses his face. He begins to gesture to the* GURU CHILDREN *to leave, but they remain oblivious. The* SOLDIERS *reach the stage and form a line right stage, their rifles held in an at-ease position. The* AGITATORS *begin to form a line, left stage, unobtrusively herding the* GURU CHILDREN *into the center.* JULIUS *grows increasingly apprehensive. He climbs to the top of the catwalk and whispers down to the* GURU CHILDREN, *gesturing wildly.* "Go home. Get out of here. You're in danger," *etc. He looks frantically from the hovering figures of the* AGITATORS *to the* SOLDIERS. *One of the* AGITATORS *now raises his arm slowly. He has a gun in his hand*] Oh, my God! Look out!

There is a sudden gunshot, followed by a blackout and a burst of gunfire. There is a rushing movement in the darkness, shouts, shots continue to sound, followed by silence. When the lights come up again, the GURU CHILDREN *are lying dead around the stage. The* AGITATORS *stand to one side, on the left, bending over the bodies, and the* SOLDIERS *stand on the right, their rifles poised. Music is heard: a tango, "Lesz Maga Juszt Is Az Enyem." The* SOLDIERS *and* AGITATORS *slowly look at each other. The* AGITATORS *raise their arms, pointing accusingly at the* SOLDIERS. *The* SOLDIERS *raise their arms pointing accusingly at the* AGITATORS. *Then the* SOLDIERS *and* AGITATORS *move slowly toward each other and break into a tango together as the lights fade to black, with a spot on* JULIUS *staring down in horror. When the lights come up again,* JULIUS *is back in the bed, asleep beside* GLORIA. *The bodies of the* GURU CHILDREN *are still on stage and remain there for the rest of the act. A tooting whistle is heard offstage, followed by an offstage voice.*

OFFSTAGE VOICE: Mailman. [*Too-toot*] Mailman.

GLORIA *rises from the bed. She leans over the sleeping* JULIUS *and reaches under the bed, removing a large, ugly pink piggy bank.*

GLORIA: Just a minute. [GLORIA *and the* MAILMAN *play the following scene as though they do not see the bodies of the* GURU CHILDREN] Come in. [*The* MAILMAN *enters. He is a sinister-looking man whose uniform is much too large for his skinny body. His hat comes down almost over his eyes*] What have you got? Anything?

MAILMAN: Yeh, three.

JULIUS *has risen to a sitting position on the bed.* GLORIA *and the* MAILMAN *play the scene as though he were not there, however; but there is a sense of furtiveness and secrecy, like two thieves.*

GLORIA: Three! Give them to me.

MAILMAN: Not so fast. Remember our deal. Half.

GLORIA: Okay, okay, half. Now give them to me.

He hands her three envelopes, which she opens hurriedly.

MAILMAN: What is it? How much?

GLORIA: Twenty-five for the paragraph on human weakness.

MAILMAN: Hurry up. I haven't got all day.

GLORIA: Take it easy. Take it easy. [*She is fumbling with the second one*] Forty-two fifty for the "Ode to a Fledgling."

MAILMAN: That makes sixty-seven fifty. Come on, come on . . .

GLORIA: Quit poking me. [*She has opened the third one*] Oh, my God! I can't believe it!

MAILMAN: What? What?

GLORIA: Two hundred and change for the "Black Prince."

MAILMAN: Two hundred and how much change?

GLORIA: Thirty-eight cents.

MAILMAN: That makes two hundred and sixty-seven dollars and eighty-eight cents. You owe me one hundred and thirty-three dollars and ninety-four cents.

GLORIA: That's a pretty big cut.

MAILMAN: You said half.

GLORIA: I know I said half, but on second thought . . .

MAILMAN: Half!

GLORIA: What did you do for it? Nothing. You make the contact, that's all. It isn't worth half.

The MAILMAN *pulls out a six-shooter.*

GLORIA: [*Frightened*] All right. All right.

MAILMAN: Don't pull any funny stuff, girlie. Don't fool around with the United States Post Office or you might get hurt.

GLORIA: If the United States Post Office knew about your little side deals . . .

MAILMAN: And who's going to tell them? Who's going to squeal . . . you? [*He brandishes the six-shooter*]

GLORIA: No, no. All right. All right. Half. But I'll have to give you a check.

MAILMAN: No checks. Cash.

GLORIA: How can I give you cash? I haven't got that much cash. You'll have to take a check.

MAILMAN: It better be good. I'm warning you.

GLORIA: [*Getting the checkbook from a drawer in the desk*] It's good. It's good. Put that thing away, it makes me nervous.

MAILMAN: Not until you give me the check. [*She hands him the check*] What . . . ? Are you trying to be funny? This check is made out to the United States Post Office! Do you want to get us both locked up? [*He tears up the check and throws it in her face*]

GLORIA: What are you doing?

MAILMAN: Make it out to me personally.

GLORIA: [*She makes out another check*] How do you spell your last name?

MAILMAN: No last names. Just make it out to Fred, the Mailman.

GLORIA: All right. Fred, the Mailman.

He takes the check and crosses to the door.

MAILMAN: Have you got anything else?

GLORIA: No.

MAILMAN: Don't try to cross me. Remember, we have an exclusive deal.

GLORIA: I haven't got anything else.

MAILMAN: What about the secret book?

GLORIA: No.

MAILMAN: No? What do you mean, no? Now listen: I want that secret book, do you understand?

GLORIA: It isn't finished yet.

MAILMAN: When's he going to finish it?

GLORIA: I don't know. Maybe never.

MAILMAN: Never! What do you mean, never? I got a guy who will pay top price for it tomorrow. He specializes in secret books. You better get him working on it, understand?

GLORIA: What can I do? He won't even let me read it. He keeps it hidden. All of his private revelations are in that book.

MAILMAN: Which is exactly why we want it. There's a lot of money in private revelations these days.

GLORIA: But he won't even take the book out until he's finished with this revelation. He only takes it out to record one of his revelations.

MAILMAN: Fucking nut. How long before this one is over?

GLORIA: How should I know? It's about war. It could go on forever.

MAILMAN: Well, you just hustle him along, understand? And remember: it's fifty-fifty.

GLORIA: Sure. Sure.

MAILMAN: And don't get any ideas in your head about reporting my side deals to the Postmaster General, because if you do . . . [*He holds the six-shooter to her head*] I'll get you before they get me.

GLORIA: All right. All right. I'm not going to cross you. [*He exits. Frightened. Muttering out loud*] Boy. That's some mailman. I never knew a mailman like him in my life. Goddamned thief. Lousy blackmailer. He's got me in deep.

The lights come up. JULIUS *is sitting on the bed.*

JULIUS: [*Staring straight out. His manner is strangely calm, distant, detached. He is like steel*] Who was that?

GLORIA: The mailman.

JULIUS: Anything for me?

GLORIA: No, nothing.

JULIUS: [*Pause. He looks at her steadily*] Are you sure it was the mailman?

GLORIA: [*Growing uncomfortable*] Yes, of course I'm sure it was the mailman.

JULIUS: And you're sure there wasn't anything for me?

GLORIA: No, nothing.

Pause. He turns away from her.

JULIUS: I don't like his looks.

GLORIA: Who?

JULIUS: That mailman. He looks very shifty to me. He's the shiftiest-looking mailman I've even seen.

GLORIA: He is shifty. He's very shifty.

JULIUS: [*Sharply*] What d'ya mean?

GLORIA: Nothing. It's just a feeling I have about him. The way he delivered the mail.

JULIUS: I thought you said there wasn't any mail?

GLORIA: There wasn't. Not for you, I mean. But there was for me.

JULIUS: Oh, yes? What?

GLORIA: I got a letter from my mother.

JULIUS: From your mother.

GLORIA: Yes.

JULIUS: What does she have to say? . . . Your mother . . .

GLORIA: She wants me to go home and live with her.

JULIUS: You mean leave me.

GLORIA: Well, if I went home to live with my mother, I guess I'd have to leave you. [*He turns away. She begins circling the trunk*] That would be a shame because I know how you feel about me. I know that I am the only person in the world who means anything to you. If I left, you might go out of your mind. You might even kill yourself. Still, I'm not so sure that I want to stay here anymore. You haven't been very nice to me lately. You're suspicious all the time. You think I am trying to steal your ideas, when the truth of the matter is I am simply interested and I want to learn. [*Pause*] Besides . . . my mother says you are nothing but a nut. She says you are getting me in deeper and deeper with your revelations. "Why does he have to have revelations?" she says. "Other men have money, he has to have revelations." Well, maybe she's right. And these seizures of yours. It isn't easy to live with a man who has seizures, you know. All everybody else sees is the revelations, they don't see the seizures. But I have to live with the seizures and I don't even understand the fucking revelations! So what am I getting out of this relationship? I don't have to be in this relationship.

JULIUS: Maybe you're right. Maybe I am nothing but a nut.

GLORIA: I didn't say it. My mother said it.

JULIUS: Maybe you'd be better off if you did go home to your mother.

GLORIA: [*Surprised*] You'd let me go? You wouldn't care if I left?

JULIUS: I sometimes wonder why you stay. You said it yourself: What are you getting out of this relationship? [*Turning slowly to her*] Why do you stay?

GLORIA: [*Hesitantly*] I stay because you need me.

JULIUS: [*Rising slowly*] Because I need you.

GLORIA: Yeh.

JULIUS: You only want to learn.

GLORIA: Yeh.

JULIUS: You're interested.

GLORIA: Yeh.

JULIUS: In my work.

GLORIA: Yeh.

JULIUS: In my revelations.

GLORIA: Yeh.

JULIUS: In my secret book.

GLORIA: Yeh. [*Suddenly*] What about the secret book?

JULIUS: *Yes. What about the secret book?!*

GLORIA: [*Pause*] Nothing. I'd like to see you finish it, that's all.

JULIUS: Oh, you'd like to see me finish it. Why? [*Answering for her*] Because you're *interested.*

GLORIA: Well, who knows? You might get it published if you finish it.

JULIUS: I might get it published.

GLORIA: Yes, you might.

JULIUS: [*Shouting suddenly*] Well, I don't want to get it published. It's never going to be published. That's why it's a secret book . . . because it's not for publication. It's *my* secret book, my own private revelations, and nobody gets to read it. Nobody! Now that we understand each other, you can go home to your mother. [*He has crossed to the desk, where he begins to assemble his things*]

GLORIA: There you go, being suspicious. [*She becomes aware of his movements. He has crossed to the trunk now, opens it and begins to remove personal items: a pair of work boots, a muffler, a cap, the objects given to him by Poe. Lastly, he removes a large, formidable-looking book. He holds it in his hands for a moment, then replaces it in the trunk*] What are you doing?

JULIUS: I'm leaving, Miss Gilbert.

GLORIA: No . . . no . . .

JULIUS: [*Closing the trunk, he crosses to her*] Yes, Miss Gilbert. I have to go now. [*He extends his hand. She appears stunned*] Goodbye. It's been a bit . . . kinky . . . eh, what? [*He crosses to the edge of the stage*]

GLORIA: You can't get out. The front door hasn't been built yet.

JULIUS: Only an invisible door of the mind, Miss Gilbert. [*He takes a breath, then steps out beyond the fourth wall. She watches, dumbstruck. From the aisle, as he leaves*] The secret book is in the trunk, Miss Gilbert. You can do what you want with it. Cheerio! [*He disappears up the aisle*]

GLORIA: Come back here! You're not supposed to leave like that! We didn't do the good-bye scene. Come back here. This isn't the way it's written. I'm supposed to leave you. You're not supposed to leave me! Come back here, you lousy motherfucker! I'm the one who's supposed to be indifferent! I'm the one who's supposed to lose interest, not you! That's the way it's written. I leave *him,* and *he* goes out of *his* mind. *He* jumps off the top of Loew's State, not the other way round. Nobody gets tired of me before I get tired of them! I have forty-inch tits! God damn it! Nobody gets tired of me! Nobody cools on me, understand? I'm the one who kicks *you* out of the box, motherfucker! Thinks he can treat me like some flat-chested ugly! I'll show you, son of a bitch! Son of worm-toothed whore! I'll take your secret book and give it to the mailman! That's what I'll do! I'll make you sweat, Esperanza! I'll make you bleed! You bastard. [*She falls on the bed, beating the mattress with her fists*]

From offstage we hear TERRY WONG FU.

TERRY: [*Off*] Yoo hoo . . . Yoo hoo . . .

GLORIA: Oh, shit! Here comes that rotten Chinese faggot.

TERRY WONG FU, *the Chinese landlord, enters. He wears a ruffled silk shirt, purple culottes, and lots of makeup.*

TERRY: [*Impatiently, as he enters*] Personne ne vient quand j'appelle! [*Eyeing the disorder in the room*] Ahh . . . la direction est fausse.

GLORIA: Why do you always come in the back way?

TERRY: It's my nature. I've come to collect the rent. Where's Julius?

GLORIA: In the bathroom.

TERRY: [*Crossing to the bathroom screen, in a sweet, singsong voice*] Ju-lius . . . I've come to collect the rent. [*No answer. Then to* GLORIA, *harshly*] What's the matter? Haven't you got it?

GLORIA: Ask him.

TERRY: [*Back to the screen*] When do you think you'll have it, Julius? [*No answer. To* GLORIA] Now look here, I was good enough to sublease this place to you at a nominal rent, and I would like to have my rent . . . on time!

GLORIA: Yes.

TERRY: [*Pause*] What do you mean, yes? [*She does not reply. He goes back to the bathroom screen*] When do you think you'll have it, Julius? [*He waits. No answer*] Now look, Julius, friendship has nothing to do with this. My stocks went down this month and I have a new roommate. [*He waits*] I have a lot of responsibilities, Julius. I have a responsibility to myself, I have a responsibility to my father, I have a responsibility to my stockbroker, and of course I have a responsibility to my new roommate. I have a lot of responsibilities. [*He waits. No answer. Then to* GLORIA] What's the matter with him? Why doesn't he answer?

GLORIA: Well, the fact is, he can't right now. He's going through another one of his seizures.

TERRY: Oh, yes. He's about due for another revelation, isn't he? What is it this time?

GLORIA: I don't know. Something to do with war.

TERRY: He's a fucking nut, that's what he is. [*Very confidentially, whispering*] You know he had it made once. He was on his way. Then he blew the whole works by flying in the face of everything. People don't tolerate that forever, you know. He's too arrogant, too egotistical. Always was. Why, even as a child at school he was the same. [*She glances at him*] You didn't know that Julius and I were at school together, did you?

GLORIA: No, I didn't.

TERRY: Yes. We were in the same Arts and Crafts class. Yes. I remember, Julius had a terrible crush on the teacher. [*Pause, then with evil deliberation*] Miss Hutchinson! [GLORIA *freezes. He then goes blithely on*] Yes, he was madly in love with her. In fact, he wrote a little poem for her, his first one, I believe. Lovely little poem . . . [*Carefully observing her reaction; she remains rigid, tense*] Let me see, how did it go?
"I knew you in heaven
And loved you in heaven
Before we were summoned to earth;
But how have I lived
These long years without knowing
This love which was born before birth?"
Pretty, isn't it?

GLORIA: [*Cautiously*] Yeh, it's okay.

TERRY: Unfortunately, he never gave it to Miss Hutchinson.

GLORIA: Oh, no?

TERRY: No. She shattered his love. Yes. By refusing him permission to leave the classroom one day. And do you know what he did? He stood up at his desk and pee'd on the floor. It was his way of saying to Miss Hutchinson "Kiss my ass," you see. [*Pause. He eyes her suspiciously, then goes blithely on again*] After class that day I saw him rip the poem from his notebook, roll it up into a ball and throw it away. Fortunately, I salvaged it. I copied it out in my own hand, signed my name to it and gave it to Miss Hutchinson. She was very touched by the sentiment. Yes. "Ode to Miss Hutchinson"!

The telephone rings.

GLORIA: Hello? . . . Oh, Marsha, hello. Look, I can't talk to you now, I'll call you back. . . . No, nothing's wrong. . . . I said I'll call you back. . . . I can't talk now. . . . No, nobody is here. . . . No . . . no, nobody is here except Terry Tulip. . . . I'll call you later. [*She hangs up.* TERRY *has become rigid*]

TERRY: What did you call me?

GLORIA: What?

TERRY: You called me Terry *Tulip.*

GLORIA: Oh . . . did I?

TERRY: Yes, you did. I distinctly heard you call me Terry Tulip. [*Pause*] Tulip. [*Pause*] My name is Terry Wong Fu!

GLORIA: I know your name is Terry Wong Fu.

TERRY: Then why did you call me Tulip?

GLORIA: Why did I call you Tulip?

TERRY: Yes. Why?

GLORIA: Well, I called you Tulip because . . . [*Pause*] Well, because you remind me of a tulip.

TERRY: I'll come for the rent tomorrow. You'd better have it! [*Before he exits he pauses and turns*] Oh, yes. There's something else before I leave. By some strange coincidence I found something in a magazine about two weeks ago. It's a little poem called . . . [*He takes a clipping from his pocket; then, lowering the boom*] "Ode to Mr. Hutchinson"! [*Pause. He watches her*] Shall I read it?
"I knew you in heaven
And loved you in heaven
Before we were summoned to earth . . ."
And so forth and so on. [*Emphatically*] Signed: Gloria B. Gilbert! [*There is a pause, then he whirls on her, melodramatically*] I know what's been going on between you and the mailman!

GLORIA: [*In a hoarse whisper*] What are you going to do about it?

TERRY: That depends. I could go to the Postmaster General.

GLORIA: No! If you do that, the mailman will think I turned him in and he'll get me before they get him!

TERRY: Yes, I know.

GLORIA: [*After a moment*] What do you want?

TERRY: I want IN.

GLORIA: In? What do you mean, IN?

TERRY: I want a piece of the action, that's what I mean.

GLORIA: How much?

TERRY: One third.

GLORIA: One third! That's too much. The mailman will never go for it!

TERRY: He'll go for it. He hasn't got much choice, has he? Neither have you.

GLORIA: [*Considers*] All right. One third.

TERRY: And something else. My name goes on everything.

GLORIA: What?!

TERRY: You heard me! *My name. By* Terry Wong Fu. I'll see you tomorrow. [*A drum roll. He exits. Electronic hum, followed by an explosion*]

GLORIA: Now I'm in for it. Goddamned blackmailing little worm. He's got me good. I'm getting in deeper and deeper. [*The telephone rings*] Hello? . . . Yes, this is Gloria B. Gilbert. . . . Who? Internal Revenue? . . . Oh . . . Hello, Mr. von Schtutt. How are you? Long time no see. . . . No, I still haven't got any money. . . . No, I'm not working. . . . How am I living? I don't know, but I'm still living. . . . How much is it now, with the fines and the interest? . . . Really? That much? . . . Well, I don't know what to say, I haven't got a cent. . . . Sell what mink coat? I haven't got a mink coat. . . . Wait, wait, let me get this straight: Your spy was hiding behind a tree in front of *my* house and he saw *me* come out wearing a mink coat? . . . That's ridiculous. He was standing behind the wrong tree. . . . I know your spies are well trained, but he was still standing behind the wrong tree. There is no mink coat. . . . An affidavit? Sure, why not? . . . When would you like me to come down? You'll come here? . . . When? . . . Today? . . . Two hours? . . . Yeh, sure, okay. Why not? Fine. . . . I'll make some coffee. . . . Okay. I'll see you. Good-bye. [*Rushing behind the screen*] Two hours! [*She returns in a moment with a mink coat bundled in her arms. She rushes around looking for a place to hide it*] Where? Where am I going to hide it! That fink, he'll find it no matter what . . . [*She has a sudden idea, crosses to the telephone and dials*] Hello, Marsha? . . . Look, how would you like to wear the mink coat for a few hours today? . . . So what if it's 98 degrees outside. How often do you get a chance to wear a four-thousand-dollar mink? . . . Well, I remember you said that you would like to know how it feels to wear it one day, so . . . today's the day! . . . I don't know where you could go

in it. Go to an air-conditioned luncheonette and have a cup of coffee. . . . Yeh, go to Goldie's. The air conditioning is so strong in there you need a fur coat. . . . No, don't thank me, it's my pleasure. Can you get here in a few minutes? . . . It has to be right now or the deal is off. . . . I can't wait two hours . . . so leave the rollers in your hair. . . . All right, good-bye. I'll see you.

There is a blackout, followed by the electronic hum and explosion. Then we hear the tango music again: "Lesz Maga Juszt Is Az Enyem" as the lights come up on

SCENE II

The emergency room of the hospital. The PSYCHIATRIST, *a young Ivy League gentleman who speaks in a decidedly Ivy League manner —i.e. without moving his jaws—is seated at a desk beneath a barred window. He is quietly observing* JULIUS, *who sits sullenly in a chair, his head bandaged. The* PSYCHIATRIST *is given to a habit of suddenly flashing his teeth in a grimacing smile. He does this for no apparent reason. There is a long pause. The music plays under the following scene.*

PSYCHIATRIST: Would you like to go over it again?

JULIUS: [*Dazed; almost to himself*] Sacrificio rito perpetrato; sacrificiis solemnibus factis: sacrificia laeta . . .

PSYCHIATRIST: Now why don't you be a good fellow and tell me what *really* happened?

JULIUS: I told you. It happened just as I told you.

PSYCHIATRIST: You climbed up the flagpole in order to warn them . . .

JULIUS: Yes.

PSYCHIATRIST: The . . . the . . . What was it you called them . . . ?

JULIUS: The Guru Children. [*Suddenly angry*] Look! Forget it! It happened just as I told you. I don't want to go over it again. What do you want me to say? What do you want me to tell you? Something you'll understand? All right. I climbed up on the flagpole and blew my bugle because I'm an illegitimate child! Okay? [*The* PSYCHIATRIST *is suddenly alert and makes a note on his pad*] What are you writing?

PSYCHIATRIST: Now that's the first real thing you've told me since they brought you in here. [*He flashes his devastating smile*]

JULIUS: [*Scowling; disgusted*] What are you grinning at?

PSYCHIATRIST: [*Dropping the smile*] Grinning? I'm not grinning.

JULIUS: [*Hostilely*] You were, you were! You were grinning! You were grinning! [*Turning his back on the* PSYCHIATRIST] "I'm not grinning" . . . If you weren't grinning, what were you doing—showing me your teeth? All right! You have very nice teeth! Don't show them to me again! [*The* PSYCHIATRIST *makes a note*] What are you writing? What are you writing now?

PSYCHIATRIST: [*He finishes writing his note, takes a deep breath, leans back in his chair, and, holding his pencil between both index fingers, peers at* JULIUS] Why are you so hostile toward my teeth? [JULIUS *stares at him*] Can it be, possibly, that you RESENT the fact that my teeth are PRETTIER than your teeth? Hm? [JULIUS *stares at him*] Is that it? Hm? Hm?

JULIUS: Your teeth are not prettier than my teeth.

PSYCHIATRIST: [*Half rising, both hands on the desk*] Oh Yes They Are! [*He sits down again*] I have just about the prettiest teeth in the land.

JULIUS: Oh, no you haven't! No, you haven't, buddy! Just take a look . . . ! [*He displays his teeth*] Look at these! Look at these teeth! Now those are teeth, baby! Those are TEETH!

PSYCHIATRIST: Well, it appears we got you to smile at last. [*Flashing his smile, then taking a deep breath*] Now! [*Referring to his notes*] According to the patrolman who brought you in here, you were up there . . . [*He glances quickly at* JULIUS *and back to his notes*] . . . shouting: "Listen to me, look up here, look at me, up here, you down there, look at me, up here." [*He leans back in his chair and looks at* JULIUS] "Look at me. UP HERE. You, DOWN THERE. Look at ME. UP HERE." [*He sucks in his breath*] Isn't that significant to you? Doesn't that tell you anything? [*Pause*] Now try to think creatively. Think poetically. Use your imagination: Me. Up here. Flagpole. You. Down there. You. Who? You others. Down there. Me up here. You down there. [JULIUS *is staring at him dully*] Up here. Flagpole. Flag. Pole. . . . Flag, country. Country, Authority . . . Pole. Pole, penis. Penis, Godhead. . . . Up. Up, sky. Sky, Heaven. Heaven, God. . . . Me. Up. Here. Where. Flagpole. . . . Pole, penis, Godhead. . . . Flag, Country, Authority. Authority, God. Me up. Up God. Flagpole. God. Me. Pole. Penis. Godhead. Now try to think creatively: Me. Godhead. Me. Pole. Me. Penis. . . . Penis, Godhead. . . . Me pole penis Godhead. . . . Me pole. Me penis. Me Godhead. . . . ME GOD! [*There is a dead silence*] All right! It's all out in the open. Everything's been exposed. You needn't feel ashamed, you can relax. . . .

JULIUS: What's out in the open? What's been exposed?

PSYCHIATRIST: The penis. There it is! [*He slams his hand on the desk*] Right there. Out in the open. Look at it, examine it, see it for what it is. Right there. Exposed.

JULIUS: I thought you were talking about God.

PSYCHIATRIST: Well . . . ! Ha ha ha . . . [*A nervous little laugh. Then he sings*]
God is my pecker
and I shall not want . . .
dum, de dum, dum . . .
[*He laughs again and gives* JULIUS *a knowing wink and a manly jab on the arm*]

JULIUS: God is my . . . !?!

PSYCHIATRIST: That's right. Peter Pork. Ha ha.

JULIUS: [*With mounting disbelief and anger*] Are you trying to tell me that God is a . . .

PSYCHIATRIST: [*Cutting him off, furiously, slamming his fist on the desk and shouting*] YES! GOD IS A PRICK! [*Shaking, his face all red, he sits down again. Speaking sternly, coldly*] Now. Let's get on with it. What's your name?

JULIUS: I can't tell you.

PSYCHIATRIST: Why not?

JULIUS: Because I'm famous.

PSYCHIATRIST: I see. [*He makes a note*]

JULIUS: You think I'm mad.

PYCHIATRIST: I didn't say you were mad.

JULIUS: You thought it.

PSYCHIATRIST: How do you know what I thought?

JULIUS: I heard it.

PSYCHIATRIST: You heard what I thought?

JULIUS: Yes.

PSYCHIATRIST: You hear other people's thoughts?

JULIUS: Yes.

PSYCHIATRIST: I see. [*He makes a note*] Tell me, Mr. . . . Mr. . . . Doe . . .

JULIUS: [*Suddenly*] How old are you?

PSYCHIATRIST: What?

JULIUS: You seem awfully young to be a psychiatrist. How old are you? Twenty-eight? Twenty-nine?

PSYCHIATRIST: That's close enough.

JULIUS: Are you married?

PSYCHIATRIST: Yes, I'm married.

JULIUS: Do you love your wife . . . ?

PSYCHIATRIST: Of course I love my wife.

JULIUS: . . . Or did you marry her for her money?

PSYCHIATRIST: Now see here!

JULIUS: Any children?

PSYCHIATRIST: [*Defensively*] Yes, one.

JULIUS: Boy or girl?

PSYCHIATRIST: Girl. Now see here! I'm asking the questions!

JULIUS: That's *your* fantasy!

PSYCHIATRIST: [*Taken back*] What did you say?

JULIUS: [*A pause. He looks at him*] Nothing.

PSYCHIATRIST: Now: You said earlier that you are illegitimate. Is that true?

JULIUS: I don't want to talk about it.

PSYCHIATRIST: What did you say?

JULIUS: I said I don't want to talk about it.

PSYCHIATRIST: Why are you suddenly speaking with an accent?

JULIUS: Accent? What accent?

PSYCHIATRIST: You're speaking with an accent. You're speaking with a decidedly—Middle European—Yugoslavian—Albanian—what is it?

JULIUS: I don't know what you are talking about,

PSYCHIATRIST: Do you mean that you are *un-aware* of the fact that you're speaking with an accent? How interesting. [*He makes a note*] That's very significant, you know. The *mo-ment*, I say, the *moment* we began talking about your childhood, you went into this . . . this . . . strange European accent. Your father —he must have been European.

JULIUS: No, he was from Tennessee.

PSYCHIATRIST: Your mother then. She was European.

JULIUS: No, she was from Cincinnati.

PSYCHIATRIST: [*Darkly*] Then why are you speaking with a European accent?

JULIUS: What European accent?

PSYCHIATRIST: [*Angrily*] You're speaking with an accent! It doesn't make any sense! Your father was from Tennessee, your mother was from Cincinnati, *and yet you are speaking with a European accent!* Now either tell me why you are speaking with a European accent or CUT IT OUT! DO YOU HEAR ME? CUT IT OUT! [*He flings himself into his chair*]

JULIUS: Perhaps the accent you hear is coming from your own collective unconscious.

PSYCHIATRIST: I DON'T BELIEVE IN THAT BULLSHIT! DON'T GIVE ME THAT BULLSHIT ABOUT THE COLLECTIVE UNCONSCIOUS! I'M A CLINICAL PSY-CHIATRIST, A SCIENTIST—NOT SOME GODDAMNED ROTTEN MYSTIC. [*With a sudden temperamental gesture he swivels his chair around so that his back is turned on JULIUS. He sits there muttering and mumbling angrily to himself*] Collective unconscious . . . Pff . . . blow it out your asshole. . . . That's what you can do with it! [*He begins to drum his fingers nervously on the desk, still mutter-ing. Gradually he begins to hum and sing to himself. The speaking, humming and singing interspersed*] Collective unconscious . . . Pff . . . ! [*Humming and singing*] Hmm hmm

hmm . . . God is my pecker . . . hmm hmm . . . [*Muttering angrily*] The next thing you know you'll be talking to me about the Soul! What's that, the soul? Ha! [*Humming and singing to himself again*] Hmm hmm . . . I shall not want . . . God is my Tricky Dick Dick . . . My little hmm hmm . . . Doo doo doo . . . [*Speaking half to JULIUS and half to the air*] Talk to me about something real, something tangible, something you can touch and taste, something you can hold in your hands . . . ! [*Once again returning to the humming and singing*] Hmm hmm . . . God is my Ding Dong . . . Ding Dong Doo doo . . . doo doo . . . Hmm hmm . . . My little thumpy humpy . . . Loo loo loo . . . Peter Porker went to pick a pecker . . . Hmm hmm hmm . . . Dingy Dongy doo Humpy hump . . . Hoo hoo . . . Hmm hmm . . . [*He swivels his chair sud-denly around again and faces JULIUS sternly, leaning his pencil at him*] Now let's under-stand each other, my friend! I will not be di-verted from the issue by your tactics. I will not be fooled by phony European accents, or by careless references to pseudo-psychiatric jargon. My eye stays on the ball. Do you un-derstand that? *My-Eye-Stays-On-The-Ball.* Now . . . [*He picks up his notebook*] You're illegitimate. But you know who your father was, is that correct?

JULIUS: Everybody knows who my father was.

PSYCHIATRIST: Everybody? How come?

JULIUS: He was famous.

PSYCHIATRIST: [*A slight sneer*] Oh, he was fa-mous, too.

JULIUS: Yes.

PSYCHIATRIST: I see. [*He makes another note*] What was he famous for?

JULIUS: Pornography. His name is synonymous with pornography.

PSYCHIATRIST: [*His head snaps up*] Not Zachery Schnadel!

JULIUS: [*With pretended hostility*] Yes. But I don't want to talk about *him*.

PSYCHIATRIST: Zachery Schnadel—just think of that. Why, he's one of my favorite authors. Well, if you're the son of Zachery Schnadel, then your name must be . . . Schnadel*son*.

JULIUS: Yes, that's right.

PSYCHIATRIST: What's your first name?

JULIUS: Schnadel.

PSYCHIATRIST: Schnadel Schnadelson?

JULIUS: Yes, that's right, Schnadel Schnadelson.

PSYCHIATRIST: The son of Zachery Schnadel. I'm very impressed.

JULIUS: Don't talk about *him*.

PSYCHIATRIST: I'll never forget his last book . . .

JULIUS: Stop talking about *him*. We were talking about me.

PSYCHIATRIST: Oh, he was great . . . absolutely great . . . !

JULIUS: ALL RIGHT! HE WAS GREAT!

PSYCHIATRIST: Zachery Schnadel!

JULIUS: ZACHERY THE GREAT!

PSYCHIATRIST: Extraordinary writer.

JULIUS: [*Wildly, flamboyantly*] Extraordinary pornographer! Wrapped in the lamb's wool of literary greatness and bursting out of his snakeskin of human excess!

PSYCHIATRIST: What did you say?

JULIUS: [*Sullenly*] Nothing.

PSYCHIATRIST: Tell me about him. Tell me about your father.

JULIUS: [*With bitterness*] You want to know, eh? [*Shouting*] YOU WANT TO KNOW?! ALL RIGHT! I'LL TELL YOU! [*He begins to pace around slowly, like an animal in a cage*] He was the pinnacle—the kingpin— the firestick—of a little *ménage à trois*. His legal wife had a pretty younger sister who would have been my aunt, except for the fact that she was my mother. [*He laughs wildly*] And we all lived happily together in the family house at La Jolla until I was sent away to school at 14.

PSYCHIATRIST: Then what happened?

JULIUS: [*Dramatically puffing on a cigarette*] Then I had *my* first book published.

PSYCHIATRIST: At 14?

JULIUS: No, 15.

PSYCHIATRIST: I see.

JULIUS: And it was a great success. But I never knew—and I will never know—whether it was a success because my name was Schnadelson—or because the book was truly great.

PSYCHIATRIST: So what did you do?

JULIUS: I ran away. I disappeared without a word.

PSYCHIATRIST: And where did you go?

JULIUS: To Europe! Yes . . . I spent four years bumming around Europe. [*He begins to speak with a slight British accent*] That entire period is fixed in my mind . . . delirious wandering. Frenzied, desperate, lost . . .

PSYCHIATRIST: I see.

JULIUS: And I had quite a talent for attracting all sorts of strange people.

PSYCHIATRIST: What kind of people?

JULIUS: Strange people. Wild, degenerate people. People who had pledged their souls to ecstasy. People whose souls were burning on the altar of exalted corruption. The heights and the depths, as it were.

PSYCHIATRIST: I see. And what happened?

JULIUS: What happened? [*He drags on the cigarette and laughs ironically*] I led this army of drunken, orgiastic revelers all over Europe. Yes. . . . All over Italy. France. Greece . . . all over Europe. God! When I think of those years, even now—I think of them with a mixture of delight and disgust. My body shivers at the memory. The heights and the depths, yes. When I think! When I think what it was like. . . . Do you know what it's like to plunge with your head in your hands, right into the center of every conceivable experience, until you are utterly consumed by the sheer power and energy of life . . . ? Flailing around in it . . . ?

PSYCHIATRIST: What was that?

JULIUS: Flailing, flailing.

PSYCHIATRIST: Oh yes—flailing . . .

JULIUS: Wrapping my limbs around it.

PSYCHIATRIST: Wrapping your limbs around what?

JULIUS: Life. Around life.

PSYCHIATRIST: Oh yes—life.

JULIUS: Like making love to some great giantess —wanting to destroy it, and crying out to be destroyed. God! When I remember! When I remember how entangled I was in that body. How I swallowed it whole and then ripped at my own gut to give it existence again—like giving birth to my own death. And then only to be swallowed by it again, and to find myself swimming around in the belly of the giantess—chewed up and broken boned and spat out again in a hundred pieces—each piece like a new seed sprouting a hundred new selves. And there was I, left to gather it all up again, left to piece it all back together again into the shell of *me*. Like a pomegranate. And all the while wanting to run away from it, and yet knowing that I couldn't.

PSYCHIATRIST: And all this happened when you were 15?

JULIUS: No, 16.

PSYCHIATRIST: How did it end?

JULIUS: It began to change when I met Sophie.

PSYCHIATRIST: Who is Sophie?

JULIUS: You don't know who Sophie is?

PSYCHIATRIST: Sophie, Sophie, no, I don't know . . . I don't think I know . . . Sophie . . .

JULIUS: My first wife.

PSYCHIATRIST: First wife. How many have you had?

JULIUS: Three. No, four.

PSYCHIATRIST: I see. [*He makes a note*] What were the others named?

JULIUS: Sophie.

PSYCHIATRIST: Sophie. All Sophie?

JULIUS: Yes. All Sophie.

PSYCHIATRIST: I see. [*Writing*] Sophie Schnadelson One, Sophie Schnadelson Two, Sophie Schnadelson Three, and Sophie Schnadelson Four. [*Suddenly reflective*] I used to know a Sophie Schnadelson. Or was it Sophie Schnadel*man*? . . . Schnadel*son*, Schnadel*man*. . . . Sophie Schnadelson. No, that doesn't sound right. Sophie Schnadelman. Sophie . . . Yes, that's it. Sophie Schnadelman. Yes. [*Musing*] Mm. Quite a girl. Yes. Quite a girl, Sophie Schnadelman. To her, God was a peppermint stick. [*He laughs to himself*] Suck, suck, suck . . . Oh, well! [*He laughs again*] I sometimes wonder what my life would have been like if I were Sir Isaac Newton. [*He looks at* JULIUS] I have a theory about Sir Isaac Newton. It's only a theory, of course, but I'm convinced that he had a ding dong about so big [*He indicates two inches with his fingers*]

JULIUS: How do you know that?

PSYCHIATRIST: I did an in-depth psychological analysis of his *Philosophiae Naturalis Principia Mathematica*. It's all there, in black and white . . . to the trained clinical eye, that is. It's quite obvious. Particularly in his Corpuscular Theory of Light. Are you familiar with it? . . . It's also known as the . . . [*He pauses in order to stress the next word*] Emission theory. [*Clearing his throat*] Well, briefly . . . Newton said that light consists of minute particles . . . *emitted* . . . from *luminous bodies* . . . and which then *travel through space*. [*He gives* JULIUS *a meaningful nod and a slow, knowing wink*]

JULIUS: Well, what has that . . .

PSYCHIATRIST: [*Interrupting*] What has that got to do with the size of his ding dong? I'll tell you. [*Speaking very clinically, and taking pauses before each significant point, nodding, winking, or looking assertively at* JULIUS] It's a question of simple compensation. In the Corpuscular Theory of Light, Newton was compensating for his own sexual inadequacy. Only a man whose own . . . *emission* . . . or: ejaculation . . . *nicht war?* . . . emission, ejaculation . . . coming from a . . . far from *luminous body* . . . yes, no? . . . and which emission and/or ejaculation not having the potency to reach its mark let *alone travel through space!* could have evolved such a theory. [*He pauses*] It's self-evident. Of course I don't mean to malign the reputation of a great scientist, but facts are facts. He was a great man, no doubt. A genius. But nonetheless, genius or no . . . his dick couldn't have been more than an inch and a half at the most. [*Pausing, reflectively again*] Yes,

I have often speculated . . . I've wondered about myself and my own genius. I'm sure that the only thing that stands between me and it is my rather formidable . . . [*He laughs*] Ahh, well . . . ! Where were we? [*Looking through his notes*] Four years in Europe . . . orgiastic revelers . . . flailing . . . belly of the giantess . . . pomegranate . . . [*Looking up at* JULIUS] and it all began to change when you met your first wife.

JULIUS: Yes. We met in Greece, and we lived together for a year on a small island just off the coast. All I remember of that year is lying in the sun; lying in the sun for one solid year until my body was so blistered and burned that I thought I would die that way, just lying there, burning to death in the rays of the sun. [*He pauses*] But I didn't die.

PSYCHIATRIST: [*Cheerfully*] No, obviously you didn't. [*Flashing his devastating smile*]

JULIUS: [*Without looking at him*] I grew new skin. You know, it's amazing, Dr. Ginzberg . . .

PSYCHIATRIST: Dr. Ginzberg? My name isn't Ginzberg.

JULIUS: . . . It's amazing, the power of the sun. It really is amazing.

PSYCHIATRIST: Why did you call me Dr. Ginzberg?

JULIUS: It will blister and scorch your entire being, melt you down to the very core of yourself . . .

PSYCHIATRIST: I don't understand why you called me Dr. Ginzberg. . . .

JULIUS: And the most extraordinary part of all . . .

PSYCHIATRIST: Just a minute . . . I want to know . . .

JULIUS: . . . The most extraordinary part of all: IT HAS THE POWER TO CAST A SHADOW!

PSYCHIATRIST: What?

JULIUS: The sun. It has the power to cast a shadow.

PSYCHIATRIST: You find that extraordinary?

JULIUS: Of course it's extraordinary. The sun. It casts a shadow.

PSYCHIATRIST: Well yes, it does . . . I mean . . . it does cast a shadow. Yes, the sun casts a shadow.

JULIUS: Extraordinary! Extraordinary! And I turned around and I looked at that shadow.

PSYCHIATRIST: Looked at it?

JULIUS: Yes. I looked at it and I said: THAT is my shadow. [*The* PYCHIATRIST *looks at him blankly*] Don't you understand? It is my shadow. It is not *me*. And yet I had been living in it as though it were me. All of my life I have been living in my own shadow, Dr. Ginzberg.

PSYCHIATRIST: *Now see here! My name is not Ginzberg!*

JULIUS: What is your name?

PSYCHIATRIST: Smith!!

JULIUS: Yes, well, Dr. Smith . . . I discovered that all of my life I had been living in my own shadow.

PSYCHIATRIST: I see. [*Then cheerfully*] Well . . . ! . . . that sounds like a positive discovery.

JULIUS: !!!?!

PSYCHIATRIST: [*With a beautiful smile*] I should think after making a discovery like that you would have decided to straighten up and fly right. So . . . ! I think we can send you home now. Just take this pill . . .

JULIUS: What pill?

PSYCHIATRIST: Only a tranquilizer.

JULIUS: I don't want to be tranquilized.

PSYCHIATRIST: I see. Well then, if you will just call this number in the morning . . . [*He hands* JULIUS *a slip of paper*]

JULIUS: What for?

PSYCHIATRIST: I'm recommending you take a few tests.

JULIUS: What kind of tests?

PSYCHIATRIST: Oh, various kinds of tests. An aptitude test, for one thing.

JULIUS: You mean they might discover I have hidden talent?

PSYCHIATRIST: You never know. How do you feel? Well enough to leave?

JULIUS: I feel lousy. I feel rotten. I feel stinking, stinking, stinking.

PSYCHIATRIST: I see.

JULIUS: YOU SEE NOTHING!!!

PSYCHIATRIST: [*Stunned. He recovers himself quickly and, with a nervous little laugh*] Well, you know, you may be right. But then— NOTHING is, in a way, potentially EVERYTHING. Therefore, you might say, in a way, that I know everything.

JULIUS: What did you say?

PSYCHIATRIST: I said . . .

JULIUS: [*Ominously*] I heard what you said. Where did you hear that?

PSYCHIATRIST: [*Uneasy*] Hear what?

JULIUS: That. What you just said.

PSYCHIATRIST: [*Beginning to sweat*] Well . . . as a matter of fact . . . it isn't quite original . . .

JULIUS: No, it isn't.

PSYCHIATRIST: A friend of mine . . . a . . .

JULIUS: A YOUNG LADY??

PSYCHIATRIST: [*Stunned*] Yes. Extraordinary young lady. She . . . she has a way of . . . formulating ideas, . . .

JULIUS: AND HER NAME IS *GLORIA!*

PSYCHIATRIST: [*Now dumbstruck. In a hoarse whisper*] How did you know her name was Gloria?

They stare at each other for a moment.

JULIUS: [*With a shrug*] I told you I could hear thoughts.

PSYCHIATRIST: [*Terrified*] She's only a casual friend. . . . I . . . I don't even see her very much any more. . . . It was strictly platonic. . . . My wife knew all about the relationship. I don't see her anymore . . . ever. . . . I don't see her, I tell you! STOP READING MY THOUGHTS! I haven't seen her in months. She's living with her mother at the moment.

JULIUS: With her mother.

PSYCHIATRIST: Yes. . . . She was my mentor, nothing more . . . a brilliant mind . . . nothing more . . .

JULIUS: A brilliant mind who likes JELLY CENTERS?

PSYCHIATRIST: Jelly centers? How do you know that? How do you know that Gloria likes jelly centers? What else do you know? Stop listening to my thoughts. Who sent you here? Stop listening to my thoughts.

JULIUS: Listening to your thoughts?

PSYCHIATRIST: My wife knew all about it, I tell you!

JULIUS: Ha!

PSYCHIATRIST: All right! My wife didn't know all about it! You were right! I didn't marry my wife for love! I married her for her money!

JULIUS: Ah!

PSYCHIATRIST: I was a poor, struggling intern with a taste for good living, and I hadn't quite recovered from the shock of my father dying broke. My wife was attractive, sophisticated, well traveled and well schooled. She was also highly gifted at needlepoint.

JULIUS: I see.

PSYCHIATRIST: So what if her father happened to be a somewhat successful businessman?!

JULIUS: Somewhat successful?

PSYCHIATRIST: All right! All right! So he was more than somewhat successful. He was a tycoon. So what!? So he was the Popsicle King. So what?! Don't you criticize me. It's to my credit that I chose to live well. It's a very romantic notion that every dedicated man must starve to death. Look at Goethe! He never left the house without wearing his white gloves, and look at all he managed to achieve. So what if my father-in-law was the Popsicle King! So what if my wife is the daughter of the Popsicle King! So what! So what! So what! I'll see you dead, Mr. Christian! I'll have you chained to the yardarm—do you understand? Hung from the mizzenmast! Fed to the sharks, Mr. Christian! [JULIUS *stares at him, dumbfounded. The* PSYCHIATRIST *now pauses, squares his shoulders and quietly returns to his chair behind the desk*] Now . . . !

JULIUS: [*After a pause, he stands as though he's suddenly heard something. He listens, then quietly he says*] Listen.

PSYCHIATRIST: What?

JULIUS: [*Quietly, still listening*] Listen, Shhh. Be quiet.

PSYCHIATRIST: [*Also whispering now*] What is it? What's the matter?

JULIUS: [*Softly*] Did you hear that?

PSYCHIATRIST: Hear what?

JULIUS: Again! Listen! Did you hear it???! [*He runs to the window*] Oh, my God! [*With growing horror*] My God! They're here!

PSYCHIATRIST: What's the matter with you?

JULIUS: They're here! The enemy has arrived! They're here!

PSYCHIATRIST: [*On the telephone*] Hello . . . get me the desk . . .

JULIUS: The enemy is here! Look! You can see them! They're burning the houses! Shattering the earth! They're here! [*He rushes to the* PSYCHIATRIST *and begins to shake him*] Listen to me! Listen to me!

PSYCHIATRIST: Where are the attendants? . . .

JULIUS: They're mowing us down like rats!

PSYCHIATRIST: This is Dr. Ginzberg in Emergency. I mean Smith—Dr. Smith! . . .

JULIUS: Stop them! Do something! Do something, I tell you! [*He runs back to the window*] Stop them! Dear God, stop them! Help us, dear God! Don't let them! Where are you? What have they done with you? Stop them, God! Don't let them! [*He rushes back to the* PSYCHIATRIST *and shakes him again, frantically*] Do something, damn you! Don't just sit there!

PSYCHIATRIST: [*Nervously singing*]
God is my pecker,
I shall not want
Ding dong doo doo . . .

JULIUS: Do something!

PSYCHIATRIST: Emergency . . . get some attendants in here, quickly, do you hear me? [*Singing*] Peter Pecker picked a peck . . . yes, quickly . . .

JULIUS: Look! They're springing out of the ground. They're flying from the trees, sweeping through like shadows. The shadow enemy is upon us! Help! Prince! Where are you, Prince?

DR. BROWN *enters quickly, followed by two orderlies. He is dressed as Julius Caesar and the orderlies are in the dress of Roman gladiators.*

DR. BROWN: All right. Take him quietly.

The Gladiator orderlies pounce upon the PSYCHIATRIST, *who is still singing his little pecker songs into the telephone. They put a straitjacket on him and lead him off, screaming.*

PSYCHIATRIST: Ho, wait! You've made a mistake! He's the one! I'm Dr. Ginzberg . . . I mean Smith!

The lights fade.

ACT II

Scene I.   The same.

DR. BROWN: Who are you?

JULIUS: Me? Nobody.

DR. BROWN: What do you mean, nobody? What are you doing here?

JULIUS: I . . . I . . . I'm looking for a job.

DR. BROWN: Oh? What sort of job?

JULIUS: Any sort of job.

DR. BROWN *looks around, sees a broom against the wall and hands it to him.*

DR. BROWN: All right. Let's see what you can do. Well, go on, go on. You didn't expect to start at the top, did you? Around here we work our way up. Come on, come on, let's see what you can do. FORWARD, HAR! Sweep-sweep-sweep-sweep. [JULIUS *sweeps as* DR. BROWN *continues*] Now to the rear . . . HAR! Sweep-sweep-sweep-sweep. And left, turn! Sweep-sweep-sweep-sweep. And right, turn! Sweep-sweep-sweep-sweep. [*The door swings open and the* PSYCHIATRIST, *still in the straitjacket and gagged now as well, comes running into the room, pursued by the* GLADIATORS] What? Why did you bring him back here? [*The* GLADIATORS *chase the* PSYCHIATRIST *around the room*] What's going on? [*Back to* JULIUS] Sweep-sweep-sweep-sweep. And hut, two-three-four. Sweep, two-three-four . . . Lock the door! He won't get away! And right, turn. And left, turn. [*The* GLADIATORS *have cornered the* PSYCHIATRIST, *who is making gagging noises, his eyes darting wildly around. To the* GLADIATORS] Can't you take care of your charges? [*To* JULIUS]

Two-three-four . . . [*To the* GLADIATORS] I'll be with you in a minute. [*To* JULIUS] Two-three-four . . . *RIGHT TURN.* Sweep-sweep-two-three—AND . . . *LEFT TURN.* Sweep-sweep-two-three—AND . . . COMP'NY, HALT! [JULIUS *stands at attention with the broom*] That was very good, young man. You show very good potential. [*The* PSYCHIATRIST *makes gurgling, gagging noises, as though trying to get* DR. BROWN'S *attention*] Quiet! [*To* JULIUS] Now, young man, before we put you to work there are a few things I'd like to make clear. [*He begins pacing around, hands behind his back. He suddenly stops dramatically, turns*] This is ROME, young man, not GREECE! [*He pauses a moment and resumes his pacing*] Social order, regulated by law . . . independent of the subjectivity of individual temperament. In Rome, young man, the personality is surrendered to the State. The energy is centered upon the State. Therein lies the very grit of Roman virtue. Now, I know you Greeks are all heroes . . . individuals who rely upon personal resources and initiative . . . Homeric heroes, all of you! Each man his own master, each man independent, exercising his own will and steering his own course, as it were . . . where a head of State cannot determine a fixed line of action without consulting and obtaining the consent of his vassals . . . where the lion is master and king, yes, but the bear and the wolf sit in council! This individuality of inclination, this personal will is, I know, the very characteristic of Greek virtue. Not so here! Here, if the lion determines that there shall be a war, the vassals go to war! So do the bears and the wolves. In short, consideration of personal values and inclinations must take a subordinate place to the principle of honor to the State, and obligation and duty of the citizen to that State. ROME, young man. Not Greece. Is that clear? [JULIUS *nods*] All right. You can start sweeping up in the third-floor ward. Take the elevator down the hall on the right. [JULIUS *exits. The* PSYCHIATRIST *makes very loud, agitated gagging noises.* DR. BROWN *turns his attention to the* GLADIATORS] Now. Why is this patient down here again? And why is he gagged?

FIRST GLADIATOR: He wouldn't stop screaming. . . .

SECOND GLADIATOR: He ran away. . . .

FIRST GLADIATOR: He kept shouting that he's Dr. Smith.

SECOND GLADIATOR: Yeh. He set up a real howl. . . .

DR. BROWN: Dr. Smith? Dr. . . . [*He hurriedly puts on his eyeglasses*] Good God! It *is* Dr.

Smith! Take the straitjacket off him immediately. And take that gag out of his mouth! Dr. Smith . . . I'm terribly sorry about this. . . . You must excuse . . .

The GLADIATORS *take the gag out of the* PSYCHIATRIST'S *mouth, but before they can remove the straitjacket the* PSYCHIATRIST *shouts out.*

PSYCHIATRIST: That young man . . . he got away. . . .

DR. BROWN: What young man? Who got away?

PSYCHIATRIST: That young man . . . the one who just walked out of here . . .

DR. BROWN: The new custodian?

PSYCHIATRIST: He's a raving maniac!

DR. BROWN: Good heavens! That nice Greek lad?

PSYCHIATRIST: He's not a Greek, he's a Jew! His name is Schnadelson!

The GLADIATORS *start off.*

GLADIATORS: We'll head him off. He won't get away.

DR. BROWN: Wait. Be careful not to cause a disturbance among the other patients. Check the third-floor ward. If he's there, post four attendants outside the door. Just let him think he's a custodian. Let him sweep-sweep-sweep. But above all . . . don't cause a disturbance among the other patients.

The GLADIATORS *exit quickly, without taking time to remove the straitjacket from the* PSYCHIATRIST.

PSYCHIATRIST: Wait! Get me out of this thing!

DR. BROWN *goes quickly to the desk and picks up a microphone.*

DR. BROWN: Attention! All entrances and exits! This is Dr. Brown. All entrances and exits: Be on the alert!

PSYCHIATRIST: Dr. Brown! Get me out of this thing!

DR. BROWN: Be on the alert. This is an escape alarm. This is an escape alarm.

PSYCHIATRIST: DR. BROWN!

Drum rolls are heard. Military music. Searchlights play across the entire theatre.

DR. BROWN: A mad Jew is loose on the premises. Repeat: This is Dr. Brown . . .

PSYCHIATRIST: I am Dr. Smith! Get me out of this straitjacket!

DR. BROWN: A mad Jew is loose on the premises. Close all entrances and exits. Repeat: A mad Jew is loose on the premises. . . .

PSYCHIATRIST: I AM NOT A MADMAN! I AM DR. SMITH.

The drums and music rise in volume as the lights fade and come up on MARSHA, *watching the television set. She has rollers in her hair and is wearing* GLORIA'S *mink coat.* ERIC VON SCHTUTT, *the Internal Revenue man, is standing at the window. He eyes* MARSHA *suspiciously. The music segues into a melange of movie military music. After a while,* VON SCHTUTT *turns sharply, crosses to the trunk and leafs through his attaché case. He eyes the mink coat all the while. Finally he crosses to* MARSHA *and begins to examine the coat; he takes out a magnifying glass, blows on the fur, etc.* MARSHA, *who is totally involved in the TV is unaware of his actions. The music on the TV now becomes very romantic.* MARSHA *unconsciously takes the Internal Revenue man's hand and caresses it, pulls him onto her lap and kisses him.* GLORIA *enters with a cup of coffee.* VON SCHTUTT *leaps to his feet, clicks his heels and smiles.* GLORIA, *visibly alarmed, offers him the coffee. He crosses to the trunk and resumes his paper work.* MARSHA *sits down at the television again, and* GLORIA *paces nervously around. She then crosses to* MARSHA.

GLORIA: [*Whispering*] Why didn't you stay in Goldie's like I told you to?

MARSHA: [*Loudly*] I'm sick of Goldie's. I waited two hours for you in Goldie's already. I'm sick of Goldie's.

GLORIA: Shhut! [*As she crosses away, she catches* VON SCHTUTT'S *eyes. He smiles and hands her a paper and pen*]

VON SCHTUTT: [*He speaks with a very heavy German accent*] And here is the affidavit. Just sign it here. [GLORIA *signs the paper*] Thank you. [*He puts the affidavit in his case and sits drinking his coffee. He continues to eye* MARSHA *suspiciously.* GLORIA *stands watching, uneasily, glancing from* VON SCHTUTT *to* MARSHA. *She then crosses quickly to the television set and turns it off*]

GLORIA: [*Sotto voce*] Get out of here, will you!

MARSHA: What are you doing? You turned it off! Don't turn it off, please! Don't turn it off!

GLORIA: I don't want to listen to that.

MARSHA: Then turn off the sound, but not the picture. Leave the picture on! [*She switches the set on again without the sound and resumes watching in silence.* VON SCHTUTT *sits watching for a moment, then with sudden deliberation, he rises and crosses to* MARSHA]

VON SCHTUTT: That's a nice fur coat you have, Miss.

MARSHA: Huh . . . ? [*Then, very guardedly*] Oh, yeh.

VON SCHTUTT: Very nice. [MARSHA *and* GLORIA *exchange furtive, worried looks*] Is it yours?

MARSHA: [*Glancing at* GLORIA, *who nods*] Yeh, it's mine.

There is a tense pause.

VON SCHTUTT: What do you do for a living?

MARSHA: I'm a keypunch operator. [VON SCHTUTT *snickers and crosses to the trunk, where he begins to make notes.* MARSHA *rises nervously*] Is there any more coffee? I'd like some coffee. [*She crosses into the kitchen. When she rises we see that the coat is very large on her. It hangs down to her ankles and the sleeves cover her hands.* VON SCHTUTT *glances smugly at* GLORIA *and snickers again.* MARSHA *returns with the coffee and sits, pretending now to watch the television set, but keeping one eye on* VON SCHTUTT]

VON SCHTUTT: [*Rising suddenly and crossing to* MARSHA] Aren't you hot?

MARSHA: Hot? No, I'm not hot.

VON SCHTUTT: It's ninety-eight degrees outside.

MARSHA: [*Shrugs and tries to sound casual*] So? [VON SCHTUTT *continues to stare at her. She becomes very uncomfortable under his gaze. Then, erupting aggressively*] So?! So?!

VON SCHTUTT: So? I'll tell you, so! How does a keypunch operator afford a five-thousand-dollar mink? Why is she wearing it in ninety-eight-degree weather! And how come it is five sizes large!

Another tense pause.

MARSHA: [*Finally*] So! [*Pause. Then trying to invent*] It so happens that . . . I didn't buy the coat myself!

GLORIA: No, it was a gift. . . .

MARSHA: Yeh, it was a gift. And I'm wearing it in ninety-eight-degree weather because . . . because . . .

GLORIA: . . . There's no law that says she can't wear a fur coat . . .

MARSHA: . . . There's no law that says I can't wear a fur coat . . .

GLORIA: . . . in hot weather . . .

MARSHA: . . . if I want to.

GLORIA: Besides, she happens to have a little cold.

MARSHA: Yeh, I happen to have a little cold.

GLORIA: And it's not five sizes too large at all. . . . It fits her . . .

MARSHA: . . . perfectly.

VON SCHTUTT *is frustrated. Angrily he crosses back to the window. The two girls relax, complacently.*

VON SCHTUTT: [*Suddenly*] Gift tax!

The girls jump.

MARSHA: Gift tax? What gift tax?

VON SCHTUTT: Gift tax. Ten percent gift tax. You said it was a gift, you have to pay gift tax. That's the law.

MARSHA: [*Unable to reply, she becomes aggressive again*] So?! So?!

VON SCHTUTT: So! What do you mean, so! Did you pay a gift tax on it on not? Yes or no? [MARSHA *looks to* GLORIA *for help, but* GLORIA *does not respond*] Be careful how you answer. I can check it out downtown in ten minutes. [MARSHA *begins to panic*] No. That's what I thought. [*He crosses swiftly to his attaché case*] I'll have to take your name and address. We'll have the coat appraised and we'll send you a bill for ten percent of the estimated value. That should be somewhere around five hundred dollars. [*He approaches* MARSHA *with paper and pencil*]

MARSHA: Now just a minute. Just a minute! . . .

GLORIA: Marsha, please . . .

MARSHA: What do you mean, please! Am I supposed to get stuck for five hundred bucks? That wasn't in the deal!

VON SCHTUTT: What deal?

GLORIA: Nothing, nothing! . . .

VON SCHTUTT: What's your full name, Miss?

MARSHA: I'm not going to take the rap for you!

GLORIA: Shut up!

MARSHA: Why should I get stuck for your coat!

GLORIA: Oh, shit! . . .

VON SCHTUTT: What was that?

GLORIA: . . . Now you've done it!

VON SCHTUTT: Hers, you say?

MARSHA: I have nothing to do with this coat . . . !

VON SCHTUTT: So!

MARSHA: It's hers! . . .

VON SCHTUTT: Ja!

MARSHA: I can prove it! . . .

VON SCHTUTT: Ja!

MARSHA: It's too big on me! . . .

VON SCHTUTT: Ja!

MARSHA: It's ninety-eight degrees outside! . . .

VON SCHTUTT: Ja!

GLORIA: Rat! Fink!

MARSHA: I'm only a keypunch operator! . . .

VON SCHTUTT: Ja! [*He is triumphant. Turning to* GLORIA, *who has collapsed on the bed*] You're in a lot of trouble, Miss Gilbert. A lot of trouble. You signed an affidavit.

GLORIA: I know, I know.

VON SCHTUTT: That's willful evasion . . . punishable by a jail term.

GLORIA: Jail term! Take the coat. Take it. Marsha, let him have the coat.

VON SCHTUTT: I'm afraid it's more complicated than that, Miss Gilbert. I have your signed affidavit here in my briefcase.

GLORIA: Well, tear it up. Can't you tear it up? . . . Look, I'll make a deal with you . . . we'll make a deal!

VON SCHTUTT: Are you trying to bribe a Revenue officer? What kind of a deal? [*He glances at* MARSHA, *then to* GLORIA, *sotto voce*] We can't talk in front of your friend.

GLORIA: Marsha . . . oh, Marsha . . . why don't you . . . uh . . . why don't you go to the bathroom?

MARSHA: Wha . . . ?

GLORIA: Why don't you go to the bathroom?

MARSHA: Because I don't have to go to the bathroom.

GLORIA: Then . . . uh . . . why don't you turn on the television sound?

MARSHA: Because you wouldn't let me turn on the television sound.

GLORIA: Look! Either go to the bathroom or turn on the sound! [MARSHA *looks at* GLORIA *in confusion, then turns on the sound: a cosmetic commercial: a man with a continental accent, backed by a symphony orchestra.* GLORIA *and* VON SCHTUTT *move into the corner and pantomime their conversation.* GLORIA *explains, he listens; she hands him the secret book, he examines it; she proposes a deal, he considers; she elaborates, he is interested, etc. It ends with a handshake. She walks him to the door, he exits*] You dumb shit! Thanks to you I'd be on my way to jail right now if I hadn't been able to make a deal with him.

MARSHA: So?! What would you have done in my place? . . . What deal?

GLORIA: Thanks to you I had to give him the production rights to the secret book!

MARSHA: What secret book?

GLORIA: Some friend you turned out to be. I ask you to come over here to wear my coat for me for a few hours, and what do you do! You turn me over to the Feds! You Goddamned dumb shit! You just cost me a fortune! [*She pushes* MARSHA *off the chair and throws herself on the bed*]

There is a blackout. The cosmetic commercial continues to a symphonic climax as the lights fade up on the Madhouse. In the darkness we hear the tinkle of an ice-cream wagon coming down the center aisle. TERRY WONG FU, *dressed as a Good Humor man, is pushing the cart. He stations himself at the foot of the stage, in a corner, and remains there throughout the following scene. From time to time he sells ice cream to the* SAINTS *and* MARTYRS *in the madhouse. Electronic music from Pierre Henri's* L'Orphée: *the voices in the ancient Greek are hushed and whispered. A flashlight picks up the figures of the patients in the Madhouse as they enter.* SAINTS *and* MARTYRS, *dressed in sackcloth, sheer, loose-fitting sheaths, tattered robes. They enter one by one and in pairs, and slowly find their way to their places. When the actors are all in place, the lights come up to full. The opening effect of the Madhouse should be that of a Renaissance painting.* ST. AMBROSE *is seated on the forestage,* ST. AUGUSTINE *is standing beside him, leaning on a staff.* ST. ANTONY *is framed on the rear platform, gesticulating with his hands as though drawing pictures in the air. At times he appears to be addressing an individual or a group.* ST. TERESA, *a young man, is leaning against a post He is like a snake, sensuously wrapped up in his own body. The chorus of* SAINTS *and* MARTYRS *are seated all over the floor, on the steps, and on boxes. They are each wrapped up in their own madness. A spastic, a mongoloid, a hysteric, a catatonic, and they form a chorus to the events in the scene, reacting individually or in a group.*

Seated downstage in a corner is JACK SINISTRE, *the Black Prince. He is remote, detached, somewhat hostile. He wears a black leather trenchcoat, black boots, sweater and trousers. He is listening to a transistor radio, which is attached to a pair of earphones. Beside him sits a small* HUNCHBACK, *who is also dressed completely in black and who acts as* JACK'S *demon, imitating him, moving when he moves, etc.*

JULIUS *appears on the rear platform, broom in hand. He stares around at the scene, then moves slowly down the steps.* ST. TERESA *sees him and moves around him, eyeing him seductively.*

ST. TERESA: We all return. Sooner or later we all return.

JULIUS *sweeps past him, moving downstage toward* AUGUSTINE *and* AMBROSE.

AUGUSTINE: Saints, martyrs and prophets, you see. Martyrs without the lions, saints without a savior, and prophets without a vision. And they have thrown away the key.

AMBROSE: [*As though coming out of a dream*] Ahhh . . . but who is Satan?

AUGUSTINE: Satan is the commander-in-chief of the fallen angels.

AMBROSE: What do we mean by angels?

AUGUSTINE: What do we mean by fallen?

There is a hysterical laugh from one of the chorus. It is picked up by the others.

AMBROSE: [*Glancing in* JULIUS' *direction and rising*] It would not be particularly surprising to encounter people who prefer never to raise the question of the existence of angels.

AUGUSTINE: Well, that is obviously a kind of defeatism, a petty, spiritual cowardice.

AMBROSE: Precisely. [*They have cornered* JULIUS *now, and their discussion is directed toward him*] But we need not go back to the Middle Ages to discover a dogmatic definition on this point.

AUGUSTINE: No, indeed.

AMBROSE: Much more recently than that the Vatican Council of 1870 fixed it in its definitive form. [*He raises his finger at* JULIUS, *who now stands between them*] "This God . . ."

AUGUSTINE: ". . . The one true God . . ."

AMBROSE: ". . . in His goodness and by His almighty power, has made out of nothing, at the beginning of time, both the one and the other creature . . . at the SAME TIME!"

AUGUSTINE: That is to say, the spiritual and the corporeal . . .

AMBROSE: The angels and the world.

Pause.

JULIUS: [*Totally at a loss for a reply*] Oh, yes. The angels and the world.

AMBROSE: [*He nods at* JULIUS. JULIUS *nods back*] And from these solemn official pronouncements it follows that the existence of the angels and their creation by God is contemporaneous with that of the visible world.

JULIUS: Oh, is it? Indeed?

AMBROSE: Yes, indeed.

AUGUSTINE: Indeed it is.

JULIUS: Hm.

AMBROSE: Modern science tries to give us an approximate date for that tremendous event . . .

AUGUSTINE: [*Interrupting in order to explain*] The Creation.

AMBROSE: Yes. Our earth is between . . . what is it? . . . two, three . . . ? [*He turns to* AUGUSTINE *for help*]

AUGUSTINE: That's correct.

AMBROSE: Yes . . . two-three thousand million years old. And our sun is as much as . . . what is it? . . . seven . . . ?

AUGUSTINE: Eight.

AMBROSE: Yes . . . eight thousand million years old. And there is nothing to prevent the Creation of the angels being connected with that of the material universe, you see.

JULIUS: Oh?

AMBROSE: No. And it even contains an interesting idea. . . . [*He smiles with amusement and looks at* AUGUSTINE. *They both begin to laugh at some private joke*]

AUGUSTINE: Yes, it does.

AMBROSE: For it provides, if we dare use the expression—*spectators* and *witnesses* to that immense revelation.

AUGUSTINE: You didn't know that, did you?

JULIUS: No, I didn't.

AUGUSTINE: But let us hasten to say that in the Council's definitions, the words "at the same time" are not meant to oblige us to believe in this simultaneity of time.

AMBROSE: Well, no, no. But what does emerge from the formulas is that *The Creation Of The Angels Took Place Before That Of Men!*

JULIUS: Ahh.

AMBROSE: Man is at most . . . what . . . five hundred thousand, six hundred thousand years old? Well, if the angels were created *at the same time . . . .*

AUGUSTINE: [*Again explaining his friend's meaning to* JULIUS] Eight thousand million years ago . . .

AMBROSE: *Then they are of much longer standing in time than we!*

Suddenly, from the rear platform, ANTONY *cries out in anguish, his arms outstretched.*

ANTONY: Make an end! Make an end! [JULIUS *turns sharply. There is a hysterical laugh from one of the mad people, picked up by several others.* AMBROSE *and* AUGUSTINE *drift off into a corner.* JULIUS *stares at* ANTONY, *who is now gesturing dramatically at imaginary people. The Good Humor man comes slowly on the stage. He hands* JULIUS *an ice-cream pop and extends his hand for payment.* JULIUS *stares at him, mechanically reaches into his pocket and hands him some change. The ice-cream man returns to his cart*] I nearly came to a resolve but did not. The nearer I come to being another man, the more repelled I am. What holds me back? What holds me back?

TERESA: [*Slithering on the floor*] What holds you back is your old trouble: wine, women and song.

ANTONY: Ahhh, the women, the women . . . they pluck at my fleshly robe and whisper softly: "Are you sending me away? Shall I never be with you again?" I must prepare for my baptism. For eight months I must prepare. The New Man must come to birth. [*There is a shriek of derisive laughter.* ANTONY *glances desperately around at his tormentors*] I want more solitude! [*Approaching* JULIUS, *as though for help*] I must chase the Devil to his lair, take up my quarters in an empty tomb, in a burial cave in the cliffs. [*He wanders off, staring out into space*] I must go farther into the wilderness, cross into the desert, build myself a monastery. [*He sinks to his knees.* JULIUS *approaches him.* ANTONY *looks up slowly*] Will you bring me food and water?

JULIUS: Sure. [*He hands* ANTONY *the ice-cream pop.* ANTONY *smiles, accepts it and returns to his place on the rear platform*]

AUGUSTINE: A cause, a cause! My kingdom for a cause! You see? Martyrs without the lions, saints without a savior, prophets without a vision.

TERESA: Oh, shut up, Augustine.

AUGUSTINE: No, no, I am right. I am right. I've seen it all. I've heard it all. I wrote the book. I know.

TERESA: Yes, yes, yes. And we all know. You've told us a thousand times.

AUGUSTINE: You think it isn't true? You think I made it all up out of my head? From the jungle . . . yes . . .

TERESA: Yes, we know. We know.

The mad people begin to laugh at TERESA's *teasing. As the laughter increases,* AUGUSTINE *becomes more frantic.*

AUGUSTINE: You think it wasn't a jungle? What do you know, you spoiled, pampered, rotten little wretch from Radcliffe? [*To* JULIUS] It was a jungle. And I rose out of it. Right up to the seventeenth floor. A glass cage in the executive suite. I rose from the jungle to the zoo. And one day, I wanted to go back to the jungle, and I found myself standing on the seventeenth-story ledge of my cage. Animals do that, you know, when their instincts are croaking the death rattle. They try to escape. [*He laughs*] But they are wise now. They seal the windows. You can't open the windows anymore. Or perhaps they don't even build them with any windows at all now. No windows. Have you noticed that is becoming the fashion? Well, it isn't fashion. They do it for a reason. They lose too many animals. All you have to do is open a window and jump . . . and you're free. Back to the jungle, where life at least has some zip to it. But no. They've sealed the windows. And so the zoo becomes a prison. From the jungle, to the zoo, to the prison . . . [*With a sweeping gesture*] . . . to the slaughterhouse.

TERESA: [*Dancing wildly around him*] To the honor of the holy and undivided Trinity . . . We decree and define that the blessed Mr. Blank Blank is a saint, and We enter his name in the roll of saints, ordering that his memory be religiously venerated every year by the Church throughout the world. . . .

There is convulsive, hysterical laughter from the others now.

AUGUSTINE: Get away from me, you rotten Radcliffe thing. What do you know!

AMBROSE: [*As though coming through a fog*] Ahh . . . but who is Satan?

AUGUSTINE: Satan is the commander-in-chief of the fallen angels.

AMBROSE: But what do we mean by angels?

AUGUSTINE: What do we mean by fallen?

The laughter subsides as they drift off into the corner. One of the inmates, a young man, rises and walks down to the ice-cream wagon, where he buys a popsicle. He hums "Taps." JULIUS walks slowly, sadly, to the window, where he stares out.

TERESA: [*To* JULIUS] What do you see?

JULIUS: [*Turning to her*] Nothing. [*He turns back to the window*]

TERESA: [*Approaching him*] You see something. I know you see something.

JULIUS *laughs, somewhat ironically.*

JULIUS: Maybe. [TERESA *looks out of the window*] I see things and hear things that other people don't see and hear.

TERESA: Doesn't everyone?

JULIUS: No.

TERESA: [*Climbing up on the bench and looking out of the window*] Tell me what it is you see and maybe I'll see it, too.

JULIUS: No, you won't.

TERESA: How do you know? Maybe I will. Where? Out there . . . ?

JULIUS: Yes.

TERESA: Beyond the gate?

JULIUS: [*Becoming interested*] Yes, beyond the gate.

TERESA: Stillness.

JULIUS: Yes.

TERESA: Emptiness.

JULIUS: Yes.

TERESA: Silence.

A tortured scream from a spastic inmate.

JULIUS: [*Pause*] But look beyond it all. There—beyond the stillness, beyond the emptiness, beyond the silence . . . what do you see?

TERESA: Gracie Mansion. [*There is a general titter of laughter.* JULIUS *moves away*] Wait, wait. Give me a chance. Maybe I'll see it. Don't get discouraged so quickly. Now—where would I look? Beyond Gracie Mansion?

JULIUS: [*Wearily*] Yes. Beyond Gracie Mansion.

TERESA: Show me. Point me in the direction.

JULIUS: There. Beyond Gracie Mansion. Inside the stillness there is movement. People. Do you see the people?

TERESA: [*Straining*] People. People. Yes, I see some people. It's the mayor and his wife. They're having a lawn party.

More laughter.

JULIUS: Forget it.

TERESA: Wait. Give me time. I'm not trying hard enough. Come back. Show me again. Now. You were saying . . . People . . . beyond the tranquillity. Movement . . . in the stillness.

JULIUS: [*Wearily*] Yes.

TERESA: Oh, I see them now! Long-toothed people, naked and dancing, with horns like devils . . .

JULIUS: What . . . ?

TERESA: Yes, I see them. Oh, they're fearful-looking creatures, aren't they?

JULIUS: No . . . no . . . machine-gun fire . . . houses burning . . . children being slaughtered . . .

ANTONY: [*Joining them. His voice and manner are now crisp, clear, lucid*] You have too much imagination, my friend.

JULIUS: [*In a daze*] What . . . ?

ANTONY: You must think in terms of ultramodern warfare—then the nightmare will go away. Ultramodern warfare takes advantage of the self-restricting powers of human imagination. It is easier to live with, as it were. [*He extends his hand quickly*] Oh, I beg your pardon, we haven't met. I am Lieutenant Colonel Antony Moore.

Wild applause from the mad people.

JULIUS: [*Extending his hand*] How do you do. I am . . . Schnadel . . . Julius . . . Schnadelson . . . Esperanza . . .

ANTONY: Esperanza. Is your name really Esperanza? That means "hope," doesn't it?

JULIUS: Yes.

ANTONY: [*Gradually going into a dreamlike state*] Hope . . .

JULIUS: I am . . . a poet.

A shriek of laughter.

ANTONY: Don't pay any attention to them. They're all mad! A poet. Then you are concerned with the four great natural passions . . . Hope . . . Joy . . . Fear . . . Grief . . . [*He raises his hand and peers off in the distance through an imaginary telescope*]

JULIUS: You were saying? [*Snapping his fingers*] Lieutenant Colonel—Lieutenant Colonel

Moore. [ANTONY *comes back into focus*] You were saying . . . something about modern warware . . . imagination . . .

ANTONY: Oh yes. Yes. Modern warfare. Ultramodern warfare, that is. Yes. In the old days, you see . . . hand-to-hand battle . . . the imagination, you see . . .

JULIUS: Yes?

ANTONY: Well . . . if you were to bayonet a child . . .

JULIUS: Bayonet a child . . .

ANTONY: You would see the spurt of blood . . .

JULIUS: Yes . . .

ANTONY: The curling up of the little body . . .

JULIUS: [*Growing increasingly dizzy*] Yes . . .

ANTONY: The look in the eyes . . .

JULIUS: The look . . . in the eyes . . .

ANTONY: But if you were to drop a bomb on a town, you would see only that you have made a hit.

JULIUS: Made a hit . . . yes . . .

ANTONY: Time and again I have dined with boy aviators—French boy aviators, British boy aviators, American boy aviators—home from their raids. They were gallant, warmhearted, courageous, kindly youths . . .

JULIUS: Kindly youths . . .

ANTONY: And they were thinking and talking not of the effects of their bombs, but only of the hit. These kindly, courageous youths were concerned only with whether they had made a hit.

JULIUS: Courageous youths . . . yes . . . made a hit . . .

ANTONY: If now and then a glimmer of vision shot before their eyes they closed their minds . . . cut off the imagination . . .

JULIUS: Courageous youths . . . closed their minds . . . yes . . .

ANTONY: As one must do in war . . . [*He turns slowly away and, raising his arm in command, shouts*] FIRE! [*There is a shrieking cry from one of the women of the chorus. JULIUS reacts with a violent movement of his body. ANTONY turns slowly back to him*] You are a poet. Esperanza. Hope. That means hope. Concerned with the four great natural passions. [*He approaches JULIUS slowly*] But the remedy lies in mortification . . . mortification of the flesh, you see. [*He slowly removes the rope belt from around his waist and offers it to JULIUS*] The great passions . . . [*Automatically JULIUS takes the rope as though hypnotized. ANTONY then raises both his arms above his head and assumes a position for flogging, offering his back to JULIUS*] Close the senses . . . [*He begins to move, contorting his body as though

being whipped. JULIUS raises the rope whip: not an act of his own will but a reflex. Then, with a cry, he restrains his arm from continuing the gesture. ANTONY continues to writhe, however, as though JULIUS were actually beating him*] Cut off the imagination . . . the look in the eyes . . . as one must do . . . in war . . .

JULIUS: Oh God, help me. Help me. Close . . . cut off . . . close the senses . . . [*The other mad people have begun to crawl forward; they watch ANTONY, laughing grotesquely; they encircle JULIUS, clinging to his legs and his arms, clutching at his body*] I am . . . a poet . . . [*A shriek of laughter again*] Close the mind . . . cut off . . . joy . . . hope . . . Esperanza . . . hope . . . cut off . . . curling up . . . the look in the eyes . . . close the mind . . . close the senses . . . imagination . . . cut off . . . help . . . help . . . HELP! Who . . . God . . . God . . . Who?! Prince! Prince! Where are you, Prince? . . . Where? Where is the Black Prince!

There is sudden panic at the sound of the Black Prince's name, and everyone, including ANTONY, rushes for cover. JACK SINISTRE, the Black Prince, slowly removes his earphones and rises. The LITTLE DEMON beside him rises, too.

JACK: Did you call me? [*JULIUS whirls around. The LITTLE DEMON approaches him, laughing. JULIUS moves quickly away in fear, and finds himself confronting JACK. He cries out in terror and collapses on the wooden bench*] Waddayawant?

JULIUS: Are you . . . are you really . . . ?

JACK: Yeh.

JULIUS: The Black Prince? [*He stares at JACK in awe*] I don't believe it. You're really . . . how can that be? I mean, how do you do Mr. . . . Mr. . . .

JACK: They call me Your Highness.

JULIUS: Your Highness.

JACK: So? Waddayawant?

JULIUS: [*Stammering*] I . . . I . . . I . . .

JACK: Talk fast. I'm a busy person.

JULIUS: Yes, fast. Yes . . . I . . . I . . . I . . .

JACK: What's the matter with this guy? Can't he talk?

AMBROSE *moves cautiously toward* JACK.

AMBROSE: Your reputation precedes you, Your Highness. You must give him a moment's time to regain his equilibrium. It isn't every day that one is confronted with the image of archetypal evil.

JACK: Get back in your corner.

AUGUSTINE: [*In a hoarse whisper*] Sit down, Ambrose. He'll kill you as soon as look at you.

JACK: What was that?

AUGUSTINE: Nothing, nothing.

TERESA *laughs hysterically.*

JACK: Shaddup, nut! [*He turns his attention back to* JULIUS] Okay. State your business.

JULIUS: I . . . I . . . I . . .

JACK: Aw, shit! [*He turns away*]

JULIUS: Wait! I need your help!

JACK *stops and turns back.*

JACK: Oh, yeh? What for?

JULIUS: [*Staring at* JACK's *left hand*] What for? . . . Well . . . I . . . ever since I can remember . . . you've been sort of . . . well . . . you've been . . . ever since I was kid . . . it's been Prince this, Prince that, you know? . . . The Black Prince . . . so I . . . well, I never thought I'd actually meet you . . . in the flesh, so to speak. . . . I thought you weren't real. . . . You see, when I was a kid . . . I used to worship you and write poems to you . . . in your praise, that is . . . and I . . . now, you see . . . I think I was in love with you. . . .

JACK: What is this crap? I have to get back to my music. [*He turns away*]

JULIUS: Wait! Your help. I need it . . . I mean, I'm not sure . . . but I think . . . [*JACK turns around again*] Yes. Your help. I need your help. That's it.

JACK: What for?

JULIUS: What for? . . . Well . . . I . . . you see . . . Yes . . .

JACK: Oh, for Christ sake!

ANTONY MOORE *steps forward with authority.*

ANTONY: To mobilize a defense. [*He delivers a snappy salute to* JACK]

JACK: Oh, yeh?

ANTONY: The enemy troops are taking over.

JACK: No shit.

ANTONY: That, Your Highness, is the word from the Advanced Guard.

JACK: [*Indicating* JULIUS *with a nod*] Him.

ANTONY: Yes. The enemy has found a new method . . .

TERESA *has begun to crawl up* JACK's *leg.*

JACK: [*Shoving her off*] Not now, baby, not now.

ANTONY: . . . a new method. One with tremendous possibilities for annihilation. This weapon is powerful enough to overcome us if we do not reply in kind.

JACK: [*To* JULIUS] Is that true?

JULIUS: Yes . . . true, yes . . . a new weapon . . . yes . . .

ANTONY: And that, Your Highness, is the long and short of it. I respectfully submit this report to you with the following recommendations for action: One: Always have more forces than the enemy, particularly at the point of attack. Two: Always march on the enemy at an angle. [*He salutes and stands at attention.* JACK *rises and turns to* JULIUS]

JACK: Have you got anything to add?

JULIUS: Add? No . . . uh . . . I mean . . . no. Angle. Yes. March at an angle. [*He salutes*]

JACK: Okay. I'm ready.

ANTONY: Then we can count on the support and leadership of Your Highness in this campaign?

JACK: You got it. Now, first . . . we've got to locate the exact position of the enemy . . . then . . .

JULIUS: Wait! Wait! Before we begin . . . I have to know something. [*JACK looks at him, waiting*] I have to ask you something. . . . Before I get involved, I want to know . . . [*He pauses*]

JACK: [*Slowly*] What do you want to know?

JULIUS: I have to know . . . It's about your hand . . . yes . . . your hand in your pocket. [*JACK stares at him*] Is it . . . is it true what they say about . . . [*He stops*]

JACK: Is it true what they say about what? My hand in my pocket?

JULIUS: [*Summoning his courage*] Yes. Is it true what they say about your hand in your pocket?

JACK: What do they say about my hand in my pocket?

JULIUS: They say . . . there's a rumor . . . there's a rumor that . . .

JACK: That I carry a bomb in this pocket, right?

JULIUS: Right. [*Pause. They stare at each other*] I . . . have to know, Prince. I have to know before I accept your help. Before I get involved.

JACK: [*Suddenly very harsh*] Before you get involved! Before you accept my help! You are involved, baby! You are involved! What makes you think you stand outside, without guilt? Who the fuck do you think you are, baby? . . . Mr. Clean!? Before he gets involved! [*He grabs* JULIUS *by the collar and lifts him with one hand*] Who the fuck do you think I am? Where the fuck do you think I come from? Why the fuck did you come here in the first place? And how the fuck did you happen to find me again? In the fucking telephone directory? You're involved, baby. You're as much involved as anybody else! You've been involved since the day you were born. And you've known it since that Saturday afternoon, twenty-five years ago, when you left the Stilwell movie theater and took the shortcut home across the broccoli field! [*JULIUS is stunned and frightened*] Okay. [*He lets* JULIUS *down*] Now, I'm not playing games. We weren't playing games then, and we're not playing games now. Everything has come full circle, Baby Julius. You're home, kid. And if you crap out now . . . it's curtains!

ANTONY: [*Suddenly urgent*] Hold it! Don't move!

JACK: [*Alert*] Whattasamatta?

ANTONY: [*A husky whisper*] We're being watched. Don't look now, but we're surrounded. The guards are watching every move we make.

Four GLADIATORS *with spears have appeared on the rear platform. Others appear from the rear of the house.*

JULIUS: The guards! What'll I do? It's me they're after. Jack! What'll I do? What'll I do, Jack? Jackie . . . Jackie, baby. It's me, Julius . . . little Julie . . .

JACK: You're still asking me for help. You'll never learn, will you?

JULIUS: They'll get me, Jack. They'll get me.

JACK: Who? Who's gonna get you, Julie? Who?

ANTONY: Be careful. They're suspicious.

JACK: Okay. Don't move. Just look natural. [*To* ANTONY] Wake them up. Quick. [ANTONY *begins to arouse the sleeping people*] Get 'em on their feet. On the double. [*They all rise, sleepily*] You! Ambrose!

AMBROSE: M-m-me?

JACK: Yeh, you. You play the clarinet, don't you?

AMBROSE: Y-y-yes, I play the . . .

JACK: Well, play something. The rest of you people . . . sit around and look like you're listening.

AMBROSE: [*Moving toward the trunk*] What shall I play?

JACK: I don't know. Play anything you like.

AUGUSTINE: [*Who is more aware than the others of what is taking place*] Yes, Ambrose. Play the Hungarian Rhapsody number 15. And let's all sit down and listen to Ambrose play. Come on, now . . . come along . . .

JACK: [*Moving aside with* JULIUS. *He says to* ANTONY] You! Stand guard. [ANTONY *takes up sentry duty, pacing back and forth across the stage, one eye on the guards.* AMBROSE *has removed a clarinet from the trunk. Music up: "Valse Vanité," a clarinet solo. It plays through the following scene between* JULIUS *and* JACK] So you want to know if it's true what they say about my hand in my pocket, eh? You still want to know. What *they* say. [*Pause*] You make me want to cry. You haven't learned shit in twenty-five years. [*Pause. He looks at* JULIUS *steadily, then says,*

not unkindly] You still don't know which end is up, kid. [*He sighs*] Okay. So you want me to go over the whole thing again. Okay. [*He sighs again*] What d'ya wanna know?

JULIUS: Is it true . . .

JACK: . . . what they say . . .

JULIUS: . . . about your hand . . .

JACK: . . . in my pocket. [*He pauses, takes out a cigar, which* JULIUS *lights.* JULIUS *then sits down and listens, fascinated*] It was true . . . once. I used to carry a bomb in this pocket. Yeh. . . . I used to carry a bomb in this pocket. For many years I carried a bomb in this pocket. For as many years as I can remember. In fact, I can't even remember how many years. But it was . . . many . . .

JULIUS: Many many.

JACK: Yeh. Many many. I must have been . . . what? . . . Five? . . .

JULIUS: No . . .

JACK: Six . . .

JULIUS: Yeh . . .

JACK: Six years old when I first started carrying it. [*During the following monologue,* JULIUS *listens as though anticipating every word*] Somebody left it lying around in a field out near Coney Island. It could have been there for a hundred years for all I know. It was a pretty old bomb. I mean, it wasn't a modern bomb. It was a very old-fashioned bomb. You know . . . makeshift. But what did I know? I was a kid. A bomb is a bomb . . . you know what I mean? To a kid, I mean. A bomb is a bomb. But it was a real bomb. This much I knew.

JULIUS: It was no sweet potato.

JACK: It was a *bomb!* So I took it and put it in my pocket. . . . [*Automatically* JULIUS *slips his left hand into his pocket*] I took that bomb with me everyplace. Everyplace I went. It never left my side. I ate with it, I slept with it, I went to school with it. [*He laughs nostalgically*] Many is the time I wanted to throw it at one of them teachers; but something in me always said, "Wait! There's a better time coming. Don't waste it on those crumbs!" [JULIUS *laughs*] And so, as I grew older I still kept it with me. All through the Marines I kept it with me. Oh, yeh, I had been introduced to more modern types of bombs by that time. You know, slick, fancy ones. But I hung on to my old bomb. I wouldn't trade it in for nothin'. Because it was mine, see? You know what I mean? It was mine.

JULIUS: [*Softly, from some distant place*] Mine.

JACK: And you know? I developed a kind of . . . affection for that old motherfucker. [*He laughs nostalgically again*] Even when I made love I kept it with me. Yeh, no kidding. Ohhh

. . . [*He laughs again.* JULIUS *laughs*] Many is the whore that nearly got that bomb right between the piano legs. [*He laughs and laughs.* JULIUS *laughs and laughs, silently, distantly*] But no. I always said, "Wait!" Something inside me always told me to wait. "There's a better time coming. Don't waste it on that bimbo." And so I waited. [*He sighs*] I went on my way . . . you know . . . making my way in the world. Some friends launched me on a good career . . . first a piece of the action— numbers, horses, a few girls, you know—and then I went legit. My friends put up the bread for the singing lessons, and before I could turn around, I'm a star. Who knows how these things happen? Fate. You know, when I think . . . [*He climbs up on the trunk*] I would be standing up there on the bandstand, the orchestra playing behind me, the people dancing . . . nice . . . on the dance floor. . . . Me wearing a three-hundred-dollar tux . . . and always with the hand. Always with the hand in the pocket . . . you know? [JULIUS *has risen. He stands as though singing in front of a microphone*] And me singing . . .

JULIUS: [*Singing*] I love you, for sentimental reasons . . .

JACK: . . . and then I would think . . . just to amuse myself, you know? I would think . . . wouldn't it be something . . . ? And BAM! [*He and* JULIUS *laugh*] Yeh, them were the days. But no. That wasn't the time or the place. I knew that. I always had good judgment. And so I quit the singing racket for awhile, I got married, had a good life . . . no complaints, you know? And one night . . . one night my wife says: "Let's go to the opera." Opera. Okay. She wants to go to the opera, we'll go to the opera. Women, you know how they get. . . . They got everything, then they want culture. So we go to the opera. And they're playing this *Lohengrin* thing, and they're singing—I mean real singing, you know?—and then comes a part when everything seems to stop. Nobody seems to move. Nobody is even breathing; and the only sound is the tenor's voice. Like magic notes. And two thousand people, like one person, breathing one breath. Suspended on the magic notes. I was like lifted into another world. My body felt like it wasn't my body, you know what I mean? And the only thing I could feel was something moving inside me . . . something very small, something I never felt before . . . like small . . . very small feathers in my chest. And the only thing I could hear is the sound of the magic notes. I felt like heaven was opening up and I was floating . . . [*He stops*] That's when it happened. Something said to me: NOW! And before I could do anything . . .

BAM! [JULIUS *leaps to his feet and makes a gesture of throwing a bomb*] It went off. Just like that. Bam! But I still remember that moment in that opera house. Those magic notes in the silence. My body floating up in the air. The feathers fluttering in my chest. It was the most beautiful moment in my life. It was the moment I saw God. [*He and* JULIUS *now stand face to face, as though in a mirror*]

AUGUSTINE: [*Naïvely*] And you threw a bomb in His face?

JACK: [*To* JULIUS] I am who I am.

ANTONY: [*Suddenly*] Look out!

JULIUS *whirls around quickly. The electronic hum is heard followed by staccato passages from "Musique Concrète." The* GLADIATORS *advance. He fights them off.* ANTONY *tries to help him.* JACK *stands off to the side, watching. The inmates rush around desperately.* JULIUS *frees himself from the* GLADIATORS *and with a motion that is almost a reflex, makes a hurling gesture with his left hand. Simultaneously, before we can see what has happened, there is an explosion. The lights go to black and then begin to flicker. A single flashlight plays across the stage and picks up flashes of the massacre of the* SAINTS *and* MARTYRS *by the* GLADIATORS. *Anguished crys, recorded, in the ancient Greek: "L'Orphée" accompanies the movement, which should be in slow motion. When the lights come up again, the inmates are lying dead all around. The* GLADIATORS *stand over them with their spears.* ANTONY *covers his eyes at the sight.* JACK *watches* JULIUS, *who is staring at the scene in horror.* JULIUS *then slowly raises his left hand and stares at it in disbelief. The tango music is heard, faintly: "Lesz Maga Juszt Is Az Enyem."*

JULIUS: [*Turning to* JACK] You . . . you . . . !

JACK: No, Julie baby . . . you! [JULIUS *backs away from* JACK] We're one, Julius. You and I are one. Shall we dance? [*He grabs* JULIUS *and drags him across the stage in a grotesque dance as the lights fade on the scene. The tango music continues as a bridge into the next scene*]

MARSHA, *wearing a nightgown, is staring dully into the television set; she then rises and begins to dance to the tango music. Voices off.* MARSHA *runs back to her chair.* VON SCHTUTT, TERRY, *and* FRED THE MAILMAN *enter, dressed in evening clothes. They are in a very gay mood.* TERRY *carries several bottles of whiskey, is smoking a big cigar and is wearing the mink coat.*

VON SCHTUTT: *Ja,* with a team like this I don't see how we can lose. If tonight was any indication, we should have all the money raised within a week. We're in, team. We're in.

TERRY: I'll drink to that.

FRED: Yeh. Let's have another drink.

GLORIA: [*To* MARSHA] Go get the ice.

MARSHA *rises sulkily and crosses to the kitchen.*

MARSHA: Just don't turn it off, okay? Don't turn it off. [*She exits into the kitchen*]

GLORIA: She's beginning to get on my nerves.

VON SCHTUTT: Why did you let her move in?

GLORIA: Because I can't live alone. I just can't be by myself, that's why. Ever since Julius left . . . left . . .

VON SCHTUTT: Who's Julius?

TERRY: [*Quickly*] Nobody.

GLORIA: A guy.

FRED: Let's drink to success.

VON SCHTUTT: Cheers!

TERRY: Bottoms up!

FRED: Skoal!

GLORIA: Kiss my ass!

VON SCHTUTT: [*Turning off the television*] Now, I don't mean to put a damper on things, but there's one little problem. This book . . . it stinks!

There is a stunned silence.

GLORIA: What do you mean?

VON SCHTUTT: Just what I said. It stinks. There's no dramatic action, the central character hasn't got any balls, and the visions and revelations stink. It's a Goddamn rotten book! [*He throws the book to* GLORIA, *who throws it to* TERRY]

TERRY: What are you giving it to me for?

GLORIA: You wrote it, didn't you?

TERRY: Oh! . . . yes . . . yes . . . but what do you expect me to do?

VON SCHTUTT: Rewrite it!

TERRY: Re . . . re . . .

GLORIA: Yeh, rewrite.

VON SCHTUTT: You've got two weeks to come up with a new book. . . . Otherwise . . .

TERRY: Two weeks! [*He looks helplessly at* FRED, *who looks angrily at* GLORIA, *who shrugs*]

VON SCHTUTT: I said otherwise . . . I'll get a new writer . . . and a new team!

TERRY: New book.

GLORIA: Don't be silly . . . new writer! . . . He can do it. Terry can do it.

FRED: Yeh, he can do it.

GLORIA: After all, it's the title and the idea they bought tonight. All we have to do is hang a new book on it.

VON SCHTUTT: Right! All we have to do is hang a new book on it.

TERRY: But . . . but . . . how? . . . what? . . . [*He looks to* GLORIA *for help*]

GLORIA: Don't ask me, you're the writer.

FRED: Go to the library.

GLORIA: Yeah, go to the library.

VON SCHTUTT: Look up everything you can find on the subject of visions and revelations. . . .

GLORIA: Yeah, visions and revelations . . .

VON SCHTUTT: You take a little bit from here, a little bit from there. Disguise it, change it. . . .

GLORIA: Muck it up a little. . . .

VON SCHTUTT: *Ja*, muck it up a little. . . . We shouldn't have to tell you how to write an original piece of material. That's your department. But as far as this book is concerned . . . [*He takes the secret book from* TERRY] . . . you can just throw it in the garbage can for all its worth. [*He tosses the book out of the window and it lands in a garbage can*] Okay. You've got two weeks, Tulips. Get cracking.

MARSHA *has returned and switches on the television sound as the lights fade on the scene. Organ music is heard: the sort that one hears in movie houses, skating rinks, etc. The* AN-NOUNCER'S *voice is heard, as the scene fades to black and the lights come up on: the Olive Room Cocktail Lounge, atop the Hotel Olive. Around the edge of the stage there are tables with masked patrons, drinking. The* EVIL WAITERS, *also masked, carry drinks across the floor. Seated at a dais table on the rear platform are* ALVIN *and his* MOTHER. ALVIN, *played by the* PSYCHIATRIST, *is a cocker spaniel. His* MOTHER, *played by* DR. WAVERLY BROWN, *is an enormous eight-foot puppet with a grotesque mask.*

EVALD THE ANNOUNCER: Welcome, ladies and gentlemen, to the "Alvin and His Mother Show," brought to you live from the Olive Room of the Hotel Olive. [*The organ music swells as the lights come up to full. A spotlight focuses on the dais*] And now the stars of our show: Alvin and His Mother! [*Canned applause. The patrons pantomime the canned applause*]

ALVIN: Thank you, Evald. Thank you, ladies and gentlemen. We have an exciting . . . [*The* PUPPET *has begun to move restlessly, poking and hitting at* ALVIN'S *sleeve*] . . . show for you tonight. But before we introduce our first guest, my mother wants to say a few words to you.

The PUPPET *rises clumsily and moves its huge arms awkwardly, raising them above its head, and lumbering around. It accidentally hits* ALVIN'S *arm and anything else that is in the the way.*

ALVIN'S MOTHER: [*To the audience, arms still raised in what appears to be a blessing, it makes strange, ugly, guttural noises*] Bluahh, vrahh, zzrahh, eeahh, bluahh, svrmmmm, csszz, mrrouvm . . .

ALVIN: My mother says: Smile, because God loves you. That's right, ladies and gentlemen: Smile, because God loves you. [*The* PUPPET *begins to make more noises*] That's fine, Mother. Thank you, Mother. Smile, because God loves you, ladies and gentlemen. . . . [*There is loud applause*] And now, ladies and gentlemen . . . [*Music up: "Honolulu Eyes," a recording. The lights change to half and a spotlight stops upstage of the dais*] . . . our first guest. An officer and a gentleman, LIEUTENANT COLONEL ANTONY MOORE!

More applause as ANTONY MOORE *steps into the spotlight. He is dressed in full officer's uniform and is very debonair and handsome. He moves around the stage while the music plays, greeting the audience with cool, poised nods, little half salutes and salutations. He then crosses to the center of the stage just before the whistling solo begins on the record; the actor then pantomines the whistling. It is done with great style and dash—cool, collected, in command of the situation. While he is whistling, four Oriental guerrillas appear with tree branches attached to their arms and legs. They carry bayonets and move stealthily toward* ANTONY MOORE, *who appears not to see them. As they approach him, they become gradually caught up with the whistling; Slowly they begin to dance; a lyrical dance, holding their bayonets above their heads and swaying with them.* ANTONY MOORE, *still without acknowledging their presence, moves quietly to the side, raises his arm, and shouts over the music.*

ANTONY: FIRE!

Rifle shots. The four guerrillas drop dead. Fanfare, loud applause, the lights come up to full.

ALVIN: Thank you, Lieutenant Colonel Antony Moore! [*"Honolulu Eyes" plays as* ANTONY *exits. Four* EVIL WAITERS *drag the bodies of the dead* GUERRILLAS *to the tables and prop them up in the chairs*] And now, ladies and gentlemen, our next two guests . . . [*The* PUPPET *begins to get restless again, swinging its arms at* ALVIN] What is it? [*It makes a few noises*] Not now. Later.

The noises become more agitated.

ALVIN'S MOTHER: Bluahh, ggrvrmm, szehitg, woenbiuahh.

ALVIN: All right, all right. [*To the audience*] My mother insists on saying a few more words to you, ladies and gentlemen . . .

Applause. The PUPPET *rises again in the same manner and repeats exactly the former salutation.*

ALVIN'S MOTHER: Bluahh, ggrvrmm, vrahh, zzradgg, egemanvrum, mrrourvm, svrmm.

Applause.

ALVIN: My mother says: And the Lord direct your hearts into the love of God. That's right, ladies and gentlemen: And the Lord direct your hearts into the love of God. Hear, hear! [*He claps his paws. More applause. The* PUPPET *sits, with a grunt*] Our next guest, ladies and gentlemen, direct from the Sacred College, His Eminence, Cardinal Black Jack Sinistre—

Music begins: "The Captain Betty Two-Step," played on a hurdy-gurdy. JACK SINISTRE *appears in the spotlight. He is dressed in full vestments of an officiating cardinal. His left hand is hidden under his cape. Attached to his shoulders is a hurdy-gurdy organ, which he plays with his right hand. On his arm there is a long leash, at the end of which is* JULIUS, *dressed as an organ grinder's monkey.* JULIUS *performs like a trained monkey, hopping, scratching, tossing peanuts in the air and catching them in his mouth. They move to the center of the stage, where* JULIUS *performs "The Monkey Dance" while* CARDINAL BLACK JACK *plays the hand organ. Enter, the chorus of* STARVING WOMEN, *masked. They move around the stage, arms outstretched, chanting, "Help!" in every language except English and Russian.*

STARVING WOMEN: Au secours! . . . Helfen! . . . Socorro! . . . Auxilio!

They circle the edge of the stage, dragging themselves, stumbling, crawling, repeating the words in a chant. EVALD THE ANNOUNCER *enters, throwing confetti and shouting.*

EVALD: It's time! It's time! Happy New Year!

The nightclub patrons shout and cheer, blow horns, kiss each other. It peters out to an awkward silence, with the STARVING WOMEN *still chanting their cry for help.* ALVIN *motions to* EVALD, *who instructs the* EVIL WAITERS *to remove the* STARVING WOMEN. *They are dragged to the tables and placed in chairs opposite the dead* GUERRILLAS.

ALVIN: Thank you, Cardinal Black Jack Sinistre. [*Music: "Clementine"*] And now, ladies and gentlemen, our next guest: The only woman to be canonized within her own lifetime, the beautiful and enchanting St. Teresa, patron saint of the Intercollegiate All-Star Women's Basketball Team! [*There is applause. The music segues into "The Yellow Rose of Texas"* as TERESA *enters, wearing a nun's habit. He is followed by five six-foot girls who are dressed in basketball uniforms. They do a basketball ballet number, which is nothing more than dribbling imaginary balls around and shooting for imaginary baskets. They carry themselves like athletes, with exaggeratedly hunched shoulders, and they all chew gum and have tough expressions on their faces. During their "dance,"* ST. TERESA, *with a benign smile, circles the stage, bestowing blessings on everyone, including the audience. The music segues into "Battle Hymn of the Republic."* TERESA *turns suddenly in a dance movement and begins a rather raucous striptease, removing the breakaway nun's habit piece by piece. The* EVIL WAITERS *and nightclub patrons whistle, cheer, call out, "Take it off!" "That's it, baby!" etc. The music changes to bazouki and oud music, slow and seductive.* TERESA, *now naked except for a beaded skirt and the nun's wimple, performs an erotic dance. Everyone slowly joins the dance.* CARDINAL BLACK JACK *watches* TERESA *lasciviously. As* TERESA *sinks to his knees in a writhing, erotic movement,* CARDINAL BLACK JACK *approaches slowly, holding a diamond necklace in the air. He dangles it before* TERESA, *who accepts it and tosses away a pair of rosary beads.* BLACK JACK *then sweeps* TERESA *up in his arms and carries him off.* JULIUS MONKEY *begins to make agitated noises, screeching and chirping wildly and hopping madly about. The giant* PUPPET *rises laboriously and lumbers forward, making weird, guttural noises and swinging blindly about.* JULIUS *continues to leap wildly and shriek, the* WAITERS *join in, trying to restore order; the patrons at the tables get caught up in the madness and begin to shriek and bellow like animals]* Mother! Come back here! Stop this! Waiters! Can't you restore order! Mother! Rrrf . . . rrrff . . . You! Monkey! Stop that! Bow-wow . . . Cardinal, can't you control your monkey! . . . Quiet! Rrrrff . . . rrrff . . . bow-wow . . . grrr . . . *[He begins to howl like a mad dog]*

EVALD *appears with a hand mike. Music: "Lo, Hear the Gentle Lark," sung by Alma Gluck.* TERRY WONG FU *sails down the center aisle, dressed as a lady coloratura soprano. He is followed by a demented page turner. They settle in a spotlight on the forestage,* TERRY *"sings" while the melee continues in the background, with everyone piled on the floor—a mass of bodies, arms and legs swinging madly.* JULIUS *stands in the center, watching it all, gradually losing his monkeylike countenance. A girl rises out of the sea of bodies, like a bird, and performs a solo dance, on point. As the "Gentle Lark"*

draws to an end, JULIUS *slowly returns to himself and, cautiously stepping over the bodies, runs off the stage and up the center aisle as the lights fade.*

Music: "The Gay Ranchero." VON SCHTUTT, FRED THE MAILMAN, *both wearing sombreros, dance down the aisle and onto the forestage, where they are joined by* TERRY. *They hand* TERRY *his sombrero, and they perform a dance in celebration of their prosperity.* GLORIA *enters, carrying a lantern. She regards them with some disgust and sits on a box, down stage left, on the forestage.* VON SCHTUTT *and* FRED *join her, sitting on boxes beside her.* TERRY *continues to dance.*

GLORIA: *[After observing* TERRY *for a moment]* Can we get this meeting started, please? *[*TERRY *joins them]* I don't know why we had to meet in this godforsaken place.

VON SCHTUTT: Obviously, Miss Gilbert, you have never attended a production meeting before. It is necessary for the creative team to isolate itself, to cut itself off from the outside world. Now, where were we?

FRED THE MAILMAN: The title.

VON SCHTUTT: Yes, the title. We're all agreed on the title. "The Revelations Revue" . . . written by Terry Wong Fu, starring Gloria B. Gilbert, directed by Fred the Mailman, and produced by Eric Von Schtutt, Field Division, Internal Revenue Service of the United States of America!

TERRY: That's pretty long billing, if you ask me.

VON SCHTUTT: You're getting yours. What are you complaining about?

GLORIA: Yeah, twelve-point Gothic! I'm the star!

TERRY: You're going above the title! Isn't that enough?

FRED THE MAILMAN: What about me? I'm as important as he is!

TERRY: No, you're not! I wrote it!

VON SCHTUTT: Quiet! Quiet! Please! We are not here to discuss billing. We're here to work on creative problems.

GLORIA: Close the Goddamned door! *[A murky light comes up on the rear stage.* JULIUS *enters, running. He is exhausted and there is blood on his face. He looks around frantically and runs off, up the aisle]* Close the Goddamned door, there's a draft.

JACK *enters, in pursuit of* JULIUS. *He carries a sword. He follows* JULIUS *off, up the aisle. Neither of the actors acknowledges the four others seated on the boxes, and the four do not acknowledge* JULIUS *and* JACK.

VON SCHTUTT: The rewrite is great. Great! I don't know how you did it, Tulips, but you've come up with the goods. We're all set to go. I've already begun to investigate the movie sale possibilities and the interest is tremendous. Tremendous! There's an awful lot of money to be made if we stick together, team. If we work together, make the necessary revisions, there's no reason at all why we can't be millionaires by next year. This is the twentieth century, right, team?

OTHERS: Right!

GLORIA: Kiss my ass!

VON SCHTUTT: Anybody can be rich. Right?

OTHERS: Right!

VON SCHTUTT: Shall we give it all we've got?

OTHERS: Why not!

VON SCHTUTT: Okay! Let's sock it to 'em, team! If it's a show they want, LET'S GIVE 'EM A SHOW! Eric Von Schtutt and Company Present: The Revelations Revue.

"The Revelations Revue" music begins: "Row-Row-Row." The lights fade on the production meeting and come up to full on the stage. Seven candlesticks line the back wall of the rear platform. They are about five feet in height and painted gold. Yellow lightbulbs serve as flames. In the center of the candlesticks stands a man dressed in a white gown with golden girdle. On his head there is a white woolly wig. His eyes are painted in red circles and in his right hand he holds seven tinselly stars. Right and left stage are the FOUR HORSEWOMEN, showgirls with elaborate headdresses: a White Horsewoman with a bow and arrow; a Black Horsewoman with a pair of scales; a Red Horsewoman with a sword; a Pink Horsewoman with a skull mask. A black moon is lowered, followed by sequined stars which float down from the ceiling. The seven STAR ANGELS appear dancing. JULIUS hides among them and disappears upstage when he spies JACK SINISTRE. JACK pushes through the line of dancing STAR ANGELS, looks around and exits.

MAN IN WHITE WOOLLY WIG: Fear not, I am the first and the last. I am he that liveth and was dead, and, behold, I am alive for evermore, amen; and have the keys of hell and of death. [*He sails off*]

The TRUMPET ANGELS appear. They do a tap dance. The WOMAN CLOTHED IN THE SUN with the Moon Beneath Her Feet appears. A crepepaper sunburst frames her head and she sits with her feet resting on a round ball, across which is printed the word "MOON." She wears a crown of 12 stones and in her arms carries an infant. She is followed by the DRAGON. JACK SINISTRE enters, still searching for JULIUS. The DRAGON tries to take the in-

fant from the SUN WOMAN; she resists, he tugs at it, she pulls it back. Finally, the DRAGON snatches the infant, raises it up, opens his jaws as though to eat it. He throws the infant into the wings. The four SWORD ANGELS appear, led by the three sixes Beasties. As they go into their number, JACK SINISTRE appears again, he catches sight of JULIUS on the catwalk and slowly approaches the left ladder. JULIUS, unarmed, stands poised, as though ready for JACK. The dancers have now formed a diagonal line across the stage. They open out with their arms toward the upstage entrance and GLORIA appears, dazzling in white satin and ostrich feathers. She dances down the line, smiling out front. When she turns, however, she sees JULIUS and JACK on the catwalk. She utters a cry, and backs away. The dancers stop their number, and observe the activity on the catwalk. The music, however, continues.

JACK: Why do you run from me, Julius? You can't get away from me. Don't you know that? You and I are one. We're of one mind.

JULIUS: [*Shaking his head, murmuring*] No . . . no . . .

JACK: You created me, Julius. I am a part of you: Jack, the Black Prince. See? It's me. [*He starts to move slowly toward* JULIUS] Let's be friends. Come, let's embrace. Take me into yourself. [*Pause*] I'll have to kill you, otherwise. You know that, don't you? Come . . . don't be an old-fashioned martyr. [*He moves toward* JULIUS *again.* JULIUS *appears to waver slightly*] Let's be one. Let's become one, you and I.

JULIUS hesitates. At that moment, ANTONY appears in the center aisle, with raised sword, and shouts up to JACK.

ANTONY: If thou touchest a hair on his sweet head, thou shalt answer to me, thou foul serpent of hell! [*He leaps to the center of the stage. The dancers scream and rush about*]

JACK: [*Raising his sword*] Enter the old fashioned hero!

ANTONY: I have lived by the sword, and it is right that I should die by the sword, and by the sword I shall die or kill thee if thou harmest him!

JACK: Well said, my friend! [*He leaps down, his sword raised, and they duel*]

The dancers hover along the edges of the stage. When ANTONY gains the advantage they cheer and press forward. When JACK gains the advantage they hiss and draw back. ANTONY now forces JACK backward off the stage, and they duel up the center aisle, with the entire company of dancers following. There is a shout, and the dancers rush back onto the stage as JACK and ANTONY *return, dueling down the center aisle and back onto the stage.* ANTONY *now gains the advantage and disarms* JACK *of his sword. There is a great cheer from the crowd.* ANTONY *picks up both swords and holds them above his head in acknowledgment of victory. At that moment,* JACK *takes out a switchblade and stabs* ANTONY.

ANTONY: [*Surprised*] I am baptised. I die. The New Man shall come to birth. [*He dies, falling at* GLORIA'S *feet*]

JACK: [*Looking up at* JULIUS] Well, what shall it be, my friend? Jesus Christ or God the Father?

The music stops.

JULIUS. Just . . . Esperanza! [*He swings down from the catwalk. At the same moment* PROFESSOR POE *appears on the rear platform.* JULIUS *glances swiftly from* POE *to* GLORIA *to* JACK. *He assumes the pose of a wrestler, confronting* JACK *squarely.* JACK *and* JULIUS *wrestle.* JACK *finally grabs* JULIUS *in a ferocious bear hug and appears to be crushing the breath out of him. The struggle reaches a climax, and the death grip gradually becomes an embrace. They relax their bodies and stand looking at each other. The other members of the company start forward slowly.* GLORIA *takes her place beside them, the parade music which was heard at the opening of the play begins and they march off*]

A RAT'S MASS

a play in one act

Adrienne Kennedy

A Rat's Mass was first presented by Ellen Stewart at the La Mama ETC, New York City, on September 11, 1969, with the following cast:

SISTER RAT .... *Mary Alice*

BROTHER RAT .... *Gilbert Price*

ROSEMARY .... *Marilyn Roberts*

And featuring Lamar Alford and Robert Stocking.

It was directed by Seth Allen. Music composed and directed by Lamar Alford. Set by Theodore S. Titolo; lighting by John P. Dodd, assisted by Steve Whitson; costumes by Ann-Marie Allen. Stage manager: June Perz.

Rosemary was the first girl we ever fell in love with. She lived next door behind a grape arbor her father had built. She often told us stories of Italy and read to us from her Holy Catechism book. She was the prettiest girl in our school.

BROTHER RAT *has a rat's head, a human body, a tail.* SISTER RAT *has a rat's belly, a human head, a tail.* ROSEMARY *wears a Holy Communion dress and has worms in her hair. Mass said in prayer voices that later turn to gnawing voices. They were two pale Negro children.*

Scene is the rat's house. The house consists of a red carpet runner and candles. The light is the light of the end of a summer day. BROTHER RAT *is kneeling facing the audience. At the far left of the house stands a procession of* JESUS, JOSEPH, MARY, TWO WISE MEN, *and a* SHEPHERD. SISTER RAT *stands at the end of the red aisle.*

BROTHER RAT: Kay within our room I see our dying baby. Nazis, screaming girls and cursing boys, empty swings, a dark sun. There are worms in the attic beams. [*Stands*] They scream and say we are damned. I see dying and gray cats walking. Rosemary is atop the slide. Exalted! [*Kneels again*] Kay within our room I see a dying baby, Nazis, again they scream. [*Stands again*] and say we are damned. Within our once Capitol I see us dying. Rosemary is atop the slide exalted.

SISTER RAT: We swore on Rosemary's Holy Communion book.

BROTHER RAT: Did you tell? Does anyone know?

The procession watches.

SISTER RAT: Blake, we swore on our father's Bible the next day in the attic.

BROTHER RAT: Did you tell Sister Rat, does anyone know? [*Kneels*] It was Easter and my fear of holy days, it was because it was Easter I made us swear.

SISTER RAT: Brother Rat, it was not Easter. It was night after Memorial Day.

BROTHER RAT: No, it was not after Memorial Day. It was the beginning of winter. Bombs fell. It was the War.

SISTER RAT: It was the War.

BROTHER RAT: Our fathers said everything was getting hung and shot in Europe. America wouldn't be safe long. [*Remains kneeling; procession marches across the house to center*]

SISTER RAT: Remember . . . we lived in a Holy Chapel with parents and Jesus, Joseph, Mary, our wise men and our shepherd. People said we were the holiest children. [BROTHER RAT

turns face front. SISTER RAT *comes down the aisle. Procession is still.* SISTER RAT *walking*] Blake, our parents send me to Georgia. It is a house with people who say they are relatives and a garden of great sunflowers. Be my brother's keeper, Blake. I hide under the house, my rat's belly growing all day long I eat sunflower petals, I sit in the garden Blake and hang three gray cats. [*Stands before* BROTHER RAT] Blake, I'm going to have a baby. I got our baby on the slide. [*Falls*] Gray cats walk this house all summer I bury my face in the sand so I cannot bear the rats that hide in our attic beams. Blake, why did the War start? I want to hang myself.

BROTHER RAT: Kay, stop sending me the petals from Georgia. Stop saying our mother says you have to go to the state hospital because of your breakdown. Stop saying you have a rat's belly.

Procession marches across sound of rats.

BROTHER *and* SISTER RAT: The Nazis! [*Marching*] The Nazis have invaded our house. [*Softer*] Why did the War start? We want to hang ourselves. The rats. [*Sound*] The rats have invaded our cathedral. [*They rapidly light more candles. Procession returns, marches to the center*] Our old Rosemary songs. Weren't they beautiful! Our Rosemary Mass. [*Procession watches; silence*] Yet we weren't safe long. [*They look at procession*] Soon we will be getting shot and hung. Within our house is a giant slide. Brother and Sister Rat we are.

SISTER RAT: Blake, remember when we lived in our house with Jesus and Joseph and Mary?

BROTHER RAT: Now there are rats in the church books behind every face in the congregation. They all have been on the slide. Every sister bleeds and every brother has made her bleed. The Communion wine.

BROTHER *and* SISTER RAT: The Communion wine. Our father gives out the Communion wine and it turns to blood, a red aisle of blood. Too something is inside the altar listening. [SISTER RAT *kneels*] When we were children we lived in our house, our mother blessed us greatly and God blessed us. Now they listen from the rat beams. [*Sound rats. They remain kneeling. Sound rats*] It is our mother.

Rosemary, Rosemary was the first girl we ever fell in love with. She lived next door behind a grape arbor her father had built. She often told us stories of Italy and read to us from her Holy Catechism book. She was the prettiest girl in our school. It is one of those Midwestern neighborhoods, Italians, Negroes and Jews. Rosemary always went to Catechism and wore Holy Communion dresses.

BROTHER RAT: Where are you going Rosemary? we say. And she says, "I have to go to Catechism." Why do you always go to Catechism? "Because I am Catholic"; then thinking, she says, "Colored people are not Catholics, are they?"

SISTER RAT: I don't think many.

BROTHER RAT: "Well I am. I am a descendant of the Pope and Julius Caesar and the Virgin Mary." Julius Caesar? "Yes, Caesar was the Emperor of all Italia." And are you his descendant? "Yes," she said.

BROTHER *and* SISTER RAT: We wish we were descendants of this Caesar, we said, how holy you are, how holy and beautiful. She smiled.

BROTHER RAT: Our school had a picnic in the country and she took my hand. We walked to a place of white birch trees. It is our Palatine, she said. We are sailing to Italy, I said. She was the prettiest girl—the only thing, she has worms in her hair.

SISTER RAT: Great Caesars my brother and I were. Behold us singing greatly walking across our Palatine, my brother holding my hand and I holding his and we are young before the War O Italia. Rosemary was our best friend and taught us Latin and told us stories of Italy. O Rosemary songs.

BROTHER *and* SISTER RAT: My sister and I when we were young before the War, and Rosemary our best friend, O Rosemary songs. Now we live in Rats Chapel. My sister and I.

BROTHER RAT *stares down the aisle.*

BROTHER RAT: It is Rosemary. [*Stares*] Did you tell? Does anyone know? Did you tell? Does anyone know? You started to cry Kay and I struck you in the face with our father's rifle. It was the beginning of summer. Just getting dark, we were playing and Rosemary said let's go to the playground. After you lay down on the slide so innocently Rosemary said if I loved her I would do what she said. Oh Kay. After that our hiding in the attic rats in the beam. Now there is snow on the playground, ambulances are on every street and within every ambulance is you Kay going to the hospital with a breakdown.

SISTER RAT: Blake, perhaps God will marry us in the state hospital. Our fellow rats will attend us. Every day I look under our house to see who is listening. [*Aisle bright. Procession marches out*] I cry all the time now . . . not sobbing . . . Blake, did we really go on that slide together? What were those things she made us do while she watched?

BROTHER RAT: We hide in the attic like rats.

SISTER RAT: I cry all the time now.

BROTHER RAT: Within every ambulance is you, Kay. Sister, all the time.

SISTER RAT: [*Sound rats*] I am waiting for you Blake under the hospital so the Nazis won't see me.

Procession marches to center.

BROTHER RAT: The rat comes to the attic crying softly within her head down. She thinks she's going to have a baby. If I were a Nazi I'd shoot her. On the slide she said, Blake I am bleeding. Now there is blood on the aisle of our church. Before rat blood came onto the slide we sailed. We did not swing in chains before blood, we sang with Rosemary. Now I must go to battle. Heil. [*Salutes procession*] Will you wait for me again at last spring? [*Procession does not answer.* BROTHER *and* SISTER RAT *fall down and light candles.* BROTHER RAT *stands. Stares down aisle*] Will they wait for me at last spring Rosemary?

ROSEMARY *comes down red aisle in her Holy Communion dress.*

ROSEMARY: Blake the Nazis will get you on the battlefield. [ROSEMARY *and* BROTHER RAT *stand before each other.* SISTER *remains kneeling*]

BROTHER RAT: Rosemary atone us, take us beyond the Nazis. We must sail to the Capitol. Atone us. Deliver us unto your descendants.

ROSEMARY: The Nazis are going to get you.

BROTHER RAT: If you do not atone us Kay and I will die. We shall have to die to forget how every day this winter gray cats swing with sunflowers in their mouths because my sister thinks I am the father of a baby. Rosemary will you not atone us?

ROSEMARY: I will never atone you. Perhaps you can put a bullet in your head with your father's shotgun, then your holy battle will be done.

The procession is at the edge of the house.

SISTER RAT: [*Kneeling*] O Holy Music return.

The procession marches to center.

ROSEMARY: Come with me, Blake.

BROTHER RAT: How can I ever reach last spring again if I come with you, Rosemary? I must forget how every day this winter gray cats swing with sunflowers in their mouths.

ROSEMARY: Perhaps you can put a bullet in your head.

SISTER RAT: I have a rat's belly.

BROTHER RAT: How can I ever again reach last spring if I come with you, Rosemary?

ROSEMARY: You must damn last spring in your heart. You will never see last spring again.

BROTHER *and* SISTER RAT: Then we must put a bullet in our heads.

Procession marches out. Silence. They stare at ROSEMARY. *Procession returns.*

PROCESSION: Good-bye Kay and Blake. We are leaving you.

BROTHER *and* SISTER RAT: Jesus, Joseph, Mary, Wise Men and Shepherd, do not leave. Great Caesars, we will be again, you will behold us as we were before Rosemary with the worms in her hair, a spring can come after the War.

PROCESSION: What Kay and Blake?

BROTHER *and* SISTER RAT: A spring can come after the War when we grow up we will hang you so that we can run again, walk in the white birch trees. Jesus, Joseph, Wise Men, Shepherd, do not leave us.

PROCESSION: We are leaving because it was Easter.

BROTHER RAT: No, no, it was not Easter, it was the beginning of June.

PROCESSION: In our minds it was Easter. Good-bye Kay and Blake. [*They walk out. A gnawing sound.* SISTER RAT *kneels,* BROTHER RAT *and* ROSEMARY *face each other. A gnawing sound*]

ROSEMARY: In my mind was a vision of us rats all.

BROTHER RAT: If only we could go back to our childhood.

SISTER RAT: Now there will always be rat blood on the rat walls of our rat house just like the blood that came onto the slide.

BROTHER RAT: Beyond my rat head there must remain a new capitol where Great Kay and I will sing. But no within my hot head I see the dying baby Nazis and Georgia relatives screaming girls cursing boys a dark sun and my grave. I am damned. No. . . . when I grow up I will swing again in white trees because beyond this dark rat run and gnawed petals there will remain a capitol.

SISTER RAT: A cathedral.

BROTHER RAT: Now within my mind I forever see dying rats. And gray cats walking. Rosemary worms in her hair atop the slide. Our Holy songs in our parents' house weren't they beautiful.

BROTHER *and* SISTER RAT: Now it is our rat's Mass. [*From now on their voices sound more like gnaws*] She said if you love me you will. It seemed so innocent. She said it was like a wedding. Now my sister Kay sends me gnawed petals from sunflowers at the state hospital. She puts them in gray envelopes. Alone I go out to school and the movies. No more do I call by for Rosemary. She made me promise never to tell if you love me she screamed you'll never tell. And I do love her. I found my father's rifle in the attic. Winter time . . . gray time dark boys come laughing starting a game of horseshoes gnawing in the beams. The winter is a place of great gnawed sunflowers. I see them in every street in every room of our house. I pick up gnawed great yellow petals and pray to be atoned.

BROTHER RAT: I am praying to be atoned. I am praying to be atoned dear God. I am begging dear God to be atoned for the Holy Communion that existed between my sister and me and the love that I have for Rosemary. I am praying to be atoned. [*He kisses* ROSEMARY. *He comes down aisle, movements more ratlike . . . voice more like gnawing*] Bombs fall I am alone in our old house with an attic full of dead rat babies. I must hide.

BROTHER *and* SISTER RAT: God we ask you to stop throwing dead rat babies.

BROTHER RAT *kneels.*

BROTHER RAT: When I asked you yesterday the day they brought my sister Kay home from the state hospital, you said God, Blake perhaps you must put a bullet in your head then your battle will be done. God, I think of Rosemary all the time. I love her. I told myself afterward it was one of the boys playing horseshoes who had done those horrible things on the slide with my sister. Yet I told Kay I am her keeper yet I told Rosemary I love her. It is the secret of my battlefield.

SISTER RAT: Here we are again in our attic where we once played games, but neither of us liked it because from time to time you could hear the rats. But it was our place to be alone, Blake now that I am home from the hospital we must rid our minds of my rat's belly. Can you see it? You did not visit me in the hospital Brother Rat. Blake I thought you were my brother's keeper.

BROTHER RAT: Everywhere I go I step in your blood. Rosemary I wanted you to love me. [*He turns—aisles bright—gnawing sound—battlefield sounds*]

BROTHER *and* SISTER RAT: God is hanging and shooting us.

SISTER RAT: Remember Brother Rat before I bled, before descending bombs and death on our capitol we walked the Palatine . . . we went to the movies. Now the Germans and Caesar's army are after us, Blake.

He goes back to ROSEMARY, *whose back is to him and starts.*

ROSEMARY: The Nazis are after you. My greatest grief was your life together. My greatest grief.

BROTHER *and* SISTER RAT: [*Look up*] Now every time we will go outside we will walk over the grave of our dead baby Red aisle runners will be on the street when we come to the playground Rosemary will forever be atop the slide exalted with worms in her hair. [*They kneel, then rise, kneel, then rise*] We must very soon get rid of our rat heads so dying baby voices on the beams will no more say we are our lost Caesars.

ROSEMARY: It is our wedding now, Blake.

BROTHER *and* SISTER RAT: Brother and Sister Rat we are very soon we must.

SISTER RAT: We are rats in the beam now.

ROSEMARY: My greatest grief was your life together. The Nazis will come soon now.

BROTHER and SISTER RAT: Every time we go out red blood runners will be on the street. [*They kneel, then rise, kneel, then rise*] At least soon very soon we will get rid of our rat heads and rat voices in beams will say no more we are your lost Caesars.

ROSEMARY: It is our wedding, Blake. The Nazis have come. [*Marching*] Brother and Sister Rat you are now soon you will become headless and all will cease the dark sun will be bright no more and no more sounds of shooting in the distance.

Marching procession appears bearing shotguns.

BROTHER *and* SISTER RAT: We will become headless and all will cease the dark sun will be bright no more and no more sounds of shooting in the distance. It will be the end.

The procession shoots, they scamper, more shots, they fall, ROSEMARY *remains.*

INVOCATIONS OF A HAUNTED MIND

a play in two acts

H. M. Koutoukas

Invocations of a Haunted Mind was first presented by Rene J. Metsch at the Elgin Theatre, New York City, on October 31, 1969, with the following cast:

> *Tupelo Hall*
> *Irving Metzman*
> *Aldo Gamuzza*
> *Uhshur P. Quietstone*
> *Kay Carney*
> *Deborah Berenholz*
> *Edward Barton*
> *Arturo Esquerra*
> *Jacque Lynn Colton*
> *Richard Williams*
> *H. M. Koutoukas*

It was directed by H. M. Koutoukas. Costumes by Maria Irene Fornés; lighting by John P. Dodd; makeup by Eileen Peterson.

ACT I

Music up. Enter DESTINY CHOICE. DESTINY
*lights a cigarette. He glances archly at the
audience.*

DESTINY: The *New York Times,* Sunday, August
17, 1969. REMEDY IS SOUGHT FOR VAM-
PIRE PERIL. Mexico City (Canadian Press)
The vampire swooped out of the dark night
sky and sank its razor sharp teeth into the neck
of its victim. This is not the opening of a horror tale, but a straight report of a nightly
occurrence in thousands of places in Latin
America. The vampire of legend and folklore
exists—in the form of a scourge in nearly a
score of Latin-American countries. A major
campaign is being mounted against a creature
that embodies what seems to be an instinctive
fear of many races in many parts of the world
even where no vampire, natural or supernatural, has been proved to exist. Actually,
the chief victims of the vampire are cattle.
Its depredations are greatly increased because
many of the bats are carriers of the disease
called paralytic rabies. Most of the animals
attacked by infected bats lose coordination,
become paralyzed, fall into a coma and
eventually die. An estimate of the loss of
cattle victimized by the vampire bat is $47
million. [*Lights up center where a man nude
begins a reverse strip, slowly and ritualistically
dressing*] United Nations Sponsors Study. A
team of international experts, working under
the auspices of the U.N. Food and Agricul-
tural Organization with assistance of funds
from the U.N. Development fund, is helping
the Mexican government research ways to
prevent such losses.

Scientists have spent years investigating the
vampire bat problem, but the team operating
in Mexico City has enabled a more compre-
hensive attack to be made than ever before.
In the last year, the scientists, working with
a group of Mexicans, have shown that much
is still not known about vampire bats.

For instance, although vampires prefer to
feed from cattle they also attack humans. But
much is unknown about the reasons for such
occurrences. Vampires appear to be attracted
to certain individuals and not to others. There
have been instances of vampires that repeatedly attacked the same child at night,
even when precautions were taken, while
ignoring others sleeping alongside him. Certain cattle in a herd are also more prone to
attack than others. Various forms of protection can be provided against paralytic rabies,
such as the use of vaccines before or after

attack. Better preventive measures are being
developed. The research now under way in
Mexico covers a study of behavior and living
conditions, probes into how paralytic rabies
is spread and methods of protection and control. The program is creating a keen knowledgeable corps of Mexican experts who will
continue to research the vampire after foreign
specialists leave. The approach is both practical in the field and scientific in laboratories.
The scientists handle the bats with familiarity
arising out of expert knowledge and capture
them in dark caves for research purposes with
a minimum of protection.

Yet even these specialists feel the strange
fascination of the vampire legends, which have
existed for thousands of years in many parts
of the world.

Vampire mythology existed in Europe,
China, India and Africa, for instance, long
before the presence of the blood-sucking vampire bats was found in the New World. Yet
a study of the legends indicates that vampires
did not assume bat form in European tales
until after their existence was known in the
Western Hemisphere. Earlier legends tended
to be concerned with flying horses, were-
wolves and other weird creatures. [*He takes
a long deep breath on his cigarette. Lights
up full on center stage. The* VAMPIRE *is now
fully dressed*]

VAMPIRE: Deep Magic Moisture Cream . . .
is a remarkable achievement of modern
science—a highly concentrated combination
of rich emollients, humectants and natural
moisturizers for extra-richness and full skin
softening, smoothing effectiveness. Yet new
Moisture Cream is uniquely refined for superb
texture, lightness, quick and easy absorption to
be completely nongreasy! You'll find it delightfully rewarding in promoting your facial care
and beauty.

Enter MRS. MARY BAKER EDDY.

MRS. EDDY: In 1935 Pamela Ashworth was living
with a family in Budapest. [*Music: Buda-
pestian Sad Folk Theme*] Teaching the daughter English in exchange for the privilege of
living with them. The family was well-to-do
and had a wide acquaintance with the upper
social echelons of Budapest.

Enter a YOUNG WOMAN *as if attending a
court function.*

YOUNG WOMAN: Mrs. L.'s sister-in-law became
a great friend of mine and invited me to stay
a month with her. She was gracious and
charming, the wife of the owner of a large
country house and estate on the border of
Czechoslovakia. So like a feudal castle—they
kept up a feudal state there.

DESTINY: She was assigned a huge, tapestry-hung room. Somehow it reminded her of a small church. It even boasted one stained-glass window, the only window of its kind in the entire house. Thanks to the promontory on which the house stood, Pamela could see the ancient Roman Catholic Church with its adjoining cemetery, as she stood at the window. For about a week she enjoyed the hunting, fishing and socializing. She met . . .

MRS EDDY: . . . all sorts of "interesting people" and the weather was perfect. One evening, Pamela's hosts entertained with a lavish dinner party which lasted until after midnight. It was 1:30 before she went to bed.

YOUNG WOMAN: . . . asleep almost before my head had touched the pillow. I awoke suddenly, unable to go back to sleep. I felt the mood of the night. It was dullish with a dim moon hiding behind the cloud-wracks. I heard a distinct scratching noise—I slowly sat up prepared to throw my slipper at some night mouse . . . I was horrified then beyond description—I shall never forget that moment. My scalp crinkled and sweat broke out on my back. The window was slightly open on the latch and the thing was apparently trying to lift the latch up. I could neither move nor scream.

DESTINY: From the room next to hers she heard the faint snoring of her hostess' uncle, Aladar. Her frantic thought was to rush to him for help.

MRS. EDDY: But this was unthinkable for she would have had to pass the stained-glass window and the shape outlined against it. The window opened and the shape leaped inside. The light was dim . . .

DESTINY: The light was dim and the horrified girl was able to discern the very distinct figure of a naked man. He did not walk.

MRS. EDDY: Nor did he run . . .

DESTINY: But he crept menacingly toward her bed.

YOUNG WOMAN: I was too paralyzed to move; sick, mad with fear. The room was full of a sickening, fetid smell; the horror crouched as if to spring, when I found my voice and screamed and screamed.

DESTINY: Uncle Aladar rushed in, and Pamela noticed he was armed—

MRS. EDDY: Alternately sobbing and shivering, she pointed shakily to the window. Everything was hazy but she was aware of hearing a shot. She also thought she heard the words . . .

DESTINY: "Good God." She was ill with shock and terror that would not go away.

YOUNG WOMAN: My kind family in Budapest took me for a holiday on Lake Balaton . . .

later, just before I was leaving Hungary for England, I received a letter from my friend.

Enter a FINE LADY.

FINE LADY: I will now tell you all I know. It sounds absurd, of course, as I write in the light of common day. When Uncle Aladar rushed into your room and you pointed to the window, he saw the figure scudding across the lawn toward the churchyard, when it disappeared over the wall. Now comes the amazing part. We saw the priest and demanded to search the churchyard vaults and grounds. He agreed but asked us not to let the peasants hear any rumors as they are so terribly superstitious. My husband and several men opened all the vaults, including that of our family, but found everything in order except that the lid of one of the coffins was open. Inside lay the shriveled up mummy of a man, dry and yellow, but with flesh on its bones. The burial date on the tablet was 1785. He was a Graf Arpad Rado. There was a fresh bullet wound on his left leg. The Rado family agreed to its incineration and the priest read the service of exorcism.

YOUNG WOMAN: If vampires are mythical, I would like to know just what it was that terrified me into a nervous breakdown from which I took so long to recover and which will leave a taint of horror in my mind forever. I can't explain a thing. I can only tell my story and leave people to judge for themselves. . . . That is why I have written this article for the *Australian Woman's Mirror* . . .

DESTINY: August 3, 1937.

YOUNG WOMAN: . . . Even now when I hear ivy tapping on the window, I feel ill.

Lights down on all but VAMPIRE.

VAMPIRE: Ontogeny recapitulates phylogeny. Ten multiplied by seven—the number of perfection.

Enter the THREE VAMPIRE WOMEN.

1ST WOMAN VAMPIRE: In weighing gold or drugs, there are twelve ounces to the pound. We measure twelve to the dozen and use twelve inches to the foot; our clocks show twelve hours. Both metric and duodecimal systems conform to the number twelve.

2ND WOMAN VAMPIRE: As diamonds and other pizeoelectric crystals which have twelve sides or axes. In their wild, natural state many fruits and vegetables grow in twelve sections.

3RD WOMAN VAMPIRE: There seems to be a natural feeling for twelve in children—as many educators can verify. Isn't this mythical? Shouldn't we capitalize upon it whatever it

DESTINY: This is an invocation for the dead and half dead. This is a moment to breach is?

the passing. A eulogy for all mankind from all mankind . . . For the dead and the half dead—from those who are just holding on . . .

MRS. EDDY: This is also an invocation and an invitation. To a tea. High, of course. For Miss Carole Lombard, Miss Amelia Earhart and our friend from South of Venezuela—Curacao Mama.

VAMPIRE: [*His eyes slant*] Voodoo woman's comin' don't you hear?

1ST VAMPIRE WOMAN: The living cannot change the dead—

2ND VAMPIRE: The living can only change until dead—

DESTINY: High tea and—

MRS. EDDY: Invocation. Garden attire if one hasn't time to change—

DESTINY: Everything has time to change.

MRS. EDDY: Or perhaps a costume indicative of national origin—

DESTINY: Dolls of all nations—

MRS. EDDY: [*A bit deaf*] Beg pardon—

DESTINY: Dolls—dolls of all nations like at the United Nations Gift Shop. It is important that we be indicative of our natural environment.

MRS. EDDY: Everything else is artifact . . . save artifact itself, which, being a creation pure and inspired, transcends all, becoming divine.

VAMPIRE: Voodoo Mama . . . do you hear sisters of darkness? She's come . . .

1ST VAMPIRE: She's coming. We can be sure. They are sure she is—

2ND VAMPIRE: The living are too sure often.

3RD VAMPIRE: We shall see what we shall see and silence is the first law—

VAMPIRE: The first law of the occult is silence— do you understand?

1ST VAMPIRE: With every stitch of taffeta on my coffin quilting . . .

Enter HARD SELL.

MRS. EDDY: This is an invocation—

HARD SELL: Oh, I'm looking for a—

DESTINY: Garden Party and High Tea—

MRS. EDDY: For Mlls. Earhart—Lombard—Mama?

HARD SELL: I guess I read the invitation right . . . to a tea and invocation—

VAMPIRE: [*Calling upon darkness*] Phaeton had left the rounded sky and turned his car toward setting: Silent Night leapt up from earth into the air like a high-stretching cone and wrapped heaven about in a starry robe spangling the welkin. The immortals moved about the cloudless Nile, but Zeus Cronides on the brows of Taurus awaited the light of toil awaiting Dawn—there is only one word—

1ST VAMPIRE: *Avanti!*

2ND VAMPIRE: I could not sleep the day through—

3RD VAMPIRE: A victim must be selected not assaulted—

VAMPIRE: The first law of the occult is SILENCE —never assault without selecting . . .

2ND VAMPIRE: Poisoned blood—poisoned blood.

3RD VAMPIRE: You will know sleep again— another day.

2ND VAMPIRE: I have known no sleep for three days—no rest.

1ST VAMPIRE: A coffin was not made to twist and turn in.

2ND VAMPIRE: No rest—

VAMPIRE: THERE IS NO REST FOR THE DAMNED!

1ST VAMPIRE: Yet you add to it?

VAMPIRE: Greed forced you to the throat of an amphetamine addict—greed denies you sleep. The damned are Spartan—

2ND VAMPIRE: Oh— oh—

3RD VAMPIRE: The damned are selective.

1ST VAMPIRE: To say the least!

The VAMPIRES *begin a chant and dance. Dextroamphetamine sulfate injection. Music and lights up. Chant:* Amphetamine Sulfate Injection.

VAMPIRE: Dextroamphetamine sulfate injection— each cc contains—

2ND VAMPIRE: Dextroamphetamine sulfate 20 mg.

1ST VAMPIRE: Benzyl alcohol 1½.

3RD VAMPIRE: Water for injection q.s.

VAMPIRE: Intramuscular! Intravenous or subcutaneous use.

1ST VAMPIRE: Indications: Central nervous stimulant for use in depressive states in the symptomatic treatment of post encephalitic Parkinsonism and as an adjunct in obesity therapy.

ALL: OBESITY THERAPY!

VAMPIRE: OBESITY THERAPY!

2ND VAMPIRE: Dosage: 0.5 to 1 cc daily, or as determined by the physician. When used in obesity, administer in morning. Anorexigenic effect cannot be expected to last for longer than 8 to 10 hours.

VAMPIRE: Warning! Therapy may mask signs of fatigue in some individuals; collapse has occurred in some cases.

3RD VAMPIRE: Side effects may include insomnia, hyperexcitability, sleeplessness, increased motor activity, dermatitis, gastrointestinal disturbances, nausea and vomiting, dry mouth, tachycardia, angina pectoris, arrhythmias, hypertension, nervousness, dyspnea, diaphoresis, anorexia, headache, diarrhea, constipation and vertigo.

VAMPIRE: Excessive dosage may produce chills, collapse and syncope. Prolonged use may result in habituation and addiction.

1ST VAMPIRE: Contraindications: States of undue restlessness, anxiety, excitement, hyperexcitability, and agitated PSYCHOTIC STATES.

2ND VAMPIRE: Use with caution in those with insomnia, hypertension, vasomotor instability, asthenia, psychopathic personality, history of agitated psychotic states, history of homicidal or suicidal tendencies, advanced atherosclerosis, coronary artery disease, hyperthyroidism, and in those hypersensitive to sympathemimetic amines.

VAMPIRE: Use cautiously in pregnancy, especially during the first trimester.

1ST VAMPIRE: Caution: Tolerance may develop after prolonged use.

VAMPIRE: Federal law prohibits without prescription.

HUNCHBACK *is the only one who sees the* VAMPIRE *as he brings chairs.* HARD SELL, MRS. EDDY *and* DESTINY *in lawn chairs.*

HARD SELL: Tupelo Our Two Acres (*Christian Science Monitor,* October 27, 1969). The steeple bush is brown and blossoms of the buttonbush have dwindled into tawny spheres that give the plant its name—Grasses fade.

MRS EDDY: So lyrical—

DESTINY: Grasses fade?

MRS. EDDY: No. Botanical terms—nature's terms in Latin.

HARD SELL: I always thought nature's terms were CASH . . . NET . . . UPON RECEIPT.

MRS. EDDY: Clearing one's head is colorful—

HARD SELL: There are those who might complain.

MRS. EDDY: They are to be prayed for—

DESTINY: There are those who would accuse—

MRS. EDDY: They only accuse us of what they fear they will be accused of—

HARD SELL: Accusation based upon fear of accusation has always had a mirrored effect—

DESTINY: Of the beaded sort?

HARD SELL: That would add to an increase of images of the sort I intended to mention.

MRS. EDDY: And so—

HARD SELL: All this makes a background for the brilliance of tupelo. The trees standing by Big Ledge near the pond have gained in crimson day by day. As the Western sun spotlights them, our world is stopped to observe, to be owned by the flare.

MRS. EDDY: Flowers! So like my poem!
> Flowers
> Mirrors of morn
> Whence the dew drop is born,
> Soft tints of the rainbow and skies—
> Sisters of song,
> What a shadowy throng
> Around you in memory rise!
> Far do you flee,
> From your green bowers free,
> Fair floral apostles of love,
> Sweetly to shed
> Fragrance fresh round the dead,
> And breath of the living above.
>> Flowers for the brave—
>> Be he Monarch or slave,
>> Whose heart bore its grief and is still!
>> Flowers for the kind—
>> Aye, the Christians who wind
>> Wreaths for the triumphs o'er ill.

You see, young man, others understand "Grasses Fade"—I understood on May the 21st, 1904, in Pleasant View, in Concord, new Hampshire.

DESTINY: There's nothing much one can say—a party's a party and a memory's a memory—unless it's the memory of a party.

HARD SELL: All of the important things are ancient but newly discovered. All that was written is rewritten on hearts needing gentle Parker Penmanship.

MRS EDDY: Old as Gilgamesh—old as the rainbows in a tear vase—

HARD SELL: Gilgamesh—is that a wine—a local booze?

DESTINY: An ancient Emperor—

MRS. EDDY: Is that a Buick?

DESTINY: Why—?

MRS. EDDY: Because if it is, then it isn't them!

HARD SELL: I think it's a Bison—

MRS. EDDY: Oh—such strange designs in cars these days—

DESTINY: One never knows when they will make a Ford that resembles a Bison—

HARD SELL: The name's commercial—

DESTINY: But the shape's not quite right.

MRS. EDDY: Unless it's a "Coup."

HARD SELL: [*To* DESTINY] And you will provide today's entertainment?

DESTINY: A simple improvisation on an ancient theme—

MRS. EDDY: Ancient themes are the newest.

DESTINY: Agreed.

MRS. EDDY: The dead have left their heritage—

VAMPIRE: We, the dead's heritage, attend this midnight tea—Sisters of darkness—a midnight tea—shall we wander with upmost discretion to the sure ways of the living?

1ST VAMPIRE: Look your best for we'll all be invisible.

2ND VAMPIRE: Does my hair look right—

3RD VAMPIRE: [*Pointing*] Look in the mirror.

2ND VAMPIRE: Why thank you. [*Looks in the mirror and sees no reflection*] Oh God—God's scabs on your tits. How could you!

1ST VAMPIRE: Nothing's too awful for a speed freak!

3RD VAMPIRE: Now don't go attacking! Remember—silent selection!

VAMPIRE: Silently sisters or they will know strange presences are not their own body odor —but the odor of the dead—we would not want to hurt tonight's festivities.

2ND VAMPIRE: They don't even believe in vampires—

VAMPIRE: And that's why we stalk their moonlit gardens nightly and when the moon is fullest attend their grandest operas.

1ST VAMPIRE: Cracking mirrors wherever we go.

3RD VAMPIRE: Come sisters—

VAMPIRE: *Desiderata.* Go placidly amid the noise and haste, and remember what peace there may be in silence. As far as possible without surrender be on good terms with all persons. Speak your truth quietly and clearly; and listen to others, even the dull and ignorant; they too have their story. Avoid loud and aggressive persons, they are vexations to the spirit. If you compare yourself with others, you become vain and bitter; for always there will be greater and lesser persons than yourself. Enjoy your achievements as well as your plans. Keep interested in your own career, however humble; it is a real possession in the changing fortunes of time. Exercise caution in your business affairs; for the world is full of trickery. But let this not blind you to what virtue there is; many persons strive for high ideals; and everywhere life is full of heroism. Be yourself. Especially, do not feign affection. Neither be cynical about love; for in the face of all aridity and disenchantment it is as perennial as the grass. Take kindly the counsel of the years, gracefully surrendering the things of youth. Nurture strength of spirit to shield you in sudden misfortune. But do not distress yourself with imaginings. Many fears are born of fatigue and loneliness. Beyond a wholesome discipline, be gentle with yourself. You are a child of the universe, no less than the trees and the stars; you have a right to be here. And whether or not it is clear to you, no doubt the universe is unfolding as it should. Therefore be at peace with God, whatever you conceive Him to be, and whatever your labors and aspirations, in the noisy confusion of life keep peace with your soul. With all its sham, drudgery and broken dreams, it is still a beautiful world. Be careful. Strive to be happy.

MRS. EDDY: [*Softly*] He was found in Old Saint Paul's Church, Baltimore; dated 1692.

ACT II

Overture up. Lights, thousands of them flicker from trees, from underwater, across the surface of water. Keening and wailing and a bit of mourning is heard for exactly three seconds.

CHORUS:
> There are those that love
> What has been left to die
> So in the silent moments
> Between melancholia and anger
> They weep to unknown places
>
> Silently as leaves turning
> Steadily as locked doors.
> Wherever they are least expected
> They go . . . those who love
> What has been left to die.
> Tears last only
>
> Till the doors close
> Then there are no more tears
> Just the waiting and wondering
> At all that cannot be.
>> Some morning morning will be mourned
>> Then we will know Assyria and
>> Babylonia more.
>
> In silence
> And wisps of hair
> Covering closed lips
> That fear night's passing
> You can hear
> You can hear

DESTINY:
> You can weep
> For hours
> That will never come
> Life that has always passed.
> In life it is always TOO LATE
>> TOO LATE
>> TOO LATE

CHORUS:
> TOO LATE . . . TOO LATE . . .
>> TOO LATE . . .

COMMUNION GIRL:
> Remembrances
> Washed into the sea
> Are not forgotten.
> Day comes and leaves
> Quickly as light across a leaf.

CHORUS:
> No moment is enough to know
> To know or not know is not enough.

AMOS:
> What of the dead—
> Shall we dare look for them
> In the place where there are not eyes?

CHORUS:
> Only the ocean is deep enough to hold our
>   terror,
> Only the sky immense enough to hold
>   our dreams.

COMMUNION GIRL:
> Terror around corners from a glance,
> One glance, a thousand changes
> The many-sided moments that are lost—
> When hope dies there is little else.
>   Can we face the dead
>   Knowing that we once loved them
>   Caress stench of unlived hopes,
> Too late—too late—too late,
> The phrase that brackets all tomorrows!

CHORUS:
> Only the ocean is deep enough to hold
>   our terror
> Only the sky immense enough to hold
>   our dreams—

Music up: Lights down as prologue draws to end. Only a faint wash of light should cross the fountain as COMMUNION GIRL *speaks.*

COMMUNION GIRL:
> Wash water with tears,
> Gently know the stars must go
> And in the going know the coming
> All else destroys the gentle threads of
>   dreams.
> Wash water with tears
> And tend the ancient fires of dreams.

PART ONE

KING OF WILLIES *appears. He is lost. His crown is tarnished, his goosie disheveled.*

MRS. EDDY:
> Threads no matter what knot
> So kings may loose their way
> Not knowing of the silver thread
> That runs gently through all lives.
> Wander till tarnish
>
> Overtakes your ecstasy,
> Wander till the moon
> No longer lights the North Star.

Music up. KING OF THE WILLIES *dives into the pool.* NYMPHS *dive from side of pool just missing him as he passes.*

VAMPIRE:
> The sea shall remember
> What the ocean has forgotten
> In an overlapping wave
> The story of a thousand pebbles.

KING, *after having swum the entire length of pool underwater, rises, goes to diving board and looks out. The* NYMPHS *all duck beneath the water.*

CHORUS:
> We have a spot at the corner of our eyes
> That misses a good deal of what
> Otherwise might become memory.

NARRATOR:
> Rush by to find we've missed
> Precisely what we've been splashing for.

CHORUS:
> Too late . . . too late . . . too late.

Sound: trumpets.

VAMPIRE:
> Yet after all else, there IS beauty
> To remind us that it isn't all just a
>   splash
> And dash for air!

The NYMPHS *all swim to form a circle in the middle of the pool, sparklers in their hands.* WILLIES *enter carrying flares. Fireworks go off as* VENUS *enters.*

CHORUS:
> There is beauty to remind us
> That things weren't always so simple.
>   A touch of Goddess
>   A taste of God
>   Leaf gone golden from
>   Love of autumn.

The WILLIES *remove the* KING'S *tattered goosie.* VENUS *gives jeweled goosie and untarnished crown to* MAIDENS *who have formed a relay line and pass it on to* KING. *The corps of* NYMPHS *form flowers about* VENUS, *while the* WILLIES *dance about the pool. The* KING *puts on his new ecstasies. Triumphant music as he lifts crown to head.*

VAMPIRE:
> We wear what we have
> Which is hardly enough
> Of an introduction to glory.
>
> Yet we wear what we have
> And if the light is right
> We are beautiful.

DESTINY:
> Sometimes—we may even
> Allow love to enter into ritual.
> But only when it behaves properly.

KING *places crown on head and does a swan dive as we hear a ten-cannon salute.* VENUS, the KING, *and* CORPS *do a water minuet. The creatures of the shore wash gracefully and dance images that edge-of-the-water creatures might have.*

MRS. EDDY:
> Never smile without a tear,
> It is not possible,
> Always haunting near the corner of the eye
> Which cannot see—
> Are those horrors that can always be
>> counted upon.

As she is exhausting PRINCE, *the* WILLIES *dance his army of uglies to death. The* PRINCE *drowns and only his cape remains above water.*

DESTINY:
> Sometimes we give value
> Through our desires,
> Requiring by doing so
> That an end come.
> Yet it is only choice
> That makes this ending endable.

VAMPIRE:
> An instant has many sides
> As does a tear
> We must laugh
> And so must we weep . . .
> To choose an end
> That justifies our tears and laughter
> May truly be glory.

CHORUS:
> Glory in a conch shell
> Weave webs and know the making
> Of gestures gone beneath our knowing
> Deep into caring for all
> That has been left to our dreams.
> Touch
> Touch
> And feel the seeing
> Of the gentle love of growing
> Sad at the loss of grace apparent
> In the dead
> In the dead
> In the dead.

The KING *dances a dance with* VENUS *as* VAMPIRE'S *voice says:*

VAMPIRE:
> Can we love the dead
> Or must we lie with memories gone stale?
> How long before rot turns to dust,
> How long before dreams go haywire?
> Kissing a memory is simple,
> Kissing rot is beyond reason.
> In the face of a love far gone
> Can we remember anything worth
>> worshiping?

She dies in his arms. Her maidens draw from him and carry her to the bottom of the pool.

CHORUS:
> Horror can always be counted on
> In a pinch.
>> When things are too beautiful
>> There's always horror to count on.
> No need to gamble
> Put your faith in horror.

Evil creatures begin plot. They push WILLIES *into the water and kidnap* VENUS. *The* KING *searches for her but the* PRINCE *reminds him of his homeland and seduces him into believing that he should return. As they leave he signals behind the* KING'S *back that the ugly creatures take over and enslave the lost souls in the pool.*

VAMPIRE:
> Terror can be a vowel
> Or crooked little finger,
> Door creek
> Or tarnished spoon,
> Light on a fallen paper,
> Sound not usual for night.

CHORUS:
> Terror.

The lost creatures are enslaved. They are dragged ashore, gasping for water, trying to return to the sea. The PRINCE *returns to plot the death of the* KING.

VAMPIRE:
> Established ritual of hate
> Imposed on blossoms
> Never left to bloom,
> Shades of lost yearning,
> Mutilated dreams.

CHORUS:
> Kill only what you can.
> Only what you know and have loved
> Is weak enough to be killed.

VENUS *overhears the plot. She seduces the* PRINCE. *They swim to the center of the pool, where she begins a tango swim so furious that he cannot keep up.*

VAMPIRE:
> Then after loving
> Little more
> Than gentle knowledge
> Of what nature
> Has in store.

The KING *gathers up his creatures, but they falter and cannot follow. They want to mourn lost beauty.*

DESTINY:
> Easy to mourn lost beauty
> Than to find new glamour.
> Easy to wear the weeds
> And close the eyes with tears.

Easy to stab the instant with memories
Of all that has gone by.

VAMPIRE:
So all "too lates" join
In one huge never-more.
Our story's sad for we know
All stories' endings.
Weeping near the ocean
We know how small a tear becomes.

CHORUS:
Only a wave
Can know the ocean.
Only a cloud
Can know the sky.
Only sadness
Remembers supper.
Only terror
Replaces lunch.

VAMPIRE:
A rock rots slower than a sweetheart.

DESTINY:
A stone lasts longer than a God.

CHORUS:
There are those that love
What has been left to die
So in the silent moments
Between melancholia and anger
They weep to unknown places.

VAMPIRE:
Yet sometimes loss of love
    Persuades great men
To instill the memory of it
    To others who need to hope.

The King walks on water.

DESTINY:
And music makes neat destruction
Of all tackiness,
Removing lines from the most wrinkled
    heads.

CHORUS:
Weep
In places where
Weeping is least expected.
Weep,
Weep.

VAMPIRE:
That love might die
Love then lives
And learns the bitter tale of hate.

*His creatures follow him into water. They swim
happily about him as he walks on water and
begins a tap dance.*

VAMPIRE:
So all the truths are truths—

DESTINY:
Until they're felt.

VAMPIRE:
Tears lead to laughter—

CHORUS:
And music erases all the mistakes
Of tackiness.

There are those that love
What has been left to die
So in the silent moments
Between melancholia and anger
They weep to unknown places.

DESTINY:
Silently as leaves turning
Steadily as locked doors.
Wherever they are least expected
They go . . . those who love
What has been left to die.

VAMPIRE:
They are those who love
What's been left do die.
They wander to where they are
Most least expected
In the silent hours
Between melancholia and anger.

CHORUS:
Weep laugh and weep
Sigh cry and love gently
For love is breakable
And there through choice only.

VAMPIRE: [*Bitterly*] Has anyone ever recovered
from seeing?

*Skyrockets fill the air. Light beams cross the
sky. A Dionysian finale. Water jets spray the
audience.*

EPILOGUE

Projection: full stage projection of JOSEPH
CINO. *Sound:* KOUTOUKAS' *voice with background music by* ROBERT COSMOS SAVAGE.

KOUTOUKAS:
He came to the altar with flowers
He came to the altar with flowers
But the preacher did not hear
No the preacher did not hear
For the preacher was singing a folksong
Not knowing the folks had all but gone.

Each man chooses the stations
That he waits at while choosing his cross
Each man chooses the stations
As each man chooses his death.

Everyone took HIS life for granted
Refused to grant logic to his joy—
                    Now that joy's gone
                    Now that joy's gone

Now that joy's gone
Now that joy's gone
No one need be bothered by his joy.

For each tomb in the graveyard there's a life that's been lived/ For each tomb there's a tear and a silence/ But most don't bring tender peace/ Before we can weep/ Aren't the living worth our tears. He came to the altar with flowers/ But the preacher was singing a folksong. Oh he walked the stations that marked his life along/ disguising his madness/ Heath his generosity— Oh he knew the sadness of joy/ Yes he knew the sadness of joy/ We can't blame Uncle Death/ For he's not kept his date with us— We can ONLY look to the places that he left/ We can only search the eyes/ Of those who had no replies/ To the sadness that guided his hand/ To the sadness that guided his hand. He went on a trip with Uncle Death— Didn't he like our land Oh didn't he like our land/ He went on a trip with Uncle Death/ And we dare not understand/ Until Uncle Death knocks on our door. He came to the altar with flowers. He came to the altar with flowers. He came to the altar with flowers.

SLAVE SHIP

an historical pageant

Imamu Amiri Baraka (LeRoi Jones)

Slave Ship was first presented by Chelsea Theater Center (Robert Kalfin, artistic director; Michael David, executive director) in association with Woodie King at the Brooklyn Academy of Music on November 19, 1969, with the following cast:

ATOWODA, *auctioneer*	*Frank Adu*
TAWA	*Gwen D. Anderson*
AKOOWA, *modern preacher*	*Preston Bradley*
IYALOSA (TSIA)	*Lee Chamberlin*
AKANO	*Bill Duke*
SEGILOLA	*Jackie Earley*
ADUFE	*Phyllis Espinosa*
OLALA	*Ralph Espinosa*
DADEMI	*Maxine Griffith*
LALU, *plantation Tom*	*Garrett Morris*
SALAKO, REV. TURNER	*Tim Pelt*
SAILOR	*C. Robert Scott*
NOLIWE	*Seret Scott*
IMANI	*Marilyn Thomas*
OYO	*Reeta White*

It was directed by Gilbert Moses. Design by Eugene Lee; choreography, Oliver Jones; music, Archie Shepp, Gilbert Moses; production coordinator, Burl Hash; sound, Paul Jaeger, Mary Lou Lehman; additional music, Leopoldo Fleming, Richard Fells, John Griggs, Bob Ralston, Michael Ridley, Charles Davis; Yoruba consultant, Mr. Ogundipe; musical director, Leopoldo Fleming; masks, Hilary Scharrad; Yoruba music consultant, Joe Comadore. Stage managers: Peter Turner, David Eidenberg, Joan Lebowitz, Laurence Cohen.

Slave Ship was subsequently transferred to Washington Square Methodist Church, New York City, where it opened on January 13, 1970.

A drama presented without intermission. The action takes place in the hold of a ship.

CAST

AFRICAN SL'AVES, *voices of African slaves*
1ST MAN, *prayer—husband of* DADEMI
2ND MAN, *curser*
3RD MAN, *struggler*

1ST WOMAN, *prayer*
2ND WOMAN, *screamer—attacked*
3RD WOMAN, *with child*

DANCERS
MUSICIANS

CHILDREN
Plus voices and bodies in the slave ship

OLD TOM SLAVE
NEW TOM, *preacher*

WHITE MEN, *voices of white men*
CAPTAIN
SAILOR
PLANTATION OWNER, *"Eternal Oppressor"*

PROPS

Smell effects: incense, dirt/filth smells/bodies
Heavy chains
Drums (African bata *drums, and bass and snare)*
Rattles and tambourines
Banjo music for plantation atmosphere
Ship noises
Ship bells
Rocking and splashing of sea
Guns and cartridges
Whips/whip sounds

Slave Ship

Whole theatre in darkness. Dark. For a long time. Just dark. Occasional sound, like ship groaning, squeaking, rocking. Sea smells. In the dark. Keep the people in the dark, and gradually the odors of the sea, and the sounds of the ship, creep up. Burn incense, but make a significant almost stifling smell come up. Pee. Shit. Death. Life processes going on anyway. Eating. These smells, and cries, the slash and tear of the lash, in a total atmos-feeling, gotten some way.

African drums like the worship of some Orisha. Obatala. Mbwanga rattles of the priests. BamBamBamBamBoom BoomBoom BamBam.

Rocking of the slave ship, in darkness, without sound. But smells. Then sound. Now slowly, out of blackness with smells and drums staccato the hideous screams. All the women together, scream: AAAAAIIIEEEEEEEEEEE. *Drums come up again, rocking rocking, black darkness of the slave ship. Smells. Drums go up high. Stop. Scream:* AAAAAAIIIIEEEEEEEE. *Drums. Black darkness with smells.*

Chains, the lash, and people moaning. Listen to the sounds come up out of the actors of Black People dragged and thrown down into the hold. AAAAIIIEEEEEEE. *Of people, dropped down in the darkness, frightened, angry, mashed together in common terror. The bells of the ship. White Men's Voices, on top, ready to set sail.*

VOICE 1: Okay, let's go! A good cargo ob black gold. Let's go! We head West! We head West. [*Long laughter*] Black gold in the West. We got our full cargo.

V-2: Aye, aye, Cap'n. We're on our way. Riches to be ours, by God.

V-1: Aye, riches riches be ours. We're on our way. America!

Laughter. There is just dim light at top of set, to indicate where voices are. African drums. With the swiftness of dance, but running into the heaviness the dark enforces. The drums slow. The beat beat of the darkness. "Where are we, God?" The mumble murmur rattle below. The drone of terror. The voices begin to beat against the dark.

W-1: Ooooooooo, Obatala!

W-2: Shango!

W-1: Ooooooooo, Obatala. . . .

Children's crying in the hold, and the women trying to comfort them. Trying to keep their sanity too.

W-3: Moshake, chile, calm calm be you. Moshake, chile. O calm Orisha, save us!

W-2: AAAIIIEEEEEEEEEE.

M-1: Quiet woman! Quiet. Save your strength for your child.

W-2: AAAIIIEEEEEEEEEE.

M-1: Quiet, foolish woman! Be quiet!

W-3: Moshake, baby, chile, be calm, be calm, it give you, ooooooo.

M-1: Shango, Obatala, make your lightning, beat the inside bright with paths for your people. Beat Beat Beat.

Drums come up, but they are walls and floors being beaten. Chains rattled. Chains rattled. Drag the chains.

We get the feeling of many, many people jammed together, men, women, children, aching in the darkness. The chains, the whips, magnify the chains and whips. The dragging together. The pain. The terror.

Women begin to moan a chant-song: African sorrow song, with scraping of floor and chains to accompaniment.

M-2: Fukwididila! Fukwididila! Fukwididila! Fuck you, Orisha! God! Where you be? Where you now, Black God? Help me. I be a strong warrior, and no woman. And I strain against these chains! But you must help me, Orisha. OBATALA!

M-3: Quiet, you fool, you frighten the women!

Women still chanting, moaning. Children now crying. Mothers trying to comfort them. Feeling of people moving around, tumbling over each other. Screaming as they try to find "a place" in the bottom of the boat, and then the long stream of different wills, articulated as screams, grunts, cries, songs, etc.

M-3: Pull, pull, break them. Pull.

W-1: Oh, Obatala!

W-3: Oh, chile . . . my chile, please please get away . . . you crush . . . !

M-3: Break . . . Break. . . .

ALL: Uhh, Uhhh, Uhhh, Uhhh, OOOOOOOOO-OOOOOOOO.

WOMEN: AAAAAIIIIIEEEEEEEEEE.

ALL: Uhhh, Uhhh, Uhhh, Uhhh, OOOOOOOOO-OOOOO.

WOMEN: AAAIIIIEEEEEEE.

Drums down low, like tapping, turns to beating floor, walls, rattling, dragging chains, percussive sounds people make in the hold of a ship. The moans and pushed-together agony. Children crying incessantly. The mothers trying to calm them. More than one child. Young girls afraid they may be violated. Men trying to break out. Or turning into frightened children. Families separated for the first time.

W-2: Ifanami, Ifanami . . . where you? Where you?? Ifanami [*Cries*] Please, oh God.

M-1: Obata . . .

Drums beat down, softer . . . humming starts . . . hummmmmm hummmmm, like old colored women humming for three centuries in the slow misery of slavery . . . hummmmmmmm hummmmmmmmmmmmmmmmmmm. Lights flash up on the faces of white men in sailor suits, grinning . . . humming voices down, humming, "hummmmmmmmmmmm . . . hummmm. . . ." Lights flash on white men in sailor suits grinning their vices . . . voices down, hummmumnin . . . hummmmmmmmmmmmmmmmmmmm mmmm. Lights to light white people are sudden, very bright and blinding. The white men begin to laugh and point, as if they were pointing at the filth, misery and degradation of the Black People. They laugh: "HHA-AAAAAHAAAHAAHAAHAAHAAHHAA-

HAHAHAHAHAHA." When they are out-lined again they are rolling in merriment. Pointing, dancing, jumping up and down. Ha-HaHa Ha hahaha Haaaa.

Laughter is drowned in the drums. Then the chant-moan of the woman . . . then silence. Then the drums, softer, then the humming, on and on in a maddening, building death-patience, broken by the screams, and the babies and the farts, and the babies crying for light, and young wives crying for their men. Old people calling for God. Warriors calling for freedom. Some crying out against the white man.

M-3: Devils! Devils! Devils! White beasts! Shit eaters! Beasts! [*They beat the walls, and try to tear the chains out of the walls*] White shit eaters.

W-3: Aiiiiieeeeeeeee.

M-1: God, she's killed herself, and the child. Oh, God. Oh, God.

Moans. Moans. Soft drums, and the constant, now almost maddening humming . . . hummmmmmmmmmmm, hummmmmmmmmmmm, hummmmmmmmmmmm . . . like mad old nigger ladies humming forever, in deathly patience . . . hummmmmmm hummmmmmm hmmm.

W-1: She strangled herself with the chain. Choked the child. Oh, Shango! Help us Lord. Oh, please.

W-2: Why you leave us, Lord?

M-1: Dademi, Dademi . . . she dead, she dead . . . Dademi . . . [*Hear man wracked with death cries, screams*] Dademi, Dademi!!!!

Hummmmmmmmmmm, Hummmmmmmmmmm, Hummmmmmmmmmm, Hummmmmmmmmm. Drums low, and moans . . . the chains, and Black People pushed against each other struggling for breath and room to live. The Black Man weeps for his woman. The Black Woman weeps for her man together in the darkness, some calling for God.

W-2: Oh, please, please don't touch me . . . Please . . . [*Frantic*] Ifanami, where you? [*Screams at someone's touch in the dark, grabbing her, trying to drag her in the darkness, press her down against the floor*] Akiyele . . . please . . . please . . . don't don't touch me . . . please. Ifanami, where you? Please help me. . . . Go . . .

M-1: What you doing? Get away from that woman. That's not your woman. You turn into a beast too.

Scuffle of two men turning in the darkness trying to kill each other. Lights show white men laughing silently, dangling their whips, in pantomime, still pointing.

M-3: Devils. Devils. Cold walking shit.

All Mad Sounds Together.

    Humming begins again. Bells of ship. Silence. And moans. And humming. And movement in the dark, of people. Sliding back and forth. Trying to stay alive, and now, over it, the constant crazy laughter of the sailors.

SAILORS: AHAHAHAHAHAHAHAHAHAHA-HAHAAAAA HHHAHAHAHAHAHAHHA HAHAH.

M-3: I kill you devils. I break these chains [*Sound of men struggling against heavy chains*] I tear your face off. Crush your throat. Devils. Devils.

W-1: Oh, oh, God, she dead . . . and the child. [*Silence. Sound of the sea . . . fades.*

[*Humming*] HMMMMMMMM HMMMMM-MM HMMMMMMMM HMMMMMMMM HMMMMMMM HMMMMMMM.

Lights on suddenly show a shuffling "Negro." Lights off . . . drums of ancient African warriors come up . . . hero-warriors. Lights blink back on show shuffling Black Man, hat in his hand, scratching his head. Lights off. Drums again. Black dancing in the dark, with bells, as if free, dancing wild old dances. BamBoom Bam Booma Bimbam Boomama boom beem bam. Dancing in the darkness . . . Yoruba Dance: Lights flash on briefly, spot on off the dance. Then off. Then on to show THE SLAVE *raggedy ass raggedy hat in hand shuffling toward the audience, shuffling, scratching his head and butt. Shaking his head up and down, agreeing with massa, agreeing, and agreeing, while the whips snap. Lights off, flash on, and the sailors, with hats changed to show them as plantation owners, are still laughing, no sound, but laughing and pointing, holding their sides, and they laugh and point.*

SLAVE: [*In darkness*] Yassa, boss, yassa, massa Tim, yassa, Boss. [*Lights up*] I'se happy as a brand-new monkey ass, yassa boss, yassa, mass' Tim, Yass, mass Booboo, I'se so happy I'se so happy I jus' don' know what to do. Yass, mas' boa, youse so han'some and good and youse hip too, yass, I'se so happy I jus' stan' and scratch my ol nigger haid. [*Lights flash on slave doing an old-new dance for the boss, when he finishes he bows and scratches*]

Lights out . . . the same hummmmmm rises up . . . with low drums, but the hum grown louder drowns it out . . . hummmmmmhum-mmmmm hummmmmmhummmmmmmmmm-mm. The laughter now drowns out the humming, the same cold, hideous laughter.

W-3: [*Whispering after death*] Moshake. . . . Moshake. . . . Moshake-chile, calm yourself, love [*Woman runs down into soft weep, with no other distracting sound, just her moaning sad cry, for her baby*]

Chains. Chains. Dragging the chains. The humming. Hummmmmmmmmmmmmmmm.

WOM: AIEEEEEEEEEEEEEEEEEEEEE.

ALL: Uhh, Uhhh, Uhhh, Uhhh, Oooooooooooooo-ooooo.

Silence.

    Soft at first, then rising. Banjos of the plantation.

SLAVE: 1: Reverend, what we gon' do when mass come? [*He sounds afraid*]

SLAVE 2: We gon' cut his fuckin' throat!

Banjos. Humming. . . . Hummmmmmmmmmm.

S-1: Reverend, what we gon' do when the white man come?

S-2: We gon' cut his fuckin' throat.

S-3: Devil. Beast. Murderer of women and children. Soulless shit eater!

S-1: Reverend Turner, sir, what we gon' do when the mass come?

S-2: Cut his Godless throat.

Lights flash up on same tomish slave, still scratching his head, but now apparently talking to a white man.

SLAVE: Uhh, dass right, massa Time . . . dey gon' 'volt.

WHVOI: What? Vote? Are you crazy?

SLAVE: Nawsaw . . . I said 'volt . . . uhhhh . . . re-volt.

Laughter now, rising behind the dialogue.

WHV: When, boy?

S: Ahhh, t'night, boss, t'night . . . they say they gon' . . . 'scuse de 'spression . . . cut you . . . uhhh fockin' . . . uhh throat . . .

V: [*Laughs*] And who's in charge of this " 'volt"?

S: Uhh . . . Reverend Turner . . . suh . . .

V: What?

S: Uhh . . . dass right . . . Reverend Turner . . . suh. . . . Now can I have dat extra chop you promised me??? [*Screams now, as soon as the lights go down*] AIEEEEEEIEIEIEIEI.

Gunshots, combination of slave ship and breakup of the revolt. Voices of master and slaves in combat.

WHVOICE: I kill you niggahs. You Black savages.

BLVOICE: White Beast. Devil, from hell. [*Voice, now, humming, humming, slow, deathly patient hum*] HUMMMMMMMMMM.

Drums of Africa and the screams of Black and White in combat. Lights flash on Tom, cringing as if he is hiding from combat, gnawing on pork chop. Voice of white man laughing in triumph. Another chop comes sailing out of the darkness. Tom grabs it and scoffs it down, grinning, and doing the dead-ape shuffle, humming while he eats.

W-3: [*Dead whispered voice*] Moshake, Moshake
. . . chile . . . calm calm. . . . We be all right,
now. . . . Moshake, be calm.

M: White beasts!

ALL: Uhh. Ohhh. Uhhh. Uhhh. Uhhh. [*As if
pulling a tremendous weight*] Uhhh. Ohhh.
Uhhh. Uhhh. Uhhh.

W: Ifanami. . . .

M-1: Dademi . . . Dademi.

W-2: Akiyele . . . Akiyele. Lord, husband, where
you . . . help me.

M: Olabumi . . . Olabumi. . . . Touch my hand
. . . woman . . .

W: Ifanami!

W: Moshake!

*Now same voices as if transported in time to
the slave farms . . . call names, English slave
names.*

ALL: [*Alternating man and woman losing mate
in death, or thru slavesale, or the aura of constant fear of separation*] "Luke. Oh, my God."

M: Sarah.

W: John. Everett. My God, they killed him.

ALL: Mama, Mama. . . . Nana. Nana. Willie,
Ohhh, Lord. . . . They done. Uhh. Uhhh. Uhh.
Obatala. Obatala. Save Us. Lord. Shango.
Lord of forests. Give us back our strength.

*Chains. Chains. Dragging and grunting of peo-
ple pushed against each other. The sound of a
spiritual. "Oh, Lord Deliver Me. . . . Oh
Lord" . . . and now cries of "JESUS LORD
JESUS . . . HELP US JESUS."*

M-1: Ogun. Give me weapons. Give me iron. My
spear. My bone and muscle make them tight
with tension of combat. Ogun, give me fire
and death to give these beasts. Sarava! Sarava!
Ogun.

*Drums of fire and blood briefly loud and
smashing against the dark, but now calming,
dying down, till only the moans, and then the
same patient humming . . . of women now, no
men, only the women ... strains of "The Old
Rugged Cross" . . . and only the women and
the humming . . . the time passing in the darkness, soft soft mournful weeping. "Jesus . . .
Jesus . . . Jesus . . . Jesus . . . Jesus . . .
Jesus . . . Jesus . . . Jesus . . . Jesus."*

*Now lights flash on, and preacher in modern
business suit stands with hat in his hand. He is
the same Tom as before. He stands at first
talking to his congregation: "Jesus, Jesus,
Jesus, Jesus, Jesus, Jesus," then with a big
grin, speaking in the pseudo-intelligent patter*

*he uses for the boss. He tries to be, in fact,
assumes he is, dignified, trying to hold his
shoulders straight, but only succeeds in giving
his entire body an odd slant like a diseased
coal shute.*

PRE: Yasss, we under-stand . . . the problem. And
personally I think some agreement can be
reached. We will be nonviolenk . . . to the last
. . . because we under-stand the dignity of
pruty mcbonk and the greasy ghost. Of course
diddy rip to bink, of vout juice. And penguins
would do the same. I have a trauma, that the
gold sewers won't integrate. Present fink. I
have an enema . . . a trauma, on the coaster
with your wife bird-shit.

W-3: [*Black woman's voice screaming for her
child again*] Moshake! Moshake! Moshake . . .
beeba . . . beeba . . . Wafwa Ko wafwa ko fukwididila

*Screams moans . . . drums . . . mournful death-
tone. . . . The preacher looks head turned just
slightly, as if embarrassed, trying still to talk
to the white man. Then, one of the Black Men,
out of the darkness, comes and sits before the
Tom, a wrapped-up bloody corpse of the dead
burned baby, as if they had just taken the
body from a blown-up church, sets corpse in
front of preacher. Preacher stops. Looks up at
"person" he's tomming before, then, with his
foot, tries to push baby's body behind him,
grinning, and jeffing all the time, showing
teeth, and being "dignified."*

PR: Uhherr . . . as I was sayin' . . . Mas' un . . .
Mister Tastyslop. . . . We Kneegrows are
ready to integrate . . . the blippy rump of
stomach bat has corrinked a lip to push the
thimble. Yass Yass Yass.

*In background while preacher is frozen in his
"Jeff" position . . . high hard sound of saxophone, backed up by drums. New sound saxophone tearing up the darkness. At height of
screaming saxophone, instruments and drums
comes voices screaming.*

M: Beasts. Beasts. Beasts. Ogun. Give me spear
and iron. Let me kill . . .

*Humming as before . . . long . . . incredible
patience, as if it would go on forever, turns
into OMMMMMMMMMMMMMMMMMMMM-
MMMMMMM: all take it up, as the climax
rise. Lights down. Ommmmm sound, mixed
with sounds of slave ship, saxophone and
drums. Sounds of people, thrown against each
other, now as if trying all, to rise, pick up.
Sounds of people picking up. Like dead people
rising. And against that the same sounds of
slave ship. White laughter over all of it.
White laughter. Song begins to build with the
saxophone and drums. First chanted.*

ALL:

> Rise, Rise, Rise
> Cut these ties, Black Man, Rise
> We gon' be the thing we are . . .

Now all sing "When We Gonna Rise"

When We Gonna Rise

> When we gonna rise/ up
> When we gonna rise/ up
>
> When we gonna rise/ up
> When we gonna rise
>
> I mean when we gonna lift our heads
>   and voices
> When we gonna show the world who
>   we really are
> When we gonna rise up, brother
> When we gonna rise above the sun
> When we gonna take our own place,
>   brother
> Like the world had just begun
> I mean when we gonna lift our heads
>   and voices
> Show the world who we really are
> Warrior-Gods, and lovers, the first
>   Men to walk this star
> Yes, oh, yes, the First Men to walk
>   this star
> How far, How long will it be
> When the world belongs to you and
>   me
> When we gonna rise up, brother
> When we gonna rise above the sun
> When we gonna take our own place,
>   brother
> Like the world had just begun.

Drum—new sax—voice arrangement. Bodies dragging up, in darkness. Lights up on the preacher in one part of the stage. He stands still jabbering senselessly to the white man. And the white man's laughter is heard trying to drown out the music, but the music is rising. PREACHER turns to look into the darkness at the people dragging up behind him, embarrassed at first, then beginning to get frightened. The laughter too takes on a less arrogant tone.

W: Moshake. Moshake.

M: Ogun, give me steel.

ALL: Uhh. Uhh. Ohhh. Uhhh. Uhhh.

Humming rising too behind. Still singing "When We Gonna Rise." PREACHER squirms, turns to see, and suddenly his eyes begin to open very wide, lights are coming up very slowly, almost imperceptibly at first. Now singing is beginning to be heard, mixed with old African drums, and voices, cries, pushing screams, of the slave ship. PREACHER begins to

fidget, as if he does not want to be where he is. He looks to boss for help. Voice is breaking, as lights come up and we see all the people in the slave ship in Miracles'/Temptations' dancing line. Some doing African dance. Some doing new Boogaloo, but all moving toward PREACHER, and toward voice. It is a new-old Boogalooyoruba line, women children all moving popping fingers all singing, and drummers, beating out old and new, and moving all moving. Finally the PREACHER begins to cringe and plead for help from the white voice.

PRE: Please, boss, these niggers goin' crazy, please, boss, throw yo lightnin' at 'em, white Jesus boss, white light god, they goin' crazy! Help!

VOICE: [*Coughing as if choking on something, trying to laugh because sight of PREACHER is funny . . . still managing to laugh at PREACHER*] Fool. Fool.

PR: Please, boss, please . . . I do anything for you . . . you know that, boss . . . Please . . . please . . .

All group merge on him and kill him daid. Then they turn in the direction of where the voice is coming from. Dancing, singing, right on toward the now pleading voice.

VOICE: HaaHaaHaaHaa [*Laugh gets stuck in his throat*] Uhh . . . now what . . . you' haha can't touch me . . . you scared of me, niggers. I'm god. You cain't kill white Jesus God. I got long blonde blow hair. I don't even need to wear a wig. You love the way I look. You want to look like me. You love me. You want me. Please. I'm good. I'm kind. I'll give you anything you want. I'm white Jesus saviour right God pay you money nigger me is good God be please . . . please don't . . .

Lights begin to fade . . . drums and voices of old slave ship come back.

ALL: Uhh. Ohh. Uhh. Ohh. Uhh. Ohh. Uhh. Ohh. [*And then the terrible humming, turning to the OMMMMMMMMMMMMMMmmmmmmmmmmm sound, broken now by the finally awful scream of the killed white voice*] AWHAWHAEHAHWAWHWHAHW.

All players fixed in half light, at the moment of the act. Then lights go down. Black.

Lights come up abruptly, and people onstage begin to dance, same hip Boogalyoruba, finger-pop, skate, monkey, dog. Enter audience, get members of audience to dance. To same music RISE UP. Turns into an actual party. When the party reaches some loose improvisation, etc., audience relaxed, somebody throws the preachers head into center of floor, i.e., after the dancing starts for real. Then black.

THE UNSEEN HAND

a play in one act

Sam Shepard

The Unseen Hand was first presented by Ellen Stewart at La Mama ETC, New York City, on December 26, 1969, with the following cast:

BLUE MORPHAN	*Beeson Carroll*
WILLIE (THE SPACE FREAK)	*Lee Kissman*
CISCO MORPHAN	*Bernie Warkentin*
THE KID	*Sticks Carlton*
SYCAMORE MORPHAN	*Victor Eschbach*

It was directed by Jeff Bleckner. Lighting by Johnny Dodd.

The Unseen Hand was subsequently presented by Albert Poland at the Astor Place Theatre, New York City, as half of a double bill with *Forensic and the Navigators,* also by the author, on April 1, 1970, with the following cast:

BLUE MORPHAN	*Beeson Carroll*
WILLIE (THE SPACE FREAK)	*Lee Kissman*
CISCO MORPHAN	*David Selby*
THE KID	*David Clennon*
SYCAMORE MORPHAN	*Tom Rosica*

It was directed by Jeff Bleckner. Settings by Santo Loquasto; costumes by Linda Fisher; lighting by Roger Morgan. Music written and played by Paul Conly on the ARP Synthesizer. Featuring Lothar and the Hand People: Paul Conly, Rusty Ford, Sam Shepard. Production stage manager: Elissa Lane. Associate producer: June Stevens.

Center stage is an old '51 Chevrolet convertible, badly bashed and dented, no tires and the top torn to shreds. On the side of it is written "Kill Azusa" with red spray paint. All around is garbage, tin cans, cardboard boxes, Coca-Cola bottles and other junk. The stage is dark. Sound of a big diesel truck from a distance, then getting louder, then passing with a whoosh. As the sound passes across the stage the beam of the headlights cuts through the dark and passes across the Chevy. Silence. Soft blue moonlight comes up slowly as the sound of another truck repeats, as before, its headlights cutting through the dark. This should be a synchronized tape-light loop which repeats over and over throughout the play—the headlights sweeping past accompanied by the sound of a truck. The lights come up but maintain a full moon kind of light. The whooshing of the trucks and the passing lights keep up. A figure slowly emerges out of the back seat of the Chevy. His name is BLUE MORPHAN. *He has a scraggly beard, black overcoat, blue jeans, cowboy boots and hat and a bottle in his hand. He is slightly drunk and talks to an imaginary driver in the front seat.*

BLUE: Say listen. Did we pass Cucamunga? Didn't we already pass it up? Listen. This here is Azusa. We must a' passed it up. Why don't ya pull up on the embankment there and let me out? Come on now. Fair's fair. I didn't stab ya' or nothin'. Nobody stole yer wallet, did they? OK. So let me out like I ask ya'. That's it. Atta' boy. OK. Good. If I had me any loose jingle I'd sure lay it on ya' fer gas money but I'd like to get me a cup a'coffee. You know how it is. Thanks, boy. [*He slowly climbs out of the back seat onto the stage, then reaches into the back and pulls out a battered guitar with broken strings*]

If ya' ever happen through Duarte let me know. Gimme a buzz or something. Drop me a line. 'Course ya' don't got the address but that's all right. Just ask 'em fer Blue Morphan. That's me. Anyone. Just ask any old body fer old Blue. They'll tell ya'. [*He pulls out an old dusty suitcase held together with rope and sets it on the ground, then a rifle.*]

I ain't been back there fer quite a spell now but they'll be able to direct ya' to the stables all right. Follow the old Union Pacific till ya' come to Fish Creek. Don't pick up no longhairs though. Now I warned ya'. OK. OK. Do what ya' like but I warned ya'. [*He pulls out a broken bicycle, a fishing rod, a lantern, an inner tube, some pipe, a bag full of bolts and other junk. He keeps taking more and more stuff out of the back seat and setting it down on the stage as he talks*]

You been driving long enough by now to tell who to pick up and who to leave lay. But if they got their thumb out you better look 'em over twice. I know. I used to drive a Chevy myself. Good car. Thing is nowadays it ain't so easy to tell the riff-raff from the gentry. Know what I mean. You can get tricked. They can fool ya'. All kinda fancy over-the-head talk and all along they're workin' for the government same as you. I mean you might not be. Like me fer instance. I'm a free agent. Used to be a time when I'd take an agency job. Go out and bring in a few bushwackers just for the dinero. Usually a little bonus throwed in. But nowadays ya' gotta keep to yerself. They got nerve gas right now that can kill a man in 30 seconds. Yup. A drop a' that on the back of a man's hand and poof! Thirty seconds. That ain't all. They got rabbit fever, parrot fever and other stuff stored up. Used to be, a man would have hisself a misunderstanding and go out and settle it with a six gun. Now it's all silent, secret. Everything moves like a fever. Don't know when they'll cut ya' down and when they do ya' don't know who done it. Don't mean to get ya' riled though. Too nice a night fer that. Straight, clean highway all the way from here to Tuba City. Shouldn't have no trouble. If yer hungry though there's a Bob's Big Boy right up the road a piece. I don't know if ya' go in fer double decker cheeseburgers or not but—Listen, tell ya' what, long as yer hungry I'll jest come along with ya' a ways and we'll chow down together. Sure. Good idea. I ain't ate since yesterday mornin' anyhow. Just before ya' picked me up. [*He starts putting all the junk back into the car*]

Sure is nice of ya' to help me out this a way. Don't come across many good old boys these days. Seems like they all got a chip on the shoulder or somethin'. You noticed that? The way they swagger around givin' ya' that look. Like ya' weren't no more than a road apple or somethin' worse. If they'd a known me in my prime it might change their tune. Hadn't a been fer the old hooch here I'd a been in history books by now. Probably am anyhow, under a different name. They never get the name straight. Don't matter too much anyhow. Least it don't hurt my feelings none. 'Course yer too young to remember the Morphan brothers probably. Cisco, Sycamore and me, Blue. The three of us. 'Course we had us a few more. Not a gang exactly. Not like these teen-age hot rodders with their Mercurys and Hudson Hornets. Least ways we wasn't no menace. The people loved us. The real people I'm talkin' about. The people people. They helped us out in fact. And vica versa. We'd never go rampant on nobody. Say, you oughta' get yer tires checked before ya' go too much further. That left rear one looks a little spongy. Can't be too careful when yer goin' a distance. A car's like a good horse. You take care a' it and it takes care a' you. [WILLIE, *the space freak, enters. He is young and dressed in super future clothes, badly worn and torn. Orange tights, pointed shoes, a vinyl vest with a black shirt that comes up like a hood over the back of his head. His skin is badly burned and blistered with red open sores. His head is shaved and there is a black hand print burned into the top of his skull. At moments he goes into convulsive fits, his whole body shaking. He staggers on stage.* BLUE *sees him and stops his babble. They stare at each other for a moment*] I suppose yer lookin' fer a handout or somethin'. [WILLIE *just stares. Exhausted, his sides heaving,* BLUE *climbs back into the back seat and disappears. His voice can still be heard*] That's the trouble with you kids. Always lookin' fer a handout. There ain't nothin' romantic about panhandlin', sonny. Ye' ain't gonna' run across the holy grail thataway. Anyhow ya' come to the wrong place. This here is Azusa, not New York City. [BLUE'S *head pops up from the back seat. He looks at* WILLIE *still standing there, panting*] "A," "Z," "U," "S," "A." "Everything from 'A' to 'Z' in the USA." Azusa. If yer thinking on robbin' me a' my worldly possessions you can take a look for yerself. I been livin' in this Chevy for twenty years now and I ain't come across no diamond rings yet. [He *disappears back down in the back seat*] 'Course if ya' just wanna' rest that's a different story. It's a free highway. Yer welcome to stay a spell. The driver's seat's mighty comfortable once ya' get used to the springs.

WILLIE: You Blue Morphan?

A pause as BLUE *slowly rises, his head coming into view.*

BLUE: What'd you call me?

WILLIE: Is your name Blue Morphan?

BLUE: Look, sonny, nobody knows my name or where I been or where I'm goin'. Now you better trot along. [He *sinks back down*]

WILLIE: I've traveled through two galaxies to see you. At least you could hear me out.

BLUE'S *head comes back into view.*

BLUE: You been hittin' the juice or somethin'? What's yer name, boy?

WILLIE: They call me Willie.

BLUE: Who's they?

WILLIE: The High Commission.

BLUE: What're ya' shakin' for? It's a warm night. Here. Have a swig a' this. It'll put a tingle in ya'. [*He offers* WILLIE *the bottle*]

WILLIE: No thanks.

BLUE: What, Apple Jack ain't good enough for ya', huh? Suppose you run in fancy circles or somethin'. Just a second, just a second. [*He climbs out of the back seat and goes around to the trunk and opens it. He starts rummaging through junk in the trunk as* WILLIE *stands there shaking*] Got a couple a Navajo blankets here in the back somewheres. Keep 'em special fer when the wind comes up. Sometimes it blows in off the San Joaquin and gets a bit nippy. Ah, here ya' go. This oughta' do it. [*He pulls out a dusty Indian blanket from the trunk and takes it over to* WILLIE] Here ya' go. Here. Well, take it. [*He offers the blanket to* WILLIE, *but* WILLIE *just stares at him, shaking and trembling*] You sure got yerself a case a the DT's there, boy. Here. Wrap this around ya'. Come on now. [BLUE *wraps the blanket around* WILLIE'S *shoulders, then notices the handprint on his head*] What's that ya' got on yer head there? Some new fashion or somethin'?

WILLIE: The brand.

BLUE: Like they do with steers, ya' mean? Who done it to ya'?

WILLIE: The Sorcerers of the High Commission. It's why I've come.

BLUE: You better come over here and sit down. I can't make hide nor hair out a what yer sayin'. Come on. Have a seat and collect yerself. [*He leads* WILLIE *over to the car, opens the front door and seats him in the driver's seat.* BLUE *climbs up on the front fender and sits*] Now what's this here High Commission stuff? Why would they wanna put a brand on yer head?

WILLIE: I can't see where I'm driving if you're going to sit there.

BLUE: Say, what's yer game, boy? Any fool can see this Chevy ain't got no wheels.

WILLIE: We used to shoot deer and strap them over the hood.

BLUE: Forget the deer. What's this brand business?

WILLIE: I've been zeroed.

BLUE: What's that mean?

WILLIE: Whenever I think beyond a certain circumference of a certain circle there's a hand that squeezes my brain.

BLUE: What hand?

WILLIE: It's been burned in. You can't see it now. All you can see is the scar.

BLUE: And this High Commission fella did this to ya'?

WILLIE: It's not a fella. It's a body. Nobody ever sees it. Just the sorcerers.

BLUE: Who's that?

WILLIE: Black magicians who know the secrets of the Nogo.

BLUE: I'll have to make a left turn on that one, sonny. I'm a simple man. I eat simple. I talk simple and I think simple.

WILLIE: That's why we need you.

BLUE: We?

WILLIE: The prisoners of the Diamond Cult.

BLUE: Just talk. I'll listen.

WILLIE: I am descended from a race of mandrills. Fierce baboons that were forced into human form by the magic of the Nogo. It was decided since we were so agile and efficient at sorting out diamonds for the Silent Ones that we could be taken a step further into human form and tested as though we were still baboons but give results in the tests as though we were human.

BLUE: What kinda' tests?

WILLIE: Mind warps. Time splits. Electro-laser fields. Dimensional overlays. Spatial projections. Force fields.

BLUE: But you think like a man?

WILLIE: And feel. This was a mistake the sorcerers had not counted on. They wanted an animal to develop that was slightly sub-human, thereby to maintain full control over its psychosomatic functions. The results were something of the opposite. We developed as superhuman entities with capacities for thought and feeling far beyond that of our captors. In order to continue their tests they needed an invention to curtail our natural reasoning processes. They came up with the Unseen Hand, a muscle contracting syndrome hooked up to the will of the Silent Ones. Whenever our thoughts transcend those of the magicians the Hand squeezes down and forces our minds to contract into non-preoccupation.

BLUE: What's that like?

WILLIE: Living death. Sometimes when one of us tries to fight the Hand or escape its control, like me, we are punished by excruciating muscle spasms and nightmare visions. Blood pours past my eyes and smoke fills up my brain.

BLUE: What do ya' want me to do about all this? I'm just a juicer on the way out.

WILLIE: You're more than that. The sorcerers and the Silent Ones of the High Commission have lost all touch with human emotion. They exist in almost a purely telepathic intellectual state. That is why they can still exert control over our race. You and your brothers are part of another world, far beyond anything the High Commission has experienced. If you came

into Nogoland blazing your six guns they wouldn't have any idea how to deal with you. All their technology and magic would be at a total loss. You would be too real for their experience.

BLUE: Now hold on there, whatever yer name was.

WILLIE: Willie.

BLUE: Yeah. Well, first off, my brothers are dead. Cisco and Sycamore was gunned down in 1886.

WILLIE: It doesn't matter.

BLUE: Well, unless yer counting on bringin' 'em back from the grave it matters a whole lot.

WILLIE: That's exactly what I'm counting on.

BLUE *jumps down from the fender and grabs the rifle. He points it at* WILLIE.

BLUE: All right, wiseacre. Out a' the car. Come on or I'll plug ya' right here on the spot.

WILLIE: You can't plug me, Blue. I don't die.

BLUE: Not ever?

WILLIE: Never.

BLUE: Then how come yer so scared to take on them High Commandos yer own self?

WILLIE: Because of the Hand.

WILLIE *goes into a violent spasm, clutching his head in agony.* BLUE *drops the rifle and goes to* WILLIE. *He pulls him out of the car and sets him on the ground.*

BLUE: Now stop jumpin' around, yer makin' me nervous. Just settle down. You want the cops to catch us?

WILLIE *writhes on the ground and screams phrases and words as though warding off some unseen terror.*

WILLIE: Wind refraction! Cyclone riff! Get off the rim! Off the rim!

BLUE: What's with you, boy?

WILLIE: The latitudinal's got us! Now! Now! Smoke it up! Smoke him! Gyration forty zero two nodes! Two nodes! You got the wrong mode! Wrong! Correction! Correct that! Step! Stop it! Modulate eighty y's west! Keep it west! Don't let up the field rays! Keep it steady on! Harmonic rhythm scheme! Harmony four! Discord! You got it! Aaah! Aaaaaaaah! Let up! Extract! Implode! Bombard the picture! The picture! Image contact! Major! Minor! Loop syndrome! Drone up! Full drone wave! Now! Oooooh! Just about! Just about! Crystallize fragment mirror! Keep it keen! Sharpen that focus! Hypo filament! Didactachrome! Resolve! Resolve! Resolve! Reverb! Fuzz tone! Don't let the feedback in! Feed it back! Keep your back up! Back it up! Reverse foilage meter! Fauna scope. Graphic tableau. Gramophonic display key. All right. All right. Now raise the horizon. Good. Moon. Planets in place. Heliographic perspective. Atmosphere checking cool. Galactic four count. Star meter gazing central focus. Beam to head on sunset. Systol reading ace in. Dystol balance. Treble boost. All systems baffled. Baffled.

WILLIE *goes unconscious.* CISCO MORPHAN *enters. He wears a serape, jeans, cowboy hat and boots, a bandana on his head, a rifle and a hand gun. He has long black hair and scraggly beard. He is younger than* BLUE *by about twenty years.*

CISCO: Still foxy as ever, ain't ya'. Better watch *out]* Well, don't ya' recognize me, boy? It's me! Cisco. Yer brother. Yer mean ornery old flesh and blood.

BLUE: Just stand back, mister. I'm gettin' rid a' this right now. [*He throws his bottle behind the car and holds his rifle on* CISCO]

CISCO: Still foxey as ever, ain't ya'. Better watch out that thing don't go off by accident. Let a gun go to rustin' like that and ya' never can tell what it's liable to do.

BLUE: It's plenty greased enough to open daylight in the likes of an imposter.

CISCO: Oh. So ya' don't believe it's really me, huh. Let's see. What if I was to show ya' some honest to God proof of the puddin'?

BLUE: Like what, fer instance?

CISCO: Like say a knife scar ya' give me fer my sixteenth birthday in Tuscaloosa.

BLUE: That'd do just fine.

CISCO: All right. Now you hold yer fire there while I get out a' my poncho.

BLUE: Just hurry it up.

CISCO *sets down his rifle and starts taking off his serape as* BLUE *holds the rifle on him.*

CISCO: Yeah, I guess yer plenty busy nowadays.

BLUE: How da ya' mean? Keep yer hand away from that pistol.

CISCO: There we go. Now. Take a looksee. [CISCO *takes off his poncho and shows* BLUE *a long star going from the middle of his back all the way around to his chest.* BLUE *examines it closely]* What ya' got to say now? Ain't that the mark ya' give me with yer very own fishing knife?

BLUE: Sure beats the hell outa' me.

CISCO: If yer satisfied why don't ya' do me a favor and lower that buffalo gun.

BLUE *lowers his rifle as* CISCO *puts his poncho back on.*

BLUE: But you and Sycamore was gunned down in the street right in broad daylight. I was there.

CISCO: You escaped. Sycamore should be comin' up any second now.

BLUE: I don't get it, Cisco. What's goin' on?

CISCO: Seems there's certain unfinished business. This must be the fella here.

BLUE: You know this looney?

CISCO: Let's take a look. He ain't dead, is he?

[CISCO *leans over* WILLIE *and looks at his face]*

BLUE: Damned if I can tell. He just shows up out a' the clear blue and starts to jawin' about outer space and High Commancheros and what all. I can't make it out.

CISCO: He came alone?

BLUE: So far. First him and then you. You know somethin' I don't, Cisco?

CISCO: All I know is that I was summoned up. Me, you and Sycamore is gonna be back in action before too long. And this here dude is gonna set us straight on what the score is.

BLUE: What score? I settled up all my debts a long time ago. I hunted down every last one a' them varmints what got you and Sycamore. I'm an old man, Cisco.

CISCO: There's other upstarts seems to be jammin' up the works. Besides, I'll be glad to see a little action for a change. I been hibernatin' for too long now. You got any grub layin' around here somewhere?

BLUE: Best I can do is Campbell's pork and beans, Cisco. Have to be cold out a' the can too. Can't make no fires on account a' the Highway Patrol.

CISCO: What's that?

BLUE: The law. Like the old Texas Rangers, 'cept they got cars now. [BLUE *goes to the car and opens the trunk. He rummages around for a can of beans]*

CISCO: Well, looks like you got yerself a nice enough campsite. What's this here rig?

BLUE: Fifty-one Chevy. Don't make 'em like this any more. Now they got dual headlights, twin exhausts, bucket seats, wrap around windshields and what all. Extra junk to make it look fancy. Don't go no better though.

CISCO *sits in the driver's seat and turns the steering wheel.*

CISCO: Must take a hefty team to pull this load. What's it made out of, iron or somethin'?

BLUE: It drives itself, boy. This here is a gasoline, internal combustion six banger. Don't need no team a horses. [*He pulls out a can of beans and walks around to* CISCO]

CISCO: I'll be damned. And this here is what ya' guide it with, I'll bet.

BLUE: You got it. Here. There's a can opener in the glove compartment.

CISCO: What's that?

BLUE: That little door over there. Ya' just push the button and she flaps open.

CISCO: I'll be damned. Keep gloves in there, do ya'? [*He opens the glove compartment and takes out a can opener and some other junk*]

BLUE: Here, ya' better let me handle it for ya'.

[BLUE *takes the can and the can opener and opens the can of beans*]

CISCO: How fast can ya' go with one a these here?

BLUE: Some of 'em'll do over a hundred mile an hour.

CISCO: What's that mean, Blue?

BLUE: That means in an hour's time if you keep yer boot stomped down on that pedal you'll have covered a hundred mile a' territory.

CISCO: Whooeee! Sure beats hell out of a quarter horse, don't it?

BLUE: You better believe it.

CISCO: What's these buttons for? [*He pulls a button and the headlights go on*]

BLUE: Don't pull that! Push that back in. You want the fuzz down on our necks? [CISCO *pushes the button back in and the lights go out*] I just get the damn battery charged so's I can listen to a little radio and you wanna go and run the damn thing down again. Here's yer beans. [*He hands* CISCO *the can of beans*]

CISCO: Thanks boy. How come yer so scared a' the law all of a sudden?

BLUE: It ain't so sudden as all that. I'm goin' on a hundred and twenty years old now. Thanks to modern medicine.

CISCO: That a fact? Sure kept yerself fit, Blue.

BLUE: Well, you live on the lam like I have for a while and you gotta keep yer wits about ya'.

CISCO: What's this radio thing yer talking about?

BLUE: That second knob on yer right. Just turn it a click. It's already set up for Moon Channel.

CISCO *turns the radio on. Rock and Roll or news or any random radio station comes on soft. It should be a real radio and not a tape.*

CISCO: I'll be damned.

BLUE: Just keep it soft.

CISCO: Where's it comin' from, Blue?

BLUE: Up there. They got a station up there now.

[*He points to the moon*]

CISCO: The moon? Yer pullin' my leg.

BLUE: Things've changed since you was last here, boy.

CISCO: How'd they get up there?

BLUE: Rocket ship. Damndest thing ya' ever did see. Taller than a twenty story office building.

CISCO: How'd they get back?

BLUE: Come right down plop in the ocean. Some of 'em stay up there, though. Don't know what they all do. I've heard tell they travel to Mars and Venus, different planets like that.

CISCO: All in a rocket ship thing?

BLUE: Yep.

CISCO: Don't they like it down here no more?

BLUE: The earth's gettin' cramped, boy. There's lots more people now. They're lookin' for new territory to spread out to. I hear tell they've sent prisoners up there too. 'Stead a sendin' 'em to jail. They don't hang no one no more. Just strand 'em high and dry on a planet somewheres in space. Probably where this critter come from.

CISCO: Wonder what's keepin' Sycamore.

BLUE: What makes ya' so sure he's comin'?

CISCO: Has to. Same as me. He's been summoned up.

BLUE: How's that work?

CISCO: Some voice wakes ya' up. I don't know. Just like you been sleepin' or somethin'. 'Fore you know it yer movin' and walkin' and talkin' just like always. Hard to get used to at first. Anyhow I'm glad I'm back.

BLUE: Me too, boy. Sure gets lonely on yer own all the time.

CISCO: Well, before you know it we'll be back together just like old times. Robbin', rapin' and killin'.

BLUE: Yeah boy!

A drunken high school cheerleader kid comes on yelling. He has a blond crewcut and a long cheerleader's sweater with a huge "A" printed on it. He holds a huge megaphone to his lips. His pants are pulled down around his ankles. His legs are red and bleeding and look as though they've been whipped with a belt. He has white tennis shoes on. He yells through the megaphone to an unseen gang of a rival high school in the distance behind the audience. He doesn't notice BLUE *and* CISCO.

KID: You motherfuckers are dead! You're as good as dead! Just wait till Friday night! We're going to wipe your asses off the map! There won't even be an Arcadia High left! You think you're all so fuckin' bitchin' just 'cause your Daddies are rich! Just 'cause your old man gives you a fuckin' full blown Corvette for Christmas and a credit card! You think your girls are so tough looking! They're fucking dogs! I wouldn't fuck an Arcadia girl if she bled out her ass hole! You punk faggots shouldn't even be in the same league as us! The Rio Hondo belongs to us! You're gonna go fucking scoreless Friday night and I'm gonna be right there cheering and seeing it all happen! Then we're gonna burn your fucking grandstand to the ground! Right to the fucking ground! Then we're gonna burn a huge "A" for Azusa right in the middle of your fucking field. Right on the fifty yard line! [*He wheels around and faces* BLUE *and* CISCO] What're you looking at? You think it's funny or something? What the fuck are you looking at? You wanna make something out of it? You wanna put your money where your mouth is? Come on! Come on! Try me! You think I'm funny looking? Come on!

BLUE: I don't know, Cisco. This used to be a quiet little highway.

KID: What'd you say, old man? What'd you say? I'll kill you if you say one more word! I'll fucking kill you!

CISCO: Better watch that kinda tongue, boy. This here's my brother Blue yer talkin' at.

KID: What're you, some hippie creep? I can smell you all the way over here! I'll kill you too! I'll kill both of you!

CISCO: Better pull yer pants up and head home, boy.

KID: Don't tell me what to do, you commie faggot! I'll fucking kill you! [*He takes a leap toward* CISCO. CISCO *draws his pistol lightning fast. The* KID *stops still.*]

CISCO: Now look, boy. I ain't in the habit of shootin' down unarmed infants, but yer startin' to grate on me. Now git home before this thing goes off. [*The* KID *crumples to the ground sobbing*]

KID: I can't! It's too late now. They grabbed me. Right after the rally. They got me and took me up Lookout Point and whipped me with a belt. They tried to paint my balls black but I wouldn't let them. I fought. I kicked. They stuck a Tampax up me. Right up me. I tried to stop them. I yelled. There were some cars. A couple cars. Girls making out with the fullback and the quarterback. But they turned their lights on and left. They could've helped. At least they could have helped me. I cheered for them plenty of times. Plenty of games. The least they could've done—Just because I couldn't make second string. I could've played Junior Varsity but I decided to be a cheerleader instead. They could've helped me. The least they could've done.

CISCO: O.K. O.K. Why don't ya just go home now and sleep it off.

KID: I can't! It's too late. My old man'll beat the shit out of me. It's after two. He won't let me use the car for a month. I can't go home. Let me stay here. Please. Let me. Please.

BLUE: Might as well. What's one more looney.

CISCO: We got business to set straight here, Blue.

BLUE: He won't get in the way. Let him stay.

CISCO: All right. But keep to yerself over in the corner there.

KID: Thanks. [*The* KID *stands up and moves upstage left*]

CISCO: And pull yer pants up, fer Christ's sake.

KID: It stings too bad.

CISCO: All right.

The KID *throws down his megaphone and starts stomping on it violently.*

KID: I'm never going to lead another cheer! Never! Not for them or anybody else! Never! Never! Never! Never! Never! Never! Never! Never! Never!

BLUE: Atta boy. Get it out a yer system.

KID: I'll just stay over near the drainage ditch there. I won't get in your way. I promise.

CISCO: Good.

KID: If those Arcadia guys come by here don't tell them where I am, O.K.?

CISCO: O.K.

The KID *turns to go off left then stops.*

KID: Oh, would you mind waking me up in the morning? I don't usually get up too easy.

BLUE: Don't worry, you'll hear the traffic.

KID: Thanks.

BLUE: Sweet dreams, boy.

The KID *goes off.*

CISCO: Boy, howdy, what'd I miss all them years?

BLUE: A whole lot, Cisco. A whole lot. Things change over night now. One day there's a President, the next day he gets shot, the next day the guy what shot him gets shot.

CISCO: No foolin'.

BLUE: Next day they outlaw guns and replace 'em with nerve gas. Stuff can turn a full grown man into a blithering fool. Then they change the government from Capitalism to Socialism because the government's afraid of a full blown insurrection. Then they have a revolution anyhow and things stay just like they was.

WILLIE *rolls over and speaks on his back lying down.*

WILLIE: Cisco?

CISCO: That's me.

WILLIE: You made it. Good. Sycamore here yet?

CISCO: Not yet. Should be soon though.

WILLIE *sits up.*

BLUE: You feelin' better now, boy? That was some awful fit ya' had there.

WILLIE: Get prepared to see worse.

BLUE: Why? You plannin' on flippin' out some more?

WILLIE: In Nogoland there's men walking around with their brains eaten out, skinless, eyes turned inside out, frozen in pictures of terror. Men walking day and night like dogs on the end of a leash. You'd be happy if the worst you saw there was "flipping out," as you say.

CISCO: What's the scoop, Willie?

BLUE: How'd you know his name?

WILLIE: Long before we turned human, the magicians introduced us to the mysteries of telepathy, Blue. Your brother is able to know and understand things that he himself won't have the answers to.

BLUE: Well, how 'bout me? Why don't ya clue me in on a few secrets?

WILLIE: It will take time. First of all you must undergo temporal rearrangement.

BLUE: I don't get ya'.

CISCO: Yeah. Keep it simple, Willie.

WILLIE: Your brain has undergone cell breakdown with age and time, Blue. We have to regroup your temporal field to make you young enough to again become sensitive to telepathic and extrasensory reception.

BLUE: Yer gonna make me young?

WILLIE: That's right.

CISCO: How 'bout that.

BLUE: I don't exactly know if I go fer that idea. I been on a long hard road fer so long now it feels kinda good to know it's drawin' to a close. Now ya want me to go through it all over again?

WILLIE: Whenever you want it, the scheme can be reversed back to your normal earth age. But for now we must transform you, for it's the only hope for the prisoners of Nogoland.

BLUE: Who are these dudes exactly? I don't even know if I like 'em yet.

WILLIE: People, like you and me but with a strange history and stranger powers. These powers could work for the good of mankind if allowed to unfold into their natural creativity. But if they continue as they are they will surely work for evil, or, worse, they will turn it on themselves and commit a horrible mass suicide that may destroy the universe.

BLUE: Well, you seem like a decent enough Joe. What've I got to lose?

WILLIE: Fine.

CISCO: Good boy.

BLUE: How do I start?

CISCO: Sit down here in front of me.

WILLIE *sits with his feet out.*

BLUE: Right here? Like this? [BLUE *sits with his feet out facing* WILLIE]

WILLIE: That's right. Now push your feet against the soles of my feet. Real hard.

BLUE: Like this? [BLUE *presses his feet against* WILLIE'S]

WILLIE: Press hard. Now grab my hands and squeeze. [BLUE *follows* WILLIE'S *directions*]

BLUE: This ain't gonna hurt, is it?

WILLIE: Not a bit. You'll feel an interior shrinkage as your organs rearrange themselves and grow stronger, but don't panic. Just push with your feet and grip my hands firmly.

BLUE: O.K.

CISCO: Hang on, Blue. Yer half way home.

WILLIE *goes into another seizure but different this time. It's as though thousands of electric volts were being transmitted from* WILLIE *to* BLUE. *It should look like waves of shock being transformed. First* WILLIE *trembles and shakes violently, then* BLUE. BLUE *gradually becomes younger until at the end he is a young man of about thirty.*

WILLIE: The truth of the spinning fire wheel! Steel brings you close! Strength in the steel! Strengthen! Electric smoking man power! The strength of a man! Power in the man! Tower of power! Texaco sucks! Texas man! Longhorn panhandle tough cowboy leather man! Send him home! Where the buffalo roam! It's daytime! It's bright day! Truth in the sun! Sun play! Mexican silver stud! Proud of his pride! Proud guy! Tall and lean and mean! Look out, Tuba City! Look out, down and out crumpled up muffled old bad guy! Here's screaming new blood! A flood of new blood screaming straight to your raggedy heart! Churning new blood flooding your mind up! Sending you zig zag straight to your heart! Aaaaaaaah! Gyrode screen! The Hand! The Hand's got me, Blue! The Hand!

BLUE: Hang on, Willie. I'll see ya' through it.

[BLUE *grips* WILLIE'S *hands tighter and pushes hard with his legs as* WILLIE *twists and grimaces trying to ward off the hand*]

WILLIE: No! No! Diminish laser count! Aaaaaah!

CISCO: Hang on, Blue! Don't let him go!

WILLIE: My brain! It's squeezing my brain!

BLUE: Hold his head, Cisco! Grab his head!

CISCO *puts both hands on* WILLIE'S *head and presses down.*

WILLIE: Gama build up! System burn! Burning! Cell damage to block unit! Can't see! Can't see! They've smoked it good this time! Black wire smoke burn! There's a fire in code D! Disorient power pack! Aaaaaaaaaaah! Fading! [*He shakes violently, then goes limp and unconscious as before.* CISCO *lowers his head to the ground as* BLUE *releases his grip.* BLUE *is now much younger than before. He stands*]

CISCO: Poor devil.

BLUE: He'll be all right in a little while. The same thing happened to him before you came. Anyway, it worked.

CISCO: What?

BLUE: I'm young. Least I feel young. I still know it's me and everything but I feel much stronger. Tough, like I used to be.

CISCO: Hot damn! We're getting close now, Blue. It won't be long. [BLUE *lets out a yell, takes a run across the stage and does a somersault*] How 'bout that. [CISCO *takes a run and does a somersault right next to* BLUE. BLUE *stands and starts singing "Rock Around The Clock."* CISCO *stands and joins him, dancing around and doing the twist and all that jive.*]

CISCO *and* BLUE: One for the money. Two for the show. Three to get ready. Now go man go. We're gonna rock around the clock tonight. We're gonna rock, rock, rock until the broad daylight. We're gonna rock, gonna rock around the clock. . . .

SYCAMORE MORPHAN *appears opposite them. They freeze.* SYCAMORE'S *very tall and slick. Dressed like Bat Masterson with black tails, black hat, black vest, white shirt with ruffled cuffs and diamond cuff links, black boots, black leather gloves and black cane with a diamond-studded handle and a pearl-handled revolver tied down to his hip in a black holster. He just stands staring at his two brothers.*

BLUE: Sycamore.

CISCO: Hey, boy. Where you been? We been waitin' and waitin'. [SYCAMORE *sidles over to* WILLIE *and pokes him with his cane*]

BLUE: Thought you was probably lost or somethin'.

CISCO: Yeah. Don't know why we'd figure that though, since you know the trails better than any of us.

Uneasy silence as SYCAMORE *moves to the Chevy and pokes it with his cane, scanning the area with his eyes. He is cold and mean. He reaches in the car and turns the radio off with a sharp snap.*

BLUE: Sure is good to see us all back together again, though. Boy howdy, how long's it been, anyhow?

CISCO: Must be goin' on a hundred some-odd years, I'll bet.

BLUE: Sure. Must be that. At least a hundred.

CISCO: Yer lookin' mighty fit, Sycamore. Just like old times.

SYCAMORE *turns to them swinging his cane.*

SYCAMORE: Was there some specific reason behind choosing a rendezvous point right on the open highway?

BLUE: This here's Azusa, Sycamore. "Everything from A to Z in the USA." Nothing hardly but rock quarries and cement factories here. All the traffic dies down at night on account of most of the vehicles is trucks carrying gravel and they don't work at night.

SYCAMORE: The sun don't rise on Azusa, huh.

BLUE: Well, sure. But we'll be out a here by then.

CISCO: Yeah, we should be long gone by mornin'.

SYCAMORE: I guess you boys know exactly where you're goin', then, and how you're gettin' there.

CISCO: Well, not exactly. But Willie's gotta set us straight soon as he comes to.

SYCAMORE: I reckon he's got you all set up with enough guns and provisions, then, huh.

BLUE: Hadn't thought a' that one.

CISCO: Well, we all got guns, ain't we? I got mine.

SYCAMORE *takes out a cheroot and lights it.*

SYCAMORE: We just meet 'em in the street, then, huh? Like old times. A showdown.

CISCO: Yeah, why not?

BLUE: I see what Sycamore's driving' at, Cisco. There's only three of us with pistols against hundreds, maybe thousands.

CISCO: So what. We used to bring a whole town to a standstill just by ridin' in. They used to roll out the carpet for the Morphan brothers.

BLUE: This ain't a town Willie's talkin' about, it's a whole country, maybe even a whole planet. We ain't in the movies, ya' know.

CISCO: So what do you suggest we do?

BLUE: Round up some more men maybe.

CISCO: Why don't we wake Willie up and ask him.

SYCAMORE: I say we forget it.

A pause as they both look at SYCAMORE.

BLUE: The whole thing?

SYCAMORE: Why not? We don't stand a chance of freeing those baboons.

BLUE: But they ain't baboons any more, Sycamore. They're human beings just like us.

CISCO: Yeah.

SYCAMORE: So what?

BLUE: They're being tortured and stuff. Brainwashed or somethin'. Experimented on.

SYCAMORE: What's that got to do with us? We're free now. We been brought back to life. What do you want to throw it away for a bunch of baboons? Look, I say we split up, go our different ways and lay low for a while. Then we meet up again in Tuba City or somewhere on the North Platte. That way it'll give us time to think things over.

CISCO: What things?

SYCAMORE: Reorganizing the gang, you pinhead. The Morphan brothers ride again, except this time in a whole different century. This time we don't make no mistakes. We stick to trains and forget about banks and post offices.

BLUE: There ain't no trains no more, Sycamore. Just planes and hovercrafts and such like.

SYCAMORE: What're you talkin' about?

BLUE: There ain't no trains to rob no more. Besides, we can't ditch Willie like that. He just give me back my youth. I can't go walkin' out on him.

SYCAMORE: No trains?

CISCO: Yeah, I feel kinda' bad about that too. I wouldn't even be here if it weren't for him. You neither, Sycamore.

SYCAMORE: No trains.

BLUE: I say we stay and see it through.

WILLIE *comes to.*

WILLIE: It's up to you. What Sycamore says is true. Why should you feel responsible for some species of hybrid in another galaxy? You could stay here and be free. Live like you want to.

CISCO: You mean you wouldn't mind of we took off on ya'?

WILLIE: I can't force you to help us. It must be left to your own conscience. All I can do is try to persuade you to come.

SYCAMORE: No trains.

BLUE: Oh, this here's my brother Sycamore, Willie.

WILLIE: I know. I'm happy you came.

SYCAMORE: They got trains where you come from?

WILLIE: They used to have a system underground but it's long been made obsolete.

SYCAMORE: It's still there though?

WILLIE: Yes. As far as I know.

SYCAMORE: And it connects to all the parts of the city where these prisoners are?

WILLIE: Yes. I think it must. Throughout the whole planet, I think.

BLUE: What you gettin' at, Sycamore?

SYCAMORE: Sounds to me like it could be used as an escape route.

CISCO: Then we're goin' then! Waaaahoooo! Attaboy, Sycamore! I always knew ya' had a soft spot.

SYCAMORE: Well, if there's no trains here we might as well go there.

BLUE: Hot dog!

WILLIE: Good. Let me show you a plan of Nogoland. [WILLIE *stands and draws a huge map with his finger on the floor of the stage. As he indicates lines different colored lines of light appear on the floor as though they emanated from the tip of his finger. The other three watch as* WILLIE *describes Nogoland and draws the map accordingly*] In the Northeastern sector is the Capitol, as you would say, contained in a transparent dome permitting temperature and atmosphere control. It is here that the Silent Ones conduct their affairs of state. Only members of the High Commission and Sorcerer Chiefs are allowed passage to and from the Capitol. Over here in the Southwestern sector are the Diamond Fields where slaves work day and night under constant guard by the soldiers of the Raven Cult.

BLUE: Who're they?

WILLIE: Fierce morons cloaked in black capes. They ride on huge black ravens which continually fly over the area, patrolling and keeping a constant eye out for the possibility of an uprising amongst the slaves. Here in the West are the laboratories of the Sorcerers of the Nogo. Here is where my friends are kept. They are also watched by Raven guards but the control is not so heavy there since the power of the Unseen Hand is believed to be security enough.

SYCAMORE: What's in the middle?

WILLIE: Huge refineries and industrial compounds for the processing of the diamonds. It is here that the biggest and best diamonds are culled out of the crop.

BLUE: What do they do with them?

WILLIE: Each year a Great Game is played with the people of Zeron, a competition of some kind. The winner is allowed to extend the boundaries of his domain into the loser's territory and rule the people within that new area. The loser must also pay off the winner with certain secret information of magical knowledge.

SYCAMORE: What about the South?

WILLIE: A vast primitive region of swamps and lagoons. We must enter Nogoland by this route since we'll surely be spotted by Raven guards if we attempt to come in from the North.

BLUE: What's up there?

WILLIE: Desert. Nothing. The sky never changes. No day and no night. No atmosphere of any kind. Not even craters to break up the landscape. We would surely be seen.

SYCAMORE: How do they get back and forth from these different areas?

WILLIE: Only certain chosen ones are allowed to travel at all. These do so by means of teleportation. They beam themselves into a chosen area by displacing their bodies.

SYCAMORE: Does this underground railroad you're talkin' about go into the South there?

WILLIE: Just about. We'll have to be extra careful once we arrive there, though.

BLUE: Why's that?

WILLIE: This region is inhabited by the Lagoon Baboon, another experiment on our race. He watches over the Lower Regions and is also controlled by the Hand.

SYCAMORE: Uh, don't anybody let on to it but we're being watched.

BLUE: What do you mean?

SYCAMORE: Don't turn around. Act like we're still talkin' about the map. He's over behind my car. I'll try to circle around behind him.

CISCO: How ya' gonna do that without him seein' ya'?

SYCAMORE: I'll go off like I'm goin' to take a leak then come up behind him. You stay here and keep talkin'. Just act natural.

BLUE: O.K.

CISCO: So ya' say this here Lagoon Baboon's an ornery critter, eh Willie?

WILLIE: Yes. Very ornery, as you say. He can eat three times his weight in human flesh in less time than it would take you to eat a donut.

SYCAMORE: Well listen, I gotta go see a man about a horse so why don't you fellas carry on here.

BLUE: O.K., Sycamore. Don't get it caught in the zipper now.

SYCAMORE *exits. The rest continue to act "natural."*

CISCO: Sounds to me like this Nogoland's a pretty depressing place. Don't they ever have no fun? No rodeos or nothin'?

BLUE: Yeah. What about that, Willie?

WILLIE: Twice a year they hold tournaments where my people are pitted against beasts from other galaxies. Also robots and androids are programmed to fight my people in the Gaming Arena.

BLUE: Where's that at?

WILLIE: Right here in the East. [*He draws another area of light with his finger*] Many of my people are slaughtered each year in the tournaments.

CISCO: Don't they ever win?

WILLIE: It has only happened once and the Silent Ones were so impressed and stunned that they allowed the man his freedom but kept him still under the control of the Hand.

BLUE: Well, what happened to him? Where's he now?

WILLIE: Right here. It is me they set free.

CISCO: You? Hot dog! You must be a mean hombre, Willie.

BLUE: But how come they let you go?

WILLIE: The Silent Ones believed I could not survive the Southland and the Lagoon Baboon. Plus they still had control over me with the Hand. They thought if I was to return to my people I would cause trouble so rather than kill me they played another game.

Voice of the KID *yelling from behind the car. He comes out into the open with his hands raised and his pants still down and* SYCAMORE *right behind him with his gun out.*

KID: Wait a minute! Wait a minute! Please. I don't mean to bother you. I just couldn't sleep and I heard you talking so I came over. I just wanted to listen.

SYCAMORE: He's heard the whole shootin' match.

CISCO: I told you once, boy. How come you didn't listen?

KID: I know, but I can help you. I want to come with you.

SYCAMORE: I say we put a bullet through his head.

BLUE: Now wait a minute, Sycamore.

WILLIE: What makes you say you could help us?

KID: I know about that kind of fighting. I learned it in school.

SYCAMORE: Come on. He's seen our whole hand.

BLUE: Hear him out.

KID: Three things: Constant movement, absolute mistrust and eternal vigilance. Movement: that is, never stay put; never spend two nights in the same place; never stop moving from one place to another. Mistrust: at the beginning mistrust even your own shadow, friendly peasants, informants, guides, contacts; mistrust everything until you hold a liberated zone. Vigilance: constant guard duty, constant reconnaissance; establishment of a camp in a safe place and, above all, never sleep beneath a roof, never sleep in a house where you can be surrounded.

CISCO: I'll be damned.

WILLIE: And how does this apply to our mission? We go to free prisoners, not to start a revolution.

CISCO: Yeah.

KID: The two are inseparable. Freedom and revolution are inextricably bound up. To free the oppressed you must get rid of the oppressor. This constitutes revolution. And the surest means to victory is guerrilla warfare. This has held true for hundreds of years.

WILLIE: Then you see no other way to liberate my people than to make war with the Silent Ones?

KID: Exactly.

SYCAMORE: Keep those hands up.

CISCO: And pull up yer pants, fer Christ's sake.

The KID *goes to pull up his pants.*

SYCAMORE: I told ya' to keep yer hands raised.

KID: Well, I can't do both.

BLUE: Let him pull up his pants, Sycamore.

SYCAMORE: This here is a spy in case you forgot. I say we plug him right here and now.

BLUE: And I say we let him pull up his doggone pants!

CISCO: What do you say, Willie?

WILLIE: I have come to find any means possible to free my people. If he has information we should listen.

SYCAMORE: O.K. But keep yer hands high, mister.

The KID *talks with his hands raised and his pants down. The others listen.*

KID: First of all you need more men. A guerrilla unit should be small but four or five is not enough to be fully effective.

BLUE: Well, let's see, there's Red Diamond.

CISCO: And Slim and Shadow. We could get them easy.

SYCAMORE: What about Fatback?

CISCO: Yeah. And then there's Sloe Gin Martin, Cat Man Kelly, Booger Montgomery, the Mouse, Mojo Moses—

KID: That's enough. Ten to fifteen is all you'll need in the initial stages. It's important to remember that what you're organizing is more than a gang of bandits. Guerrilla warfare is a war of the masses, a war of the people. The guerrilla band is an armed nucleus, the fighting vanguard of the people. It draws its great force from the mass of the people themselves. Bandit gangs have all the characteristics of a guerrilla army, homogeneity, respect for the

leader, valor, knowledge of the ground and often even good understanding of the tactics to be employed. The only thing missing is support of the people and inevitably these gangs are captured and exterminated by the public force.

WILLIE: But the people you speak of, the masses, in this case are all held prisoner.

KID: Then you must liberate a few for reinforcements.

BLUE: How?

KID: Hit and run, wait, lie in ambush, again hit and run, and thus repeatedly, without giving any rest to the enemy. The blows should be continuous. The enemy ought not to be allowed to sleep. At every moment the impression ought to be created that he is surrounded by a complete circle.

SYCAMORE: Keep those hands high.

WILLIE: Go on.

KID: Acts of sabotage are very important. It is necessary to distinguish between sabotage and terrorism, a measure that is generally ineffective and indiscriminate in its results, since it often makes victims of innocent people and destroys a large number of lives that would be valuable to the revolution. Sabotage should be of two types: sabotage on a national scale against determined objectives, and local sabotage against lines of combat. Sabotage on a national scale should be aimed principally at destroying communications. The guerrilla is a night combatant. He thrives in the dark, while the enemy is afraid of the dark. He must be cunning and able to march unnoticed to the place of attack, across plains or mountains, and then fall upon the enemy, taking advantage of the factor of surprise. After causing panic by this surprise he should launch himself into the fight implacably without permitting a single weakness in his companions and taking advantage of every sign of weakness in the enemy. Striking like a tornado, destroying all, giving no quarter unless the tactical circumstances call for it, judging those who must be judged, sowing panic among the enemy, he nevertheless treats defenseless prisoners benevolently and shows respect for the dead.

BLUE: Now I say we let him pull his pants up.

CISCO: Yeah, let him, Sycamore. What the hell.

SYCAMORE: All right. Pull 'em up but nice and slow.

The KID *very slowly bends down and goes to pull up his pants. He gets them halfway up then suddenly kicks* SYCAMORE *in the balls and grabs his gun.* SYCAMORE *falls on the ground holding his crotch and groaning. The* KID *holds the gun on all of them.*

CISCO: What the hell!

KID: All right! Now up, all of you! Get your hands up! Don't try anything or I'll shoot. Honest I will. All I'll have to tell the cops is I caught a bunch of subversives right in the act. They wouldn't think twice. In fact they'd probably call me a hero. [*They all raise their hands*]

SYCAMORE: I told you! I told ya' we shoulda' killed the bastard.

KID: He's right, you know.

BLUE: Well, you sure disappointed me, boy.

KID: Why? What do I owe you?

BLUE: Here I thought you was gonna lead us on to victory and all.

CISCO: Yeah, me too. The way you was talkin'. . . .

KID: Shut up! Don't say anything more or I'll kill all of you! I mean it.

CISCO: Ya' really ought to pull yer pants up though. It don't look right.

KID: Shut up!

CISCO: I mean we're your prisoners and you got yer pants pulled down like yer about to get whooped or something.

The KID struggles to pull up his pants with one hand while he holds the gun on them with the other. He gets them up around his waist and hangs on to them with one hand.

KID: You better shut up!

WILLIE: Don't tease him.

CISCO: That's right. He's had a rough night.

BLUE: What you gonna' do now, boy? How ya' gonna go fer help?

KID: We'll wait until morning. There'll be plenty of trucks.

BLUE: Yer gonna' tell 'em you captured a bunch a' subversives single handed, huh?

KID: That's right! And everything else too. How you were planning to take over Azusa.

SYCAMORE starts laughing hysterically, then screams with pain, then back to laughter. The others join in laughing except for WILLIE, who watches.

SYCAMORE: Azusa!

CISCO: That's a good one! "Everything from A to Z in the USA." Yeah boy!

In the background the old "C" "A" "F" "G" Rock and Roll chords are played to the KID's speech.

KID: Shut up! Shut up! I'll kill you all! I'll kill you! This is my home! Don't make fun of my home. I was born and raised here and I'll die here! I love it! That's something you can't understand! I love Azusa! I love the foothills

and the drive in movies and the bowling alleys and the football games and the drag races and the girls and the donut shop and the High School and the Junior College and the outdoor track meets and the parades and the Junior Chamber of Commerce and the Key Club and the Letterman's Club and the Kiwanis and the Safeway Shopping Center and the freeway and the pool hall and the Bank of America and the Post Office and the Presbyterian [*They laugh louder and louder as KID keeps on*] church and the Laundromat and the liquor store and the miniature golf course and Lookout Point and the YMCA and the Glee Club and the basketball games and the sock hop and graduation and the prom and the cafeteria and the principal's office and Chemistry class and the country fair and peanut butter and jelly sandwiches and the High School band and going steady and KFWB and white bucks and pegger pants and argyle socks and madras shorts and butch wax and Hobie boards and going to the beach and getting drunk and swearing and reading dirty books and smoking in the men's room and setting off cherry bombs and fixing up my car and my Mom, I love my Mom most of all. And you creeps aren't going to take that away from me. You're not going to take that away from me because I'll kill you first! I'll kill every one of you if it's the last thing I do!

They stop laughing. WILLIE goes into a trance, speaking a strange ancient language. The others watch.

WILLIE: Od i gniht tsal eht sti fi uoy fo eno yreve llik lli. Tsrif ouy llik lli esuaceb em morf yawa taht ekat ot gniog ton eruoy. Em morf yawa taht ekat ot gniog tnera speerc uoy dna. Lla fo tsom mom ym evol i mom ym dna rac ym pu gnixif dna sbmob yrrehc ffo gnittes dna moor . . .

KID: Shut up, you! Shut up!

WILLIE: . . . snem eht ni gnikoms dna skoob ytrid gnidaer dna gniraews dna knurd gnitteg dna hcaeb eht ot gniog dna sdraob eiboh dna xaw hctub dna strohs sardam dna skcos elygra dna stnap reggep dna skcub etihw dna bwfk dna . . . [*The KID fires the pistol into WILLIE but WILLIE keeps on speaking and getting very weird*] . . . ydaets gniog dna dnab loohcs hgih eht dna sehciwdnas yllej dna rettub tunaep dna riaf yrtnuoc eht dna ssalc yrtsimehc . . .

KID: Shut up! [*The KID fires again. WILLIE keeps on*]

WILLIE: . . . dna eciffo slapicnirp eht dna airetefac eht dna morp eht dna noitaudarg dna poh kcos eht dna semag . . . [*The KID empties the gun into WILLIE but WILLIE con-*

tinues, accumulating incredible power from the language he speaks] ... Ilabteksah eht dna bulc eelg eht dna acmy eht dna tniop tuokool dna esruoc flog erutainim eht dna erots rouqil eht dna tamordnual eht dna hcruhc nairet-ybserp eht dna eciffo tsop eht dna acirema fo knab eht dna llah loop eht dna yaweerf eht dna retnec gnippohs yawefas eht dna bulc snamrettel eht dna bulc key eht dna ecremmoc fo rebmahc roinuj ...

The KID *screams and holds his hands to his ears. His whole body twitches and writhes as* WILLIE *did when the hand grabbed him.*

KID: Stop it! Stop it! I can't—No! No more! Stop!

WILLIE: ... eht dna sedarap eht dna steem kcart roodtuo eht dna egelloc roinuj eht dna loohcs hgih eht dna pohs tunod eht dna slrig eht dna secar gard eht dna semag llabtoof eht dna syella gnilwob eht dna sievom ni evird eht dna sllihtoof eht evol i ...

KID: No! No! My head! My brain! Stop it! [*He falls to the ground holding his head and writhing, screaming for mercy*]

WILLIE: Asuza evol i. Dnatsrednu tnac uoy gnihtemos staht. Ti evol i. Ereh desiar dna nrob saw i. Emoh ym fo nuf ekam tnod. Emoh ym si siht. Uoy, llik lli. Lla noy llik lli. Pu tuhs! Pu tuhs! Free! Free! Free! Free! Free! Free!

[WILLIE *goes into an elated dance as the* KID *screams on the floor. Very gradually dayglo painted ping pong balls start to fall from the ceiling passing through black light as they fall and bouncing on the stage as* WILLIE *screams "Free" over and over again and dances*]

BLUE: Willie! What's goin' on!

WILLIE: I have discovered their secret! The Hand is in my control! I have the Hand! We are free! Free! Free!

KID: My brain! I can't stand it!

WILLIE: My people are free! Nogoland is exploding! The Silent Ones are dying! Look! Look at the sky!

As they look up at the sky more and more ping pong balls fall, dayglo strips of paper flutter to the ground. CISCO *joins* WILLIE *in his dance and yells "free" with him.* SYCAMORE *and* BLUE *look at the sky.* SYCAMORE *takes off his hat and catches the balls and throws them up in the air.* BLUE *joins in.*

CISCO: Free! Free! Yipeee! Wahoooo! Alaman left and swing her low! Catch her on the backside and watch her glow!

BLUE: Then we don't have to go to no other galaxy after all. We can stay right here!

SYCAMORE: We're free! Free!

KID: No! My brain!

WILLIE: It was all in my brain the whole time. In my mind. The ancient language of the Nogo. Right in my brain. I've destroyed them by breaking free of the Hand. They have no control. We can do what we want! We're free to do what we want.

BLUE: Let's have us a party, Willie.

CISCO: Sure, we'll invite the old gang. You can call them all back, Willie. You've got the power.

WILLIE: So have you. Do it yourself. Do whatever you want. I've got to leave.

BLUE: How come?

SYCAMORE: You just got here, I thought.

WILLIE: My people need me now more than ever. Now we can start to build our own world.

BLUE: What's a' matter with this one?

WILLIE: I am a visitor here. I came for help. This is your world. Do what you want with it.

CISCO: But we're strangers too. We're lost, Willie.

WILLIE: Good luck.

BLUE: Wait!

WILLIE *exits. The* KID *is frozen in an attitude of terror.*

SYCAMORE: Well of all the damn nerve. He just used us.

CISCO: What're we gonna' do now?

BLUE: Anything.

CISCO: Stop talkin' like him, dammit. We're in some pickle, Blue. It's gonna' be mornin' and here we are stuck in some other century in some hick town called Azusa somewheres.

BLUE: "Everything from A to Z in the USA." That's us all right.

CISCO: Stop saying that over and over all the time!

SYCAMORE: What do you mean, "That's us all right"?

BLUE: Now they got us thrown in to boot.

CISCO: And I ain't so sure they're gonna go fer the idea. He sure didn't.

SYCAMORE: What're we gonna do with him anyway?

CISCO: I say we plug him.

BLUE: He's free like us.

SYCAMORE: Free to kill us, ya' mean.

CISCO: Yeah, or turn us in to the law.

BLUE: If you waste him there's gonna be a dozen more to take his place. Look at him. He's as good as dead anyway.

CISCO: He's right, Sycamore.

SYCAMORE: I don't know. Can't seem to think straight. Who runs this town anyhow? That's the dude to go to. Straight to the top.

BLUE: The mayor?

SYCAMORE: The mayor.

BLUE: He runs the cops. The governor runs the mayor.

SYCAMORE: The governor. What's his name?

BLUE: Congress runs the governor. President runs the Congress.

SYCAMORE: What's his name? We gotta get outa' this.

CISCO: We could hide in the drainage ditch.

SYCAMORE: Yeah, we could sit it out. We ain't done nothin' wrong.

CISCO: We could change our names. Get a haircut, some new threads. Blend right in.

SYCAMORE: That's it. That's the ticket. I could get me an office job easy enough.

CISCO: Sure. Western Union. Pacific Gas and Electric. Plenty of places.

SYCAMORE: Settle down with a nice little pension. Get me a car maybe.

CISCO: Yeah boy, And one a' them lawnmowers ya' sit on like a tractor.

SYCAMORE: Sure. We could fit right into the scheme a' things. Don't have to bust our balls for nobody. What do ya' say, Blue?

BLUE: Whatever you boys want. I'm gonna be long gone by mornin'.

CISCO: What do you mean, Blue?

BLUE: I'm leavin'. I been hangin' around this dump for twenty years. Seems about time to get the lead out. [*He moves toward the car and pulls the suitcase out of the back seat*]

CISCO: But where you gonna go? What you gonna' do?

BLUE: I'll answer them questions when they come up. Right now I just gotta move. That's all I know.

CISCO: Well, let me come with ya' then. Please, Blue.

BLUE: All right.

CISCO: Sycamore? You comin'? We oughta' stick together since we're brothers and all.

SYCAMORE: Naw, thanks anyway. Think I'll stay awhile.

CISCO: All right. So long then.

BLUE: Sorry it didn't work out like you want, Syc. . . .

SYCAMORE: Don't matter. Seemed unreal from the start anyhow.

BLUE: Yeah. I know what you mean.

SYCAMORE: You boys go ahead on and take care, ya' hear. Don't worry about me.

CISCO: Good luck, Syc.

SYCAMORE: Yeah. You too.

BLUE: Peace.

BLUE *and* CISCO *exit.* SYCAMORE *looks down at the* KID, *still frozen grotesquely. He stares at the* KID's *face and slowly becomes older and older just with his body. He turns to the Chevy and talks to an imaginary driver as* BLUE *did in the beginning.*

SYCAMORE: [*In ancient voice*] Well now. Well. Sure is decent of ya' stoppin' so late of an evenin' fer an old wreck like me. Yes sir. Mighty decent. Cars get to rollin' by here, eighty, ninety, a hundred mile an hour. Don't even see the landscape. Just a blur. Just a blue blur. Can't figure it. Wouldn't hardly call it a vacation now, would ya'. Screamin' out to Desert Hot Springs, back to Napa Valley. Don't even see the country. Not to speak of. Most folks is too scared, I guess. That's what it mounts up to. A certain terrorism in the air. A night terror. That's what's got 'em all locked up goin' so fast they can't see. Me, I'm slow by nature. I got nothin' agin' speed now, mind yo'. I've done plenty a speed in my time to know the taste good and well. Speed's a pleasure. Yes sir. Naw, that ain't it. Mind if I grab yer back seat here so's I can curl up? Feet are awful dogged. Good. Mighty kind. Mighty kind. [*He opens the door of the Chevy and slowly climbs in the back seat. The lights fade slowly as he gradually disappears in the back while he talks*] It's just a hankerin' to take stock a' things. A man's gotta be still long enough to figure out his next move. Know what I mean? Like in checkers, fer example. Can't just plunge in. Gotta make plans. Figure out yer moves. Make sure they're yer own moves and not someone else's. That's the great thing about this country, ya' know. The fact that you can make yer own moves in yer own time without some guy behind the scenes pullin' the switches on ya'. May be a far cry from bein' free, but it sure comes closer than most anything I've seen. Me, I don't yearn fer much any more but to live out my life with a little peace and quiet. I done my bit, God knows. God knows that much. There comes a time to let things by. Just let 'em go by. Let the world alone. It'll take care of itself. Just let it be.

As SYCAMORE *disappears the lights fade out. Guitar music accompanies ending speech.*

BLUEBEARD

a melodrama in three acts

Charles Ludlam

Bluebeard was first presented by The Ridiculous Theatrical Company at La Mama ETC, New York City, on March 26, 1970, with the following cast:

SHEEMISH	*John Brockmeyer*
MRS. MAGGOT	*Eleven*
KHANAZAR VON BLUEBEARD	*Charles Ludlam*
GOOD ANGEL	*James Morfogen*
BAD ANGEL	*Fredrick "Dude" Teper*
SYBIL	*Black-Eyed Susan*
RODNEY	*Bill Vehr*
MISS CUBBIDGE	*Lola Pashalinski*
LAMIA "THE LEOPARD WOMAN"	*Mario Montez*
HECATE	*Lohr Wilson*
HER TRAIN	*James Morfogen, Fredrick "Dude" Teper*

It was directed by the author. Settings by Christopher Scott and Sam Yahn; lighting by Leandro Katz; costumes by Mary Brecht. Music and sound by David Scott.

ACT ONE: THE EAVESDROPPER

*Scene: The alchemical laboratory of Dr. Blue-
beard, located on an island off the coast of
Maine. The house is a lighthouse still in use.
Revolving light, test tubes and other laboratory
equipment including an operating table.
SHEEMISH, the butler, and MRS. MAGGOT, the
housekeeper, are dusting and sweeping. MRS.
MAGGOT bumps the table, causing a test tube
to fall and break.*

Scene 1.   SHEEMISH, MRS. MAGGOT

SHEEMISH: Now see what you've done! Clean it
up at once. For if Khanazar, the Bluebeard,
finds anything broken, he will surely send you
to the House of Pain.

MRS. MAGGOT: [*Terribly frightened*] No, no, not
the House of Pain!

SHEEMISH: [*Sadistically*] Yes, yes, the House of
Pain. If I should mention the fact that you
broke this little glass tube, I'm sure the master
would send you to the House of Pain.

MRS. MAGGOT: [*More frightened*] No, no, not the
House of Pain! Please, Sheemish, don't tell, I
beg of you.

SHEEMISH: [*Calculatingly*] Very well. I will not
tell . . . as long as you realize that I am doing
you a favor . . . and that I will expect a favor
in return.

MRS. MAGGOT: Anything, I'll do anything you
ask, but please, please do not tell.

SHEEMISH: Replace the little glass tube. Substitute something for the sticky liquid inside. Do
this quickly, for the good ship *Lady Vain* will
dock here at three o'clock this afternoon, drop
off a female passenger and return to the mainland. We must prepare the guest room for
tonight . . . and the bridal chamber for tomorrow.

MRS. MAGGOT: You mean he's found another,
another [*She begins to weep*] . . . ?

SHEEMISH: Say it, Mrs. Maggot! Wife! Say it:
Wife! Wife! Wife!

MRS. MAGGOT: I can't. I can't bear to say it.
[*Falling to her knees*] Lord of my prayers!
God of my sacrifice! Because you have done
this thing, you shall lack both my fear and my
praise. I shall not wince at your lightnings nor
be awed when you go by.

SHEEMISH: Curse not our god, Khanazar, the
Bluebeard.

MRS. MAGGOT: Why should I not curse him who
has stolen from me the gardens of my childhood?

SHEEMISH: Remember the House of Pain and
hold your tongue. You have replaced the little

glass tube. It looks exactly as it did before the
little accident. Even the liquid is the same
color and viscosity. You and I are the only
ones who know. Come, the guest room. And,
Mrs. Maggot, forget about the past.

MRS. MAGGOT: Since the operation I can't remember it anyway.

SHEEMISH: And think as I do, of the future.

MRS. MAGGOT:
    The future is so very far.
    The present is what must be feared.
    For we are slaves of Khanazar,
    And dread the wrath of the Bluebeard.

Scene 2.   LAMIA THE LEOPARD WOMAN

*Enter LAMIA THE LEOPARD WOMAN, wearing
more leopard than the costume designer
thought advisable.*

Scene 3.   KHANAZAR THE BLUEBEARD

BLUEBEARD: [*Entering and seeing* LAMIA] I
thought I told you never to come to this side
of the island again? [*Draws gun and fires.
Lamia runs out*] Give up your passions, Bluebeard, and become the thing you claim to be.
Is to end desire desire's chiefest end? Does sex
afford no greater miracles? Have all my perversions and monstrosities, my fuckings and
suckings led me to this? This little death at the
climax followed by slumber? Yet chastity
ravishes me. And yet the cunt gapes like the
jaws of hell, an unfathomable abyss; or the
boy-ass used to buggery spread wide to swallow me up its bung; or the mouth sucking out
my life! Aaagh! If only there were some new
and gentle genital that would combine with
me and, mutually interpenetrated, steer me
through this storm in paradise! [*The sound of
a foghorn*] They said I was mad at medical
school. They said no third genital was possible. Yang and yin, male and female and
that's that. [*Laughs maniacally*] Science suits
a mercenary drudge who aims at nothing but
external trash. Give me a dark art that
stretches as far as does the mind of man; a
sound magician is a demigod.

Foghorn again.

*Scene 4.   GOOD ANGEL, BAD ANGEL,
BLUEBEARD*

GOOD ANGEL:
    On, Bluebeard, lay these thoughts aside,
    And think not on them lest it tempt thy
        soul

And heap God's heavy wrath upon thee.
Take half—one sex, that's all—for that
　is nature's way.

Foghorn.

BAD ANGEL:
Go forward, Bluebeard, in that famous art
Wherein all nature's treasure is contained:
Be thou on earth as God is in the sky,
Master and possessor of both sexes.

Exit ANGELS.

Scene 5.　BLUEBEARD

BLUEBEARD:
Love must be reinvented, that's obvious.
Sex to me no longer is mysterious
And so I swear that while my beard is blue,
I'll twist some human flesh into a
　genital new.

*Scene 6.　BLUEBEARD, SHEEMISH,
MRS. MAGGOT*

SHEEMISH: Master, Master.

BLUEBEARD: [*Enraged*] Swine! How dare you enter my room without knocking? [*Lashes whip*] Have you forgotten the House of Pain?

SHEEMISH: [*Clutching his genitals*] No, no, not the House of Pain! Mercy, Master.

BLUEBEARD: How can I show you mercy when I am merciless with myself? I see in you nothing but my own failure; another experiment down the drain.

SHEEMISH: [*On his knees pathetically*] Forgive me. [*Whimpers*]

BLUEBEARD: Aaagh, get up. Tell me what you want.

SHEEMISH: The good ship *Lady Vain* has docked here on the rocky side of the island.

BLUEBEARD: [*Anticipating*] Yes . . .

SHEEMISH: There are two women . . .

BLUEBEARD: [*In ecstasy*] Ah, resolve me of all ambiguities. Perform what desperate enterprises I will!

MRS. MAGGOT: And a man.

BLUEBEARD: Huh? A man? There is no man! [*Lashes her with whip*] You are mistaken, there is no man.

Loud knocking at the door.

MRS. MAGGOT: It's them.

SHEEMISH: [*Correcting her*] It is they.

BLUEBEARD: [*Looking through spy hole*] Sybil said nothing about a man. [*Loud knocking,*

howling wind and the sound of rain] Go away! Go away! Leave me in peace!

*Scene 7.　BLUEBEARD, SHEEMISH, MRS.
MAGGOT, RODNEY PARKER, SYBIL,
MISS FLORA CUBBIDGE.*

RODNEY'S VOICE: Baron Bluebeard, please open the door!

BLUEBEARD: Leave me alone! Go away!

SYBIL'S VOICE: Dear Uncle, please let us in for the love of God. It's bitter without.

BLUEBEARD: [*Aside*] And I am bitter within!

MISS CUBBIDGE'S VOICE: We'll catch our death of cold!

MRS. MAGGOT: [*In confusion*] What should we do, Master?

SHEEMISH: [*Calling down from a lookout point*] We must let them in for their ship, the *Lady Vain,* its sails big-bellied, makes way from our port. I think it will go down in the storm.

BLUEBEARD: Aagh, very well, come in then. But you can't stay. [*Opens the door*]

Enter SYBIL, RODNEY *and* CUBBIDGE, *wet.*

SYBIL: [*Rushing to Bluebeard*] Oh Uncle Khanazar, my dear Uncle Khanazar, why wouldn't you let us in? How glad I am to see you. Who would have thought of you?

BLUEBEARD: Why, Sybil, I hope you always thought of me.

SYBIL: Dear Uncle, so I do; but I meant to say of seeing you—I never dreamed I would while you were quartered here at . . . at . . . what is the name of this island anyway?

BLUEBEARD: [*Lying*] I don't believe it has a name. I've never thought to give it one.

RODNEY: The sailors called it "The Island of Lost Love."

SYBIL: It's true our ship was almost lost in the fog.

RODNEY: And we are in love.

BLUEBEARD: [*Aside*] Grrrr!

SYBIL: Oh, excuse me, Uncle, this is my fiancé, Rodney Parker.

BLUEBEARD: [*Icily*] Howdyedo?

RODNEY: [*Running off at the mouth*] Sybil has told me so much about you. She says you were the great misunderstood genius at medical school. But that you suddenly gave it all up, threw it all away to live here in almost total seclusion. . . .

SYBIL: [*Interrupting*] And this is Miss Cubbidge, my beloved traveling companion and tutor.

MISS CUBBIDGE: [*Shaking his hand violently*] I am incensed to meet you, Baron Bluebeard.

Sybil told me that you were with her father at medical school when the terrible fire . . .

BLUEBEARD: [*Flaring up*] Don't squeeze my hand! I work with my hands. [*Then politely*] If you will excuse me. I expected only one guest. [*Turning to* MRS. MAGGOT *and* SHEEMISH, *who bow with sinister smiles*] Now there are extra preparations to be made. Mrs. Maggot and Sheemish will show you to your rooms. [*Kisses* SYBIL'S *hand, shakes* MISS CUBBIDGE'S *hand and ignores* RODNEY'S *hand*] We will sup when the moon rises over Mount Agdora. [*Exits*]

RODNEY: Did you see that? I offered him my hand, but he refused it.

SYBIL: I'm sure Uncle Khanazar meant nothing by it. He's so involved in his work and he's unused to human companionship.

Scene 8. *SYBIL, RODNEY, CUBBIDGE, MAGGOT, SHEEMISH*

RODNEY: [*Aside to* SYBIL] What about these serving people he keeps around here?

SYBIL: [*Aside to* RODNEY *and* CUBBIDGE] Yes, of course. [*Then strangely*] But then they hardly seem human, do they?

MRS. MAGGOT: [*Dykey*] This way to the washroom, ladies. Follow me to the washroom, ladies.

MISS CUBBIDGE: Shall we wash away that which we acquiesced during our long adjunct? I refer, of course, to the dust of travel.

SYBIL: Until dinner, Rodney dear.

RODNEY: Sybil, there is something that I must discuss with you.

SYBIL: Excuse me until then, dear Rodney, I must freshen up. [*Throws him a kiss and exits*]

Scene 9. *RODNEY, SHEEMISH*

RODNEY: Ah, I'm convinced of it! Sybil is in love with him.

SHEEMISH: With whom?

RODNEY: Excuse me, I was thinking aloud. Thinking, thinking, thinking, that's all I ever do. My head thunders with thinking. I must stop thinking. I needs must shout it. [*Very loud*] Why did she come here? To look for him. Nothing I could do but she must come to look for him. I think this jealousy will drive me mad!

SHEEMISH: Shall I tell you between our two selves what I think of it? I'm afraid she'll get little return for her love; her journey to this foggy island will be useless.

RODNEY: [*Overjoyed*] But what is the reason? Do tell me, Sheemish, what makes you take such a gloomy view of the situation?

SHEEMISH: His feelings are cold.

RODNEY: [*Enraged again*] You think he will betray her innocent love?

SHEEMISH: He has no heart, that man.

RODNEY: But how could a gentleman do such a vile thing?

SHEEMISH: I have been his servant on this island 19 years and I will say this—just between us—that in my master, Baron Khanazar, the Bluebeard, you see the vilest scoundrel that ever cumbered the earth, a madman, a cur, a devil, a Turk, a heretic, who believes in neither Heaven, Hell, nor werewolf: he lives like an animal, like a swinish gourmet, a veritable vermin infesting his environs and shuttering his ears to every Christian remonstrance, and turning to ridicule everything we believe in.

RODNEY: But surely there's nothing between them. He wouldn't marry his own niece, Sybil. What a ridiculous idea! [*Laughs*]

SHEEMISH: [*Ominously and with candor*] Believe me, to satisfy his passion he would have gone further than that, he would have married you as well and her dog and cat into the bargain. Marriage means nothing to him. It is his usual method of ensnaring women! [*Sound of footsteps*] But here he comes taking a turn in the palace. Let us separate—what I have spoken I have spoken in confidence. I am his slave, but a master who has given himself over to wickedness is a thing to be dreaded. If you repeat a word of this to him, I will swear you made it up.

Exit RODNEY.

Scene 10. *SHEEMISH, BLUEBEARD*

BLUEBEARD: I have been in my laboratory putting things in readiness, for I have found the ideal subject for my next experiment . . . or should I say my next work of art?

SHEEMISH: [*With dread*] Oh, Master.

BLUEBEARD: What is it?

SHEEMISH: I'm afraid. I'm afraid. I'm afraid. [*Leaps into* BLUEBEARD'S *arms*]

BLUEBEARD: [*Throwing him off*] Down, down, you fool. Never mind the disagreeable things that may happen. Let us think of the pleasant ones. This girl is almost the most charming creature imaginable. Add to that a few of my innovations! I never saw two people so devoted, so completely in love. The manifest tenderness of their mutual affection inspired a like feeling in me. It affected me deeply.

My love began as jealousy. I couldn't bear to see them so happy together; vexation stimulated my desire and I realized what a pleasure it would give me to disturb their mutual understanding and break up an attachment so repugnant to my own susceptibilities.

SHEEMISH: Have you no desire for Miss Cubbidge?

BLUEBEARD: She is not without a certain cadaverous charm. [*Footsteps*] Shhh! Quickly, the spy hole, see who it is.

SHEEMISH: The sun is in my eyes, but I know the sound of her footsteps. It is only Mrs. Maggot.

Scene 11.   MRS. MAGGOT, SHEEMISH

MRS. MAGGOT *and* SHEEMISH *bring on a table and chairs. Then they set the table for dinner.*

MRS. MAGGOT: [*Carrying in a platter*] Yum, yum, yum . . . I'm nibbling . . . yum . . . mutton good! Lovely . . . yum . . . yum . . . yum.

SHEEMISH: It is the first time meat has been seen in the palace in 19 years.

MRS. MAGGOT: Twenty for me! Twenty years and never any meat. I've withered. You fed yourself on the fat in your hump, didn't you? Ach. Ouf. [*She is seized by a violent coughing fit*] Swallowed the wrong way.

SHEEMISH: Heaven has punished you, glutton. Stop, before you eat the knives and the tablecloth.

MRS. MAGGOT: My illness, not my sin! Look, Sheemish, a chicken! Ah, the drumstick! [*With her mouth full*] Those who have a stomach, eat; those who have a hump, glue themselves to keyholes.

SHEEMISH: Watch what you say to me. My hump contains a second brain to think my evil thoughts for me. It hasn't forgotten the broken test tube and our little secret.

MRS. MAGGOT: You must teach me to spy through keyholes. Which eye does one use, the right or the left? They say in time one's eye becomes shaped like a keyhole. I prefer eavesdropping. There, see my ear, a delicate shell. [*She shows her ear trumpet*]

SHEEMISH: When others are present you are as deaf as a bat—but when we are alone you are cured and hear perfectly.

MRS. MAGGOT: It's a miracle! Look at that pork chop!

SHEEMISH: [*Grabs her and throws her onto the table. Climbing on top of her, he forces a huge piece of meat into her mouth*] Here, glutton, eat this! Someday your mouth will be full of

maggots and greenish pus. [*Laughter of the dinner guests is heard off*] But here come the guests to dinner. Let us have a truce until the next time that we are alone.

MRS. MAGGOT: Peace!

Scene 12.   MRS. MAGGOT, SHEEMISH, BLUEBEARD, RODNEY, SYBIL, MISS CUBBIDGE

The dinner guests and BLUEBEARD *enter.* MRS. MAGGOT *and* SHEEMISH *just manage to get off the table in the nick of time.* MISS CUBBIDGE *enters on* BLUEBEARD'S *arm,* SYBIL *on* RODNEY'S *arm.*

BLUEBEARD: Work, work, work. I have thought of nothing else these 19 years. My work, my work, and nothing else.

SYBIL: Beware, Uncle, all work and no play makes Jack a dull boy.

MISS CUBBIDGE: True, Sybil, but all play and no work makes Jack a mere toy.

BLUEBEARD: No danger there. I never cease in my experimenting. My dream is to remake Man. A new man with new possibilities for love.

SYBIL: "Love for a man is a thing apart. 'Tis woman's whole existence."

MISS CUBBIDGE: [*Applauding*] Lord Byron!

BLUEBEARD: Won't you all be seated? [BLUEBEARD *seats* MISS CUBBIDGE *at the table.* RODNEY *seats* SYBIL]

MRS. MAGGOT: [*To* SYBIL] Why, dearie, what an unusual locket.

SYBIL: Yes. It's Lapis Lazuli. My Mother gave it to me the night she died when the terrible fire . . .

MISS CUBBIDGE: [*Interrupting*] Don't, Sybil. . . .

SYBIL: I never knew my mother.

RODNEY: Strange, all the places are set to one side of the table.

BLUEBEARD: That is because of a little surprise I have for you. There will be an entertainment tonight while we are taking our evening meal, a little play I wrote myself.

SYBIL: What, a play?

RODNEY: Jolly!

MISS CUBBIDGE: Wrote it yourself? You've a touch of erosion, I see, Baron. And yet you studied medicine?

BLUEBEARD: I write for amusement only.

MISS CUBBIDGE: Were you indoctrinated? I mean, did you receive the Doctorate? On what theme did you write your dissipation? Which degree did you receive?

BLUEBEARD: I received the third degree.

MRS. MAGGOT *places a platter of meat on the table.*

RODNEY: This meat looks delicious.

BLUEBEARD: [*Having a seizure*] Meat? Meat? [*Turning on* MRS. MAGGOT] You dare to serve them meat?

MRS. MAGGOT: Eh?

BLUEBEARD: [*In a blind rage*] Take it away at once, blockhead! Do you want to ruin my experiment? [*He throws the meat at* MRS. MAGGOT *and then leaps up on the dinner table like a wild man, roaring*] What is the Law?

MRS. MAGGOT and SHEEMISH: [*Bowing before him as though he were an idol on an altar, they link their arms together and chant, swaying back and forth rhythmically*] We are not men. We are not women. We are not men. We are not women. His is the hand that makes. We are not men. We are not women. His is the House of Pain. We are not men. We are not women. That is the Law!

BLUEBEARD: [*Rolling his eyes savagely*] Now get out! [*Turning on the guests*] All of you!

MISS CUBBIDGE: [*Horrified*] What about dinner?

BLUEBEARD: I've lost my appetite!

RODNEY: What about the play?

BLUEBEARD: I detest avant-garde theater.

Scene 13.   BLUEBEARD, MISS CUBBIDGE, SYBIL, RODNEY, SHEEMISH, MRS. MAGGOT, LAMIA

The face of LAMIA THE LEOPARD WOMAN, *appears at the window.*

RODNEY: Look, there's a face at the window!

MISS CUBBIDGE *screams.* SYBIL *faints in* RODNEY'S *arms.* BLUEBEARD *fires his revolver at* LAMIA: Tableau vivant. The curtain falls.

ACT II

Scene 1.   SYBIL, RODNEY

SYBIL: Rodney, you have come to speak to me about my letter to you.

RODNEY: Yes, you could have told me face to face. People living in the same house, even when they are the only people living on a deserted island, as we are, can be further apart than if they lived 50 miles asunder in the country.

SYBIL: I have thought much of what I then wrote and I feel sure that we had better . . .

RODNEY: Stop, Sybil . . . do not speak hurriedly, love. Shall I tell you what I learned from your letter?

SYBIL: Yes, tell me if you think it is better that you should do so.

RODNEY: I learned that something had made you melancholy since we came to this island. There are few of us who do not encounter, every now and again, some of that irrational spirit of sadness which, when overindulged, leads men to madness and self-destruction. Since I have loved you I have banished it utterly. Do not speak under the influence of that spirit until you have thought whether you too can banish it.

SYBIL: I have tried, but it will not be banished.

RODNEY: Try again, Sybil, if you love me. If you do not . . .

SYBIL: If I do not love you, I love no one upon earth. [*Sits quietly, looking into his face*]

RODNEY: I believe it. I believe it as I believe in my own love for you. I trust your love implicitly, Sybil. So come, return with me to the mainland and let us make an early marriage.

SYBIL: [*Strangely, as if in a trance*] No, I cannot do so.

RODNEY: [*Smiling*] Is that melancholy fiend too much for you? Sybil, Sybil, Sybil.

SYBIL: [*Snapping out of it*] You are noble, good, and great. I find myself unfit to be your wife.

RODNEY: Don't quibble, Sybil.

SYBIL: [*Falling to her knees*] I beg your pardon on my knees.

RODNEY: I grant no such pardon. Do you think I will let you go from me in that way? No, love, if you are ill, I will wait till your illness is gone by; and if you will let me, I will be your nurse.

SYBIL: I am not ill. [*Her hands stray unconsciously to her breasts and yoni*]

RODNEY: Not ill with any defined sickness. You do not shake with ague, nor does your head rack you with aching; but yet you must be ill to try to put an end to all that has passed between us for no reason at all.

SYBIL: [*Standing suddenly*] Mr. Parker . . .

RODNEY: [*Deeply hurt*] If you will call me so, I will think it only part of your malady.

SYBIL: Mr. Parker, I can only hope that you will take me at my word. I beg your forgiveness and that our engagement may be over.

RODNEY: No, no, no, Sybil. Never with my consent. I would marry you tomorrow, tomorrow or next month, or the month after. But if it cannot be so, then I will wait . . . unless . . . there is some other man. Yes, that! and that alone would convince me. Only your marriage to another man could convince me that I had lost you. [*He kisses her on the lips*]

SYBIL: [*Turning away and surreptitiously wiping away the kiss*] I cannot convince you in that way.

RODNEY: [*Prissily wipes his lips on a lace hanky, and carefully folds it and replaces it in his breast pocket, relieved*] You will convince me in no other. Have you spoken to your uncle of this yet?

SYBIL: Not as yet.

RODNEY: [*Anxiously*] Do not tell him. It is possible you may have to unsay what you have said.

SYBIL: No, it is not possible.

RODNEY: I think you must leave this island. The foggy air is no good for you. You need the sun, I think. You've grown so pale. You need a change.

SYBIL: Yes, you treat me as though I were partly silly and partly insane, but it is not so. The change you speak of should be in my nature and in yours. [*Rodney shakes his head and smiles. Aside*] He is perfect! Oh, that he were less perfect!

RODNEY: I'll leave you alone for 24 hours to think this over. I advise you not to tell your uncle. But if you do tell him, let me know that you have done so.

SYBIL: Why that?

RODNEY: [*Pressing her hand*] Good night, dearest, dearest Sybil. [*Exits*]

Scene 2. SYBIL, BLUEBEARD

BLUEBEARD: What, Sybil, are you not in bed yet?

SYBIL: Not yet, Uncle Khanazar.

BLUEBEARD: So Rodney Parker has been here. I smell his cologne in the air.

SYBIL: Yes, he has been here.

BLUEBEARD: Is anything the matter, Sybil?

SYBIL: No, Uncle Khanazar, nothing is the matter.

BLUEBEARD: He has not made himself disagreeable, has he?

SYBIL: Not in the least. He never does anything wrong. He may defy man or woman to find fault with him.

BLUEBEARD: So that's it, is it? He is just a shade too good. I have noticed that myself. But it's a fault on the right side.

SYBIL: [*Deeply troubled*] It's no fault, Uncle. If there be any fault, it is not with him.

BLUEBEARD: Being too good is not one of my faults. . . . I am very bad.

SYBIL: [*Starry-eyed*] Are you bad? Are you really bad?

BLUEBEARD: When I am good, I am very, very good; but when I'm bad, I'm not bad. I'm good at being bad. . . . I do it well.

SYBIL: [*Again as if in a trance*] Tonight, at dinner, your words carried me away . . . [*Their lips almost meet but she yawns, breaking the spell, and he yawns sympathetically*] . . . But I am yawning and tired and I will go to bed. Good night, Uncle Khanazar.

BLUEBEARD: Good night, Sybil. [*Aside*] And rest, for a new life awaits you!

Exit SYBIL.

Scene 3. BLUEBEARD, MISS CUBBIDGE

MISS CUBBIDGE: Oh, excuse me. I didn't realize that the parlor was preoccupied. [*Starts out*]

BLUEBEARD: Come in, Miss Cubbidge. I do not desire to be alone.

MISS CUBBIDGE: No, I think I'd better go and leave you to your own devices.

BLUEBEARD: Please stay. I think I know what you are thinking.

MISS CUBBIDGE: I'll do my own thinking, thank you; and my own existing.

BLUEBEARD: Miss Cubbidge, I don't think you like me.

MISS CUBBIDGE: I can sympathize with neither your virtues nor your vices.

BLUEBEARD: What would you say if I told you that I need a wife?

MISS CUBBIDGE: I do not believe in sudden marriages.

BLUEBEARD: People often say that marriage is an important thing and should be much thought of in advance, and marrying people are cautioned that there are many who marry in haste and repent at leisure. I am not sure, however, that marriage may not be pondered over too much; nor do I feel certain that the leisurely repentance does not as often follow the leisurely marriages as it does the rapid ones. Why, you yourself might marry suddenly [*kneeling before her on one knee*] and never regret it at all.

MISS CUBBIDGE: My health might fail me under the effects of so great a change made so late in life.

BLUEBEARD: Miss Cubbidge, how can you live without love?

MISS CUBBIDGE: It is my nature to love many persons a little if I've loved few or none passionately, Baron Bluebeard.

BLUEBEARD: Please, call me Khanazar; and may I call you . . .

MISS CUBBIDGE: [*Shyly*] Flora.

BLUEBEARD: Ah, Flora! It is only possible to be alone with you in nature. All other women destroy the landscape; you alone become part of it.

MISS CUBBIDGE: [*Aside*] Could any woman resist such desuetude? [*Giggling*] Why, Baron Blue . . .

BLUEBEARD: [*Interrupting*] Khanazar.

MISS CUBBIDGE: [*Giggling*] Khanazar.

BLUEBEARD: Flora, you are part of the trees, the sky; you are the dominating goddess of nature. Come to me, Flora, you lovely little fauna, you.

MISS CUBBIDGE: [*Recovering herself*] Mr. Bluebeard, I shall certainly not come to you.

BLUEBEARD: [*Suddenly*] Look, do you see what it is I am holding in my hand?

MISS CUBBIDGE: [*Alarmed*] A revolver!

BLUEBEARD: Take it, press it to my temple and shoot, or say you will be mine.

MISS CUBBIDGE: [*Frightened with the revolver in her hand*] I can't shoot you, but I cannot be yours, either.

BLUEBEARD: It is one or the other. Blow my brains out. I will not live another day without you.

MISS CUBBIDGE: Recuperate your gun at once. It isn't loaded, is it?

BLUEBEARD: Pull the trigger! There are worse things awaiting Man than death.

MISS CUBBIDGE: To what do you collude?

BLUEBEARD: All tortures do not matter . . . only not to be dead before one dies. I will not live without your love. [*He pretends to weep*]

MISS CUBBIDGE: Don't weep, Baron Bluebeard . . . er . . . Khanazar. 'Tisn't manly. Try to be more malevolent.

BLUEBEARD: Marry me, marry me, Flora, and make me the happiest man on earth.

MISS CUBBIDGE: How can I marry you?

BLUEBEARD: [*Hypnotically*] Easily. Just repeat after me. I, Flora Cubbidge . . .

MISS CUBBIDGE: I, Flora Cubbidge . . .

BLUEBEARD: Do solemnly swear . . .

MISS CUBBIDGE: Do solemnly swear . . .

BLUEBEARD: To take this man, Baron Khanazar von Bluebeard, as my lawful wedded husband . . .

MISS CUBBIDGE: To take this man, Baron Khanazar von Bluebeard, as my lawful wedded husband . . .

BLUEBEARD: To love, honor, and obey; for better or for worse; for richer or poorer; in sickness

and in health; from this day forward . . . [*He begins to undress her*]

MISS CUBBIDGE: To love, honor, and obey; for better or for worse; for richer or for poorer; in sickness and in health; from this day forward . . .

BLUEBEARD: Until death us do part.

MISS CUBBIDGE: Till death us do part.

BLUEBEARD: [*Licentiously*] I may now kiss the bride.

MISS CUBBIDGE: What about your vows?

BLUEBEARD: Don't you trust me?

MISS CUBBIDGE: I do. I do. I do.

They begin to breathe heavily as they undress slowly. They move toward each other, wearing only their shoes, socks, stockings and her merry widow. They clinch and roll about on the floor making animal noises.

BLUEBEARD: Was ever woman in this manner wooed? Was ever woman in this manner won?

MISS CUBBIDGE: [*Aside*] There are things that happen in a day that would take a lifetime to explain.

There follows a scene of unprecedented eroticism in which MISS CUBBIDGE *gives herself voluptuously to* BARON VON BLUEBEARD.

BLUEBEARD: In my right pants pocket you will find a key. It is the key to my laboratory. Take it. And swear to me that you will never use it.

MISS CUBBIDGE: I swear! I must return to Sybil at once. She sometimes wakes up in a phalanx.

BLUEBEARD: Won't you sleep here tonight, with me?

MISS CUBBIDGE: No, I can't sleep in this bed. It has cold, wet spots in it. Good night, Baron . . . husband.

BLUEBEARD: Good night, Miss Cubbidge.

MISS CUBBIDGE: Please don't mention our hymeneals to Sybil. I must find the right words to immure the news to her.

BLUEBEARD: Believe me, I'll confess to none of it.

MISS CUBBIDGE: Thank you. I believe that you have transformed me to a part of the dirigible essence. You have carried me aloft and I believe I am with Beatrice, of whom Dante has sung in his immortal onus. Good night. [*Exit*]

Scene 4. BLUEBEARD

BLUEBEARD: It is a lucky thing for me that I did not take the vows or this marriage might be binding on me as it is on her. I cannot sleep tonight. There is work to be done in my laboratory. Good night, Miss Cubbidge, wherever you are. And good night to all the ladies who do be living in this world. Good night, ladies. Good night, sweet ladies. [*Exits into laboratory*]

Scene 5. *RODNEY PARKER, LAMIA THE LEOPARD WOMAN, MRS. MAGGOT*

Entering surreptitiously, MRS. MAGGOT *crosses lighting the candelabra.*

LAMIA: SHHH! Take care or the deaf one. . . . She hears nothing of what you shout and overhears everything that you whisper.

RODNEY: What is it that you wish to tell me?

LAMIA: He is mad, I tell you, mad! And he will stop at nothing.

RODNEY: Who?

LAMIA: The Bluebeard, Khanazar. If you love that girl, convince her to leave this island at once.

RODNEY: But why?

LAMIA: Look at me. I was a woman once!

RODNEY: But you are a woman. So very much a woman. You are all woman.

LAMIA: No, no, never again will I bear the name of woman. I was changed in the House of Pain. I was a victim of his sex-switch tricks and his queer quackery.

RODNEY: Quackery—Sybil told me that he was a brilliant physiologist.

LAMIA: Even in Denmark they called him a quack. He wasn't satisfied with sex switches. He wants to create a third genital organ attached between the legs of a third sex. I am an experiment that failed.

RODNEY: [*Seductively*] You look like a woman to me.

LAMIA: I wish I could be a woman to you. [*Aside*] Perhaps when Bluebeard is defeated I will. [*Aloud*] He uses the same technique on all his victims. First he married me. Then he gave me the key to his laboratory, forbidding me to ever use it. Then he waited for curiosity to get the better of me. All women are curious.

RODNEY: Men marry because they are tired, women because they are curious.

LAMIA: Both are disappointed.

RODNEY: Does he ever use men for his experiments?

LAMIA: At first he did. Sheemish was the first. But when that experiment failed he turned to women. We are all experiments that have failed. He has made us the slaves of this island.

RODNEY: [*Realizing*] The Island of Lost Love.

LAMIA: Save yourself and save the woman you love. Take the advice of the Leopard Woman and go.

RODNEY: How did a nice girl like you get mixed up in a mess like this?

LAMIA: I was entertaining in a small bistro nightclub called The Wild Cat's Pussy. I was billed as Lamia the Leopard Woman. It was only 14 beans a day but I needed the scratch. I sang this song: [*Sings*]
Where is my Leopard Lover?
When will I spot the cat for me?
I'm wild when I'm under cover.
Where is the cat who will tame me?
Where is my wild cat lover?
Leopard hunting is all the rage.
Where is my wild cat lover?
I'm free but I want to be caged.
If you dig this feline,
Better make a bee-line.
I've got the spots to give men the redhots
Where is my wild leopard hunter?
I'm game if you'll play my game.
Where is that runt cunt hunter?
I'm wild but I want to be tame.

After I sang my set, he signaled and I sat at his table. He ordered a Tiger's Milk Flip. He was into health food. No woman can resist him, I tell you.

RODNEY: He seduced you?

LAMIA: Worst, worst, a thousand times worst. I didn't know if I was coming or going. He has a way with women.

RODNEY: Sybil, great Scott no. Either you're jesting or I'm dreaming! Sybil with another man? I'll go mad.

LAMIA: His idealism . . . his intensity . . . the Clairol blue of his beard! His words carried me away. He had a strange look in his eyes. I felt strange inside. He and I were total strangers! If you love her, get her off this island before it is too late.

RODNEY: No, not Sybil. I am ashamed to listen to you. Yet she admires him so. . . . I have gone mad!

LAMIA: He came closer . . . closer. "Submit," he said, "in the name of science and the dark arts. Submit. Submit."

RODNEY: [*In a panic*] Sybil is with him now. You are lying.

LAMIA: If you think I am lying, look. [*She lifts her sarong*] Look what he did to the Leopard Woman's pussy.

RODNEY: Eeeccht! Is that a mound of Venus or a penis?

LAMIA: [*Perplexed*] I wish I knew.

RODNEY: No, no, he can't do that to Sybil. I must kill him. What am I saying? This is madness. But what consolation is sanity to me? The most faithful of women is after all only a woman. I'll kill you. No, I am mad.

LAMIA: Go and stop him. Save her from the fate that has befallen me.

RODNEY: I will kill myself! No, I will kill her! Oh, God, it is impossible. I have gone mad! [*He runs out*]

Scene 6.   *LAMIA*

LAMIA: [*Sings*]
>I've lost my leopard lover.
>A world of made is not a world of born.
>Bluebeard will soon discover
>Hell hath no fury like a woman scorned.

Scene 7.   *LAMIA, SHEEMISH*

LAMIA: [*Calling after him*] Rodney! Rodney! Rodney! He is gone.

SHEEMISH: [*Appearing out of the shadows*] Are you afraid of being alone?

LAMIA: [*Fanning herself with a leopard fan*] How stifling it is! There must be a storm coming.

SHEEMISH: I heard you telling the secrets of the island to Rodney [*Spits*] Parker.

LAMIA: [*Furiously*] Sneaking little eavesdropper! How dare you?

SHEEMISH: I love you.

LAMIA: [*Fanning herself*] What awful weather! This is the second day of it.

SHEEMISH: Every day I walk four miles to see you and four miles back and meet with nothing but indifference from you.

LAMIA: Your love touches me but I can't return it, that's all.

SHEEMISH: [*Accusing*] But you came four miles here to tell the secrets of the island to Rodney [*Spits*] Parker.

LAMIA: You are a bore.

SHEEMISH: [*Twisting her arm*] You are in love with him!

LAMIA: [*In pain*] Yes, its true. If you must know. I do love him. I do! [*Aside*] For all the good it will do me. He loves Sybil.

SHEEMISH: [*Taking her in his arms roughly and humping her like a dog*] I want you.

LAMIA: [*Fighting him*] You stupid, vulgar, deformed nincompoop! Do you think I could

ever fall for such a one as you? You are as ugly as sin itself. Besides, our genitals would never fit together.

SHEEMISH: [*Groping her*] We can work it out.

LAMIA: Evil cretin! God will punish you. [*She breaks away*]

SHEEMISH: God will not punish the lunatic soul. He knows the powers of evil are too great for us with weak minds. Marry me!

LAMIA: I'd rather blow a bald baboon with B.O. and bunions than marry a monster! [*Exit LAMIA in a huff*]

SHEEMISH: [*Following her*] Lamia, be reasonable!

Scene 8.   *BLUEBEARD, SYBIL*

SYBIL *is seated at the spinet. She plays dramatic music.* BLUEBEARD *moves slowly, approaching her from behind. His eyes are ablaze. She senses his approach. She plays with greater emphasis. Her shoulders are bare. He begins kissing them. The music she is playing rises to a crescendo. She stops playing suddenly.*

SYBIL: This is ridiculous!

BLUEBEARD: [*Swinging a key on a chain back and forth before her eyes as though hypnotizing her*] Here is the key to my laboratory. Take it and swear to me that you will never use it.

SYBIL: [*In a trance*] Yes, Master!

BLUEBEARD: Ah, my darling, my own one. You will be my wife.

SYBIL: Yes, Master!

BLUEBEARD: You will be the loveliest of all wives. [*Aside*] When I am through with you.

SYBIL: Yes, Master.

BLUEBEARD: I am about to perform the *magnum opus*. The creation of a third genital organ will perhaps lead to the creation of a third sex. You will be my ultimate masterpiece of vivisection! [*He kisses her*]

Scene 9.   *BLUEBEARD, SYBIL, CUBBIDGE*

MISS CUBBIDGE: [*Entering*] Sir, what are you doing with Sybil there? Are you making love to her too?

BLUEBEARD: [*Aside to* CUBBIDGE] No, no, on the contrary, she throws herself at me shamelessly, although I tell her that I am married to you.

SYBIL: What is it you want, Miss Cubbidge?

BLUEBEARD: [*Aside to* SYBIL] She is jealous of my speaking to you. She wants me to marry her, but I tell her it is you I must have.

MISS CUBBIDGE: [*Incredulous*] What, Sybil?

BLUEBEARD: [*Aside to* CUBBIDGE] The impressionable little creature is infatuated with me.

SYBIL: [*Incredulous*] What, Miss Cubbidge?

BLUEBEARD: [*Aside to* SYBIL] The desperate old maid has got her claws out for me.

MISS CUBBIDGE: Do you . . .

BLUEBEARD: [*To* MISS CUBBIDGE] Your words would be in vain.

SYBIL: I'd . . .

BLUEBEARD: [*To* SYBIL] All you can say to her will be in vain.

MISS CUBBIDGE: Truly . . .

BLUEBEARD: [*Aside to* CUBBIDGE] She's obstinate as the devil.

SYBIL: I think . . .

BLUEBEARD: [*Aside to* SYBIL] Say nothing to her. She's a madwoman.

SYBIL: No, no, I must speak to her.

MISS CUBBIDGE: I'll hear her reasons.

SYBIL: What . . .

BLUEBEARD: [*Aside to* SYBIL] I'll lay you a wager she tells you she's my wife.

MISS CUBBIDGE: I . . .

BLUEBEARD: [Aside to CUBBIDGE] I'll bet you she says I'm going to marry her.

MISS CUBBIDGE: Sybil, as your chaperone I must intercept. It is past your bedtime.

SYBIL: Dear Miss Cubbidge, I have been to bed but I got up because I have insomnia.

MISS CUBBIDGE: So I see. Sybil, I must ask you to leave me alone with *my* husband. The Baron and I married ourselves in an improvident ceremony earlier this evening.

BLUEBEARD: [*Aside to* SYBIL] What did I tell you? She's out of her mind.

SYBIL: Dear *Miss* Cubbidge, are you sure you are feeling all right? Are you ill?

MISS CUBBIDGE: [*Indignantly*] I've never felt more supine in my life. Sybil, it does not become a young *unmarried* woman to meddle in the affairs of others.

BLUEBEARD: [*Aside to* CUBBIDGE] She thinks she is going to marry me.

SYBIL: It is not fit, *Miss* Cubbidge, to be jealous because the Baron speaks to me. I am going to be his wife.

BLUEBEARD: [*Aside to* CUBBIDGE] What did I tell you?

SYBIL: Baron, did you not promise to marry me?

BLUEBEARD: [*Aside to* SYBIL] Of course, my darling.

MISS CUBBIDGE: Baron, am I not your wife, the Baroness von Bluebeard?

BLUEBEARD: [*Aside to* CUBBIDGE] How could you ask such a question?

SYBIL: [*Aside to the audience*] How sure the old goat is of herself!

MISS CUBBIDGE: [*Aside to the audience*] The Baron is right, how pig-headed the little bitch is!

SYBIL: We must know the truth.

MISS CUBBIDGE: We must have the matter abnegated.

SYBIL *and* MISS CUBBIDGE: Which of us will it be, Baron?

BLUEBEARD: [*Addressing himself to both of them*] What would you have me say? Each of you knows in your heart of hearts whether or not I have made love to you. Let her that I truly love laugh at what the other says. Actions speak louder than words. [*Aside to* CUBBIDGE] Let her believe what she will. [*Aside to* SYBIL] Let her flatter herself in her senile imagination. [*Aside to* CUBBIDGE] I adore you. [*Aside to* SYBIL] I am yours alone. [*Aside to* CUBBIDGE] One night with you is worth a thousand with other women. [*Aside to* SYBIL] All faces are ugly in your presence. [*Aloud*] If you will excuse me, there's work to be done in my laboratory. I do not wish to be disturbed. Good night, ladies. [*Exits*]

Scene 10. *SYBIL, MISS CUBBIDGE,*
SHEEMISH

SHEEMISH: [*Appearing out of the shadows*] Poor ladies! I can't bear to see you led to your destruction. Take my advice, return to the mainland.

SYBIL: I am she he loves, however.

MISS CUBBIDGE: It is to me he's married.

SHEEMISH: My master is an evil sadist. He will do you irreparable harm as he has done to others. He wants to marry the whole female sex so that he can take them to his laboratory and . . .

Scene 11. *SYBIL, MISS CUBBIDGE,*
SHEEMISH, BLUEBEARD

BLUEBEARD: [*Popping back in*] One more word . . .

SHEEMISH: My master is no evil sadist. He means you no harm. If you ladies think he can marry the whole female sex, you've got another think coming. He is a man of his word. There he is—ask him yourself.

BLUEBEARD: What were you saying, Sheemish?

SHEEMISH: [*Aside to* BLUEBEARD] You know how catty women are. I was defending you . . . as best I could.

BLUEBEARD: [*To* SYBIL *and* MISS CUBBIDGE] She who holds the key to my heart holds the key to my laboratory. [*Exit*]

Scene 12.   MISS CUBBIDGE, SYBIL. SHEEMISH

MISS CUBBIDGE: [*Aside*] Then he is my husband, for he gave me the key.

SYBIL: [*Aside*] The key, I have the key! It is me he loves after all. [*Loud*] Good night, Madame. If you have the key, you are his wife.

MISS CUBBIDGE: Good night, Sybil. If it is to you he gave the key, you are his bethrothed.

[*They both exit laughing*]

Scene 13.   SHEEMISH, MRS. MAGGOT

MRS. MAGGOT: [*Entering excitedly*] I overheard laughter. It is the first time laughter has been heard on this island in 19 years. Who was laughing? Who is it that knows a single moment of happiness on the Island of Lost Love?

SHEEMISH: It was not with joy you heard them laughing, but with scorn. Bluebeard has got the young woman and her governess fighting like cats in the alley.

MRS. MAGGOT: I thought they always swore by each other.

SHEEMISH: It's at each other that they swear now. He's married both of them!

Scene 14.   SHEEMISH, MRS. MAGGOT, SYBIL

MRS. MAGGOT: Look, here comes the young one carrying a candle, her long black hair unloosed, her lips slightly parted. A lovely flower that blooms for just one hour.

SHEEMISH: A sleepwalker, a somnambulist.

MRS. MAGGOT: Her eyes are open.

SHEEMISH: But their sense is shut. I believe he has mesmerized her. Let us conceal ourselves, I will keep my eyes peeled.

MRS. MAGGOT: And I my ears. I can't wait to find out what happens next! [MRS. MAGGOT *and* SHEEMISH *hide*]

SYBIL: I can control my curiosity no longer. I must see what lies behind the door to my lover's laboratory. I know he has forbade me ever to use this key. But how can I stand the suspense? Should not a woman take an interest in her husband's work? [*She unlocks the door with her key and opens it.* BLUEBEARD *awaits her*]

MRS. MAGGOT: Shouldn't we try to save her?

SHEEMISH: Would you prefer to take her place in the House of Pain?

MRS. MAGGOT: No, no, not the House of Pain.

Scene 15.   SYBIL, BLUEBEARD, SHEEMISH, MRS. MAGGOT

BLUEBEARD: I trust you have kept your coming here a secret.

SYBIL: Baron!

BLUEBEARD: Curiosity killed the cat. [*Aside*] But it may have a salutary effect on the pussy. Look into my eyes, my little kitten, and repeat after me. [*Hypnotizing her*] I, Sybil, do solemnly swear to take this man, Baron Khanazar von Bluebeard, as my lawful wedded husband.

SYBIL: I, Sybil, do solemnly swear to take this man, Baron Khanazar von Bluebeard, as my lawful wedded husband.

MRS. MAGGOT: [*Moving her ear trumpet like an antenna*] I hear someone coming. Just in time! Rodney Parker will save her from the fate worse than death!

SHEEMISH: [*Aside*] My rival, Rodney Parker! Now I will have my revenge. [*To* MRS. MAGGOT] Detain him!

BLUEBEARD: To love, honor and obey . . .

MRS. MAGGOT: Oh, cruel! Don't ask me that. I won't do it. Anything but that.

SYBIL: To love, honor and obey.

SHEEMISH: Even the House of Pain? The test tube! Master, Master . . .

BLUEBEARD: For better or for worse; for richer or for poorer . . .

MRS. MAGGOT: I'll do it.

BLUEBEARD: In sickness and in health . . . from this day forward . . .

SYBIL: For better or for worse; for richer or for poorer . . . in sickness and in health, from this day forward . . .

Scene 16.   SHEEMISH, MRS. MAGGOT, SYBIL, BLUEBEARD, RODNEY

RODNEY *rushes onto the stage, mad.*

RODNEY: Where is he? Where is he?

SHEEMISH *roughly throws* MRS. MAGGOT *into* RODNEY.

MRS. MAGGOT: Eh?

BLUEBEARD: Until death us do part.

SYBIL: Until death us do part.

> BLUEBEARD *blows out the candle and kisses* SYBIL.

RODNEY: [*Shaking* MRS. MAGGOT *violently*] Where is Bluebeard?

MRS. MAGGOT: Eh?

RODNEY: Aagh! [*He throws* MRS. MAGGOT *aside*]

BLUEBEARD: [*Pressing* SYBIL *to him, demented*] And now, ye demons, ere this night goes by, I swear I'll conjure or I'll die!

RODNEY: [*Sees* BLUEBEARD] Damn you, Bluebeard! Damn your soul!

SYBIL: Rodney! Ah! [*She faints*]

> BLUEBEARD *catches her and quickly carries her into the laboratory.* MRS. MAGGOT *trips* RODNEY, *then* SHEEMISH *and* MRS. MAGGOT *follow, slamming the door in* RODNEY'S *face and locking it.* RODNEY *beats on the door and shouts.*

Scene 17.   RODNEY

RODNEY: Open the door, you pervert! You invert, you necrophiliac! Open up! Bluebeard! Bluebeard! BLUEBEARD!

Curtain

ACT III

Scene 1.   BLUEBEARD, SYBIL, SHEEMISH, MRS. MAGGOT

There is no lapse of time between Act II and Act III. The scene changes to the interior of BLUEBEARD'S *laboratory. Enter* BLUEBEARD *carrying* SYBIL *in his arms. He walks with a hesitant step, looking from side to side, his cheeks quivering, contracting and expanding, his eyes intently focused.* SHEEMISH *and* MRS. MAGGOT *scurry about taking care of last-minute details. There is an air of great anticipation.*

RODNEY'S VOICE: [*Offstage*] Bluebeard! Bluebeard! Bluebeard! Open this door or I'll break it down! [*Loud knocking*] Bluebeard!

BLUEBEARD: [*Laughing*] That door is lined with double-duty quilted zinc. No mortal arm can break it down. Even a man whose heart

is pure and has the strength of ten could not break it down. But a delicate girl with just enough strength to lift a powder puff to her white bosom can open it . . . if she has the key. [*More loud knocking*] Sheemish, take the girl to the operating rom, bathe her and prepare her for surgery.

SHEEMISH: No, Master, please don't ask me to do that. Anything but that.

BLUEBEARD: And be gentle with her. I want no marks left on her lily-white body. If you so much as bruise her, you and I will make an appointment for a meeting here in the House of Pain, hum?

SHEEMISH: No, no, not the House of Pain! [*He carries* SYBIL *off*]

Scene 2.   BLUEBEARD, MRS. MAGGOT

BLUEBEARD: Mrs. Maggot, bring in the frog, the serpent and the hearts, hands, eyes, feet, but most of all the blood and genitals of the little children. Bring in the serpent first. I need it to trace a magic circle.

MRS. MAGGOT: Eh?

BLUEBEARD: Perhaps your hearing would be improved by a vacation. [*He covers her ears and whispers*] In the House of Pain.

MRS. MAGGOT: No no, not the House of Pain!

> [*She quickly hands him a bottle of blood and a paintbrush*]

BLUEBEARD: [*Laughs*] Thank you. Now leave me. Go and assist Sheemish. [MRS. MAGGOT *lingers*] Is there something that you want, Maggot?

MRS. MAGGOT: Yes, Master.

BLUEBEARD: Well, what is it?

MRS. MAGGOT: The lapis lazuli locket the girl is wearing. May I have it?

BLUEBEARD: Yes, take it, scavenger!

MRS. MAGGOT: Do you think she will mind?

BLUEBEARD: No, she will not mind. She will remember nothing of her former life after the operation. Now get out. [*Kicks her in the ass*]

MRS. MAGGOT: Thank you, thank you, Master. [*Exit*]

Scene 3.   BLUEBEARD

BLUEBEARD: [*Enscribing a circle of blood*] Now by the powers that only seem to be, With crystal sword and flame I conjure thee. I kiss the book; oh come to me! Goddess of night: Hecate!

The sound of a gong is heard and a high-pitched cock crow that sometimes breaks from the most refined throat. HECATE *appears in a flash of light and a puff of smoke.*

Scene 4. *BLUEBEARD, HECATE*

HECATE: [*Wearing a blue beard*] Who summons the Slave of Sin?

BLUEBEARD: [*Laughing quietly aside*] Not for nothing I have worshiped the Dark One. [*To* HECATE] I called, Hecate; I, Khanazar von Bluebeard.

HECATE: How dare you? Don't you know that torture is the price you pay for summoning the Slave of Sin?

BLUEBEARD: All tortures do not matter: only not to be dead before one dies.

HECATE: What is it you want of me, my fool?

BLUEBEARD: Look, here are my books written in blood, there my apparatus. For 19 long years I've waited and worked for this moment. In there, on the operating table, swathed in bandages, a new sex, waiting to live again in a genital I made with my own hands! [*Maniacally*] With my own hands!

HECATE: What about your own genitalia?

BLUEBEARD: The male genital organ is but a faint relic and shadow, a sign that has become detached from its substance and lives on as an exquisite ornament.

HECATE: And what do you want of me, my fool?

BLUEBEARD: Good fortune.

HECATE: Do not seek for good fortune. You carry on your forehead the sign of the elect.
> Seek, probe,
> Details unfold.
> Let nature's secret
> Be retold.

If ever you mean to try, you should try now. [*She vanishes*]

There is a roll of thunder. Dramatic music from Bartok's Castle of Bluebeard *begins to swell.* BLUEBEARD *dons surgeon's coat, gloves and mask and enters the House of Pain.* MRS. MAGGOT *and* SHEEMISH *close the doors after him. There is the sound of loud knocking at the door.*

Scene 5. *MRS. MAGGOT, SHEEMISH*

MRS. MAGGOT: Look, Sheemish, the lapis lazuli locket. The Master said I could have it. Pretty, ain't it?

SHEEMISH: What's with you and that locket? [*A bloodcurdling scream issues from the laboratory. We may be sure that it is* SYBIL *writhing under the vivisector's knife. Both* SHEEMISH *and* MRS. MAGGOT *freeze for a moment in terror and clutch their own genitals in sympathy*] Listen, he has begun the operation.

There is another bloodcurdling scream. Again MRS. MAGGOT *and* SHEEMISH *freeze and clutch their genitals.*

RODNEY'S VOICE: [*Off*] What are you doing in there, you monster? [*He beats loudly on the door.* SYBIL *screams again off*] Open the door or I'll tear your heart out! [*Knocks loudly*]

Scene 6. *BLUEBEARD, MAGGOT, SHEEMISH*

BLUEBEARD: [*Rushes on*] The test tube! The test tube. Everything depends upon the sticky liquid now. [*He snatches the test tube and hurries back to his work*]

MRS. MAGGOT *and* SHEEMISH *exchange a guilty look. Another scream is heard. Suddenly* MISS CUBBIDGE *and* RODNEY *burst into the room.* MISS CUBBIDGE *brandishes the key.*

Scene 7. *MRS. MAGGOT, SHEEMISH, RODNEY, MISS CUBBIDGE*

MISS CUBBIDGE: I could control my curiosity no longer.

RODNEY: I'll see to it that he goes to the guillotine. That will shorten him by a head.

MISS CUBBIDGE: He robbed me of my maidenhead. So it's not his head I'll see cut off him! I want him decalced.

Another scream is heard.

RODNEY: Let me at him. I'll maim the bloody bugger.

SHEEMISH: Don't be a fool. The girl is on the operating table. If you interfere now, she'll lose her life.

MISS CUBBIDGE: [*Aside*] With Sybil out of the way, the Baron will be mine alone. [*Aloud*] We must save her no matter what the danger.

SYBIL *screams again.*

RODNEY: I can't stand it. I'm going in there.

SHEEMISH: Are you crazy?

RODNEY: Yes, I'm crazy.

SHEEMISH: Can't you understand that we are powerless against a supernatural enemy?

Scene 8. *BLUEBEARD, MISS CUBBIDGE, RODNEY, MRS. MAGGOT, SHEEMISH*

BLUEBEARD: The time has come. The final stage of transmutation must be completed. Mars, God of War, and Venus, Goddess of Love, are conjunct in the twelfth house. The house of change and transformation. Scorpio, which rules surgery and the genitalia, is at the zenith. This is the horoscope I have been waiting for. The signs are in perfect aspect. The third genital will be born under the most beneficent stars that twinkle in the heavens. Sheemish, bring in the girl, or should I say "subject"?

MISS CUBBIDGE: Khanazar, you have deceived me. I . . .

BLUEBEARD: Quiet! I have no time to talk to an idiot.

RODNEY: If anything goes wrong with this experiment, I swear I'll kill you.

BLUEBEARD: I have already sworn upon the cross to enter into this experiment for life and for death.

SHEEMISH *carries on* SYBIL, *who is wrapped in bandages like a mummy.*

Scene 9. *RODNEY, SYBIL, SHEEMISH, MISS CUBBIDGE, MRS. MAGGOT, BLUEBEARD*

BLUEBEARD: Gently, gently! Be careful, you fool.

MISS CUBBIDGE: [*Gasps*] Is she . . . is she . . . dead?

BLUEBEARD: [*Listens to* SYBIL'S *heart and genital through stethoscope*] No, she is not dead. She's just resting, waiting for new life to come.

There is the sound of thunder and flashes of lightning. MRS. MAGGOT *and* SHEEMISH *light candles, incense. There are science-fiction lighting effects.*

RODNEY: Is it a new life or a monster you are creating, Baron Prevert?

BLUEBEARD: The word is "pervert." I believe in this monster as you call it.

RODNEY: So, this is the House of Pain.

BLUEBEARD: How do you know when you unlock any door in life that you are not entering a House of Pain? I have thought nothing of pain. Years of studying nature have made me as remorseless as nature itself. All we feel is pain. But we must take risks if we are to progress.

RODNEY: How could you? How could you?

BLUEBEARD: Do you know what it feels like to be God, Parker?

RODNEY: [*Spits in* BLUEBEARD'S *face*] I spit in your face.

BLUEBEARD: Do you think that the envenomed spittle of 500 little gentlemen of your mark, piled one on top of the other, could succeed in so much as slobbering the tips of my august toes? [*He turns his back on* RODNEY *and, with the assistance of* SHEEMISH, *begins unwinding the bandages that envelop* SYBIL. *When she is completely nude except for her fuck-me pumps, the genital begins to move*]

BLUEBEARD: Look, it's moving. It's alive. It's moving. It's alive! It's alive!

SYBIL *moves like the bride of Frankenstein, with stiff, jerking movements of the head and neck. First she looks at* SHEEMISH *and screams with horror, then she looks at* BLUEBEARD *and screams with horror, then she looks at her new genital and growls with displeasure.*

Scene 10. *LAMIA, RODNEY, SYBIL, MRS. MAGGOT, SHEEMISH, MISS CUBBIDGE, BLUEBEARD*

LAMIA: [*Enters and crawls over toward* SYBIL *with catlike stealth and examines the third genital*] Now no man will ever want her! Rodney is mine. [*She leaps toward* RODNEY. BLUEBEARD *fires on her and she falls.*]

BLUEBEARD: I told you never to come to this side of the island again.

SHEEMISH: [*Kneeling over* LAMIA'S *body*] You killed the woman I love.

BLUEBEARD: [*Going to her also, feeling her pulse*] Woman—I wouldn't say she was a woman. She was a leopard, a wild cat. I couldn't make my leopard love me.

SHEEMISH: You killed the woman I love. Now you must die. [*He moves toward* BLUEBEARD *threateningly*]

BLUEBEARD: [*Backing away*] No, Sheemish, no! Remember the House of Pain!

SHEEMISH: I no longer fear pain. My heart is broken. [*He seizes* BLUEBEARD *by the throat*]

RODNEY: [*Looking at* SYBIL'S *genital*] No man will ever want her?

MISS CUBBIDGE: [*To* MRS. MAGGOT] What are you doing with the lapis lazuli locket? Sybil's mother gave it to her the night she died when the terrible fire . . . Sybil's real mother had a strawberry birth mark on her left knee cap.

RODNEY: I need never be jealous again!

MISS CUBBIDGE: Margaret, Margaret Maggot? Maggie!

SHEEMISH *releases* BLUEBEARD *in amazement.*

MRS. MAGGOT: The fire? Margaret Maggot? It's all coming back to me. I am Maggie Maggot. [*Turning on* BLUEBEARD] What have you suffered for that child that you dare to tear her from me without pity? Sybil is my daughter. I am her real mother. If you give me back my child, I shall live for her alone. I shall know how to tame my nature to be worthy of her always. My heart will not open itself to anyone but her. [*On her knees*] My whole life will be too brief to prove to her my tenderness, my love, my devotion.

BLUEBEARD: [*Kicking her over*] I detest cheap sentiment.

MISS CUBBIDGE: This exploits women!

MRS. MAGGOT: Women want an answer!

They seize BLUEBEARD, *tie ropes to his wrists and stretch him across stage.* LAMIA *rises and begins strangling him slowly.*

BLUEBEARD: Lamia! I thought you were dead.

LAMIA: My dear, didn't you know? A cat has nine lives.

SYBIL: [*The monster speaks haltingly*] Stop . . . in . . . the . . . name . . . of love. The human heart . . . who knows to what perversions it may not turn, when its taste is guided by aesthetics?

The women drop the rope. LAMIA *releases* BLUEBEARD. *The sound of the ship's foghorn is heard offstage.*

SHEEMISH: [*Looking out the spy hole*] The *Lady Vain!* The *Lady Vain!* The *Lady Vain* has weathered the storm!

MISS CUBBIDGE: [*To* BLUEBEARD] I am leaving this moment. Tomorrow I shall be far away. I shall have forgotten everything that happened yesterday. It's enough to say that I will tell nobody, nobody. If, as I hope, you regret the words that escaped you, write to me and I shall despond at once. I leave without rancor wishing you the best, in spite of all. I am carrying your child. Would that your son will be your good angel. [*Hands him the key to the laboratory*] Adieu! Come, Margaret, Sybil, Rodney. We must return to normalcy. [*They exit. There is the sound of a foghorn*]

Scene 11. BLUEBEARD, LAMIA, SHEEMISH

BLUEBEARD: [*In a rage. Shaking his fists at the heavens*] I curse everything that you have given. I curse the day on which I was born. I curse the day on which I shall die. I curse the whole of my life. I fling it all back at your cruel face, senseless fate! [*Laughing*] With my curses I conquer you. What else can you do to me? With my last breath I will shout in your asinine ears: Be accursed, be accursed! Be forever accursed! I'm a failure, Sheemish, I'm a failure.

SHEEMISH: But, Master, you have heart, you have talent.

BLUEBEARD: Heart! Talent! These are nothing, my boy. Mediocrity is the true gift of the gods. [*Exit*]

Scene 12. SHEEMISH, LAMIA

SHEEMISH: Come, let us do the best we can, to change the opinion of this unhappy man. [*Exit with* LAMIA]

GERTRUDE or WOULD SHE BE PLEASED TO RECEIVE IT?

a mystery

Wilford Leach

Gertrude was presented by Ellen Stewart and the ETC Company at La Mama ETC, New York City, on September 9, 1970, with the following cast:

GERTRUDE	*Murrell Gehman*
ERNEST, *her dog*	*William Finley*
ISADORA	*Ceil Smith*
ANGEL	*John Braswell*
GUESTS	*Nancy Heikin, Donald Harrington, Margaret Benczak*

It was staged by John Braswell and Wilford Leach. Music by Ben Johnston; orchestrations and musical direction by James Cuomo. Masks and props by Richard Laws; set pieces and stage by Peter Murkett; costumes by Nancy Reeder. Production stage manager: Michael O'Rand.

Enter an ANGEL, *on the wind or a wire.*

ANGEL: Well, as anybody knows, everything is very well worked out from bottom to top. Anybody knows that: how well everything is worked out from bottom to top and not at all well worked out from top to bottom. Anybody knows, for example, that there are rocks at the bottom of everything and they just are . . . they just sit there and they are, and then there are plants next and they both are and they grow, and then there are animals and they are and they grow and also they sense, and then there is Man, who is and grows and senses and reasons, and, well then, there are angels.

    Well, anybody knows that when you come to angels you can't come at them from the bottom to top.

    Anybody could tell you that angels are, for example, but on the other hand, everybody isn't so sure, and as to whether they grow or don't grow, well, that's a pretty interesting question itself, if you're interested in it, but right now the interesting thing is that you can't come at angels from the bottom. You have to work from the top down. Now, on the one hand, anybody could think it would be very nice not to be and not to grow or sense. Anybody could think it would be very nice not to have to reason and just to do as the angels do; they just *know*. They do do that; they just know anything. Anybody would think it would be nice just to know anything and not to reason anything out, but on the other hand, anybody can be wrong and they often are and this is an example because it isn't. It isn't very pleasant, I can tell you, always to know a good deal more than you understand.

    Now, for example, now at this moment, here I am and I know that; anybody could know that or most anybody could, anybody could know that about anything they can see, like anybody can right this minute. And *anybody* could know what the mystery was about in a mystery play when it is concluded because that's the way a mystery play is; there's always a conclusion at the end. Everybody always gets together in one place at the end and one of them is the one and the others aren't and the detective comes to that conclusion and that's the ending. Well, anybody could know all that. Anybody could know here I am; they could see me and figure that out, but, well, an angel can't. He can be very interested in everything, but until he *knows* something, he doesn't know it. In the meantime, he can be very interested in everything.

    And I am.

ANNOUNCER: Gertrude is in her garden with Ernest, her dog.

Distant thunder. A pale sun. Music.

CHORUS: [*Singing*] She sighs, she sighs and she says.

GERTRUDE: [*Singing, musing*] Well, I hope this isn't an electric storm blowing up, but I'm afraid it is. It will certainly wash the grass seeds away. If the birds don't do it, then the rain does and there's always a lot of noise that shakes the windows and makes the window shades roll up so you can't reach them. What could any of that mean? What does it mean?

ERNEST *bothers her.*

ANNOUNCER: [*Speaking, always*] Ernest, her dog, is often a great deal of trouble.

GERTRUDE *throws a stick and* ERNEST *runs after it.*

GERTRUDE: [*Singing*] It must be going to storm because whenever I'm in this mood it always storms or vice versa. I think it must be going to storm because I feel this way. And I did want to go to the post office to see if I have any letters in my box. I certainly do like to have a box because I can go in and get any letters that come in on Sunday and I never can stand to think there are letters in the post office and I can't open them. Well, a storm is coming up and I suppose something will be hit or something will get blown down. It is certainly disappointing how something like the clothesline could stay there so long and get blown down. I certainly would like to know why that is. I'm reminded of a little incident that happened to a lady I knew once who was wife to a man who worked for the plant where they take nitrogen out of the atmosphere instead of mining it in Peru, where they have a good many seagulls. She had her front door open and the back door open and was in the kitchen and lightning came in and right out of the room. She said it gave her a very definite feeling. She said she had never thought until then about astrology, but now that she thought about how the planets affected people, now she thought the weather was the way the earth affected people. It's very seldom that anyone gets that close to lightning without being hit by it; so when they have something to say about it, it is certainly interesting to listen to them; but that's the trouble when it happens to somebody else; you never can really tell from what they say anything about it.

    But then I've had a good many experiences and I would like to know what they mean. I would like to think they mean something, but does something mean anything? It certainly takes a lot of effort to think it means something, and generally I'm not so sure.

Now, about the weather; why does it do that? Will it or won't it, and why does this or that happen? Who can say? Is it so or isn't it so? It probably is so but, on the other hand, maybe it isn't. Who knows? Who knows? God knows. Well, I hope he does.

ANNOUNCER: She goes away but will presently go for a walk with Isadora, her companion, and Ernest, her dog.

Sign: "Scene 1—Gertrude Defies the Elements. Morning. A phone booth is nearby. An electric storm approaches. The ANGEL observes and is interested."

GERTRUDE: [*Speaking*] I am not expecting a telephone call but I would be pleased to receive one.

Music.

ISADORA: [*Speaking*] Well, Gertrude, here we are out walking your dog, Ernest, and the wind certainly is blowing nicely. The wind certainly is blowing nicely and I certainly do wish I had my scarves. If I didn't know how much Ernest loves me, I'd think he'd run off with one of my scarves.

ANGEL: [*Singing*] The wind blew it. It ble-e-e-ew it. Where is it?

The wind blows harder. ERNEST digs a hole and sits under a bush.

ISADORA: [*Speaking*] I do believe the wind has blown your dog, Ernest, away and, oh, Gertrude, don't you even care?

ANGEL: [*Singing*] Save them. Sa-a-a-a-a-a-a-a-a-a-ave them. From the Elec. Tric. Storm. Where is it? Do they see?

Heat lightning and distant thunder.

ISADORA: [*Speaking*] I'm certain the wind has blown your dog, Ernest, away and, oh, Gertrude, something should be done about it.

An ominous storm glowers. Thunder.

ANGEL: [*Singing*] Isa. Dora. Gertrude and. Ernest her dog. Do. They. See. It?

The storm threatens but goes away.

GERTRUDE: [*Speaking*] Isadora, what are you talking about?

ANGEL: [*Singing, looking after the storm*] They do not see. It. Yet. But I do.

ANNOUNCER: Gertrude finds Ernest under a gorse bush.

GERTRUDE and ERNEST dance. ISADORA watches, annoyed.

ISADORA: Gertrude, I don't think we should go any further in this direction because that man who opens and closes the drawbridge has a big dog and besides, I'm beginning to think an electric storm may be coming up or I'm being looked at. What do you think?

GERTRUDE: I think I heard a phone ring.

ISADORA: No, I'm sure you couldn't have heard a phone ring. You were just annoyed.

GERTRUDE: Annoyed at what?

ISADORA: Because Ernest generally pays so much more attention to me than he does to you.

GERTRUDE: Why, I never even thought about it, Isadora.

ISADORA: Well, of course you're right when you say that whenever we're sitting down it's always my lap he jumps up on and goes to sleep on, but you know animals just sense things and you mustn't be upset. I mean, animals are just that way, they like some people more than others and I just love everything, that's just the way I am, and he senses it. Did you say something?

GERTRUDE: No.

ANNOUNCER: A storm is on its way.

ANGEL: I'm watching it.

ISADORA: What did you say?

GERTRUDE: Nothing.

ISADORA: You said something.

GERTRUDE: I didn't say anything. I thought I heard something.

ISADORA: Do you think it's that big dog that belongs to that man and he's going to run out and attack us? I knew we shouldn't go so far in this direction.

GERTRUDE: No, it sounded like a phone. And we aren't going in that direction any longer now, Isadora . . . we're going in this direction now, so I'm sure we won't be bothered by that dog.

ISADORA: Do you think a bull may have gotten loose from someplace and is in the bushes watching us?

GERTRUDE: No, I think it was probably just the wind in the trees and just now I felt a drop of rain.

Rain. Opens umbrella.

ISADORA: Oh, I'm certain it's an electric storm and the center rod of this umbrella will attract the lightning. I'm also afraid of thunder and rain and wind and tumbling rocks, hurricanes and glaciers.

Thunder.

ANNOUNCER: The storm is now nearby.

ANGEL: I see it, do they see it?

GERTRUDE: There, I heard a phone again.

ISADORA: It's probably television in the air. Oh, I tell you, I am frightened at the way they just

let television loose in the air all the time. All
of that radio in the air all the time before was
bad enough, but just think of how it is now
with all of those ultra-high frequencies and
color and educational frequencies just flying
loose.

Thunder. Rain. Phone rings.

ISADORA: Don't answer it!

Storm grows worse.

ANNOUNCER: Gertrude and the dog face into the
wind, which blows harder.

GERTRUDE: [*Speaking*] There, I knew I heard a
phone ring and over there is an outdoor telephone booth.

ISADORA: [*Speaking*] But think, think, Gertrude,
of wind and rain and storms and glaciers,
tidal waves and television in the air, and notice
how your dog, Ernest, doesn't go near it. You
know they know what is good for them and
what isn't! Oh, Gertrude, please, Gertrude, I
beg of you, Gertrude, don't answer the telephone in this electric storm or you'll certainly
get struck in the ear by lightning!

The telephone continues to ring.

GERTRUDE: [*Speaking*] But I never can stand to
hear a phone ring and not know what is on it.

ANNOUNCER: Gertrude answers it. It is about
how some lady would like to call on her about
insurance.

ANGEL: [*Speaking, watching* GERTRUDE] I find
her very interesting.

*Sign: "Scene 2—The Temptation of Gertrude.
Night. The* ANGEL *fears that a sudden appearance might alarm* GERTRUDE, *so he calls
on her first in a dream as she sleeps." A tap
dance with magic flowers that appear and
vanish.* GERTRUDE *is in her bed, sleeping. A
crescent moon.*

ANGEL: [*Singing*]
    Ah, love, if you hear whisper of wings
    And sweet musick enters at your
        window,
            Sighing: Pity me.
    No birdie small from the gorse bush
        does call
    But an angel perched in your maple
        tree
            Sighing:
            Je vous en prie: Pity me.

GERTRUDE, *still asleep, sits up to listen.*

GERTRUDE: [*Singing*]
    Ah, winds, ah, winds,
    Ah, east wind blowing in spring,
    Go tell the sad pheasant
    April showers kiss the flowers
    But wet feathers are sore unpleasant.

    With a heigh and a ho and a bother,
        bother,
    If it isn't one thing, it's another.
[*She lies down*]

ANGEL: [*Singing*]
    Ah, love, now the south wind doth
        blow
    And stirs the curtains of your bed
            Sighing: Pity me.
    My flocks feed not, my ewes breed
        not.
    'Tis Corydon perched in your maple
        tree
            Crying:
            Je vous en prie: Pity me.

GERTRUDE: [*Singing*]
    Ah, winds, ah, winds,
    Ah, south wind blowing in summer,
    Go tell the poor dove
    Spring alas is just past
    So 'tis both too sad and too hot for
        love.
    So with a heigh and a ho and a
        bother, bother,
    If it isn't one thing, it's another.

ANGEL: [*Singing*]
    Ah, love, so now 'tis fall
    Like the moths at the screens
            Whisp'ring: Pity me.
    The flowers die away, and birdies fly
        away
    And an angel perched in your maple
        tree
            Asking: *Je vous en prie:* Pity
            me.
    And now, 'tis winter
    And sweet musick taps at the storm
        windows
            Faintly: Pity me
    But to look, go not; up the window,
        throw not,
    'Tis only crows in your bare maple
        tree
            Cackling:
            Shall nothing
            Shall nothing
            Shall nothing
            Lie on thee except earth?

GERTRUDE: [*Singing slowly*]
    Ah, winds, ah, winds
    Ah, north, south, east, west wind
    With a hey nonny, nonny,
    Je vous en prie:
    Pity me.

The dream fades away.

ANNOUNCER: Another Scene 2: Isadora talks in
her sleep.

ISADORA *is in her bed and rises, sleepwalking.*

ISADORA:

> Don't tell me it's daylight already,
> God damn me, no.
> Those are the north lights,
> That's not the sun,
> Take away the sun.
> No, give me a Mad Moon
> Shining at three
> A.M.
>
> Don't sing me those old songs,
> That's old stuff.
> God damn me, no.
> Give me that new beat.
> That's not the new!
> Take away the old,
> Up there's a Mad Moon
> Shining at three
> A.M.
>
> That's the old-style hemline,
> Take it away, what a bore.
> That's the old kind of dance,
> Take it away,
> Don't dance it anymore.
> I loved your Ford coupé,
> Your model A,
> I loved your rumble seat
> But take it all away!
> Your coupé, take it away,
> Your Model A,
> Your rumble seat,
> Take it away,
> Take it all away!
> It's last year's model,
> *You're* last year's model!
> Take it away!
>
> Take away the sun.
> Take away those old songs.
> Give me the new beat.
> Take me away in a fast car,
> Take me away
> Somewhere, someplace,
> Take me away
> Someplace, somewhere, someplace
> Somewhere in this world
> It's just three A.M.
> And that's the place
> Somewhere, someplace,
> For me!
> Under that Mad, Mad Moon,
> Shining at three A.M.
> Singing at three A.M.
> Sinning at three
> A.M.

Sign: "Scene 3—Gertrude Arranges a Picnic. Afternoon. GERTRUDE *arranges a picnic at the seashore for the* ANGEL *and the* Pope, *during which a heated theological debate ensues.* ER-NEST *is there.* ISADORA *is someplace else. This scene will not be performed but there will be*

a Scarf Dance instead." A dance by ERNEST *with one of* ISADORA'S *scarves.*

Sign: "Scene 4—The Mad Scene from 'Gertrude.' " Twilight.

ANNOUNCER: Ernest is very playful.

ERNEST *hides under a gorse bush. Enter* ISA-DORA *and* GERTRUDE *walking. A "Mad Moon" is overhead. As the scene progresses,* ISADORA *begins to growl, snarl and bark.*

ISADORA: Well, Gertrude, here we are out walking again and the wind certainly is blowing nicely and I'm certainly glad I have my scarves. [*A storm threatens*] The wind is blowing nicely, but this heat lightning certainly makes me nervous. Grrr.

GERTRUDE: Here, Ernest, Ernest, Ernest.

ISADORA: I'm sure it's that very large moon that makes him act that way. He kept me awake all last night barking out of the window. Woof Woof.

GERTRUDE: I didn't hear him.

ISADORA: [*Sharply*] Of course not. You were having a very interesting dream.

GERTRUDE: Here, Ernest, Ernest, Ernest. [*She whistles*]

ANNOUNCER: Gertrude finds Ernest under a gorse bush. Ernest is very playful. [GERTRUDE *and* ERNEST *play while* ISADORA *looks on, annoyed. The storm threatens intermittently; thunder, etc.*] Presently they continue their walk.

ISADORA: Gertrude, do you notice anything strange about Ernest? Grrrrr. Woof Woof.

GERTRUDE: No.

ISADORA: Gertrude, it may be my imagination, but I think Ernest is frothing at the mouth. Grrrr. Gertrude, I'm quite sure Ernest is frothing Woof, Grrrr, at the mouth and I do believe he's mad. Gertrude, Ernest is certainly frothing at the mouth and certainly mad, aren't you going to do anything about it? Snarl, Grrrr, Grrr. Gertrude, Ernest is stark raving mad Woof Grrrr and presently will bite us all. Something most definitely must be done about him immediately. Help, help, save us! Mad dog! Mad dog! Help, help!

ANNOUNCER: Ernest is taken away to the Humane Society. Isadora sings.

ERNEST *goes off very slowly as if being led away, looking back sadly.*

ISADORA: [*Singing as he goes*] I shall never forget Ernest in his bath, his sad, frightened eyes, his sad sad eyes, so helpless, so trusting. And when we took him out he was so glad that he would roll on the carpet until he was tired and had to close those sad eyes, his trusting, sad eyes. Oh, Ernest was a good dog, Ernest was good, he was good, and if there is anything more beautiful than a boy and his dog, I don't know what it is. Oh, what does a dog want, what does he always want, whenever you sit down he comes to you and always wants something from you; oh, what does a dog want, what does a little dog always want?

ANNOUNCER: Presently she continues.

ISADORA: [*Singing*] Oh, I shall never forget Ernest at the refrigerator door, his sad, anxious eyes, his sad eyes. Whenever he ate his little supper he always washed his dish. Oh, Ernest was a good dog, Ernest was good, he was good, and I shall never forget of an evening how he'd sit and look at the victrola.

GERTRUDE *and* ISADORA: [*Singing*] Oh, what does a dog want, what does he always want, why does a dog care, why is it he always cares, and why does he always come to you and what can he want, what does a little dog always want?

Sign: "Scene 5—Gertrude entertains in the Arboretum. Sunset just at daybreak." Sun and moon.

ANNOUNCER: They move about.

ISADORA, GERTRUDE, *the* ANGEL *and guests walk around slowly with fans.*

CHORUS: [*Singing*] Here we are in the arboretum and now it is summer now and the days are so long now that it is sunset just at daybreak, just at daybreak it is sunset, and now it is summer here, and shortly each one of them will leave because it is sunset now and summer now and too hot oh too hot now to sit or to stand or go in or go out but only to move about until each one of them will leave. And now it is summer here and too hot oh too hot to sit or to stand except to move about.

ANNOUNCER: Gertrude meditates on madness.

GERTRUDE: [*Singing*] Yes, here we are in the arboretum and now it is summer now and the days are so long so very very long in the summer; days become so long that it is sunset just at daybreak, just at daybreak it is sunset, so of course it grows too hot and there is always heat lightning, so that at a sunset just at daybreak one is put to thinking, to meditating, to thinking on all that has ever happened and though heat lightning is nothing to be afraid of, because it never does anything; now thinking, now mediating on lightning and rain and thunder and falling rocks and tidal waves and electric storms, now thinking, now meditating on those elemental things, all those elements outside, all those outside elements to be coped with, I find I don't fear them.

CHORUS: [*Singing*] Thinking on all that has ever happened I find I don't fear them as much as

that a million people may go mad at any moment now, once again a million suddenly mad ones, and all the forces inside of each one of them, the forces inside them, the elemental forces inside of each one of them suddenly let loose into a sudden universal madness, a universal disorder, a sort of universal psychic disorder!

ISADORA: [*Speaking; crying out*] Like Ernest . . . !

GERTRUDE: Like Ernest.

ISADORA: [*Singing*] This heat lightning makes me nervous—and I'm so hot I can't breathe. . . . I want to go for a ride out in the country with my scarves blowing. [*Speaking*] There! I heard an auto horn, oh, perhaps it was David or Mark or Cliff or Edward to take me for a ride . . . [*Singing*]

Oh, we'll ride out in the country with
    my scarves blowing,
Oh, we'll ride and the little breezes
    will make it cool.
With the top down, we'll ride and
    ride through the country
With the little breezes blowing my
    scarves.

Enter a handsome, tall tennis player in whites.

ISADORA: [*Speaking*] Oh yes, it is David or Jeff, so excuse me, all. Good night, good night, it is certainly David or Jeff, good night, good night, or Mark, or Ernest.

GERTRUDE *and* ANGEL: [*Speaking*] Good night Good night Good night Good-bye.

Exit ISADORA *with the young man.*

ANNOUNCER: They move about.

GERTRUDE: [*Singing*] Did you hear a phone ring?

ANGEL: [*Singing*] No.

GERTRUDE: [*Singing*] Oh . . . Did you hear the sound of a bicycle in the driveway?

ANGEL: [*Singing*] No.

GERTRUDE: [*Singing*] Didn't you see anything?

ANGEL: [*Singing*] Where?

GERTRUDE: [*Singing*] Out of the corner of my eyes I thought I saw something—over there.

ANGEL: [*Singing*] Oh yes, over there is something. But here is now, everyone knows here is now, so of course over there is sometime else. Ah, I see a gentleman in your future, Gertrude, intelligent, proud, businesslike and artistic. And I see you take his hand as you walk down the lane of a little exotic orchard and turn out of sight.

GERTRUDE: [*Singing*] What do I have on?

ANGEL: [*Singing*] Pale green.

GERTRUDE: [*Singing*] Yes, I am fond of green, so perhaps it is me. The gentleman, what does he look like?

ANGEL: [*Singing*] Short (or tall), somewhat thin.

GERTRUDE: [*Singing*] . . . with gold wings?

ANGEL: [*Singing*] I glimpsed him only for a moment, of course, but let me think—yes . . . yes . . . I do believe he did have golden wings.

GERTRUDE: [*Speaking*] Then I'm sure it isn't me.

ANGEL: [*Speaking; disappointed*] No?

GERTRUDE: [*Speaking*] Wings would complicate an already difficult thing.

ANGEL: [*Speaking*] No, your way lies differently now that I think of it. [*Singing; viciously*] I see you alone now in a house with a thousand windows, standing on a stool, pulling the shades down. It thunders, a thousand shades go flapping up all at once, and the days are so long that it is today and tomorrow at once, and it is so hot that even with the shades drawn to darken the rooms, the discontented cherubs climb down from the wallpaper because they have begun to shrivel and grow wrinkled. And those grasshoppers which were eating the cherub's garlands have turned their attention to the begonia and geranium and devoured the blossoms of the century plant. While you spray them with a tiny Flit gun. And since there's nothing else to do, you're in your bath and a man who has been hiding behind the shower curtain suddenly reaches out and yanks out your tongue with a clever pair of patented pliers and smiles as he runs down the stairs because you can't cry after him. And in the house with a thousand windows, each with shades to be pulled down, the sun comes in, and it would be nice to have a glass of water, but nobody remembers in which room the sink is.

GERTRUDE: [*Speaking*] Well, that certainly is interesting and all of that must certainly be dealt with when it comes up.

ANGEL: I really must say I'm disappointed at the day this turns out because I thought perhaps it was a Mystery Play with a detective and a solution. Everybody knows in every Mystery Play there has to be a detective and a solution, or if not, then there has to be temptation and despair. That's the trouble with a Mystery Play: if it isn't very pleasant with a detective and a solution, it turns out to be the kind that has to have temptation and despair.

GERTRUDE: It's no fault of yours, of course.

ANGEL: No.
         Well.
         Good night.

GERTRUDE: Good night.

Music.

CHORUS: [*Singing*] Now in the summer when the days are so long now that it is sunset just at daybreak it certainly would be nice if every beginning and middle had its Conclusion.

ANNOUNCER: Gertrude, or Would She Be Pleased to Receive It?

CHORUS: [*Singing*] It would be a nicer way if every kind of thing had that, if only sunset were an ending and conclusion so it wouldn't be so hot, and if every kind of ending had a conclusion, if every ending was a Conclusion.

ANNOUNCER: Gertrude, or Would She Be Pleased to Receive It?

CHORUS: [*Singing*] It's hot and the day is long in the summer sunset just at daybreak and never any conclusion to it even here in the arboretum.

DRACULA:SABBAT

a play in two acts

Leon Katz

based on the novel Dracula *by Bram Stoker*

Dracula:Sabbat was first presented by the Judson Poets' Theatre at the Judson Memorial Church, New York City, on September 13, 1970, with the following cast:

DRACULA	*Duane Tucker*
HIS ATTENDANTS	*Charles Richetelle, Rhea Pearlman*
COVEN	*Pia Piro, Schaja Wainsztajn, J. Wellington Gorgal, Arabella Colton, Curtis Carlson, Luba Ash, Marina Stefan, Quaid Smith, Anne Oehlschlaeger, Marlene Willoughby, Earnest Gray, David Tice, Vincent Mosso, David Leopold, Sandy Ratcliff*
RENFIELD	*Theo Barnes*
VAMPIRES	*Marlene Willoughby, Arabella Colton, Sandy Ratcliff*
LUCY	*Crystal Field*
MINA	*Florence Tarlow*
DR. SEWARD	*Tim Kincaid*
DR. VAN HELSING	*William Pardue*
ARTHUR	*Richmond Hoxie*
VOICE OF DRACULA	*Duane Tucker; Sandy Ratcliff*

It was directed by Lawrence Kornfeld. Music by John Herbert McDowell. Costumes by Joyce and Jerry Marcel; lighting by Beverly Emmons; masks by Ralph Lee; set by David Barabas. Production stage manager: Richard Lipton.

A NOTE FOR THE DIRECTOR

Nietzsche explains in *The Birth of Tragedy* that the spectators dream the tragic chorus and the chorus in turn dreams the legend. In this version of *Dracula,* the audience is assumed to be on a psychedelic trip; it hallucinates a coven performing the rite of the Witches' Sabbath, and the coven in turn evokes the Dracula legend.

At the beginning of the performance, a Speaker —who is heard through loudspeakers situated at random under the audience's seats—explains to the audience that it is now dead, that it will experience the visions common to the recently dead in their journey out of the Self, and eventually reenter the realm of ordinary reality ("game existence"). The Speaker, throughout the performance, whispers into the ear of the audience advice, instructions, comfort as prescribed in the *Tibetan Book of the Dead* to guide them and help them endure their journey. (The version of instructions from the *Tibetan Book of the Dead* used in this production is adapted from Timothy Leary's Westernization of these instructions in his volume *The Psychedelic Experience.*)

There is an intimate relation between the Sabbath and the Dracula legend. The scenes of the legend are "born" each time out of the ongoing Sabbath and are themselves part of the continuity of the rite. The script avoids overspecifying the staging of the transitions so that the structuring of the spectators' experience may grow out of the particular terms of each separate production of the play.

ACT I

PREPARATION

Blank stage. A circle of white light on stage floor. After a long time, a Voice is heard through speakers situated under the theatre seats. The Voice is quiet, neutral, as though whispering into each spectator's ear.

SPEAKER:
>Listen carefully.
>It is as though you are dead.
>This will be the hour of your death
>   and rebirth.
>Not the death of the body, but of the self.
>Take advantage of this temporary death to
>   seek illumination. [*A long silence*]
>
>You are face to face with the clear light.
>All things are void.
>Remain in this state.
>Do not fear it.

>Hold on to this moment
>Of void,
>Of nonself. [*A long silence*]
>
>If you are slipping back,
>If you are again falling into contact with
>   the self,
>You will begin to see figures.
>Do not be frightened.
>These visions are your own thoughts.
>They exist only within you.
>
>During this journey through your visions,
>Relax.
>Merge with them.
>Be neither attracted by them nor repulsed.
>Enter into the world of your hallucinations
>   with good grace.
>Remain calm.
>Remember the teachings.

Three or four figures appear. They drape an altar, and put a crucifix, bowl and chalice on it. One of them sits center stage. He pulls a mask over his head: a huge goat head. He lights a candle between his horns. All other lights go out. The lighted goat head alone is visible. Otherwise, darkness and silence.

INTROIT

Extremely slow. Low, almost inaudible hissing. The COVEN *(a minimum of twelve who, with the* SATAN-PRIEST, *make up the celebrants of the Witches' Sabbat) assembles from all parts of the theatre. They carry lighted incense tapers. They move toward the goat head at the altar. As they approach in very slow procession,*

SPEAKER:
>Answer us
>Old Horned One
>Provender
>And power
>Are yours
>Come to us
>God of Blessings
>Come
>Among us
>Bring us death
>Greatest
>Father
>Let us know
>The one
>Clear
>Light

The COVEN *is seated in a perfect circle around the goat head. A harsh down-spot on the goat. He smashes the crucifix. Spot off. The* COVEN *stomps the crucifix, rends it, scatters the pieces.*

They are in motion, soundless ecstasy. They cluster around the now-invisible form of the goat. They have covered themselves with lengths of black cloth. They are one. They lurch away from the center (now in blue light) and reveal: a black object (made up of some of the COVEN's bodies) which passes for a coach. Seated in front of it is a black-cloaked figure, face invisible. Standing in front of it is RENFIELD, a solicitor, holding a portmanteau and wearing an overcoat. (This revelation of the first scene should appear to materialize out of the massed body of the COVEN)

THE CASTLE ROAD

THE COACHMAN: The Englishman?

RENFIELD: Yes. Renfield.

THE COACHMAN: You are expected.

The COVEN is now a group of townspeople moving anxiously about the perimeter of the scene. Muffled whispers during the rest of this scene, in which only these words audible:

TOWNSPEOPLE: Ordog—pokol—stregoica—vrolok—vlkoslak—

A WOMAN approaches RENFIELD.

WOMAN: Do you know what day it is?

RENFIELD: Yes. The fourth of May.

WOMAN: But do you know what day it is?

A MAN: The Eve of St. George's Day.

WOMAN: Do you know where you are going?

RENFIELD: To the castle of Count Dracula.

ANOTHER WOMAN: [*Runs up to him and kneels*] Do not go. At least, wait a day or two before starting.

RENFIELD: [*Raising her up*] It is imperative. I must go.

The WOMAN gives him a crucifix.

WOMAN: Wear this. [*She makes the sign of the cross*]

The Townspeople point two fingers at him, making the sign of the cross. RENFIELD mounts. The COACHMAN cracks a fantastically long whip. The COVEN falls flat on the floor. The coach is in motion, though remaining in place. The journey of the coach is done with light and sound and the motions of the COVEN. The coach passes wolves (the COVEN, hunched on floor, covered with their black cloths, holding lighted tapers to the sides of their heads, like eyes). Blue flames flicker— when they are behind the COACHMAN, he is revealed to be transparent (black cheesecloth form with no one inside it. Note: the actor

has slipped behind the "coach" proper. At the end of the scene, he will be back in place, behind the cheesecloth form). During the journey, the SPEAKER recites from the Tibetan Book of the Dead.

SPEAKER:
Strange sounds, weird sights, disturbed
   visions may occur.
Do not impose your will on them.
Do not fear them.
They are old friends.
Blood-drinking demons, machines,
   monsters, devils,
Exist nowhere but in your own skull.
The motto is peace, acceptance.
The key is inaction, merging.

The wolves begin to howl. The horses rear. The COACHMAN reins in the horses, dismounts, goes out of sight. RENFIELD is ringed by wolves. Their howling terrifies him.

RENFIELD: [*Calling*] Coachman. They're upon us. They're here. [*He feels strangled by the encroaching circle*]

The COACHMAN returns. With a gesture, as though brushing them aside, he causes the wolves to fall back. They flatten on the stage floor, extinguish their tapers (their eyes). Absolute silence.

COACHMAN: We have arrived. Come in.

RENFIELD takes his portmanteau from the coach, and goes in. The COACHMAN turns, and walks to stage center. He is wearing the goat's head.

THE LIGHTING OF TORCHES

From behind him, the goat's torch is lighted, as the coach figures separate. The COVEN collects six torches and pans (of water). They light their torches from the goat's candle, and stand them upright in the pans, which are arranged like footlights. The coffin boxes are shifted about for the next scene. Under this torch preparation,

SPEAKER:
You are in the magic theatre of heroes
   and demons.
Devils, sorcerers, infernal spirits.
The werewolf, the vampire, the witch.
The whole divine theatre of figures are
   aspects of yourself.
The whole fantastic comedy takes place
   within you.
Do not become attached to the figures.
Do not be afraid of them.
Recognize them.

Six of the COVEN lie prone in front of the torches, feet toward audience, heads upstage. The actor wearing the goat head removes it: he is DRACULA. RENFIELD enters for scene, without coat or portmanteau. A down-light at center is put on. The scene begins.

THE CASTLE

DRACULA: I am Count Dracula. I bid you welcome to my house. Come in. The night air is chill, and you must needs eat and rest. [REN-FIELD *comes toward him*] I pray you, be seated, and sup how you please. You will, I trust, excuse me that I do not join you. [*He uncovers the dish for* RENFIELD, *who sits. He pours for* RENFIELD. *The goblet and dish are the altar's chalice and bowl*] My coachman has told me of your experiences on the road. I must remind you that we are in Transylvania, and Transylvania is not England. Our ways are not your ways. You know something of what strange things there may be already. Tomorrow you must tell me of London, and of the house you have procured for me. I am glad that it is old and big, and that it has a chapel of old times. We Transylvanian nobles love not to think that our bones may lie among the common dead. You have brought the deed? [RENFIELD *takes it from his breast pocket and gives it to him.* DRACULA *regards the papers*] For some years past, I have longed to go to your great England. I long to go through the crowded streets of your mighty London, to be in the midst of the whirl and rush of humanity, to share its life, its change, its death, and all that makes it what it is. I trust you will forgive me, but I have much work to do in private this evening. You will, I hope, find all things as you wish. This will be your room. Retire when you please. [*He leaves*]

RENFIELD *sits motionless, then rises and goes to his bed. He removes his coat. The six figures lying prone rise slightly and hunch forward.* RENFIELD *stops.*

RENFIELD: Who is there? Who is there?

The six plunge the torch flames into the pans of water. Black light throughout theatre. In niches against the walls of the theatre, SIX VAMPIRE WOMEN appear, luminous in black light. They and RENFIELD'S *shirt are prominent. They advance toward* RENFIELD, *who freezes in (formal) posture of fear.*

VAMPIRE I: Go on.

VAMPIRE II:
    You are the first, and we shall follow.
    Yours is the right to begin.

VAMPIRE III:
    He is young and strong.

VAMPIRE II:
    There are kisses for us all.

VAMPIRE III:
    How dare you cast your eyes on him.
    Back, I tell you.

Light above. DRACULA *appears aloft in a long black cloak, reaching to floor of stage. He is an immensely long apparition.*

DRACULA: [*To* VAMPIRE III] Love him.

VAMPIRE III: Yes, I can love. You know it from the past. Is it not so? [*She is standing over* RENFIELD, *who is now reclining*]

VAMPIRE II: Are we to have nothing tonight?

VAMPIRE III: Back to your own place. Your time has not yet come.

DRACULA: [*To the other vampires*] Wait. Have patience. On the voyage, he will be yours. [*To* VAMPIRE III] Embrace him.

VAMPIRE III *lies on* RENFIELD'S *body and fastens her teeth in his neck. (This is performed as a gentle, loving gesture)* RENFIELD *exhales deeply. The green and purplish light seeps back, replacing the black light.*

THE BANQUET

Solemn, but matter of fact. DRACULA *moves to stage level and puts on the goat's head. Meanwhile, without disturbing their positions (prone, she on him),* RENFIELD *and the VAM-PIRE are borne to center stage and laid on the altar. The VAMPIRE rises and rejoins the COVEN.* DRACULA *brings to the altar a sack with a form inside it. He removes a dead baby from the sack. The ritual preparation of the baby is done over* RENFIELD'S *body. As the blood drips on his face, he grunts with pleasure, drinking drops of blood, writhing. Blood from the baby is put into the chalice. Urine and dung are squeezed out of the baby's body and put into the chalice. The segmented body is distributed to the COVEN. They eat the flesh and drink the brew from the chalice. A rhythmic tremor begins to run through the COVEN. As they respond to it more and more, they rise, and gradually fall into the pattern of,*

THE WITCHES' ROUND

The Round is danced by the whole COVEN alternately facing in and out from a circle, hands clasped and heads turned so that they might see each other. The pattern of the dance can be either a circle or a more complicated form, swastika or other. Staggered gait, jerky movements, which induce a shift of conscious-ness so that psychic contact can be made with inner life. The dance produces "magical" re-active effects on the dancers. When the dancers are possessed by the spirit, they are capable of acrobatic and muscular feats absolutely impossible in their normal state. Frenzy.

THE VOYAGE

Lentissimo, lentissimo, lentissimo. Overhead, on levels that exploit the full height of the playing area (or on an arrangement of planks connecting ladders of different heights), the six men of the COVEN *represent sailors—in the lookout, at the wheel, on the masts, on the deck—all facing in one direction, into the wind. On the stage floor—belowdecks—boxes.* RENFIELD *is still lying on the altar-coffin. Pans of dry ice near the boxes cover the floor of the stage with mist (if possible, much of the stage is enveloped in mist). Rhythm of the scene is established by the creaking of the ship (excruciatingly slow, audible on speakers) and synchronized motion of the crew. The helmsman at the wheel, the mate beside him, and the other sailors hang limp in their positions —dead. They flop gently with the roll of the ship. As the* SPEAKER *drones on very softly, hypnotically, reading instructions from the* Book of the Dead, *one by one the coffins— their glass-paneled sides now facing the spec-tators—are slowly, slowly illuminated, re-vealing the sleeping* DRACULA *and* VAMPIRES. *And severally, at random, they rise from their coffins and move somnambulistically about the mist-covered stage floor. The scene is devoted —literally—to putting the spectators to sleep. It is a calculated exercise in hypnosis.*

SPEAKER: [*Throughout scene*]
You imagine a voyage of the dead.
The figures before you are lifeless.
You have slipped back into self-isolation.
The people around you are robots.
The world is a façade, a stage set.
You are a helpless marionette,
A plastic doll in a plastic world.
Cold,
Feelingless,
Wooden,
Waxen.
You are unable to feel.
You say: I am dead.
I will never live and feel again.
Do not force feeling by action, by shouting,

Do not be attracted to your old self.
Merge with the feeling of oneness of all
life and all matter.

DRACULA *climbs to the upper levels on which the sailors are hanging limply, and beckons them down from their perches. They join the drifting movement of the* VAMPIRES *below.* DRACULA, *with a gesture, instructs them to drag ashore the boxes. They go off with the boxes (and the pans of ice).* DRACULA *and the* VAMPIRES *drift off too.* RENFIELD, *alone, rises. He is bewildered, then terrified. He cries out:*

RENFIELD: Master. [*He jumps off the altar, and screams in desperation*] Don't leave me. [*He falls to the ground. An endlessly prolonged scream from* RENFIELD]

THE CHURCHYARD

LUCY *and* MINA *are sitting on the altar box. White lawn dresses. Sunset, then night. Lovely English churchyard, out of Trollope. (Sug-gest in lights.)*

LUCY: His eyes were beautiful. When I first saw them, they were red and terrible, but when I looked closely, they were beautiful. I suppose I walked here to the churchyard. I didn't quite dream. It all seemed to be real. I only wanted to be in this spot—I don't know why, but I was afraid of something—I don't know what. I suppose I was asleep, but I remember passing through the street and over the bridge. And I heard dogs howling as I went up the steps. Then there is a memory of something long and dark with red eyes, just as I see his, and something very sweet and very bitter all around me at once. And then I sank into deep green water, and everything seemed to pass away from me. My soul seemed to go out from my body, and float about in the air. Then there was an agonizing feeling, as if I were in an earthquake, and I came back and found you shaking my body. I saw you crying, "Lucy." I saw you before I heard you or felt you.

MINA: It will be dark soon.

LUCY: No, let me stay. I want to be here alone, and go back alone.

MINA *leaves.* LUCY *lies down on the altar-box. She remains there throughout the next episode.*

THE MADMAN

First part of scene, realistic. After DRACULA'S *entrance, same presentational style as in earlier scenes.* RENFIELD *in a cage, the size of a room.*

With him, DR. SEWARD *and two* GUARDS. RENFIELD *screams—continuation of scream at end of his last scene. Lights up.*

SEWARD: Overpower him.

RENFIELD: I beg you, don't put me into a jacket. I won't harm you. I have no hatred for you. You don't understand. [SEWARD *nevertheless signals to the* GUARDS] No! Don't tie me! I'm abandoned, I'm suffering. I won't make you suffer with me. [*They tie him into a strait-jacket.* RENFIELD *is quiet. He speaks gently*] The blood is the life. I must do for myself now. He's gone from me. He won't help me. [*He weeps quietly*]

SEWARD: Who won't help you? Who is He?

RENFIELD: I must have life. I must do for my-self now. Will you give me sugar?

SEWARD: For what?

RENFIELD: For crumbs.

SEWARD: What will you do with them?

RENFIELD: Feed them to flies.

SEWARD: And the flies?

RENFIELD: To spiders.

GUARD: We give him no more sugar.

SEWARD: What harm is there in it?

GUARD: He feeds the spiders to sparrows, then eats the sparrows himself.

OTHER GUARD: He eats them alive. He vomits up the feathers.

RENFIELD: [*Laughs*] Bother all that. I'm sick of all that rubbish.

SEWARD: You want no more sugar?

RENFIELD: Give me a cat. Let me have a cat . . . a kitten?

SEWARD: You're laughing at us.

RENFIELD: [*Suddenly*] SH!

SEWARD: What is it?

RENFIELD: AH . . . [*Silence. A long sliver of* DRACULA'S *face—as though seen through a door crack—is projected, the full height of the stage, behind* RENFIELD'S *cage. In frenzy*] He has come!

SEWARD: [*To* GUARDS] Control him.

RENFIELD: No, I will be still!

SEWARD: You said you were like Enoch. Why?

RENFIELD: Because he walked with God.

SEWARD: Have you a soul?

RENFIELD: I don't want to talk to you. You don't count now. My Master is at hand!

SEWARD: You don't care about spiders any more either?

RENFIELD: [*Screaming*] Don't torment me! Go!

SEWARD: [*To* GUARDS] Stay close to him.

Faint suggestions of bat's wings above, which RENFIELD *follows with his eyes. Then the*

projection of DRACULA'S *face dims, and* DRACULA *himself is visible above the cage, his cloak falling to the floor in Beardsley folds. Specks of light swirling amid blue-toned stage light. They dart about. Flitting shadows of small bat forms.*

RENFIELD: I am here to do your bidding, Master. I am your slave, and you will reward me, for I shall be faithful. Do not pass me by. Let me join you now.

DRACULA: Soon.

RENFIELD: I shall be patient. I can wait.

DRACULA: You shall have gifts.

RENFIELD: They are life to me.

DRACULA: You shall be of my household.

RENFIELD: [*In paroxysm, screaming*] I want to be with you! I'll frustrate them. They shan't murder me by inches. I'll be with my Lord and Master. [*He beats his head against the bars of his cage*]

The GUARDS *rush in, then* SEWARD.

SEWARD: Stop him.

GUARD: [*To the other*] The chains.

They chain him to either side of the cage so that he is in center of cell, preventing him from getting close to the bars. RENFIELD *is on his knees, head bowed, immobolized, weeping quietly.* SEWARD *regards him, then motions to the* GUARDS *to leave. The three exit.*

RENFIELD: [*Weeping. Talking quietly. In misery*] I shall be faithful. Now that you are near, I shall be patient. I will pray to you, and for the life to come. Will you embrace me?

DRACULA *raises his arms—hugely extended. like wings. His cloak enfolds the entire cage.*

THE RITE

Swirling specks of light continue. DR. VAN HELSING, DR. SEWARD, ARTHUR HOLMSWOOD *and* MINA. MINA'S *white dress,* SEWARD'S *and* VAN HELSING'S *white coats,* ARTHUR'S *white suit. Acting style is patently nineteenth century, but not to be done as parody. For the most part, they speak in anxious whispers. All through the scene with the four visitors and* LUCY *on her bed (the altar), the* COVEN, *flat on their stomachs, completely covered by their black cloths, crawl onto the stage (so that the floor of the stage looks alive with dark living things). The four in white take no notice of them. More huge projections of* DRACULA *appear one after the other on different parts of the stage. In all of them, his eyes are fixed on the four gathered about* LUCY. VAN HELSING *goes to* LUCY. SEWARD *follows him.*

VAN HELSING: [*Heavy Dutch accent*] It is not too late. Her heart beats, though but feebly. [*He goes to* ARTHUR] She is very, very bad. [ARTHUR *sits, almost fainting*] Nay, my child. Do not go on like that. You are to help her, you can do more for her than any that live and your courage is your best help.

ARTHUR: What can I do?

VAN HELSING: Come, you are a man, and it is a man we want. She wants blood, and blood she must have or die.

ARTHUR: If you only knew how gladly I would die for her, you would understand—

VAN HELSING: Good boy. In the not so far off, you will be happy you have done all for her you love. Come now and be silent. You shall kiss her once whiles I bring over the table. Friend John, help to me. [*Both look away while* ARTHUR *bends over* LUCY *and kisses her. Aside to* SEWARD] He is young and strong and of blood so pure that we need not defibrinate it. [*The transfusion is performed. Silence during the passage of the blood from one to the other, except for breathing, audible on speakers (continues to end of scene). To* SEWARD] It is enough. You attend to him, I will look to her. [SEWARD *dresses* ARTHUR'S *wound*] The brave lover, I think, deserve another kiss, which he will have presently. [*To* ARTHUR] You have saved her life, and you can rest easy in mind that all that can be is. She shall love you none the less for what you have done. [*To all of them*] Now we may begin. [*He takes a great bundle of white garlic flowers from his case. To* MINA] These are for you, Miss Mina.

MINA: Oh, dear Dr. van Helsing.

VAN HELSING: Yes, my dear, but not to play with. These are medicines. You will put them about Miss Lucy's room. You will make pretty wreath and hang him around her neck so that she sleep well. Oh, yes. They are like the lotus flower, make her trouble forgotten. It smell so like the waters of Lethe.

MINA: Oh, Professor, I believe you are only putting up a joke on us. Why, these flowers are only common garlic.

VAN HELSING: [*Sternly*] No trifling with me! There is grim purpose in all I do. And I warn you that you do not thwart me. Take care, for the sake of the others, if not for your own. [*While* MINA *puts the wreaths about,* VAN HELSING *takes a crucifix from his case*] And this most of all, to protect her from any. [*He places the crucifix upright at* LUCY'S *head on the altar. They all kneel*] God. God. God. What have we done, what has this poor thing done that we are so sore beset? Is there fate among us still, sent down from

the pagan world of old, that such things must be, and in such a way? How are all the powers of the devil against us? We must see and act. Devils or no devils, or all the devils at once, it matters not. We fight him all the same. In your name, in your father's, in your holy ghost's. [*They rise*] Come. [*To* MINA] You will watch outside the door, and see to Miss Lucy during the night. May all be prevented.

They leave. Muttered words, unintelligible sounds, are heard simultaneously with the sounds of breathing emanating from the speakers. The stage lighting (the green and purplish tints) again embraces the whole theatre. It is supplanted gradually by black light. The VAMPIRES, *in their niches around the walls, alternately appear and fade out of sight. (This continues until the Rite begins.) A projection of* DRACULA *appears behind the altar, towering over the figure of* LUCY.

DRACULA'S VOICE: [*To* LUCY] Nosferatu.

She rises. Sounds of wolves howling. The swirling points of light, the flitting shadow of bat forms. LUCY *rids the room of all the protective talismans. While she is engaged in this, the* SPEAKER *recites.*

SPEAKER:
  You are now preparing visions of sexual acts.
  Desire and anticipation seize you.
  You wonder what sexual performance is expected of you.
  Withhold yourself from action or attachment.
  If you try to join the orgy you are hallucinating,
  You will experience possessive desire and jealousy,
  You will suffer stupidity and misery.
  Be neither attracted nor repulsed by your sexual hallucinations.

The Rite begins. LUCY *stands on the altar facing the crucifix and disrobes.*

LUCY: Enter in, to this altar, my Master, my Lord. Protect me, in your embrace, from the violent, the treacherous, the hypocrites, the liars. [*The men of the* COVEN, *who are still prone on the floor, still completely covered in their black cloths, rise and sit in a wide ring facing the altar.* LUCY *lifts the crucifix from its place and lays it flat on the altar. She rises with the goat mask in her hands, a torch alight. The back of the goat mask faces us. As the* COVEN *lights its torches from the goat's, they chant in response to* LUCY] Come my Lord who has suffered wrong

COVEN: My Lord who has suffered wrong

LUCY: The Proscribed God of ancient days

COVEN: Proscribed of ancient days

LUCY: Unjustly driven out of heaven

COVEN: Driven out of heaven

LUCY: The implanter of seed in the earth

COVEN: Seed of the earth

LUCY: God of my body and my blood

COVEN: Body and blood

The torches are again ringing the altar. The COVEN sits outside the ring, their backs to the altar. DRACULA, cloaked, has appeared upstage of the altar, and facing upstage. (The projection of him dims before his appearance on stage.) The COVEN begins the singing of the Gloria. The text is sung backwards. LUCY places the goat mask on DRACULA. She unfastens his cloak, which drops to the floor. He is still facing upstage. He is naked, covered with glistening black hair, like an animal. His torso is human, his legs and feet those of a goat. LUCY, with ceremonious gravity, kisses his backside. He turns, and faces forward. Two men of the COVEN fasten an enormous dildo on him. LUCY is elevated by the two men for her ritual impregnation (this is ceremonial, there is no sexuality in the action). She is then placed on her back on the altar, and lies on the crucifix. Two black candlesticks are put at the head of the altar, which she grasps. She is outspread. The Mass is then performed on her body. The Credo is chanted backwards by the GOAT-PRIEST. He deposits the Host—a black compost—on her loins. He sets it aflame; it bakes on her loins. LUCY moans in ecstatic pain. Bats, toads and insects are deposited on her body (they are attached to long fishing poles held by the COVEN). Prayers are said over these offerings by the GOAT-PRIEST. At the conclusion of the prayers, the offerings are "flown" from LUCY's body. The sacrament is distributed to the COVEN while the Agnus Dei is sung backwards. At the conclusion of the sacrament, LUCY raises the crucifix from the altar and, holding it aloft, cries out.

LUCY: I defy you, Jesus, I, the priestess of this rite, whose body is now both altar and offering, to strike me with lightning and turn my flesh to dust this moment, before the eyes of my faithful coven, if your power is greater than my Lord's and Master's. [*As part of the ritual, all look up expectantly and wait. After a long pause, they scream their pleasure at Jesus' defeat. LUCY smashes the crucifix to bits*]

My Lord Satan is redeemed. I give myself to my Lord. My Lord and Master, your bride is hungry for your embrace.

The torches are again doused suddenly. The lighting is again green and purplish, and fills the theatre. The same atmosphere which preceded the rite (the flitting bat forms, etc.) is recovered. The VAMPIRES move again through the audience toward the stage, gasping, making whispering and sucking noises. LUCY is lifted and put on her back on the altar. The GOAT-PRIEST moves to the foot of the altar and stands before LUCY, his back to us, a huge, naked animal figure. When the VAMPIRES have reached the stage, and the whole COVEN is moving again as in the Voyage scene (narcotic movement), the GOAT-PRIEST removes his mask. His hovering presence excites LUCY. He touches her. LUCY's sounds blend with the low breathing and sucking sounds of the COVEN. DRACULA mounts her and buries his face in her neck. LUCY cries out, a triumphant, impassioned cry. MINA bursts into the room holding a lamp. The COVEN falls flat on the floor and remains motionless. LUCY turns to MINA with a wild, mocking look and laughs outrageously. MINA screams, drops the lantern with a crash and runs out. LUCY lies back, and, rubbing her body, her breasts, her loins, with the sheer pleasure of longing, urges:

LUCY: My lover. My lover. Embrace me. Again.

DRACULA's body covers hers. He buries his teeth in her neck. She is in bliss.

ACT II

THE DEATH OF LUCY

The COVEN sits in a semicircle, facing upstage, dressed in long black robes and holding tapers. One of the COVEN, standing center, puts a mask of LUCY on a cross-braced pole. The mask has the face of a vampire. The flowing garments of the vampire are hung from the cross-bracing. In the dim light, the effigy of LUCY is borne about the stage. It moves faster and faster, until it appears to take on motion of its own. A nightingale singing outside; the face of DRACULA, dimly perceived, is projected on the back wall. The projection covers the wall. The effigy of LUCY, now floating, now flying, is borne to the altar, where it is laid, as though sleeping. The four white ones —MINA, ARTHUR, DR. VAN HELSING and DR. SEWARD—group for a formal deathbed scene. Again, the actors perform formally in Victorian idiom, but not parodistically.

VAN HELSING: She is dying. [MINA, *weeping, goes to* SEWARD, *who supports her*] Wake that poor boy, and let him come and see the last.

SEWARD: [*Seats* MINA, *and raises* ARTHUR. *To* ARTHUR] Come, my dear fellow, summon all your fortitude.

ARTHUR *approaches* LUCY'S *bed.* LUCY'S *heavy breathing is heard on the speaker.*

LUCY: [*Her voice emanates from inside the altar-coffin, from below the effigy*] Arthur! My love. I want you with me. Kiss me.

As ARTHUR *bends over her,* VAN HELSING *swoops upon him, grabs him by the neck, and hurls him across the room.*

VAN HELSING: Not for your life! Not for your living soul, and hers!

LUCY'S *breathing (over the speaker) becomes a spasm of rage. She moans, but almost inaudibly.* LUCY *extends her hands toward* VAN HELSING. (*NOTE: the hands are extended from below the effigy.*)

LUCY: [*To* VAN HELSING] Thank you, my true friend. My true friend and his. Oh, guard him from me, guard him and give him peace.

VAN HELSING *kneels beside her.*

VAN HELSING: I swear it. [*To* ARTHUR] Come, my child, take her hand in yours and kiss her on the forehead but once.

ARTHUR *kisses her forehead.*

LUCY: [*Suddenly, in the voice of the Priestess of the Rite*] Embrace me. Love me. Love me. Kiss my mouth. Take my body. Kiss me. [VAN HELSING *tears* ARTHUR *out of her embrace. A great cry*] Give me my lover.

ARTHUR: Let me go to her!

VAN HELSING: Courage!

A long sigh is heard on the loudspeaker. Then LUCY'S *breathing stops.*

ARTHUR: [*La Bohème*] LUCY! [*He falls across her body*]

VAN HELSING *goes to the bed, and bends over* LUCY.

VAN HELSING: It is over. She is dead. [VAN HELSING *leads* ARTHUR *to a seat, where he sobs, beyond comfort*]

MINA: [*Approaches* LUCY] We thought her dying whilst she slept, and sleeping when she died. She is restored in death. Her end is peace.

VAN HELSING: It is only the beginning. Friend John, bring me postmortem knives. We must cut off her head, and take out her heart. [*Sensation among the other three*] It is I that shall operate, and you must only help. When she is entombed, we shall uncover her, and do what we must.

SEWARD: But why?

VAN HELSING: I have good reason for all.

ARTHUR: In God's name, what does it mean? Are we mad? Or what sort of horrible danger is there?

VAN HELSING: It is for your dear girl's sake. Come, now we must pray for her soul.

The four leave.

THE SORCERESS' SACRILEGE

The COVEN, *robed in black and holding their lighted tapers, make up a procession. They take up the coffin on which* LUCY *is lying, and proceed, while chanting the Burial Service, to the back of the stage, where the coffin is raised high and lowered three times, then placed on a platform. As the procession is about to lift the coffin, the effigy of* LUCY *lying on it is raised high so that she appears to swoop into the air. The effigy is moved about as though it is enraged.* LUCY, *in the voice of the High Priestess of the Rite, cries out (above the chant of the Burial Service, and accompanying the procession) a curse against the four in white.*

LUCY: I call on the lightning to strike their bodies and wither their flesh. Let my Master empty their veins of blood and leave them without desire, dead to every desire. Let their veins shrivel and their bodies lie in agony, in eternal drought. Let them scream with the pain of hunger and thirst forever, and never know, never, that hunger and thirst are their pain. I call on my Master to bring me toads, to bring me crawling things to eat, to bite, to crush, to bleed, to drink, and may he let *them*—those whom I hate—see me and loathe me and vomit at the sight of me, and be damned forever not to know that the blood is the life, that the kiss of blood is joy, that the joy of life is my Master's.

Very slowly, during the procession and the curse, the projection of DRACULA'S *face at the rear of the stage dissolves into a matching projection of the goat head, so that the features of the one are individually and precisely replaced by the features of the other. At the end of the procession and the curse, the* COVEN *flings off its black robes and claps on demon masks. Their bodies are naked, but painted with viscera, organs, veins and arteries, glistening with slime and blood. The masks are of Tibetan demons; the wrists and ankles of the* COVEN *members have bracelets and anklets attached so that each body's silhouette reflects that of an Oriental demon's. Some of the*

COVEN *drag on a sack and throw it onto* LUCY's *coffin. Others set up an uneven line of torches across the stage. In place of her effigy (which disappeared behind the coffin)* LUCY *rises from the coffin—vampire* entière. *She dumps the contents of the sack onto coffin and floor; a mass of toads (presumably) swollen with blood. The* COVEN *freezes, facing her. She lifts several toads and bites into them. The blood spurts; the* COVEN *goes wild. She throws a handful into the midst of the* COVEN, *which they grab and eat. The* COVEN *leaps and tumbles over the torches, screaming. The* COVEN *grows wanton. It reaches delirium. It passes beyond its delirium to the rite's climactic image of ecstatic unification. When it reaches this final state, which is blissful, throbbing.*

SPEAKER:

> The motor of the heart merges with the
>   pulsing of all life.
> The heart breaks,
> And red fire bleeds into all living beings.
> All living beings are throbbing together.
> You are at last divested of robot clothes
>   and limbs.
> Every cell in your body is singing
>   its song of freedom.
> The entire universe is in harmony,
> Freed from your censorship,
> Freed from your control.
> You are a joyful part of all life,
> Ecstatic, orgiastic, blissful unity.

[*A long pause. The unified pulsation of the* COVEN *is suddenly broken*]

> You are afraid.
> The self, an island in this throbbing life,
> Screams, STOP.

THE MURDER

VAN HELSING'S *voice is heard (from loudspeaker on stage).*

VAN HELSING: Unlock the tomb! [*The torches are doused and the* COVEN *falls flat. The brilliant red of the previous scene changes to cold blue—a dank, dark stage. Silence.* VAN HELSING *leads in the four, each carrying a lantern. He carries a crucifix before him.* SEWARD *carries a bag. The* COVEN *crawls out of sight; hissing sounds are heard on the speaker. The four stand looking about, silent. Suddenly the effigy of* LUCY *swoops up from behind her coffin, brushes them and disappears.* MINA *screams*] Have no fear from Miss Lucy, or for her. She is young as Undead, and she will heed. [LUCY *laughs uproariously (over stage speaker).* VAN HELSING *gives the crucifix to*

SEWARD] Seal up the door of the tomb with this crucifix. So, she will stay.

Suddenly, a down-spot illuminates the vampire LUCY, *standing quietly, far upstage, in the shadows.* VAN HELSING *gasps, and points to her. The other three fall back in astonishment, and* SEWARD *holds the crucifix over them.*

LUCY: [*With voluptuous grace*]
Come to me, Arthur. Leave these others and come to me. My arms are hungry for you. Come, and we can rest together. Come, my lover, come.

[*As she and* ARTHUR *begin to move toward one another,* VAN HELSING *grabs the crucifix and springs between them*]

VAN HELSING: Stay. [LUCY, *with a cry of rage leaps behind her coffin. To* ARTHUR] Answer me. Am I to proceed? Or do you falter?

ARTHUR: [*Falling to the ground*] Do as you will. There can be no horror like this ever, any more.

VAN HELSING: [*Still holding the crucifix toward the coffin, to keep the invisible* LUCY *at bay*] Light the candles. [SEWARD *takes two candles from the bag, lights them and places them on two coffins. To* MINA] Hold our cross. [*She takes it, and* VAN HELSING *takes from the bag a wooden stake about three feet long and gives it to* SEWARD. *He keeps for himself a heavy hammer.* ARTHUR *is given an ax,* MINA *a wreath of garlic. While distributing these things*] A moment's courage, and it is done. [*To* SEWARD] Take this stake in your hand, ready to place the point over the heart. [*To* ARTHUR] When the moment is here, strike in God's name, that the Undead may pass away. Yours is the blessed hand that shall strike the blow to set her free. [LUCY, *with a yell of rage, tries to leap over the coffin to escape.* VAN HELSING *prevents her, catches her by the hair, and flings her full-length on the coffin*] Arthur. Now! [LUCY *screams, tosses her head trying to get out of* VAN HELSING'S *grip.* VAN HELSING, *still holding her hair, pulls her head up high, and cries out to* ARTHUR *over* LUCY'S *screams*] Now! For our God! [*In an instant* ARTHUR, *already beside* VAN HELSING, *swings the ax and slices off* LUCY'S *head. NOTE: A standard Grand Guignol and magician's stunt simple to execute. (1) The coffin is placed narrow end to audience (after funeral procession two scenes back). (2) It is elevated on platform with concealing skirt. (3) The instant* LUCY *as vampire falls onto its surface,* VAN HELSING *is in front of coffin, concealing her falling* through. *He holds her hair (all that is visible for an instant), and during the tussle with her, drops his hand below surface of coffin, and grabs the false head.* LUCY *goes through false bottom, and leaves the stuffed body (duplicate of hers) to roll out headless. The force of the blow tips the coffin over, and* LUCY's *body falls onto the stage floor.* ARTHUR *takes* LUCY's *head from* VAN HELSING, *and* MINA *rushes to it with the wreath of garlic. To* SEWARD] Hold firm! [*As* SEWARD *grabs the rolling body and rights it, and presses the stake directly to the heart,* VAN HELSING *drives the stake in with repeated blows of his hammer. Blood is spurting from* LUCY's *severed head, her neck, her heart. While* ARTHUR *holds the severed head,* MINA *stuffs* LUCY's *mouth with garlic. When the four have finished, they come forward, join hands, and speak to the audience one after the other (Don Giovanni epilogue).* The ordeal was fearful, but none of us did falter.

ARTHUR:
Mine was the hand that sent her to the stars,
The hand of him that loved her best.

MINA:
Now our Lucy takes her place among the other angels.

SEWARD: Her captive soul is free.

The four then walk in procession. During their processional,

SPEAKER:
You were terrified by the radiant red light,
With a terrible ripping of fibers and veins,
You tore your roots out of the body of life.
The throbbing stopped.
The ecstasy ceased.
Your plastic doll body hardened and
    stiffened into its angular form.

Now you walk
Outside the stream,
Isolated,
Impotent,
Miserable.

THE BETRAYAL

In the dark, RENFIELD's *scream. Lights up; he is in his cell. From far side of stage, the four are walking toward his cell. As they approach it and climb to its stage level,* RENFIELD *is in breathless prayer, choking back tears.*

RENFIELD: Why do you leave me here to suffer this death? Why do you leave me with these demons of righteousness? I am not of their world. Believe me, believe I am not as they are, I am not of them. I am of your body and your blood. I am at one with you. I have no substance but your substance. I have no will but

yours. I believe in your body and your spirit. I believe in your blood. I hunger and thirst for you. I hunger and thirst. Cast me aside, tread on me, I will do what you will, and shout your praise. My Master, I am your tears, I weep your blood, I am a lake of tears. [*He hears the approach of the visitors behind him*] Save me, my Master! The righteous are here.

The four enter.

SEWARD: Visitors.

RENFIELD *looks up, but does not respond to* SEWARD. *For a long time he stares at* MINA.

RENFIELD: [*To* MINA] Why are *you* here?

VAN HELSING: Only to talk with you.

RENFIELD: No need. [*Again, to* MINA] Why are *you* here? I don't care for pale people. I like them with lots of blood in them. Yours seems to have run out. You have bad dreams. You dreamed you coupled with my Master, and that He clapped your face to His body, and made you drink from the gash in his side. You dreamed this many times. [*To* SEWARD] You made light of Him. But I warned you.

SEWARD: Of what?

RENFIELD: Of what is in her face. Touch a cross to it. [VAN HELSING *takes a crucifix from his pocket. He touches it to* MINA's *forehead. She screams with pain*] She is one of us. Like the other, whom you destroyed.

MINA: [*Falling to her knees*] Unclean! Unclean!

RENFIELD: She belongs to you. She should not be one of us. But He has taken her too.

VAN HELSING: Who is *He?*

RENFIELD: My Master.

VAN HELSING: Who is your Master?

RENFIELD: S-sh-h-h-h. He will hear you.

VAN HELSING: And if he does?

RENFIELD: It is not just that He should pass me by, and choose her. [*He screams*] It is not just! [*He is calm*] She will follow him.

MINA: My God, protect me!

VAN HELSING: When he comes, we will be waiting.

RENFIELD: He will not come again.

VAN HELSING: Where is he?

MINA: [*With closed eyes*] In his grave. He is asleep in his own earth. Cold. Dark. He is on a road. I am inside his body.

RENFIELD: [*Screams*] Master, don't abandon me!

MINA: I am inside his body. I am being carried in darkness. There is silence. No, there are shuffling steps. Darkness, but there are points of light. Lanterns. My way is being lighted.

RENFIELD: The gypsies carry Him. They are not afraid of Him. They are taking Him away.

VAN HELSING: Away?

RENFIELD: From me.

VAN HELSING: Where are they taking him?

RENFIELD: [Screams] Away! [Calm] To His own land. He is going home.

MINA: [Screams] I will not go!

VAN HELSING: What road is he on?

RENFIELD: I won't tell you. He is my Master.

VAN HELSING: What road?

RENFIELD: Back to the sea.

VAN HELSING: The port?

RENFIELD: [Waits, then he nods] To the port. Five miles from. Five miles from. [He is trembling] At Whitby.

VAN HELSING: [To the other visitors] Come.

They leave quickly. RENFIELD, alone, shouts after them.

RENFIELD: You cannot catch Him. He is greater than all of you.

THE MAGIC CIRCLE

The figures onstage are in silhouette. Some of the COVEN are in the shape of a grotesque horse, on which MINA rides. VAN HELSING leads the horse, ARTHUR and SEWARD follow. The four wear long white traveling cloaks. The procession moves onstage in a wide circle. The rest of the COVEN are formless forms (covered in their black cloths) on the periphery of the circle. They move restlessly, like great sleeping beasts. Their sounds are whispers, hisses. The stage floor begins to fill with mist (continues to the end). The lighting of the scene (after the silhouetted journey on the horse) comes in gradually, filling the stage with indefinable anxieties.

SPEAKER: [During the silent procession]
    In confusion and bewilderment
    You look at your fellow voyagers and
        friends
    And sense that they cannot understand you.
    You think: "I am dead! What shall I do?"
    And in misery wonder if you will ever
        return.
    You feel oppressed, squeezed,
    Held within a cage or prison,
    Trapped within a magic circle.
    These are signs that you are struggling to
        return.
    Do not struggle.
    Your reentry will happen by itself.
    Only recognize where you are.
    Recognition will lead to your liberation.

VAN HELSING brings the travelers to a halt.

VAN HELSING: Is this the road?

MINA: [Whose eyes remain shut throughout the episode] Not yet.

They continue in silence. They stop.

VAN HELSING: Have we found the road?

MINA: Not yet.

They continue in silence. They stop.

VAN HELSING: Is it here?

MINA: Not yet. [They continue in silence] Stop. He will pass here.

The horse is led to one side. MINA is taken off.

VAN HELSING: Build the fire. [A fire is set at the rear of stage center. MINA is seated center stage, on a box] Draw the circle. [ARTHUR and SEWARD, with their feet, describe a wide circle on the ground, with MINA at its center. During the drawing of the circle, the COVEN, on the periphery, begin to emerge, bit by bit, from their coverings. They are wearing the Oriental demon masks. They are dimly visible, but the eyes of all of them are phosphorescent. One by one, the women vampires become discernible among the demon figures, but faintly] Take the Host. [He holds up the bowl. The men each take wafers. They cross themselves, then crumble the wafers around the edge of the circle. Standing at the fire in the rear of the stage, to MINA] Will you not come over to the fire? [MINA starts to go, but stops before reaching the edge of the circle] Why not go on?

MINA: I cannot.

ARTHUR: [At a different point outside the circle, to MINA] Will you come to this side? [She starts again, but stops] Go on.

MINA: I cannot.

SEWARD: [At a different point outside the circle, to MINA] Will you come here? [She tries again, but stops] Come.

MINA: I cannot.

VAN HELSING: She is safe. If she cannot leave the circle, none whom we dread may enter. [VAN HELSING gives ARTHUR and SEWARD crosses] Make your ambush.

ARTHUR and SEWARD go off together. VAN HELSING joins MINA in the center of the circle. The COVEN outside the circle become somewhat more agitated; they cluster around the horse momentarily, then leave him again. The horse rears and moans.

VAMPIRES: Come, sister. Come to us. Come. Come.

VAN HELSING: What is around us?

MINA: [Eyes still closed] Wolves. Snakes. Great dogs. Some. Flying things.

VAN HELSING: And spirits such as Lucy's?

MINA: [*Doesn't answer for a moment*] Yes.

VAMPIRES: Come, sister. Come. [*They laugh*]

VAN HELSING: They cannot touch you. [*He starts for the fire*]

MINA: Take care. Don't go there. Here you are safe.

VAN HELSING: I have the cross. It is for you that I fear.

MINA: There is none safer in all the world from them than I am.

VAMPIRES: You are one of us. Come to us. Come, sister. Come to us.

The COVEN *cluster again around the horse. Sharp, hissing sounds. They swirl around the horse. He bridles, trembles, moans. He begins to fall.*

VAN HELSING: [*Inside the circle*] What is happening?

MINA: They have fastened on the horse. [VAN HELSING *moves toward the horse*] It is too late. His life is almost gone.

The horse sinks to the ground and lies still.

VAN HELSING: Did they drain his blood?

MINA: No. He died of terror.

They are silent.

VAN HELSING: Are they coming?

MINA: They are almost here.

VAN HELSING: [*Rises*] Make ready. [*He brings two lighted torches from the fire to* MINA. *She stands in the center of the circle, holding the torches.* VAN HELSING *goes out*]

THE SACRIFICE

Slow and deliberate. The episode is performed as a grave, utterly unimpassioned ritual.

SPEAKER: The gypsies came up the road bearing the coffin of the Master. [*The line of gypsies, carrying lanterns, precedes the coffin, which is mounted on wheels. They pull it with ropes*] There was a struggle. The protectors of the coffin abandoned Him. [VAN HELSING, SEWARD *and* ARTHUR *come out of ambush and attack the cart and the gypsies. The gypsies slash at them with knives; the three men protect themselves with their implements: the hammer, the stake, the ax.* ARTHUR *mounts*

the cart and rips open the lid of the coffin. The Gypsies run away. The COVEN *disperses gradually. The rest of the ritual is done almost in silence, the indistinct and inarticulate sounds of the* COVEN *and on the speaker fading out*] The body was disinterred. [DRACULA *is lifted from the coffin and placed on the ground before the fire*] The heart was impaled. [*The stake is hammered, soundlessly and deliberately, through* DRACULA'S *heart*] The head was severed. [*The ax is brought down on* DRACULA'S *neck slowly, and passes through the neck effortlessly*] The Master revealed Himself. [*The severed head and body are lifted and impaled on a post center stage, directly behind the fire. But in transit from ground to post, the head becomes the Goat's head, and the body, an empty goatskin*] He was burned, so that He might not return. [MINA *puts the torches to the goatskin. The effigy is aflame. While it burns, the entire* COVEN *emerges quietly, dressed in black, as at the beginning of the play. They form a broken pattern of figures all over the stage. They observe the burning. The Four Actors remove their traveling cloaks. They are dressed like the rest of the* COVEN. *The whole* COVEN, *without changing positions, clasps hands*] He is remembered. [*The entire* COVEN *very slowly forms a circle, clasping one another closely. During this movement, the final instruction is read over the loudspeaker to the audience*]

It is almost time to return.
Choose your future self with care.
A vision of your new self is forming.
Recognize it.
When you return to game-existence
Try to follow the pleasant delightful visions.
If you return in panic, a fearful state will follow.
If you return in radiance, a happy state will follow.
Whatever you choose,
Choose impartially,
Without attraction or repulsion.
Go back to game-existence with good grace.
Voluntarily and freely.
Remain calm.
Remember the teachings.

The COVEN *extends its hands to the spectators, and takes one or two steps toward them.*

THE RICHEST GIRL IN THE WORLD FINDS HAPPINESS

a play for all occasions

Robert Patrick

The Richest Girl in the World Finds Happiness was first presented by Ellen Stewart at La Mama ETC, New York City, on December 24, 1970, with the following cast:

SINGER	*Mary Sterling*
MADALAYNA	*Jeffrey Herman*
STAR	*John Albano*
GIRL	*Marilyn Roberts*

It was directed by the author. Music by Mary Sterling. Jewelry by Kenneth Wyrtch.

It was subsequently revised and presented by Ellen Stewart at the Bowery Follies on February 5, 1972, with Pichulina Hampi as Madalayna and Kathy McAlpine as the Singer. Music by Preston Wood, Steve Fisher, Ms. McAlpine and the author.

To Charles Terrell

NOTE: This piece is played with no scenery, and therefore is adaptable not only to the stage but to any situation in which a celebratory entertainment is appropriate. The line "It's Christmas, too," should be altered to fit the occasion; for instance, "It's Harold's Birthday, too," or "It's Lena and Vernon's third anniversary, too," or "It's Buddy Poppy Day, too." As no settings are required, the costuming should be as elaborate as possible. Of course, if you have the $500,000 necessary to build the sets described in the dialogue, feel free.

SINGER:

Theatre, theatre, theatre,
Rhymes with "creator,"
and every critic claims
the theatre and its games
create to some extent
all outside event.
And people are always descending
to ask for a happy ending.
So we present to you tonight
an incident that turns out right,
a story that begins
as happily as it ends.
And though not repetitious,
even the center is delicious.
And the title of our story, we confess,
is, "The Richest Girl in the World
    Finds Happiness."

SINGER *exits and* MADALAYNA, *a maid, enters with a feather duster.*

MADALAYNA:

Here we are, all in ease
in the swellest of millionaire's colonies:
delightful Deal, New Jersey,
where the stars are starry, the furze
    is furzy.
It's a joy to lady-in-waiting,
watching the beautiful people mating.
Any moment we anticipate
a suitor, and he *is* a date.
The handsomest movie star is due
to make a proposal to you-know-who.
She's awaiting him in the conservatory;
it's the golden end to a gilded story,
and soon the headlines will be unfurled:
The Handsomest Star Gets the Richest Girl in the World!

The STAR, *in leather jacket glittering with studs, enters with great clumping of boots.* MADALAYNA *quivers in anticipation. He rings an imaginary doorbell and she vibrates to its*

tone. *Gaining control of herself, she opens the door. He slowly removes his jacket and drops it in her arms. She falls to her knees.*

STAR: How do you do, Madalayna?

MADALAYNA: [*To audience*] I'm a very valued retainer.

STAR: Your mistress expects me, I believe?

MADALAYNA: She's in the conservatory, reading Congreve.

STAR: [*Sticks some letters in her mouth*] I took the liberty to bring in the mail.

MADALAYNA: Can you find the conservatory?

STAR: Without fail. [*He exits*]

MADALAYNA:

Now let me see. Be still, my heart,
or I can't tell the letters apart.
Con Ed. Bell Tel. The A. & P.
Saks Fifth Avenue. A. T. & T.
It's the everyday mail one always
    expects:
the first of the month dividend
    checks.
But—oh!—What's this? Special Delivery?
Oh, all of a sudden I'm shaky and
    shivery.
I dassn't open it. Yes, I must.
Oh, if this is what I think, I'll bust.
It is! Nom Yo Harengya Kyo.
Oh, whatever will I doe?
I'm approaching a status hysterica.
My mistress is voted Miss America!
And she may at this moment be vowing to wed.
And she won't break a promise; she's
    such a straight head.
The conservatory. I must make haste.
It's the worst problem I've ever faced.
She wanted this so; it'll make her
    whole spring.
What else can you give the girl who
    has everything? [*She exits*]

THE RICHEST GIRL *and the* STAR *enter immediately.*

GIRL:

Oh, Geoffrey, darling, I'm on the
    verge
of tears because you want us to
    merge.
How on Earth could I ever refuse
    you?
But before I answer, just to amuse
    you,
let me show you around the place.

STAR:

Geraldine, come face to face
and answer me in this exquisite setting.

GIRL:

> Oh, come take a look at what you're
>   getting.
> We're in the conservatory, as you
>   know;
> let's take the tour; it's my favorite
>   show.
> Every room is unique and rare,
> imported by Pan-Am from every-
>   where.
> When you see it, I know your flesh'll
>   crawl; they did a TV special,
> where I, like Grace Kelly or Jacque-
>   line Kennedy,
> exhibited it in all its infinity,
> showing all my virginals and spinets,
> and they called it "Sixty Sets in Sixty
>   Minutes."

She leads him away with a grand gesture.
MADALAYNA *enters immediately.*

MADALAYNA:

> They're not here—Have I got the
>   wrong conservatory?
> No, there's the moneytrees in their
>   platinum amphorae.
> They must be somewhere else—but
>   since the expansion,
> there's twelve hundred rooms in this
>   motherfucking mansion.
> I've got to be fast or her dreams will
>   all come true
> and collapse in a nightmare—and
>   that will never do!
> Yoo hoo! Yoo hoo! Yoo hoo!

She exits, waving the letter. STAR *and* GIRL
enter immediately, reverently.

GIRL:

> And this is the Indian temple that is
>   known as Shalimar.
> I had it brought over tile by tile by
>   tile by tile by tile by tile by tile;
>   that's how women are.

STAR:

> It makes a truly lovely early-morning
>   breakfast nook.
> I'm glad you had the sun put there;
>   I love the way you look.

GIRL: We could roller-skate to the other side of
the house where I keep the Moon.

STAR: Very well, if that's your whim—but I want
my answer soon!

They exit. MADALAYNA *enters immediately,
throws herself down and presses her ear to the
floor.*

MADALAYNA:

> I'd swear I heard a footfall—but
>   there are 28 doors out of here.

> Perhaps I can follow her perfume—
>   if the gardenias don't interfere.
> Oh, I'm efficient, I'm loyal, I'm fast and I'm
>   funny
> And he wants to marry her for her money.

Sings:

> Oh, honey, gold is good,
> But it ain't like a good man.
> Gold don't get old the way I do.
> I can't compete with it; you don't want me;
> You wanna be free to find another girl
> Who comes complete with it.
> Willin' to work for you my baby,
> Willin' to save,
> Willin' to bear your children! Anything!
> Willin' to be your slave!
> But not if you're in love with somethin'
> Slick and hard and cold.
> Be good as gold to you, you know I do,
> But there's somethin' scared inside of you
> Says, "Nuthin's as good as gold!"
> No, no, no, no, no, nothin's good
> If nothin's as good as gold.

She exits, sniffing like a bloodhound. STAR *and*
GIRL *enter immediately.*

STAR: [*Dipping holy water from font, crossing
himself with it*] This cathedral is truly stunning, my dear; tell me, where is it from?

GIRL: [*Dipping water from font, dabbing it behind her ears*] I got it with coupons from all
of the servant children's bubble-gum.

STAR: Won't you tell me here in the sight of
What's-His-Name that you're mine?

GIRL: Not in the ruins of Ravenna, dear—it's
much too Byzantine.

STAR: Well, doesn't your mansion include a Vene-
tian canal, romantic and pleasant?

GIRL: Of course, you silly boy. Right this way.
Whaddaya think—We're a peasant?

They exit. MADALAYNA *enters immediately,
somewhat fatigued.*

MADALAYNA:

> I've looked in the Javanese treasury
>   and the Babylonian salon.
> In the Paraguayan kennel I tripped
>   over a sleeping faun.
> I've checked the Bessarabian terrace,
>   the Austrian observatory.
> (Venus is in Scorpio; Heaven protect
>   this story.)
> In the Lithuanian library they had
>   riffled through *Romeo and Juliet.*
> Oh, dear, I haven't dredged the E'hi-
>   opian lily pool yet.
> I peeked in the Gothic game room,
>   which is somnolent and sinister,
> and that reminded me the guests
>   here often include a minister.

If they elope to the Chaldean chapel,
    it truly will be *finisterre.*
[*To audience*] That's French for "End of the
world."

MADALAYNA *exits. Singer wanders across for
no good reason, singing.*

SINGER:
    Oh, it's nice to have a man around
      the house,
    but it's nice to have a house around
      the man.
    And if he ever happens to become all
      homesick, then
    it's nice to have a hallway he can
      keep his hometown in.
    One way to keep a man at home
    is to make home big enough to roam,
    and a girl who owns half the free
      world's radium
    can always build a wing on, and
      bring on Yankee Stadium.
    He's a lot less likely to wander
    if even getting to the door involves a
      caravan;
    one way to keep a man around the
      house
    is to always keep a house around the
      man. And out.

SINGER *exits.* STAR *and* GIRL *enter immediately. He needs to urinate.*

GIRL: Darling, you seem a bit tense. Is it something I've said or done?

STAR: No, I was looking for a—well, you know. Tell me, is there one?

GIRL: Why, of course, don't be bashful—the men's wing is right through here.

STAR: [*Looking through doorway. Looks up*] How very attractive. Who did the graffiti?

GIRL: Michelangelo, dear. [*She shoves him through door and they exit.* MADALAYNA *enters immediately, hushed*]

MADALAYNA:
    Perhaps I'd do better to stand in one
      spot and wait.
    No! I'd rather trust in chance than
      trust in fate.
    I *could* toss the I Ching to "ahsk"
      where they are. Is that too much
      to "ahsk?"
    Naw. I'm just feeling mystic because
      I'm in a Melanesian mosque.

She exits. STAR *and* GIRL *enter immediately. He is on his knees.*

STAR: I won't go up another step.

GIRL: But I wanted to show you Heaven.

STAR: [*Gets up*]
    I insist you agree to marry me; I will
      not be André Previn.

    I want your answer now, in this fabulous scenery we're amid.

GIRL: Well, I'm not the first girl to be swept off her feet here on the Great Pyramid.

STAR: Then your answer is—

GIRL: Yes!

He places a huge diamond ring on her finger.

STAR: You've made me the most ecstatic of men, my sweet.

GIRL: No, your suite's over there in the Tower of London. Let's go get something to eat.

They are about to exit when MADALAYNA *enters, waving the letter. She is exhausted.*

MADALAYNA: Mistress, at last I've found you. You look happy. Am I too late?

GIRL: Madalayna, we've something to tell you.

STAR: [*Idly*] This Pyramid is *great.*

GIRL: I have agreed to marry this gentleman.

MADALAYNA:
    Aiyeeee! I have failed in my duty.
    Madame, if I may be first to call you
      so, read this tribute to your
      beauty.

She hands the GIRL *the letter and hides her face. The* GIRL *skims the letter.*

GIRL:
    Wow-dow, I'm Miss America. How
      happy can I be?
    I'm awfully glad that you're both
      here to share this thrill with me.

MADALAYNA:
    But-but-but-but but-but-but-but but-
      but you're not a Miss.
    The contest is this evening. They
      won't put up with *this!*

She indicates the puzzled STAR.

GIRL:
    My dear, this side of the house is
      over the International Date Line.
    Did you think I could ever miss? Get
      a load of that fate line.

GIRL *extends her palm.* STAR *and* MADALAYNA *examine it.*

STAR:
    I don't know if you've ever examined your hand with any great
      totality,
    but here's a line assures you and your
      mate youth, beauty, and immortality.

GIRL: And yesterday they discovered oil here in the West salon. [*She indicates a line in her palm*]

MADALAYNA: I do like working here; there's always something going on.

GIRL:

> And now I have an announcement to
> make. I've beauty, love, and
> health,
> so I really don't need anything else.
> I want to give my wealth
> to all the poor children of the world.
> Please don't fret and fawn.
> Take that message to all of my news-
> papers. Now! Begone.

MADALAYNA *exits hurriedly.*

STAR: Oh, darling, do you think that's wise?
Perhaps they'll overeat?

GIRL: But everything always turns out for the
best.

STAR: [*Reassured*] If you say so, my sweet.

MADALAYNA *reenters, hurriedly.*

MADALAYNA:

> Madam, to honor your wedding, the
> poor children asked me to say
> they want to give all your money
> back, and happy wedding day.

GIRL:

> All of you out there listening, you
> see, it's really true;
> the happiness you give away *does*
> come back to you.

STAR:

> And the moral of our story is one
> you all can guess:
> the richest girl in the world is the one
> who finds true happiness.

SINGER *enters and they all begin a spirited
gavotte.*

SINGER:

> How truly it is written that happi-
> ness is found
> only by those who are truly happy all
> the year around.
> The secret of serenity is one we all
> possess:
> the richest girl in the world is the one
> who finds true happiness.

MADALAYNA: You must have faith in Providence
and 'twill dispell your gloom.

GIRL: Whenever I feel it start to rain, I move to
another room.

STAR:

> This is the only secret your study will
> impart:
> the true sense of well-being comes to
> the untroubled heart.

GIRL: Possessions are as nothing; Madalayna, call
the car.

STAR: Do your best to brighten the corner where
you star.

GIRL: Now let our servant sing out what we
would all profess:

MADALAYNA: The richest girl in the world is the
one who finds true happiness.

GIRL: And don't forget it.

STAR: The richest girl in the world is the one who
finds true happiness.

GIRL: And holds on to it.

SINGER: The richest girl in the world is the one
who finds true happi—

MADALAYNA: [*Interrupting*] Oh, Madam. There
is one other thing I forgot to tell you.

GIRL: What's that?

MADALAYNA: It's Christmas, too:

SINGER:

> This is the end of our story, an-
> other's starting soon.
> Niagara Falls is coming to them for
> their honeymoon.

ALL:

> You must have wealth within you or
> wealth could not mean less.
> The richest girl in the world is the
> one who finds true happiness.
> Happy ending to you.
> Happy ending to you.
> Happy ending forever.
> Happy ending to you.

*They dance off, singing, "La, la, la" or "The
richest girl in the world is the one who finds
true happiness."*

*Additional note: The songs in this piece may
be spoken with great spirit if music is not
practical.*

LINE
a play in one act

Israel Horovitz

Line was first presented by Ellen Stewart at the Cafe La Mama ETC, New York City, on November 29, 1967, with the following cast:

FLEMING	*Paul Haller*
STEPHEN	*Israel Horovitz*
MOLLY	*Ann Wedgeworth*
DOLAN	*John Cazale*
ARNALL	*Michael Del Medico*

It was directed by James Hammerstein. Assistant director: Bonnie Frindel.

A revised version was subsequently presented by The New Comedy Theatre (Jerry Schlossberg, James Hammerstein, Israel Horovitz and Albert Poland) at the Theatre De Lys, New York City, as one half of a double bill with *Acrobats,* also by the author, on February 15, 1971, with the following cast:

FLEMING	*John Randolph*
STEPHEN	*Richard Dreyfuss*
MOLLY	*Ann Wedgeworth*
DOLAN	*John Cazale*
ARNALL	*Barnard Hughes*

It was directed by James Hammerstein. Additional staging by Grover Dale. Production designed by Neil Peter Jampolis. Production stage manager: Robert Vandergriff. Presented by special arrangement with Lucille Lortel Productions, Inc.

Editors' note: The version of *Line* as performed at the Theatre De Lys follows. For the original version see *First Season,* a collection of the author's plays published by Random House, Inc., 1968.

For My Father

"Sleep with dogs, wake with fleas."
(Webster, or somebody like that.)

SCENE: *A line.*

TIME: *Now.*

As the audience enters the theatre, FLEMING
*is standing behind a fat white strip of ad-
hesive tape that is fixed to the stage floor. The
play has begun. He is waiting . . . waiting . . .
waiting. The stage is without decoration other
than* FLEMING *and the line. The lighting is
of that moment when late night turns to early
morning: all pinks and oranges and, finally,
steel-gray blue.* FLEMING *checks and rechecks
his feet in relation to the line. He is clearly
first there, in first place. He steps straight
back now and again, testing his legs and the
straightness of the line that will follow.* FLEM-
ING *has carried a large war-surplus duffle
with him, full of beer, potato chips, whatever
he might need for a long-awaited long wait.
Back to the audience, he reaches into the bag
and takes something out. He stands, hands
penis-high, in a small pantomime of urination.
He turns again to the line and reveals that
he has peeled a banana. He eats it. His feet
are planted solidly at the line now, yet his
body breaks the rigidity, revealing his exhaustion. He is waiting . . . waiting . . . waiting.
He dips again into the bag and produces a
bag of potato chips, a can of beer (flip-top)
and a rather nice cloth napkin, which he tucks
into his shirt-top. He opens the beer, eats the
chips, drinks, belches and does it all again. His
feet never move from the mark now. He leans
back and sings, softly at first.*

FLEMING: [*Singing*]
Take me out to the ball game.
Take me out to the park . . .
Buy me some peanuts and what's-his-
     name . . .
I don't care if you neverwhat-do-you-
     call-it.
Take me out to your ball game . . .
Buy me lots of your stuff . . .
Dum diddy dumm-dumm diddy dumm
     diddy dumm . . .
That's where I want to be-ee-ee!

[*He drinks, belches and spills potato chips all
over the place*]

Buy me some peanuts and what's-his-
     jacks . . .

I don't care if I never get back . . .
And I'll root-toot-toot for the home
     thing . . .
Root 'til my voices run dry . . .
If you'll take me out to the ball game,
I'll never want to go haome!

[STEPHEN *enters quietly. He watches* FLEMING
carefully. FLEMING *senses* STEPHEN'S *pres-
ence. He stops singing and, waiting for* STE-
PHEN *to speak, does nothing. Neither does*
STEPHEN. FLEMING *gets on with it. Singing
carefully now*]
Take me out to the ball park . . .
Take me right out there now . . .
Buy me some peanuts and crackerthings . . .
I won't care if I diddy-dumm-dumm
For I dumm-dumm . . .

STEPHEN *cuts him off with a soft question.*

STEPHEN: Is this a line? [FLEMING *stares directly into* STEPHEN'S *eyes, but doesn't answer*]
Excuse me, mister. Is this a line? [*After
studying* STEPHEN'S *clothing and manner,*
FLEMING *rechecks his feet and turns from*
STEPHEN, *facing straight ahead*] Is this a
line, huh?

FLEMING: [*Does a long, false take*] What's it
look like?

STEPHEN: [*Walking over, leaning between* FLEM-
ING'S *legs, he literally caresses the tape*] Oh,
yeah. There it is. It's a line all right. It's a
beautiful line, isn't it? I *couldn't* tell from
back there. I would have been earlier if I
had started out earlier. You wouldn't think
anyone would be damn fool enough to get
up this early. Or not go to bed. Depending
on how you look at it. [FLEMING *stares at*
STEPHEN *incredulously*] Oh, I didn't mean
you were a damn fool. [*Pauses*] Not yet. Nice
line. Just the two of us, huh?

FLEMING: What's it look like? What's it look
like?

STEPHEN: That's all you ever say, huh? "What's
it look like?"—"What's it look like?" [*Pause*]
Must be nice.

FLEMING: Huh?

STEPHEN: Being first. Right up front of the line
like that. Singing away. Singing your damn
fool heart out. I could hear you from back
there. Singing your damn fool heart out. You
like music? [FLEMING *turns his back to* STE-
PHEN, *who now begins to talk with incredible
speed*] I'm a music nut myself. Mozart. He's
the one. I've got all his records. Started out
on seventy-eight. Moved up to forty-fives.
Then I moved on to thirty-three and a third
when I got to be thirteen or so. Now I've
got him on hi-fi, stereo and transistorized snap-
in cartridges. [*Displays a portable cartridge*

tape recorder] I've got him on everything he's on. [*Pause*] Must be nice. [*Pauses*] Want to trade places?

FLEMING: You yak like that all the time?

STEPHEN: [*Peeks over* FLEMING'S *shoulder at the line*] That's a good solid line. I've seen some skimpy little lines in my day, but that one's a beauty. [*Whistles a strain from* The Magic Flute] That's Mozart. Want me to whistle some more? Or we could sing your song. "Take Me Out to the Ball Game." I know most of your pop songs from your twenties, your thirties and your forties. I'm bad on your fifties and sixties. That's when I started composing. And, of course, that's when Mozart really started getting in the way. But, have it like you will—just name that tune. 'Course, don't get me wrong. I'd rather be whistling my own songs any day of the week. Any night, for that matter. Or whistle Mozart. *The Magic Flute. Marriage of Figaro.* Go on. Just "Name That Tune." I can sing it in Italian, German, French, or your Basic English. Hell, if he could knock them out at seven, I should be able to whistle at thirty, right? Christ, I am thirty, too. Not thirty-two. Thirty *also.* Three-o. Thirty. 'He was thirty-five. Around the age of Christ. What hath God wrought? [*Pauses, arms out and feet pinned together as in crucifixion*] God hath wrought iron! [*Pauses. Waits to see if* FLEMING *has crumbled yet. Sees* FLEMING'S *confused, but still on his feet, so* STEPHEN *continues*] Thirty-five. That's how old he was. He thought he was writing his funeral music all right. He was, too. Isn't that something, to have that kind of premonition? That's what you call your young genius. The only real genius ever to walk on this earth, mister. Wolfgang Amadeus Mozart. W-A-M. [*Yells at* FLEM-ING'S *face*] WAM! WAM! WAM! [FLEMING, *thunderstruck, turns and overtly snubs* STE-PHEN, *who is perched, ready to take first position if* FLEMING *falls.* FLEMING *stays afloat, so* STEPHEN *takes his wallet out of his pocket and studies its contents carefully. He pokes* FLEMING] You want to read my wallet?

FLEMING: Huh?

STEPHEN: [*Begins to unfold enormous credit-card case*] You want to read my wallet? You can read my wallet and I'll read your wallet. You can learn a lot about people from their wallets. Avis cards. Hertz cards. American Express. Air Travel. Bloomingdale's. Saks'. Old phone numbers. Bits and scraps. Contraceptives. Locks of hair. Baby pictures. Calendars. Business cards and the ladies. Business ladies have cards. ID cards. Not the ladies,

I mean. I mean the men who own the wallets who you're learning about, right?

FLEMING: [*Sings*]

Take me out to the ball game,
Take me out to the park.

STEPHEN: Hey. Don't turn your back on me, huh? Let me read your wallet. I've read mine before. I read my wallet all the time. Hey, will you? Here. Take my wallet, then. You don't even have to let me read yours. [*Forces his wallet into* FLEMING'S *hands.* FLEMING *is absolutely astonished*] That's it. Go on. Read. [FLEMING *obeys, wide-eyed*] There. See that ID card? That lets you know who I am, right away. See? Stephen. Steve. Or Stevie. Gives you a choice, even. And where I work. See that? Now look at the pictures. My kids. That one's dead. That one's dead. That one's dead. That one's dead. There are more. Don't stop. More pictures. [STE-PHEN *leaves the wallet in* FLEMING'S *hand and begins a wide circle around him, almost coaxing* FLEMING *out of line*]

FLEMING: How'd you lose all those kids?

STEPHEN: Lose the kids?

FLEMING: Dead. All these dead kids? [*Sees that the pictures are lithographs of Mozart*] Hey! Those are drawings!

STEPHEN: Who said they were kids?

FLEMING: [*Waits, staring*] Oh, boy. Here we go. [*Sings, after jamming* STEPHEN'S *wallet back into* STEPHEN'S *pocket*]

Take me out to the ball game,
Take me out to the park,
Buy me some peanuts and cracker-
    things . . .
[STEPHEN *joins in. In unison*]
We don't care if we never get back.
[FLEMING *stops*]

STEPHEN:

For it's a root, root, root for the
    home . . .
[*Stops. Asks*]
Do you really think this line is for a ball game? Huh? There's no ball game around here. I mean, I wouldn't be here if there was a ball game. Ball games aren't my kind of stuff. I loathe ball games, myself. You like ball games?

FLEMING: [*At this point, the situation has gone beyond* FLEMING'S *comprehension, and his confusion surfaces like a rubber duck*] Who are you?

STEPHEN: That's why I gave you my wallet. If everybody would just pass their wallets around, sooner or later something would happen, right?

FLEMING: Yeah.

STEPHEN: Can you imagine if you met the President and he gave you his wallet to read? You'd know everything about him. Or the Mayor. Kings. Ballplayers, even. Read *their* wallets. Boy, would you know it all soon enough. Scraps of paper that held secrets they forgot were secrets. Meetings they were supposed to make. Locks of hair. Pictures of babies they forgot they had. Names. Addresses. ID cards. Secret money hidden in secret places. You'd know everything, wouldn't you? [STEPHEN *has* FLEMING *going now. He increases the speed of his delivery, eyes flickering, hands waving, watching* FLEMING'S *terrified responses*] You see, friend, all those up-front people are fakes. Fakes. There's never been a real first place . . . never a real leader. Except you know *who.*

FLEMING: Who?

STEPHEN: War heroes? All frauds. If there had been one really efficient war, we wouldn't be here, would we?

FLEMING: I'm first. All I know is I'm first.

STEPHEN: First. It's just a word. Twist the letters around, you get strif. God backwards. Dog. Split the first three letters off the word therapist, you get two words: the rapist. Spell Hannah backwards, you get Hannah. Spell backwards backwards, you get sdrawkcab. I tell you, show me one of your so-called winners, and let me have one look at his wallet; just one. I'll never have to count the money, either. There's never been a real first before. Never. I know, friend. I know. See that line? Turn it on end, you know what you've got? A number one. But how do you hang on to it? How do you really hold it, so you're not one of those wallet-carrying, secret-compartment fakes like all of them? Answer that question and I'd let you follow me in. You could be second.

FLEMING: What do you mean "second"? I'm first. I'm right at the front.

STEPHEN: For the moment.

FLEMING: Don't get any smart ideas.

STEPHEN: The only conclusions I draw are on men's room walls. Now if you'd shut up for a while, I'll sing my wallet. [STEPHEN *sings his Hertz card. Lyric to* Eine Kleine Nachtmusik] "This nontransferable Hertz charge card entitles the person named to use Hertz Rent-A-Car service under the terms of the Hertz Rental Agreement on a credit basis. Where you desire to make immediate payments, the card enables you to rent without deposit. Payment for rentals charged is due within ten days after the billing date. This card is subject to invalidation and modification without notice and is the property of the Hertz system. . . . [MOLLY, *a plump woman, wanders onto the stage.* STEPHEN *sees her; he continues the Hertz lyric, but changes the melody to a tacky love song.* STEPHEN *stops* MOLLY *as she crosses the stage*] Hey. You looking for a line, lady?

MOLLY: Line?

STEPHEN: That's right. This is a line. You're third. Number three. There used to be just two of us here. Me and Fleming. This is Fleming. Who are you?

FLEMING: How'd you know my name, huh? How'd you know my name?

STEPHEN: [*To* FLEMING] I read your wallet.

[*To* MOLLY] You're third. That's not too bad. You won't have to wait long.

FLEMING: [*Checks to see if* STEPHEN *has stolen his wallet, then screams*] You didn't read my wallet! Nobody's read my wallet, except me!

MOLLY: [*Joining the line*] Third? I'm third, huh? How long have you been waiting?

STEPHEN: About nine and a half minutes. Fleming must have been here all night. Were you here all night, Fleming? He looks it, huh?

FLEMING: How the hell did you know my name? How'd you know?

MOLLY: Third place. How soon do they open?

STEPHEN: You'll probably see a crowd before that. There's always a crowd. The crowd that says, "Maybe there won't be a crowd, let's go anyway." That crowd. You'll see that crowd, won't she, Fleming?

FLEMING: How'd you know my name? How'd you know my name?

STEPHEN: Fleming, don't be a bore! What's your name? Mine's Stephen.

MOLLY: Molly. I'm Molly.

STEPHEN: Hello, Molly. Glad you're third. Fleming, this is Molly.

MOLLY: Hello.

FLEMING: Hey, kid. Hold our places in line. Come here, m'am. [*Takes her aside, whispers*] That kid's crazy. Watch out. He's one of them freaky weirdos. He's been saying crazy things to me.

STEPHEN: [*Moves into first position*] I can't guarantee your places. The crowd's going to come sure as hell and I can't guarantee anybody's place. The fact is, Fleming, I'm first now.

FLEMING: What?

STEPHEN: I'm first. [*Straddles the line*] Look at me. I'm up first. Up front. Front of the line.

MOLLY *jumps into second position.*

MOLLY: You could have held our places. Nobody else is here.

STEPHEN: It's just not right. Besides, Fleming wouldn't hold anybody's place. You can tell that just from looking at him. He's never held anybody's place in his life.

FLEMING: [*Enraged, but trying to maintain control*] Kid, I've been standing there all night. All night. Waiting. Waiting in the front of the line. The very front. Now I think you'd better let me get right back up there. [*As* FLEMING *continues,* DOLAN *enters and walks toward the line. He carries an artists' canvas-topped portable stool*] Just step back one pace and let me in there. [DOLAN *quietly steps into line behind* MOLLY. *To* DOLAN] I'm up front.

DOLAN: [*Sitting*] Huh?

FLEMING: I'm first. That kid just took my spot. You're fourth.

DOLAN: I don't mean to argue, but I count third. You're fourth.

FLEMING: Hey. Listen. That kid grabbed my place. I waited all night up front. Right at the front of the line.

DOLAN: I don't want to argue, but you're not getting in front of me, pal, so skip it.

FLEMING: Skip it? Bull, I'll skip it. [*Walks up to* STEPHEN] Give me back my place, kid, or I'll knock you out of it. [STEPHEN *drops to the floor in a lotus position.* FLEMING *stares, again astonished*] Get up!

DOLAN: I hate to argue, but get out of the front, Mac! The kid was up front and I'm third. The lady's second.

MOLLY: He was up front, actually.

DOLAN: Well, he can go second if you want him to, lady. I'm third.

ARNALL *enters and walks directly into the line.*

ARNALL: Molly?

MOLLY: Arnall. Here I am.

ARNALL: You think I can't see you? You saved my place?

MOLLY: [*To* DOLAN] I was saving his place, sir. We had an arrangement.

DOLAN: Not that I want to run things, but that's too bad. No place was saved. He can go fourth.

FLEMING: I'm fourth! For Christ's sake what am I saying? I'm *first.*

ARNALL: [*Jumps into fourth position*] I'm fourth.

MOLLY: I'm second.

DOLAN: I'm third.

STEPHEN: [*After the stampede, to* DOLAN] Obviously, I'm first. My name's Stephen. Who are you?

DOLAN: [*Shaking* STEPHEN's *hand*] Dolan's what they call me. How long you been waiting?

STEPHEN: About 12 and a half minutes.

ARNALL: Jesus. If I could have found my clean shirts, Molly . . . if I could have found where you hid them . . . I would have been here half an hour ago. I would have been first.

FLEMING: I've been here all night.

ARNALL: [*Considers it*] How come you're fifth? [*Pause for a take from* FLEMING] You're not even in line. Why aren't you first?

FLEMING: I *am* first. God damn it! I *am* first. That crazy kid grabbed my place. How'd you know my name, kid?

ARNALL: Fleming?

FLEMING: How the hell do *you* know?

ARNALL: [*Pulls* FLEMING's *T-shirt neck to his eyes*] It's written on your undershirt.

FLEMING *spins around trying to read the label.*

STEPHEN: I read your undershirt.

FLEMING: [*To* DOLAN] Look, I've been here all night. You know that's true. [*To* MOLLY] You saw me here, lady. You know I was first.

MOLLY: You stepped out of line. [*To* ARNALL] He stepped out of line, Arnall.

ARNALL: Serves you right, then, Fleming. If I could have found my clean shirt, I would have been first. My dumb wife hides my dumb shirts. Isn't that terrific? She hides my shirts. I could have been first by half an hour. But she hid my shirt. You know where I found it? [*Simply*] I couldn't find it.

FLEMING: [*After rapt attention to* ARNALL's *shaggy-shirt story. Furiously*] This is ridiculous. I was first. All night. [*To* ARNALL] I just took your wife aside to warn her about that crazy kid. He jumped the line. He jumped in front. That's not fair, is it? I was here all night.

DOLAN: You're fifth. There's plenty here for five. You'll get your chance.

FLEMING: [*To* ARNALL] That's not the point. God damn it. There's only one first and I waited up all night. All night in the line all by myself. And he took it away from me. Now, that is definitely unfair.

ARNALL: [*Completely against* FLEMING's *problem*] I hate to go anywhere at night with the shirt from the day still on. You never know what kind of germs you come in contact with during the day. You never can tell, can you?

STEPHEN: Life's full of dirt.

ARNALL: Our place is full of dirt. My wife never cleans. If it were up to her, we'd be up to our lips in dirt. Day and night. That's why I'm late. What movie's playing?

FLEMING: [*He's had it!*] Movie?

ARNALL: I thought we were going to the movies, Molly?

MOLLY: Arnall, don't cause a scene!

STEPHEN: Your shirt looks terrific, Arnall.

ARNALL: Looks are deceptive. Hospitals look clean, don't they? But if you ever ran a check for germ count, oh boy, wouldn't you get a score? After all, people come there—to hospitals—because they're ridden with germs. Take an old building full of germ-ridden people, paint it stark white, you got yourself a place that looks clean, but underneath that look, there's just a white hospital—full of germ-ridden people.

STEPHEN: How do you feel about that, Fleming? Do germ-ridden people disturb you too?

FLEMING: Don't get smart with me, kid. I was waiting here a long time before you, and you know it. [*To* DOLAN] He's trying to distract your attention from the fact that he *took* first place . . . he didn't earn it. No, sir. *I* earned it. I waited up for that place. He took it!

DOLAN: Well, I don't want to be the one who starts any arguments, but he *is* in first place, and he was in first place when I first got here.

STEPHEN: Fair *is* fair, Fleming!

FLEMING: [*Yells*] Don't "fair" me, kid, or you'll have a fat lip to worry about!

DOLAN: Now listen to me, Fleming.

FLEMING: [*Screams*] What do *you* want?

DOLAN: [*Screams*] LOWER YOUR VOICE!

ARNALL: Easy, Dolan, easy.

DOLAN: [*To* FLEMING] Look, I don't want to start any trouble, but it seems to me if you want to be first, be first. Move the kid. If you want to be second, be second. Move his old lady. [*And with that,* DOLAN *(Mister Niceguy), nearly strangles* ARNALL. *He catches himself before* ARNALL *dies. He brushes* ARNALL's *jacket and smiles. To* ARNALL] And don't you—God damn it—"easy" me. I'm nice and easy all the time. I'm Mister Niceguy. Get it? Mister Niceguy.

ARNALL: Move *who?*

DOLAN: Your old lady.

FLEMING: Your old lady.

ARNALL: You can't do that.

DOLAN: And why not?

FLEMING: And "why not" is right.

ARNALL: [*Archly*] She's second. She's in line. That's the way things are. She's in second place. She can beat you there.

FLEMING: [*Has an original thought*] Hell, she did! I spent the night in first. Right up there at the white line. Got my sack here with food and drink. I'm prepared. Prepared to be first. God damn it! Not second. Not third. Not fifth. I'm prepared for first. But, mind you, if I want to move your old lady and be second, I'll just move your old lady and be second. Just like that.

ARNALL *steps out of line into* FLEMING's *way, as* FLEMING *pretends to move toward* MOLLY. FLEMING *quickly jumps into line in* ARNALL's *spot.* FLEMING *is now fourth.*

ARNALL: [*Stunned*] Hey. Hey, you dirty sonofabitch. Sonofabitch. You took my place. He took my place. What the hell is this? Get out of line, Fleming. Move out, Fleming. You took my place!

FLEMING: [*Laughing*] That's what a woman does to you, what'syourname. That's what a woman does.

ARNALL: [*Humiliated*] Stop laughing, you sonofabitch!

FLEMING: [*A mule giggling*] That's what a woman does to you.

ARNALL: [*Walks up to* MOLLY, *squares off*] He's right! [*He slaps* MOLLY *on the hand*]

MOLLY: [*Amazed and furious*] Arnall. Arnall. Damn you. How could you? [*She chases him, slapping his head.* DOLAN *and* FLEMING *quickly move up one space, laughing*]

DOLAN: [*A jock's scream of victory*] I'm second. I'm second.

FLEMING: [*A neat imitation*] I'm right behind you.

ARNALL: [*Giving the proof of the pudding*] Now look, you bitch. Now look. We're both out. They moved up. You moved up, you sons of bitches. You snuck up.

DOLAN: You stepped out.

STEPHEN: [*Whispers*] Out of line, out of luck!

DOLAN: [*Picks it up*] Out of line, out of luck!

FLEMING: [*Instinct*] Out of line, out of luck.

ARNALL: Out of line, out of luck? That's supposed to be funny, huh? That's supposed to be a joke?

FLEMING: Who said that?

ARNALL: You said that. "Out of line, out of luck!"

FLEMING: [*A bit boggled, but giddy*] Well, then . . . that's right! That's what a woman does to you, Arnall. You lose your place.

MOLLY: You made me do that, Arnall. You made me do that.

ARNALL: [*Too heavy for him*] Shut up, you bitch. You start first with the shirts, now my place, now your place. Just shut up . . . I've got to think.

STEPHEN: [*Sings*] *"Se vuoi venire nella"*—I'm first.

FLEMING: Don't be smart, kid. I don't forget easily. You'll get yours.

STEPHEN: I got mine. I'm first! [*Sings*]
    Se vuoi venire nella mia scuola,
    La capriolo le insegnero.
That's a song my mother taught me. I'll never forget it, either. [*Sings*]
    Se vuoi venire . . . etc.

FLEMING: Forget it.

MOLLY: [*Sidling up to* STEPHEN] Your mother?

ARNALL: Stay away from him, Molly.

MOLLY: Shut your dumb mouth, Arnall. Just shut up. [*To* STEPHEN] Is she young? [*She puts a foot on* FLEMING'S *bag. Her leg is Mrs. Robinson's*]

STEPHEN: [*A sweaty Benjamin*] Metza-Metz. [*He sings*]
    Se vuoi venire nella mia . . .

MOLLY: [*Interrupts*] You've got a pretty face, you know that?

ARNALL: Molly! For crying out loud.

MOLLY: [*To* STEPHEN] Don't pay any attention to him.

ARNALL *walks to the other side of the stage and sits.*

STEPHEN: I'll pay attention to whom I choose. To *who* I choose? Whatever I choose. You know what I mean.

MOLLY: I was saying that you have a pretty face.

STEPHEN: Yes, you were.

MOLLY: Good bones. Strong bones in your face. Like James Dean.

STEPHEN: James Dean?

MOLLY: The movie star. The one who got killed in his Porsche. That's who you look like. James Dean.

FLEMING: Who's James Dean? A movie star?

DOLAN: Killed in his what?

STEPHEN: Is James Dean still dead?

MOLLY: Don't make jokes about James Dean. He was a beautiful boy. And I'm telling you that you remind me of him.

STEPHEN: I wasn't trying to be funny.

MOLLY: I always wanted to make love with James Dean.

FLEMING: Holy Jesus!

DOLAN: Shut up. [*He wants to hear*]

STEPHEN: Why didn't you?

MOLLY: I never met him, silly. He's a movie star. And then he got killed. If I could have met

him, I would have made love to him. If I had been Marilyn Monroe, I'd have played with him.

FLEMING: Monroe? Joltin' Joe's missus?

MOLLY: I could have made him happy. [*Pauses*] I could make you happy.

STEPHEN: I don't have a Porsche.

MOLLY: It's very warm here, don't you think? Don't you think it's very warm here?

STEPHEN: [*Unbuttoning his shirt, just a few buttons*] Yeah. I can't remember a time this hot. It makes you want to take all your clothes off, doesn't it?

MOLLY: [*She takes his hand in hers*] All your clothes.

STEPHEN: Unbearable.

MOLLY: Unbearable.

MOLLY *and* STEPHEN: Torture. [*They kiss, a long, deep passionate kiss. Suddenly they break apart and dance off, in a comically insane minuet*]

STEPHEN: [*Sings. Optional: he sings in German, French, Italian or English, although Italian is preferred*]
    Should he, for instance, wish to go dancing,
    He'll face the music, I'll lead the band, yes.
    I'll lead the band.
    And then I'll take my cue, without ado,
    And slyly, very, very, very, very, very slyly.
    Using discretion, I shall uncover his secret plan.
    Subtly outwitting, innocent seeming,
    Cleverly hitting, planning and scheming,
    I'll get the best of the hypocrite yet,
    I'll beat him yet!

As STEPHEN *sings,* DOLAN *and* FLEMING *talk.* ARNALL *walks forward quietly to watch* MOLLY *and* STEPHEN *as they dance. All are astonished.*

FLEMING: [*Almost a whisper*] You've got to hand it to that kid.

DOLAN: Shh. Her old man's watching.

FLEMING: It's disgusting.

DOLAN: [*Watching the lovers*] What's disgusting?

FLEMING: Her old man's watching like that. It ain't natural.

DOLAN: Yeah. It certainly ain't natural.

FLEMING: Sonofabitch. You've got to hand it to that kid. I never would have guessed.

DOLAN: I had a woman once in a car.

FLEMING: What happened?

By now, their attitudes should reveal that MOLLY *and* STEPHEN *are copulating-by-dance.*

DOLAN: The usual thing.

FLEMING: That's all?

DOLAN: Yeah.

FLEMING: Oh.

DOLAN: I've never had a woman in a line.

FLEMING: Me neither.

DOLAN: It's funny watching like this, ain't it?

FLEMING: Yeah.

DOLAN: I'd rather be doing it.

FLEMING: Yeah.

They both continue to stare goggle-eyed.

DOLAN: I'm getting horny.

FLEMING: Yeah.

DOLAN: Yeah.

FLEMING: Yeah.

The "yeahs" start to build in a crescendo as the lovers reach their first climax.

ARNALL: [*From nowhere*] Yeah.

DOLAN: Yeah. Yeah.

ALL: Yeah! Yeah! Yeah! *Yeah!!! Yeah!!!*

STEPHEN: [*Sings his orgasm*]
"Piano," "Piano," "Piano."

After they dance, MOLLY *takes first!* STEPHEN *sings again, exhausted, but "dances her" out of first place, tired, but not to be beaten.*

FLEMING: He's doing it again!

DOLAN: I can't take much more of this!

FLEMING: What are we going to do?

DOLAN: You figure it out, pal. I know what I want. [*He jumps forward and grabs* MOLLY. *Sings*]
I want a girl
Just like the girl
That married dear old Dad . . .

ARNALL *tries to jump into first position, but* STEPHEN *does a terrific baseball slide into first.* ARNALL *is forced into the slot* DOLAN *vacated: second.* FLEMING *is stunned.*

STEPHEN: I'm still first. I'm still first!

ARNALL: [*To* MOLLY] Bitch. Bitch. You bitch!

STEPHEN: [*To* ARNALL] You're second. You were nowhere. You were nowhere.

FLEMING: What happened?

ARNALL: He slid into first.

FLEMING: Yeah. But what happened?

In the meantime, DOLAN *and* MOLLY *are dancing as* DOLAN *sings. Note: after each*

"dance," MOLLY *calmly attempts to return to first and brush her hair, but a new man takes her to dance with him.*

DOLAN: [*Singing happily*]
She was a pearl
And the only girl . . . etc.

Over his song, the dialogue continues.

FLEMING: [*Finally realizing*] This is terrible. I got to move up.

STEPHEN: You didn't move up. You didn't move in. Fleming, you disappoint me. [*He lies down on the floor and goes to sleep*]

FLEMING: [*To* ARNALL] You just let your old lady do that? I mean, does she do it all the time?

ARNALL: All the time. All the time.

FLEMING: That's terrible. That's a terrible thing. You must get embarrassed.

ARNALL: It doesn't hurt any more. Not after all these years.

FLEMING: Why don't you throw her out?

ARNALL: Why? She's predictable.

FLEMING: Predictable?

ARNALL: Consistent. I never have any surprises with Molly. She's pure. All bad.

FLEMING: That's good?

ARNALL: Surprises hurt. You should know that. Look how hurt you were when you didn't move up. Or "move in." You were surprised and hurt, right?

FLEMING: That's bad.

ARNALL: Right. My philosophy is quite simple. Never ever leave yourself open for surprises, and you'll never be surprised. Surprise brings pain, pain is bad. No surprise, no pain. No pain, no bad. No bad, all good. [*Proudly*] I've got it made.

DOLAN: Da-ah-aahd!

ARNALL: [*After a pause*] They're finished now. Want to take a whack at it?

FLEMING: What?

ARNALL: Go on. Go ahead. Have a bash. Have a go at it. It'll do you good. Go on. I don't mind.

FLEMING: You sure?

ARNALL: Positive.

FLEMING: Do you mind if Dolan holds my place in line?

ARNALL: Of course not.

FLEMING: Hey, Dolan.

DOLAN: What?

FLEMING: Hold my place in line, will you? I'd like to have a bash.

DOLAN: Have a what?

FLEMING: Have a go at it. That's what her old man calls it. Hey, Dolan. Hold my place, will you?

DOLAN: [*Slides into* FLEMING'S *place and falls there*] Go get it.

FLEMING *stares at* DOLAN, MOLLY, ARNALL, *and the lot again. He grabs* MOLLY *and drags her upstage slightly; he "counts" a fox-trot beat. He sings his song and they dance.*

FLEMING: One two three—one two three—one two three—and—
    Take me out to the ball game,
    Take me out to the park,
    Buy me some peanuts and crackerjacks,
    I don't care if I never get back,
    For it's . . .

As *he continues his song, the dialogue does not stop.*

DOLAN: I like the way you think, Arnold.

ARNALL: You mean my little philosophy?

DOLAN: [*A bit confused*] Yeah, I guess you could call it that. Your little philosophy. I like the way you think, Arnold.

ARNALL: *Arnall.* [*Spells it, then goes on like a house on fire*] A-R-N-A-L-L. My mother wanted to call me Arthur. My father liked Nathan. Thought it was strong. My grandmother liked Lloyd, after Harold Lloyd. So they took the A-R from Arthur, the N-A from Nathan, the L-L from Lloyd, and called me Arnall. What do you want?

DOLAN: I want to tell you how touched I am. I have a little philosophy myself. I call it the Under*dog* Philosophy.

ARNALL: Under*dog*?

DOLAN: Did you ever hear of Arnold Palmer? Arnold Palmer is the world's richest golfer. He always looks like he is going to lose, but he almost never loses. He's the world's richest golfer.

ARNALL: I don't get it.

DOLAN: Everybody wants to be first, right?

ARNALL: Right.

DOLAN: Now you can be obvious about it. Just jump right in like the kid and yell and brag about being first. Or about deserving to be first. What I mean is you got to stand back a little. [DOLAN *has walked* ARNALL *around in a circle and is about to take second place*] Maybe in second place for a while. Then when nobody's looking, you kind of sneak into first place. But first you got to build up everybody's confidence that you're really one hell of a nice guy. You smile a lot. You say nice things all the time like, "Great night for a line," or, "Terrific wife you've got there,

Arnall, kid." Then, when everybody likes you . . . you sneak up.

ARNALL: I still don't get it.

DOLAN: [*Now in second place*] You notice I'm second in line? You notice I was second to make it with your wife. Second in this line to make it . . . right?

ARNALL: Right.

DOLAN: There you are.

ARNALL: Why do you call that Under*dog*?

DOLAN: The easiest way to kick a dog in the balls is to be underneath him. Let him walk on top of you for a while. Take good aim. And . . .

ARNALL: I get it.

FLEMING *and* MOLLY *waltz into view, and then off.*

DOLAN: Good boy. Terrific wife you got there, Arnall. Kid. Great night for a line. [ARNALL *is crying*] What's the matter?

ARNALL: My philosophy is quite simple. Never ever leave yourself open for surprise and you'll never be surprised. Surprise brings pain. Pain is bad. No pain, no bad. No bad, all good. I've got it made. [*Weeping now*] I've got it made.

DOLAN: You've got to learn to take it easy, Arnall. You're making a wreck of yourself with all that unhappiness. You got to get happy.

ARNALL: I have a real philosophy, real philosophy. I'm supposed to be gleeful. All the time. I didn't know. I really didn't know. I knew she had friends.

DOLAN: Certainly she had friends. She's very friendly.

ARNALL: But I thought they were just friends.

DOLAN: [*Checking* FLEMING] They'll be done soon.

ARNALL: I can't stand it. I can't stand it.

ARNALL *rushes to* FLEMING *and* MOLLY. *He taps* FLEMING *on the shoulder, "cutting in."* FLEMING *nods and moves into line.*

FLEMING: [*Realizing*] Hey, I didn't finish. I didn't finish. I didn't finish. I didn't finish.

DOLAN: Hop in line. You can be third.

FLEMING: But I didn't finish! Didn't you see?

DOLAN: See? Of course I saw. You were doing it with his old lady. Right in front of his eyes!!!

FLEMING: You did it in front of his eyes.

DOLAN: Jesus, don't remind me.

FLEMING: I didn't finish. For Christ's sake, I'm hornier than ever.

STEPHEN: What took you so long?

FLEMING: Shut up, kid. Shut up before I finish with *you.*

ARNALL: [*Tapping out a bunny-hop beat*] Molly. It's me, Arnall. Your husband.

MOLLY: [*Shocked*] Arnall? What the hell are you doing?

ARNALL: [*Dancing the bunny hop*] I'm doing it. With you. My wife. A surprise, Molly! A surprise!

MOLLY: You've lost your place in line. You stepped out of line!

ARNALL: [*Tapping away*] I couldn't stand it. Watching all those others doing it with you. It drove me crazy. It made me want you, Molly. I really want you.

MOLLY: [*Tapping with him*] Oh, Arnall. You're such a bore.

ARNALL: [*Humming "Tiptoe Through the Tulips" before he speaks*] Please, Molly. Please.

MOLLY: [*They're dancing now*] Well, you're doing it, aren't you?

ARNALL: [*Hums "Tiptoe" and dances a bit*] I am. Oh. I am. Oh, I like it, Molly. I like it.

MOLLY: [*Bored sick*] Hurry up, Arnall. Hurry up.

ARNALL: [*Stops*] Shall I sing?

MOLLY: [*Angry*] Just hurry up, Arnall. Just hurry up.

ARNALL: [*Singing*]
And when you kiss me
In the moonlight . . .
On a June night—
Will you marry me?
Just tiptoe through the tulips—
With me. [*Exits*]

DOLAN: [*Pauses*] Now that's the way it should be. A man and his wife. That's a beautiful thing. Great night, huh?

STEPHEN, *helping* ARNALL *and* MOLLY *gain speed, sings his wallet.*

STEPHEN: [*To "Tiptoe" tune*]
Saks' card and a Hertz card and an
Avis card
And a Un-ih-Card Card
Diners Club and a Chemical New York.

DOLAN: That's a beautiful sight, isn't it?

FLEMING: It's terrible. *Terrible.* I never finished.

DOLAN: Just wait, Fleming. Let the husband finish first. That's decent enough. Then you can finish. You can start from scratch.

MOLLY: Hurry up, Arnall.

FLEMING: Yeah, Arnall. Hurry up.

ARNALL'S *erection and song begin to die offstage.*

STEPHEN: [*A dirge; sings*]
That one's dead. That one's dead.
That one's dead. That one's dead.

DOLAN: Sing a happy song, kid. For Christ's sake. That part of your wallet depresses the hell out of me.

STEPHEN: [*He sings again*]
Henry Brown, insurance man.
Harry Schwartz, the tailor.
Alvin Krantz, delivery service.
My Uncle Max, the sailor.
Franklin National Savings Bank.
[MOLLY *and* ARNALL *bunny-hop onto stage with gusto*]
Doyle and Dave and Berubach.

DOLAN: That's nice. That's got a beat.

STEPHEN: [*Stops. Speaks*] He's ready! He's ready!

ARNALL: [*Screams*] Surprise, Molly! Surprise!

DOLAN: That's a beautiful thing.

ARNALL *collapses in* MOLLY'S *arms.*

ARNALL: Were you surprised, Molly?

MOLLY: Let me go, Arnall.

FLEMING: No. Not yet. Not yet. I never finished. [FLEMING *grabs* MOLLY]

MOLLY: Hey.

FLEMING: [*Explaining; a whiny child*] I never finished.

MOLLY: Take the gum out of your mouth.

FLEMING: [*Putting the gum behind his ear*] Oh.

ARNALL: What place am I in?

DOLAN: Third.

STEPHEN: Last.

ARNALL: I'd rather be third.

STEPHEN: You're in last place.

DOLAN: Shut up, kid. Don't listen to the kid. You're third. Two from the front. You did very well. I watched you all the way.

ARNALL: It's been a long time. My legs are all rubbery. I'm very nauseous. I've got to practice up a little. A little practice and I'd be better.

DOLAN: You did good.

ARNALL: I'll practice up some.

FLEMING: [*Sings*]
Take me out to the ball game,
Take me out to the park . . .

They dance off.

ARNALL: Oh, God! Him again.

DOLAN: Don't watch. Have a beer. You'll cool down. You'll feel better. Terrific wife, great night. [*Pours beer into* ARNALL'S *mouth*]

FLEMING: [*Offstage. Continues song at a more rapid speed*]

Buy me some peanuts and crackerjacks,
I don't care if I never get back . . .

DOLAN: You feeling any better now?

ARNALL: [*Screams*] I want it again.

DOLAN: You what?

ARNALL: I want it again. Molly's mine. I want
it again. I liked it.

DOLAN: You'll get sick again, pal. You know
it makes you sick.

ARNALL: I like it. I like it.

FLEMING *and* MOLLY *dance back on—past*
ARNALL: *They stop in front of* DOLAN.

DOLAN: Fleming. [*No answer*] Fleming! [*No
answer*] Fleming. [DOLAN *reaches over with
his foot and kicks* FLEMING *a hard one on the
behind.* FLEMING *wheels around dazzled*]

FLEMING: What's the matter?

DOLAN: [*Flatly*] Her old man wants it again.

FLEMING: [*Overlapping*] He had it already.

DOLAN: [*Overlapping*] He wants it again.

STEPHEN: [*Wise ass*] He wants it again.

FLEMING: [*Angrily*] I heard Dolan.

DOLAN: [*Flatly*] He wants it again.

ARNALL: [*Cockily*] I want it again.

FLEMING: [*As though no one knows. To* MOLLY]
Your old man wants it again.

MOLLY: [*A pronouncement*] I want the boy.

DOLAN: [*Senses the unjust*] But your old man
wants it.

MOLLY: [*A solid pronouncement*] I want the
boy.

DOLAN: [*Realizing he might move up one big
space*] She wants you.

STEPHEN: [*Exhausted with the understanding of
the complicated moment*] I heard her.

MOLLY: [*Moving in*] I want you, boy.

STEPHEN: [*Holding his eyes*] I heard you.

ARNALL: [*Overlapping*] She likes them young.

FLEMING: [*Overlapping*] What about me?

DOLAN: You had two chances.

FLEMING: I didn't finish.

DOLAN: You had two chances.

FLEMING: I was almost finished. Some bastard
kicked me!

DOLAN: Two chances. I only had one. The kid
only had one.

FLEMING: The kid took two.

DOLAN: Two on one chance. He's a kid.

ARNALL: She likes the young ones. She always
likes the young ones.

MOLLY: Come here, boy.

STEPHEN: [*Pretends to be engrossed in his wallet*] American Express. Chemical New York.

Unicard. My library card! [STEPHEN *is pulled
out by* MOLLY. DOLAN *jumps up into first
position.* FLEMING *jumps over* ARNALL]

DOLAN: I'm first! I'm first.

STEPHEN: You made me lose my place.

MOLLY: You have such a wonderful bone structure.

ARNALL: She always always likes them young.
[STEPHEN *knows he's out for now. He laughs.
He and* MOLLY *dance off, singing together in
harmony*] I'm last, last, last. *Last damnit!*

DOLAN: You're third. [*To* FLEMING] Tell him
he's third.

FLEMING: You're third.

ARNALL: I'm last. There are only three of us.
One, two, three. Three is me. I'm last.

DOLAN: Two over there. Those two. The kid
and your terrific wife.

FLEMING: [*Counting on his fingers*] That makes
five.

DOLAN: You're two from the front and two
from the back. Two from the first and two
from last. You're the average.

STEPHEN *sings lightly now as he and* MOLLY
dance. ARNALL *tells his story to the world.*

ARNALL: I would like to tell the story of my
marriage. I worked hard every night. I knew
she had friends, but I never knew they were
doing it. [*Pauses*] That's the story of my
marriage.

There is a shaggy-dog silence.

DOLAN: As first man, I say that Arnall gets a
chance to do it again as soon as the kid is
finished.

STEPHEN: [*Screams the ending of his song*]
"Piano."

DOLAN: The kid is finished.

FLEMING: Have a bash, Arnall.

ARNALL: I'll lose my place in line. Never mind.

DOLAN: Stay put, then. Fleming? You want a
whack at it? You want a third, uh, try?

FLEMING: I'm second. It ain't worth it now. You
want another one, Dolan? Huh? Why don't
you have a go at it? Give it another bash.

DOLAN: You're pretty obvious, Fleming. Pretty
obvious. Did anybody ever tell you how dumb
you are? Did anybody ever take the time to
tell you just how really dumb and stupid you
really are?

FLEMING: [*After a hideously long pause*] You
think I don't know? You think I'm too stupid
to know how dumb I am? Brains ain't everything, you know. I ain't exactly at the end
of the line. It ain't over yet.

STEPHEN *walks to the opposite side of the line and squares off with* DOLAN *eye to eye.* STEPHEN *speaks with simple authority.*

STEPHEN: The line's facing the wrong way.

DOLAN: [*Incredulously*] What the hell are you talking about, kid?

STEPHEN: [*To all; an announcement*] The line's facing the wrong way. [*To* DOLAN] The line's facing the wrong way. I'm first. [STEPHEN *and* DOLAN *eye each other for a full half-minute with terrifying tension. Nobody moves.* STEPHEN *smiles a frozen smile.* DOLAN *wipes his hands with a handkerchief, checking everyone in line. As* DOLAN *checks to one side,* MOLLY *quickly sneaks around into second place, behind* STEPHEN. DOLAN *does a take.* ARNALL *quickly slides around, following* MOLLY. *He's now third in* STEPHEN's *line.* DOLAN *does a full take. Then* DOLAN *turns to* FLEMING *and signals* FLEMING *to "take it easy," to wait, to rest.* FLEMING *nods agreement. Suddenly, as soon as* FLEMING's *settled down,* DOLAN *races into fourth place in* STEPHEN's *line.* FLEMING *sees and races after him, ending up last. When* STEPHEN's *line is settled, the very instant, in fact, that* STEPHEN's *line is full,* STEPHEN *steps over the line into the true first position. He smiles. All others freeze, staring at him.* MOLLY *breaks and jumps into second*]

MOLLY: I'm second!

DOLAN *bolts into third.*

DOLAN: I'm third!

FLEMING: [*Leaping into fourth*] I'm fourth!

ARNALL: [*Limping into last*] I'm last. Bitch-damn-crap! I'm really last now.

DOLAN: [*Overlapping*] Oh, man. That was rotten, kid. Really and truly filthy rotten.

FLEMING: [*Overlapping*] That kid is no good. I told you that kid was no good.

ARNALL: [*Overlapping*] Always the young ones. I'm sick of it. Sick of it. Sick of the young ones getting to be first.

DOLAN: [*Screams*] We'll get him, Arnall!

FLEMING: Not finished. Not first! We'll get him. [*Screams*] We're gonna get you, kid!

ARNALL: [*Whining*] Cuckolded. Cuckolded. I'm a buffoon. [*Screams*] A buffoon!!!

MOLLY: [*Desperately sexual; caressing with her voice*] You have the face of a president. A movie star. A senator. You have a Kennedy's face. A beautiful face.

FLEMING: [*Overlapping*] Breathe the air now, kid. Breathe it deep! We're gonna get you!

DOLAN: [*Overlapping*] Third. First to goddamn third!

ARNALL: [*Overlapping*] Last. Really last. This time there's no question.

STEPHEN: [*A maniacal scream*] SHUT UP, IDIOTS!!!

FLEMING: Who the hell are you calling "idiot"???

STEPHEN: All of you. Idiots. Fools. Lemmings. Pigs. Lint.

DOLAN: Lint?

MOLLY: Lint?

ARNALL: Lint?

FLEMING: Lint?

STEPHEN: [*A bit embarrassed by a weak word choice*] Lint.

FLEMING: Oh boy. Oh boy. That's the limit. We're gonna have your ass, kid.

STEPHEN: It's too late, idiots. I've won. I'm in first and anyone who isn't in first is an idiot. We've got nothing in common, so why talk about it?

DOLAN: We've all got something in common, kid. And don't you forget it, either.

STEPHEN: What's that, Dolan???

DOLAN: We've all been at his terrific wife. Whatever she's got, we've got.

FLEMING: That's true. We're like a club. Whatever she's got, we've got. [*Does a huge "take" to* ARNALL] What's she got?

STEPHEN: They're right, damn you. You let them all have you. Even your husband.

ARNALL: [*Hopefully*] Molly?

MOLLY: Nobody had me.

FLEMING: Nobody but all of us!

MOLLY: Nobody had me.

STEPHEN: [*Turns sharply about to* MOLLY] Everybody had you . . . everybody.

MOLLY: Nobody had me.

DOLAN: She's crazy, too. [*To* ARNALL] You've got a crazy wife, mister.

MOLLY: Nobody had me, get it? Nobody. *I* had all of you. *I* did the doing. Not you. *I* made the choices. You all wanted to be first, what kept you from it, huh? What kept you? [*Pushes* STEPHEN *over the line, out of first place, viciously. He falls to one side. Shocked*] I'm first now. *Me!*

STEPHEN: [*Wandering, confused*] You pushed me. She pushed me.

MOLLY: I'm first now!

DOLAN: She's crazy. You've got a crazy wife, mister. This is a terrible night.

STEPHEN: Don't flatter yourself, Molly. Not for a second. You've screwed your way to first and you'll be screwed right out of first. That's the way it's always been and that's the way it's always going to be. This line's my last, Molly. You really think I'm going to let you come in first?

MOLLY: I am first. I am first. And I'm not moving. I screwed my way to first and now I'm resting.

Maybe this is my last line too. Look who's first. Just look who's first. Me. Molly. Just where I knew I'd be from the moment I saw this line.

FLEMING: You got yourself a real bitch for a wife there, Arnall. A real bitch.

ARNALL: I know. I know.

MOLLY: I know what you've been thinking all night. Here we are, four big shots. One woman in line. Might as well roll her over, just to kill time. That's what you're always thinking. That's what every line's about, right? And you think in any other place you'd never give me a look . . . but . . . as long as we're all killing time together . . . why not? 'Course, under *normal* conditions, she'd never be good enough for me. Well, I've got a piece of news for you all: under any conditions, none of you is good enough for me. Not a one of you!

STEPHEN: [*Crosses to her*] Molly. You're good enough for me.

MOLLY: Go to the back of the line, boy. You didn't satisfy me. You didn't make it. You didn't thrill me. You need experience. You make love like a child.

STEPHEN: What about my beautiful bones?

MOLLY: Go to the back of the line.

DOLAN: That's telling the wise-ass kid. Go to the back of the line, kid. You heard the lady.

MOLLY: Don't gloat. Don't lick your lips. I could have done better with an ape than with you.

FLEMING: Terrific, Molly. An ape, Dolan. An ape.

MOLLY: Are you the one with the beer and the gum who's too old and tired to finish?

FLEMING: What's that supposed to mean?

ARNALL: Molly? Molly? Is it me?

MOLLY: Don't be a bore, Arnall. You couldn't satisfy a carney.

DOLAN: You've run out. If none of us satisfied you, who did?

MOLLY: None of you. Simple as that. I am an unsatisfied woman still looking for a man. You all failed.

DOLAN: I've had better than you, tubby, and I mean some real beauties. And they've screamed for more. Screamed for more!

MOLLY: More money? Okay. Sure. I can understand that.

FLEMING: I've had models.

DOLAN: Screw your models. I had one in a car once.

FLEMING: Yeah. You told me.

MOLLY: I'm first. I'm unsatisfied. I've had four men. One three times. One unfinished. And I'm unsatisfied.

ARNALL: Don't let her get to you. Don't let her get you going. She'll drive you all crazy. Make

surprises. Ruin all your philosophies. She'll hide your shirts.

MOLLY: Arnall, you're such a bore.

STEPHEN: [*Whispers to her*] I've got something to tell you.

MOLLY: To the back of the line, sonny. You lost. You're last . . . move.

DOLAN: You're out of line completely, kid. She's right. When the crowds come, you'll be left out altogether.

STEPHEN *wanders to stage-right portal.*

MOLLY: I hope there's a man in the *crowd*. One man.

ARNALL: You see what I mean? She won't let up now. Now that she's first, she'll just keep pouring it on.

DOLAN: She's worse than *my* old lady. Much worse. My old lady's a dog, but nothing like yours. Yours is the biggest dog of all. Queen dog. Yeah. She's the biggest dog of all. How'd you get stuck with her, anyway?

ARNALL: She picked me up at a party. I was at a party. The lights were dim. I felt a hand sneak between my legs. I was only thirty-one. It was Molly. She taught me everything I know. I don't know anything either.

STEPHEN: [*A proclamation*] When I make love to a woman, I never shut my eyes. Never. I watch. I watch and I listen to every movement she makes.

FLEMING: [*Embarrassed*] Shut up.

DOLAN: [*Wants to hear STEPHEN's "secret"*] You shut up, Fleming.

STEPHEN: I listen to every movement she makes. So that every time I move, I understand her response. One little wiggle to the left, one little wiggle to the right and I get a response I remember. I make notes. I have a whole loose-leaf binder filled with notes and half another filled as well. All kinds of notes. How to wiggle front and back. How short women respond. How tall women respond. How certain ethnic groups respond.

MOLLY: What did you learn from me, little boy?

STEPHEN: [*His guise has worked. He knows it. He sets up his next line carefully, ready to strike. He moves into position close to MOLLY*] Never screw an ugly, greedy slob like you. Always to follow my natural desire. Only screw who I want, when I want. If I had followed my natural desire, I never would have screwed you. Not once. Not twice. Certainly not three times. It was all an incredible waste of my incredibly valuable time. That's what I wanted to tell you.

MOLLY: [*Explodes*] You little squirt. You little jerk. [*She charges at him in a rage. He knocks her aside and regains first position.* MOLLY *is out of line*]

STEPHEN: [*With a flourish*] Gentlemen, I am first again.

FLEMING: You've really got to hand it to that kid. Go on, Dolan. Hand it to the kid.

DOLAN: [*He is standing on* STEPHEN'S *toes*] Nice work, kid.

ARNALL: [*A small bitch*] I'm not last. You're last, Molly. I'm ahead of you. You're last.

DOLAN: [*Ruefully*] Nice work, kid.

STEPHEN: Say it again, Dolan.

DOLAN: Nice work, kid. [*He pushes* STEPHEN *violently offstage.* DOLAN *takes first.* STEPHEN *falls into the audience*] Look who's first now, will you?

STEPHEN: You pushed me. He pushed me. Hey, he pushed. Did you see him??? That's not fair, Dolan.

DOLAN: I'm first.

FLEMING: [*Jumps forward*] I'm second.

ARNALL: [*Jumps forward*] I'm third.

MOLLY: I'm fourth.

STEPHEN: [*Starts walking up the aisle*] I'm out.

DOLAN: In every crowd, there's a winner. A winner. I waited back there. I hung in. Look at me now.

STEPHEN: [*From the back of the theatre*] You broke the rules, Dolan.

DOLAN: What rules?

STEPHEN: [*From another aisle*] He pushed me.

DOLAN: *She* pushed you.

STEPHEN: [*Screaming*] She's a woman! That's different!

FLEMING: That's true, Dolan. It's different when it's a woman. Especially *that* woman.

ARNALL: You see, Molly's always breaking rules. She breaks everything. Dishes. Cups. Saucers.

MOLLY: Just shut your dumb mouth, Arnall.

FLEMING: Yeah. Shut up, Arnall. We got to figure this out.

DOLAN: What's to figure out? I'm up front. Head of the line. I won. That's pretty simple.

FLEMING: Yeah, but you pushed the kid. We sort of had an unwritten rule here. I mean, none of us did any pushing.

DOLAN: You want to push me, Fleming?

FLEMING: Hey, look. Don't start that stuff! I'm a hell of a lot tougher than you, pal. You want to start that stuff and that's the kind of stuff you'll get. You know what I mean?

STEPHEN: [*Walking back to the stage*] I'd hate to see you start a fight over me, Fleming. It's probably better that I just stay right out of line. You people can handle things on your own. You don't need me.

FLEMING: Yeah, I suppose.

DOLAN: What the hell are you trying to do, kid? You're gonna just *let* me stay in first? You ain't gonna trick me out of it?

STEPHEN: [*Standing facing stage*] You don't trust people. That's your trouble, Dolan. You think everybody's out to get you all the time, don't you?

DOLAN: I don't think of anybody but NUMBER ONE. I hung in back there in second all that time. I knew what I was doing. I've watched you up there. I knew when to strike. I knew when my iron was hot. I waited it out. I'm first. That's simple, isn't it?

STEPHEN: [*Leaning on the stage*] There are ways of getting to first that are acceptable and ways of getting to first that are unacceptable. Women and children excluded, of course.

FLEMING: That's right.

DOLAN: What's right?

FLEMING: The thing he said about women and children. That's always the way about women and children.

STEPHEN: Women and children first.

FLEMING: Women and children first.

STEPHEN: Dolan's not a women.

FLEMING: Dolan's not a children.

ARNALL: Dolan's none of those things.

MOLLY: Dolan's nothing.

STEPHEN: Everybody's something.

FLEMING: Not Dolan!!! [FLEMING *pushes* DOLAN *violently offstage and takes first*] Holy Christ! I'm in first place!

ARNALL: I'm second.

MOLLY: [*Jumping up*] I'm third.

DOLAN: [*Crawling back onstage*] For Christ's sakes. For crying out loud. Fleming pushed me.

STEPHEN: You changed the rules. You pushed first.

DOLAN: She pushed first.

FLEMING: Holy Christ! I'm really in first place. I'm first guy. Top dog. [*And he pushes* DOLAN *offstage again*]

DOLAN: He pushed me right out of first place.

MOLLY: [*She pushes* ARNALL] Be a winner, Arnall. [*She pushes* ARNALL *so hard, he clobbers* FLEMING *right out of first place.* ARNALL *is first now*]

FLEMING: Hey. Hey. Hey. [DOLAN *crawls back onto the stage and* FLEMING *crashes into him* —DOLAN *flies offstage again*]

ARNALL: I didn't do that. She did that. She pushed me so hard I pushed you. I didn't push you. Honest to God, I didn't push you. Here. Take it back. [ARNALL *walks right out* of first place, trembling. *He leads* FLEMING *by the hand back into first place.* MOLLY *stands frozen. Astonished.* DOLAN *crawls back onstage and into second*]

FLEMING: I'm first again.

DOLAN: I'm second. Hah! I'm second.

ARNALL: [*Slipping, mincing into third, in front of an astonished* MOLLY, *he says simply*] I'm third.

MOLLY: Arnall, you damn dumb fool. Look what you did. Look what you did, you damn dumb dummy.

ARNALL: I gave that to you, Fleming. I gave you first. But you've got to protect me.

FLEMING: From what?

ARNALL: Her.

FLEMING: Why?

ARNALL: Please, Fleming?

FLEMING: Why?

MOLLY: Damn you, Arnall. Damn you. [*She beats him, like a child swatting a mosquito*]

ARNALL: See? See what I mean? I need help, Fleming. Help me, Fleming.

FLEMING: [*He walks to* MOLLY *and talks to her, reasonably*] Now look, m'am. I don't want to hurt a lady. I've never hurt a lady.

ARNALL: She's no lady.

DOLAN: [*Jumps into first, incredulously*] I'm first again!

Everybody freezes, out of line, as DOLAN *stands alone.*

FLEMING: Now, just wait a God-damned minute!

DOLAN: I'm first, first!

FLEMING *clobbers* DOLAN.

ARNALL: This is awful. [*Jumps in first*]

MOLLY: This is your fault, Arnall. [*Pushes* ARNALL *out*]

STEPHEN: [*From the audience; giggling*] I'd say it was Dolan's fault.

DOLAN: Knock it off, kid.

STEPHEN: Hell, I'll knock it off. If you hadn't broken the rules and pushed me, we'd be in a perfectly straight line. This is chaos, friends. Chaos.

ARNALL *dashes into first place.*

ARNALL: I'm first. I'm first! [DOLAN *slams* ARNALL *to the ground*]

DOLAN: No, you're not. I am. I'm first.

STEPHEN: Keep it up. Keep it up.

MOLLY: [*Attacking* DOLAN, *she kicks his testicles*] Move out of there. Move.

They all end up in a horrible fist fight, ending with DOLAN *hitting* MOLLY *fiercely. . . .* ARNALL *crawls in and bites* MOLLY'S *leg.*

FLEMING: [*Astonished*] You hit her. You hit her!

STEPHEN: See? See what you have? Chaos. Pure, plain and simple. Chaos.

FLEMING: You're God-damned right it is, kid. God-damned right. [FLEMING *has* DOLAN'S *arm pinned*] Help the kid back in the line. Go on.

DOLAN: Are you crazy?

FLEMING: I've seen this happen before. Help him back!

STEPHEN: [*Walking into line, into first*] Anybody mind my being first?

DOLAN: I held back, damn it! I waited! What is this????

FLEMING: [*Screams at* DOLAN] Don't!

DOLAN: [*Frightened*] Okay. Okay. [DOLAN *suddenly lurches for first.* FLEMING *grabs him and beats him with three quick, terrifying punches*] Ughhh. Ahhh. Ughhh.

FLEMING: I said "Don't" and I mean "Don't"! Everybody hear me? Huh? Everybody hear me clear.

DOLAN: [*Whipped*] I'm second.

FLEMING: Okay. I'll stay in third. 'Til we get straightened out. You, Arnall, you get fourth. And you, you fat bitch, you started this pushing business. You get in fifth.

ARNALL: [*Like a three-year-old child*] I'm not last. You're last, Molly. I'm ahead of you. You're last.

FLEMING: Everybody shut up! [*Pauses*] Okay, kid. What do we do now?

STEPHEN: Shut up and listen. [*He presses the "on" button on his tape recorder and Mozart's* Eine Kleine Nachtmusik *fills the theatre*] Can you feel him? Mozart. *Eine Kleine Nachtmusik.* The Allegro. He was younger than me when he wrote this. A baby. The Allegro. Then Andante. Then Minuet. Then Rondo.

ARNALL: Austrian, right? Isn't he Austrian, Stephen?

STEPHEN: That's Mozart, for Christ's sakes! It's Mozart. I'm not first. I'm second. Stop. Please. This is crazy. This is a crazy thing. [STEPHEN *turns off the recorder*]

FLEMING: You're the crazy thing.

ARNALL: [*Really spooky*] You know how he died, Stephen? Singers came in and sang him to death. His Requiem, Stephen. They sang while he died.

STEPHEN: [*Staring at the Mozart he sees ahead of him*] It's not true. It's not true.

ARNALL: But I was there, Stephen. I saw it. I heard it.

STEPHEN: [*Weeping*] Stop it. Stop it.

ARNALL: I was there, Stephen. He was writing the percussion up until the last. Boom-boom.

Boom-boom. [ARNALL *marches singing, "Boom-boom"*]

STEPHEN: I'm losing my mind.

MOLLY: Arnall. You weasel, Arnall.

ARNALL: Boom-boom. Just shut up, you bitch. Just shut up. Boom-boom.

STEPHEN: No! This isn't happening! I'm first. Look at me. I'm first. I earned this, I know I did!

FLEMING: Bullshit, you did! We'll get you, kid.

DOLAN: We'll get you, kid.

ARNALL: Want me to sing it, Stephen? The Requiem? Want me to sing the Requiem now? [*He sings like a choirboy. "La-ah cree-mo-so, Day-es-lela," etc. He continues the Requiem and STEPHEN seems totally hypnotized. He walks toward STEPHEN and then past him. He moves around past DOLAN and FLEMING, who stare wide-eyed. He swings around again, softly singing, heading straight for first place*] Boom-boom. Boom-boom. It could be lovely, Stephen. Lovely. I'll sing . . . [*Checks, sees*] . . . and Dolan . . . boom-boom . . .

DOLAN: [*Taking a nod from ARNALL*] Boom-boom . . . boom-boom . . .

ARNALL: . . . and FLEMING . . . boom-boom . . .

FLEMING: [*Confused; follows with his voice*] Boom-boom . . . boom-boom . . .

ARNALL: will do their work . . . BOOM-BOOM . . . BOOM-BOOM . . . BOOM-BOOM . . .

DOLAN *and* FLEMING: BOOM-BOOM . . . BOOM-BOOM . . .

ARNALL: BOOM-BOOM . . . BOOM . . . BOOM . . . BOOM-BOOM . . .

STEPHEN *grabs his neck in anguished pain. He screams a most hideous scream and falls forward onto his face. He writhes on the floor, sobbing in agony. ARNALL walks quietly into first place.*

FLEMING: [*After a huge pause*] That's terrible. I'll never sing with you again, Arnall.

DOLAN: Holy Jesus Christ!! Will you look at that????

STEPHEN *is silently staring from the floor. He sees ARNALL. He stands slowly; almost berserk now. He lunges at ARNALL, grabbing his throat.*

STEPHEN: You little twirp. You little plucked chicken. You step back, Arnall. You're playing with fire, Arnall. Fire. You move now or I'm going to strangle you, Arnall. You'll be dead, Arnall.

ARNALL: Please, Stephen. Please. I only want Molly. I don't want first. Only Molly. Please, Stephen. Please???

But STEPHEN'S *too far gone. He squeezes* ARNALL'S *throat.*

STEPHEN: You move or I'll kill you, Arnall. Do you believe me? [ARNALL *and* STEPHEN *stare at each other. A long hold*]

ARNALL: [*Defeated*] Yes.

STEPHEN: Back of the line, Arnall.

FLEMING: Yeah, Arnall. Back of the line. I can't see what the kid is saying when you're standing there. You're blocking me from the kid.

DOLAN: That ain't right, Arnall. Move back, Arnall.

FLEMING: Move back, Arnall.

MOLLY: [*Fiercely*] You heard them! Move!!!

ARNALL *walks slowly to the end of the line. Broken. Defeated.*

FLEMING: [*Breaking the horrific silence of* AR-NALL'S *total humiliation*] What's next, kid?

STEPHEN: The end. I beat all of you, not with luck, but with genius. There's only one person to beat, and you can't see him in this line. I can see him in this line. [STEPHEN *is now screaming at the place in front of him*] I'll beat you. I'll die youngest, the best. And after I'm gone you'll see I can take it with me! [STEPHEN *turns on the recorder to an unbearable volume and slides the machine across the stage. It lands, blaring and staring up at a startled* ARNALL. *Slowly, carefully,* STEPHEN *picks up the line—that white piece of tape that is first place itself—and eats it, like a berserk strand of spaghetti.* ARNALL *picks up the tape recorder and smashes the "off" button, as though swatting an insect*]

ARNALL: [*In the now-deafening silence; carefully*] You *are* crazy! You are an insane, horrible child. [ARNALL *draws a deep, deep breath*]

STEPHEN: [*He's swallowed the tape by now*] How dare you, you cuckolded little nothing!!! You let your wife—your fat, horrible wife—screw on the street while you do nothing more than watch. She screws and you watch. And tomorrow you'll crawl in bed beside her with your chubby clean-but-sweaty little body begging for a whore's kisses!!!

MOLLY: You animal! You animal! Hit him, Arnall! Hit him!

ARNALL: We're much older than you are, son. You could show some respect.

STEPHEN: [*The final insult follows*] Maybe I hate you most, Arnall. Just maybe. [*Like a bullet*] You're a loser, Arnold.

FLEMING: It's okay, Arnall, you can hit him. Boom-boom. Boom-boom.

STEPHEN: I won! I did it! I did it. I did it. I won. I won. [*Chasing them all*] Come on, Arnall.

It's okay now. Hit me. Scratch my eyes out. Kill me.

ARNALL: Me?

STEPHEN: You. Anybody. Come on. Let's get on with it.

DOLAN: We're gonna get you, kid.

STEPHEN: Do it, Dolan. Do it.

FLEMING: Go on, Arnall. Get him. Boom-boom.

MOLLY: Hit him, Arnall. Boom-boom. [MOLLY *gets the recorder and gives it to* ARNALL]

ARNALL: Me?

DOLAN: Kill him, Arnall. Boom-boom.

ARNALL: Me?

DOLAN *and* FLEMING: Kill him, Arnall. Boom Boom.

STEPHEN: [*He laughs maniacally*] I can take it with me. I finally won! [STEPHEN *kneels; head up, eyes closed—waiting to be killed.* DOLAN, FLEMING *and* MOLLY *chant, "Boom-Boom," over and over, urging* ARNALL *to kill* STEPHEN]

ARNALL: You son of a bitch. You son of a bitch!!! [ARNALL *takes tape recorder and raises it to kill* STEPHEN. *He stops, as* MOLLY *shrieks. They all stop and jump back one step*]

STEPHEN: [*Opens his eyes; stands, amazed*] What's wrong? Why are you stopping? Somebody's got to kill me.

ARNALL: Us?

FLEMING: Kill him?

MOLLY: Kill him?

STEPHEN: You've got to kill me. I've got to die first. Please . . . please . . . please . . . please . . . please . . .

DOLAN *walks into first position, but of course the line is gone.* DOLAN *is astonished.*

DOLAN: [*A whine*] Where's the line?

FLEMING: The line! Where is it?

ARNALL: The line!

MOLLY: Arnall! The line's gone.

ARNALL: Where'd it go?

STEPHEN: [*Burps a little, smiles*] I ate it.

FLEMING: What?

STEPHEN: I ate it. [*He groans*]

MOLLY: He ate it. He ate it?

FLEMING: He ate it. He ate it?

DOLAN: He ate it?

ARNALL: He *ate* it?

STEPHEN: I ate it.

MOLLY: See? I'm right. He *is* crazy. He's really crazy.

FLEMING: I told you that, lady. I told you that the second you walked up. He's really crazy.

STEPHEN: What is this? I'm supposed to die! [*He's stunned, as it appears that he isn't going to die after all*]

MOLLY: He wanted us to beat him so he'd die so there'd be a dead kid in first. And we were supposed to just watch.

ARNALL: How could we watch a thing like that?

FLEMING: Why not? We've been watching everything else.

MOLLY: Oh, my God! What if I'm pregnant?

ARNALL: Pregnant? Molly. A son? A son, Molly?

FLEMING: But I didn't finish!

MOLLY: He finished. The way it counts.

FLEMING: [*Pointing to* STEPHEN] You see, Arnall? They never really forget the first one.

ARNALL: What?

DOLAN: Jesus! What a wife you've got there. What a rotten night! [*To* STEPHEN] Give us back the line, kid. They're going to open soon and we need a line.

MOLLY: They'll open and we won't have a line. [*Steps behind* STEPHEN] And I'm only second.

ARNALL: I'm right beside you.

FLEMING: Me too.

DOLAN: For crying out loud! We're all second!

FLEMING: This looks very phony. Give us back our line, Steve.

MOLLY: Please, Stephie. Please.

ARNALL: Give it back, Steven.

DOLAN: Cough it up, *Stephen.* Steve, Stevie. Cough it up.

STEPHEN *begins to gag and choke. The line begins to appear.*

FLEMING: Hey. The line.

DOLAN: There it is!

MOLLY: The line.

ARNALL: He *did* eat it.

DOLAN *grabs the line from* STEPHEN'S *mouth and runs across stage.*

DOLAN: He took it with him.

They all freeze, as STEPHEN *rises, dazzled.*

STEPHEN: I didn't take it with me. I didn't go anywhere. Damn it all. I'm not dead. [STEPHEN *begins to go through a series of contortions like a woman in labor*]

DOLAN: [*Standing victoriously; his own line on the floor*] I'm first. I had to wait for my chance, but I'm first. Had to wait. Wait. Hang back. But I'm first.

STEPHEN *gags again and a second piece of tape appears: another line.* FLEMING *grabs the line and stares at it as a moron might, then follows* DOLAN'S *example, setting his line down.*

FLEMING: I'm first! Finally, I'm first! I should be first. I was the first one here. Fair's fair.

STEPHEN *retches as he stands up.* MOLLY *steps forward and kisses* STEPHEN *full on the lips. She comes away with a piece of line as her reward, between her teeth.* STEPHEN *is now a dispenser. He walks mechanically, emitting sounds like a berserk Coca-Cola machine.*

MOLLY: [*Setting her line down: her first*] He gave me first. He made me first. He gave me first place.

FLEMING, MOLLY *and* DOLAN *now stare dreamy-eyed with victory.* ARNALL *slaps* STEPHEN *on the back and a line falls into his hands.*

ARNALL: [*After placing his line upstage right*] Molly. Darling. I'm first. I didn't want to be first. I never wanted first. But I'm first. And I like it, Molly! First is good.

STEPHEN *still walks like a machine, puking up a final scrap of line. He grabs it and just as he places it on the floor downstage center, he sees the others in their victory. He understands and casually throws his line away, exits.*

THE PLAY IS OVER

NOTES ON ENDING OF PLAY

STEPHEN *"eats" the line by picking it up from the floor on his speech, "I can take it with me!",* then holds it up in the air like spaghetti, eating it slowly, covered by ARNALL's speech. He then holds the original piece of tape in his mouth through his "cuckolded little twirp"

speech. As soon as MOLLY calls him "Animal!", the group rushes at STEPHEN, who then charges headlong into the chaos, quickly taking the tape from his mouth and dropping it on the floor. Each person then "palms" a fresh piece of white ribbon into his hands. When STEPHEN prostrates himself on the floor after screaming, "I'm supposed to die," he waits for MOLLY's "Dead kid in first" speech, then draws himself to his knees, facing the audience, crying. He holds his hands to his face, palming the first piece of tape into his mouth. As soon as FLEMING says, "We're all second," STEPHEN begins to act labor pains and nausea. At DOLAN's "Cough it up," he vomits (or gives birth to) the first piece of line. STEPHEN then becomes a machine, mechanically jerking about on his feet, raising one arm at a time and "goose-stepping" slightly, as a dispenser. Each person in turn places his hands to STEPHEN's mouth as STEPHEN shrieks a vomit sound. Each pulls his hands away after placing an end of their ribbon in STEPHEN's teeth. The effect is that the line has come out of his mouth. MOLLY kisses STEPHEN, placing one end of the ribbon in her mouth, the other in STEPHEN's. They pull back from each other slowly, STEPHEN's arms straight out as he cries. The line is then MOLLY's. Each person goes straight to his "first-place" position, makes his speech about winning, then freezes. During MOLLY's speech, STEPHEN staggers upstage, bends over crying, and palms the final piece of ribbon from his pocket (shirt pocket) into his mouth. He makes several machinelike sounds, before "vomiting" up his final piece of line. He throws the tape on the floor, only after carefully studying the frozen figures in their first-place positions.

RAINBOWS FOR SALE

a play in one act

John Ford Noonan Jr.

Rainbows for Sale was first presented by Norman "Speedy" Hartman at the Old Reliable Theatre Tavern, New York City, as half of a double bill with *The Mulberry Bush* by Phoebe Wray, on September 22, 1969, with the following cast:

YOUNG MAN .... *Alan Causey*
JOCKO .... *Neil Flanagan*

It was directed by Ken Hill. Lighting by David Adams.

It was subsequently revised and presented by Fatboy Productions, Inc., at the Provincetown Playhouse, New York City, May 6, 1971, with the following cast:

YOUNG MAN .... *Kevin Conway*
JOCKO STONE HALSEY .... *Kevin O'Conner*
RECRUITS .... *Alan Arkush, Joey Rosenbaum, Anthony DeNardo, Roderick Grant, Bruce Marisak,*
Sam Smalls, Alston Campbell, Joe Guardino, Charlie Gilmore, Larry Fishman, Al Lantini

It was directed by Michael Cannon. Set design by Karl Eigsti; lighting design by John P. Dodd; costume design by Carole Martin. Production stage manager: Nancy Panzarella.

In honor of my oldest friend, Robert Emmet McGannon, the "Chief"

Lights up. Hanging from back wall, a brightly colored banner which reads: "LEXINGTON FIREHOUSE #11." Upstage right, two chairs. Upstage left, trashcan with broom leaning against it. Downstage center, a portable podium on wheels. Behind it stands a YOUNG MAN, *smiling out over the audience.*

YOUNG MAN: Gentlemen, on behalf of the entire *Lexington Number Eleven Company,* I welcome you to the finest and newest firehouse facility and all-purpose social club in all the Bronx and ask only that—[*Suddenly stopping, stepping back from podium, surveying its placement, moving it stage left, returning behind podium, clearing throat*]

Yes, Gentlemen, I give you our new firehouse auditorium recently stuck in the gut of the sky and I ask you: what better place in all the world to hear an address of such monumental meaning as you are about to witness than—[*Suddenly stopping, stepping back from podium, surveying placement, moving now stage right, returning behind podium, clearing throat*]

Yes, you have been beckoned here this wondrous Wednesday morn to hear of the joys of becoming a fireman and, so doing, to sign your—[*Suddenly stopping, stepping back from podium, surveying placement, returning it to its original position, returning behind podium*]

Morning, Gents, top of the morning to you. Let me start out by introducing myself, "first things first" as my old friend The Duke, John "Duke" Wayne, used to warn me! I'm Jocko Stone Halsey, . . . Jocko Stone Halsey, . . . Jocko Stone Halsey, . . . Jocko Stone Halsey, . . . Jocko Stone Halsey, Jocko Stone Halsey . . . [*Stepping back, the smile of success on his face (as if by repeating name he has somehow convinced himself of being the person so named), returning behind podium*]

How do, Boys, how do you do, . . . name's Jocko Stone Halsey, firehouse legend in my day, and I can't thank you guys enough for the enormous response you've shown to my coming here today. Must be at least a hundred, a hundred twenty-five of your scrubbed faces looking awe-struck my way. Well, let me only say that—[*Sounds back of auditorium.* YOUNG MAN *suddenly grabs broom, sweeping stage.* JOCKO STONE HALSEY *enters singing*]

JOCKO: [*Singing*]
Got us rainbows, rainbows for sale
Two for a nickel, five for a dime.
Come get your bendin' curves of color,
Gift of the rainbow boys, anytime.

Got us purples and greens and wild blues,
The full works for a dime.
Hang 'em on your arms, friends,
Compliments of the rainbow boys, anytime.

[*Takes off coat, stops, looks about;* YOUNG MAN *sweeping, not looking up*] What else can you call it—a coincidence, a real coincidence. [*Pulling off his coat, dropping it in one of the seats. Swings his arms*] Feel . . . fantastic! [*Rubbing his hands vigorously, moving . . . now in front of the stage, placing his foot on it, testing its strength*] Jew wood! [*Getting up the stage, hands on hips, his back to* YOUNG MAN, *looks around*] Beamed roof . . . cinder-block siding . . . mesh-gut windows, regular bag of Sheeny tricks they used getting this place up. [*Moving stage left, testing the floor*] Four-ply board, the creeps, four, oughta be six, even eight, you expect big people to move on it comfortable. [*Rubbing his face, laughing to himself*] What the hell else can you say? [*Looking up, loudly*] Endo, old buddy, know something? The place's built over where you and me used to sell our rainbows, over the very ground we did our colors—a coincidence! [*Laughing*] Couple of walking pissers we were, huh? [*Blessing himself*] Think about you, old buddy, everyday, really do! No reason you had to go out the way you did, none at all—a raw deal all the way down the line. [*Laughing, moving on*] Then out of nowhere, after all those years and tears and half-drunk beers, get a chance like this! [*Moving upstage, continuing to test the wood*] Sheeny creeps! [*Stopping, looking at the* YOUNG MAN *sweeping, moving on*] Kid, you the janitor here? [YOUNG MAN *doesn't look up, sweeping on. Suddenly notices another piece of sweeping, rushes to it, moistens finger, picks it up. Laughing*] All wrapped up in keepin' the place clean, aren't ya? Real nice. [YOUNG MAN *still doesn't look up.* JOCKO *crosses to him. Loudly*] Kid, I asked were you the janitor here, don't you hear so well?

YOUNG MAN: [*On his search for sweepings*] Ah, there you are, you little mother. . . . [*Moistening his finger, picking a sweeping from the floor. Moving on*] Today's an especially big day that it is, the most crucial since we opened this new auditorium six months ago. . . . [*Moving on*] Got to have the place spotless perfect for the big event. One Mr. Jocko Halsey's soon upon us to deliver words of untold import, so as you could guess—[JOCKO *suddenly laughing loudly,* YOUNG MAN *charging on*] Sir, your deep laugh bespeaks a richly comic nature and if only I had the time, oh, how I would love to join in such richness, but as you can see—[*Suddenly stopping, spots another sweeping*]

Ah, another sweet mother. . . . [*Continues search*] Got to hurry, hurry, hurry!

JOCKO, *again laughing loudly, crosses to* YOUNG MAN, *taps him on the shoulder.*

JOCKO: [*Laughing on*] Kid, listen . . . with the serious way you work, I'm impressed! But why don't you slow down for a minute?

YOUNG MAN: Haven't time, I'm sorry. [*Starting to move, but* JOCKO *grabs him by the shirt and, lifting him to standing position, begins to brush off* YOUNG MAN's *clothes*]

JOCKO: Kid, come on, you're going to mess up all those nice clothes you got on. . . .

YOUNG MAN: [*Starting to move, but* JOCKO *grabs him again*] Sir, can't you see I'm simply too busy?

JOCKO: [*Laughing, continuing to brush* YOUNG MAN's *clothes*] You look like a nutty monkey or somethin', chargin' around like that. Got to learn to take it easy. [*Completes brushing off the* YOUNG MAN. *Holding him firmly by the shoulders*] There, that's better. . . . [*Laughing loudly, playfully tapping* YOUNG MAN *on shoulder*] Kid, I don't mean to make fun or nothing, but that's sure a funny outfit you're wearing for being a janitor!

YOUNG MAN: [*Starting to move, but again* JOCKO *restrains him*] Sir, wouldn't you be dressed as best you could if today were one of the big events of your entire life?

JOCKO: [*Sudden silence, as* JOCKO *quickly examines his own clothes. With a tone of slight bewilderment he attempts to cover with friendly laughter*] Yeah, I know what you mean. . . . [YOUNG MAN *looking directly at* JOCKO, *laughing warmly*] All right, kid, don't you like my clothes?

YOUNG MAN: [*Laughing on*] You know something, you are really strong, wow!

JOCKO: What are you talking about?

YOUNG MAN: When you held me just now, boy, could I feel how strong you were!

JOCKO: [*Sudden beaming smile*] Oh, yeah? Well, thanks, kid. Nice of you to mention, real nice, but then I guess it is pretty obvious . . . huh? [*Again playfully tapping* YOUNG MAN's *shoulder*] Know something, kid? I like you already.

YOUNG MAN: [*Also beaming with smile*] Mind if I feel your muscle?

JOCKO: [*Instantly flexing his arm, laughing*] It's all yours, kid!

YOUNG MAN: [*Feeling* JOCKO's *arm*] Wow! Do physical people ever terrify you, sir?

JOCKO: Huh?

YOUNG MAN: The fear that out of nowhere a person one day might attack you and really mess you up?

JOCKO: [*Again playful tap to* YOUNG MAN's *shoulder*] Hey, anyone bothers me I could break their back if I wanted to, shatter it good, so what!

YOUNG MAN: Yeah, so what! . . . 'Cause I'm not afraid either. Fact is, I used to be a timid sort, very, but then just the other day, after I finished work here . . . you know, I was in the early evening walking over on Delancey Street . . . you know, when all of a sudden, out of nowhere these two gigantic negroid men—

JOCKO: Kid, got any idea who put this place up? [*Looking at ceiling*] Looks like a Sheeny job to me. Just look how thin them beams are. Probably don't even meet specification!

YOUNG MAN: [*Excitedly continuing*] As I was saying, these two immense black mothers stab out at me in the dark. Well, believe it or not, you know what I said? "Okay, Niggers, say a prayer you know karate, 'cause you've had it," and quick as you can flick your eyes, those bastards swooshed off, becoming night itself.

JOCKO: [*Looking up at ceiling, waving a finger near his temple to suggest daffiness*] Hey, Endo, just like the old lady!

YOUNG MAN: But then again this Negro business fits incredibly with— [*Suddenly stopping*] What'd you say? Sir, what'd you just say?

JOCKO: Done a top job gettin' the place ready, kid, tops! [*Rubbing his hands together*] Just think of it: After all those years and tears and half-drunk beers, finally get a chance like this!

YOUNG MAN: [*Pause, staring at* JOCKO] Clock's tick-tocking, hands moving, got to get back to work! Time for hopscotching hydrants and back on the street where your kind belong, old man, good-bye! [*Going back to his search for sweepings*]

JOCKO: [*Suddenly caught by a thought, rushes to the* YOUNG MAN, *lifts him again to an upright position. Speaking excitedly*] Hey, kid, I almost forgot! [*Laughing loudly, extending his hand to* YOUNG MAN] Jocko Stone Halsey, greatest chief Lexington Eleven ever had, retired '58 . . . standing before you. . . . Come on, kid, what's the matter, you want to see my I.D.?

YOUNG MAN: You're Jocko Stone Halsey? . . . You sure? . . . You can see the embarrassment all over my face, can't you. Go on, tell me, I don't mind.

JOCKO: Hey, come on, could happen to anybody.

YOUNG MAN: You mean to tell me it was you all along while I was, you know . . . like a nutty monkey charging all—holy mother of mothers, are you mother enough to still mother me? . . . [*Shaking* JOCKO'S *hand*] Aren't dressed the way I counted on, not at all!

JOCKO: Hey, kid, who knows, but it's me, Jocko Stone Halsey, standing before you!

YOUNG MAN: Counted on a famous old chief for some legitimate sartorial splendor.

JOCKO: Sort of skipped my mind, not mentioning my name straight off.

YOUNG MAN: Counted on a famous old chief to be dressed so elegantly, done up in threads so glorious that . . .

JOCKO: Come on, nothing more than a coincidence . . . my forgetting!

YOUNG MAN: Some coincidence, huh? [*Shaking hands*] Sir, this is one of the greatest pleasures in my whole life, I mean that!

JOCKO: Kid, you're a pisser, no kiddin', a regular pisser, pleasure to meet you.

YOUNG MAN: Jocko Stone Halsey, shattering . . . absolutely shattering . . .

JOCKO: Really got this floor good and clean for me didn't you? Kid, I tell you, I'm touched, no kidding, deeply moved. . . .

YOUNG MAN: You're touched? . . . Come on, what about how I feel, huh, what about me? Me?

JOCKO: Famous people make you nervous, huh, kid? Come on, tell me, tell me how much you heard about me? [*No response*] Can't you see it already, THE JOCKO STONE HALSEY AUDITORIUM . . . my name in big bold letters stretched across the front of the building? [*No response*] Only right I should get my name on something after all the dues I've paid, right, kid? [*Touching his head, patting his hair*] Kid, do I feel fantastic! [*Looking at* YOUNG MAN, *who is staring, quickly pulling his hand from his head, then staring at his hand*] Sorry, kid, is something the matter? [*Looking back at his hand*] Come on, out with it, what's the problem?

YOUNG MAN: Why do you keep patting your hair?

JOCKO: Does it matter?

YOUNG MAN: Sir, do you have any means of identification?

JOCKO: What!

YOUNG MAN: It's really important to me to know Jocko Sto— . . . I mean, you, that you are, you know—

JOCKO: [*Breaking into laughter*] What's the matter, kid, you haven't done a study of the pictures in the coffee room? [*Laughing on*] 'Cause I'm hanging there, upright corner, '33 to '58, set in goldplate . . .

YOUNG MAN: Sir, they've taken those pictures down.

JOCKO: Woulda loved my picture, kid, was a real ladies' man in my day. . . .

YOUNG MAN: Would have known who you were right away if it had been there . . . except it wasn't.

JOCKO: Bet you're pretty good with the ladies yourself, aren't you? [*Continuing to look about auditorium*] What's the matter, kid, don't you want to talk about it?

YOUNG MAN: Sir, what do you say—

JOCKO: Picture was mine, Jocko's, was the best I ever took, yeah, the best. [*Pause, they look at each other*] Hey, kid, bet you never knew old Jocko could yell so loud, huh?

YOUNG MAN: Sir, I don't mean to upset you or anything. It's just that—

JOCKO: Still want to see my I.D., don't you?

YOUNG MAN: Today has the makings of one of the truly big events of my entire life, so I'm afraid—

JOCKO: Cut the big words—want to see it, right? [*Reaching into his back pocket, withdrawing wallet. Nervously searching for I.D., several seconds of silence . . . can't find it*]

YOUNG MAN: Sir, is something the matter?

JOCKO: [*Handing* YOUNG MAN *wallet*] Here, kid, you have a look, I forgot my glasses. . . .

YOUNG MAN: [*Taking wallet*] Sure [*Starting search*] What's wrong with your eyes?

JOCKO: Don't need glasses, really don't . . . except on . . . on, ah . . . on very close work, understand?

YOUNG MAN: Old age, part of getting on.

JOCKO: Me get old? What a joke!

YOUNG MAN: I'm hardly old enough to shave. . . . [*Pulling out piece of paper, unfolding it*] Cho Chin Laundry . . . May, 1961. Sir, did you ever pick your wash up?

JOCKO: [*Laughing nervous*] If I didn't, it's too late, right? It's gone . . . so what! Old Chink's probably dead by now.

YOUNG MAN: Sure carry a lot of money, don't you?

JOCKO: Kid, you got any ideas of robbing me, you'll get your ass wiped, understand?

YOUNG MAN: Sir, I really hope you're shucking me 'cause if you're not, I may—

JOCKO: Kid, I was only joking. Humor helps me relax.

YOUNG MAN: I understand. [*Continuing search of wallet*]

JOCKO: Just keep searching, kid, you'll find them. [YOUNG MAN *continuing to search*] Come on, kid, just the I.D.'s, Okay? [*Several more sec-*

onds of searching] Hey, what are you doing . . . memorizin'? [*Finally* YOUNG MAN *hands wallet back to* JOCKO . . . *not speaking, looking at* JOCKO, *smiling*] Well?

YOUNG MAN: That's some wallet you got there. . . .

JOCKO: Sure, sure . . . but what about the I.D.s?

YOUNG MAN: Was that a picture of your wife?

JOCKO: Huh?

YOUNG MAN: In your wallet, under the obituary slips and behind the girlie shots, that's your wife, isn't it?

JOCKO: Sure.

YOUNG MAN: Didn't even know it was there, did you?

JOCKO: Nope.

YOUNG MAN: Aren't you going to have a look?

JOCKO: It's old.

YOUNG MAN: She's very pretty. You must be proud.

JOCKO: It was shot a long time ago.

YOUNG MAN: Maybe after we're finished, I could help you clean it up. [*Pause*] The wallet, we could clean it up, put it in some sort of order?

JOCKO: Just like her tubes, scrape it clean, huh?

YOUNG MAN: Guess you'll never get to using the Trojan prophylactic with the fuzz tip under the cross of Easter palm leaves?

JOCKO: Huh?

YOUNG MAN: Not much fun, are they, Trojan prophylactics? Like a strapped-in dog on a muzzle I always felt slipping my thing to a lady. What about you?

JOCKO: Didn't mess up my obituary slips, did you?

YOUNG MAN: Still behind the girlie shots.

JOCKO: Obituary slips are no easy trick keeping in order.

YOUNG MAN: You are Jocko, aren't you?

JOCKO: Think I'd be different?

YOUNG MAN: I'm not disappointed at all, not one bit!

JOCKO: Jocko Stone Halsey's never been one to let people down. [*Pause*] Do I let you down?

YOUNG MAN: You must be kidding. [*Laughing warmly*] I'd like to keep you around as long as I can . . . I feel that honored. . . . I'm emanating a strong sense of awe over your presence, aren't I?

JOCKO: [*Suddenly yelling in direction of ceiling*] Hey, Endo . . . just like the old lady! [*Again waving finger near temple to suggest daffiness*]

YOUNG MAN: What'd you say, sir, what'd you just say?

JOCKO: Thirteen years of sitting, doing nothing, then bam! . . . get a chance like this! [*Taking hold of* YOUNG MAN'S *shoulders*] Really appreciate the cleaning up you've done, kid. Place looks real nice. . . .

YOUNG MAN: [*Suddenly sights another sweeping on the floor, rushes to it, bends down*] Ah, you little mother, you. . . .

JOCKO: [*Laughing*] Kid, you're beautiful. . . .

YOUNG MAN: [*Checks watch*] Clock's tick-tocking, hands moving, 10:28 . . . 34, sir!

JOCKO: Huh?

YOUNG MAN: Thirty-two minutes till you negotiate the threat of unknown faces? [JOCKO *staring, not speaking*] The lecture to the recruits, sir, the speech?

JOCKO: [*Laughing*] Relax, will you? I don't go till noon.

YOUNG MAN: I was told 11 o'clock, sir, 11 on the button.

JOCKO: In the letter I was told 12, the invitation said noon!

YOUNG MAN: Sir, they did say 11 o'clock sharp!

JOCKO: They who, who said 11 sharp?

YOUNG MAN: Don't know his name. He wasn't a fireman. [*Pause*] Sir, is something the matter?

JOCKO: After all these years, finally THE JOCKO STONE HALSEY AUDITORIUM, and still they can't get things straight!

YOUNG MAN: The guy who told me 11 was wearing a blue suit, medium height, brown hair, not too short, not too long, just about right. Ring a bell?

JOCKO: Probably one of the Sheeny creeps who put the building up.

YOUNG MAN: Sir, you're sure the letter said noon?

JOCKO: What do you mean, am I sure? Don't you think I can read?

YOUNG MAN: Don't have the letter with you, do you?

JOCKO: Left it home . . . threw it away, so what!

YOUNG MAN: Yes, of course . . . except that it leaves us shrouded in quite something of a mystery, wouldn't you say? [*Checking watch*] 10:29:47, sir.

JOCKO: Got to learn to speak simpler, kid. [*Suddenly* JOCKO *moves toward* YOUNG MAN]

YOUNG MAN: Sir, did I say something wrong?

JOCKO: One of them, aren't you, kid, one of the educated who couldn't make it in the thinker's big time so you just scooted down the ladder, right? [*Taking* YOUNG MAN *by shoulder*] Kid, it's okay, fine, no worry. Firehouse's a great place for melting people together, mean, you keep cleaning the place like this, no one gives two craps how goddamn messed up you are inside your nut, get me?

YOUNG MAN: Do I make you uncomfortable or something, sir?

JOCKO: Get along good with everybody, mean, don't you figure that's why I'm here, huh, why I was brought in to talk to the recruits and get my name across the front of that building, huh?

YOUNG MAN: Yes, and I'm here to help you. Some assignment they threw my way, huh?

JOCKO: Help you're going to give me, is it?

YOUNG MAN: Why, when you think of all the people they could've chosen for today, you've—

JOCKO: Kid, what's your name?

YOUNG MAN: Jocko Stone Halsey, greatest chief Lexington Number 11 ever had, retired '58, standing before you!

JOCKO: Jocko Stone Halsey, that's a laugh and a half.

YOUNG MAN: [*Laughing*] Only trying to be funny, sir. Said yourself humor helps you relax.

JOCKO: Kid, you educated types don't manage so good at firehouse work, mean, no wonder you're tryin' so extra hard to keep busy!

YOUNG MAN: [*Tapping* JOCKO's *shoulder*] I'm hardly better than you, sir. Relax, relax. [JOCKO *violently punches* YOUNG MAN's *arm, knocking him down*] If it'll help, I'll let you punch me. I don't mind!

JOCKO: [*Rubbing his hands together*] What do you say we get things ready, huh?

YOUNG MAN: Everything is ready, sir. . . . I've been here since dawn.

JOCKO: [*Looking at the podium, laughing loudly*] Kid, nobody ever tell you about positionin' a speakin' box? [*Crossing downstage toward the podium*]

YOUNG MAN: Stage is set in perfect order, sir, a truly proper arrangement, no need to move anything!

JOCKO: Kid, you and my old lady'd get along famous, no kiddin! [*Daffiness gesture; behind podium to push it, but* YOUNG MAN *blocks him*]

YOUNG MAN: I don't mean to be in any way disrespectful, sir, but my experience at arranging stages for speaking engagements, lectures, debates, et cetera, is so extensive and illustrious that . . .

JOCKO: I wouldn't know. You're in the way.

YOUNG MAN: Really know what I'm up to, sir. Why don't you want to put me and my gift to good use?

JOCKO: Sorry about hitting you, kid. You're in the way.

YOUNG MAN: If you'll only give me a minute, sir, I could explain why my approach to presenting speakers to proper advantage is so soundly based beyond even the vaguest shadow of a—

JOCKO: We'll talk about it later, kid. You're in the way. [JOCKO *starts to push podium, but* YOUNG MAN *blocks him*]

YOUNG MAN: Sir, I'd like to return the podium to its proper position. Please move!

With a tremendous surge of strength, JOCKO *rolls the podium forward, knocking the* YOUNG MAN *out of the way and onto the floor.*

JOCKO: You educated types sure have trouble getting the message. . . . [*Pushing podium across stage*] . . . 'cause the first rule in speaking to people is you gotta take advantage of the proper side of the stage, know what I mean? Topmost important the angle you go at them from. Now, you take your really top speakers down through history and you notice—

YOUNG MAN: Okay, okay, your way's okay, A-1, super-terrific, just so long as you put me to—

JOCKO: Forget it. Down the pages of history, your Roose—

YOUNG MAN: Long as you put me to proper advantage, put—

JOCKO: Your Roosevelts, your Jimmy Walkers, your Lou Gehrigs—

YOUNG MAN: Put my gift to good use and in that—

JOCKO: Your great people at speakin', get me?, and you notice their topmost concern is always—

YOUNG MAN: [*Crawling after* JOCKO] Got to let me set it, won't you, let me exer— [*Starting to rise, but* JOCKO *keeps him to floor, pressing* YOUNG MAN's *fingers down with the tip of his shoe*] Please, sir, I'm dreadfully terrified of a fracture.

JOCKO: [*More pressure on* YOUNG MAN's *fingers*] We like each other, don't we kid?

YOUNG MAN: With a background like mine at presenting people to proper advantage, what can liking each other possibly have to do with the monumental task at hand!

JOCKO: [*Pressure all the while continuing*] Really can't stop your talking, can you? Never stop, and my old lady's exactly the same way with her big mouth blabbing hour on—

YOUNG MAN: My hand! [*Screaming*] You're acting just like Captain Quinn, really are, stupid Captain Quinn! [JOCKO *immediately releases hold on* YOUNG MAN'S *fingers*] Was beginning to wonder, wonder if you'd ever let go. . . . [*Jumping to feet*] You're one tough mother for a man of your years. [*Rubbing fingers*] Wow!

JOCKO: Who'd you say, kid, who'd you say that was?

YOUNG MAN: Captain Quinn.

JOCKO: Old Quinn, huh? Real interesting . . .

YOUNG MAN: Two weeks ago Thursday he came stumbling in here like an overworked ox and tried to—

JOCKO: Bad enough another chief, but to invite some worthless captain, a goddamn insignificant captain, why— [JOCKO *pushes the two chairs over onto floor and starts for podium*]

YOUNG MAN: Relax, sir. He was a much, much different sort than you! Why, when—

JOCKO: [*In front of the podium, clearing his throat*] Gentlemen, don't have to mention how much I appreciate your getting me away from the old lady for a morning, know what I mean? [*Nervous laugh*] That opening remark always kills 'em, fractures their gut, puts 'em on the floor. . . . Anyway, I won't be long with my— [*Stops. turns to* YOUNG MAN] Kid, you're lying, aren't you, about Quinn being here, aren't you? Mean, his name ain't on the building yet.

YOUNG MAN: If it's come time for rehearsing speeches, better move my chairs, don't you think?

JOCKO: [*Turning back to podium*] Now, as to why you guys been invited here is real plain, simple, being offered the greatest poss—

YOUNG MAN: [*Crossing to* JOCKO *with chairs*] Here, sir, at least sit down so you can relax a bit before you have—

JOCKO: [*Turning around*] Huh? [*Pause*] Kid, please, huh?

YOUNG MAN: Sir, I brought you the chairs as you wanted. [*Measuring placement*]

JOCKO: Thanks, kid, real thoughtful of you!

YOUNG MAN: [*Bending over, moving seats under* JOCKO] You're set, sir, you can continue with your speech.

Smiling, JOCKO *sits down.*

JOCKO: Kid, don't you understand a speaker can't talk sitting down? . . . [*Jumping back up, pushing chairs away*] I didn't ask for no chairs so why would you— [*Suddenly stopping, again rubbing his hands vigorously, taking a deep breath*] Gentlemen, know something? If I was still chief of Lexington Number 11 here—know what? They'd retire me, understand? [*Slamming the podium*] I'd get

close to 11,000 retirement pay. I mean, get 69 hundred as it is. But do nothing and get 11,000, that's nothing to laugh at. [*Pause*] Now, you take your really top speakers down through history and you see— [*Suddenly stopping*]

YOUNG MAN: Sir, you sound a bit disoriented. Maybe I could offer some helpful suggestion or two and in that—

JOCKO: [*Laughing nervously*] Not to mention the small things like the food and beddin' at Lexington number 11's best in all the Bronx, and the friends, why, the buddies you make—

YOUNG MAN: Sir, I'd truly like to help you with your speaking!

JOCKO: [*Imitating* YOUNG MAN] "Sir, I'd truly like to help you with your speaking." [*Looking up at ceiling, circling hand about temple*] A pisser, Endo, this kid's a real pisser! . . . Hey, speaking's my forte, my special excellence, I mean, man got a natural ability like that, no need of preparing or getting ready for anything, understand? . . . Just get up there and knock 'em dead, right? Ever seen—what's his name, Gehrig, yeah, Iron Man Lou Gehrig— big Lou got ability, no need of anything else, right, just do it, right? . . . Now, you take your best speakers of all time, don't matter when, you always notice that they speak from a right position. And in that way they—

YOUNG MAN: We're on the left, sir!

JOCKO: The left? [*Pause*] A left position, aren't we, you and I, the left! [*Pushing podium to correct side*] That's it, isn't it? That's what you want, for me to get all shook up . . . to get, like you say, disorientated, right? . . . Yes, sir, you educateds are all the same. Ain't for shit at nothing but getting in the way of people who got some real talent for something! [*Setting podium*] Now this is the right, right?

YOUNG MAN: Sir, everytime you move that podium, please bear in mind that you alter not only it, but the terrifying delicate relation it has to the recruits attending in that—

JOCKO: [*Clearing throat, behind podium*] Gentlemen, handle a hose, swing an axe, you're a fireman, greatest job in the world, not to mention—

YOUNG MAN: 10:36:50, sir, clock's tick-tocking, hands moving.

JOCKO: Then you take your hours which are really something because [*Scratching at his scalp*] really something because [*Again scratching*] you work a lot while everyone else is asleep. [*Stopping, sneaking a look at the sweaty hand he scratched his scalp with*] Next, you take your, ahm . . . [*Again sneaking a look at that hand*] ahm . . . gentlemen, see this hand, this sweat-dripping paw? Was told 35 years ago I didn't keep it out of my hair, I'd only speed the fall, go bald, see, 'cause my hair started to shed early. . . . Well, look, still got plenty left, mean it ain't thick full, but— [*Laughing*] Kid, wanna show you something, come here!

YOUNG MAN: [*Crossing to* JOCKO, *laughing*] I'm sorry, sir, what's up? [*They look at each other, but* YOUNG MAN *can't stop laughing*] You must admit, sir, to the humor of our situation, what with me wanting to help out after . . . you know, and then your being absolutely, you know, unable to even attempt your speech to —[*Tapping* JOCKO *on the shoulder*] We are a very funny pair, you and I, impossibly comic . . .

JOCKO: Okay, out! . . . [YOUNG MAN *laughing on*] I mean it, blow!

YOUNG MAN: [*Moving chairs*] Got to set my chairs first, then I'll be more than happy—

JOCKO: [*Pushing the* YOUNG MAN] Out! You, out, out, out!

YOUNG MAN: There, everything's arranged to your proper advantage. Guess you can handle it from here. Good luck! Jocko Stone Halsey. [*Jumps from stage, starts up aisle to exit*]

JOCKO: Kid, wanna know what I was going to show ya? [*The* YOUNG MAN *turns around and moves back toward* JOCKO. *Stepping up on the stage slowly*] Kid, come on, before they float away, wanna *show* ya somethin! [JOCKO *taps* YOUNG MAN *on shoulder with his free hand*] Know what they are, kid? [*Holding up his hand*] Hair, fallen strands, dead. [*Mumbling as he counts*] One—

YOUNG MAN: I just knew you'd never let me go. . . .

JOCKO: One . . . three . . . seven, *nine, kid, nine* beauties I itched out of my head just now. And know what else? Must be a good 40 years at least—

YOUNG MAN: Thirty-five. [*Pause*] Thirty-five years ago everyone warned you that if you didn't leave it alone, it would only—

JOCKO: Kid, you're okay, nice sense of comedy . . . was more like 35, wasn't it, right?

YOUNG MAN: Right!

JOCKO: Thirty-five years ago my hair started falling on me, see, and everybody 'round the firehouse saw me itching, you know, a shock, you itch, and so, they warn me, don't stop itching, my hair'll go in no time. Well, they were wrong, huh? I mean, ain't thick full, but take a look, not that many thin spots for a guy my age, understand? [*Laughing*] I mean, they predicted wrong, right? [*Nervously starting to move*] But that ain't all, kid, see, 'cause not only am I no skinhead like they predicted. I keep a count of the loss, no kiddin', count every dead strand I can, just so there be no arguing about how goddamn wrong they were, understand, except none of 'em living anymore, which is another kinda big point for old Jocko, okay? [*Blessing himself, looking up*] Everyday, Endo, everyday! [*Moving on*] Kid, know how you read them advertisements for hair-saving where they claim a man got 100,000, tops 120,000 hairs in his head? Lotta crap 'cause old Jocko passed the 200,000 mark nine years, twelfth of last month, was Minnie's birthday how I remember, my old lady, and this very day I'm nearing the 280,000 mark and still going strong, understand? Here, I'll give you [*Pulling a small notebook out of his back pocket*] . . . the precise tabulations, 2-7-8-4-7-8 plus. . . . How many I say I lost today?

YOUNG MAN: Nine . . .

JOCKO: . . . 9 plus 2-7-8-4-7-8 . . . ?

YOUNG MAN: 278487!

JOCKO: [*Mumbling to himself*] God bless you educateds . . . 2-7-8-4-8-7, kid, got it all here in the book, which ain't to mention the thousands I never known about, showers, sleepin', know what I mean? [*Putting book back in his pocket. Moving downstage left, motioning*] Kid, wanna show you somethin'. [YOUNG MAN *moves to him*] To keep your real accurate count, gotta search out places where the light shafts are best, understand? Now watch this. Keep your eye on the spotlight beam right over my head. [*Bending forward, shaking his hair with one hand and extending the other to catch any falling strands*] Did you see that one, kid? See, there's another . . . a third . . . see that one, bent like wire, floats different . . . [*Standing up, counting those others that have landed in his hand, mumbling*] One . . . five, plus the three we caught in the light is eight, which brings the grand total to [*Again taking out his notebook*] . . . 8 plus 2-7-8-4-8-7 . . . [YOUNG MAN *starts to answer, but* JOCKO *stops him. Laughing, putting the notebook back in his pocket*] Know what, kid? Gonna forget these, [*Opening his hand, letting the hairs fall*] understand, sort of a good luck thing for today's lecturing, huh! [*Suddenly changing gears*] To this day, kid, the whole thing's been driving my old lady kooks! . . . See, we got this place up in Connecticut, Westport, long ranch job, real nice, with lots of them pine and spruce needle shrub forming a privacy row behind the flowers, which, let me tell ya, ain't really necessary, see, 'cause we got a good eight, ten acres out back 'fore you come to the next place, understand? But the old lady yapped privacy, know what I mean? Privacy this, privacy that, for so goddamn long I just went out one day, dug the holes, dropped the shrub in so she'd finally turn off. [*Laughing*] Okay? And guess what I told her, kid? 'll really bust ya up. Told her, Minnie—that's her name—Minnie, all them shrubs doing is keeping the porcupine and deer from pissing the grass brown. [*Laughing*] But listen to this: know what she does? Bows her head, and mumbles something 'bout can't be sure wild animals do that—piss or crap—'cause we never see 'em in person, wow! Not much in the humor department, my Minnie, is she, not to mention she gettin' to look like a kicked-around balloon couple hundred people tromped on marching in a parade or somethin', understand? [YOUNG MAN *checking his watch,* JOCKO *totally involved in completing his story, moving on, laughing loudly*] Like I said, the falling hair drives her kooks. See, I take a walk out back every morning, real early, nothin' like it, out back by the shrubs I told ya I planted before, okay? Now, I don't know if you're up on this, kid, but pine, spruce . . . your thick-heavy willow, sometimes even your rich leaf oak, they're your really top makers of light shafts, and as you know [*Laughing*] a top shaft of light and Jocko's there like a magnet, okay? So every morning I'm out back flapping out my head, making a count of the day's loss, and old Minnie's sitting in the living room watching me through the bay window, twiddling her pudge-fingers, nervous sweat, the whole works, like somebody's momma watching so Johnny don't pull his, [*Gesturing toward his privates*] know what I mean? Can feel her over my shoulder when I bend down and bury my longest dead hairs in the moss under the pines 'cause, I don't know, [*Laughs*]. They been mine the longest, understand, watching me like a hawk till I get up and, turning, wave at her which makes her smile which I can hardly see 'cause the bay glass's so fogged with the 85-degree thermostat she gotta have, yap, yap, 85 goddam degrees, looking like a slop-painted—I don't know—coconut face, ya see, smiling when I wave, [*Laughing*] smiling, not knowing how I dream of clenchin' my wavin' paw and splatterin' her dyin' mug once and for all. [*Pause*] Marriage isn't no responsibility means a man gotta sit watchin' a baby wrinkle, gotta get bent by the saggin' ass he promised 50 years ago got strapped to his back, understand, yappin', on and on, like it'll never turn off . . . else it's that goddamn smile, through dry, crinklin' lips liable to flash nothin' but gums 'cause she's always forgettin' her bridges in that pink sauce crap that hangs from one end

of the house to the other. [*Laughing strangely*] One day ya roll over in bed and bam, like outa nowhere with no warning, there's an empty grocery bag leanin' against ya somebody forgot to throw away . . . [*Suddenly looking at ceiling, scratching his head*] Endo, buddy, why'd ya kick off and leave me with nothing [*Again scratching his head*] with nothing! [*Looks slowly at his hand, mumbling the count of new lost hairs*] One . . . three, six, seven, seven more, kid, [*Laughing*] seven, bringin' the grand tabulation to [*Reaching into his pocket and once again pulling out the little notebook, mumbling*] . . . 2-7-8-4-8-7 plus 7 is 2-7-8-4-9-4. [*Putting the book away*] Used to be so proud, kid, my Minnie was showcase, greatest looker in all the Bronx, top to bottom. Then, bam . . . [*Bowing his head*] so unexpected like, not a breath of warning. [*Mumbling on, pause.* YOUNG MAN *laughing*] What's so funny?

YOUNG MAN: I'm losing my hair too. Look! [*Playfully flapping at his head, checking for falling strands*] It had to happen, someone like you finally showing up, it just had to happen! You and I, sir, we're going to eat these recruits alive . . . 'cause you and I, sir, we've got the makings of a real team!

JOCKO: [*Sudden, quick move, laughing loudly, looking up*] Endo, place built right over the spot we sold rainbows. [*Clearing his throat, suddenly singing a song*]
    Got us rainbows, rainbows for sale
    Two for a nickle, five for a dime.
    Come get your bendin' curves of
        color,
    Gift of the rainbow boys . . . any-
        time!

    We got us purples and greens and
        wild blues,
    The full works for a dime.
    Hang 'em on your arms, friends,
    Compliments of the rainbow boys . . .
        anytime!

Humming the song's tune, moving on, periodic dance steps—suddenly stopping, noticing something on the ground, bending over.

YOUNG MAN: That we could both be losing our hair, why, that's more than mere coincidence, much much more. Destiny's the word, destiny. [*Suddenly noticing* JOCKO *bending over*] Sir, that's okay, that's my job!

JOCKO: [*Rising, laughing, holding out his finger*] Kid, missed a sweepin' after all. . . . [*Swinging away, throwing the sweeping into the air, laughing on*] Kid, watch it dive like a dead strand, cuttin' the curve of our rainbows . . . [*Moving to the podium, staring straight ahead*]

Kid, didn't you hear—even once—somebody mention a little something about my name on the building? THE JOCKO STONE HALSEY AUDITORIUM in big bold letters across the front?

YOUNG MAN: [*Moving to* JOCKO] I've heard it mentioned many times, THE JOCKO STONE HALSEY AUDITORIUM. Fact is, it's all anyone in the firehouse business talks of, day and night, THE JOCKO HAL—

JOCKO: [*Punching* YOUNG MAN *hard, knocking him down*] Then what was Quinn, what was Captain Quinn doing here two weeks ago Thursday, looking for a place to piss!?

YOUNG MAN: [*Jumping to feet*] Your suit's gotten wrinkled from all your punching. [*Moving in on* JOCKO] I'm going to press you off now. . . . [*Nearing*] Then you'll be smart-looking just like me.

JOCKO: [*Turning away, moving on*] Shoulda gotten you outa here, but no, not old Jocko, let things go on, like I shoulda stuck my old lady out to farmin' in one of them homes, understand? [*Rubbing his hands together*] Well, all that's changin', 13 years on my ass, waitin', doing nothin', and now we're gonna get a little action, know what I mean? [*Looking around the stage*] Kid, wanna get rid of them chairs? Liable to distract from my speakin' . . . and don't give me none of your big-word yappin', please, 'cause you oughta been outa here long ago. . . . [YOUNG MAN *crosses to the chairs.* JOCKO *moves around, passes by him and slaps him on the back*] Kid, you're okay, a regular pisser, [*Again gestures with his hand to suggest daffiness*] mean, you get me all worked up, but you're okay. [YOUNG MAN *starts to drag chairs backstage,* JOCKO *is still moving*] Not so much noise, kid, pick 'em up, come on, up! [*Suddenly humming the rainbow song*] . . . two for a nickle, five for a dime.
　　Come get your bendin' curves a
　　　　color . . .
[*Humming some more, moving on*] Gunna have to leave in a second, kid, action time, understand? [*Moving on, waving his arms*] Air's startin' to clear, Endo, old buddy, Old Jocko's gunna be ready this time. . . .

YOUNG MAN: It's absolutely shattering you've stuck with your hair 35 years. . . . Gives me and my sort great hope, yes, sir, great hope! [*Setting chairs backstage*] My humble opinion is, the trashcan doesn't look natural at all where it is, not at all!

JOCKO: Wanna get rid of the trashcan, kid? Don't look so good where it is. [*Moves on, rubbing his hands.* YOUNG MAN *drags the trashcan offstage*] Not so much noise, kid, pick it up!

YOUNG MAN: [*Continues to drag trashcan*] Can't, sir, too heavy!

JOCKO: Then carry it! [*Moving quickly back to the podium, clearing his throat*] Been waitin' for you guys, thought you'd never show. [*Laughing*] Pleasure to see your loving faces. [*Starts to reach for his head. Suddenly stops himself*]

YOUNG MAN: Trashcan in position, sir. . . .

JOCKO: Gentlemen, I'll be frank with you, only way I know how. Can tell by the looks on your faces you're the lost type [*Laughing*] . . . which really ain't even a matter of lookin' 'cause you weren't lost, you wouldn't be here. . . .

YOUNG MAN: Clock's tick-tocking, sir, 10:43:17.

JOCKO: Being lost's okay, see, 'cause I was the same way once. That's why being a fireman's so great.

YOUNG MAN: I wouldn't tell them that if I were you, Jocko.

JOCKO: 'Cause it gives ya time to put yourself in order.

YOUNG MAN: They'll laugh your ass right out of here.

JOCKO: Listen, I'll tell ya a story 'bout me and Endo, an old buddy of mine, greatest hook-and-ladder driver Lexington number 11 ever had. Now, it all has to do with . . . ahm . . . No reason you had to go out the way you did, Endo, a raw deal all the way down the line. [*Suddenly spins around, looking about the stage*] Real good job, kid. You can leave now. [*Turning back, facing out*] See, Endo and me, we were real close, best buddies . . . which I guess is why we was firemen, 'cause there was no one else close to us, I mean you know how an old lady gets after a while. . . . [YOUNG MAN *moves quickly downstage, behind* JOCKO *at the podium*] Firehouse's that place in the world where ya . . . you know . . .

YOUNG MAN: Sir, I'll have to take over now.

JOCKO: Don't interrupt me now. . . . See, firehouse's the kinda place where ya get away from what's bothering—

YOUNG MAN: [*Violently grabbing the edge of the podium*] Sir, you're a dead duck without me to set you up for these recruits. Out of my way! [YOUNG MAN *starting to push podium.* JOCKO *jumps in front of it.* YOUNG MAN *starts to push podium harder, shoving* JOCKO *backwards*]

JOCKO: Right when I was about to find my speakin' point, you gotta start— [YOUNG MAN *shoves him back again*] . . . Don't you understand? I'm findin' my speakin' point . . . [YOUNG MAN *shoves him back again*] Kid, you know how strong I am, gunna snap your back you don't stop it.

YOUNG MAN: Captain Quinn, Mendowski, Propp, O'Toole, been marching 'em through here, never listening to me, every one of them falling on their faces. . . . Shatner, the chief before you?—but us, me and you, we're going all the way down the line, out of the way!

JOCKO: About to knock the bastards dead, right on top of my speaking point, and you gotta—

YOUNG MAN: Sir, you're on top of nothing. Out of the way!

JOCKO: Aren't you familiar with the top speakers of history, the Roosevelts, the Stevensons, the—

YOUNG MAN: Success's a matter of presenting oneself to proper advantage. . . . Out of the way!

JOCKO: The great speakers, the Jimmy Walkers, the Lou Gehrigs, the people who— [YOUNG MAN *pushes past* JOCKO *and returns podium to original position center stage*] Those exceptional few who knew what real speaking was about, who had a gift for delivering up just the right word so's even the dumbest of dum-dums got the message loud and true.

YOUNG MAN: [*Getting behind podium*] Gentlemen, boys, friends, . . . Jocko Stone Halsey's the name, huffing and bluffing's the game. I'll be simple and brief to the point as I know how! Jocko Stone Halsey, Jocko Stone Halsey, I'm Jocko Stone Halsey.

JOCKO: What'd you say, kid, what'd you just say?

YOUNG MAN: Yes, I, Jocko Stone Halsey, do humbly admit to being an old man . . . with hair floating from me like winter snow, with fears that shake me beyond description and cardboard tales better left as lies. I, Jocko Huff-and-Bluff, do—

JOCKO: A very, very bum imitation, kid. Why not one you're up to? Ed Sullivan you could handle, John Wayne's even easier.

YOUNG MAN: I, Jocko Huff-and-Bluff, offer you the life of being a fireman . . . with the hours that never pass and the friends who, laughing, never listen and the wives forever turning away, the silence a shape to fill the lacks, you both your whole lives long have let—

JOCKO: [*Loudly booing*] Worst pretending I ever seen, boo . . . boo. Bring on the next joker!

YOUNG MAN: I, Jocko Stone Halsey . . .

JOCKO: . . . Want my money back if this— [*Continued booing*]

YOUNG MAN: I offer you my crumbling body, my dying arms, [*Raising arms*] fleeting heart, offer my dreams that never even once came true, . . . passing today before you as would a

waxen mummy in a museum visited only by people with nothing more to do, . . . passing this hour before you like a rotting, crumb—

JOCKO: Over the line, kid. Cut it!

YOUNG MAN: Like a rotting, crumbling, shit-stinking, piss-thin pair of fire boots everyone forgot to bring in during a wild winter storm, . . . passing before you this second like the beaten, half-bagged bluff of a muffled fart bland beyond ever even stink—

JOCKO: [*Rushing to* YOUNG MAN] That's it, isn't it, kid, what you want, isn't it, to confuse me so bad that you get to deliver the speech, you to be the man everyone listens to when the recruits march through that door and—

YOUNG MAN: Yes, I stink so bad anyone with even half a nose left could smell—

JOCKO: Just love to be me, wouldn't you, to be the center of attention, wouldn't you?

YOUNG MAN: I, Jocko Stone Halsey, . . . Jocko Stone Halsey . . . Jocko Stone Hal—

JOCKO: Needle jammed, kid. Spit it out!

YOUNG MAN: I, Jocko Stone—

JOCKO: Kid! Kid! [*Shaking* YOUNG MAN *to silence him*] Kid, . . . no one wants to hear it!!

YOUNG MAN: [*Turning from podium*] Sir, we're almost ready, really are! [*Moving chairs*] You and I, sir, we turn this last corner together, hand in hand, or we're down the drain for good, yes, for us this is it! But they don't listen, Quinn, Mendowski, the ones who came before, . . . none of the stupid, goddamn bastards, mean, I'm the answer to a name on a building 'cause I understand what it is to take proper advantage of things, to squeeze from my one gift enough goodness so that it can be said in the end, "That man put himself to some sort of use, somehow made a mark," mean, how long can the shit come flying at us . . . old man, before we go all the way to the wall and turn and jam the bastards downtown and up—so, so easy to understand and you, sir, I'm sure follow my every word. . . . [*Moving to* JOCKO] You do, don't you? [*No response*] I mean, what I've been saying, you and me hand in hand taking a stand, . . . they couldn't follow, but I can tell, the moment you came in something happened between us, we, so to speak, you and me, we showed the markings of a real team. [*No response*] Sir, if you're scared beyond even talking, let's forget the recruits and just take the building, the room, the floor, the podium, something, each other's hands, anything, so that we at least *take*—

JOCKO: But, listen, kid, listen. You can't take me.

YOUNG MAN: But— [*Takes hold of* JOCKO'S *hand*]

JOCKO: Let me go, please, kid. I gotta go it alone.

YOUNG MAN: But you know there's no way alone is any good—[*Pulling harder on* JOCKO'*s hand*]

JOCKO: I gotta make them see I ain't finished.

YOUNG MAN: But you and me, we gotta make it together hand in hand or we're permanent down the drain—

JOCKO: [*Finally escaping hold of* YOUNG MAN] But, kid, I'm so much closer to the drain than you, so much nearer the distance. I gotta go the rest of the route myself. Brings to mind most vivid that September of 1941 when the great Lou Gehrig, first-base player for the legendary Yankees of New York, went strolling to home plate and, with half the world weeping tears for the truth they wanted not to hear, the great Iron Man announced that he was ravaged by an illness that left the end-of-the-line last stop but a few short months away. But Iron Man Old Lou had enough courage of spine left to stand proud and admit he had to go the rest of the way by himself.

YOUNG MAN: You do have to go it alone, don't you?

JOCKO: How else? I'm Jocko Stone Halsey. No gravestone in my backyard, no crutches, no canes, no pennies in my eyes, no death warrants out on my name. Let me enter my own house justified, let me earn my name on a building. Well, what do you say, kid?

YOUNG MAN: You're a pisser, Chief Halsey, a legitimate pisser, far and away the biggest of them all.

JOCKO: Thanks, kid, thanks.

YOUNG MAN: Know what? I'm going to get myself a brush and some paint and start stenciling your name over the front door, yes, sir. THE JOCKO STONE HALSEY AUDITORIUM. [*Checking watch*] 10:51:27, sir, the recruits'll be here any minute. Good luck.

[*Starts toward door*]

JOCKO: [*Yelling after* YOUNG MAN] Hey, kid, you forgot to tell me your name.

YOUNG MAN: Jocko Stone Halsey!! [*Exits*]

JOCKO: Endo, Endo, Endo, old buddy. [*Yelling at ceiling*] Just like the old lady, that kid, huh? Just can't stop with the yappin' . . . yap, yap, yap, yap, yap, yap! [*Gets behind podium, clears his throat*] Gentlemen, real pleasure to see . . . to see . . . to see [*Slams podium, steps back, trying a second time*] Gentlemen, don't have to mention how much I appreciate your getting me away from the old lady for a morning, know what I mean? [*Laughing to himself*] Always kills 'em, fractures their guts, puts 'em on— [*Suddenly stops, stepping back, trying a third time*] Gentlemen, to be a fireman, to be a battler of blazes requires that a man be . . . that a man be . . . that a man be— [*Once again slams podium and, turning away, yells toward ceiling*] To be a fireman, that's a real laugh and a half . . . huh, Endo, huh? When I think of you, old buddy, and how we could've been together again today, could've stayed best pals through all these years . . . why, there was no reason you had to go out the way you did, none at all, a raw deal all the way down the line. Can still picture it like it was only yesterday, that fateful day of the great fire over on Delancey Street, can still picture it all. [*Laughing*] There you were, danglin' out of the warehouse window, smoke weavin' all around you, screamin', "Chief, Chief, there's this woman up here won't leave till she finds all her clothes." What could I say, you know? Who the hell can think of somethin' to say at a time like that? It was hilarious. First off, all the boys workin' the fire started laughin'. 'Member Jimmy Alexander, was my best hose man, got the shakes so bad he couldn't keep the goddamn thing in his hand, water sprayin' every which way, hittin' everybody. That started it 'cause then a coupla the other boys began laughin' so hard they fell down in the street, lyin' there sloppin' around in the hydrant water. Then there were these old people from the neighborhood, cluttering up the streets, mostly Polacks and Guineas, standin' around with these dumb expressions on their faces, mouths hangin' open like they were watchin' a baby bein' delivered or somethin'. Soon as they saw my boys floppin' around in the streets, they started laughin' too, got louder and louder, these skinny Wop kids runnin' around, makin' wise remarks, "Give her your clothes and let's see what you look like," . . . "Ass on fire," . . . "Flamin' pussy for sale," . . . things like that. Wow, was it hilarious, so, so hilarious. [*Laughs, reaches for his hair, stops himself*] Was cruel, too, very, very cruel, all those people screamin' and you chargin' down the ladder backwards with that blubbery old hag flopped over your shoulder, naked, nothin' on. Just couldn't laugh, old buddy. Out of all those people standin' there I was the only one who couldn't laugh. Just turned away and looked across the street. Was this old Guinea frozen in the door of his store lit up by the flames from the fire and his front window next to him shinin' like a mirror. I'll never forget this, but in that window there was this reflection of you comin' down the ladder through the smoke, wobblin' back and forth like crazy, the laughin' gettin' stronger and stronger, that dumb Wop the worst of them all, till he finally spit in the street and went inside. Wanted to kill the bastard. That's what musta made me turn around. Woulda gone after him and killed him in his own store, understand? Anyway, it was the very second the Guinea turned me around that you fell from half up the ladder and hit the street. The sound, an awful splatterin' like ground meat against a butcher's block, and the old lady on top of you like a big, swollen baby, the two of you just lyin' there, everyone jumpin' around like mad, pointin' at you like it was some kind of freak show or somethin'. And all of a sudden, like out of nowhere, I started laughin' too. Me, your best friend laughin', couldn't stop, didn't know what to do. Louder and louder I roared on till I finally fell in the street water. Then by the time I came to, they'd carted you away, and old Alexander and Skoski were carryin' me to the truck. The whole way home and the day following too, all I wanted was to apologize for laughin' at you like all the rest, to tell I was sorry, and have you take my hand and explain how you understood that line between funny and sad, and that you would've done the same if things'd been the other way around. But I told Minnie about it, stood right up to her, starin' her dead in the eyes, told her, "The only thing that ever really mattered in my whole life is smashed and gone." Yup, my very words. And know what she says? Know what? "I understand what it must be like." . . . Understand? How the hell could she know, the jealous hag. Figured out she was jealous, right? I mean, what else? How would you feel your best friend gets done in by an old hag lyin' on his face. [*Slams the top of the podium, yells*] Hey, kid, where are they, huh? Where? I'm waiting for those recruits. Endo, why'd you kick off and leave me with nothin'? We were close, buddy, so, so close, with somethin' miles beyond a lady's understanding, and that dried-up excuse for a wife dares tell me she understands what it must be like. Minnie, you're out to pasture the second I get home, mean it. You shoulda let things be, but not you, oh no. Yap yap yap yap yap yap. [*Suddenly messes up his hair, violent gestures*] Dive, you bastards, dive, and leave my head alone! [*Crosses back to podium, clearing his throat*] Gentlemen, to be a fireman, to be a battler of blazes, requires that a man be brave and courageous and honorable and good and strong, but most important, it gives him a chance to form bonds, to build links with others . . . like with me and my Endo, who went out such a great and lasting hero. Oh, if only you coulda seen the two of us together. Me and my buddy Endo, we were the love boys of Guinea-town, yes sir, always on the move, chasing down the Wop-ladies on Freemont Street, givin' it to 'em good . . . always on Friday night, 'member, Endo? Bet your ass, every Friday night after our shift was over, we'd take off for old Freemont Street . . . always around the time one of the boys was taking the week's garbage out to the incinerator. See, in those days we had the big Friday fire to burn the week's junk and always around the time we were leaving, the thing'd be startin', no flames yet, just swirls of spark, smoke, this whizzin' buzz soundin' like fryin' do-do . . . [*Laughs*] and we'd get over to Freemont Street, and there they'd be, crowd of Guinea ladies waitin' for us, hangin' out windows, crawlin' the streets everywhere, everyone of 'em cryin', beggin' to be taken. Old Endo always got a good one, was a mover, but Jocko, well most times he got stuck with a fat stump of a thing. Among friends such matters are understood, and anyway good, plump things . . . you know, so why not, huh? We were very very close, okay, they were kicks, fat pigs to laugh about. [*Yells*] Hey, kid, where are they? I'm waitin'. . . . I was bigger than Endo, understand, better face, straighter teeth . . . so it wasn't like I wasn't gettin' what I wanted, . . . understand? Soon as we finished 'em we'd take off back for the firehouse, leavin' the bags flat. Boy, what a sight, Endo and me down the street, arm in arm, swiggin' away, dizzy drunk, screamin' our asses off. [*Laughs*] Then about halfway there, always happened about halfway, mean, never gave it any thought . . . halfway, I'd get this pain in my stomach from havin' to go. Man drinks, he pisses, right? And I'd scream, "Endo, Endo, have to stop," but the bastard wouldn't stop, yellin' back, "Jocko, save it, save it," makin' me run faster and faster till we got back to the firehouse, me screamin' with pain. . . . We'd run out back, near right where I'm standin' now, no kiddin' . . . a coincidence. The fire'd be blazin' away. Endo'd yell, "Go," and wow, we'd start peeing away into the flames. Shoulda seen it, clouds of smoke swirlin' around us, shootin' on and on like there was no end, screamin'. And if the light was right, like it most often was, all these strange colors would drift up the shafts of whizzin' steam, us shootin' on and on, colors all over the place, greens, yellows, purples, these wild, wild blues . . . [*Laughs*] and we'd be chasin' em, gettin' pee all over each other, grabbin' at those crazy colors and havin' them disappear in our hands, yeah, the two of us. . . . [*Singing*]

Got us rainbows, rainbows for sale
Two for a nickel, five for a dime.
Come get your blendin' curves of color,
Gift of the rainbow boys, . . . anytime!

[*Turns from the podium, moving, humming the tune of the song. Crosses to the center-stage chairs, sits down, humming on, laughing, yelling loudly*] Come on, kid, bring 'em on, I'm ready. . . . Come on, where are they, the recruits? Bring 'em on! [*Humming, punching the air as though the* YOUNG MAN *were there*] That's for to distract my concentration, you and my Minnie! . . . Come on, I'm *waiting*, THE JOCKO STONE HALSEY AUDITORIUM, I'm waiting.

YOUNG MAN: [*Entering in a rush*] The recruits, sir, they're here!

At the back of the hall, doors open and recruits come forward.

THE BASIC TRAINING OF PAVLO HUMMEL

a play in two acts

David Rabe

The Basic Training of Pavlo Hummel was first presented by the New York Shakespeare Festival (Joseph Papp, Producer) at the Public Theatre, New York City, on May 20, 1971, with the following cast:

PAVLO HUMMEL	*William Atherton*
YEN	*Victoria Racimo*
ARDELL	*Albert Hall*
FIRST SERGEANT TOWER	*Joe Fields*
THE COMPANY	
CAPTAIN SAUNDERS	*Edward Cannan*
CORPORAL FERRARA	*Anthony R. Charnota*
PARKER	*Peter Cameron*
BURNS	*Stephen Clarke*
RYAN	*John Walter Davis*
HALL	*Bob Delegall*
GRENNEL	*Tom Harris*
HINKLE	*Edward Herrmann*
KRESS	*Earl Hindman*
PIERCE	*Robert Lehman*
HENDRIX	*D. Franklyn Lenthall*
MICKEY	*Frederick Coffin*
MRS. HUMMEL	*Sloane Shelton*
CORPORAL JONES	*Garrett Morris*
SERGEANT BRISBEY	*Lee Wallace*
MAMASAN	*Christal Kim*
SERGEANT WALL	*John Benson*
PARHAM	*Bob Delegall*
LINH	*Hoshin Seki*
ZUNG	*Victoria Racimo*
FARMER	*Hoshin Seki*

It was directed by Jeff Bleckner. Settings by David Mitchell; costumes by Theoni V. Aldredge; lighting by Martin Aronstein. Associate producer: Bernard Gersten. Production stage manager: Dean Compton.

ACT I

TIME AND PLACE

The United States Army—1965-1967

A radio is playing American pop music in the darkness; and the lights rise immediately. PAVLO *is dressed in army fatigues. He wears sunglasses, though by the lighting it is clearly close to dusk. The music is not loud and* PAVLO *moves slightly, influenced by its rhythm. The wall that indicates the shanty is tin. Perhaps Budweiser beer labels mark a section of it. The wall is far upstage. It has a shelf of beer bottles, cans. Before it is a large barrel, military green; it is being used as a table. Beside it is a crate, also military green. Using it as a chair, a drunken G.I. sits slumped over the top of the barrel.* YEN, *a Vietnamese girl, moves about, trying to make some contact with* PAVLO. MAMASAN, *an older Vietnamese woman dressed in peasant garb, stands in the background, watching closely.* YEN, *pronounced "Ing," wears purple silk pajamas, slacks and pullover top. She sort of pursues* PAVLO, *trying to get him to take a drink of beer, trying to calm him down.*

PAVLO: [*Dealing with everyone as he speaks*] Did I do it to him? The triple-Hummel. [*A sort of shudder runs through his shoulders: he punches*] A little shuffle and then a triple boom-boom-boom. Ain't I bad, man. Gonna eat up Cleveland. Gonna piss on Chicago. [*Banging with his palms on the side of the barrel*]

YEN: Creezy, creezy.

PAVLO: Dinky dow!

SOLDIER: [*Disturbed by banging, looking up, but deeply drunk*] Les . . . go . . . home. . . .

YEN: Pavlo boucoup love. Sleep me all time. . . .

PAVLO: Did I ever tell you, whore? Thirteen months a my life ago—you listenin' to me, Stoner? [*Again, banging on the barrel*] I had this girl Joanna Sorrentino. Little bit a guinea-woppin' bitch, and she was my girl. I lived with my mother and we had a cat, you know, so we had a kitty box, which is a place for the cat to shit. Yeh.

YEN: Talk "shit." I can talk "shit". Numba ten talk. [*Touching him*]

PAVLO: Ohhhh, damn that Sorrentino, what she couldn't be taught. And that's what I'd like to do—look her up—"Your face, Sorrentino, I don't like your ugly face!" Did I ever tell you about my ole lady, Stoner? Me mudda. Did I ever speak her name?

YEN: Mudda you, huh, Pavlo? Very nice.

PAVLO: And now I'm the guy who's been with the Aussies. I HAD TEA WITH 'em. IT WAS ME THEY CALLED TO—"HUMMEL, MEDIC! [*With a fairly good Australian accent*] The dirty little blighters blew me bloody arm off." [*Jumping about, animated*] You see what she did, she wrote Joanna a letter. My ole lady wrote Joanna a letter callin' her a dirty little slut who should stay away from her good little son. Poor Joanna, a slut. Jesus Christ, no way. And when I found out, see, I wailed, I cried, baby, big tears, I screamed and threw kitty litter and cat shit all up in the air, screamin' over and over, "Happy Birthday, Happy Birthday," I don't know why except it seemed like I wasn't ever gonna get old. You listenin' to me, Fuckface? [*Banging the barrel. Maybe moving close to the drunken G.I., lifting his head to speak directly to him. And there is joy in this*] She called that sweet little church-goin' girl a whore. To be seen by her now, oh, she would shit her jeans to see me now, up tight with this little odd-lookin' whore, feelin' [*Maybe moving to* YEN *now, grabbing her*] good, and tall, ready to bed down. [*The grenade hits with a loud clump, having been thrown by a hand that merely flashed between curtains and everyone looks without moving*] GREEEEENADE!

And by now PAVLO *has moved. He has the grenade in his hand, and there comes the explosion, loud, extremely loud, and the lights go black, go red, or blue, the girl screams, the bodies fly. And a soldier,* ARDELL, *a black man in a uniform that is strangely unreal, perhaps gray in color, or perhaps khaki, but with black ribbons and medals. He wears sunglasses, bloused boots. He appears distantly, far upstage, at the center. A body detail is moving in the side at the instant he speaks, two men carrying a stretcher. They wear fatigues, helmets.*

ARDELL: You want me, Pavlo? You callin'? Don't I hear you? Yeh, yeh, that the way it happen sometimes. Everybody hit, everybody hurtin', but the radio ain't been touched, the dog didn't feel a thing; the engine's good as new but all the people dead and the chassis a wreck, man. [*The stretchermen have come in to remove the body of the dead G.I. The body of the girl and of* MAMASAN *have vanished in the explosion. The radio has continued to play until the point where* ARDELL, *speaking, has turned it off*] Yeh, yeh, some mean motherfucker, you don't even see, blow you away. Don't I hear you callin'? [*Pivoting, moving swiftly down center stage*] Get off it. Bounce on up here. [*And* PAVLO, *leaps to his feet, runs to join* ARDELL]

PAVLO: Pfc Pavlo Hummel, RA-74-313-226

ARDELL: We gonna get you your shit straight. No need to call me Sir.

PAVLO: Ardell . . . ?

ARDELL: That's right. Now what's your unit. Now shout it out!

PAVLO: Second of the Sixteenth; First Division. BIG RED ONE.

ARDELL: Company.

PAVLO: Echo.

ARDELL: C.O.?

PAVLO: My company commander is Captain M. W. Henderson. My battalion commander is Lieutenant Colonel Roy J. S. Tully.

ARDELL: Platoon?

PAVLO: Third.

ARDELL: Squad.

PAVLO: Third.

ARDELL: Squad and platoon leaders.

PAVLO: My platoon leader is 1st Lieutenant David R. Barnes; my squad leader is Staff Sergeant Peter T. Collins.

ARDELL: You got family?

PAVLO: No.

ARDELL: You lyin', Boy.

PAVLO: One mother; one half brother.

ARDELL: All right.

PAVLO: Yes.

ARDELL: Soldier, what you think a the war?

PAVLO: It's being fought.

ARDELL: Ain't no doubt about that.

PAVLO: No.

ARDELL: You kill anybody?

PAVLO: Yes.

ARDELL: Like it?

PAVLO: Yes.

ARDELL: Have nightmares?

PAVLO: Pardon.

ARDELL: What we talkin' about, Boy?

PAVLO: No.

ARDELL: How tall you? you lyin' motherfucker.

PAVLO: Five-ten.

ARDELL: Eyes.

PAVLO: Green.

ARDELL: Hair.

PAVLO: Red.

ARDELL: Weight.

PAVLO: 152.

ARDELL: What you get hit with?

PAVLO: Hand grenade. Fragmentation-type.

ARDELL: Where about it get you?

PAVLO: [*Touching himself*] Here. And here. Mostly in the abdominal and groin areas.

ARDELL: Who you talkin' to? Don't you talk that shit to me, man. Abdominal and groin areas, that shit. It hit you in the stomach, man, like a ten-ton truck and it hit you in the balls, blew 'em away. Am I lyin'?

PAVLO: [*Able to grin; glad to grin*] No, man.

ARDELL: Hurt you bad.

PAVLO: Killed me.

ARDELL: That right. Made you dead. You dead, man; how you feel about that?

PAVLO: Well . . .

ARDELL: DON'T YOU KNOW? I THINK YOU KNOW! I think it piss you off. I think you lyin' you say it don't. Make you wanna scream.

PAVLO: Yes.

ARDELL: You had that thing in your hand, didn't you? What was you thinkin' on, you had that thing in your hand?

PAVLO: About throwin' it. About a man I saw when I was eight years old who came through the neighborhood with a softball team called the Demons and he could do anything with a softball underhand that most big leaguers can do with a hardball overhand. He was fantastic.

ARDELL: That all?

PAVLO: Yes.

ARDELL: You ain't lyin'.

PAVLO: No. [*A whistle and figures move behind* PAVLO *and* ARDELL, *a large group of men in fatigues without markings other than their name tags and U.S. Army. There are a good number of them. And on a high drill instructor's tower, dimly lit at the moment, is a large Negro sergeant. A captain observes from the distance. A corporal prowls among them, checking buttons, etc.*] Who're they?

ARDELL: Man, don't you jive me. You know who they are. That Fort Gordon, man. They Echo Company, 8th Battalion, Third Training Regiment. They basic training, baby.

PAVLO: [*Removing Pfc stripes and 1st Division patch*] Am I . . . really . . . dead . . . ?

ARDELL: Damn near, man; real soon. Comin' on. Eight more weeks. Got wings as big as streets. Got large, large wings.

PAVLO: It happened . . . to me. . . .

ARDELL: Whatever you say, Pavlo.

PAVLO: Sure. That grenade come flyin', I caught it, held it.

ARDELL: New York, huh?

PAVLO: Manhattan. 231 East 45th.

ARDELL: Okay. Now we know who we talkin' about. Somebody say "Pavlo Hummel," we know who they mean.

SGT. TOWER: GEN'LMEN! [*As the men snap to parade rest and* PAVLO, *startled, runs to find his place among them*] You all lookin' up here and can you see me? Can you see me well? Can you hear and comprehend my words? Can you see what is written here? Over my right tit-tee, can you read it? Tower. My name. And I am bigger than my name. And can you see what is sewn here upon the muscle of my arm? Can you see it? ANSWER!

THE MEN: No. [*The men all stand in ranks below the tower*]

SGT. TOWER: No, what? WHAT?

THE MEN: NO, SERGEANT.

SGT. TOWER: It is also my name. It is my first name. SERGEANT. That who I am. I you Field First. And you gonna see a lot a me. You gonna see so much a me, let me tell you, you gonna think I you mother, father, sisters, brothers, aunts, uncles, nephews, nieces, and children—if you got 'em—all rolled into one big black man. Yeh, Gen'lmen. And you gonna become me. You gonna learn to stand tall and be proud and you gonna run as far and shoot as good. Or else you gonna be ashamed; I am one old man and you can't outdo no thirty-eight-year-old man, you ashamed. AM I GONNA MAKE YOU ASHAMED? WHAT DO YOU SAY?

THE MEN: Yes, Sergeant!

SGT. TOWER: NO! NO, GEN'LMEN. No, I am not gonna make you ashamed. SERGEANT, YOU ARE NOT GONNA MAKE US ASHAMED.

THE MEN: SERGEANT, YOU ARE NOT GONNA MAKE US ASHAMED.

SGT. TOWER: WE ARE GONNA DO EVERY-THING YOU CAN DO AND DO YOU ONE BETTER!

THE MEN: WE ARE GONNA DO EVERY-THING YOU CAN DO AND DO YOU ONE BETTER!

SGT. TOWER: YOU A BUNCH A LIARS. YOU A BUNCH A FOOLS! Now you listen up; you listen to me. No one does me one better. And especially no people like you. Don't you know what you are? TRAINEES! And there ain't nothin' lower on this earth except for one thing and we all know what that is, do we not, Gen'lman?

THE MEN: Yes . . . , Sergeant!

SGT. TOWER: And what is that? [*Pause*] You told me you knew! Did you lie to me? Oh, no, nooo, I can't believe that; please, please, don't lie. Gen'lmen, did you lie?

THE MEN: Yes, Sergeant.

SGT. TOWER: No, no, please. If there something you don't know, you tell me. If I ask you something and you do not know the answer, let me know. Civilians. That the answer to my question. The only creatures in this world lower than trainees is civilians, and we hate them all. All. [*Quick pause*] And now . . . and finally . . . and most important, do you see what is written here? Over my heart; over my left tit-tee, do you see? U.S. ARMY. Which is where I live. Which is where we all live. Can you, Gen'lmen, can you tell me you first name now, do you know it? [*Quick pause*] Don't you know? I think you do, yes, I do, but you just too shy to say it. Like little girls watchin' that thing just get bigger and bigger for the first time, you shy. And what did I tell you to do when you don't know the answer I have asked?

THE MEN: What is our first name?

SGT. TOWER: You! . . . You there! [*Suddenly pointing into the ranks*] You! Ugly! Yeah, you. That right. You ugly. Ain't you. You TAKE ONE BIG STEP FORWARD. [*And it is* PAVLO *stepping forward*] I think I saw that you were not in harmony with the rest of these men. I think I saw that you were looking about at the air like some kinda fool and that malingering, Trainee, and that intol'able. So you drop, you hear me. You drop down on you ugly little hands and knees and lift up you butt and knees from off that beautiful Georgia clay and you give me TEN and that's pushups of which I am speaking. [PAVLO *begins the push-ups:* TOWER *goes back to the men*] NOW YOU ARE TRAINEES, ALL YOU PEOPLE, AND YOU LISTEN UP. I ask you WHAT IS YOUR FIRST NAMES, YOU TELL ME "TRAINEE"!

THE MEN: TRAINEE!

SGT. TOWER: TRAINEE, SERGEANT!

THE MEN: TRAINEE, SERGE—

SGT. TOWER: I CAN'T HEAR YOU!

THE MEN: *TRAINEE, SERGEANT!*

SGT. TOWER: AND WHAT IS YOUR LAST NAMES? YOU OWN LAST FUCKING NAMES?

THE MEN: (A CHORUS OF AMERICAN NAMES)

SGT. TOWER: AND YOU LIVE IN THE ARMY OF THE UNITED STATES OF AMERICA.

THE MEN: AND WE LIVE IN THE ARMY OF THE UNITED STATES OF AMERICA.

SGT. TOWER: WITH BALLS BETWEEN YOUR LEGS! YOU HAVE BALLS! NO SLITS! BUT BALLS, AND YOU— [*Having risen,* PAVLO *is getting back into ranks*]

THE MEN: AND WE HAVE BALLS BE-TWEEN OUR LEGS! NO SLITS, BUT BALLS!

SGT. TOWER: [*Suddenly back to* PAVLO] Ugly! Now who told you to stand? Who you think you are, you standin', nobody tole you to stand. You drop. You drop, you hear me. [*And* PAVLO *goes back into the pushup position*]

SGT. TOWER: What your name, Boy?

PAVLO: Yes, sir.

SGT. TOWER: Your name, boy!

PAVLO: Trainee Hummel, sir!

SGT. TOWER: Sergeant.

PAVLO: Yes, sir.

SGT. TOWER: *Sergeant.* I AM A SERGEANT!

PAVLO: SERGEANT! YOU ARE A SER-GEANT!

SGT. TOWER: All right. That nice; all right, only in the future, you doin' pushups, I want you countin' and that countin' so loud it scare me so I think there some kinda terrible, terrible man comin' to get me, am I understood?

PAVLO: Yes, Sergeant.

SGT. TOWER: I can't hear you!

PAVLO: Yes, Sergeant! Yes, Sergeant!

SGT. TOWER: All right! You get up and fall back where you was. Gen'lmen. You are gonna fall out. By platoon. Which is how you gonna be doin' most everything from now on—by platoon and by the numbers—includin' takin' a shit. Somebody say to you, ONE, you down; TWO, you doin' it; THREE, you wipin' and you ain't finished, you cuttin' it off. I CAN'T HEAR YOU!

THE MEN: YES, SERGEANT.

SGT. TOWER: I say to you SQUAT, and you all hunkered down and got nothin' to say to anybody but HOW MUCH? and WHAT COLOR, SERGEANT?

THE MEN: Yes, Sergeant.

SGT. TOWER: You good people. You a good group. Now I gonna call you to attention and you gonna snap-to, that's heels on a line or as near it as the conformation of your body permit; head up, chin in, knees not locked; you relaxed. Am I understood?

THE MEN: Yes—

SGT. TOWER: AM I UNDERSTOOD GOD-DAMNIT, OR DO YOU WANT TO ALL DROP FOR TWENTY OR—

THE MEN: YES, SERGEANT! YES, SER-GEANT!

ARDELL: PAVLO, MY MAN, YOU ON YOUR WAY.

CORPORAL: PLATOOOON! PLATOOOON!

SGT. TOWER: I GONNA DO SOME SINGIN', GEN'LMEN, I WANT IT COMIN' BACK TO ME LIKE WE IN GRAND CANYON—

CORPORAL: TEN-HUT!

ARDELL: DO IT, GET IT!

SQUAD LEADERS: RIGHT FACE!

SGT. TOWER: —AND YOU MY MOTHER-FUCKIN' ECHO!

CORPORAL: FORWARD HARCH!

SGT. TOWER: LIFT YOUR HEAD AND LIFT IT HIGH!

THE MEN: —LIFT YOUR HEAD AND LIFT IT HIGH—

SGT. TOWER: ECHO COMPANY PASSIN' BY!

THE MEN: ECHO COMPANY PASSIN' BY!

ARDELL: [*And the men are going off in groups during this*] MOTHER, MOTHER, WHAT'D I DO?

THE MEN: MOTHER, MOTHER, WHAT'D I DO?

ARDELL: THIS ARMY TREATIN' ME WORSE THAN YOU!

THE MEN: THIS ARMY TREATIN' ME WORSE THAN YOU!

SGT. TOWER: LORD HAVE MERCY I'M SO BLUE.

THE MEN: LORD HAVE MERCY I'M SO BLUE!

THE MEN: IT EIGHT MORE WEEKS TILL WE BE THROUGH! IT EIGHT MORE WEEKS TILL WE BE THROUGH! IT EIGHT MORE WEEKS TILL WE BE THROUGH!

And all the men have marched off in lines of four or five in different directions, giving a sense of large numbers, a larger space and now, out of this movement, comes a spin off of two men, KRESS *and* PARKER, *coming down the center of the stage, yelling the last lines of the song, marching, stomping, then breaking and running stage left and into the furnace room. There is the hulk of the belly of the furnace, the flickering of the fire.* KRESS *is large, muscular, with a constant manner of small confusion as if he feels always that something is going on that he nearly, but not quite, understands. Yet there is something seemingly friendly about him.* PARKER *is smaller; he wears glasses.*

KRESS: I can't stand it, Parker, bein' so cold all the time and they're all insane, Parker. Waxin' and buffin' the floor at 5:30 in the morning is insane. And then you can't eat till you go down the monkey bars and you gotta eat in ten minutes and can't talk to nobody, and no place in Georgia is warm. I'm from Jersey. I can jump up in the air, if there's a good wind.

I'll land in Fort Dix. Am I right so far? So Sam gets me. What's he do? Fort Dix? Uh-uh. Fort Gordon, Georgia. So I can be warm right? Down South, man. Daffodils and daisies. Year round. [*Hollering*] But am I warm? Do you think I'm warm? Do I look like I'm warm? Jesus H! Even in the goddamn furnace room, I'm freezin' ta death!

PARKER: So, what the hell is hollerin' like a stupid ape gonna do except to let 'em know where we at?

KRESS: [*As* PAVLO *enters upstage, moving slowly in awe toward the tower, looking*] Heat up my blood!

ARDELL: [*To* PAVLO] What you doin' strollin' about like a fool, man, you gonna have people comin' down all over you, don't you know—

OFFICER: [*Having just entered*] What're you doing, walking in this company area? Don't you know you run in this company area? Hummel, you drop, you hear me. You drop!

PAVLO *goes into pushup position and starts to do the ten pushups.*

ARDELL: [*Over him*] Do 'em right, do 'em right!

KRESS: Why can't I be warm? I wanna be warm.

PARKER: Okay, man, you're warm.

KRESS: No; I'm not; I'm cold, Parker. Where's our goddamn fireman, don't he ever do nothin' but pushups? Don't he ever do nothin' but trouble!

PARKER: Don't knock that ole boy, Kress, I'm tellin' you; Hummel's gonna keep us laughin'!

KRESS: Yesterday I was laughin' so hard. I mean, I'm stupid, Parker, but Hummel's *stupid.* I mean, he volunteers to be fireman 'cause he thinks it means you ride in a raincoat on a big red truck and when there's nothin' to do you play cards.

PARKER: Yeah! He don't know it means you gotta baby-sit the goddamn furnace all night, every night. And end up lookin' like a stupid chimney sweep!

KRESS: Lookin' what?

PARKER: [*As* PIERCE *enters at a jog, moving across the stage toward* ARDELL *and* PAVLO, *the officer having exited after the order*] Like a goddamn chimney sweep!

PAVLO: Where you goin'?

PIERCE: [*Without hesitating*] Weapons room and furnace room.

PAVLO: [*Getting to his feet*] Can I come along?

PIERCE: [*Still running, without looking*] I don't give a shit. [*He exits,* PAVLO *following as* ARDELL *is drifting the opposite direction*]

PAVLO: . . . great . . .

KRESS: Yeh? Yeh, Parker, that's good. Chimney sweeps!

PARKER: Yeh, they were these weird little men always crawlin' around, and they used to do this weird shit ta chimneys. [PIERCE *and* PAVLO *enter. They have their rifles.* PIERCE *is a trainee acting as a squad leader. He has a cloth marked with corporal stripes on his left sleeve*]

PIERCE: At ease!

KRESS: Hey, the Chimney Shit. Hey, what's happenin', Chimney Shit.

PAVLO: How you doin', Kress?

KRESS: Where's your red hat, man?

PAVLO: What?

PARKER: Ain't you got no red fireman's hat?

PAVLO: I'm just with Pierce, that's all. He's my squad leader and I'm with him.

PARKER: Mr. Squad Leader.

PAVLO: Isn't that right, Pierce?

PARKER: Whose ass you kiss to get that job, anyway, Pierce.

PIERCE: At ease, trainees.

KRESS: He's R.A., man. Regular army. Him and Hummel. Lifer morons. Whata they gonna do to us today, anyway, Mr. Actin' Sergeant, Corporal. What's the lesson for the day: first aid or bayonet. I love this fuckin' army.

PIERCE: The schedule's posted, Kress!

KRESS: You know I don't read, man; hurts my eyes; makes 'em water.

PAVLO: When's the gas chamber, that's what I wanna know?

KRESS: For you, Chimney Shit, in about ten seconds when I fart in your face.

PAVLO: I'm all right. I do all right.

KRESS: Sure you do, except you got your head up your ass.

PAVLO: Yeh? Well maybe I'd rather have it up my ass than where you got it.

Slight pause: it has made no sense to KRESS *at all.*

KRESS: What?

PAVLO: You heard me, Kress.

KRESS: What'd he say, Parker? [*There is an element of frenzy in this*] I heard him, but I don't know what he said. WHAT'D YOU SAY TO ME, HUMMEL?

PAVLO: Just never you mind, Kress.

KRESS: I DON'T KNOW WHAT YOU SAID TO ME, YOU WEIRD PERSON!

PARKER: [*Patting* KRESS] Easy, man, easy; be cool.

KRESS: But I don't like weird people, Parker. I don't like them. How come I gotta be around him? I don't wanna be around you, Hummel!

PAVLO: Don't you worry about it, I'm just here with Pierce. I just wanna know about the gas chamber.

KRESS: It's got gas in it! Ain't that right, Parker! It's like this goddamn giant asshole, it farts on you. THHPPBBBZZZZZZZZ! [*Silence*]

PAVLO: When is it, Pierce?

KRESS: Ohhhhh, Jesus, I'm cold.

PAVLO: This ain't cold, Kress.

KRESS: I know if I'm cold.

PAVLO: I been colder than this. This ain't cold. I been a lot colder than—

KRESS: DON'T TELL ME IT AIN'T COLD OR I'LL KILL YOU! JESUS GOD ALMIGHTY I HATE THIS MOTHER ARMY STICKIN' ME IN WITH WEIRD PEOPLE! DIE, HUMMEL! Will you please do me that favor! Oh, God, let me close my eyes and when I open them, Hummel is dead. Please, Please. [*He squeezes his eyes shut, clenches his hands for about two seconds and then looks at* PAVLO, *who is grinning*]

PAVLO: Boy, I sure do dread that gas chamber.

KRESS: He hates me, Parker. He truly hates me.

PAVLO: No, I don't.

KRESS: What'd I ever do to him, you suppose.

PARKER: I don't know, Kress.

PAVLO: I don't hate you.

PARKER: How come he's so worried about that gas chamber, that's what I wonder.

PAVLO: Well, see, I had an uncle die in San Quentin. [KRESS *screams*] That's the truth, Kress. [KRESS *screams again*] I don't care if you believe it. He killed four people in a fight in a bar.

PARKER: Usin' his bare hands right?

PAVLO: You know how many people are executed every damn day in San Quentin? One hell of a lot. And every one of 'em just about is somebody's uncle and one of 'em was my Uncle Roy. He killed four people in a barroom brawl usin' broken bottles and table legs and screamin', jus' screamin'. He was mean, man. He was rotten, and my folks been scared the same thing might happen to me; all their lives, they been scared. I got that same look in my eyes like him.

PARKER: What kinda look is that?

KRESS: That really rotten look, man. He got that really rotten look. Can't you see it?

PAVLO: You ever steal a car, Kress? You know how many cars I stole?

KRESS: Shut up, Hummel! You're a goddamn chimney sweep and I don't wanna talk to you because you don't talk American, you talk Hummel! Some goddamn foreign language!

PARKER: How many cars you stole?

PAVLO: Twenty-three.

KRESS: Twenty-three!

PARKER *whistles*.

PAVLO: That's a lotta cars, huh?

PARKER: You damn betcha, man. How long'd it take you, for chrissake? Ten years?

PAVLO: Two.

PARKER: Workin' off and on, you mean.

PAVLO: Sure. Not every night, or they'd catch you. And not always from the same part of town. Man, sometimes I'd hit lower Manhattan, and then the next night the Bronx or Queens, and sometimes I'd even cut right on outa town. One time, in fact, I went all the way to New Haven. Boy, that was some night because they almost caught me. Can you imagine that. Huh? Parker? Huh? Pierce? All the way to New Haven and cops on my tail every inch a the way, roadblocks closin' up behind me, bang, bang, and then some highway patrolman, just as I was wheelin' into New Haven, he come roarin' outa this side road. See, they must a called ahead or somethin' and he come hot on my ass. I kicked it, man, arrrrgggggg-hhhhh . . . ! 82 per. Had a Porsche; he didn't know who he was after; that stupid fuzz, 82 per, straight down the gut, people jumpin' outa my way, kids and businessmen and little old ladies, all of 'em, and me kickin' ass, up to 97 now, roarin' baby sirens all around me so I cut into this alley and jump. Oh, Jesus, Christ, just lettin' the car go, I hit, roll, I'm up and runnin' down for this board fence, up and over, sirens all over now, I mean, *all over*, but I'm walkin' calm, I'm cool. Cops are goin' this way and that way. One of 'em asks me if I seen a Porsche go by real fast. Did *I* see—

KRESS: Jesus-goddamn—the furnace room's smellin' like the gas chamber! [*Rising to leave,* PARKER *following*]

PARKER: That's right, Hummel. That's right. I mean, I liked your story about your really rotten uncle Roy better than the one about all the cars.

KRESS: Les go get our weapons, will ya?

PARKER: Defend our fuckin' selves. [*As they exit the furnace room, and* PAVLO *stands thinking.* PIERCE *is quiet*]

PAVLO: I'll see . . . you guys later. [*Half calling, half to himself as they are gone.*] Hey, Pierce, you wanna hear my General Orders; make sure I know 'em okay? Like we're on guard mount and you're the O.D. . . . You wanna see if I'm sharp enough to be one a your boys. O.K.? [*Snapping to attention*] Sir! My first general order is to take charge of this post and all government property in view, keeping always on the alert and . . .

PIERCE: Gimme your eighth, Hummel.

PAVLO: Eighth? No, no, lemme do 'em 1, 2, 3. You'll mess me up.

PIERCE: That's the way it's gonna be, Hummel. The man comes up to you on guard mount, he's gonna be all over you—right on top a you yellin' down your throat. You understand me? He won't be standin' back polite and pretty lettin' you run your mouth.

PAVLO: Just to practice, Pierce. I just wanna practice.

PIERCE: You don't wanna practice shit. You just wanna stand there and have me pat your goddamned head for bein' a good boy. Don't you know we stood here laughin' at you lyin' outa your ass? Don't you have any pride, man?

PAVLO: I got pride. And anyway, they didn't know I was lyin'.

PIERCE: Shit.

PAVLO: And anyway, I wasn't lyin', it was storytelling. They was just messin' with me a little, pickin' on me. My mom used to always tell my dad not to be so hard on me, but he knew.

Whistle blows loudly from off.

PIERCE: Let's go.

PAVLO: See, he did it to me, 'cause he loved me. I'm R.A., Pierce.

PIERCE: You got a R.A. prefix, man, but you ain't regular army.

PAVLO: They was just jumpin' on me a little; pickin' on me.

Again the whistle.

PIERCE: That whistle means formation, man.

PAVLO: They're just gonna draw weapons; I already got mine.

PIERCE: That ain't what I said, Jerkoff!

PAVLO: Well, I ain't goin' out there to stand around doin' nothin' when I can stay right here and put the time to good use practicin' D and D.

Again the whistle, the men are gathering, we hear their murmuring.

PIERCE: You ain't no motherin' exception to that whistle, Hummel!

PAVLO: You ain't any real corporal anyway, Pierce. So don't get so big with me just because you got that hunk a thing wrapped around you—

PIERCE: Don't you mess up my squad, Hummel! Don't you make me look bad or I'll get you your legs broken.

PAVLO: [*As the whistle blows and* PIERCE *is leaving and gone*] I bet you never heard a individual initiative.

Whistle again as soldiers rush in to line up in formation at Parade Rest while SGT. TOWER *climbs to stand atop the platform.*

ARDELL: They don't know, do they? They don't know who they talkin' too.

PAVLO: No.

ARDELL: You gonna be so straight.

PAVLO: So clean.

SGT. TOWER *notices that someone is missing from formation he turns, descends, exits.*

PAVLO: Port Harms! [*And he does it with only a slight and quickly corrected error*]

ARDELL: Good, Pavlo. Good. [*Slight pause*] Order Harms!

PAVLO *does it. There is some skill in the move.*

PAVLO: Okay . . .

ARDELL: RIGHT SHOULDER . . . HARMS . . . !

And PAVLO *does this, but again there is the head flinch, the rifle nicking the top of his helmet. His back is toward the group and* SGT. TOWER *enters, watches for a time.*

PAVLO: Goddamn it. Shit. [*Again the rifle back to order*] RIGHT SHOULDER HARMS.

ARDELL: RIGHT SHOULDER . . .

PAVLO: HARMS! [*Again it is not good*]

PAVLO: You mother rifle. You stupid fucking rifle. RIGHT SHOULDER, HARMS. [*He tries*] Mother! Stupid mother, whatsamatter with you? I'll kill you! [*And he has it high above his head. He is looking up*] Rifle, please. Work for me, do it for me. I know what to do, just you do it.

ARDELL: Just go easy. Man . . . just easy. It don't mean that much. What's it matter?

SGT. TOWER: What you doin', Trainee?

PAVLO: [*Snapping to attention*] Yes, Sir! Trainee Pavlo Hummel, sir.

SGT. TOWER: I didn't ask you you name, Boy. I asked you what you doin' in here when you supposed to be out on that formation?

PAVLO: Yes, sir.

SGT. TOWER: No, I don't have no bars on my collar, do you see any bars on my collar?

PAVLO: No . . . no . . .

SGT. TOWER: But what do you see on my sleeve at about the height a my shoulder less a little, what do you see?

PAVLO: Stripes, Sergeant. Sergeant stripes.

SGT. TOWER: So how come you call me "sir"? I ain't no sir. I don't want to be no sir. I am a sergeant. Now do we know one another?

PAVLO: Yes, Sergeant.

SGT. TOWER: That mean you can answer my question in the proper manner, do it not?

PAVLO: I was practicin' D and D, Sergeant, to make me a good soldier.

SGT. TOWER: Ohhhhhhh! I think you tryin' to jive this ole man, that what you doin'. Or else you awful stupid because all the good soldiers is out there in that formation like they supposed to when they hear that whistle. Now which?

PAVLO: Pardon, Sergeant?

SGT. TOWER: Which is it? You jivin' on me or you awful stupid, you take your pick. And lemme tell you why you can't put no jive on the ole Sarge. Because long time ago, this ole Sarge was one brand-new, baby-soft, smart-assed recruit. So I see you and I say "What that young recruit doin' in that furnace room this whole company out there bein' talked at by the CO? And the answer come to me like a blast a thunder and this voice sayin' to me in my head, "This here young recruit jerkin' off, that what he doin'," and then into my head come this picture and we ain't in no furnace room, we in that jungle catchin' hell from this one little yellow man and his automatic weapon that he chained to up on top of this hill. "Get on up that hill!" I tell my young recruit. And he tell me, "Yes, Sergeant," like he been taught, and then he start thinkin' to hisself, "What that ole Sarge talkin' about, 'run on up that hill'? Ah git my ass blown clean away. I think maybe he got hit on his head, he don't know what he's talkin' about no more—maybe I go on over behind that ole rock—practice me a little D and D." Ain't that some shit the way them young recruits wanna carry on? So what I think we do, you and me, long about 2200 hours we do a little D and D and PT and all them kinda alphabetical things. Make you a good soldier.

PAVLO: I don't think I can, Sergeant. That's night time, Sergeant, and I'm a fireman. I got to watch the furnace.

SGT. TOWER: That don't make me no never mind. We jus' work it in between your shifts. You see? Ain't it a wonder how you let the ole Sarge do the worryin' and figurin' and he find a way. [*Turning, starting to leave*]

PAVLO: Sergeant, I was wondering how many pushups you can do. How many you can do that's how many I want to be able to do before I ever leave.

SGT. TOWER: Boy, don't you go sayin' no shit like that, you won't ever get out. You be an ole, bearded, blind, fuckin' man pushin' up all over Georgia.

PAVLO: [*And* PAVLO, *speaking immediately and rapidly, a single rush of breath, again stops* SGT. TOWER] And I was wondering also, Sergeant Tower, and wanted to ask you—when I was leaving home, my mother wanted to come

along to the train station, but I lied to her about the time. She would have wanted to hug me right in front of everybody. She would have waved a handkerchief at the train. It would have been awful. [*And* SGT. TOWER *now leaves, is gone.* PAVLO *calls*] She would have stood there, waving. Was I wrong?

CORPORAL: TEN HUT! FORWARD HARCH!

The men begin to march in place. PAVLO, *without joining them, also marches.*

SGT. TOWER: AIN'T NO USE IN GOIN HOME.

THE MEN: [*Beginning to march and exit*] AIN'T NO USE IN GOIN' HOME.

SGT. TOWER: [*At the side of the stage*] JODY GOT YOUR GAL AND GONE.

THE MEN: JODY HUMPIN' ON AND ON.

SGT. TOWER: AIN'T NO USE IN GOIN' BACK. [*And* PAVLO, *in his own area, is marching away*]

THE MEN: JODY GOT OUR CADILLAC.

CORPORAL: AIN'T NO MATTER WHAT WE DO.

ALL: JODY DOIN' OUR SISTER TOO.

CORPORAL: COUNT CADENCE, DELAYED CADENCE, COUNT CADENCE COUNT!

ALL: 1—2—3—4. 1,2,3,4. 1234. HEY!

All are gone now except PAVLO *who comes spinning out of his marching pattern to come stomping to a halt in the furnace room area while* ARDELL *drifts toward him, and toward the audience.*

ARDELL: Oh, yeh; army train you, shape you up, teach you all kinds a good stuff. Like bayonet. It all about what you do you got no more bullets and this man after you. So you put this knife on the end a your rifle, start yellin' and carryin' on. Then there hand to hand. Hand to hand, cool. It [PAVLO *is watching, listening*] all about hittin' and kickin'. What you do when you got no gun and no knife. Then there CBR. CBR: chemical, biological and radiological warfare. What you do when some mean motherfucker hit you with some kinda chemical. You [ARDELL *mimes throwing a grenade at* PAVLO] got green fuckin' killin' smoke all around you. What you gonna do? You gotta git on your protective mask. You ain't got it?

PAVLO: [*Choking*] But I'm too beautiful to die. [*Rummaging about in the furnace room*]

ARDELL: But you the only one who believe that, Pavlo. You gotta be hollerin' loud as you know how, "GAS." And then, sweet lord almighty, little bit later, you walkin' along, somebody else hit you with some kinda biological jive. But you know your shit. Mask on.

PAVLO, *having found a mask, is putting it on, waving his arms.*

PAVLO: GAS! GAS! GAS!

ARDELL: You gettin' it, Pavlo. All right. Lookin' real good. But now you tired and you still walkin' and you come up on somebody bad— this boy mean—he hit you with radiation.

PAVLO *goes into a tense, defensive posture.*

PAVLO: Awww. [*Realizing his helplessness*]

ARDELL: That right. You know what you do? You kinda stand there, that what you do, whimperin' and talkin' to yourself, 'cause he got you. You gotta be some kinda fool, somebody hit you with radiation, man, you put on a mask, start hollerin', "Gas." Am I lyin', Pavlo? What do you say?

PAVLO: Aww, no. . . . No, man—No, no.—I did not! No, no.

And there has been toward the end of the above a gathering of a group of soldiers in T shirts and underwear, T shirts and trousers in the barracks area. PAVLO, *muttering in denial of the radiation, crosses the stage hurriedly, fleeing the radiation, running into* PARKER *who grabs him, spins him.*

KRESS: The hell you didn't!

PARKER: You been found out, Jerkoff. [*Kneeling behind* PAVLO *to take a billfold from his pocket*]

PAVLO: No.

KRESS: We got people saw you. Straight honest guys.

PARKER: Get that thing off your face. [*Meaning the mask*]

BURNS: The shit I didn't see you.

PARKER: You never saw a billfold before in your life, is that what you're tryin' to say? You didn't even know what it was?

KRESS: Is that what you're tryin' to say, Hummel.

PAVLO: No.

KRESS: What are you tryin' to say?

PAVLO: I'm goin' to bed. [*Moving toward his bed but stopped by* KRESS]

KRESS: We already had two guys lose money to some thief around here, Shitbird, and we got people sayin' they saw you with Hinkle's billfold in your pudgy little paws.

HINKLE: [*Deep Southern drawl, as* PARKER *hands him the billfold he found on* PAVLO] Is that right, Hummel?

PAVLO: I was just testin' you, Hinkle, to see how stupid you were leavin' your billfold layin' out like that when somebody's been stealin' right in our own platoon. What kinda army is this anyway, you're supposed to trust people with your life, you can't even trust 'em not to steal your money.

PARKER: Listen to him.

PAVLO: That's the truth, Parker. I was just makin' a little test experiment to see how long it'd be before he'd notice it was gone. I don't steal.

KRESS: What about all them cars?

PAVLO: What cars?

PARKER: The New Haven caper, Jerk-off. You know.

PAVLO: Ohhh, that was different, you guys. That was altogether different.

KRESS: Yeh, they were cars and you couldn't fit them in your pocket.

PAVLO: Those people weren't my friends.

PARKER: You don't steal from your friends. That what you're sayin'? Kress, Hummel says he don't steal from his friends.

KRESS: [*Jumping up on* PAVLO'S *bed, standing, walking about*] Don't that make his prospects pretty damn near unlimited?

PAVLO: Hey! Kress, what're you doin'?

KRESS: What?

PAVLO: I said, "What're you up to?" You're on my bed.

KRESS: Who is?

PAVLO: You are. You are.

KRESS: Where?

PAVLO: Right here. You're on my bed. That's my bed.

KRESS: No it isn't. It's not anybody's. It's not yours, Hummel.

PAVLO: It is too.

KRESS: Did you buy it?

PAVLO: Get off my bed, Kress!

KRESS: If you didn't buy it, then how is it yours, Ugly!

PAVLO: It was given to me.

KRESS: By who?

PAVLO: You know who, Kress. The army gave it to me. Get off it.

KRESS: Are you going to take it with you when you leave here? If it's yours, you ought to be planning on taking it with you. Are you?

PAVLO: I can't do that.

KRESS: You're taking people's billfolds; you're taking their money; why can't you take this bed?

PAVLO: Because it was just loaned to me.

KRESS: Do you have any kind of papers to prove that? Do you have papers to prove that this is your bed?

PAVLO: There's proof in the orderly room; in the orderly room, or maybe the supply room and you know it. That bed's got a number on it somewhere and that number is like its name and that name is by my name on some papers somewhere in the supply room or the orderly room.

KRESS: Go get them.

PAVLO: What do you mean?

KRESS: Go get them. Bring them here.

PAVLO: I can't.

KRESS: If they're yours, you can.

PAVLO: They're not my papers, it's my bed. Get off my bed, Kress. [KRESS *now kneels down, taking a more total possession of the bed*] Goddamn it, Kress. GODDAMN IT! [*Silence:* KRESS *has not moved, seems in fact about to lie down*] All right. Okay. You sleep in my bed, I'm gonna sleep in yours. [*Everyone stands around watching as* PAVLO *charges off toward where* KRESS'S *bed is located*]

KRESS: [*Rising a little, tense, looking off, as all look in the direction* PAVLO *has gone*] No, Hummel. [*Warning in* KRESS'S *voice*]

PAVLO: The hell I ain't, Kress.

KRESS: No. No. I strongly advise against it. I do strongly so advise. Or something awful might happen. I might get up in the middle of the night to take a leak and stagger back to my old bed. Lord knows what I might think you are . . . laying there. Lord knows what I might do. [*Slight pause*]

PAVLO: [*Yelling from off*] Then get out of my bed.

KRESS: You don't understand at all, do you, Shitbird! I'm sleeping here. This is where I'm going to sleep. You not going to sleep anywhere. You're going to sit up, or sleep on the floor, whatever. And in the morning, you're going to make this bed. This one. Because if you don't it'll be unmade when Sgt. Tower comes to inspect in the morning and as we've already discussed, there's papers somewhere in one room or another and they show whose bed this is.

PAVLO: [*Entering enough to be seen at the edge of the stage*] GODDAMN YOU, KRESS, GET OUT OF MY BED! GET OFF MY BED! GET OUT OFF IT!

Whistle blows and everyone scrambles to firing range. There is the popping of many rifles firing as on the back platform, at the very rear of the set, three or four of the men are in firing positions; others stand behind them at port arms until SGT. TOWER *calls* "CEASE FIRE" *and the firing stops. The men who have been firing put their rifles*

on their shoulders to be cleared. SGT. TOWER *walks behind them tapping each on the head when he has seen the weapon is clear. The men leap to their feet.* SGT. TOWER *then steps out in front of them, begins to pace up and down.*

SGT. TOWER: GEN'LMEN! IT GETTIN' TOWARD DARK NOW AND WE GOT TO GET HOME. IT A LONG LONG WAYS TO HOME AND OUR MOTHERS' GOT SUPPER READY WAITING FOR US. WHAT·CAN WE DO? WE GOT TO GET HOME FAST AS WE CAN. WHAT CAN WE DO? DO ANYBODY HAVE AN IDEA? LET ME HEAR YOU SPEAK IF YOU DO. I HAVE AN IDEA. ANYBODY KNOW MY IDEA? LET ME HEAR YOU IF YOU DO.

PAVLO: Run . . .

BURNS: Run?

SGT. TOWER: WHAT?

MORE MEN: RUN!

SGT. TOWER: I CAN'T HEAR YOU.

THE MEN: WHAT?

SGT. TOWER: RUN!

THE MEN: RUN!

SGT. TOWER *and* THE MEN: RUN! RUN! RUN! RUN! RUN! PORT HARMS—WHOOO! DOUBLE TIME! WHOOO! [*They have been running in place. Now* SGT. TOWER *leads them off. They exit running, reappear, exit again, reappear, spreading out now, though* PAVLO *is fairly close behind* SGT. TOWER, *who enters once again and at a point down stage where he turns to* PAVLO *entering, staggering, leading*]

SGT. TOWER: FALL OUT!

PAVLO *collapses, the others struggle in, fall down.*

PIERCE: FIVE GODDAMN MILES! [*All are in extreme pain*]

KRESS: MOTHER-GODDAMN BITCH—I NEVER RAN NO FIVE GODDAMN MILES IN MY LIFE. YOU GOTTA BE CRAZY TO RUN FIVE GODDAMN MILES . . .

PARKER: I hurt. I hurt all over. I hurt, Kress. Oh, Christ.

PIERCE: There are guys spread from here to Range 2. You can be proud you made it, Parker. The whole company, man; they're gonna be comin' in for the next ten days.

PARKER *yells in pain.*

KRESS: Pierce, what's wrong with Parker?

PARKER: SHIT TOO, YOU MOTHER!

KRESS: It'll pass, Parker. Don't worry. Just stay easy. [*And a little separate from the others,* PAVLO *is about to begin doing pushups. He is very tired. It hurts him to do what he's doing*] Oh, Hummel, no. Hummel, please. [*He is doing the pushups, breathing the count softly*] Hummel, you're crazy. You really are. He really is, Parker. Look at him. I hate crazy people. I hate 'em. YOU ARE REALLY CRAZY, HUMMEL. STOP IT OR I'LL KILL YOU. [PAVLO, *saying the number of pushups, stopping, pivoting into a sit-up position*] I mean, I wanna know how much money this platoon lost to that thief we got among us.

PIERCE: Three hundred and twelve dollars.

KRESS: What're you gonna do with all that money?

PAVLO: Spend it. Spend it.

KRESS: Something gonna be done to you! You hear me, Weird Face? You know what's wrong with you? You wouldn't know cunt if your nose was in it. You never had a piece a ass in your life.

There is a loud blast on a whistle.

PAVLO: Joanna Sorrentino. Joanna Sorrentino ga' me so much ass my mother called her a slut.

KRESS: YOU FUCKING IDIOT!

Again the whistle.

PIERCE: Oh, Christ . . .

PAVLO: Let's go. LET'S GO. LET'S GET IT.

KRESS: Shut up.

PAVLO: Let's GO, GO, GO—

Moving right all exit.

KRESS: SHUT YOUR MOUTH, ASS HOLE!

PAVLO: LET'S—GO, GO, GO, GO, GO, GO, GO . . . [*Yelling, leading, yelling*]

As a light goes on at the opposite side of the stage, there are two soldiers with pool cues at a pool table. There are no pool balls. The game will be pantomime. One of them is the CORPORAL. *They use a cue ball to shoot and work with.*

HENDRIX: You break.

CORPORAL: Naw, man, I shoot break on your say so, when I whip your ass, you'll come cryin'. You call. [*Flipping a coin as* PAVLO *comes running back to get his helmet*]

HENDRIX: Heads.

CORPORAL: You got it.

PAVLO, *scurrying off with his helmet, meets* SGT. TOWER *entering from opposite side.*

SGT. TOWER: Trainee, go clean the day room. Sweep it up.

PAVLO: Pardon, Sergeant? I forgot my helmet . . .

SGT. TOWER: Go clean the day room, Trainee.

As at the pool game, HENDRIX *shoots break.*

CORPORAL: My . . . my . . . my . . . Yes, sir. You're gonna be tough all right. That was a pretty damn break all right. [*Moving now to position himself for his shot*] Except you missed all the holes. Didn't nobody tell you you were supposed to knock the little balls in the little holes?

PAVLO: [*Entering*] Sergeant Tower said for me to sweep up the day room.

2ND SOLDIER: And that's what you do—you don't smile, laugh or talk, you sweep.

CORPORAL: You know what buck a ball means, Trainee?

PAVLO: What?

CORPORAL: Trainee's rich, Hendrix. Can't go to town, got money up the ass.

PAVLO: Sure I know what "buck a ball" means.

CORPORAL: Ohh, you hustlin' trainee motherfucker. New game. Right now. Rack 'em up!

HENDRIX *moves as if to re-rack the balls.*

PAVLO: You sayin' I can play?

CORPORAL: Hendrix, you keep an eye out for anybody who might not agree Trainee can relax a bit. You break, man.

PAVLO: I'll break.

CORPORAL: That's right.

PAVLO: You been to the war, huh? That's a 1st Division Patch you got there, ain't it? [*Shooting first shot, missing, not too good*]

CORPORAL: That's right.

PAVLO: Where at?

CORPORAL: How many wars we got?

PAVLO: I mean exactly where.

CORPORAL: [*Lining up his shot*] Di An. Ever hear of it?

PAVLO: Sure.

CORPORAL: Not much of a place but real close to Da Nang. [*He shoots, watches, moves for the next shot*]

PAVLO: You up there too?

CORPORAL: Where's that?

PAVLO: By Da Nang. [CORPORAL *is startled by* PAVLO *knowing this. He shoots and misses here. He stands now facing* PAVLO] I mean, I thought Di An was more down by Saigon. D Zone. Down there. They call that D Zone, don't they?

CORPORAL: You're right, man, you know your shit. We got us here a map-readin' motherfucker, Hendrix. Yeh, I was by Saigon, Hummel.

PAVLO: I thought so.

CORPORAL: Your shot. [*He has moved off to the side and* HENDRIX, *who has a hip flask of whiskey*]

PAVLO: [*Moving for his shot*] Bed Red One, man, I'd be proud wearin' that. [*And he shoots*] Shit. [*Having missed*]

CORPORAL: [*Moving again to the table*] Good outfit. Top kinda outfit. Mean bastards, all of 'em. Every place we went, man we used ta tear 'em a new asshole, you can believe me. [*Shooting, making it, he moves on*] I'm gonna win all your damn money, man. You got your orders yet for where you go when you're finished with basic?

PAVLO: No.

CORPORAL: Maybe if you're lucky, you'll get infantry, huh? Yeh, yeh, I seen some shit, you can believe me. [*And during the following long speech, he moves about the table, shooting, shooting, running the table, as he speaks*] But you go over there, that's what you're goin' for. To mess with them people, because they don't know nothin'. Them slopes; man they're the stupidest bunch a people anybody ever saw. It don't matter what you do to 'em or what you say, man they just look at you. They're some kinda goddamn phenomenon, man. Can of bug spray buy you all the ass you can handle in some places. Insect repellent, man. You ready for that? You give 'em can a bug spray, you can lay their 14-year-old daughter. Not that any of 'em screw worth a shit. [*Slight pause*] You hear a lot a people talkin' Airborne, 173rd, 101st Marines, but you gotta go some to beat the 1st Division. I had a squad leader, Sergeant Tinden. He'd been there two goddamn years when I got there, so he knew the road, man; he knew his way. So we was comin' into this village once, the whole company, and it was supposed to be secure. We was Charlie Company and Alpha'd been through already, left a guard. And we was lead platoon and lead squad and comin' toward us on the path is this old man, he musta been a hundred, about three foot tall and he's got this little girl by the hand and she's maybe a half-step behind him. He's wavin' at us, "Okay, okay, G.I." And she's wavin', too, but she ain't sayin' nothin', but there's this funny noise you can hear, a kind of cryin' like. [*He still moves about, shooting, speaking, pausing, judging which shot to take*] Anyway, I'm next to the Sarge and he tells this ole boy to stop, but they keep comin' like they don't understand, smilin' and wavin', so the Sarge says for 'em to stop in Vietnamese and then I can see that the kid is cryin'; she's got big tears runnin' outa her eyes, and her eyes are gettin' bigger and bigger and I can see she's tuggin'

at the old man's hand to run away but he holds her and he hollers at her and I'm thinkin', "Damn, ain't that a bitch, she's so scared of us." And Tinden, right then, man, he dropped to his knees and let go two bursts— first the old man, then the kid, cuttin' them both right across the face; man, you could see the bullets walkin'. It was somethin'. [*In silence he sets and takes his last shot. He flops the cue onto the table*] You owe me, man; thirteen bucks. But I'm superstitious, so we'll make it twelve. [*As* PAVLO *is paying*] That's right. My ole daddy—the last day he saw me —he tole me good—"Don't you ever run on nobody. Boy, or if you do I hope there's somebody there got sense enough to shoot you down. Or if I hear you got away, I'll kill you myself." There's folks like that runnin' loose, Hummel. My ole man. You dig it. [*And* PAVLO *is staring at him*] What the fuck are you lookin at?

PAVLO: I don't know why he shot . . . them.

CORPORAL: Satchel charges, man. The both of them, front and back. They had enough T.N.T. on 'em to blow up this whole damn state and the kid got scared. They was wearing it under their clothes.

PAVLO: And he knew . . .

CORPORAL: That's right. Been around; so he knew. You ready, Hendrix? [*They are moving to exit*]

HENDRIX: Ain't that some shit, Hummel. Ain't that the way to be.

Far across the stage, PARKER *is crouching in dimness, peering toward where* PAVLO *is. Nearby,* KRESS *is with three or four other soldiers crouching among the beds.*

PARKER: Dear Mother. It was the oddest thing last night. I sat near my bunk, half awake, half asleep . . .

CORPORAL: You keep your ear to the ground, Hummel, you're gonna be all [*Exiting*] right. We'll see you around.

PAVLO: Just to see and to move; just to move. [*Miming with his broom or just his hands the firing of a rifle while* ARDELL *stares at him across the table and lunges suddenly backwards, rapidly hauling the table off*]

PARKER: Yes, yes, good Mother, I could not sleep, I don't know why. And then for further reasons that I do not know, I happened to look behind me and there . . . was a space ship, yes a space ship, green and golden, good Mother, come down to the sand of our Georgia home. A space ship. [*He is referring to* KRESS *and the others as they hide. He speaks loudly, flamboyantly.* KRESS *kneels downstage with a blanket.* PAVLO *wanders nearer, nearer*] And out of it, leaping they came, little green men no larger than pins. "Good Lord in Heaven," said I to myself. "What do they want? Sneaking among us, ever in silence, ever in stealth." Then I saw Hummel. Hummel is coming, said I. I will ask Hummel, said I to myself. Hummel is coming. [KRESS *and the others are stationed as if near a door through which* PARKER *is looking and toward which* PAVLO *is now moving as if to enter the barracks*] THIEF!

And PARKER *flicks a switch to shut off lights.* PAVLO *enters. Blanket is thrown over him. He is dragged to the floor. They beat and kick him, calling him "thief." He cries out. Squirms. A second blanket is thrown on him, a mattress. It is his own bedding they are using, and as they beat and kick him, a whistle blows. All but* PAVLO *go running out, grabbing rifles and helmets as they go to form up for bayonet practice.* SGT. TOWER *is there.*

PAVLO: [*Emerging from beneath the blankets—no one is there*] Didn't I do enough pushups. How many do you have to do? Ardell!

ARDELL: You got to understand, Pavlo, it fun sometimes to get a man the way they got you. Come down on him, maybe pivot kick. Break his fuckin' spine. Do him, man. Do . . . him . . . good.

SGT. TOWER: [*Standing atop his platform, bayonet in hand*] You got to know this bayonet shit, Gen'lmen, else you get recycled, you be back to learn it all again. Eight more beautiful weeks in the armpit a the nation. Else you don't get recycled, you get killed. Then you wish for maybe half a second you been recycled. Do you know the spirit of the bayonet is to kill? What is the spirit of the bayonet?

THE MEN: [*While* PAVLO *stirs about and* PIERCE *enters the barracks*] To kill!

SGT. TOWER: You sound like pussies. You sound like slits.

THE MEN: TO KILL!

PAVLO is still on the floor; does not see PIERCE, *who is disheveled and a little drunk.*

SGT. TOWER: You sound like pussies.

MEN: TO KILL! [*Freeze*]

PIERCE: [*To* PAVLO, *who grabs inside his footlocker for a book*] Look at you. Ohhh, you know how much beer I hada drink to get fucked up on 3.2 beer? Hummel, look at me. You think it's neat to be squad leader? It's not neat to be squad leader. [PAVLO *has been pretending to read from the little book he has gotten from his locker*] I hear you got beat up this afternoon.

PAVLO: I got a blanket party.

PIERCE: You're in my squad and other guys in my squad beat you, man; I feel like I oughta

do somethin'. I'm older, see. Been to college a little; got a wife. And I'm here to tell you, even with all I seen, sometimes you are unbelievable, Hummel.

PAVLO: I don't care. I don't care.

PIERCE: I mean, I worry about you and the shit you do, man.

PAVLO: You do what you want, Pierce.

PIERCE: I mean, that's why people are after you, Hummel. That's why they fuck with you.

PAVLO: I'm trying to study my code a conduct, Pierce, you mind. It's just not too damn long to the proficiency test. Maybe you oughta be studyin' your code a conduct too, instead a sneakin' off to drink at the PX.

PIERCE: I wanna know how you got those rocks down your rifle. It's a two-mile walk out to the rifle range, and you got rocks in your barrel when we get there. That's what I'm talkin' about.

PAVLO: I don't know how that happened.

PIERCE: And every fight you get into, you do nothin' but dance, man. Round in a circle, bobbin' and weavin' and gettin' smacked in the mouth. Man, you oughta at least try and hit somebody. Jesus Christ, Hummel, what's wrong with you? We're in the shower and I tell you to maybe throw a punch once in a while, step with it, pivot, so you try *it* right there on that wet floor and damn near kill yourself smashin' into a wall.

PAVLO: Fuck you, Pierce.

PIERCE: Fuck you, Hummel.

PAVLO: You know somethin', Pierce. My name ain't even really Pavlo Hummel. It's Michael Hummel. I had it legally changed. I had my name changed.

PIERCE: You're puttin' me on.

PAVLO: No, no, and someday, see, my father's gonna say to me, "Michael, I'm so sorry I ran out on you," and I'm gonna say, "I'm not Michael, Asshole. I'm not Michael anymore." Pierce? You weren't with those guys who beat up on me, were you?

ARDELL: Sometimes I look at you, I don't know what I think I'm seein', but it sooo simple. You black on the inside. In there where you live, you that awful hurtin' black so you can't see yourself no way. Not up or down or in or out.

PAVLO *begins making his bunk and bayonet begins.*

SGT. TOWER: [*Having descended from the platform, moves among the men*] There ain't no army in the world got a shorter bayonet than this one we got. Maneuverability. It the only virtue. You got to get inside that big long knife that other man got. What is the spirit of the bayonet?

THE MEN: TO KILL!

SGT. TOWER: You sound like pussies.

THE MEN: TO KILL!

SGT. TOWER: You sound like slits!

THE MEN: TO KILL!

SGT. TOWER: EN GARDE!

THE MEN: AGGGH!

SGT. TOWER: LONG THRUST, PARRY LEFT . . . WHOOOOOO!

THE MEN: [*They make the move; one of them stumbling, falling down, clumsy, embarrassed*] AGGGH!

SGT. TOWER: Where you think you are? You think you in the movies? This here real life, Gen'lmen. You actin' like there ain't never been a war in this world. Don't you know what I'm sayin'? You got to want to put this steel into a man. You got to want to cut him, hurt him, make him die. You got to want to feel the skin and muscle come apart with the push you give. It come to you in the wood. RECOVER AND HOLD!

THE MEN: AGGGH! [*And the men make the move. They yell and growl with each thrust. Another falls down, gets up*]

SGT. TOWER: EN GARDE!

THE MEN: AGGGH!

SGT. TOWER: Lookin' good, lookin' good. Only you ain't mean. [*Men growl*] How come you ain't mean? [*Men growl again*] HORIZON-TAL BUTT STROKE SERIES, WHOOO [*They make the move, much more complicated this time. There is the thrust, recovery, then upper-cutting butt stroke, horizontal butt stroke and finally the downward slash. The growling and yelling is louder this time*] Look at you; look at you. Ohhh, but you men put into my mind one German I saw in the war. I got one bullet left, don't think I want to shoot it, and here come this goddamned big-assed German. "Aggggghhhh," I yell to him and it a challenge and he accept. "Aggggghhhh," he say to me and set hisself and I just shot him. Boom! Ohhh, he got a look on his face like I never saw before in my life. He one baffled motherfucker, Jim.

Without command, the men begin to march.

ARDELL: ONCE A WEEK IT GET TO TOWN . . .

Singing, marching, beginning immediately after "Jim."

THE MEN: THEY SEE ME COMIN' THEY ALL LAY DOWN.

ARDELL: IF I HAD A LOWER I.Q. . . .

All are marching now, exiting.

THE MEN: I COULD BE A SERGEANT TOO.

SGT. TOWER: LORD HAVE MERCY, I'M SO BLUE.

THE MEN: LORD HAVE MERCY, I'M SO BLUE.

SGT. TOWER: IT SIX MORE WEEKS TILL I BE THROUGH.

The earliest off are PIERCE, BURNS, IST SOLDIER.

THE MEN: IT SIX MORE WEEKS TILL WE BE THROUGH.

SGT. TOWER: SOUND OFF!

THE MEN: I—2—

BURNS, PIERCE, IST SOLDIER *enter barracks area, still singing as others are still exiting, and these three men set up the crap game on a footlocker.*

SGT. TOWER: SOUND OFF.

Others enter barracks; PAVLO, HINKLE.

THE MEN: 3—4. CADENCE COUNT. I—2—3—4. I—2. 3-4. [*The counting ends, new scene begins*]

PAVLO: [*Talking to* HINKLE. *A crap game goes on nearby*] Can you imagine that, Hinkle? Just knowin'. Seein' nothin' but bein' sure enough to gun down two people. They had T.N.T. on 'em; they was stupid slopeheads. That Sergeant Tinden saved everybody's life. I get made anything but infantry, I'm gonna fight it, man. I'm gonna fight it. You wanna go infantry with me, Hinkle. You're infantry and good at it, you're your own. Man, I'm gonna wear my uniform everywhere when I'm home, Hinkle. My mother's gonna be so ex-cited when she sees me. She's just gonna yell. I get nervous when I think about if she should hug me. You gonna hug your mother when you get home?

HINKLE: My mom's a little bitty skinny woman.

PAVLO: I don't know if I should or shouldn't.

HINKLE: What's your mom like?

PIERCE: You tellin' him about your barn house exploits, Hinkle?

HINKLE: Oh, no.

PIERCE: Hinkle says he screwed sheep. He tellin' you that, Hummel?

PARKER: How about pigs, Hinkle?

HINKLE: Oh, yeh.

KRESS: I'm tellin' you, Parker, it was too much; all that writin' and shit, and runnin' around. They ain't got no right to test you. Proficiency test, proficiency test; I don't even know what a proficiency is—goddamn people—crawlin' and writin'—I'm tellin' you they ain't got no right to test you. They get you here, they mess with you— [*He is in a near frenzy, talking rapidly*] they let you go. Who says they gotta test you?

PIERCE: [*Who has the dice and is laying down money*] Who's back, man? I'm shootin' five.

KRESS: I got so nervous in hand-to-hand, I threw a guy against the wall. They flunked me for bein' too rough.

PIERCE: Who's back man?

KRESS: I'll take three. [*Putting down money. PARKER drops a couple of ones*] I get re-cycled, I'll kill myself, I swear it. [*As PIERCE is shaking the dice, saying over and over, "Karen loves me, Karen loves me"*] I'll cut off my ear.

PIERCE: [*Throwing the dice*] Karen says I'm GOOD!

KRESS: Goddamn! Shit! How they do it again, Parker?

PARKER: Pierce, you're incredible.

KRESS: Parker!

PARKER: They add up your scores, man; your P.T. plus your rifle, plus the score they got today. Then they divide by 3. You lettin' it ride, Pierce. [*Throwing down a five*]

PIERCE: Karen loves me.

KRESS: Where they get the 3? [*Putting in money*]

PARKER: There's three events, man.

PIERCE: [*Throwing the dice*] Karen say, "I know the *road!*"

KRESS: You fucking asshole!

PARKER: Goddamn it, Pierce!

PIERCE: Who wants me? Back man's got no heart. Shootin' twenty I come for 11—double or nothin'. Whose twenty says I can't come for all out of the gate . . .

A soldier enters on the run.

GRENNEL: Tower's right behind me; he's got the scores.

General commotion as SGT. TOWER *strides across the stage and enters their area.*

PIERCE: TENHUT!

All come to attention before their bunks.

SGT. TOWER: AT EASE! [*Men to parade rest*] Gen'lmen. It's truth and consequences time. The sad tidings and the [*Handing a paper to PIERCE for him to post on the board*] glad tidings. You got two men in this platoon didn't make it. They Burn and Kress. They gonna have to stay here 8 more weeks and if they as dumb as it look, maybe 8 more after that and 8 fuckin' more. The rest a you people, maybe you ain't got no spectacular qualities been endowed upon my mind, but you goin' home when you figured. [*Turning and leaving*]

PIERCE: TENHUT!

SGT. TOWER: [*Exiting*] Carry on.

The men are silent a moment: KRESS *stands at or near the center.*

PIERCE: Lemme holler . . . just one . . . time, lemme holler . . .

HINKLE: Mother, mother, make my bed!

A SOLDIER: [*At the bulletin board*] Me! My name! Me!

PIERCE: AGGGGGGGGHHHHHHHHHHHHHHHH HHHHHHHAAAA!

PARKER: Lemme just pack my bags!

HENDRIX: [*Entering with civilian clothes, shirt, trousers on a hanger, hat on his head*] Lookee lookee—

HINKLE: What're them funny clothes?

PIERCE: CIVILIAN CLOTHES! CIVILIAN—

HINKLE: CI-WHO-LIAN?

PIERCE: PEOPLE OUTSIDE, MAN! THAT'S WHY THEY AIN'T ALL FUNNY AND GREEN, BECAUSE YOU'RE OUTSIDE WHEN YOU WEAR 'EM. YOU'RE BACK ON THE BLOCK. BACK IN THE WORLD!

PAVLO: DON'T NOBODY HEAR ME CALLIN' "KRESS"? [*He has said the name a few times during the yelling. He is atop his own bed*] I think we oughta tell him how sorry we are he didn't make it. I'm gonna. I'm gonna tell him. I'm sorry, Kress, that you're gonna be re-cycled and you're not goin' home. I think we're all sorry. I bet it's kinda like gettin' your head caught in a blanket, the way you feel. It's a bad feelin', I bet, and I think I understand it even if I am goin' back where there's lights and it's pretty. I feel sorry for you, Kress, I just wanna laugh, I feel so sorry—[*And KRESS pushes him off the bed, leaping after him. PAVLO staggers backward*] Sonofabitch, what're you—SONOFABITCH! [*Swinging a wild right hand; they flail and crash about, KRESS grabbing PAVLO's wrist, snapping the arm up into a hammer lock*]

KRESS: Down. [*Then lifting*] Don't you hear me? Down, I'm sayin'. Don't you hear me? [*Then easing down*] Thata boy . . . Called crawlin' . . . [*PAVLO has been thrown to the floor, while PIERCE has been seized by HINKLE and another soldier who keep him from going to PAVLO's aid*] You got the hang of it . . . now . . . Crawlin' . . . Yeh. Now I'm gonna ask you something? Okay?

PAVLO: . . . Okay . . .

KRESS: What I'd like to know is who is it in this platoon steals money from his buddies? Who is it don't know how to talk decent to no-body? and don't have no goddamn friend? Who is that person? You tell me, Hummel? The name a that person passed his test today by cheatin'. [*Twisting the arm*]

PAVLO: I don't . . . know . . . [*The whole of this is furious; both men are wild*]

KRESS: Who? [*Working the arm*]

PAVLO: No— [*And the arm is twisted again*] Stop him, somebody. Pierce. You're my squad leader, Pierce. Ohhhh . . . Pierce, please . . . Aggghhhh . . . Pierce . . .

KRESS: WHO?

And PAVLO *yells.*

PIERCE: Ease off a little . . .

KRESS: I CAN'T HEAR YOU!

PIERCE: Kress, I—

PAVLO: HUMMEL!

KRESS: WHAT? WHAT?

PAVLO: HUMMEL! HUMMEL!

KRESS: WHAT?

PAVLO: HUMMEL! HUMMEL! He did 'em. All of those things. All of 'em. He cheated. He cheated. HUMMEL! HUM—

PIERCE: Kress, goddamn it. GODDAMN IT!

Leaping to lift KRESS *away from* PAVLO.

KRESS: [*Leaving* PAVLO, *pulling free of* PIERCE] What? What you want, Corporal? Don't mess with me, man. [*Staring at* PIERCE *who is now between him and* PAVLO] Don't mess with Kress. Not when he's feelin' bad. He'll kill ya, honest to God. He'll pee in your dead mouth. [PAVLO *rushes at* KRESS, *howling*]

PIERCE: Nooooooooo. [*Seizing* PAVLO]

PAVLO: I'm all right. I'm all right. I do all right!

PIERCE: Will you listen to me, man; you're goin' home, not Kress. You got him.

PAVLO: Fucking asshole!

PIERCE: Will you listen? [*Shoving* PAVLO *back toward center stage. Scolding him, blocking his pursuit of* KRESS, *backing him up*] You gotta learn to think, Hummel. You gotta start puttin' 2 and 2 together so they fit. You beat him; you had ole Kress beat and then you fixed it so you hadda lose. You went after him so he hadda be able to put you down.

PAVLO: I just wanted to let him know what I thought.

PIERCE: No, no!

PAVLO: He had no call to hit me like that. I was just talkin'—

PIERCE: You dared him, man.

PAVLO: You shoulda stopped him, that's the problem. You're the squad leader. That's just this whole damn army messin' with me and it ain't ever gonna end but in shit. How come you're a squad leader? Who the fuck are you? I'm not gonna get a chance at what I want. Not ever. Nothin' but shit. They're gonna mess with me—make a clerk outa me

or a medic or truck driver, a goddamn moron —or a medic—a nurse—a fuckin' Wac with no tits—or a clerk, some little goddamn twerp of a guy with glasses and no guts at all. So don't gimme shit about what I done, Pierce, it's what you done and done and didn't— [*And during this whole thing,* PIERCE, *Squad Leader, has moved about straightening the bunk, and footlockers disturbed by the fight, and* PAVLO, *in growing desperation, has followed him. Now* PIERCE, *in disgust, starts to leave*] That's right; keep on walkin' away from you duties, keep—

PIERCE: You're happy as a pig in shit. I don't know why I keep thinkin' you ain't.

PAVLO: I am not.

PIERCE: Up to your eyeballs!

PAVLO: I'm gonna kill myself, Pierce! [*It bursts out of him*]

PIERCE: If you weren't in my squad, I'd spit in your face . . .

PAVLO: Fuck you, fuck you, fuck you. [*Rocking backward, bowing then forward*] I hate you goddamn people!

ARDELL: I know.

PAVLO'S *bending carries him down to the floor.*

PAVLO: Ardell. [*At his footlocker,* PAVLO *rummages about*]

ARDELL: I know. I know. All you life like a river and there's no water all around—this emptiness—you gotta fill it. Gotta get water. You dive, man, you dive off a stone wall [PAVLO *sits, canteen and paper bag in his hands*] into the Hudson River waitin' down dark under you, for a second, it's all air . . . so free . . . do you know the distance you got to fall? You think you goin' up. Don't nobody fall up, man. Nobody.

PAVLO: What is it? I want to know what it is. The thing that Sergeant saw to make him know to shoot that kid and old man. I want to have it, know it, be it.

ARDELL: I know.

PAVLO: When?

ARDELL: Soon.

PAVLO: If I could be bone, Ardell; if I could be bone. In my deepest part or center, if I could just be bone. [*Taking a container from the bag, he takes pills, washes them down with water, while* SGT. TOWER, *already on the platform speaks and* PAVLO *crawls under the covers of his bunk*]

SGT. TOWER: Now I'm gonna tell you gen'lmen how you find you way when you lost. You better listen up. What you do, you find the North Star and the North Star show you true north accurate all year round. You look for the

Big Dipper and there two stars at the end a
that place in the stars that look like the bowl
of the dipper and they called the pointer. They
them two stars at where the water could come
out of the dipper if it had some water and out
from them on a straight line you gonna see this
big damn star and that the North Star and it
show you north and once you know that, gen'l-
men, you can figure the rest. You ain't lost
no more.

THE MEN: [*From the darkness*] YESSSS, SER-
GEANT!

SGT. TOWER: I hope so. I do hope so . . .

PIERCE, PARKER, *others, set up card game
on footlocker.*

KRESS: [*Passing bunk where* PAVLO *is a lump
beneath his blanket*] I wonder what the
fuckin' chimney shittin' shit is doin' now?

HINKLE *settles curiously on the bunk next
to* PAVLO.

PARKER: You gonna see me, Pierce? [*Talking
even as they set the card game up*]

PIERCE: And raise you.

PARKER: Ten ta one, he's under there jerking
off!

HINKLE: [*Bending near to* PAVLO] No, no, he's
got this paper bag and everything smells
funny. Y'all some kind of acrobat, Hummel?

KRESS: He's got some chick's bicycle seat in a
bag man.

HINKLE: And the noises he's makin'.

PIERCE: Poor pathetic motherfucker.

KRESS: He ain't pathetic.

PIERCE: He is too.

PARKER: Under there pounding his pud.

KRESS: You musta not seen many pathetic people,
you think he's pathetic.

PIERCE: I seen plenty.

PARKER: Call.

PIERCE: Full boat. Jacks and threes! [*Laying
down his cards*]

PARKER: Jesus Goddamn Christ.

HINKLE: I was wonderin' can ah look in you
all's bag, Hummel? [*Reaching under the
blanket to pick up the bag*]

PARKER: Jesus Goddamn Christ.

HINKLE: Ohhhh . . . it's . . . you been sniffin'
airplane glue . . . [*And he laughs, "Ha, Ha,
Ha," turns toward the others*] Hummel's been
sniffin' airplane glue.

KRESS: [*From his bed*] ATTAWAY TO GO,
HUMMEL.

HINKLE: An' where's all the aspirins . . . ? [*Holding the bottle*]

PAVLO: Tum-tum, Pavlo.

HINKLE: You all kiddin' me.

PAVLO: No.

HINKLE: Y'all ate 'em?

PAVLO: Yeah!

HINKLE: Hey, y'all. . . . [*To* PAVLO] Was it full?

PAVLO: [*Attempting to sit up, flops back down*]
Tippy top.

HINKLE: Hummel just ate— [*Examining the
bottle*] 100 aspirins. Hummel just ate 'em.

KRESS: Attaway to go, Hummel.

PARKER: Nighty-night.

HINKLE: [*Moving toward* PIERCE] Won't it
hurt him, Pierce?

KRESS: Kill him probably.

PARKER: Hopefully.

KRESS: Hinkle, ask him did he use chocolate
syrup?

HINKLE: He's breathin' kinda funny, Pierce,
don't you think?

KRESS: Hummel does everything funny.

PIERCE: [*Beginning to deal*] Five cards, gen'lmen;
jacks or better.

HINKLE: Pierce.

PIERCE: Hummel, you stop worryin' that boy.
Tell him no headache big enough in the
world, you're gonna take a hundred aspirins.
[*Slight pause:* KRESS *begins imitating* PAVLO's
odd breathing] How come everybody's all
the time bustin' up my good luck.

BURNS: Shit, man, he took a hundred aspirins,
he wouldn't be breathing period.

RYAN: Sounds like a goddamn tire pump.

BURNS: Hummel, TENHUT!

PIERCE: Hummel, you just jivin' cause you don't
know what else to do or did you eat them
pills?

BURNS: Tryin' to blow himself up like a balloon
. . . drift away. Float outa the fort.

PARKER *begins to imitate* KRESS *imitating* PAV-
LO's *breathing.*

RYAN: He's fakin', man.

BURNS: How you know?

RYAN: They'd kill you like a bullet.

HINKLE: Get over here, Pierce!

Throwing down his cards, PIERCE *goes to the
bed.*

KRESS: How come the army don't throw him out,
Parker?

PARKER: Army likes weird people, Kress.

KRESS: I hate weird people.

PARKER: Sure you do.

KRESS: Weird chimney shittin' friendless, gutless
cheatin'—

PIERCE *is examining* PAVLO. PAVLO *makes a sound and then begins to cough, to sputter.*

PIERCE: [*Realizing what is true*] NOOO! NOT IN MY SQUAD, YOU MOTHER. GET UP. [*He is trying to get* PAVLO *to his feet; the* 1ST SOLDIER *is helping*] YOU SILLY SONOFA-BITCH. We got to walk him. [PAVLO *is feebly resisting, saying "no, no"*] Hinkle, double-time-it over the orderly room.

HINKLE: [*Making for the door*] Right.

PIERCE: Tell 'em we got a guy over here took a hundred aspirins, they should get an ambulance.

HINKLE: [*Turning to head for the door*] Right.

KRESS: Hinkle!

HINKLE: [*Hesitating, turning back, to face* KRESS] Yeh!

KRESS: Pick me up a coke on your way back.

And HINKLE *leaves.*

PIERCE: [*Working with the aid of another soldier*] Hold him steady, I think we oughta get him outside, more air.

ARDELL: [*Standing over near the base of the platform*] Pavlo, look at you. You gonna have ambulances and sirens and all kinds a good shit. Ain't you somethin'? It gonna be a celebration. C'mon over here [*As if his voice draws them, they lug* PAVLO *toward the tower; they lay him down, remove all clothes from him but his underwear and T shirt*] Look at you. You got people runnin' around like a bunch a fools. That what you wanted? Yeah, that what you want! They sayin', "Move him. Lift him. Take his shirt off." They walkin' you around in the air. They all thinkin' about you, anyway. But what you doin' but cryin'. You always think you signifyin' on everybody else, but all you doin' is showin' your own fool self. You don't know nothin' about show-boatin', Pavlo. You hear me? Now you get on up off that floor. You don't get up, man, I blow a motherfuckin' whistle up the side a you head. I blow it loud. YOU THINK YOU GOT A MOTHERFUCKIN' WHISTLE IN YOUR BRAIN. [PIERCE *and the other soldier have turned away, frozen.* PAVLO *has jumped. Everything he does is performed in the manner of a person alone, as if* ARDELL *is a voice in his head. The light perhaps suggests this.* KRESS, *all others, are frozen as when* HINKLE *left*] I'm tellin' you how to be. That right. [PAVLO *slumps back down*] Ohhh, don't act so bad; you actin', man. What you expect, you go out get you head smokin' on all kinds a shit, sniffin' that goddamn glue. then fallin' down all over yourself. Man, you lucky you alive, carryin' on like that. [PAVLO *is doubled over*] Ain't doin' you no good you

wish you dead, 'cause you ain't, man. You know you do. Get on up. [PAVLO *takes a deep breath and stands*] You go on in the latrine now, get you a bromo, you wash off you face . . . [PAVLO *exits*] Then get you ass right back out here. And you don't need no shave, man, you ain't got no beard no ways. [*He sees* PAVLO's *uniform lying on the floor*] What kinda shit this? Your poor ole Sarge see this, he sit down on the ground and he cry, man. Poor ole Sarge, he work himself like he crazy tryin' ta teach you so you can act like a man. An' what you do? [*Turning suddenly toward the door through which* PAVLO *exited*] PAVLO! You diddlin' in there, you take this long. And you bring out you other uniform. We gonna shape you up. [PAVLO *enters carrying military dress uniform in clothing bag which he hangs on the tower*] It daytime, man, you goin' out struttin'. You goin' out standin' tall. You tear it open. Trousers first, man. Dig 'em out. [PAVLO, *having selected the trousers, moves as if to put them on*] NOOOO! Damnit, ain't you got no sense at all? [*He has rushed to* PAVLO, *lifted the trouser bottoms from off the floor*] You drag 'em all over the floor like that, man, they gonna look like shit. Get up on this footlocker! [*Pulling a footlocker into place.* PAVLO, *standing on the footlocker* ARDELL *has placed before him, puts on the trousers. Now* PIERCE *and the other soldier move to help* PAVLO *dress. All is ease and grace now*] That right, that it. Make 'em look like they got no notion at all what it like ta be *dirty*. Be clean, man. Yeh. [PIERCE *has moved before* PAVLO, *pulling down on the cuffs, pulling the crease tight*] Now the shirt. [*It is a ritual now,* PAVLO *must exert no effort whatsoever as he is transformed. Everything is done for him*] Lemme look you brass over. [*Soldier moves to the jacket*] Ain't too bad. It do. Lemme just touch 'em up a little. You put on you tie. Make you a big knot. Big knot make you look tall. [*He is brushing with his handkerchief at the brass*] Where you boots? [*Finished with the jacket,* PIERCE *and other soldier move to boots*] Where you boots? An' you got some shades? Lemme get you some shades. [*Walking backwards*] And tuck that tie square. Give her little loop she come off you throat high and pretty. [*As* ARDELL *exits, beginning the song,* PAVLO *sits on the footlocker, back to audience, and* PIERCE *and the other soldier each kneel to put on a boot*]

PAVLO: HUT . . . HOO . . . HEE . . . HAW . . . IF I HAD A LOWER I.Q.

THE MEN: [KRESS *and all sing*] IF I HAD A LOWER I.Q.

ARDELL: I COULD BE A SERGEANT TOO!

THE MEN: I COULD BE A SERGEANT TOO!

Across the back of the stage, two men march.

ARDELL: LORD HAVE MERCY, I'M SO BLUE.

The two men do an intricate drill team step.

THE MEN: IT FOUR MORE WEEKS TILL I BE THROUGH.

The two men spin and stomp their rifles, exit.

ARDELL: You gonna be over, man, I finish with you. [*Reentering with the sunglasses as* PAVLO *stands up, now fully dressed*] You gonna be the fat rat, man; you eatin' cheese. [ARDELL *moves about* PAVLO, *examining him, guiding him toward the tower which* PAVLO *will climb and stand upon and then* ARDELL *will move to join him*] OVER BABY! Ardell can make you straight; you startin' ta look good now; you finish up, you gonna be the fattest rat, man; eatin' the finest cheese. Put you in good company, you wear that uniform, you go out walkin' on the street, people know you, they say, "What that?" Somebody else say, "Man, he straight. He look good." Somebody else say, "That boy got pride." Yeh, baby, Pavlo, you gonna be over, man. You gonna be that fat fat rat, eatin' cheese, down on his knees, yeh, baby, doffin' his red cap, sayin' "yes, Massa." You lookee out there. [*They are both atop the tower,* ARDELL *a little behind* PAVLO *and gesturing outward, pointing.* PAVLO *stands. He has sunglasses on*] Who you see in that mirror, man? Who you see? That ain't no Pavlo Hummel. Noooo, man. That somebody else. An' he somethin' else. Ohhh, you goin' out on the street, they gonna see you. Ardell tellin' you and Ardell know. You back on the block an' you goin' out struttin'. An' they gonna cry when they see you. You so pretty, baby, you gonna make 'em cry. You tell me you name, you pretty baby!

PAVLO: [*Snapping to attention*] PAVLO MOTHERHUMPIN' HUMMEL!

Blackout.

ACT II

CAPTAIN *and* SGT. TOWER *are upstage facing out.* PAVLO *still stands on the tower, with other soldiers in formation below.* MICKEY, PAVLO'S *brother, stands downstage, looking out as if into a mirror, combing his hair.*

CAPTAIN: As we enter now the final weeks of your basic training, I feel a certain obligation as your company commander to speak to you of the final purpose of what has gone on here. Normally this is more difficult to make clear. Pleiku, Vietnam is the purpose of what we have done here. A few nights ago, mortar and machine gun fire in a sneak attack in the highlands killed 9 Americans and wounded 140 serving at our camp there in Pleiku. In retaliation, a bombing of the North has begun and it will continue until the government of Hanoi, battered and reeling, goes back to the North.

SGT. TOWER: Company fall out.

The TROOPS *scatter. Music starts from* MICKEY'S *radio.* PAVLO *descends. Picks up duffle bag, AWOL bag.*

PAVLO: Hey, Mickey, it's me. I'm home! [MICKEY, *in T shirt, slacks, shoes, combs hair*] It's me. I'm home, I'm home, I'm home.

MICKEY: Whata you say, huh? Hey, hey, what happened? You took so long. You took a wrong turn, huh? Missed your stop and now you come home all dressed up like a conductor. What happened? You were down in that subway so long they put you to work? Huh? Man, you look good though; you look good. Where were you again?

PAVLO: Georgia.

MICKEY: Hot as a bitch, right?

PAVLO: No. Cold.

MICKEY: In Georgia?

PAVLO: Yeh, it was real cold; we used to hide out in the furnace room every damn chance we ever got.

MICKEY: Hey, you want a drink? Damn, that don't make much sense, does it?

PAVLO: What?

MICKEY: They send you to Georgia for the winter and it's like a witch's tit. Can you imagine that? A witch's tit? Eeeeeggggggg. Put ice on your tongue. That ever happens to me, man, I'd turn in my tool. Ain't you gonna ask about the ole lady? How's she doin' and all that, cause she's doin' fine. Pickin' and plantin' daisies. Doin' fine. [*And* PAVLO *laughs softly, shaking his head, taking the drink* MICKEY *has made him*] Whatsa matter? You don't believe yo-yos can be happy? Psychotics have fun, man. You oughta know that.

PAVLO: I just bet she's climbin' some kinda wall and she's pregnant again, she thinks, or you are or me or somebody.

MICKEY: Noo, man, noo, it's everybody else now. Only nonfamily.

PAVLO: [*Laughing, loudly*] That's me and you! Nonfamily moutherfuckers!

MICKEY: All the dogs and women of the world!

PAVLO: Yeh, yeh, all the guys in the barracks used to think I was a little weird so I'd—

MICKEY: —you are a little weird— [*Slight pause*]

PAVLO: Yeh, yeh, I'd tell 'em, "You think I'm weird, you oughta see my brother, Mickey. He don't give a big rat's ass for nothin' or nobody."

MICKEY: And did you tell 'em about his brains, too. And his wit and charm. The way his dick hangs to his knees—about his 18 thou a year? Did you tell 'em all that sweet shit?

PAVLO: They said they hoped you died of all you got.

MICKEY: [*Has been dressing throughout: shirt, tie, jacket*] How come the troops were thinkin' you weird? You doin' that weird stuff again. You say "Georgia" and "the army." For all I know you been down town in the movies for the last three months and you bought that goddamn uniform at some junk shop.

PAVLO: I am in the Army.

MICKEY: How do I know?

PAVLO: I'm tellin' you.

MICKEY: But you're a fuckin' liar; you're a fuckin' myth maker.

PAVLO: I gotta go to Vietnam, Mickey.

MICKEY: Vietnam don't even exist.

PAVLO: I gotta go to it.

MICKEY: Arizona, man; that's where you're goin'. Wyoming.

PAVLO: Look at me! I'm different! I'm different than I was! [*This is with fury*] I'm not the same anymore. I was an asshole. I'm not an asshole anymore. I'm not an asshole anymore! [*Slight pause*] I came here to forgive you. I don't need you anymore.

MICKEY: You're a goddamn cartoon, you know that.

PAVLO: [*Rapidly. A rush of words*] I'm happier now than I ever was, I got people who respect me. Lots of 'em. There was this guy Kress in my outfit. We didn't hit it off . . . and he called me out . . . he was gonna kill me, he said. Everybody tried to stop me because this guy had hurt a lot of people already and he had this uncle who'd taught him all about fightin' and this uncle has been executed in San Quentin for killing people. We went out back of the barracks. It went on and on, hitting and kicking. It went on and on; all around the barracks. The crowd right with us. And then . . . all of a sudden . . . this look came into his eye . . . and he just stopped . . . and reached down to me and hugged me. He just hugged and hugged me. And that look was in all their eyes. All the soldiers. I don't need you anymore, Mickey. I got real brothers now.

MICKEY: You know . . . if my father hadn't died, you wouldn't even exist.

PAVLO: No big thing! We got the same mother; that's shit enough. I'm gonna shower and shave, okay? Then we can go out drinkin'.

MICKEY: All those one night stands. You ever think of that. Ghostly pricks. I used to hear 'em humpin' the ole whore. I probably had my ear against the wall the night they got you goin'.

PAVLO: [*After a slight silence*] You seen Joanna lately?

MICKEY: Joanna?

PAVLO: Joanna. My ole girl. I thought maybe she probably killed herself and it was in the papers. You know, on account of my absence. But she probably did it in secret.

MICKEY: No doubt.

PAVLO: No doubt.

MICKEY: Ain't she the one who got married? I think the ole lady tole me Joanna got married and she was gonna write you a big letter all about it. Sure she was. Anyway, since we're speaking of old girls and pregnant people, I've got to go to this little party tonight. Got a good new sweet young thing and she thinks I'm better than her daddy. I've had a run a chicks lately you wouldn't believe, Pavlo. They give away ass like Red Cross girls dealin' out donuts. I don't understand how I get half a what I get. Oh, yeh, old lady comes and goes around here. She's the same old witch.

PAVLO: I'm gonna go see Joanna. I'll call her up. Use the magic fuckin' phone to call her up.

MICKEY: I'll give you a call later on.

PAVLO: I'll be out, man. I'll be out on the street.

MICKEY: You make yourself at home. [*Exits*]

Soldiers suddenly appear far upstage, marching forward as ARDELL, *off to the side, counts cadence; other soldiers appear at various points about the stage.*

ARDELL: HUT . . . HOO . . . HEE . . .

SGT. TOWER: SAW SOME STOCKIN'S ON THE STREET . . .

THE MEN: WISHED I WAS BETWEEN THOSE FEET.

SGT. TOWER: WISHED I WAS BETWEEN THOSE FEET. HONEY, HONEY, DON'T YOU FROWN.

THE MEN: I LOVE YOU DRUNK AND LAYIN' DOWN.

SGT. TOWER: STANDIN' TALL AND LOOKIN' GOOD. WE BELONG IN HOLLYWOOD. [*Atop the tower as the men come to a stomping halt*]

THE MEN: WE BELONG IN HOLLYWOOD.

SGT. TOWER: Take five, Gen'lmen, but the smoking lamp is not lit.

PAVLO *is there, off to the side, disheveled, carrying a pint whiskey bottle. He undresses, speaking his anger, throwing his uniform down. The men are relaxing a little.*

PAVLO: Stupid fuckin' uniform. Miserable hunk a green shit. Don't we go to good bars—why don't you work for me? And there's this really neat girl there sayin' to me how do I like bein' a robot? How do I like bein' one in a hundred million robots all marchin' in a row? Don't anybody understand about uniforms? I ain't no robot. You gotta have braid . . . ribbons and patches all about what you did. I got nothin'. What's so complicated? I look like nothin' cause I done nothin'. [*In his T shirt and underwear, he kneels now with the bottle*]

SGT. TOWER: Gen'lmen, you best listen up real close now even though you restin'. Gonna tell you little bit about what you do you comin' through the woods, you find a man wounded in his chest. You gotta seal it off. That wound workin' like a valve, pullin' in air, makin' pressure to collapse that man's lung; you get him to breathe out and hold his breath. You apply the metal foil side a the waterproof wrapping of the first aid dressing, tie it off. Gonna hafta tie it extra; you use your poncho, his poncho, you get strips a cloth. You tear up you own damn shirt, I don't care. You let that boy have his lung. You let him breathe. AM I UNDERSTOOD?

THE MEN: YES, SERGEANT!

SGT. TOWER: FALL IN! DISMISSED!

The troops go; leaving PAVLO *alone, in his underwear, near or on the bed.*

PAVLO: I wanna get laid. . . , bed. . . . bottle. [*Pause*] I wanna get laid! I wanna get laid, phone! You goddamn stuck-up motherin' phone. Need a piece of ass, phone, need a piece of ass. Bed. Lemme walk on over to that phone. Lemme crawl on over to that phone. Lemme get there. Gonna outflank you. Goddamn army ant. Thas right. Thas right. Hello, Joanna [*Dialing now, he has crawled to the phone*] This is Pavlo, Joanna, hello. Certainly of course. I'd be glad to screw your thingy with my thingy. BSZZZZZZZ . . . BBBBBBBBZZZZZZZZZZZZZZZ . . . BBBZZZ . . .

WOMAN: [*On the phone*] Hello?

PAVLO: BBBZZZZZZZZZZZZZZZZZZZZZ . . .

WOMAN: Hello?

PAVLO: Little bitty creature . . . hello, hello. . . . .

WOMAN: Who is this?

PAVLO: Hollering . . . hollering . . . poor creature . . . locked inside, can't get out, can't—

WOMAN: Pavlo?

PAVLO: Do you know me? Yes. Yes, it is me, Pavlo. Pavlo Hummel . . . Joanna . . . And I am calling to ask how can you have lived to this day away from me?

WOMAN: Pavlo, listen.

PAVLO: Yes. I am. I do.

WOMAN: Pavlo: this isn't Joanna.

PAVLO: What?

WOMAN: This is Mrs. Sorrentino, Pavlo. Joanna isn't here.

PAVLO: What?

WOMAN: I said, "Joanna isn't here," Pavlo. This is her mother; may I have her call you?

PAVLO: What?

WOMAN: I said, "May I have her call you?" She's married, Pavlo. Or did you just call to say "hello"?

PAVLO: Who is this?

WOMAN: Pavlo, what's wrong with you?

PAVLO: Who are you? I don't know who this is. You get off the line, goddamn it, you hear me, or I'll report you to the telephone company. I'll report you to Bell Telephone. And G.E., too. And the Coke Company and General Motors. [*The* WOMAN *hangs up the phone*] You'll be hurtin', Baby. I report you to all those people. Now you tell me where she is. Where is she?

Behind him a light pops on, a table lamp. His mother, a small, dark-haired woman, plump, fashionably dressed, has been there all the while, sitting in the dark and listening, visible only as a figure in a chair. She begins to speak almost at the same instant that the light goes on. At first tentative, she then gains confidence, gathers speed, tells her story as if she is simply thinking it.

MRS. HUMMEL: In Stratford, Connecticut, Pavlo. Pregnant more than likely. Vomiting in the morning. Yes . . . trying . . . to . . . get . . . rid of . . . it. . . . Hello, Pavlo . . . I wrote you that . . . I wrote you. [*Silence*] Hello . . . Pavlo. I wrote you she was married. Why are you calling? Why? [*Silence*] Pavlo? Listen, are you finished on the phone and could we talk a minute? I don't want to interrupt . . . I only have a few . . . few things to say. They won't take long. I've been working since you've been gone. Did you know? Doing quite well. Quite well indeed. In a department store. Yes. One of the smaller ones. Yes. And we had an awful, awful shock there the other day and that's what I want to tell you about. There's a woman, Sally Kelly, and Ken was her son, in the Army like you now, and he went overseas last August. Well I talked to Sally when I went in at noon and she was in the lunchroom writing a little card to Ken and she let me read it. She knew that you were in the army so she said she was sure I knew the way it was consolation to write a little note. Then about 5:45, I was working on the shoes and I saw two Army officers come up the escalator and talk to one of the other clerks. I never gave them another thought and at 6:00 o'clock Sally came through and went down the escalator and made a remark to me and laughed a little and went on down. In about fifteen more minutes, I was waiting on a lady and she said to me, "Isn't that terrible about the lady's son who works downstairs?" I said, "Who?" She said, "The lady who works at your candy department just got word her son was killed in Vietnam." Well, I was really shook when I heard that and I said, "Oh, you must be mistaken. She just went downstairs from her supper hour and I talked to her and she was fine." She said, "Well, that's what I heard on the main floor." Well, I went right to the phone and called the reception desk and they said it was true. This is what happened, this is what I want to tell you. The officers had gone to Sally's house but no one was home so they talked to the neighbors and found out Sally worked at the store. So they went up to our receptionist and asked for our manager. He wasn't in so they asked for one of the men and Tommy Bottle came and they told him, they needed his help because they had to tell one of the employees that her son was killed in Vietnam. Tommy really got shook as you can imagine and he took the officers to Mr. Brenner's office and closed the door. While they were in there, Sally came out of the lunchroom and came downstairs. Joyce, the girl who is the receptionist knew by this time and Sally laughed when she went by and said that she better get to work or something like that. Joyce said later on that she could hardly look at her. Anyway, Tommy called the floorman from first floor to come up and he told him what had happened and then he had to go back down to 1st floor and tell Sally she was wanted in Tommy's office. She said, "Oh, boy, what have I done now?" By the time she got to the fourth floor, the office door was open and she saw the two Army men and said, "Oh, dear God, not Kenny." [*Pause*] A mother . . . and her children should be as a tree and her branches . . . A mother spends . . . but she gets . . . change. You think me a fool . . . don't you. There are many who do. [*Pause*] He joined to be a mechanic and they transferred him to Infantry and he was killed on December 1st. So you see . . . I know what to expect. I know . . . what you're trying to do.

PAVLO: Who . . . was . . . my father? Where is he?

MRS. HUMMEL: You know that.

PAVLO: No, I want you to tell me.

MRS. HUMMEL: I've already told you.

PAVLO: No, where is he now? What did he look like?

MRS. HUMMEL: I wrote it all in a letter. I put it all in an envelope, I sealed it, mailed it.

PAVLO: I never got it.

MRS. HUMMEL: I think you did.

PAVLO: No!

MRS. HUMMEL: No, you had many fathers, many men, movie men, filmdom's great—all of them, those grand old men of yesteryear, they were your father. The Fighting 76th, do you remember? Oh, I remember, little Jimmy what a tough little mite, he was and how he leaped upon that grenade, did you see? my god what a glory, what a glorious thing with his little tin hat.

PAVLO: My real father!

MRS. HUMMEL: He was like them, the ones I showed you in movies, I pointed them out.

PAVLO: What was his name?

MRS. HUMMEL: I've told you.

PAVLO: No. What was his name? I don't know what it was.

MRS. HUMMEL: Is it my fault you've forgotten?

PAVLO: You never told me.

MRS. HUMMEL: I did. I whispered it in your ear. You were three. I whispered the whole thing in your ear!

PAVLO: Lunatic!

MRS. HUMMEL: Nooooo!

PAVLO: Insane hideous person!

MRS. HUMMEL: [*Slight pause*] I've got to go to bed now. I have to get my rest. [*Her back is turned. She is walking*]

PAVLO: [*Stopping her*] I picked this girl up in this bar tonight and when I took her home and got her to the door and kissed her, her tongue went into my mouth. I thought that meant she was going to let me in to her apartment. "Don't get hurt," she said "and get in touch when you get back, I'd love to see you." She knew I was going overseas, did you? And then the door was shut and all I wanted to say was, "What are you doing sticking your tongue in my mouth and then leaving me, you goddamn stuck-up motherin' bitch." But I didn't say anything.

MRS. HUMMEL: Yes . . . well . . . I'll . . . [*Pause*] . . . see you in the morning . . . Pavlo . . . [*And she leaves*]

ARDELL: [*Who has been watching*] Oh, man, how come? You wanted to get laid, how come you didn't do like the ole Sarge told you steada gettin' all tore up with them walkin' blues? Take you a little money, the old Sarge say, roll it up long ways, put it in your fly, man, so it stickin' out. Then go on walkin' up and down the street that green stickin' right outa your fly. You get laid. You got that money stickin' outa your fly, you get laid. You get your nut! How come you didn't do that?

OFFICER: [*Who has been standing on rear platform at parade rest*] And the following will depart conus 12 August 1966 for the Republic of Vietnam on assignment to the 23rd Field Hospital. Thomas. Simpson. Horner. Hinkle. Hummel.

PAVLO: I don't wanna be no medic!

The bar music starts, YEN and older Vietnamese woman entering from one side of the stage, BRISBEY calling from the other and then entering, his bed on wheels pushed onstage by two soldiers, while ARDELL has hauled off the footlocker on which the phone had sat, revealing a pile of clothes, PAVLO's jungle fatigues which he immediately starts getting in to. YEN is at the bar. All this happens nearly simultaneously, BRISBY calling "PAVLO," YEN entering, music starting.

YEN: Hey, G.I. cheap Charlie, you want one more beer.

JONES: [*Offstage*] One bomniba, one beer.

BRISBEY: Pavlo.

YEN: [*As JONES, in a bright colored walking suit, enters*] EEEEEEaaaaaa? What you talk? One bomniba, one beer. Same—same, huh? I no stand. What you want?

JONES: [*Pursuing her; both are playing yet both have real anger*] You gimme boucoup now?

YEN: Boucoup what? I don't know what you want. Crazy G.I., you dinky dow.

BRISBEY: PAVLO!

PAVLO: [*Who is and has been dressing into jungle fatigues*] I'm in the can, Brisbey, I'll be there in a minute.

ARDELL: He be there, Brisbey.

JONES: You got lips as fat as mine, you know that, ho?

YEN: *Toi cum biet!*

JONES: Shit, you don't know.

YEN: Shit. I can say, too. I know. Shit. [*And he is reaching for her*] No. We fini. Fini. You no talk me no more, you numba fuckin' ten. [*And she bounces away to sit on a crate and look at sheet music, as BRISBEY speaks to PAVLO*]

BRISBEY: Do you know, Pavlo? I saw the metal point of that mine sticking up from the ground just under my foot—I said, "That's a mine. I'm stepping on a mine." And my foot went right on down and I felt the pin sink and heard the first small . . . pop. I jumped . . . like a fool. And up she came right outa the ground. I hit at it with my hand as if to push it away, it came up so slow against my hand . . . Steel . . . bits . . . of dirt . . .

PAVLO: I'm off duty now, Brisbey. [*Having listened reluctantly*]

ARDELL: Ole Brisbey got himself hit by a Bouncin' Betty. That a kind of land mine, you step on it, she jump up to about right here [*Indicating his waist*] then she blow you in half. That why she got that name. Little yellow man dug a hole, put it in, hoped he'd come around. He an old man, damn near; got seventeen years in the army; no legs no more, no balls, one arm.

As a small Vietnamese boy comes almost running across stage to grab PAVLO's hand and guide him into the whorehouse, bar area, and leave him there.

BOY: HEY, G.I. SHOW YOU NUMBA ONE!

PAVLO: [*To JONES who is sitting there drinking a beer*] Hey, what's goin' on?

JONES: What's happenin', man?

MAMASAN: [*The elderly Vietnamese woman, returning*] Hello, hello! You come my house, I am glad. Do you want a beer? I have. Do you want a girl? I have. Number one girl. Number one. You want?

PAVLO: [*Pointing to MAMASAN*] You?

MAMASAN: No, no I am Mamasan. But I have many girl. You see, maybe you like. Maybe you want short-time, huh? Maybe you want long-time. I don't know, you tell me. All number one. [*JONES laughs*]

JONES: Man, don't you believe that ole lady, you just gotta get on and ride. Like her. [*Indicating YEN*] I been. And I'm restin' to go again; an' I don't think it any kinda numba one; but I been outa the world so *damn* long. I jus' close my eyes an' jive my own self—"That ain't no dead person," I say, "that ain't no dead Ho jus' 'cause she layin' so still. I saw her walk in here." I mean, man, they so screwed up over here. They got no nature. You understand me, Bro? They got no nature, these women. You—how long you been over here?

PAVLO: Not long; couple weeks.

JONES: You new then, huh?

PAVLO: Yeh.

JONES: You wanna go? [*Reaching out, toward YEN who is across the room, calling to her*] Hey, Ho! C'mon over here!

YEN: You talk me?

JONES: Yeh, baby, you, c'mon over here. You wanna go, man?

PAVLO: What about the V.D.? [*Taking a seat*]

JONES: [*Big laugh*] What about it?

YEN: [*Who, approaching with a beer, has heard*] I no have. I no sick. No. No, sweat, G.I. You want short-time me, no sweat.

JONES: Shit, Ho, you insides rotten. You Vietnamee, ain't you? Vietnamee same-same V.D.

YEN: No! No sick. [*As* JONES *grabs her, pulls her near, then sets her down on* PAVLO'S *lap*] What you do? No.

JONES: [*Holding her in place*] I'm jus' tryin' ta help you get some money, baby. I be you sportsman. Okay. [*She has stopped her struggle, is sitting nicely on* PAVLO'S *lap*] You just sit on down an' be nice on the man's lap, pretty soon, he ain't gonna be worried 'bout no V.D. If you jus' . . . sorta shift . . . [*He demonstrates*] every now and then. Okay . . . [*She is still now and he turns his attention to* PAVLO] Now, lemme tell you 'bout it, lemme tell you how it is. It be hot, man. I come from Georgia, and it get hot in Georgia, but it ain't ever been this kinda hot, am I lyin'? An' you gonna be here one year and that 365 days, so you gonna sweat, now do you think I'm lyin'?

PAVLO: [YEN *has been messing with him, rubbing under his shirt*] I ain't never sweat so much.

JONES: So that's what I'm sayin'. You gonna be here and you gonna sweat. And you gonna be here and you gonna get V.D.? You worried about sweatin'? Ahhhhh. You grinnin'. So I see I have made my meanin' clear. [YEN *has been rubbing* PAVLO'S *thigh*] How you feelin' now? She kinda nice, huh? She kinda soft and nice.

PAVLO: Where you work?

JONES: [*Laughs*] Don't you be askin' me where I work. That ain't what you wanna know. I gotta get you straight, gotta get outa here, buy myself some supplies. My ole mom all the time tellin me, "Don't you go near that PX. You get blown away for sure. Them V.C.'s gotta wanna get that PX."

PAVLO: [*To* YEN] What's your name?

YEN: Name me Yen.

PAVLO: Name me Pavlo. Pavlo.

YEN: Paaa-blo.

PAVLO: How much?

JONES: Lord, she says his name, he loves her.

YEN: You want short-time: I ask Mamasan. [*She is getting up, but* MAMASAN *has been watching*]

MAMASAN: [*Approaching*] OK. OK. Yen numba one. I am happy. 500 peas.

JONES: Two-hundred.

MAMASAN: She very beautiful.

JONES: Two-fifty.

MAMASAN: Four hundred; can do. No sweat.

JONES: Mamasan, who you think you jivin'?

MAMASAN: Yen boucoup boyfriend! She very love!

JONES: Two-fifty.

MAMASAN: [*To* PAVLO] Three hundred twenty. You, huh? Three hundred twenty.

JONES: Pavlo, give her 300, tell her things is tough at home, she don't know.

MAMASAN: [*As* PAVLO *hands her the money*] No, no, I talk you 320!

JONES: AND I TALK HIM 300, MAMASAN, 300.

Slight silence.

MAMASAN: [*Softly, whiney, to* PAVLO] G.I. You be nice, you give Mamasan 10 peas more. G.I.? Ten peas very easy you!

PAVLO: [*To* JONES] How much *is* 10 peas, man?

JONES: Eight cents, or about—

PAVLO: Eight cents! Eight cents. Over 8 goddamn stupid cents I'm still standin' here!

JONES: [*As* PAVLO *is giving more money to* MAMASAN] Man, no.

MAMASAN: [*Patting him on the back*] Okay, okay. You numba one—

YEN: [*Taking* PAVLO *by the hand toward the bed*] I show you.

JONES: [*As he leaves*] Oh man, deliver me from these green troops; they makin' everybody fat but me. [*The whistle blows loudly, and the troops come roaring into formation for instructions; they face the tower*]

SGT. TOWER: [*His voice booming*] GEN'LMEN! [*And his voice stops* PAVLO, *who comes to attention near the bed.* YEN *has jumped onto the bed. And as* SGT. TOWER *continues his speech, she comes around front of* PAVLO, *unbuttons his pants, unbuttons his shirt, takes his pants down, all this as* SGT. TOWER *gives instructions. He is holding up a rifle*] This an M-16 rifle, this the best you country got, now we got to make you good enough to have it. You got to have feelin' for it, like it a good woman to you, like it you arm, like it you rib. The command is *Right Shoulder . . . HARMS!* At the command, HARMS, raise and carry the rifle diagonally across the body, at the same time grasping it at the balance with the left hand, trigger guard in the hollow of the bone. Then carry the left hand, thumb and fingers extended to the small of the stock, and cut away smartly and everything about you, Trainee, is at the position of attention. RIGHT SHOULDER. HARMS!

THE MEN: [*Performing it*] 1—2—3—4. [PAVLO *also yells and performs the drill in pantomime*]

SGT. TOWER: You got to love this rifle, Gen'lmen, like it you pecker and you love to make love. You got to care about how it is and what can it do and what can it not do, what do it want and need. ORDER. HARMS!

THE MEN: 1—2—3—4.

SGT. TOWER: RIGHT SHOULDER. HARMS!

THE MEN: [PAVLO *with them, yelling also*] 1—2—3—4.

CORPORAL: FORWARD HARCH!

PAVLO *pulls up his trousers and marches.*

SGT. TOWER: AIN'T NO USE IN GOIN' HOME . . .

THE MEN: AIN'T NO USE IN GOIN' HOME . . .

PAVLO'S *marching is joyous.*

SGT. TOWER: JODY GOT YOUR GAL AND GONE . . .

THE MEN: JODY HUMPIN' ON AND ON . . .

Something of PAVLO'S *making love to* YEN *is in his marching.*

SGT. TOWER: AIN'T NO USE IN GOIN' BACK . . .

THE MEN: JODY GOT OUR CADILLAC.

CORPORAL: LORD HAVE MERCY, I'M SO BLUE.

THE MEN: IT TWO MORE WEEKS TILL I BE THROUGH.

CORPORAL: Count cadence, delayed cadence, count cadence—count. [*And the men, performing delayed cadence, exit.* PAVLO *counts with them, marching away beside the bed, around the bed, leaping upon the bed as the counting comes to its loud end, and* BRISBEY, *who has been on-stage in his bed, all this while, calls to* PAVLO]

BRISBEY: Pavlo!

PAVLO: Just a second, Brisbey!

BRISBEY: Pavlo!

PAVLO: [*Crosses toward* BRISBEY] Whatta you want, Brisbey?

BRISBEY: Pavlo, can I talk to you a little?

PAVLO: Sure.

BRISBEY: You're a medic, right?

PAVLO: Yeh.

BRISBEY: But you're not a conscientious objector, are you? So you got a rifle.

PAVLO: Sure.

During the following, PAVLO *busies himself with* BRISBEY'S *pulse and chart, straightening the bed, preparing the shot he must give* BRISBEY.

BRISBEY: I like the feel of 'em. I like to hold 'em.

PAVLO: I'm not gonna get my rifle for you, Brisbey.

BRISBEY: Just as a favor.

PAVLO: No.

BRISBEY: It's the only pleasure I got any more.

PAVLO: Lemme give you a hypo; you got a visitor; you can see him before you sleep.

BRISBEY: The egg that slept, that's what I am. You think I look like an egg with a head? [PAVLO *is preparing the needle; there is a figure off in the shadows*] Or else I'm a stump. Some guys, they get hit, they have a stump. I am a stump.

PAVLO: What about your visitor; you wanna see him?

The figure steps forward.

BRISBEY: Henry?

SGT. WALL: It's me, Brisbey, how you doin'? [*He is middle-aged, gray-haired, chunky*]

BRISBEY: Henry, Henry, who was the first man 'round the world, Henry? That's what I want to know. Where's the deepest pit in the ocean? You carryin'? What do you have? .45? You must have a blade. Magellan. Threw out a rope. I ever tell you that story? Gonna go sleepy-bye. Been trying to get young Pavlo Hummel to put me away, but he prefers to break needles on me. How's the unit? You tell 'em I'll be back. You tell 'em, soon as I'm well, I'll be back.

SGT. WALL: I'm off the line . . . now, Brisbey. No more boonies. I'm in Supply now.

BRISBEY: Supply? What . . . do you supply? [*Slight pause, as if bewildered, thinking, yet with bitterness, with irony*] If I promise to tell you the secret of life, Henry, will you slit my throat? You can do it while I'm sleeping.

PAVLO: Don't he just go on?

BRISBEY: Young Hummel here, tell him who you love. Dean Martin. Looks at ole Dino every chance he gets. And "Combat." Vic Murrow, man. Keeps thinkin' he's gonna see himself. Dino's cool, huh. Drunk all the time.

PAVLO: That's right.

BRISBEY: You fucking asshole. Henry. Listen. You ever think to yourself, "Oh, if only it wasn't Brisbey. I'd give anything. My own legs. Or one, anyway. Arms. Balls. Prick." Ever . . . Henry?

Silence.

SGT. WALL: No.

BRISBEY: Good. Don't. Because I have powers I never dreamed of and I'll hear you if you do, Henry, and I'll take them. I'll rip them off you.

Silence.

SGT. WALL: You'll be goin' home soon. I thought . . . we could plan to get together . . .

BRISBEY: Right. Start a softball team.

SGT. WALL: Jesus Christ, Brisbey, ain't you ever gonna change? Ain't you ever gonna be serious about no—

BRISBEY: I have changed, Motherfucker. You blind or somethin' askin' me if I changed. You get the fuck outa here, hear me? [WALL *is leaving, having left a pint of whiskey*] You take a tree, you cut off its limbs, whatta you got? You got a stump. A living feeling thinking stump.

PAVLO: You're not a tree, Brisbey.

BRISBEY: And what terrible cruelty is that? Do you know? There is responsibility. I want you to get me that rifle. To save you from the sin of cruelty, Pavlo. [As PAVLO *is moving with alcohol, cotton, to prepare the shot*] You are cruel, Pavlo . . . you and God. The both of you.

PAVLO: Lemme do this, man.

BRISBEY: [As PAVLO *gives the shot*] Do you know . . . if you were to get the rifle, Pavlo, I'd shoot you first. It's how you'll end up anyway. I'd save you time. Get you home quicker. I know you, boy.

PAVLO: Shut up, man. Relax . . .

BRISBEY: You've made me hate you.

PAVLO: I'm sorry. I didn't mean that to happen.

BRISBEY: No, no, you're not sorry. You're not. You're glad it's me, you're glad it's not you. God's always glad that way because it's never him, it's always somebody else. Except that once. The only time we was ever gonna get him, he tried to con us into thinkin' we oughta let him go. Make it somebody else again. But we got through all that shit he was talkin' and hung on and got him good—fucked him up good—nailed him up good . . . just once . . . for all the billion times he got us.

PAVLO: Brisbey, sometimes, I don't think you know what you're sayin'. [*Officer enters upstage left, carrying clip board*] Grennel.

GRENNEL: [*Appearing from the back, far upstage*] Yes, sir.

CAPTAIN: Go get me Hummel. He's down with Brisbey.

BRISBEY: I keep thinkin', Pavlo, 'bout this kid got his hand blown off, and he kept crawlin' round lookin' for his fingers. Couldn't go home without 'em, he said, he'd catch hell. No fingers. [PAVLO *shakes his head, mutters, "Brisbey, Brisbey"*] I keep think' about ole Magellan, sailin' round the world. Ever hear of him, Pavlo? So one day he wants to know how far under him to the bottom of the ocean. So he drops over all the rope he's got. 200 feet. It hangs down into a sea that must go down and down behind its end for miles

and tons of water. He's up there in the sun. He's got this little piece of rope dangling from his fingers. He thinks because all the rope he's got can't touch bottom, he's over the deepest part of the ocean. He doesn't know the real question. How far beyond all the rope you got is the bottom?

PAVLO: Brisbey, I'm gonna tell you somethin'. I tried to kill myself once. Honest to God. And it's no good. You understand me. I don't know what I was thinkin' about. I mean, you understand it was a long time ago and I'd never been laid yet or done hardly anything, but I have since and it's fantastic. I just about blew this whore's head off, it was fantastic, but I'd killed myself, it'd never a happened. You see what I'm saying, Brisbey? Somethin' fantastic might be commin' to you, you don't know about it.

GRENNEL: [*Entering*] Hummel. Man, the Captain wants to see you.

PAVLO: Captain Miller? Captain Miller! [*Leaving*]

BRISBEY: Pavlo!

GRENNEL: [As *he wheels* BRISBEY *off*] How you doin', Brisbey?

PAVLO: [*Rushing up to the* CAPTAIN, *standing with his clipboard*] Sir. Pfc Hummel reporting as ordered.

CAPTAIN: Good afternoon, Hummel.

PAVLO: Good afternoon, sir.

CAPTAIN: Are you smiling, Hummel?

PAVLO: Excuse me, sir.

CAPTAIN: Your ten-forty-nine says you're not happy at all; it says you want a transfer out of this unit because you're ashamed to serve with us. I was wondering how could you be ashamed and smiling simultaneously, Hummel.

PAVLO: I don't know, sir.

CAPTAIN: That's not a very good answer.

PAVLO: No, sir.

CAPTAIN: Don't you think what you're doing here is important? You helped out with poor Brisbey, didn't you?

PAVLO: Yes, sir.

CAPTAIN: That's my point, Hummel. There are people alive who would be dead if you hadn't done your job. Those invalids you care for, you feed them when they can't. You help them urinate, defecate; simple personal things they can't do for themselves but would die without. Have you asked any one of them if they think what you are doing is important or not, or if you should be ashamed?

Pavlo: Yes, sir . . . more or less. But . . . I . . . just . . . think I'd be better off in squad duty.

Distant firing and yelling are heard, to which neither the Captain *nor* Pavlo *respond. There is a quality of echo to the sounds and then there is a clattering and a young Negro Pfc appears at the opposite side of the stage in full combat gear except for his helmet which is missing. He has come a few steps onto the stage and he crouches.*

Soldier: Damn, baby, why that ole Sarge gotta pick on me?

Pavlo: I'm regular army, sir; I'm going to extend my tour.

Captain: You like it here, Hummel?

Soldier: Damn that ole Sarge. I run across that field I get shot sure as hell. [*He breathes*] Lemme count to five. Lemme do it on 5. [*As he tenses, preparing*]

Captain: How many days left in your tour, Hummel?

Soldier: Lemme do it like track and field.

Pavlo: I enlisted because I wanted to be a soldier, sir, and I'm not a soldier here. Four nights ago on perimeter guard, I tried to set up fields of fire with the other men in the bunker—do you know what I mean, sir? Designating who would be responsible for what sector of terrain in case of an attack? And they laughed at me; they just sat on the bunker and talked all night and they didn't stay low and they didn't hide their cigarettes when they smoked or anything.

Soldier: FIVE! [*And he runs, taking no more than two steps before a loud explosion hits and he goes down and bounces and rolls onto his back, slamming his fist into the ground in outrage*] DAMN IT! I KNEW IT! I KNEW IT! I KNEW IT!

Captain: You want the V.C. to come here?

Pavlo: I want to feel, sir, that I'm with a unit Victor Charlie considers valuable enough to want to get it. And I hope I don't have to kill anyone; and I hope I don't get killed.

Soldier: [*Still trying but unable to rise*] Medic? Medic? Man, where you at? C'mon out here to me! Crawl on out here to me.

Pavlo: But maybe you can't understand what I'm saying, sir, because you're an R.O.T.C. officer and not O.C.S., sir.

Captain: You mean I'm not regular army, Hummel.

Pavlo: An R.O.T.C. officer and an O.C.S. officer are not the same thing.

Captain: Is that so, Hummel?

Pavlo: I think so, sir.

Captain: You want to get killed, don't you, Hummel?

Pavlo: No, sir. No.

Captain: And they will kill you, Hummel, if they get the chance. Do you believe that? That you will die if shot, or hit with shrapnel, that your arm can disappear into shreds, or your leg vanish, do you believe that, Hummel—that you can and will, if hit hard enough, gag and vomit and die . . . be buried and rot, do you believe yourself capable of that . . . ?

Pavlo: Yes . . . sir. I . . . do . . .

Soldier: Nooooooo! [*Quick pause*] Ohhh, shit, somebody don't help me, Charlie gonna come in here, cut me up, man. He gonna do me.

Captain: All right, Hummel. [*Sitting down at the desk*]

Soldier: Oh, Lord, you get me outa here, I be good, man; I be good, no shit, Lord, I'm tellin' it.

Captain: All right . . . you're transferred. I'll fix it. [Captain *salutes, pivots, exits.* Pavlo *moves to change into combat gear in darkening light. He finds the gear in a footlocker in the bar area*]

Soldier: What's happenin'? I don't know what's happenin'! [*The light goes and the soldier is alone in the jungle, in a center of silver; it is night, there are sounds*] Hummel, c'mon. It's me, man, Parham; and I ain't jivin', mister. I been shot. I been truly shot. [*He pauses, breathing, and raises his head to look down at himself*] Ohhhh, look at me; ohhh, look at my poor stomach. Ohhhh, look at me, look at me. Oh, baby, stop it, stop bleedin', stop it, stop it; you my stomach, I'm talkin' to you, I'm tellin' you what to do, YOU STOP IT! [*His hands are pressing furiously down on his stomach. And he lies in silence for a moment: only his breathing*] SOMEBODY GET ME A DUSTOFF! Dustoff control, do you hear me? This here Pfc Jay Charles Johnson Parham. I am coordinates X-Ray Tango Foxtrot, Lima . . . Do you hear me? I hurtin, baby; hear me. Don't know what to do for myself; can't remember; don't know what it is gone wrong . . . requesting one med-evac chopper. I am one litter patient; gunshot wounds; stomach. Area secure, c'mon hear me; this ole nigger . . . he gonna die. [*And he freezes, sensing presences behind him and he twists his head to see. They stand up, one with a rifle pointing*]

1st v.c.: Hello, G.I.

Soldier: Oh, no. Oh, no. No.

1st. v.c.: Okay. Okay. [*Very sing-song*]

2nd v.c.: You number one.

Soldier: Get away from me! I talkin' to you, Charlie, you get away from me! You guys get away from me! MEDIC! ME—

*They say "okay, okay," "You numba one."
And at a nod from the V.C. with the weapon,
his partner has jumped forward into a sitting
position at the head of the soldier, one leg
pinning down each shoulder, the hands, grasping under the chin, cocking the head back,
stuffing a rag into the mouth. There are only
the sounds of the struggle as the other V.C.
crouches and holds a knife over the* SOLDIER'S
*eyes. He stares at it, his feet moving slowly
back and forth.*

1ST V.C.: Numba one, you can see, G.I.? Airplane
  me . . . Vietnam. Have many bomb. Can do
  boom-boom, you stand! [*He moves the knife
  up and down*] Same-same you, many friend
  me, fini. Where airplane now, G.I.? Where
  very gun? [*And he places the blade against*
  SOLDIER'S *chest and* SOLDIER, *behind his gag
  begins to howl and begins to flail his pinioned
  arms and beat his heels furiously upon the
  ground*] Okay, okay . . . ! An di dow! [*Until
  the knife goes in and they rise up to stand over
  him as he turns onto his side and pulls himself into a knot as if to protect himself, knees
  tight to his chest, arms over his head. They
  unbuckle his pistol belt and take his flack vest
  and his billfold from his pocket and are working at removing his shirt when they both
  straighten at a sound and then seize his fallen
  rifle and run to disappear.* PAVLO *appears,
  moving low, accompanied by a second American,* RYAN]

RYAN: Man, I'm tellin' you let's get outta here.

PAVLO: [*Pointing*] No, no. There [*He has a large
  belt hooked over his shoulder. He moves toward
  the body*] Just look. [RYAN *is following*] Hey,
  man . . . hey . . . Ohhhhh . . . look at him.

RYAN: It's Parham.

PAVLO: Man, he's all cut . . .

RYAN: Pavlo, let's get outta here . . . ! [*And he
  starts to move off*] What the hell's it matter?

PAVLO: I'll carry him.

RYAN: I ain't worried about who has to carry
  him, for Chrissake, I wanna get outta here.
  [*As* PAVLO *hands his rifle*] I'm gonna hustle
  over there to the side there. [*On the move*]

PAVLO: Nooooooo . . .

RYAN: Give you some cover.

  RYAN *is gone, leaving* PAVLO *with the body.
  His task is as follows: The circular belt is
  placed under the buttocks of the man, one
  length along his back, the other across his legs
  so that two loops are formed—one on either
  side of the man's hips. The carrier then lies
  down with his back to the dead man and he
  fits his arms through the two loops. He then
  grasps the man's left arm with his own right
  hand and rolls to his right so that the man*

*rolls with him and is on his back. He then rises
to one knee, keeping the body pressed tightly
to his own. As* PAVLO *begins this task,* ARDELL
is there, appearing as RYAN *departs.*

ARDELL: How many that make?

PAVLO: What's that?

ARDELL: Whatta you think, man? Dead bodies!

PAVLO: Who the hell's countin'?

ARDELL: Looooookeeeee. Gettin' ta *beeeee bad!*

PAVLO: This one's nothin'. When they been out
  here a couple days, man, that's when it's interesting—you go to pick 'em up they fall apart
  in you hands, man. They're mud; pink mud;
  like turnin' over a log; all maggots and ants.
  You see Ryan over there hidin' in the bushes.
  I ain't hidin' in no bushes. And Parham's glad
  about that. They're all glad. Nobody wants to
  think he's gonna be let lay out here.

ARDELL: Ain't you somethin'.

PAVLO: I'm diggin' it, man. Blowin' people away.
  Cuttin' 'em down. Got two this afternoon I
  saw and one I didn't even see—just heard him
  out there jabberin' away—[*And he makes a
  sound mimicking a Vietnamese speaking*] And
  I walked a good goddamn 20 rounds right over
  where it sounded like he was: he shut up his
  fucking face. It ain't no big things.

ARDELL: Like bringing down a deer . . . or dog.

PAVLO: Man, people's all I ever killed. Ohhhh, I
  feel you thinkin', "This poor boy don't know
  what he's doin'; don't know what he got into."
  But I do. I got a dead boy in my hands. In a
  jungle . . . the middle a the night. I got people
  maybe 10 feet away, hidin'—they're gonna
  maybe cut me down the minute I move. And
  I'm gonna . . . [*During all this he has struggled to load the body like a pack on his back.
  Now he is rising. Is on his knees*] . . . take this
  dead thing back and people are gonna look at
  me when I do it. They're gonna think I'm crazy
  and be glad I'm with 'em. I'm diggin'— [*The
  Vietcong comes streaking out from hiding
  place*] Ryan, Ryan, Ryan! [*The Vietcong,
  without stopping, plunges the knife into* PAV-
  LO'S *side and flees off.* PAVLO *falls, unable, because of the body on his back, to protect himself*] What happened?

ARDELL: The blood goin' out a hole in your guts,
  man, turn you water.

PAVLO: He hit me . . .

ARDELL: TURN YOU INTO WATER! Blood
  goin' in the brain make you think—in you
  heart make you move, in your prick makes you
  hard, makes you come. YOU LETTIN' IT
  DROP ALL OVER THE GROUND!

PAVLO: I won't . . . I'll . . . noooooo . . . [*Trying
  to free himself of the body*] Ryan . . .

ARDELL: The knowledge comin', baby. I'm talkin' about what your kidney know, not your fuckin' fool's head. I'm talkin' about your skin and what it sayin', thin as paper. We melt; we tear and rip apart. Membrane, baby. Cellophane. Ain't that some shit.

PAVLO: I'll lift my arm. [*He can't*]

ARDELL: AIN'T THAT SOME SHIT.

PAVLO: Nooooooo . . .

ARDELL: A bullet like this finger bigger than all your fuckin' life. Ain't this finger some shit.

PAVLO: RYAN.

ARDELL: I'm tellin' you.

PAVLO: Nooooo.

ARDELL: RYAN!

PAVLO: [*As* RYAN *comes running on with a second soldier*] RYAN!

ARDELL: Get on in here. [*They struggle to free* PAVLO *from the body. He flails, yelling in his panic as* SGT. TOWER *comes striding on and mounts the stairs to his tower*]

PAVLO: Ryan, we tear. We rip apart. Ryan, we tear.

SGT. TOWER: [*As they move* PAVLO *off*] You gonna see some funny shit, Gen'lmen. You gonna see livin' breathin' people disappear. Walkin' talkin' buddies. And you gonna wanna kill and say their name. When you been in so many fights and you come out, you a survivor. It what you are and do. You survive.

A body detail removes PARHAM'S *body from the stage.*

ARDELL: Thin and frail.

SGT. TOWER: Gen'lmen, can you hear me?

THE MEN: [*From off. Only* ARDELL *is there below the tower, listening*] Yes, Sergeant.

SGT. TOWER: I saw this rifle one time get blown right outa this boy's hands and him start wailin' and carryin' on right there how he ain't ever goin' back on no line, he'll die for sure he don't have that one rifle in all the world. You listenin' to me, gen'lmen. I'm gonna tell you now what you do when you lost and it black black night. The North Star show you true North accurate all year round. You gonna see the big dipper and two stars on the end called the pointer and they where the water would come on outa that dipper if it had water in it, and straight out from there is this big damn star and once you know North you ain't lost no more!

PAVLO *has appeared, rising up from the back of the set, walking slowly as in a dream, looking at* SGT. TOWER, *yelling in response to him.*

PAVLO: YES, SERGEANT! [*An explosion hits;* PAVLO, *yelling, goes down again*]

ARDELL: What you sayin'? YES SERGEANT. What you sayin'? [*Perhaps also having fallen with the explosion*]

PAVLO: YES, SERGEANT! [*Struggling to rise, as distantly, downstage, drifting,* YEN *enters and moves soundlessly to a place to kneel*]

ARDELL: Ask him what about that grenade come flyin'? How come if you so cool, if you such a fox, you don't know nothin' to do with no grenade but stand there—holdin' it—get your abdominal and groin area blown to shit.

PAVLO: I don't know what you're talking about!

ARDELL: You walkin' talkin' scar, what you think you made of?

PAVLO: I got my shit together.

ARDELL: How many times you gonna let 'em hit you?

PAVLO: As many times as they want.

ARDELL: That man up there a fool, Jim.

PAVLO: Shut up.

ARDELL: You ever seen any North Star in your life?

PAVLO: I seen a lot of people pointin'. [PAVLO *is on the move toward* YEN *now*]

ARDELL: They a bunch a fools pointin' at the air.

PAVLO: I want her, man. I need her. [*In some way touching her*]

ARDELL: Where you now, man? You with her? What you doin'?

PAVLO: I'm with her, man.

ARDELL: You . . . in . . . her . . .

PAVLO: . . . soon . . . [PAVLO *is taking her blouse off her*]

ARDELL: Why you there . . . ?

PAVLO: I dunno . . . jus wanna . . .

ARDELL: You jus gonna ride . . .

PAVLO: I jus' wanna . . .

ARDELL: There was one boy walkin' . . .

PAVLO: I know, don't talk no shit. [*Seizing her, embracing her*]

ARDELL: Walkin' . . . singin' . . . soft, some song to himself, thinkin' on mosquitoes and coke and bug spray until these bushes in front of him burst in fire and his fine young legs break in half like sticks . . .

PAVLO: Leave me alone! [*Rising, trying to get off his own trousers*]

ARDELL: At 7 his tonsils been cut out; at 12 there's appendicitis. Now he's 20 and hurtin' and screamin' at his legs, and then the gun come back. It on an fixed traversing arc to tear his yellin' fuckin' head right off.

PAVLO: Good; it's Tanner; it's Weber. It's Smith and not Pavlo. Minneti, not Pavlo. Klaus and Weber, YOU. Layin' there, lookin' at me. NOT Pavlo, not ever.

ARDELL: You get a knife wound in the ribs.

PAVLO: It misses my heart. I'm clean.

ARDELL: You get shrapnel all up and down your back.

PAVLO: It's like a dozen, 15 bee stings, all up and down my back.

ARDELL: And there's people tellin' you you can go home if you wanna. It's your second wound. They're sayin' you can go home when you been hit twice and you don't even check. You wanna go back out, you're thinkin', get you one more gook, get you one more slopehead, make him know the reason why.

PAVLO: [*Whirling, scooping up a rifle from the floor*] That's right. They're killin' everybody. They're fuckin' killin' everybody! [*The rifle is aimed at* ARDELL]

ARDELL: Like it's gonna make a difference in the world, man, what you do; and somethin' made bad's gonna be all right with this one more you're gonna kill. Poor ole Ryan get's dinged round about Tay Ninh, so two weeks later in Phu Loi you blow away this goddamn farmer . . .

FARMER: [*Waving in the distance*] Okay, G.I., okay. [*The farmer wears Vietnamese work clothes, conical hat*]

ARDELL: And think you're addin somethin' up.

PAVLO: I blew him to fuckin' smithereen's. He's there at 20 yards, wavin'.

FARMER: Okay, G.I., okay. [*He sways in the distance, appearing to approach*]

PAVLO: *DUNG LYE. DUNG LYE.* [*This is "Stop" in Vietnamese*]

ARDELL: You don't know he's got satchel charges.

PAVLO: I do.

ARDELL: You don't know what he's got under his clothes.

PAVLO: I do. He's got dynamite all under his clothes. And I shoot him. [*Gunshot, as* PAVLO, *having pushed* ARDELL *aside, fires. He will fire two more times: two more gunshots*] I fuckin' shoot him. He's under me. I'm screamin down at him. RYAN. RYAN. And he's lookin' up at me. His eyes squinted like he knows by my face what I'm sayin' matters to me so maybe it matters to him. And then, all of a sudden, see, he starts to holler and shout like he's crazy, and he's pointin' at his foot, so I shoot it. I shoot his foot and then he's screamin' and tossin' all over the ground,

so I shoot into his head. I shot his head. And I get hit again. I'm standin' there over him and I get fuckin' hit again. They keep fuckin' hittin' me. [*Explosion and* PAVLO *goes flying forward*] I don't know where I'm at. In my head . . . It's like I'm 12 . . . a kid Ardell, it's going to happen to meeeeeee? [*He is on the ground where he has been knocked, crawling*]

ARDELL: What do you want me to do?

PAVLO: I don't want to get hit anymore.

ARDELL: What do you want me to do?

PAVLO: Tell me.

ARDELL: He was shot . . . layin' down under you, what did you see?

PAVLO: What?

ARDELL: He was squirmin' down under you in that ditch, what did you see?

PAVLO: I saw the grass . . . his head. . . .

ARDELL: Noooooooooo.

PAVLO: Help me. I saw the grass, his head. . . .

ARDELL: Don't you ever hear?

PAVLO: I want out, Ardell, I want out.

ARDELL: When you gonna hear me?

PAVLO: What are you tryin' to tell me? I saw blood . . . bits of brain. . . .

ARDELL: Noooooooooooo!

PAVLO: The grass, the grass. . . .

ARDELL: When you shot into his head, you hit into your own head, fool!

PAVLO: What? Noooo.

ARDELL: IT WAS YOUR OWN.

PAVLO: NOOOOOOOOOO! [*As* ARDELL *has turned to leave*] Don't leave me you sonofabitch, I don't know what you're saying. [ARDELL *has stopped, back turned, far upstage*] JIVE MOTHERFUCKIN' BULLSHIT! [ARDELL *is leaving and gone*] and I stood . . . lookin' . . . down . . . at that black, black Hudson river . . . ; there was stars in it . . . I was 12 . . . I remember. . . . [*He is turning toward* YEN *who is kneeling, singing*] I went out toward them . . . diving . . . down . . . [*He is moving toward* YEN, *crawling*] They'd said there was no current, but I was twisted in all that water, fighting to get up . . . all my air burning out, couldn't get no more . . . [*He is moving toward* YEN] and I was going down, fighting to get down. I was all confused, you see, fighting to get down, thinking it was up. I hit sand. I pounded the bottom. I thought the bottom was the top. Black. No air. [*As the* OFFICER *enters, striding swiftly*]

OFFICER: YES! [*He carries a clipboard on which he writes as* PAVLO *runs up to him.* YEN, *though she remains kneeling, stops singing.* PAVLO *salutes*]

PAVLO: Sir! I've just been released from Ward 17, gunshot wound in my side and I've been ordered back to my unit, Second of the 16th, 1st Division, and I don't think I should have to go. This is the third time I been hit. I been hit in the ribs and leg and back . . . I think there should be more trainin' in duckin' and dodgin', sir. I been hit by a knife, shrapnel and bullets.

OFFICER: Could you get to the point?

PAVLO: That is the point. I want to know about this regulation sayin' you can go home after your second wounding?

OFFICER: Pardon, Hummel?

PAVLO: I been told there's this regulation you can go home after your second wound. When you been hit twice, you can go home.

OFFICER: Hummel, wouldn't you be home if you were eligible to be home?

PAVLO: I don't know, sir; but I wanted to stay the first two times, so I don't know and I was told I had the option the second time to go home or not, but I never checked and if I passed it by, sir, I'd like to go back and pick it up.

OFFICER: You didn't pass it by; there's no such regulation.

PAVLO: It was a sergeant who told me.

OFFICER: These orders are valid.

PAVLO: Could you check, sir?

OFFICER: I'm an expert on regulations, Hummel. These orders are valid. You've earned the Purple Heart. Now, go on back and do your job. [*Raising his hand to salute, pivots, exits as* PAVLO *is about to salute*]

ARDELL: No! No!

PAVLO: I do my job. [SGT. WALL *enters the bar, calling to* YEN *who moves quickly to the bar area where she pets him and then moves to prepare a drink for him*]

SGT. WALL: Come here, Pretty Piggy, we talk boucoup love; okay? Make plans go my home America.

YEN: Sow.

SGT. WALL: No lie.

SGT. TOWER: [*In a kind of brooding, mournful rage atop his tower as* PAVLO *stands before him, looking up*] Gen'lmen, lemme tell you what you do, the enemy got you, he all around you. You the prisoner. You listenin', gen'lmen?

ARDELL: [*All despairing sarcasm*] Yes, Sergeant.

SGT. TOWER: You got to watch out for the enemy. He gonna try to make you feel alone and you got no friends but him. He gonna make you mean and afraid; then he gonna be nice. We had a case with them North Koreans, this group a American P.O.W.s, one

of 'em was wounded so he cried all night. His buddies couldn't sleep. So, one night his buddies picked him up, I'm tellin' you, they carried him out the door into that North Korean winter, they set him down in the snow, they lef' him there, went on back inside. They couldn't hear him screamin' the wind was so loud. They got their sleep. You got to watch out for the enemy.

PAVLO *pivots away from* SGT. TOWER *and into the bar, where* MAMASAN *greets him.* YEN *is with* SGT. WALL *who wears civilian clothes: flowered, short-sleeved shirt and trousers.*

MAMASAN: Paaablooooo . . . how you-you. I give you beer, okay?

PAVLO: [*Unmoving, rigid*] Mamasan, Chow Ba.

SGT. WALL: . . . so who," he says, "was the first motherfucker to sail 'round the world? Not Vasco da Gama." I don't know what he's sayin'. "Who was the first motherfucker to measure the ocean?" [*He is loud and waving his arms*] I don't know! He wasn't even asking. MAMASAN! MAMASAN! ONE BEER! ONE BEER, ONE SAIGON TEA! [*And he reaches now to take* YEN'S *hand and tug her gently around to his side of the table, drawing her near to sit on his lap*] Come here; sit down. No sow. Fini sow. Beaucoup love Co Yen. Beaucoup love. [*His hand on her breast, as she nibbles his ear*]

YEN: I think you maybe papasan America. Have many babysan?

SGT. WALL: No . . . no.

YEN: I think you sow.

SGT. WALL: No lie, Yen. No wife America, no have babysan. Take you, okay?

PAVLO: Sarge! [*Slight pause as* SGT. WALL *looks up to* PAVLO] Listen; I don't have too much time, I got to go pretty soon; how long you gonna be talkin' shit to that poor girl? I mean, see, she's the whore I usually hit on, I'm a little anxious, I'd like to interrupt you, you gonna be at her all fuckin' night. I'll bring her back in half an hour.

SERGEANT: Sorry about that. Sorry—

PAVLO: I didn't ask you was you sorry?

SERGEANT: This little girl's my girl.

PAVLO: She's a whore, man—

SERGEANT: We got a deal, see, see; and when I'm here, she stays with me.

PAVLO: You got a deal, huh?

SERGEANT: You guessed it, Pfc.

PAVLO: Well, maybe you shoulda checked with me, you shoulda conferred with me maybe before you figured that deal was sound.

SERGEANT: You have been informed.

PAVLO: But you don't understand, Sarge, she's the only whore here who move me.

SERGEANT: My baby.

PAVLO: You rear-echelon asshole!

SERGEANT: [*Beginning to rise*] What's that?

PAVLO: Where you think you are, the goddamn PX? This the garbage dump, man, and you don't tell me nothin' down here let alone who I can hit on, who I can't hit on, you see what I'm sayin', to you, Fuckface.

YEN: Paablo . . . no, no . . .

PAVLO: You like this ole man.

YEN: [*Moving to face* PAVLO *and explain*] Can be nice, Paablo . . .

PAVLO: Old man. Papasan. Can do fuck-fuck maybe one time one week. Talk, talk. Talk. No can do boom-boom. PAPASAN. NUMBA FUCKIN' TEN!

YEN: Shut up. Paablo, I do him. Fini him. Do you. Okay. [*Angry at his stupidity*]

PAVLO: Shut up?

SERGEANT: You heard her.

PAVLO: Shut up? [*His hand twisting in her hair. She yells*] I don't know who you think this bitch is, Sarge, but I'm gonna fuck her whoever you think she is. I'm gonna take her in behind those curtains and I'm gonna fuck her right side up and then maybe I'm gonna turn her over, get her in her asshole, you understand me? You don't like it you best come in pull me off.

SERGEANT: [*Switchblade popping open in his hand*] I ain't gonna have to, PUNK.

PAVLO *kicks him squarely in the groin. The man yells, falls.*

PAVLO: The fuck you ain't. Hey . . . were you ready for that? Were you ready for that, ole man? Called crawlin', you gettin' [*Dragging the man along the ground, shoving him*] the hang of it, you ole man. Get up, get up. [*The man moans as* PAVLO *lifts him*] I want you gone, you mother, you understand. I don't wanna see you no more. You gonna disappear. You are gonna vanish. [*He flings the old man,* SGT. WALL, *away.* WALL *staggers, falls, and* PAVLO *picks the knife off the floor, goes for a beer as* SGT. TOWER *begins to speak and* WALL, *grenade in hand, circles*]

SGT. TOWER: This a grenade, Gen'lmen. M2 fragmentation, 5.5 ounces, composition B, time fuse, 13 feet a coiled wire inside it like the inside a my fist a animal and I open it and that ANIMAL LEAP OUT TO KILL YOU. Do you know a hunk a paper flyin' fast enough cut you in half like a knife, and when this baby hit, 15 meters in all directions, ONE

THOUSAND HUNKS A WIRE GOIN' FAST ENOUGH!

ARDELL *enters, joining* PAVLO *who celebrates.*

PAVLO: Did I do it to him, Ardell? The triple Hummel? Got to be big and bad. A little shuffle. Did I ever tell you? Thirteen months a my life ago.

YEN: Paaaabiloooo, boucoup love!

PAVLO: Thirteen months a my life ago. [SGT. WALL, *pulling pin on the grenade is there in the corner, beginning to move*] What she did my ole lady, she called Joanna a slut and I threw kitty litter, screamin'—cat shit— "happy birthday!" She called that sweet church-goin' girl a whore. To be seen by her now, up tight with this odd-lookin' whore, feelin' good and tall, ready to bed down. Feelin'—

The grenade lands, having been thrown by SGT. WALL *moving in a semi circle, and fleeing.* PAVLO *drops to his knees seizing the grenade, looking up in awe at* ARDELL. *The grenade is in* PAVLO'S *hands in his lap.* Oh Christ! *The explosion is there, now loud, it is a storm going into darkness and changing light. Silence. Body detail enters as* ARDELL, *looking at* PAVLO *lying there begins to speak. The body detail will wrap* PAVLO *in a poncho, put him on a stretcher, carry him to* ARDELL.

ARDELL: He don't die right off. Take him 4 days, 38 minutes. And he don't say nothin' to nobody in all that time. No words; he just kinda lay up and look and when he die, he bitin' on his lower lip, I don't know why. So they take him, they put him in a blue rubber bag, zip it up tight and haul him off to the morgue in the back of a quarter-ton where he get stuck naked into the refrigerator long with the other boys killed that day and the beer and cheese and tuna and stuff the guys who work at the morgue keep in the refrigerator except when it inspection time. The bag get washed, hung out to dry on a line out back a the morgue. [*Slight pause*] Then . . . lemme see, well, finally, he get shipped home and his mother cry a lot and his brother get so depressed he gotta go out and lay his chippie he so damn depressed about it all; and Joanna, she read his name in the paper, she let out this little gasp and say to her husband across the table, "Jesus, Jimmy, I used to go with that boy. Oh, damn that war, why can't we have peace? I think I'll call his mother." Ain't it some kinda world? [*Laughing*] Sooooooooo . . . that about it. That about all I got to say. Am I right, Pavlo? Did I tell you true? You got anything to say? Oh, man, I know you do, you say it out. [*Slight pause as* ARDELL *moves to uncover* PAVLO] Man, you don't say it out, I don't wanna know you. Be cool as you wanna be, Pavlo! Beee cool; leeme hear you . . . You tell it to me: what you think of the cause? What you think a gettin' your ass blown clean off a freedom's frontier? What you think a bein' R.A. regular army lifer?

PAVLO: [*Softly, with nearly embarrassed laughter*] Sheeeeee . . . ittttt . . . Oh, lord . . . oh . . .

ARDELL: Ain't it what happened to you? Lemme hear it.

PAVLO: . . . Shit!

ARDELL: And what you think a all the "folks back home," sayin' you a victim . . . you a animal . . . you a fool . . .

PAVLO: They shit!

ARDELL: Yeh, Baby; now I know you. It all shit.

PAVLO: It all shit!

ARDELL: You my man again.

PAVLO: It shit.

ARDELL: Lemme hear it! My *main* man.

PAVLO: SHIT!

ARDELL: Main motherfuckin' man.

PAVLO: OH, SHIT!

ARDELL: GO!

PAVLO: SHIT!

ARDELL: GET IT! GET IT!

PAVLO: SHHHHHHHHHIIIIIIIITTTTTTTT-ttttttt!

As the howl continues into silence four men enter carrying the aluminum box of a coffin, while two other men go across the back of the stage doing the drill, the marching and twirling rifles that were done at the end of the first act. They go now, however, in the opposite direction, and the coffin is placed beside PAVLO.

ARDELL: That right. How you feel? You feel all right? You gotta get that stuff outta you, man. You body know that and you body smart; you don't get that outta you, it back up on you, man, poison you. [*The four men are placing* PAVLO *in the coffin*]

PAVLO: But . . . I . . . am dead! [*The men turn and leave. There is no precision in anything they do. All is casual, daily work*]

ARDELL: Real soon; got wings as big as streets; got large large wings. Comin' on. [*Slight pause*] You want me to talk shit to you? Man, sure, we siftin' things over, ain't we. We in a bar, man, back home, we got good soft chairs, beer in our hands, go-go girls all around; one of 'em got her eye on you, 'nother one thinkin' little bit on me. You believe what I'm sayin'. You *home*, Pavlo. [*Pause*] Now . . . you c'mon and you be with me . . . We gonna do a little singin'. You be with me. Saw some stockin's . . . on the street . . . [*Silence*]

PAVLO: Saw some . . . stockin's . . . on . . . the street . . .

ARDELL: [*Slight pause*] . . . wished I was . . . between those . . . feet . . .

PAVLO: Wished I was between those feet! [*Slight pause*]

ARDELL *and* PAVLO: [*Together*] Once a week, I get to town, they see me comin', they jus' lay down . . .

ARDELL: Sergeant, sergeant, can't you see . . .

PAVLO: Sergeant, sergeant, can't you see . . .

ARDELL: All this misery's killin' . . . me . . .

PAVLO: All this misery's killin' . . . [ARDELL *lets the coffin close; it thuds*]

ARDELL:
Ain't no matter what you do . . .
Jody done it . . . all to you . . .
[*Slight pause:* ARDELL *is backing away*]
Lift your heads and lift 'em high . . .
[ARDELL *turns, begins to walk away*]
Pavlo Hummel . . . passin' by . . .
As ARDELL *disappears upstage, the coffin stands in real light.*

COUNTRY MUSIC

a comedy in two acts

Michael Smith

Country Music was first presented at Theatre Genesis, St. Mark's Church in-the-Bowery, New York City, on December 16, 1971, with the following cast:

BOPPO	*Dwight Marfield*
BABY	*Melissa Linden, John Albano*
PETEY	*Nevele Adams*
LOUISE	*Barbara Eda-Young*
MARCUS	*Charles Stanley*
ANDY	*Beeson Carroll*
BILLY HAWS	*Bill Hart*

Direction and lighting by the author. Setting by Jerry Marcel. Costumes by Joyce Marcel. Audio and light control by Burton Greenhouse. Production stage manager: Scott Burton.

The music called for in the text should be selected from the piano works of Beethoven. Sometimes, as indicated, it is performed live offstage left, sometimes recorded and played over speakers in the audience area.

The kitchen of an old farmhouse in New England. The setting is realistic and detailed. The room is plain and pleasant, comfortable and cluttered with living, a warm, friendly, personal place where people are at ease, where good work is done easily. A large table, six chairs. A big old wood-burning stove. Wood. Windows upstage and right, a view of meadows and woods. A rocking chair. Downstage right a door to the outside; outside it a small porch. A tree. The leaves have fallen. Upstage right an open doorway to the pantry. Up center a counter with a sink set into it and a pump. Upstage left a door leading to the rest of the house. The house has no electricity or running water. There is no light in the kitchen except what spills in the windows from outside and, later, candles. The "natural" light might fill the entire theatre. Bucolic scenery could be painted on all the walls. The sky would be blue and the audience seated on grass.

ACT I

Late November, early evening. The light outside is bright blue. A big ticking clock says 5:20. A very old man, BOPPO, is sitting in the rocking chair asleep. After the audience is settled he wakes with a start.

BOPPO: What? What? [*Louder*] What?

He listens. Silence. He looks around the darkening room. He closes his eyes and starts to drift off but wakes again. He sits as if paralyzed for a time, abstracted. Pulling himself together, he gets up creakily, goes to the stove, puts in some wood, adjusts the flue, looks in a large stewpot on the back of the stove. BABY (SUZY) comes to the outside door, all bundled up in warm clothing, and lets herself in. She is four or five years old.

There you are. I thought I was abandoned. Such a funny dream. Here, let's get out of those heavy things. [*Sits, takes off her outer clothes during the following*] Did I tell you my story about Gran'daddy Gopher? I'll tell it again. Far out in the middle of the oak wood Gran'daddy Gopher lived in a snug and cozy gopher hole all by his lonesome self. You know much about gophers? Troublesome critters. I had a pet gopher once bit off one of my toes. Some pet. My friend Pete Byers said I was in love with that gopher. Anyway. Gran'daddy warn't so much alone in the old times, had a big busy family, and even after his Missy split, the little ones kept on coming round. He had an outrageous cellar full of seeds and stuff. It warn't long though till the little ones got big and got off into

other things, and pretty soon he didn't see a soul for a month of Sundays. Heavy was the old rat's heart. Full were still his cellars but empty his days dragging down the dog-end of his . . . There. Too warm in here for all those heavy wraps. I'm ready to move to a tropic isle, lie around bare-ass all winter in the sun. I can feel the long nights closing in on us and hear the icy blast arattling at the door. Gotta get myself together, get myself away. You wanna come along? Where do we wanta go? Then one evening when he was waiting for the first snow to fall and getting really depressed he decided to put on a show. This was all in his head, you understand. He invited everyone he'd ever loved, his Missy, and the kids, and quite a few others too. Come on in. And all of them came to see his show, and this is what they saw.

PETEY, *a strikingly handsome, small-boned man in his middle 20s, comes in the up left door carrying a lighted match. He is dressed in an extravagantly decorative style—satins, velvets, beads, etc.*

PETEY: Is it always this dark?

BOPPO: Darker, much darker. This is daylight. It's only five o'clock.

In fact the blue light is gradually failing. The match goes out. PETEY strikes another and lights two candles on the table.

PETEY: What's happening? Where are the people?

BOPPO: Did I meet you up here before?

PETEY: No, I've never been here before.

BOPPO: How'd you like the bus?

PETEY: I'm still speeding.

BOPPO: It takes a couple of days. Or a couple of years. How long you staying?

PETEY: I don't know. Have you seen Marcus?

BOPPO: I been here since the Stone Age. You stoned, man?

PETEY: I guess I'm tired. It sure is cold.

BOPPO: Cheery up, I'll tell you a story.

PETEY: I don't think I could sit still for a story right now. I don't mean to be rude.

BOPPO: Go ahead, *be* rude. I'm not forming any opinions. I'm glad of somebody else to talk to. This is my favorite time, to feel the slowness of the light leaving, leaving. Also it's the evening of the year, and my life, and we're on our own, and we will or won't get through.

PETEY: Is that supposed to cheer me up?

BOPPO: Yes.

PETEY: What are you doing here? Are you somebody's friend?

BOPPO: I'm the gran'daddy of this baby. [PETEY *is getting it on with* BABY] And it's my house. Put in that pump myself summer of '87, '34, '51, first time the spring run dry since I was your age. I mean her age. How old are you?

PETEY: Four.

BOPPO: And such a good little girl. I didn't say that.

PETEY: Yes, isn't she. How old are you?

BOPPO: I'm not as old as I look. I'm not really old, I'm just run down.

PETEY: You need somebody to take care of you.

BOPPO: You take me on, boy? I got a swell set-up down in Florida, one a them superdeluxe new trailer things down beside the slough. I got a 50-horse hydroplane. And there's this place, we can dump the others out if you want, get some of your younger friends up here. What do you say?

PETEY: I'm already engaged.

BOPPO: And I won't last forever. No telling what I've got socked away in the building and loan. You'd be surprised the fun we could have.

PETEY: I wish *some*body would show me a good time.

BOPPO: Voilà!

LOUISE, *mother of* BABY, *pops out of the pantry, laughing. She is a beautiful woman about 30, matter-of-fact in her manner, warm in her ways. She holds a bunch of carrots. During the ensuing scene she washes and cuts up the carrots and various other vegetables, making a salad.*

LOUISE: Take it easy, Bops.

PETEY: There you are. I thought I was abandoned.

LOUISE: Don't be mean to Boppo. [*She is affectionate to the old man*] You have a good nap?

BOPPO: I had a sex dream.

LOUISE: Really? A wet dream?

BOPPO: No, I woke up.

LOUISE: Were you young?

BOPPO: You don't have to be young to be horny. [*Reaches out and pinches* PETEY, *who squeaks and jumps*] Your friend's a little jumpy.

LOUISE: Give him a chance, he just got here.

PETEY: Do you have any reds?

LOUISE: Is it that bad?

PETEY: Where's Marcus?

LOUISE: I don't know. Haven't you seen him?

PETEY: No, Andy picked me up in the jeep and then split off into the woods. Then I didn't see a soul till you popped out of the pantry.

LOUISE: I think they're up to something. I don't know what.

BOPPO: I can guess.

PETEY: Anybody can guess.

BOPPO: Then I won't.

PETEY: Who else is here?

LOUISE: Just us and the two of you.

BOPPO: The two of him?

LOUISE: He's with Marcus.

BOPPO: Really.

PETEY: Let's drop it.

LOUISE *drops a lettuce.* BOPPO *drops a log he was about to put into the stove.* PETEY *jumps to help them but gets confused about which first, so they both pick up their own things.*
Let's drop it.
Repeat.
Let's drop it. I think I'll go for a walk before it's dark.
Fetches and puts on a coat.
He didn't know I was coming.

He goes out the door, stands a moment on the porch looking at the dying light, then walks off. Conversation has continued within.

LOUISE: That city really freaks people over. This time he nearly citied out.

BOPPO: Is that it?

LOUISE: I don't know. He's in a heavy scene with Marcus. I suppose they're breaking up.

BOPPO: He seems like a nice boy.

LOUISE: Do you want to help with this dinner?

BOPPO: No. I'm keeping the stove going for the bread.

He rocks. It's nearly dark outside. More candles have been lit near BOPPO. *A piano is played in the other room, off left.* LOUISE *makes salad,* BABY *colors. After the music ends* MARCUS *comes in from the other room, puts on a coat, smiles at* LOUISE *and* BABY *and* BOPPO, *and goes outside without saying anything, shutting the door behind him.* MARCUS *is amiable looking, of indeterminate age, dresses in dark, soft clothes. On the porch he meets* ANDY, *father of* BABY, *just arriving carrying a flashlight that's not on.* ANDY *is virile and big, mid-30s, wears farm work clothes.*

MARCUS: [*Softly*] Far-out. Night.

They clasp each other affectionately. For a moment they appreciate the night. Then MARCUS *goes out right, and* ANDY *comes into the kitchen.*

ANDY: [*Entering*] Incredible night. Did you see it? I found a place to watch the sunset.

LOUISE: Really? Where?

ANDY: Up on the ridge in back of the meadow, down at the far end. Up in the woods. You go straight up through a lot of boulders and birches, and just over the top there's a little bowl, like a natural theatre. The trees are spaced out on the far side of it like a park, beech, black cherry, hemlock, spruce, goosefoot maples, oak, and silver birch, falling away down the mountain like a garden, and over them all the sunset. I'll take you up there tomorrow. [*He's taken off his jacket and work boots and is washing up at the sink.* ANDY'*s talk is slow*] Incredible. We could make it into a theatre, but it already is a theatre. Free show, continuous. I don't need a lot of psychology. No explanations—over and over is good enough for me. [*He goes to* BABY *and makes contact*]

BOPPO: I got a letter from Pete Byers. He's let himself get sick. His lungs are gone bad, says he can't get a good breath.

ANDY: Too many cigarettes. Too many fears. Couldn't let it all out; I remember him. He used to talk to me like I was a dog.

BOPPO: He was such a nice boy.

ANDY: So was I.

LOUISE: You still are.

ANDY: I'm not up to anything, I'm just digging the sunset. It may not amount to anything, but sometimes I get a feeling, when I'm alone, I don't know what it is, bursting from my chest, clean wild spirit of the light, we're mutually thrilled, me and it. I throw back my arms and take huge breaths of it, striding along through the leaping trees. Or else I'll sit there in it perfectly still, humming to the pure vibration. Nothing could be finer. [*He takes two freshly baked loaves of bread out of the oven*] When do we eat?

LOUISE: In a little while.

ANDY *takes one of the hot loaves to* BOPPO, *who smells it appreciatively.*

ANDY: Did you do the grapes?

LOUISE: No.

ANDY: Let's do them tonight after dinner. It's getting earlier every day; it keeps catching me by surprise. I never paid attention to it before this year. I don't know how I missed it. All the electric lights. Night doesn't make any difference. The moon is nothing but a decoration and a symbol. This is really weird. No moon to speak of for practically two weeks.

BOPPO: By then there's snow.

ANDY: Outasight. Meantime the nights get really long. I need a few indoor projects.

LOUISE: Is Marcus going to stay all winter?

ANDY: I hope so.

LOUISE: What about Petey?

ANDY: I don't know.

LOUISE: When does the action stop?

ANDY: I guess it doesn't. Anyway I like it. I don't mean their broken hearts, but maybe something else will happen.

LOUISE: I hope so.

ANDY: I thought you wanted isolation, rest, whole blank months.

LOUISE: No, I left that somewhere. I don't know what I want. I want to be on good terms with whatever actually happens.

BOPPO: It's all blank anyway.

LOUISE: It's all blank anyway.

The front door blows open in a howl of wind. ANDY *and* LOUISE *jump to shield the candle flames.* BOPPO *shuts the door. All of them, chilled, go shivering to the stove.* LOUISE *stirs the soup. They sing, softly, in close harmony.*

SONG:
> Bubble soup and crackle flames
> Warm our skins and save our brains
> All our hopes reside in thee
> Heat of sun in holy tree
>
> Vegetable garden gift
> Good God's light transliterate
> In thy praise our voices lift
> Miracle we celebrate
>
> Bubble soup and crackle flames
> Warm our skins and feed our brains
> All our hope abides in thee
> Sun incarnate in a tree

LOUISE: Do we have a gun?

ANDY: No.

BOPPO: I had a dandy gun, kept it on me fer years. I really got a kick outa that gun.

ANDY: I saw a fox up the mountain, trotted right by me fifty feet away, jaunty as can be.

BOPPO: I could hit a silver dollar at fifty yards but I sure never shot a living thing. I been a vegetarian for fifty years, saves me a mess of karma. We got plenty to be scared of, winter and comets and each other, no need to be scared of the animals. Doesn't do to cross a gopher, though. Pete Byers got plumb jealous of that gopher; it was pitiful. It was plain ridiculous if it didn't make him such a misery. I caught it too. Finally the gopher got uptight and bit off my toe. Poor paranoid Pete, I was sleeping with him every night but he thought I dug the rat.

ANDY *and* LOUISE *have begun embracing, lightly and casually at first, gradually getting more into it, aware only of each other, as* BOPPO *goes on talking, until finally they are simply standing there making love.* BOPPO *has continued:*

I was really mad about the toe. I had a complete set of stuff till then. I was 18 and just beginning to feel perfect, really feeling it come

together. It warn't an important toe, but
without it I felt off balance. That was the
beginning of the end. Next I'd lose a tooth,
and my hair would start falling out, and—
what else? God knows. Actually I held together pretty well. I don't know what become
of the gun. I think Pete hocked it, that's what
I thought, but I never asked him. He wouldn't
give me a straight answer, he'd think I was
fucking with our heads, or *I* would, or I
would be. Anyway it's gone. I don't care, I
don't want a gun, I outgrew it. I transcended
it. I am reclassified! [*Pause*] Ahem. [*No reaction*] Gone. [*To* BABY] Pretty soon he's
all alone again, they comes and goes and the
little ones grows. It won't stay the same. Soon
the food'll be on the table, he's feelin' stronger
at the thought. Fat gold loaves and plenty of
soup. Gran'daddy Gopher loved that hour
best when the day was gone but full night
hadn't taken hold.

LOUISE *and* ANDY, *without breaking their
concentration on each other, quietly leave the
room.*

I'm still trying to do the same old things, but
not in such a hurry. Only some of it will
happen anyway. Do you want to come sit on
your Gran'daddy's lap? [*She does or doesn't*]
The show goes on.

PETEY *and* MARCUS *have come to the porch
holding hands and, letting go, enter the
kitchen. They take off their coats, hang them
up, and go to the stove to get warm.*

MARCUS: Boppo, this is Petey.

BOPPO: We've met.

PETEY: He means in another life.

BOPPO: Imaginary.

PETEY: I understand you perfectly.

BOPPO: Why not?

PETEY: [*To* MARCUS] We're some kind of old
friends. Anything can happen; it's wonderful.
What have you been doing?

MARCUS: Growing hair.

PETEY: Slow work.

MARCUS: But steady.

PETEY: We think you're a little self-centered.

MARCUS: We who?

PETEY: Your grandfather and I.

BOPPO: I'm not *his* grandfather.

PETEY: I've been miserable without you. Sure I
have a good time, but a big piece is missing
out of the center. You're a big piece. I brought
you a bunch of mail; it's upstairs. I don't
know what to tell people you're doing.

MARCUS: What have you been doing?

PETEY: Oh, you know, you don't want to hear
the details—don't get me started. I got the

floor done and finished the new curtains; that
was a bunch of changes. Am I bringing in
too much madness?

MARCUS *smiles at him.*

I really like it here, I'm glad I came. All that's
in another world. Here it's just you and me—

BOPPO: —and me, and her—

PETEY: —and them. There I'm surrounded by
mirrors. Here I can look outside and actually
see something. [*Goes to window and looks
outside into the dark*] Real darkness. I don't
know what to talk about. I don't know what's
available. Blonds. Bad karma. Hundreds of
naked bodies blistering in the sun. Who has
the *next* next move? Who said anything about
forever? I'm not one of your admirers. I'd
like to get to know you. I can't stop talking.
I could appreciate a down. Doesn't anything
ever happen here?

MARCUS *has gone into the other room. Now
piano music abruptly begins.* PETEY *stops
talking. Gradually he begins to dance and
goes very far out into it. Music and dancing
ends.*

So what if that's behind me now. I must have
had enough—you never know it at the time.

MARCUS *comes in again.*

That's behind me now. That's behind me now.

MARCUS: Let's not talk.

PETEY *comes to him and embraces him.* MAR-
CUS, *abstracted at first, gradually gets in
touch with what he's doing. They kiss. It's
dark outside; the kitchen is lit only with
three or four candles. The night is still.* MAR-
CUS *and* PETEY *embrace with increasing passion. After a long time—*

BOPPO: This has kept him occupied through the
long November nights. What do you want
to talk about? [*Has an open conversation with
BABY if she will*] Let me go on with my story.
Everyone else is getting it on. Do you mind
me telling you all this? Other animals were
tramping and scampering around his house,
look outside you might see anything, or anyone, kind of one, thing of a kind, in any light.

BABY *leaves the room.*

Between the moons he stayed at home, there's
a time for dreams and visions, let the darkness take your soul, how else you know you
got one?

*Piano music, tape-recorded, fills the theatre.
He speaks over and with it, with long pauses.*
MARCUS *and* PETEY *quietly leave the room.
Strange things happen during the music.*

He still felt lonely sometimes, but what can
you expect? At least he wasn't alone. Sometimes he *was* alone, the others were asleep

or off someplace taking a break. Is there someone else in the house? Sometimes he woke in
the night in the wild arms of panic, body
aching and sluggish, and found he was on his
own, cut off, the others are all asleep, dreaming, and he's cut out of time, can't even count
on the modern conveniences, all he can hope
for is the dawn, salvation eventually rising
out of the desert. At least he's snug in his bed
in his snug little hole. But his terror is complete. Nothing happens but that.

*Music continues. Music ends. Pause. He
laughs.* MARCUS *and* LOUISE, *also laughing,
come in from the other room carrying candles.
They talk while laughing.*

LOUISE: . . . "an extended scene" . . .

MARCUS: . . . over the radio . . .

LOUISE: . . . between bars . . .

MARCUS: . . . of the moon! [*Whoops of laughter*]

BOPPO: [*Laughing*] . . . full of witches . . .

LOUISE: . . . which witness? . . .

BOPPO *and* MARCUS: . . . both of them . . . both
of them . . .

BOPPO *and* MARCUS *and* LOUISE: . . . all of
them! . . . [*General laughter.* LOUISE *goes
back to work on her salad.* MARCUS *starts
setting the table*]

MARCUS: I don't know what's so funny.

BOPPO: I've gotta go someplace.

MARCUS: I thought you loved it here.

BOPPO: Sure. I love it everywhere. I'd like a
little right now, but you're all tired. I'm a
little tired myself today. We'll see what
happens.

LOUISE: Let's just sit around and talk, for a
change. Nothing has to happen. Let's change
the subject.

MARCUS: I finished another picture.

LOUISE: Can I see it?

*He takes it from his pocket and gives it to
her. It's about the size of a large postage
stamp. She holds it near the light and examines it with a magnifying glass.*

Wow! That's fantastic! It's just like last night.
They're actually twinkling.

MARCUS: Very subtle effect.

LOUISE: I'll say! [*They laugh*] It's really beautiful.

BOPPO: Lemme see.

MARCUS: Pass it on.

LOUISE *hands picture and magnifying glass to*
BOPPO.

LOUISE: Did you ever make grape jelly?

MARCUS: No, not me myself. I've seen people
do it.

LOUISE: I know it's possible.

MARCUS: We should do something with the
grapes.

LOUISE: I want to know if you can use honey
in place of sugar.

MARCUS: Why not?

LOUISE: Maybe it won't jell.

BOPPO: Dynamite!

Stars all over the theatre.

MARCUS: We can try, and then if it doesn't,
we'll put in some glue.

LOUISE: First dinner.

BOPPO: It's like a postage stamp from Heaven.
With the glass it *is* Heaven.

LOUISE: Sure.

MARCUS: What are we drinking?

LOUISE: I got some cider.

He gets a gallon jug of it from pantry.

MARCUS: I'm getting hungry.

PETEY *comes in.*

BOPPO: [*Lecherously*] Me too. [*Pause*]

PETEY: Keep talking.

BOPPO: Pete Byers and I used to make cider.

LOUISE: Now Boppo.

BOPPO: The press is still there in the barn.

PETEY: Does it work?

BOPPO: Sure. And there's apples all over the
trees.

PETEY: We should make some.

LOUISE: Definitely.

BOPPO: There's a tree of Spies outside the back
door, and Cortlands around the barn, and
down below the meadow, those are Jonathans.

PETEY: Really, we should do it.

LOUISE: Really, I agree. We can't start until
daylight.

MARCUS *has poured himself a tiny bit of the
cider and now tastes it. They all watch him.
He looks around.*

MARCUS: Heaven.

BOPPO: Thank you.

PETEY: What do you mean?

BOPPO: We appreciate apples.

PETEY: I think I'll leave and come in again. Keep
talking. [*He leaves*]

BOPPO: Pete Byers and I used to . . .

PETEY: [*Sticking his head back in, interrupting*]
Not you.

MARCUS: It's about a princess who got locked in
a tower and waited for a prince to come and
he never did.

PETEY *nods and rewithdraws.*

I know what he likes.

LOUISE: I should hope so.

ANDY: [*Coming in; to* LOUISE] I'm getting hungry.

MARCUS: Me too.

LOUISE: Grapes after dinner, cider tomorrow.

ANDY: You have to do cider every day.

MARCUS: I'm willing.

ANDY: Once we get it going we can all take turns.

LOUISE: Let's get it going.

BOPPO: One, two, three, four.

The talk takes on a steady, not too fast rhythm. Dinner preparation accelerates.

MARCUS: Five.

ANDY: Who's the fifth?

LOUISE: I'm the mother.

MARCUS: I'm another.

ANDY: There's the baby. I'm its Dad.

MARCUS: I get six.

LOUISE: O.K., six.

MARCUS: Just in case.

ANDY: What do you mean, you're another?

LOUISE: He was joking.

BOPPO: Ho ho ho.

MARCUS: I was joking.

BOPPO: Ha ha ha.

LOUISE: You know exactly what he means.

ANDY: Are you angry?

BOPPO: What about?

LOUISE: What about?

MARCUS: What about?

LOUISE: Not at all, I like it too.

ANDY: Now where's Petey?

MARCUS: Let him be.

ANDY: Can't we go faster?

BOPPO: O.K. by me. [*Accelerando. Piu moto*]

MARCUS: Over the wind wood flung up a shadow . . .

LOUISE: [*In unison*] . . . flung up a shadow . . .

ANDY: That was the moment I thought I was free.

BOPPO: Saw by the clock it was time for my supper . . .

ANDY: . . . hungry hungry hungry (etc.) . . .

MARCUS: . . . taking it easy . . .

LOUISE: The salad's ready.

ANDY: Bread's on.

MARCUS: Soup's coming up.

LOUISE: Come to the table, Boppo, dinner's ready.

BOPPO: Yum yum.

MARCUS: Oh, I forgot napkins.

ANDY: I want chopsticks.

MARCUS: For soup?

ANDY: Sure.

LOUISE: [*Calling off*] Petey. Petey.

MARCUS: Do you want chopsticks, Louise?

LOUISE: Bring a whole handful.

ANDY: Did you remember to put in anti-freeze?

LOUISE: Yes, it's all done. Worry no more.

MARCUS: Is it that cold?

Freeze. They are seated at the table with dinner before them. In an abrupt silence PETEY *enters dressed and made up as a woman, beautiful and rather exotic in this setting. He takes his place at the table. No one takes any notice of his appearance. There is a long silence in which they all exchange ambiguous, possibly paranoid looks.*

PETEY: [*To Louise*] Honey, would you pass the honey?

BOPPO: No brown rice?

MARCUS: It's in the soup.

During this scene they eat dinner. The rhythm is very much slower and spacier.

PETEY: [*To* MARCUS] Do they like me?

ANDY: We don't have people here we don't like.

PETEY: Which we?

ANDY: Any of us.

LOUISE: Which they?

ANDY: The collective singular.

PETEY: What do you like about me?

BOPPO: You're inherently groovy.

Elaborate fake horse sounds off right: whinnying, hoof stamping, snorting, etc.

BILLY'S VOICE: Whoa, boy, settle down now, easy, big fella, take it easy, atta boy— (etc.)

BILLY HAWS *enters. He's the nearest neighbor, a young ruin given to broad hick manners and cruddy cowboy clothes. He is wildly drunk. He crashes into the room.*

ANDY: Howdy, Billy. Git yerself some grub.

BILLY: Gittin' lonely.

MARCUS: Evening, Billy.

BILLY: [*Peering at* PETEY] Who's that? Never mind. Take it easy, fella. Oops. [*He almost goes out the door. He gets it shut and sits at the table. To* PETEY] Evenin', ma'am. [*To* ANDY] Who's the tootsie roll? [*To* PETEY] Excuse me. [*Reaches across and tears off a hunk of bread*] No meat?

LOUISE: You know we don't eat meat.

BILLY: I want some meat.

PETEY: We don't like meat.

BILLY: I'd like some meat.

ANDY: Which we?

LOUISE: The house.

BOPPO: I'm getting crazy.

ANDY: For meat?

BOPPO: Something, I don't know, excitement.

PETEY: Please.

BOPPO: Yes, meat.

LOUISE: That's nonsense.

ANDY: What kind?

PETEY: Raw, bloody, warm, familiar, friendly, agreeable, free, fantastic . . .

BOPPO: [*With* PETEY] . . . yeah, yeah (etc.) . . .

BILLY: . . . fuckers . . .

MARCUS: Whose Boppo is he?

BOPPO: I'm the fairy grandfather. [*Spotlight on him. Others applaud. Spotlight out*] Why not say it?

ANDY: You all alone down there, Billy?

BILLY: All alone.

LOUISE: Are you warm enough?

BILLY: I'm hot. [*Pulls open his shirt*] Can't get any air in here. Excuse me, ma'am.

PETEY: Hey, take it easy.

MARCUS: Miss, Miss. Pass the butter. [PETEY *does*] Tell us a little about yourself.

PETEY: I'm an entertainer.

BOPPO: [*Sarcastic*] I know, Marleen Dietrich.

PETEY: I get off work in an hour.

BILLY: Just me and the chickens.

LOUISE: Pass the butter.

ANDY: You get any eggs?

BILLY: Yesterday I got one.

ANDY: That's enough.

BILLY: I guess. I'm gittin' a little spaced out.

ANDY: You gonna stick it through the winter?

BILLY: I guess. I stuck it this long. I'm O.K., I guess.

BOPPO: What about you folks?

BILLY: What about you folks?

An awkward pause.

LOUISE: What?

ANDY: Far as I know.

LOUISE: Certainly.

MARCUS: What?

PETEY: I think it's weird.

MARCUS: I love it.

PETEY: I hate it.

MARCUS: I know what you mean.

BILLY: I got no place else to go.

MARCUS: And you can't stay here.

LOUISE: Who?

ANDY: Anybody else comin' up to visit you?

BILLY: Naw, winter's another number, you'll see.

ANDY: I don't know if I want to.

BILLY: So what?

PETEY: [*To* MARCUS] You have any idea how long you're staying?

LOUISE: [*To* ANDY] What's this all about?

ANDY: We'll talk about it later.

LOUISE: We can talk about it now. There isn't any secret.

ANDY: I just don't know what I think.

LOUISE: Well, do you want to move back to the city?

ANDY: Let's talk about it later.

BOPPO: Sometimes Gran'daddy'd catch himself dozing off.

LOUISE: It makes me feel very funny.

ANDY: Me too. Let's change the subject.

BOPPO: Did I miss something?

MARCUS: [*To* PETEY] Well, partly it depends on you. Everything depends on everything else. I don't know what I'm doing. What's happening?

BILLY: [*Shivers*] Brrr!

LOUISE: You said it!

ANDY *puts more wood in the stove, looks out the window.*

BOPPO: Could be snow in that wind.

ANDY: It's clear as crystal. I like the cold.

LOUISE: I wouldn't want to sleep alone.

ANDY: Me neither. [*Goes and stands behind her chair and touches her*]

BILLY: The soup's great.

MARCUS: This is the best restaurant in town.

BILLY: I could stand some meat.

LOUISE: Don't start that again.

BILLY: Maybe I better go.

LOUISE: No, Billy, I didn't mean to sound so sharp. I just get tired of that meat conversation.

PETEY: We don't even like to talk about it.

LOUISE: It's really good you're here.

ANDY: You could come for dinner every night. Why don't you start doing that?

BILLY: I don't know.

LOUISE: No sense in being lonely.

ANDY: Nights coming on so early, cold coming in—

PETEY: You're cute.

MARCUS: I'll walk you back—

LOUISE: We'd dig it.

BILLY: [*Getting up*] Excuse me, ma'am. Nice of you folks to have me over. Thanks for the grub. [*Leaves. On the porch outside he takes a deep breath, stretches, smiles, and saunters off. Meanwhile:*]

MARCUS: By the time she'd been in the tower fifteen or twenty years, she hardly ever felt she was trapped any more. Then one day while she was dusting the front hall she discovered by accident that the door wasn't actually locked. But that eliminates the story.

PETEY: I don't know how I feel about it.

ANDY: That's not very much help, is it?

LOUISE: Let it go.

ANDY: No time for anything, here or anywhere.

MARCUS: [*Senselessly hysterical*] Time!? Time!?

LOUISE: But everything gets done.

MARCUS: [*Blowing the character*] Don't talk to me about time!

LOUISE: I don't need the plans.

MARCUS *is glaring about like a maniac.*

ANDY: Hey, take it easy!

Abrupt silence. ANDY *reaches out to touch* MARCUS, *who cringes.*

MARCUS: [*Through clenched teeth*] Keep talking.

PETEY: I was riding my bicycle down Second Avenue in heavy traffic and suddenly some dude on the sidewalk says to me, "Wow! I haven't seen you in fifteen years!" He went right on, and by the time I could stop—

LOUISE: You both must have looked completely different.

PETEY: I wouldn't have recognized myself.

ANDY: What were you dressed as?

PETEY: Oh, just something I found in the closet.

MARCUS *throws himself over backward in his chair.* ANDY *goes to him and tips the chair upright, holding* MARCUS *into it.* MARCUS *moans and grunts and thrashes around. The conversation has continued without a pause.*

LOUISE: That's a charming story.

BOPPO: What more can you ask?

LOUISE: And quite becoming.

PETEY: Yes, I thought so.

BOPPO: Lucky you can appreciate it.

LOUISE: It's a lucky moment in a lucky life. But what's happening now?

BOPPO: Shh. Watch.

PETEY: Then what did he say?

ANDY: Something about right of way. I knew it would work itself out.

PETEY: What, for the baby?

ANDY: Sure.

PETEY: I really can't think ahead at all.

LOUISE: Is everyone being very quiet?

ANDY: That's what I mean. I mean there's no need to, and you do.

LOUISE: Or am I going deaf?

She beats on the stove a few times with the poker. PETEY *has fetched from the pantry a small bottle of soda. He covers* MARCUS'S *chest and shoulders with a dishtowel. First shaking the bottle, he now pops it open right in* MARCUS'S *face, spraying him.* MARCUS *is immediately himself again and resumes eating.*

PETEY: [*To* ANDY] Why don't you come up and see me sometime?

ANDY: What?

PETEY: You're such a big beautiful man. You really turn me on.

LOUISE: I guess I'm O.K.

BOPPO: I wouldn't do a thing like that. But then I'm not doing it.

ANDY: Neither am I. [*Resumes his seat*] Is there anything for dessert?

PETEY: Fruit. [PETEY *and* LOUISE *clear the table*]

BOPPO: Sometimes he'd get so frustrated he could scream.

LOUISE: You just need something to do.

The conversation gets very relaxed and slow.

PETEY: Do you have an iron?

LOUISE: You have to heat it up on the stove.

PETEY: Is it a lot of trouble?

BOPPO: It's the latest thing.

ANDY: Do you hear people talking somewhere else in the house?

LOUISE: Don't be silly.

ANDY: Where's the baby?

BOPPO: [*Calling off*] Suzy! Suzy!

BABY *enters now costumed as a small bear and goes out the front door and into the woods. Conversation has continued.*

PETEY: Do you have a tent? Maybe I'll sleep outside in a tent.

LOUISE: We have everything you need. She's all right. Who wants coffee?

PETEY: I really love being here.

MARCUS: Yes, it's exciting at first. Such a change.

PETEY: I feel right at home.

LOUISE: Are you being sarcastic?

PETEY: No.

LOUISE: Do you want coffee?

PETEY: Yes, please.

LOUISE: Anybody else?

MARCUS: I'd like some tea.

LOUISE: What kind?

MARCUS: Oops.

ANDY: Sassafras.

BOPPO: Lapsang soochong.

PETEY: Can I have tea instead of coffee?

LOUISE: I guess no one wants coffee. [*She makes tea in a teapot*]

PETEY: I'm never going back to the city. I hope I never set foot there again.

BOPPO: I'm with you, beautiful.

LOUISE: What were we talking about?

ANDY: I think Marcus has stopped talking.

PETEY: [*Snide*] His lips are sealed. [MARCUS *makes a face at* PETEY, *who moves closer to him. They hold hands*]

LOUISE: Well, it's very relaxing. I'm about ready for bed.

PETEY: Isn't there anything to do?

ANDY: The grapes.

LOUISE: Oh, O.K., let me drink my tea.

ANDY: It's not going to wake you up.

BOPPO: We can put speed in the jelly.

LOUISE: Anyway, I'm not convinced we should do it tonight. Night is the time for sleep. We can do grapes in the morning and cider in the afternoon and sleep at night. That leaves plenty of time for love. A perfect life.

ANDY: Me too.

PETEY: Me too.

BOPPO: Me too.

LOUISE: Then it's settled.

ANDY: What kind of a day was that?

LOUISE: Perfect.

PETEY: I'm exhausted.

ANDY: You'll really sleep tonight.

PETEY: I always sleep.

ANDY: But this is different.

PETEY: I hope so. I was getting too crazy. I couldn't take much more of it.

ANDY: Well, I hope you stay forever. That's out front.

PETEY: That's really good.

LOUISE: I do too. Don't get confused about that.

PETEY: I sometimes do get confused. Sometimes I think it's the whole point. But that's ridiculous.

BOPPO: What?

LOUISE: Nothing, Boppo.

BOPPO: Don't think you're putting anything over on me.

LOUISE: I don't know what you're talking about.

PETEY: I do.

BOPPO: You were prettier before. But so was I.

PETEY: Isn't it awfully early to go to bed?

BOPPO: Let's just take a break and see what happens.

ANDY: Anybody can do anything.

MARCUS *has risen, picks up* PETEY *in his arms.* PETEY *holds a candle.* MARCUS *carries him out the up left door.*

PETEY: This is wonderful!

They are gone.

BOPPO: [*To* ANDY] Yes, that's a nice thing to pretend.

During this they extinguish all lights except two candles on the table, clean up dinner dishes, etc.

LOUISE: I feel this sequence drawing quickly to a close. I still don't know what you're up to.

ANDY: We'll talk about it later.

LOUISE: I wish you'd talk about it now.

ANDY: It isn't clear yet in my mind, it still keeps changing.

LOUISE: Is something about to happen?

ANDY: Yes, well, I wouldn't be surprised. Maybe you're making it happen. I haven't said a word.

LOUISE: Who brought in these vibes?

ANDY: Petey, they flew in along with him, or whoever that woman is, or they were here, I don't know.

LOUISE: Do you think this house is haunted?

ANDY: Sure. It sure isn't empty.

LOUISE: Are you taking me with you?

ANDY: Do you want to come?

LOUISE: I want to go wherever you go. Forever.

ANDY: I don't want to go anyplace without you, except sometimes walks in the afternoon. And sometimes dreams. Good night, Boppo. [*Exits with candle*]

LOUISE: Wait for me. Good night, Boppo, have a good night. [*She comes over and kisses him and follows* ANDY *out.* BOPPO *rises and comes and looks out the door at the audience*]

BOPPO: This is the intermission. [*He goes upstairs, taking the last candle. The house is dark. The audience is in starlight*]

ACT II

Early morning in late spring. During the interval dawn has come, the sun has risen; and during this act the audience area is brightly but not harshly lit—somewhat more brightly than the stage. The clock has continued to run and now reads about 7. It's a beautiful day. Birds are singing. There's a bush of flowers beside the front porch. Sunlight is streaming in the windows, and the kitchen looks cheery and inviting. In fact the whole theatre is delightful.

As the audience is returning from intermission, piano music is heard from off left. After the audience is in, the music ends and MARCUS *comes in wearing a long, luxurious robe in an archaic style. He is now much older and has become an elegant, faded, slightly ghostly eccentric. He almost never speaks. The actor must play against this image so that* MARCUS's *presence is much more forthright and vigorous than his appearance would suggest, and a quite different person is sometimes seen looking out from his eyes.*

He opens the door and goes out on the porch into the sunlight. He yawns and stretches and looks about. BABY, *now a full-grown bear, comes in from off right and rubs against* MARCUS's *leg. He absently scratches her head. She playfully starts nuzzling him in the crotch. He starts to pull away, then relaxes and enjoys it.*

BOPPO *comes in up left looking just the same as he did in Act 1. He goes to the stove and pokes it up.* BABY *lumbers in the door, followed by* MARCUS, *leaving the door open. Sunlight streams in.*

BOPPO: Morning, Baby.

BABY: [*Gruff*] What's happening? [*Lies down in a corner*]

BOPPO: Morning, Marcus. Morning, Boppo, I hope you slept well. Why, thank you, Marcus, I certainly did; and how's about yourself now? Not so hot, I keep hearing voices, makes me a mite jittery. You young folks gotta settle down, quit fuckin' around with your heads. I been thinking about some changes. Don't pay, I tell you, no sir! How 'bout some coffee? [MARCUS *sits in the rocking chair and rocks, smiling to himself. To* BABY] Did I tell you the story about Gran'daddy Gopher? One of my favorites. [*To* MARCUS] I bet you got a mess of stories to tell if you ever get it together. One thing leads to another, just let it all hang out. Remember the old-time funky talk? [*Brings him a cup of coffee*] I don't know what went wrong, we just blew it. He's over in Hawaii now, got a place up on the side of a volcano, Mauna Loa, or one of them. I got a postcard a few years back. Nothing was happening. This is one of the slow times. You have to expect it after all that beauty and misery.

MARCUS: Sounds like a Beethoven symphony.

BOPPO: Well, I miss it. That's a lovely way to wake up, you playin' on the piano. I really love it when you play. Pete Byers could only play *Für Elise*. Lovely, but too short.

Silence awhile while he does things and MARCUS *rocks.* LOUISE *comes in, yawning. She is much older and has come to look like a low comedienne, perhaps Imogene Coca; but she feels herself to be the same character as she was in Act 1. This would be a good time to mention that none of these character changes are foreshadowed in what goes before. She laughs, then stops herself.*

Morning, Louise.

LOUISE: Morning, Boppo. Morning, Marcus.

BOPPO: Morning, Louise.

She laughs, then stops herself and goes out on the porch.

Coffee's on.

LOUISE: [*On the porch*] It's a beautiful day. So clear. There's not a cloud in the sky. You can see the depth of the air, so clear and deep it's blue, but the blue itself is nowhere, only in the deep, clear distances. It's the same blue as the sound of bees. And the same yellow. It's all the same!

BOPPO: Anybody going into town?

LOUISE: [*Coming back in*] What do you mean, town? Why do you keep asking that?

BOPPO: Touchy.

LOUISE: Maybe Andy. I don't know what he's up to.

BOPPO: It's all in your mind. Don't be afraid of it.

LOUISE: I'm so nervous I'm grinding my teeth.

BOPPO: You young folks better take it easy. I don't know how long you can take it.

LOUISE: Oh, Boppo!

BOPPO: [*Laughing*] Reminds me of the time Pete and I— Never mind, but it was really funny. Whenever I think of it I laugh out loud.

LOUISE: Honey, it's all uncomfortable. I'm not saying anything.

BOPPO: It's only a matter of money.

LOUISE: We're not dreaming, we're really ready to spend.

BOPPO: Every blue angel is a blue devil in disguise.

LOUISE: I don't care. I don't mind.

BABY: Grrr.

BOPPO: There's more than enough.

LOUISE: Isn't that generous? I mean it. What am I, out here all by myself? Take it easy, Louise. What do you want, what do you really want?

BOPPO: A little fun. Ha.

PETEY *comes in, now a plain, even dowdy woman in her forties, with the effect of no makeup, in faded shirt and pants, her hair in a bun. Looks depressed.*

How'd you sleep, honey?

PETEY: I lay awake all night with out-of-focus sex fantasies. I couldn't get away from . . . I couldn't get together with . . .

BOPPO: Tell your dreams before breakfast, they won't come true.

PETEY: They don't come true anyway.

BOPPO: Get out.

PETEY *leaves.*

LOUISE: It's an old Sufi awakening.

BOPPO: All the sexiest people are turning out to be incompetents.

LOUISE: But they dress beautifully. We're surrounded by incredible personalities.

BOPPO: If it doesn't work, don't do it. Remember that as you course through life.

LOUISE: But nothing works.

BOPPO: What are we, vamping?

LOUISE: Are you talking to me, or are you talking to yourself?

BOPPO: Myself. This is when the old gopher got spaced out, in the morning. You with me, Baby? The show is still going on.

PETEY *again, same but not depressed, just himself in depressing makeup. He carries clothing and a makeup case. He sits at the table, center, facing the audience. During what follows he changes his makeup and costume and becomes not pasty glamorous but breathtakingly beautiful. Talk continues.*

LOUISE: I can't keep track of what's going on.

BOPPO: You're over by the pump, I'm watching the pot.

LOUISE: It's flattering enough, but I'd like it if it was also art.

PETEY: Stop talking.

After a very long pause in which nothing happens but PETEY *putting on makeup,* MARCUS *goes into the other room and stumbles through* Für Elise. *During the music* ANDY *comes in and very slowly has the following short conversation with* LOUISE. *He is much older than in* Act 1.

ANDY: We'd better split. How soon can you get everything together?

LOUISE: It's all done.

ANDY: Are you cool?

LOUISE: Sure.

ANDY: I hate to go.

LOUISE: Me too.

ANDY: Last night it was so pleasant, I could feel it coming, summer, singing, and we have to go.

LOUISE: I know. Look outside.

ANDY *slowly goes out on the porch and sits in the sunlight drinking something hot from a mug. Music ends.* MARCUS *comes in and sits.*

PETEY: It's time for a big monologue and I just don't think I can get into it. My whole body is tingling. I feel a horrible emptiness, a wonderful wild longing feeling, here in my chest. [*To* MARCUS] Can I touch you?

MARCUS: Of course.

PETEY: I'm almost ready. Then I'll wait a little longer. Anticipation—I feel it in my cock, decoration, not perversion. It's an old, uninteresting concept, surrounding yourself with pretty things. I want everyone wide awake, then we'll drowse off together. I'll wear anybody's jewels. But I have to bring me own, otherwise betimes I end up alone—I mean plain. The same with love. Trust your affinities. Consider, sisters, the people's many ideals of beauty. We're only trying to be beautiful. And it's skin deep *too.* I sound like a flapper. It isn't easy to have confidence in anything if you live in the real world.

LOUISE: There's fresh coffee, if you want it.

PETEY: I'd love some cocaine.

BOPPO: Help yourself.

PETEY *goes into the pantry and is heard snorting.*

LOUISE: What *is* this scene?

BOPPO: [*To* PETEY, *off*] You should always taste it first, it might be poison.

PETEY: [*Off*] That's a weird thing to say. [*Snorts*] How can you tell?

BOPPO: You can tell.

PETEY: [*Coming in*] I'm a foolishly trusting person. [*Sniffs*]

BOPPO: The bitter that kills the critter.

PETEY: [*Sits and resumes transformation. Pause*] I'm totally anodized. I don't know if I like it.

BOPPO: We all know cocaine isn't worth it.

MARCUS *gets up and goes into the other room.*

PETEY: My love.

LOUISE: I'm not going to be hurried, I'm nervous enough as it is. [*Laughs, stops herself*]

BOPPO: As the sun rose higher in the sky he felt the energy coming down into his cozy hole. The energy fell down out of the sky onto the ground and rolled and flowed into the low places and down the softly curving tunnel into his snug and cozy hole and filled it up until he nearly drowned in it.

ANDY: [*From porch*] Louise. [*She laughs, stops herself, goes out on the porch*]

BOPPO: He felt it rising wild around him and in him and felt the panic flashing. The first time they set off an atom bomb some of them thought there would be a chain reaction, remember the chain reaction, atom to atom it all becomes energy. We would say that the earth had exploded. We had transformed ourself into a very sun. We had become God. I've always had a taste for drama. But it didn't work.

LOUISE: [*Looking at the landscape*] It all seems to refer to something else, but it's difficult to figure out what that something else is.

ANDY: That's enough; I don't want to get overstimulated.

LOUISE: I thought it was a place to rest, but it's a place with a very high concentration of good vibes, a place to get yourself together if you're already together.

ANDY: You just have to be lucky in your friends and stars.

LOUISE: [*Laughs, stops herself; pause; then she laughs freely. Then*] I guess I like head trips.

BOPPO: We're all human here.

ANDY: We're all human.

Piano music, recorded. MARCUS *enters, now recognizable as Beethoven.* PETEY *has completed his transfiguration and rises, beautiful, from the table. The music is a dance.*

PETEY: Don't tease her, Petya. You can see she's unhappy enough without that.

MARCUS: She's much too zealous, always meddling in other people's affairs. All summer long she's given Anya and me no peace—afraid a romance might develop. What business is it of hers? Besides, I've given no occasion for it; I am far removed from such banality. We are above love!

PETEY: And I suppose I am beneath love. [*In great agitation*] Why isn't Leonid here? If only I knew whether the estate had been sold or not! The disaster seems to me so incredible that I don't even know what to think, I'm lost. . . . I could scream at this very instant . . . I could do something foolish. Save me, Petya. Talk to me, say something. . . .

MARCUS: Whether or not the estate is sold today —does it really matter? That's all done with long ago; there's no turning back, the path is overgrown. Be calm, my dear. One must not deceive oneself; at least once in one's life one ought to look the truth straight in the eye.

PETEY: What truth? You can see where there is truth and where there isn't, but I seem to have lost my sight, I see nothing. You boldly settle all the important problems, but tell me, my dear boy, isn't it because you are young and have not yet had to suffer for a single one of your problems? You boldly look ahead, but isn't it because you neither see nor expect anything dreadful, since life is still hidden from your young eyes? You're bolder, more honest, deeper than we are, but think about it, be just a little bit magnanimous, and spare me. You see, I was born here, my mother and father lived here, and my grandfather. I love this house, without the cherry orchard my life has no meaning for me, and if it must be sold, then sell me with the orchard . . . [*Embraces* MARCUS *and kisses him on the forehead*] And my son was drowned here . . . [*Weeps*] Have pity on me, you good, kind man.

MARCUS: You know I feel for you with all my heart.

PETEY: But that should have been said differently, quite differently . . . [*Takes out her handkerchief and a telegram falls to the floor*] My heart is heavy today—you can't imagine. It's so noisy here, my soul quivers at every sound, I tremble all over, and yet I can't go to my room. When I am alone the silence frightens me. Don't condemn me, Petya . . . I love you as if you were my own. I would gladly let you marry Anya, I swear it, only you must study, my dear, you must get your degree. You do nothing, fate simply tosses you from place to place—it's so strange. . . . Isn't that true? Isn't it? And you must do something about your beard, to make it grow somehow . . . [*Laughs*] You're so funny!

MARCUS: [*Picks up the telegram*] I have no desire to be an Adonis.

PETEY: That's a telegram from Paris. I get them every day. One yesterday, one today. That wild man has fallen ill again, he's in trouble again . . . He begs my forgiveness, implores me to come, and really, I ought to go to Paris to be near him. Your face is stern, Petya, but what can one do, my dear? What am I to do? He is ill, he's alone and unhappy, and who will look after him there, who will keep him from making mistakes, who will give him his medicine on time? And why hide it or keep silent, I love him, that's clear. I love him, love him . . . It's a millstone round my neck, I'm sinking to the bottom with it, but I love that stone, I cannot live without it. [*Presses* MARCUS'S *hand*] Don't think badly of me, Petya, and don't say anything to me, don't say anything . . .

MARCUS: [*Through tears*] For God's sake, forgive my frankness: you know that he robbed you!

PETEY: No, no, no, you mustn't say such things! [*Covers his ears*]

MARCUS: But he's a scoundrel! You're the only one who doesn't know it! He's a petty scoundrel, a nonentity—

PETEY: [*Angry, but controlling himself*] You are 26 or 27 years old, but you're still a schoolboy!

MARCUS: That may be!

PETEY: You should be a man, at your age you ought to understand those who love. And you ought to be in love yourself. [*Angrily*] Yes,

yes! It's not purity with you, it's simply prudery, you're a ridiculous crank, a freak—

MARCUS: [*Horrified*] What is she saying!

PETEY: "I am above love!" You're not above love, you're just an addlepate, as Firs would say. Not to have a mistress at your age!

MARCUS: [*In horror*] This is awful! . . . What is she saying! . . . [*Goes quickly toward the door*] This is awful! . . . I can't . . . I won't stay here . . . [*Goes out, but immediately returns*] All is over between us! [*Goes out*]

PETEY: Petya, wait! You absurd creature, I was joking! Petya!

Loud crash offstage. Music ends. ANDY comes in from the porch.

Alone at last!

ANDY: What do you mean?

PETEY goes out after MARCUS. BILLY HAWS comes in from right looking the same as he did in Act 1.

How do, Billy?

BILLY: Perfection.

BOPPO: Made it through the winter.

BILLY: Do you have a *Farmer's Almanac*?

BOPPO: In the pantry.

BILLY: [*Comes back looking in book*] Who else is here?

BOPPO: Just us and the two of you.

BILLY: I been awful alone down here. I see people running in the field sometime, playing and singing, and conversations under the window. My flesh is dirt, and the rich dirt smell comes up in my house. Spring's wet smell wakes me up. And here I am. [*Looks up. LOUISE comes in from the porch*] When are you going?

LOUISE: Now. [*Goes out left*]

BOPPO: Set awhile.

BILLY: I do believe I will.

BOPPO: What are you planting?

BILLY: Tomatoes.

PETEY comes in up left. ANDY goes out up left. MARCUS comes in up left. PETEY and MARCUS are dressed for travel in the style in which they played the Chekhov scene.

MARCUS: Let's get out of here.

PETEY: Do you have everything? This is all there is. Goodbye, dear friends, goodbye. It's a wild feeling, freedom, but just a feeling, but that's enough. I'm wild to get back to the city.

MARCUS has put his palms together and bowed to BOPPO and BILLY and BABY Hindu-fashion.

MARCUS: Let's get out of here!

They go out and off right. Sound of car doors and car starting and driving away.

BILLY: 'Fore long you'll be on your own, like me.

BOPPO: I reckon.

BILLY: It's better.

BOPPO: You're bitter. I'm not going to get bitter.

BILLY: I'm not bitter. That's *your* head. I'm lonely, sure, man, and spaced out, it's spring, I need a little change, get it on with my friends. I'm going down for the week; anything I can bring you back?

BOPPO: No, I'm fine.

BILLY: But the in-betweens are grand, no hassles, get as crazy as you want—

ANDY and LOUISE enter in high spirits. They are dressed for travel and carry suitcases. BILLY rises.

I'll ride along with you folks if you'll have me.

LOUISE: Sure, come along.

ANDY: Do we have everything?

BILLY: I need to stop off down at my place a minute.

LOUISE: I'm leaving most of it here. I leave whole lives behind, whole sets of equipment.

ANDY: Maybe we're too modern.

LOUISE: Can such a thing be?

BILLY: I'll get Floyd to feed the chickens.

LOUISE: I guess the baby can take care of herself.

ANDY: Well, I hope so.

LOUISE: I know Boppo can.

BILLY: Anybody *can.*

ANDY: Remember Baby Suzy—

LOUISE: And now—

BILLY: Yes, my lady, weep a nostalgic tear.

LOUISE: Watch out now.

BILLY goes out on the porch.

ANDY: There are flies in here. Those are the first flies. I'm glad I don't have to kill them.

LOUISE: Shh. Boppo's asleep. Look.

They step aside to reveal BOPPO asleep in the rocker as at the beginning of the play, bathed in a magical glow.

ANDY: Let's not wake him up—let's just go.

LOUISE: He'll think it was all a dream.

ANDY: Well, it might as well be.

He kneels and touches his forehead to BOPPO's feet. LOUISE does the same.

LOUISE: Let's get this show on the road.

They leave. Sound of car doors and car starting and driving away. As it drives away all the lights in the theatre go smoothly out except the magic radiance around BOPPO and a spotlight, previously unnoticed, on the sleeping bear BABY. BABY rises simply, as in a dream steps out of the bear costume, and is revealed to be a tender and charming young prince.

BABY: Fabulous. What can art offer but pleasure to the subtle senses? Sleep, old friend, and dream of me, and in the dream I am your heart's desire.

A buzzing as of bees begins imperceptibly and very softly and smoothly increases until at the end it is very loud.

You wake—[BOPPO *opens his eyes*]—and sleep again. [BOPPO *sleeps*] In the dream, I am your simple friend, nothing has happened, we're afloat in love. You wake—[BOPPO *opens his eyes*]—and look what's happened, I'm really here. We're really here. Let's go to a movie. Afterwards you're tired. It's late, and you fall asleep in the car coming home. [BOPPO *sleeps again*] It's all right, I'm driving. I don't want to be repetitious or get on your nerves. I'm probably going back to school. Sleep, I've got you. [*Beethoven with the bees*] I've been watching, I'm beginning to understand, it's strange and yet simple, you think of something and it's here, but I'm *really* here. I get off work in just a few minutes.

He stops talking and smiles radiantly at BOPPO. *Sound very loud.* BOPPO *smiles in his sleep.*

Lights, music, sound out.

Conventional bows.

SATYRICON

a play in two acts

Paul Foster

Satyricon was first presented by The Play-House of the Ridiculous at La Mama ETC, New York City, on May 20, 1972, with the following cast:

PETRONIUS	*David Lucas*
NERO	*Charles Stanley*
TIGELLINUS	*Gary Feldman*
ENCOLPIUS	*Russel Krum*
GITON	*Robin Pennings*
ACHILTO	*Jacques Brouwers*
PANNYCHIS	*Herndon Ely*
PRIAPUS	*Sara Allen*
AGRIPPINA	*Marie Antoinette*
TRIMALCHIO	*Paul Zegler*
FORTUNATA	*Monica Manz*
AMALTHEA	*Deborah Rush*
QUARTILLA	*Agosto Machado*
HYPNOS	*Richard Laws*
PENETRACION	*Benton Quinn*
THE VERMILLION SNAKE	*Carolyn Lord*
THE GREEN GIANT	*Harvey Fierstein*
SARAH LEE	*Diane Gude*
BACCHANTS	*Silvie Papernik, Allan Thomas, Susan Tobias & Company*

It was directed by John Vaccaro. Lighting by John Patrick Dodd; costumes by Richard Laws; set by Joseph Peroni. Production stage manager: Frank Schmidt.

TIME

A.D. 65, the night of the Priapus Revels

PLACE

The Temple of Priapus at the bottom of the Palatine Hill where the swamps drain into the storm sewers (the Cloaca Maxima), Rome

ACT I

The proscenium arch encloses the acting arena in two gigantic furry goat legs. High in the center hang the furred testicles of the goat god, PRIAPUS. *On them a high perch. The scarlet flammeum (hymen-veil) hangs in the center. The dressing room is onstage. All preparations are in view of the audience behind the flammeum. A platform from which* PETRONIUS *directs the devotions to the goat god. Bare-breasted girls dance and sing rutting wails. The flammeum is torn. Shrieks! It reveals the altar of* PRIAPUS: *a gorged amber phallus with fossilized flowers and bones. Girls ritually sponge it down to begin the revels.* PRIAPUS *swings down from his perch. He speaks through a large fallopian horn. Sounds and voices overlay each other.*

PRIAPUS: ". . . And in the twelfth year of Nero's reign, Publius Tacitus said heaven marked that crime-stained year with tempest and pestilence! Executions abounded in the city. Many are accused of treason. But at night, the Temple of Priapus echoed with singing and blazed with lights. Nero, corrupted by every lust, natural and unnatural, gave the ultimate devotion to the Goat God, Priapus. By the side of the emperor was a man of enormous wit and imagination, Gaius Petronius. He alone was master of dissipations and pleasure. He arranged for Nero to go through a formal wedding ceremony with a boy. The emperor put on the bridal veil. Everything was public which even at a natural union is hidden by night. Petronius was worn out by the spectacle he was compelled to arrange. The next day, after Priapus Night, there were riots in the streets. Many noble Romans fell, one after another, including Petronius. . . ."

PETRONIUS *places the fabulous myrrhine glass on the phallus altar.*

PETRONIUS: The myrrhine glass to hold the love juices.

ACHILTO: When we're done, this glass could fertilize the world.

PRIAPUS: [*Begins again*] To the blasé emperor, smartness and elegance were what Petronius approved. So Tigellinus, who hated him as a rival hedonist, denounced him for treason. Petronius wrote out a list of Nero's debaucheries giving the secret names of each male and female bed partner and the details of every novelty. Petronius refused to wait, so he went to his room with his razors, he prepared his wrists and he quietly . . ."

QUARTILLA, *with a snake wig, gilded eyelids, blue stiletto fingernails.*

QUARTILLA: THE SUN SETS ON ETERNAL ROME!

BACCHANTS: NIGHT!

A great mirror reflects a powerful offstage light which bathes the stage in deep red. PRIAPUS *swings up to his perch.*

QUARTILLA: Overhead, the billion-yeared planets are seated. The tickets are numbered in light-years. Mars farts and destroys a galaxy. Venus giggles and scrapes her chair. *Hush!* The ingenue Earth, a young little thing, makes her debut. She calls it . . . *Eternal* Rome.

BACCHANTS: The set is Rome with seven hills. We're at the bottom of all seven.

QUARTILLA: It's damp and funky down here.

ENCOLPIUS: The swamps drain in the sewers down here.

ACHILTO: You come here for one thing . . .

BACCHANTS: HEAD!

QUARTILLA: The Cloaca Maxima! The temple of Priapus! And I am Quartilla, the priestess of Priapus!

Cacophonous music and shouts come from the walls themselves and rise to a crescendo and frenzy. Strange musical instruments hung in the goat fur are beaten and blown and strummed. A large dish is carried on, a big fish on it. Several hump the fish. It unzips. A fantastic girl comes out. Melons are carried on and humped in the Persian style. Unified shouts before the song.

BACCHANTS:
MEAT! MEAT!
MEAT! MEAT!
MEAT!
Can anybody give us
what we want?
We want bread! Like
hell we do!
WE WANT MEAT!
Lip-smacking, bone-
cracking MEAT!   [*Shouts*]
There ain't nothing   I'M HUNGRY!
like MEAT!

There ain't nothing like MEAT!

ME TOO!

Don't be a meat tease,
Swing me that meat.

I want some eatin'
MEAT!

I'm beggin' you, please
Don't tease me with
greasy meat.

I want rock-hard meat!

Don't be a meat tease,
Swing me that meat,
Sling me that meat.

WANT SOME FAT-
BACK!

I wanna wrap my teeth
around SOME
MEAT!

I want some MEAT!

Owww! Hard meat!
Sick of selling it,
I want it free.
Give me some more,
Stuff it up every pore,
GIMME HARD
MEAT!

I can't dance the meat
dance
Without MY MEAT!

KILL NERO!

I wanna suck those
Roman bones
And tongue that Ro-
man meat.

KILL NERO!
VAE TYRANNIS!

Smack my lips and
moan,
Sucking bones and
meat.

Crack his joint,
Suck his juicy bones!
Rip a joint
Make me moan.

KILL NERO!

Don't be a meat tease,
Swing me that meat,
Sling me that meat.

Hmm, juicy joints're
good lickin'.
Slap it on the block.
Hmmm, I hear some-
thing rippin',
I'm too busy to stop.

TIGELLINUS: [*On the platform*] I AM TIGEL-
LINUS! The emperor is a god. He will arrive
at the bacchanal in another form. You must
guess what god he is. If you guess wrong, I
check off your name for the lions, for Nero's
amusement.

Laughter, derisive farts, shouts.

BACCHANTS: No! No! We're allowed to do whatever we want on Priapus Night! Ask Petronius!
He's the Arbiter!

TIGELLINUS: Ask Petronius! He arranged the
amusements for tonight. Not me.

BACCHANTS: Kill Petronius!

ENCOLPIUS: I am Encolpius! Tigellinus arranged
this! Not Petronius!

TIGELLINUS: Oh, yes, Petronius loves us all. Then
why does he boil us in sarcasm in his filthy
book? He hates this republic!

ACHILTO: We are not a republic. We are *Imperial* Rome! Petronius cares enough to blast
that lie! You still believe it.

TIGELLINUS: I am a patriot!

ACHILTO: You suck!

TIGELLINUS: Whatever Encolpius says, Achilto
will agree! They're lovers!!

BACCHANTS: LOVERS!! FORNICATI!!

*Blasts of laughter, obscene pantomime, hoots,
thrown garbage.*

PANNYCHIS: I'm Pannychis, Petronius' daughter!

BACCHANTS:
Liar! Liar!
He don't have a daughter!
Vagina Maxima!
Show us your tits!

Jeers. The fish is humped in derision. AMAL-
THEA *dances with a knife.*

AMALTHEA: I am Amalthea, the oracle woman!
I prophesy Nero will be RRRRRRRIIIIPED!
On Priapus Night we can do anything! We'll
cut and puncture his body! Insult his memory!!
[*Wild cheers*] The Claudian Dynasty is swept
away! EXIT, NERO CAESAR!!

BACCHANTS: *FELICITER!! FELICITER!!*

PETRONIUS: I am Gaius Petronius!

*A massive outcry, drums, gongs, an avalanche
of anger.*

BACCHANTS: Feed us! Feed us! MEAT! MEAT!
MEAT!

TIGELLINUS: Fantasies of a debauched mind!
You're hungry and Petronius gives banquets
every night!

BACCHANTS:
Why does Nero let us go hungry?!

PETRONIUS: I'll let Tigellinus explain that. He's
close to the emperor.

PANNYCHIS: WHY IS THERE NO BREAD?!

TIGELLINUS: There's plenty of bread.

PANNYCHIS: There's no jobs to pay for it!

TIGELLINUS: Ah, well, we have to control infla-
tion.

PANNYCHIS: The prices are still high. We can't
buy it!

TIGELLINUS: That's why there's plenty of bread.
[*They hold* TIGELLINUS]

QUARTILLA: Let him alone. I dig him.

SARAH LEE: He's a mess!

QUARTILLA: Big shoulders're not important to me.
I get horny over brains.

SARAH LEE: Oh, honey, if you get horny over *his*
brains, you'll be sterile.

PRIAPUS: Petronius, give them wine! Entertain us!

Loud marching drums at once.

ACHILTO: Encolpius, what is it?

GITON *and* ACHILTO: Encolpius, what is it?

ENCOLPIUS: Achilto! Giton, come on!

GITON: Pannychis, come on!

The four climb up to the platform with PE-
TRONIUS. *Parade on a large dish of red meat.
A big haunch on it. Attack it, chew it, and
voraciously hump it.*

ENCOLPIUS: A TRIUMPHAL PARADE! All the
might and power, pomp and pageantry, diversity, grandeur and richness, the panoply of
corruption of Imperial Rome itself. A parade
of the rare, the perverse, the exquisite, the bestial and swiny, an unfurlment of the mightiest
empire on this sphere. Drums and pipes,
brasses and flags, banners and bunting, fasces,
slaves and courtesans with eggplant-purple
eyes, eunuchs, captives and patrician knights,
the glut of humanity; Cretans, Greeks, Afri-
cans, Egyptians, cages of beasts and birds, lit-
ters of Periclean statuary, Phidian treasures,
the raw and moving life of heaven and earth,
the nude, the deformed, the grotesque, the
beautiful and the sublime, plundered and
ripped from the genius, the heart and mind
and soul of the civilized and barbaric world.

PENETRACION: ENTER THE RULER OF THE
WHOLE HUMAN RACE, NERO CAESAR!

A sustained whispering hiss as NERO *ejacu-
lates from the meat haunch. He presses a scent
bottle to his nose.*

NERO: What god . . . are we today?

*Barking, braying, howling yes-men, eager to
answer for their lives.*

BACCHANTS:
    Zeus!
    Hercules!
    Apollo!
    Pluto!
    Bacchus!
    Priapus!
    Atlas!

A voice hangs in the silence.

You're a pig's ass. [*Drops the haunch*]
And you're a good fuck.

NERO: I am Minerva! Arrest three men on my
left! Get the handsome ones. Cover them with
oil! Set them into wall sockets in the palace!
Light them for the banquet to my celestial
mother, Venus! I am a god and cannot die!
[*Giggling*] You hear them buzz, Tigellinus?
Like smoked bees.

PENETRACION: Señor, your mother, Agrippina!

NERO: How did she escape?! Hide me! I'm not
here! [NERO, *crawl back into the haunch,
head in, butt out*]

AGRIPPINA *enters, a strong, sensual woman in
a towering wig which needs attendants to hold
it upright with bamboo poles.*

AGRIPPINA: Romans, lovers! I am Agrippina, the
Emperor's mother! Son, kiss your mother.

They drag him out. NERO, *give her a cautious
peck.*

BACCHANTS: Kiss her!

AGRIPPINA, *grab him and tongue him deep
down.*

NERO: Mother, stop. I can't control myself when
you do this. *MOTHERRR!* The vulgate.
They're all watching. Turn your heads, dirty
voyeurs!

BACCHANTS: *Pantomimi!* ROMULUS! REMUS!
LUPA!

AGRIPPINA: They want us to play their good old
favorite. You play Romulus. I'll play the wild
she-wolf. And . . . *you* play Remus.

PENETRACION: Señora, you want me do Rimus?
I do Rimus.

AGRIPPINA: *Remus!*

PENETRACION: You pay me money? I work for
living.

AGRIPPINA: Hmm, what's your stock in trade?

PENETRACION: Nine inches. Every inch a piece of
gold.

AGRIPPINA: *The Founding of Rome!*

NERO: When a nation gets started this way, it
can only lead to trouble. [NERO *and* PENETRA-
CION *go under her like the babies on her teats.*
AGRIPPINA, *wail like a wild she-wolf, then
abruptly slap* NERO.]

AGRIPPINA: That's for the tiger you put in my
bed, you bitch!

NERO: It was just a pussy cat! A surprise. [*Slap
him again*] They told me it was defanged!

AGRIPPINA: You almost killed me!

NERO: Mother, how could you think that?

AGRIPPINA: I'd be torn to pieces if it wasn't for
Germenicus.

NERO: What did he do to my tiger?!

AGRIPPINA: He killed it!

NERO: He killed my surprise?! I hope you repri-
manded him.

AGRIPPINA: I gave him a tongue lashing for two hours. I'm exhausted. He never even said thank you.

NERO: Don't feel bad, dear. I bought you a greenhouse of flowers. Next to the serpentarium. Go. Smell them.

AGRIPPINA: Another "surprise," son?

NERO: Mother, go! I am a god! I command you, go! Get her out of here, quick!

PENETRACION *carries her off laughing.*

AGRIPPINA: A god? A god? He's crazy as his father. [NERO *circle nervously*]

NERO: I'm bored. PETRONIUS! Where is he? He's the only one who's any fun. He believes I'm a god. He said he'd be here in this, this glory hole of the Empire. Oh, my nerves are shot. SHOT!!! Where is he?! He knows when I'm nervous I need *excitement!* I need *glamour!* I'M BORED!!! AND MY NERVES ARE SHOT!!! [*Work yourself up. Pull your hair. Pull yourself to the floor, hysterical*] STOP IT! STOP IT! OH! FUCKLESSNESS!!! STOP IT!!!

PETRONIUS: I'm up here.

PENETRACION: [*Point to the haunch*] His Imperial Majesty, Nero!

PETRONIUS: [*Slow take*] He's done it again.

NERO: What's the matter, Petronius? Don't you think I could change my form if I wanted to?

PETRONIUS: Control yourself. Look at you.

NERO: I don't know what you're talking about.

PETRONIUS: You know what you do when you ride around in that litter with Agrippina and the curtains all shut.

NERO: I don't know what you mean.

PETRONIUS: Sticky stuff all down your tunic.

NERO: Well, she pretends she's asleep!

QUARTILLA: You keep doing that and you'll go blind.

NERO: I don't believe it. [*Instant blackout. NERO shriek*]

PETRONIUS: And how is Agrippina?

NERO: Rotting, I hope.

PETRONIUS: Nice family.

NERO: Oh, we're not so bad as families go.

PETRONIUS: Let's see, there was your Uncle Julius, he was stabbed to death in the Senate. Then there was your Uncle Octavius, he was poisoned by his wife—that's your sweet old grandmother, Livia. Your dear cousin Caligula was poisoned, then stabbed 68 times and then strangled and then flung down the steps. Ahh, then poor Claudius, your father. Agrippina fed him hemlock so you could have the throne.

NERO: Yes, we've had our little ups and downs, but what family doesn't? [*Pause*] Do you like my new Pretorian Guard? He's Spanish.

PETRONIUS: What's his name?

NERO: Penetrácion.

PANNYCHIS: I don't get the point.

GITON: Of course *you* don't.

NERO: Petronius, come down here. Aren't you going to bow to your emperor?

PETRONIUS: Nero, I don't think a descendant of two Consuls of Rome, the Arbiter of Taste to the Patrician House of Claudius, the ex-governor of Bithynia, a leader of the Roman Knights, and a confident of the Imperial Senate should have to bow.

NERO: [*To* PENETRACION] Do you think she'd bow if both her legs were broken?

PETRONIUS: Actually, I didn't recognize you. Your usual dress is a dress.

NERO: DRESS?!! I BECOME A GODDESS!! It's a religious duty. [*Straight out*] I can't help it. When you're divine you can't control these things.

SARAH LEE: We understand.

NERO: EVERY MONTH I HAVE THE WOMAN'S CURSE, DON'T I, PENETRACION?!

PENETRACION: *Si, Señor.*

NERO: I CHANGE INTO A GODDESS!!

PETRONIUS: NERO! Control yourself! You are the Commander in Chief of the Military Forces. Now conduct yourself like an officer and a lady.

TIGELLINUS: How dare you!

NERO: Thank you, Tigellinus. Petronius, do you know Tigellinus?

PETRONIUS: Yes. Intensely.

BACCHANTS *chant "MEAT!"*

PENETRACION: Señor, the peasants are nervous.

NERO: Why are they nervous? They're not gods.

PANNYCHIS: They're stifled and they can't breathe!

NERO: I'm not stifled.

PANNYCHIS: You're not breathing!

NERO: [*Very tight smile*] Sweeeeet child.

PANNYCHIS: You are sick!

NERO: Then, dear child, if *I* am sick, God must stamp out mental health. Who is that disgusting brat? Write her name down. She's dead.

PETRONIUS: Nero, stop this! Use your common sense!

NERO: A sovereign *never* stoops that low.

TIGELLINUS: Give the word. I'll kill every second man here. I'll make it an amusement for you.

NERO: Yes, I like that. Tigellinus, give the order.

PETRONIUS: Nero, my dove, this game is so crude. It's not for you. You are too sensitive.

NERO: Yes, I am sensitive.

PETRONIUS: You are a poet.

NERO: Yes, I am a poet.

PETRONIUS: You play the harp!

NERO: Like a pro!

PETRONIUS: You actually sing!

NERO: Of course I do. What key am I in?

PETRONIUS: What's the difference, just sing!

NERO: [*Talk-song*] I am a sensitive poet, with a very, very delicate nature. A tender nature. Can't stand to see a flower trod on, I weep. And I'm a sucker for animals, way down deep. A lion never goes hungry around me if there's a Christian to be found around me.

TIGELLINUS: Kill every second man. It's what would happen in any war.

NERO: War's a game fit for an emperor, but it's not fit for a poet?

PETRONIUS: And you are a poet.

NERO: You bet your ass I am. I'm a poet.

PETRONIUS: Now here's another game, a divination game. This boy.

NERO: Oh, I like this game.

PETRONIUS: Don't touch. He's sacred meat. We'll open his lovely body, we'll read his entrails.

NERO: Prepare the sacred meats!

GITON: HEY! WHAT'RE YOU DOING?! STOP! STOP!

PETRONIUS: Ready, Nurse?

NERO: Ready, Doctor.

PETRONIUS: Cut and sing!

The talk-song ends with the "Great Bonesaw Oratorio" in B minor.

BACCHANTS: Ready the scalpel. Ready the bonesaw. Ready the suture. We're about to read the future. The scalpel. The bonesaw. The bonesaw! The bonesaw!

GITON is gutted open. Out pour jewels, opals, emeralds, rubies, moonstones, pearls, topazes on an accordion-pleated cloth. Music rises as they cascade out. All see it as an artful diversion and applaud.

PETRONIUS: Emerald eyes, topaz teeth, a ruby heart, a prince's stone among the bones and coral meat. Jewels! The divination is favorable! Nero will live forever!

BACCHANTS: FOREVER! THE BONESAW! FOREVER! THE BONESAW! FOREVER

AND EVER, THE BONESAW! THE BONESAW! THE BONESAW! FOREVER!

Song ends. All help GITON.

PETRONIUS: Get out of that costume, quick.

NERO: [*Very excited*] How did you do that?! Teach me to read prophecies like that.

TIGELLINUS: Fake! A penny forecast by a mynah bird!

PETRONIUS: I'll take you to Amalthea, the oracle woman. She'll teach you, but you must go and get dressed properly.

NERO: Come with me. I need somebody to braid the hair under my arms. You're supposed to entertain me. Tigellinus is bucking for your job. Tigellinus is coming, aren't you, Tiggy?

TIGELLINUS: Yes! Yes!

NERO: Well, are you coming or are you *not* coming?

PETRONIUS: Yes.

NERO: Yes? Yes, what?

PETRONIUS: Yes, I am not coming. I've heard about your list of missing persons.

NERO: What list?

PETRONIUS: A list I heard you left at the butcher shop.

NERO: Well, I've heard about your list too!

PETRONIUS, *feign ignorance.*

TIGELLINUS: You know what lisst!

PETRONIUS: He said "list," Tigellinus, not "lisp." [*To* NERO] He's the only person I know can get a sibilant S on a vowel.

TIGELLINUS: YOU WROTE OUT A LIST OF NERO'S DEBAUCHERIES! All Rome is laughing at him. Some stupid satire you call *Satyricon*. It's filthy.

NERO: Tiggy, shut up. Petronius, you can be *so* acid, so *unspeakably* evil, so . . . [*Now they just hold each other and laugh, to* TIGGY'S *horror*] . . . absolutely divine.

TIGELLINUS: It's shocking! It embarrasses the empire!

NERO: This is a shocking empire. Now listen, you closet critic, get this straight! Petronius is my friend. He gives me pleasure, which is more than you do.

TIGELLINUS: Divine Nero, ask those street boys. They're in his filthy book. So are you, but he's disguised you so you won't know.

NERO: Those boys? They're harmless chickens.

TIGELLINUS: Yes, but a chicken with the teeth of a dog, disguised with the cunning of a tiger, the claws of an eagle, and with the ears of a rabbit, hiding behind the smile of a chicken. Ask them! They're playing with treason.

NERO: Tell me, who am I? What allegory am I? Where am I in his book?

ENCOLPIUS: [*A fast snow job*] You're not in it.

ACHILTO: It's about Petronius himself.

GITON: Sometimes he's a poet.

PANNYCHIS: Or Trimalchio, the rich man.

ACHILTO: Sometimes he's me or Encolpius or Giton or . . .

NERO: NOW, JUST A MINUTE!!

ACHILTO: Even his daughter, Pannychis, is in it. But you're not.

NERO: Daughter? He doesn't have a daughter! She's not his daughter!

GITON: Of course she is.

NERO: Is he sometimes her too?

PANNYCHIS: Maybe. I never saw us together.

TIGELLINUS: Nonsense! Nero, this book is about you!

NERO: Tiggy, put all their names on your list for being in his book when I'm not.

TIGELLINIUS: Who are these boys?

PETRONIUS: My story is about them. Encolpius loves Giton. Achilto is his competition.

TIGELLINUS, *scrunch your face.*

NERO: Your normal Roman love affair.

TIGELLINUS: Disgusting!

NERO: Oh, come off it, Tiggy. Everybody experiments when they're young. Didn't you?

TIGELLINUS: I tried it once. I didn't like it.

NERO: I tried it once. I liked it.

TIGELLINUS: How do boys get started in this kind of love?

PETRONIUS: By asking questions.

TIGELLINUS: Shall we leave? I have some new games for you.

PETRONIUS: Tiggy thought of something *new?* Impossible! Even his dreams are secondhand. If a thought ever wandered into his brain, it would die of loneliness.

TIGELLINUS: You best watch your ass, Petronius! Think about tomorrow!

PETRONIUS: Oh, tomorrow and tomorrow and tomorrow . . . CREEPS!

NERO: STOP IT!

TIGELLINUS: Consider that food for thought!

PETRONIUS: Frozen food.

NERO: STOP IT! You know why I came. Give me the glass.

TIGELLINUS: The glass! Be quick about it!

NERO: [*Exploding*] *STAAATAZIT, BRRRRR-UTA FACIA!*

PETRONIUS: What glass, Nero? What glass? I have many glasses. Every patrician has a glass.

Every slave has a glass. *What* glass, Nero? [*Whisper*] Beg me.

NERO: SWINE! CLOD! MAGGOT! [*Immediate switch without a breath*] Oooooooooh, loveohprinceohsweetangelcherubchild, the sapphireglasstheglassofkingsmadebykingsenvyof kings . . . divine, Petronius. The glass cut from a single sapphire. The glass so fragile the least sound will break it. SWINE! SCUMBAG! YOU BITCH TO MAKE ME CRAWL! [*Immediate switch*] Ooooooh, how I envy that glass, my glittering, my flaming Petronius.

PETRONIUS: I know. [*Pause*] Nero, my dove, why are you afraid of me? I'm only a voluptuary.

NERO: Oh, epigrams! You writers are all so conflict-motivated.

PETRONIUS: A sleek-headed man is not dangerous.

NERO: A touching maneuver. I've heard it said that beavers, when hunted down, will bite off their own balls and spit them in front of the hunter to show submission.

PETRONIUS: Noooo, my dove, my chick, we are only phagocytes. Nature's garbage collectors.

NERO: Hmm, very pretty, I'm sure.

PETRONIUS: Go. Clean your body. When you return, I'll have Amalthea read you prophecies and I'll give you the myrrhine glass.

NERO: A bargain! HEIGH-HO, EVERYONE! WE'RE OFF TO THE TUBS! Lift me in, Penetrácion.

PENETRACION, *lift* NERO *into a litter. Just as they begin,* AGRIPPINA *huffs on, her arm in a great bandage.*

AGRIPPINA: Where is he?! WHERE IS HE?! Thanks for the flowers. Look at that! Asps!

NERO: What's asps?

AGRIPPINA: He asks what's asps. SNAKES!

NERO: Oh, Motherrrr, you're so hard to please. Now, I have a new barge I want you to test for me. Go to the Lucrine Lake.

AGRIPPINA: Another surprise, son?

NERO: Agrippina, don't be paranoid. Just go! I am a god. I command you.

AGRIPPINA: Why can't I ride in that litter with you anymore?

NERO: GO! Drag her off! And shave the hairs on her lip!

As before, PENETRACION *carries her off, laughing.*

AGRIPPINA: A god?! A god?! Just like his father, CRAZY!

NERO, *prepare to exit. The Sylva Fornicata forms, a Rousseau-like forest. As the change takes place.*

TIGELLINUS: You just sawed off the branch you're sitting on, Petronius.

PETRONIUS: I've already lived, Tiggy.

TIGELLINUS: TIGELLINUS!

PETRONIUS: I've already lived, *Tiggy*. My chapter is written in the skies, in heliotrope, to turn to the sun. I've only to figure out the ending. Now, you run along and flush the dirt off your body. I've got to select a color of ink that suits immortality. And you know I will. It's style, Tiggy. ENCOLPIUS! ACHILTO! GITON! PANNYCHIS! WHAT COLOR, YOU BEAUTIES?!

ALL FOUR: HELIOTROPE!

NERO: Tigellinus, fill your pen. We're adding a new name to our shopping list for the butcher.

TIGELLINUS: Shall I write it in heliotrope?

NERO: Yes. Yes, that would be a nice color. Milk the donkeys! I want a bath as soon as I arrive! [*Exit*]

Forest set moved into place by BACCHANTS *made up in exotic masks with intense avaricious eyes. A hum of vibrating phalli.*

PETRONIUS: It's in this time I set my story. Three young boys and a girl begin a journey. And Rome? Well, Rome has two choices. A violent revolution or forget it all in pleasure. Rome didn't revolt, and neither did I.

PRIAPUS *swings down from the high perch.*

PRIAPUS: A woods where I live, infested with divinity!

PANNYCHIS: [*On a Rousseau-red couch*] Why don't you love me? I love your eyes. They're purple.

GITON: Go away. You're too young.

PANNYCHIS: NO! It's not your eyes! *I loathe them!* They're mud color and they're crossed. *Your eyes are ugly!* It's your hair I love, Giton. Curled and thick. It hangs there, ripe.

GITON: You're gawky and you got freckles. [*Laugh at her*]

PANNYCHIS: It's not your hair! Your hair's grotesque, it's sludge, it's scales. *A goat has better hair!* It's your mouth I love. Red. A puckered fire. Kiss me, Giton.

GITON: You steal souvenirs from my dressing room. I know you do.

PANNYCHIS: I HATE YOUR MOUTH! It's your arms I love. [GITON *gives whooping laugh*] Your arms are so ugly! They're not arms, they're roots! They're warts! I HATE YOUR ARMS! Kiss me. Tell me lies. Lay your head in my lap, then how sweet would I sing and speechify on. [ACHILTO, *run on, sweep up* GITON *and pull him behind the red couch. Four legs stick up from behind the couch.*

Spastic movements and guttural sounds] It *is* his arms I love.

ENCOLPIUS, *wrap your arm in a cloak for a fight and shout a fester of language.*

ENCOLPIUS: ACHILTO! You meat-rack whore! You bastard! As soon as I turn my back you snatch my boy! And you, Giton! I feed you, I put clothes on your back and you run off with my best friend!

GITON: I defended myself, but he forced me!

ACHILTO: [*Taunt him, push him down*] When I showed him this, he begged me! He whined, he cried, it's the biggest thing he ever saw! He was fantastic! He wouldn't let me go!

ENCOLPIUS: [*Overthrow him, strike him*] I can't stand your whorish face!

ACHILTO: Don't be stupid! Did I damage him?! Is he broken?!

ENCOLPIUS: We split! We divide our things right now! Our friendship is over!

ACHILTO: Then we divide everything! In half! Even him! [*Raise a sword over* GITON'S *head*]

PANNYCHIS: Don't touch him!

BACCHANTS:
    Priapus, throw him out!
    Drag him behind the couch again!
    Do it! Do it!
    Share him!
    Petronius, get us in the action!

ACHILTO: Ahh, the poor boy, look at his innocent face. It's the face of a poet. He inspires me. He's my muse.

ENCOLPIUS: Achilto, get your hands off his ass and go find your own muse!

PRIAPUS: Quartilla, stop the fight! They desecrated my temple! I want a sacrifice!

QUARTILLA: You have defecated the temple!

PRIAPUS: DESECRATED, YOU DAMN MUTATE!

ENCOLPIUS: What's so sacred about an orgy?!

PRIAPUS: Sacrilege!

BACCHANTS: Sacrilege! Sacrilege!

PRIAPUS: Quartilla, you are my priestess. Who are these boys?!

QUARTILLA: I never saw them before.

PRIAPUS: Petronius, who in hell are they?!

ENCOLPIUS: I'LL KILL HIM!

PETRONIUS: Encolpius, stop it.

PRIAPUS: For this outrage, I want my sacrifice. A virgin. Seize them!

BACCHANTS, *seize them.* SARAH LEE, *ravish* GITON.

GITON: Quartilla, help, get this creature off me! Help!

QUARTILLA: Sarah Lee! Get off him or I'll deck you! This is supposed to be a sacred ritual. Is he all right?

GREEN GIANT: He was kissed unconscious.

SARAH LEE: Was I really terrible?

GITON: Have you ever made love to her?

GREEN GIANT: Yes. At gunpoint.

PRIAPUS: You desecrated my woods!

QUARTILLA: Sacrilege!

PRIAPUS: To purify my temple, I demand a sensorium! A virgin sacrifice!

SARAH LEE: Let me sacrifice him?

PRIAPUS: I SAID A VIRGIN!

QUARTILLA: Who does he belong to?

BACCHANTS: ME!

QUARTILLA: Come here. Pannychis gets him.

[QUARTILLA, *take* PANNYCHIS. *Kiss her arms and stomach and body*]

GITON: Quartilla, she's too young.

QUARTILLA: If you're big enough, you're old enough.

SARAH LEE: Then I get *him*. [SARAH LEE, *throw* ACHILTO *over your shoulder*]

GREEN GIANT: SARAH LEE! When you finish, you won't forget you belong to me . . . SARAH LEE! Ahh, my ruin's just been eveninged.

PRIAPUS: Prepare the sacrifices. Lift the sacred meats. Worship Priapus with your bodies! [*Place the flammeum over* PANNYCHIS' *head. A ceremonial lifting of* PANNYCHIS *and* GITON. PRIAPUS, *get into the costume of a glassine vermilion snake*] Worship Priapus with all the secret dreams you tell lies about and throw away in towels. Give me all the creams and musics of love. Heavy breathing, the cries, the sweats, the milks, the tongues and nipples and cheeks, the kisses and licks and sucks and splits. All the skins of your body, touched and rubbed and opened and entered and pleasured!

BACCHANTS:
Everything alive is fertilized!
All life begins with a touch!
The pollen, the semen, the petal, the bud!
The flower opens!
[GITON, *lift the flammeum from* PANNYCHIS]
All life begins with love!
Love is pleasure!

GITON, *rip the flammeum. All shriek! The Saturnalia begins:* BACCHANTS, *roll in positions of gymnastic love.* GITON'S *dream on stage level. Dim out. The stage is hung with billowing gauzes.* GITON *and* PANNYCHIS *sleepwalk through them. Hazy veils of incense glide across the lacy glow. A snake charmer plays a shawm. Above the forest orgy, a rickety rope suspension bridge leading to a dark cave above.* NERO *and* PENETRACION *crawl across it.*

PRAIPUS: Sssh. Nero's back. A rickety rope across an abyss. Listen.

PETRONIUS: Amalthea will show him how she receives prophesies.

NERO: Penetrácion, are you sure this bridge is safe?

PENETRACION: Sssh! Don't worry. You are a god and cannot die.

NERO: Never mind that bullshit. Is this bridge safe?

PENETRACION: It's the only way to get to the cave of the mysterious oracle woman, Amalthea.

NERO: Oww, damn! I broke a fingernail.

PENETRACION: SSSH!

AMALTHEA *sits in a cage of sticks, hanging above center stage in the shadows. She has a young and beautiful but insane face.*

NERO: Amalthea, tell me how you make prophecies.

AMALTHEA: First . . . they drive me wild and crazy on laurel leaves. They drug me. [*Long pause. She begins to swing in the cage higher and higher*]

NERO: Don't worry about it. It's adrenalin that's hard to handle.

AMALTHEA: They bring me a man. He looks like your guard. He says he is the God Priapus. Then there is . . . A RUSHING THROUGH ALL THE GALLERIES! DOORS BANG, WINGS SWISH IN MY FACE, THE LIGHT VANISHES! The God Priapus comes to me in this violet hour. And I speak prophecies. [AMALTHEA, *continue to swing in the stick cage as a large* VERMILION SNAKE *coils across the stage toward the sleepwalking* GITON *and* PANNYCHIS. *It entwines them as they copulate.* ENCOLPIUS *and* ACHILTO *wind the* SNAKE *around them in a Laocoön*]

PETRONIUS: Giton's dream. Gorgeous snake, tell this poet who made the whizzing world?

VERMILION SNAKE: Sssssssssssssssss. I will not.

PETRONIUS: Sweet snake, tell me.

VERMILION SNAKE: Move me not, I will not tell you. Sssssssssssssssss.

NERO: Go on, Amalthea. [NERO *and* PENETRACION *mime her above*]

AMALTHEA: I remember . . . nothing. I see . . . nothing. The glitter of his jeweled body comes to me, naked and dripping wet. He stands before me. His legs spread apart. An athletic giant! His chest is deep, his hips are narrow, his hard stomach arches toward me. His powerful legs flex. He licks his lips . . . he reaches his great arm down under my back. He lifts me in an arch. MY HEAD FALLS

BACK! HE KNEELS DOWN! His knees spread apart . . . he shoves my legs before him.

NERO: Go on, Amalthea! You witch!

AMALTHEA: I hear nothing. I feel the heat grow from the thick black hair of his body. I smell him! He spreads over me, stiff and taut, and inches his way up my stomach. He places my hand . . . [*Hysterical*] My tongue is thick! I CAN'T GO ON!

NERO: Don't stop! I'll have you whipped!!

PETRONIUS: Gorgeous snake, tell me. Look at the night, drugged with divinity, combing her black hair for you. Look at the cold stars and comets and sparks embracing space for you.

VERMILION SNAKE: ssssSSSSSSSSS! Rocks. Lunatic and old, like your silly poetry.

PETRONIUS: Without our poetry we won't know who we are.

VERMILION SNAKE: I know who I am. I'm alive. And I'm beautiful.

AMALTHEA: He throbs and beats in my hand! He is so thick I can't get my hand around him! MY FINGERS STRETCH FULL LENGTH! I CAN'T MEASURE HIM!! I . . . I'M AFRAID! His bushy eyes hold my eyes. He squirts thick oil. He works it up and down the shaft of his body. He locks his eyes on mine!! I can smell the musk of his body. He smiles! His teeth shine! His massive legs stretch! [*Difficult to breathe*] They move over me. They slide into position. He spreads over me. Wet and slippery. Hard as iron. HE ENTERS MY BODY! HE CLAMPS HIS BROWN EYES SHUT! HE THROWS BACK HIS HEAD! HIS BODY STRAIGHTENS . . . [*Tight in the vise embrace of the* SNAKE]

GITON: MY HEAD IS A BURNING CITY!!

NERO: Go on! I'll tear you apart by horses!!

PETRONIUS: Jeweléd snake, groaning, tossing in the whirling zodiac, *tell me!*

VERMILION SNAKE: Sssss. If you love me, come here, let me fondle you.

AMALTHEA: . . . he opens his massive mouth. He sucks in my lips and tongue. He moans without control. My eyes roll in my head. I look over his shoulder. His back muscles power his body up and down inside me. HIS LIPS! SLIP UP AND DOWN! IN A RAGE! HE STIFFENS! HIS CHEST! HIS LEGS! THE SWEAT! A SOLID ROCK! HE REARS! LIKE A HORSE! HE PLUNGES DOWN! I SCREAM! I SHRIEK MY PROPHECY! THE WINDS RUSH! DOORS SLAM! THE ORACLE SPEAKS FROM THE GODS!!

PETRONIUS: You know nothing. You're a child.

VERMILION SNAKE: SSSSSSS! And with the yearning of the moth for a star.

ENCOLPIUS, *chase a giant white moth of flash paper. It flies to a candle and bursts to a bright phosphorescence! The dream ends. The* VERMILION SNAKE *sheds his skin and slinks away.*

AMALTHEA: And . . . I remember nothing . . . gentle him, my handsome Pretorian Guard. Caress the emperor.

PENETRACION, *cradle the unconscious* NERO *off.* PANNYCHIS, *follow the* SNAKE. ACHILTO, *kiss the sleeping* GITON.

ENCOLPIUS: Petronius, who are you talking to?

PETRONIUS: Giton, I think. Or to his dream.

ENCOLPIUS *sees* GITON *where the* SNAKE *left him,* ACHILTO *over him.*

ENCOLPIUS: GITON! ACHILTO! YOU SNEAK! YOU BASTARD! YOU WHORE! YOU SEWER! YOU FILTH! GET UP!

All scatter excited while ENCOLPIUS *and* ACHILTO *fight.*

BACCHANTS:	ACHILTO: Man, you
Oh, oh, fight!	are tough to take!
Punch up!	You're possessive,
High-cussout!	you're jealous, you're
Evil!!	hysterical! [*Hit him,*
A bitch out!	*push him*] You're a
Word fester!	drag!!
Take Pannychis!	
She's a virgin!	ENCOLPIUS: WHAT
Take Encolpius!	CAN YOU OFFER!
Take Achilto!	Your famous crotch?!
He's too big!	That horse-sized ob-
What could you do	scenity?! You're a
with it?!	freak, a monster.
I'd think of some-	You're a mutation,
thing!	half-horse, *you're a*
Split him in half!	*jackass!* It's obscene!
	ACHILTO: [*Takes up a*
	big knife] We share
	him, half and half!
	Which half do you
	want?!
	PANNYCHIS: Achilto,
	stop! Share him, don't
	kill him!
	ENCOLPIUS: I WON'T
	SHARE HIM!
	ACHILTO: EVERY-
	BODY SHARES ON
	PRIAPUS NIGHT!

Silence for the line.

ENCOLPIUS: TO HELL WITH PRIAPUS!! I WON'T SHARE HIM!!

Stunned silence.

PETRONIUS: You fool. What did you say?

BACCHANTS: SACRILEGE!!

PRIAPUS: [*Next to the amber phallus*] I won't forget this, Petronius. One of you will pay for it. Giton, choose.

ENCOLPIUS: Giton, come over here!

GITON: *I* will decide who I want! [*Without hesitation*] Achilto. And Pannychis.

ACHILTO: Come on, let's split.

ENCOLPIUS *is stunned.* GITON, ACHILTO *and* PANNYCHIS *run off laughing.*

BACCHANTS:

Priapus, give us a break!
Give us a break, we're tired!
I can't get it up anymore!
It's raining! The roof leaks!
A break! A break! A break!

Pound the floor in protest.

PRIAPUS: RAIN! RAIN! RAIN! FLUSH THE TEMPLE CLEAN! [PRIAPUS, *pound drums and thunder sheets and send rain. All disperse except* PETRONIUS *and* ENCOLPIUS. *They stand alone in the rain mist, a cardboard over their heads. Offstage a powerful light shines through the mist and makes a real and very beautiful rainbow*]

PETRONIUS: Comedy. Tragedy.

ENCOLPIUS: They'll lie in bed and laugh at my loneliness. Everything's gone. Priapus is a capricious god.

AGRIPPINA, *huff on, dripping wet. The giant wig trailing behind on the floor.*

AGRIPPINA: Where is he?! Where is he?! The damn boat broke in half. I swam ashore. My wig saved me, it floats. What's he trying to do, drown me? Why is it raining in here? HE'S AT IT AGAIN! HE'S TRYING TO DROWN ME AGAIN!! HE CAN'T DO THIS!! I'M THE QUEEN! I'M THE QUEEN!

PRIAPUS: Agrippina, get off the stage. Everybody take a break! Be back in ten minutes! Cruise the lobby! Stretch your legs! Stretch anything! I'm getting excited. Agrippina, get on the couch!

AGRIPPINA: I never made it with a god before.

PRIAPUS: That's okay, I never made it with a queen before.

CURTAIN

ACT II

Opener is played against an invisible curtain of nitrogen gas coming from the front lip of the stage. Projections on this inert gas will appear as a hologram, a movie in midair. It is erased *when* QUARTILLA *dances holes through it.* QUARTILLA *in a four-sided Janus mask, her body in a split costume: half-boy, half-girl. She speaks through her four faces, turning in careful lighting so a clothed and nude girl, a clothed and nude boy all speak in a single body. She is sequined.*

QUARTILLA: Look into Circe's secret ball. [*Turn*] Trimalchio's pleasure dome! [*Turn*] I go against the grain of your brain. [*Turn*]

BACCHANTS: Trimalchio's sensorium!

QUARTILLA: In the dark room of your mind. [*Turn*] Where's stored the remembrance of things long ago. [*Spin*] CRY! WEEP! WAIL! RANT!

BACCHANTS: Trimalchio's feast! Trimalchio's pleasure dome! Trimalchio! Trimalchio! Trimalchio!

PRIAPUS *swings down. He zippers himself into an upholstered suit of plastic neon tubes so he looks like a fat electric eel. He kicks the debris from first act.*

PRIAPUS: Garbage! Why can't I have a temple in the nice end of town? Up on one of the hills, next to Jupiter's and Saturn's elegant temples. I'm down here with the swamps and malaria. Garbage and noise, garbage and noise! GARBAGE AND NOISE! Petronius, start. Where is he? [SARAH LEE *moves the cardboard.* PETRONIUS *and* ENCOLPIUS *lie together*] What did you program for us?

PETRONIUS: [*Obviously lying*] What did I program? Well, ah . . . I wrote it down on something.

BACCHANTS: Never happened! SSSSSSSSSSSSSS!

SARAH LEE: He was back there with Encolpius. What were you two doing?

PETRONIUS: I . . . I wrote it all out. On the last page, I wrote "curtain." I worked like a mad man. Pages and pages. It had a beautiful girl and a beautiful boy, and . . . *then,* there was a knock at the door. Everybody was gone. Nobody was here. I went to the door, and . . . there was a green-fanged man! With . . . with a greased love curl on his head.

ENCOLPIUS: He made my blood run cold!

PETRONIUS: And he came closer and closer and . . .

ENCOLPIUS: I saw it too!

PETRONIUS: And . . . and then he snatched the papers from my hand and ran away!

SARAH LEE: Who was he?!

PETRONIUS: Who was he? Who do you think he was?

GREEN GIANT: Not . . . NOT . . .

PETRONIUS: Ummhmm.

BACCHANTS: AAAAAHHHHH! Doctor Caligari Frankenstein Dracula!

PETRONIUS *combining* SARAH LEE *and the* GREEN GIANT *into a unisexual.*

PETRONIUS: [*Sings*]
> A green-fanged man
> With a greased love curl
> Makes your blood run cold,
> He's a dirty old . . . vampire!!
> Aaaahhhhh!
> Doctor Caligari Frankenstein Dracula!

> His claw scratches his love curl,
> A blood-curdling laugh,
> The laboratory bubbles and hisses,
> He kisses the pretty young things on
>   the neck.
> Aaaahhhhh, velvetine skin,
> The bats flap on the cauldron rim,
> Pure love, Doctor Caligari Frankenstein
>   Dracula!

> He'll experiment on them
> And combine the best of both of them,
> He'll make them flexible,
> A unisexual!
> Aaaaahhhh! Doctor Caligari Frankenstein
>   Dracula!

> She screams! He cries!
> He licks her body,
> He licks his body.
> They like it but they don't know why.

> I dig her arms. I dig his chest.
> I dig her tits. I dig his cock.
> I dig her ass. I dig his head.
> I glue them all together.
> I'm gonna make 'em better,
> The best of both forever.

> He's a dirty old vampire,
> Aaaahhhh!
> Doctor Caligari Frankenstein Dracula!

PRIAPUS: All right, Petronius, quit stalling. Where's the program?

SARAH LEE: He was back there on an old mattress with Encolpius. I didn't see any papers.

PETRONIUS: I wrote it *on* Encolpius. And now I need to copy it. I need some fresh skin.

All surround SARAH LEE.

SARAH LEE: Oh no, oh no . . .

BACCHANTS: He needs some skin! He needs some skin! [*All grab* SARAH LEE *and write all over her body with lipstick. They scrawl up her legs and arms and belly*]
    Hold still!

SARAH LEE: WHAT ARE YOU DOING TO ME?

PETRONIUS: [*Licking her*] I'm erasing a mistake.

GREEN GIANT: Sarah Lee, stretch it out. I can't read in the fat rolls.

ALL: READ THIS!

PETRONIUS: NERO GETS MARRIED!

BACCHANTS:
> The poor girl.
> Who's he gonna marry? I can't read it.
> Sarah Lee, stretch it out!

SARAH LEE: Go to hell! This library's shut down! [SARAH LEE *puts on a robe.* PRIAPUS *is now in the* TRIMALCHIO *costume*]

TRIMALCHIO: The bride.

Flutes, candles, incense, finger cymbals. A creature veiled from head to toe in the scarlet flammeum.

BACCHANTS:
> The *flammmeummmm.*
> The hymen-veilll.
> Of the virgin briiiiiiide.

TRIMALCHIO: The groom. Thunder. [*A Celotex horse is rolled on. It opens and a live horse comes from it*] Do you take this bride to be your lawful wedded wife? [*Thunder, whinny*] Do you take this horse to be your lawful wedded husband?

NERO, *throw off the veil.*

NERO: Indeed I do.

TRIMALCHIO: I now pronounce you horse and wife. Kiss the bride.

All throw wheat at the couple.

TIGELLINUS: How dare you marry the emperor to a *horse!*

NERO: Oh, Tiggy, what do you know about love uptown? Petronius, I'm so happy.

PETRONIUS: You make a beautiful bride.

NERO: How did you know Thunder was my secret fantasy?

PETRONIUS: It's my job.

AGRIPPINA, *huff on.*

AGRIPPINA: I'm late! I'm late at my own son's wedding. [*Sees Thunder*] Ohh, he *is* beautiful.

NERO: MOTHER! STOP IT! Don't you dare upstage my wedding!

AGRIPPINA: That's the thanks I get. I ran all the way to be on time.

NERO: Well, *you're late!*

AGRIPPINA: I had to shop. I told the clerk my son was getting married. I wanted something for his bride, in size 112. What can you buy for a horse? A bed jacket, table linens, what? Here, take some sugar for Thunder.

NERO: A!G!R!I!P!P!I!N!A!!!! G!O!!!!

QUARTILLA: That's terrible. She's your mum.

NERO: [*Clenched teeth*] I know she's my mum. I tried to *drown* her in kisses and *smother* her in hugs, but nothing works. Now I'm going to *burn* her, I mean, warm her with this cloak. Go home and try it on, Agrippina. It's a present. Take it, don't be paranoid.

AGRIPPINA: Another surprise? Who made this cloak, Medea?

NERO: THROW HER OUT!

TRIMALCHIO: TEAR THE MAIDENHEAD!

Flammeum ripped. NERO *shrieks.*

NERO: Oh, that felt good. Good-bye, Penetrácion. I'm sorry but I found Thunder now.

PENETRACION: Don't worry about me.

NERO, *lead Thunder off. All throw wheat and shout.*

BACCHANTS: *FELICITER! FELICITER!*

GITON, ACHILTO *and* PANNYCHIS *enter, dazed.*

ENCOLPIUS: Giton? Pannychis . . . what happened? You look so strange. What did Achilto do to you?

BACCHANTS:
He turned them on.
He blew their minds.

ENCOLPIUS: He made a threesome! You hated it, didn't you?

GITON *and* PANNYCHIS: We liked it.

ENCOLPIUS: What did he make you do?

GITON: We never saw anything like it.

PANNYCHIS: He showed us everything . . .

GITON *and* PANNYCHIS: Bigger and bigger and bigger . . .

GREEN GIANT: He's not the noblest Roman of them all, but he's the biggest.

ENCOLPIUS: YOU PIG!

ENCOLPIUS *and* ACHILTO *fight.* BACCHANTS *shout with them and pull them apart. A fanfare for the entrance of great trays of overstuffed food.*

BACCHANTS: FOOD! FOOD! STOP THE FIGHT!

PETRONIUS: You can't start the feast until your wife gets here.

TRIMALCHIO: I don't have a wife.

PETRONIUS: You don't? What do you do for aggravation?

SARAH LEE: I want to play the wife!

We see QUARTILLA *preparing to play* FORTUNATA.

PETRONIUS: No, Quartilla is playing Fortunata. FORTUNATA, COME OUT HERE! Wait'll you see her.

BACCHANTS: FORTUNATA!

TRIMALCHIO: What's she look like?

SARAH LEE: She puts her lipstick on with a shovel. Her perfume will bruise your nose.

GREEN GIANT: What do you care? She's rich.

The fight erupts again. BACCHANTS *pull them apart.*

BACCHANTS: STOP THE FIGHT! WE'RE GONNA EAT!

ENCOLPIUS: Why did you go away with him?!!

GITON *and* PANNYCHIS: We can't explain it.

FORTUNATA *staggers on under a load of body jewels.*

BACCHANTS: LET'S EAT, WE'RE HUNGRY!

TRIMALCHIO: Fortunata, give me something. I'm having a fat attack.

FORTUNATA: Not you, Trimalchio. You're larded. He's a junkie for food. I caught him with a needle mainlining of a leg of lamb.

TRIMALCHIO: Well then, just pat me all over with butter.

FORTUNATA: Oh, food, food! I bathed myself in yak milk, I perfumed my arms, I put on all my jewels.

SARAH LEE: Now she's playing hard to get.

FORTUNATA: No, I'm not. I want *him!* [FORTUNATA *and* SARAH LEE *both grab* ACHILTO]

ENCOLPIUS: What's he got that everybody wants him?! He's a bastard!

SARAH LEE: I love him too much to share him. This is no ordinary love. It's divine and forever. It's a Frenchfried love, with a side of baked macaroni and cheese.

FORTUNATA: Your love sounds like a menu. Gluttons! Eat what you want. I'll have a little cracker and delicate pâté.

TRIMALCHIO: You won't get fat that way. You eat to get fat, everybody knows that. Tell her.

PETRONIUS: My friend Apicius invented a delicacy by stuffing pigs with figs. He calls it pâté.

The fight erupts again. BACCHANTS *stop it.*

ENCOLPIUS: YOU PIG! GITON, WHAT ATTRACTS YOU TO HIM?!

PETRONIUS: Achilto, give them the anatomy lesson of the Apicius pigs!

BACCHANTS *stuff* FORTUNATA *and* TRIMALCHIO *with food. Their costumes inflate larger and larger. They are stuffed into two enormous round balls. Funnels of food are stuffed into them. Their costumes inflate more and more. A long cloak is placed over* ACHILTO. *He stands upright between them on their shoulders and makes a giant phallus. Back-projection of an X ray of a stomach gluttonizing and digesting.*

ACHILTO: [*Sings*]	BACCHANTS: [*Speak*]
Hands spread,	To make delicate
Eyes wide,	pâté, they hold the
Mouth wide open,	pig between their
I got size, size, size.	legs. They stuff a

Conquest by quantity,
That's me, big me.
Oh, they come from
half the planet to see
Amber and furs from
Germany,
Wines and cedars and
silks,
Perfumes and drugs
from Syria.
Incense and laudanum,
roses and myrrh
from Persia,
Transparent flowers of
silk from China,
Pepper and herbs, ti-
gers and pearls,
Indigo and elephants,
Diamonds and ame-
thysts from India.

If you got it,
Show it.
Make it big,
Let it grow,
Let it show,
Let 'em know
You got size, size, size,
You got size, size, size.

Asses from Egypt, ala-
baster and glass,
Citron and purple dyes
from Africa,
Apes and ivory,
Fertile green turtles
from Ethiopia,
Jades from Asia,
Linen and gold, silver
and ham,
Copper and tin,
Cocks and corks and
horses
And Spanish fly from
Spain.
Wine and wheat,
Oysters and eunuchs
from Gaul.
From Britain I showed
them boars.
From Turkey I showed
them whores and
honey,
And figs and fish and
foul and fragrance,
And peacock tongues
and money,
And carpets and jewels
and oils and un-
guents.

funnel in the gullet
and grind away.

They fatten the liver
with figs. They force-
feed the pig until he
swells and swells.
The liver distends,
his legs bloat with
fat, the waist swells
until it is one big bag
of food. He becomes
an insatiable glutton.

His liver gets larger
and larger, his stom-
ach is a storage bin.
His only purpose in
life is to grow a giant
irritated liver.

From Greece I showed
them emeralds and
art,
Roses and gold, drugs
and silks,
Furs and marbles and
cinnabar,
Parchments and
Smyrna figs,
And the quiet beauty
of a marble hand.

His misery is insignif-
icant to the delicacy
of his liver and the
pleasure it gives to
aristocratic bellies.

*Pâté is passed around. All scoop up handsful.
It evolves into a sensuous gluttony of touching
and kissing.*

BACCHANTS: Ummmmmmmm, it's good, it's rich,
it's fatted, it's slick, liverdip, ummmmmmmmm-
mmmm.

As the scene reaches its peak, TIGELLINUS
enters. TRIMALCHIO *and* FORTUNATA *unzip
the costumes.* ACHILTO *jumps down. The
scene dissolves.*

TIGELLINUS: Don't anybody leave. The emperor
is getting married again.

PETRONIUS: Giton, Encolpius, go! I didn't arrange this. He's up to something dangerous.
Get away!

ENCOLPIUS: Where, Petronius?!

PETRONIUS: Anywhere!

ENCOLPIUS, GITON, ACHILTO *and* PANNYCHIS:
[*Sing*]
Emigration to where?
Where to go?
Where's the dream gone?
Where's the rainbow?
Change your name.
Change your way of dressing.
Change your way of talking.
Change your language.
Change your occupation.
Change your nation.
Where to go?
Where's the dream gone?
Where's the rainbow?
Who do I worship?
Who am I?
What's my country?
Where am I?
Dislocation.
Everything is new and strange to me.
Nothing's where it used to be.
Running from wars and poverty, in-
sanity,
To another country. Where?

PETRONIUS: Why is Nero getting married again?

NERO *enters pregnant, a pillow under his
bridal dress.*

NERO: I HAD TO! THIS CHILD NEEDS A
NAME!

PETRONIUS: Nero, this is the product of a diseased mind!

NERO: DON'T SHOUT AT A PERSON IN MY CONDITION! [PENETRACION *and* SARAH LEE *are wrapped together. He pulls them apart*] Oh, marry me, Penetrácion? Make me an honest woman. Stop their vicious gossip.

PENETRACION: Señor, please, please don't make me do this.

NERO: OH, GODS! GODS! I'm not even married, and-I-think-I'm-going-to-be-a-widow-already. KILL HIM! KILL HIM!

BACCHANTS: [*Up thumbs*] NO! NO! *VIVAT! VIVAT! VIVAT!*

NERO *gives a limp wave for silence. Long pause. His thumb hangs in the air.*

NERO: Tiggy, what is "live" spelt backwards? [*Both do a short giggle. Down thumbs*] Die. [*Great storm of protest from* BACCHANTS. *A frothing rage from* NERO] IF YOU DON'T MARRY ME, I'LL KILL MYSELF!

PENETRACION: Señor, don't! You're a mother now! Think of our baby!

NERO, *pull the horse pillow out from under the dress and beat* PENETRACION *with it.*

NERO: YOUR BABY! YOUR BABY! THAT'S ALL I HEAR! YOUR BABY! [NERO, *chew the horse pillow*] OOOWWWW! I'M SO NERVOUS! MY NERVES ARE SHRRREE-EEEEEDDEDDD! I'LL NEVER FORGIVE YOU! NEVER! [*Hit him with the horse pillow again*] NEVER! NEVER! Penetrátion, MARRY ME!! [*Abrupt change*] Look at the poor thing. He's got my eyes. He's got your hoofs. We could be so happy.

PENETRACION: Ooh, señor, how would it look to the guys in the barracks?

NERO: We won't tell them. They don't have to know everything. I'll shave every day. We'll keep them guessing. Marry me.

PENETRACION: Ooh, what would the sergeant think if he knows I married a man who's pregnant with a 400-pound horse?

NERO: It might start a new fad. It could become all the rage. *Marry me!*

PENETRACION: NO!

NERO: I'm gonna slap you with a cactus! MARRY ME!

PENETRACION: *No! Nada! Imposible!*

NERO, *draw a knife. Screams, shouts.*

PRIAPUS: Petronius, stop him before he murders the audience!

PETRONIUS: He's deranged! He's got so crazy I can't stop him anymore!

PRIAPUS: INVENT SOMETHING! THROW HIM INTO A FIT!

NERO, *stab the pillow. Feathers everywhere. Run through the aisles, screaming.*

NERO: MY BABY! MY BABY! MY BABY! WHAT HAVE I DONE?! TELL THAT WOMAN TO STOP LAUGHING AT ME OR I'LL HIT HER WITH MY BABY!

PETRONIUS: NERO! COME UP HERE! You're acting insane.

NERO: I am *not* insane! I am *very* nervous, but I am *not* insane! If you put a glass plate in my head, you'd see an ant kingdom running around in there. But they're all doing *one thing* in there!

PETRONIUS: What is happening in there?

NERO: THEY ARE BURNING THE QUEEN ANT IN THERE! THAT IS WHAT IS HAPPENING IN THERE!

PETRONIUS: NERO! COME UP ON THE STAGE!

NERO: I don't have to do anything. I am a god and an emperor and a mother! With that kind of power I could start a war or send this whole room to bed without supper!

PETRONIUS: Now, look . . . my dove, you have a delicate psyche. We're your friends.

NERO, *come up on the stage.*

NERO: I don't have any friends.

PETRONIUS: You have Tigellinus.

NERO: Of course. Tiggy is my friend. I have Tiggy as a friend. DO YOU KNOW HOW BORING TIGGY IS?! [*Whines*] Why doesn't anybody love me?

PENETRACION: Señor, you are loco. When they catch you, they gonna put you in a soft room.

NERO: Did you hear? He sassed God!

TIGELLINUS: [*One long evil hiss*] Thiss-ssnakess-sspeech-hass-sslit-hiss-throat.

NERO: I am getting very *nervous!!*

PRIAPUS: Hurry up, Petronius!

PETRONIUS: It could be nerves . . . or it could be . . . epilepsy.

NERO: Epilepsy? Me?

PETRONIUS: All the great leaders had it. Caesar, Alexander . . .

NERO: Come on, I don't believe it.

PETRONIUS: Even Caligula had it.

NERO: CALIGULA! He's my hero! *I* want an epileptic fit! Stage it for me!

PETRONIUS: It'll be terrible what we'll see. A fit is a mental electrical storm.

BACCHANTS: DO IT! DO IT! STAGE IT FOR HIM!

PETRONIUS: Call the goddess Hypnos with the veil of sleeeeep!

QUARTILLA *runs nude across the stage trailing a veil behind her. She is blindfolded. Wind constantly plays on her. The veil is always in violent motion.*

HYPNOS: Rome rules the world. The world is gathered in one brain. The ruler of the world is having a fit. The world is afflicted.

NERO *falls to the floor in a screaming fit.* BACCHANTS *in head masks of shark jaws and double rows of serrated teeth. They dance around* NERO *and whisper in rondo.*

BACCHANTS: 1. Rumors, whispers, secrets, plots, intrigues, codes, messages, confessions, writings on the walls at night.

2. Conspiracies, denunciations, briberies, incriminations, associations, allegations.

3. Spies, informers, murders, exiles, poisons, suicides, assassinations, strangulations.

4. *Vae Tyrannis!*
Vae Tyrannis!
Vae Tyrannis!

HYPNOS: Nero is frightened. The guards are doubled. The guards are tripled. The walls are manned. The Forum's guarded. Rome's arrested. Nero is frightened from his skin. *His bones leave his body! Lightning rips the air! HE COUGHS UP HIS SKELETON!!*

Lightning cracks. Stop. The mood breaks.

NERO: Wait a minute. This isn't working.

PETRONIUS: Get the feel of it! Get into it!

All, at once.

HYPNOS: A fit is a mental electrical storm!

BACCHANTS: *Lightning rips the air!* HE COUGHS UP HIS SKELETON!

NERO *falls to the floor. He shrieks! He separates from his skeleton. The flesh and bones thrash apart in a fit.*

PETRONIUS: THE EMPERORS OF IMPERIAL ROME!!

BACCHANTS:	NERO:
Caesar!	Stabbed to death in Congress!
Augustus!	Poisoned by his wife, Livia!
Caligula!	Assassinated!
Claudius!	Poisoned by his wife, Agrippina!
Galba!	Murdered!
Otho!	Cannibalised!
Vitellius!	Pitchforked!
Domitian!	Flung down the steps!
Commodus!	Strangled!
Nero!?	[*Pause*]

NERO: NERO NOTHING! I won't die. I'll be plucked off the earth by a giant white bird

and flicked into the diamond galaxies of the sky.

BACCHANTS: NERO!!!???

HYPNOS: Nero, suicide.

BACCHANTS:
Nero butchers his family for treason!
He jumps on his pregnant wife, Poppaea!
He castrates a boy who looks like Poppaea and marries him!
He stabs his mother, Agrippina, in the womb!
He rapes his 14-year-old brother, Britannicus!
A world gone to hell in a teapot!

ENCOLPIUS: Good God, let's escape.

ACHILTO: Hide in the sewers.

PETRONIUS: STAY HERE! HELP ME! "HE CONDEMNS A YOUNG BOY AND GIRL." SAY IT!

PANNYCHIS: He condemns a young boy and girl. The gibbet. The noose is around their necks. The young boy and girl are virgins. SEE! THEIR BODIES ARE HAIRLESS!

GITON: Virgin death is a bad omen, forbidden by law. The executioneer rapes them with the noose around their necks. They are strangled. Their bodies flung on the Gemonian Steps. The crowd cowers and devours their bodies.

PANNYCHIS: Escape to the sewers.

ACHILTO: They flow to the sea.

ENCOLPIUS: We'll take a ship.

GITON: A storm is coming.

BACCHANTS: A FIT IS A MENTAL ELECTRICAL STORM!

ENCOLPIUS: ESCAPE TO THE SEA!

BACCHANTS: THE VIRGINS ARE RAPED AND HUNG! HIS THOUGHTS STAMPEDE!

ENCOLPIUS, GITON, ACHILTO *and* PANNYCHIS *rise upward and outward on a telescope crane, floating sea-blue banners behind them. Lightning cracks. Thunder sheets.*
  NERO *trembles and speaks rapidly, breathless in terror as the crane erects. He gets on it. Images pack and jam on each other.*

NERO: The virgins are led to the gibbet. The steps creak. My knees buckle. My legs sweat. I start to piss. He ties my hands behind my back. He smiles. He pats my ass. I can't help myself. I wink. The crowd laughs! *He puts the rope around my neck!* IT'S BIG! IT'S ROUGH! IT SCRATCHES MY NECK! IT BURNS MY THROAT! OH, GOD! VIRGIN DEATH!! FORBIDDEN BY LAW!! THE ANCIENT LAW!! Oh, my God, the long arm. Here it comes. The fist! [*The crane telescopes out*] HERE IT COMES! HE'S

GREASED HIS ARM!! HE'LL FUCK THE SKY!! THE CROWD LAUGHS! WHY DO THEY LAUGH?! THEY SHAKE THE TRAPDOOR UNDER MY FEET! STOP!! STOP!! DON'T RATTLE IT LOOSE!! CUT THE ROPE!! VIRGIN DEATH!! THEY LAUGH!! Oh, God, Oh, God, here he comes. THE EXECUTIONER!! HE'S GREASED HIS ARM! HE'S GREASED HIS FIST! WHY IS IT GREASED?! THEY LAUGH! THEY WINK! WHY??!! YOU CAN'T DO IT!! IT WON'T WORK!! CUT THE ROPE!! GOD! GOD! GOD! GOD! GOD! HE MUST SATISFY THE ANCIENT LAW!!! THE TRAPDOOR TREMBLES! STOP!! THE ARABS! THE BERBERS! THE TURKS! THE ARABS! "ALLAH WILL BE BORN FROM A MAN!!!" STOP!! STOP!! A FIST AS BIG AS ALLAH'S HEAD!!! IT WON'T WORK!!! THE ARM!! HERE IT COMES! HERE IT COMES! HERE IT COMES! HE SATISFIES THE ANCIENT LAW!!!!! THE CROWD LAUGHS! THE TRAPDOOR OPENS!! IT OPENS!! IT OPENS!! IT OPENS!!! IT OPENS!!!! IT OPENS!!!!! PACKED! RAMMED! LOADED! FITTED! LOCKED TOGETHER! THE ROPE CONTRACTS! THE ARM SPREADS! THE TRUMPETS SCREAM!! MY KNEES BUCKLE!! THE TRUMPETS SCREAM!! MY KNEES BUCKLE!! THE TRUMPETS SCREAM!! GOD IS BORN!!!!! PRIAPUS!! EROS!! ALLAH!! ALLAH!! THE ARM!! THE FIST!! ALLAH!!!!! ALLAH!!!!! AL-LAH!!!!! ALLAH!!!!! ALLAH!!!!! [NERO *falls. The orgasm completed. A twitching muscle spasm. The crane begins to retract. The storm fades. Soft music*]

PETRONIUS: Go! Go! Get away! Escape from this falling, dying world. It's soured to madness.

BACCHANTS *run off, leaving the chaos of a long party strewn across the stage.*

ENCOLPIUS: Come with us.

PETRONIUS: I can't. I'm in this world even though its flavor is gone and it's creaking to a halt and it's tongue's removed by *this maniac.* Its zodiac declines and falls and soon the earth's ready for another layer of extinct footprints she'll lay next to *Tyrannosaurus rex,* the Romans.

ENCOLPIUS: WHY?! WHY GODDAMN IT?!

ACHILTO: Why can't we stay and burn it down?! BURN EVERYTHING!

PETRONIUS: Burn everything? Nothing left to light the way? No books of counsel and reason? Nothing but the club in the long night of centuries.

GITON: I . . . I can't run away and leave.

PANNYCHIS: We'd rather sit by the road and wait for the night to come.

PETRONIUS: [*Song-speech*] There was a man who drove to work one day. He saw a boy and a girl sitting by the road, beading leather work. Hitchhike to nowhere. The next day he saw more of them, and the next day more, sitting by the road, waiting for the night to come. Soon he couldn't get through at all. The street lights went out. No one fixed them. The road holes got bigger. No one patched them. The cities, like people unloved, were abandoned. They collapsed from within and from without and withered away.

ENCOLPIUS: Come with us.

PETRONIUS: Go! I can't bear to be serious for too long. Run! This crazy man is waking up. Run!

ACHILTO: Come on! To the sewers!

PETRONIUS: Good-bye! Good-bye, Encolpius!

ENCOLPIUS *stops. He turns. They look at each other.*

ENCOLPIUS: Petronius, I want . . .

ACHILTO: COME ON! ENCOLPIUS! [*They run off. They do not say good-bye*]

PETRONIUS: Good-bye, you beautiful . . . beautiful . . . [*He stops. He lowers his hand*] Good-bye. [*He goes slowly to the platform*] Have they gone?

PRIAPUS: They sailed off in the distance and disappeared in a storm at sea, and I never saw them again.

PETRONIUS: He's waking up. He'll want to be amused. Give me an idea, Priapus!

PRIAPUS *laughs and swings up to the perch.* TIGELLINUS *and* PENETRACION *cradle* NERO's *head in their laps. They pass the head from lap to lap.*

TIGELLINUS: Take his head.

PENETRACION: You take it. It's like cradling a loaded bomb.

TIGELLINUS: How do you defuse it?

PENETRACION: Soak it in water.

NERO: [*Fitfully*] Damn Turks . . . where's his arm? . . . Did he marry me?

TIGELLINUS: No, he didn't.

NERO: He won't marry me? He won't marry me? *That is very funny.* KILL HIM! Tigellinus, stab Penetrácion. [AGRIPPINA *comes on, singed, slapping out the smoldering cloak*] Agrippina, you ruined your cloak, ooooh.

AGRIPPINA: YOU AND YOUR DAMN SURPRISES!

NERO: You're so hard to please. You don't like the barge!?

AGRIPPINA: NO!

NERO: I had it made special for you!

AGRIPPINA: I bet you did.

NERO: You don't like the pussy I put under your bed?

AGRIPPINA: The pussy had claws!

NERO: You don't like the flowers I sent?

AGRIPPINA: The flowers had asps!

NERO: You don't like the cloak?

AGRIPPINA: NO!!

NERO: You don't like any of my surprises?!

AGRIPPINA: Your goddamn barge broke in half!

NERO: Yes, I heard that.

AGRIPPINA: Your flowers bit me!

NERO: Yes, I heard that.

AGRIPPINA: Your pussy clawed me!

NERO: I heard that too.

AGRIPPINA: Your cloak burned the house down!

NERO: Yes, I heard that.

AGRIPPINA: I must be *brilliant* to be alive!

NERO: I didn't hear *that*. KILL HER!

AGRIPPINA: THEN STAB HERE WHERE I GAVE HIM BIRTH!!

> TIGELLINUS, *stab her in the womb. An abrupt, mad cheerfulness.*

NERO: It's morning, Petronius! Your festival night is finished! [*They exit*]

> PETRONIUS *is alone, writing the last entry in his book. As he writes,* ENCOLPIUS *crawls on, dripping wet.*

PETRONIUS: Now I, Petronius Arbiter, have seen lost, Achilto, Encolpius, Giton, Pannychis, those addicts of dreams. Their hot pursuit for pleasure snuffed and out. Like a swarm of damaged birds, lost and wandering in a storm at sea, crying down the empty night, "Rome is lost! Rome is lost!"

ENCOLPIUS: PETRONIUS! GITON'S GONE! HE'S RUN AWAY!

PETRONIUS: [*Continue as before. You do not hear him. He is not there*] And Encolpius, alone and lost, wanders slowly down the beach of the phalli fetishes, drenching wet, and cries out . . .

ENCOLPIUS: PETRONIUS! WHAT'S TO HAPPEN TO ME?!

PETRONIUS: Priapus, what shall I do?!

PRIAPUS: I'll help the one who lives. You're on your own. *Decide!* [PRIAPUS, *laugh through the speakers.* PETRONIUS, *clap your hands over your ears to shut the laughter out. Continue writing.* GITON *and* PANNYCHIS, *masked and gilded, dance toward him in slow pantomime. Hidden from us, they cut his wrists and bind them in golden tissues and strands of snow lilies*] Decide, Petronius! It's dawn!

PETRONIUS: Gone, those addicts of dreams, every taste jaded, they suffocate in ecstacy. [*To dancers*] Let me bathe them in warm water. No, let me bathe them in silver pots of warm perfume. I hate heroics, but I love luxury. [NERO *is carried on in a litter*] Divine Nero, you couldn't stay away.

NERO: "Divine" Petronius, no, I couldn't. Where's the glass?

PETRONIUS: [*Laughing*] The glass? I thought you came back to see me.

NERO: You remember I told you you could live as long as you give me pleasure. You don't please me anymore.

TIGELLINUS: Tomorrow you must be dead. Your name is on the list.

PETRONIUS: You finally got around to it.

NERO: If you give me the glass, I'll take your name off the list.

PETRONIUS: Bless you, you did make a list.

TIGELLINUS: And your name's right on top. In heliotrope.

PETRONIUS: It's the wrong color for pig Latin, Tiggy. Well, I thought it over.

NERO: And?

PETRONIUS: And it's not worth the price. But I'll let you look at it, and if you beg me, I'll let you sip spiced wine from it. There. [NERO *takes the fabulous glass from the altar*] Careful, pet, the least vulgar slurping will shatter it. But you're too refined to do that.

NERO: Oh, Petronius, this wine is impeccable. Your taste is perfect. You were my best teacher in luxury.

PETRONIUS: In the history of manners there never was a worse student than you.

NERO: You mean I flunked the course?

PETRONIUS: Hands down. [PETRONIUS *raises his arms. They see his slashed wrists and the blood falling from his flowered wounds*]

TIGELLINUS: You cheated! You're killing yourself!

NERO: Oh, Tiggy, shut up. You don't know style when you see it. How dull life will be when you're gone, Petronius. Between the assassins and the puritans, I don't know who will do me in. Thank you for the glass.

PETRONIUS: Sssh. A sound could shatter it.

> *Pause. Silence as* NERO *drinks.* PETRONIUS, *lift your bleeding arm and pluck a single string of a harp. The glass shatters in* NERO'S *mouth.*

NERO: [*Whisper*] You bitch. Burn this pen! BURN IT! Burn it to the ground! BURN IT! [TIGELLINUS *lights a torch*] Set fire to the whole city! Start it in your house! BURN IT DOWN!

TIGELLINUS: The mobs will blame me! They'll tear me apart!

NERO: Well then, Tiggy, you better add your name to the list to make it neat and complete. START THE FIRES!! [*Blazing red light begins to bathe the stage*] Lift me in. Get me to the Palatine quick before the fires spread. [*Pause*] What are you writing, Petronius, more amusements? They'll burn in the fires. [*For a moment, very sincere*] Good-bye, Gaius Petronius, Arbiter.

PETRONIUS: Good-bye, Lucius Domitius Nero, Emperor of Rome.

NERO: Oh, how I miss Agrippina on these little trips. [NERO *is littered off*]

PETRONIUS *advances through the broken and abandoned debris strewn across the stage, reading from his book.*

PETRONIUS: . . . and then, Encolpius, alone and lost and drenching wet, wanders slowly down the ancient beach and wonders sadly at the great work of the sea, encircled by the phalli fetishes . . . my life is leaving . . . going cold, far away as the Arctic star . . . Encolpius, half-drowned, half-crawling, walks down the ancient beach . . . [*He breaks off mid-sentence.* PRIAPUS *leads on* ACHILTO, *masked and gilded*]

ENCOLPIUS: PETRONIUS! WHAT'S TO HAPPEN TO ME?! GITON'S GONE!

PETRONIUS: [*Sings*]	PRIAPUS: [*Speaks*]
Where are they now, I cried,	. . . and then he met . . . a young Greek sailor . . .
All your anger and your greatness?	
But a moment ago You boasted of your pride and power,	
And yet, what are you now?	
And yet, we scheme and hope,	
Stuffing our foolish hearts with dreams,	
Scrimp and plan our lives	. . . a boy of flashing gold . . .
As though we had a thousand to live.	
Why, why?	. . . he stares at Encolpius . . . their eyes lock . . . he walks to him . . .
One little day ago,	
Somewhere in this world,	
Someone waits for someone,	
Never doubting his return,	
Or somewhere a someone	
You kissed good-bye,	
Never doubting his return.	. . . his legs like a god . . . measuring the earth with muscled calipers . . . they smile and they touch . . .
He sailed away in a silver ship.	
To think our every human hope	
Must someday come to this,	
This end of great ambitions,	
This poor drowned body of our dreams,	
And this was once a man,	. . . and they touch . . . and they touch . . . and they touch . . . they touch . . . yes.
This thing that floats now merely?	

ENCOLPIUS: Ooh! Thank you! Petronius!

The stage is ablaze in flashing red light, brighter and brighter. PETRONIUS *continues to advance, the blood pouring from his flowered wrists, and the music pulsing and climbing.*

BIOGRAPHIES

Information was furnished by the playwrights, except where otherwise indicated. The years indicated in parentheses in the *major works* classification denote the year each work was *written,* which may not coincide with the year of its first production or publication.

ABBREVIATIONS USED

b., date and place of birth
p., parents' names
fo., father's occupation
m., marriage
d., divorce
c., children
ed., education
po., occupations prior to writing
mw., major works
av., avocations
in., influences
ma., mailing address

BARAKA, IMAMU AMIRI (LeRoi Jones). *b.* October 7, 1934, Newark, New Jersey; *p.* Coyt L. and Anna Lois (Russ) Jones; *fo.* post office supervisor; *ed.* Newark Rutgers, Howard University, New School of Social Research, Columbia University; *po.* taught poetry at New School, taught drama at Columbia and literature at University of Buffalo, Visiting Professor at San Francisco State; *mw.* Plays: *Dante* (1962), *Dutchman** (1964), *The Baptism, The Toilet, Jello, Experimental Death Unit #1* (1965), *Black Mass* (1966), *Mad Heart, Slave Ship* (1967), *Great Goodness of Life* (1968), *Junkies Are Full of Shh . . . , Bloodrites* (1970) *Baraka* (1971); Books: see Bibliography;

av. founded Black Arts Repertory Theater School, Harlem, 1964; Spirit House, Newark, 1966; Newark political organizer for United Brothers, 1967, and Committee for United Newark, 1968; and member of International Coordinating Committee of Congress of African Peoples; *in.* revolutionary African nationalism; *ma.* c/o Ronald Hobbs Literary Agency, 211 East Forty-third Street, New York, New York 10017.

*Awards: Dutchman (Obie, Best American Play, 1964). Whitney Fellow, 1963. Guggenheim, 1965. Yoruba Academy Fellow, 1965.

BIBLIOGRAPHY:
Plays: *Dutchman* (William Morrow, 1964). *The System of Dante's Hell* (Grove Press, 1965). *The Baptism* (Grove Press, 1966). *The Toilet* (Grove Press, 1966). *Four Black Revolutionary Plays* (Bobbs-Merrill, 1969), includes *Experimental Death Unit #1, Great Goodness of Life, A Black Mass, Mad Heart. Baraka* in *Spontaneous Combustion Plays,* edited by Rochelle Owens (Winter House, 1972).
Books: *Preface to a Twenty-Volume Suicide Note* (Totem Corinth, 1961). *Blues People* (William Morrow, 1963). *The Dead Lecturer* (Grove Press, 1963). *Home* (William Morrow, 1965). *Black Music* (William Morrow, 1967). *Tales* (Grove Press, 1968). *Black Magic Poetry* (Bobbs-Merrill, 1969). *In Our Terribleness* (Bobbs-Merrill, 1970). *Black Fire* (co-edited with Larry Neal; William Morrow, 1968). *Raise Race Rays Raze: Essays Since 1965* (Random House, 1971). *The Life and Times of John Coltrane* (William Morrow, 1971). *African Congress* (William Morrow, 1971). *The Creation of the New-Ark* (William Morrow, 1972).

BARSHA, TONY (Anthony Richard Barsha). *b.* March 7, 1938, Los Angeles, California; *p.* Leon and Helen (Pollack) Barsha; *fo.* film producer and director; *m.* Yen Leung, 1966; *c.* Lili Nadja; *ed.* U.C.L.A. (B.A., Theatre Arts, Motion Pictures); *po.* film editor, writer, director, actor, formed Keystone Theatre Company group; *mw.* Plays: *The Trunk, The Pattern* (1966), *Smash, The Hawk* (with Murray Mednick) (1967), *A Vision Piece, Aleph* (with Ralph Gibson) (1969), *Forgotten American, Tragedy of Homer Stills* (1970); *av.* director, filmmaker, director of theatre workshop at Brooklyn House of Detention; *in.* Mack Sennett, Artaud, Black Elk, I.W.W.; *ma.* 39 First Avenue, New York, New York 10003.

BIBLIOGRAPHY:
The Hawk: An Improvisational Play (Bobbs-Merrill, 1968).

BOVASSO, JULIE (Julia Bovasso). *b.* August 1, 1930, Brooklyn, New York; *p.* Bernard Michael and Angela (Padovani) Bovasso; *fo.* teamster; *m.* George Ortman, 1951; *d.* 1958; *m.* Leonard Wayland, 1959; *d.* 1964; *ed.* City College New York; *po.* founder of Tempo Theatre* (1953–58), which introduced Genet, Ionesco, de Ghelderode to U.S. in professional productions, wrote for newspapers and magazines, actress; *mw. Moondreamers* (1963), *Gloria and Esperanza* (1968), *Down by the River Where Waterlilies Are Disfigured Everyday, Monday on the Way to Mercury Island, Shubert's Last Serenade* (1971), *The Final Experiment* (1972); *av.* actress, director, painter, teaches in theatre departments at New School and Sarah Lawrence; *in.* Genet, Carl Jung; *ma.* c/o Howard Rosenstone, William Morris Agency, 1350 Sixth Avenue, New York, New York 10019.

*Awards: Julie Bovasso (Obie, Best Actress for *The Maids,* Tempo Theatre, 1955); Tempo Theatre (Obie, Best Experimental Theatre, 1955); *Gloria and Esperanza* (Obie, Best Play, 1969); Julie Bovasso (Obie, Best Actress for *Gloria and Esperanza,* 1969); Julie Bovasso (Obie, Best Direction for *Gloria and Esperanza,* 1969); *Schubert's Last Serenade* (PBC National Radio Award, 1972); Rockefeller Foundation Playwriting Grant, 1969. New York State Council on the Arts Public Service Grant, 1970; Guggenheim Fellow Creative Writing in the Theatre, 1971.

BIBLIOGRAPHY:
Shubert's Last Serenade in *Spontaneous Combustion Plays,* edited by Rochelle Owens. (Winter House, New York, 1972.)

BULLINS, ED (Edward Artie Bullins). *b.* July 2, 1935, Philadelphia, Pennsylvania; *po.* founder of Black Arts West, San Francisco, Cultural Director of Black House, Oakland, California; *mw.* Plays:

How Do You Do (1964), *Clara's Ole Man,** *A Son Come Home,** *The Electronic Nigger** (1966), *In the Wine Time* (1968), *Goin' A Buffalo* (1969), *The Duplex* (1970), *The Fabulous Miss Marie* (1971), *Dialect Determinism* (1972); *av.* editor of *Black Theatre,* co-founder and resident playwright of New Lafayette Theatre, Harlem; *ma.* 2349 Seventh Avenue, Harlem, New York, New York 10030.

*Award: *Clara's Ole Man, A Son Come Home, Electronic Nigger* (Vernon Rice Award, Outstanding Achievement in Off Broadway Theatre, 1968).

BIBLIOGRAPHY:
Black issue of *The Drama Review* (No. 40) edited by Ed Bullins. *Five Plays by Ed Bullins* (Bobbs-Merrill, 1969), includes *Clara's Ole Man, In the Wine Time, Goin' A Buffalo, A Son Come Home, Electronic Nigger. The Duplex: A Black Love Fable in Four Movements* (William Morrow, 1971). *Dialect Determinism* in *Spontaneous Combustion Plays,* edited by Rochelle Owens (Winter House, 1972).
    Information compiled from above sources and an autobiographical form on file with Bobbs-Merrill (New York).

DREXLER, ROSALYN (Rosalyn Selma Bronznick). *b.* November 25, 1926, Bronx, New York; *p.* George B. and Hilda (Sherman) Bronznick; *fo.* pharmacist; *m.* Sherman Drexler, 1946; *c.* Rachel, Danny; *po.* lady wrestler (under name of Rosa Carlo, "The Mexican Spitfire"), masseuse, playground director, waitress at Schrafft's, sculptress, singer; *mw.* Plays: *Home Movies** (1961), *The Line of Least Existence* (1967); Short Story: "Dear"* (*Paris Review,* 1966); Novels: *I Am the Beautiful Stranger* (1965), *One or Another* (1970), *To Smithereens* (1972); *av.* painter, singer, freelance feature writer; *in.* Nathaniel West, Machado DeAssis; *ma.* c/o Georges Borchardt, 145 East Fifty-second Street, New York, New York 10022.

*Awards: *Homes Movies* (Obie, Distinguished Playwriting, 1964); "Dear" (Humor Award for Fiction). Guggenheim and Rockefeller Grants.

BIBLIOGRAPHY:
Plays: *Line of Least Existence and Other Plays* (Random House, 1967), including *Home Movies, The Investigation, Hot Buttered Roll, Softly, and Consider the Nearness, The Bed Was Full.*
Novel: *I Am the Beautiful Stranger* (Grossman, 1965; Dell, 1967). *One or Another* (Dutton, 1970; Dell, 1971). *To Smithereens* (New American Library, 1972).

EYEN, TOM (Thomas Lee Eyen). *b.* August 14, 1941, Cambridge, Ohio; *p.* Abraham and Julia (Farhad) Eyen; *fo.* restaurateur; *m.* Lisa Giraudeaux, 1967; *c.* Jacque; *ed.* Ohio State; *po.* press-agent assistant for Max Eisen and Dorothy Ross, N.Y.C.; *mw.* Plays: *Frustrata, the Dirty Little Girl with the Red Paper Rose Stuck in Her Head, is Demented, The White Whore and the Bit Player, My Next Husband Will be a Beauty* (1964), *Why Hanna's Skirt Won't Stay Down, Miss Nefertiti Regrets* (1965), *Give My Regards to Off Off Broadway* (1966), *Court, Sarah B. Divine, Grand Tenement and November 22nd* (1967), *Kama Sutra: An Organic Happening, Who Killed My Bald Sister Sophie?* (1968), *The No Plays, Caution: A Love Story, Eye in New York* (1969), *The Fully Guaranteed Fuck-Me Doll, What Is Making Gilda So Gray?, The Dirtiest Show in Town* (1970); *av.* swimming, surfing; *in.* Jerome Robbins, Barbara Harris, Nichols and May, Julius Monk; *ma.* c/o Marian Searchinger, Creative Management Associates, 600 Madison Avenue, New York, New York 10022. Awards: Rockefeller Grant, 1967. Guggenheim Fellow, 1970.

BIBLIOGRAPHY:
White Whore and the Bit Player in *New American Plays,* Vol. II (Hill and Wang, 1965). *Sarah B. Divine! and other plays by Tom Eyen,* edited by Michael Feingold (Winter House, 1972), including *Three Sisters from Springfield, Ill.* (trilogy), *Areatha in the Ice Palace, Kama Sutra, White Whore,. Death of Off-Broadway,* others.

FORNES, MARIA IRENE (Mary Irene Fornés). *b.* May 14, 1930, Havana, Cuba; *p.* Carlos and Carmen (Collado) Fornés; *fo.* government clerk; *po.* factory worker, interpreter, export clerk, waitress at Stouffer's, painted flowers on trays, textile designer, opened envelopes; *mw.* Plays: *The Widow* (1960), *Tango Palace* (1961), *The Successful Life of 3,** *Promenade** (one-act version, 1963), *The Office* (1964), *A Vietnamese Wedding, Molly's Dream* (1967), *Dr. Kheal, The Red Burning Light* (1968), *Promenade* (full length, 1969), *Aurora* (1972); *av.* director, creates costumes and props, travel; *in.* production of Beckett's *Waiting for Godot* (Paris, 1954), production of Joyce's *Ulysses in Nighttown* (New York, with Zero Mostel, directed by Burgess Meredith), *The Goon Show,* Ionesco; *ma.* 1 Sheridan Square, New York, New York 10014.

* Award: *The Successful Life of 3* and *Promenade* (Obie, Distinguished Playwriting, 1965). Whitney Foundation Grant, 1961–62. Rockefeller Foundation Grant, 1971. Guggenheim and New York State Council on the Arts Grants, 1972.

BIBLIOGRAPHY:
Tango Palace, The Successful Life of 3 in *Playwrights for Tomorrow,* Anthology (University of Minnesota Press, 1966). *Promenade* in *The Bold New Woman,* Anthology (Fawcett, 1966). *The Successful Life of 3* in *Eight Plays from Off Off Broadway,* edited by Michael Smith (Bobbs-Merrill, 1966). *Promenade* in *The New Underground Theatre,* Anthology (Bantam, 1968). *Dr. Kheal* in *The Best of Off Off Broadway,* edited by Michael Smith (Dutton, 1969). *Tango Palace* in *Concepts of Literature,* Anthology (Prentice-Hall, 1971). *Promenade and Other Plays* (Winter House, 1971).

FOSTER, PAUL. *b.* October 15, 1931, Pennsgrove, New Jersey; *p.* Eldridge and Mary (Manning) Foster; *fo.* lawyer; *ed.* Rutgers (B.A., English Lit.), New York University Law School, St. John University Law School; *po.* co-founder of La Mama ETC in 1962; *mw.* Plays: *Hurrah for the Bridge** (1963), *Balls, The Recluse* (1964), *The Madonna in the Orchard* (1965), *The Hessian Corporal* (1966), *Tom Paine* (1967), *Heimskringla* (1969), *Satyricon* (1970), *Elizabeth 1st* (1971); *av.* whale preservation; *ma.* 193 Orchard Street, New York, New York 10002.

*Awards: *Hurrah for the Bridge* (Irish Drama Prize, 1967). *Tom Paine* (New York Drama Critics Circle Award, 1968, Galway Cup, Ireland, 1969), Rockefeller Grant, 1967–69. New York State Council on the Arts Grant, 1972.

BIBLIOGRAPHY:
Balls (Bobbs-Merrill, 1966). *Tom Paine* (Grove Press, 1967). *The Madonna in the Orchard* (Breakthrough Press, 1971). *Tom Paine and Other Plays* (Winter House, 1973).

GUARE, JOHN (John Edward Guare). *b.* February 5, 1938, New York City; *p.* John Edward and Helen (Grady) Guare; *fo.* N.Y. Stock Exchange; *ed.* Georgetown University (A.B., English, 1960); *po.* car parker, garbage man, cabana boy, machinist in Good Humor factory, reader for publishing house, advance man for stock tour, sold honeymoons; *mw.* Plays: *To Wally Pantoni, We Leave a Credenza* (1964), *Day for Surprises* (1965), *Loveliest Afternoon of the Year* (1966), *Muzeeka** (1967), *Cop Out** (1968), *Home Fires* (1969), *The House of Blue Leaves** (1966–70), *Two Gentlemen of Verona* (1971, adaptation and lyrics; music by Galt MacDermot); Screenplay: *Taking Off* (with Milos Foreman, 1970); *in.* Broadway productions of *Gypsy, The Homecoming,* Old Vic production of *A Flea in Her Ear,* Strindberg; *ma.* c/o Andrew Boose, Greenbaum, Wolff and Ernst, 437 Madison Avenue, New York, New York.

*Awards: *Muzeeka* (Obie, Distinguished Playwriting, 1968); *Cop Out* (New York Drama Critics'

Circle, Most Promising Playwright, 1969); *The House of Blue Leaves* (Obie, Best Play; New York Drama Critics' Circle, Best American Play; Outer Circle, Best Playwriting, 1970). *Two Gentlemen of Verona* (Tony Award, Best Musical; New York Drama Critics' Circle Award, Best Musical, 1972).

BIBLIOGRAPHY:

Three by John Guare (Grove Press, 1970), includes *Muzeeka, Cop Out, Home Fires. Day of Surprises* in *Best Short Plays of 1970,* Stanley Richards, editor (Avon, 1970). *The House of Blue Leaves* (Viking, 1972).

GURNEY, A. R. (Albert R. Gurney, Jr.) *b.* November 1, 1930, Buffalo, New York; *m.; c.* four; *ed.* Williams College (B.A. English) Yale School of Drama (M.F.A., Playwriting); *po.* Professor of Literature at M.I.T.; *mw.* Plays: *The Rape of Bunny Stuntz* (1966), *The Golden Fleece* (1967), *The David Show* (1968), *The Love Course* (1969), *Scenes from American Life** (1971); *av.* sports; *in.* classical French drama, Yale Drama School, childhood; *ma.* c/o Claire Degener, Sterling Lord Agency, 660 Madison Ave., New York, New York 10022.

* Award: *Scenes from American Life* (Drama Desk Award, 1971).

BIBLIOGRAPHY:

The Love Course in *Best Short Plays of 1970,* Stanley Richards, editor (Avon, 1970). *Three People* in *Best Short Plays of 1955–56,* Margaret Mayorga, Editor (Beacon, 1956). *Turn of the Century* in *Best Short Plays of 1957–58,* Margaret Mayorga, Editor (Beacon, 1958). *Scenes from American Life* (Samuel French, 1970).

HEIDE, ROBERT (Robert Heitke). *b.* May 9, 1939, Irvington, New Jersey; *p.* Ludwig and Olga (Straefle) Heitke; *fo.* tool and die manufacturer; *ed.* Northwestern University (B.A., Speech, 1962); *po.* factory worker, dialogue writer for MGM, taught for East Harlem Youth Employment Service, production assistant for Living Theatre and Stratford; *mw.* *Hector, West of the Moon* (1964), *The Bed* (1965, incorporated into Warhol's *The Chelsea Girls* film, 1966), *Statue, Why Tuesday Never Has a Blue Monday** (1966), *Moon* (1967), *At War with the Mongols* (1970), *Split Level* (1972); *av.* collecting pop Americana and twentieth-century American history; *in.* Edward Albee, Julian Beck and Judith Malina, Alvina Krause, Stella Adler, Uta Hagen, existentialist playwrights; *ma.* 84 Christopher Street, New York, New York 10014.

*Award: *Why Tuesday Never Has a Blue Monday* (National Catholic Theatre Award, 1969).

BIBLIOGRAPHY:

Moon in *The Best of Off Off Broadway,* edited by Michael Smith (Dutton, 1969). *Why Tuesday Never Has a Blue Monday* (Breakthrough Press). *At War With the Mongols* in *New American Plays* (Vol. 4), edited by William M. Hoffman (Hill and Wang).

HOFFMAN, WILLIAM M. (William Moses Hoffman). *b.* April 12, 1939, New York City; *p.* Morton and Johanna (Papiermeister) Hoffman; *fo.* caterer; *ed.* City College New York (Phi Beta Kappa, Latin); *po.* worked in laundromat, wrote liner notes for rock albums, movie scripts, book reviews for *Library Journal* and *Status* magazine; *mw.* Plays: *Thank You, Miss Victoria* (1966), *Goodnight, I Love You, Saturday Night at the Movies* (1966), *Spring Play, The Masked Dances* XX (1967), X X (1968), *From Fool to Hangman, A* X *Quick Nut Bread to Make Your Mouth Water* (1970), *Buddha!* (1972, musical); *av.* editor of New American Plays Series (Hill and Wang), poet; *in.* Beethoven, Bach, Balinese temple music, sun, Byrd Hoffman; *ma.* c/o Gilbert Parker, Curtis Brown, Ltd, 60 East 59th Street, New York, New York 10022.

BIBLIOGRAPHY:

Plays: *Thank You, Miss Victoria* in *New American Plays,* Vol. 3 (Hill and Wang, 1970). *From Fool to Hangman* in *Meal* (Hunter College Press, 1970). *Goodnight, I Love You* XX (Breakthrough Press, 1973). X X in *More* X *Plays from Off Off Broadway,* edited by Michael Smith (Bobbs-Merrill, 1972). *A Quick Nut Bread to Make Your Mouth Water* in *Spontaneous Combustion Plays,* edited by Rochelle Owens (Winter House, 1972).

Poetry: *The Cloisters* (a song cycle, music by John Coregliano, G. Schirmer, 1968). *Thirty-One New American Poets,* edited by Ron Schreiber (Hill and Wang, 1970). *Fine Frenzy,* edited by Baylor E. Stokes (McGraw-Hill, 1972).

HOROVITZ, ISRAEL (Israel Arthur Horovitz). *b.* March 31, 1939, Wakefield, Massachusetts; *p.* Julius Charles and Hazel Rose (Solberg) Horovitz; *fo.* attorney; *m.* Doris Keefe, 1960; *c.* Rachael, Matthew, Adam; *ed.* Harvard College (B.A., 1961), Fellow, University of London at the Royal Academy of Dramatic Art, London, England (M.A., 1963), The City University of New York (Ph.D., 1972); *po.* stage manager, stagehand, carpenter, film director, film critic for *Eye Magazine,* art critic for *Craft Horizons Maga-*

zine, literary critic for *Village Voice* and *Magazine Littéraire* (Paris); *mw.* Plays: *The Indian Wants the Bronx** (1966), *It's Called The Sugar Plum** (1967), *Rats** (1968), *Line** (1968), *Morning* (originally entitled *Chiaroscuro*) (1968), *Leader** (1969), *The Honest-to-God Schnozzola** (1969), *Dr. Hero* (1970), *Acrobats* (1971), *The Wakefield Plays: A Triology—Alfred the Great, Our Father's Failing,* and *Alfred Dies* (1971–72); Screenplays: *Alfredo* (United Artists, 1968), *The Strawberry Statement** (MGM, 1969–70), *Camerian Climbing* (MGM, 1970), *Believe in Me* (MGM, 1971, originally entitled *Speed Is of the Essence*), *The Sad-Eyed Girls in the Park* (Columbia Pictures, 1972), *Acrobats* (Stuart Films, 1972); Fiction: *Capella* (a novel, Harper & Row Publishers, Inc., New York: 1972); Poetry: *Spider Poems and Other Writings* (Harper & Row Publishers, Inc., New York: 1972); *av.* contributing editor, *Magazine Littéraire,* Paris ("Words From New York: La Chronique de Israel Horovitz"); Professor of English, The City College, New York; regular contributor, *Village Voice; ma.* c/o Mary Dolan, Gloria Safier (literary) Agency, 667 Madison Avenue, New York, New York 10021, or c/o Martonplay, 33 avenue Champs-Elysées, Paris, 8e, France; or c/o Margaret Ramsay, 14a Godwin's Court, London, W1, England.

*Awards: *The Indian Wants the Bronx* (Obie Award, Vernon Rice—Drama Desk Award, and *Jersey Journal* Best Play Award, 1968–69); *It's Called The Sugar Plum* (*Plays & Players* Best Foreign Play Award, England, 1969–70); *Leader* and *The Honest-to-God Schnozzola* (Obie Award, 1969–70); *Show Business* Grand Award, Best American Playwright (1969–70, for *Rats* and *Line*); *The Strawberry Statement* (Cannes Film Festival, Prix de Jury, 1970–71); Award in Literature, American Academy of Arts and Letters (1972–73).

Honors: First American to be chosen as Playwright-in-Residence, Royal Shakespeare Company, Aldwych Theatre, London (1965); Fellowship in Playwriting, Rockefeller Foundation (1968, and again in 1969); Fellowship in Playwriting, New York State Council on the Arts (1972–73).

BIBLIOGRAPHY:
First Season (includes *Line, The Indian Wants the Bronx, It's Called the Sugar Plum,* and *Rats,* plus introduction by Horovitz, Random House, 1968); *Rats* in *Collision Course,* (ed.) Edward Parone (Random House, 1968); *The Indian Wants the Bronx,* in *Best Short Plays— 1969,* (ed.) Stanley Richards (Chilton, 1969; Avon Books, 1970); *The Indian Wants the Bronx* (Dramatists Play Service, 1969); *Rats* (DPS, 1969); *It's Called the Sugar Plum* (DPS, 1969); *Morning* in *Morning, Noon and Night* (Horovitz *et al*, Random House, 1969); *Acrobats* (in *Show Magazine,* May 1970); *Morning* (Samuel French, 1970); *Trees and Leader*

(DPS, 1970); *Acrobats* in *Best Short Plays of 1970,* (ed.) Stanley Richards (Chilton, 1970, Avon Books, 1971); *The Honest-to-God Schnozzola* (Breakthrough Press, 1971); *Play for Trees* (*Scholastic Voice,* May 1972); *Capella* (Harper & Row, 1972); *Spider Poems and Other Writings* (Harper & Row, 1972); *The Indian Wants the Bronx,* in *Best Plays of the 1960's* (ed.) Harold Clurman (Dell, 1972); *Le Première* (translated by Claude Roy, Gallimard, Paris, 1972); *Schnozzola* (translated by Jean-Paul Dellamotte, Gallimard, Paris, 1972); *L'Indien Cherche le Bronx* et *Sucre D'Orge* (Gallimard, Paris, 1972).

KATZ, LEON. *b.* July 10, 1919, New York City; *p.* Bernard and Rose (Koslow) Katz; *fo.* grocer; *m.* Sadell Kasmere, 1941; *c.* Elia, Fredric; *ed.* City College of New York (B.S.S., 1940), Columbia University (M.A., 1946, Ph.D., 1952, English and Comparative Lit.); *po.* teacher, director, actor, TV drama critic, radio film critic, TV writer; *mw.* Plays: *The Three Cuckolds, Finnegans Wake* (from Joyce, 1950), *Amerika* (from Kafka, 1958), *Dracula:Sabbat, Toy Show* (1970), *Swellfoot's Tears* (1971) *The Making of Americans* (from Stein, 1972); Teleplays: *Confrontation** (1969, N.E.T.), *Biography: George Washington* (1971, N.E.T.); Screenplay: *Lee* (1968, unproduced); *in.* Stein, Chekhov, Joyce, Artaud, Strindberg; *ma.* 5742 Northumberland Street, Pittsburgh, Pennsylvania 15217.

*Award: *Confrontation* (N.E.T. Award, Outstanding Contribution to Television, 1969).

BIBLIOGRAPHY:
The Three Cuckolds in *Classic Theatre,* Vol. I, edited by Eric Bentley (Anchor Books).

KENNEDY, ADRIENNE (Adrienne Lita Hawkins). *b.* September 13, 1931, Pittsburgh, Pennsylvania; *p.* Cornell W. and Etta (Haugabook) Hawkins; *fo.* social worker; *m.* Joseph C. Kennedy, 1953; *d.* 1966; *c.* Joseph, Adam; *ed.* Ohio State (B.S., Education, 1953); *po.* mother; *mw.* *The Pale Blue Flower* (1956), *Funnyhouse of a Negro** (1962), *The Owl Answers* (1963), *A Rat's Mass* (1965), *A Lesson in Dead Language* (1966), *A Beast's Story* (1967), *In His Own Write* (with John Lennon and Victor Spinetti), *Sun* (1969); Screenplay: *Funnyhouse of a Negro* (unproduced, with Pablo Ferro, 1971); *av.* collects letters from famous people; *in.* Edward Albee, Tennessee Williams, the Bible; *ma.* 100 York St., New Haven, Conn. 06511.

*Award: *Funnyhouse of a Negro* (Obie, Distinguished Playwriting, 1964).

BIBLIOGRAPHY:
The Owl Answers in *New American Plays,* Vol. II (Hill and Wang, 1962). *A Lesson in Dead*

Language in *Collision Course,* edited by Edward Parone (Random House, 1968). *Funnyhouse of a Negro* in *Best Short Plays* (Avon, 1969). *Cities in Bezique* in *Contemporary Black Drama* (Scribners). *Sun* in *Spontaneous Combustion Plays,* edited by Rochelle Owens (Winter House, 1972).

KOUTOUKAS, H. M. (Haralimbus Medea Koutoukas). *b.* June 4, 1947, aboard *Île de France; p.* Hartabie and Agnia (Daily) Koutoukas; *fo.* import/export; *m.* Countess Olivera Sajkovitch, 1965; *d.* 1965; *ed.* Middletown College, New School for Social Research; *po.* kept in many places, invented Camp, chamber theatre for penthouses, newspaper theatre; *mw. The Cargo Cult, The Last Triangle,* * *Only a Countess May Dance When She's Crazy, Turtles Don't Dream or Happy Birthday, Jesus* (1964), *Medea, Michael Touched Me, Pomegranada* (1965), *Letter from Colette* (1966), *Two Camps* (1967), *Tidy Passions, Tender Tales, Jews Should Be Well Done, Negroes are Negroes* (1968), *Last Night I Dreamt I was Julie Bravado, Invocations of a Haunted Mind* (1969); *av.* the sacrifice of noble youth, the cobra cult; *in.* memorials of things gone by; *ma.* 87 Christopher Street, New York, New York 10014.

*Awards: *The Last Triangle* (National Arts Club Award, 1964); special Obie Award "for the style and energy of his assault on the theatre in both playwriting and production," 1966.

KRAUSS, RUTH (Ruth Ida Krauss) *b.* July 24 or 25 (hour of midnight), 19??, Baltimore, Maryland; *p.* Julius and Blanche (Rosenfeld) Krauss; *fo,* artist, inherited fur business; *m.* Crockett Johnson, *circa* 1950; *ed.* dropped out of elementary school, graduate of Parsons' School of Fine and Applied Arts, attended Columbia University and New School (studied under Kenneth Koch and Frank O'Hara); *po.* anthropologist (lived with Blackfeet Indians and worked with Ruth Benedict), violinist; *mw.* Plays: *A Beautiful Day,* other poem plays (1963); Books: see Bibliography; *av.* swimming; *in.* Koch, O'Hara, surrealist French, Spanish poets, new German poets, modern American poets; *ma.* 24 Owenoke Road, Owenoke Park, Westport, Connecticut 06880.

BIBLIOGRAPHY:
Children's Books: *A Hole Is to Dig, The Carrot Seed, I'll Be You, I Can Fly, A Moon or a Button, Open House for Butterflies* (Harper and Row.) *The Cantilever Rainbow,* collection of poems and theatre poems (Pantheon, 1965). *There's a Little Ambiguity Over There Among the Bluebells,* theatre poem collection (Something Else Press, 1969). *If Only,* poem mono-

logue (Toad Press, 1969). *Under Twenty,* poem collection (Toad Press, 1971). *Somebody Else's Nut Tree,* tales from children (Bookstore Press, Lenox, Mass., 1971). *The Little King, The Little Queen, The Little Monster,* 3 plays for children (Toad Press 1972).

LEACH, WILFORD (Carson Wilford Leach). *b.* August 26, 1929, Petersburgh, Virginia; *p.* C. W. and Louise Leach; *fo.* auto salesman; *ed.* College of William and Mary (B.A., 1949), University of Illinois (M.A., 1954, Ph.D., 1957); *po.* teacher at Hollins College, University of Illinois; *mw.* Plays: *Gertrude* (1959), *Zodiac of Memphis Street* (1964), *In 3 Zones* (1966), *Camilla, The Damask Drum, Demon* (1970); Directed film: *The Wedding Party* (1966); *av.* co-director of La Mama ETC Company, teaches film and theatre at Sarah Lawrence; *in.* movies, Gertrude Stein, Berliner Ensemble; *ma.* c/o La Mama, 74 East Fourth Street, New York, New York 10003.

LUDLAM, CHARLES. *b.* April 12, 1943, New York City; *p.* Joseph and Marjorie (Braun) Ludlam; *fo.* plasterer; *ed.* Hofstra University (B.A., Dramatic Literature); *po.* actor, director; *mw.* Plays: *Big Hotel, Conquest of the Universe* or *When Queens Collide* (1967), *Turds in Hell* (with Bill Vehr, 1968), *Bluebeard* (1969), *Eunuchs of the Forbidden City* (1971); *in.* Lord Dunsany, Ronald Firbank, J. K. Huysmans; *ma.* c/o New Arts Management, 100 Fifth Avenue, New York, New York 10011.

* Awards: Ridiculous Theatrical Comany (Obie, 1961); *Bluebeard* (2nd Prize, Bitef Festival, Belgrade, 1971); Guggenheim, 1971.

BIBLIOGRAPHY:
Turds in Hell in *TDR,* Vol. 14, No. 4.

McNALLY, TERRENCE (Michael Terrence McNally). *b.* November 3, 1939, St. Petersburg, Florida; *p.* Shubert Arthur and Dorothy Katherine (Rapp) McNally; *fo.* Schlitz beer distributor; *ed.* Columbia University (B.A., English, 1961); *po.* newspaper reporter, tutor for children of John Steinbeck, stage manager at Actors' Studio; *mw.* Plays: *And Things That Go Bump in the Night* (1964), *Sweet Eros, Witness, Tour, Noon* (1968), *Cubi-Si, Next* (1969), *Bad Habits, Where Has Tommy Flowers Gone?* (1971), *The Tubs* (1972); *in.* Shakespeare, Mozart, Albee's *Zoo Story,* Beckett, Pinter, contemporary American playwrights; *ma.* c/o William Morris Agency, 1350 Sixth Avenue, New York, New York 10019.

BIBLIOGRAPHY:
And Things That Go Bump in the Night in *Playwrights for Tomorrow: A Collection of Plays,*

Vol. I (University of Minnesota Press, 1966). *Tour* in *Collision Course,* edited by Edward Parone (Random House, 1968). *Sweet Eros, Next and Other Plays* (Random House, 1969).

MEDNICK, MURRAY. *b.* August 24, 1939, Brooklyn, New York; *p.* Sol Joseph and Betty (Greenstein) Mednick; *fo.* motion picture projectionist; *m.* Amy Herman, 1963; *d.* 1966; *ed.* Brooklyn College; *po.* waiter, dealer in exotic imports, member of Heavy Metal Kid rock group, taught playwriting at Theatre Genesis; *mw.* Plays: *The Box* (1965), *The Mark of Zorro, Guideline* (1966), *Sand, The Hawk* (with Tony Barsha) (1967), *Willie the Germ, The Hunter* (1968), *The Shadow Ripens* (1969), *The Deerkill** (1970), *Cartoon* (1971); *av.* musician; *in.* Theatre Genesis, Artaud, Genet, Céline; *ma.* 475 First Street, Brooklyn, New York 11215.

*Awards: *The Deerkill* (Obie, Distinguished Playwriting, 1970); Rockefeller Grants, 1968, 1972; Poetry Award, National Council on the Arts, 1968.

BIBLIOGRAPHY:

The Hawk: An Improvisational Play (Bobbs-Merrill, 1968). *The Hunter* (Bobbs-Merrill, 1969). *The Deer Kill* (Bobbs-Merrill, 1971). *Three Poets* and *Cartoon and Other Plays* (Bobbs-Merrill, in preparation).

MELFI, LEONARD (Leonard Anthony Melfi). *b.* February 21, 1935, Binghamton, New York; *p.* Leonard and Louise (Gennarelli) Melfi; *fo.* roadside tavern keeper; *ed.* St. Bonaventure (1954–57); *po.* carpenter, refinished furniture, waiter at Village Gate, ticket taker at Eighth St. Playhouse, N.Y.C.; *mw.* Plays: *Lazy Baby Susan* (1962), *Birdbath, Ferryboat* (1965), *Niagara Falls* (1966), *Times Square, The Shirt* (1967), *Halloween, Stimulation, Jack and Jill* (in *Oh! Calcutta!*), *Having Fun in the Bathroom, Stars and Stripes, Night, The Breech Baby, Wet and Dry* (1968), *Alive, The Jones Man* (1969), *Cinque* (1970), *Beautiful, Sweet Suite* (1971), *The Delaware Water Gap, Lake Success* (1972); Screenplays: *Mortadella* (1971, Carlo Ponti, U.A.), *Times Square, To Forget Palermo; av.* songwriter, painter; *in.* Ellen Stewart, Nan and Gay Talese, Elaine Dundy; *ma.* 320 East Seventy-third Street, New York, New York 10021.

BIBLIOGRAPHY:

Encounters: Six One-Act Plays by Leonard Melfi (Random House). *Night* in *Morning, Noon and Night* (Random House, 1969). *Stars and Stripes* in *Collision Course,* edited by Edward Parone (Random House, 1968). *Cinque* in *Spontaneous Combustion Plays,* edited by Rochelle Owens (Winter House, 1972).

NOONAN, JOHN FORD. *b.* October 7, 1943, New York City; *p.* John Ford and Rita (McGannon) Noonan; *fo.* dentist; *m.* Marcia Lunt, 1962; *d.* 1965; *c.* Tracy Walker, Ian Christopher; *ed.* Brown University (B.A., 1964), Carnegie Tech (M.A., 1966); *po.* taught at Buckley Country Day School, stagehand at Fillmore East; *mw.* Year *Boston Won the Pennant* (1969), *Rainbows for Sale* (1970), *Good-by and Keep Cold* (1971), *Older People* (1972); *av.* music listening; *in.* all my close friends; *ma.* 233 W. Fourth Street, New York, New York 10014.

BIBLIOGRAPHY:

Year Boston Won the Pennant (Evergreen, Grove Press, Inc., 1970).

OPPENHEIMER, JOEL (Joel Lester Oppenheimer). *b.* February 18, 1930, Yonkers, New York; *p.* Leopold and Kate (Rosenwasser) Oppenheimer; *fo.* retail merchant; *m.* Rena Furlong, 1952; *d.* 1960; *m.* Helen Bukberg, 1966; *c.* Nicholas Patrick, Daniel Eben, Nathaniel Ezra, Lemuel Shandy Davin; *ed.* Cornell School of Civil Engineering, University of Chicago, Black Mountain College; *po.* ran advertising type shop, editor of poetry magazines, director of St. Mark's Church-in-the-Bowery Poetry Project (1966–68); *mw.* Plays: *The Great American Desert* (1960), *Like a Hill* (1961), *Miss Right* (1962), *The Perfect Detonator* (1965), *Bad Times in Bummersville* (1968, with Bummers Co.); Poems: see Bibliography; *av.* military history, pornography, sports; *in.* William Carlos Williams, Miles Davis, Franz Kline, Li Po, Pierre Vidal, Browning, Van Gogh; *ma.* c/o Karen Hitzig, Wender and Associates, 1545 Broadway, New York, New York, 10036.

BIBLIOGRAPHY:

Play: *The Great American Desert* (Grove Press, 1966).
Poetry: *The Dancer* (Jargon, 1951). *The Dutiful Son,* collection (Jargon, 1956). *The Love Bit,* collection (Totem/Corinth, 1961). *In Time,* collection (Bobbs-Merrill, 1969). *Sirventes on a Sad Occurrence* (Perishable Press, 1967). *Treatise* (Brownstone Press, 1966).

OWENS, ROCHELLE (Rochelle Bass). *b.* April 2, 1936, Brooklyn, New York; *p.* Maxwell and Molly (Adler) Bass; *fo.* postal clerk; *m.* David Owens, 1956; *d.* 1960; *m.* George Economou, 1962; *po.* lot saleswoman for Parke-Bernet Galleries, store detective, shoe inspector for Jonas, perfume tester for whaling company, camp counselor; *mw.* Plays: *Futz** (1959), *String Game, Homo* (1964), *Istanbul* (1965), *Beclch* (1966), *He Wants Shih* (1968), *Kontraption, The Karl Marx Play* (1971), *Baal Shem* (1972); *av.* poet, creates collages, practices self-hypnosis; *in.* Gerard Manley Hopkins, Grimm fairy tales, the Bible; *ma.* c/o Elisabeth Marton, 96 Fifth Avenue, New York, New York 10011.

*Awards: *Futz* (Obie, Distinguished Playwriting, 1967); Guggenheim Fellow (1971).

BIBLIOGRAPHY:

Poetry: *Not Be Essence That Cannot Be* (Trobar Press, 1960). *Four Young Lady Poets* (Totem/Corinth Press, 1961). *Salt and Core* (Black Sparrow Press, 1968). *I Am the Babe of Joseph Stalin's Daughter* (Kulchur Press, 1972).

Plays: *Futz and What Came After,* collection of five plays by Rochelle Owens (Random House, 1968), includes *Futz, The String Game, Beclch, Istanboul, Homo. The Karl Marx Play* in *Best Short Plays of 1971,* edited by Stanley Richards (Avon). *Kontraption* in *Scripts Magazine,* Vol. I, No. 1. *He wants Shih* in *Spontaneous Combustion Plays,* edited by Rochelle Owens (Winter House, 1972) including plays by Bovasso, Bullins, Hoffman, Baraka, Terry, Kennedy, Melfi.

PATRICK, ROBERT (Robert Patrick O'Connor). *b.* September 27, 1937, Kilgore, Texas; *p.* Robert Henderson and Beulah (Jo) (Goodson O'Conner Durkee Hawkins Bobo Henson) O'Connor; *fo.* oil-field worker, electric lineman; *ed.* Caffe Cino; *po.* manager of miniature golf course, doorman at Caffe Cino, swept stage for Tom O'Horgan, autopsy typist; *mw.* Plays: *Haunted Host* (1964), *Golden Circle* (1965), *Camera Obscura* (1967), *Joyce Dynel** (1968); *av.* astrology, feature editor for *Sybil Leek's Astrology Journal; in.* Shaw, Jean Kerr, Herman Wouk, Johnny Mack Brown, June Allyson, Maggie Dominic, Joe Cino, Justice Society of America, W. H. Auden, Ayn Rand; *ma.* c/o La Mama, 74 East Fourth Street, New York, New York 10003.

*Award: *Joyce Dynel* (*Show Business* Award, Best Play, 1968–69).

BIBLIOGRAPHY:

Action in *Yale/Theatre,* edited by Ren Frutkin, Vol. 2, No. 2. *See Other Side* in *Yale/Theatre,* edited by Ren Frutkin, Vol. 2, No. 2. *Camera Obscura* in *Collision Course,* edited by Edward Parone (Random House, 1968). *Golden Circle* in *New American Plays,* Vol. III (Hill and Wang). *Robert Patrick's Cheep Theatricks!,* collection including *Joyce Dynel, Haunted Host,* others, edited by Michael Feingold (Winter House, 1972).

PRIDEAUX, JAMES (James Priddy). *b.* August 29, 1927, South Bend, Indiana; *p.* Lloyd and Beulah (Shirey) Priddy; *fo.* portrait photographer; *ed.* Ball State Teachers College, University of Michigan; *po.* typist, usher at Radio City, assistant director of audiovisuals of Foreign Policy Association, tour guide at *New York Times,* secretary at Henry St. Playhouse; *mw.* Short Story: *The Cow on the Way to Delphi* (1964); Plays: *The Bench, Ain't It Awful About Marie Antoinette?* (1965), *Postcards* (1966), *The Last of Mrs. Lincoln* (1967), *Lemonade, The Autograph Hound* (1969), *Under MacDougal* (1970); Screenplay: *Martha in Paris* (unproduced, collaboration with Katharine Hepburn, 1969); *av.* travel, collects history; *in.* The Playwrights Unit; *ma.* Eagle's Nest Road, Hurley, New York 12443.

RABE, DAVID (David William Rabe) *b.* March 10, 1940, Dubuque, Iowa; *p.* William and Ruth (McCormick) Rabe; *fo.* shipping dock, meat packing, teacher; *m.* Elizabeth Pan, 1969; *ed.* Loras College (B.A., English); *po.* egg carrier, bellhop, parking lot attendant, substitute teacher; *mw.* Plays: *The Basic Training of Pavlo Hummel** (1971), *Sticks and Bones, The Orphan* (1972); *av.* Playwright in Residence and Playwriting Consultant at Villanova University; *in.* Virginia Woolf, James Jones, Arthur Miller, Open Theatre production of *The Serpent; ma.* c/o Public Theater, 425 Lafayette Street, New York, New York 10003.

*Awards: *The Basic Training of Pavlo Hummel* (Obie Award, Distinguished Playwriting; Drama Desk Award, Most Promising Playwright; Variety Poll, Most Promising Playwright, 1971). *Sticks and Bones* (Tony Award, Best Play; Outer Critics Circle Award, Best Play, New York Drama Critics Circle, Citation, 1972).

RIBMAN, RONALD (Ronald Burt Ribman). *b.* May 28, 1932, New York City; *p.* Samuel and Rosa (Lerner) Ribman; *fo.* lawyer, businessman; *m.* Alice Rosen, 1967; *c.* James Wyatt; *ed.* Brooklyn College, University of Pittsburgh (B.B.A., M.A., English Literature, Ph.D., English); *po.* assistant professor of English at Otterbein, salesman for coal company, poet; *mw.* Plays: *Harry, Noon and Night* (1965), *Journey of the Fifth Horse** (1966), *Ceremony of Innocence* (1968), *Passing Through from Exotic Places* (1969), *Fingernails Blue as Flowers* (1971), *A Break in the Skin* (1971); Teleplay: *Final War of Olly Winter* (*CBS Playhouse,* 1967); *in.* Thomas Mann, Kafka, T. S. Eliot; *ma.* c/o American Place Theatre, 111 West 46th Street, New York, New York 10036.

*Award: *Journey of the Fifth Horse* (Obie, Best Play 1966).

BIBLIOGRAPHY:

Journey of the Fifth Horse in *Journey of the Fifth Horse and Harry, Noon and Night,* two plays by Ronald Ribman (Little, Brown and Co., 1967). *Final War of Olly Winter* in *Great Television Plays,* edited by William I. Kaufman (Laurel Edition, Dell, 1969).

SHEPARD, SAM (Samuel Shepard Rogers). *b.* November 5, 1943, Fort Sheridan, Illinois; *p.* Samuel Shepard and Jane (Schook) Rogers; *fo.* Air Force officer, Spanish teacher; *m.* O-Lan Johnson, 1969; *c.* Jesse Mojo; *po.* actor with Bishop's Company Repertory Players, waiter at Village Gate, horseshit remover and hot walker at Santa Anita; *mw.* Plays: *Cowboys, Rock Garden* (1964; excerpt later included in *Oh! Calcutta!*), *Chicago,* * *Icarus' Mother** (1965), *Fourteen Hundred Thousand, Red Cross,** *La Turista** (1966), *Forensic and the Navigators, Melodrama Play* (1967), *Shaved Splits* (1968), *Operation Sidewinder, The Unseen Hand* (1970), *Mad Dog Blues, Cowboy Mouth* (with Patti Smith), *Back Bog Beast Bait* (1971); Screenplay: *Zabriskie Point* (1969, with Antonioni and others, MGM); *av.* rock; *in.* Mick Jagger, Charles Mingus, Sr., Little Richard; *ma.* c/o Toby Cole, 234 West Forty-fourth Street, Sardi Building, New York, New York 10036.

* Awards: *Chicago, Icarus' Mother, Red Cross* (Obie, Distinguished Playwriting, 1966); *La Turista* (Obie, Distinguished Playwriting, 1967); *Forensic and the Navigators, Melodrama Play* (Obie, Distinguished Playwriting, 1968). Rockefeller, Guggenheim and OADR Grants.

BIBLIOGRAPHY:
Five Plays by Sam Shepard (Bobbs-Merrill, 1967), includes *Chicago, Icarus' Mother, Red Cross, Fourteen Hundred Thousand, Melodrama Play. Cowboys #2* in *Collision Course,* edited by Edward Parone (Random House, 1968). *Forensic and the Navigators* in *The Best of Off Off Broadway,* edited by Michael Smith (Dutton, 1969). *Operation Sidewinder: Play in Two Acts* (Bobbs-Merrill, 1970). *Unseen Hand and Other Plays by Sam Shepard* (Bobbs-Merrill, 1971), includes *The Holy Ghostly, Back Bog Beast Bait, Forensic and the Navigators. Mad Dog Blues and Other Plays by Sam Shepard,* edited by Michael Feingold (Winter House, 1972), includes *Cowboy Mouth, Rock Garden, Cowboys #2.*

SMITH, MICHAEL (Michael Townsend Smith). *b.* October 5, 1935, Kansas City, Missouri; *p.* Lewis Motter and Dorothy (Pew) Smith; *fo.* retail merchant (dry goods, women's clothing); *ed.* Yale; *po.* journalist, reporter for *London Evening Standard* (New York office), *Daily Express,* assistant film editor for television film company, photographer; *mw. I Like It* (1963), *The Next Thing*

(1965), *More. More. I Want More!* (with Johnny Dodd and Remy Charlip), *A Dog's Love* (1966), *Forspiel Mach Marienstein* (with Johnny Dodd and Ondine), *Captain Jack's Revenge* (1970), *Peas, Tony, Country Music** (1971); *av. Village Voice* critic, anthology editor, manager of Sundance Theatre, Bucks County, Pa., lighting designer, director, member board of directors Theatre Genesis, plays keyboard instruments, chamber music; *in.* Ionesco, Chekhov, Strauss, American history, J. S. Bach; *ma.* 236 East Fifth Street, New York, New York 10003.

* Award: *Country Music* (Obie, Distinguished Direction, 1972).

BIBLIOGRAPHY:
The Best of Off Off Broadway (Dutton). *Eight Plays from Off Off Broadway* (with Nick Orzel, Bobbs-Merrill). *Theatre Trip* (Bobbs-Merrill). "The Good Scene" in *TDR,* Vol. 10, No. 4. *More Plays from Off Off Broadway* (Bobbs-Merrill).

STARKWEATHER, DAVID. *b.* September 11, 1935, Madison, Wisconsin; *p.* Walter S. and Norma (Shroyer) Starkweather; *fo.* wholesale radio and TV; *ed.* University of Wisconsin (B.A., Speech, 1957); *po.* actor, manager, driver for touring theatre company; *mw.* Plays: *The Family Joke* (1962), *You May Go Home Again, So Who's Afraid of Edward Albee?* (1963), *Owey Wishy Are You There?* (1964), *The Assent, The Wish House* (1967), *The Poet's Papers* (1968), *A Practical Ritual to Exorcise Frustration After Five Days of Rain* (1969); *av.* editor of *New York Visitors' Reporter; in.* Cino, Martha Graham, Japanese theatre; *ma.* 340 West Eleventh Street, New York, New York 10014.

BIBLIOGRAPHY:
The Poet's Papers in *New American Plays,* Vol. III (Hill and Wang, 1970).

STEIN, GERTRUDE. *b.* February 3, 1874, Allegheny, Pennsylvania; died July 27, 1946, Paris France; *p.* Daniel and Amelia (Keyser) Stein; *ed.* Radcliffe (Psychology major, 1893–97), Johns Hopkins (Medicine, 4 years) "bored by exams," no degrees; *mw. Ada, Autobiography of Alice B. Toklas, Bee Time Vine, Before the Flowers of Friendship Faded,* "Birthplace of Bonnes," *Blood on the Dining Room Floor, Brewsie and Willie,* "Capital Capitals," *Composition as Explanation, Dr. Faustus Lights the Lights,* "An Elucidation," *Everybody's Autobiography,* "The Fifteenth of November," *Four in America, Four Saints in Three Acts,* "The Gentle Lena," *The Geographical History of America, Geography and Plays,* "The

Good Anna," "Gypsies in Spain," "Have They Attacked Mary He Giggled," *How to Write, Ida,* "If You Had Three Husbands," *Lectures in America, Life and Death of Juan Gris, A Long Gay Book, Lucy Church Amiably, The Making of Americans, Many Many Women, Matisse, Picasso and Gertrude Stein,* "Melanctha," "Mildred's Thoughts," *Moral Tales, The Mother of Us All, Mrs. Reynolds,* "Normal Motor Automatism," "One," *Operas and Plays, Paris France,* "Patriarchal Poetry," "Portrait of F. B.," *Portrait of Mabel Dodge at the Villa Curonia, Portraits and Prayers,* "Precoisilla," "Reflections on the Atomic Bomb," "Rooms," "Saints in Seven," *Stanzas in Meditation,* "Susie Asado," "Talks to Saints in St. Remy," *Tender Buttons,* "They Must Be Wedded. To Their Wife," "Things As They Are (*Quod Erat Demonstrandum*)," *Three Lives, The First Reader,* "A Valentine for Sherwood Anderson," *Useful Knowledge, Wars I Have Seen,* "The Work," *The World Is Round, Yes Is for a Very Young Man.*

BIBLIOGRAPHY:

As Fine As Melanctha (Yale University Press, New Haven, 1934), *Autobiography of Alice B. Toklas* (Harcourt, Brace and Co., New York, 1933. John Lane the Bodley Head, London, 1933), *Bee Time Vine* (Yale University Press, New Haven, 1953), *Brewsie and Willie* (Random House, New York, 1946), *Composition as Explanation* (The Hogarth Press, London, 1926. Doubleday Doran and Co., Inc., New York, 1928), *Everybody's Autobiography* (Random House, New York, 1937), *Four in America* (Yale University Press, New Haven, 1947), *The Geographical History of America* (Random House, New York, 1936), *Geography and Plays* (The Four Seas Co., Boston, 1922), *How to Write* (Plain Edition, Paris, 1931), *Ida, A Novel* (Random House, New York, 1931), *Last Operas and Plays* (Rinehart and Co., Inc., New York, 1949. Pittsburgh Press, Pittsburgh, 1970), *Lectures in America* (Random House, New York, 1935), *Lucy Church Amiably* (Plain Edition, Paris, 1930), *The Making of Americans* (Contact Editions, Paris, 1925. Albert and Charles Boni, New York, 1926. Harcourt, Brace and Co., New York, 1934, abridged edition), *Mrs. Reynolds* (Yale University Press, New Haven, 1952), *Narration* (University of Chicago Press, 1935), *A Novel of Thank You* (Yale University Press, New Haven, 1958), *Painted Lace* (Yale University Press, New Haven, 1955), *Paris France* (Charles Scribner's Sons, New York, 1940), *Picasso* (Charles Scribner's Sons, New York, 1939), *Portraits and Prayers* (Random House, New York, 1934), *Selected Writings of Gertrude Stein* (Random House, New York, 1946), *Stanzas in Meditation* (Yale University Press, New Haven, 1956), *Tender Buttons* (Claire Marie, New York, 1914), *Things As They Are* (The Banyan Press, Pawlett, Vermont, 1951), *Three Lives* (The Grafton Press, New York, 1910. The Modern Library, Inc., New York, 1933), *To Do: A Book of Alphabets and Birthdays,* Yale University Press, New Haven, 1951), *Unpublished Works of Gertrude Stein* (8 vols., 1957 facsimile ed., Books for Libraries, Inc., Select Bibliography Reprint Revue (Freeport, New York, 1957), *Useful Knowledge* (Payson and Clarke Ltd., New York, 1928), *Wars I Have Seen* (Random House, New York, 1944), *What Are Masterpieces* (The Conference Press, Los Angeles, 1940), *The World Is Round* (Camelot, Avon Books, New York, 1971).

Information compiled from above sources.

TAVEL, RONALD. *b.* May 17, 1941, Brooklyn, New York; *p.* George and Florence (Sterns) Tavel; *fo.* diamond setter; *ed.* Brooklyn College (B.A., Philosophy and Literature, 1960), University of Wyoming (M.A., Philosophy and Literature, 1961); *po.* freelance tutor, taught at Wyoming University, shill for freak show at Coney Island; *mw.* Poem: *The True Story of Billy the Kid* (1964); Novel: *Street of Stairs* (1963); Plays: *Indira Gandhi's Daring Device* (1965), *Gorilla Queen* (1966), *Arenas of Lutetia* (1967), *Boy on the Straight Back Chair** (1968), *Bigfoot* (1970); Screenplays: *Horse, Screentest* (Warhol, 1965); *av.* comic books and films; *in.* Victor Hugo, Lord Byron, Warhol, Jack Smith; *ma.* 1095 East 53rd Street, Brooklyn, New York 11234.

* Award: *Boy on the Straight Back Chair* (Obie, Best Play, 1968). Rockefeller grant, 1971.

BIBLIOGRAPHY:

Life of Lady Godiva in *New Underground Theatre,* edited by R. T. Schroeder (Bantam). *Gorilla Queen* in *Best of Off Off Broadway,* edited by Michael Smith (Dutton, 1969). *Vinyl Visits an F.M. Station* in TDR. Vol. 14, No. 2. *Bigfoot and Other Plays by Ronald Tavel* (Winter House, 1972). *Canticle of the Nightingale* (Breakthrough Press, 1972).

TERRY, MEGAN. *b.* July 22, 1932, Seattle, Washington; *ed.* University of Washington (B. Ed.), University of Alberta, Banff School of Fine Arts, Yale; *po.* actress with Seattle Repertory Playhouse, set and costume designer, director, taught art at Banff, founding member of Open Theatre (1963), painter; *mw.* *Ex-Miss Copper Queen on a Set of Pills* (1958), *The Magic Realist* (1962), *People vs. Ranchman* (1963), *The Gloaming, Oh My Darling, Calm Down, Mother, Keep Tightly Closed in a Cool, Dry Place* (1965), *Viet Rock,*

Comings and Goings (1966), Jack-Jack, Key Is on the Bottom (1967), Massachusetts Trust, Home (1968), The Tommy Allen Show, One More Little Drinkie (1969), Approaching Simone* (1970), Frankenstein, Pro Game (1971), "Choose a Spot on the Floor" (with JoAnn Schmidman), Grooving, Brazil, Fado: You're Always with Me, Don Juan, Madwoman with Carrot (1972); av. founding member of Women's Theatre Council and New York Theatre Strategy (1971), studies "living" American English, fishing; in. Aristophanes, Bugs Bunny, all the Irish writers, Strindberg, Gertrude Stein; ma. c/o Elisabeth Marton, 96 Fifth Avenue, New York, New York 10011.

*Award: Approaching Simone (Obie, Best Play, 1970). Rockefeller and OADR grants.

BIBLIOGRAPHY:

Viet Rock and Other Plays by Megan Terry (Simon and Schuster, 1967), includes Comings and Goings, Keep Tightly Closed in a Cool, Dry Place and In the Gloaming, Oh My Darling. Ex-Miss Copper Queen on a Set of Pills in Playwrights for Tomorrow, Vol. 1. (University of Minnesota Press, 1966). Sanibel and Captiva in Spontaneous Combustion Plays, edited by Rochelle Owens (Winter House, 1972). Approaching Simone (Feminist Press, 1972).

VAN ITALLIE, JEAN-CLAUDE. b. May 25, 1936, Brussels, Belgium; p. Hughes Ferdinand and Marthe Mathilde Caroline (Levy) van Itallie; fo. stockbroker; ed. Harvard (B.A., History and Literature, 1958); po. carhop, display assistant at Bond's Department Store (Washington, D.C.), editor of Transatlantic Review, researcher at CBS-TV, scriptwriter for public affairs programs at CBS and NBC; mw. Plays: War (1963), Almost Like Being, I'm Really Here, The Hunter and the Bird (1964), America Hurrah* (1965), Where Is de Queen? (1966), The Serpent,* Thoughts on the Instant of Greeting a Friend on the Street (with Sharon Thie, 1968), Eat Cake (1970); teleplay: Take a Deep Breath (N.E.T., 1968); Screenplay: Three Lives for Mississippi (unproduced, based on novel by William Bradford Huie); Book: To India: A Journal (1972); in. Artaud, Beckett, Marat/Sade (play); ma. c/o Bridget Aschenberg, International Famous Agency, 301 Sixth Avenue, New York, New York 10019.

*Awards: America Hurrah (Vernon Rice Drama Desk, Outer Circle Critics Award, Jersey Journal Award Best Play, 1966-67); The Serpent (Obie presented to the Open Theatre, 1969).

BIBLIOGRAPHY:

I'm Really Here in New Underground Theatre, edited by R. J. Schroeder (Bantam). Almost Like Being in TDR, Vol. 9, No. 4. Where Is de Queen? in Playwrights for Tomorrow, collection (University of Minnesota Press, 1967). Thoughts on the Instant of Greeting a Friend on the Street in Collision Course, edited by Edward Parone (Random House, 1968). America Hurrah (Pocket Books, Inc., 1969). The Serpent (Atheneum, 1969). To India: A Journal (Winter House, 1972).

WILSON, LANFORD (Lanford Eugene Wilson). b. April 13, 1937, Lebanon, Missouri; p. Ralph and Violetta (Tate) Wilson; fo. aeronautical engineer; ed. Southwest Missouri State, San Diego State, University of Chicago; po. dishwasher, reservation clerk, furniture salesman, riveter, package designer, waiter, ad layout man, subscription departments at Phoenix Theatre and N.Y. Shakespeare Festival; mw. Plays: So Long at the Fair, Home Free (1963), Sand Castle, Ludlow Fair, Balm in Gilead (1964), Sex Is Between Two People, This Is the Rill Speaking, Gingham Dog, Madness of Lady Bright (1965), Days Ahead, Rimers of Eldritch,* Wandering (1966), Untitled Play (1967), Lemon Sky (1968), Serenading Louie, One Arm (adaptation from T. Williams) (1970), Sextet (Yes), The Great Nebula in Orion (1971), The Family Continues, Victory on Mrs. Dandywine's Island (1972); Libretto: Summer and Smoke (opera based on play by T. Williams, 1971); in. The Glass Menagerie (production at Southwest Missouri State College), The Lesson (at Caffe Cino), You May Go Home Again (at Cino), Next Time I'll Sing to You (Phoenix Theatre) and What Happened (Judson Poets'); ma. Box 891, Sag Harbor, New York 11963.

*Award: The Rimers of Eldritch (Best Play, Vernon Rice Drama Desk Award, 1966).

BIBLIOGRAPHY:

Balm in Gilead and Other Plays (Hill and Wang, 1965). Gingham Dog (Hill and Wang, 1969). Rimers of Eldritch and Other Plays (Hill and Wang, 1967). Lemon Sky (Hill and Wang).

BIBLIOGRAPHY

Abel, Lionel. *Metatheatre: A New View of Dramatic Form.* New York: Hill and Wang, 1963.

Aldo, Rostagno, with Julian Beck and Judith Malina. *We, The Living Theatre.* New York: Ballantine Books, 1970.

Artaud, Antonin. *The Theatre and Its Double.* New York: Grove Press, 1958.

Atkinson, Brooks. *Broadway.* New York: Macmillan, 1971.

Barba, Eugenio. "A Theatre of Magic and Sacrilege," *TDR,* Vol. 9, No. 3.

Bentley, Eric. *The Theatre of Commitment.* New York: Atheneum, 1967.

Blau, Herbert. *The Impossible Theatre: A Manifesto.* New York: Macmillan, 1964.

Bowers, Faubion. *Japanese Theatre.* New York: Hermitage, 1952.

Braun, Edward (ed.). *Meyerhold on Theatre.* New York: Hill and Wang, 1969.

Brecht, Bertolt. *On Theatre* (John Willett, ed.) New York: Hill and Wang, 1964.

Brecht, Stefan. "LeRoi Jones' Slave Ship," *TDR,* Vol. 14, No. 2.

Brook, Peter. *Empty Space.* New York: Avon (Discus), 1969.

Brustein, Robert. *Revolution as Theatre, Notes on the New Radical Style.* New York: Liveright, 1971.

———. *Seasons of Discontent.* New York: Simon and Schuster, 1967.

———. *The Theatre of Revolt: An Approach to the Modern Drama.* Boston: Little, Brown, 1964.

———. *Third Theatre.* New York: Alfred Knopf, 1969.

Burke, Kenneth. *Philosophy of Literary Form.* New York: Vintage, 1957.

Carpenter, E. S., and McLuhan, Marshall (eds.). *Explorations in Communications.* Boston: Beacon, 1960.

Chaikin, Joseph. "The Open Theatre," *TDR,* Vol. 9, No. 2.

———. "Interview Fragments," *TDR,* Vol. 13, No. 3.

Chiari, J. *Landmarks of Contemporary Drama.* London: Herbert Jenkins, 1965.

Cohen, Marshall. "Theatre '67," *Partisan Review,* XXXIV: 3.

Cohn, Ruby. "Theatrum Mundi and Contemporary Theatre."

Coigney, Martha W., and Leabo, Judith R. and Karl (eds.). *Theatre,* Vols. I, II, III. New York: International Theatre Institute, 1968–69–70.

Cordell, R. L., and Matson, L. "Off Broadway Theatre," in Colby, V., *American Culture in the Sixties.*

Corrigan, Robert W. (ed). *Comedy.* San Francisco: Chandler, 1965.

——— (ed.). *Tragedy: Vision and Form.* San Francisco: Chandler, 1965.

Cruse, Harold. *The Crisis of the Negro Intellectual.* New York: William Morrow, 1967.

Currie, R. Hector. "The Energies of Tragedy: Cosmic and Psychic," *Centennial Review,* Vol. XI.

Dan, Isaac. "Ronald Tavel: Ridiculous Playwright," *TDR,* Vol. 13, No. 1.

Downer, Alan S. (ed.). *American Drama and Its Critics.* Chicago: University of Chicago, 1965.

Esslin, Martin. *Brecht: The Man and His Work.* Garden City: Doubleday (Anchor Books), 1971.

———. *Theatre of the Absurd.* Garden City: Doubleday (Anchor Books), 1969.

———. *Reflections, Essays on Modern Theatre.* Garden City: Doubleday, 1971.

Feldman, Peter. "Director's Notes: Keep Tightly Closed," *TDR,* Vol. 10, No. 4.

Fraser, G. S. (ed.). *The Modern Writer and His World.* Baltimore: Penguin, 1964.

Gassner, John. *Directions in Modern Theatre and Drama: An Expanded Edition of Form and Ideas in Modern Theatre.* New York: Holt, Rinehart and Winston, 1965.

———. *Form and Idea in Modern Theatre.* New York: Holt, Rinehart and Winston, 1956.

———. *Theatre at the Crossroads.* New York: Holt, Rinehart and Winston, 1960.

Gayle, Addison Jr. (ed.). *The Black Aesthetic.* Garden City: Doubleday, 1971.

Golden, Joseph. *Death of Tinkerbell: The American Theatre in the Twentieth Century.* Syracuse: Syracuse University Press, 1967.

Gorelick, Mordecai. *New Theatres for Old.* New York: Samuel French, 1957; New York: Dutton, 1962.

Gottfried, Martin. *Opening Nights. Theatre Criticism of the Sixties.* New York: G. P. Putnam's Sons, 1969.

———. *A Theater Divided, The Postwar American Stage.* Boston: Little, Brown, 1969.

Grotowski, Jerzy. *Toward a Poor Theatre.* New York: Simon and Schuster, 1970.

Huizinger, Johan. *Homo Ludens.* Boston: Beacon, 1955.

Ionesco, Eugene. *Notes and Counter Notes; Writings on the Theatre by Eugene Ionesco* (trans. by Donald Watson). New York: Grove Press, 1964.

Kerr, Walter. *Tragedy and Comedy.* New York: Simon and Schuster, 1968.

———. *The Decline of Pleasure.* New York: Simon and Schuster, 1968.

———. *Thirty Plays Hath November, Pain and Pleasure in the Contemporary Theatre.* New York: Simon and Schuster, 1970.

Khan, Hazrat Inayat. *The Sufi Message of Hazrat Inayat Khan.* Vol. 2: *The Mysticism of Sound, Music, The Power of the Word, Cosmic Language.* London: Barrie and Rockliff, 1960.

King, Kenneth. "SuperLecture," in *The Young American Writers* (Richard Kostelanetz, ed.). New York: Funk and Wagnalls, 1967.

Kirby, E. T. (ed.). *Total Theatre: A Critical Anthology.* New York: Dutton, 1969.

Kirby, Michael. *The Art of Time.* New York: Dutton, 1969.

———. *Happenings: An Illustrated Anthology.* New York: Dutton, 1965.

Knapp, Bettina L. *Antonin Artaud, Man of Vision.* New York: Avon, 1971.

Kostelanetz, Richard. *The Theatre of Mixed Means.* New York: Dial Press, 1968.

Kott, Jan. *Theatre Notebook: Nineteen Forty-seven to Nineteen Sixty-seven.* Garden City: Doubleday, 1968.

Lahr, John. *Up Against the Fourth Wall, Essays on Modern Theatre.* New York: Grove Press, 1970.

Lawter, Paul (ed.). *Theories of Comedy.* Garden City: Doubleday, 1964.

Leary, Daniel J. "Theatre of Dislike: Contemporary Drama," *Catholic World,* CCV (July).

Lebel, Jean-Jacques. "On the Necessity of Violation," *TDR,* Vol. 13, No. 1.

Lewis, Allan. *American Plays and Playwrights of the Contemporary Theatre.* New York: Crown, 1965.

Lewis, Emory. *Stages. The 50-Year Childhood of the American Theatre.* Englewood Cliffs, N.J.: Prentice-Hall, 1969.

Living Theatre. "The Avignon Statement," *TDR,* Vol. 13, No. 3.

———. "*Paradise Now* Notes," *TDR,* Vol. 13, No. 13.

Lukacs, George. "The Sociology of Modern Drama," *TDR,* Vol. 9, No. 4.

Lumley, Frederick. *New Trends in Twentieth-Century Drama: A Survey Since Ibsen and Shaw* (3rd ed.). New York: Oxford University Press, 1967.

Mandel, Oscar. *A Definitional Tragedy.* New York: New York University Press, 1961.

Marechal, Judith R. "Off Broadway: A Limited Engagement," *TDR,* Vol. 10, No. 1.

Mead, Margaret. "Art and Reality," *College Art Journal,* No. IV (May 1943).

Menagh, H. Beresford. "A Way of Separating Theatre from Rite," *Educational Theatre Journal,* XIX: 2.

Mueller, William R., and Jacobson, Josephine. "The Absurd Quest," *Kenyon Review,* XXIX: 2.

Neff, Renfreu. *The Living Theatre.* New York: Bobbs-Merrill, 1970.

Novick, Julius. *Beyond Broadway, The Quest for Permanent Theatres.* New York: Hill and Wang, 1969.

Orzel, Nick, and Smith, Michael (eds.). *Eight Plays from Off-Off Broadway.* New York: Bobbs-Merrill, 1966.

Pasolli, Robert. "The New Playwrights Scene of the Sixties," *TDR,* Vol. 13, No. 1.

—————. *A Book on the Open Theatre.* Indianapolis: Bobbs-Merrill, 1970.

Peacock, Ronald. *The Art of Drama.* London: Routledge and Kegan Paul, 1957.

Phelps, Lyon. "Brecht's *Antigone* at the Living Theatre," *TDR,* Vol. 12, No. 1.

Price, Julia. S. *The Off-Broadway Theatre.* New York: Scarecrow Press, 1962.

Raphael, D. D. *The Paradox of Tragedy.* Bloomington, Ind.: Indiana University Press, 1960.

Reed, Ishmael (ed.). *19 Necromancers from Now.* Garden City: Doubleday, 1970

Roose Evans, James. *Experimental Theatre from Stanislavsky to Today.* New York: Universe Books, 1970.

Saint-Denis, Michel. *Theatre: The Rediscovery of Style.* New York: Theatre Arts, 1969.

Schechner, Richard. *Public Domain, Essays on the Theatre.* New York: Avon, 1970.

Schroeder, Robert J. (ed.). *The Coffee House Theatre: Off-Off Broadway and the New American Stage.* New York: Funk and Wagnalls.

Shah, Sayed Indries. *Oriental Magic.* London: Octagon Press, 1956.

Sharpe, Robert Boies. *Irony in the Drama: An Essay on Impersonation, Shock and Catharsis.* Chapel Hill, N.C.: University of North Carolina Press, 1959.

Shattuck, Roger. *The Banquet Years.* Garden City: Doubleday, 1961.

Silvestro, Carlo (ed.). *The Living Book of the Living Theatre.* Greenwich, Conn.: New York Graphic Society, 1971.

Smith, Michael. *The Best of Off Off Broadway.* New York: Dutton, 1969.

—————. *Theatre Trip.* Indianapolis: Bobbs-Merrill, 1969.

—————. "The Good Scene," *TDR,* Vol. 10, No. 4.

Sontag, Susan. "Film and Theatre," *TDR,* Vol. 11, No. 1.

—————. *Styles of Radical Will.* New York: Dell, 1970.

—————. *Against Interpretation and Other Essays.* F. S. & G., 1966.

Southern, Richard. *The Seven Ages of the Theatre.* New York: Hill and Wang, 1961.

Steiner, George. *The Death of Tragedy.* New York: Alfred Knopf, 1961.

Stanislavski, Constantin. *My Life in Art* (trans. by J. J. Robbins). Cleveland: World (Meridian), 1968.

Styan, J. L. *The Dark Comedy: The Development of Modern Comic Tragedy.* London: Cambridge University Press, 1962.

Tse-tung, Mao. *Talks at the Yenan Forum on Literature and Art.* Peking: Foreign Languages Press, 1962.

Tynan, Kenneth. *Curtains.* New York: Atheneum, 1961.

—————. *Tynan Right and Left.* New York: Atheneum, 1967.

van Itallie, Jean-Claude. "Playwright at Work: Off Off Broadway," *TDR,* Vol. 10, No. 4.

Wager, Walter (ed.). *The Playwrights Speak.* New York: Delacorte.

Weales, Gerald. *The Jumping Off Place. American Drama of the Sixties.* London: Macmillan, 1969.

Weissman, Philip. *Creativity in the Theatre: A Psychological Study.* New York: Basic Books, 1965.

Wellwarth, George E. *The Theatre of Protest and Paradox: Developments in the Avant-Garde Drama.* New York: New York University Press, 1964.

ADDITIONAL READING

Adler, Gerhard. *The Living Symbol.* Princeton, N.J.: Princeton University Press, 1961.

Aesop's Fables.

Aldridge, Alan. *The Beatles Illustrated Lyrics,* Vols. I and II. New York: Seymour Lawrence Books–Delacorte Press, 1969 and 1971.

Andersen, Hans Christian. *Fairy Tales.*

Barnes, Clive, and Mitchell, Jack. *Dance Scene: U.S.A.* Cleveland: World, 1967.

Baum, L. Frank. *The Wizard of Oz.*

Black Theatre magazine.

Blum, Daniel (rev. by John Kobal). *New Pictorial History of the Talkies.* New York: Grosset and Dunlap, 1970.

Brown, Norman O. *Life Against Death.* Middletown, Conn.: Wesleyan University Press, 1959.

Bruce, Lenny. *How to Talk Dirty and Influence People.* Chicago: Playboy Press, 1967.

Bullfinch's Mythology. New York: Random House (Modern Library)

Campbell, Joseph. *The Hero with a Thousand Faces.* New York: Pantheon Books, 1949.

Carson, Richard. *Fashions in Hair, The First 5,000 Years.* New York: Hillary House, 1971.

Cavendish, Richard. *Black Arts, An absorbing account of witchcraft, demonology, astrology and other mystical practices through the ages.* New York: G. P. Putnam's Sons, 1967.

Cohen, John (ed.). *The Essential Lenny Bruce.* New York: Ballantine Books, 1967.

Colum, Padraic. *Orpheus, Myths of the World.* New York: Macmillan, 1930.

Compton, Michael. *Pop Art.* London: Hamlyn Publishers Group, 1970.

Crone, Rainer. *Andy Warhol.* New York: Praeger 1970.

Daniels, L., and Peck, J. (eds.). *Comix: A History of Comic Books in America.* New York: Outerbridge and Dienstfrey, 1971.

Dent, T. C., and Schechner, R. (eds.). *Free Southern Theatre by the Free Southern Theatre.* Indianapolis: Bobbs-Merrill, 1969.

Deren, Maya. *Divine Horsemen, The Living Gods of Haiti.* New York: New York Book Collectors Society, 1952.

Dille, Robert C. (ed.). *The Collected Works of Buck Rogers in the 25th Century.* New York: Chelsea House, 1969.

Eisen, Jonathan (ed.). *The Age of Rock, Sounds of the Cultural Revolution,* Vols. I and II. New York: Random House (Vintage) 1969 and 1970.

Eros magazine.

Escher, M. C. *The Graphic Work of M. C. Escher.* New York: Ballantine Books, 1971.

Estrin, Marc (ed.). *reCreation: Some Notes on What's What and What You Might Be Able to Do About What's What.* New York: Dell (Delta), 1971.

Everson, William K. (ed.). *A Pictorial History of the Western Film.* New York: Citadel Press, 1969.

Frazer, James G. *The Golden Bough.* London: Macmillan.

Golden Age of Comics (series). Franklin Square, N.Y.: Nostalgia Press.

Goodstone, Tony (ed.). *The Pulps, Fifty Years of American Pop Culture.* New York: Chelsea House, 1970.

Graves, Robert. *The White Goddess.* New York: Random House (Vintage), 1958.

Green, Abel, and Laurie, Joe Jr. *Show Biz: From Vaude to Video.* New York: Henry Holt, 1951.

Griffith, Richard, and Mayer, Arthur (eds.). *The Movies.* New York: Simon and Schuster, 1970.

Grimm's Fairy Tales.

Horan, J. D. *Pictorial History of the Wild West.* New York: Crown.

I Ching or Book of Changes. Princeton, N.J.: Princeton University Press (Bollingen Series XIX), 1970.

InterView magazine.

Janov, Arthur. *The Primal Scream, Primal Therapy: The Cure for Neurosis.* New York: G. P. Putnam's Sons, 1970.

Jung, Carl G. *Man and His Symbols.* Garden City: Doubleday, 1971.

Levin, Martin (ed.). *Hollywood and the Great Fan Magazines.* New York: Arbor House, 1970.

Lupoff, Dick, and Thompson, Don (eds.). *All in Color for a Dime.* New Rochelle, N.Y.: Arlington House, 1970.

Marvel, Eleanor, and Radin, Paul (eds.). *African Folk Tales and Sculpture.* New York: Pantheon Books (Bollingen), 1952.

McCrindle, Joseph F. (ed.). *Behind the Scenes: Theatre and Film Interviews from the Transatlantic Review.* New York: Holt, Rinehart and Winston, 1971.

McLuhan, Marshall. *Understanding Media.* New York: McGraw-Hill.

Meltzer, R. *The Aesthetics of Rock.* New York: Something Else Press, 1970.

Millett, Kate. *Sexual Politics.* New York: Avon (Equinox Books), 1971.

Moussinac, Leon. *The New Movement in the Theatre.* New York: Benjamin Bloom, 1967.

New York Review of Books, The.

Ovid.

Pauwels, L., and Bergier, J. *Morning of the Magicians* (trans. by Rollo Myers). New York: Avon, 1969.

Performance magazine.

Plays and Players magazine.

Rags magazine.

Rolling Stone.

Rouse, W. H. D. *Gods, Heroes and Men of Ancient Greece.* New York: New American Library (Signet Key Book), 1962.

Rudhyar, Dane. *Astrology of Personality.* New York: Doubleday, 1970.

Sanderson, Ivan T. *Invisible Residents.* Cleveland: World, 1970.

Schafer, George, and Cruz, Nan. *The Kingdom of Mescal.* Berkeley, Calif.: Shambala Publications, 1970.

Schreiber, Hermann and Georg. *Vanished Cities* (trans. by Richard and Clara Winston). New York: Alfred Knopf, 1957.

Schutz, William C. *Joy, Expanding Human Awareness.* New York: Grove Press, 1969.

Scripts magazine.

Shipman, David (ed.). *The Great Movie Stars, The Golden Years.* New York: Crown Publishers, 1970.

Stewart, Mary. *The Crystal Cave.* Greenwich, Conn.: Fawcett Crest Book, 1971.

TDR. (The Drama Review, Tulane Drama Review)

Tolkien, J. R. R. *The Hobbit.* New York: Ballantine, 1969.

———. *Lord of the Rings.* 3 vols. New York: Ballantine, 1969.

Village Voice.

Waite, Arthur E. *The Pictorial Key to the Tarot.* Hyde Park, N.Y.: Universal Books, 1959.

Weston, Jessie L. *From Ritual to Romance.* New York: Doubleday (Anchor), 1957.

White, T. H. *The Once and Future King.* New York: G. P. Putnam's Sons, 1958.

Wilmot-Buxton, E. M. *Told by the Northmen; Stories from the Eddas and Sagas Retold by E. M. Wilmot-Buxton.* London: George G. Harrap, 1949.

Yale/Theatre magazine.

Yeats, William Butler. *A Vision.* New York: Macmillan (Collier Books), 1969.